ANXIETY
AND THE
ANXIETY DISORDERS

ANXIETY
AND THE
ANXIETY DISORDERS

Edited by

A. Hussain Tuma
Jack Maser
National Institute of Mental Health

LEA LAWRENCE ERLBAUM ASSOCIATES PUBLISHERS
Hillsdale, New Jersey   London

Lawrence Erlbaum Associates, Inc., Publishers
365 Broadway
Hillsdale, New Jersey 07642

Library of Congress Cataloging in Publication Data
Main entry under title:

Anxiety and the anxiety disorders.

Bibliography: p.
Includes index.
1. Anxiety.   I. Tuma, A. Hussain.   II. Maser, Jack D.
[DNLM: 1. Anxiety.   2. Anxiety Disorders.   WM 172 A6365]
RC531.A58 1985   616.85′223   85-6924
ISBN 0-89859-532-0

10 9 8 7 6 5 4 3 2 1

Printed in the United States of America

Contents

List of Contributors

Thomas M. Achenbach, Ph.D., Professor of Psychiatry and Psychology, Section of Child, Adolescent, and Family Psychiatry, Department of Psychiatry, 1 South Prospect Street, University of Vermont College of Medicine, Burlington, Vermont 05405

W. Stewart Agras, M.D., Professor of Psychiatry and Director, Behavioral Medicine Program, Department of Psychiatry, School of Medicine, Stanford University, Stanford, California 94305

Hagop S. Akiskal, M. D., Professor of Psychiatry, Director, Affective Disorders Program, University of Tennessee Center for Health Sciences, 66 North Pauline Street, Suite 633, Memphis, Tennessee 38163

E. James Anthony, M.D., Professor and Director, Division of Child Psychiatry, Harry Edison Child Development Research Center, Washington University, 363 North Taylor Avenue, St. Louis, Missouri 63108

David H. Barlow, Ph.D., Professor of Psychology and Co-Director, Center for Stress and Anxiety Disorders and Department of Psychology, State University of New York at Albany, Albany, New York 12222

Aaron T. Beck, M.D., University Professor of Psychiatry, Department of Psychiatry, University of Pennsylvania School of Medicine, 133 South 36th Street, Room 602, Philadelphia, Pennsylvania 19104

Samuel H. Blumberg, M.A., Department of Psychology, University of Delaware, Newark, Delaware 19711

Thomas D. Borkovec, Ph.D., Professor of Psychology, Department of Psychology, 417 Bruce V. Moore Building, Pennsylvania State University, University Park, Pennsylvania 16802

Jean-Philippe Boulenger, M.D., Visiting Associate, Unit on Anxiety and Affective Disorders, Biological Psychiatry Branch, National Institute of Mental Health, Building 10, Room 3S239, NIH Reservation, Bethesda, Maryland 20205

Gregory Carey, Ph.D., Assistant Professor of Medical Psychology in Psychiatry, Department of Psychiatry, Washington University School of Medicine, 4940 Audubon Avenue, Box 8134, St. Louis, Missouri 63110

xi

Erminio Costa, M.D., Chief, Laboratory of Preclinical Pharmacology, William A. White Building, Room 101, NIMH, St. Elizabeth's Hospital, Washington, D.C. 20032

Thomas Detre, M.D., Senior Vice President for Health Sciences, and Director, Western Psychiatric Institute and Clinic, 3811 O'Hara Street, University of Pittsburgh, Pittsburgh, Pennsylvania 15261

Joel E. Dimsdale, M.D., Associate Professor of Psychiatry, Department of Psychiatry, Harvard University, Massachusetts General Hospital, Boston, Massachusetts 02114

Marshall Edelson, M.D., Ph.D. Professor of Psychiatry, Department of Psychiatry, 25 Park Street, GB Room 617, Yale University School of Medicine, New Haven, Connecticut 06519

Robert N. Emde, M.D., Professor of Psychiatry, Department of Psychiatry, University of Colorado Health Sciences Center, 4200 East Ninth Avenue, Denver, Colorado 80262

Colonel Joseph C. Finney, M.D., Ph.D., Chief, Department of Psychiatry, Hays Hospital, Fort Ord, California 93941

Edna B. Foa, Ph.D., Professor of Psychiatry, Behavior Therapy Unit, EPPI, Temple University School of Medicine, Henry Avenue and Abbotsford Road, Philadelphia, Pennsylvania 19129

Allen J. Frances, M.D., Associate Professor of Psychiatry, Department of Psychiatry, The New York Hospital-Cornell University Medical Center, 525 East 68th Street, New York, New York 10021

Rachel Gittelman, Ph.D., Professor of Clinical Psychology, New York State Psychiatric Institute, and Columbia University, College of Physicians and Surgeons, 722 West 168th Street, New York, New York 10032

Byron Good, Ph.D., Assistant Professor of Medical Anthropology, Department of Social Medicine and Health Policy, Harvard Medical School, 25 Shattuck Street, Boston, Massachusetts 02115

Jack M. Gorman, M.D., Assistant Professor of Clinical Psychiatry, New York State Psychiatric Institute, and Columbia University, College of Physicians and Surgeons, 722 West 168th Street, New York, New York 10032

Jeffrey Gray, Ph.D., Professor and Head, Department of Psychology, Institute of Psychiatry, University of London, De Crespigny Park, Denmark Hill, London SE5 8AF, England

Mardi J. Horowitz, M.D., Professor of Psychiatry, Department of Psychiatry, Langley Porter Neuropsychiatric Institute, University of California, San Francisco, California 94143

Thomas Insel, M.D., Staff Psychiatrist, Clinical Neuropharmacology Branch, NIMH, Building 10, Room 3D41, NIH Reservation, Bethesda, Maryland 20205

Carroll Izard, Ph.D., Unidel Professor of Psychology, Department of Psychology, University of Delaware, Newark, Delaware 19711

Assen Jablensky, M.D., D.M.Sc., Senior Medical Officer, Division of Mental Health, World Health Organization, 1211 Geneva 27, Switzerland

Frederick Kanfer, Ph.D., Professor of Psychology, Department of Psychology, University of Illinois, 603 East Daniel, Champaign, Illinois 61820

Donald F. Klein, M.D., Professor of Psychiatry, Director of Research, New York State Psychiatric Institute, and Columbia University, College of Physicians and Surgeons, 722 West 168th Street, New York, New York 10032

Arthur Kleinman, M.D., M.A., Professor of Medical Anthropology at the Faculty of Arts and Sciences, and Professor of Psychiatry, Department of Social Medicine and Health Policy, Harvard Medical School, 25 Shattuck Street, Boston, Massachusetts 02115

Gerald L. Klerman, M.D., George Harrington Professor of Psychiatry, and Director, Stanley Cobb Research Laboratories, Department of Psychiatry, Bullfinch 3, Massachusetts General Hospital, Fruit Street, Boston, Massachusetts 02114

Michael J. Kozak, Ph.D., Assistant Professor of Psychiatry, Behavior Therapy Unit, EPPI, Temple University School of Medicine, Henry Avenue and Abbottsford Road, Philadelphia, Pennsylvania 19129

Malcolm Lader, M.D., Ph.D., Professor of Clinical Psychopharmacology, Institute of Psychiatry, University of London, De Crespigny Park, Denmark Hill, London SE5 8AF, England

Peter J. Lang, Ph.D., Graduate Research Professor, Department of Clinical Psychology, University of Florida, J. Hillis Miller Health Center, Box J165, Gainesville, Florida 32610

Jack D. Maser, Ph.D., Chief, Psychopathology and Clinical Methods Section, Clinical Research Branch, National Institute of Mental Health, 5600 Fishers Lane, Room 10C24, Rockville, Maryland 20857

Barbara Melamed, Ph.D., Professor of Psychology, and Director, Behavioral Medicine and Fear Clinic, Department of Clinical Psychology, J. Hillis Miller Health Center Box J165, University of Florida, Gainesville, Florida 32610

Robert Michels, M.D., Barklie McKee Henry Professor and Chairman, Department of Psychiatry, The New York Hospital-Cornell University Medical Center, 525 East 68th Street, New York, New York 10021

Neal E. Miller, Ph.D., Professor Emeritus and Head, Laboratory of Physiological Psychology, Rockefeller University, 1230 York Avenue, New York, New York 10021

Susan Mineka, Ph.D., Associate Professor of Psychology, Department of Psychology, University of Wisconsin-Madison, Madison, Wisconsin 53706

Dennis L. Murphy, M.D., Chief, Clinical Neuropharmacology Branch, NIMH, Building 10, Room 3D41, NIH Reservation, Bethesda, Maryland 20205

Robert M. Post, M.D., Chief, Biological Psychiatry Branch, National Institute of Mental Health, Building 10, Room 3N212, NIH Reservation, Bethesda, Maryland 20205

Judith Godwin Rabkin, Ph.D., M.P.H., Associate Professor of Clinical Psychology in Psychiatry, New York State Psychiatric Institute, and Columbia University, College of Physicians and Surgeons, 722 West 168th Street, New York, New York 10032

S. Rachman, Ph.D., Professor and Director, Clinical Psychology Program, Department of Psychology, The University of British Columbia, 2075 Westbrook Mall, Vancouver, B.C., Canada V6T 1W5

D. Eugene Redmond, Jr. M.D., Associate Professor of Psychiatry, Department of Psychiatry, Yale University School of Medicine, 333 Cedar Street, New Haven, Connecticut 06510

Peter P. Roy-Byrne, M.D., Medical Staff Fellow, Unit on Anxiety and Affective Disorders, Biological Psychiatry Branch, NIMH, Building 10, Room 3S239, NIH Reservation, Bethesda, Maryland 20205

Irwin G. Sarason, Ph.D., Professor, Department of Psychology, University of Washington, Seattle, Washington 98105

Richard I. Shader, M.D., Professor and Chairman, Department of Psychiatry, Tufts University School of Medicine, 171 Harrison Avenue, Boston, Massachusetts 02111

M. Katherine Shear, M.D., Assistant Professor of Psychiatry, Department of Psychiatry, The New York Hospital-Cornell University Medical Center, 525 East 68th Street, New York, New York 10021

Lawrence J. Siegel, Ph.D., Associate Professor of Pediatrics, Department of Pediatrics, University of Texas Medical Branch, Galveston, Texas 77550

Charles D. Spielberger, Ph.D., Professor and Director, Center for Research in Behavioral Medicine and Community Psychology, Department of Psychology, University of South Florida, Tampa, Florida 33620

Robert L. Spitzer, M.D., Professor and Chief, Biometrics Research Department, New York State Psychiatric Institute, and Columbia University, College of Physicians and Surgeons, 722 West 168th Street, New York, New York 10032

Peter Stokes, M.D., Professor of Psychiatry, and Chief, Division of Psychobiology, The New York Hospital-Cornell University Medical Center, 525 East 68th Street, New York, New York 10021

Auke Tellegen, Ph.D. Professor of Psychology, Department of Psychology, University of Minnesota, Minneapolis, Minnesota 55455

A. Hussain Tuma, Ph.D., Chief, Clinical Research Branch, National Institute of Mental Health, 5600 Fishers Lane, Room 10C24, Rockville, Maryland 20857

Thomas Uhde, M.D., Chief, Unit on Anxiety and Affective Disorders, Biological Psychiatry Branch, NIMH, Building 10, Room 3S239, NIH Reservation, Bethesda, Maryland 20205

Eberhard H. Uhlenhuth, M.D., Professor and Acting Chairman, Department of Psychiatry, Box 411, University of Chicago Medical School, 950 East 59th Street, Chicago, Illinois 60637

Bernard J. Vittone, M.D., Medical Staff Fellow, Unit on Anxiety and Affective Disorders, Biological Psychiatry Branch, NIMH, Building 10, Room 3S239, NIH Reservation, Bethesda, Maryland 20205

Herbert Weiner, M.D., Professor of Psychiatry, and Chief of Behavioral Medicine, Neuropsychiatric Institute, University of California, Los Angeles, 760 Westwood Plaza, Los Angeles, California 90024

Myrna M. Weissman, Ph.D., Professor of Psychiatry, and Director, Depression Research Unit, and Department of Psychiatry, Yale University School of Medicine, 904 Howard Avenue, Suite 2A, New Haven, Connecticut, 06519

Janet B. W. Williams, D.S.W., Associate Professor of Clinical Psychiatric Social Work in Psychiatry, Biometrics Research Department, New York State Psychiatric Institute, and Columbia University, College of Physicians and Surgeons, 722 West 168th Street, New York, New York 10032

Theodore P. Zahn, Ph.D., Research Psychologist, Unit on Psychophysiology, Laboratory of Psychology & Psychopathology, NIMH, Building 10, Room 4C118, NIH Reservation, Bethesda, Maryland 20205

Preface

The 1980s have been called the decade of anxiety. Not only is this true of the popular press, but students of behavior and psychopathology have contributed to the rather sudden reemergence of anxiety as a respectable and fascinating field of investigation. At one time, the psychological journals abounded with studies on anxiety, and the leading theory of mental illness in psychiatry held that neurotic anxiety underlay nearly all psychopathology. Then, for no obvious reason, anxiety research suddenly ebbed in the psychological research literature.

If the number of grant applications received by the National Institute of Mental Health (NIMH) can serve as a guide, the major preoccupation of the research community in the 1950s and 1960s was with schizophrenia, and in the 1970s with the affective disorders. Some four years ago we anticipated that a significant surge of research interest in the anxiety disorders would develop in the 1980s. Today, that prediction seems more plausible to us than ever.

A review of anxiety research supported by the NIMH in 1981 revealed a relative dearth of both a knowledge base and an active research interest in the construct and nature of anxiety and its pathological manifestations. In order to stimulate the field, the Clinical Research Branch of the NIMH's Division of Extramural Research Programs initiated a series of activities with the aims of assessing the state of current knowledge, sensitizing the field to specific questions requiring collaboration among researchers, and identifying major theoretical and methodological directions in the area of anxiety disorders. A second aim, represented in this volume, was to disseminate this information in the hope of serving the needs of investigators, educators, students, clinicians, and other groups for which this area holds some interest.

The task began in 1982 with a small group of consultants to the staff of the Clinical Research Branch, who provided encouragement and advice on undertaking a major state-of-the-art review of the field. The consultants agreed on the importance of a major conference for identifying research issues and discussing future directions. That meeting was followed by a full year of planning the specific content areas to be reviewed and selecting participants on the basis of their contributions to basic biological and psychological research relevant to anxiety and to the study of its pathological manifestations. Nineteen basic and clinical researchers were commissioned to write a series of issue-oriented critical analyses of the literature to serve as background documents for a three-day conference on anxiety and anxiety disorders that was held at the Sterling Forest Conference Center, Tuxedo, New York, in September, 1982.

This volume is a culmination of more than two years of planning, literature reviews, writing, conference discussions, revising of original papers, and integrating the material for final publication. It is not a collection of disconnected papers written independently by scholars or observers; it is a series of interrelated statements about research on anxiety and the anxiety disorders written by many of the leading investigators currently active in this field. By the time the final manuscripts were submitted, most of the participants had read each other's preliminary chapters and could refer to them in their own contributions. Often the intense discussions held at the Sterling Forest Conference were carried over and incorporated into the final versions of individual chapters. There is, therefore, more "cross talk" between chapter writers than is usually found in an edited book of this type.

At the conference, the role of the discussants was to assist in further defining major scientific issues and in identifying research data and information felt to be relevant but missing from specific reviews provided to them. Many of the discussants used the opportunity to present their views of the field in far greater detail than what they had presented at the meeting.

For these reasons the book is not the proceedings of a conference. Although the conference was a forerunner of *Anxiety and the Anxiety Disorders*, the book stands on its own as a summary of research and thinking about anxiety.

While the NIMH sponsored the conference and covered most of its costs, we acknowledge with pleasure the financial contribution of Hoffman-LaRoche, Inc. for making it possible for some of the participants, especially those from Europe, to attend. Medicine in the Public Interest provided invaluable administrative support.

Dr. Martin Katz, past Chief of the Clinical Research Branch, met with us for many hours over the 8 months of planning, and his ideas and sage advice contributed significantly to the success of the meeting. Dr. Lyle Bivens, Deputy Director of the Division of Extramural Research Programs and Dr. Herbert Pardes, Director of the NIMH at that time gave us the administrative support that was needed. Moreover, Dr. Pardes welcomed the opportunity to address the conference participants and to signal the Institute's endorsement of and support for the goals of the meeting. Dr. Ellen Simon Stover was also helpful in the early stages of our planning, and Elizabeth Breckinridge in the later stages. Clerical assistance from Mrs. Dona McLemore and Mrs. Karen Kemp, of the NIMH staff, was invaluable. At the conference we found the staff at Sterling Forest Conference Center exceptionally willing to help solve the problems that invariably occur despite the best of plans.

Clearly, our heartfelt appreciation and congratulations go to the individual chapter authors whose scientific work and scholarship are embodied in this book. Their enthusiasm and cooperation made this publication possible.

Our publisher, Lawrence Erlbaum and his staff, particularly Art Lizza, were most helpful and accommodating at every step. We are very pleased to bring this aspect of our programmatic efforts to a conclusion and hope that clinical researchers concerned with anxiety and the Anxiety Disorders will find this publication an aid in their work.

The Editors

February 1985

Introduction and Overview of Selected Issues[1,2]

A. Hussain Tuma and
Jack D. Maser

SIGNIFICANCE OF THE PROBLEM

The various roles of anxiety in human behavior and in psychiatric disorders have long been recognized by psychologists, psychiatrists, and psychophysiologists. The instrumental survival value of anxiety must be acknowledged to be as essential in human experience as that of pain. Research attention to the biological, behavioral, and experiential components of anxiety has, however, waned in the past several decades. Much of the early impetus to examine the source and roles of anxiety in psychiatric disorders came from psychoanalytic writings, particularly those of Freud and his students based on case histories and clinical observations of individuals. Significant contributions also were made by behavioral psychologists concerned primarily with the treatment of fears and phobias, particularly in children. World military conflicts and catastrophies provided opportunity for field studies of stress and anxiety under naturalistic conditions, but these efforts were not, for the most part, systematic, broad gauged, or coordinated. Clearly, there is a pressing need to explore biological, psychological, and behavioral components of anxiety; to develop valid models that can bring these phenomena under laboratory control; and to construct theories that accommodate and summarize existing knowledge while simultaneously serving a heuristic function.

[1]The opinions expressed here are those of the authors and do not necessarily represent the position of the National Institute of Mental Health. Requests for reprints should be addressed to either author, Clinical Research Branch, NIMH, Room 10C24, 5600 Fishers Lane, Rockville, Maryland 20857.

[2]In highlighting some of the conceptual and methodological issues, the authors often paraphrased or quoted from papers in this volume and from discussions at the 1983 Sterling Forest Conference.

A few of the fundamental questions that need to be answered are: What constitutes an anxiety response? What are its neurological, psychological, and behavioral components? Is this response expressed differently at different stages of human development? How is it modified by cognitive, neuroendocrine, and social environmental influences? Are there basic individual differences in vulnerability to pathological forms of anxiety? What are the critical factors that contribute to these individual differences, and what are the biological and psychological mechanisms that may be involved in causing such differences? Can the emergence of pathological anxiety response be prevented or modified; by what mechanisms and under what circumstances? What role, if any, does anxiety play in such other psychiatric disorders as depression, schizophrenia, schizoaffective disorders, anorexia nervosa, sleep pathologies, and sexual dysfunctions. These and similar questions that flood this area of research represent the concerns of the community of researchers whose work is reported in this volume.

BACKGROUND

The primary goal of this introduction is to provide background information about this volume. It is intended to serve as a guide that may facilitate understanding of this book's structure and content. The chapters that follow are grouped into several basic and clinical sections. Each section is a collection of leading investigators' reviews of major findings, theoretical positions, substantive and methodological issues, and suggested approaches for future research. The reviews do not aspire to be comprehensive; emphasis is on covering major research efforts rather than being exhaustive. Similarly, this introduction highlights a few selected issues and refers to only some of the chapters as illustrative examples; no attempt is made at complete coverage of every important topic contained in this volume.

In addition to those scientists who prepared reviews of their respective areas of research, many others were asked to serve as formal discussants of the review papers. As many of these discussants committed their ideas to paper, their chapters not only came to provide a critique and a different point of view but, evolved into complementary theoretical statements meant to have broader impact and become more than "mere" discussions. All authors were encouraged to cross-reference each other's material and relate it to other represented areas. This book, therefore, is a more thorough and complete presentation of ideas and data than what transpired at the Sterling Forest Conference (see Preface).

The fundamental orientation of the editors and conference organizers has been clinical. Our central concern is with the data, theories, and research strategies that may help define anxiety and illuminate its etiology, diagnosis, and classification. Concern with strategies for the treatment of anxiety is limited here to their potential for understanding this class of disorders.

Anxiety and the Anxiety Disorders begins with a substantial coverage of basic research in the neurobiology, neuropsychology, psychology, and psychobiology of anxiety in animals and humans. The emphasis on basic research is deliberate. It stems from the editors' conviction that progress in resolving clinical problems depends on knowledge in the biological, psychological, and sociocultural sciences. The clinical studies that follow cover a spectrum of epidemiological, cross-cultural, psychosomatic, developmental, treatment, and psychodynamic approaches, each with its own database, theoretical constructs, and methodological issues. Four chapters on the assessment of anxiety in both children and adults present a considerable range of opinion, instruments, and psychometric attitudes that seem vital to the researcher wishing to investigate anxiety and the Anxiety Disorders. The volume ends with several chapters on diagnosis and classification. It is our hope that the issues discussed throughout this volume will capture the interest of the research-oriented reader and will lead to increased productivity in this area of psychopathology. We turn now to a discussion of some of these issues.

ANIMAL STUDIES AND ANIMAL MODELS

Given the prominence of laboratory animal research, particularly the development of animal models for the study of human health problems, several authors in this volume have stressed the importance of developing appropriate animal models for human anxiety, both normal and pathological.

In Chapter 10, the history of the use of animal models in psychology and psychiatry is traced from Pavlov (1927), Liddell, Gantt, Masserman and Maier (1930s and 1940s) to the more recent work of Wolpe (1958), McKinney (1974), Seligman (1974, 1975), Akiskal and McKinney (1975), and Suomi and Harlow (1977). The theoretical models invoked by these workers are based on either important features of mental disorders or etiological contrasts with anxiety and other disorders of affect. Full-fledged animal models for phobias, Obsessive-Compulsive Disorder, or generalized anxiety states do not yet exist. Although animal research has illuminated important features of these disorders, Dr. Mineka concludes that research on subhuman species has had a marginal impact on understanding the origin of signs and symptoms and their mediating mechanisms in humans.

Conditioning has been the mechanism most often considered, but, as an adequate explanatory model of etiology, conditioning is too simplistic. Even complex forms of conditioning leave out many factors, including early childhood experiences and variables related to a sense of control and mastery. The conditioning literature virtually ignores predispositional and genetic factors.

Based on clinical observation of separation anxiety in human and animal infants, Klein sees a need for animal models of human psychopathology. He suggests the possibility of repeated inbreeding of animals to produce models of separation anxiety. If successful, such inbreeding may provide clinically useful analogues of human anxiety. This suggestion clearly is based on a genetic conception of anxiety-proneness or vulnerability.

Compelling as some of these arguments may be, the reader should consider Kanfer's admonition about the limitations of animal models in understanding human anxiety. In briefly reviewing the history of mind-body interaction from Descartes through Darwin and the functionalism and behaviorism in American psychology, Chapter 11 asserts that, ". . . contributions of cognitive and symbolic variables that modify simple input-output relationships play a significant role in maintaining human anxiety." However, "To date, these cognitive factors have not yet been investigated or perhaps are beyond reach in the animal laboratory." Thus, our current understanding of human anxiety is hampered by difficulties in generalizing across species with vastly different CNS structures and functional capacities. Chapter 11 bluntly challenges the ecological validity of findings that are based on contrived laboratory situations. The laboratory seldom closely approximates the complexities of living with which organisms in the natural environment must cope. One goal for the next generation of researchers is to facilitate making laboratory settings more representative of human experience.

We fully acknowledge the importance and contributions of animal models of fear and anxiety, and believe that animal models of Anxiety Disorders have greater face validity than most current models of other psychiatric disorders. Nevertheless, we would argue that human and animal researchers too often ignore ethological considerations. Laboratory guinea pigs (of all species) have evolved into different environmental niches, and each species probably derives a unique meaning of the world from its phylogenetic heritage and life experience. In some species, the sense of smell is more highly developed than in others, whereas cognitive sophistication in conceptualizing abstract ideas and probabilities that certain events will occur (e.g., death) appears to differ across species. The perception of electric shock that different species of animals might have is likely to vary depending on the functional adaptations that have evolved due to environmental pressures and the particular past history of a given member of that species. Primarily because the database in ethology is so limited, one cannot be certain of the range of restrictions that must be placed on conclusions derived from animal models of behavior.

CONTINUITY VERSUS DISCONTINUITY

A variety of anxiety states can be readily identified. These may range from hypoanxiety, where the individual seldom, if ever, experiences anxiety, to "normal" anxiety, where the emotional response is proportional to the perceived risk or danger. Normal anxiety is a state that acts as a positive motivating force towards adaptive coping. The range of anxiety response may further include a state of acute fear, discomfort, and tension that seems to be incongruent with conscious reality and that reduces effective cognitive functioning (e.g., stage fright, school phobia). Still more severe and debilitating are those states that call for clinical treatment and even hospitalization. Finally, there is a state of panic or terror that may exacerbate a disorder (e.g., depression) or be the basis for another disorder (e.g., agoraphobia).

Whether these conditions simply represent a different degree of severity along a single dimension or are qualitatively different categories of anxiety is the core of the continuity/discontinuity issue. This issue surfaces throughout the book in the context of co-morbidity and diagnostic categories and in the very conception of and distinction between normal and pathological anxiety. Zubin (1968, 1978) pointed out that the dichotomy between continuity and discontinuity models was artifactual. It is the state of the art in the field that determines whether the categorical or the dimensional view is most widely accepted.

Klein argues rather persuasively for the discontinuity model in the classification of Anxiety Disorders. He articulates an ongoing contrast in research strategy. Some investigators hold to a continuity model of normal to pathological anxiety, a belief most often grounded in their training and the populations with which they deal. For similar reasons, other researchers hold to a model that assumes pathological anxiety to be qualitatively different from normal anxiety. This difference in viewpoint leads to differences in research strategies and interpretations of the data.

Tellegen believes that we tend to converge on prototypes, but in so doing we may err by mistaking a small sample prototype for a junction or break in the continuum. There is a danger, at least for the purpose of studying naturally occurring variations and patterns of co-variation, to focus on prematurely and narrowly defined prototypes. To accomplish this purpose, studies of substantial numbers of relatively unselected "normal" and "ill" subjects are required. If this strategy is used, the distinctiveness of a categorical entity may at least become less hypothetical.

A recent attempt to reconcile the continuity and categorical perspectives is seen in Achenbach and Edelbrock (1983) and Achenbach (this volume), in which a taxonomy of profile patterns is derived from the Child Behavior Checklist.

How productive the continuity-discontinuity issue will be for the field is not yet clear, but it is generating useful research on mechanisms of psychopathology and on classification of disorders. For this reason alone it is a significant issue, and the reader will encounter it throughout the book.

THE ASSESSMENT OF ANXIETY

Only a few contributors to this volume appear satisfied with the instruments currently in use to assess anxiety, and our observation is that the field can benefit from new, creative approaches. The question of how to measure and diagnose anxiety properly seems inextricably bound to the researcher's conception of the phenomenon of anxiety.

Issues concerning assessment emerge directly from the three systems definition of the anxiety response (Lang, 1964, 1968, 1978, this volume) that seems to be adopted widely by the community of researchers and throughout this book. Consequently, these issues fall in the domains of: (a) verbal reports of the experience of anxiety, fear, dread, panic, worry, obsessions, guilt, inability to concentrate, lack of self efficacy, insecurity, and the like; (b) avoidance behavior, escape, hypervigilance, dysfunctional immobility, compulsive mannerisms, and deficits in attention, performance, and control; and (c) patterns of visceral and somatic activation as in increases in heart rate, blood pressure, sweating, generalized muscle tension, and concomitant biochemical changes. Data are slowly accumulating on when the various measures come together and when they are discordant. The occasions when the systems desynchronize and the sequence in which desynchrony occurs might be predictive of certain future events (Rachman & Hodgson, 1974).

Given that data from the three subsystems of anxiety response intercorrelate to only a limited degree and given that the variables underlying anxiety response in the three subsystems interact with each other, it follows that concomitant sampling and measurment in all three response systems is mandatory. If we accept the proposition that our research goals are to identify and understand the specific discrepancies and the specific links across data from the three systems, a single or even multiple measures within any one subsystem will, by definition, be inadequate.

Although assessment in all three subsystems faces certain conceptual and technical difficulties, those in the physiological domain seem less problematic, possibly due to conceptual and methodological advances in that and related fields. A wide variety of physiological and biological measures have been used in studies of emotions. These have been applied to both somatic and visceral physiology and include: measures of epinephrine, norepinephrine, and their metabolites; gastric motility, secretion, and blood supply to the gut; increments in heart rate, blood pressure, respiration rate, muscle tension, skin temperature, galvanic skin response; and changes in facial muscles by electromyography and facial expression. Issues concerning central nervous system (CNS) measures of anxiety on the biochemical and electrophysiological levels are discussed at length in several chapters and are highlighted elsewhere in this Introduction.

Assessment of behavioral aspects of the anxiety response receives only indirect attention in this volume. Behavioral assessment of anxiety has been the topic of several publications (e.g., Barlow, 1981; Hersen & Bellack, 1981) and is typically attended to in the context of behavioral treatments of Anxiety Disorders, particularly in the context of assessing treatment outcome. The measures usually include performance tests and direct observations of specific behaviors by trained observers in either a laboratory-type setting or a natural environment. Behaviors that are assessed include frequency, intensity, and pervasiveness of phobic avoidance and escape; time spent on ritualistic behaviors and compulsive mannerisms; decrement in performance especially along dimensions of attention, memory, and other cognitive processes. Psychometric properties (e.g., internal consistency, test-retest reliability, external validity, sensitivity, and specificity) of the available measures are, for the most part, not adequately established or known.

The area that receives perhaps most concern in this volume is the assessment of subjective experience by means of verbal reports, as in the use of symptom checklists, rating scales, interviews and questionnaires. Although there may be some fundamental philosophical issues concerning rules of evidence that should govern the study of human experience, the most immediate and practical issue is how to objectively measure subjective experience. Objective measurement will not proceed very far until the defining properties of feeling states and emotions are specified and agreed upon. What would be a useful definition of the phenomenology of personal experience? How might self-reports be calibrated and adjusted in order to make them more precise? What factors in the relationship between a clinical interviewer and the interviewee can be manipulated to maximize the accuracy of self-reports? What could be done to assure the inclusion of both positive and negative perceptions? If anxious or phobic subjects suffer from a "deficit" in self-efficacy, how can the impact of such self-perceptions on their reports be accounted for and measured? Would it be helpful to carry out comparative studies of self-reports in several settings or contexts with the goal of identifying similarities and dissimilarities in self-report information given to a physician, psychologist, spouse, or employer?

Worry is one type of cognition frequently mentioned by authors in this book, and much of Chapter 25 is devoted to the topic. Worry may play an adaptive role, but our concern is with its maladaptive aspect. In this regard, worry appears conceptually related to several other intrusive mental events: obsessive thoughts and hallucinations. At the very least, such aberrant cognitions are a source of suffering for the victim and are often the symptom that brings the individual into a clinic. There is relatively little in the literature on the measurement of worry, and this topic should be given more attention by cognitive researchers.

Given the possibility that current self-report instruments can assess experience only at a certain threshold of awareness, then what can be done to assess experiences that may fall below that threshold in one or another context and thus may not be reported? What is lacking is a methodology that allows the measurement of unconscious cognitions and motivations. Are there methods that can be adapted from the field of information processing to meet such a need? For example, consider panic attacks as a psychological reaction to the content of one's thoughts. Psychodynamic and cognitive researchers may well be interested in exploring the regularity of specific cognitive content that precedes the onset of panic attacks. Perhaps the first several attacks begin with a feeling of dread or anxiety, followed by an interval that is increasingly filled with mental elaboration that rises to a crescendo of terror. Therefore, what may appear to the clinician as a "spontaneous" panic state may be the endstate of the foregoing cognitive/affective process. The future may witness the emergence of new techniques to measure such phenomena.

To some degree this technology already exists. For example, "thought sampling" (see Chapter 9), in which people perceive a stimulus at various time intervals, has been used by cognitive assessors. The types of cognitions that emerge in agorophobics are often danger related, particularly when the stimulus is associated with an anxiety-arousing event. Also reported are thoughts dealing with how to cope in the situation, including the incapacitating thought that the individual is helpless.

Some authors hold that adequate measures of the anxiety experience are currently available and that greater systematic use of such existing measures as the MMPI-derived scales (Chapter 35) and the Spielberger state-trait measure (Chapter 8) is needed. However, many clinical investigators contributing to this volume seem to believe that current instruments do not correspond to clinical observations, and they are often insufficiently sensitive to current theories of anxiety.

Another set of issues concerns the level of descriptive detail required for answering such specific questions as whether or not Panic Disorder and agoraphobia represent extreme degrees of anxiety or are categorically (qualitatively) different phenomena. For example, can the mental content of the experience of a "spontaneous" panic attack be specified, and can the data gathered be sufficiently detailed to be suitable for testing dimensional and categorical diagnostic concepts? Both self-report measures and behavioral measures of panic are distinctly lacking. For purposes of obtaining rational answers to the issue of qualitative versus quantitative distinctions among disorders, appropriately fine-grained measures would help avoid forcing the data into one or the other conceptual framework.

A related feature of unbiased assessment would be to avoid narrowly focused and hierarchically-structured approaches. This would entail the use of multivariate approaches and the utilization of a wider range of information in assessing co-morbidities such as anxiety and depression, and the cooccurrence of Generalized Anxiety Disorder with specific phobias and Somatoform Disorders. Another desirable feature is that sources of data should include not only the subject's self-report, physiological, and behavioral data, but also data from significant other observers of the subject (e.g., parents, spouse, peers, teachers, co-workers, and employer).

An approach to assessment on which virtually all authors seem to agree is a developmental multivariate one that concurrently assesses subjective experience, physiological events, and behavioral responses along with data from significant others. Detailed examination of intercorrelations among these domains of data under different conditions, as in the case of laboratory intervention (e.g., lactate infusion) in one domain and observation of pattern, timing and nature of change in other domains, seems most promising. Such assessments under naturalistic settings and also under various psychological and biological therapeutic conditions repeated over time will provide data likely to address some of the questions concerning the psychobiological mechanisms of anxiety response.

DEVELOPMENT AND ANXIETY

Is there a continuity of anxiety states from childhood to adult life? Are persons who have had an extraordinary level of childhood fears more prone to adult anxiety disorders than children with more ordinary fears? Subsumed under these broad questions are several issues that merit further consideration and investigation. For instance, can we state precisely the definition and assessment of the phenomenon of anxiety and anxiety disorders in children at various stages of their affective, cognitive, and social development? Do children evidence one or more patterns of behavioral responses in the face of anxiety-provoking situations? Are there buffers or protective factors in normal coping with stress that guard against pathological sequella of anxiety, and when these buffers are missing can coping be taught? Is there a relationship between a particular personality structure (e.g., compulsive, hysterical, etc.) and the type of Anxiety Disorder that develops? Not just in childhood, but across the age span, are there critical points of vulnerability for the emergence of anxiety-based psychological and somatic problems? What is the role of cognitive processes, including learning, in emotional development and, inversely, what is the role of anxiety in the formation of cognitive schema, and more broadly, personality formation?

In order to address these questions, prospective, longitudinal studies of children with and without pathological anxiety are necessary. Certainly at the Sterling Forest conference there was unanimous agreement on the need for longitudinal research on children at various degrees of risk for emotional disorders, including pathological anxiety. Repeated, multifaceted assessments of these children over time may be the best means to ascertain the stability of symptom expression, record the presence of positive and negative behaviors, and measure their biological concomitants. In this regard, there is a serious lack of normative developmental data on the emotions and on potential modifiers of emotional responding (e.g., parental behavior, peer interactions). Accurate knowledge of the course of an illness, both in its natural and in its treated states, would be a significant contribution to understanding these disorders and their relationship to other illnesses. Consideration of how different classes of variables in childhood, adolescence, middle age, and old age modify coping strategies will provide insight into the various forms these disorders may take throughout the lifespan.

Unfortunate, frightening, and sometimes tragic events occur in life. For the researcher, this means that not all stressful situations need to be artificially contrived in laboratory settings. Among the researchers that view stressful events in living as scientific opportunities are Melamed and Siegel. In Chapter 19 they specifically discuss fears in such normally occurring anxiety-provoking experiences as hospitalization, going to school, and visits to the dentist. Particularly important for current theoretical notions is the fact that the first two of these experiences usually involve separation from parents or caretakers. Psychosomatic and stress researchers have also capitalized on natural situations in which anxiety is expected to occur: combat, parachute jumping, presenting cases at grand rounds, and undergraduate public speaking classes. The reader is referred to Chapters 16, 17, and 18, which illustrate further studies on somatic changes induced by stressful, life events.

CO-MORBIDITY

The issue of co-morbidity—or more accurately at the present state of our knowledge, similarity and overlap of symptoms—in psychiatric disorders is both fascinating and problematic. Not infrequently, two or more different disorders will co-occur in the same individual, but this fact alone does not constitute a need for research unless it is reported in an unexpectedly high percentage of cases. In such instances, the phenomenon becomes theoretically attractive, because some fundamental questions about common etiological mechanisms and possible overlap among diagnostic criteria may emerge.

One area in psychiatric nosology for which considerable suggestive evidence is emerging is the co-morbidity between Anxiety Disorders and Depressive Disorders. Many clinicians have written about this phenomenon, and some have even incorporated it into their theoretical formulation of the Affective Disorders (Lewis, 1938) in order to accommodate the clinical experience where depression is encountered as a frequent complication of Anxiety Disorders and anxiety symptoms as common elements of primary depressive illness. Sir Martin Roth (1959) was the first to report that over half a sample of patients suffering phobic anxiety-depersonalization syndrome also exhibited "brooding gloom reminiscent of reactive depression."

To the extent that psychiatric diagnosis and classification continue to be based on syndromal, phenomenological data alone, symptoms such as tension, fear, anxiety, worry, avoidance behavior, and the like will continue to appear as prominent features of a variety of conditions, including those currently classified as Anxiety Disorders, Affective Disorders, psychosomatic disorders, sleep, eating and sexual disorders, and alcoholism, among others. Many of these symptoms represent general organismic responses to external threats and/or to concomitant internal psychobiological events. As such, they constitute a general symptom or index of disturbance that several disorders may have in common, and not necessarily a unique or specific feature that characterizes a particular disorder.

The current excitement and interest in the similarity between Anxiety Disorders and depression is the result of the convergence of suggestive data from disparate clinical and laboratory sources, mainly over the past two and a half decades. These data tend to come from several domains including: (a) the domain of symptoms (e.g., in patients with major affective illness, anxiety is almost always a prominent symptom); (b) the clinical course of syndromes (e.g., a substantial proportion of Panic Disorder and Obsessive Compulsive Disorder patients have a lifetime incidence of depression); (c) with regard to neurobiological characteristics or "markers" (e.g., both obsessive compulsive and panic-anxious patients have significantly blunted growth hormone response to clonidine, an abnormality that is consistently reported in depressive patients; (d) epidemiological family studies of depression (e.g., anxiety disorders are common in both depressed probands and their first degree relatives); and (e) in responses to treatment (e.g., patients with Panic Disorders and agoraphobia and also depressives have very similar responses to tricyclic antidepressant and monoamine oxidase inhibitor medications).

Despite the seemingly strong evidence for the reported co-occurrence of Depressive and Anxiety Disorders, many issues and problems lead to uncertainty, ambiguity and controversy in this area. These issues include: (a) lack of adequate operational definition and quantification of anxiety in its various normal and pathological forms; (b) lack of appropriate and accurate instruments for measuring anxiety in normals and others for measuring pathological anxiety in patients; (c) dependence on symptom patterns, verbal reports, or biological events *alone*, without concurrent reference to data in the other two domains; (d) the DSM-III hierarchical rule regarding the primacy of the diagnosis of depression when symptoms of both depression and anxiety coexist (see Chapter 40).

In addition to these definitional, design, diagnostic, and measurement issues, there are other basic substantive issues that need to be addressed. For example, does the overlap or relationship between anxiety and depression contribute to the severity of depression? Does the close relationship between the clinical symptoms of anxiety and depression suggest that they share some of the same biological systems and/or neural circuitry? Some investigators conclude that panic disorders, with or without agoraphobia and major depressive illness, simply represent different expressions of the same underlying biological disturbance. Should this prove to be the case, then what are the cognitive and perceptual mechanisms that may explain some of the different manifestations of similar biological substrates? Chapter 14 describes cultural variables that too often are overlooked. Other investigators emphasize the differences between anxiety and depression, citing data from identical twin studies and sleep studies. Such studies suggest genetic and psychophysiological differences between these forms of psychopathology; consequently, they hold that Panic Disorder and Major Depressive Disorder represent separate psychobiological conditions. Should this be the case, then what type of research approaches are necessary to disentangle current data and provide clearer differentiation among these and related disorders?

The NIMH Epidemiologic Catchment Area Program reported on co-morbidity in a recent paper by Boyd et al. (1984). Based on the Diagnostic Interview Schedule (DIS), these investigators tested the DSM-III exclusion rule that a diagnosis not be made if the symptoms are "due to" another disorder. For example, Agoraphobia, School Phobia, Panic Disorder, Generalized Anxiety Disorder, and Obsessive Compulsive Disorder are not given as the primary diagnoses if their respective criteria are presumed to be due to Major Depression. The same hierarchical rule appears to apply to Simple Phobic Disorder, although Major Depression is not specifically mentioned, but it does not apply at all to Post-traumatic Stress Disorder. Clearly, use of this rule has at least two problems. First, the clinician may not be able to decide whether an obsessive behavior is due to depression or the depression is due to an obsessive behavior. Second, epidemiological data are potentially distorted by a hierarchical rule that by definition "suppresses" real phenomena. In this volume, Weissman's Chapter 13 provides considerable epidemiological data on the Anxiety Disorders.

Incidently, the co-morbidity likelihood or odds ratio for Agoraphobia and Panic Disorder has implications for etiology. If further survey data replicate (and extend) these findings, we may then conclude that there are in the community many agoraphobics without Panic Disorder, and perhaps a number of these have never had panic attacks. Should this be so, it suggests that two groups of agoraphobics may exist. One group originates from panic's "driving" the agoraphobic into an avoidance response; in the other, panic plays little or no role in avoidance behavior.

The issue of co-morbidity also has implications for research on the role of anxiety in a variety of other psychopathological conditions mentioned earlier. Less discussed in this volume (and clearly less documented) is the possible co-morbidity of anxiety and Personality Disorders, anxiety and Somatoform Disorders. Clinical lore holds that many persons with chronic, generalized anxiety have disorders of personality, a dictum apparently based in psychoanalytic theory but not sufficiently investigated beyond the case study method. An individual with a personality in which particular defense mechanisms predominate may be more vulnerable to certain anxiety disorders. Coping styles can be measured by researchers, and to the extent that these can be related to psychological defenses, this may be a means of assessing the relationship between personality type and anxiety disorder.

Not discussed at all are such issues as: (a) the intensity and pattern of anxiety and panic as a prominent feature of psychotic states; (b) the role of neurobiological events associated with anxiety in effecting the pathogenesis, course and outcome of somatic diseases; and (c) psychological consequences of biological abnormalities in somatic disorders that resemble those seen in anxiety states.

Current data and controversy with regard to the "co-morbidity" of anxiety and panic with other psychological and somatic disturbances have profound implications for the type of research designs and strategies needed in descriptive and experimental psychopathology. It is vital that these strategies take into account the many issues that are articulated throughout this volume and be responsive to the need for theoretical formulations that attempt to integrate what currently seem to be divergent data.

BIOLOGY OF ANXIETY

Studies on the biological aspects of anxiety seek to uncover the mechanisms by which neuropharmacologic, neuroanatomic or neurophysiologic stimuli increase or decrease anxiety. So much has been published in the past two decades in the neurosciences that researchers are hard pressed just to keep abreast of developments in their relatively narrow areas of expertise. This information explosion may lead one to forget that much of neuroscience is focused on monoamines (5-HT, NE, and Dopamine), which collectively represent less than 1% of CNS synapses. Many anxiogenic and anxioletic compounds have been found, but there is little doubt that many more exist. The discovery of anxiolytic drugs has fostered interest in the neurochemistry of anxiety, and, as our knowledge of brain biochemistry expands, it continues to suggest new pharmacotherapeutic compounds. None of these drugs is entirely selective for anxiety, and no single neurochemical system or neuroanatomical locus has been shown to mediate the effects of all anxiolytic drugs. Nevertheless, as a number of chapters demonstrate, major steps toward a neurochemical anatomy of anxiolytic drug action have already been taken. It is important to remember that the biology of anxiety is not necessarily the biochemistry of drug action. A variety of drugs have also been described as anxiogenic. Lactate, beta-carboline, isoproterenol, caffeine, and yohimbine produce anxiety states that may differ phenomenologically, physiologically, or neurochemically. Further study of the mechanisms of action of these compounds may shed light on the biologic origin of symptoms underlying different syndromes within the Anxiety Disorders.

The individual chapters address a number of technical and theoretical problems in the interpretation of this literature, but we will discuss only one here: central and peripheral events in the generation of panic attacks.

Isoproterenol is an anxiogenic agent that induces a panic-like anxiety state not unlike that induced by sodium lactate. However, very little, if any, isoproterenol crosses the blood-brain barrier. If it acts only or predominately on tissue outside the central nervous system, from where does the sensation and experience of panic arise? This question is a reminder that the CNS does not act in isolation from events that are spatially distant from it. With this in mind, assume for a moment that panic is the experiential result of the brain's reaction to a sudden dysfunction or change in the respiratory, circulatory, or thermoregulatory system. Especially if the change is subtle, and even if it triggers a variety of other physiological counteractions, all of these events may be below the individual's level of awareness. In such a case, the search for the cause of the panic would be difficult indeed. Some drugs might alleviate the anxiety state by their central actions, others by their peripheral actions. Neuroscientists are likely to follow their training and interest in the brain and ignore or play down the possible peripheral activity of compounds known for their central mechanisms of action. Clinicians might well describe the panic as spontaneous or unpredictable.

It may not be too fanciful to presume further that, after a series of panic attacks, the brain has become conditioned to respond with anxiety to even one or just a few of the peripheral changes. In Pavlovian terms this feedback from the periphery would be a conditioned stimulus (CS). Drugs like yohimbine or isoproterenol could produce their anxiogenic effects by activation of this CS, and the results would only mislead the investigator. Before we can have more confidence in our conclusions, a strategy must be devised to separate peripheral and central actions of these drugs.

It is of some interest that DSM-III defines disorders of anxiety by their behavioral manifestations (including self-reports and gross observation of certain psychophysiological events). Biologically oriented researchers have learned much about the neural and endocrine events underlying anxiety and its disorders, but this information has thus far contributed little to diagnosis, nosology or the nomenclature.

BIOLOGICAL MARKER

A biological marker may be defined as a structural and/or functional sign of a relatively specific disorder. The individual may express the marker symptomatically, or it may be present under subclinical conditions; it may be latent or carried in the individual's gene pool to be transmitted to his or her offspring. The marker may be etiologically implicated, or it may be an indirect result of the disease. The important point is that markers, when known, indicate the presence of or strong potential for disorders, and when specific, they are useful in differential diagnosis.

Mental health professionals have few such markers on which they can rely (e.g., as in Down's syndrome or phenylketonuria). In the anxiety disorders area, there are candidates for biological markers (e.g., lactate-induced panic, sleep patterns, and drug responsivity), but none seem to have better validation than behavior per se. It is safe to say that none of these putative markers are generally agreed upon, nor are we aware of any that are in routine use across clinical settings.

NEURAL & NEUROHORMONAL MECHANISMS

In this volume, Chapter One attempts to clarify the long-running controversy regarding the role of norepinephrine (NE) in those behavioral and biochemical changes induced by the learned helplessness paradigm. In so doing, Gray's logic and understanding of the data lead to the conclusion that the neural circuitries of anxiety and neurotic depression overlap. Still unaddressed are the relationship between psychotic depression and anxiety, the relation of anxiety to "toughening up" as an adaptation to stress, and whether drugs that block NE transmission increase the organism's sensitivity to anxiogenic stimuli. Nevertheless, the conclusion is reached that anxiety and depression overlap, a belief shared by many others.

Another chapter (2) argues that synapses releasing GABA regulate anxiety: Anxiety is reduced by enhanced activity of GABAergic neurons. Limbic structures, septum and amygdala in particular, are the suspected sites of ths GABA activity. Further research is needed at these sites, as well as research on the physiological role of the benzodiazepine recognition site. The function of the Diazepam Binding Inhibitor (DBI) needs clarification, since within the structure of this polypeptide may lie an endogenous anxiogenic or anxiolytic fragment.

No less complex than the role of neurotransmitters in anxiety is that of the hypothalamic-pituitary-adrenocortical (HYPAC) system. The multiple neuroendocrine HYPAC axes regulate hormonal release from the brain, pituitary, and peripheral glands. The great majority of clinical studies on the HYPAC system have been with samples of depressed patients, and similar information on non-depressed, well-diagnosed anxiety disorder patients lags far behind. Chapters 3, 16, and 17 provide overviews on what is known at the basic level and point out how research on stress has provided much of what is known in this area. One question that intrigues us is the potential for overlap in HYPAC function for anxiety and depression.

If multiple hormones are to be measured within one neuroendocrine axis, response patterning may help discriminate subgroups of depression and identity patients with both anxiety and affective symptomatology. It would be a significant step forward to understand what happens to the functioning of HYPAC subsystems in recovery or remission. Can the subsystem provide early signs of relapse? Once again, longitudinal studies, if the data existed, could reveal hormonal changes across the life span and give clinical investigators a baseline against which patient data could be evaluated.

ETIOLOGICAL IMPLICATIONS OF TREATMENT STUDIES

In their critical review of the etiological implications that one can draw from pharmacological treatments of anxiety, Klein, Rabkin and Gorman (this volume) conclude that their extensive search was not overly revealing. Redmond's review of the neurochemical basis of anxiety and anxiety disorders is somewhat more optimistic. This may be because the basic research approach of Chapter 28 seeks a more direct answer to the question of which neurochemical mechanisms are involved in anxiety. Such optimism is tempered by the expanding number of chemical compounds implicated in fear behavior. The field has moved from relatively simple notions of epinephrine and norepinephrine involvement to serotonin, adenosine, benzodiazepine receptors, GABA, and opioid peptides. Neither the various hormonal axes (e.g., the hypothalmo-pituitary-adrenal system) nor patterns of psychophysiological responding (e.g., blood pressure, skin resistance, cardiorespiratory systems) have been integrated at all with studies of central nervous system receptors.

Discussions of the pharmacological approaches to treatment bring up again the need for better definition and measurement of panic and anxiety by combining self-reports with behavioral and physiological measures and by utilizing graphics and computerized on-line technologies. There is value in using provocative pharmacological and psychological procedures in the laboratory to evoke anxiety and panic (e.g., lactate, carbon dioxide, psychological stress procedures, including imagery). It is clear that Klein's work on pharmacological dissection has clarified the nature of anxiety reactions by demonstrating that panic attacks play an etiological role in the development of agoraphobia. There is also the possibility of using reactions to the aforementioned provocative measures as independent, more or less objective indexes of treatment effectiveness, in addition to their current use in identifying etiological links or mechanisms. The use of amphetamine-like agents to turn off obsessional behavior is one such example that needs further investigation.

There is a need for better understanding of the effects of anxiolytic drugs on specific behaviors (e.g., punished behavior) in animals. This information would clarify the neurophysiological effects of these drugs and the mechanisms by which drugs alter behavior in normal and disease states. The fact that acquired behavioral patterns in anaimals can be modified or obliterated by anxiolytic drugs is important in studying the combined use of drugs and behavioral approaches to treatment of anxiety disorders. The question of whether or not there is an endogenous ligand of the GABA system or other modulators that interact with anxiolytic or anxiogenic drugs is an important area of research that is already ongoing and needs to be fostered.

Also, if tricyclics or monoamine oxidase inhibitors are, in fact, more effective than benzodiazepines in reducing some forms of human anxiety, then research should focus on the specific neurophysiological effects of these drugs and identify the specific mechanisms of their action. Hypotheses about neural mechanisms involved in producing anxiety-like behavior in the laboratory animal can then be tested on humans exhibiting similar states by using drugs known to alter particular neurotransmitters and observing any modification in the anxiety state.

Assuming that the efficacy of the benzodiazapines is due to their capacity to interfere with an anxiogenic compound in some neural circuit, then it is conceivable that people who have too much of an endogenous anxiogenic will manifest generalized anxiety. Therefore, they can conceivably benefit from benzodiazapine antagonists. This etiological model illustrates the possibility of unraveling the pathophysiology of panic by means of specific pharmacological challenges, tests or treatments that would work on one or another biologic circuit—serotonin, norepinephrine, etc. Generalized anxiety is viewed as an extremely heterogeneous group that could be further differentiated by means of pharmacological or behavioral dissection.

A great deal of the early research on the etiology of anxiety disorders occurred in the context of treatment studies. Thus, if the researcher's strategy was to compare outcomes after two or more treatments, say drug versus behavior therapy, it was likely that the result allowed inferences about the biological or learned components of the disorder (or their interaction). This tradition is reviewed and exemplified in Chapter 23. In a treatment context, Foa and Kozak attempt to relate Lang's theoretical position to clinical phenomena. They conclude that the development of psychopathology cannot be derived from knowledge of treatment outcome, but that data on the process of therapy can illuminate the impairments that underlie emotional disorders. Chapter 25 considers the paradox of treatment-induced anxiety observed among chronically anxious persons. If it were understood why a standard progressive relaxation procedure should generate an anxiety response in some patients, the etiology of anxiety in those cases might be better understood.

Whether the method of intervention is pharmacological or behavioral, they both may impact the neurophysiological processes in remarkably similar ways. For instance, by preventing the reuptake of norepinephrine, tricyclic drugs may initially aggravate the anxiety state but subsequently lead to postsynaptic undersensitivity and decreased autonomic nervous system activity. Likewise, exposure therapies are distinctly unpleasant and may even increase the subject's anxiety level when first introduced, yet in bombarding or flooding the noradrenergic system, they may ultimately lead to better synaptic homeostatis by lowering sensitivity and thereby reducing the impact of previously anxiety-provoking stimuli.

The last point exemplifies the need for a theoretical approach that is truly psychobiological, comprehensive and integrative. The editors hope that this volume will facilitate meeting this need.

The issues highlighted in this Introduction were meant to be illustrative. Several areas of research were either briefly mentioned or not mentioned at all. The developmental, longitudinal approach to the study of anxiety is neither fully utilized nor extensively represented in this volume. Similarly, sophisticated cross-cultural studies are seldom done, and the concepts embodied by this approach are not adequately represented in other areas of research reported on here. Chapters 14 and 39 are notable exceptions. We believe that the contributions of psychoanalytic theory in general, and particularly those concerning psychological defense mechanisms, warrant further attention. We need to know considerably more about psychological processes and mechanisms that mediate not only experiential and behavioral events, but also physiological events and the specific feedback loops that moderate human functioning at each level.

BASIC BIOLOGICAL AND PSYCHOLOGICAL RESEARCH APPROACHES TO ANXIETY

A. Neurobiology of Anxiety

1

Issues in the
Neuropsychology of Anxiety

Jeffrey A. Gray
University of Oxford

The purpose of this paper is to draw attention to a number of researchable issues in the neuropsychology of anxiety. Now, what is an "issue" in any subject depends upon one's point of view: it is theories which throw up questions, theories for which data pose problems. So, to sharpen perception of some issues, I shall start by presenting an outline of a theory of the neuropsychology of anxiety that has been developed in detail elsewhere (Gray, 1982a, 1982b).

A THEORY OF ANXIETY: THE ROLE OF THE LIMBIC SYSTEM

The Antianxiety Drugs

Progress in the study of the biological basis of anxiety has been critically dependent on the availability of drugs that, clinically, reduce human anxiety. By studying the behavioral changes produced by these drugs in experimental animals, it has been possible to establish a reasonably good understanding of the psychological nature of anxiety. Furthermore, by studying the physiological pathway by which the drugs produce their effects on behavior, it is possible to attack the problem of the neural basis of anxiety. I have reviewed the behavioral effects of the antianxiety drugs (benzodiazepines, barbiturates, and alcohol) elsewhere (Gray, 1977). Many hundreds of studies have been conducted, in species ranging from goldfish to chimpanzee. There is rarely any need to qualify a description of the behavioral effects of the antianxiety drugs with respect to species. Thus, assuming that the behavioral changes produced in animals by the antianxiety drugs are

5

indeed due to a reduction in anxiety, we may conclude that anxiety, and its neural basis, are phylogenetically relatively old.

However, the assumption that the antianxiety drugs reduce anxiety in animals cannot be made lightly. Support for this assumption comes from a consideration of the nature of the changes that the antianxiety drugs in fact produce in animal behavior (Gray, 1977). Although very diverse experimental paradigms have been used to describe these changes both within and between species, it is fairly simple to summarize them in an economical formula, as outlined below.

The antianxiety drugs counteract the behavioral effects of three classes of stimuli: stimuli associated with punishment, stimuli associated with the omission of expected reward ("frustrative nonreward"), and novel stimuli. Furthermore, they counteract all the major kinds of behavioral change produced by these stimuli, i.e., inhibition of ongoing behavior (and especially instrumental, that is, reinforced, behavior); increased attention to environmental, especially novel, stimuli; and an increased level of arousal (Gray, 1977). Finally, antianxiety drugs do *not* affect behavior elicited by other classes of reinforcing stimuli, including primary punishment and primary frustrative nonreward. These findings are summarized in Fig. 1. This figure illustrates the postulate that there is a behavioral inhibition system (BIS) upon which the antianxiety drugs act to produce their behavioral effects. The BIS is activated by the adequate inputs listed to the left of the figure and produces the outputs listed to the right. *Ex hypothesi,* activity in the BIS constitutes anxiety. According to this view, and in less technical language, anxiety in animals consists of a central state elicited by

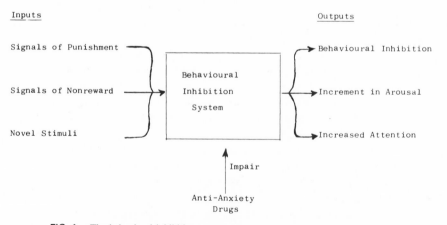

FIG. 1. The behavioral inhibition system.

threats of punishment, frustration or failure, and by novelty or uncertainty. This formulation is clearly plausible as a description of anxiety in humans, thus providing grounds for supposing that anxiety exists in animals, and in a form closely comparable to that taken by the human emotion.

The Brain and Anxiety

This evidence, then, suggests that it is possible to study the physiological basis of anxiety in experimental animals. There are two main ways in which this has been done. The first concentrates on an anxiolytic drug as drug. It asks, for example, how the drug affects neurons, whether it acts on specific receptors, and so on. The second way is more indirect: It concentrates on the behavioral effects of the drug, and attempts to find other manipulations of the brain which produce similar effects. The two approaches are complementary; each alone suffers from inevitable limitations.

Important advances in the direct study of antianxiety drug action have come from the demonstration of a receptor for the benzodiazepines located on neural membranes (Braestrup & Nielsen, 1980), and the establishment of a probable relation between this receptor and the inhibitory neurotransmitter, gamma-aminobutyric acid (GABA) (Guidotti, Toffano, & Costa, 1978). Furthermore, facilitation of GABA-ergic transmission is produced by the barbiturates as well as by the benzodiazepines (Barker & Ransom, 1978). But, if antianxiety action depends on facilitated GABA-ergic transmission, a proposition for which the psychopharmacological evidence is in any case equivocal (Gray, Quintero, & Mellanby, 1983; Thiébot, Jobert, & Soubrié, 1979) this is likely to be only at specific and critical points in the brain (Gray, 1979).

The more indirect, behavioral approach to the problem suggests that such a critical site of antianxiety drug action is likely to lie in the limbic system. The structures most strongly implicated are the septo-hippocampal system and its afferents and efferents (Ciba Foundation, 1978). There is substantial overlap between the profile of behavioral change observed after septal and hippocampal lesions, on the one hand, and administration of antianxiety drugs on the other (Gray, 1982a). This pattern of results has given rise to the hypothesis that the antianxiety drugs act in some way on the septo-hippocampal system to produce those changes that are critical for their antianxiety effects. One possibility is that the antianxiety drugs act on critical afferents to the septo-hippocampal system. There is evidence to support this possibility with respect to two pathways: the noradrenergic afferents to the septo-hippocampal system from the locus coeruleus, and the serotonergic afferents from the raphe nuclei.

Activity is increased in both these pathways by stress and this increase is counteracted by antianxiety drugs (Lidbrink, Corrodi, Fuxe, & Olson, 1973). Furthermore, destruction of either pathway, most often produced by local injection of a specific neurotoxin, gives rise to certain critical behavioral changes also seen after injection of antianxiety drugs (Gray, 1982a). It is possible, therefore, that the critical action of the antianxiety drugs that underlies their antianxiety behavioral effects consists in a reduction in the flow of noradrenergic and serotonergic impulses to the septo-hippocampal system under conditions of stress. This hypothesis is not in conflict with the biochemical and neurophysiological evidence indicating that these drugs enhance GABA-ergic transmission. Such enhancement might inhibit the firing of cells in the locus coeruleus and/or the raphe nuclei, both of which probably receive GABA-ergic afferents. Enhanced GABA-ergic inhibition acting presynaptically at the terminals of these neurons is a further possibility (Gray et al., 1984).

If we accept this hypothesis, it is possible to gain further insight into the nature of anxiety by asking what functions are performed by the septo-hippocampal system and its noradrenergic and serotonergic afferents. There is general agreement that the septo-hippocampal system acts in some way as a comparator (Ciba Foundation, 1978), but the particular tasks to which this function is applied are in dispute. I have reviewed the evidence that concerns these issues, and have attempted to wed the notion that the septo-hippocampal system functions as a comparator to the hypothesis that it forms a critical node in the neural substrate of anxiety. I therefore finish this section with a brief outline of the ensuing theory.

A Theory of Anxiety

The theory (Gray, 1982a, 1982b) maps the functions of the BIS, as outlined in Fig. 1, on to the septo-hippocampal system and connected structures, but at the same time it proposes specific ways in which these brain regions act so as to respond appropriately to the adequate stimuli for anxiety (i.e., the inputs listed to the left of Fig. 1). The theory allots functions to the septal area and hippocampus themselves; to the ascending noradrenergic and serotonergic afferents to these regions; to the Papez circuit, i.e., the outflow from the subicular area (itself in receipt of afferents from area 1 of *cornu ammonis* (CA), i.e., the hippocampus) to the mammillary bodies in the hypothalamus, to the anterior thalamus, to the cingulate cortex and back to the subicular area; to the neocortical input to the hippocampus from the entorhinal area of the temporal lobe; to the prefrontal cortex, which projects to the entorhinal area and cingulate cortex; and to the particular pathways by which these structures are interrelated. The central task of this overall system is to compare, quite generally, actual with expected stimuli. The system functions in two modes. If actual stimuli are successfully matched with expected stimuli, it functions in "checking" mode, and behavioral control remains with other (unspecified) brain systems. If there is discordance between actual and expected stimuli or if the predicted stimulus is aversive (conditions jointly termed "mismatch"), it takes direct control over behavior, now functioning in "control" mode.

In control mode, the outputs of the BIS (Fig. 1) are operated. First, there is an immediate inhibition of any motor program which is in the course of execution. Second, the motor program that was in the course of execution at the time that "mismatch" was detected is tagged with an indication which, in English, might read "faulty, needs checking." This has two further consequences. (a) On future occasions the relevant program is executed with greater restraint (more slowly, more easily interrupted by hesitations for exploratory behavior, more readily abandoned in favor of other programs, and so on). (b) The tagged motor program is given especially careful attention the next time it occurs, that is to say, the system exercises with particular care its basic function of checking predicted against actual events. It is supposed that in performing this function the system is able to subject each stimulus in the environment to an anlysis that ranges over many dimensions (e.g., brightness, hue, position, size, relation to other stimuli). The dependencies between the subject's responses and behavioral outcomes can similarly be subjected to this type of multidimensional analysis (e.g., a turn in a rat's T-maze can be classified as left-going, white-approaching, alternating, moving along the longitudinal axis of the room that surrounds the maze). Third, the system initiates specific exploratory and investigative behavior designed to answer specific questions that arise from the operation of the comparator (e.g., is it left-going or white-approaching in a T-maze that gives rise to mismatch?). Among the environmental stimuli for which the system commands a special search in this way, an important class is constituted by those which themselves predict disruption of the subject's plans, i.e., stimuli that are associated with punishment, nonreward, or failure.

It is further supposed that the system is able to identify certain stimuli as being particularly important and requiring especially careful checking. In this connection the role played by ascending monoaminergic inputs to the hippocampus is of particular importance. Physiological experiments have shown that impulses coming from the entorhinal cortex to the hippocampus and thence to the subicular area must pass through a "gate" in the dentate gyrus and area CA 3 of the hippocampus proper. With stimulus repetition, such impulses either habituate quickly or become consolidated and enhanced (Segal, 1977a, 1977b). It seems, furthermore, that impulses are more likely to pass the dentate-CA 3 gate if they are associated with events of biological importance to the animal, such as those associated with the delivery of food or foot-shock (Segal, 1977b). Segal (1977a) has, in addition, shown that the passage of impulses in the hippocampal formation is facilitated by the simultaneous stimulation of either noradrenergic or serotonergic inputs to the hippocampus. The action of noradrenergic afferents in particular can apparently be characterized as increasing the signal-to-noise ratio of hippocampal neurons, thereby allowing them to respond more effectively to sensory information (of neocortical origin) entering the system from the entorhinal cortex. In accordance with these data, the author's theory of anxiety attributes to the noradrenergic and serotonergic afferents to the septo-hippocampal system the role of labeling such sensory information as "important, needs checking," as outlined above.

Applied to human clinical syndromes, this theory of anxiety can explain most naturally the symptoms of obsessive-compulsive neurosis (Rachman & Hodgson, 1979), especially those that involve excessive checking of potential environmental hazards. In this respect it contrasts with earlier theories of anxiety based on animal experiments, which have usually found their most natural application to phobic symptoms. However, phobic symptoms can also be readily understood within the present theory, which attributes them to the inhibition of motor programs. Pharmacotherapy of anxiety is seen as depending essentially on a reduction in the intensity of noradrenergic and serotonergic signals reaching the septo-hippocampal system; this, given the theory outlined above, would tend to diminish the subject's tendency to check the environment for threat. The effectiveness of behavior therapy in cases of anxiety (Mathews, 1978) is seen as depending on manipulations of schedules of presentation of phobic stimuli which maximize the rate of habituation (Watts, 1979); the critical site of habituation, according to the theory, lies in the hippocampal formation (Vinogradova, 1975).

In man, a particularly important role is apparently played by the prefrontal and cingulate regions of the neocortex. Destruction of each of these areas has been used successfully in the treatment of anxiety (Powell, 1979). Within the present theory, the role of these regions is twofold. First, they supply to the septo-hippocampal system information about the subject's own on-going motor programs; this information is essential if the septo-hippocampal system (together with the Papez circuit) is to generate adequate predictions of the next expected event to match against actual events. Second, they afford a route by which language systems in the neocortex can control the activities of the limbic structures which are the chief neural substrate of anxiety. In turn, these structures, via subicular and hippocampal projections to the entorhinal cortex, are able to scan verbally coded stores of information when performing the functions allotted to them in the theory outlined above. In this way, it is possible for human anxiety to be triggered by largely verbal stimuli (relatively independently of ascending monoaminergic influences), and to utilize in the main verbally coded strategies to cope with perceived threats. It is for this reason, if the theory is correct, that lesions to the prefrontal and cingulate cortices are effective in cases of anxiety that are resistant to drug therapy (Powell, 1979).

THE ISSUES

The theory of anxiety briefly sketched above has wide ramifications (Gray, 1982b, 1982c). I pick out here only a few of the issues to which it gives rise.

The Role of GABA

There is abundant evidence that the two major classes of antianxiety drugs, the benzodiazepines (Haefely, Pieri, Polc, & Schaffner, 1981) and the barbiturates (Barker & Ransom, 1978; Olsen, 1981), both enhance GABA-ergic inhibition; similar observations have been made with ethanol (Nestoros, 1980; Ticku, 1980). It is unclear, however, whether this neurochemical change underlies the specifically anxiolytic effects of these agents. The ubiquitous distribution of GABA-ergic neurons and receptors throughout the central nervous system makes enhanced GABA-ergic inhibition a strong candidate for the critical change underlying sedative and/or anticonvulsant, rather than anxiolytic, drug action (Gray, 1979), especially since the latter is characterized by the highly specific behavioral changes captured in Fig. 1. Thus, one must ask whether anxiolytic action per se is mediated by enhanced GABA-ergic inhibition; and, if so, whence comes its behavioral specificity?

There is indeed evidence to implicate GABA in the anxiolytic effects of the benzodiazepines. Billingsley and Kubena (1978) were able to reverse the disinhibitory effect of benzodiazepine treatment on punished instrumental responding (a classic test of anxiolytic action; see Fig. 1) with the GABA antagonist, picrotoxin; and Soubrié, Thiébot and Simon (1979) report that picrotoxin itself increased the inhibitory effect of punishment. In my laboratory, Quintero has confirmed the effect of picrotoxin described by Soubrié et al.; and, though she failed to obtain a reliable blockade of the disinhibitory effect of chlordiazepoxide on punished responding using picrotoxin, she was able to produce such a blockade using the more specific GABA antagonist, bicuculline (Gray, Quintero, & Mellanby, 1983). In other experiments Buckland has shown that the inhibitory effect of nonreward (as tested by extinction of a previously food-rewarded running response in the straight alley) is reduced by chlordiazepoxide (see Fig. 1) and that this action of the drug, too, is blocked by either picrotoxin or bicuculline (Gray et al., 1984). We also used entry into a changed arm in a T-maze as a test of the reaction to novelty (see Fig. 1). Normal rats choose the changed arm about 75% of the time, chlordiazepoxide reduces this to about 50% (i.e., random choice), and picrotoxin (but not bicuculline) reverses the effect of chlordiazepoxide (Gray et al., 1983).

The results of experiments in which GABA-ergic inhibition is facilitated have been more equivocal. The GABA-receptor agonist, muscimol, has been reported to disinhibit punished responding (an anxiolytic effect) when injected into the ventricles (Guidotti, Baraldi, Leon, & Costa, 1980; see also Costa, this volume) but not systemically (Gray et al., 1983, 1984; Thiébot, Jobert, & Soubrié, 1979). It is customary to dismiss the latter observation on the grounds that muscimol penetrates the blood-brain barrier only poorly (Baraldi, Grandison, & Guidotti, 1979). However, systemic injections of the drug are sufficient to affect the hippocampal slow-wave response to electrical stimulation of the septal area

(Mellanby, Gray, Quintero, Holt, & McNaughton, 1981) and the response to stimulus change in the T-maze (Gray et al., 1983, 1984), in both cases in an anxiolytic direction, so it is not clear why they should fail to affect punished responding. In our hands muscimol also failed to affect behavior inhibited by nonreward in either the straight alley or the Skinner box (Gray et al., 1984). These results appear to suggest a stronger role for GABA in mediating anxiolytic effects on responses to novelty than on responses to stimuli associated with punishment or nonreward. However, Hodges and Green (1984) have found that chronic systemic treatment with the GABA-transaminase inhibitor, ethanolamine-0-sulphate, which elevates brain GABA levels, increases punished responding, and potentiates the disinhibitory effects of chlordiazepoxide on both punished and nonrewarded responding.

On balance, then, evidence that benzodiazepine-induced anxiolytic effects can be blocked by GABA antagonists is nicely complemented by evidence that facilitated GABA-ergic inhibition has anxiolytic effects. The problems that remain appear to be of a purely pharmacological nature—for example, the variable ability of picrotoxin or bicuculline to be the better antagonist of benzodiazepines and muscimol, or of systemic muscimol to exert anxiolytic effects (Gray et al., 1983, 1984; Mellanby et al., 1981). However, this harmonious picture is marred when we extend the compass of our review to include the barbiturates. These compounds are only marginally less effective as clinical anxiolytics than the benzodiazepines (Rickels, 1978), and the behavioral effects of the two classes of drugs are barely distinguishable in relevant animal experiments (Gray, 1977). Like the benzodiazepines the barbiturates enhance the electrophysiological effects of GABA (Barker & Ransom, 1978), apparently after binding to part of the supramolecular complex (of which the GABA receptor is a part), though to the picrotoxinin rather than the benzodiazepine receptor (Olsen, 1981). Yet our efforts to block the electrophysiological (Mellanby et al., 1981) or the behavioral (Gray et al., 1983, 1984) effects of sodium amylobarbitone with either picrotoxin (which is also bound by the picrotoxinin receptor) or bicuculline have been completely without success. Thus it may be the case that (a) enhanced GABA-ergic inhibition has anxiolytic effects; (b) the benzodiazepines have anxiolytic effects by virtue of the enhanced GABA-ergic inhibition they produce; (c) the barbiturates enhance GABA-ergic inhibition; yet (d) the barbiturates have anxiolytic effects by some other route (perhaps in addition to the GABA-ergic one).

Accepting this rather muddy conclusion for the present, we pass on to the second question identified at the start of this section: What is the origin of the behavioral specificity of anxiolytic drug action? Several answers have been offered to this question, none of them fully satisfactory.

Two suggestions call upon receptor heterogeneity as the solution to the problem. The first (Klepner, Lippa, Benson, Sano, & Beer, 1979) arose in the course of biochemical studies of the benzodiazepines. Klepner and his co-workers proposed that there are two types of benzodiazepine receptors, and that anxiolytic action is linked to only one of them. This "Type I" receptor is thought to be unrelated to GABA receptors, whereas the other, "Type II" receptor, has a close relation to the GABA system (Braestrup & Nielsen, 1980). The distinction between Type I and II benzodiazepine receptors is not universally accepted. Even if it were, Klepner et al.'s proposal suffers from two major disadvantages: The purest concentration of their Type I receptors is in the cerebellum, a structure which, on other grounds, is most unlikely to be related to anxiety; and the evidence, summarized above, that GABA plays a significant role in the anxiolytic action of the benzodiazepines makes it unlikely that this action is exerted by way of the receptor that is not related to GABA.

The second suggestion of receptor heterogeneity as the basis of the specificity of antianxiety action turns on the evidence for a novel type of GABA receptor (Bowery et al., 1980). This "$GABA_B$" receptor is insensitive to the agonists, muscimol and isoguvacine, and antagonist, bicuculline, to which the classical $GABA_A$ receptor is sensitive; in contrast, the $GABA_B$ receptor is sensitive to an agonist, baclofen, which does not act at the $GABA_A$ receptor. Furthermore, the $GABA_B$ receptor appears to be linked to a calcium channel (Dunlop & Fischbach, 1981; Fung & Fillenz, described in Gray et al., 1984) rather than a chloride channel (sensitive to the action of picrotoxin) as is the $GABA_A$ receptor. Fung and Fillenz (in Gray et al., 1984) have shown that (a) benzodiazepines potentiate the action of GABA at the $GABA_A$, but not the $GABA_B$ receptor; (b) these drugs mimic the action of GABA at the $GABA_B$, but not the $GABA_A$ receptor; and (c) both receptors probably co-exist on noradrenergic terminals in the hippocampus. This heterogeneity of GABA receptors raises the possibility that the specificity of anxiolytic drug action depends upon action at one or the other type of receptor (Gray et al., 1983, 1984). The evidence summarized above (relating to the blockade of benzodiazepine effects by bicuculline and picrotoxin and the partial mimicry of anxiolytic action by muscimol) clearly implicates the $GABA_A$ receptor in anxiolysis. But there is also some (albeit limited) evidence for an involvement of the $GABA_B$ receptor: Punished responding may be disinhibited by a combination of muscimol and baclofen (both administered systemically), although neither drug on its own reliably produces this effect (Gray et al., 1984). Thus, this solution to the problem also lacks viability.

An alternative possibility has been suggested by Haefely (Haefely, Polc, Pieri, Schaffner, & Laurent, 1983). He points out that GABA-ergic cells frequently appear to play a critical role in negative feedback loops. These cells are often activated by firing in long-axoned neuronal pathways and provide recurrent inhibition to keep that firing within bounds. This type of system operates, for example, in the hippocampus, where recurrent inhibition is probably provided by GABA-ergic basket cells. In such a feedback loop, the GABA-ergic neurons might fire only if the principal cells for which they provide feedback are themselves excited. If we now assume that the anxiolytic effects of the benzodiazepines are due to an enhancement of the inhibitory action of GABA, this enhancement can only take place at synapses where GABA transmission is occurring; and this transmission can, in turn, take place (on the arguments advanced above) only in systems where the related principal cells are themselves firing. In this way, benzodiazepines would selectively dampen activity in anxiety-related brain systems, not because these drugs have a special affinity for such systems, but because it is in these systems that (given appropriate anxiogenic stimulation) neuronal firing of a kind with which they interact is currently taking place. (Parallel arguments can be produced to account for the other effects produced by the benzodiazepines, e.g., their anticonvulsant action.)

If it is correct that the hippocampus plays an important role in anxiety, as proposed by Gray (1982a, 1982b), the foregoing arguments lead one to expect the benzodiazepines to enhance recurrent inhibition in this structure. Haefely et al. (1981) review several studies in which such effects have been demonstrated. A further possibility is that benzodiazepines might enhance GABA-ergic transmission in the larger feedback loop comprising the hippocampal formation and the septal area. Operation of this loop has been implicated in some of the behavioral (Gray, Feldon, Rawlins, Owen, & McNaughton, 1978) and electrophysiological (Rawlins, Feldon, & Gray, 1979) effects of the anxiolytic drugs; and there is evidence for a GABA-ergic synapse in the hippocampo-septal limb of the loop (McLennan & Miller, 1974).

These suggestions are obviously only tentative at present. For the moment, we must conclude that the basis for the specificity of the antianxiety action of the benzodiazepines and other anxiolytic drugs remains an open question.

The Opiate Connection

The theory developed by Gray (1982a, 1982b) allots a critical role in anxiety to the ascending noradrenergic fibers that originate in the locus coeruleus. A similar conclusion has been reached by Redmond (1979). This convergence of views is encouraging, as is the independence of the data bases from which they derive. But juxtaposition of these two data bases poses an interesting problem worth both experimental and clinical attention.

Gray's (1982a) theory is based in the first instance upon the behavioral effects of the antianxiety drugs. These reduce responses to stimuli associated with unconditioned painful stimuli, but not responses to pain itself (Gray, 1977). Conversely, opiates, such as morphine, reduce pain reactions, but have no effect on responses to stimuli associated with pain, as in the classic Geller-Seifter conflict test of anxiolytic drug action (Geller, Bachman, & Seifter, 1963; Hodges & Green, 1984). These findings demonstrate a strong double dissociation between anxiolytic and analgesic drugs, and so speak against any close connection of central opiate mechanisms with anxiety.

The data and arguments marshaled by Redmond (1979), in contrast, suggest just such an opiate connection. The starting point for Redmond's analysis is the observation that electrical stimulation of the locus coeruleus gives rise to fear-like behavior in conscious monkeys. This observation leads him to attribute to the noradrenergic fibers originating in this nucleus a role as a general "alarm" system activating structures throughout the neuraxis that mediate anxious behavior. Gray (1982a, 1982b) comes to a virtually identical conclusion in the light of evidence that (a) antianxiety drugs reverse the stress-induced increase in turnover of central noradrenaline (Lidbrink et al., 1973), and (b) lesions of the dorsal ascending noradrenergic bundle (which carries locus coeruleus efferents destined for the limbic system and neocortex) partially mimic the behavioral effects of antianxiety drugs. Given the evidence (considered above) that these drugs act by enhancing GABA-ergic inhibition, these two sets of data can be brought into neat alignment by taking into account the many reports of GABA receptors both in the locus coeruleus itself (references in Gray, 1982a) and at noradrenergic terminals in the forebrain, including the hippocampus (Bowery et al., 1980; Fung & Fillenz in Gray et al., 1984).

However, a further strand in Redmond's (1979) analysis of the neural basis of anxiety consists in the observation that many of the symptoms of opiate withdrawal resemble those of anxiety states, though in a particularly intense form. Furthermore, it is possible to control the symptoms of opiate withdrawal by administering clonidine (Gold, Pottash, Sweeney, & Kleber, 1979), an alpha-adrenergic agonist which reduces locus coeruleus activity, apparently by way of boosted auto-receptor-mediated feedback inhibition. Since the locus coeruleus contains opiate receptors (Pert & Snyder, 1973), these observations may be accounted for by postulating that opiates depress locus coeruleus activity and that the anxiety symptoms seen in the opiate withdrawal syndrome are due to rebound hyperactivity in locus coeruleus neurons when opiate-induced inhibition is removed (Gold & Fox, 1982; Redmond, 1979). It follows from this account that both endogenous and exogenous opiates should reduce anxiety, and there is some evidence that exogenous opiates indeed have this effect (Mirrin, Meyer, & McNamee, 1976). However, I do not find this evidence as convincing as do Gold and Fox (1982).

How is this contradiction to be resolved: Do opiates reduce anxiety, or are they unrelated to anxiety? It may be that this question is framed too generally to receive—perhaps even to merit—an answer. The solution to the problem may require recognition of the fact that there are diverse symptoms of anxiety and not all of these symptoms are mediated by identical mechanisms. Conceivably, the opiates (endogenous or exogenous) are unrelated to some symptoms of anxiety (those, for example, that are modeled in animals by a Geller-Seifter conflict schedule), but are antagonistic to others (those that appear in the opiate withdrawal syndrome).

One way in which such diversity could come about is as follows. There is evidence for inhibitory receptors on locus coeruleus neurons of three types: GABA receptors (probably associated with benzodiazepine and picrotoxinin receptors), opiate receptors, and alpha-adrenergic auto-receptors. Now suppose that opiate receptors are situated in the main on locus coeruleus cells which send their efferents into the spinal cord (i.e., those located caudally), but not on cells that contribute to the dorsal ascending noradrenergic bundle (located more rostrally). Similarly, suppose that GABA receptors and their associated supramolecular complexes are situated in the main on locus coeruleus cells that contribute to the dorsal bundle, rather than those destined to descend in the cord. This hypothesis predicts that opiates would affect primarily somatic symptoms of anxiety, which appears to be the case, judging from the opiate withdrawal syndrome; while anxiolytics, such as the benzodiazepines, would affect more purely psychological aspects of anxiety, as measured, for example, by a conflict test in animals or by self-ratings of anxiety in patients. Although this account is at present post hoc, it is easily open to experimental test, anatomically (by observation of the precise distribution of opiate and GABA receptors in the locus coeruleus), behaviorally (by observation of the different symptoms of anxiety after appropriate drug treatment in animals), and clinically (by similar observations in patients). Such experiments might also extend to alpha-antagonists such as clonidine. If alpha-receptors are present on all locus coeruleus cell-bodies, such drugs would be expected to reduce opiate-sensitive and anxiolytic-sensitive symptoms equally well.

Anxiety and Depression

The relation between the neural bases of anxiety and depression remains enigmatic. In part the enigma stems from the fact that the term "depression" seems to refer to a whole continuum of illnesses ranging from neurotic depression at one pole to psychotic depression at the other (Gray, 1982a, 1982b; Roth, 1979). Neurotic depression includes many symptoms (e.g., agitation, self-reported anxiety) that are identical to those seen in states of anxiety, whereas psychotic depression involves symptoms (e.g., motor retardation, delusional beliefs) that are quite unlike anxiety (Roth, 1979). A second reason lies in the paucity of clear animal models of human depression (of either kind) in contrast to the many well-established tests of anxiety in animals. A third source for this enigma may lie in the ambiguities that surround the action of antidepressant drugs: These are seen by some (Schildkraut, 1965) as *increasing* central monoaminergic activity, but more recently by others (Stone, 1979; Sulser, 1978) as *decreasing* it. (Antianxiety drugs almost certainly act in the latter way, so resembling antidepressants according to the Sulser-Stone hypothesis, but being their mirror image according to Schildkraut's.)

The animal model of depression with the best claims to validity is probably that of helplessness consequent upon exposure to uncontrollable stress (Maier & Seligman, 1976). This model has been the subject of much controversy, concerning the nature of the psychological changes to which uncontrollable stress gives rise, the brain mechanisms that mediate these changes, and the relation of either to human depression. Recent evidence makes it clear that regimes of uncontrollable stress (e.g., repeated unpredictable and inescapable footshock) give rise to both lowered activity levels and difficulties in associating instrumental responses with outcomes (Jackson, Maier, & Rapoport, 1978), thus confirming both rival hypotheses concerning the nature of the psychological changes caused by uncontrollable stress (Maier & Seligman, 1976; Weiss, Glazer, & Pohorecky, 1976). In addition, uncontrollable stress causes anorexia, weight loss, reduced aggressiveness and competitiveness, loss of grooming and play behavior, and sleep disturbances, all of which may be mapped with some degree of plausibility onto human depressive symptoms (Weiss et al., 1982). It is also clear that at least some of these behavioral changes after uncontrollable stress are paralleled by changes in central monoaminergic, and especially noradrenergic, function (Weiss et al., 1976; Weiss, Bailey, et al., 1982), and a good case can be made that the behavioral changes are mediated by the neurochemical ones. Given the evidence for changed monoamine function in human depression, the apparent role of central noradrenegic mechanisms in helplessness is further support for the validity of the model. Finally, Sherman and Petty (1982) have shown that helplessness can be reversed by chronic but not acute administration of tricyclics, monoamine oxidase inhibitors, or atypical antidepressants, but not by a range of other drugs, thus paralleling the pharmacological profile of human depression.

Let us accept for the purposes of this discussion that "helplessness" (shorthand for the full range of behavioral changes that occur after uncontrollable stress rather than just the cognitive changes emphasized by Seligman, 1975) is indeed a valid model of human depression. What light does this conclusion throw upon the relation between anxiety and depression? To be able to answer this question we need to know (1) whether helplessness is a model of neurotic or psychotic depression; (2) whether helplessness is mediated by decreased or increased forebrain release of noradrenaline, and perhaps other monoamines; and (3) whether antidepressant therapy depends upon a net increase or a net decrease in monoaminergic transmission. Ambiguity surrounds each of these issues.

In favor of an identification of helplessness with psychotic depression (Gray, 1982a, chap. 12) are some of the symptoms that characterize helplessness, especially weight loss and inactivity, since these mark out the psychotic pole of the neurotic-psychotic depression continuum (Roth, 1979). This appears to have been Weiss's position until recently. Weiss now identifies helplessness with neurotic depression, on the grounds that animals appear to be tense and anxious after exposure to uncontrollable stress regimes (Weiss et al., 1982). Little guidance can be gained from the data reported by Sherman and Petty (1982) on the sensitivity of helplessness to drug treatment, since they obtain positive results both with monoamine oxidase inhibitors (which are clinically effective in states of neurotic depression and even anxiety; Paykel, Parker, Penrose, & Rassaby, 1979), and with tricyclics (which appear to be most effective in psychotic depression).

What of the second question: Is helplessness mediated by increased or decreased forebrain release of noradrenaline? Most of the research on this issue has come from Weiss's laboratory. This group originally favored the view that uncontrollable stress reduces central noradrenaline function, so giving rise to lowered activity levels. This hypothesis was based on observations of lowered whole-brain levels of noradrenaline after appropriate stress regimes (Weiss et al., 1976). Difficulties arose from the lack of any other evidence supporting a role of central noradrenergic mechanisms in the promotion of movement (Gray, 1982a). Recently, however, Weiss has espoused exactly the opposite hypothesis: that helplessness is due to reduced release of noradrenaline in the forebrain, consequent upon lowered auto-receptor (alpha-adrenergic) mediated inhibition in the locus coeruleus. This hypothesis is based on the observation that the lowered levels of noradrenaline to which uncontrollable stress gives rise are confined to the region of the locus coeruleus. Furthermore, it is supported by a number of experiments in which the alpha-agonist, clonidine, and the alpha-antagonist, piperoxane, were infused into the ventricles near the locus coeruleus in conjunction with appropriate behavioral paradigms (Weiss et al., 1982). An important advantage of this change in Weiss's position is that it allows him to treat the dorsal ascending noradrenergic bundle in the same way as Redmond (1979) and Gray (1982a), that is, as mediating behavioral inhibition under conditions of threat, an approach which is supported by much other evidence.

The position adopted by Weiss et al. (1982) is nicely complemented by evidence from Petty and Sherman's laboratory implicating as a nodal structure in helplessness the hippocampus (e.g., Petty & Sherman, 1981). These investigators have used a variety of methods that converge upon the conclusion that helplessness is mediated by increased activity in the hippocampal formation that is itself consequent upon a reduction in GABA-ergic inhibition in this structure. If we now put together Weiss's and Petty and Sherman's views and the data upon which they are based, we can see helplessness as being similar to anxiety as this emotion is comprehended by Gray (1982a) and Redmond (1979). In both cases there is a hypothesized central state that is due to enhanced hippocampal function consequent upon an increased noradrenergic input to this and other regions of the forebrain. The increased noradrenergic input may be due to reduced locus coeruleus auto-receptor-mediated inhibition (Weiss), or to reduced GABA-ergic presynaptic inhibition of noradrenaline release (Petty and Sherman, combined with ideas developed in the section on GABA, above), or to both; and it may be combined with decreased GABA-ergic control of intrinsic hippocampal neurons (Petty and Sherman).

If we are to identify in this way the neural mechanisms that mediate helplessness and anxiety, respectively, coherence demands two further assumptions. First, Weiss et al. (1982) must be right in their claim that helplessness models neurotic rather than psychotic depression. Second, the antidepressant drugs must exert their therapeutic effect by causing a net reduction in noradrenergic transmission (by way of receptor desensitization), as proposed by Sulser (1978) and

Stone (1978), rather than an increase as proposed by Schildkraut (1965). It would still remain mysterious, however, that some symptoms of activity in this overall system are sensitive to increased GABA-ergic inhibition produced by the antianxiety drugs, while others are sensitive to decreased noradrenergic receptor sensitivity produced by antidepressants. A clue to this mystery may lie in the observation from Petty and Sherman's laboratory that lorazepam or diazepam will prevent the development of helplessness if given before exposure to uncontrollable stress but will not reverse helplessness once it is induced, whereas antidepressants given chronically reverse helplessness after it is established (Petty, pers. comm. 1982).

If the above arguments are correct, we have animal models of anxiety and neurotic depression which share much of the same neural circuitry, and are in line with the close relationship between the clinical symptoms of these two conditions (Roth, 1979). On the other hand, we would then have no well-validated model of psychotic depression at all. On the contrary assumptions, that helplessness is a model of psychotic depression (Weiss et al., 1976), very different arguments can be marshaled. But, since I have pursued that line of thought elsewhere (Gray, 1982a, chap. 12), I shall forebear to do so now.

Toughening Up and its Inverse

Part of the evidence cited by Weiss et al. (1976) in support of a noradrenergic basis for helplessness relates to the phenomenon of "toughening up": whereas acute exposure to uncontrollable stress causes helplessness, chronic exposure (over 15 consecutive days) eliminates helplessness. At the same time, whereas whole-brain levels of noradrenaline were reduced after a single session of inescapable shock that gave rise to helplessness, the animals exposed to 15 sessions of inescapable shock had normal levels of noradrenaline accompanied by elevated activity of tyrosine hydroxylase, the rate-limiting enzyme in noradrenaline synthesis. One natural interpretation of these findings is that helplessness is due to insufficient release of noradrenaline (the transmitter being temporarily exhausted), while toughening up reflects increased synthesis of noradrenaline, so preventing exhaustion of the transmitter (Weiss et al., 1976).

The change of view adopted by Weiss et al. (1982) concerning the neural basis of helplessness (too much forebrain noradrenaline release taking the place of too little) must necessarily affect their interpretation of toughening up. This is now seen as reflecting a rise in tyrosine hydroxylase activity and thus in noradrenaline levels in the locus coeruleus, followed by a rise in auto-receptor-mediated inhibition in that nucleus, and a consequent fall in noradrenaline release in the forebrain.

This change of view makes it much easier to bring Weiss's work into line with certain other phenomena that may also be regarded as instances of toughening up. Chen and Amsel (1977), for example, showed that inescapable foot-shock delivered over several days before rats were trained to run in an alley for a food reward led to a rise in resistance to extinction of the running response when food was withheld. We may describe this finding as an increase in resistance to the behaviorally disruptive effects of nonreward consequent upon exposure to a regime of chronic uncontrollable stress, just as Weiss's findings may be described as an increase in resistance to the disruptive effects of shock consequent upon exposure to a similar regime. Now if we try to interpret Chen and Amsel's (1977) findings in the light of the Weiss et al. (1976) model, we would need to say that the rise in resistance to extinction observed by these workers was due to a rise in forebrain noradrenergic transmission. But a rise in resistance to extinction is produced, not by enhancing central noradrenergic function, but rather by destruction of the dorsal ascending noradrenergic bundle (Mason & Iversen, 1979; Owen, Boarder, Gray, & Fillenz, 1982). In contrast, if we interpret Chen and Amsel's findings on the later Weiss et al. (1982) model, everything falls into place. In line with the effect of dorsal bundle destruction on resistance to extinction (an increase), we now state that Chen and Amsel's chronic stress regime led to a fall in forebrain noradrenaline release.

 If helplessness is a model of anxious or neurotic depression (Weiss et al., 1982), we may interpret the experiments on toughening up as showing that chronic stress causes decreased susceptibility to anxiety. Two well-established laboratory phenomena fit neatly into this generalization: the partial reinforcement extinction effect and the partial punishment effect. In the first of these, exposure to unpredictable nonreward on a partial reinforcement schedule gives rise to increased resistance to extinction; in the second, exposure to unpredictable foot-shock on a partial punishment schedule gives rise to increased resistance to punishment. Furthermore, there is cross-tolerance between the two varieties of stress: a partial reinforcement schedule increases resistance to punishment and a partial punishment schedule, resistance to extinction (Brown & Wagner, 1964). It will be clear from Fig. 1 that reduced sensitivity (increased resistance) to punishment or nonreward are both indices of reduced anxiety within Gray's (1982a, 1982b) theory.

A further set of phenomena that fits the generalization that chronic exposure to stress reduces susceptibility to anxiety consists in the effective treatment of a number of symptoms of anxiety (phobias, obsessions, compulsions) by exposure, either for a sufficiently long time on one occasion (flooding) or on a sufficiently large number of repeated occasions (desensitization therapy), to the stimuli the patient finds anxiogenic (Mathews, 1978).

Juxtaposition of these different data bases brings out a potential clinical hazard. The major alternative to behavioral treatments of anxiety (which achieve a high rate of cure; Mathews, 1978) is drug treatment (which is palliative only). But what happens if behavioral and drug treatments are combined? Assuming that the parallels between toughening up, the partial reinforcement and partial punishment effects, and behavioral treatments of anxiety are real, we may give an answer to this question (Gray et al., 1982). If medications are administered during training on either a partial reinforcement or a partial punishment schedule, antianxiety drugs prevent the development of increased resistance to extinction or punishment (Davis, Brookes, Gray, & Rawlins, 1981; Feldon & Gray, 1981; Feldon, Guillamon, Gray, De Wit, & McNaughton, 1979). Depending on the parameters of the experiment, and particularly the inter-trial interval, this block-ade by the antianxiety drugs of the increased behavioral tolerance for stress normally produced by exposure to intermittent nonreward or punishment may be total or limited to the case in which testing is conducted in the absence of the drug (i.e., state-dependent). But, since the aim of pharmacotherapy is to leave the patient drug-free as well as symptom-free, the clinical implications are the same in either case: medication with anxiolytic drugs may reduce the long-term curative effects of behavior therapy. This potential hazard needs much more clinical research directed to it, but such clinical data as exist suggest that it may be a real one (Gray 1982a, pp. 450–452).

Recently, while studying the behavioral effects in the rat of the beta-blocker, propranolol, Salmon and I have demonstrated a phenomenon that may be the inverse of toughening up (Salmon, 1983). Clinically, propranolol is reported to have anxiolytic effects (Tyrer, 1976), as both Redmond's (1979) and Gray's (1982a) theories of anxiety predict that it should. However, these effects appear to be mediated peripherally rather than centrally, as both Redmond and I would predict. In agreement with these clinical observations, Salmon and I have found anxiolytic-like effects of propranolol in the rat. For example, the drug disinhibited responding during the nonrewarded components of a multiple schedule of inter-mittent reward and extinction in the Skinner box, and it impaired responding on a schedule of differential reinforcement of low rates of response (DRL), both effects that are also produced by classical anxiolytics (Gray, 1977). Furthermore, disinhibition of responding during extinction was also produced by practolol, a beta-blocker that barely crosses the blood-brain barrier, suggesting a peripheral locus of action as in the clinical case. (Notice the complex interactions between feeling and cognition that one must attribute to the rat to make sense of these observations. The animal's brain must detect nonreward centrally, send efferent signals to the autonomic nervous system, receive afferents informing it of the consequent peripheral autonomic disturbance, and alter behavior accordingly—much as postulated long ago in the James-Lange theory of emotion.)

Although it was encouraging to find anxiolytic effects of propranolol in these experiments with the rat, the effects were small and disappeared rapidly with continued drug treatment. Further experiments disclosed the reason for this rapid disappearance of the drug effect. In one of these experiments (Salmon & Gray, in press; see Fig. 2), we injected propranolol either just before or some time after a daily session of training on a DRL schedule. The animals injected after the session grew steadily better at DRL than controls. This effect is opposite in sign to the usual anxiolytic one, so we may call it "anxiogenic." The animals injected before the session, in contrast, barely differed from uninjected controls,

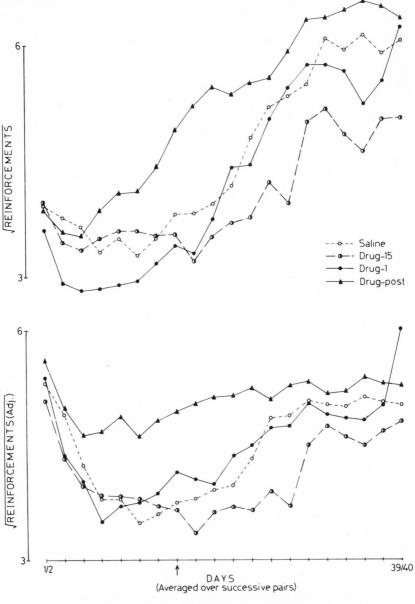

FIG. 2.   The effects on reinforcements received of propranolol HCl, 5 mg/kg, injected intraperitoneally either 5–8 minutes before (in the Drug-1 and Drug-15 conditions) or immediately after (in the Drug-post condition) daily sessions of training on a DRL-20 schedule. Drug injections started on Day 15 (arrow) for the Drug-15 group, but on Day 1 for the other two drug conditions. Above: square-root transformed data. Below: same data after covariance for the effects of drug treatment on response rate. Note increase in reinforcements received by animals drugged *after* the daily session, and the decrease in the Drug-15 group. From Salmon & Gray, in press.

and they were greatly inferior to the animals injected with the same amount of drug after the session. One may conclude that propranolol has two effects. The first builds up with repeated administration, it is independent of the presence of the drug in the bloodstream at the time of testing, and it is anxiogenic in sign. The second is an acute, anxiolytic-like effect. The first, chronic, effect presumably reflects some kind of adaptation to repeated administration of the drug, receptor desensitization, for example; we do not yet know if it is central or peripheral in origin. If these inferences are correct, the process of adaptation to repeated propranolol administration is the inverse of toughening up: there is a gradual build-up of an increased susceptibility to anxiety. Such a process might represent a major clinical hazard attached to treatment with beta-blockers, but I know of no clinical evidence relating to this issue.

On a more hopeful note, other recent experiments in my laboratory suggest that it is possible to mimic the beneficial effects of chronic exposure to stress (i.e., toughening up) by a course of nonstressful, electrical stimulation of the septal area (driving the hippocampal theta rythm) in free-moving rats (Holt, 1982; Holt & Gray, 1983). Such stimulation, delivered before the animal has any behavioral training or testing, gives rise to increased resistance to extinction, increased resistance to conditioned suppression of barpressing (to a stimulus associated with footshock), and less baseline suppression when barpressing is punished in the presence of a distinctive stimulus. These effects are all observed weeks after the end of the course of septal stimulation, and may be interpreted as a long-term reduction in susceptibility to anxiety. Of course, the therapeutic possibilities of this technique in humans are at present remote, but further investigation of its neurochemical and neurophysiological basis may provide clues to more practical ways of boosting long-term resistance to anxiety.

The Anxious Personality and its Converse

Not everyone, faced with equally anxiogenic stimuli, becomes clinically anxious. Those that do tend to have a particular kind of personality, and their personality is determined to a degree that accounts for at least 50% of the relevant variance by genetic factors (Fulker, 1981).

The correct description of the personality that predisposes to anxiety is controversial. Eysenck (1967) has argued powerfully for the existence of two separate sets of causal factors that underlie two orthogonal personality dimensions known as "neuroticism" and "introversion-extraversion"; anxious individuals are then construed as being both introverts and neurotics. In opposition to this position, I have argued that one should rotate these two Eysenckian dimensions by about 30°, so producing an account in which the anxious individual is high on the one dimension of trait anxiety (Gray, 1970, 1981). In terms of the theory sketched earlier in this paper, such an individual has a highly reactive behavioral inhibition system (Fig. 1). This, in turn, might arise from an excessively active ascending monaminergic input to the septo-hippocampal system or from other similar physiological causes. I will not recount again the arguments that support my revision of Eysenck's theory, but the interested reader is referred to Gray (1981). Rather, continuing the policy adopted throughout this paper of adopting a definite theory so as to highlight the issues that arise from it, I shall suppose that this revision is correct.

Since one needs, not two, but at least three orthogonal dimensions in which to capture the different personality attributes that are related to psychiatric phenomena (Eysenck & Eysenck, 1976), locating one pole of a dimension is insufficient to define it fully. The question arises, where are we to place the opposite pole of the dimension I have called above "trait anxiety" (Gray, 1983)? There appear to be two major possibilities.

First, the opposite pole of this dimension may predispose people toward primary psychopathy (Hare & Cox, 1978). Such individuals appear to be specifically poor at developing anticipatory anxiety (as measured by passive avoidance behavior) when errors are punished by electric shock, a form of behavior that is the mirror image of one of the defining characteristics of anxiety as pictured in Fig. 1.

The second possibility is that the opposite pole of trait anxiety is associated with a high susceptibility to the development of psychotic depression. According to this view (Gray, 1982a), psychotic depression is due (as postulated by Schildkraut, 1965; see the section on the relation between anxiety and depression, above) to functional exhaustion of central monoaminergic systems (especially noradrenergic systems and especially those in the hypothalamus and midbrain) and is thus the physiological opposite of anxiety (characterized by high noradrenergic activity, especially in the forebrain). In accordance with this hypothesis, electroconvulsive therapy (which is the antidepressant treatment most specific for the psychotic variety of depression) appears to enhance central monoaminergic function rather generally, with the ascending noradrenergic pathways playing a nodal role in this phenomenon (e.g., Green & Deakin, 1980; Modigh, 1976).

It is to be noted that primary psychopaths and psychotic depressives both occupy the same region of Eysenck's 3-space, that is, they are extraverted, stable, and psychotic, opposite in all respects to the introverted, neurotic, nonpsychotic individual who is prone to anxiety. Thus the two hypotheses sketched above are not necessarily mutually exclusive. It is possible that primary psychopaths and psychotic depressives share important psychophysiological predispositions and that some further factor determines which of the two relevant conditions is eventually displayed. If so, one might expect a genetic relationship between these two conditions, as evidenced, say, by an unusually high incidence of psychopaths among the kin of psychotic depressives and vice versa. I know of no data that speak to this prediction; but it should not be too difficult to gather them.

CONCLUSION

It will be clear that the theory of anxiety (Gray, 1982a, 1982b) which has given rise to these reflections is wide ranging. The issues to which it has directed us include the following.

What is the role played by GABA in mediating the antianxiety action of anxiolytic drugs? Does GABA play the same role with respect to all the different classes of anxiolytic drugs? How is the behavioral specificity of effect of the anxiolytic drugs produced? (With regard to the latter question, we do not even know whether we should be seeking the answer in the neurochemistry of the brain or in the situation in which we test our subjects.) How can the evidence that opiates reduce anxiety be reconciled with the equally compelling evidence that they do not? (One possibility is that these drugs act only upon some cells in the locus coeruleus, particularly those with descending efferents destined for the spinal cord.)

The questions enumerated so far are relatively specific. But much more general questions also arise. What is the relation between anxiety and depression? Is there one relationship between anxiety and neurotic depression and a rather different one between anxiety and psychotic depression? Is "helplessness" a model of neurotic or psychotic depression (if either)? And is helplessness mediated by increased or decreased forebrain release of noradrenaline? How do anxiety and depression relate to the adaptation to stress that Weiss et al. (1976) describe as "toughening up"? How does toughening up relate to changes in the functioning of central noradrenergic neurons? How do antianxiety drugs interact with the stress regimes that give rise to toughening up? And—a clinically important question—how do anxiolytic drugs interact with the exposure to stress which constitutes the heart of most forms of behavior therapy? Do drugs (like propranolol) which block noradrenergic transmission produce an adaptation of the opposite kind (giving rise to increased sensitivity to anxiogenic stimuli) to that seen in toughening up? Can one mimic toughening up by appropriate stimulation of the brain, as suggested by Holt's (1982; Holt & Gray, 1983) experiments? If so, does this fact have any potential implications for future therapeutic stratagems?

At a still more general level, one comes to questions of the kind that have so occupied Eysenck (1967). What traits, psychological and physiological, predispose one to anxiety? How can one best describe the personality of such susceptible individuals? What is the opposite (in a dimensional sense) of the personality that predisposes to anxiety? Two possible answers to this question, each with some plausibility, are at first sight startlingly different: a primary psychopath or a psychotic depressive (Gray, 1983). Might the primary psychopath and the psychotic depressive have some kind of genetic relationship?

Some of these questions are old, some are new. All of them (I believe) are researchable; I hope that this paper will stimulate others to embark on the needed research.

2 Benzodiazepine/GABA Interactions: A Model to Investigate the Neurobiology of Anxiety

E. Costa, M.D.
National Institute of Mental Health

INTRODUCTION

Though neither the existence of the neurotransmitters nor the role of transmitter receptors in brain function were known in Sigmond Freud's time, he suggested that one day "paths of knowledge will be opened up leading from organic biology and chemistry to the field of neurotic phenomena." During the past three decades some fundamental "paths of knowledge" were opened and through them we have learned that studies of drug effects on behavior and on neurochemistry can yield important information on the mechanisms that regulate brain function in health and disease. In the case of anxiety, a pharmacological link between neuro-chemistry and behavior was established by the anxiolytics.

In the development of this class of drugs, benzodiazepines first occupied a prominent position as a treatment agent and later as an important experimental tool. Similar to many other centrally acting drugs, benzodiazepines also came into existence by serendipity. About 25 years ago (Sternbach, 1983), these drugs were introduced into clinical psychiatry because of their low toxicity and potent anxiolytic properties, which were obtained in the absence of overt sedation. Over the years, attempts were made to elucidate the neurochemical basis of their therapeutic activity, but these attempts failed to uncover a selective interaction with a specific neurotransmitter that could be related to their therapeutic action (Costa & Greengard, 1975). When links were detected between the known actions of benzodiazepines and changes in the activity of cholinergic, serotonergic, and catecholaminergic pathways, the dose levels required to document such interactions were greater than those prescribed in clinical psychiatry and used in behavioral tests in animals (Guidotti, 1978). Hence, for over a decade while

27

descriptive pharmacology of benzodiazepines flourished, data on the mechanism of action of these drugs were practically nonexistent.

The real progress in the understanding of the mechanism of action of benzodiazepines occurred when independent investigations in Haefely's (Haefely et al., 1975) and our laboratories (Costa, Guidotti, & Mao, 1975; Costa, Guidotti, Mao, & Suria, 1975) established a close connection between the therapeutic action of the anxiolytics and their capability to facilitate transmission in gamma-aminobutyric acid (GABA) synapses. With the discovery by Braestrup and Squires (1977) and by Möhler and Okada (1977) that specific high affinity binding sites for the benzodiazepines are located in crude synaptic membranes prepared from brain, a number of possibilities whereby benzodiazepine recognition sites can interact with GABAergic transmission was suggested (Costa, Guidotti, & Toffano, 1978). The high affinity binding of benzodiazepines acquired significance immediately after its discovery because of its role in modulating GABAergic synaptic function (Costa & Guidotti, 1979). It was soon shown that not only the affinity whereby various benzodiazepines bind to their synaptic recognition site relates to their pharmacological potency (Braestrup & Squires, 1978; Möhler & Okada, 1978a, 1978b), but also that some ligands for benzodiazepine recognition sites could increase the number of GABA recognition sites (Guidotti, Toffano, & Costa, 1978). Immediately after its discovery many investigators believed that the benzodiazepine binding site was a site for the physiological action of a yet unknown transmitter different from GABA (Marangos et al., 1979; Möhler, Polc, Cumin, Pieri, & Kettler, 1979); today there is near unanimity in accepting the hypothesis that the benzodiazepine recognition site is part of the supramolecular organization that forms the GABA receptor (Costa, 1983; Costa & Guidotti, 1979; Costa, Guidotti, & Mao, 1975; Costa, Guidotti, Mao, & Suria, 1975).

This view has received wider acceptance after several lines of independent investigations have indicated that in many instances synaptic transmission includes the participation of multiple chemical signals, some of which are transduced into a stimulus for the postsynaptic cells, others only act as modulators (Cuello, 1982). Accordingly, in GABAergic transmission, the release of GABA would be transduced into an activation of the chloride (Cl^-) channels located in the membrane of the postsynaptic cell, while putative ligands for the benzodiazepine recognition site (Costa, 1982) can facilitate or disfacilitate the action of GABA on the Cl^- channels (Study & Barker, 1981). Although the type of response appears to depend on the characteristics of the ligand that occupies the benzodiazepine recognition site, none of the benzodiazepines tested to date has activated the Cl^- channel in the absence of GABA (Haefely, Polc, Pieri, Schaffner, & Laurent, 1983).

Three classes of benzodiazepine recognition site ligands have been described, each class has a different pharmacological profile, and each binds with high affinity to the benzodiazepine recognition sites. A group of effectors (including among others, flunitrazepam, diazepam, oxozepam, and zopiclone) that are anxiolytics facilitates GABAergic transmission; another group with anxiogenic activity reduces GABAergic transmission (this group includes, methyl (beta-CCM) and ethyl (beta-CCE)-beta-carboline-3-carboxylate; beta-carboline-3-carboxylate methylamide (beta-CCMA); methyl-4-ethyl-6,7-dihydroxy-beta-carboline-3-carboxylate (DMCM); still another group shows antagonistic activity toward the actions of benzodiazepines and beta-carboline-3-carboxylate esters. This last group is devoid of intrinsic activity and fails to change GABAergic transmission. It includes an imidobenzodiazepine (RO 15–1788) (Haefely, Bonetti, Burkard, Cumin, Laurent, Möhler, Pieri, Polc, Richards, Schaffner, & Scherchlicht, 1983) and propyl-beta-carboline-3-carboxylate.

Whether the benzodiazepine recognition site has a physiological function besides that of mediating the action of drug ligands has been a source of considerable discussion. A definition of this problem helps to solve the important question of whether the benzodiazepine/GABA model is suitable to investigate the neurobiology of anxiety. At present, considerable controversy surrounds the interpretation of the mechanisms mediating the pharmacological responses elicited by various ligands of benzadiazepine recognition sites.

A number of investigators believe that anxiolytic benzodiazepines act as agonists of a specific recognition site, and that anxiolytic benzodiazepines facilitate the operational gain of GABAergic transmission by increasing the Bmax of high affinity GABA recognition sites (Costa, 1982). Since benzodiazepines are the agonists of a drug receptor, these investigators reserve the nomenclature of reverse agonist (Haefely, 1983) for those ligands that elicit anxiety by decreasing the operational gain of GABAergic transmission (Braestrup, Honore, Nielsen, Petersen, & Jensen, 1983). Finally, this group of investigators has termed "benzodiazepine recognition site inhibitors" those compounds that antagonize the action of anxiogenic and anxiolytic ligands for benzodiazepine recognition sites, but fail to modify GABAergic transmission (Haefely, Polc, Pieri, Schaffner, & Laurent, 1983). Many investigators do not readily accept such a classification and believe that an appropriate nomenclature can be proposed only when it is known for certain that the benzodiazepine recognition site is a drug receptor, or when direct information exists on the mode of action of physiological natural agonists for the recognition site of benzodiazepines (Costa, 1983).

The present exposition is prefaced by some behavioral considerations to help bridge biochemical and behavioral models of anxiety. It is necessary to create a background that allows us to study the biochemical substrates regulating the expression of this behavioral trait. Therefore, on a faint background of behavioral/ pharmacological considerations, experiments are presented that establish the anxiolytic action of benzodiazepines as dependent on their ability to modify GABA receptor function. This review further attempts to elucidate how studies of the benzodiazepine recognition site and of its endogenous effector(s) have established a new avenue to study the neurobiology of anxiety. We also consider how and why the interaction of benzodiazepine with GABA receptors is becoming a source of biochemical marker(s) of anxiety.

BEHAVIORAL MODELS OF ANXIETY

Anxiety is a subjective emotional state characterized by feelings of impending danger or fear, which cannot objectively be measured in animals; existing reliable models to study anxiety rely on indirect approaches. One such approach holds that the behavioral responses elicited by anxiogenic or anxiolytic compounds may be taken as a reference index and the neurochemical changes elicited by them may be screened as possible biochemical markers of anxiety. Currently, several studies that use the behavioral approach focus on the most important category of anxiolytic and anxiogenic drugs, the benzodiazepines and the 3-carboxylate esters of beta-carbolines, respectively (Braestrup et al., 1983).

The effectiveness of benzodiazepines as anxiolytic drugs has prompted a number of studies on their essential pharmacological profile as related to their ability to reduce anxiety. The behavioral methodology that has emerged has been used to obtain information on biochemical and neurophysiological mechanisms that can be related to anxiety. Thus, the various ligands of benzodiazepine recognition sites have become interesting tools to explore the neurobiological basis of anxiety. The validity of all the research patterned on this principle rests on the answer given to the question of whether rodents experience anxiety following the injections of drugs that are anxiogenic in man. Though it is unde-cided whether this parallelism is operative, the currently accepted compromise is that those rodent behaviors that are specifically elicited by compounds that are anxiogenic in humans can represent a starting point to assess correlations between neurochemical and behavioral parameters in animals. However, this leaves an important number of open questions, including that concerning the validity of the inference that the neurochemical changes elicited by benzodiaze-pines are an indication of the neurochemistry operative in generating anxiety.

Aggressiveness

The discovery that benzodiazepines exert a taming effect in vicious monkeys prompted a number of investigators to claim that benzodiazepines decrease aggressiveness (Krsiak, 1979). However, a close look at the data of acute exper-iments suggests that very often fighting behavior is reduced only by those doses of benzodiazepines that will incapacitate motility. After repeated daily admin-istrations of benzodiazepines the difference between motor impairment and antiaggressiveness becomes clearer (Simon & Soubrié, 1979). Since benzodi-azepines appear to selectively inhibit certain components of aggression, and since in some cases benzodiazepines have been reported to facilitate aggression

(Guaitani, Marcucci, & Garattini, 1971), more information is needed to resolve these contradictions. Hence, neurochemical changes associated with facilitation or inhibition of aggression cannot be taken at this time as a focal point for studying the neurochemical correlates of the anxiolytic action of benzodiazepines.

Social Interaction and Novelty

Frequently the degree of anxiety induced by novelty has been assessed by the duration of exploratory behavior or the frequency of social interactions; benzodiazepines reportedly enhance both parameters (File, 1980b; Noland & Parkes, 1973). Benzodiazepines also enhance the number of transitions from a safe to a more fearful environment and shorten the latency time for entering an unknown test box (Crawley, Marangos, Paul, Skolnick, & Goodwin, 1981). Taken together these data suggest that benzodiazepines attenuate the emotional factors that limit exploratory activity. However, such an interpretation of the data is questionable, because the behavioral changes elicited by benzodiazepines when the animals attempt to cope with novelty may derive from a reduction in the ability to retain information (Nicholson & Wright, 1980). Benzodiazepines given to rodents placed in a Y maze reduce the tendency to alternate their choice of the right and left arms of the Y on successive trials (Iwahara, Oishi, Yamazaki, & Sakai, 1972). Since areas of the frontal cortex are innervated by dopaminergic axons and contain a high density of benzodiazepine binding sites (Möhler & Okada, 1978a, 1978b), it can be suggested that the activation of these sites by endogenous ligands and drugs can modulate the afferent dopaminergic tonus. The reduction in Y maze alternation may reflect an impairment of cognitive function associated with changes in the activity of meso-frontal dopaminergic innervation.

Benzodiazepines are known to stimulate feeding in rats and mice (File, 1980a). This action could be related to stimulation of hypothalamic GABAergic centers (Kelly & Grossman, 1979) by reducing satiety and consequently inhibiting food intake (Morgan, 1974). However, because the intensity of the feeding response peaks when the rodents are offered highly palatable and novel food in a novel environment, the anxiety-relieving action may participate in the increase of food intake elicited by benzodiazepines. Though it is possible to accept any of these behavioral patterns changed by novelty as an operant behavior associated with some degree of anxiety, the measurement of neurochemical changes associated with changes in the pattern of feeding behavior is an ambiguous way to search for the neurochemical markers of anxiety.

Punishment

A mild electric shock inhibits ongoing behavior (Aron, Simon, Larousse, & Boissier, 1971), and this behavioral output suppression is in turn inhibited by benzodiazepines (Aron et al., 1971). Hence, such a conflict paradigm allows for the behavioral expression of the anticonflict activity (Geller & Seifter, 1960) of benzodiazepines, and usually there is a high degree of correlation between binding affinity of a benzodiazepine to specific brain recognition sites and its anticonflict potency. The antipunishment effect of benzodiazepines not only is rather specific, but it depends markedly on the relationship between the organism and the consequences of its response. Accordingly, putative endogenous ligands for benzodiazepine recognition sites should be investigated for the various components of the conflict situation, including those thought to be benzodiazepine insensitive. For instance, beta-carboline derivatives can cause a proconflict action (Corda, Blaker, Mendelson, Guidotti, & Costa, 1983) in rats and anxiogenic responses in man (Braestrup, Schmiechen, Neef, Nielsen, & Petersen, 1982). If food or water reward or shock is involved, it is important to exclude that a change in appetite, thirst, or pain threshold has modified the operant behavior following the injection of a ligand of the benzodiazepine recognition sites.

Usually the paradigms used to test proconflict or anticonflict action of compounds include an appetitive stimulus that is coupled with an aversive stimulus. Depending on the relative intensity of the two stimuli, the animal will exhibit varying degrees of responsiveness to drugs. Predictability of drug responsiveness and other exogenous stimuli is optimized when thirst is used as an appetitive stimulus and electric shock as punishment (Vogel, Beer, & Clody, 1971). In this test, water-deprived rats are placed in a chamber with a water source (for details see Corda et al., 1983). In the absence of punishment, water-deprived rats lick the water spout almost without interruption for the test duration (3 minutes). The testing apparatus can be set that after 3 seconds of licking, the rats receive through the water spout an electric shock lasting 1 second. When the stimulus intensity is set at .8 to 1 mA, the drinking behavior is completely suppressed (Corda et al., 1983). Under the influence of anxiolytic benzodiazepines, the rat typically continues drinking despite this severe punishment.

Anticonflict Action of Benzodiazepines

The benzodiazepine capability to lessen the behavioral inhibition elicited by punishment is termed "anticonflict" action. The intensity of the anticonflict action of benzodiazepines is dose related and, as seen in Table 1, can be blocked by two antagonists of the benzodiazepine recognition sites, which are themselves devoid of any action. These two compounds are RO 15–1788 (ethyl-8-fluoro-5,6-dehydro-5-methyl-6-oxo[4H]imidozol(1-5a)-(1-4)benzodiazepine-3-carboxylate) (Haefely, Polc, Pieri, Schaffner, Laurent, 1983) and CGS 8216 (2 phenyl pyrazolo (4,3-c) quinolin-3-(5H)one); they are practically devoid of intrinsic activity when given in dosages that are 10–15 times those that inhibit the anticonflict action of benzodiazepines. However, when the two antagonists are given in very high doses to thirsty rats, the compounds can evince a slight proconflict action, i.e., though they are thirsty, they stop drinking for a shock

TABLE 1
Reduction of the "Anticonflict" Action of Diazepam by
the Benzodiazepine Receptor Antagonist, RO 15–1788

	Licking Periods per 3 Minutes[a]	
Treatment	Saline	Diazepam (.5 mg/kg i.v.)
Saline	5.5 ± 2.4	26 ± 3.3[b]
RO 15–1788 (2 mg/kg i.v.)	6.3 ± 1.8	8.1 ± 1.5

[a]Current intensity 1 mA.
[b]$p < .01$ when compared with saline-treated animals. RO 15–1788 (Haefely, Bonetti, Burkard, Cumin, Laurent, Möhler, Pieri, Polc, Richards, Schaffner and Scherschlicht, 1983) binds with high affinity to neuronal benzodiazepine recognition sites, lacks intrinsic activity and acts as a specific benzodiazepine antagonist.

intensity that fails to suppress behavior in saline-treated thirsty rats. Moreover, RO 15–1788 given intravenously in moderate dosages (about 10 mg/kg) can facilitate the onset and prolong the duration of convulsions elicited by isoniazid, an inhibitor of glutamic acid decarboxylase, which lowers the availability of GABA at GABAergic synapses (Corda, Costa, & Guidotti, 1982).

Proconflict Action of 3-Carboxylate Esters of Beta-Carboline

Many 3-carboxylate esters of beta carbolines bind with high affinity to the benzodiazepine recognition site, but they differ from the benzodiazepines because of several important characteristics. For instance, flunitrazepam binds to the recognition sites in a covalent manner when the binding occurs in the presence of an ultraviolet light of given characteristics (Möhler, Richards, & Wu, 1981). Crude synaptic membranes to which flunitrazepam is bound irreversibly fail to bind ^{3}H-diazepam or other ^{3}H-benzodiazepines by an extent corresponding to that of the irreversibly bound flunitrazepam (Hirsch, 1982; Karobath & Supavilai, 1982). In contrast, the binding of ^{3}H-3-carboxylate esters of beta carbolines is unimpaired (Hirsch, 1982). As shown in Table 2, this finding indicates that the binding of various ligands to the benzodiazepine recognition site, though very similar, is not identical.

Anxiolytic benzodiazepines preferentially relieve convulsions due to an impairment of GABAergic transmission (Costa, Guidotti, Mao, & Suria, 1975). They also increase the Bmax of the high affinity GABA recognition site (Costa & Guidotti, 1979), whereas the affinity of benzodiazepine recognition sites is increased by GABA (Tallman, Thomas, & Gallager, 1978). RO 15–1788 and CGS 8216 fail to relieve anxiety, bind to the benzodiazepine recognition site in

TABLE 2
Potency of Beta Carboline-3-
Carboxylic Acid Ester
Derivatives on the Proconflict
Test

β-Carboline	ED_{30} (mg/kg i.v.)
β-CCM	.10
DMCM	.14
β-CCE	.18
FG 7142	1.8

The ED_{30} dose causing 30% suppression of punished behavior was estimated by log probit analysis of
responses to at least four doses injected 10 minutes before
the test.

a GABA independent manner, and fail to increase or decrease the Bmax for
GABA binding (Haefely, Bonetti, Burkard, Cumin, Laurent, Möhler, Pieri, Polc,
Richards, Schaffner, & Scherschlicht, 1983). The derivatives of beta-carbolines-
3-carboxylate facilitate convulsions (Cowen, Green, Nutt, & Martin, 1981) caused
by a partial impairment of GABAergic transmission (Polc, Ropert, & Wright,
1981). They also reduce the increase in affinity of benzodiazepine recognition
sites elicited by GABA and block the increase in the Bmax of GABA binding
induced by anxiolytic benzodiazepines (Braestrup & Nielsen, 1981; Braestrup
et al., 1982).

Those 3-carboxylate esters of beta-carboline that cause anxiety in man can
also facilitate the onset of behavioral inhibition by a punishment of an intensity
that is not sensed by saline-treated rats (Corda et al., 1983); this facilitation is
termed a "proconflict" action; that is, the drugs cause a conflict behavior that
did not exist without the drug. The beta-carboline derivative FG 7142 (beta-
carboline-3-carboxylic acid ethylester methyl amide), which produces panic anxiety in man (Dorow, Horowski, Paschelke, Amin, & Braestrup, 1983), also
depresses drinking in thirsty rats (Corda et al., 1983) when the aversive stimulus
delivered to the drinking spout has a subthreshold intensity (see Table 2). FG
7142 fails to change behavioral suppression when the shock is set at a higher
intensity and fails to reduce drinking when drinking is not paired with shock.
However, before accepting the parallel that human anxiolytic compounds cause
suppression of a specific type of punished behavior in the animal test of Vogel
et al. (1971), other ligands of benzodiazepine recognition sites that are not
anxiogenic must be shown to fail in the suppression of punished behavior. We
tested the benzodiazepine antagonists RO 15–1788 and CGS 8216 (Bernard,
Bergen, Sobisky, & Robson, 1981) and found that both compounds failed to
evince an anticonflict or a proconflict action, but (as seen in Table 3) they

TABLE 3
Antagonism by RO 15–1788 of the
Proconflict Action of FG 7142

	Licking Periods per 3 Minutes	
Treatment	Saline	FG 7142
Saline	22 ± 2.1	9.6 ± .8[a]
RO 15–1788	21 ± 2.2	21 ± 2.9

[a]$p < .01$ when compared to saline-treated animals. RO 15–1788 (2 mg/kg) and FG 7142 (4 mg/kg) were injected i.v. 10 minutes before the test. Each value is the mean of 6–10 animals per group. RO 15–1788 is the specific blocker of benzodiazepine recognition site (Haefely, Bonetti, Burkard, Cumin, Laurent, Möhler, Pieri, Polc, Richards Schaffner and Scherschlicht, 1983) and FG 7124 is a derivative of beta-carboline endowed with anxiogenic activity in man (Dorow et al., 1983).

antagonized the proconflict action caused by FG 7142 and the anticonflict action of benzodiazepines.

Role of GABA in the Anticonflict and Proconflict Action of Benzodiazepine Recognition Site Ligands

The data of Tables 1 and 3 show that the proconflict action of the beta-carboline derivatives and the anticonflict action of diazepam are specifically mediated through a binding to the benzodiazepine recognition site, since they are completely antagonized by RO 15–1788. We may ask whether the proconflict and anticonflict action is related to a facilitation of GABAergic transmission. The anticonflict effect of benzodiazepines is potentiated and mimicked by the i.c.v. injection of muscimol, a GABA receptor agonist (Cananzi, Costa, & Guidotti, 1980). Bicuculline and picrotoxin, which reduce GABA receptor function, curtail or completely inhibit the anticonflict action of diazepam (Stein, Wise, & Belluzzi, 1975). These findings suggest an involvement of GABA receptors in the control of behavioral inhibition induced by punishment, and they are consistent with the theory that the anxiolytic action of benzodiazepines is mediated through facilitation of GABAergic transmission (Costa, Guidotti, & Mao, 1975; Costa, Guidotti, Mao, & Suria, 1975).

To verify whether a down regulation of GABAergic transmission participates in the proconflict action of the 3-carboxylate esters of beta carboline, we studied whether the proconflict action of these drugs could be changed by compounds known to impair GABAergic transmission. We used isoniazid in doses that decrease the GABA content of various brain areas by inhibiting the activity of glutamic acid decarboxylase. Table 4 shows that 150 mg/kg i.p. of isoniazid failed to change licking punished by a low intensity shock. When this dose was given 30 minutes before FG 7142, it potentiated by fivefold the action of this anxiogenic drug.

Since higher doses of isoniazid may cause convulsions after 40-minutes latency, the potentiation of the anticonflict action of FG 7142 by isoniazid could be considered a nonspecific response elicited by subconvulsant doses of a convulsant. However the lack of specificity could be ruled out by showing that a subconvulsant dose of strychnine failed to change the punished behavior (Stein et al., 1975; Corda, unpublished). Hence, these results are consistent with the possibility that also the proconflict action of the 3-carboxylate esters of beta-carboline is associated with a down regulation of GABAergic transmission. This suggestion agrees with studies showing that beta-carboline 3-carboxylates block the enhancement of high affinity GABA binding elicited by benzodiazepines (Guidotti, Corda, Wise, Vaccarino, & Costa, 1983; Skerritt, Johnston, & Braestrup, 1983), decrease the ^{3}H-GABA binding to synaptic membranes (Concas, Salis, Serra, Corda, & Biggio, 1983), and antagonize the inhibitory effect of GABA on the firing rate of hippocampal pyramidal cells (Polc et al., 1981).

To consolidate the view that a down regulation of GABAergic transmission could be operative in the regulation of punished behavior, Lal and Shearman (1980) studied whether metrazol, which is known to be anxiogenic in man and which is reported to act on GABA receptors, could evoke a proconflict action.

The data of Table 5 show that metrazol inhibits punished behavior and unlike benzodiazepines and 3-carboxylate esters of beta carbolines, the action of metrazol is resistant to the inhibitory action of RO 15–1788. Although metrazol is chemically unrelated to the 3-carboxylate esters of beta-carbolines, its pharmacological profile on punished behavior is seen as similar to that of the beta-carboline derivatives. Since in electrophysiological experiments metrazol

TABLE 4
Facilitation by Isoniazid of the Suppression of Punished
Behavior Elicited by FG 7142

	Licking Periods per 3 Minutes	
Treatment	Saline	Isoniazid
Saline	23 ± 1.5	22 ± 1.8
FG 7142 (.5 mg/kg i.v.)	21 ± 1.8	13 ± .96[a]
FG 7142 (1.25 mg/kg i.v.)	22 ± 1.6	5.5 ± 2.1
FG 7142 (2.5 mg/kg i.v.)	13 ± 1.4	—

[a]Isoniazid (150 mg/kg i.p.) was injected 40 minutes before the test. FG 7142 was injected intravenously 10 minutes before the test. Punishment was a .3 mA shock delivered to the water spout. FG 7142 is an anxiogenic drug in man (Dorow et al., 1983).

TABLE 5
Action of Metrazol on Punished Behavior

	Licking Periods per 3 Minutes	
Treatment	Saline	RO 15–1788
Metrazol (15 mg/kg i.p.)	11 ± 1.2	11 ± 1
Metrazol (20 mg/kg i.p.)	9 ± .96	10 ± .83
Saline	23 ± 2.1	22 ± 1.8

RO 15–1788 (6 mg/kg i.v.) and metrazol were injected 20 and 15 minutes before the test, respectively. Shock intensity was .3 mA.

antagonizes the postsynaptic inhibition mediated by GABA by acting on Cl^- channels, one can infer that anxiogenic action in humans and punished behavior regulation in rodents are related to GABAergic function. In the test proposed by Vogel et al. (1971), using low current intensity, metrazol in doses that would cause anxiety in humans and which were one-third or less of those required to induce convulsions mimicked the proconflict effect of the 3-carboxylic esters of beta carboline. However, unlike the beta-carboline derivatives, the action of metrazol cannot be antagonized by RO 15–1788 (Table 5) because the drug modifies GABAergic transmission by acting at a site that is after the benzodiazepine recognition site. Hence the results obtained using punishment as a probe to study modulation of behavior by GABAergic mechanisms indicate that GABA transmission can be modulated by the so-called recognition site of benzodiazepines. To sum up, according to the intrinsic properties of the ligand used to test the role of the benzodiazepine recognition sites, one can elicit the following specific profiles of pharmacological activities: (1) ligands that possess anticonflict action (benzodiazepines) may relieve anxiety in humans; (2) ligands that possess proconflict action may cause panic anxiety in humans (beta-carboline-3-carboxylate derivatives); and (3) high affinity ligands that appear pharmacologically inert can block the anxiogenic or the anxiolytic action of the two classes of benzodiazepine recognition site ligands mentioned above and produce a proconvulsant action when GABAergic transmission is down regulated (Corda et al., 1982).

From the above studies it appears clear that using a conflict test one cannot answer the question whether or not benzodiazepine recognition sites are drug receptors devoid of physiological significance or physiological receptors subserving the action of endogenous effectors. This question can be answered only when an endogenous ligand is found that mimics the action of benzodiazepines or that of beta-carbolines. It is tempting to infer as a working hypothesis that a complete spectrum of behavioral states, ranging from anticonflict or proconflict, could be elicited by endogenous agonist(s) of benzodiazepine recognition sites. The molecular mechanism of this behavioral action would consist of physiological modulation of a subunit of GABAergic receptors capable of amplifying or restricting the number of GABA recognition sites available to GABA released into the synaptic cleft.

Primate Behavior in the Study of the Biological Basis of Anxiety

Using male adult rhesus monkeys restrained in chairs under ketamine anesthesia and allowing them to adapt to this condition for at least 24 hours, Ninan, Insel, Cohen, Cook, Skolnick, & Paul (1982) studied the action of the 3-carboxylate ethyl ester of beta-carboline (beta-CCE) alone or in association with the benzodiazepine antagonist, RO 15-1788. They observed the behavior of the monkeys, measured cortisol, epinephrine and norepinephrine blood levels, and monitored heart rate and blood pressure. Tackycardia, increase in blood pressure, and elevation in blood levels of epinephrine, norepinephrine, and cortisol followed the injection of beta-CCE. In addition, the monkeys exhibited vocalization, defecation, urination, penile erection, and intense behavioral agitation. These effects were abolished by RO 15-1788, leading Ninan et al. (1982) to believe that all these responses were related to the stimulation of central mechanisms that are modulated by benzodiazepine recognition sites. They proposed that monkey responsiveness to injection of beta-CCE is a reliable and reproducible model of human anxiety and, as such, can be a valuable model in studying anxiety and stress in a variety of human diseases. Finally, they concluded that these experiments demonstrated that the benzodiazepine recognition sites and the interacting GABA receptor complexes are located in the monkey's brain and are important for the behavioral and physiological expression of anxiety, which could be estimated by measuring blood levels.

I believe that the experiments discussed above merely confirm Haefely, Polc, Pieri, Schaffner, & Laurent (1983) report that RO 15-1788 antagonizes the effects of beta carboline-3-carboxylate derivatives. The model proposed by Ninan et al. (1982) is an artificial one, which fails to deal with the physiology of the receptor complex as it is involved in anxiety. In addition, there is the possible participation of peripheral GABAergic mechanisms in the responses elicited by beta-CCE. Recent experiments (Kataoka, Gutman, Costa, & Guidotti, 1983) have shown the existence of functional GABAergic mechanisms within the adrenal medulla.

One interpretation of the data summarized in Table 6 is that GABA functions as an autocoid regulating cholinergic modulation of chromaffin cells. GABA produced and released (by acetylcholine (?) or histamine (?)) from a selected population of chromaffin cells could modulate medullary cell responsiveness to acetylcholine (released from splanchnic axons) and perhaps to histamine, enkephalins and other endocoids (secreted by splanching terminals or medullary cells).

TABLE 6
GABAergic Mechanisms in Primary Cultures of Bovine Chromaffin
Cells from Adrenal Medulla*

1. GABA is present in primary culture of chromaffin cells and is secreted in the medium.
2. Some chromaffin cells contain glutamic acid decarboxylase (histochemical evidence).
3. Chromaffin cells contain high and low affinity GABA recognition sites.
4. Chromaffin cells contain benzodiazepine recognition sites.
5. Bicuculline, 10^{-6}M facilitates the release of catecholamines elicited by ACh added to the primary cultures of chromaffin cells.
6. In anesthetized dog the quaternary (N) derivative of bicuculline injected intravenously (1 mg/ kg i.v.) facilitates the release of catecholamines from adrenal medulla elicited by electric stimulation of the severed splanchnic.

*For details see Kateska, Gutman, Guidotti, Panula, Wrobleski, Cosenza-Murphy, Wu and Costa (1984).

Since there is reason to believe that all of these factors are functionally operative in regulating the adrenal medullary output of the catecholamines, which are responsible for blood pressure and heart rate effects of beta-CCE, one would tentatively suggest that some of the factors recorded in the experiments by Ninan et al. (1982) are only a reflection of the medullary function stimulated "directly" by the beta-CCE.

THE GABA RECEPTOR COMPLEX

Several lines of independent investigations have created a consensus of opinion that GABAergic transmission participates in the anticonvulsant and anxiolytic action of benzodiazepines (Costa, 1983). The evidence implies that the benzo-diazepine recognition site interacts with specific GABA receptor sites (Costa & Guidotti, 1979). Since the benzodiazepine recognition site is easily accessible to investigation, several lines of evidence suggest that it is intimately connected with the Cl^- channel of the GABA receptor. Though the conformational changes induced in the benzodiazepine recognition sites by the various ligands have not yet been unveiled, the transducer function that is regulated by these changes appears to be the GABA-regulated Cl^- ionophore. Unlike the recognition sites for transmitters, the conformational changes elicited by various ligands on the benzodiazepine recognition sites do not seem to act directly on a specific trans-ducer mechanism but require the release of GABA to express an action. Hence on the basis of all established evidence, it is confirmed (as early suggested by us) that the benzodiazepine recognition site does not subserve a specific trans-mitter function but operates through GABAergic mechanisms (Costa & Guidotti, 1979). Activation of the benzodiazepine recognition sites by anticonflict drugs probably amplifies the operation of the GABA receptor system, whereas occupancy of these sites by proconflict drugs restricts GABA receptor operation. The molecular mechanism operative in this modulation of the Bmax of GABA recognition sites is not precisely known (Guidotti et al., 1983). Certainly the activation of benzodiazepine recognition sites by anxiolytics modulates GABA-mediated changes of Cl^- currents across postsynaptic membranes. The crucial result of benzodiazepine recognition site activation by anticonflict ligands is an increase in the time in which the Cl^- channel remains open (Study & Barker, 1981). Thus, we can suggest that benzodiazepine recognition site activation by anticonflict ligands indirectly regulates Cl^- channel operation via modification of GABA receptors. Though all the GABAergic synapses are potential targets for injected benzodiazepines, the level of activation of a given GABAergic synapse by the injected benzodiazepine depends largely on the level of synaptic activity operative in that GABAergic synapse. If we assume that benzodiazepine recognition sites are the physiological sites of action of an endogenous ligand, and not casual receptors for the mediation of drug actions, then it would become relevant to insert the type of synaptic action of benzodiazepines into the larger puzzle of synaptic transmission. In this larger view of the problem we should be mindful that there are two classes of GABA receptors (Olsen et al., 1980), which can be differentiated by their ability to be coupled or not with benzodiazepine recognition sites—$GABA_A$ and $GABA_B$ receptors. $GABA_A$ receptors are susceptible to benzodiazepine modulation and are activated by muscimol and not by baclofen. In contrast, $GABA_B$ receptors are muscimol resistant, cannot be modulated by benzodiazepines, but can be activated by baclofen (Bowery et al., 1980). There are also two types of benzodiazepine recognition sites: one that has been termed "central," which is clonazepam sensitive, and another termed "peripheral," which is clonazepam resistant, and binds with high affinity 4'-chlordiazepam (RO 5–4864) (Syapin & Skolnick, 1979).

However, it has been found that peripheral benzodiazepine recognition sites are located in the brain, perhaps on glial cells (Gallager, Mallorga, Oertel, Henneberry, & Tallman, 1981). They have a functional role in brain because RO 5–4864 is capable of causing convulsions (Weissman et al., 1983). It is not known whether both types of benzodiazepine sites are linked to GABA receptors, but it does not appear that any benzodiazepine recognition site is linked to $GABA_B$ receptors. Recent evidence (Majewska, Chuang, & Costa, 1983) suggests that RO 5–4864 binds with high affinity to a benzodiazepine recognition site located in glial cells, which is linked to a $GABA_A$ site that is not coupled with a Cl^- channel, but coupled with phospholipase A_2. Hence it could be proposed that there are two types of $GABA_A$ receptors. A $GABA_{A1}$ that is linked to the Cl^- channels is coupled to a benzodiazepine recognition site that binds RO 15–1788 but not RO 5–4864. The function of this benzodiazepine recognition site is that of modulating GABA action on the Cl^- channel; the action of benzodiazepines is specifically blocked by RO 15–1788. A $GABA_{A2}$, which is linked to a phospholipase A_2, is coupled to a benzodiazepine recognition site that binds RO 5–4864 but not RO 15–1788. The function of this benzodiazepine recognition site is that of facilitating the stimulation of phospholipase A_2 by GABA and causing the accumulation of prostaglandin D_2; the action of benzodiazepines is blocked by RO 5–4864 which is devoid of intrinsic activity of $GABA_{A2}$ receptors. If the evidence discussed above is projected into the current concept on the functioning of synapses, we must suggest that there are at least two types of regulatory recognition sites and two effectors in GABA "A1" synapses: the GABA effector site is linked to the Cl^- channel that functions as its transducer; in contrast, the benzodiazepine recognition sites are linked indirectly to GABA recognition sites and they require GABA to act. They function by modulating the action of GABA on the Cl^- channel. GABA "A2" receptor is not a synaptic receptor and functions by activating phospholipase A_2 located in the glial cell membrane. The benzodiazepine recognition sites enlarge the action of GABA by stimulating the formation of prostaglandin D_2. The function of this $GABA_{A2}$ receptor is unknown and could be mediated by arachidonic acid and prostaglandin D_2 functioning as second messengers. This and other studies of GABAergic receptors support the contention that multiple chemical signals may participate in the communication transfer at $GABA_A$ synapses.

The "Barbiturate Shift"

It is presently believed that $GABA_{A1}$ receptors are supramolecular entities that include several functional subunits. In addition to the Cl^- ionophore, GABA and benzodiazepine recognition site, the GABA receptor may include a protein kinase (Wise, Guidotti, & Costa, 1983) and a coupler protein called GABA modulin (GM) (Guidotti et al., 1982). A complete understanding of the molecular interaction that makes these subunits operative and how this operation links with that of Cl^- ionophores is still lacking, however, it is known that the Cl^- ionophore includes a number of modulatory sites that mediate the action of picrotoxin, metrazol, and some barbiturates; probably also these sites may have endogenous effectors that function in GABAergic transmission.

In order to gain some understanding of the properties of the Cl^- channel, particular attention has been paid to the action of those barbiturates that are believed to facilitate GABA function by acting on the Cl^- channel (Olsen, 1981). Since benzodiazepine binding depends on Cl^- concentrations, Braestrup, Honore, Nielsen, Petersen and Jensen (1983) have studied the effect of $10^{-3}M$ pentobarbital on the affinity of ligands for the benzodiazepine recognition sites. For instance, the affinity of beta-CCM for the benzodiazepine binding site is reduced by pentobarbital, while that of flunitrazepam is enhanced by about twofold (30° Cl^- containing buffer). The capacity of barbiturates to modulate benzodiazepine recognition sites has been termed the *barbiturate shift*. Table 7 shows the barbiturate shift for some of the benzodiazepine recognition site ligands. In the examples of Table 7, the "barbiturate shift" value partially predicts pharmacological efficacy. A low "barbiturate shift" value appears to characterize proconflict action; a high "barbiturate shift" value typifies anticonflict action. From this data it appears that sites in the Cl^- channel of the GABA receptors participate in the benzodiazepine induced modification of GABA receptor function. It is conceivable that the overall pharmacological efficacy of a ligand for benzodiazepine recognition sites may not depend on a specific coupling mechanism, but may reflect many aspects of the complex GABA receptor function.

The "GABA Shift"

Another method to probe interactions between various components of the GABA receptors is the *GABA shift*. This term refers to the ability of added GABA to produce a change in direction of the binding characteristics of various ligands for the benzodiazepine recognition sites. Table 8 shows that the three classes of benzodiazepine recognition site ligands can be differentiated by the GABA shift. Moreover, the three classes of benzodiazepine recognition site ligands have a different photoaffinity labeling ligand ratio. They differ functionally with regard to their modality to link to the proteins that form the recognition site, and are associated with a difference in the intrinsic activity of the compound as documented by the response in the conflict test. The relationship between binding,

TABLE 7
Barbiturate Shift[a] For a Number of Ligands
for Benzodiazepine Recognition Sites

Compound	Barbiturate Shift
Anticonflict Drugs	
Diazepam	3.14
Lararepam	1.83
Triazolam	1.71
Antagonist Drugs	
Without Intrinsic Activity	
RO 15–1788	1.09
CGS 8216	.93
Proconflict Drugs	
DMCM	.56
FG 7142	.51
β-CCM	.50

$$^a\text{Barbiturate shift} = \frac{IC_{50} \text{ per pentobarbital}}{IC_{50} + \text{pentobarbital } 10^{-3}M}.$$ (See Braestrup et al., 1983)

TABLE 8
Photoaffinity Labeling Ratio (PALR) and GABA Shift For Various Ligands
of Benzodiazepine Recognition Sites

Type of Drug	Compound	GABA Shift[a]	PALR[b]
Anticonflict	Flunitrazepam	2.4	2
	Diazepam	2.3	2.2
	Clonazepam	2.1	1.5
Antagonist	RO 15–1788	1.2	.10
	CGS 8216	.86	.12
Proconflict	Beta-CCM	.81	.11
	DMCM	.60	.093

[a]IC_{50} for ^{3}H-flunitrazepan $\dfrac{\text{without GABA}}{\text{with GABA}}$

[b]log IC_{50} for ^{3}H-Beta-CCE $\dfrac{\text{in photoaffinity-labeled membrane}}{\text{not photoaffinity-labeled membrane}}$

DMCM = (6,7-dimethoxy-4-ethyl-beta-carboline-3-carboxylic acid methyl ester

βCCM = (beta-carboline-3-carboxylic acid methyl ester)

βCCE = (beta-carboline-3-carboxylic acid ethyl ester)

GABA shift, and conflict test allows us to infer the existence of a correlation between benzodiazepine/GABA interaction and operant behavior in animals studied in a conflict situation.

GABA-Modulin

As mentioned earlier, when ^{3}H-GABA is incubated with crude synaptic membrane preparations, it binds to two populations of specific GABA "A" recognition sites (Toffano, Guidotti, & Costa, 1978). These two populations of GABA binding sites are also present in membranes of cloned cell cultures (NB$_{2A}$ and C6) (Baraldi, Guidotti, Schwartz, & Costa, 1979), and do not appear to be artifacts of preparing crude synaptic membranes from brain. One population of sites has a high affinity (20 to 30 nM), the other a low affinity (120–200 nM) for ^{3}H-GABA. Only the high affinity population of binding sites is down regulated by the addition of the endogenous basic protein located in synaptic membranes and in membranes of cloned cell preparations that include GABA receptors in their membranes (Baraldi et al., 1979; Toffano et al., 1978). We have purified this protein to homogeneity and termed it *GABA modulin* (GM) (Guidotti et al., 1982). The properties and the amino acid composition of this protein are reported in Tables 9 and 10.

If the concentration of free GABA present in brain preparations were to be present in vivo, one has the impression that there must be specific mechanisms regulating receptor availability for GABA released by nerve impulses. One such mechanism appears to be the modulation of high affinity GABA recognition site

TABLE 9
Characteristics of GABA-Modulin (GM)

Molecular Weight	~ 16500
Thermostable	yes
Basic	yes
A polypeptide	yes
Different from myelin basic protein	yes
Inhibits high affinity ^{3}H-GABA binding allosterically	yes
Inhibits ^{3}H-diazepam binding	no
Binds ^{3}H-GABA	no
Binds ^{3}H-Benzodiazepines	no
Is a substrate of cAMP-protein kinase	yes (stoichiometry = 4)
Is a substrate of Ca^{2a} dependent protein kinase	yes (stoichiometry = 1)
GABA content	undetectable
Phospholipid content	undetectable
Loses biological activity after cAMP dependent phosphorylation	yes
Loses biological activity after Ca^{2+}-dependent phosphorylation	no

by GM. The amino acid composition of GM is similar to the small molecular weight myelin basic protein (SMBP), and like this protein, GM can be phosphorylated by cyclic-adenosine monophosphate (cAMP) and Ca^{2+} dependent protein kinases (Wise et al., 1983).

The chromatographic behavior of SMBP is similar to that of GM. However, this basic protein can be extracted from subcellular fractions that are enriched with postsynaptic synaptosomal membranes and are devoid of myelin (Vaccarino, Costa, & Guidotti, 1983). Table 11 shows that the amino acid composition of SMBP differs substantially from that of GM. Other differences between these two proteins are also reported in Table 11. Finally, GM and not SMBP inhibits the Bmax of high affinity ^{3}H-GABA binding when added to purified preparations of crude synaptic membranes (Guidotti et al., 1982). Other basic proteins, such as various types of histones and high molecular weight myelin basic protein (obtained from M. Kies, NIMH) fail to affect ^{3}H-GABA binding (Guidotti et al., 1982). Taken together, this evidence allows a working hypothesis that GM functions as a coupler protein in GABA receptors. Probably this protein, through phosphorylation and dephosphorylation, mediates the interactions of GABA and benzodiazepine recognition sites (Wise et al., 1983). When GM is phosphorylated by cAMP, dependent enzymes fail to inhibit the Bmax of high affinity GABA recognition sites. This change in GM function fails to occur following phosphorylation with Ca^{2+} dependent protein kinase. The Ca^{2+} dependent protein kinase phosphorylates only one amino acid residue per molecule of GM, whereas the cAMP dependent enzyme phosphorylates four amino acids residues per GM molecule. The GM with four phosphorylated residues loses its biological activity, whereas the GM with only one phosphorylated residue retains its capability to inhibit Bmax of GABA binding. In order to better

TABLE 10
Amino Acid Composition of GABA-
Modulin Extracted from Synapto-
somes of Rat Brain

Residue	Mean Value of the Relative No. of Amino Acid Residues per Mole
Asx	10(10,11)
Thr	7(6,8)
Ser	12(11,13)
Glx	14(13,16)
Pro	11(9,13)
Gly	15(14,16)
Ala	11(10,12)
Cys	0
Val	5(4,6)
Met	2(1,3)
Ile	4(4,5)
Leu	7(6,8)
Thy	2(2)
Phe	5(4,5)
Lys	11(10,12)
His	5(4,5)
Arg	10(9,12)
Trp	—
Total	131

The protein was analyzed with a Hitachi 835 automatic amino acid analyzer. The values are calculated on a 17000 δ molecular weight. The value is the average of 8 analyses; in parenthesis upper and lower values obtained.

understand the relationship between phosphorylation and biological activity, a partial tryptic digestion of GM phosphorylated with the two enzymes was performed (Wise et al., 1983). The tryptic digests of the two products appear to be very different. Data reported in Table 12 clearly show that the two enzymes phosphorylate completely different sites. The fragment that is phosphorylated by the Ca^{2+} dependent enzyme is different from each of the four fragments that are phosphorylated by the cAMP dependent enzyme. It remains to be ascertained whether or not the phosphorylation occurs always in the serine residue; it would not be surprising if, in the case of the Ca^{2+} dependent protein kinase, a fragment with a tyrosine residue were to be phosphorylated. The action of GM on ^{3}H-GABA binding appears to be rather specific for the specific binding of dopamine; norepinephrine (NE), muscarinic antagonists (QNB), opiates, imipramine and benzodiazepines failed to be changed by GM (Guidotti et al., 1982). Moreover the specificity of GM is further supported by the GM inhibition of the GABA-elicited facilitation of benzodiazepine binding, by the benzodiazepine-elicited

TABLE 11
Differences between GABA-Modulin and Small Myelin Basic Protein
from Rat Brain

	GABA-modulin (GM)	Small Myelin Basic Protein (SMBP)
Subcellular distribution	Synaptosomes	myelin
Molecular weight (SDS-PAGE)	17,000	15,500
Total amino acid residues	131	125
Major differences in amino acid residues		
Glx	14	7
Arg	10	17
Lys	11	7
Ser	12	15
Mobility toward cathode on urea-acidic PAGE	Lower	Higher
Retention time on reverse phase HPLC (μ Bondopack C18)	53.6	48.6
MW of major fragment after cyanogen bromide treatment	13,000	13,500

TABLE 12
HPLC Separation of Tryptic Fragments of Phosphorylated GM Using
Ca^{2+} or cAMP-Dependent Protein Kinase

GM Phosphorylation Conditions	HPLC Retention Time of Phosphorylated Fragments				
cAMP-dependent protein kinase	9	—	21	26	30
Ca^{2+}-dependent protein kinase	—	19	—	—	—
Peptide	1	II	III	IV	V

ODS 10 gradient 0–50%; .1% TFA acetonitrile in 180 min.

facilitation of GABA binding, and by the lack of action of GM on the facilitation of GABA or benzodiazepine binding induced by pentobarbital (Costa & Guidotti, 1979; Guidotti et al., 1982). These findings suggest that GM may participate in the modulation of GABA binding when a number of ligands stimulate benzodiazepine recognition sites. The putative mechanism is depicted in Fig. 1. We have adopted as a working hypothesis the view that protein kinase and GM are functionally linked to GABA receptor function. This is supported by experiments showing that GM can be phosphorylated in vitro while still located in brain

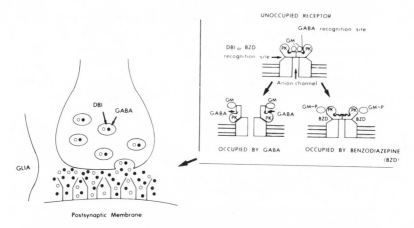

FIG. 1.   Schematic representation of a GABAergic synapse. The primary trans-
mitter-cotransmitter hypothesis proposes a presynaptic terminal containing GABA
and the endogenous benzodiazepine effector (DBI). In the insert a view of the
postsynaptic GABA/benzodiazepine receptor complex in three different states:
unoccupied, occupied by GABA and occupied by benzodiazepines (BZD). The
binding of GABA to its recognition site is partially impaired by the presence of
GABA-modulin (GM) in proximity of the recognition site (see unoccupied receptor
and receptor occupied by GABA). Benzodiazepines, presumably through activation of a protein kinase (PK), remove GM molecules from the GABA recognition
site thus helping GABA to bind. When bound, GABA allows chloride ions to
flow through the anion channel, inhibiting nerve signals.

membranes by the addition of Ca^{2+} or cAMP. However, the functional characterization of the role of cyclic-guanyl monophosphate (GMP) in GABA receptor function has not yet been completed.

ENDOGENOUS LIGANDS FOR THE BENZODIAZEPINE
RECOGNITION SITE

Strictly connected to the concept that the benzodiazepine recognition sites do
not directly modulate a transducer system but are coupled to the function of the
GABA/Cl$^-$ ionophore/transducer complex is the question of the physiological
role that those benzodiazepine recognition sites may exert and whether there is
an endogenous effector for these sites. The opinions in the field are divided
about this issue. One school of thought believes in the existence of an endogenous
effector for the benzodiazepine recognition sites; whereas another designs and
interprets experiments as if the endogenous effector did not exist. In fact, the
latter group of scientists studies the mode of action of benzodiazepines as if
these drugs were binding to a site located on the GABA receptor, which is devoid

of physiological significance. The lack of intrinsic pharmacological action of RO 15–1788 is used as evidence against the existence of an endogenous effector. We take exception to this conclusion and hold that the lack of action of RO 15–1788 in normal GABAergic synapses is in line with the concept that there are multiple signals in GABAergic synaptic transmission. If the benzodiazepine recognition sites reflect the site of action of the co-transmitter chemical signal involved in GABAergic transmission, then it is not surprising that the occupancy of a co-transmitter binding site by RO 15–1788 can be physiologically silent when GABAergic transmission is in balance. Co-transmitters change the gain of the system, but do not activate the transducer that is linked to the receptor (Costa, 1982).

Since there is no electrogenic signal generated in the postsynaptic membrane by agonists of benzodiazepine recognition site, the postsynaptic cell is not stimulated and no effect should be expected from the blockade of the benzodiazepine recognition site. Only if the function of a given GABAergic synapse is out of balance is there an overt activation of the benzodiazepine recognition site. In these cases there is an action associated with the blockade of benzodiazepine recognition sites by RO 15–1788. Presumably, only when GABAergic synapses are out of balance is there an important spontaneous secretion of the endogenous effector of benzodiazepine recognition sites. Through the secretion of the endogenous effector the altered GABAergic synaptic function is balanced, presumably because the gain at GABA synapses is amplified or reduced.

Historical Perspectives

Since the discovery of specific high affinity binding sites for benzodiazepines, much effort has gone into the search for endogenous effectors of these sites. Two approaches have been followed: extraction of specifically acting endogenous brain components and functional evaluation of previously studied brain components. Both approaches study modifications of high affinity ligand binding to benzodiazepine recognition sites to define the potency of putative ligands. Then these ligands are used in tests directed to evaluate anticonvulsant-proconvulsant or proconflict-anticonflict activities.

Purines were the first candidates for a natural ligand of benzodiazepine recognition sites (Marangos et al., 1979). Although their potency is a thousandfold smaller than that of the benzodiazepines, the combined in vivo concentrations of inosine and hypoxanthine in tissues are in a range sufficient to occupy a reasonable number of benzodiazepine recognition sites. Though the behavioral testing of inosine has shown this compound to be similar to benzodiazepines in antagonizing metrazol seizures (Skolnick, Syapin, Paugh, Moncada, Marangos, & Paul, 1979), these experiments have created confusion by showing that inosine reverses the sedative effect of diazepam in mice. A role of purines as endogenous effectors of benzodiazepine recognition sites became questionable after Lapin

(1981) demonstrated that inosine and hypoxantine are low potency, nonspecific, nonselective anticonvulsants, and therefore, their antimetrazol action cannot be related to their binding to benzodiazepine recognition sites. Nevertheless, benzodiazepines antagonize caffeine and theophylline-induced convulsions (Marangos, Matino, Paul, & Skolnick, 1981), which are mediated by an action on specific adenosine receptors. Rather than speculate on a physiological role of purines as effectors of the benzodiazepine recognition sites, these compounds may act to modify benzodiazepines via an action on adenosine receptors.

Melatonin and the melatonin metabolite N-acetyl-5-methoxy-kynurenamine (Marangos, Patel, Hirata, Sondhein, Paul, Skolnick, & Goodwin, 1981) have good affinity for benzodiazepine recognition sites and for this reason have been considered as putative endogenous ligands. Melatonin is anticonvulsant and sedative (Albertson, Petersen, Stark, Lakin, & Winters, 1981). If melatonin were to be the endogenous effector, one would have to assume that benzodiazepines act by mimicking the action of melatonin. In addition, another putative ligand of benzodiazepine recognition sites is a tryptophan derivative, the dipeptide tryptophan-glycine. The compound produces sedation and augments the anticonvulsant effects of diazepam (Velucci & Webster, 1981). More recently, D-thyroxine was shown to have high affinity for the benzodiazepine recognition sites (Nagy & Lajtha, 1983); however, this compound has not been found in tissue in sufficient concentrations to be considered an endogenous effector. These potential physiological ligands of benzodiazepine recognition sites are not considered valid because they fail to fulfill one or more of the essential prerequisites for a putative effector.

In considering whether or not benzodiazepines can mimic or antagonize an endogenous effector that physiologically regulates the level of anxiety through the modulation of a GABAergic mechanism, we are proposing that benzodiazepines act in a manner similar to that of morphine. That is, they mimic an endogenous effector. It appears that this analogy extends to the presence in both systems of two configurations of effectors (agonist-antagonist). In our laboratory, the existence of an endogenous effector for the benzodiazepine/GABA receptor complex was inferred from observations made while studying endogenous factors that modify the interaction between GABA and benzodiazepines (Massotti, Guidotti, & Costa, 1981). We noticed that the Kd for ^{3}H-diazepam binding to GABA free crude synaptic membranes, prepared from rat brain, was reduced by about 50% when the membranes were repeatedly washed with low concentrations of detergent. It was soon discovered that the synaptic membranes contained a peptide that produced a dose-related increase in the Kd of diazepam binding without affecting the Bmax. Subsequently, several partially purified brain preparations, capable of displacing ^{3}H benzodiazepines from their binding sites, were isolated in other laboratories. Although these studies have failed to identify the endogenous ligand of benzodiazepine recognition sites, which is presumably responsible for the control of anxiety, they have focused attention on a number of high affinity ligands, such as the beta-carboline-3-carboxylic esters (Braestrup & Nielsen, 1981), which are currently an important tool to study the biochemical pharmacology of anxiety.

Isolation of an Anxiogenic Brain Peptide That Displaces ^{3}H-Diazepam From High Affinity Recognition Sites

Using binding affinity and Vogel's testing procedure (Vogel et al., 1971) we have been successful in isolating and characterizing a natural brain peptide that has affinity for benzodiazepine recognition sites (Guidotti et al., 1983). This basic brain peptide has 103 amino acids (1.1×10^4 dalton) and is termed DBI (diazepam binding inhibitor) because it displaces ^{3}H-diazepam from its binding sites (Table 13).

Experiments carried out to establish the sequence of the amino acids that are constituents of this purified peptide revealed that its N-terminal amino acid is blocked. The presence of 2-methionine residues in the molecule allowed for the generation of three fragments following cyanogen bromide treatment. The sequence of the carboxy terminal fragment and a partial sequence of the middle fragment were performed (Guidotti et al., 1983). The two amino acid sequences that

TABLE 13
Amino Acid Composition of Diazepam Binding Inhibitor (DBI) Purified From Rat Brain

Residue	Number of Residues
Asparagine/aspartate	10
Threonine	7
Serine	10
Glutamate/glutamine	12
Proline	3
Glycine	6
Alanine	8
Cysteine	0
Valine	4
Methionine	2
Isoleucine	3
Leucine	7
Tyrosine	4
Histidine	3
Phenylalanine	3
Lysine	19
Arginine	3
Tryptophan	1
Total	105

emerged are unique. The concentrations of DBI in brain was about 10–25 μM; less than 1 μM of DBI was found in peripheral tissues. Benzodiazepines and ^{3}H-beta-carboline are displaced by DBI competitively, K_1 1 to 4 μM. Because DBI inhibits ^{3}H-beta-carboline binding more effectively than ^{3}H benzodiazepines, the question arose whether the endogenous effector possessed anxiogenic rather than anxiolytic action. To answer this question, DBI was injected intraventricularly into thirsty rats subjected to the thirst conflict test. The compound failed to display anticonflict action, and actually antagonized the anticonflict action of benzodiazepines. In addition it lowered the threshold for the suppression of punished behavior evidencing a clear proconflict action, which could be blocked by RO 15–1788.

The data of Table 14 suggest that DBI may function as a naturally occurring anxiogenic compound; however, the question of whether DBI represents a physiologically relevant endogenous co-transmitter operative in GABAergic transmission remains unanswered by these experiments. If DBI has any relationship to GABAergic transmission, it might be the peptide precursor of the endogenous effector.

CONCLUSIONS

The above material encourages us to believe that the function of some GABAergic synapses is somehow related to an endogenous mechanism that regulates anxiety. The exact location of these synapses still eludes our search, but we suspect that the septum, and amgydaloid nuclei should be investigated thoroughly. Anxiety may be lessened by a facilitation of GABAergic function; reduction of GABAergic function facilitates anxiety. A continuum of behavioral states ranging from tension and panic to relaxation and calm can be brought about by various chemicals

TABLE 14
Action of Diazepam Binding Inhibitor (DBI) on the Vogel Behavioral
Paradigm of the Thirsty Rat

	Licking Periods/3 min ± S.E.			
	Vehicle		*DBI*	
Test	*Without Diazepam*	*With Diazepam*	*Without RO 15–1788*	*With RO 15–1788*
Anticonflict[a]	5 ± .8	21 ± 1.4	3 ± 1.1	5 ± .9
Proconflict	23 ± 1.4	21 ± 1.05	8 ± 1.2	18 ± 1.8

[a]Anticonflict uses high intensity shocks (1 mAmp). Proconflict uses low intensity shocks (.3 mAmp).

acting as ligands of benzodiazepine recognition sites. Whether or not this recognition site for benzodiazepines located on GABA receptors has a physiological role is still controversial. Certainly the demonstration of a physiological effector that is stored in neurons may help to resolve this puzzle. Along this line, our laboratory has shown that a brain peptide (DBI) can displace various ligands from the benzodiazepine recognition site and can cause a proconflict action in rats.

Currently, we believe that DBI, with its 104 amino acids, is a polyprotein that functions also as precursor for a smaller peptide that acts at specific receptors as a physiological ligand. This belief is substantiated by the large molecular weight of DBI and the large number of Lys-Arg; Lys-Lys bonds present in the amino acid sequence of DBI, which usually denotes signals for protease cleavage. We cannot say whether in this peptide there also exists an anxiolytic compound and whether there are anxiogenic or anxiolytic fragments that have a functioned role. On the basis of the data presented, we can hope that by continuing to study the regulation of GABAergic transmission, we may uncover the mechanisms that regulate anxiety and may provide interesting biochemical markers to sutdy anxiety states in man.

3 The Neuroendocrinology of Anxiety

Peter E. Stokes
New York Hospital–Cornell Medical Center

INTRODUCTION

In this chapter I review aspects of neuroendocrine function concentrating on those areas that have been studied in relation to anxiety or closely related affect states. The entire field of neuroendocrinology has not been explored in relation to states of anxiety, but certain neuroendocrine functions have been studied. Consequently, this chapter focuses on them. There is also the problem of defining anxiety. Much of the neuroendocrine study to date has been in relation to contrived or naturally occurring situations which induce a state referred to in the literature as "arousal" or refer to a neuroendocrine response occurring within a "stressful condition" that is implicitly, often with considerable face value, equated with anxiety. In this chapter I concentrate on human data rather than animal data.

The classical neuroendocrine system embodies all secretions of the anterior and posterior lobes of the pituitary gland. These hormones include the releasing hormones elaborated in the hypothalamus and the pituitary hormones they release. Many of the pituitary hormones act on peripheral endocrine glands in turn releasing other hormones which act on selected or all tissue cells (see Williams, 1974). The various neuroendocrine axes of the systems are seen in Fig. 1.

I have chosen to concentrate on certain neuroendocrine axes because they are more extensively studied and the problems and questions that need further attention are largely highlighted by that work. The hypothalamic-pituitary-adrenocortical (HYPAC) system is emphasized because of its classic relevance to arousal, responsiveness to appropriate stimuli, and its more recently appreciated

53

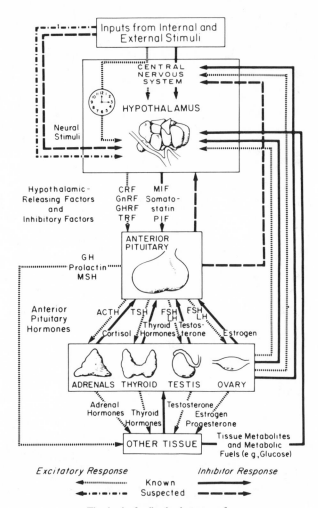

Excitatory Response   Inhibitor Response

◀·············   Known   ━━━━▶

◀·■·■·■·■   Suspected   ■━■━■▶

The basic feedback character of the neuroendocrine system is suggested in the schema above, indicating the relationship among its components: the central nervous system, hypothalamus, anterior pituitary, and target glands and tissues. Hormone secretion is regulated by a balance of stimulatory and inhibitory effects.

FIG. 1. From Krieger, 1981, p. 126.

and extensively studied activation in depression, an affect state akin to anxiety, apprehension and even fear.

The HYPAC System: Introduction and Brief Historical Background

Interest in neuroendocrine function in association with psychological stimuli started over one-half century ago. In 1922 Uno, following up the work of others, in particular Cannon (1922; Cannon & DeLa Paz, 1911) and Pavlov, reported on the effects of general excitement and fighting on the ductless glands of rats. Uno also observed an increase in pituitary weight. In 1936 Selye reported his first work showing adrenocortical enlargement and thymus involution in rats who were restrained (wrapped in towels) but had no physical injury. Herrington and Nelback in 1942 confirmed the adrenocortical hypertrophy in rats subjected to the psychological perturbation of cage vibration and noises (bells and air blasts). The work of Elmadjian (1955), Elmadjian and Pincus (1945, 1946) and that of Long (1947) in the 1940s further supported these findings.

Increased interest in the effects of psychological stimuli on neuroendocrine function, with focus continuing on the pituitary adrenocortical axis, occurred during the 1950s. Christian (1955) found a direct correlation between crowding and adrenal hypertrophy in caged mice, and this was confirmed in rats living in the wild by Barnet (1958) and Christian and Davis (1956), in wild deer by Welch (1962) and in monkeys under laboratory conditions by Mason, Harwood & Rosenthal (1957). These observations made the additional important point that the pituitary adrenocortical changes observed in relation to laboratory contrived stimuli (crowding) were similar to the results observed under conditions occurring in nature. Further support for the psychogenic origin of the adrenal hypertrophy observed in the experiments on crowding is found in the work of Bronson and Eleftheriou (1963). Among strains of fighting mice, mere exposure of the submissive or previously defeated mouse to the dominant one produced as much adrenocortical activation as actual fighting (Bronson & Eleftheriou, 1964, 1965). Thus the concept of strain or constitutional differences and the role of expectancy and prior experience, now considered important in human studies of psychogenic activation of the adrenal cortex, are highlighted in these earlier animal studies.

A few human studies, starting in the 1940s, gave parallel results to the animal data summarized above. Elevations in urinary 17-ketosteroids were observed in test pilots by Pincus and Hoagland (1943), and in 1953 Thorn, Jenkins, Laidlaw, Goetz & Reddy reported that urinary 17-hydroxycorticosteroids (17OHCS) increased in the nonphysically stressed coxswain as well as the oarsmen of the Harvard Racing Crew during race days. Mason's extensive work with monkeys (Mason et al., 1957) and humans (Mason & Brady, 1964) provided extensive data demonstrating the importance of novelty or first experiences, uncertainty or unpredictability, and expectancy or anticipation especially of something unpleasant, in the subsequent psychological activation of the pituitary adreno-cortical system. In the mid-1950s the direct chemical measurement of plasma 17OHCS was a further spur to investigation of psychologically appreciated life events as effective stimuli to the activation of the pituitary adrenal system (Bliss, Migeon, Branch, & Samuels, 1956; Fransson & Gemzell, 1955; Price, Thaler, & Mason, 1957).

Paralleling the animal and human studies was the increasing understanding of the control mechanism for the pituitary adrenal axis. The work of Harris (1956), building on the earlier work of Scharrer and Scharrer (1939), was com-pelling in demonstrating the importance of an intact hypothalamus and the hypo-thalamic-pituitary portal capillary system for adrenocortical function. This micro-portal system allows transport of factors from hypothalamic secretory neurons of the brain to the endocrine axis starting in the anterior lobe of the pituitary and continuing, via the release of adrenocorticotrophic hormone (ACTH), into the systemic circulation to the adrenal cortex. The importance of this demon-stration of the extremely intimate relationship between the nervous system and the endocrine system is still often not fully appreciated, even though four decades earlier Cannon and DeLa Paz (1911) demonstrated emotional stimulation of adrenal medullary secretion via the sympathetic nervous system.

The interrelationship of the nervous and endocrine system can be thought of in a heuristically useful manner as comprising three degrees of combined neuronal and glandular function. The most "neural" degree is that exemplified by a pre-synaptic and postsynaptic neuron when the former secretes a neurotransmitter to alter the activity of the postsynaptic neuron on which it connects. An example of the most "endocrine" degree and of classic endocrine function is seen in the hypothalamic secretory nerve cell that elaborates and releases a hormone, cor-ticotropin releasing hormone (CRH), into a portion of the circulatory system (hypophyseal portal system). Corticotropin releasing hormone, transported through this portal system, alters the activity of particular anterior pituitary cells that are not in direct contact with the secretory nerve cells in the hypothalamus. In turn, these pituitary cells or corticotrophs elaborate and secrete ACTH into the macro-circulation, thus stimulating the adrenal cortex. An intermediate degree might be exemplified by the hypothalamic (or higher CNS) neurons that synapse on the hypothalamic secretory cells that elaborate CRH. The neuroendocrine system can then be thought of as a third effector system of the central nervous system (CNS), after the long recognized motor and more recently recognized autonomic systems (Cannon, 1922; Mason, 1970).

Frankenhaeuser has extensively studied the sympathetic nervous system and the HYPAC axis. She considers the former perhaps a quicker reacting system and the latter a more protracted response system (see Frankenhaeuser, 1978, 1980 for reviews). Her extensive work over the past quarter century has related the activity of the autonomic nervous system to the perception of emotional arousal in humans. She has examined psychophysiological changes and reactions to infusions of adrenalin in attempts to replicate endogenous activation of the sympatho-adreno-medullary (SAM) axis and also has examined in detail how the endogenous SAM axis responds to relaxation *versus* participation or performance demands (Frankenhaeuser & Rissler, 1970). In addition, she has related personality characteristics (e.g., Type A personality) to psychophysiological response patterns (1975; Frankenhaeuser, Lundberg & Forsman, 1980) and has demonstrated remarkable interindividual and gender-related differences in sympathomedullary axis activity patterns within experimentally controlled or naturally occurring circumstances (1978).

From this work she has concluded that an event that is *perceived* by the individual as emotionally arousing (whether pleasant or unpleasant) will activate the sympatho-adreno-medullary system. Furthermore, attenuation of the SAM response occurs only when the initially arousing event or stimulus is no longer perceived as arousing; i.e., the attenuation is not just related to the number or frequency of exposures per se (1962). Consequently she considers that stimuli which are novel for that individual (i.e., deviate from the ordinary input load or level for stimuli) are those that will induce a SAM response. Those perceived events that are considered part of the "usual" environment do not activate the system. Thus, there are distinct and *necessary* cognitive processes that precede activation of the SAM axis: perception, followed by identification as "usual" or "unusual," and if considered arousing, then a response occurs in the SAM axis. She points out that we do not fully understand how the adrenomedullary hormones work to alter behavior.

It is also apparent that infusion of these hormones does not fully develop the spontaneous behavioral picture that occurs with an arousing stimulus. There is evidence that these peripheral hormones can get into some brain regions, especially around the base of the brain at the area of the tubero-infundibulum. Is it possible that these hormones proceed from this area into the third ventricle and then get distributed elsewhere in the CNS? There is increasing evidence for interaction of the SAM and HYPAC axes, and as usual, the interaction may go both ways.

Thus alteration in peripheral epinephrine secretion may be associated with changes in HYPAC activity secondary to those peripheral catecholamines and not only via concurrent central changes in control of HYPAC function. The HYPAC system may also influence SAM axis activity. Some evidence exists that tissue levels of cortisol may modulate the availability of synaptic biogenic amines (Maas & Mednieks, 1971). If this is true then increasing levels of cortisol in the CNS could result in alteration of biogenic amine neurotransmitters that control the sympathetic nervous system's outflow and hence adrenomedullary secretion.

I have not discussed the sympatho-adreno-medullary system in great detail because it is discussed elsewhere in this symposium, but I did want to refer to some of this work and cite Frankenhaeuser's extensive studies in this area.

STUDIES OF THE HYPAC AXIS IN ANXIETY

In the past 30 years, the study of HYPAC function has documented repeatedly the activation of this system in normals in contrived laboratory situations such as stressful interviews (Bliss et al., 1956; Hertzel, Schotistaedt, Grace, & Wolff, 1955), dramatic war movies (Wadeson, Mason, Hamberg, & Handlon, 1963), or the use of a pursuit meter (Hoagland, Bergen, Bloch, Elmadjian, & Gibree, 1955). In most instances the HYPAC activation was mild, with occasional persons showing somewhat more pronounced responses. It was also demonstrated that the level of HYPAC activity could be lowered, at least in some subjects, by using stimuli generally considered psychologically non-arousing or quieting: viewing nature films, sitting quietly in a comfortable room, or during induction of a hypnotic trance (Handlon et al., 1962; Persky, Grosz, Norton, & McMurty, 1959; Sachar, Fishman & Mason, 1965). Subsequent induction of anxiety during the trance state was associated with increased plasma 170HCS concentration indicative of HYPAC activation in women but was not observed in men (Grosz, 1961; Persky, Grosz, Norton & McMurty, 1959).

Thus, it became apparent that HYPAC activity could be increased or decreased by particular stimuli, and that many but not all subjects responded to some degree. Demographic differences such as gender were often significantly correlated with the response observed. This gender difference is apparently mediated from within the CNS portion of the HYPAC system since there is no evidence that the response of the pituitary-adrenocortical portion of the system is significantly different in males or females as far as potential response of adrenocortical steroidogensis to adequate stimuli (Koslow, Stokes, Mendels, Ramsey, & Casper, 1982). Other demographic differences such as age and body weight have recently been shown to be correlated with HYPAC activity (Stokes et al., 1984). Sufficient attention was not always given to these variables and their potential effects on the character or degree of spontaneous or stimulated output of the HYPAC system.

Naturally occurring life situations have been another area of study of HYPAC reactivity. It is not particularly surprising that life events that are generally considered emotionally arousing would be found associated with increased HYPAC activity. All of the situations studied have, more or less, incorporated the concepts and psychological sets mentioned previously that were found to be associated with HYPAC activation. These studies include, for example, apprehension before surgery (Fransson & Gemzell, 1955; Price, Thaler, & Mason, 1957), before examinations (Hodges, Jones, & Stockham, 1962; Jensen & Ek, 1962; Venning, Dyrenfurth, & Beck, 1957), novelty effects, such as found in normals on the first day of admission to a hospital as volunteers for a research project (Mason, Sachar, Fishman, Hamburg, & Handlon, 1965), or in inexperienced aircraft flight crews (Hale, Duffy, Ellis, & Williams, 1964).

Mason emphasized the significant individual differences in response to these situations. His comment raises the question of potential trait or state characteristics that might predispose differential response to apparently identical stimuli. These trait/state characteristics could be either psychological or endocrinological. Regarding the latter there could be inherent differences in the qualitative or quantitative reactivity or the neuroendocrine system to a particular stimulus. This issue has to date been inadequately studied in states of anxiety, although Bliss, Migeon, Branch, & Samuels (1956) were unable to demonstrate response differences between normals and schizophrenic subjects, given standard provocative tests of HYPAC function. Recently, considerable investigative interest has been aroused by the possibility that a neuroendocrine abnormality ("blunted" thyroid stimulating hormone [TSH] response to thyroid releasing hormone [TRH]) found in some depressed patients with major affective disorder may be a trait marker of vulnerability to depression (Loosen, Kistler, & Prange, 1983).

The psychological contributions to individual response variability (the individual variability of response to a stimulus with face value of strong affective impact) were reported in a study of parents of dying children. This situation provided a stimulus with face validity of strong affective impact. Wolff, Friedman, Hofer, & Mason (1964) hypothesized that the individuals with "more effective" psychological defenses were those with the lowest HYPAC response to the impending loss of a child to a fatal illness. This hypothesis was supported by the correlation found between a clinical rating and the observed HYPAC function, measured by 24-hour excretion of 170HCS. Individuals were considered effectively defended if they showed "little or no overt distress (*affect*), or little or no impairment in *function* and demonstrated the ability to mobilize further defenses in superimposed acutely stressful experiences." These and similar data (Fox, Murausku, Bartholomay, & Giffords, 1961) were a beginning effort to quantify and operationalize assessments of interindividual response patterns, but only in supposed normals.

Most of the studies discussed above dealt with the endocrine response to a single acute event. However, Mason's group studied helicopter ambulance medics in combat (Bourne, Rose, & Mason, 1967, 1968), and Hofer, Wolff, Friedman, & Mason (1972a, 1972b) reported on long-term (up to 2 years) bereavement in parents who lost a child to fatal illness. The former study found relatively little day-to-day change in urinary 170HCS excretion within an individual pilot and found 170HCS excretion was unrelated to flying days. In the study of bereaved parents there was evidence of anticipatory HYPAC activation prior to the loss of their child in only a few of the 36 parents studied. At 6 months and 2 years after the death of their child, those parents in the highest and lowest quartiles of 170HCS excretion could be distinguished by their level of interview measured grief, but it was not possible to predict the level of HYPAC activity in the entire sample from the activity and intensity of the observed grief per se. Although almost all parents showed less intense grief at the 2-year follow-up, the group mean 170HCS excretion was not significantly different either at 6 months or 2 years, and individuals had similar excretion at both visits ($r_s = .80$).

In contrast to the studies in normals, up to 1970 little had been done with patients diagnosed as anxious with the exception of early work by Perskey et al. (1956). Almost all the studies of reactivity of the HYPAC system were situational studies of normal persons carried out in laboratory sessions or in relation to naturally occurring life events with generally conceded face validity for being significant stimuli for emotional arousal and anxiety. In summary, the investigations of the HYPAC system up to about 1970 had demonstrated clearly the reactivity of this system to psychological stimuli. However, the degree of response showed marked individual variation ranging from undetectable to modest whether in the laboratory or in naturally occurring life-threatening situations.

By the early 1970s a parallel interest in neuroendocrine function was developing, slowly at first, in a related sphere of psychopathology. In contrast to the lack of neuroendocrine data regarding pathological states of anxiety, considerable data had accumulated by this time on HYPAC function in depression (Carroll, 1972; Stokes, 1972). It is clear from this work that the HYPAC system (Stokes et al., 1984) is very reactive to states of pathological depressive affects. Increased plasma cortisol levels, cerebrospinal fluid (CSF) cortisol, 24-hour urinary-free cortisol excretion, abnormally flattened and elevated circadian rhythm of plasma cortisol, and resistance to the dexamethasone suppression test (DST nonsuppression) have been repeatedly demonstrated in 30% to 60% of patients with major affective disorder, depressed.

As one who initially began studying the psychoendocrinology of anxiety but quickly switched to depression and other pathological affective states, it appears to me that two major problems exist in regard to the endocrine study of anxiety. First is the difficulty of defining pathological anxiety, and second is the lack of readily available and well-defined cases for study. Depression, on the other hand, has become a more recognized public health problem because of its prevalence, severity, association with suicide and sometimes homicide, and the frequent need for hospitalization. The definition of depression has been increasingly operationalized as seen in Feighner criteria (Feighner, Robins, Guze, Woodruff, Winokur, & Munoz, 1972), and the research diagnostic criteria (RDC; Spitzer, Endicott, & Robins, 1978). Similar work is needed in the psychobiological approaches to anxiety. In fact, a continuing point of interest to all of us is how to obtain separate and useful measures of depression and anxiety. Perhaps the question of whether these behaviors can effectively be separated in an operationalized and useful way (Foa & Foa, 1982) needs to be addressed first so that a similar accumulation of data is available about patients with anxiety. Interestingly, schizophrenia has a relatively large neuroendocrine data base in large part because of the public health characteristics which are similar to those described above for pathological depression.

A difficulty with most of the human studies discussed previously is that anxiety is not operationally defined and often is not defined at all except by the biological responses that are quantitated. A good example is the report by Bridges, Jones, and Leak (1968) on a "comparative study of four physiological concomitants of anxiety" in normal students taking an examination. It was observed that systolic blood pressure, heart rate, plasma cortisol concentration, and urinary adrenaline showed an increase over control concentrations, but the authors note that "the response each [variable] makes seems to be as much related to intrinsic sensitivity of activation as it is to the degree of *anxiety* (italics mine) experienced" (p. 143). In fact, no quantification of anxiety was presented in the study nor were other psychological measures. The point is that anxiety, which most of us would agree might be present in many of those normal students, is perhaps different from pathological anxiety in both quality and quantity. Consequently we are left without a good operational definition of the psychological aspects of the biological changes observed. We therefore lack the data needed to compare situational "anxiety" in normals with pathological anxiety and the endocrine concomitants in both cases. A problem is that appropriate instruments for measuring anxiety in normals may not be adequate for measuring anxiety in patients and vice versa. More attention to this problem is needed.

The importance of considering multiple biological variables simultaneously to "estimate the individual's total pattern of responsiveness to a stress (stimulus)" was pointed out by Bridges and his co-workers (1968), a suggestion voiced also by Mason (1968). The latter's research team noted that assigned role in a group (Bourne et al., 1968) or interactions between individuals in a group of normals in an anxiety-producing situation (Mason et al., 1965) play a significant part in determining the effect of that stress on HYPAC stimulation as measured by 17OHCS excretion. The variation in HYPAC response to what on the surface would appear to be a significantly anxiety-provoking stimulus, hospital admission prior to elective surgery, is well demonstrated in two studies. In the first study (Czeisler et al., 1976) plasma cortisol concentration was measured every 20 minutes via indwelling catheter for 24 hours immediately prior to surgery. Only one of the four patients, a woman, showed any difference in circadian pattern from the five comparison normal volunteers. She showed an abnormally flat, but not abnormally elevated, plasma cortisol curve throughout the day; more reactivity to environmental stimuli as shown by cortisol pulses; and one clearly elevated pulse to greater than 27 μg/dL shortly before awakening at 0430 hours. All four patients showed a major secretory pulse superimposed on their endogenous pulsatile circadian pattern at the time of preoperative preparation (body shaving and an enema). However, most episodes of cortisol secretion that were observed in the five normals and four patients could not be reliably correlated with environmental stimuli, with the sometime exception of the insertion of an intravenous (IV) catheter.

The second study was that of Knight et al (1979). These investigators measured cortisol production rate in 25 children 2 weeks before and on the day of hospital admission for elective surgery. Four groups of children emerged based on defense effectiveness scores and cortisol production rates. Contrary to expectation, one group had lower cortisol production after hospital admission and found the hospital apparently less distressing than either the clinic or home setting studied before admission. The authors concluded that stress does not necessarily produce distress but depends on how the evidence is interpreted. This is consistent with previous reports in adults without diagnosable psychiatric illness awaiting surgery. During this time it appeared that personality type and psychological defense mechanisms were associated with, or perhaps determined, the response of the HYPAC system (Katz, Weiner, Gallagher, & Hellman, 1970; Price et al., 1957).

Tennes, Downey, and Vernadakis (1977) studied urinary cortisol excretion in 8-hour samples from 1-year-old infants. Interest centered on the "stress" imposed on the infant by having the mother leave the infant for 1 hour. No difference was observed in urinary cortisol on the "stress" day as compared to a prior control day. However, it is possible that the design was faulty. The 1-hour stress response of increased cortisol production may have been obscured by pooling it with 7 hours of essentially normal secretion. Of greater interest is that "fearful" or "fussy" children had higher cortisol levels than children classified as "happy" or "indifferent." The children who were classified as fearful or fussy because of their attempt to follow the mother, who cried at her departure or ran to her when strangers approached, had chronically higher urinary cortisol levels than infants without this behavior. These observations need replication and extension in larger numbers of subjects and suggest "that it is necessary to consider both impact of an emotion-arousing event upon the biochemical response, and the readiness of the individual to respond to the event as determined by his psychological state." I would suggest again that the subject's physiological state (e.g., time in circadian cycle, preceding output of the neuroendocrine axis under study, etc.) may help determine the response. These data, though in a few subjects, have the exciting possibility of being an example of how the HYPAC system can be "programmed" early in life through the interaction of heredity and early environmental factors (including perhaps intrauterine ones) to react to perturbing stimuli. Excess hormone productions, repeatedly induced, could impact on the developing CNS and play a role in subsequently altered behavior (Levine, Haltmeyer, Karas, & Denenberg, 1967).

Remarkable differences in neuroendocrine response have been recorded by Rose and Hurst (1975) among 18 young normal volunteers who underwent intravenous catheterization on two separate occasions. Both growth hormone (GH) and plasma cortisol responses decreased on the second occasion as expected, but GH responses were much more variable than cortisol responses and individuals who listed more symptoms after their first catheterization had significantly greater cortisol and GH plasma concentrations during that experience. Thus, the patterns of hormone response to a discrete stimulus are different between hormones and between individuals.

Recently Williams et al. (1982) have shown that subjects with so-called Type A (coronary prone) behavior were hyper-responsive on both cardiovascular and several neuroendocrine measures to the stimuli of mental work (arithmetic) and sensory intake (reaction time). The Type A subjects had greater concentration of blood cortisol, norepinephrine and epinephrine than did Type B subjects during mental work. They also had increased testosterone, and for subjects with positive family history for hypertension, increased cortisol during sensory intake as compared to Type B subjects. These findings are compatible with those of Tennes et al. (1977), Rose and Hurst (1975), and with the proposal of Mason (1968) that a single neuroendocrine system does not respond in isolation to a significant behavioral stimulus, but rather as a component of a broadly orchestrated multiple neuroendocrine response pattern.

More investigation of this hypothesis is needed, especially now that the technology for multiple simultaneous hormone analyses is available. Prospective studies beginning at infancy or in childhood are indicated. Subhuman primate models can potentially provide rich data by using self-contained, continuous biological sampling techniques, and appropriate concomitant behavioral observations across the life span of the animal. Data within individuals of a social group obtained over time and across comparable subjects at similar times are needed and potentially available. Obviously, attention could then be given to systematic experimental perturbation of the social group at various times in its development to observe the effect of uncertainty, expectancy, apprehension or fear on these multiple neuroendocrine measures.

In recent years there has been a return to the study of patients with diagnosed anxiety disorders. This is appropriate and needed. As physicians and psychiatrists it is useful for us and for psychologists to examine carefully the experiments of nature that are available to us in the form of disease states.

Curtis, Buxton, Lippman, Nesse, and Wright (1976) stated that clear activation of the HYPAC system occurs with stimuli of sufficient magnitude, stimuli generally referred to as "stressors." Stressors with the face value of being rated as severe, such as combat or being in a war zone with potential threat of death, can be less effective stimuli in some instances than are certain novel situations with high levels of uncertainty or expectancy. The lack of HYPAC response in some individuals exposed to apparently very disturbing circumstances has been ascribed to the effectiveness of psychological defenses, a psychological contribution to inter-individual response variability (Bourne et al., 1968). In seven patients with circumscribed, specific, severe phobias of physical objects Curtis et al. (1976) were unable to find any HYPAC activation when patients were abruptly presented with their phobic object. The lack of HYPAC activation remained constant even when the phobic object was pressed on them with the "flooding technique" (Gelder & Marks 1966; Marks, 1972). This lack of HYPAC response occurred in spite of subjective reports of severe discomfort and the experimenter's observation that the patient looked and acted anxious "with screaming, weeping, fine and gross tremors, cringing, shying or running away, startling at slight sounds or movements, clammy hands and goose flesh" (Curtis, Nesse, Buxton, & Lippman, 1978, p. 370). These sessions were often described by the patients as the most frightening experience of their life. In contrast, the HYPAC system did show some increase in activity in response to the novelty aspect of the first visit to the laboratory for what was known to the patient as a control, no treatment session, with blood sampling only. The second control session showed less HYPAC activation consistent with an adaptational response.

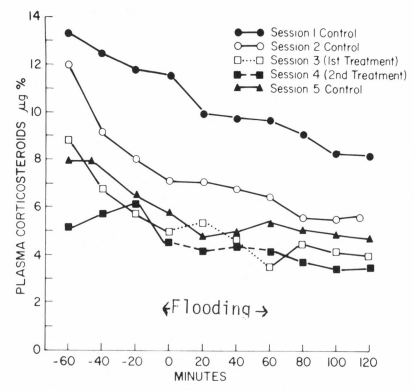

Mean plasma cortisol levels over five sessions, all during evening hours. Time adjusted so that 0 corresponds to beginning of each patient's treatment hours.

FIG. 2.   From Curtis et al., 1976, p. 105.

Lack of HYPAC activation in the face of clear anxiety or fear is a provocative finding. The blood sampling occurred after 20 minutes. Collection was sufficiently frequent so that with the long (60 minutes) half-life of plasma cortisol, a secretory burst would have produced a detectable rise in plasma concentration. It is very unlikely that the response to flooding was so delayed that it occurred more than 2 hours after the flooding stimuli began. All past data supports the belief that the HYPAC response to an acute stimulus is prompt (Ader & Friedman, 1968; Dunn, Scheving, & Millet, 1972; Mason et al., 1957; Persky, Grinker, Hamburg et al., 1959). However, the timing and frequency of sampling is important, as shown by the fact that after electroconvulsive therapy, increased plasma cortisol is seen at 15 and 30 minutes (Stokes, 1972; Stokes, Pick, Stoll, & Nunn, 1975), but not at 5 minutes after this form of treatment (Whalley, et al., 1982).

Curtis et al. (1976) suggest that HYPAC activation may not be a part of phobic anxiety, an interesting and testable possibility. They further suggest that the HYPAC response to phobic anxiety may attenuate with time and after many exposures to the phobic object. This would be analogous to the observed extinction of the vasodilator component of the defense reaction in cats after repeated exposure to dogs. The behavioral response remains, like the behavior Curtis observed when his patients were presented with their phobic objects. This is an ideal experimental technique for observing the response of multiple neuroendocrine axes. Curtis, Nesse, Buxton, & Lippman (1979) have reported that some of these patients demonstrated GH responses in the absence of HYPAC activation—a fact that supports the concept that the flooding technique is not physiologically inert.

This is reminiscent of the differential responsiveness between GH and the HYPAC system reported by Rose and Hurst (1975) after repeated intravenous catheterizations. Are the individuals with growth hormone response during flooding also those who reported the greatest number and severity of symptoms in the repeated IV catheterization studies of Rose and Hurst? Specific patterns of neuroendocrine activity may occur during flooding and subside in a specific manner in patients that respond well to treatment; i.e., these patterns might be predictors of treatment outcome or adequacy. Careful prospective observations of behavior, including the multi-vantage technique described by Katz, Robins, Croughan, Secunda, & Swann (1982) using video as well as at the scene observer ratings, could be profitably applied here.

Curtis et al. (1978) repeated this study on six additional subjects during the morning hours when HYPAC activity is normally increased. They again failed to observe HYPAC activation. Plasma cortisol concentration fell gradually and normally throughout the morning session from about 0900 to 1200 hours. It is very striking that 3 out of 6 patients did not meet onset criteria (Weitzman et al., 1971) for HYPAC secretory episodes during any of the six treatment periods. The 3 patients were studied during the morning hours when endogenous HYPAC activity is prominent. Here are clear experimental data showing marked emotional arousal without concurrent HYPAC activation, but with an occasional GH response. This obviously needs, and is amenable to, further investigation.

I am struck by the relative lack of uncertainty for the phobic subjects in Curtis et al.'s (1978) experiment. Each subject was carefully told that the five-session experiment would consist of two adaptation sessions followed by two treatment sessions and a final post-treatment session. Treatment would be given during the second of 3 hours in sessions 3 and 4. In view of the relationship of uncertainty or unpredictability to HYPAC activation it is possible that these patients would have shown different neuroendocrine function had they not been told when the flooding session would occur. Curtis and co-workers note the clinically evident autonomic responses that occur during flooding, and it is probable that adrenal medullary response and plasma epinephrine were high. This is a further area for additional investigation and could provide information on the gender differences reported by Frankenhaeuser et al. (1978). These investigators have shown that during examination stress, adrenaline and 3-methoxy-4-hydroxy-phenylethylene glycol (MHPG) are significantly *more* elevated in male high school students compared to their female counterparts.

The HYPAC system has been examined from another perspective in patients with anxiety disorder diagnoses. The dexamethasone suppression test (DST) is a measure of sensitivity of the HYPAC system to inhibition by increased circulating and tissue (brain and pituitary) corticosteroid concentration. Normal subjects show HYPAC inhibition in about 90% of cases. Plasma cortisol levels fall below 5 μg/dL throughout the day after a dose of 1 mg dexamethasone has been given the evening before at 2300 hours. Thirty to 60% of patients who meet criteria for primary major affective disorder show nonsuppression of the HYPAC axis (Carroll, Feinberg, Greden, Tarika, Albala, Haskett, James, Kronfol, Lohr, Steiner, DeVigne, & Young 1981; Stokes et al., 1984). The nonsuppression is state related and returns to normal when the depression lifts.

It has been observed that depressive illness can exist without obvious depressed mood, and some have suggested that patients with agoraphobia may also have a depressive syndrome. Schapira, Kerr, and Roth (1970) have reported that patients with agoraphobia are more vulnerable to affective disorder. Curtis, Cameron, and Nesse (1982) suggested that if depressive illness, agoraphobia, and panic disorder were all variants of a common disorder, then the incidence of the DST nonsuppression should be similar for these syndromes. Schlesser, Winokur, and Sherman (1980) reported normally suppressing DSTs in 7 patients having anxiety neurosis, but no details of their current behavioral states were given. Curtis et al. (1982) found only 3 out of 20 (15%) anxiety disorder patients who showed nonsuppressing dexamethasone suppression tests. All 3 subjects were agoraphobic with panic attacks and all had additional disorders often associated with DST nonsuppression (two were alcohol abusers, one had concomitant major affective disorder, depressed). Lieberman et al (1983) reported none of

10, and Sheehan et al (1983) 6 out of 51 patients with panic attacks had DST nonsuppression. The DST aspect of HYPAC function in patients with anxiety disorder is apparently consistent with that reported in normals. However, the reports to date have only used one post-dexamethasone plasma sample at 1600 hours, a procedure that may be less sensitive than other techniques (Carroll et al., 1981; Stokes et al., 1984).

GROWTH HORMONE AND PROLACTIN SECRETION

The experiments with GH response to flooding, though very interesting, must be taken as preliminary. The GH system is a difficult one to study from the psychoneuroendocrine viewpoint because (as Curtis found in his studies) the system is labile and generally considered a "stress responsive" neuroendocrine axis (Brown & Heninger, 1976a; Brown & Heninger, 1976b; Brown & Reichlin, 1972; Greene, Conron, Schalch, & Schreiner, 1970; Kurokawa et al., 1971; Syvalahti, Lammintausta, & Pekkarinen, 1976). Consideration of the GH axis for use in psychological studies raises some technical endocrine considerations. It is definitely easier to study any endocrine axis if interest is in knowing only whether there is excessive and persistent, adequate (i.e., normal) or inadequate hormone secretion. Regarding GH, this is the question in endocrine patients who may suffer from acromegaly or dwarfism. If one wishes to quantitate the GH response more finely, the difficulties increase considerably. Growth hormone response to normal effective stimuli is inhibited (via negative feedback) by its own plasma level at the time of stimulus presentation. Gender, menstrual status, age, prior food intake, drug ingestion, body weight, and perhaps recent weight change can all influence growth hormone response markedly. This is especially true if the stimulus used is not maximal (Koslow, et al., 1982). All but one of Curtis et al.'s (1979) nine female patients were pre-menopausal; two patients were men. There is no information given about when patients last ingested a meal or how long they were "drug free" and from what medications. While some of these questions may sound picayune, they are necessary when complex studies are pursued in this field.

The history of psychoneuroendocrine and psychobiological studies in general is severely pock-marked with the exploded "new findings" of yesterday. Researchers in this area are well advised to proceed cautiously and to rely on carefully controlled studies with sufficient sample size. They must require that attempts at replication are at least as carefully designed and executed. Curtis commented about the elevated (greater than 5 ng/ml) initial GH values in the control sessions for some of his patients. He concluded that these elevations did not influence GH response to flooding since 8 out of 11 patients showed the response; of these, 7 out of 8 responded in both flooding sessions. This was a greater response frequency than had been noted in previous studies. The fact that GH responses tended to increase during the second flooding session is of interest in regard to patterns of multiple endocrine measures. Curtis had previously reported that HYPAC responses (plasma cortisol), which were initially minimal, tended to diminish after the first flooding exposure.

In contrast, prior experiments in normals showed a decreased frequency of GH response after the first exposure to a repeated "stressful procedure" (Brown & Heninger, 1976a) or after the first hour of a single multi-hour stress (Rose & Hurst, 1975). This could be an example of the differences in psychoneuroendocrine responses between "stressed" normals and patients with pathological anxiety. Curtis notes that the degree of affect manifested by the subject may have less relationship to GH response than personality variables, which were thought to be significant in earlier studies of GH response to psychological stimuli in nonpsychiatric patients. These personality variables include field dependence or the Nowlis egotism factor (Brown & Heninger, 1976a), Type A behavior (Friedman & Roseman, 1971), and measures of social engagement (Greene, Conron, Schalch, & Schreiner, 1970; Kurokawa et al., 1971). These possibilities warrant further examination with adequate attention given to the potential differences between normals studied in contrived or naturally occurring stressful situations and studies of patients with pathological anxiety.

The complexity of the GH response system has recently been reemphasized (Wehrenberg, Baird, & Ling, 1983). Either exogenously or endogenously induced chronic hypercortisolemia is associated with cessation of somatic growth. Growth hormone release is inhibited in these hypercortisolemic patients in response to stimuli that are known to increase GH release through mediation of CNS pathways (Krieger & Glick, 1972; Martin, 1973). This fact has been difficult to reconcile with the recent reports showing that corticosteroids act on pituitary tissue in vitro to increase gene transcription and increase GH release. The new studies by Wehrenberg et al. demonstrate that corticosteroids enhance pituitary GH release in vivo in response to exogenous growth hormone releasing factor (GHRF). This means that corticosteroids like cortisol apparently act to inhibit GH response within the CNS and simultaneously can enhance the response at the level of the pituitary. Consequently, studies that induce HYPAC response with hypercortisolemia may enhance or inhibit the potential GH response in the same experiment. This depends on the relative impact of the induced hypercortisolemia on the brain areas involved in control of GH release versus the impact of GH on the pituitary gland at the same time.

It must be born in mind that the mechanism(s) for the double effect of corticosteroids is not known. Corticosteroids may influence synaptic availability of neurotransmitters necessary for neural activation of hypothalamic neurosecretory neurons. Secretion of GHRF and other releasing factors may govern other pituitary hormones (Maas & Medniek, 1971), but this activity is still controversial (Lieberman, Stokes, Fanelli, & Klevan, 1980). At any rate the neurotransmitter control of hypothalamic releasing factors is very complex. Releasing factors seem to have multiple neurotransmitter inputs and brain control loci within the hypothalamus and outside as well, probably in the limbic system and brain stem. These complexities coupled with an incomplete understanding of the identified control mechanisms make present work in psychoendocrinology a relatively crude attempt to adequately describe, much less fully comprehend, the synthesis and activity of multiple hormonal axes within the neuroendocrine system.

This in no way is meant to diminish Mason's (1968) farsighted call to explore the psychoendocrine field in its full scope. Rather, it is aimed at emphasizing what he also said was a necessary first step in pursuing the goal of understanding neuroendocrine organization. We must first understand the various *separate* neuroendocrine axes that make up this apparent system. We are still in the latter phase, in part because we are increasingly able to measure more of the activity of each axis. As additional hormone assays become available, we observe ever more complex control of hormone release and greater interaction between hormones than anticipated.

Prolactin, considered another stress responsive hormone, has been examined by investigators interested in behavior; relatively good assays for prolactin have been available for about 10 years. Though relatively little work has been done with prolactin in regard to anxiety per se, somewhat more has been done in regard to various stimuli considered to be "stressful." Various physical stressors will induce prolactin release in apparently healthy normal controls as shown when prolactin was secreted in association with growth hormone during induced motion sickness (Noel, Suh, Stone, & Frantz, 1972).

There are conflicting reports about the response of prolactin to psychic stimuli, Noel, Dimond, Earll, and Frantz (1976) examined prolactin, GH and thyroid-stimulating hormone (TSH) release in 14 young healthy males prior to and immediately after their first military training parachute jump. Mean plasma concentrations for each hormone were unchanged in samples obtained twice, 13 days and 3 days before the jump, and three times on the day of the jump. However, all three hormones showed a significant increase in mean plasma concentration in samples taken immediately after landing from the uneventful parachute jump. The investigators concluded that psychological factors were responsible and noted such signs of apprehension on the afternoon of the jump as sweating palms, tremulousness, and verbalization of anxiety. No formal psychological assessments were made however. Other factors known to be capable of increasing prolactin, GH, and TSH levels, such as cold exposure and physical exertion, were not present in this procedure. Ground temperature was 65°F, the jump was from only 1200 feet, and the men had no difficulty collapsing their parachutes and sitting quietly awaiting venipuncture immediately after landing. What is potentially more interesting than the significant increases observed in group mean plasma levels for each hormone is the question of what happened to each individual's pattern of hormone response. It is clear from the distribution of the individual prolactin responses that the significant elevation of the group mean is due mainly to the large increase observed in five individuals. The same observations can be made about the GH and TSH responses after the jump.

With this kind of data appropriately analyzed we can begin to approach a description of the simultaneous "synthesized" psychoneuroendocrine pattern that exists in normals. With the use of appropriate psychological measures it is then possible to relate these integrated patterns to observations in patients with pathological anxiety and other disorders. For example, Noel et al. (1976) found a significant inverse correlation between prolactin and the time elapsed after landing but did not find a significant correlation for GH or TSH. Aside from the known differences in plasma disappearance rate of these hormones, this finding suggests differences in the dynamics of secretion as well. The importance of multiple sampling, at least until the full response dynamics are known for each neuroendocrine axis, is evident. However, the psychic origin of the stimulus for these hormone secretions would have been further revealed if the experiments had included age- and weight-matched experienced parachute jumpers.

PROLACTIN: FIRST PARACHUTE JUMP (14 MEN)

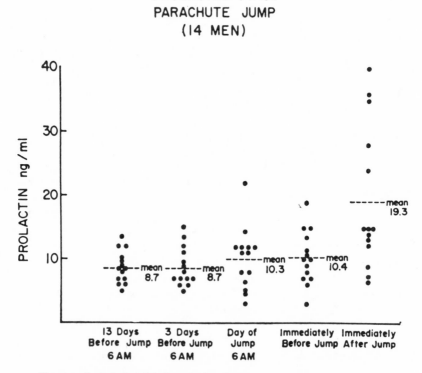

Plasma prolactin before and after parachute jump.

FIG. 3.   From Noel et al., 1976, p. 544.

Nesse, Curtis, Brown, & Rubin (1980) reported that eight severe phobics showed no prolactin response in spite of the intense anxiety experienced during flooding treatment, as described above. The absence of a prolactin response was surprising in view of the reported intensity of the emotional response of these patients, and previous studies suggesting that psychic stimuli were sufficient for prolactin release (Konincyx, 1978). I agree with Curtis' conclusion that these data suggest that the neuroendocrine responses to psychic stimuli are not "general." This is supported by his finding of GH changes (and small cortisol changes) in the same subjects. I am not as convinced as he, however, that these changes relate to the nature of the stressor or stimulus, but rather suspect that they relate to the character of the "transducer," i.e., the subject's genetic, experiential, and current state. The observations of Miyabo (1977) address this point. He observed that prolactin was elevated during a frustrating mirror drawing test, but only in neurotic females, not in neurotic men or controls of either sex. Other recent evidence also suggests that patterns of neuroendocrine response relate to the condition of the transducer. Physically trained subjects had higher prolactin and cortisol levels and lower anxiety levels at the conclusion of a session of psychosocial stress than did physically untrained subjects (Sinyor, Schwartz, Peronnet, Brisson, & Seraganian, 1983). These data support Mason's idea that the nonspecificity of neuroendocrine stress responses need to be reevaluated.

Before leaving prolactin, an interesting observation has recently been made about the effect of meditation on prolactin release. Jevning, Wilson, & Vanderlaan (1978) reported that prolactin levels increased significantly starting at the end of a 40-minute period of transcendental meditation. This finding was not observed in well-matched controls, who rested with their eyes closed in the same environment. Sleep was monitored by standard electroencephalographic techniques and could not explain the differences observed.

TSH RESPONSE TO TRH

Thyroid-stimulating hormone response to TRH has been extensively studied in recent years. Evidence recently reviewed by Loosen et al. (1983) shows that some euthyroid depressed patients have reduced (i.e., "blunted") TRH-induced TSH response. Such blunting appears to be a trait-related finding, at least in some patients. These same investigators have further shown that blunting of TSH response is not specific to depression and shows reasonable test re-test reliability, and that these patients apparently have disturbed feedback inhibition within the thyroid axis. Mason et al. (1972) had previously shown that there are small but highly consistent increases in plasma TSH in each of eight normal men during a 20-minute interval immediately prior to participating in an exhausting exercise session for the first time. These findings are consistent with those of Johansson, Levi, and Lindstedt (1970), who reported on an extensive series

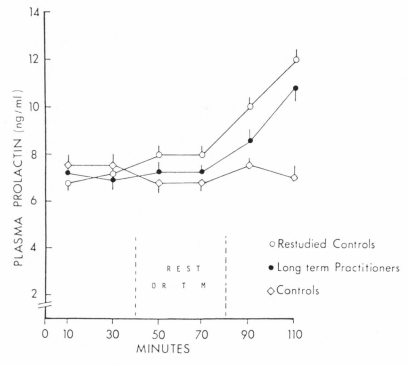

Plasma prolactin levels (mean ± SE) before, during, and after TM in short-term (restudied controls) and long-term practitioners and before, during, and after rest in controls. Note the increase in both TM groups following meditation.

FIG. 4.   From Jevning et al., 1978, p. 330.

of studies of thyroid responses to emotional stimuli in normals. Mason observed that there was no TSH response to the anticipation of a subsequent similar trial that took place after a 7-week period of heavy physical conditioning. He suggested, and I would agree, that the lack of anticipatory TSH response on the second test was probably due to the absence of a novelty effect. However, after nearly 2 months of intensive physical training these young men had almost certainly changed in their attitude of confidence about their ability to cope with the repeat test. In other words the transducer had changed in at least two ways from test 1 until the time of test 2.

In the severely phobic patients studied by Curtis et al. (1979) no change was observed in TSH levels during the intensive anxiety associated with flooding treatment, in spite of increases in GH and, to a lesser degree and frequency, cortisol. These differences again appear between patients and normals. Whether these differences are the result of different stimuli or relate to individual subject differences (physiological and/or psychological) is not clear at this time.

PITUITARY/GONADAL AXIS

The pituitary gonadal system is also responsive to stimuli perceived as significant to the organism. Considerable data in animals show a rather profound and prolonged decrease in plasma testosterone (Ducharme, Tache, Charpenet, & Collu, 1982). It is not totally clear that the testosterone change is due only to the decreased activity of the hypothalamic-pituitary-gonadal axis. Perhaps this change is secondary to increased peripheral metabolism or disposition of testosterone or to primary alterations in testicular secretion of testosterone occurring under stressful conditions independent of circulating and normal luteinizing hormone (LH) (Aono et al., 1976; Ellis et al., 1976). Similar reductions in plasma testosterone have been observed in humans under both physical and psychological stress (Davidson, Smith, & Levine, 1978). Mason showed that during shock avoidance sessions in monkeys, urinary testosterone, androsterone, and etiochoanolone were reduced (Mason, Kenion, Collins, Mougey, Jones, Driver, Brady, & Beer, 1968; Mason, Tolson, & Robinson, 1968) and Rose, Bourne, Poe, Mougey, Collins, & Mason (1969) reported that soldiers in basic training and special forces personnel awaiting expected combat in Viet Nam had lower urinary testosterone, epitestosterone, androsterone, and etiochoanolone.

One of the clearest demonstrations of the profound decrease in plasma testosterone that can occur in humans under psychological stress was demonstrated in the study of Kreuz, Rose, & Jennings (1972). These investigators studied healthy young men entering and going through Officer Candidate School. This study is important because it clearly demonstrated, probably for the first time, the effect of chronic emotional and mental stress on circulating testosterone in normal humans. It is important to note that only by implication can we assume that the hypothalamic-pituitary-gonadal axis was inhibited to an extent equal to the observed one-third decrease in circulating plasma testosterone. Only 1 out of 18 men studied did not show a decrease in plasma testosterone concentration during the early (most stressful) phase of training. No separate appraisal of his psychological makeup or status was presented. Kreuz et al. (1972) had controlled for the potential effects of circadian variation of plasma testosterone, and the possible effects of change in diet, sleep, and season of the year. The authors felt that the effects of extensive physical activity were not the cause of the suppression of testosterone concentration observed in early phases of training. However, their level of physical activity and physical training prior to their entry into Officer Candidate School is unknown. In view of the previously discussed differences in psychoneuroendocrine reactivity in aerobically trained and nontrained healthy individuals, it is possible that an initial increase in physical activity contributed to the diminished plasma testosterone observed. Plasma cortisol levels were significantly increased during the initial phase of Officer Candidate School consistent with the characteristic response of the HYPAC system to perceived stress; simultaneous plasma testosterone levels were low. Subsequent similar studies could be pursued with characterization of psychoneuroendocrine findings before entry into Officer Candidate School and include measures of follicle-stimulating hormone (FSH), LH and other neuroendocrine axes in order to obtain a more complete picture of neuroendocrine reactivity to this form of stress in healthy normals.

Increases in plasma testosterone have been reported in young healthy males who were "successful" (i.e., were winners) in a tennis competition or upon graduation from medical school (Mazur & Lamb, 1980). In contrast, "winners" in a lottery showed no such rise in plasma testosterone. It appears that when young healthy men are successful and achieve a rise in status through their own efforts (but not passively, as in a lottery), and have an associated feeling of elation, then there is a rise in their testosterone levels over the next 1 or 2 days. This interesting study needs replication with additional neuroendocrine measures. Additional questions to ask include whether or not HYPAC function changes accompany increases in testosterone; if so, are the HYPAC changes up or down? Is there any increase in aggressivity or assertiveness consistent with the reported increase in aggressiveness of young prisoners, which was thought to be related to testosterone (Kreuz & Rose, 1972)? Studies of the effect of positive stimuli and pleasant emotions have thus far not been forthcoming (Miller, 1982).

Another recent report (Houser, 1979) attempted to relate FSH, LH and plasma testosterone in five young healthy, male adults to mood and behavior changes. A repeated measures design with samples taken three times weekly over a 10-week period was used. In view of the small number of subjects the study is necessarily of a pilot nature. No evidence of a consistent within-subject relationship was observed between affect, behavior, and hormonal measures. However, it would be expecting too much to have found significant correlations. These were normal individuals whose range of mood was relatively small and alterations of affect and behavior that do relate to mood may be dependent on multiple hormone systems. The advantage of studying pathological states as compared to that of normals is that the affect states are pronounced, and at least in some cases, patients can be studied during both illness and periods of recovery.

Studies of menstrual function and affect have been reported, but very few studies have used adequate controls. Janowsky, Berens, & Davis (1973) suggested that in 11 college age normal volunteers studied, the activation of the renin angiotensin system might underlie increases in psychopathology. During the premenstrual phase of the cycle, "negative affect" was found to be associated with increased body weight and an increased potassium/sodium ratio in 24-hour urine collections. However, these associations may be coincidental or epiphenomenal since there is no evidence that angiotensin alters behavior and aldosteronomas have not been associated with severe mood changes.

Abplanalp, Livingston, Rose, & Sandwisch (1977) studied 21 healthy young women during one menstrual cycle to see if cortisol or GH responsivity to psychological stress was correlated with estrogen levels. Blood samples of estradiol, progesterone, cortisol, and GH were obtained three times per week. Participation in a "mildly stressful" interview occurred on one day of the study. Anxiety state and hormone levels were measured pre- and post-interview. Half of the subjects were interviewed during the menstrual phase and the other half during the periovulatory phase. Neither anxiety levels nor hormone levels proved to be correlated with the menstrual phase, but both cortisol and GH were significantly related to the level of anxiety reported after the interview. The women who showed significant endocrine response had higher post-interview anxiety levels than did the endocrine nonresponders, although the two groups did not differ in regard to anxiety levels before the stress interview. The relationship was not marked for those women who were responders on both endocrine measures (GH and cortisol). Whether this double endocrine response is a measure of anxiety induced by the interview or reflects a differential pattern of neuroendocrine response is not answered by this study, but is an interesting and testable question.

A similar study testing multiple neuroendocrine axes could answer this question. Lahmeyer, Miller, and DeLeon-Jones (1982) carefully demonstrated that young healthy females had very few symptoms as a function of menstrual cycle. The study demonstrated that daily 24-hour urine pregnantriol excretion allows adequate identification of phases of the (ovulatory) menstrual cycle. The assay is therefore suitable for studies involving psychopathology and biological correlates of the menstrual cycle. There was a significant increase in water retention and weight gain during the premenstrual phase, confirming the earlier work of Janowsky et al. (1973). Women reported an increase in all symptoms during the premenstrual interval. More studies are needed among women with complaints of menstrual cycle symptoms and comparison with carefully selected and studied normals, like those of Lahmeyer et al. (1982).

CONCLUSION

In summary I would like to stress several points. The neuroendocrine system is a third and most recently recognized component of the nervous system. Its multiple neuroendocrine axes have central releasing hormones, pituitary hormones, and in some cases peripheral hormones. The neuroendocrine system in humans is rapidly reactive to emotional stimuli and to many stimuli that are anxiety arousing or diminishing. Investigations have focused on the HYPAC system and suggest that neuroendocrine responses to anxiety-provoking stimuli are generally excitatory to that system, but the response varies with the individual's perception of the stimulus. The response may be modified if he or she experiences this as a single individual or as part of a group. Demographic factors are important and need to be assessed along with hormonal measures. Neuroendocrine studies in anxiety have not been as extensive as in depression or schizophrenia because of a decreased ability to characterize anxiety in terms of disease state. Anxiety is thought to be less common and/or severe compared to other psychological disorders such as depression or schizophrenia.

In the past, investigators have concentrated on studying normal animals or humans under contrived or natural stimulus conditions that have face validity for being anxiety producing. Relatively little neuroendocrine study of naturally occurring disease states of pathological anxiety in humans have been done until recently, with the notable past exception of Persky's work a quarter century ago. The description and operational quantitation of pathological anxiety has not received the intensive clinical study accorded to the related area of depressive affect. More work is needed in the field of anxiety, with attempts at separation of measures of anxiety from other affect states, especially depression.

In future neuroendocrine studies, multiple hormones need to be measured within one neuroendocrine axis. This will allow greater certainty of the hormonal changes observed: do these changes reflect an overall modification in the function of this axis, or is it just an effect on one hormone from outside factors (e.g., increased hepatic metabolism)? We should be more aware and exploitative of our ability to measure multiple hormones within multiple neuroendocrine axes simultaneously. Only in this manner can we test the concept that "patterns" of neuroendocrine response may discern different populations within otherwise apparently homogeneous groups. Applied to patient groups these patterns may provide indicators of prognosis, choice of therapy, need for further treatment, or diagnosis. Patient groups need to be studied while sick and again after recovery, or, if not recovered, at a repeat session later in time. Longitudinal studies are needed. Much more is needed in regard to test re-test reliability not only of biochemical assays per se, but of their results in relation to the clinical syndrome and total biological condition. In short, we need to pay attention to the stimuli, to the receiver-transducer (the subject), and the neuroendocrine correlates of behavioral output.

4

Benzodiazepines, Anxiety and Catecholamines: A Commentary

Malcolm Lader
University of London, U.K.

The biology of anxiety and anxiety disorders has been a relatively neglected area of research, despite its obvious involvement and the plethora of physical manifestations and symptoms associated with them. One aspect which has been researched rather extensively is the psychophysiology of anxiety, but this is essentially a refinement of clinical observation to use physiological measures as monitors of psychological state. Biological theories of anxiety for most of this century were overshadowed by psychological ones, especially those of psychoanalysis, because of the pivotal role afforded to anxiety in both the early and later theoretical systems of Freud. Later behavioral theories became influential especially in the United Kingdom where behavioral methods of treatment were early on the scene.

The advent of effective pharmacotherapy for a disorder is not only of practical utility but of theoretical interest in that it should help to elucidate underlying mechanisms. However, in order to do this, the mechanisms of action of the drug should be known, at least in outline. The introduction of the benzodiazepines represented a step forward in the treatment of anxiety states with respect to both increased efficacy and decreased toxicity as compared with the barbiturates. But the lack of any clear pharmacological mode of action hindered progress in studying the biological aspect of anxiety. All this has changed in the last few years. The discovery of the benzodiazepine receptor has given an enormous fillip to basic research in this area, and developments are beginning to be seen in the clinical area as well. Some of the older problems can now be readdressed, for example the role of catecholamines in anxiety.

This chapter will comment on three outstanding reviews concerning the biological substrates and concomitants of anxiety. Costa's chapter discusses in detail the recent exciting work on GABA and benzodiazepine receptors, using biochemical interactions as the basis for a model of some neurobiological aspects of anxiety. The second by Gray attempted the Sisyphean task of presenting not only a coherent behavioral model of anxiety, but of relating the various complex elements of that model to neurophysiological functions and neuroanatomical structures. Stokes's critical review of the neuroendocrinology of anxiety focuses on the hypothalamic-pituitary axis. Although the three papers have in common the axis of neurobiology, they cover an extremely wide area in coruscating detail.

One impression of the three papers is the amount of progress during the past decade. The advent of more selective antianxiety agents led to the search for specific receptors in the brain mediating their action. However, their biochemical pharmacology has proved to be complex with an interaction between benzodiazepine and GABA receptors still undergoing analysis, as recounted by Costa. The search for the endogenous ligand at the benzodiazepine receptor proceeds apace but no convincing candidate has yet emerged, raising the possibility either that there is no ligand—the benzodiazepine receptor being nonphysiological—or that the ligand is something very simple such as the chloride ion itself. Both possibilities are unlikely.

The Costa and Gray papers in particular base much of their theoretical exegesis on the action of the benzodiazepines in anxiety. Thus, Gray states, "Progress in the study of the biological basis of anxiety has been critically dependent on the availability of drugs which, clinically, reduce human anxiety. . . . Furthermore, by studying the physiological pathway by which the drugs produce their effects on behavior, it is possible to attack the problem of the neural basis of anxiety." Two assumptions are implicit: First, that benzodiazepines reduce anxiety to a substantial extent—it is pointless using marginally effective drugs as analytical tools; second, that anxiety is specifically the target of benzodiazepine action, and not something more diffuse such as emotion in general or that elusive substrate, "arousal." I urge caution with respect to both assumptions, and, in addition, would ask the proponents of theories of anxiety to specify what they mean by "anxiety."

The tide of opinion, particularly in the United States, is toward "splitting" anxiety syndromes into a series of different syndromes, as found in the *Diagnostic and Statistical Manual* (*DSM-III*). Although this move has been much less pronounced in Europe and some "lumping" may be taking place in the revision of *DSM-III*, for research purposes it is essential that such distinctions are kept. Certainly, it is an eminently tenable hypothesis that different mechanisms, biochemical, physiological and anatomical, mediate generalized anxiety, normal and abnormal, phobic anxiety, panic attacks and post-traumatic anxiety states. Of these, I would envisage generalized anxiety as being most amenable to biochemical, neuropsychological and neuroendocrinological theorizing in that it is a sustained state in humans with a wealth of physiological markers. However, many behavioral models of anxiety are more convincing as analogues of phobic anxiety, social anxiety, and stress responses (e.g., Kornetsky, 1977; McKinney, 1974).

My second and most detailed point concerns the effectiveness of the benzodiazepines. Several reviews have surveyed clinical trials of benzodiazepines and most concur in confirming the effectiveness of this class of compounds as anxiolytics (e.g., Greenblatt & Shader, 1978; Rickels, Downing, & Winokur, 1978; Rosenbaum, 1982), although dissentient voices have been raised (e.g., Solomon & Hart, 1978). Thus, in a detailed review of the pharmacotherapy of anxiety with benzodiazepines, Greenblatt and Shader (1978) state: "Despite the elusive, evanescent, and relatively nonspecific manifestations of clinical anxiety as well as the methodologic problems in reliable and relevant quantitation, most clinicians and investigators seem to agree that benzodiazepine derivatives are more consistently effective than placebo in well-controlled, short-term trials of anxiolytic drug therapy" (p. 1382). Of 25 such trials reviewed, 18 showed strong benzodiazepine-placebo differences, 4 a trend and 3 no difference. However, I was concerned with the question, How great are benzodiazepine-placebo differences?

As a starting point, I surveyed the literature from mid-1977 to mid-1982, 5 years, and selected double-blind placebo-controlled studies of tranquilizers administered to anxiety patients and using the Hamilton Anxiety Scale. This observer rating scale is so well established that almost all clinical trials of new tranquilizers in the United States and United Kingdom employ it routinely. My search was not exhaustive, concentrating on the Anglo-Saxon literature in which the Hamilton Anxiety Scale was used. Twenty-one trials met my criteria. The published data from these trials were pooled to give mean values before treatment and those at the end of 4 weeks in patients on the test benzodiazepine, the placebo and, in some trials, the standard benzodiazepine, usually diazepam or lorazepam.

Failure to take proper cognizance of drop-outs has led to some biased conclusions concerning the efficacy of benzodiazepines. In particular failure to compensate for placebo dropouts due to inefficacy markedly underestimates the effectiveness of benzodiazepines. Accordingly, dropouts were compensated for in this manner: dropouts due to failure to respond or to intolerable side effects were allocated a notional score at the end of treatment the same as the mean initial score; dropouts due to successful resolution of symptoms before 4 weeks were allocated a notional score equal to half the mean 4-week value for the group from which they dropped out. Both these procedures are arbitrary, the second even more than the first, but successful dropouts were rare.

The mean values are shown in Table 1. No statistical conclusions can be drawn because published accounts do not usually include useful estimates of variance, but as most of the constituent trials showed, drug-placebo difference was also significant. However, one can comment on the clinical significance of the results. First, the mean initial Hamilton Score is about 29. Eighteen to 20 is usually used as the threshold criterion of severity for inclusion in a trial and

TABLE 1
Mean Hamilton Scores Before and After 4 Weeks of Administration of
Placebo, Standard or Test Benzodiazepine

	N	Pre-Score	4-Week Score
Placebo	960	28.7	22.4
Standard	753	30.5	17.3
Test Drug	1017	28.8	14.1

the maximum score of the scale is 60 (Hamilton, 1959). Thus, 29 represents moderate severity in clinical terms. In those studies giving some indication of variation among patients with respect to initial Hamilton Score, the range was restricted, and the variation between studies was also not great.

Improvement with placebo was limited, with a mean decrease of only 6 units. There was great variation between trials for placebo effects. After 4 weeks, patients were still on average above the usual threshold severity criterion. In other words, they were still eligible for inclusion in a trial of anxiolytics. Improvement with the test drug was over twice as great as with placebo and psychopathology scores were halved. Even so, a score of 14 is quite high putting patients into the "probably anxious" range of the population, although drug treatment is usually not indicated at this level. But the patients are not "cured." The standard drug, which one might have expected to have been the best, was actually marginally less effective than the test benzodiazepines, although the chance finding of a slightly higher initial score in this group makes interpretation difficult. A final score of 17 is almost in the clinically anxious range.

Most trials employed one or more self-rating instruments, but lack of standardization made it impossible to draw more than a general impression from the data. That is, the benzodiazepine tranquilizers seem less effective compared with placebo when self-ratings are used, than when a trained observer rates the patient. Indeed, it seems that all treatments, placebo as well as active medications, are rated more conservatively by the patients than by their doctors.

Further trials documenting the limited effectiveness of benzodiazepines continue to appear. For example, Shapiro and his co-workers (Shapiro, Struening, Shapiro, & Milcarek (1983), in a 6-week double-blind trial comparing diazepam and placebo in 224 neurotic and anxious outpatients, found very little therapeutic effect attributable to the drug beyond the first week. Thus, we have a situation where a group of drugs are regarded by clinicians as effective agents, are highly successful commercially, and yet on detailed appraisal are not anxiolytic panaceas.

My next point is less easy to document and concerns the specificity of action, biochemical and clinical, of the benzodiazepines. Biochemical data attest to the specific nature of the binding of benzodiazepines to widespread sites in the brain. A few studies suggest that such binding subserves a physiological purpose, for example, the convulsive threshold is raised (Paul, Syapin, Paugh, Moncada, & Skolnick, 1979). One may conclude quite reasonably that benzodiazepines act specifically at receptor sites in the brain. However, this does not imply clinical selectivity. Too often, one action of a drug class is singled out for study and too little attention paid to its spectrum of efficacy. In the case of the benzodiazepines, accepted indications include the treatment of insomnia, muscle spasm, and some forms of epilepsy, as well as the mitigation of anxiety. But as well as these clinical uses, evidence exists that the benzodiazepines lessen anger, hostility, and aggression (Bond & Lader, 1979), and patients report lessening of some hedonic feelings, such as pleasure and eager anticipation. Thus, the possibility cannot be discounted that benzodiazepines clinically are fairly non-specific drugs lessening emotion in general, perhaps by diminishing its physiological-substrate, sometimes called "arousal" (Lader, 1975). Hypotheses based on the action of benzodiazepines may therefore be more relevant to emotion in general than to anxiety in particular. The null hypothesis, epistemologically, is that effects are nonspecific so the onus remains with the proponents of such hypotheses to disprove the null hypothesis and to show specificity of action of the benzodiazepines in man as anxiolytics.

Even if this specificity could be established, a further caveat should be lodged. Drug action does not equate with mechanisms of the pathological process. Thus, elucidation of the mode of action of a diuretic does not greatly help understand congestive cardiac failure. Also, symptomatic treatments (among which surely are the benzodiazepines) may not throw much light on the pathogenesis, as opposed to the symptom mediation, of clinical conditions. We can treat parkinsonism with L-Dopa; we know little of the processes leading to the decay of dopaminergic neurons in the basal ganglia.

Stokes concentrated on the neurohypophysial mechanisms accompanying anxiety. I should like to draw attention to the catecholamine systems in anxiety as they provide a common thread running from peripheral concomitants of anxiety, and the induction of anxiety-like states, to central pathways from the locus coeruleus and other nuclei to the cerebral and other cortices (Redmond, 1979).

The earlier work on sympathomimetic agents and the induction of anxiety, both in normal subjects and in patients with anxiety and related disorders, has elucidated many aspects but left others far from clear. Thus, Tompkins and his associates (Tompkins, Sturgis, & Wearn, 1919) found that 5 mg of adrenaline intramuscularly markedly increased symptoms of anxiety in soldiers with "irritable heart syndrome" (Da Costa's syndrome, neurocirculatory asthenia), but not in normal control soldiers, although both groups developed physiological changes following the injection. This early study has been replicated in its essentials many times (Pitts & Allen, 1980).

Much of the later literature was involved with detailed discussions of the role of the investigator and the expectation of the subject in influencing the onset of anxiety symptoms. This culminated in the suggestion that the undoubted propensity of diagnosed anxious patients to develop anxiety after adrenaline administration lay in the learned association during their illness, with feelings of physiological change, e.g., palpitations or tremor. Thus, when palpitations and tremor were induced by the adrenaline, the anxious patients, because of previous secondary interoceptive conditioning, feel psychologically anxious because no prior association had been established (Tyrer, 1976, p. 98). Some studies have shown that only those patients with histories of autonomic symptoms and anxiety attacks develop anxiety on infusion or injection of adrenaline (Lindemann & Finesinger, 1938, 1940; Vlachakis, DeGuia, Mendlowitz, Antram, & Wolf, 1974).

Adrenaline has both alpha- and beta-adrenergic actions, although the latter predominate. Isoprenaline (isoproterenol), a selective beta-adrenergic agonist, was used by Frohlich, Dustan, & Page (1966) and Frohlich, Tarazi, & Dustan (1969), who defined the so-called "hyperdynamic beta-adrenergic circulatory state." This is a labile hypertensive state with multiple anxiety symptoms, hypersensitivity to isoprenaline injections, and relief of symptoms with a beta-blocker such as propranolol.

One of the effects of adrenaline administration is the marked production of lactate. Lactate is also produced during exercise and several studies have shown that this production is excessive in anxious patients (e.g., Cohen & White, 1950; Holmgren & Strom, 1959; Kelly & Walter, 1968). Pitts & McClure (1967) followed these lactate findings by infusing lactate into anxious patients and normal controls, using double-blind precautions. Thirteen of 14 patients and 2 of 10 controls had typical acute anxiety attacks during the infusion. No subject in either group had such attacks during control infusions. Grosz & Farmer (1969) trenchantly criticized the study, particularly the theoretical interpretations, but other workers convincingly replicated the main findings (Fink, Taylor, & Volavka, 1969; Kelly, Mitchell-Heggs, & Sherman, 1971). Thus, in summary, beta-adrenergic agonists (adrenaline, isoprenaline) or metabolic products of their action (lactate) will produce anxiety symptoms and anxiety attacks in patients with anxiety neurosis, but not in matched normal controls.

Recently, lactate infusions have been used as a possible means of differentiating subgroups of anxiety disorders. The American Psychiatric Association's *DSM-III* classification system (1980) makes a distinction between phobic states with and without panic, panic states and generalized anxiety disorder. This is based, at least in part, on more than two decades of extensive work by Donald Klein (1964, 1967), who has shown that panic states, but not anticipatory anxiety, is improved by antidepressants such as imipramine rather than by standard antianxiety treatment. Kelly et al. (1971) reported that lactate-induced panics in anxious patients were prevented by the prior administration of monoamine oxidase inhibitors. Based on this, current investigations are evaluating the usefulness of lactate infusions in distinguishing various subgroups of anxiety states (Appleby,

Klein, Sachar, and Levitt, 1981). Biochemical controls are incorporated in these studies, and it seems that plasma adrenaline levels significantly differentiated between patients who panicked and controls (who did not); noradrenaline and cortisol levels did not distinguish the groups. This area of research will surely continue to be fruitful.

Finally, although I have urged caution in the interpretation of data and the erection of theoretical superstructures, I do not wish to imply depreciation in any way of the value of the experimental studies that have been carried out. Right across the board, biochemical, pharmacological, behavioral, and physiological studies have widened our understanding of anxiety and anxiolytics. New initiatives concerning benzodiazepine agonists, antagonists, and inverse agonists will surely increase our therapeutic options.

B. Cognition, Emotion, and Psychophysiology

5 Cognitive Processes, Anxiety and the Treatment of Anxiety Disorders

Irwin G. Sarason
University of Washington

The cognitive perspective views the behavior of people as products of thoughts, understandings, ideas, and interpretations concerning themselves and their environments. This point of view, which emphasizes the ways in which individuals process, evaluate, and respond to stimuli has become the successor to behaviorism as the dominant influence in many areas of psychology. Whereas behaviorism emphasized behavior as an outcome of environmental influences, cognitive psychology looks for causes of behavior not only in the environment but also within the individual. Cognitive theorists have replaced stimulus-response psychology with an input-output psychology that pays attention to transformations taking place between perceived stimulus and behavioral response, including control processes often captured through introspection. In recent years, cognitive psychologists have given special attention to *hot cognitions,* by which is meant thoughts and decisions that have high affective importance to the person.

Cognitive behavior therapy, while overlapping conceptually with cognitive psychology, has grown out of clinical research rather than the experimental laboratory. It emphasizes the interdependence of the overt and the covert and the need for persons to develop self-control over their lives. Clinicians who work along cognitive lines have sought to change behavior by changing specific thought patterns. For example, for some dental patients the cognitions of anticipation of pain might be modified and recast as anticipation of no longer having a toothache; for highly test-anxious students fear of flunking out at the end of the school year might be altered to planning how to study tonight; and for angry acter-outers thoughts about how to get back at their tormenters might be changed to thoughts focused on the undesirable consequences of acting out.

Evidence gathered in the laboratory and in clinical settings has demonstrated the important roles that cognitive processes play in both maladaptive and adaptive behavior. A person's usual train of thought and habitual mental set can be viewed as assets or as vulnerability factors that interact with characteristics of situations to produce either adaptation or maladaptation. For example, in anxiety disorders, precipitating events elicit or magnify underlying personal preoccupations (such as fear of negative consequences) and give rise to uncertainty about outcomes, hypervigilance, and concern over potential dangers. As a result, the anxious individual may continuously scan situations for potential danger signals and because of looking for these signals, might not pay full attention to the task at hand.

COGNITIVE PROCESSES AND ANXIETY SYNDROMES

Although it has often been said that distortion of reality characterizes psychotics but not neurotics, considerable evidence now indicates that disorders of thinking, less gross and more limited than in psychosis, are important features of anxiety disorders. People with these disorders are prone to think in extreme terms about certain types of situations, such as those in which personal danger is a possibility, although a quite remote one. An unexpected noise in the house could be burglars breaking in and the noise of children playing in the street could give rise to visions of a hit-and-run accident. The anxious person is prone to anticipate rejection, humiliation, and deprecation by strangers as well as friends. These expectations of censure and harm can result in continual bodily mobilization for danger.

An example of the cognitive difficulties experienced by people with anxiety disorders is furnished by the obsessive person who experiences intense anxiety when having to cross the street and who actually might be unable to attempt a crossing. Most people would use the following train of thought:

1. Streets are safe for crossing at green lights or when free of traffic.
2. This street has a green light or is free of traffic.
3. Therefore this street can be crossed.

The obsessive person's thinking, on the other hand, might go this way:

1. Streets are safe for crossing at green lights or when free of traffic.
2. This street has a green light or is free of traffic, but the light may change suddenly or a car may suddenly appear.
3. Therefore this street is not safe for me to cross.

Research studies of obsessives have revealed several categories of unreasonable beliefs and assumptions (Rachman & Hodgson, 1980). In addition to a preoccupation with achieving certainty, obsessives believe that they (1) should be perfectly competent, (2) must avoid criticism or disapproval, (3) will be severely punished for their mistakes and imperfections.

Obsessives often believe that thinking certain thoughts or performing certain rituals will help avoid the disastrous outcomes they imagine are just around the corner. They adhere to arbitrary rules that they must follow carefully (for example, stepping on every seventh crack on the sidewalk). Rule making is seen in other anxiety disorders; for example, a phobic might think "If I go into the elevator it might get stuck and I might suffocate, so I must not use the elevator." Unfortunately these "protective" thoughts and rituals become very intrusive, cause psychic strain, and can interfere with ongoing activity.

There are two general problems in a cognitive analysis of anxiety disorders: the diversity of phenomena subsumed under anxiety disorders and the multiplicity of components in most anxiety syndromes.

Diversity of Anxiety Disorders

The anxiety disorders cover a broad range of human problems. Whereas obsessives experience repetitive, troubling intrusive thoughts, compulsives exhibit repetitive overt behavior presumably based on dysfunctional cognitions. In phobias unrealistic fear of certain objects, activities, or situations predominates. In generalized anxiety disorders the major features are motor tension, autonomic hyperactivity, apprehensive expectation, and vigilance for danger signals. Questions that need investigation include the similarities and differences among anxiety disorders with regard to the psychological filters people employ in attending or not attending to stimuli produced by environmental events or by their own bodily and psychological reactions, the schemas or sets of assumptions individuals bring to life situations, and people's concepts of what constitutes appropriate, reasonable, or effective ways of handling situations. A clearer picture of those suffering from anxiety disorders should focus not just on finding these differentiating characteristics of the various anxiety disorders, but also on individual behavior patterns and histories. It requires information about their characteristic cognitive styles, their life experiences—both in the recent and distant past—that are associated with the salient cognitive and clinical features and the cognitive factors involved in particular coping processes.

To better understand the anxiety disorders it is necessary to explicate the specific cognitive processes involved in specific maladaptive thoughts, images, and behavior. George Kelly (1955), a pioneer in the development of the cognitive approach to clinical problems, was among the first to recognize one roadblock that must be overcome in applying this approach.

A person is not necessarily articulate about the constructions he places upon his world. Some of his constructions are not symbolized by words. . . . Even the elements which are construed may have no verbal handles by which they can be manipulated and the person finds himself responding to them with speechless impulse. Thus, in studying the psychology of man-the-philosopher, we must take into account his subverbal patterns of representation and construction. (1955, p. 16)

The importance of such processes, those that are preverbal or that function automatically (that is, outside awareness), is increasingly being recognized, and these now seem to be ripe for expanded empirical investigation. It is at least conceivable that the diversity of symptoms in anxiety disorders can be understood through a combined attack on both the thoughts of which people are aware (for example, "I'm terribly worried") and those that have either gone on automatic pilot, so to speak, or that are now forgotten but in the past initiated a train of maladaptive thoughts.

Multiple Components of Anxiety

Anxiety disorders by definition either have anxiety as their predominant symptom, as in generalized anxiety disorder (GAD), or the anxiety is related to the person's attempts to master some disturbing symptom such as a phobia or obsessive-compulsive behavior. In addition to the 2% to 4% of the population that may at some time fit the anxiety disorder diagnosis, a far greater number experience anxiety that is occasionally or mildly incapacitating.

In spite of the general agreement that anxiety is an important aspect of human life, there is wide disagreement about its definition. Typically it is discussed as being such a complex experience as to make scientific investigation difficult or impossible. If there were such a thing, perhaps the modal definition of anxiety would be in terms of an unpleasant emotional state or a condition marked by apprehension. In 1972, Spielberger defined anxiety as "an unpleasant emotional state or condition which is characterized by subjective feelings of tension, apprehension, and worry, and by activation or arousal of the autonomic nervous system" (p. 482). More recently, Leary (1982) offered this definition of anxiety: "Anxiety refers to a cognitive-affective response characterized by physiological arousal (indicative of sympathetic nervous system activation) and apprehension regarding a potentially negative outcome that the individual perceives as impending (p. 99)."

These definitions are typical and perhaps better than most but they still include many terms that have low inter-rater reliability. For example, how much agreement is there about what an emotional or affective state is, what subjective feelings of tension are, and what the referents are for the concepts of activation and arousal? Although the general concept of anxiety has been researched extensively, many of the findings have been conflicting and confusing. Contributing to this confusion have been definitions of anxiety that are not only difficult to apply reliably but also are too broad with regard to both what anxiety is and how it functions in affecting performance.

During recent years, several writers have adopted a slightly different approach. They have focused on the components of anxiety syndromes and on the correlations that might or might not exist among these (Lang, 1969, 1979, this volume; Rachman, 1978). At any given time, people can be characterized by their observable behavior (e.g., hand washing), their thoughts (e.g., worries), and their bodily reactions (e.g., heart rate). For a given individual, these components might or might not be correlated. Since little is known about the degree of synchrony or desynchrony that may exist among components for particular disorders, this approach could be of considerable value both in increasing reliability and in adding to an understanding of the relationships involved in anxiety disorders. Therefore, a study of these components should have high priority in research on anxiety.

As pointed out earlier, the cognitive component of anxiety includes personal beliefs, construals, assumptions, and expectations about how the world works and one's role in the world. Cognitive theorists view human beings as information processors who respond to the environment based on the data they receive, how they interpret it, and available problem-solving strategies. How information is acted upon is the result of the interaction between personal characteristics and environmental events. Personal factors include residues of earlier life experiences; self-assessment of personal skills, talents and inadequacies; and coping skills. The environment provides a variety of opportunities, constraints, and demands for some action. The joint contributions of personal resources and personal interpretations and situational requirements determine overt behavior.

Although all people think about their personal capabilities in relation to the task at hand, anxious individuals seem to become overly preoccupied with these thoughts. Thoughts such as "I don't know what to do now" can be self-defeating if the person really has the wherewithal to handle the situation. Anxious self-preoccupation arouses emotions that interfere with the perception and appraisal of events, producing errors in estimating the possibility of danger, loss (of love, job, money, reputation), and probability of attaining goals.

One type of cognition that may be particularly relevant to psychophysiological and other conditions, as well as to anxiety disorders, consists of perceptions and thoughts about one's bodily processes. A person's physical and psychological condition may be a joint function of his or her state of physiological arousal, how that arousal is perceived and interpreted, and the contributions these perceptions and interpretations may make to the heightening of bodily arousal. Cognitive styles influence what people pay attention to in the psychological and bodily aspects of their lives, and because of their influence over how symptoms are presented, they may be related to clinical observations.

COGNITIVE ASSESSMENT

Finding out about style and content of thought is of obvious relevance to the cognitive approach to anxiety. Cognitive assessment is needed to provide information about thoughts that precede, accompany, and follow maladaptive behavior. It also can provide information about the effects of treatment procedures intended to modify behavior and how someone thinks about a problem.

Efforts to assess the thoughts and ideas that pass through people's minds is a relatively new development. Cognitive assessment can be carried out in a variety of ways (Kendall & Korgeski, 1979). Questionnaires have been developed to sample thoughts, for example, after an upsetting event has taken place. "Beepers" have been used as signals to subjects to record their current thoughts at certain specific times (Klinger, Barta, & Maxeiner, 1981). There are also questionnaires to assess the directions people give themselves while working on a task and their personal theories about why things happen as they do. All of these procedures have been used in research on the cognitive component of anxiety. However, they are limited because of the possible confounding of self-presentational styles with the cognitions reported by subjects.

In some cases, distortion is created by subjects' defensiveness and their need to present themselves in a particular light, either favorable or unfavorable. In other cases, subjects may not be able to provide accurate accounts of their cognitions. Despite the limitations of self-reports, the data they provide are valuable as indicators of individual difference variables and as dependent variables that may reflect clinical treatment, experimental manipulations, or events of everyday life. One type of study that might have valuable clinical implications would be comparisons of cognitive assessments made among various diagnostic groups. This type of research might provide clues to the types of thoughts most in need of or amenable to cognitive interventions.

An example of cognitive assessment is provided by Krantz and Hammen's (1979) study of distortions in thinking that play roles in depression. Their work grew out of research and theory suggesting that depression-prone individuals tend to commit certain errors in thinking that stimulate feelings of depression. Krantz and Hammen developed a questionnaire consisting of several stories. The stories dealt with interpersonal relationships and themes concerning activities and the achievement of goals. For each story, the subjects answered questions pertaining to the central character's feelings, thoughts, and expectations. The answers were scored for various types of distorted thinking, such as the tendency to draw a general conclusion either from a single incident or no evidence whatever, and failure to attend to relevant aspects of a situation.

On the basis of the subjects' interpretations of the central character, Krantz and Hammen were able to show that those who were depressed were more likely to make certain types of thinking errors than were nondepressed subjects. Their findings, together with those of other reseachers, suggest that persons with depressive tendencies are particularly prone to accept more responsibility in difficult situations than they should, feel more self-blame, and expect the worst to happen. There is also evidence that couples who experience marital disorder have more maritally related irrational beliefs than do better adjusted couples (Eidelson & Epstein, 1982). Similar studies with anxiety disorders might yield valuable insights into how obsessives, compulsives, phobics, and generally anxious people deal cognitively with various types of problems. There is already evidence that groups differing in anxiety symptoms differ in their irrational beliefs and dysfunctional cognitive styles, with high anxiety being associated with high levels of irrational beliefs. Furthermore, cognitively oriented therapy is associated with positive changes in these characteristics. For example, Smith (1983) showed that clients who received rational-emotive therapy had significant pre-to-post-therapy decrements in irrational beliefs and desires (e.g., "I want everyone to like me"). In addition there were decrements in emotional distress.

Test Anxiety

Research with clinical cases as well as surveys of normal populations have shown that, perhaps in most instances, people do not experience anxiety and irrational beliefs across the board. This fact has led to investigation of a variety of specific situational anxieties, including anxiety about taking tests and being evaluated, about social situations, about going to the dentist, as well as a variety of phobic reactions. Studies of situationally delimited anxiety have been popular because with them it becomes possible to relate indices of specific anxieties to measures of how subjects actually behave in the defined situational contexts. Test anxiety illustrates this approach.

As mentioned earlier, anxiety is usually defined as a complex state that includes cognitive, emotional, behavioral, and bodily components. Most anxiety measures reflect this inclusive definition by yielding only one global score. An instrument, Reactions to Tests (RTT), has recently been created to assess separately the multiple components of a person's reactions to test situations (Sarason, 1984). It consists of four factor analytically derived scales:

Tension ("I feel distressed and uneasy before tests")
Worry ("During tests, I wonder how the other people are doing")
Test-Irrelevant Thought ("Irrelevant bits of information pop into my head during a test")
Bodily Reactions ("My heart beats faster when the test begins").

While these scales are positively intercorrelated, the correlations are low enough to justify comparisons among them concerning their predictive value. When the RTT was related to performance on a difficult digit-symbol task under evaluative conditions, the Worry scale was more consistently related to performance and post-performance reports of cognitive interference than were the other scales. The Tension scale approached the Worry scale as a predictor of performance.

There is growing evidence that worry and self-preoccupation are among the most active ingredients of anxiety (Breznitz, 1971). This seems to be especially true for situations that lead to performance evaluations. Anyone who has taken examinations knows that worrying about one's level of ability, failure, and what other students might be doing interferes with effective performance. While thoughts that reflect worry have undesirable effects, thoughts that are directed to the task at hand are helpful. The Cognitive Interference Questionnaire was developed by Sarason and Stoops (1978) to assess the degree to which people, while working on important tasks, have thoughts that interfere with concentration while working on important tasks. These task-irrelevant thoughts have a particularly detrimental effect on highly test-anxious students.

In a recent study (Sarason & Basham, unpublished paper), subjects were given first the RTT, then a series of general information questions and finally a modification of the Cognitive Interference Questionnaire. In this revised version, called the Thought Occurrence Questionnaire or TOQ, there are three parts. The first part asks about thoughts related to the task just performed. The second part asks about "thoughts not about that task." The third part, a single item, asks about the degree to which the subject's mind wandered while working on the task.

Scale II of the RTT, the Worry scale, was found to correlate most highly with part 1 of the TOQ. Scale III of the RTT, Test Irrelevant Thoughts, correlated most highly with parts 2 and 3 of the TOQ. These findings suggest that the scales of the RTT can be used to predict the type and degree of interfering thoughts that actually occur to an individual in an evaluative situation.

The RTT also has been used in relating physiological measures taken during stressful situations to verbal reports of typical personal reactions under stress. Burchfield, Sarason, Sarason, and Beaton (unpublished study) examined the relationship of the RTT to physiological indices gathered while college students worked on items of the type found on intelligence tests. The Tension and Worry scales were significantly correlated with skin conductance (GSR) and finger tip temperature changes during performance. There were no significant correlations with electromyographic (EMG) changes. The Test-Irrelevant Thinking and Bodily Reactions scales were unrelated to all physiological change measures. More studies dealing with relationships among test anxiety, performance variables, and physiological measures are needed in order to assess the degree of desynchrony that may exist among them.

Research on social anxiety, while less extensive than research on test anxiety, is consistent with the findings presented above. Socially anxious people become upset or disturbed by others' scrutiny or remarks or merely because others are present. They suffer from heightened self-awareness and become embarrassed easily. Worry over being evaluated in social situations has been shown to be the most important active ingredient of social anxiety (Leary, 1982; Smith, Ingram, & Brehm, 1983).

Worry and Anxiety

Might the concept of anxiety be defined primarily or exclusively in terms of interfering worry and self-deprecation? Such a definition would be consistent with what we know about the relationships among test anxiety, self-preoccupation, and performance. It would, however, not be consistent with the widely held view that physiological arousal is a major component of anxiety in general and that the anxious response to stress involves hypermobilization of physiological resources. Perhaps this physiological view of anxiety needs some rethinking, at least in relation to the test-type situations. For example, in an extensive literature review, Holroyd and Appel (1980) concluded that the cognitive aspects of test anxiety may be its most active ingredients, and that no relationship has been demonstrated between test anxiety and physiological activity.

Would it be reasonable to conclude that the problem of anxiety, or at least the problem of test anxiety, is simply a problem of worry and interfering thoughts? At this stage of our knowledge the answer would have to be negative. For one thing, we know very little about these interfering thoughts (Borkovec, Robinson, Pruzinsky, & DePree, 1983). For example, we have little data about where worries come from and what people do about them. Do persistent painful worries go underground, that is, become unconscious? To what extent are conscious worries either in part or entirely symbolic of past worries that have been transformed in some way by what Freud called the psychic apparatus? How are worries and other interfering cognitions related?

There is another reason for resisting any temptation to reduce anxiety to a collection of worries and off-target thinking; the fact that anxiety as presently conceptualized is a complex concept is not a sufficient reason for dismissing this view as a confusing or misleading one. Instead, its complexity is a sufficient reason to separate its components for investigation in order ultimately to put them together again in an effort to better understand the wide range of human experience. Intensive research is needed to relate presumed components of anxiety to specific behavioral and clinical criteria. Assessing the components poses challenges because of pitfalls in operationalizing them. For example, Morris, Davis, and Hutchings (1981) developed questionnaire items to assess Worry and Emotionality aspects of anxiety. Their Emotionality scale includes items that refer to both general tension level ("I feel panicky") and specific body reactions ("I am so tense that my stomach is upset"). The items in the Emotionality scale of Spielberger's (1980) Test Anxiety Inventory also refer to both general tension and bodily reactions. The bodily reactions items seem quite a bit less ambiguous than the tension items. However, people who describe their reactions in terms of general tension may or may not differ in their physiological reactions from those who emphasize their worries. Do the phrases "I am tense" and "I am worried" simply differ semantically, or do they refer to different phenomenological and bodily experiences? The Tension scale of the Reactions to Tests may, to a degree, be a "semantic factor": that is, a factor that reflects ways of saying things like "I get worried when I have to take a test."

To the extent that statements such as "I feel tense" are simply a way of saying, "I am worried," the distinction between worry and emotionality becomes blurred. Although the concepts of emotions and emotionality are often discussed in terms of their physiological components, it would be a mistake to think of worry and emotionality as uncorrelated factors. The analysis of most emotional states in daily life almost requires identification of the thoughts that contribute to their arousal. It would be worthwhile to put on the anxiety research agenda further exploration of the interrelationships among classes of cognitive and bodily processes, such as types of worries, level of actual autonomic arousal, and persons' perceptions of their bodily states. Perhaps when we clarify the concepts of emotion, tension, and affect—that is, make them less ambiguous—we will be in a better position to come to grips with the problem of anxiety. A better understanding of specific types of worries and cognitive styles and their relationships to behavior and bodily processes can contribute to the needed clarification.

The assessment approaches described in this section, while as pointed out not problem-free, are instructive and useful because they show that it is possible to devise indices of cognitive characteristics that relate in a meaningful way to specific behavioral and performance criteria. Research that contributes to the development of profiles of cognitive characteristics is needed. Such profiles need not—indeed, probably should not—be limited to the worry dimension that seems so important in test anxiety. While profiles of worries would quite likely be useful from both assessment and treatment planning standpoints, there is a need also for measures of stylistic variables, such as the tendencies to deny or exaggerate one's anxiety or to be hypervigilant for danger signals.

Experimental Approaches to Decreasing Worry.   Researchers have looked not only at the components of anxious behavior and worry, but also have studied experimental manipulations by which a person's proneness to self-preoccupation generally and to worry in particular can be decreased. In one experiment, subjects differing in test anxiety were given the opportunity to observe a model who demonstrated effective ways of performing an anagrams task (Sarason, 1973). Using a talk-aloud technique, the model displayed several types of facilitative thoughts and cognitions. The major finding was that highly test-anxious subjects benefited more from the opportunity to observe a cognitive model than did those low in test anxiety. Cognitive modeling might have considerable potential in instructional and therapeutic programs as a means of demonstrating the differences between adaptive and maladaptive cognitions and the negative aspects of maladaptive attentional habits. Sarason and Sarason (1981) found that cognitive modeling was a valuable component of a social skills program for non-academically oriented high school students, and that test-anxious students benefited more from the cognitive modeling than did other students.

Another approach to self-preoccupation is simply to instruct subjects to maintain a task focus. In a recent experiment, 180 undergraduate students differing in RTT Worry scores worked on difficult anagrams (Sarason, 1983). The instructions for the anagrams task were contained in the test booklet. The attention-directing and reassuring communications were given by the experimenter after the subjects had read the task instructions, which included the achievement-orienting message. The subjects were told that performance on the anagrams task was a measure of the ability to do college-level work. After this communication, the subjects were given one of the following: an attention-directing condition, reassurance, or no additional communication. Subjects under the reassurance condition were told not to be overly concerned about their performance on the anagrams. The experimenter made such comments as "don't worry" and "you will do just fine." Subjects under the attention-directing condition were told to absorb themselves as much as possible in the anagrams task and to avoid thinking about other things. The experimenter said, "Concentrate all your attention on the problems," "Think only about the anagrams," and "Don't let yourself get distracted from the task." High-worry subjects under the control condition performed poorly compared to the other control subjects. High-worry subjects in the attention-directing and reassurance groups performed well. However, consistent with previous evidence, the study showed that reassuring instructions have a detrimental effect on people who are not worriers. Non-worry subjects in the reassurance group performed poorly. Non-worriers take the reassuring communication at face value; i.e., they take the task lightly and lower their motivational level. The attention-directing condition had all of the advantages that reassurance has for high-worry subjects with none of the disadvantages for low-worry subjects. The performance levels of all groups that received the attention-directing instructions were high.

After the anagrams task, all the subjects responded to the Cognitive Interference Questionnaire (CIQ), which provided a measure of the number and type of interfering thoughts experienced in that particular situation. Cognitive interference under the attention-direction condition was consistently low. The high cognitive interference of the high-worry groups under the control condition is similar to previous findings concerning highly test-anxious subjects. The performance and CIQ scores were reanalyzed in terms of other Reactions to Tests scales, in order to provide information about the possible interactions of the experimental conditions with the scores on the other scales. None of these additional analyses revealed statistically significant results. The results of this study support an attentional interpretation of anxiety and worry and suggest that simply calling subjects' attention to the need for task-oriented behavior can have a salutary effect on their performance and decrease intrusive thoughts.

Evidence is increasing that the interfering effects of anxiety on behavior can be significantly reduced through attentional training (Wise & Haynes, 1983). This therapeutic approach may be helpful not only in evaluation anxiety but in other types of anxiety-related problems. For example, Grayson, Foa, and Steketee (1982) have found that obsessive-compulsives, when they were helped to focus attention on their ruminations and rituals, showed significant degrees of habituation.

Cognitive Therapeutic Approaches

In addition to experimental studies that investigate how to alter cognitive patterns, there are several well-developed therapeutic approaches that make use of cognitive techniques. These can be generally divided into cognitive-behavioral and cognitive-psychodynamic approaches. Cognitive-behavioral therapists seek to change behavior by changing specific thought patterns. Cognitive-behavioral therapy (often also simply called cognitive therapy) is typically more concerned with *how* to change maladaptive cognitions than why the cognitions arose in the first place. While for some practical therapeutic purposes why questions may not be crucial, they are germane to a general understanding of the content of thoughts and the way in which that content influences behavior. Cognitive-psychodynamic writers have given particular emphasis to current cognitions as intrapsychic and developmental products and attempt to analyze the cognitive histories of their patients and the varying strengths and degrees of accessibility of particular types of thoughts. This approach directs attention to the cognitive residues of early experiences that are like ashes in the fireplace, seemingly inert but actually smoldering.

The cognitive-behavioral and cognitive-psychodynamic therapeutic approaches are not necessarily in conflict with each other. In fact, there is a reason to believe that they are complementary. Both approaches require further specification of how systems of cognitions function, how seemingly disparate thoughts might come to be linked, how these linkages change over time, and the relationships among cognitions, bodily processes, and behavior.

Cognitive-Behavioral Approaches

Exposure Therapy.   Perhaps the most traditionally behavioral of the cognitive-behavioral therapies are those based on the principle of exposure to anxiety-provoking situations and thoughts. Much research has been carried out in which clients are exposed to feared stimuli and prevented from making an avoidance or escape response. In this work the client is strongly urged to continue to attend to the anxiety-eliciting stimuli, despite the initial stressful effects this usually entails. From a behavioral perspective, the exposure allows the anxiety to extinguish because no catastrophic outcome ensues. The individual, no longer avoiding the situation, experiences it until eventually its negative excitatory characteristics cease.

Exposure therapy has been used particularly in treating both phobic and obsessive-compulsive disorders. Exposure to feared stimuli may be either imaginal or in vivo. In in vivo exposure the individual experiences the actual feared situation rather than imagining it under the therapist's direction. A critical element of the treatment is motivating the client to maintain contact with the actual noxious stimuli or with their imagined presence until he or she becomes used to them. This might mean, for example, either exposing a compulsive hand washer to dirt until hand washing, and later the hand-washing urge, no longer occurs. Exposure could also be to imagine dirt, perhaps first thought of as some household dust and later as particularly noxious dirt, such as vomit or feces. The therapist's task is to identify all components of the stimulus that evoke an avoidance or escape response and continue exposure until the evoked response no longer occurs.

The exposure principle is employed in the cognitive-behavioral techniques. In systematic desensitization a series of fear-arousing stimuli, carefully graded from mild to strongly fearful, are used. Only when a client is comfortable with one level of fear-producing stimuli is the next, slightly stronger stimulus introduced. Implosive therapy refers to therapist-controlled exposure to the imaginal re-creation of a complex high-intensity fear-arousing situation. Flooding is rapid in vivo exposure that begins at an intense level.

Exposure treatment of phobias and obsessive-compulsive disorders has produced consistently good results with lasting improvements for up to several years (Barlow & Wolfe, 1981; Marks, 1981). The longer the exposure to the critical stimulus, the better the results. How well exposure treatment works depends on the motivation of the client and on specific factors in his or her life. For example, when compulsive rituals are triggered by home cues (which is true in many cases), treatment needs to be conducted in the home setting. When compulsives receive in vivo exposure therapy in their homes, their task is to avoid compulsive responding when evoking stimuli are present. If the client refrains from his or her compulsive behavior in the presence of the stimuli, the level of anxiety decreases immediately after exposure and the decrease is usually maintained in the presence of the compulsion-evoking stimuli as long as 1, or even 6 months, later (Biran & Wilson, 1981). The most common reason for failure to improve is not complying with treatment instructions, particularly for clients to seek exposure to fear-arousing stimuli on their own.

An important task for future research is identifying the basis of exposure's effectiveness. When a client "gets used to" an upsetting stimulus, what is going on? The explanation could be the strictly behavioral principle of extinction or it could have distinctly cognitive elements. For example, a more cognitive explanation for the effectiveness of exposure treatment is that as clients observe their ability to handle a little exposure to upsetting stimuli and note how their anxiety level subsides, they gain confidence in themselves and develop the courage to persist in efforts to overcome their problems.

Many of the exposure therapies started out to be strongly behavioral in emphasis. Cognitive elements were restricted to imagining anxiety-provoking situations in order to allow the fear responses to extinguish. As these therapies have developed, increasing emphasis has been placed on their cognitive aspects and on their use as a way of changing how a person thinks in particular types of situations.

There is increasing recognition of the fact that changes in behavior can lead to changes in cognitions, and that these changes can, in turn, modify overt behavior. As a consequence, it is not possible to draw a sharp line between purely cognitive and behavioral therapies. Both employ learning concepts, although more behaviorally oriented therapists emphasize efforts to directly change overt behavior, and more cognitively oriented therapists emphasize the thoughts that influence overt behavior. Both types of therapists see themselves as educators of a special kind. Over 30 years ago, Dollard and Miller (1950) expressed this idea:

> . . . we view the therapist as a kind of teacher and the patient as a learner. In the same way and by the same principles that bad tennis habits can be corrected by a good coach, so bad mental and emotional habits can be corrected by a psychotherapist. There is a difference, however. Whereas only a few people want to play tennis, all the world wants a clear, free, efficient mind. (p. 8)

Modeling.   Another cognitive-behavioral therapy whose focus is somewhat different from the exposure therapies is modeling. Modeling is often employed by the therapist to demonstrate for the patient how a dreaded situation can be handled. In this way, modeling provides information about how to handle the situation when exposure begins. In addition to its roles in providing information and contributing to disinhibition, modeling can function in the acquisition of new skills and response capabilities. This is especially true in participant modeling, which is often more effective than modeling alone. In participant modeling, a therapist models a response and then provides corrective feedback as the client models the same behavior. In addition to the information provided by the modeled behavior, the client also receives guidance on his or her own performance. Participant modeling works especially well with complex behaviors, such as behavior in certain social situations. When indicated, the therapist might model ways of thinking (e.g., problem-solving strategies) instead of, or in addition to, overt behaviors. This emphasis on cognitive factors in modeling is, like that in the exposure therapies, a current trend. Originally modeling dealt almost exclusively with the observation of motor behavior. Currently, however, the modeling of cognitions and effective ways of thinking about situations is probably the most emphasized part of the field.

The Role of Self-Efficacy. Bandura's (1978, 1982) concept of self-efficacy has received increasing attention as a likely explanation for the effectiveness of exposure, modeling, and several other therapies. According to Bandura, when behavior change occurs, it is noticed and interpreted by the individual. Positive changes, even if achieved in the face of great personal discomfort, lead to favorable self-evaluations and result in such self-statements as, "I may have more on the ball than I thought." One aspect of cognitive assessment that is certain to receive attention in the future is the assessment of self-efficacy beliefs and the expectations people have concerning their ability to perform particular tasks. Whereas negative self-referential statements, such as "No one is interested in me," seem to have an interfering effect on ongoing behavior, statements indicative of self-efficacy, such as "I can do it," seem to contribute to a relatively anxiety-free task orientation. Behavioral achievements change both self-perceptions and personal expectations and the behavior of significant others who notice the behavioral changes. At the same time, increases in self-efficacy enable the individual to consider behavioral avenues that previously may have seemed impossible.

COGNITIVE RESTRUCTURING

According to cognitive-behavioral theorists, thinking disturbances that occur only in certain settings or in relation to specific problems are often the primary sources of anxiety. This would be true of obsessive and phobic individuals. These types of thoughts include unrealistic appraisals of situations and consistent overestimation of their dangerous aspects; the degree of harm and the likelihood of harm may both be exaggerated. These thoughts can be viewed as vulnerability factors that interact with the characteristics of situations. From this point of view, precipitating events (the situation) elicit or magnify an underlying attitude of fear (the vulnerability factor) and give rise to hypervigilance for signs of danger and/or other components of the anxiety syndrome. As this attitude strengthens, danger-related thoughts become more easily activated by less specific, less avoidable situations ("If you look for it, you're sure to find it"). As a result, the anxious individual may continually scan internal and external stimuli for danger signals.

Cognitive therapists with a behavioral orientation work on the problem as presented by the patient and are concerned with specifically identifying and changing the thoughts involved in the maladaptive behavior. Since many of these thoughts appear to function automatically, feelings such as the dread, apprehension, and intense fear characteristic of anxiety disorders often arise in the absence of rational problem solving when certain environmental triggers occur. Cognitive therapists help patients to (1) become aware of their automatic thoughts through improved self-monitoring skills, and (2) do specific things to control them. An element common to many cognitive therapies is cognitive rehearsal, through which the client is encouraged to rehearse mentally adaptive approaches to problematic situations.

A therapeutic approach that stresses the cognitive side of the cognitive-behavior therapy spectrum is *cognitive restructuring*. In cognitive restructuring, the client is instructed to identify irrational thoughts associated with specific problematic situations, to question and dispute them, and to think about the situation more rationally. Verbal persuasion, direct challenges, cognitive rehearsal of more adaptive, less anxiety-provoking thoughts, and rehearsal in the therapy session, as well as in homework assignments, may be used to bring about changes in thinking which presumably have behavioral consequences. By means of cognitive restructuring, people are encouraged to develop more realistic appraisals of themselves and others (Ellis, 1970; Goldfried, 1977). For example, when taking an examination a person might think, "This test is hard. Everyone else seems to think it's simple. They all must know a lot more than I do." Such thoughts are likely to lead to a high degree of anxiety. A cognitive therapist would help the client concentrate on a more adaptive type of thought such as, "I studied hard. I'll just try to answer one question at a time. If I don't know the answer, I'll go on to the next one. No reason for panic. Even people who do well don't know the answer to every question."

While a number of positive findings concerning cognitive restructuring have been reported in the literature, there also have been negative ones (Wilson, 1982). Part of the problem is probably the lack of standardization of restructuring procedures and methodological flaws in some studies, such as not including attention control groups in research designs. An additional problem has been a lack of clarity about subject and therapist characteristics. Cognitive restructuring studies have not explored possible interactions between therapist and client characteristics. This observation is, of course, not peculiar to cognitive restructuring, cognitive therapies, or any other therapeutic approach. The important general point, familiar to all therapy researchers, is that there are very few empirical studies that are sufficiently complex to permit firm conclusions about the effectiveness of specific therapeutic elements.

Further research is needed on the dynamic interrelationships over time between cognitive and behavioral change (Miller & Berman, 1983). Progress in the application of cognitive therapies has been so rapid that several important topics have been relatively untouched. Three such neglected topics are the developmental histories, interactions among cognitions, and strength and accessibility of cognitions (Sarason, 1979). Cognitive-behavior therapists have had notable success in their efforts to eliminate specific symptoms and strengthen specific classes of adaptive behavior or thought. The therapeutic successes that have been attained should not detract attention from larger questions about the relationships between present thoughts and behavior and past thoughts and behavior, or from that between past and current environmental events.

The common vague, yet troubling, psychological problems that burden many people (e.g., a general feeling of malaise and dissatisfaction with one's social relationships and role in life) have yet to receive the attention they deserve. The amorphous complaints of large numbers of anxiety neurotics have thus far been a stumbling block to behavioral clinicians because of the difficulty of isolating the specific anxiety-eliciting stimuli.

Cognitive-Psychodynamic Approaches

A review of the gamut of psychodynamic therapies is beyond the scope of this paper. However, it is important to note that cognitive processes are receiving more and more attention among psychodynamic therapists. Arieti (1980), Barnett (1980), and Bieber (1980) are among a growing number of psychoanalysts who emphasize the need to study the development, formation, content, interconnections, and dynamic effects of ideas. This emphasis is related to the belief that psychoanalysis has in the past been too preoccupied with vaguely defined drives, instincts, and urges. As a consequence, psychoanalytic theorists have neglected ideas as major components of inner reality and as dynamic forces. Arieti (1980) has succinctly expressed this position.

> Freud stressed how we tend to suppress and repress ideas which elicit anxiety. But we psychiatrists and psychoanalysts have suppressed or repressed the whole field of ideas, that is, cognition. We have repressed it apparently because it is anxiety provoking. As a matter of fact, as we shall see later, there would be very little anxiety in the human being without ideas or precursors of ideas. But psychoanalysts have for a long time preferred to think that cognition deals with those so-called conflict-free areas and therefore does not pertain to psychoanalysis. The contention of cognitive psychoanalysts is that very few conflicts, and only elementary ones, would exist in the human being if he were not able to think, to formulate ideas, old or new, to assimilate them, make them part of himself, face and compare them, distort them, attribute them to others, or finally, repress them. (p. 5)

Whereas the cognitive-behavioral orientation has spawned a variety of novel therapeutic procedures, the cognitive-psychodynamic orientation is usually applied within traditional psychotherapeutic frameworks, emphasis being placed on how patients' thoughts are clustered, the linkages between thoughts and emotions, and the genesis of these linkages. However, it is noteworthy that a growing number of clinicians employ both behavioral and psychodynamic concepts in their work (Goldfried, 1982).

Barnett's (1980) meshing of cognitive elements with a noninstinctual psychodynamic approach illustrates what would appear to be a salutary development in the field of psychotherapy. He sees the self-concept as a special case of the organization of cognitions related to the personal meanings attached to events and interpersonal relationships. From this perspective, the self can be seen in terms of templates that guide a person's systems of knowing and ways of interpreting reality. The work of psychotherapy is identifying and modifying the templates. While cognitive-psychodynamic approaches are in many ways appealing and complementary to cognitive-behavioral ones, they have not yet led to controlled empirical evaluations of their basic concepts.

RESEARCH ISSUES AND NEEDS

At several points throughout this chapter I have commented on the present state of knowledge concerning cognitive approaches to anxiety. In this concluding section I would like to summarize in the form of an agenda for research some points already made and make a few suggestions implied, perhaps, but not stated explicitly earlier.

The Need for a Component Analysis of Anxiety.   Concepts of what anxiety is have changed over the years, seemingly as do styles in automobile models. Anxiety conceived as drive, instinctual energy, and emotion has at various times been "in" and not so "in." Anxiety as a product of cognitive factors seems to be "in" today. Perhaps fashions have changed so easily because anxiety as a concept is too vague and lacks solidity. Because anxiety is almost always regarded as being multidimensional, it is easy for theoreticians to shift their focus of attention from one dimension to another. As argued at the outset, a component analysis of anxiety is sorely needed. This paper has been about its cognitive component, but cognitions alone are not the whole story of anxiety. The finding in several studies that worries and autonomic responding are not correlated very highly is but one of the pieces of evidence suggesting the need for multidimensional studies.

Cognitive Anxiety as a Vulnerability Factor.   By cognitive anxiety is meant the troubling thoughts, such as worries, that people report having. While there may be wide individual differences in the frequency and correlates of worries and their levels of accessibility to awareness, we all know what worries are and can recognize them in ourselves and often in others. The worries of the anxious person are distressing preoccupations and concerns about impending or anticipated events. The worries of those who are anxious tend to be future-oriented in contrast to depressed people, for example, who tend to be preoccupied with the past.

The concept of stress plays a key role in a cognitive analysis of worries. Stress can be understood in terms of perceived performance demands, a person's awareness of the need to do something about a given state of affairs. These demands are evoked by situational challenges and can lead to either task-relevant or task-irrelevant cognitions. From this point of view, the most adaptive response to stress should be task-oriented thinking which directs the individual's attention to the task at hand. The task-oriented person is able to set aside unproductive worries and preoccupations. The self-preoccupied person, on the other hand, becomes absorbed in the implications and consequences of failure to meet situational challenges. Anxious people worry about their perceived personal incompetence and possible difficulties they may be called upon to confront. Their negative self-appraisals are unpleasant, and because they are self-preoccupying, they also detract from task concentration. Since many anxious people describe themselves as being tense and feel that something terrible will happen, even though they may not be able to specify the cause of their worry, these self-preoccupations are likely to create cognitive interference that precludes an orderly, task-oriented approach to situational requirements. In this way worry proneness can be regarded as a vulnerability factor.

Vulnerability refers to how likely a person is to respond maladaptively to specific situations. The range of vulnerability associated with particular aspects of cognitive anxiety needs to be determined. In general, the greater the stress the less vulnerability a person needs to have before maladaptive behavior occurs. The less the stress, the greater the vulnerability needed to produce maladaptation. As more is learned about relationships among cognitive vulnerability factors, stress, and maladaptation, it may become possible to develop hypotheses about the mechanisms involved.

A vulnerability approach to cognitive anxiety may have implications for prevention. At the very least we need to know more about the prevalence of cognitive vulnerabilities, such as significantly preoccupying worries. The range of human maladaptation is wide, and most failures in functioning are not serious. However, not infrequently, little problems lead to big ones. Freud attributed anxiety to the failure of defense mechanisms. Some contemporary writers might say that anxiety is experienced when coping resources are not adequate to situational challenges. However one phrases it, these resources or defenses counter tendencies toward vulnerability. Anxiety is common, not rare, and when it occurs it has observable effects on performance and takes a subjective toll in the form of personal unhappiness. Perhaps knowledge acquired in the study of relatively minor problems, such as test or social anxiety and their treatment, will have something to contribute to improving personal adjustment for a large neglected segment of the population.

A Recognition of Levels of Cognitive Anxiety.   As pointed out earlier, cognitive-behavioral writers have directed their attention to those personal concerns that are accessible to the individual, while cognitive-psychodynamic writers preoccupy themselves with unconscious processes. There are growing signs that both schools of thought are moving to recognition of the need to study the entire range of accessibility (Bowers & Meichenbaum, in press; Goldfried, 1982; Meichenbaum & Gilmore, in press). One divergence in usage of the anxiety concept is employment of it by some as a hypothetical mediator between experience and behavior and by others as an observable symptom. Can a fruitful theoretical formulation be devised to handle these seemingly disparate approaches?

The Relationships Among Anxiety and Other Conditions. The practical need to classify can seductively lead us to think of the currently popular classifications as being real and distinct categories, which they may not be. There is considerable evidence already available indicating significant overlaps among a variety of disorders, for example, among people suffering from anxiety and depression. Foa et al. (1983) reports a correlation of .60 between anxiety and depression in a group of obsessive-compulsives. While the size of the correlation could be expected to vary as a function of the types of patients studied, it would be interesting to carry out studies in which people are categorized primarily in terms of dimensional variables, such as cognitive styles, worries, and preoccupations. The point of this work need not be the replacement of traditional diagnoses with cognitive profiles, but rather that these profiles may provide information about differential vulnerabilities to particular stressors and also might have value in predicting the efficacy of different clinical interventions.

Loneliness and shame provide additional examples of human experiences that overlap with anxiety. Lonely people experience social isolation, often because of deficits in social skills (Peplau & Perlman, 1982). They tend to be shy, introverted, and reluctant to take interpersonal risks and frequently are described as suffering from social anxiety. As mentioned earlier, there is evidence that socially anxious people may generally be less able to concentrate or focus their attention effectively in social situations. They seem to dwell on their actions to a greater degree than do people who are not lonely. Because of self-preoccupations about their lack of social appeal, their ability to take effective social initiatives is low. Shame also is often involved in difficulties in taking initiatives. People who are ashamed about something they have done or experienced in the past avoid situations and actions that would bring humiliation. They suffer from an accentuated painful state of self-awareness (Wurmser, 1981).

What is common to anxiety, depression, loneliness, and shame are self-preoccupying cognitive intrusions that involve self-devaluation and self-debasement. Comparative studies of people with these types of problems would provide information about the similarities and differences in cognitions and cognitive processes among them. In addition, they might contribute to identifying cognitive categories that are not now clearly in focus. There is another similarity that seems important. While anxiety, depression, loneliness, and shame occur in varying forms and degrees, they affect large numbers of people. While the most severe disorders, understandably perhaps, have received the most clinical and research attention, more must be known about the sometimes debilitating problems of living that are experienced daily by millions of people.

Need for More Sophisticated Studies of Therapeutic Effectiveness. Despite widespread recognition that studies of the effectiveness of a therapeutic procedure require much more than treated and untreated groups, the research literature does not reflect the needed levels of sophistication and complexity. This state of affairs characterizes both behavioral and psychodynamic studies. Although behavioral studies may be somewhat easier to interpret than psychodynamic ones because of their more explicit dependent measures, studies from both points of view rarely permit partialing out the effects of the therapist; his or her personality; confidence in, and enthusiasm about his or her therapy; ability to provide social support and interpersonal responses to the particular client; and other factors often described as being nonspecific. Until the effects of these types of variables are systematically incorporated into research designs, there will continue to be much heat and little light regarding controversies about ways of helping people over their problems.

CONCLUSIONS

This paper has been about the hypothesis that specific types of thoughts and ways of thinking and problem solving are key elements in the experience of anxiety. The purpose of this paper was to direct attention to (1) the contributions of cognitions to all aspects of life and (2) the gaps in our knowledge about the specifics of those contributions. The gaps may be due as much to conceptual limitations in relating cognition to other aspects of life—such as mood, emotion, and affect—as to imperfect knowledge of thought processes per se. One impediment to understanding these specifics of human thought and problem solving is the creation of concepts of cognition that are not veridical with personal experience. By studying problems representative of real-life situations and keeping close to our data, we may be able to avoid some of the excesses that have marked other theoretical approaches and, at the same time, help people achieve well-being and more personal control over their lives.

6 Emotion Theory and the Role of Emotions in Anxiety in Children and Adults

Carroll E. Izard
Samuel H. Blumberg
University of Delaware

We view anxiety as a complex multidimensional phenomenon that always involves a pattern of emotions and interactions of emotions with cognitions and actions and sometimes with physiological needs. And, of course, it involves the neurochemical processes subserving the emotion and the other components of anxiety. Each of these various components or aspects of anxiety is addressed in one or more chapters of the present volume. The present chapter focuses on emotions and the pattern of emotions in anxiety.

Much of the theory and research on anxiety makes little use of the recent advances made in the science of emotions. Several factors contribute to this situation. First, a number of investigators with roots in the behavioristic tradition (e.g., Lang, this volume; Mandler, 1975) focus on response and cognitive characteristics of emotion and deliberately ignore or discount the importance of the feeling states or emotion components of anxiety. Second, many who acknowledge anxiety to be an emotion (e.g., Levitt, 1967) show little interest in the emotion concepts. Third, investigators who frame their definition and study of anxiety in essentially cognitive terms (e.g., Sarason, 1972; this volume) never relate their work to the major theories of emotion or research bearing on these theories. This fact holds even when the emotion theory and research deals with fear, which is sometimes equated with anxiety. Fourth, with few exceptions (see Schwartz, 1982) psychophysiological studies of anxiety have ignored somatic indices that might have kept this line of investigation vigorous and more closely related to emotion research. Fifth, some though not all (Gray, 1983; this volume) of neuroscience research on anxiety runs at right angles to emotion theory and research. Finally, anxiety theory and research has been particularly unconcerned with the rapidly growing body of knowledge on the development of emotions (Izard & Malatesta, in press; Lewis & Michalson, 1983).

Thus, a close look at the psychology of anxiety reveals little of current emotion theories and emotion research. Yet, perhaps no one participating in this volume, and probably no one at all, would deny that anxiety and emotion are related. An effort is needed to juxtapose research and theory on emotions as basic biosocial processes and anxiety as a determinant of human problems and psychopathology. It is not necessary to repeat recent surveys of emotion theories (Izard, Kagan, & Zajonc, in press; Plutchik, 1980). It is appropriate to review the major issues in contemporary emotion theories, with special reference to anxiety. This constitutes the first section of this chapter. The second section discusses some cognitive theories of anxiety and related research. The third section presents theory and evidence for viewing the affective symptomatology of anxiety as a pattern of emotions. The final section summarizes recent evidence that this differential emotions theory distinguishes between anxiety and depression in children.

ISSUES IN EMOTION THEORIES, WITH SPECIAL REFERENCE TO ANXIETY

A review of the theories of emotions reveals four major issues that can have an important influence on an investigator's efforts to conceptualize problems and formulate hypotheses for empirical test. The issues concern (a) the activation of emotions, (b) the components of emotions, (c) the relationship of emotions and cognition, and (d) the role of emotions in behavior and in the development of personality and psychopathology. The following analysis of these issues raises a number of unanswered questions, but it will show that different theoretical positions can lead to different problems, hypotheses, measurements, and inferences. The discussion may also suggest ways of framing studies that compare the predictive and explanatory power of the different theoretical positions.

The Activation of Emotions

A source of confusion in emotion research has resulted from a failure to distinguish consistently between models of emotion activation and theories of emotion. The former focus on the problem of the generation of emotion. Various theorists have conceived the production of emotion in terms of linear causal relationships (Arnold, 1960; Lazarus & DeLongis, 1983; Mandler, 1975), additive functions (Schachter, 1971), sensory feedback (Tomkins, 1962, 1980), and complex feedback loops that are modulated by genetically influenced receptor thresholds and selectivity (Candland, 1977; Izard, 1977).

It is important to recognize that a model of emotion activation is only one aspect of emotion theory. The latter is concerned not only with the generation of emotions but with their functions in evolution, biology, motivation, human development, personality traits, social behavior, and the etiology and symptomatology of psychopathological conditions, such as anxiety and depression.

Early work on emotions reflected little interest in the problem of emotion activation. Darwin's (1872) famous principles were the result of his observations of emotion expressions and his effort to explain their origins in phylogeny and their production in living species. Spencer (1855) and Wundt (1907) seemed to have taken for granted the notion that emotions arise as a function of consciousness and concerned themselves more with the characteristics of emotion experience and its relationship to cognitive processes.

Emotion as a Result of Sensory Feedback.   James (1884, 1890) presented the first really influential model of emotion activation, and his notion of the differential qualitative effects of sensory feedback remain a part of some contemporary formulations (Izard, 1971; Leventhal, 1980; Tomkins, 1962). He proposed that, contrary to popular thought, *"bodily changes follow directly the perception of the exciting fact, and that our feeling of the same changes as they occur is the emotion"* (James, 1890, p. 449). James' use of the term perception here is ambiguous; he failed to distinguish between cognitive processes involved in the "perceptions" that result when "we lose our fortune" and when "we meet a bear." In fact, these two examples of "perception" fall at nearly opposite ends of a continuum of complexity of perceptual-cognitive processes, and thus they may generate emotions through different neural pathways and structures. In the wild, the sense impression or percept of a bear can lead to escape behavior with little or no inferential process (cf. Zajonc, 1980), but "perception" of a loss of fortune involves complex cognitive processes, including memory and anticipation.

In the original statement of his model, James described "bodily changes" resulting from both somatic and autonomic nervous system activities. The association of his work with that of Lange (1885/1922), however, led to the "James-Lange" theory that made the "bodily changes" synonomous with visceral activities. Later, on the basis of physiological experiments, Cannon (1929) argued that emotion, or rather emotion expression or "emotional behavior," was independent of visceral feedback. This led to widespread rejection of the feedback hypothesis of emotion activation, but two disparate approaches revived it. F. H. Allport (1924), Jacobsen (1929), Tomkins (1962), and Izard (1971) drew attention to somatic feedback, which was not considered by Cannon, and Schachter (Schachter & Singer, 1962) and Mandler (1975) held that undifferentiated arousal (autonomic nervous system activity) contributes to emotion experience, given certain mediating cognitive processes. The somatic factor was highlighted in Tomkins' (1962) claim, phrased essentially like James', that awareness of facial feedback is the emotion.

Tomkins (1962), following Spencer, Darwin, and James, posits a number of innate emotions, and he explains their activation in terms of a single principle— "the density of neural firing or stimulation." For example, a sudden and rapid increase in the rate of neural firing activates startle, a less rapid increase produces fear, and a still less rapid increase activates interest. Thus, according to Tomkins, a particular gradient of neural firing over time produces a particular pattern of neuromuscular activity in the face and the facial feedback is sensed as a specific emotion experience. Tomkins' model ignores the differential involvement of various brain structures in different emotions (see Section B). The same overall density of neural firing may activate very different emotions if the neural activity differentially involves limbic structures that are differentially involved in, say, anger and fear.

The sensory feedback models of emotion activation do not readily explain the activation of anxiety, if anxiety is considered as a unitary phenomenon (see Lazarus & Averill, 1972). This is so because there is no evidence to indicate that anxiety can be represented physiologically by a specific autonomic or somatic response pattern (Izard, 1972). In the absence of such an anxiety-specific pattern, one could not expect patterned sensory feedback to be the activator of the anxiety state. However, sensory feedback could figure as an activator of anxiety experience, if anxiety experience is considered as a pattern of emotions that do have specific neuromuscular patterns (facial expressions) (Ekman, Friesen, & Ellsworth, 1972; Izard, 1971).

Emotion as a Function of Cognition.   Arnold (1960) presented a comprehensive theory of emotion, including a model of emotion activation that became the cornerstone of contemporary cognitive theories of emotion. She maintains that emotions arise *only* as a consequence of perception and appraisal and that the latter two processes are different. She defined perception as the "integration of sense impressions" and appraisal as an "integrative sensory function," but the distinction proved difficult to clarify and most later cognitive models have ignored it. Lazarus (Lazarus, Kanner, & Folkman, 1980) describes the cognitive antecedents of emotion as involving "learning, memory, perception, and thought" (p. 192) and Plutchik's (1980) model of "cognitive-emotional" functioning involves short- and long-term memory, evaluation, and prediction. The case is similar for the positions of Schachter (1971) and Mandler (1975).

A variation of the appraisal model described by developmental psychologists ascribes emotion or motivation to information processing (Hunt, 1965). Positive affect arises from the assimilation of information; negative affect arises from difficulty or failure in assimilating information. In particular, negative emotion is activated by incongruity or discrepancy between the perceived object and a previously established schema or central representation of the object. (The incongruity hypothesis was first described by Hebb, 1946, who later discounted it, Hebb, 1949). Explanation of emotion activation by the assimilation-discrepancy model requires either the assumption of innate schemas or the acquisition and storage of schemas in memory before emotion can be elicited. This position, as presented by Bronson (1968), Kagan (1974), Schaffer (1974) and others, holds that emotion is a function of the matching (assimilation) or mismatching (discrepancy) of the products of perceptual processes with learned schemas already existing in consciousness.

Leventhal (1980) holds that some form of cognitive process is always "active along with—if not prior to—emotion." However, he recognizes that the accompanying or preceding cognitive processes can vary from "minimally processed pre-attentive perception" to a "more deeply processed and specific schematic or conceptual code. (p. 193)" Leventhal's position is, in this respect, similar to that of Arnold.

Emotion as a Result of Arousal Plus Cognitive Evaluation.   Schachter and Singer (1962) proposed that undifferentiated and unexplained arousal leads to a cognitive evaluation or unbiased search for explanation. The search leads to a label that determines the quality of the emotion experience. In this formulation it is cognition involving symbolic processes that determines the quality of emotion. This model, similar to that of Mandler (Mandler & Watson, 1966), generated considerable research on cognitive manipulation of the labeling process under various experimental conditions, but the only direct tests of the model were recent experiments that were intended to be replications of the original Schachter-Singer study (Marshall & Zimbardo, 1979; Maslach, 1979). Both these experiments failed to replicate the original, and the data suggested that undifferentiated, unbiased arousal leads to a negatively biased search and to predominantly negative emotion labels and experiences. Schachter and Singer and Marshall and Zimbardo subsequently debated the merits of the original study and the failures to replicate its findings (Marshall & Zimbardo, 1979; Schachter & Singer, 1979).

Since the early studies of Wolf and Wolff (1942), Funkenstein (1955), and Ax (1953), there have been a few successful demonstrations of emotion-specific autonomic nervous system (ANS) activity. That the more frequent failures of such efforts may have been due to ineffective methods of eliciting specific emotions in the laboratory is suggested by the recent successes of Schwartz (1982) and Ekman, Levenson, & Friesen (1983). Taken together, these studies present a serious challenge to all theories that assume undifferentiated ANS arousal as the necessary physiological basis of emotion.

Need for a Multifactor Model of Emotion Activation.   Each of the foregoing models attempts to explain the activation of emotion on the basis of a single critical variable—density of neural firing (stimulation) or cognitive appraisal or as a function of arousal plus appraisal. The first two of these principles (stimulation and cognitive appraisal) offer reasonable explanations of the activation of some of the emotions under certain circumstances. For example, stepping into quicksand in a swamp on a dark night can elicit fear, as can a hostile remark that is appraised as an ominous threat.

Although there is no experimental evidence that bears directly on Tomkins' model, some developmental studies raise questions about its usefulness. Precisely the same painful stimulus (diphtheria-pertussis-tetanus inoculation) activates different emotion expressions in different infants of the same age (Izard, Hembree, Dougherty, & Spizzirri, 1983).

There is ample anecdotal and experimental evidence to indicate that cognitive processes trigger emotions. James (1890) called attention to the power of imagery to elicit emotions. Experimental evidence for the correctness of James' observation has come from the work of Fridlund and Schwartz (1979), Izard (1972), Lang (1979), and Schwartz, Fair, Salt, Mandel, and Klerman (1976).

Thus, the crucial issue is not whether cognitive processes activate or trigger emotions, but whether there are other activating processes. Current evidence suggests that there are. The concept of emotion threshold, which is related to the concept of biological preparedness (Seligman & Hager, 1972), helps account for individual differences in emotion responsiveness and for species-related and age-related differences in emotion activation in relation to particular stimuli. McDougall's (1923) notion that the "nervous system is peculiarly fitted to respond" affectively to certain sensory data and not to others helps explain why some stimuli, but not others, elicit a particular emotion. Strangeness (Emde, Gaensbauer, & Harmon, 1976) and heights (Campos & Sternberg, 1980) are often effective stimuli for fear in the second half year of life.

A satisfactory model of emotion activation must be multifactor or multidimensional and must allow for developmental changes in emotion and emotion-cognition processes. All the potentially relevant factors are not independent and all may not be operative on all occasions or at all stages of development. The following factors or concepts must be taken into account: neurochemical processes (Costa, this volume; Gray, this volume; Redmond; this volume); selectivity of receptors (Izard, 1971; McDougall, 1923); biological preparedness or genetically determined thresholds (Bowlby, 1973; Gray, 1971; Izard, 1971); noninferential sensory-perceptual or preattentive processes (e.g., uninterpreted sense impressions) (Izard, 1971; McDougall, 1923); density of neural firing or stimulation gradients (Tomkins, 1962); feedback from physiological arousal or ANS activity (Mandler, 1975; Schachter, 1971); feedback from facial patterning and activity of the somatic system (Izard, 1977; Leventhal, 1980; Tomkins, 1962); immediate, nonreflective, cognitive appraisal or evaluation (Arnold, 1960); thought, memory (and higher order cognitive processes) (Lazarus, 1974; Lazarus, Kanner, & Folkman, 1980). Perhaps considerable empirical research in relation to each of the foregoing concepts is in order before the multifactor model of emotion activation is formalized. In any case, a viable and comprehensive model will have to be a complex one. Insofar as anxiety is an emotion or pattern of emotions, the same holds true for its activation.

The Components of Emotions

Failure to recognize that emotions involve processes in different systems has been a source of confusion and controversy. Some of the early views of emotion (e.g., Lange, 1885/1922) held that emotion was essentially vasomotor reaction, and emphasis on the study of visceral changes has been continued by many investigators (Gasonov, 1974; Mandler, 1975). Other investigators have focused almost exclusively on neural structures and pathways (Flynn, 1967; Gellhorn, 1961, 1964, 1965; Lindsley, 1951, 1970; MacLean, 1972), hormones and neurotransmitters (Brady, 1970; Davis, 1970; Frankenhaeuser, 1979; Mason, 1975; Schildkraut, 1974) observable behavior, particularly facial expression (Ekman et al., 1972), or subjective experience (Russell, 1979). While these specialists have made significant contributions to the field, they have typically presented information on only one system or component of emotion. They often leave open the question whether emotion has really been measured, since they present no evidence of concomitant emotion processes in other systems. Most emotion theorists now define emotions as having three components—neurophysiological-biochemical, behavioral-expressive, feeling-experiential. Each component can be viewed as a system that organizes (noncognitive) information from other life systems. Therefore, it is evident that the subject of emotions and the study of anxiety are interdisciplinary in nature, and that the study of different component systems requires different conceptual tools and different methodologies for the study of highly different variables.

The Neurophysiological-Biochemical Level. The neurophysiological domain includes anatomical and physiological studies of brain structures and neural pathways involved in emotions. This research has shown that the limbic system and certain limbic structures such as the hypothalamus, hippocampus, amygdala, septum, and cingulate gyrus are differentially involved in different emotions (Gellhorn, 1965; MacLean, 1972). The evidence seems to support the notion that the neural substrate for a given emotion consists of complex interconnections among structures, and that different pathways may be involved in activation/amplification processes and inhibition/attenuation processes (Adams, 1979; Delgado, 1971; Isaacson, 1974).

The biochemistry of emotions includes psychoendocrinological and psychopharmacological studies of hormones and neurotransmitters involved in the limbic and limbic-neocortical processes in emotions. These studies have found that any of five neurotransmitters or any of hundreds of different chains of these transmitters may be involved in emotions. The existing evidence does not show strong relationships between a specific hormone and a specific emotion. However, a number of studies have suggested that the corticosteroids are implicated in stress (Frankenhaeuser, 1979; Selye, 1979), dopamine in anger (Kety, 1972), the monoamines in depression (Davis, 1970; Schildkraut, 1974; Schildkraut & Kety,

1967), norepinephrine and serotonin in anxiety (Gray, this volume), and gamma-amino buteric acid (GABA) in anxiety (Costa, this volume). The trend in psychopharmacology, psychoendocrinology, and psychophysiology is toward a search for profiles or patterns of neurophysiological functions underlying an emotion or a pattern of emotions (Mason, 1975; Schwartz, 1982). The neurophysiology and biochemistry of anxiety are considered in the first section of the present volume.

In psychophysiological research on emotions, the question as to what functions should be measured has been debated for years and still cannot be given an unqualified answer. Even the choice among neurophysiological systems has not proven simple. The pros and cons of measuring autonomic versus somatic functions have been discussed by several investigators (Izard, 1977; Mandler, 1975; Obrist, Light, & Hastrup, 1982). Evidence suggests tht the best approach is to take multiple measures of two or more systems (Lang, this volume; Schwartz, 1982). At present, facial EMG, with electrodes on combinations of muscles that produce a particular expressive pattern, and observer-based measurement of the action of such muscles (Ekman & Friesen, 1978; Izard, 1979; Rusalova, Izard, & Simonov, 1975; Schwartz, Fair, Greenberg, Freedman, & Klerman, 1974; Schwartz et al., 1976) provides the best independent evidence of emotion-specific neurophysiological activity. Hoffman (1982) suggested that even the complex affective-cognitive phenomenon of empathy, at least in infants and children, is best indexed by facial behaviors. Even with measurement of facial muscle activity, however, it is necessary to show that the facial actions are involuntary or spontaneous if one wants to infer genuine emotion.

There is scant evidence of emotion-specific autonomic nervous system functions (Obrist et al., 1982), but the dearth of such evidence may be due in part to the paucity of studies using a multilevel systems approach in a search for patterns or profiles of autonomic activities in relation to emotion experience and activities of the somatic nervous system (Ekman et al., 1983; Schwartz, 1982).

The Behavioral-Expressive Level.   In the past decade, research on facial expressions of emotions experienced a renaissance that has been spreading to the whole field of emotion investigation. Robust evidence for Darwin's (1872) century-old hypothesis of the innateness and universality of the expressions of several discrete emotions (Eibl-Eibesfeldt, 1972; Ekman et al., 1972; Izard, 1971) sparked this upturn. The emergence of ethology as a vigorous discipline and a Nobel award to its leaders (who claimed Darwin as their intellectual progenitor) fanned and fueled the spark. The fact that facial expressions are observable behaviors that can be analyzed in terms of anatomical patterns of muscle actions that produce reliably identifiable appearance changes and the rapid growth of interest in nonverbal communication gave additional impetus to this area. The confluence of these forces resulted in an increasingly wide acceptance of facial patterns as the best single index of the presence of emotion, particularly with regard to emotions in infants and young children where cultural influences on expressive behavior are minimal and more readily sorted out when present. Facial behaviors occupy a unique place in emotion and hence in emotion research. They are involved in the neurophysiological processes of emotion and central to their social or communicative aspect.

"Felt Emotion"—Subjective Experience, Feeling. James (1890) argued that the ultimate verification of the existence of emotion depended on the self-report of the subject. He made a point of lasting value, and indeed, the self-report scales to be discussed in a later section have proved valuable tools. Self-report scales are generally of two sorts—ratings on dimensions such as pleasantness, tension, and acceptance (Schlosberg, 1954) or on adjectives that define discrete categories of emotion experience, such as happy, sad, angry, afraid (Izard, 1972). Both types have high reliability and the support of numerous validity studies.

While it is generally accepted that emotion has an experiential or feeling component that can be measured only via self-report, it is not always clear whether self-reports relate more to words or thoughts *about* emotion, which may be important in their own right, or to genuine emotion experience. Another problem with self-reports is that of timing—because they are reflective, they are influenced by learning and memory. Finally, unlike some of the measures of the other two components (biological, behavioral), self-report has to be considered as a joint function of affective and cognitive processes. The strength of self-report data will depend largely on evidence that they correlate in predictable ways with activity of the other components of emotion and help predict or account for behavior subsequent to emotion-eliciting events.

Emotion and Cognition

Many of the early life scientists, like people in general, assumed that thinking and feeling were different but related processes. Spencer (1890) maintained that "only in those rare cases in which both its terms and its remote associations are absolutely indifferent, can an act of cognition be absolutely free of emotion." Defining cognition to include perceptual processes, he went on to argue that "no emotion can be *absolutely* free of cognition" (pp. 474–75). Wundt (1907) departed from Spencer with an even more dramatic statement on the issue, maintaining that affect follows directly from sensory processes and *precedes* cognition.

James (1890), like Spencer and Wundt, recognized that emotion and cognition involve different processes. He thought that without emotions one would have to "drag out an existence of merely cognitive or intellectual form" (p. 453). His discussion of the interaction of emotion and cognition could have been the framework for the recent research on imagery-induced emotion. He thought that memory for a felt emotion, its particular quality of consciousness, was poor. "We can remember that we underwent grief or rapture, but not just how the grief or rapture felt" (p. 474). However, the mind can easily compensate for this deficiency of memory by use of imagery. "That is, we can produce, not remembrances of grief or rapture, but new griefs and raptures, by summoning up a lively thought of their exciting cause" (p. 474).

Zajonc (1980), taking his inspiration from Wundt, argued that it is necessary to modify the typical information processing model that begins with feature discrimination. New models must allow for important occasions wherein affect precedes what is typically described as cognition. The need for the study of emotion-cognition relationships is beginning to be recognized by experimental, social, and cognitive psychology.

Emotions, Behavior, Personality, and Psychopathology

Most biosocial theorists consider emotions as having important motivational functions that influence personality development and the course of psychopathology. Most cognitively oriented theorists do not focus on emotions as key constructs in the understanding of normal or abnormal behavior but Lazarus (1968) and Plutchik (1980) are exceptions.

Biologists made the first scientific contributions to the study of emotions, and they conceptualized emotions as significant factors in behavior and adaptation. Darwin (1872) emphasized the signal functions of emotion expressions, noting that "They serve as the first means of communication between mother and infant; she smiles approval, and thus encourages her child on the right path, or frowns disapproval. We readily perceive sympathy in others by their expression; our sufferings are thus mitigated and our pleasures increased; and mutual good feeling is thus strengthened" (p. 364). He also recognized functional relationships between emotion, cognition, and action. He observed that in anger "The excited brain gives strength to the muscles, and at the same time energy to the will" (p. 239).

Although the study of emotion has not been a central theme in biology, the topic continues to be pursued by a few contemporary neuroscientists. They, like their predecessors, typically assume functional relationships between emotion and adaptive behavior, and they focus their research on delineating the brain mechanisms, neural pathways and neurotransmitters associated with different emotions or emotional behaviors (e.g., Delgado, 1971; Gellhorn, 1961; Gray, this volume; Hamburg, 1963; Mason, 1975; Schildkraut, Davis, & Klerman, 1968). For example, they have suggested that the amygdala, a limbic structure, and dopamine, a neurotransmitter, are implicated in anger or aggressive behavior (Hamburg, Hamburg, & Barchas, 1975; Moyer, 1971) and that the septo-hippocampal system is a critical substrate of anxiety (Gray, 1983; this volume).

Theories that view emotions as motivational (Dienstbier, 1979; Izard, 1977; Plutchik, 1980; Tomkins, 1962) see them as direct and immediate determinants of cognitive and motor behavior. Most of the studies that support this premise have induced emotions experimentally, and in some cases the results are ambiguous because the investigators failed to test for the effects of the emotion induction on subjective experience. Nevertheless, these studies provide rather robust support for the direct effects of emotion on attention, learning, memory, and social behavior.

Some theories view emotion primarily as response, but they do not necessarily trivialize the role of emotions in influencing behavior. Although Lazarus (1968, p. 209) takes the "perspective of emotions as response," he argues that emotions are sometimes "integral aspects of the effort to cope with potential harm." He also argues that coping or adaptation results in "lowered levels of emotional response." Lazarus et al. (1980) take a position similar to that of the emotion-as-motivation theorists in maintaining that positive emotions, like negative ones, can signal the need for coping. Further, they argue that "coping activity can be *aroused* and *sustained* . . . by positively toned emotions" (p. 207, emphasis added), which can also act as "breathers" (temporary relief from stress) and "restorers" (aids in recovery from stress).

A few theorists have attempted to apply their conceptual framework to the broad issues of personality development, defense mechanisms, and psychopathology. Izard (1972; Izard & Schwartz, in press) has presented an empirical analysis of the affective component of anxiety and depression in terms of reliably identifiable patterns or combinations of discrete emotions (Izard, 1972). Plutchik, Kellerman, and Conte (1979) have argued for a relationship between specific ego defense mechanisms and specific emotions and that diagnostic personality types are derived from particular defensive styles. Tomkins (1963) has presented a well-reasoned explanation of paranoid tendencies and paranoid schizophrenia in terms of the emotions of fear and shame.

SOME COGNITIVE CONCEPTIONS OF ANXIETY AND RELATED RESEARCH

Like the cognitive model of emotion activation, cognitive conceptualizations of anxiety assume that some kind of cognitive process is essential as a cause or mediator (Lazarus & Averill, 1972; Mandler, 1972). This is clearly the case for cognitive theorists who acknowledge an emotional component in anxiety, for they hold that appraisal or evaluation is a necessary antecedent of emotion (e.g., Lazarus & DeLongis, 1983).

Mandler (1975, 1980) has presented a general model of emotion and a specific model of anxiety. For Mandler (1980), anxiety is a "concatenation of visceral arousal with the cognition of helplessness" (p. 234). More specifically, anxiety results when (a) interruption of ongoing cognition and action leads to ANS/ visceral activity and (b) unavailability of situation-relevant thought/actions (adequate coping techniques) leads to the perception of helplessness. Lazarus and

Averill (1972) have criticized Mandler's model of anxiety as simplistic, as being like the frustration-aggression hypothesis with anxiety substituted for aggression. That is, Lazarus & Averill reject any single-cause model. It should also be noted that Mandler's model actually lacks specificity. It is very similar to Seligman's (1975) learned helplessness model of depression. Mandler (1980) considers the problem as a nonproblem, describing the hopelessness of depression as the generalization of the helplessness of anxiety.

For Lazarus (Lazarus & Averill, 1972), anxiety is a fear-related emotion, which like other emotions is a function of appraisal—appraisal of a threat that is largely symbolic. The appraisal that leads to anxiety is also seen as anticipatory and as involving uncertainty. Lazarus and Averill distinguish anxiety, also considered a complex response syndrome, from fright (more stimulus bound), separation distress (which can be seen as a stage of the grief syndrome), and instrumental fear (better described in terms of goal-directed responses to concrete, unambiguous cues of danger).

Spielberger's model (1972; this volume) of state anxiety is clearly in the tradition of the appraisal model, and he includes cognitive, affective, and behavioral responses in his conception of the anxiety process. More than most investigators in this tradition, however, he emphasizes the motivational or dynamic functions of the feeling component of anxiety.

Appraisal models of emotion and anxiety activation can explain one way that anxiety is generated—perception of threat or worrisome problems. This is not unlike Freud's (1926/1959) classical attribution of anxiety to perceived danger. However, appraisal models cannot readily explain anxiety that stems from interactions of physiological need states and emotion, emotion-emotion conflicts, or the interaction of needs, emotions, and cognitions.

The cognitive formulations of anxiety have guided much research. For example, research on test anxiety has shown that text-anxious individuals are not less intelligent than others, but that they exaggerate and personalize threats of evaluation (Mandler & Sarason, 1952; L. G. Sarason, 1956; S. B. Sarason, 1972; Sarason & Minard, 1962; Watson & Friend, 1969). As a result, test-anxious individuals perform worse when they are informed that their intelligence is being evaluated than when that information is not provided (S. B. Sarason, 1960; S. B. Sarason, 1961).

Related research has shown that evaluative conditions elicit autonomic reactivity (Berry & Martin, 1957) and self-criticisms (Doctor & Altman, 1969; Phares, 1968) from test-anxious persons. Wine (1971) pointed out that rather than attending to the task, test-anxious people selectively attend to irrelevant and interfering variables, such as worry and self-criticism, that impede performance.

Attribution theory, a social-psychological variant of cognitive theory, has been inspiring a good deal of research in the emotion domain (Weiner & Graham, in press). This research includes studies of anxious individuals, particularly test-anxious individuals. According to Weiner et al. (1971), low test-anxious individuals attribute success to their own ability and effort—an internal attribution. They persist following failures, because they attribute the failures to lack of effort—an unstable attribution. In contrast, high test-anxious individuals attribute successes to external factors—task difficulty and luck—and attribute failures to a stable internal factor—lack of ability. So high test-anxious individuals are resistaht to engaging in achievement-related activities.

As already noted, another field of research—learned helplessness—has generated a similar theory. The reformulated learned helplessness model (Abramson, Seligman, & Teasdale, 1978) maintains that attributing successes to external, unstable, and specific causes, and attributing failures to internal, stable, and global causes lead to subsequent expectations of lack of control. This maladaptive set of attributions, according to this theory, produces feelings of helplessness and loss of self-esteem leading to depression.

The attribution models for anxiety and depression are very similar. Both consider two dimensions of attributions—internality and stability—to be relevant to maladaptive behavior. The depression model adds a third dimension—globality. Both of these theories maintain that the attribution styles lead to particular emotions, but they do not indicate what determines which of several emotions result. In particular, what determines the emergence of fear and anxiety versus sadness and depression?

In one of the few attribution style studies that investigated discrete emotions, Arkin, Detchon, and Maruyama (1982) found that particular types of attributions were related to particular discrete emotions. For subjects who perceived themselves as failures on a task, fear was positively correlated with causal attributions related to task difficulty and luck. Also for the perceived failure subjects, sadness correlated negatively with causal attributions related to effort and trait attributions related to ability at the task. For all subjects, sadness was positively correlated with trait attributions concerning task difficulty. Neither of the attribution style theories explains this pattern of correlations with emotion experiences.

Sadness and fear were both correlated with a measure of cognitive interference that assessed the extent of task-irrelevant thoughts during the task. Arkin et al. (1982) considered this an anxiety measure. Interest, joy, surprise, disgust, anger, and shame were also related to several of the attributions and to the cognitive interference measure.

Of particular interest was the finding that high test-anxious subjects experienced the most shame when they failed a difficult task, while low test-anxious subjects experienced the most shame after failing an easy task. The explanation provided by the investigators was that the low test-anxious subjects were "quite reasonable" in feeling more shame after failing a task on which they should have been able to perform well. High text-anxious subjects felt more shame "when failing the difficult task because they felt unable to control their anxiety (cognitive interference) and viewed this as contributing to their failure" (p. 1122).

In other words, the investigators suggested that particular attributions cause anxiety and the anxiety can cause shame. The data were correlational, but the explanation devised goes to great lengths to keep shame (the emotion variable) as the end-product in a chain of cognitive events (anxiety being considered purely cognitive). Likewise, the authors state that "cognitive interference clearly had a strong impact on negative affect (distress, anger, fear, shame)" (p. 1120).

Even from a cognitive viewpoint one could argue that negative emotions are caused by maladaptive attributions. For example, thinking that one has no ability on a task could produce negative emotions.

From the standpoint of differential emotions theory, one would argue that, at the phenomenological level, ongoing emotion influences attributions which interact with particular patterns of emotion variables to produce anxiety. Through biological factors, socialization, or conditioning, individuals may become predisposed to particular emotions in certain situations (Buechler & Izard, 1980; Izard & Malatesta, in press; Izard & Tomkins, 1966). The interaction between emotions, attribution style, and particular situations then determines the likelihood of depression or anxiety. If one was predisposed to emotion blends with fear as a primary element, one would be more likely to feel anxiety, while a predisposition to sadness blends would lead to depression.

This formulation allows for variation across situations both in terms of the syndrome experienced (anxiety or depression) and the emotion pattern of the syndrome. Stattin and Magnusson (1980) have conducted research supporting the position that anxiety varies across situations. They asessed the consistency and stability of 15-year-olds' reactions to anxiety-inducing situations over a 6-month period. The subjects rated their reactions to 12 imaginary situations involving threat of punishment, threat of pain, inanimate threat, and ego threat. The list of reactions was nervousness, worry, insecurity, depression, panic, hand shaking, difficulty swallowing, heart rate increase, perspiration, and stomach trouble. In accord with the hypotheses, it was found that the rank-order of response was relatively consistent for individuals over a 6-month period. There was also greater consistency for similar situations than for dissimilar situations. That is, the pattern of responses over time were more consistent for perceptually similar than perceptually dissimilar situations.

In a similar study, Magnusson and Stattin (1981) found that the variance accounted for in the response patterns by persons was 33.3% for boys and 26.1% for girls. The variance accounted for by person-situation interactions was 13.6% for boys and 15.4% for girls. This indicates individual differences in anxiety states within situations and intrapersonal differences in anxiety states across situations.

Individuals' actual patterns of responses were not reported by Magnusson and Stattin, because their variables had no independent meaning. It would be worthwhile to investigate the actual patterns of variables that influence coping strategies, such as emotions and attributions.

THE DIFFERENTIAL EMOTIONS THEORY OF ANXIETY AND RELATED RESEARCH

Differential emotions theory holds that anxiety can be analyzed phenomenologically in terms of patterns of emotions and emotion-cognition or affective-cognitive relationships. It recognizes the importance of the neurochemical substrates of anxiety and the probable role of genetic factors, particularly in determining emotion thresholds. The theory does not deal directly with biological variables, but it argues that such variables might be better understood with cross-disciplinary and cross-specialty research aimed at a closer interface of neurophysiological, cognitive, and emotional factors. Whereas the theory recognizes all these components of anxiety, it focuses on the emotions, which still receive a disproportionately small amount of attention by students of anxiety. This is so despite the fact that emotion concepts and variables are coming into prominence in developmental psychology (Campos & Barrett, in press; Izard & Malatesta, in press) and are making inroads into social and cognitive psychology (Clark & Fiske, 1982; Izard, Kagan, & Zajonc, in press).

Differential emotions theory has been described in detail previously (Izard, 1977) as has its conception of anxiety (Buechler & Izard, 1980; Izard, 1972). This section begins with a summary of some essential elements of the theory and its conception of anxiety. Finally, the results of several studies will be presented to support this theory of anxiety.

In differential emotions theory each fundamental emotion is defined by unique neurophysiological, expressive, and phenomenological components. The neurophysiological component of an emotion is an innately programmed pattern of electrochemical activity. The expressive component involves, primarily, characteristic facial expressions along with some bodily responses. The phenomenology of an emotion is the quality of the sensed experience, the feeling state.

The emotions system is viewed as the principal motivational system for human beings. The emotions are seen as adaptive and motivating organizers of experience and behavior. Each discrete emotion plays a role in an individual's development of coping skills, exploration, and creative abilities. The emotions system interacts with the homeostatic, drive, perceptual, cognitive, and motor systems in controlling awareness by selectively focusing perception.

In addition to emotions there are three other motivational systems. First is the biological maintenance or physiological needs system, which includes hunger, thirst, sex, pain, and elimination. The second motivational system consists of interactions among emotions, physiological needs, perceptions, and cognitions. The third system consists of affective-cognitive structures—stable trait-like phenomena resulting from the repeated occurrence of particular patterns of affective-cognitive interactions. These affective-cognitive structures can develop into complex personality traits, such as introversion and anxiety.

The phenomenology of anxiety consists of a variable pattern of emotions and affective-cognitive structures. A pattern of emotions is defined as an interactive set of emotions, in which one of them, the key emotion, is experienced more intensely than the others. The emotions in the pattern are causally linked; that is, the activation of one of them, particularly the key emotion, increases the likelihood that the others in the set will be activated. When a particular pattern is experienced frequently, it can become a stable personality trait or a stable response to particular situations.

Fear is the key or essential element in the pattern of emotions in anxiety. Other affects (e.g., pain) or affective-cognitive structures (e.g., guilt-aggression fantasies) form the remainder of the pattern. Research with adults (Bartlett & Izard, 1972; Izard, 1972) indicates that interest, anger, guilt, shame, and shyness are variable elements in the pattern of emotions in anxiety. Any of the above emotions can be experienced along with fear in an anxiety pattern.

The variable patterns of anxiety clearly show that anxiety is not a unitary phenomenon. Both within and between individuals there are neurophysiologically, phenomenologically, and motivationally different "anxieties." The particular anxiety or pattern of emotions and affective-cognitive structures that an individual experiences depends upon situational and personological variables, including parental patterns of socialization of fear and sadness.

Thus, anxiety refers to a variety of feeling states and associated cognitions and action tendencies. One way to specify types of anxiety is by analyzing the patterns of emotions experienced by individuals. For example, when Toddler X gets lost in a department store, she experiences a pattern including fear and anger—fear over a sudden realization of being in strange surroundings without familiar faces nearby, alternating with moments of anger in protest over mother's failure to keep up with her. If the fear prevails the anxiety will mount, whereas the gradual predominance of anger will counteract the fear and nullify or ameliorate the anxiety. In the same situation Toddler Y will experience a pattern of emotions including fear and sadness. The continued dominance of fear would lead to efforts to escape the strange situation and the alternating moments of sadness might lead to appeals for help. If the sadness becomes predominant and help does not lead to a successful resolution of the problem, depressive-like withdrawal behavior may ensue.

Besides describing the various phenomenological characteristics of anxiety, the pattern of emotions and affective-cognitive structures provide a basis for predicting an individual's motivations, cognitions, and actions. On the grounds that anxiety takes various forms at the level of emotion, cognition, and action tendencies, it is assumed, as indicated earlier, that there are some corresponding differences at the neurophysiological-biochemical level.

According to differential emotions theory, fear is a fundamental emotion that motivates escape or avoidance behaviors. Anxiety, being a complex pattern of emotions, can motivate a number of behaviors. For example, a fear-interest pattern of anxiety may motivate cautious exploration. An 8–9-month-old infant's response to strangers exemplifies this type of anxiety. Rather than withdrawing from a stranger, an infant may tentatively approach, especially if the infant's mother is near (Gaensbauer, Emde, & Campos, 1976). This fear-interest motivated approach to a stranger allows learning to occur that would not be possible for an infant motivated solely by fear.

These patterns of emotions distinguish anxious from depressed adults, who tend to report emotion patterns with sadness as the key emotion (Izard, 1972). The other emotions in the depression pattern were variable but tended to be ranked in the following order: self-directed hostility, shame, anger, fear, and guilt. Interest and joy were inversely related to depression. The motivations of anxious and depressed adults can be predicted to differ based on the composition of the patterns of their emotions. An anxious person, for example, may experience interest and be motivated to explore cautiously, while a depressive is unlikely to feel much interest and therefore is unlikely to try to learn.

A recent study (Blumberg & Izard, 1983) indicated that depressed 10- and 11-year-olds experience a pattern of emotions similar to that of adult depressives. The major difference between the patterns found for adults and children was that instead of sadness, anger was the emotion reported to be most frequent for depressed children. Sadness tended to be ranked second, particularly for depressed girls for whom patterns of emotions were more similar to the average adult pattern than were boys'. While anger can play an important role in adult depression (e.g., Abraham, 1968; Rado, 1968), it tends to remain secondary to sadness.

The anger of depressed children may motivate their behavioral differences from depressive adults. For example, the concept of masked depression (e.g., Toolan, 1974) emerged as a result of the realization that many children with conduct disorders also present symptoms of depression. Puig-Antich (1982) found that depressed boys often developed subsequent conduct disorders, suggesting that depression led to conduct disorder. Also, Carlson and Cantwell (1980) found that the 39% false positive scores on a self-report measure of depression in children was accounted for by a variety of conduct and physical disorders, which indicated the need for care in distinguishing these syndromes.

In a study comparing anxious and depressed 7–17-year-old children, Hershberg, Carlson, Cantwell, and Strober (1982) found differences from adults. Unlike anxious adults, no anxious children met *DSM-III* (*Diagnostic and Statistical Manual*-Third Revision, American Psychiatric Association, 1980) criteria for secondary depression. Depressed children, however, did report many anxiety symptoms (as do depressed adults). Poor school performance, appetite and sleep disturbances, lack of energy, and somatic complaints were equally common to the anxious and depressed groups. Depressed children received higher scores on the Children's Depression Inventory (CDI) (Kovacs & Beck, 1977)—a self-report measure of depression—and reported more dysphoric mood, anhedonia, low self-esteem, and suicidal ideation. The most frequent symptoms of anxiety were fears of being alone, crowds, darkness, school, tests, failure, and new situations. Hershberg et al. state that although primarily anxious children did not exhibit a "diagnosable depressive syndrome . . . 20%–30% had dysphoric mood and low self-esteem as symptoms." The investigators hypothesized that secondary depression may occur after prolonged periods of anxiety.

These studies indicate that understanding developmental processes may be essential in understanding the development of anxiety and depressive disorders. In particular, the Hershberg et al. (1982) study indicated that the coincidence of anxiety and depression may be a function of aspects of development, and the Blumberg and Izard (1983) study suggested that emotion experience in depression may change during preadolescent development.

Blumberg and Izard (1983) hypothesized that highly anxious children, like adults, have variable patterns of emotions with fear as the key emotion in the pattern. In contrast, they predicted that highly depressed children would report a pattern with sadness and anger as the key emotions. The Trait scale of the State-Trait Anxiety Inventory for Children (STAIC) (Spielberger, Edwards, Lushene, Montuori, & Platzek, 1973) was selected as the measure of A-Trait. The CDI (Kovacs & Beck, 1977) was used to assess level of depression. The children's patterns of emotions were assessed with the Differential Emotions Scale-IV (DES-IV) (Izard, Dougherty, Bloxom, and Kotsch, 1974)—a self-report measure of the fundamental emotions of interest, joy, surprise, sadness, anger, disgust, contempt, fear, shame, shyness, guilt and the emotion blend of self-directed hostility. Teachers rated the children on the Emotions-Behavior Inventory (EBI) (Lelwica, Izard, & Blumberg, 1983). This newly developed scale consists of global ratings of the frequency of discrete emotions followed by ratings of the frequency of behaviors that indicated to the teacher the presence of a particular discrete emotion.

The children were administered the CDI and DES-IV on two occasions; and, they were administered the STAIC only at the second occasion. The 12 DES-IV and EBI scales were entered into multivariate regression analyses as predictors of the Time 2 STAIC and CDI scores. There were no significant differences for the four sex-grade groups, so the data were collapsed across sex and grade. The multiple correlation coefficients (R) for the DES-IV with the STAIC and CDI were .82 and .78 ($ps < .001$), respectively. The multiple Rs with the EBI as the predictor were .31 and .34 ($ps < .01$). This suggests that patterns of emotion variables can effectively predict these measures of trait anxiety and depression.

Based on differential emotions theory, Izard's (1972) depression and anxiety research with adults, and Blumberg and Izard's (1983) depression research with children, two hierarchies of emotion scales were used as predictors. The depression hierarchy consisted of the following order of emotions scales: sadness, self-directed hostility, shame, anger, fear, guilt, shyness, disgust, contempt, interest, joy, and surprise. The anxiety hierarchy was arranged as follows: fear, interest, guilt, sadness, shame, anger, disgust, contempt, shyness, self-directed hostility, joy, and surprise.

The STAIC and CDI were correlated ($r = .58$, $p < .01$). To analyze their independent relationships with the DES-IV, both were entered as criteria in a step-down regression analysis using the same hierarchies as previously.

The results of these analyses are presented in Tables 1 and 2. While sadness was an important predictor of both the STAIC and CDI, it is noteworthy that interest and joy only contributed additional variance to the prediction of the Children's Depression Inventory. Self-directed hostility and anger also contributed to the prediction of CDI scores. Fear was not related to the CDI (after the STAIC was partialed out) but was the largest predictor of the partialed STAIC. Guilt, sadness, and shame predicted additional variance in the STAIC. Altogether, the DES-IV accounted for 49.8% ($p < .001$) of the variance remaining in the STAIC after the CDI was partialed out and 43.6% ($p < .001$) of the variance in the CDI after the STAIC was partialed out.

One could argue that the relationships between the DES-IV with the STAIC and CDI are due to the content similarity of the items in these measures. To test this hypothesis, four raters familiar with differential emotions theory assessed the content of the items in the CDI and STAIC. When items with emotion content were removed from the STAIC and CDI, their relationships with the DES-IV

TABLE 1
Regression of the Differential Emotion Scales on the Children's
Depression Inventory (CDI)

Differential Emotion Scale Hierarchy	Variance Accounted for In:		
	CDI	CDI With STAIC Partialed Out	Non-Affect CDI
Sadness	43.9%***	12.18%***	39.48%***
Self-Directed Hostility	7.07***	6.05***	7.05%***
Shame			
Anger	1.19**	1.08 **	1.29**
Fear	1.96**	2.49[a]	1.45**
Guilt			
Shyness			
Disgust			
Contempt			
Interest	2.9**	3.11***	2.65***
Joy	4.07***	3.94***	4.19***
Surprise			

*$p < .05$
**$p < .01$
***$p < .001$

[a]The variance accounted for by these variables is a statistical artifact resulting from a suppression effect, so caution should be used in interpretations.

TABLE 2
Regression of the Differential Emotion Scales on the State-Trait Anxiety
Inventory for Children (STAIC)

Differential Emotion Scale Hierarchy	Variance Accounted For In:		
	STAIC	STAIC With CDI Partialled Out	Non-Affect STAIC
Fear	42.1%***	22.78%***	38.05%***
Interest		1.09[a]	
Guilt	6.9***	1.75***	5.6***
Sadness	13.9***	6.02***	8.89***
Shame	3.3***	2.33***	4.81***
Anger			
Disgust			
Contempt			
Shyness			
Self-Directed Hostility			
Joy			
Surprise			

*$p < .05$
**$p < .01$
***$p < .001$
[a]The variance accounted for by these variables is a statistical artifact resulting from a suppression effect, so caution should be used in interpretations.

remained virtually unchanged (see Tables 1 and 2). All the raters in this study expressed difficulty with the task because several items on the STAIC contain the phrase "I worry," and it was not clear whether this phrase reflected the discrete emotion fear. Thus, several fear items may have been left in the STAIC. It is noteworthy, though, that guilt, sadness, and shame contributed to the prediction of the STAIC without items on the STAIC related to these emotions.

In the EBI anxiety hierarchy, fear and guilt were significant predictors, although the variance accounted for by guilt was not significant when the CDI was partialled out of the STAIC. In the EBI depression hierarchy, the sadness, self-directed hostility, and shyness scales were significant CDI predictors. Sadness and shyness remained significant as predictors after the variance attributable to the STAIC was partialled out.

To evaluate the efficacy of emotion variables as predictors of future depression, the Time 1 DES-IV and EBI were used as predictors of the Time 2 CDI. To control for stability of the CDI, the Time 1 CDI was partialled out of the Time 2 CDI. The multiple R between the Time 1 DES-IV and the partialled Time 2 CDI was .22, $p < .018$. Fear and joy were significant predictors. The relationship between the EBI and CDI at Time 1 was essentially the same as their Time 1–Time 2 relationship. When the Time 1 CDI was partialled out of the Time 2 CDI, the EBI did not account for any of the remaining variance in the

Time 2 CDI. Thus, at least for the measure of depression, the predictive validity of the EBI seemed to be a function of EBI concurrent validity and CDI stability.

These results tend to support the differential emotions view of anxiety and depression, because different patterns of emotions significantly predicted the unique variances in these two syndromes. Also, that the hypothesized patterns of specific emotions were related to the two syndromes (rather than anxiety simply correlating with fear and depression with sadness) supported the hypothesis that these syndromes involve complex interactions between emotions.

ACKNOWLEDGMENTS

This work was supported in part by NSF Grant BNS 811832 to Carroll E. Izard.

7

The Cognitive Psychophysiology of Emotion: Fear and Anxiety

Peter J. Lang, Ph.D.
University of Florida

The present paper is an exploration of response organization in fear and anxiety. It includes a discussion of how information about physiological mobilization and action are represented in memory, their relationship to semantic knowledge, and a speculation as to their significance in the cognitive processing of emotion. It is argued that psychophysiological responses are integral to the expression of clinical anxiety and that their activation plays a significant role in mediating other syndromal behaviors.

WHAT ARE THE DATA OF ANXIETY?

For most patients the basic datum of anxiety is their feeling state, i.e., a direct experience or internal apprehension, requiring no further definition. In some cases even the most careful clinical inquiry may elicit from the patients no more elaborate description of their disorder. Nevertheless, feeling states are completely private and represent a poor data resource for the clinician preparing to undertake treatment. Their unavailability to the community of observers appears to deny any possibility of scientific investigation. However, most patients show peculiarities of behavior and will themselves describe a variety of symptoms associated with their feeling of fear or dread that are more yielding to objective analysis. Several investigators have undertaken the factor analysis of these symptom reports (e.g., Buss, 1962; Hamilton, 1959). Buss concluded that observed and reported symptoms of anxiety fell into two primary domains of complaint (originally proposed by Eysenck, 1961): (1) *autonomic overreactivity*—physiological events such as sweating, flushing, shallow breathing; subjective reports of heart palpitations, intestinal discomfort, aches and pains; (2) *conditioned*

131

anxiety—restlessness, worry, and muscular tension. Buss reported that "distractibility" surprised him by loading on the conditioned anxiety factor, suggesting the possibility that visceral feedback might somehow interfere with attentiveness. In a subsequent study of manifest anxiety test items, Fenz and Epstein (1965) and Fenz (1967) reported three factors in anxiety, of which autonomic overreactivity again accounted for the majority of the variance. The Eysenck-Buss conditioned anxiety factor was divided into two subfactors: symptoms of striate muscle tension (including aches and pains, twitching and shaking), and a third factor called feelings of anxiety, which contained inability to concentrate, worry, compulsive mannerisms, insecurity, sleep and relaxation disturbances, and feelings of fear or panic.

The above investigators did not consider the validity of symptoms in accomplishing their analyses. Fenz and Epstein used only test items and Buss mixed external observation and subjective report of symptoms. Autonomic reactivity is implicated importantly in these studies, but not directly measured. Other investigators (e.g., Lader & Wing, 1966) have done the appropriate polygraph research and do report a high degree of spontaneous and reactive sympathetic arousal in anxious patients. However, it is not clear from these data if and how the different symptom phenomena interrelate. Are feelings of anxiety really independent from autonomic reactivity? Do the different factors covary within individuals? Are reports of visceral symptoms or muscle tension related to objective physiological events?

Such queries are clearly pertinent, even if we consider the symptom report itself to be the objective data of anxiety. However, clinicians and researchers sometimes cast the patient in the role of observer of his/her own behavior. It is then important also to inquire how accurate and reliable is the information the patient provides. Clinical lore has it that patients are poor witnesses to their own emotional responses, and the available research literature is in agreement with this suggestion. For example, Mandler and his associates (Mandler, Mandler, Kremen, & Sholiton, 1961; Mandler, Mandler, & Uviller, 1958) undertook an extensive investigation of the relationship between reports of visceral anxiety and actual response of autonomically mediated organ systems (e.g., heart rate, sweat gland activity). Correlations between verbal report of visceral symptoms and physiology were seldom significant and often not even positive. Sarason (this volume) reports similar low or incongruous correlations in studies of test-anxious subjects. Interestingly, in one experiment he found a clearer relationship between measured visceral responses and reports of worry than between such physiological events and reports of perceived visceral symptomology. Analogous results have been obtained in studies of phobia, in which report of fear experience intensity, actual avoidance, and visceral arousal have all been monitored while the subject confronted his phobic object (Barlow, Mavissakalian, & Schofield, 1980; Lang, 1964; Leitenberg, Agras, Butz, & Wincze, 1971; Sartory, Rachman, & Grey, 1977). Correlations between verbal report of fear and other measures of fear rarely accounted for more than 10% of the total experimental variance.

These results should not be taken to mean that people who report feelings of phobic distress do not generally show more avoidance and sympathetic arousal than people who do not ascribe to such feelings. Research confirms these phenomena as the objective fear symptom set with which we should be concerned. However, these responses do not necessarily appear coincidentally in time, nor do all anxious patients show these behaviors to the same extent. Rachman and Hodgson (1974) have referred to the out-of-phase character of anxiety symptoms as emotional desynchrony, noting that therapeutic intervention often modulates subsystems of anxiety at different rates. For example, it is not unusual for a phobic patient, treated by behavioral methods, to show a reduction in objective avoidance behavior prior to reports of change in feelings of fear (Lang, 1964, 1968). Klein (1981, this volume) reported an analogous desynchrony in drug-augmented therapy: Among agoraphobic patients with panic attacks, the drug treatment regimen resulted in a dramatic reduction in requests for assistance and support from ward personnel long before the patients acknowledged any lessening of experienced anxiety, and apparently independent of changes in anticipatory avoidance.

In addition to these phasic differences, there also appear to be different behavioral topographies between subjects and between types of fear (Lang, 1977). The latter phenomena are recognized obliquely in the third revision of the *Diagnostic & Statistical Manual of the American Psychiatric Association* (*DSM-III*) (1980). Thus, the diagnostic criteria for agoraphobia include, "the individual has marked fear of and thus avoids being alone or in public places." The criteria for social phobia also specify "persistent, irrational fear of," but only require a "compelling desire to avoid"—rather than actual avoidance of social situations. A fear pattern often fails to include any palpable fear data in one or more subsystems (language response, gross motor action, physiology), yet we still make the anxiety diagnosis. Thus, the anxious patient may show no marked avoidance or behavioral deficit (the patient is said to be "coping"), may report no feelings of distress (the patient is said to be "stoic," or "denying his feelings," or "alexithymic"), and may not even display a clear physiology of arousal (*la belle indifference*). It is also likely that there are individuals who, because they report no feelings of distress and betray no performance deficit, will never receive a diagnosis of anxiety. Nevertheless, these individuals show a persistent anxiety pattern of sympathetic arousal in specifiable social performance settings. This latter behavioral topography may represent the optimal premorbid condition for psychosomatic illness.

To return to the original question: What are the data of anxiety? I propose here that they are measurable responses which fall into three general categories of behavior: (1) *Verbal report of distress,* i.e., reports of anxiety, fear, dread, panic, and associated complaints of worry, obsessions, inability to concentrate, insecurity, and the like. At this primary data level no assumptions are made about the reality of underlying "states of feeling." However, the absence of a "feeling" premise should not be taken to devalue verbal report as a data source.

As for other complaints, the patient is not treated here as an observer (in this case of a phenomenon that has no objective, validating referent), rather the reports themselves are considered to be part of the primary response of anxiety. (2) *Fear related behavioral acts.* Included here are the observable acts of anxiety and fear—avoidance, escape, hypervigilance, dysfunctional immobility, compulsive mannerisms; deficits in attention, performance, and control. (3) *Patterns of visceral and somatic activation.* For the most part anxiety and fear are associated with sympathetic arousal, and the physiological data of anxiety are such events as heart rate and blood pressure increases, sweating, and generalized muscle tension. However, individual patterns of response are highly varied, and in some phobic reactions, e.g., fear of blood and mutilation, autonomic tonus may be predominantly vagal rather than sympathetic (Sartory, 1981, p. 217).

Because the three data subsystems in anxiety are only loosely coupled, presenting a variable configuration within and between subjects and fear contexts, it is important in both clinical and research investigations that all three of the above response systems are sampled. The assumption that a single measure of fear is sufficient for diagnosis and analysis is currently not tenable. This apparent disarray in the data base is also the primary challenge to the theorist who seeks to explain the nature of anxiety.

IS ANXIETY AN EMOTIONAL STATE OR AN AFFECTIVE DIMENSION?

The study of emotion has traditionally begun with the analysis of reported feelings. Human beings describe a host of different affects as attested to by the immense natural language vocabulary of emotion. The substantive reality of the internal states designated by this language is a fundamental premise of lay psychology. However, because human experience is private (unavailable to external observation) and because there are wide individual differences in descriptions of specific affects, there is no generally accepted theory of emotional life. Scientific efforts have generally been directed to the goal of reducing the number of affects to some fundamental list of emotions. A focused affective lexicon would specify states having historical, cross-cultural stability, as well as ontogenetic and/or phylogenetic continuity and significance. An underlying assumption here seems to be that the diversity of affective reports is partially attributable to vagaries of language and that much of the specificity in reported feelings is semantic and superficial to the substantive emotions. Research efforts have generally followed one of two complementary paths: (1) Researchers have analyzed affective language responses in a variety of situations, and using regression or multidimensional scaling techniques, attempted to isolate a few basic emotional factors that underlie and organize the semantic diversity, or (2) investigators have sought to redefine fundamental affects in terms of either observable behavioral dispositions or physiological patterns.

Language, Mood, and Emotion

Over the previous three decades, a number of investigators have studied affective language as it relates to the concept of mood. Moods and emotions are viewed as overlapping categories, with moods understood to be somewhat less intense but more persistent states of feeling.[1] Utilizing factor analysis, McNair and Lorr (1964) determined that there were seven basic moods: anxiety-tension, anger, depression, vigor, fatigue, friendliness, and confusion. Other investigators have offered similar lists of 6 to 12 independent monopolar factors (e.g., Izard, 1972; Nowlis & Nowlis, 1956; Ryman, Biersner, & La Rocco, 1974). These data have been used to buttress theories of discrete emotional states, such as those proposed by Izard (1972) and Ekman (1973, 1983), and formal mood scales (e.g., *The Profile of Mood States* [*POMS*], McNair, Lorr, & Droppleman, 1971) are commonly used in assessment research with patients.

Despite broad acceptance of the approach, factor lists have not proved stable across investigators. Furthermore, critics of this work argue that, "When measures of individual monopolar factors have been developed, they have been found to be moderately, or occasionally highly, intercorrelated rather than independent as had been assumed" (Russell, 1980, p. 1171; see also Russell & Mehrabian, 1977), and that monopolarity might be attributable more to rating formats (Meddis, 1972) or other methodological factors (Russell, 1979), rather than to a fundamentally discrete nature of emotional states. In fact, when bipolar affects are hypothesized, statistical analysis radically restricts the list of emotions to two or three dimensions of response (Eysenck, 1961; Mehrabian & Russell, 1974; Russell & Mehrabian, 1977). The major proportion of variance is invariably accounted for by two scales: one associated with activation (arousal-quiescence) and the other with valence (pleasure-displeasure). Russell (1980) has proposed a circumplex model of affect, modeled on Schlosberg's (1952) and Schaefer and Plutchik's (1966) earlier views, in which affective ratings are

---

[1]McNair and Lorr (1964) describe a mood as an "organismic state definable in terms of antecedent inducing operations and the correlated behavioral consequences" (p. 620). Thus, instructions to prepare a speech for immediate delivery to an unfamiliar audience might be expected to induce in a subject the mood of tension-anxiety, described as nervous, on edge, panicky, anxious, with a correlated increase in restless pacing. "Mood states and emotional states are viewed as overlapping categories" (p. 621), differing only in persistence (more so for moods) and intensity (greater in emotions). Physiological distinctions between moods are not assumed" (p. 620) and while behavioral acts are referenced in the definition, efforts at compiling a list of moods have generally been restricted to the analysis of language, specifically descriptor adjectives, which subjects are asked to employ in assessing their emotional stage.

arranged in a circle defined by these two axes (e.g., pleasure [0 degrees], high arousal [90 degrees], displeasure [180 degrees], sleepy [270 degrees]). In this view, fear and distress fall on the circumference of the model in the lower right quadrant.

The amount of verbal report data accommodated by the bidimensional view is impressive. Furthermore, this approach is consistent both with the way laymen appear to implicitly conceptualize affect and with studies of the affective structure of the English language (Russell, 1980). Nevertheless, there is a small but significant proportion of experimental variance that seems to be neglected by the two-factor model. In Osgood's original studies of the semantic differential he found a third dimension, "potency," which represented variance unaccounted for by activity or evaluation. Russell and Mehrabian (1974, 1977) also reported a third dimension, which they called dominance-submission. Russell (1980) later dismissed these findings because the additional scale accounted for less variance and because, he argued, it has more to do with "perceived aspects of the antecedents or consequences of the emotion rather than the emotion per se" (p. 1171). Nevertheless, the measurement of dominance has sometimes proved crucial in making the simpler, bipolar model work. For example, anger and fear situations were both shown to involve high arousal and low pleasure ratings. Discrimination between them depended on the subject's dominance ratings, which were low in fear and high in response to the anger context (Mehrabian & Russell, 1974; see also Miller et al., in preparation). It is important to note here that the scales underlying this dimension heavily involve words such as "controlling," "autonomous," "in control," "guided." Thus, Russell and Mehrabian's dominance dimension seems to be more generally relevant to the rater's sense of self-control or of environmental control, rather than implying only social dominance (although that may also be included).

In summary, research on the language of emotion suggests that human beings can discriminate and reliably describe several emotional states or moods, one of which could be called anxiety-tension or fear. Other studies suggest that many of these factors (including anxiety) are highly intercorrelated and that the underlying mathematical structure of reported affect is simpler, involving only two or three bipolar dimensions of response (arousal, valence, control), and that the affective states might best be represented as combinations of values on these dimensions. From this semantic perspective, fear and anxiety are most parsimoniously and reliably described as states of high arousal, negative valence, and low dominance or control.

Physiology and Expressive Behavior

Emotional States.   The view that physiological patterns (both somatic [postural] and visceral) were fundamental in defining emotional states was advocated by William James (1884), who also proposed a theory of experienced affect which profoundly influenced the subsequent study of emotion. James suggested that the experience of emotion was itself the conscious perception of a defining physiological response pattern. This precipitated a broad search for such fundamental patterns, with some researchers reporting success and others, failure.

Wolf and Wolff (1943, 1947) were among the early investigators who obtained dramatic evidence for a differentiated physiology in emotions. They observed the stomach of a laboratory employee, whose medical condition had required a chronic gastric fistula. They noted differences between emotional states in motility, secretion, and blood supply of the gut: The gastric wall became pale and the blood supply was reduced when the subject appeared apprehensive and frightened; a state of anger seemed to be associated with a stomach lining engorged with blood.

A broader physiological differentiation of fear and anger became a focus of research in the 1950s and 1960s. Funkenstein, Greenblatt, and Solomon (1952), Ax (1953), Schachter (1957), and Wenger et al. (1960) examined the hypothesis that two general emotional states existed: an aggressive, hostile, "anger-out" condition, associated with the urinary excretion of metabolites of norepinepherine, and a state described variously as fear, timidity, depression, or "anger-in," associated with the excretion of metabolites of epinepherine. As both neurotransmitters are always present in the body and active in any condition of arousal, Ax (1962) suggested that an epinepherine-norepinepherine response ratio be used, based on polygraph measurement of various visceral and somatic responses, whose neurochemical innervation implied dominance of one state or the other. A mainly epinepherine response, presumably associated with fear, would include marked increment in heart rate, systolic blood pressure, and respiration rate; an emphasis on norepinepherine, to be expected with aggression or anger, would place an additional emphasis on greater muscle tension and increment in diastolic blood pressure.

Evidence in support of this dichotomy has not always been easy to obtain (e.g., Frankenhaeuser, 1971; Levi, 1965, 1975). Supporters of the specific-states view argue that replication difficulties are due to problems of measurement (few investigators have an employee with a gastric fistula; there are no noninvasive, continuous blood pressure monitors available for research or clinical use), or to the failure to employ potent emotion-instigating techniques as were applied, for example, by Ax. (To evoke fear, Ax's (1953) subjects were connected by electrodes to laboratory machinery that appeared to be dramatically malfunctioning. In addition, a clearly incompetent technician suggested that they might suffer accidental electrocution.)

Graham and his associates (Graham, 1972; Graham, Kabler, & Graham, 1962) finessed the affect-induction problem by using hypnosis to facilitate the evoking of vivid emotional attitudes. They observed significant increment in diastolic pressure when subjects were encouraged to feel that they were under threat and "had to be ready for anything" (anger-out?); on the other hand, when instructed to feel attacked and "helpless to do anything about it" (fear?), the same subjects showed skin temperature increases. Roberts and Weerts (1982) studied the physiological response of subjects who vividly imagined scenes they reported to be anger or fear inducing. While both scene types prompted increase in heart rate and systolic blood pressure, diastolic blood pressure increases were observed uniquely in response to anger images, similar to those previously found for an anger exposure situation by Ax (1953).

James's hypothesis about the role of visceral feedback was not limited to the viscera (1890). He also emphasized the importance of posture and facial expression in the generation of affective experience. Gellhorn (1964) echoed James, commenting on the richness of neural innervation of the face and speculating on the influence of facial afferents on affect generators in the hypothalamus. Based on the formal analysis of video-taped facial expressions, Ekman (1973) has defined five discriminable affective states, which appear to have considerable cross-cultural stability. Schwartz and colleagues (Schwartz, Brown, & Shern, 1980) have reported patterns of facial muscle action potentials consistent with the appropriate emotional expression during affective imagery. Ekman (1983) has also reported new data suggesting that facial expressions may be associated with a broader emotional differentiation. Actors and laboratory personnel were both instructed to assume various face poses (directed facial action task) and asked to relive vividly previous emotional experiences. Preliminary results suggested that at least some emotional expressions may be associated with specific visceral patterns.

Dimensions of Emotion.   While data have slowly accumulated for the specific pattern view, an even more robust behavioral and psychophysiological literature developed supporting the hypothesis that the emotions were physiologically non-specific and best described in terms of a few fundamental affective dimensions. James's distinguished early antagonist was the physiologist W. B. Cannon, whose second point in his (Cannon, 1927, 1939) famous rebuttal of James's theory denied the key role assigned to autonomic patterning, contending that *the same visceral changes occur in very different emotional states and in nonemotional states.* Many researchers embraced Cannon's view, presenting evidence that suggested that the emotions were simply highly energized behavior. They further proposed that the physiology of the emotions was best understood as different levels of a general state of activation or arousal (e.g., see Duffy, 1941, 1962, 1972; Lindsley, 1951, 1952). From this perspective, emotion is not conceived to be a group of specific states; rather it is held to be the expression of a continuous dimension of behavior.

During the 1950s, the dimension of arousal was identified with Hull's (1933) concept of drive, the propellor construct for all behavior. Furthermore, Spence & Spence (1966) considered anxiety to be the premier example of high drive, a view that accommodated itself well to the Freudian *zeitgeist* in clinical psychology and psychiatry. With this impressive theoretical lineage, anxiety became a dominant concept in general psychology and in abnormal psychology. Thus, anxiety was at once a primary individual difference characteristic or trait, the energizer of a host of diverse behaviors (much as Freud had proposed), as well as a state of feeling, a reaction to or perception of one's own high arousal (Speilberger, 1972).

While the conglomerate concept (anxiety-drive-arousal) has broad explanatory powers, it cannot alone account for the diversity of emotional expression. Many activation theorists have looked to behavioral data to define a second dimension of emotion, determining direction of response. This later component was primary for the animal behaviorist Schneirla (1959) who, emphasizing phylogenetic continuity, held that all behavior could be located on a dimension of approach-avoidance (the direction determined primarily by stimulus intensity). Both Lindsley (1951) and Duffy (1941, 1972) proposed that both the dimensions of direction and arousal were fundamental to the interpretation of behavior. Neurophysiological research has also accommodated to this view: Since Papez (1937) the brain stem (reticular system and hypothalamus) has been assigned energizing functions, while the differentiation of affects has been the province of the limbic system and the higher cortical centers (e.g., see Grey, this volume; Routenberg, 1968).

Social psychology has also been dominated by two-factor theory: Stanley Schachter (1964) led his field in strongly advocating the unidimensional nature of physiological arousal in emotion. He proposed that specific affective experiences and direction of response are determined by the person's appraisal of that arousal in the environmental context of its occurrence. Thus, what are seen to be the same states of sympathetic activation result in anger, if one has just been verbally abused; in fear, if confronted by danger; or perhaps in no affective experience at all, if one has just completed a run around the block. Lazarus (1968) and Mandler (1975) have expressed similar views of the role of cognitive appraisal in emotional states.

In addition to direction and arousal, a third dimension, control, has emerged from behavioral research on emotion. Human performance generally improves with increases in arousal until some optimal level is reached. Subjects then show performance deterioration, manifested by a reduction in fine control or disorganization of the response sequence. This so-called Yerkes-Dodson law has frequently been invoked to explain the performance deficits of trait-anxious subjects (Denemberg, 1964). D. O. Hebb (1946, 1949) suggested that disruption of an organized behavioral sequence might itself be the occasion of an emotion, with arousal being secondary to the abortive response. Thus, the monkey's fright reaction to a model of a primate head occurs because the sculptured face cues a normal social response (e.g., grooming); however, the usual sequence of behavior cannot be completed because there is no living, second monkey present. The animal's brain responds to disruption of the "phase sequence" with a state of general excitation. The behavioral acts, flight or attack, occur because they can potentially terminate the state of disturbance. A similar view of emotion was taken by advocates of the famous frustration-aggression hypothesis, who saw aggressive behavior (or some other affect) as a consequent of a blocked goal-directed behavior (e.g., Berkowitz, 1978). The importance of such program-disruption in emotion has also been underlined by Mandler (1975).

In summary, although the evidence for a simple dimension of arousal, a general "release of energy into various internal physiological systems" (Duffy, 1972) seems strong, a parallel body of evidence continues to grow that supports the seemingly incompatible thesis of specific physiologies for specific emotional states. Overall, the study of the behavioral and physiological evidence for differentiated affective states has seemingly arrived at two incompatible, but independently supported, conclusions (rather like the wave and particle theories of light). On the one hand, much evidence supports the view that emotion can be understood in terms of one, two, or at the most three dimensions of response, i.e., a dimension of behavioral intensity, underscored by an underlying, general state of physiological arousal, a directive valence dimension, involving mainly approach or withdrawal, and finally, perhaps, a dimension of control or degree of disruption in the behavioral sequence. On the other hand, evidence has been obtained that emotional states are explicit, individual patterns of expressive behavior (each perhaps associated with a unique physiology). In this latter regard, I have not touched upon the support for the pattern view evident in studies of human sexuality (e.g., Geer, Morokoff, & Greenwood, 1974), or the clear indications of stimulus-specific, ontogenetically timed emotional patterns that are revealed in studies of animal ethology (Tinbergen, 1951) and the early development of human infants (Emde, 1980; Izard, 1972; Sroufe, Waters, & Matas, 1974).

IS ANXIETY A RESPONSE?

It is of compelling interest that the two metatheoretic positions—affective dimension and emotional state—should appear both in studies of the language of feelings and in the broader explorations of emotion physiology and behavioral response. I would argue that the parallel emergence of these overviews is evidence that both have merit, and rather than being incompatible, they represent different perspectives on the same phenomena. It is proposed here that emotions (including pathological affect) are fundamentally to be understood as behavioral acts. Furthermore, in the sense that specific actions have their own physiology and behavioral topography, many emotional acts will be similarly individual in pattern. However, it is also obvious that all contexts and behaviors can be judged for affective tone, and that few events will receive a zero rating! *Emotional states are grouped together because of shared response dimensions.* As a pragmatic matter, both laymen and scientists classify an action as emotional when it is judged to approach the extreme ends of the three affective dimensions that have consistently emerged from a varied research literature, i.e., arousal, valence, and control.

It is likely that the specificity of emotional acts developed phylogenetically from basic survival tasks, e.g., feeding and search for food, fighting for territory and access to sexual partners, escape from or defense against predators, sexual approach or display. While the purpose and pattern of these behaviors are necessarily highly individual, it is not unreasonable to expect that several general affective postures might emerge, with some continuity in the mammalian phylum and consistency within species. Furthermore, the generative behaviors would all share the characteristics of sustained directional posture, approach or avoidance; the requirement of general energy mobilization or suppression of activity; and because survival depends on their smooth execution, control or disruption of the behavioral sequence would be in all cases of critical importance.

This speculation presumes a three-level hierarchical organization in emotion, ascending from specific context bound acts (e.g., subroutines for attack, vigilance, or escape), to larger emotional programs, such as fear or anger, that may vary in the specific acts included, but still show relative response stereotypy across situations, to broad dimensional dispositions (the parameters of intensity, direction, and control), that apply descriptively to all emotional behavior. From this perspective we expect psychological phenomena related to emotion, such as reinforcement effects, transfer of training, generalization, and the information structure of memory to reflect all three of these aspects of response organization.

As for any environmental transaction, all emotional behaviors involve both the reception of information and the execution of an action program. However, it is clear that there is no consistent state of attention nor any unique behavioral act that covaries consistently either with the patient's judgment that he/she is afraid or with the observer's diagnosis of anxiety. Fear is associated with vigorous action, agitated pacing or headlong flight; as well as passive defense, immobility, and helplessness. Similarly, an anxious state can involve keen attention, hypervigilance, and continuing watchfulness for threat; or it can be a condition of internal preoccupation, distractibility, and blunted attention to the environment.

The answer to the discontinuity between data systems in fear (which we described at the outset of this paper) and an explanation of what links together the varied domains of anxious acts should be a primary goal of our research. It is clear that this will require analysis at all three levels of potential, affective response organization. It is of particular importance to determine how anxiety and fear states are represented in memory, to determine how emotion drives cognitive processing, and what specific information (about stimuli or responses) mediates between the different contexts in which anxious behavior is expressed.

ANXIETY AND MEMORY

The classic psychoanalytic view of cognition and anxiety emphasized the phenomenon of "repression," a presumed mental mechanism through which thoughts evocative of an anxious state were prevented from entering working memory, thus permitting the patient to maintain emotional equilibrium in the face of associative or environmental prompts to affective expression. Despite many efforts to test this hypothesis, its scientific status remains curiously murky (Holmes, 1974). In contrast, more recent research emphasizing the fluidity of affective memory (rather than the barriers to the spread of association) has been remarkably successful. Human beings appear to show an easy susceptibility to the induction of emotions, even when they are negative, and quite mild mood states can have a widespread impact on the content of conscious memory and memory processing.

Recent research suggests that an anxious mood can itself act as a cue for the recall of other thoughts and behaviors, which were acquired remotely in time and context, but acquired when the patient was in a similar affective state. Increased understanding of such emotion-state-dependent learning and memory may help us to account for the persistence across diverse settings of such anxiety-related, nonproductive responses as worry, obsessive thoughts, compulsive rituals, and negative self-evaluation.

DO NEGATIVE AND POSITIVE EMOTIONS CUE
DIFFERENT MEMORIES?

Some of the most relevant work on the problem of emotion and memory has been accomplished by Gordon Bower and his associates (e.g., Bower, 1981; Bower & Cohen, 1982). An experimental paradigm used by these investigators involved the induction of an emotional state through hypnotic instructions to relive a previous affective experience (either happy or sad), and the subsequent learning and recall of lists of unrelated words. Thus, in a typical study subjects learned two lists of words—List A first, then List B—and were subsequently tested for recall of List A. Different subject groups experienced different pre-word-task emotions according to prearranged patterns (e.g., Happy, A; Sad, B; Happy, Recall A, *or* Happy, A; Sad, B; Sad, Recall A). It was determined that subjects who were in congruent moods during learning (List A) and recall (List A) remembered the words better than if acquisition and remembrance occurred in different affective states. Furthermore, if List B was learned in a noncongruent mood (e.g., the subject was sad when learning B, but happy when learning A and at recall of A), subjects showed optimal memory for List A. Bower (1981) suggests that "their different learning moods isolated the two lists, thus reducing interference from List B when trying to recall List A" (p. 131). The poorest memory scores were obtained when mood at recall of A was congruent with the emotional experience during List B learning, and different from that experienced at List A acquisition. In this "interference condition . . . recall of the target List A suffers because the recall mood evokes memories of the wrong List B rather than the Target List A" (p. 131).

Bower (1981) has further shown that these apparent state-dependent memory effects obtain even when subjects recall actual, extra-laboratory experiences. For example, subjects recalled more previously rated unpleasant events from an "emotional diary," when they were later recalled in an induced unpleasant mood (with the same pattern holding for the recall of pleasant events in a pleasant mood). Subjects also showed mood congruence effects in their recall of childhood memories. Another experiment demonstrated a kind of state-dependent selective learning, in which subjects acquired more information about characters in a narrative who were in a similar mood to their own (happy or sad) at the time the subjects read the material.

Much of the work by Bower and his colleagues depends on the validity of hypnotically induced moods, the hope that hypnosis does not have other confounding effects on memory, and the representativeness of a subject population that is made up exclusively of hypnotically susceptible subjects. Given our uncertain understanding of these factors, questions may be raised about the relevance of this work for natural experience. However, other investigators have used different mood induction procedures and obtained similar results. For example, Teasdale and Fogarty (1979) used an induction method developed by Velten (1968), in which subjects read and thought about a series of self-referent statements evocative of a consistent affective content (e.g., for depression, "Looking back on my life I wonder if I have accomplished anything really worthwhile"; "I feel downhearted and miserable"). Following mood induction, they measured the subjects' latency of retrieval for pleasant and unpleasant memories, and obtained results analogous to Bower's: that is, reaction times were shorter when there was congruence between the affective valence of the memorial content and the valence of affective state at recall.

In addition to these studies of memory and learning, other investigators have explored the effects of mood congruence on response initiation. Isen, Shalker, Clark, and Karp (1978) gave subjects small gifts to produce a positive mood state, and then evaluated their degree of satisfaction with various possessions in an apparently unrelated consumer survey. These "happy" subjects reported greater satisfaction than controls with their automobiles, television sets, and other purchases. More recently, Isen, Means, Patrick, and Nowicki (1982) have been studying the effect of mood valence on risk-taking behavior. Preliminary results suggest that subjects in a positive mood tend to take more chances than controls, but only when probability of a negative outcome is low. Thus, in this limited sense, they behave more bravely. Rachman (1978) has commented on the independence of courage and fear in phobic patients, some of whom, despite their intense distress, accept exposure treatments and confront phobic objects and situations. The Isen et al. (1982) data imply that such procedures depend on the subject being in a positive mood just prior to the treatment manipulation, and also on a demonstration (modeling) that the probability of an aversive consequence is low.

While there is little work on mood valence and memory in anxious patients, there is an increasingly large literature evaluating memory, response initiation and appraisal in nonpatient depressed subjects and in depressed patients (see Kovacs & Beck for a review, 1979). In general, depressed subjects are much more likely to recall past failures than successes, provide negative rather than positive appraisals of stimuli, and are reluctant to initiate approach responses. It is not surprising that the presence of depressed mood in a predominantly phobic or obsessive symptom picture is a negative prognostic sign for treatment (Foa, Grayson, & Steketee, 1982; Marks, Rachman, & Hodgson, 1980).

IS EMOTIONAL MEMORY A SEMANTIC NETWORK?

In a previous theoretical discussion of emotional imagery and its memory storage, I suggested that affect might be represented propositionally and organized in network form (Lang, 1977, 1979). Bower's interpretation of emotion-dependent learning and recall (and presumably of other related behaviors) is also based on a network theory of associative memory (Bower, 1981; Gilligan & Bower, 1984):

> An event is represented in memory by a cluster of descriptive propositions. These are recorded in memory by establishing new associative connections among instances of the concepts used in describing the event. The basic unit of thought is the proposition; the basic process of thought is activation of a proposition and its concepts. The contents of consciousness are the sensations, concepts, and propositions whose current activation level exceeds some threshold. Activation presumably spreads from one concept to another, or from one proposition to another, by associative linkages between them. A relevant analogy is an electrical network in which terminals correspond to concepts or event nodes (units), connecting wires correspond to associative relations with more or less resistance and electrical energy corresponds to activation that is injected into one or more nodes (units) in the network. Activation of a node can be accomplished either by presentation of the corresponding stimulus pattern or by prior activation of an associated thought. (Bower, 1981, p. 134)

Bower holds that there are distinct emotions, e.g., joy, fear, depression. Each emotion has a specific node or unit in memory "that collects together many other aspects of the emotion that are connected to it by associative pointers," e.g., expressive behaviors such as overt approach or avoidance, facial expressions; visceral patterns of response; verbal labels for emotions; descriptions of evocative situations; and meaningful appraisals of contexts and responses (See Fig. 1;

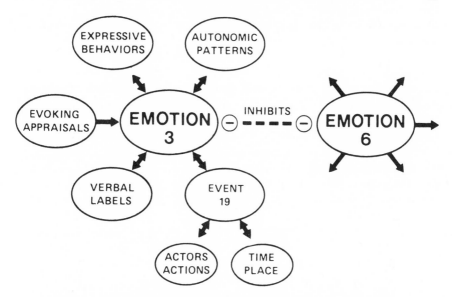

FIG. 1.   Small fragment of the connections surrounding a specific emotion node or unit. Bidirectional arrows refer to mutual exchange of activation between nodes. An inhibitory pathway from Emotion 3 to Emotion 6 is also shown (from Bower, 1981).

Bower, 1981). The associative network of the emotion is in turn related to the larger domain of general associative memory. It is held that relatively high relational strength obtains between the emotion network and information from general memory pertaining to events that occurred contiguous with emotional expression. Thus, later activation of an emotion node will cause activation to spread throughout the structure of memory, raising connected memories above the threshold of conscious thought and expression. In effect, emotion represents a coincidental retrieval cue along with stimulus context, and in circumstances where the external stimulus cues are weak or not present, its effect will be palpable, priming memories of events that occurred when the organism was in a similar affective state. "In contrast, if the mood is altered between learning and recalling . . . recall suffers because the benefits of intersection from two search cues are absent" (Bower, 1981, p. 136).

Bower's (1981) theory states that specific emotion nodes can be activated by "physiological or symbolic verbal means," and that "the emotion unit then transmits excitation to those nodes that produce the pattern of autonomic arousal and expressive behavior commonly assigned to that emotion" (p. 135). To date, Bower's group has not studied affect instigation techniques themselves, nor have they provided much in the way of manipulation checks on the presumed emotions that result. We do not know what specific behaviors, beyond the verbal labels, were produced by his procedure. It is reasonable to question whether there is a specific emotion node that must be activated before emotional behavior occurs, or whether it is the central representation of the relevant behaviors themselves (verbal, overt acts, and physiological pattern) which are, in aggregate, both "the emotion" (see Lang, 1984) and the individual and collective mediators of the state-dependent effects. If the latter is true, then mood congruence effects are more likely to be expressed across a dimension of responding (arousal, valence, and perhaps control) than confined to the boundaries of a particular emotional state. Furthermore, emotions that are similar in valence and/or arousal (i.e., share postural and visceral response components) will be synergistically augmenting of behavior associated initially with only one state. Emotions would be reciprocally inhibiting associated memories only if they involved mutually exclusive patterns of response.

WHAT RESPONSES CUE PLEASANT AND UNPLEASANT MEMORIES?

While the importance of response commonalities and differences in emotion is not stressed, Bower (1981) has provided preliminary evidence suggesting that state-dependent memory may follow a circumplex model, i.e., if the affect during recall is more nearly adjacent to the emotional state during the original learning, on Schaefer and Plutchik's model (1966), retention scores are better than if the two mood states are 180 degrees from each other (e.g., opposite). The mood and memory congruence paradigm may prove to be extremely useful in comprehending the synergistic and inhibiting properties of emotional states on learning and memory. Furthermore, it could be used to tease out the specific response structures that are the carrier spores of this phenomenon.

Recent research by Laird, Wagener, Halal, and Szegda (1982) suggests that a program for facial expression could be part of such a mediating code in memory that might account for valence modulated state-dependent memory effects. In these experiments subjects first read either an "anger" story (about the killing of dolphins) or a happy story (humor by Woody Allen). They were later instructed to assume various positions of the facial muscles, corresponding to their configuration in emotional expression, i.e., either a frowning or smiling visage, and recall trials were conducted. On the basis of an independent test, subjects were divided into the groups depending on whether, in an ambiguous situation, their self-reports of affect were more consistent with external emotional cues (labels on abstract pictures) or their own facial expression at the time of viewing.

The external cue group failed to show any interaction between manipulated facial expression at recall and story content. However, the group that had previously been shown to be more congruent in facial expression and affective report showed significantly better recall of the humorous story while smiling, and better recall of the "anger" story while frowning.

In a subsequent experiment, Laird's group explored more subtle relationships between memory content and facial expression. The verbal material to be recalled was all negative in valence, but was designed to instigate three different affects: fearful incidents; incidents descriptive of annoyance or anger-inducing contexts; and finally, sad material, descriptive of loss and isolation. The material was recalled while subjects' faces were positioned in standard sad, fearful, or angry expressions. Again, only subjects previously shown to be more face congruent than external cue congruent in their affective judgments showed differential recall. This face congruent group showed the expected significant interaction between facial expression and the type of affective content they recalled, e.g., recall of fear content was best when the subjects were posed in the matching, fearful facial expression.

The above materials are provocative and certainly encourage the thesis that facial expression is one of the mediators of mood congruent memory, at least within a subsample of expression sensitive subjects. However, other factors have also been implicated. For example, Riskind (1983) provides evidence that overall posture, "slumped" or upright, may facilitate recall of sad or happy material, respectively. It must also be noted that in the Laird study, no effort was made to control for sympathetic arousal, which could well have been different for both contents and expression, and could have accounted for the subtle differences in negative valence. Indeed, as is shown below, other experiments suggest that patterns of arousal may in themselves mediate otherwise unrelated memories. Thus, mood congruence effects could be facilitated either by valence responses such as facial expression or by visceral arousal patterns, or perhaps by an interaction of these parameters.

IS AROUSAL A CUE FOR MEMORY RETRIEVAL?

Clark and associates (Clark, Milberg, & Ross, 1983) have recently undertaken a series of experiments designed to determine whether physiological arousal is the critical mediator of mood congruent memory effects. They propose "that information about changes in autonomic arousal that accompany moods may be part of how a mood is stored in memory and that changes in arousal that reoccur with subsequent moods may be part of what primes affectively-toned material stored earlier" (p. 633).

In one test of the hypothesis, subjects first learned a list of unrelated phrases while experiencing enhanced arousal and a second list, while relaxing in a normal state. Later they were given a recall test for both lists under ostensible conditions of visual distraction. The arousal condition that preceded the learning of one list involved stepping up and down repeatedly on a cinder block (which produced palpable heart rate and blood pressure increases). The relaxation task that preceded the other study list simply required subjects to rest in a lounge chair (with no cardiovascular pressor effect). Orders of lists and arousal tasks were counterbalanced. All subjects were asked to recall both lists. According to random subgroup assignment, recall was preceded by one of two conditions: arousal—subjects viewed a sexually explicit film; relaxation—subjects viewed a film about a chimpanzee learning sign language. The results were as predicted: When subjects were aroused by the sex film at recall, they best remembered the list that was learned after the cinder block step test. Furthermore, when subjects recalled the lists after viewing the sign language film, memory was better for the phrases originally learned after relaxation than it was for the list previously learned after exercise arousal. This effect is interesting particularly because of the marked difference in the arousal task from learning to recall phases (e.g., step test and sexual stimulation). This change in induction procedure would appear to greatly reduce the possibility that commonalities in stimulus information could account for these data.

The above results are reminiscent of similar phenomena in the animal-conditioning literature (see the review in this volume by Mineka). For example, Fonberg (1956) reported that dogs first trained to make leg lifts to avoid a shock or to make head-shaking movements to airpuffs showed a reemergence of these specific behaviors during the subsequent administration of an increasingly difficult appetitive discrimination procedure (this latter paradigm is Pavlov's classical method of inducing experimental neurosis in animals). As with the research of Clark and associates (Clark et al., 1983), the mediating commonality between the two different experimental procedures appears to be the arousal state that both paradigms elicit. Thus, a response learned in the first context was reactivated in the second. Both human and animal studies suggest that information about arousal responses is represented in memory and that such action information is a key mediating element in state-dependent learning.

The broad impact of the above phenomena is indicated in a subsequent experiment by Clark's group (1983). They evaluated the proposition that arousal might act to potentiate positive judgments in an opinion survey. Subjects first listened to a story under one of two "distracting" conditions: the high arousal cinder block step test, or a low arousal task—subjects were seated, placing cardboard disks on a string. All subjects subsequently were tested for story recall, and then given either no feedback of results or positive feedback (e.g., "You really did very well! Your score is way above the norm," p. 642). Another experimenter then administered the opinion survey concerning student views of their university. It was found that subjects who were both aroused at story learning, and received positive feedback of results, rated the university more favorably than did the other experimental groups. The authors "believe this occurred because information about arousal is part of what is stored when people store memories of positive experience. Consequently, extra arousal at the time of a positive mood may result in a greater number of positive memories coming to mind" (p. 644). Presumably, similar results might be obtained for negative memories, although this was not tested. It is noteworthy that Bartlett and Santrock (1979) found that their state-dependent memory effects were dramatically reduced when subjects received relaxation instructions prior to mood induction. Clark et al. (1983) suggest that the relaxed state inhibited the arousal component of mood induction and reduced the number of mediating cues available. Differences between the mediational properties of anxious and depressive moods may depend on different intersections of the variables of valence and arousal.

DOES EMOTIONAL EXCITATION TRANSFER FROM ONE EMOTIONAL STATE TO ANOTHER?

The research previously reviewed suggested that affect information (about arousal *or* about valence) may mediate otherwise unrelated memories over fairly long time spans. A related line of investigation also merits consideration in the context of anxiety studies: There is the possibility that the experience and expression of different emotions are themselves modified by close sequential evocation. In the first experiment considered from the Clark group, sexual arousal appeared to be linked to (i.e., contained overlapping information with) exercise arousal, as attested to by the obtained memory effects. Another phenomenon predictable from the hypothesis of a shared response structure in memory is that emotions with such information base commonalities will be synergistic or mutually augmenting in effect.

Zillmann (1980, 1983) has reported extensive research on this theme. His work suggests, first, that residual excitation from physical exercise can intensify subsequently induced anger and anger behavior (Zillmann & Bryant, 1974; Zillmann, Katcher, & Milavsky, 1972) or sexual excitement (Cantor, Zillmann, & Bryant, 1975). Thus, like Clark, Zillmann and colleagues specifically implicate a general arousal factor. Furthermore, between-emotion transfer has been shown. Both Zillmann's group (Zillmann, Bryant, Comisky, & Medoff, 1981) and Donnerstein and Hallam (1978) report that prior sexual arousal can potentiate aggression. Such excitation transfer appears to be independent of hedonic tone. Thus, Mueller and Donnerstein (1981) have demonstrated that sexual arousal can also facilitate positive social behavior, and Zillmann (1980, 1983) reports that both positive arousal and disgust at sexual material can prime the enjoyment of music, humor, or drama.

The above studies suggest that valence factors may be completely dominated by arousal information in a transfer situation. However, when specific response structures are examined more closely, this inference must be tempered. Thus, Hoon, Wincze, and Hoon (1977) examined an opposite prediction, i.e., Wolpe's theory that different emotional states (specifically, sexual arousal and anxiety) are reciprocally inhibiting rather than mutually facilitating. Female subjects were

alternately exposed to three video tapes depicting (1) anxiety content—the after-
math of tragic automobile accidents, "including occupants' death cries"; (2) erotic
content—a nude couple engaged in foreplay; (3) neutral content—a travelogue
of Nova Scotia. Heart rate and vaginal blood flow were recorded continuously
during stimulus presentation. When preexposed to the erotic content, subjects
showed a more rapidly diminishing vaginal blood flow during the subsequent
anxiety stimulus than was observed when the neutral stimulus was next in the
sequence. This appears to be in accord with reciprocal inhibition theory. However, when preceded by the anxiety stimulus, vaginal blood flow during a subsequent erotic tape was significantly greater than when the erotic stimulus followed
the neutral travelogue. In this latter circumstance, the interaction between affective states was synergistic rather than mutually inhibiting (see Fig. 2).

The Hoon et al. (1977) heart rate data were not clearly interpretable, and in
any event, heart rate is, by itself, inadequate for the assessment of a general
state of arousal or energy mobilization. Thus, as in many of these experiments,
a general arousal factor may be inferred, but its actual response structure goes
unspecified. It is worth adding, however, that response synergy between anxiety
and sexual arousal has been observed in males by Barlow, Sakheim, and Beck
(1983), who reported that fear of electric shock prompted increases in tumescence
when these subjects were subsequently stimulated by erotic material. Further

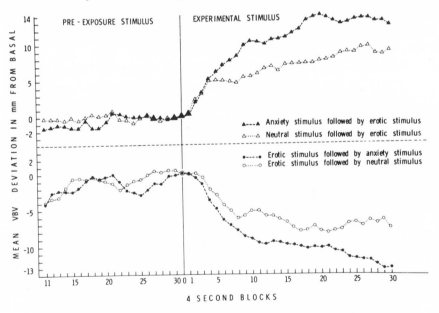

FIG. 2.   Mean vaginal blood volume (VBV) deviation in millimeters (mm) from
basal levels across 4-sec blocks during four sequences of stimulus exposure. In
this experiment pre-exposure to an anxiety-provoking videotape potentiated a
greater subsequent sexual response to an erotic videotape (from Hoon, Wincze,
& Hoon, 1977).

research is clearly needed to define those properties of emotional states that result in mutual augmentation or inhibition.

THE INFORMATION TAXONOMY OF EMOTIONAL MEMORY

Response Information

In developing an information-processing model of emotion and emotional imagery, I suggested (Lang, 1977, 1979, 1984) that the information structure of an emotion could be construed to contained response information. Furthermore, while many of its propositional details might enjoy semantic representation, response information was basically part of a deeper code, which was represented fundamentally as action programs for efferent expression.

The importance of response information in the memorial representation of an emotion cannot be minimized. To paraphrase Sperry's (1952) argument in an effort to reorient the thinking of his neurophysiological colleagues, the brain did not develop to its present complexity, teleologically directed toward a perceptual, contemplative organism. If purpose can be lent to phylogenetic history, the value of the brain and its nervous elaboration is to organize action and response. Aggregations of nervous tissue function increasingly throughout evolution to extend the flexibility and variation of behavior. Thus, much more is to be learned by an emphasis on the consequent, efferent side of the S-R equation than by considering perception in isolation or by viewing internal information transfers as ends in themselves. In this overview sense, we are very much in sympathy with Weimer's (1977) motor theory of mental processing, i.e., that an important goal of psychology is to "successfully integrate acting and perceiving, something that has never before been done by either behaviorism or cognitive psychology," or even, "the mind is intrinsically a motor system" (p. 272). We are not suggesting a return to Watsonian "muscle memory" (1930), but we are advocating a view of memory transfers or cognitive processes as fundamentally parts of programs for efferent expression.

Zajonc and Markus (1984) have recently proposed a view of emotion very similar to ours in its emphasis on response components as key units in memory. We cheerfully join with them in commending this approach to the field: "We propose that since affect contains a significant motor component and since cognition, too, contains such a motor component . . . , a focus on the motor system as serving representational and mnestic functions provides a particularly fruitful alternative for the investigation of the interaction of affect and cognition" (Zajonc & Markus, 1984, pre-publication abstract).

Our broadside for the virtues of a response-oriented view would be of little value unaccompanied by some coherent plan of attack on the nature of response structure in emotion. The first task is clearly to determine what response features are represented in associative memory (i.e., at the level of higher cortical functioning) that can provide the mediating code in such phenomena as mood-dependent memory, excitation transfer, or in the pan-behavioral effects of generalized anxiety and depression.

I originally proposed (Lang, 1977) that response components from the three data systems in emotion must enjoy separate memorial representation—otherwise, how could they show both unique patterns across situations, as well as so much desynchrony over time? However, it seems likely that this was not true in phylogenetic history, nor does it appear to be a phenomenon of early ontogenetic development. Primitively, the physiology of an emotional act was probably no more than the "real time" housekeeping requirements of the act itself. However, when organisms developed in complexity, such that resources could be mobilized prior to behavior, in anticipation of action, or even tried out in imagination, there evolved separate representation of the logistic physiology and of the act itself because of the superior survival value conferred by better preparation for response.

Two response systems became three systems with the evolutionary development of natural language. It is reasonable to presume that natural language first came into being as a second control system for behavior (Pavlov, 1941), permitting more refined differentiation of acts and providing pointers during inhibition, such that delayed responses were not lost with the advent of new, distracting stimuli from the environment. At its inception language was tied inexorably to active behaviors. This association between action and language is evident in the ontogeny of human beings. Thus, in the famous Ivanov-Smolenski paradigm (1927, 1949), described by Luria (1957), children who have only recently acquired language can readily be trained to press on a ball with their hands, and to simultaneously say the word, "press." However, these same young children (or older, brain-damaged children) have great difficulty, despite much instruction and demonstration, saying "press" at the same moment that they release the ball. At this early age, language and action are one. Later in the developmental sequence language becomes detached from overt acts. In the adult expressive language of emotion (e.g., I hate your guts!), act and language retain their intimate association. As professional actors report, the mere mouthing of such lines sometimes causes the viscera to follow. On the other hand, the pseudoperceptual language of feelings can be expressed in contexts that include no other emotional responses (Lang, 1978). Affective judgments are represented semantically and are subject to associative modification quite independently from the behavior and physiology of an affective response.

It is more difficult to define the separate structures of physiological mobilization and overt behavioral acts. The distinction also begins in such phenomena as inhibition and anticipation. Subjects delaying a response show a distinctive psychophysiology, as do subjects waiting for a stimulus to occur. Their visceral and somatic patterns are in some ways like those of an overt action, and in other ways unique. Thus, Chase, Graham, & Graham (1968) reported that heart rate increased, after a warning tone and before a subsequent "GO" signal, when the required action was a physically demanding series of leg lifts. However, when "GO" signaled only a rapid reaction time, involving a very small motor movement of the finger, heart rate decelerated over the preceding interstimulus interval, with the slowest beat at the onset of the response signal. Without dwelling on the microphysiology of baroreceptor action, vagal release, or sympathetic innervation (e.g., see Obrist, 1981), this difference can be construed as a consequence of the subject being assigned a dual task: Attention to a stimulus signal and preparation for action at the signal's occurrence. Graham and Clifton (1966), Obrist (1981), Lang, Ohman, & Simons (1978) are among the many investigators who have found that an attentional set is accompanied by a decrease in heart rate and/or muscle tension. On the other hand, large muscle movement itself requires a different pattern of cardiovascular activity. When only minimal response is to be required, e.g., finger reaction time, the interstimulus interval reflects mainly the attentional task; however, when a gross muscle act is to be called up, the cardiovascular mobilization process dominates the interval. We have recently observed a similar phenomenon in classical conditioning, in which conflict between attention and preparation for action appears to be implicated, and in which the task that dominates the CS-UCS interval varies between individuals.

Using cluster analysis, Hodes, Cook, and Lang (in preparation) found that a sample of classically conditioned normal subjects were readily divided into three distinct groups, depending on CS-UCS interval heart rate change during conditioned response acquisition: Accelerators, moderate decelerators, and decelerators (see Fig. 3; the conditioned stimuli used in this experiment were colored slides and the UCS was an aversive noise). These different heart rate responses indicate the subjects were engaged in different cognitive processes, and that only the accelerators clearly learned to respond emotionally to the CS. This hypothesis derives from contemporary views of learning (Rescorla, 1978) which suggest that classical aversive conditioning may involve the acquisition of two basic types of responses: (1) learning an association between stimuli; i.e., that two stimuli have a temporal relationship; (2) learning to get ready for, perhaps to avoid, a signaled aversive event. Subjects tend to emphasize in their performance one or the other of these two responses. Psychophysiological research has shown that when the attentional task is dominant (i.e., stimulus association) heart rate deceleration characterizes the CS-UCS interval; emphasis on the aversive quality of the signaled event will prompt mobilization for escape and heart rate acceleration (e.g., see Obrist, 1981). We believe that even if actual avoidance is gated out by instructions, the preparatory physiology remains as an atavism of the primitive "fight or flight" response.

Some support for this general view was obtained from analysis of the subjects' post-conditioning affective judgments of the slides used in the Hodes et al. experiment. As can be seen in Fig. 4, the accelerators found the slides that had been followed by shock to be less pleasant (reduced in valence), more arousing,

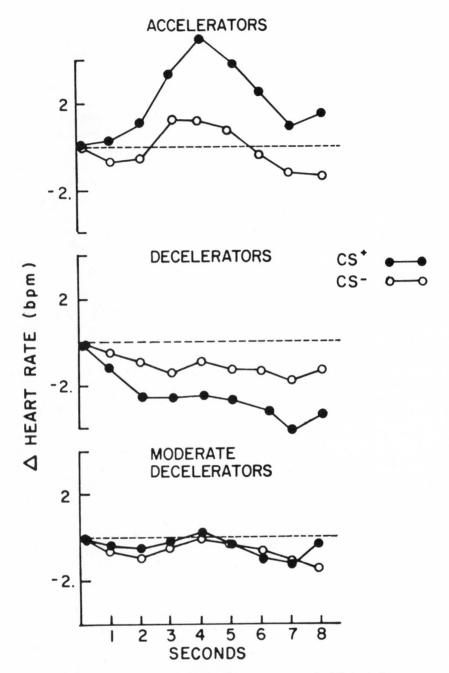

FIG. 3.   Results of the cluster analysis of heart rate responses for 148 classically conditioned subjects. Data were taken during the response acquisition phase of the experiment from the interval beginning at conditioned stimulus onset (a slide photo) and ending at the onset of the unconditioned stimulus (CS + , noise). Three groups were defined: *Accelerators, Decelerators,* and *Moderate decelerators* (from Hodes, Cook, & Lang, in preparation).

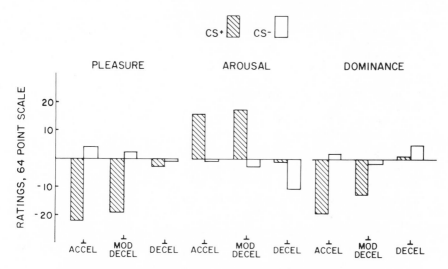

FIG. 4.   Change in affective ratings of colored slides from before to after classical conditioning. Some slides were followed by aversive noise (CS +) during conditioning and others (CS −) had no aversive sequelae. The rating method employed was the self-assessment manikin (SAM), in which subjects adjusted a computer display to provide scaled affective judgements. Three bipolar scales were rated: pleasure-displeasure, arousal-calm, dominance-submission (Lang, 1980). The SAM method is highly correlated with the semantic differential estimate of these dimensions, as used by Mehrabian and Russell (1974) (from Hodes, Cook, & Lang, in preparation).

and to generate less of a feeling of dominance or control (i.e., subjects showing predominant CS-UCS acceleration were more afraid). In contrast, the pure decelerators showed little change in their affective experience of the slides as a function of conditioning. It is interesting to note that the accelerators also differed significantly from the decelerators in electrodermal extinction. That is, the accelerators were strongly orienting to the shocked slides, long after the decelerators had ceased to make this distinction between shocked and unshocked pictures. Finally, the moderate decelerators seemed to show both a physiological middle ground, and less three-systems concordance. They are like the accelerators in their affective judgments, but their physiology, including the electrodermal data, is closer to the decelerators.

Thus, we see in the results of this conditioning study a model of the system discordance observed in many anxious patients. In this case it occurs because the same context prompts two actions (attention and avoidance) which have incompatible physiologies. Some subjects go one way, some the other, while a third group shows evidence of both types of processing, but in different response systems! One of the difficulties in the psychophysiological analysis of information processing (either at the level of classical conditioning or the imagery of fearful experiences) lies in this fact that several acts or preparations for action may be occurring simultaneously, and the researcher (or clinician) can be hard pressed to sort them out.

Stimulus and Meaning Information

It is clear that information about stimuli and their significance is a fundamental part of the associative aggregate that constitutes an affective response disposition. Indeed, several theories of emotion emphasize stimulus attributes as the primitive organizing elements in understanding the varied gamut of emotional behavior. As previously suggested (Lang, 1970), these views fall into three basic categories: (1) the view that affective responses grew out of differential responding to stimulus intensity. For example, Schneirla (1959) holds that intense stimuli intrinsically prompt avoidance and states of high arousal, whereas weak stimuli occasion approach and low arousal. Sokolov (1963) (see also Graham & Clifton, 1966; Lacey, 1967) proposes an analagous view in the domain of attention. Based primarily on studies of auditory input, they view the attentive set as either orienting, receptivity to moderate environmental stimuli, or defense, a shutting down of stimulus analyzers in the face of high intensity. (2) Various theories of novelty have also been offered as explanations of emotion. Hebb's (1949) approach is basically a novelty theory, emphasizing, as we previously noted, the disruption of acts by incongruous or inappropriate stimuli. Kagan (1974) views the reactions of infants to abrupt, unexpected events as a precursor of adult emotional responsivity. From this perspective, the startle reflex could be taken as an ontogenetic or phylogenetic model of the emotional response. Stimuli with rapid onset (short rise time) occasion widespread somatic and visceral reactions, disrupt ongoing behaviors or cognitions, and prompt a transient loss of control (e.g., Ison & Hoffman, 1983). (3) Finally, there is the view held by ethologists, that certain complex stimuli are phylogenetically prepotent, or prepared for specific emotional response. The continuity of affective stimuli, for example within primates, is cited as support: Both monkey and man appear to react with emotion to snakes, eye contact, strangers, physical touching, various facial expressions, looming stimuli, and so forth, with these S-R bonds appearing at consistent stages of ontogenetic development, having minimal opportunity for previous learning. This approach to the origins of phobia has been taken by Seligman (1975) and pursued by Öhman in the conditioning laboratory (1979). Berkowitz (1983) has similarly argued that "aversive stimulation evokes an instigation to aggression *independently of how the afflicted individual might interpret his or her sensations.*"

It seems likely that some relationships between specific stimuli and perhaps equally specifiable response patterns are "firm wired" in the brain. It is also clear that a great variety of other stimuli find their way into an associative memory network through learning; and finally, that in human beings these S-R relationships, whatever their origin, are surrounded by a semantic penumbra of meaning.

In theories that presume the substantive reality of the internal subjective life, meaning information has loomed large. Schachter (1964) held that emotions occurred when the essentially neutral input about physiological arousal was interpreted in the context of the person's appraisal of the meaning of the stimulus, e.g., "I'm aroused; there's a bear over there; bears eat people; therefore, I'm afraid and will behave fearfully." James' original view implied a similar sequence, but rather than external stimulus context, the pattern of physiological events was the focus of appraisal. Schachter's view has been cogently criticized by many theorists, some of whom still regard conscious feelings as a datum of emotion (e.g., Berkowitz, 1983; Lang, 1970; Leventhal, 1980; Zajonc, 1980; Zillmann, 1983). The arguments against it include evidence that emotional responding often precedes evidence of appraisal, that arousal patterns are not unidimensional, and that emotional behavior may occur despite reports of conflicting appraisals (e.g., the patient "knows" that beetles aren't dangerous, but still panics at the sight of one).

On the other hand, most students of human emotion believe meaning information to be important, and hold that it must be considered in any general theory of emotion. However, if we presume that an emotion is represented in memory as network of information, in which response, stimulus, and meaning information are all associatively related, many of the problems in appraisal theories appear to be bypassed. Conscious evaluation is simply not a necessary part of primary emotional processing in a network theory. We are no longer required to view the influence of visceral patterning only through the lens of conscious appraisal. I can do no better than quote Berkowitz (1983) on this point:

The network analyses of emotions recently advanced by Lang (1979), Leventhal (1980) and Bower (1981) generally maintain that a particular emotional experience is a construction of expressive-motor reactions, ideas and memories (and not an inference made from one's own behavior and other situational cues). The activation of any one of these components presumably evokes the other parts of the network. Thus, where Schachter believed that thoughts affect emotions primarily by determining what label is applied to one's physical sensations, the present theorizing suggests that situationally evoked thoughts can have a priming effect. In essence, they can activate emotional expressive-motor reactions, ideas and memories that can either intensify or weaken the expressive-motor responses, ideas and recollections elicited by the aversive event. All this takes place, moreover, even if the suffering person does not label his or her sensations. (p. 1141)

AN INFORMATION-PROCESSING VIEW OF FEAR AND ANXIETY

My own recent research on emotion has focused on the study of fear, particularly its pathological manifestation in phobia. The specificity of context and response in this disorder is great, and cognition and behavior remain relatively stable in the absence of any real nociceptive events. Thus, considering the transient character of most emotional states (that affects must be, so to speak, caught on the fly, if indeed they are to be examined at all) phobia is a valuable, stable preparation for the study of pathological emotion. The goal of our work has been to define the data structure in long-term memory that forms the information base for phobic behavior, and to understand the conditions under which this information is or is not accessed and processed.

Our working theory presumes the emotion memory structure to contain three categories of information that we have just outlined: (1) information about prompting external stimuli and the context in which they occur; (2) information about responding in this context, including expressive facial or verbal behavior, overt acts of approach or avoidance, and the visceral and somatic events that support attention and action; and (3) information that elaborates or defines the meaning of the stimulus and response data.

We propose (Lang, 1977, 1979, 1984) that emotion information is coded in memory in the form of propositions, and that these propositions are organized into associative networks of the general sort first described by Quillian (1966) for semantic knowledge and later adapted to accommodate other types of information (e.g., Anderson & Bower, 1974; Kieras, 1978). However, we view this information structure as three-dimensional: The foundation plane contains the efferent code and motor programs, which in turn project upward and define a fundamental stimulus code (the concrete, action imagery described, for example, by Paivio (1971)). The top plane is a true semantic network, which may include natural language representations of deeper level concepts, in addition to the logically derived meaning propositions. We presume that associative bonds extend between code levels as well as within planes.

The information network of an emotion is a sort of prototype or schema, which, when a critical number of propositions are accessed (through a match to environmental stimuli or internal association, or both), is processed as a unit. It is reasonable to assume as in Anderson's ACT theory (1976) that the prototype network is associated with a production system (Newell, 1973). The production system is both an information analysis program (i.e., the emotional image) and a program for response generation. Its activation is roughly equivalent to the cognitive work of emotional expression. Somato-visceral efferents and action are the output events occasioned by the production system processing of response information.

The network is the declarative knowledge of a phobia and the procedural knowledge (test programs, motor plans) is in the production system. Phobic expression is produced when a sufficient number of input concepts match those in the network. As a working hypothesis we currently presume that the probability of a phobic production is determined by the number of matching propositions, irrespective of their taxonomic category (stimulus, response, meaning) which are present in short-term memory. Obviously, network activation is most likely when the phobic individual is confronted by the actual phobic object, which presumes a near-perfect stimulus match. However, phobic emotions may also be elicited by degraded input—pictures of the phobic object, verbal descriptions of context, and the like. It is important to remember that the information stored in memory is presumed to be conceptual and not iconic. A variety of media can be the vehicles of information input to the network and the production system. Furthermore, degraded stimulus matches may be as effective in prototype activation as exposure if other propositions (response or meaning), are simultaneously instigated. For example, reduced stimulus cues will still prompt a full phobic reaction in a subject who is otherwise aroused or in a context where fear stimuli are expected.

Phobic reactions are characterized by unusually coherent, stable emotion prototypes (high association value and high propositional interdependency within the network). Activation spreads with unusual rapidity through a phobic network, and total network activation can be occasioned by a limited number of concept matches. Fear production will often occur under what appear to be minimal, external instigating conditions. An example of a possible phobic network prototype is presented in Fig. 5.

Is the Image the Message?

Emotional imagery is widely remarked in dreams, in anticipation of affective events, as aesthetic experience, and as a vehicle of therapeutic change (e.g., Singer, 1974). From the perspective of phenomenological investigation, images are sensory events in the mind, pictures presented to the mind's eye, which may be transient and unclear or so vivid as to approach the status of hallucinations. It is a surprising fact that despite the compelling nature of this hypothesis, experimental psychology has uncovered almost no evidence that the ability to report imagery or the vividness of individual images relate to sensory memory (e.g., see Strosahl & Ascough, 1981). For example, several investigators have failed to find that self-described good imagers remember more accurately or in more detail previously observed visual materials than do people who maintain they have few if any images at all.

On the other hand, studies of the psychophysiological events in imagery have shown positive relationships between responses observed during perception and those observed while subjects image. The probability of finding this relationship between verbal report and physiological responses is increased when the subjects studied are people who say they have vivid imagery. Thus, a number of researchers have examined tasks that require highly stereotyped cyclical eye movements (such as visual tracking of an oscillating pendulum or cathode ray tube display) and demonstrated that during recall of this task good imagers tend to regenerate eye movements that have a dominant frequency similar to that of the perceptual display (Brady & Levitt, 1966; Brown, 1968; Deckert, 1964; Weerts, Cuthbert, Simons, & Lang, in preparation). From the perspective presented here the above phenomenon is attributable to the fact that subjects coded response information

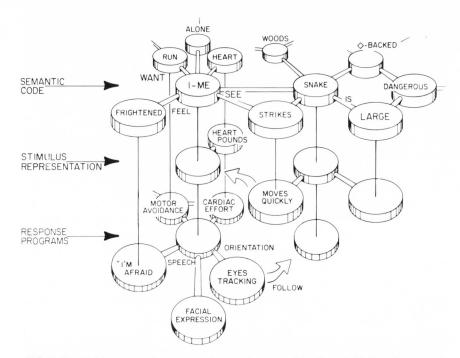

FIG. 5. The phobia prototype is a conceptual network of propositionally coded information, related by association, which has as functional output a visceral and somato-motor program. The prototype may be activated as a unit by instructional, media, or objective sensory input, which contains information matching that in the network. The above phobia prototype could be rendered in descriptive, narrative English text as follows: "I am in a wooded area, when I see a large snake. It appears to be moving towards me. There's a diamond pattern on its back. This could be a dangerous snake. My eyes jump in my head, following a quick, striking movement. My heart starts racing. Snakes are unpredictable. "I'm afraid!" I say it aloud, but nobody is there to hear me. I'm alone and very frightened. I want to run."

Propositions in the network are represented by the round nodes, containing the concept name, and the labeled stems that show the links between concepts. In the notation proposed by Kintsch (1974), the stems indicate predicators and the round nodes are their arguments e.g., (Is, Snake, Large). No attempt is made here to indicate all propositions or all possible connections. However, it is suggested that certain propositions are strongly bonded to others, and may thus be keys to the broad recruitment of the network, with its action subprograms. For example, as a basic stimulus representation (Moves, Snake, Quickly) may have a primitive, high-probability connection to (Pounds, I-Me, Heart), which in turn unlocks the other fear-response propositions, prompting rapid prototype activation.

The model is presented here in Tinkertoy form to illustrate three basic levels in the brain code. The semantic code is the high-level language which includes three broad classes of information—stimulus, meaning, and response propositions. Stimulus information may also enjoy a more fundamental representation as primary, action-defined, input concepts. The base representation of the entire network is the efferent code that organizes responding. Concepts may or may not be represented across levels. Network activation can theoretically begin with any set of concepts and move within or between structural levels. Similarly, mediation between different emotion networks (as in state-dependent learning) could be carried by concepts of any type—stimulus, response, meaning—or at any of the three levels of the structure.

The view taken here is that the deep structure of the prototype is an action set. Although the prototype can be described in a natural language, and the semantic level may be processed with some degree of independence from the rest of the memory architecture, an affective network is functionally organized to generate efferent output. Thus, the processing of conceptual emotional information (in imago or in vivo) always involves some degree of visceral and motor outflow.

160

into an associative memory network during the original perception. Subsequent image processing involves the accessing of the entire network (including both the stimulus and response information). While the image is a cognitive production, processing of response information initiates associated motor programs. In imagery, the final action commands of these programs are gated out or inhibited. However, there is always a certain amount of efferent leakage. Thus, a sub-overt pattern of motor responses apes many of the original sense organ and postural adjustments of the specific stimulus-orienting task. It is our view that this same motor regeneration process underlies emotional imagery. In this case, however, the efferent pattern is even more elaborate, representing the prototype of the emotion action set.

In a series of experiments we have explored the effects of inducing emotional imagery through textual descriptions of affect-arousing scenes (Lang, Kozak, Miller, Levin, & McLean, 1980; Lang, Levin, Miller, & Kozak, 1983; Miller et al., in preparation). On the assumption that the text or image script can be a stimulus for prototype concept matches, we have varied the propositional content of these materials. One manipulation involves presenting an auditory description of an encounter with the phobic object, and including or excluding information about the responses that occur in that context: "Your heart is pounding as you begin to speak." "Your muscles tense; you press backward." Another procedure utilizes training programs that encourage subjects to focus on either stimulus or response information in their imagery. The results of these experiments have been very clear: The inclusion of a response emphasis encourages response processing, resulting in a psychophysiological pattern of efferent activity during imagery that duplicates in topography (albeit at lower amplitude) the affective responses observed with actual stimulus confrontation. Phobic subjects imaging phobic scenes show significant increases in heart rate, skin conductance, and respiratory rhythm, in pattern similar to what they actually do when faced with the real phobic context. In general, we have found that subjects are most likely to develop an affective response to imagery instructions: (1) when response processing is encouraged (as described above); (2) when self-reported good imagers are used as subjects; and (3) particularly when networks of high associative coherence are tapped (as with phobics). Contrary to the emphasis on stimulus information prompted by subjective theory, emotional imagery has been found to be much more of a response process, and in this it is consistent both with the notion that affect is basically an action set and that memory representations of psychophysiological events figure importantly in cognition.

Matching Concepts in Memory

As mentioned previously, we are exploring the hypothesis that the number of input matches to network concepts determines the probability of an affective production. This view predicts that improved stimulus matches should be as effective as the response matches encouraged in the above studies of emotional text processing, in evoking the psychophysiology of affect. To test this assumption McLean (1981) presented subjects with realistic emotional playlets that they were to use as a prompt to an imagery experience. The scenes included, for example, an actor playing a clumsy laboratory attendant, who removed a live, ostensibly poisonous snake from a cage a few feet from the subject, and then struggled, almost unsuccessfully, to reconfine it. Under these circumstances the conceptual match of stimulus information to affective view prototype is nearly perfect. Even though the subjects were clearly preinstructed that all aspects of the scenario were staged and not real (the snake was harmless and the actor skilled), we nevertheless observed the same context-specific physiology of emotion that we had previously noted with response concept matching in our studies of emotion-inducing text. We have not yet attempted to deceive our subjects, but we presume that consonant meaning information would have a further enhancing effect. The data are at this point consistent with the view that any concept match increases the probability of network activation.

In addition to our basic research in emotional imagery, we are also studying the imagery of anxious and phobic patients in the context of clinical treatment. The information-processing view has prompted us to develop the concept of functional imagery. A functional image is held to be one that can mediate a response change in the target reality context described by the image. Our preliminary clinical work suggests that such functional imagery occurs (regardless of subjects' verbal reports of vividness or arousal) only if the relevant response information in the network is processed.

It is clear that subjects can respond to an image script with alternative processing modes. A subject may be instructed to simply report what events the text describes, or even just to comment on its lexical properties, and unless he is severely phobic, no affective response will be observed. Imagery implies, in our view, a different processing mode, one that includes the regeneration of response code, i.e., total network production. We already have data that the patients who profit from imagery therapies (that is, become less anxious or frightened after treatment) are those patients who can be shown to generate functional images, i.e., appropriate affective response topographies are observed during image induction in therapy (Lang, Melamed, & Hart, 1970). Furthermore, our recent results suggest that it is specifically fear patients who regenerate response code during a pre-therapy assessment who have the best prognosis for treatment (Levin, Cook, & Lang, 1982; see Fig. 6). It is not yet clear how the imagery experience comes to modify emotional behavior. However, that regeneration and at least partial processing of response code are critical elements suggests that subjects could be accomplishing "off line" processes of extinction or reconditioning that normally only occur in objective settings of response evocation. In any event, these results show that imagery procedures derived from the present model may be extremely useful both in distinguishing among different pathological states

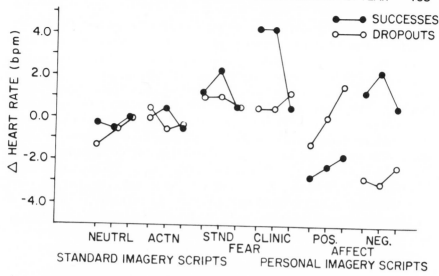

FIG. 6.   A comparison of pretreatment heart rate change scores for patients who successfully completed therapy ($N = 19$) and those who discontinued therapy prior to successful outcome ($N = 5$). These clients were seen at the Psychology Department Clinic, University of Wisconsin. Patients were provided scripts and instructed to vividly imagine six scene types: *Neutral* situations (e.g., relaxing at home in an easy chair); *action* scenes that were nonaffective but included vigorous activity (e.g., bike riding); *standard fear* scenes (e.g., locked in a sauna); scripts prepared with the patients collaboration describing the *clinical fear* context; two other personal scripts, one referring to an outstanding positive life experience (pos.) and the other an unpleasant, but nonclinical fear context (neg.). The heart rate data are change scores from pre-scene rest. Three data points are shown for each scene: the 30-second period during which the scripts were orally presented; the subsequent 30 seconds of imagery; and a 30-second recovery time, which began immediately after the patients were told to stop imagining the scene. In the average patient, neutral material prompted little change in heart rate. Action and negative affects occasioned acceleration, while patients tended to decelerate during positive affect scenes. These latter effects were dramatically larger in patients who responded positively to behavior therapy intervention (e.g., flooding, desensitization, coaching, and modeling) (from Levin, Cook, & Lang, 1982).

of anxiety and also in providing a firmer basis for estimates of prognosis and treatment selection.

THE ANXIETY DISORDERS: DIFFERENCES IN AFFECTIVE MEMORY STRUCTURE

The phobias are unique among anxiety disorders for several reasons. First, the stimulus information is explicit and reliable; second, the response pattern appears to be built around active avoidance. In a recent experiment comparing focal phobics and socially anxious subjects (Lang et al., 1983), we found overt avoidance tended to occur more frequently in focal phobics facing their own fear object than in socially anxious subjects similarly confronting their primary stress. Differences between these fear types were even clearer when physiological responses were examined. We found little distinction between the arousal physiologies of socially anxious subjects and phobics when both gave speeches to an unfamiliar audience (both groups showed marked visceral activation during this social-performance task); however, when these same two groups viewed phobic fear stimuli, socially anxious subjects stayed relatively calm, but the specific phobics showed a progressive increase in heart rate the closer they were to their phobic object—an increase paralleled by a higher probability of avoidance. Thus, the psychophysiology of phobia looks very much like preparation for flight, whereas the arousal response of socially anxious subjects, although quite high in amplitude, was more general in pattern and less explicit in affective meaning. These group differences in psychophysiological response were also apparent in their fear imagery and in anticipation of threat. Overall, severe phobics showed more three-systems (affective report, physiological and behavioral) concordance across contexts of emotional instigation than did comparably distressed socially anxious subjects.

We infer from the above phenomena that the information network of a phobia is, in general, more stable and coherent than that of social anxiety. Furthermore, we believe that this property of network coherence is related to a general ability to vividly imagine both new and previously experienced events. In several studies focal phobics have reported images to be more vivid, to involve more movement, and to be more closely related to content in arousal response than was observed for socially anxious subjects (Bardach & Weerts, 1980; Lang et al., 1970; Weerts & Lang, 1978). We are not suggesting here that phobics are better imagers than normals, but only that among the anxiety disorders studied, they generate the most stable, vivid, and representative imagery. Furthermore, as we have previously argued (Lang, 1979), what is reported subjectively as an image has much more to do with the organization of responses than it has to do with pictures in the mind's eye. The phobic image is a highly focused psychophysiological memory structure and a prototype affective response disposition. It may be that the effect of high network coherence in phobia is to restrict the association of its related arousal response processes and thus limit their influence on other memory content, relative to the spread or transfer of such excitation in other anxiety disorders.

The differences we have observed between socially anxious subjects and focal phobics have reappeared with some consistency across experiments, but the effect has often been too subtle for statistical significance and seldom dramatically large. This may be because socially anxious subjects were selected according to their degree of speech fear. We inadvertently included in the sample focal speech phobics (who may be no different from other specific phobics in imagery), as well as members of a more broadly, socially anxious population (who are presumed to have a relative imagery deficit). In recent clinical applications of a new imagery assessment technique, we have found even more dramatic differences in imagery ability between focal phobics and a population of agoraphobics. Perhaps even more than the socially anxious (with whom they are sometimes diagnostically confused), agoraphobics show much less affective network coherence, and considerably less context specificity of the consequent anxious behaviors. Although some stimulus and response information is recurrent across fear induction settings, the associative generality of the arousal response pattern is again much greater than that of focal phobia. It is expected that these patients will report less vivid images, show a less responsive physiology in imagery, be less concordant across a three-systems assessment, and be less consistent in the anxiety induction contexts to which they respond. Furthermore, as the associative structure is more diffuse, and less accessible to any therapeutic intervention, agoraphobia is more persistent and prognosis is poorer than for focal phobia.

The results of a psychophysiological imagery assessment of agoraphobic and other phobic patients is presented in Fig. 7 (McNeil, Melamed, Cuthbert, & Lang, 1983). It will be noted that the physiological response to affective imagery is significantly less for the agoraphobics than for the other phobics. Agoraphobics report themselves to image less vividly. We have also observed that agoraphobics have a higher incidence of dropping out from therapy, whereas focal phobics more frequently continued therapy to a successful resolution. Research accomplished by other investigators (Barlow, Mavissakalian, & Schofield, 1980) supports this general view, suggesting that agoraphobics have a less concordant three-systems structure, and that this may be related to this group's poorer prognosis. Epidemiological studies (Agras, Sylvester, & Oliveau, 1969) are also consistent with our analysis, showing that focal phobias are relatively short-lived, while agoraphobia persists in the population, with peak prevalence late in adult life.

An Anxiety Disorder Continuum

It is proposed that the anxiety disorders may be distributed along a continuum of affective memory organization. The continuum is defined by the degree to which arousing, negatively valent responses (and perhaps also disruption of control) are linked associatively to coherent affect networks; or viewed from the other direction, the degree to which these affective response dispositions float in memory, and are prompted by many stimuli, transferring their excitation to a great variety of other memory structures. Proceeding from most to least along the continuum of network coherence, the order of nosology is as follows: focal

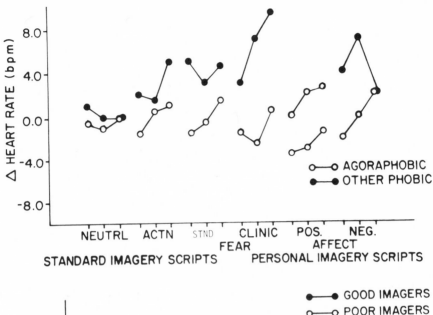

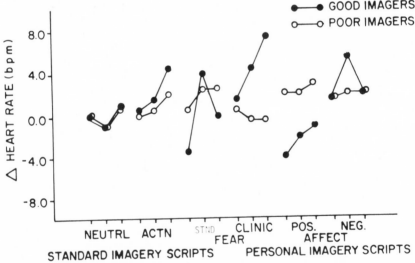

FIG. 7.   Pretreatment imagery assessments conducted at the Fear Clinic, University of Florida Health Center. Agoraphobics ($N = 5$) tend to show less acceleration during action and negative affect scenes than other phobics ($N = 7$), and less deceleration to positive material. When the sample was regrouped according to imagery questionnaire scores (in which subjects describe the vividness of their imagery in normal experience), a similar pattern is apparent, in which good imagers ($N = 8$) are more consistently responsive than poor imagers ($N = 4$) (from McNeil, Melamed, Cuthbert, & Lang, 1983).

phobia, obsessions and compulsions; social anxiety; agoraphobia; panic and generalized anxiety states.[2] Generalized anxiety would appear to represent the condition of maximum associative fluidity of affective response structures. It is for these patients that the research on state-dependent learning may be most relevant. Their behavior seems consistent with the notion of an underlying affective response program, which mediates associated anxious thoughts, worries and the like, across disparate contexts and environments. Such a mechanism could account for Gentil and Lader's (1978) report that anxiety patients have more frequent dreams of being attacked, or Butler and Mathews' (1983) finding that anxiety patients overestimate the probability of many threatening events (both social and physical). The presence of the proposed mediating physiology already has general documentation: Lader and Wing (1966) and Hart (1974) are among the many who have shown that anxiety patients generate more spontaneous sympathetic responses, even at rest. We have already noted the high frequency of visceral and somatic symptom reports in this population (Buss, 1962; Hamilton, 1959).

A variety of clinicians tend to view cognitive and physiological response mechanisms as separate domains of symptomology, and as independent treatment targets (e.g., Ellis, 1971; Meichenbaum, 1977). However, our own studies of affective imagery and the research on emotional state-dependent learning argue something quite different. They suggest that the psychophysiology of emotion is represented in associative memory and is in this sense no less cognitive than a verbal report. Furthermore, the evidence suggests that the response program of an emotion can be either highly differentiated or general in its representation. It can serve either as a focus for specific, content-bound acts (as in phobia) or as the mediator of a spectrum of syndromal behaviors that may appear in any setting. It is important here to remind ourselves that response information does not need to exert a central influence through interoceptive or exteroceptive feedback from peripheral afferents. We do not need to assume a homunculoid self that assesses acts after they occur. There is every reason to believe that the action program itself (or a particular subroutine, such as a pattern of visceral activation) is associatively linked to other information in the brain. While subsequent feedback may support, confirm, or modify ongoing emotional processing, it is not necessary to the instigation or persistence of affective responses or their associations.

---

[2]It is not obvious where post traumatic stress syndrome or somataform disorders would fit in this scheme. The former are very like phobias in the vividness of evoked imagery, but differ in that the affective response is less clearly cued by specific external stimuli. Somataform disorders involve highly organized response structures, but these are not closely linked to semantic information. Some of these latter patients could be called alexithymic (Nemiah, Freyberger, & Sifneos, 1976), and at least in this sense, they have less organized anxiety networks.

The Parameters of Fear and Anxiety

Viewed from the present perspective, there is much work to be done. We need to determine more precisely the responses that serve as affect mediators and the level of specificity at which they are represented in associative memory (subroutine, program, or parameter). We need to know much more about the general dimensions of emotion:

1. What defines valence? Is facial expression a fundamental component, or has the face, like language, become detached from affect by the needs of social communication? Should we be considering attentional sets such as orienting and defensive reflexes (Sokolov, 1963)? Is there a general underlying response pattern for approach and avoidance?

2. Arousal is a similarly confusing concept. When we look at emotional acts there are great differences in the peripheral physiology. Is Obrist's (1981) concept of active and passive coping a good model on which to begin the analysis of the varied fear physiology? Zillmann (1983) has presented interesting data suggesting that excitation transfer occurs best when the preceding emotion has had some time to dissipate, i.e., the arousal state is present but moderate, perhaps undemarcated by verbal labels or other cues. He also finds that excitation transfer is less when subjects are in good physical shape, apparently because recovery from arousal is rapid, and the optimal physiological state for affect mediation is passed through too quickly. The background arousal levels (Lader & Wing, 1966) of most anxious subjects are moderately elevated and may be optimal for excitation to transfer. In trait-anxious patients (Speilberger, 1972) mild environmental prompts to very different emotions (anger, sexuality, etc.) could activate somatic or visceral response elements held in common with the anxious state, thereby mediating associated negative memories, feelings of inadequacy or helplessness, which then continually reattach themselves to new contexts and situations. This is consistent with the view that the genetic component of trait anxiety may be a somewhat higher background level of visceral activity, which in this way provides ideal soil for generalized anxiety states to grow (Eysenck, 1961; Torgenson, 1979).

3. We also need more information on how control-dominance may be represented in memory. Feelings of being out of control are clearly a preeminent theme in anxiety and panic disorders. We need to know if this is truly an independent dimension of affect with its own psychophysiology, or whether it can be understood, as some argue (Russell, 1980), as "meaning" information that can be associated with various interactions of valence and arousal.

The significance of valence, arousal, and control as parameters of anxiety is extensively documented in research already reviewed. However, as a concluding comment it is worth considering that these dimensions also provide a natural classification of methods used in the treatment of anxiety disorders. That is to say, therapists either attempt to reduce arousal through drugs or relaxation training (Klein, 1981; Wolpe, 1958); or try to modify the valence of negative contexts by, for example, providing success experiences in the aversive context and by reinterpreting the meaning of negative situations (e.g., Ellis, 1971; Meichenbaum, 1977); or they focus on training the subject in self-control, efficacy, and competency by teaching skills and modeling (Bandura, 1977; McFall & Twentyman, 1973). It may well prove that the most effective therapy will not be similarly unimodal, but will depend on careful consideration of all three affective parameters.

CONCLUSIONS: ON BASIC SCIENCE AND APPLIED RESEARCH

In conclusion, let me suggest some more specific projects for future research that I believe will significantly advance our understanding of clinical anxiety and fear. It seems clear that we should extend the study of emotion-dependent learning and excitation transfer to anxiety patients. The arguments made here suggest that the mediation of memories through affective state may be more generalized in anxious subjects than in normals. It is important that we confirm the evidence that imagery is best in phobics, and that it is reduced in quality as the hypothesized network coherence lessens and the diagnosis of generalized anxiety becomes more appropriate. We should test the hypothesis that excitation transfer occurs more easily in anxiety, that valence may be less significant in inhibiting generalizations between arousal states in anxious patients than in normals, and that positive affective arousal as well as aversive activation may potentiate worry and negative self-reference in high-trait-anxious subjects.

Basic research on memory and affect is already significantly advanced. Parallel progress in the study of pathological emotion can be achieved if these paradigms and strategies are applied in research on anxiety. We need to know more about the organization of memory networks and the conditions that encourage or limit "spread of activation" (e.g., see Ratcliff & McKoon, 1981). Furthermore, it is important to determine whether these phenomena are altered in any fundamental way when affective contents are processed. In this effort it will be necessary to carefully monitor the psychophysiology of patients, as the evidence is now strong that the representation of physiological events figures strongly in cognitive life. Finally, it may be important also to consider suspending our traditional subjectivist theory of the patient, i.e., that the mind is a collection of private purposes, in which the cognitive mechanism is held to intentionally disguise, conceal, and distort behavior. As Laird et al. (1982) said in concluding their paper on facial expression and state-dependent recall, "Perhaps many of the emotion/memory relationships that have previously been thought to reflect self-protective or self-aggrandizing purposes may instead arise from essentially undirected organizational properties of memory" (p. 656).

ACKNOWLEDGMENTS

The work was supported in part by NIMH grant MH 37757.

8 Anxiety, Cognition and Affect: A State-Trait Perspective

Charles D. Spielberger
University of South Florida, Tampa

The complexity and multifaceted nature of anxiety phenomena are clearly reflected in the excellent papers contributed to this volume by Izard, Lang and Sarason. Given the wide range of topics that are covered and the limitations in space for discussion in this brief chapter, it is not possible to do justice to the work of these distinguished contributors to theory and research on emotion, anxiety, and the anxiety disorders. Each has worked productively in this field for more than a quarter century, and has made many important contributions to the conceptualization and assessment of anxiety as a psychobiological construct.

Izard, Lang and Sarason approach the problem of anxiety from their own unique theoretical perspective, and with different research objectives. Consistent with their diverse theoretical views and research interests, each investigates different aspects of anxiety phenomena, using methods that are particularly suited to his individual orientation. While all three recognize the importance of cognition and physiological arousal, Izard regards the pattern of emotions as the most fundamental aspects of an anxiety state, and Sarason emphasizes the centrality of worry cognitions. Lang has historically focused on the psychophysiology of anxiety, but his current views assign cognitions and memory a critical role in anxiety arousal.

In addition to important differences in their theoretical conceptions and research methods, Izard, Lang and Sarason also differ in terms of their implicit epistemological assumptions about the nature of anxiety. The phenomenology of emotional experience is basic to Izard's conception of anxiety as a variable pattern of fundamental emotions. From Lang's strong behavioral orientation, introspective reports are merely verbal behaviors that bear no necessary relationship to unobservable internal states or conditions. Although Sarason has previously taken a position nearer the middle of the phenomenological-behavioral continuum, his current views seem to reflect movement toward Lang's position, with increasing emphasis on cognition and behavior, and correspondingly less interest in affective feeling states.

The three papers also differ with regard to the emphasis given to individual differences in anxiety as a personality trait. Over the years, Sarason has pioneered research on the assessment of the impact of individual differences in anxiety, and especially test anxiety, on performance and learning. Although Izard and Lang seem to accept the state-trait distinction, the assessment of individual differences in trait anxiety receives relatively little systematic attention. Trait differences are implicitly recognized by Lang in the careful attention that he gives to differences in the presumed nature of stored cognitions and memories associated with different types of anxiety disorders. Similarly, Izard's research on differential patterns of emotion in childhood attempts to predict differences in trait anxiety from self-reports and teachers' ratings of the patterns of emotions experienced by fifth- and sixth-grade school children.

In the preceding paragraphs, I have attempted to highlight a number of important differences in the theoretical and philosophical assumptions, and in the research interests and methods, that characterize the anxiety research of Izard, Lang and Sarason. Later in this chapter, I comment in greater detail on each of the papers. Prior to examining them individually, however, I briefly review the evolution of anxiety as a psychological construct and introduce a conceptual frame of reference that identifies the major classes of variables generally considered in anxiety research. The particular variables emphasized in the three papers are then evaluated within the context of this conceptual model.

CONCEPTIONS OF ANXIETY: STATE-TRAIT-PROCESS

Contemporary theories of anxiety have their historical roots in the philosophical and theological views of Pascal and Kierkegaard, and in Darwin's naturalistic conception of fear as a fundamental emotion. Within the framework of his theory of evolution, Darwin (1872) observed that the potential for experiencing fear was an inherent characteristic of both animals and humans. For Pascal and Kierkegaard, and for contemporary existential philosophers and therapists, anxiety is a distinctively human condition that results from the self-conscious capacity to discern the irrational contingencies of life, the "possibility of freedom," and the ultimate threat of non-being (May, 1977).

Darwin believed that fear reactions were instinctive, and that the essential characteristics of these reactions in both humans and animals had evolved over countless generations through a process of natural selection. On the basis of his sensitive naturalistic observations, Darwin noted that manifestations of fear generally included rapid heart palpitations (tachycardia), dilation of the pupils, increased perspiration, erection of the hair, dryness of the mouth, changes in voice quality, and peculiar facial expression. Within the framework of his theory of evolution, the adaptive function of fear was to arouse and mobilize the organism for coping with external danger.

Many of the attributes of fear described by Darwin are also found in Cannon's (1929) "fight-or-flight" reaction, and in the "alarm" reaction that occurs in the initial phase of Selye's (1956) General Adaptation Syndrome. But Darwin placed a greater emphasis on the observable physical and behavioral manifestations of fear, whereas Cannon and Selye, who worked mainly with laboratory animals, were concerned primarily with the physiological and biochemical changes that occurred within the body.

Sigmund Freud was the first to attempt a systematic explication of the meaning of anxiety within the context of psychological theory. In 1894, Freud conceptualized anxiety neurosis as a discrete clinical syndrome to be distinguished from neurasthenia and subsequently proposed a critical role for anxiety in the formation of neurotic and psychosomatic disorders. For Freud, anxiety was the "fundamental phenomenon and the central problem of neurosis" (1936, p. 85), and understanding anxiety was "the most difficult task that has been set us," a task whose solution required "the introduction of the right abstract ideas, and their application to the raw material of observation so as to bring order and lucidity into it" (1933, p. 113). The complexity of this task and Freud's personal commitment are reflected in the fact that his theoretical views on anxiety evolved over a period of nearly 50 years, were continually modified, and were never regarded as complete. Given the preeminence of Freud's contributions to our understanding of the nature of anxiety and the anxiety disorders, it is surprising that citations of his work are conspicuously absent in all three of the preceding papers.

First and foremost, Freud regarded anxiety as "something felt"—an unpleasant emotional state or condition of the human organism. This emotional state was characterized by "all that is covered by the word 'nervousness', apprehension and anxious expectation," and it also included behavioral and physiological components (Freud, 1924). An anxiety state was distinguishable from other unpleasant emotions such as anger, sorrow, or grief, by a unique combination of phenomenological and physiological qualities, giving it special "character of unpleasure" which, though difficult to describe, seemed "to possess a particular note of its own" (Freud, 1936, p. 69). The subjective, phenomenological qualities of anxiety—the feelings of tension, apprehension and dread, and cognitions of impending danger—were emphasized by Freud, whereas the behavioral manifestations and the physiological (efferent) discharge phenomena, although considered an essential part of an anxiety state that contributed to its unpleasantness, were of little theoretical interest.

In his early formulations, Freud theorized that anxiety resulted from the discharge of repressed sexual energy (libido). When blocked from normal expression, libido accumulated and was subsequently transformed into "free-floating anxiety," or other psychological or physical symptoms that were anxiety equivalents. Freud subsequently modified this view to emphasize the critical role of anxiety as a response to the presence of danger—either from the external environment or from internal thoughts or feelings. In this later conception of anxiety, the perceived presence of danger evoked an unpleasant emotional reaction that served to warn the individual that some form of adjustment was necessary. The nature of anxiety as an emotional state and Freud's emphasis on the adaptive utility of anxiety as a danger signal are quite similar to Darwin's conception of fear.

Freud's danger signal theory of anxiety calls attention to two potential sources of threat—the external world and a person's own internal impulses. If the source of danger is in the external world, and the anxiety reaction is proportional in intensity to the magnitude of the external danger, the anxiety is said to be objective, i.e., the greater the external danger, the more intense the resulting objective anxiety reaction will be. When the perception of danger from one's own unacceptable (forbidden) internal impulses evokes an emotional reaction, this is called neurotic anxiety.

For Freud, objective anxiety was synonymous with fear; both terms refer to the unpleasant emotional state that is aroused when a person anticipates injury or harm from a real (objective) danger. In other words, if a real danger in the external world is accurately perceived as threatening, this will result in an anxiety (or fear) reaction that is proportional in intensity to the actual danger. Thus:

$$\begin{matrix} \text{External} \\ \text{danger} \end{matrix} \rightarrow \begin{matrix} \text{Perception} \\ \text{of danger} \end{matrix} \rightarrow \begin{matrix} \text{Objective} \\ \text{anxiety} \end{matrix}$$

Like objective anxiety, neurotic anxiety is also a danger signal, but the source of danger stems from the individual's own repressed sexual and aggressive impulses, not from an external danger. When these impulses are associated with painful punishment during childhood, they are often repressed. When a partial breakdown of repression leads to the renewed perception of danger from derivatives of the repressed impulses, a neurotic anxiety reaction will occur. Thus, neurotic anxiety involves a complex sequence of events in which derivatives of internal impulses evoke an anxiety reaction that signals the danger of further punishment if the impulses are expressed. Since the memory of the original punishment remains repressed, neurotic anxiety is experienced as "free-floating" or "objectless."

According to Freud, punishment for the expression of normal sexual and aggressive impulses, especially during childhood, may result in objective anxiety being converted into neurotic anxiety. Consider, for example, the sequence of events involved in the etiology of neurotic anxiety when a child is punished for aggressive behavior: (1) The child feels angry because his mother gives a younger sibling more attention and expresses his anger in aggressive behavior directed against the sibling. (2) He is immediately punished for his misdeed and accurately perceives his mother as a source of external danger. (3) On later occasions, whenever the child has angry thoughts or feelings that might instigate aggressive behavior likely to be punished by his mother, he will feel apprehensive about the possibility of being punished, i.e., objective anxiety. This sequence of events may be diagramed as follows:

Angry	(1)	Aggressive	(2)	External	(3)	Objective
Feelings	$\rightarrow$	behavior	$\rightarrow$	danger	$\rightarrow$	anxiety
				(Punishment)		

Although objective anxiety can be a useful signal to help a child avoid punishment by inhibiting the expression of angry impulses, severe punishment of aggressive acts can result in the conversion of objective anxiety into neurotic anxiety. The process of converting objective anxiety into neurotic anxiety involves the following sequence of events: (1) It begins when internal cues associated with previously punished behaviors arouse objective anxiety; (2) since objective anxiety is experienced as unpleasant, this may result in the repression of internal cues (i.e., thoughts or memories associated with the previously punished behaviors may be banished from awareness); (3) since repression is never final or complete, a breakdown in repression may permit derivatives of repressed thoughts (i.e., fragments or symbolic representations of traumatic events) to erupt into awareness; (4) these derivatives may then serve as danger signals that evoke neurotic anxiety reactions. This process is diagramed below:

Internal	(1)	Objective	(2)	Repression of
cues	$\rightarrow$	anxiety	$\rightarrow$	internal cues

Breakdown in	(3)	Derivatives of	(4)	Neurotic
repression	$\rightarrow$	repressed thoughts	$\rightarrow$	anxiety

Freud's distinction between neurotic and objective anxiety (fear) is useful as a conceptual framework for clinical practice and raises a number of provocative theoretical issues, but it is difficult to evaluate and verify in empirical research. Evaluation and verification would require a sensitive assessment of the magnitude of the danger associated with the evoking stimulus and precise measurement of the intensity of the anxiety reaction. The distinction also implies that fear (objective anxiety) and neurotic anxiety have different response properties, which would need to be operationally defined and measured.

In essence, Freud's concepts of neurotic and objective anxiety define anxiety as a complex psychobiological process with cognitive, affective, and behavioral components. In reviewing and commenting on process definitions of anxiety, I have previously made the following suggestion (Spielberger, 1972a):

The concept of anxiety-as-process implies a theory of anxiety that includes stress, threat, and state and trait anxiety as fundamental constructs or variables. The development of a comprehensive theory to account for anxiety phenomena must begin with a definition of the response properties of anxiety states. After these properties are conceptually identified, appropriate procedures for measuring them must be constructed. (p. 489)

Specifying the nature of anxiety as an emotional state (S-Anxiety) is thus an essential first step in formulating a meaningful theory of anxiety. But there is still much ambiguity, conceptual confusion, and wide disagreement with regard to how anxiety should be defined, as the readers of this volume will no doubt discover. Nevertheless, most definitions of anxiety refer to "an unpleasant emotional state or a condition marked by apprehension," as Sarason has noted in his chapter. Consistent with this prevailing convention, and with Freud's conception of anxiety as "something felt," I have proposed, as a conceptual definition of S-Anxiety, that it consists of subjective, consciously perceived, feelings of tension, apprehension, nervousness, and worry, accompanied by or associated with activation and arousal of the autonomic nervous system (Spielberger, 1966, 1972a, 1975a, 1975b, 1979).

Another important characteristic of anxiety as an emotional state is that S-Anxiety may vary in intensity and fluctuate over time as a function of the stresses that impinge on an individual. The intensity of an anxiety state may be measured by self-report scales such as Zuckerman's (1960; Zuckerman & Lubin, 1965, 1968) Affect Adjective Check List or the S-Anxiety scale of the State-Trait Anxiety Inventory (Spielberger, 1983, 1984), which assess the feelings experienced by a person at a particular moment in time, or by changes in physiological responses such as heart rate, blood pressure, and muscle action potential that reflect activation of the autonomic nervous system.

Research on stress and anxiety phenomena has now established that it is essential to distinguish between S-Anxiety as a transitory emotional state and relatively stable individual differences in anxiety proneness as a personality trait (T-Anxiety). Although S-Anxiety is occasionally experienced by everyone, there are substantial differences among people in the frequency and the intensity with which these states are experienced. The concept of trait anxiety refers to these individual differences in the tendency to see the world as dangerous and threatening, and in the frequency that S-Anxiety is experienced over long periods of time (Spielberger, 1972a, 1972b, 1979).

It should be noted that dispositions to experience T-Anxiety are reactive and remain latent until activated by the stress associated with a specific danger situation. Research has shown that persons who are high in T-Anxiety are more prone to perceive greater danger in their relationships with other people, responding to these threats with greater elevations in S-Anxiety than persons low in anxiety-proneness, especially in situations that involve threats to self-esteem (Spielberger, 1972b, 1975a, 1977, 1979). In contrast, persons who are high or low in trait anxiety do not appear to differ in their reactions to physical dangers such as the threat of electric shock (Hodges & Felling, 1970; Hodges & Spielberger, 1966) or imminent surgery (Spielberger, Auerbach, Wadsworth, Dunn, & Taulbee, 1973).

State and trait anxiety were first empirically identified by Cattell and Scheier (1958, 1961) in their factor analytic studies more than a quarter of a century ago. Since that time, these constructs have been assessed in numerous investigations of anxiety phenomena. Indeed, the State-Trait Anxiety Inventory alone has been used to measure anxiety in more than 2000 studies since it was published in 1970 (Spielberger, 1984).

A state-trait-process model of anxiety derived from the foregoing theoretical analysis and research findings (Spielberger, 1966, 1972a, 1972b, 1975a, 1975b, 1976, 1979) is diagramed in Fig. 1. Based on Freud's (1936) danger-signal theory of anxiety and Lazarus' (1966) conception of stress and coping, this model identifies the major classes of variables generally encountered in anxiety research. Each box in the diagram represents a critical element in the anxiety process, linking external stressors with state and trait anxiety, other internal mediators of anxiety reactions, and behavior. The arrows in the diagram refer to the hypothesized interactions among the components of the model and the possible influence of one element on another.

As can be seen in Fig. 1, the arousal of an anxiety state may be initiated by either external stressors or internal stimuli, e.g., thoughts, memories, feelings. Any stimulus or situation that is perceived or appraised as threatening will evoke

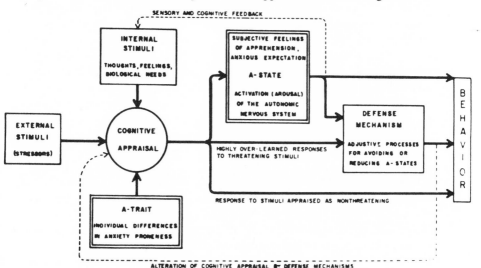

FIG. 1.   A state-trait-process model of anxiety. The model posits two anxiety constructs, state anxiety (A-State) and trait anxiety (A-Trait), and specifies the relationships between these constructs, external and internal stressors, cognitive appraisal of threat, and psychological defense mechanisms. Reprinted from Spielberger (1972a) with the permission of Academic Press, Inc.

an S-Anxiety reaction, irrespective of the real (objective) danger. The intensity and duration of this reaction will be proportional to the amount of threat the situation poses for the individual and the persistence of the evoking stimuli. The objective characteristics of a situation, the thoughts, memories, and feelings that are elicited or recalled, and the individual's coping skills and previous experience in dealing with similar circumstances all contribute to the appraisal of a situation as more or less threatening.

Individual differences in trait anxiety also contribute to threat appraisals. Although situations that involve objective physical danger are interpreted as threatening by most people, circumstances in which personal adequacy is evaluated are more likely to be perceived as threatening by people who are high in T-Anxiety than by those with low trait anxiety. In general, people high in trait anxiety are more vulnerable to being evaluated by others because they tend to be low in self-esteem and lack confidence in themselves.

High levels of state anxiety are experienced as extremely unpleasant and motivate behavior designed to eliminate or reduce the anxiety. Two obvious ways of reducing the anxiety aroused by an external danger are simply to avoid the source of danger or to modify the environment so the danger is reduced or eliminated. But people also adjust to stressful situations by engaging in unconscious psychological maneuvers or defenses that alter the way they see a situation without modifying the situation itself.

Psychological defense mechanisms modify, distort, or render unconscious the feelings, thoughts and memories that would otherwise provoke anxiety. To the extent that a defense mechanism is successful, a stressor will be appraised as less threatening, and there will be a corresponding reduction in the intensity of state anxiety. Although defense mechanisms are prominent in persons who suffer from anxiety disorders, there are relatively few measures available to assess them. The construction and development of objective measures for assessing psychological defenses should be given high priority in future research.

COMMENTS ON THE IZARD, LANG AND SARASON CHAPTERS

My comments on these chapters are offered in the context of the state-trait-process conception of anxiety described in the preceding section. Since Izard gives greater attention than the others to the nature of anxiety as an emotional state, his paper is considered first. Of the three papers, Sarason's deals most explicitly with the concept of trait anxiety and his paper is considered next. The wide range of anxiety phenomena considered by Lang makes it especially difficult to review his paper within the limits of the available space. Therefore, my comments focus largely on Lang's efforts to integrate the exciting current work on state-dependent learning and memory with anxiety research.

Izard's conception of emotions and their effects on behavior appears to be firmly grounded in principles of evolution, and highly consistent with Darwin's views on the nature of emotion. In defining emotions as innately programmed, motivating and adaptive organizers of experience, Izard calls our attention to the existence of a number of fundamental emotions and to patterns of human emotional experience that consist of variable combinations of fundamental emotions. Clearly, individual emotions rarely, if ever, occur in isolation.

I share Izard's view that emotions can be best understood within the context of their evolution as adaptive motivators and organizers of behavior, and his conviction that emotions must be analyzed in phenomenological terms, taking into account their unique neurophysiological and expressive components. But I strongly disagree with his definition of anxiety as a variable pattern of fundamental emotions. There are two basic issues of contention, namely, the criteria for defining the fundamental emotions and the specification of a finite list of emotions that meet these criteria.

For Izard, there are 10 fundamental emotions: Fear, anger, interest, joy, surprise, sadness, disgust, contempt, shyness (shame), and guilt. But firm empirical support for Izard's conception of fundamental emotions is lacking and other theorists have different views regarding the particular emotions they consider to be basic or "fundamental." My own list of basic emotions would currently include, but would not necessarily be limited to, anger, curiosity, and anxiety.

Anxiety is defined by Izard as a variable pattern of emotions that includes fear as the essential component, with interest, anger, guilt, shame, and shyness as the other components. However, the difference between Izard's conceptions of anxiety and fear and definitions of these constructs employed by other investigators may be largely semantic. For example, evidence of overlap between Izard's definition of fear and my own concept of S-Anxiety can be noted in examining the specific items that operationally define these concepts in Izard's Differential Emotions Scale (DES) and the State-Trait Anxiety Inventory (STAI). Essentially the same adjectives that are used to measure fear in the DES (afraid, fearful, scared, tense, uneasy) are among those employed to assess state and trait anxiety with the STAI.

A major methodological limitation in Izard's work stems from the fact that the DES subscales that he uses in assessing his 10 fundamental emotions are each comprised of only three items. From a psychometric perspective, the resulting measures are likely to be highly unstable. Moreover, the DES inquires about how frequently a particular feeling was experienced "during the past week," thus confounding trait (frequency) and state (intensity) concepts in a single measure. In contrast to the 3-item DES subscales, the STAI S-Anxiety and T-Anxiety scales each consist of 20 items, with explicit instructions to report the intensity and the frequency of specific feelings.

In Sarason's chapter, he appropriately criticizes prevailing definitions of anxiety as being too broad and difficult to apply, and containing vague terms that defy reliable assessment. Noting the diversity of the phenomena typically sub-sumed under the anxiety disorders, Sarason recommends a careful analysis and assessment of the cognitive processes that are characteristic of individuals suf-fering from different types of anxiety disorders. On the basis of the literature and his own research findings, he notes that anxious persons "continually scan situations for potential dangers," and that their thought processes are critically determined by habitual expectations of censure and rejection, and by irrational beliefs about personal adequacy and self-worth.

There is strong clinical and empirical support for Sarason's view of the centrality of cognition in the evocation and maintenance of anxiety states, and in determining their influence on learning, problem solving, and performance. Izard's conception of anxiety as a variable pattern of emotions, Freud's Danger Signal Theory, and the State-Trait-Process Theory discussed earlier in this chap-ter also emphasize the critical role of cognitive processes in anxiety. But these theories consider the phenomenology of anxiety—the unpleasant feelings of tension, apprehension, nervousness, and fear—to be the basic, distinctive, and unique defining properties of anxiety as an emotional state.

In using terms such as "hot cognitions," "emotional distress" and "painful worries," Sarason acknowledges unpleasant, disturbing feelings as a component of anxiety, but the nature of these feelings and their relation to the other three major components of anxiety identified in his paper (cognitions, bodily reactions, and behavior) are left largely unspecified. Moreover, Sarason's ambivalence and reluctance to accept the legitimacy of unpleasant feelings as a component of anxiety are reflected in his comments on the results of recent experiments with his Reactions to Tests (RTT) and Cognitive Interference Questionnaire (CIQ). Apparently, Sarason would prefer to reinterpret feelings of anxiety in terms of cognition processes and bodily reactions as is suggested in the following quotation:

> Do the phrases "I am tense" and "I am worried" simply differ semantically, or do they refer to different phenomenological and bodily experiences? . . . . To the extent that statements such as "I feel tense" are simply a way of saying, "I am worried" the distinction between worry and emotionality becomes blurred.

The state-trait distinction is explicitly recognized by Sarason (1978) in his research on test anxiety, which he defines as a situation-specific personality trait. The Test Anxiety Scale (TAS), which Sarason introduced more than 25 years ago (Sarason, 1958; Sarason & Ganzer, 1962), inquires about the thoughts and feelings experienced during examinations, but does not provide independent assessments of worry and emotionality as components of test anxiety (Spielber-ger, 1980). In contrast, the RTT, CIQ, and the Thought Occurrence Question-naire (TOQ) described by Sarason in this volume are concerned primarily with the assessment of the cognitive aspects of anxiety. In attempting to assess worry cognitions and other thoughts that occur while a person is actually performing on a task, Sarason has conceptually and operationally extended the state-trait distinction to the assessment of cognitive processes.

Lang is centrally concerned with understanding the nature and organization of cognitive and physiological responses in fear and anxiety, which he views as complex "conglomerate" concepts. He poses a series of provocative questions with regard to the basic phenomena of anxiety, and identifies what he considers to be three fundamental underlying dimensions (arousal, direction, and control) on the basis of which these phenomena can be categorized and objectively measured. The scope of the laboratory and clinical studies that he reviews, his efforts to integrate recent developments in cognitive psychology with research on fear and anxiety, and his own studies of pathological fear as manifested in phobic patients are truly impressive.

The cutting edge of Lang's research focuses on how anxiety responses are stored in associative memory and subsequently aroused in persons who suffer from different types of anxiety disorders. Based on his assumptions about the specificity of the organization of cognitive-psychophysiological events in memory, Lang proposes a continuum of anxiety disorders. One extreme is anchored by focal phobias, in which the stored cognitive-psychophysiological content is highly specific and limited. Generalized anxiety states, in which the underlying affective response programs are associatively linked to many different cues and assumed to "float in memory," define the other extreme, with obsessions and compulsions, social anxiety, and agoraphobia falling at intermediate positions on this continuum.

The notion that cognitive and psychophysiological aspects of emotion are stored in networks of associative memory as action-programs that can be activated by a variety of stimuli is an exciting conceptual contribution to the understanding of phobias and other types of anxiety disorders. Evidence cited by Lang from studies of state-dependent learning, demonstrating that emotional states at the time of learning can have substantial influence on the recall of previous events, provides impressive support for his major thesis, as does his own research on the effects of induced emotional imagery on the response processing of phobic patients.

I strongly agree with Lang's conclusion that studies of emotion-dependent learning should be given a high priority in future research on anxiety and the anxiety disorders. In addition to clarifying the basic nature of anxiety as a complex psychobiological response, investigations of the associative networks that link cognitive and physiological components of anxiety would seem to have extremely important implications for the treatment of patients suffering from anxiety disorders. There is, however, a curious incongruity in Lang's conception of anxiety that seems to reflect limiting epistemological assumptions that have an adverse impact on his measurement operations.

At the beginning of his chapter, Lang states: "For most patients the basic datum of anxiety is their feeling state, i.e., a direct experience of internal apprehension, requiring no further definition." Thus, Lang explicitly acknowledges that the feelings associated with an anxiety state are its unique defining property, a view that is quite consistent with the conceptions of anxiety as an emotional state discussed in the preceding section of this chapter. Nevertheless, Lang concludes that "feeling states are completely private and represent a poor data source for the clinician preparing to undertake treatment." As a consequence of the implicit epistemological bias reflected in this statement, Lang tends to ignore anxious feelings or attempts to redefine them in cognitive or psychophysiological terms.

Given the impressive evidence from Lang's research and studies of state-dependent learning that emotions can influence information processing and retrieval, should we not try to obtain sensitive measures of the unique feeling qualities that are associated with emotional states? While Lang accepts verbal reports of fear and dread as "part of the primary response of anxiety," he reports very little information about the assessment of emotional feelings in his own research, and seems to place much greater faith and emphasis on cognitive, physiological, and behavioral responses.

SUMMARY

Papers on cognition, emotion and the psychophysiology of anxiety by Carroll Izard, Peter Lang and Irwin Sarason were reviewed in this chapter. Differences in the theoretical and philosophical assumptions and in the research objectives and methods that have characterized the work of these distinguished contributors to theory and research on emotion, anxiety, and the anxiety disorders were examined within the context of a state-trait-process conceptual model. The evolution of fear and anxiety as psychological constructs and Freud's Libido and Danger Signal Theories of anxiety were also briefly discussed.

9 Theoretical Perspectives on Clinical Anxiety

Aaron T. Beck
University of Pennsylvania

MYSTERIES OF ANXIETY

In attempting to understand the phenomenon of anxiety, we might start by considering some typical anecdotes of individuals who are smitten with this malady.

A world renowned pianist on a concert tour abroad suddenly discovers to his chagrin that his hands begin to shake and his fingers stiffen as he sits down to play before an audience. Moreover, he finds his heart is racing so fast he is afraid it will burst.

A brilliant young woman going out for the first time with a man she admires finds that her "mind goes blank" and when she starts to speak her words come out as a whisper—without a sound.

A physician observing a mutilated body is overwhelmed with feelings of nausea, faintness, shortness of breath, and his mind is full of images of being disgraced.

A paradoxical aspect of the above scenarios is that what the individual most desperately wants not to happen is exactly what does happen. Any satisfactory explanatory model of anxiety should be able to explain these paradoxes. It would certainly be most useful to us in understanding the plight of these individuals and attempting to help them if we could identify a specific cause or mechanism and then prescribe a specific treatment, as medical science has done for phenylketonuria and tuberculosis. However, in the light of our present knowledge, it seems unlikely that a complex phenomenon like anxiety will be decipherable by a simple code, that it will be reducible to a specific derangement of hormones or neurotransmitters, to an aberrant stimulus-response connection, or to an irrational cognition.

Rather, anxiety is more likely to surrender its secrets if we stop viewing it simply as a disease with a specific etiology and begin to study it from a number of perspectives. If we acknowledge at the start that no one perspective will yield the correct or only explanation, we may then get a composite picture that will begin to make sense out of this puzzling problem and may point the way to solving it.

Several inferences may be gleaned from the examples just presented. First, the symptoms run counter to important goals: They seem powerful enough to interfere with the person's career or highly valued interpersonal objectives as well as devastating the person's morale. Second, the symptoms may appear in many forms and involve different systems: the motor system (stiff and trembling fingers) in the case of the pianist; primarily parasympathetic innervation (faintness and nausea) in the case of the physician; and mental and vocal inhibition of the college student.

Each of the theories of anxiety represents a particular perspective of this state. The various perspectives should attempt to cast some light on why a problem that is potentially so devastating can be so universal and also take so many different forms. Depending on his perspective, the investigator will look for certain types of data, select instruments to obtain and measure these data, and make inferences and generalizations on the basis of what he finds. Thus, the neurochemical perspective may lead the researcher to assay metabolites of hormones or neurotransmitters and present explanations of anxiety based on the result. Operating from a psychopharmacological perspective, the investigator will observe what drugs precipitate panic attacks and which relieve or prevent them and will build a theory based on those findings.

The behavioral perspective consists of the study and conceptualization of anxiety in terms of molar behavior such as avoidance and measures of autonomic responses prior to and following behavioral interventions. The cognitive perspective will focus on the individual's cognitive appraisals and their influence on his behavior and affect. The developmental and psychodynamic perspectives will concentrate on data from childhood and observe the progressions of early patterns into the clinical anxiety appearing later in life.

It should be clear from the foregoing that no particular perspective has an exclusive claim on the domain of anxiety or is likely to provide a complete explanation. To avoid the type of reductionism that is inherent in the commitment to a single perspective, investigators would do well to be familiar with the other perspectives. An even greater service would be performed, however, by combining several approaches simultaneously (for example, the neurochemical, pharmacological, behavioral, cognitive, and developmental) and specifying commonalities from one perspective to the next.

The first perspective attempts to place the construct of anxiety in the broad context of the evolution of our species. This perspective is relevant to the question of how a condition that seems to be so maladaptive could have eluded the workings of natural selection or, alternatively, how this condition represents a pattern that was selected by evolutionary mechanisms on the basis of its adaptational value. The proposal is advanced that the nonadaptiveness of the anxiety disorders is due to the fact that although our environment has changed over the millennia, our innate protective mechanisms have remained the same. Next, looking at anxiety in terms of individual functions, I examine how the patterning of symptoms is an expression of protective and defensive functions that are normally adaptive. Further I explore how specific patterns of symptoms may be analyzed as specific strategies for dealing with danger. Proceeding from an affective perspective, I compare the antecedents of anxiety with those of anger, joy, and sadness and also explore the relationship of these "normal" reactions to the "abnormal states" of anxiety disorders, paranoid disorders, mania, and depression. Finally, the cognitive perspective is used to show how a shift in formal information processing can lead to the affective behavioral and autonomic aspects of anxiety.

These above perspectives are by no means exhaustive and have been chosen to illustrate how different views of the condition of anxiety will provide different explanatory models. In addition to the perspectives to be discussed, the anatomical, pharmacological, neurochemical, and interpersonal perspectives all provide important data and models for understanding anxiety.

AN EVOLUTIONARY PERSPECTIVE

The first perspective on clinical anxiety represents an attempt to understand this disorder not as a disease but as a basic biological mechanism that apparently has had survival value (see Plutchick, 1980). Since the term "anxiety" is generally applied to a subjective experience, I use the term "fear" to apply to the cognitive-behavioral component of the response to perceived danger (Beck, 1976).

A reasonable argument may be mustered to support the proposition that fear must have had a significant evolutionary advantage to have persisted in our behavioral repertoire. In order to have continued in the gene pool for thousands of generations and remained as ubiquitous as any type of human experience, fear and anxiety must have contributed in significant ways to adaptation to a dangerous environment. Their value, however, may have diminished as our environment has changed over the millennia. In many ways we may be like animals in a zoo: Our innate repertoire has not changed since we roamed the plains and forests, but the environment has changed. The types of threats humans encounter have shifted from those directed primarily at our physical well-being to those directed at our psychological well-being. But we are genetically pro-grammed to react in terms of the more primitive threats that our distant ancestors faced in the early development of the species. Although we become as fully mobilized in reaction to threats as did our forebears in the wild, we are now caged in by all kinds of social constraints and restraints that prevent this mobi-lization (e.g., fight or flight) from being translated into action.

In primitive environments, anxiety could have served a very useful purpose. If an individual perceived his environment as threatening and himself as vul-nerable, then an anxiety response would be valuable in spurring him to protect himself or to get away from the threatening situation. The problem is that contemporary homo sapiens has to deal less with the physical threats of a pri-mitive environment than with psychosocial threats. Although the individual becomes fully mobilized to flee in the face of psychosocial threats (for example, to being devalued for poor performance), this response is generally not acceptable or adaptive. So humans become mobilized for action when action is inappropriate and, consequently, like an animal in the zoo, we tend to suffer a variety of psychological and physical ailments resulting from a mismatch between our innate patterns of adaptation and our current environment.

Another factor that may contribute to the persistence of anxiety through the millennia is the survival value of anxiety in the form of false alarms (false positives) in response to danger rather than insufficient alarms (false negatives). We can continue to live with false positives, but we may not survive after false negatives. The saying "Evolution favors anxious genes" seems to have real truth value. The evolutionary perspective allows us to identify common denominators of the responses to threat in a variety of species. The further understanding of these behavioral patterns in anxiety may be promoted by studying the reactions to threat of nonhuman animals in their natural habitats (see Marks, 1969). Further evidence may be obtained through ethological investigations of animal patterns and comparing them to human patterns.

A FUNCTIONAL PERSPECTIVE

Symptoms and Systems

We can now turn from a consideration of the phylogenetic aspect of anxiety to a focus on the individual and specifically on the operation of the various systems that facilitate adaptation to the environment. It is notable that the specific classes of *symptoms* associated with anxiety correspond to the *functions* of specific systems and subsystems: cognitive (or information processing), affective, behav-ioral, and physiological (including sympathetic and parasympathetic subsys-tems). These systems do not function autonomously, but are integrated into a master program, serving the basic requirements of the organism. The master system is programmed to carry out certain objectives (e.g., self-preservation, feeding, and breeding) and coordinates the specific systems in order to implement that master plan.

The clinical symptoms of anxiety disorders represent an excessive activity of these systems. Since an anachronistic pattern of response is activated in response to a perceived danger, we get symptoms instead of adaptation. Moreover, the specific patterns of protective responses (e.g., fight, flight, freeze, or faint) differ from each other even though the same apparatus (anatomical, neural, behavioral) is employed.

Under normal conditions the patterning of the specific activities of the systems changes as the organism switches from one function to another, depending on the demands of the situation and the master program. Operation of the apparatus proceeds according to a comprehensible design under control of the cognitive component. The cognitive or information-processing component draws on peripheral and central sensory systems to construct meaningful patterns at the perceptual level. It integrates inputs, selects an appropriate plan, and thus activates the rest of the behavioral, affective, and physiological systems.

When the organism is confronted with a threat, the cognitive system processes information about the threatening situation and the available coping resources, determines whether a clear and present danger exists, and sets in motion the sequence of affective, behavioral, and physiological responses. The affective system, specifically subjective anxiety, spurs protective action by enhancing the sense of urgency. The behavioral system consists of a variety of motor patterns and selective inhibitions, while the physiological system provides autonomic components that "service" the motor apparatus.

The presumed lack of concordance (desynchrony) of various measures of anxiety may be explained on the basis of the different levels of activation of the various systems, which are tapped by these measures (see Barlow & Beck, 1984; Lang, 1979). The expectation that these systems should co-vary in a uniform fashion is based on a simplistic notion of the nature of the response to danger. It seems more likely that in order to prepare to deal effectively with dangers, the systems contribute in varying degrees—depending on the specific stage of the response and the strategy that is selected. The patterning of the systems changes as the sequence shifts from sounding an alert, to defining the danger, to assessing and selecting appropriate coping strategies, to mobilizing the appropriate motor apparatus, and to providing appropriate autonomic innervations to support the mobilization. The operation of the master system and the component systems continues to shift as feedback is integrated. Hence, the relative contribution of each system and subsystem fluctuates from one moment to the next.

Take, for example, a blood phobic. Prior to entering a blood bank, his muscles are tense, his blood pressure is raised, and he can think only of running away.

As he enters the room and feels the needle in his arm, his blood pressure drops precipitously and he thinks he is dying. If the investigator takes into account such continually changing relationships, it is likely that the samples of cognition, affect, behavior, and physiological activities will fit into a more comprehensible pattern.

The coupling of the autonomic and somatic nervous systems reflects the kind of strategy that is selected (flight, freeze, faint). A major function of the autonomic activity is to facilitate motor activity through regulating blood supply, metabolism, and temperature. The type of autonomic innervation, thus, is contingent on the specific behavioral pattern (approach, avoid, escape) rather than on the affect (anxiety, anger, love). Consequently, a specific combination of autonomic and motor patterns will be used for escape, a different combination for freezing, and still different for fainting. However the subjective sensation—anxiety—will be approximately the same for each strategy.

The activation of the somatic nervous system and the autonomic nervous system is consistent with the specific cognitive set. Thus a hypervigilant set (preparation for flight, fight, or defense) may be reflected in a rigid posture ("freezing") and an increase in blood pressure and heart rate, whereas a "helpless" set may be manifested in a slump or an actual fall associated with a drop in heart rate and blood pressure. An active, coping set is generally associated with sympathetic nervous system dominance, whereas a passive set, triggered by what is perceived an an overwhelming threat, is often associated with parasympathetic dominance (as in the case of the blood phobic, cited previously). In either case the subjective experience of anxiety is similar.

It should be emphasized that a person manifests the same type of physical response in reaction to a psychosocial threat as to a physical threat. The same motor and autonomic patterns, such as defensive stiffening, sweating, pulse and blood pressure changes, occur in anticipation of making a speech as in anticipation of armed attack. Similarly, a psychosocial *or* a physical threat may lead to the same sympathetically dominant inhibition of action (muscular rigidity, blocking, muteness). The shock of bad news or of losing blood from a wound may lead to muscular flaccidity and loss of postural control, and ultimately fainting, usually associated with parasympathetic dominance.

The profound mobilization of the systems is usually counterproductive in the ordinary situations of psychosocial threat. An individual with test anxiety or public speaking anxiety becomes fixated on the "ultimate disaster": poor performance, failing or being rejected. Thoughts of failure or rejection, though extraneous to the immediate performance task, are central to the "danger" and are consequently exaggerated. Simultaneously, concentration, planning, recall relevant to the task are "extraneous" to the danger and consequently blocked. It should be emphasized that fear-induced blockage of selective focus and memory retrieval is an active process. During panic, there appears to be a corresponding selective inhibition of reflective activity and reality testing.

Primitive "Strategies"

The phenomenon of anxiety represents but one of many separate automatic "strategies" for dealing with threat and thus can be best conceptualized within the total framework of the organism's responses to danger. In the broadest sense, these strategies include not only patterns generally associated with anxiety, but also the class of hostile behaviors associated with anger. Cannon (1929) formulated the well-known paradigm of the "fight-flight reaction" to designate the basic physiological patterns of response to threat. The individual, however, is endowed with a much broader range of specific protective mechanisms, each designed to deal with specific dangers. These other protective responses range from defending against entry of noxious substances to defending against an external blow, inhibiting one's own actions, and fainting. A more comprehensive label than Cannon's for the survival strategies would be the "Fight-Flight-Freeze-Faint Reaction."

I apply the label "primal responses" to these protective behaviors because (1) they represent an initial line of defense against threat, (2) they are primitive in that they may be observed in other primates, and (3) they are automatic, non-rational and to a large extent, involuntary. One group of primal protective reactions consists of discrete reflexes designed to ward off or eject potentially harmful agents. These reflexes include eyeblink, gagging, sneezing, coughing, bronchospasm, vomiting, and diarrhea. A more complex set of reflexive behaviors is designed to defend against trauma to the body as a whole. The response to such threats includes such actions as ducking, dodging, flinching, retracting, and stiffening. Threats of losing one's balance or being submerged in deep water activate a reflex clutching or grabbing. The sudden perception that one is at the edge of a cliff activates a recoiling or stiffening response.

The instant automatic responses described above consist of discrete reflexes involving the somatic nervous system: eyelid reflex, sneezing, coughing, flinching, and fainting. Although carried out by "voluntary" muscles, these reflexive actions are automatic and involuntary. Their adaptational value depends on their speed and their ability to bypass the slower-acting volitional processes.

Another type of response, geared to counteract less imperative threats, is mediated by the slower-acting autonomic nervous system. This set of defense operations includes nausea, vomiting, and diarrhea. These responses have a more gradual onset and build-up than reflexes such as coughing and gagging, which are designed to neutralize more vital threats—namely blockage of the airway. The more gradual gastrointestinal responses can provide adequate protection against the danger of absorption of irritating substances without requiring immediate action.

Freezing.   Inhibition of action by muscular rigidity, blocking, or aphonia is associated with sympathetic dominance. Muscular and vocal inhibition may reflect a pattern of self-protection. Vocal inhibition appears to be derived from a primitive "silencing" or "stilling" strategy such as avoiding being observed by a predator. Muscular flaccidity and loss of postural control is associated with parasympathetic dominance.

Fainting.   Many people show a rather curious response to receiving injections, withdrawal of blood, and piercing injuries—or upon observing these traumas occurring to others. They evidence a pronounced drop in blood pressure, profuse sweating, and faintness. This fainting response, markedly present in "blood phobias," may best be understood as an archaic mechanism designed to minimize blood loss (and possibly reduce mobility) when a person is subjected to a penetrating unavoidable attack. This response also occurs in many people when they perceive (or misperceive) a threat as overwhelming and themselves as defenseless and vulnerable.

Flight.   In contrast to fainting and freezing, flight is a "voluntary" response in that the actions are under voluntary control. However, it seems likely that the autonomic and motor mobilization for flight is involuntary or automatic; what is voluntary is the ability to utilize the state of mobilization or else to inhibit such actions.

Anxiety Reduction Mechanism.   The most familiar type of primal response depends on the generation of unpleasant subjective sensations that prompt a volitional, intentional action designed to reduce danger. The wide variety of voluntary actions instigated by anxiety fall into this category. Thus, the arousal of anxiety when a driver feels that he is not in complete control of the car prompts him to reduce his speed until he again feels in control. Similarly, the sense of faintness or dizziness experienced when climbing or approaching the edge of a cliff prods an individual to get a better grip or to back off to a safer position.

Another type of "protective" reaction associated with anxiety is illustrated by panic attacks. This condition is generally characterized by a fear of an impending internal disaster (heart attack, stroke, mental derangement) and a sense of loss of control over physical and mental functions. The sense of being unable to direct one's thinking and behavior may reflect an inhibition of higher level cognition and is a particularly disabling feature. Moreover, since the person attributes the symptoms to some dangerous internal disturbance, he is at a loss how to eliminate it and is swept by a sense of helplessness. Some types of panic attack may be viewed as an alarm evoked to warn of an overwhelming danger and as a stimulus to escape from the situation and to seek help or refuge. Other types of panic attack are also evoked in the face of an "overwhelming" external threat. This condition is seen when a phobic individual is suddenly exposed to a phobic situation. For example, an individual with claustrophobia may have a catastrophic reaction (feeling of being suffocated) when put in a closed space. Hence, the solution is simple: get out of the situation and stay out. The need for help is not as imperative as when the individual feels threatened by an overwhelming internal "danger," as in the agoraphobic syndrome.

AN AFFECTIVE PERSPECTIVE

The anxiety disorders may be viewed as being on the same continuum as "normal" cognitive-affect-behavioral responses to life situations. If we examine four basic emotions (affects), we can identify specific settings in which they occur. Thus, sadness appears to be evoked when there is a perception of loss, a defeat or deprivation—frequently in the form of unfulfilled or disconfirmed positive expectations (disappointment or disillusionment). The usual consequence is to withdraw the investment in the particular source of disappointment. Elation, in contrast, follows from a perceived gain and this is likely to reinforce activity toward achieving a goal. In contrast to sadness and gladness, which are related to positive goals, anxiety and anger are aroused in response to threats. Anxiety is evoked when the individual is concerned about the outcome of being vulnerable (namely, being hurt or killed), and he or she consequently is impelled to withdraw. In contrast, the focus of anger is not on the individual's vulnerability, but is directed to the offensive qualities of the threat. Consequently, the behavioral inclination is to expunge the threat by attack.

The clinical syndromes appear to represent exaggerated forms of the normal emotional reactions. For example, in depression the sense of defeat or deprivation, the sadness, and the withdrawal of interest in previous goals are intensified and prolonged. In mania, in contrast, there is a heightened investment in expansion. Anxiety disorders are characterized by a generalized and intensified sense of vulnerability and a consequent automatic mobilization for self-defense or escape. Similarly, in paranoid disorders, the perception of being mistreated is generalized across all situations and leads to anger and a mobilization to counterattack.

Anxiety is a dramatic experience that generally overshadows other components of the response to threat. We experience an intensely unpleasant emotion in response to danger and are strongly moved by the experience of anxiety to take steps to reduce it and to prevent its recurrence. Furthermore, in analyzing psychopathological disorders such as panic attack, we are inclined to highlight the unpleasant experience of anxiety as the central, overriding factor in the disturbance. Anxiety, however, is not *the* pathological process in so-called anxiety disorders any more than the skin rash or fever represents the pathological process in yellow fever.

Humans are constructed in such a way as to ascribe great significance to the experience of anxiety so that we will be impelled to take measures to reduce it. But we should not allow nature's mechanism for dramatizing the feeling of anxiety mislead us into believing that this most salient subjective experience plays the pivotal role in the anxiety disorders.

Anxiety operates as an "attention-getter." It forces attention away from our preoccupations and directs it to this unpleasant subjective experience. The experience is generally sufficiently unpleasant to spur the individual to terminate it. He does this by adopting a shift in behavior, e.g., from advancing into an unsafe area to pulling back from it. Also, by alerting the individual to the notion that he can be hurt, anxiety induces him to curb reckless action or to initiate defensive behavior.

The role of anxiety may be likened to that of pain. The experience of pain impels us to do something in order to stop the pain: This may be achieved by terminating whatever activity is producing an injury. However, pain is not the disease (e.g., a fracture, appendicitis) or the primary lesion. Similarly, anxiety is not the cause of a disturbance. In the anxiety disorders, the unremitting generation of this affect represents a perseverative, ineffective way to impel the organism to reduce the danger that is activating the anxiety response. However, when the problem is not an actual danger but a misperception or exaggeration of the danger, the generation of anxiety is a futile, counterproductive mechanism for instigating remedial action.

The locus of the disorder in the anxiety states is not in the affective system but in the *hypervalent cognitive schemas* relevant to danger that are continually presenting a view of reality as dangerous and the self as vulnerable (Beck, 1963). These "fear schemas" (cognitive structures utilized to process information relevant to danger) interact with environmental and internal stimuli to yield frightening interpretations. The degree of anxiety is proportional to the degree of misperceived danger. This concept leads us to consideration of anxiety disorders from a cognitive perspective.

A COGNITIVE PERSPECTIVE

Since information processing is assigned a primary role in activating affective and behavioral functions, it is valuable to focus specifically on this system. The cognitive content in normal anxiety or clinical anxiety is centered around the notion of danger. When an anxious individual considers a problematic situation, he may be drawn to consider the most negative consequences. Although it may be adaptive under some circumstances to anticipate the "worst possible case," the patient with clinical anxiety is fixated on ideas of extreme outcomes and therefore becomes over-prepared to deal with physical or social threats. Although it is conceivable that this extreme anticipation ("catastrophizing") might occasionally be adaptive in providing a "preview" of a possible outcome, this mobilization thwarts realistic problem solving in most situations.

The antecedent of anxiety may be an automatic thought or a visual image relevant to danger. The patient may become so immersed in the image that he believes to some degree that the noxious event is actually occurring. It should be noted, however, that a person may have a cognitive set relevant to danger without necessarily experiencing any spontaneous thoughts or images relevant to danger. For example, when a patient states that he is feeling tense for no apparent reason, the cognitive set may be identified through introspection. By focusing on the thoughts that occur in association with the experience of anxiety, the patient is able to provide information that indicates the nature of his cognitive set (Beck, 1963).

In situations of presumed danger, the cognitive channels are cleared of "irrelevant" data in favor of perception, cognition, and recall of data relevant to the danger. Thus, there is not only a selective enhancement of stimulus configurations relevant to danger, but also a selective suppression of data that are not congruent with the perceived danger.

This mechanism is obviously counterproductive when the danger is of personal devaluation rather than physical attack. An individual with test anxiety or public speaking anxiety may become fixated on his vulnerability to the "ultimate" threat; for example, failing or being rejected. Although fears of ultimate failure or rejection are extraneous to the immediate requirements of the task, they are central to the perceived threat and are, consequently, magnified in terms of the primitive response to danger. Concentration, reasoning, and recall relevant to performance are thus inhibited since they are not congruent with the fantasized danger.

The blockage of concentration and memory retrieval is an active process found notably in test anxiety and panic disorder. Thus, the panicky individual is prevented from devising and applying strategies to cope with danger because the mechanisms for reasoning and reflective thinking are inhibited. The inhibition of higher level cognitive processes is one of the key problems in panic disorders and may explain why the patient has difficulty in "reasoning his way out of the panic." Even though he knows prior to the attack that it is not dangerous, he is unable to apply this knowledge once the attack has started.

The controlling cognitive content triggers (a) the motor components specifically designed for coping with danger (e.g., flight, freeze, or faint), (b) the physiological component (specifically, the autonomic nervous system) that facilitates the action of the specific motor component, and (c) the affective component, specifically anxiety. Continuous anxiety, inhibitions, and palpitations when there is no objective threat may be attributed to the continuous processing of situations as dangerous. Since the individual's concept of the dangerousness of the problematic situation is erroneous or exaggerated, there is no possibility for developing or applying coping skills because there is no objective danger for which the coping will be appropriate. Hence the individual continues in a state of inappropriate mobilization.

Normal reactions as well as clinical syndromes are conceived as being mediated by primal cognitive processes, analogous to Freud's concept of the primary process. Thus, the primal conceptualizations of situations tend to be global, and relatively crude. Higher level cognitive processing is more specific and refined and, when functioning properly, provides a reality testing and correction of the global, primal conceptualizations. These corrective functions, analogous to Freud's concept of the secondary process, appear to be impaired in psychopathology. Consequently, the usual "ceiling" over anger, anxiety and elation has become attenuated as is the "floor" under sadness. Concomitant with the weakening of higher level cognitive processes, the primal responses escalate, leading to a full-blown psychopathological syndrome.

Research Studies of Cognition in the Anxiety Disorders

In a study of 10 patients with "free-floating" anxiety, Beck (1970) found a meaningful correlation between the patient's cognitions and fluctuations in his level of anxiety. The major theme in these cognitions was the concept of personal danger. Beck, Laude, and Bohnert (1974) studied 32 cases of anxiety neurosis and noted that 27 of these cases had visual fantasies, as well as automatic thoughts relevant to the theme of danger. The dominant theme in the individuals' cognitions related to imminent danger involving physical well-being or loss of bodily or mental control. The most prominent themes evolved around the fears of dying, social rejection, disease, and failure. Similar themes were reported by Mathews and Shaw (1977) in a smaller sample of patients with anxiety neurosis. Sewitch and Kirsch (1984) reported naturalistic evidence for the predominance of threat-related thoughts associated with anxiety.

Other studies including control groups indicated a link between anxiety and cognitive content associated with danger. Gentil and Lader (1978) found that the theme of danger differentiated the dream content of anxious patients from those of normal controls. Finlay-Jones and Brown (1981) found that severe life events or threats classed as "dangers" differentiated anxiety patients from cases of depression who had a higher proportion of events relevant to loss. Butler and Mathews (1983) found that anxious individuals overestimated the subjective personal risk of a number of items relevant to personal harm. The results are not completely conclusive in terms of the anxiety syndrome, since a group of depressed patients who also scored higher in anxiety than did the anxiety patients also overestimated the subjective personal risk. Finally, Hibbert (in press) reported that patients with generalized anxiety disorder showed a dominance of themes of danger associated with the experience of anxiety.

SUGGESTIONS FOR FUTURE RESEARCH

The various perspectives presented in this chapter can provide a framework for future research that may provide useful data relevant to the diagnosis, treatment, and prevention of clinical anxiety.

Many ethological studies have shown patterns of reactions to threats in animals that closely parallel those observed in humans. Developmental studies have shown that the responses of human infants to strangers or ledges are similar to those observed in nonhuman animals (Marks, 1969). Both the types of threats evoking a fear response and the specific patterns or strategies should be studied further in human and nonhuman species. Such studies should cast light on the difference between an adaptive and nonadaptive response.

The systems perspective can be usefully employed by making concomitant observations of various systems in a threat situation as shown by Barlow and Beck (1984). Specific experiments designed to activate the threat response may allow sampling the blood to determine neuroendocrine changes, making physiological recordings, and correlating these findings with sampling of self-reported mood and cognitive set.

Further, the effect of specific interventions (behavioral, cognitive, and pharmacological) on these systems may clarify their interactions. Simons, Garfield, and Murphy (1984) conducted such a study of depression treated with drugs or with cognitive therapy. They found that not only did successful cognitive therapy produce changes in dysfunctional attitudes and information processes but successful pharmacotherapy produced the same changes in cognitive processing. Their findings suggest that therapeutic approaches derived from different perspectives may have a common site of action.

The affective perspective can cast light on the mechanisms of anxiety by comparing this state with other states that are instigated by threat or other stressors. The similarities and contrasts with normal states such as sadness, anger, and euphoria as well as depression, paranoid state, or mania may give valuable clues about specific antecedent conditions most likely to instigate a particular state. Furthermore, experimental activation of anxiety or depression in individuals prone to these conditions can provide valuable insights. In view of the frequent association between depression and anxiety, studies of the relationships, overlaps, and distinguishing features of those disorders should be especially fruitful.

The cognitive perspective has a broad range of applicability. Studies of automatic thought aroused in response to danger or loss can explore the specificity of particular cognitive sets to specific reported affects. Investigators of the relationship of imagery to anxiety in generalized anxiety disorders, panic disorders, agoraphobia, and specific phobias can explore the cognitive structure of these conditions. Furthermore, the identification of the specific "cognitive profile" of anxiety may help to differentiate this disorder from other conditions such as depression as well as delineate the subtypes of the anxiety disorders.

CONCLUSION

The understanding of clinical anxiety can best be promoted by studying this condition from a variety of perspectives. No one perspective is likely to provide an adequate explanation of clinical anxiety but a combination of different approaches can help to fit together the various pieces of the puzzle. It is essential that investigators recognize the limitations and nonexclusivity of their own perspectives as well as recognize the contributions emerging from other vantage points. A major pitfall that needs to be avoided is biological or psychological reductionism. A variety of research studies using a number of different models is most likely to advance our knowledge of the causes and treatment of clinical anxiety.

C. Learning and Animal Models

10 Animal Models of Anxiety-Based Disorders: Their Usefulness and Limitations

Susan Mineka
University of Wisconsin–Madison

The study of emotions such as fear and sadness in animals dates back at least to Darwin (1872), whereas the study in animals of their more extreme "neurotic" counterparts such as phobias, anxiety, and depression did not begin until some years later (e.g., Pavlov, 1927). In the 1930s and 1940s there was a large spurt of interest in this country in Pavlov's so-called "neuroses of the experiment," as work began on this topic in many now well-known laboratories, e.g., Liddell, Gantt, Masserman, N. R. F. Maier. This early work on what became known as experimental neurosis received a fair amount of attention and was clearly influential in establishing the foundations of behavioral approaches to the etiology of neurotic disorders, as well as behavioral therapeutic approaches for their treatment. Unfortunately, however, this early work was largely unsystematic and not very focused toward documenting whether real similarities existed between the animal disorders and supposedly parallel human disorders. Instead, in most cases each investigator explored the effects of one or more conditioning paradigms (often discovered accidentally) that seemed to produce disturbed behavior in their animals, without systematically manipulating various aspects of the procedure to determine what the critical features were, and without attempting to demonstrate compelling phenotypic or functional similarities to the symptoms of neurotic disorders in humans.

As a consequence of this failure to systematically investigate the causal factors in the development of experimental neuroses, and to demonstrate compelling similarities to human neurotic disorders, the use of animal models for psychopathological disorders fell into disfavor for a good many years. Recent work on animal models has, however, been more successful because investigators have attempted to document similarities in symptomatology, etiology, and therapy between the animal model and the human disorder (e.g., McKinney, 1974;

Seligman, 1974, 1975; Wolpe, 1958). Thus, for example, Wolpe attempted to demonstrate the similarity between his cats' phobic responses to the boxes in which they had been shocked and anxiety-based disorders in humans. He made a case for a common etiology (classical conditioning of fear or anxiety) and a common therapy (extinction of anxiety through counterconditioning). Seligman also attempted to demonstrate the similarity between symptoms of the learned helplessness phenomenon in animals and certain kinds of depression in humans. He has argued for a common etiology (exposure to uncontrollable life events producing feelings of helplessness) and therapy (learning or relearning a sense of control).

This kind of recent work on animal models has been of major significance in reestablishing the importance that animal work can contribute to theory and practice in clinical psychology and psychiatry (e.g., Akiskal & McKinney, 1975; Seligman, 1974, 1975; Suomi & Harlow, 1977). However, it can also be argued that strict adherence to the criterion approach exemplified by Wolpe, Seligman, and McKinney may also be unnecessarily restrictive. For most disorders, compelling full-fledged animal models that meet all of the criteria do not exist, and they are not likely to in the near future. Nevertheless, there are many very interesting "mini-models" (Marks, 1977) which help illuminate many different aspects of the symptomatology, or the etiology, or the therapy for these disorders. What is meant here by mini-models is simply conditioning phenomena that cannot, in and of themselves, account for the origin of the disorder in all cases, the full range of symptoms of the disorder, or the complete mechanisms through which therapy produces its beneficial effects. Instead, these conditioning phenomena should each be thought of as one step in a complex sequence or interaction of events that may be involved in the etiology, maintenance, or therapy for the disorder. And although they may not illuminate every feature or symptom of these disorders (at least in part because humans have cognitive capacities that are different from and often exceed those of even the highest nonhuman primates), they can and do illuminate many of the most prominent and cardinal features of the disorders.

The present review constitutes an attempt to integrate and discuss a variety of conditioning phenomena, studied mostly in animals, that bear on issues relating to the etiology, maintenance, and therapy of the three primary anxiety-based disorders—phobias, obsessive-compulsive disorders, and generalized anxiety states, in that order. For each disorder there is first a discussion of the extent to which animals show symptoms similar or parallel to those seen in humans with these three diagnoses. Following the discussion of symptomatology, there is a review of conditioning phenomena of relevance to an understanding of the etiology and maintenance of each disorder. Special attention is directed to discussing a range of experiential variables occurring prior to, during, or following a conditioning experience that can affect the level of anxiety that is conditioned in the first place, or that is maintained over time. Finally, the discussion of each disorder concludes with a review of conditioning phenomena of relevance to an understanding of the mechanisms through which various behavioral therapeutic approaches produce their beneficial effects for people with that disorder.

PHOBIAS

Symptomatology

The dominant approach to understanding the symptomatology of fear and anxiety in recent years derives from Lang's three-systems approach (1968, 1971). Lang and later Rachman (1976, 1978; Rachman & Hodgson, 1974) argued that fear is best thought of as a set of three only loosely related systems (cognitive/verbal, behavioral avoidance, and psychophysiological), rather than as a hard phenomenal "lump" as in the more traditional view. It has now been well established that there is often a considerable degree of discordance between these three response systems, especially under conditions of low arousal, and that treatments designed to reduce "fear" often have their effect on one (or two) response systems well before they affect the others (e.g., Hodgson & Rachman, 1974; Rachman & Hodgson, 1974). Therefore in the review that follows, an attempt is made to carefully indicate which of the three response systems is being modeled.

In the recent *DSM-III* (1980), a phobia is defined as a persistent and recognizably irrational fear of an object or situation, associated with a compelling desire to avoid that object or situation, and with significant distress from the disturbance. By these criteria, do phobic fears exist in animals? Although some of the criteria cannot be directly confirmed with animals, it does seem that some animals' fears have a distinctly phobic quality. As one example, for years it has been noted that many primates demonstrate an intense fear of snakes and snake-like objects that clearly leads to intense disturbance in a snake's presence and to behavioral avoidance (e.g., Haselrud, 1938; Hebb, 1946; Joslin, Fletcher, & Emlen, 1964; Yerkes & Yerkes, 1936). Until recently, however, no systematic attempts had been made to determine how persistent this fear is, or how difficult it is to modify. Therefore, not even an indirect assessment of how irrational or out of proportion the fear is could be made.

These issues have been addressed recently by Mineka, Keir, and Price (1980) and Mineka and Keir (1983) who reported results of attempts to extinguish an intense fear of snakes in wild-reared rhesus monkeys.[1] These monkeys had all met a criterion of showing an intense fear of snakes both by indices of behavioral avoidance and behavioral disturbance. They were then subjected to at least 12 sessions of a flooding-like procedure (7 in the first month and 5 six months

---

[1]Laboratory-reared monkeys do not show any significant fear of snakes. (See below).

later). In each session they were exposed to a real snake for a series of 1–8-minute trials. Trials were terminated after they reached for a food treat on the far side of the snake (although there was a 60-second minimum trial duration). Sessions ended when they reached a criterion of reaching rapidly for the food treat on the far side of the snake on four consecutive trials. Not too surprisingly given the results of previous less systematic attempts to modify snake fear in primates (e.g., Murray & King, 1973; Schiller, 1952), all monkeys reached this criterion on every session. Unlike in previous studies, however, a number of signs of the monkeys' behavioral disturbance in the presence of the snake were also monitored and no significant changes in these disturbance behaviors were found across the 12 flooding sessions. In spite of the fact that these monkeys showed significant changes in behavioral avoidance (and even avoidance showed complete spontaneous recovery over the 6-month follow-up interval), there were no changes in the behavioral disturbance component of the fear (which is considered to be most similar to the verbal/subjective component of the fear in the three-systems approach) in spite of some 4–11 hours of exposure to the snake. This would certainly seem to qualify for the *DSM-III* requirement that the fear be persistent. In addition, by inference, these results would also suggest that the fear is irrational, since the monkeys had safely reached for the food in the presence of the snake on many dozens of trials, and with rapid latencies on at least 48 trials. In other words, they "knew" they were not in any real danger and yet they continued to show intense signs of behavioral distress in the presence of the snake.

Although many of the examples of mini-models discussed below probably do not qualify as being of phobic intensity, there are numerous examples of intense fears in animals that do so qualify (cf. Wolpe's, 1958, description of his cats' phobic fears of the boxes in which they had been shocked; and Masserman's, 1943 and 1953, descriptions of his cats' and monkeys' phobic fears. While these investigators did not take a three-systems approach to fear, or use the *DSM-III* criteria, their animals' reactions would probably have qualified in the same general way that Mineka et al.'s, 1980, monkeys did).

Etiology and Maintenance

Original Classical Conditioning Model.   For years the textbook example for the origins of fears and phobias has been Watson and Rayner's (1920) case of Little Albert, who developed an intense fear of white rats and other white furry objects as a result of having the presence of the rat (conditioned stimulus-CS) paired with the sounding of a loud gong (unconditioned stimulus-US) seven times. So began the theory that most humans' fears and phobias are simply examples of classically conditioned fear responses. Wolpe (1958) further perpetrated this view with his studies of cats and humans where he tried to draw close parallels between the intense, generalized and long-lasting fears that he conditioned in his cats with electric shock, and the phobic fears he treated in his practice. Unfortunately, because of an unyielding adherence (e.g., Wolpe, 1971) to Hull's outmoded theory of extinction (cf. Gleitman, Nachmias, & Neisser, 1954), and a related failure to separate conceptually classically conditioned fear and avoidance learning paradigms, Wolpe's theory proved to be oversimplified both in terms of facts and in terms of theory. Wolpe maintained that classically conditioned fears should not (and do not) extinguish because autonomically based responses, such as fear, generate little reactive inhibiton (I_R), and because every time an animal or person is taken out of an anxiety-eliciting situation drive reduction occurs, thereby reinforcing the fear response. Hull's theory of extinction and of the importance of drive reduction in classical conditioning has not been supported by data and has been considered outmoded for years. Furthermore, it is now generally accepted that classically conditioned fears in the laboratory do extinguish in a moderate number of trials, even when an intense US has been used (Annau & Kamin, 1961). Thus, Wolpe's model of why phobic fears do not easily extinguish was not supported by the animal conditioning literature, either from an empirical or from a theoretical standpoint.

Avoidance Learning Model.   Although the suggestion that avoidance learning might be involved in phobias was made a number of times before Wolpe's influential model (e.g., Dollard & Miller, 1950; Mowrer, 1947), the conceptual and theoretical distinctions between the two were not clearly spelled out for some time. Perhaps as a result of the surge of interest in avoidance learning in the 1950s and the resulting rise in popularity of a two-process theory of learning that emphasizes the interactions between classically conditioned fear responses and instrumentally reinforced escape and avoidance responses, interest in an avoidance model of phobias increased in the 1960s. For example, Eysenck and Rachman (1965) noted the parallels between the renowned high resistance to extinction of avoidance responses conditioned in the laboratory (e.g., Solomon, Kamin, & Wynne, 1953) and the definitional characteristic of phobias, which is that they are notoriously resistant to change (until, of course, they get treatment with a behavior therapist!). Thus, the avoidance model had an obvious advantage over the straightforward classical conditioning model because it could seemingly account for behavioral persistence in a more compelling fashion.

Although this avoidance model has had its share of popularity, it too has come under attack from many sides since 1970. Some of these criticisms seem more compelling than others. For example, Costello (1970) argued against the model on the grounds that conditioned avoidance responses are adaptive but that phobias are not. However, others (e.g., Powell & Lumia, 1971) have argued that adaptiveness is not an inherent characteristic of a response, but rather a characteristic that derives from the context in which the response appears; therefore the use of more neutral criteria for evaluating animal models seems desirable (Abramson & Seligman, 1977). Costello further argued that the two-process theory of avoidance learning on which Eysenck and Rachman's model was based had been found to be faulty, thus questioning the validity of the model itself. However, it again seems that the avoidance model could in theory be a good one, even if there has been an evolution in thinking about the theoretical mechanisms used to account for avoidance learning (see Mineka, 1979a, for a related argument). In other words, the crucial criteria on which the model should be evaluated are whether the known features of conditioned avoidance responses seen in the laboratory resemble the known features of naturally occurring human phobias.

In this regard Seligman (1971) made a more telling theory-free criticism when he noted that phobics generally go to great lengths to avoid their phobic stimulus (the presumed CS in an avoidance paradigm), whereas animals trained to avoid aversive stimulation in the laboratory are trained to avoid the US, not the CS. In fact, in spite of a number of attempts in the literature to train animals to avoid CSs (for aversive USs) there have apparently been no successful attempts to do so (see Mineka, 1979a, 1979b; Seligman, 1971, for reviews). We see here a significant and important difference in a crucial feature of avoidance learning as studied in the laboratory and in naturally occurring phobias. The same feature mismatch seems to apply to the suggestion of Rachman and Hodgson (1980) and others who have conceptualized phobias as *passive* avoidance responses wherein the organism learns to avoid the US by refraining from making some active response as a result of contingent punishment. Again, in the passive avoidance learning literature there is no model for avoidance of the CS.

Hodes (1983, personal communication) has argued that one possible explanation for why there is no laboratory model for avoidance of the CS stems from the arbitrary nature of the CS-US relationship in laboratory avoidance paradigms. In phobias the CS-US relationship is generally less arbitrary, i.e., the phobic object (CS) is often the direct source of the US. For example, a germ phobic not only avoids germs per se, but thereby also avoids the possible illness that the germs might cause, and a snake phobic not only avoids snakes per se, but thereby also avoids the possible bite the snake might inflict. By contrast, the relationship between a light or tone CS and a shock US in a laboratory avoidance paradigm is very arbitrary, since the light or tone is not itself the source of the shock US. This line of argument would suggest that perhaps a closer laboratory analogue to avoidance of the CS could be obtained if the CS and US had a less arbitrary relationship, with the CS actually being the source of the US. (See also discussion of preparedness below.)

A second feature of avoidance learning and phobias that appears to be dissimilar stems from an analysis of what exactly is so highly resistant to extinction in each case. In phobias, the cardinal characteristic is the level of subjective distress that is evoked by the presence or the thought of the phobic object or situation, and secondarily the avoidance behavior that this in turn engenders, and the accompanying disruptions to the person's life. In other words, even if we accept that the three components of fear in Lang's (1968, 1971) system are only loosely coupled, it is very unlikely that we would diagnose someone as having a phobia if they consistently avoided an object or situation about which they expressed no major subjective distress. By contrast, with avoidance responses conditioned in the laboratory, what is so notoriously highly resistant to extinction and even stereotyped is the motor avoidance response itself. Indeed, it is now well known that Solomon et al.'s (1953) early informal observations that well-trained dogs become nonchalant about the whole traumatic avoidance situation were indeed correct. Animals who are well trained at avoidance responses show a marked (although not complete) decline in their fear of the CS, as assessed in an independent situation where the avoidance response itself was not used as the index of fear (Kamin, Brimer, & Black, 1963; Linden, 1969; Mineka & Gino, 1980; Starr & Mineka, 1977). This decline in the component of fear that is akin to the subjective distress component is not simply a result of the increased amount of exposure to the nonreinforced CS that they have had with their string of successful avoidance responses (Starr & Mineka, 1977). Instead, it seems that some aspect of the added sense of control and/or predictability over US offset that comes with extensive training is responsible for this drop in independently assessed fear of the CS (Cook, Mineka, & Trumble, in preparation; Starr & Mineka, 1977). It often seems that this sense of control or predictability is precisely what is missing for phobics, and may, in turn, be what maintains their high level of subjective distress. This may be because the lives of phobics are not conducted in a shuttlebox or a jump-up box and they inherently have less control and predictability. Nevertheless, there seems to be a salient feature mismatch here: What is so notoriously difficult to change in phobias is the intense and irrational subjective distress itself, whereas the laboratory analogues of the subjective distress component diminish quite rapidly in laboratory avoidance settings, without a comparable loss in avoidance response strength (Mineka & Gino, 1980).

A diehard avoidance modeler could still argue that phobics' subjective distress can often be held at a minimum if they manage to avoid their phobic object or situation, and conversely that an animal's fear of the CS returns as soon as its avoidance response is blocked (Baum, 1970; Mineka, 1979b; Solomon et al., 1953). However, one then returns to the problem raised by Seligman regarding the difference in what is being avoided (CS versus US), and to the difference in the degree to which a sense of control and predictability is inherent in the general nature of avoidance responses as studied in the laboratory versus in naturally occurring phobias.

Prepared Classical Conditioning Model.   At least in part as a result of some of these problems discussed above with the avoidance model, the trend in recent years has been to think of many phobias once again as instances of classically conditioned fear responses. Many new ideas and findings about classical conditioning, and about fear, have been incorporated into this model that were not part of the Watson and Rayner or Wolpe models. In a now classic paper on phobias Seligman (1971) argued that there are five crucial features that make phobias dissimilar to classically conditioned fear responses as traditionally studied: (1) the above discussed differences in the ease of extinction of the two; (2) that most phobias that are acquired through traumatic conditioning are acquired in only one trial, whereas only a very few laboratory studies have ever demonstrated one trial fear conditioning (see Campbell, Sanderson, & Laverty, 1964, for a classic exception); (3) that where traumatic conditioning has been known to have occurred, there was often a long delay between the appearance of the CS (and now the phobic object) and the presumed trauma (US), and yet traditionally classical conditioning has not been thought to occur with very long CS-US intervals; (4) that phobias do not generally occur to a random class of objects that might be expected to have been paired with trauma, but rather to a selected class of objects (e.g., snakes and spiders, but not electric outlets and stoves); (5) that phobias are notoriously irrational and cannot be talked away, whereas conditioned fear responses in human subjects are often quite sensitive to cognitive information about changes in CS-US contingencies (instructed extinction).

Seligman proposed that all five of these dissimilarities could be accounted for if one took a broader view of classical conditioning. In particular, he proposed that phobias be thought of as examples of "prepared classical conditioning" (see Seligman, 1970; Seligman & Hager, 1972, for extensive discussions of the preparedness concept). Prepared associations, of which taste aversion conditioning is the prototypic example, were thought to be characterized by (1) their relatively high resistance to extinction; (2) 1–2 trial conditioning; (3) conditioning that bridges long CS-US intervals of several hours; (4) their selectivity, i.e., only certain CS-US combinations condition with these parameters; (5) their irrationality or inability to be talked away. (See Seligman, 1970, and Seligman & Hager, 1972, for a discussion of the origin of these postulated characteristics.) Seligman further proposed that the stimuli which are "prepared" for association with aversive events are stimuli that were probably dangerous or threatening to our evolutionary ancestors. Therefore our ancestors, who acquired fears of these objects easily and who maintained them for prolonged periods, may have had a selective advantage in the struggle for existence over their contemporaries who did not acquire these fears so easily, or for whom the fears, once acquired, extinguished quite rapidly.

Although Seligman's preparedness (1970) theory as a complete alternative to general process learning theory has been subject to a great deal of criticism (e.g., Rozin & Kalat, 1971; Schwartz, 1974; Shettleworth, 1972), within the limited realm of what it has to say about models of phobic disorders it has fared much better. This has largely been the result of the ingenious work of Öhman and his co-workers in Sweden and Norway. In an elegant and now well-known series of experiments Öhman and co-workers have investigated the characteristics of human electrodermal conditioning to stimuli that are known to be the common objects of phobias (primarily snakes and spiders), as opposed to more arbitrary everyday stimuli that are rarely the objects of phobias (flowers, mushrooms, geometric objects). Conditioning to snakes and spiders is thought to be an example of Seligman's "prepared associations," whereas conditioning to flowers or geometric figures is thought to be an example of Seligman's "unprepared," or even "contra-prepared associations." In this series of experiments (e.g., Öhman, Ericksson, & Olofsson, 1975; Öhman, Frederikson, & Hugdahl, 1978a, 1978b; Öhman, Frederikson, Hugdahl, & Rimino, 1976) testing Seligman's hypothesis that phobias are examples of "prepared classical conditioning," they have used primarily mild electric shock as a US, and electrodermal responses as an index of fear in nonphobic human subjects. They have found that CRs to common phobic stimuli (vivid slides of snakes and spiders) extinguish very slowly if at all, and are not affected by cognitive instructional variables. Although these investigators have not generally found significant differences in rate of acquisition between "prepared" and "unprepared" stimuli, they have found robust conditioning with only one CS-US trial using prepared CSs, but not using unprepared CSs. More recently they have extended their work to include finger-pulse-volume responses and found parallel results. In at least one study they have also found significant ratings of unpleasantness of the stimuli following conditioning to prepared, but not to unprepared, CSs (Öhman et al., 1975), thus extending their findings beyond the psychophysiological response system in Lang's three-systems model.

Öhman and his colleagues have further shown in several different ways that this "prepared" conditioning that occurred with snakes and spiders as CSs was not merely a result of the subjects simply being predisposed to show larger responses to the prepared stimuli, or of these CSs simply being more salient/prepotent. First, by using a discriminative conditioning paradigm where both the CS$^+$ and CS$^-$ are either prepared or unprepared, their results are based on superior discrimination of prepared CS$^+$s and CS$^-$s, not simply on a greater CR to a prepared CS. (This also controls for possible nonassociative sensitization effects.) Second, in a nonaversive conditioning paradigm, conditioning with snakes and spiders did not show these characteristics of superior conditioning, thus demonstrating that snakes and spiders are only "prepared" to be associated with aversive consequences (Öhman et al., 1976). And very recently Hodes (1981) and Cook (1983) in Lang's laboratory have demonstrated the importance of the use of shock as a US. When they used loud noise as a US, even though it supported an equally large UR, they did not find comparable results to those of Öhman, but they did with the use of shock. Thus, it seems that there is something selective about the use of a tactile US that results in the superior conditioning to these prepared stimuli. (In fact, the cognitive associations between both snakes and spiders and painful bites may play a role here.) (See LoLordo, 1979, and Schwartz, 1974, for a discussion of the importance of the double-dissociation experiment in these matters.) Furthermore, when slides of guns and electric outlets (which are clearly salient and potentially dangerous objects, but which were not present for our evolutionary ancestors) have been used as CSs, the conditioning was more like that seen with "unprepared" stimuli than like that seen with "prepared" stimuli (Hodes, Cook, Öhman, & Lang, in preparation; Hugdahl & Kärker, 1981). The possible importance of evolutionary factors in the superiority of snakes and spiders as CSs for aversive conditioning is thus supported.

Although Öhman's results do not provide support for Seligman's theory as a whole, they do lend some support to Seligman's hypothesis that phobias may best be thought of as examples of "prepared" classical conditioning, i.e., conditioning that may obey somewhat different laws from those traditionally studied by learning theorists (e.g., Pavlov, 1927). The idea is certainly not new that fear conditions more easily to some objects than to others, or that fear of some objects may even be relatively "innate" or spontaneous, i.e., require no special experience to manifest itself (e.g., Bregman, 1934; Hebb, 1946; Yerkes & Yerkes, 1936). What is new with the Seligman (1970, 1971) approach is the idea that the other laws of conditioning (e.g., rate of extinction, CS-UCS delays which can be bridged, sensitivity to cognitive manipulations) may vary directly with the selectivity and rate of acquisition measures. So, for example, although many have noted that fear is very easily conditioned to selected objects, no one has systematically investigated whether such conditioning is also always highly resistant to extinction, insensitive to cognitive manipulations, and able to bridge long CS-UCS delay intervals. Öhman and his colleagues' results are the only firm evidence to date demonstrating that fear conditioning in nonphobic humans to some selective common phobic objects—snakes and spiders (and most recently angry faces, Öhman & Dimberg, 1978)—is highly resistant to extinction and insensitive to cognitive instructional variables.

Finally, it should also be noted that a more neutral stance with regard to the theoretical interpretation of Öhman's work can also be taken by simply talking about it as a case of "selective associations" (LoLordo, 1978, 1979) or as a case of the belongingness principle (Rozin & Kalat, 1971; Thorndike, 1932). Thus, one does not have to accept the notion that the reason why snakes and spiders show superior conditioning with aversive USs resides in our evolutionary past. The reasons for the superior conditioning might, for example, reside in onto-genetic factors and yet still qualify for the label "selective associations" (see Mackintosh, 1974, for one such argument; see Delprato, 1980, for a review of the ontogenetic factors that might be involved.) Furthermore, this more neutral approach also does not predict that the "laws" of learning will covary in any systematic fashion with the selectivity of the association. On the negative side this means that Öhman and his colleagues might not have made this interesting set of predictions regarding the characteristics of conditioning to phobic stimuli, and therefore that some of the fruitful discoveries from their laboratory might not have occurred. On the other hand, some of the predictions of the preparedness approach have not yet proved as useful when it comes to retrospective analysis of already existing phobias (cf. de Silva, Rachman, & Seligman, 1977; Rachman & Seligman, 1976). Thus, for example, de Silva et al. did not find that phobias for "prepared" stimuli as rated by the experimenters (who considered the evolutionary history of man in developing their rating scale for preparedness) had been any more rapidly acquired or were any more persistent than were phobias for unprepared stimuli. From this standpoint a more neutral stance of discussing "fear-relevant" versus "fear-irrelevant" stimuli may be a more appropriate tack to take. (This is, in fact, what Öhman and his colleagues have done in their more recent publications.)

At a minimum it seems safe to say that the work of Öhman and his colleagues has made a very important contribution by rekindling interest in conditioning models of phobias, models which to this point had never been especially compelling precisely because of the nonarbitrary nature of the stimuli involved, the very high resistance to extinction of the fears, and the irrationality of the fears (Costello, 1970; Rachman, 1977, 1978; Seligman, 1971). There are, nonetheless, a number of kinds of limitations in the preparedness model that prevent it from providing a wholly satisfactory model for the etiology of phobias. One limitation stems from the fact that with the exception of Öhman et al. (1975), all of the research supporting a preparedness account has involved only autonomic indices of fear, and even among autonomic indices the results with heart rate often differ considerably from the results with electrodermal responses (e.g., Öhman et al., 1978a). And as discussed at the outset, the physiological fear response system often shows a considerable degree of discordance with the other two fear response systems. To a large extent this limitation stems from appropriate ethical concerns that do not allow for conditioning of truly phobic responses in human subjects. Nevertheless, it is a limitation insofar as it limits knowledge of whether the same characteristics of conditioning with prepared or relevant stimuli would hold with the other two response systems.

A second limitation of the preparednes model that also leaves it an incomplete account is that prepared CRs are usually not as inextinguishable as phobias are generally thought to be (although as discussed below the behavior therapy literature has clearly shown that with forced exposure most phobias do diminish rapidly in intensity). In fact, a common observation in people's accounts of the origins of their phobias is that after the first signs appeared they gradually got worse over time rather than better.[2] The question then arises whether there are

---

[2] The same observation also clearly applies to many cases of posttraumatic stress disorder, a new *DSM-III* category of Anxiety Disorders.

phenomena in the conditioning literature that could account for such increases in intensity over time in the absence of further traumatic conditioning. The answer suggested below is yes, although not all of the conditioning phenomena to be discussed below have previously been considered before in this framework.

How to Account for Increases in Fear, or Failures to Extinguish?   The first and perhaps most familiar attempt to account for increases in fear is Eysenck's incubation theory (1968, 1976, 1979). Briefly, Eysenck has argued that in some cases a fear CR may be sufficiently noxious so as to serve as a US and to further reinforce conditioning, even in the absence of a true US. Although this account has a considerable degree of appeal, the experimental evidence supporting the idea that fear CRs actually do increase or incubate over time in the absence of further conditioning trials is extremely sparse (see Bersh, 1980; Mineka, 1979a; and other reviews of Eysenck's 1979 *Behavioral and Brain Sciences* review for discussion of this evidence—or rather lack thereof). Although the possibility exists that some, as yet unidentified, parameters may yet be found to be critical in establishing a robust incubation phenomenon (e.g., perhaps the use of prepared or fear-relevant CSs), at the present time it appears to be far too fragile a phenomenon to account for the majority of cases where fears and phobias gradually increase in intensity over time.

A second category of conditioning phenomenon more likely to be involved is the reinstatement and inflation phenomena first explored by Rescorla. In the original reinstatement paradigm Rescorla and Heth (1975) found that once a fear CR had been fairly well extinguished, exposure to the US alone was sufficient to substantially reinstate the fear CR. Although subsequent research has raised questions about the generality of this effect unless the US is given in the original conditioning context (e.g., Bouton & Bolles, 1979), it does seem to be a robust phenomenon at least if the same context is used for the inflation experience as for testing. Furthermore, at least one study (Rescorla & Heth, 1975) also showed that the US need not be the same as the original US used in conditioning, i.e., a klaxon could be used to reinstate a fear CR established with electric shock. The implications of this work on reinstatement for phobias should be obvious: If a person has had some "nonreinforced" exposures to his phobic object and shows extinction, chance encounters with a traumatic event, even of a different sort than that involved in the original conditioning, may be sufficient to reinstate the fear.

The remaining question is whether related phenomena might also be used to account for cases where the intensity of the fear actually increases over time. The first and most obvious in this regard is the postconditioning inflation phenomenon. Rescorla (1974) found that following conditioning with a US of a moderate intensity, postconditioning experience with a US of greater intensity resulted in an inflated CR. Used to support a S-S view of conditioning, Rescorla argued that the inflation experience altered the animal's representation of the original events involved in conditioning and that this in turn resulted in a change in the performance of the CR so that it matched the new representations. More recently, Hendersen and Blaccioniere (submitted) have shown that this inflation effect can be exaggerated if a long delay intervenes between the original conditioning experience and when the inflation experiences occur. In particular, they argued that some forgetting of the characteristics of the original US occurs over a long interval (60 days in their case), and that this forgetting leaves the memory trace more malleable to change. With regard to phobias, the inflation experiments suggest an account whereby once a phobic fear has begun to develop, later exposures to traumatic events of greater intensity could alter the level of fear in an upward direction. Hendersen and Blaccioniere's results further suggest that the likelihood of this happening increases with the passage of time.

In addition, there are several other conditioning phenomena studied in recent years that may also be relevant to understanding the pronounced resistance to change, and even increases, in the intensity and generality of phobic fears. First, Levis and Boyd (1979) have argued that many phobic stimuli can be thought of as serial CSs and they have shown that when avoidance responses are trained with serial CSs, there is greatly pronounced resistance to extinction. Although their model is primarily an avoidance model and their experiments have generally used an avoidance paradigm, their results suggest that extinction of a fear CR may be prolonged with the use of a serial CS.

Second, there is also good evidence that the specificity of conditioned fears decreases over time. In particular, Hendersen, Patterson, and Jackson (1980) have shown that although shortly after conditioning, an animal may remember precisely the object of its fear (e.g., an air blast), the specificity of this anticipation or fear declines markedly over a several month interval. The animal remembers its fear of the CS, but confuses that fear with other fears (e.g., of electric shock). One consequence of this forgetting is that a more conservative strategy is taken after the long-term retention interval and fear/avoidance behavior may be elicited in contexts in which it would not have appeared shortly after conditioning. A similar account might apply to apparent increases over time in the number of situations in which phobic fears arise and provoke avoidance behavior as the specificity of the original conditioning memory trace is gradually lost. (Exactly how likely this account is depends on whether results parallel to those of Hendersen et al. can be found in the human conditioning literature, since humans probably have more detailed and accurate representational systems.)

Third, although conditioned fears are well remembered (even though as discussed above their specificity may decrease), there is also evidence that conditioned *inhibitors* of fear (CSs) are not well remembered (Hendersen, 1978; Thomas, 1979). Specifically, these investigators found that CS⁻s lost their fear inhibitory properties over a several month interval. By analogy, a phobic might acquire safety signals or CS⁻s that facilitate discrimination of fearful versus safe places or events early in the acquisition of their phobia. However, with the passage of time the CS^+s would be likely to retain their excitatory properties, but the CS^-s would be likely to lose their inhibitory properties. This in turn may lead to a loss of discrimination between fearful and safe places or events, and a concomitant increase in generalization of fears.

Fourth, there is also increasing evidence alluded to above that a sense of lack of control or helplessness can clearly lead to increased levels of fear. Since Mowrer and Viek's (1948) classic demonstration of "fear from a sense of help-lessness," there have been several other demonstrations that greater levels of fear are conditioned with uncontrollable as opposed to controllable aversive events (Brennan & Riccio, 1975; Desiderato & Newman, 1971; Mineka, Cook, & Miller, 1984; Osborne, Mattingly, Redmon, & Osborne, 1975; Starr & Mineka, 1977). Furthermore, there is also some evidence that a general history of control over one's environment reduces emotionality. This was first reported in rats by Joffe, Rawson, and Mulick (1971) who found that rats reared in an environment where they could control delivery of food, water, and lights were later less emotional in an open field test than were rats reared in yoked uncontrollable environments.

Two recent, as yet unpublished, studies confirm and extend this finding that a sense of mastery can reduce fear in infant monkeys (Mineka, Gunnar, & Champoux, submitted). In these studies two groups of infant monkeys— Masters—were reared in controllable environments where they could control delivery of their food, water, and treats. Two other Yoked groups of infants lived in identical environments and had exposure to the same positive reinforcers; however, their response manipulanda were inoperative and their reinforcers were delivered automatically every time a Master group monkey successfully operated its manipulandum. In one replication of the experiment there was also a No Stimulation Control group that did not have access to the variety of reinforcers that the Master and Yoked groups had. Between 7 and 9 months of age all the monkeys were subjected to fear tests with a fear-provoking mechanical toy monster, as well as playroom tests in a novel situation to assess fear and explor-atory tendencies. In both replications of the experiment there was clear-cut evidence that the Master group monkeys showed more approach responses to the fear-provoking toy monster than did the Yoked and No Stimulation monkeys, and were far more eager to enter and explore the novel, initially frightening playroom situation. It seems that a generalized expectancy of control or a sense of mastery can indeed have profound effects on an animal's reaction to fear or anxiety-provoking situations. This is obviously a way in which personality var-iables stemming from a person's experience with control or mastery over his/ her environment may influence or interact with the development and maintenance of phobic fears. It is also possible that the higher incidence of phobias in women than in men might, in part, be a function of differences in the experience of gaining a sense of control over the environment in the course of development.

How to Account for Phobias with no Known Traumatic Conditioning History? One potentially serious limitation of all the models or mini-models that has not been discussed so far stems from the fact that some investigators have found that only a relatively small proportion of phobias seem to have involved a traumatic conditioning history, at least that the person can recollect (e.g., Marks, 1977; Murray & Foote, 1979; Rachman, 1978; Rimm, Janda, Lancaster, Nahl, & Dittman, 1977). These findings seem to pose a serious problem for any of these conditioning models insofar as they seriously limit the proportion of cases for which the models can account. There are, however, a number of points that need to be made about these criticisms. First, some more recent findings from Sweden (Öst & Hugdahl, 1981) suggest that well over 50% of severely phobic patients do recall direct traumatic conditioning experiences. These investigators have argued that the earlier studies of Murray and Foote (1979) and Rimm et al. (1977) found such low proportions of phobic subjects to recall direct traumatic conditioning experiences because of their use of analogue college student subjects as opposed to severely phobic patients. Thus, to the extent that Öst and Hugdahl's (1981) findings can be replicated in other countries, there is support for the proposition that direct conditioning models are useful for at least a slight majority of cases of severe phobias. Milder phobias seem more likely to be acquired in other ways (see below).

In addition, there are three other phenomena in the conditioning literature that begin to give models for the cases in which there is no recall of direct traumatic conditioning. The first is a suggestion made by a number of theorists over the years who have demonstrated that anxiety states can be conditioned without a traumatic or aversive US if the organism is in a state of frustration or conflict over appetitive events. For example, Wolpe (1958) noted the induction of anxiety in many of the classic experimental neurosis experiments occurred simply through the use of "ambivalent stimulation." In addition, many theorists (e.g., Amsel, 1971; Brown & Wagner, 1964; Gray, 1979; and Mowrer, 1960) have noted the similarity between the emotional states induced by aversive USs and frustration induced by withdrawal or withholding of anticipated appetitive reinforcers. Indeed, Brown and Wagner (1964) demonstrated a cross-tolerance for the persistence that had developed in the face of punishing aversive stimuli such as shock and frustration over withholding of appetitive events. Thus, phobic patients may have no recollection of a traumatic conditioning history simply because their anxiety may have been conditioned on the basis of conflict or frustration over appetitive events. Although there is no apparent research on this topic, it seems plausible that memories for such states of conflict or frustration may be less vivid or accurate than those for traumatic incidents.

A second phenomenon of relevance to this issue of phobias without a traumatic conditioning history is second-order conditioning, which some years ago Rizley and Rescorla (1972) proposed may be involved in the origins of some phobias.

Although this idea was not entirely new, dating back at least to Dollard and Miller's (1950) famous book, their logic and their experiments were new. The most obvious problem with a proposal that second-order conditioning might be involved is that it still requires a conditioning history. However, what Rizley and Rescorla demonstrated is that second-order CRs once established become independent (functionally autonomous) of their origins. In particular, they found that after second-order conditioning has occurred the first-order CR can be extinguished without affecting the magnitude of the second-order CR. They were primarily interested in this and related results (e.g., Rescorla, 1973) because it seemed to establish second-order conditioning as being S-R rather than S-S in nature. For purposes of the present discussion, however, it suggests the possibility that some phobias may be cases of second-order CRs (albeit probably to prepared or fear-relevant CSs). In particular, people may have no recollection of a traumatic conditioning history simply because the first-order CR and conditioning experience upon which the phobia was originally based have long since extinguished and been forgotten. Such an hypothesis should be further explored in the context of the prepared conditioning model discussed above and in the vicarious conditioning model discussed below.

Third, and perhaps most important in terms of the actual number of cases that it may be expected to account for, is the phenomenon of observational or vicarious conditioning. It has been suggested for over a decade that some fears and phobias may be learned vicariously (see Bandura, 1969; Marks, 1969, for early reviews of this topic), and this idea has gained increasing popularity in recent years due to increasing recognition of the relatively large number of cases that cannot be accounted for by a traditional conditioning account (Murray & Foote, 1979; Rachman, 1977, 1978). Unfortunately, the evidence to support this hypothesis has been meagre at best. Of the dozen or so studies that have examined observational learning of fear in humans, all have been single session laboratory experiments with no tests for context specificity or persistence of the fears once acquired. Furthermore, none have used anything other than autonomic measures of fear even though these indices of fear do not always correlate highly with the other two primary components of fear—subjective distress and behavioral avoidance. Finally, only one study has begun to examine the issue of how the nature of the CS may influence the ease of conditioning and/or resistance to extinction. Yet with direct conditioning there is considerable evidence to suggest that some fear-relevant CSs show better conditioning with aversive USs than do other fear-irrelevant CSs.

Somewhat surprisingly there are also very few studies of observational conditioning of fears in animals. Yet, as with humans, there has been considerable speculation that observational conditioning is prominently involved, at least for primates, in the origins of certain pronounced fears that exist across a wide number of species. In particular, there has been considerable speculation that the well-known fear of snakes exhibited by many primate species is based on observational conditioning (e.g., Joslin, Fletcher, & Emlen, 1964). Recent data strongly support the viability of this hypothesis by showing the social transmission of snake fear from wild-reared rhesus monkeys' mothers to their adolescent offspring, and even among unrelated monkeys who barely know each other (Mineka, Davidson, Cook, & Keir, 1984).

In their first study of observational conditioning, Mineka et al. used as observers six adolescent/young adult rhesus monkeys who had been living all their lives in a nuclear-family laboratory environment with their wild-reared parents, who all had a pronounced fear of snakes, presumably as a result of their experience in the wild some 20 years earlier. The observer offspring, like nearly all laboratory-reared monkeys, did not show any fear of snakes prior to observational conditioning. During each of six sessions of discriminative observational conditioning, the adolescents observed their wild-reared parents behave fearfully in the presence of real, toy, and model snakes for a short period of time, and behave nonfearfully in the presence of a variety of neutral objects. The adolescents were tested by themselves for their fear of snakes in a different situation, and showed nearly asymptotic levels of fear after only 8 minutes of exposure to one of their parents behaving fearfully in the presence of the snake stimuli. By the end of the six sessions their fear as indexed both by behavioral avoidance and behavioral disturbance was statistically indistinguishable in intensity from that of their parents (although there was some suggestion that the parents showed more fear or disturbance behaviors in the presence of the real snake). Furthermore, there were no signs of diminution in the intensity of the fear over a 3-month follow-up interval.

Thus it seems that a very strong and persistent phobic-like fear can be acquired in a very short period of time through observation alone. Two other aspects of these results are also noteworthy. First, the levels of disturbance behaviors shown by the parental models to the snake stimuli during the conditioning sessions were highly correlated (.986) with the levels of disturbance shown by the observers in the posttest. Although genetic and other common experiential factors may have played a role in this high correlation, it may also have implications regarding the possibility of prevention of fears. In particular, it suggests that parents who have strong fears or phobias should avoid confronting their phobic object as much as possible in the presence of their children. Although one might expect that such avoidance, especially if it were obvious, might suffice to instill a fear in the children, these results suggest that the level of disturbance exhibited by the parental model is more important than behavioral avoidance per se. This suggestion stems from the observation that although all the models showed virtually complete and equivalent behavioral avoidance, it was their level of disturbance that correlated so highly with the level of fear conditioned in their offspring. To the extent that parents can prevent themselves from exhibiting their fear in a dramatic way, they may be able to help prevent the observational conditioning of fear in their children, or at a minimum to reduce the extent of such conditioning. A further question of interest regarding the issue of prevention will be whether observational learning of safety will interfere with the later observational conditioning of fear.

The second noteworthy aspect of this paradigm stems from more recent findings concerning the role of the parent-child relationship in producing such conditioning. In a recent study (Cook, Mineka, Wolkenstein, Laitsch, submitted) it has been found that learning can and does occur with unrelated adult model-observer pairs who had known each other only by having been previously housed in cages in the same room. The results suggest that the learning occurs just as rapidly but that there is slightly more variability in the results. That such learning occurs in unrelated monkeys who had never lived together seems quite striking. And as in the previous study there were very high correlations between the level of disturbance exhibited by the models during conditioning and by the observers in the posttest. Because these monkeys were unrelated, unlike in the previous study, this further supports the suggestion made above that there is very close modeling by an observer of the level of disturbance exhibited by the model. In addition, the finding of comparably high correlations in both studies can be taken to imply that the high correlations in the first study were not simply the result of genetic or common experiential factors.

Final Comments and Limitations.   It seems that all the mini-models discussed thus far give a fairly compelling picture of how many humans' fears and phobias may emerge and be maintained or even increase over time. No one has yet tried to see the extent to which all of the conditioning phenomena discussed above (e.g., preparedness, serial CSs, inflation, reinstatement, lack of control, and second-order conditioning) may interact with each other, or whether any of these same phenomena can be demonstrated with the recent observational conditioning paradigm of Mineka, Davidson, Cook, & Keir (1984). It seems likely that such an undertaking could result in a very compelling full-fledged animal model of at least certain kinds of human phobias.

However, the last question that has to be addressed concerns whether such mini-models, or even a full-fledged one, are relevant to all kinds of human phobias. Some theorists (e.g., Mathews, Gelder, & Johnston, 1981) have argued that such models are minimally relevant for understanding the origins of agoraphobia, and perhaps social phobias as well. Since these two kinds of phobias account for a majority of cases seen in treatment clinics, this would seem to be a fairly serious limitation. Although it is clearly the case that the relevance of these models for social phobias and agoraphobia has been less well worked out, an argument can be made that they are relevant.

First, there is some suggestion that a preparedness account such as discussed above may be applicable to social phobias. Öhman and Dimberg (1978), for example, found superior conditioning to angry faces as CSs than to neutral or happy faces as CSs. Given the parallel between these results and his earlier ones with snakes and spiders as fear-relevant stimuli, these authors have suggested that such conditioning may be involved in the origins of social phobias. Marks (1977) has further suggested that there may be critical periods in development when organisms are especially prone to acquiring fears of neutral stimuli, including social stimuli, when and if they are paired with innately fear-releasing stimuli such as threatening facial expressions (see Sackett, 1966, for results suggesting the existence of a maturational system that results in threat faces becoming innate releasing stimuli for fearful behavior in 2–3-month-old rhesus monkeys).

With regard to agoraphobia the primary problem for a conditioning model has been thought to be similar to one of those discussed above for simple phobias, i.e., in the majority of cases there was no obvious precipitating trauma. Instead it seems that the majority of agoraphobics report that their first acute anxiety or panic attack came "out of the blue," and that their fear of open public places generalized more-or-less quickly to other related situations, and often intensified to the original situation. They also frequently report that they were under considerable general life stress at the time of the first attack. (See Mathews et al., 1981, for a review of recent results.) Thus, the primary problem for a conditioning model seems to be the lack of a precipitating trauma (US) in most cases. In addition, the majority of agoraphobics do not come from families with an agoraphobic, and so the opportunity for observational conditioning of agoraphobic behavior cannot be used to account for these cases either.

How problematic these data are for a conditioning account is at least in part a function of how strictly one adheres to a traditional Pavlovian framework. A majority of studies have supported an S-S (as opposed to S-R) view of first-order conditioning and this would suggest the necessity of a clearly identifiable US for conditioning to occur. It is also well known in the conditioning literature that there are a wide variety of interoceptive USs that can elicit very strong anxiety responses, and yet may be difficult to identify (e.g., Razarn, 1961). Thus, the simple failure of an identifiable exteroceptive US to be present in the majority of cases of onset of agoraphobia does not seem to be a major problem if one considers that there may well have been an unidentified interoceptive US. Indeed a recent study of Öst and Hugdahl (1983) is quite consistent with this suggestion. They found that 81% of severely agoraphobic patients could recall having had a panic attack in the situation about which they subsequently became phobic, although only a small number of these could identify a specific US that had precipitated the first panic attack. They argued that their results were highly consistent with a conditioning view of the acquisition of agoraphobia, and in doing so clearly did not believe that the absence of a memory of an overt identifiable US in a majority of cases was inconsistent with the conditioning model.

According to this model, following the initial panic attack, the person shows anxiety both to the situation in which it occurred and to the possibility that another attack may occur (fear of fear). While the fear of fear concept has no clearly identifiable analogue in the conditioning literature, it does resemble to some extent the serial CS issue that has been discussed most recently by Levis and Boyd (1979). These authors showed that the early portions of a CS in an avoidance paradigm very rapidly elicited sufficient fear to motivate a short latency escape/avoidance response, and thereby protected the later portions of the CS from extinction. Whenever long latency responses were made, the exposure to the longer duration of the CS seemed to elicit greater fear, and reconditioned the fear again to the earlier portion of the CS. In a similar vein, Zielinski (1979) noted that the very short latency avoidance responses that tend to occur in well-trained animals, even without a serial CS, may be considered to be a model for avoidance of fear, motivated by something like fear of fear.

Although this model of the possible origins of agoraphobia seems plausible, it cannot be said to account for all the other complexities of the disorder, which in many ways make it more like generalized anxiety states than like simple phobias. While such conditioning factors may play a prominent role, other factors that need to be taken into account are (1) high levels of generalized fearfulness or anxiety in agoraphobia-prone individuals, (2) high levels of nonspecific background stress factors leading to generalized anxiety, (3) personality styles that are avoidant and dependent rather than involving active coping and self-reliance, (4) an association with external locus of control and a resultant tendency to attribute initial anxiety attacks to external situations rather than to internal factors. (See Mathews et al., 1981.) In other words, a more complex psychological modeling approach discussed by Öhman (1981) and others seems especially necessary when it comes to accounting for the origins of agoraphobia.

Therapy

In the past 25 years two highly effective forms of treatment for phobias have emerged—systematic desensitization and flooding or exposure therapy. Each of these forms of therapy has a clear-cut animal model and it seems safe to say that animal work in this area has had a significant impact both on the initial and on the later developments of these two forms of therapy. This section reviews the development of these two forms of therapy and how they grew out of the conditioning literature, as well as some of the more recent experimental data that have relevance for a current understanding of the mechanisms through which they may produce their therapeutic effects. (See Foa & Kozak, this volume, for a review of the human literature on the effects of these techniques and their possible modes of action.)

Systematic Desensitization.   The idea of using counterconditioning techniques to extinguish fears has as long a history as conditioning models of phobias themselves (e.g., Guthrie, 1935; Jones, 1924; Watson & Rayner, 1920), but it was not until Wolpe's reciprocal inhibition therapy developed in the 1950s that such ideas became popular in the treatment of phobias. As stated earlier, Wolpe (1958) developed his ideas about the importance of reciprocal inhibition because of his adherence to a Hullian model of extinction. Autonomic responses like fear and anxiety were not believed to generate sufficient reactive inhibition to allow extinction to occur, and removal of the organism from the situation in which the fear/anxiety has occurred constituted drive reduction and thereby further reinforced the fear. Therefore, Wolpe predicted that a simple extinction paradigm would not work in reducing intense fears and might even produce increases in fear. He also claimed that his work with cats confirmed this belief, i.e., their fear of boxes in which they had been shocked did not extinguish through simple exposure. As a consequence of these beliefs Wolpe argued that a response that is mutually inhibitory of anxiety must be used to countercondition the anxiety. For his cats he chose eating and for his patients he chose deep muscle relaxation. These counterconditioning ideas were combined with Guthrie's threshold idea for extinction in which the animal or person is exposed to stimuli of gradually increasing intensity, making sure that high levels of anxiety are never elicited so that anxiety is never the last response to have occurred in the situation. Wolpe used a direct animal modeling approach and first tried out his ideas with his phobic cats. Feeding the cats in boxes of gradually increasing similarity to the originally conditioning box resulted in rapid and permanent reductions in fear. He then successfully expanded these attempts to the treatment of phobic patients, using relaxation instead of feeding as the response reciprocally inhibitory of anxiety; hierarchies of imagined stimuli that elicited varying degrees of anxiety were used as the analogue of the boxes of varying degree of similarity to the conditioning box.

Over the years since the publication of Wolpe's first book on this topic (1958), systematic desensitization therapy has become known as a highly effective form of treatment for most kinds of phobias other than agoraphobia (see below and Foa & Kozak, this volume). However, Wolpe's original ideas about why and how his therapy worked have not fared as well. The idea that muscle relaxation is necessary because it reciprocally inhibits anxiety has not held up. Some studies have questioned the importance of relaxation at all (see Leitenberg, 1976, for a review), and have even shown that the occurrence of fear during the stimulus presentations is predictive of a good outcome rather than a bad one (Lang, Melamed, & Hart, 1970). The general consensus today is that, in part, relaxation simply serves to ensure that the person will expose himself to the feared situation because his level of arousal will be low enough to prevent an avoidance response from being precipitated. In addition, it has been suggested that desensitization works simply because it allows extensive exposure to the feared situations (in vivo or in imagination) to occur at a low level of arousal; this may facilitate habituation or extinction of the fear (Lader & Mathews, 1968; Mathews, 1971).

It is interesting to note that somewhat similar conclusions have been reached regarding the necessity and effectiveness of counterconditioning procedures in the reduction of fears in animals. There is some evidence that using a hierarchy of CSs of gradually increasing intensity may be more effective, and that the use of feeding as a competing response may have a slight facilitatory effect. However, these effects are by no means enormous and their current interpretation is more akin to current views in the desensitization literature than to Wolpe's original reciprocal inhibition therapy, i.e., feeding as a competing response and/or the use of a hierarchy of stimuli probably facilitate exposure to the CS and therefore facilitate extinction of fear by reducing arousal and the likelihood of avoidance. (See Wilson & Davison, 1971, for a review of the relevant animal literature.)

Flooding or Implosion Therapy. Around 1965, some years after the successful advent of systematic desensitization techniques, a number of investigators began to experiment with the more straightforward extinction or flooding techniques that had earlier been rejected as being dangerous because they might produce increases in fear (e.g., Gelder et al., 1973; Marks, Boulogouris, & Marset, 1971; Stampfl & Levis, 1967; see Marks, 1972, for a review of early studies, and Foa & Kozak, this volume, for a review of more recent studies). It is interesting to note that the development of these techniques coincided approximately with the time discussed above when avoidance models for the acquisition and maintenance of phobias were becoming popular (e.g., Eysenck & Rachman, 1965; Stampfl & Levis, 1967). As with the rationale for the development of systematic desensitization techniques stemming out of Wolpe's reliance on a Hullian model of classical fear conditioning and extinction, the flooding or implosion model developed from ideas that were then current about the extinction of avoidance responses.

Masserman (1943) had first reported the effectiveness of what he called an environmental press in overcoming experimental neuroses in cats. With this procedure he forced the cats, through the use of movable barriers, to get closer and closer to the food box where they had been punished. He reported that their anxiety at first increased but gradually subsided and that other neurotic behaviors also rapidly diminished in intensity. This procedure was found to be one of the most effective that he tried in "curing" his cats of their experimental neuroses.

In the avoidance learning literature, Solomon, Kamin, and Wynne (1953) reported the first attempt to facilitate the extinction of avoidance responses through the use of flooding or response-blocking techniques in highly trained dogs. They found such a procedure to be only moderately effective, but they did not test different parameters, such as increasing the number or durations of the response-prevention trials. Other early reports (e.g., Page, 1955; Page & Hall, 1953; Polin, 1959; Weinberger, 1965) suggested that some combination of prolonged forced CS exposure and response blocking could be quite effective in facilitating avoidance response extinction. The presumed mechanism for these effects derived from the currently popular two-process theory of avoidance learning. The argument was that the forced exposure to the CS allowed fear extinction to occur, thereby reducing the source both of motivation and of reinforcement for the avoidance response. A parallel mechanism was thought to account for the early reports of the effectiveness of flooding or implosion therapy for phobias: By forcing the phobic patients to fully confront images of their phobic objects, anxiety would mount at first, but then gradually subside and extinguish, thereby removing the motivation for their phobic avoidance behavior.

The effectiveness of flooding or response-prevention techniques in hastening avoidance response extinction and in the treatment of phobias increased in the late 1960s and early 1970s as the importance of certain parametric variables began to be explored. The single most important variable in both situations has been found to be the duration of exposure to the feared stimulus, with increasing effectiveness being found with greater exposure durations (see Baum, 1970; Marks, 1972; Mineka, 1979b, for reviews of the animal and human studies on this variable). Other variables of importance in both cases involve facilitating exposure through increased exploration of the feared situations, and the presence of a nonfearful social partner (Baum, 1970; Marks, 1972).

Although these flooding techniques derived out of a two-process avoidance framework, and their presumed mechanism was thought to be fear reduction, the techniques have stood the test of time far better than the theory and presumed mechanism of straightforward fear reduction. Coulter, Riccio, and Page (1969) first suggested that response-prevention might facilitate avoidance extinction through the learning of a competing response (e.g., freezing) rather than through fear reduction. Shortly after, Baum (1970) reviewed evidence suggesting that although fear reduction may play a role, it is certainly not a necessary precursor of avoidance extinction. In fact, animals who have undergone flooding may still show considerable fear even though their avoidance response strength has been greatly reduced (Mineka & Gino, 1979). In a comprehensive review of four current theories of the effects of flooding on avoidance response extinction, Mineka (1979b) concluded that none is completely adequate. This may in part be because different learning processes mediate the effects of flooding with different kinds of avoidance responses and, in particular, that fear extinction may be more central to the extinction of some kinds of avoidance responses than to others. However, it seems clear that fear extinction is rarely, if ever, necessary as a precursor of avoidance response extinction, although of course with continued exposure to the CS once avoidance responding has stopped, fear may continue to decline to the zero or near zero point.

As an understanding of how flooding of avoidance responses may produce its effects becomes increasingly complex, a parallel phenomenon has occurred in the human literature on the flooding of phobias. In that literature as well, it has been found that not all aspects of the fear diminish at equal rates. Using Lang's (1968, 1971) three-systems model, it seems that one of the most common reports is that "the first beneficial effect of flooding is an ability to control unwanted responses at the behavioral level. Autonomic and subjective signs of distress, associated with nonavoidance, are then gradually extinguished over a period of days, weeks or months." (Hodgson & Rachman, 1974, p. 321; see also Rachman, 1978.) Thus, the human parallel with conclusions in the avoidance learning literature is quite strong if the behavioral avoidance component of the phobia is taken to be analogous to the learned behavioral avoidance response in the laboratory. Furthermore, as discussed above in the section on Symptomatology, parallel results have also been found when strongly ingrained phobic-like fears of snakes have been altered in rhesus monkeys through a flooding-like procedure (Mineka et al., 1980; Mineka & Keir, 1983). Again, changes were produced in behavioral avoidance without accompanying changes in behavioral disturbance (although it is unknown whether even more prolonged exposure would eventually have resulted in such changes in these monkeys, or whether making receipt of food treats contingent on suppression of behavioral disturbance would have resulted in such changes.)

In conclusion, it seems that flooding techniques that were developed out of an avoidance framework can be highly effective when certain parameters are taken into account. However, the original attractive simplicity of the two-process account of these results has proved misleading, both in the case of avoidance responses conditioned in the laboratory, and in the case of treatment of phobias. Nevertheless, it does seem that the ultimate goals in treating phobias are still well met by these procedures in that they get the person to stop avoiding the phobic objects, and eventually fear extinction is likely to follow as is the case with avoidance learning. Thus, in spite of the sometimes misleading parallels that have been drawn between conditioned avoidance responses and phobias (see above), the model for therapy has proved to be a very fruitful one. This may be because the issue of whether it is the CS or the US that is being avoided (the CS in the case of phobias and the US in the case of avoidance responses) is not as important in developing a model for therapy where the more important resemblances are that in each case there is fear, and a persistent, well-trained response that serves to escape or avoid that fear.

Finally, it should also be noted that although flooding therapy most obviously derives out of an avoidance framework, its effectiveness is also predicted by a contemporary non-Hullian classical conditioning framework as well. Here flooding therapies simply involved prolonged exposure to the CS (phobic object), thereby allowing fear extinction to occur. Although such a view does not appear to focus as much on the avoidance components of phobias, it does derive in a straightforward way from the more recent prepared classical conditioning models of phobias discussed above. And if the three-systems approach to fear is taken concurrently, the discordance or desynchrony between the different response systems that emerges in extinction is even expected (Gantt, 1953).

OBSESSIVE-COMPULSIVE DISORDERS

Symptomatology

In the *DSM-III* the diagnostic criteria for obsessions are "recurrent, persistent ideas, thoughts, images, or impulses that . . . are experienced as senseless or repugnant." The diagnostic criteria for compulsions are "repetitive and seemingly purposeful behaviors that are performed according to certain rules or in a stereotyped fashion . . . [and are] designed to produce or prevent some future event or situation. . . . The act is performed with a sense of subjective compulsion." In their comprehensive book on obsessive-compulsive disorders Rachman and Hodgson (1980) gave very similar definitions. They defined an obsession as "an intrusive, repetitive thought, image or impulse that is unacceptable and/or unwanted and gives rise to subjective resistance," and they defined compulsions as "repetitive stereotyped acts" (p. 10) that may be partly unacceptable and are "regarded by the person as being excessive and/or exaggerated" (p. 11). They also argued that a three-systems approach was as useful for obsessive-compulsive disorders as for phobias in that these disorders tend to manifest three loosely coupled sets of symptoms—subjective, behavioral, and psychophysiological. Given these few background comments, what can be said about parallel symptomatology in animals? Because one does not have access to animals' thought processes there is no close animal model for obsessions. Also given that the majority of people who have these disorders have both obsessions and compulsions, one cannot have a full-fledged animal model for the combined obsessive-compulsive disorder. Nevertheless there are several animal phenomena that do seem to resemble compulsive acts, and there is evidence that these acts are mediated by central states such as anxiety and frustration that may be quite similar to the mood states experienced by obsessive-compulsives when they experience a compulsion to perform their ritual. Therefore, the failure to model obsessions per se has not meant that useful animal models have not developed for at least certain features of obsessive-compulsive disorders.

The first classic example that has been cited frequently as a model for compulsive behaviors is the famous demonstration of Solomon et al. (1953) of traumatic avoidance learning in dogs. They noted that as the avoidance response became well learned it occurred with very short latencies and became more and more stereotyped in nature. The animals also showed progressively fewer overt signs of anxiety as the response became more stereotyped, and these stereotyped responses persisted for hundreds of trials even in the absence of further exposures to the US.

A second example that has also been cited of compulsive behavior in animals is N. R. F. Maier's (1949) classic work on fixations in rats. Maier reported that rats developed very strong fixations after being repeatedly forced to jump from a Lashley jumping stand to solve an insoluble discrimination problem. He argued that the behavior showed a compulsive quality in that the animals continued to make the fixated response even after the problem had been made soluble and they gave behavioral indications that they knew the correct response, e.g., an animal with a right position fixation might orient to the left and now correct side, but nonetheless jump off to the right side. Maier (1949) wrote, "This property of the fixation makes it appear as a form of compulsion. The animal executes an unadapted response even though it knows better" (p. 43).

Third, it has long been noted that primates subjected to a variety of stressful procedures often engage in stereotypic behavior. *Stereotypy* is generally defined as any repetitive behavior involving patterned and rhythmic locomotor movement, and it must occur at least three times before it is scored. A related behavior known as *ritualistic* behavior is defined as idiosyncratic nonlocomotor stereotyped actions, such as picking the teeth for prolonged periods, or strumming the mesh of the cage. Such stereotypic or ritualistic behavior is especially characteristic of monkeys with abnormal rearing histories, but is also known to occur in nearly all monkeys under periods of stress. For example, in one study young adult rhesus monkeys who had lived together all their lives were subjected to a series of eight 4-day separations (Mineka, Suomi, & Delizio, 1981). During these separations their distress or anxiety manifested itself primarily by high levels of stereotypic and ritualistic behavior, and this tendency increased across repeated separations. In fact, by the eighth separation five of the six monkeys were spending over half of their observed time engaged in highly agitated stereotypies.

And finally, displacement activities observed in a broad range of species under situations of conflict or high arousal may bear some resemblance to compulsive behaviors. For example, Holland (1974) has argued that displacement activities often involve grooming or nesting, and thus may resemble the obsessional's indulgence in washing and tidying rituals. Furthermore, Holland noted that displacement activity occurs under situations of frustration or high conflict between drives, and thus may resemble the situations of intrapsychic conflict often thought to be characteristic of obsessive-compulsives. In sum then, there are at least four kinds of rigidly stereotyped behaviors in animals that bear some resemblance to compulsive or ritualistic behavior in humans. Two of these (well-trained avoidance responses and abnormal fixations) have been studied in learning contexts and can be said to be induced by the training situation. The other two (primate stereotypies and displacement activities) appear to be innate responses to stress or conflict and do not appear to have the same degree of a learned component.

Etiology and Maintenance

Anxiety-Reduction Theory. For years a dominant theory of obsessive-compulsive behavior has been the anxiety-reduction theory (e.g., Dollard & Miller, 1950; Metzner, 1963; Nemiah, 1967; Rachman & Hodgson, 1980; Teasdale, 1974; Walton & Mather, 1963). Rachman and Hodgson remarked that "although most of the evidence on which these views are based consists of unsystematic clinical impressions, the degree of unanimity among writers is impressive" (p. 170). Although the details of the different theories vary slightly, the essence of each is that anxiety, often elicited by obsessive thoughts, motivates the performance of the compulsive ritual and that the ritual is strengthened or reinforced by the reduction in anxiety that ensues. The analogy to Miller's and Mowrer's two-process theory of avoidance learning is obvious: the CS (obsession) which elicits fear motivates the performance of the avoidance response (compulsive ritual) which removes the source of fear and is thereby reinforced by fear/anxiety reduction. Rachman and Hodgson have suggested that the correctness of this theory is enhanced considerably if one expands the term anxiety to include a mood state often described by patients as discomfort rather than anxiety per se.

What evidence is there to support the anxiety/discomfort reduction theory and its avoidance learning model? In the past 12 years several studies have been conducted by Rachman and Hodgson and their colleagues which support the proposition that most, although not all, obsessive-compulsive behaviors do fit well within this model (see below for a discussion of the exceptions). In their first experiment (Hodgson & Rachman, 1972) on 12 obsessive-compulsive cleaners they found clear-cut evidence that subjective anxiety-discomfort significantly increases following contact with a contaminated object, and significantly decreases following completion of the washing ritual. If the patients were not allowed to carry out the ritual following contamination there was a slight spontaneous decrease in anxiety/discomfort over the next half-hour period. Somewhat surprisingly, given earlier suggestions in the literature and clinical lore that interruption of a ritual would lead to a marked increase in anxiety (e.g., Dollard & Miller, 1950; Mandler & Watson, 1966), they found no evidence that interruption of the ritual once it had started caused an increase in anxiety.

In a second experiment on obsessive-compulsive checkers (Röper, Rachman, & Hodgson, 1973) similar, but not identical, results were found. Provoking an urge to check was followed by a significant increase in anxiety/discomfort, although not as great an increase as in the study with the compulsive cleaners. Similarly, completion of the checking ritual was followed by anxiety reduction, but 5 of the 12 patients reported an increase in anxiety on at least 1 of 3 occasions (accounting for a total of 7 out of 36 of the occasions studied experimentally). In a follow-up study on more compulsive checkers studied in their homes, Röper and Rachman (1976) found similar results, with 2 out of 12 patients reporting an increase in anxiety/discomfort after performance of the ritual some of the time. They also found that the presence of the experimenter significantly reduced the duration of the checking rituals, and was associated with the rituals being more effective in reducing anxiety.

It seems that both obsessive-compulsive checkers and cleaners experience marked increases in anxiety upon provocation, although the increases tend to be greater in compulsive cleaners. In addition, both experience marked decreases in anxiety after completion of their ritual, although the drops are sharper for compulsive cleaners than for compulsive checkers, and there are a minority of instances where the checking rituals are followed by increases rather than decreases in anxiety/discomfort. In both cases the anxiety reduction that follows completion of the ritual is more marked than the small spontaneous decays that occur over a half-hour interval if the ritual is prevented. However, in neither case is there evidence that interruption of a ritual leads to increases in anxiety over that already provoked.

Relevant Findings in the Avoidance Learning Literature.   As discussed above, well-trained avoidance responses can be markedly resistant to extinction, and this persistence can be potentiated by the use of serial CSs (Levis & Boyd, 1979). In fact, with serial CSs animals are known to make short latency responses to early portions of the stimulus and thereby manage to avoid later portions of the CS which elicit higher levels of anxiety (Boyd & Levis, 1976; Levis & Boyd, 1979). It would seem that the obsessive thoughts and feelings that pre- cipitate compulsive rituals could also often be characterized as being serial in nature, with these people showing a strong tendency to perform the ritual at the earliest signs of anxiety and thereby avoid potentially higher levels of anxiety/ discomfort later. For example, an obsessive-compulsive cleaner who has just touched a potentially contaminated doorknob will seek to wash immediately rather than wait for the dirt to have a chance to spread to other parts of his body and/or his environment. The longer he has to wait the greater the magnitude of his anxiety is likely to be, and probably the more extensive the cleaning ritual will have to be as well.

Teasdale (1974) has also reviewed several other aspects of the avoidance learning literature that are relevant to an understanding of obsessive-compulsive disorders. First, he has noted that higher rates of avoidance behavior are usually maintained when there are no explicit signals indicating that shock is about to occur (Sidman, 1955). With such unsignaled (Sidman) avoidance paradigms, animals learn to perform their response at fairly regular intervals and are able to postpone shocks indefinitely (although performance is not always perfect). However, the typical finding is also that they perform the response considerably more frequently than is necessary. Teasdale has suggested that compulsive ritu- alistic behavior can also be considered to be avoidance behavior that is often under poor or minimal stimulus control, which may account in part for its frequency of occurrence. In particular, as Mather (1970) suggested, obsessive- compulsives may have an especially difficult time discriminating between appro- priate and inappropriate stimuli, e.g., the difference between safe dirt and lethal germs. As would be expected from the avoidance learning literature, the absence of well-defined S^Ds would be expected to result in higher rates of responding.

A second point made both by Teasdale (1974) and by Rachman and Hodgson (1980) is that avoidance learning and efficient performance of an avoidance response are facilitated by the presence of good safety signals or feedback stimuli. These can be either in the form of an especially salient avoidance response itself (providing good proprioceptive feedback) or in the form of an exteroceptive feedback stimulus delivered immediately after the response is made (Bolles, 1970; Denny, 1971; Mowrer, 1960; Weisman & Litner, 1969, 1972). In the currently popular safety-signal revision of the two-process theory of avoidance learning, such safety or feedback signals are thought to acquire fear inhibitory properties and actually become sources of positive reinforcement. Furthermore, it seems to be the informational properties of the avoidance response or feedback stimulus rather than the response per se that is the important variable (Cook, Mineka, & Trumble, in preparation; Mineka, Cook, & Miller, 1984; Starr & Mineka, 1977). Therefore according to this theory, when such fear inhibitory stimuli are lacking, learning and performance will be less efficient because the transition from fear-motivated responding at the outset of training, to safety motivated responding will not occur as rapidly, if at all. (See also Delprato & McGlynn, in press, for a discussion of the relevance of safety-signal or approach-withdrawal theory to the maintenance of anxiety disorders).

Teasdale (1974) has suggested that compulsive rituals can be characterized as not having good feedback or safety-signal properties and that this may contribute to their high rate of occurrence. For example, because much of the dirt or contamination that precipitates a cleaning ritual is invisible to begin with, it follows that the effects of the cleaning ritual are invisible as well. Similarly, since many of the dangers that precipitate checking rituals are invisible (e.g., gas leaks) or unknown sources of future danger, the rituals themselves do not generate very effective feedback about their success. As Rachman and Hodgson (1980) stated, "checking rituals are prolonged and associated with excessive doubting because they are designed to anticipate, and indeed to prevent, some future event, and hence can have no end point, no obvious conclusion. . . . [They have] no assurance that the task is finished (i.e., that the perceived danger has been removed). At best, the risks are diminished" (p. 134).

It is also well known that noncontingent presentations of safety signals have a marked effect on decreasing rates of free operant (Sidman) avoidance responding, just as noncontingent presentations of excitatory fear stimuli have marked effects on increasing rates of responding (e.g., Rescorla & LoLordo, 1965). It seems likely that obsessive-compulsives may not have many thoughts or situations that have acquired strong fear inhibitory properties (CS^-s), and yet do have many thoughts and situations that have acquired strong fear excitatory properties (CS^+s). Thus their rates of responding/ritualizing may be expected to often increase over baseline levels when they encounter some object or situation that raises their anxiety level. Unfortunately, however, in the absence of good fear inhibitors (which as discussed above are easily forgotten when compared to fear excitors, cf. Hendersen, 1978), their rates of ritualizing would be expected to go below baseline levels less often. In addition, there is some evidence that fear inhibitors must be more specific to produce their inhibitory effect on avoidance responding than fear excitors to produce their facilitatory effects. For example, LoLordo (1967) found that CS^+s for loud noise facilitated Sidman avoidance responding for shock, but CS^-s for loud noise did not inhibit responding for shock. Thus, it might be expected that many fearful situations could increase rates of ritualizing, but relatively few thoughts or situations would be sufficiently specific in their inhibitory properties to have dampening effects.

In a related vein, Teasdale (1974) and others have also suggested that the literature on punishment of avoidance responding may have relevance to an understanding of obsessive-compulsive behavior. Administration of occasional "free" shocks may increase rates of avoidance responding (e.g., Sidman, 1966), and delivery of punishing shocks contingent on avoidance responding is more likely to enhance resistance to extinction of the response rather than to hasten extinction (see Brown, 1969, for one comprehensive review of this literature). This latter so-called vicious circle phenomenon has been the subject of considerable theoretical controversy over the years, and at the present time there does not seem to be a completely satisfactory resolution. Nevertheless, one popular account that captures part of what occurs states that the punishing shocks increase the animal's fear or anxiety level, and since the animal has previously been trained to make a particular response to reduce fear, it continues to make that same response, even though such responding now leads to shock rather than shock avoidance. With regard to obsessive-compulsive behavior the above findings suggest that random or contingent presentations of noxious stimulation may contribute to the persistence and high rate of performance of the compulsive rituals. Such noxious stimulation might occur in many forms, such as criticisms from friends or family members, the aversive consequences of excessive performance of the ritual itself (e.g., painful bleeding hands), the state of conflict or arousal often engendered by performance of the ritual, and the occasional increases in anxiety seen after the performance of checking rituals in a minority of cases. In this latter case, there may also be something analogous to Herrnstein's (1969) avoidance paradigm where animals learn to make responses that reduce shock frequency, although never to zero. In other words, individuals who experience increases in anxiety following completion of their ritual may well be avoiding even higher levels of anxiety that would be experienced if they did not perform the ritual at all.

A final set of findings may be discussed with respect to the issue of the wide variety and generality of situations in which compulsive behaviors tend to occur. The avoidance models of obsessive-compulsive behavior have sometimes been criticized for being unable to account for the broad range of situations in which cleaning or checking rituals occur since, after all, avoidance responses are usually only trained in one context. There is very little literature on the extent to which such responses would still occur in widely differing contexts. (Rescorla & LoLordo,

1965, or Solomon & Turner, 1962, showed that independently established excitatory CSs could immediately acquire control over previously established avoidance responses—but these tests were only made in the original avoidance context.)
There are, however, several findings in the animal literature that bear on this
question. They demonstrate that very specific responses learned in response to
an emotional state, such as fear or frustration in one situation, often occur again
in very different situations when a similar emotional state is elicited in the animal
for different reasons.

In one well-known example that has been cited by other authors writing on
related issues (e.g., Teasdale, 1974; Wolpe, 1958), Fonberg (1956) first trained
dogs to make leg-lifting avoidance responses to avoid shock and/or airpuffs. The
dogs were later put through a Pavlovian discriminative appetitive conditioning
procedure designed to induce experimental neurosis by making the discrimination
increasingly difficult (the original procedure of Shenger-Krestovnovika in Pavlov's laboratory for inducing neurosis). As the dog's behavior became increasingly neurotic, Fonberg observed that the previously trained leg-lifting avoidance
response began to occur with considerable frequency, even though no more
discriminative stimuli (S^{D}s) for the response were presented. In addition, "shaking off" movements occurred in the dogs who had previously been conditioned
to avoid airpuffs into the ear. Thus, a response trained to relieve fear or anxiety
based on aversive stimulation, such as shocks and airpuffs, reemerged in a
different situation when the dogs were induced to experience an anxious, aroused
state through an entirely different procedure (conflict, frustration, or loss of
predictability over the appetitive discriminative conditioning procedure, cf. Mineka
& Kihlstrom, 1978).

The second example of a phenomenon of relevance to the issue of the variety
and generality of the situations in which obsessive-compulsive behaviors occur
has not previously been discussed in this context. In this famous experiment
from the frustration and persistence literature, Ross (1964; see also Amsel, 1971,
for a pertinent description) first trained hungry rats to make highly distinctive
responses (jumping hurdles or climbing) under a partial reinforcement schedule
for food reward in a short black-sided box. According to Amsel's theory of
frustration and persistence (e.g., 1971), during this initial training these animals
would be expected to have anticipatory feelings of frustration counterconditioned
to jumping or climbing responses, thus building a basis for persistence in future
frustrating situations such as extinction. In the second phase of the experiment,
the animals were trained under thirst drive to run down a long narrow white
runway to obtain water reward on a continuous reinforcement schedule (thereby
receiving no frustration experience associated with running for water reward).
In the third phase when this running response for water reward was put on an
extinction schedule, the jumping and climbing responses from the first phase
reemerged, even though there were no more hurdles or the appropriate box out

of which they might climb. Thus, the highly distinctive responses that had been conditioned to feelings of frustration under one drive state and in one stimulus context reemerged for the first time in a different context and under a different drive state when similar feelings of frustration occurred there for the first time. Related findings were also reported by Amsel and Rashotte (1969) who found the reemergence of idiosyncratic rituals when their animals were trained in one situation under conditions of frustration and later frustrated for the first time in a different situation. As discussed by Amsel (1971), such findings may be a model for frustration-produced regression in that they show animals spontaneously regressing back to earlier learned patterns of behavior when frustrated in new situations. In addition, the Ross, Rashotte, and Amsel results seem relevant to an understanding of obsessive-compulsive behavior insofar as they provide a model for the occurrence of ritualized kinds of behavior across a wide variety of situations, given that a similar emotional state is elicited in each and that a particular response has been conditioned to occur in the presence of that emotional state in the past.

In sum, it seems that there exist a number of findings in the conditioning and avoidance learning literatures that provide useful insights into the maintenance and persistence of obsessive-compulsive behaviors. It should be acknowledged that the language of the anxiety-reduction theory has been maintained in this discussion of these findings. Others, such as Carr (1974), have suggested that a more useful tact may be to use more cognitive terminology such as that used by Seligman & Johnston (1973) in their cognitive theory of avoidance learning. Thus, Carr argued both that obsessive-compulsives make abnormally high subjective estimates of the probability of undesired outcomes, and that situations where there are potentially harmful outcomes generate anxiety. Compulsive behaviors develop and occur as ways to reduce threat by lowering the probability of unfavorable outcomes. Although Carr's terminology is somewhat different than that used in the previous discussion, in reality his model does not seem significantly different. He also states that "the chosen strategy (i.e., the ritualistic behavior) is reinforced by anxiety reduction and is always successful in averting the unfavorable outcome" (p. 316). Furthermore, Carr's model does not appear to make different predictions about characteristics of obsessive-compulsive behavior, and is even less able than the anxiety reduction model to explain the stereotyped nature of compulsive responses, or the cases where compulsive behaviors are sometimes followed by elevations in anxiety.

Origins of Obsessive-Compulsive Behavior.   The discussion to this point has really focused on the issue of the maintenance and persistence of obsessive-compulsive behavior once it is established, rather than on the issue of how it originates. Such an emphasis reflects the state of the literature on this topic because there is not a great deal known about the origin of such disorders. As summarized by Rachman and Hodgson in their comprehensive book on the topic

(1980), there is little evidence in most cases for a specific traumatic conditioning history that would provide a basis for the beginning of the disorder. Nor is there much evidence to support a role for direct vicarious or observational conditioning in most cases, because the incidence of the same disorder in family members, especially in the children of obsessive-compulsives, is not especially high. Thus, although direct or vicarious learning may play a role in a small proportion of cases, it does not seem to be critical in the majority. Where it does play a role, Rachman and Hodgson suggest that the observational learning is likely to be of general behavior patterns such as timidity and overdependence, which contribute to a personality style that may be especially prone to the development of obsessive-compulsive behavior, rather than learning of specific compulsive behaviors per se.

Current evidence seems to suggest that there is an important genetic contribution in the origins of this disorder, but only in the sense that there is a "general emotional oversensitivity or neuroticism" (Rachman & Hodgson, 1980, p. 38). With or without this very general predisposition toward neuroticism of some sort, obsessive-compulsive disorders vary considerably in mode of onset. Rachman and Hodgson found that the estimates of number of cases where there was a precipitating incident varied from 56% to 90%. These precipitating incidents were usually of a general nature and did not often qualify in the sense of a traumatic avoidance learning incident, e.g., sexual and mental difficulties, pregnancy, illness or death of a relative, and frustration and overwork. In a study of their own, Rachman and Hodgson found that there was a much higher proportion of cleaners (75%) than of checkers (27%) who reported a sudden onset of the disorder. They suggested that direct conditioning may be more likely to play a role in the origins of cleaning compulsions, given their greater likelihood of sudden onset, and that vicarious or instructional learning may play a greater role in checking compulsions with their typically more gradual onset. However, these suggestions must be seen as tentative given the paucity of evidence for a clear-cut role for either direct or vicarious conditioning in most cases.

Several other issues related to etiology do bear some discussion. First, Beech and Perigault (1974) have suggested that people who develop obsessive-compulsive disorders may be prone to a high level of arousal (consistent with findings of high neuroticism), which may make them especially susceptible not only to classical or avoidance learning contingencies, but also to pseudoconditioning, one-trial learning, and poor habituation. They reported the results of some experiments on obsessive-compulsives that were supportive of each of these three propositions, although they acknowledged that other neurotics often showed parallel results, i.e., the differences emerged in comparisons with normals rather than with other neurotics.

Second, de Silva, Rachman, and Seligman (1977) discussed the relevance of the preparedness concept, discussed above for phobias, for understanding the distributions of kinds of obsessive-compulsive thoughts and behaviors. Obsessive thoughts about dirt and contamination associated with compulsive washing are, for example, so common among obsessives as to make their occurrence clearly nonrandom. In their study of 69 phobic and 82 obsessional patients, de Silva et al. (1977) did find the content of a great majority of phobias and obsessions to be rated as "prepared" in the sense that they were judged to have "probably been dangerous to pretechnological man under not uncommon circumstances." However, in this retrospective study they did not find any relationship between the degree of preparedness of the phobia or the obsession and the mode or speed of onset of the disorder, or severity of the disorder, or of therapeutic outcome. Thus, at the present time the importance of these findings seems to be limited to the observation that certain objects or situations are much more likely to become the subject of phobias or obsessive-compulsive behaviors than others. Whether a carefully done prospective study would reveal any relationship of this factor to speed of onset, persistence, or resistance to change is unknown at the present time.

Finally, Rachman and Hodgson (1980) have made an interesting distinction between the kind of avoidance learning that is involved in obsessive compulsive cleaning and checking that could have implications for understanding their etiology. They have suggested that obsessive-compulsive cleaning is most often characterized by passive avoidance, and that obsessive-compulsive checking most closely resembles active avoidance. Compulsive cleaners, like phobics, go to great lengths to passively avoid places, people, and objects that might be dirty or contaminated. The washing rituals themselves can be seen as escape responses to remove dirty or contaminated material. Compulsive checkers can be seen engaging in their rituals in an attempt to forestall some unpleasant event, such as the occurrence of harm to one's self, one's family, or even strangers. Checking rituals are in this sense more akin to active avoidance where the animal responds in anticipation of an upcoming aversive event in order to prevent it. It should be noted that this distinction is not an absolute one in that there can be an active avoidance element with cleaning rituals (preventing disease to oneself or family), and a passive avoidance element with checking rituals (staying away from situations that are likely to provoke the obsessive thoughts that lead to the rituals). Nevertheless, it may have some interesting implications regarding differential etiology of these two most common subtypes of obsessive compulsive disorders. In particular, Rachman and Hodgson (1980) suggest that cleaners may have a history of punishment (passive avoidance training) and overprotection by parents leading to a pattern of passive avoidance and fearfulness rather than active coping. Checkers, by contrast, may be more likely to come from families that were overly critical and set excessively high standards. This, in turn, may engender an excessive concern with causing harm to others and resultant learning of active avoidance behaviors that are aimed at prevention of such harm.

Summary and Conclusions.   It seems that there are only hints or clues as to the origins of a high proportion of obsessive-compulsive disorders. The extent to which preparedness, opportunities for passive or active avoidance learning, pseudoconditioning, and other related phenomena play a direct role is unknown. However, regardless of the exact etiology, once the disorder has begun the anxiety/discomfort reduction theory accounts to a large degree for its persistence, and even the frequent instances of increasing severity over time. As discussed above, there are a wide variety of findings in the conditioning and avoidance learning literatures, which when considered together, give a plausible account of many of the fundamental features of these disorders: their stereotyped nature, their high rate of occurrence, their persistence, their appearance in a wide variety of situations, and their compulsive nature.

Therapy

Although Wolpe (1958) originally intended his reciprocal inhibition therapy (systematic desensitization) to be effective for all anxiety-based disorders, research over the years has clearly demonstrated it to have limited usefulness in the treatment of obsessive-compulsive disorders (see Rachman & Hodgson, 1980, for a review). In fact, until the early 1970s there were no clearly successful treatments available for a majority of cases when the disorder was of moderate to severe intensity. With the advent of the use of flooding or response-prevention techniques in the treatment of phobias, systematic research was also initiated on the use of such techniques in treating obsessive-compulsive disorders. The results have been impressive in that a high proportion of patients with a moderate to severe disorder show marked improvements in relatively short periods of time (e.g., Foa & Goldstein, 1978; Mills, Agras, Barlow, & Mills, 1973; Rachman, Hodgson, & Marks, 1971; Rachman, Marks, & Hodgson, 1973). (See Foa & Kozak, this volume, and Rachman & Hodgson, 1980, for reviews.)

Given the support for the anxiety-reduction avoidance model of obsessive compulsive disorders, it is not surprising that there are strong parallels in the factors known to be effective in hastening extinction of avoidance responses and in alleviating obsessive-compulsive disorders. As discussed in the section on therapy for phobias, there is now a large literature demonstrating that response-blocking or flooding techniques can be highly effective in eliminating, or at least in hastening the extinction of, well-trained avoidance responses (see Baum, 1970; Mineka, 1979b; Riccio & Silvestri, 1973, for reviews). However, it is also equally apparent that the simple two-process account of how these techniques work is oversimplified: fear extinction does not always precede or mediate avoidance response extinction. The point emphasized in the discussion of phobias was that avoidance responding may be reduced while there are still moderately high levels of fear, and this seems to parallel a common finding in the treatment of obsessive-compulsives, i.e., the rituals may stop or be reduced before the urges and anxiety have disappeared.

In addition, there is another and opposite finding in the animal flooding literature that has its parallel in the literature on therapy for obsessive-compulsive behaviors. Using a one way jump-up avoidance training procedure, Mineka, Miller, Gino, & Giencke (1981) found that a small amount of flooding had significant effects on reducing fear, but no significant effect on hastening avoidance response extinction. They argued that fear may not play a very important role in the maintenance of this easily learned, stereotyped, and highly persistent type of avoidance response, making moderate reductions in fear unlikely to affect avoidance responding. They noted the parallel to certain cases of obsessive-compulsive disorders where fear or anxiety may be quite low in spite of the marked persistence of a compulsive ritual, cases where Rachman and Hodgson describe the rituals as having become functionally autonomous of their origins in anxiety reduction. Walton and Mather (1963) described two such interesting cases of long-standing obsessive-compulsive disorders where the treatment that was effective in reducing anxiety left the obsessive-compulsive behaviors unchanged. This may parallel the situation described by Mineka et al. (1981) where a treatment that was effective in reducing fear left the somewhat stereotyped jump-up response intact.

A further issue of interest concerns parallels in the factors known to enhance the effectiveness of flooding in hastening avoidance response extinction and in curing obsessive-compulsive disorders. In the avoidance learning literature, as in the human flooding literature, a number of variations in flooding techniques have been tried, e.g., whether or not the response is allowed to occur, whether long or short CS exposures are used, and whether or not CS termination is response-contingent. The results of these studies have not been wholly consistent (e.g., Polin, 1959, versus Berman & Katzev, 1972). However, in reviewing the relevant literature Mineka (1979b) concluded that the bulk of the evidence suggested that although total amount of nonreinforced CS exposure is an important variable, response-prevention per se also seems to facilitate extinction of at least certain kinds of avoidance responses, perhaps by allowing the learning of competing responses. Similarly, in their review of the literature on flooding therapy for obsessive-compulsive disorders, Rachman and Hodgson (1980) concluded that the majority of studies have suggested an important role for the response-prevention aspect of the treatment, i.e., the prevention of the ritual following provocation of the urge. Indeed, in at least one study Mills et al. (1973) found that exposure to contaminating objects alone, without response-prevention, was ineffective in reducing the frequency of compulsive behavior and, in fact, produced some increases in the behavior. Although their results were inconclusive by themselves because the patients did not receive very extensive exposure, the bulk of the evidence does seem to support the conclusion that exposure plus response-prevention are the essential features of an effective therapy. As noted above, in most cases the same two variables have generally been shown to be most important in maximizing the effectiveness of flooding, both in hastening avoidance response extinction and in reducing fear of the CS itself (Mineka & Gino, 1979; but see also Miller, Mineka, & Cook, 1982, for different results with jump-up avoidance responding). In both cases it seems that two important things happen during the treatment: habituation or extinction of the fear or anxiety elicited by the obsessive thought begins, and some new way of responding is acquired that replaces the old avoidance response or compulsive ritual. In both instances there is evidence that these two changes may not proceed at exactly the same rate, producing desynchrony between the three fear response systems.

GENERALIZED ANXIETY DISORDERS

Symptomatology

To qualify for a diagnosis of generalized anxiety disorder in the *DSM-III* system an individual must have had more or less continuous signs of anxiety for at least one month, and the symptoms must include ones from three of the following four general categories: motor tension, autonomic hyperactivity, apprehensive expectations, and vigilance/scanning. Strictly speaking, there are probably no precise animal models of the full range of symptoms of generalized anxiety states by these criteria. Nevertheless, there are a number of examples in the animal literature of emotional states that share many of these features and discussion of them is warranted.

It is somewhat ironic that many of the best examples of symptoms resembling generalized anxiety states come from the experimental neurosis literature, given the number of critiques made of that literature for not paying close attention to symptom similarity. In fact, if some of the experimental neurosis paradigms from Pavlov's, Gantt's, and Liddell's laboratories had ever been studied systematically enough, a good animal model for generalized anxiety disorders might well exist. These investigators consistently found patterns of behavior characterized by extreme agitation, hypersensitivity, restlessness, rapid respiration and heart beat, muscular tension, piloerection, mydriasis, distractibility, and inability to perform previously learned responses (see Broadhurst, 1970, 1973; Mineka & Kihlstrom, 1978, for reviews of this literature). Such symptoms were often apparent outside the experimental situation and often persisted for many months following the termination of any of the experimental procedures. In some cases, such as Gantt's famous dog Nick, the symptoms even continued to increase and worsen over time. Thus, although these experiments were not performed with *DSM-III* diagnostic criteria in mind (and in fact many of the investigators never tried to tie their "experimental neurosis" to any particular subtype of neurosis), it does seem that some of these animals fit the prototype described in the *DSM-III* (see Cantor, Smith, French, & Mezzich, 1980, for the concept of psychiatric diagnosis as prototype categorization, and Mineka, 1982, for a discussion of applications of this to animal modeling). In particular, these animals showed clear signs of the first two symptom categories: motor tension and autonomic hyperactivity. Apprehensive expectations, such as anxieties and fears, would also seem to be inferable from their behavior toward the experimenters and experimental situations. Finally, symptoms of vigilance and scanning would also seem to be inferable from their hypersensitivity, distractibility, and difficulty performing even simple learning tasks.

A second widely studied phenomenon in the primate literature that shares some of the features of generalized anxiety states is the response to social separation. Both human and nonhuman primate infants respond to separation from their mothers (or other primary attachment objects) with an intense response of protest characterized by extreme agitation and general panic (Bowlby, 1973; Mineka & Suomi, 1978). Their behavior can become quite frantic, as indicated by extremely high levels of vocalization, locomotion, and stereotypy. During this protest phase there are sleep disturbances, heart rate and body temperature changes (e.g., Reite, Short, Seiler, & Pauley, 1981), and rapid activation of the pituitary adrenal system as indexed by elevations in plasma cortisol (Coe & Levine, 1981). This intense period of protest and agitation is seen by Bowlby (1973, 1980) as a prototype of anxiety, and there is some reason to believe that primate infants, like human infants, can come to anticipate an impending separation and show signs of separation anxiety (Baysinger & Suomi, in Suomi, Kraemer, Baysinger, & DeLizio, 1981). Such protest responses to separation are not confined to infant monkeys, but rather occur in adolescent and young adult monkeys as well. For example, as described in the section on obsessive-compulsive behaviors, Mineka et al. (1981) found high levels of protest and agitation upon separation in 3–5-year-old monkeys who had lived together all their lives. Thus although separation protest differs from generalized anxiety states in a number of ways (e.g., it is usually of limited duration such as 1–3 days and it has a clear-cut precipitant), the symptoms themselves bear considerable resemblance to those of panic attacks and generalized anxiety states.

Etiology

Any discussion of the etiology of generalized anxiety states must start with an acknowledgement of the contribution of a reasonably strong genetic predisposition (see Lader & Marks, 1971; Slater & Shields, 1969, for reviews). There is also a large animal literature involving selective breeding experiments, which shows that emotional reactivity related to fear and anxiety depends to some extent on genetic factors (see Fulker, D. W., 1981; Gray, 1971; Rosenthal, 1971; for reviews). Nevertheless, it is clear that experiential factors also play a strong role in determining who will and who will not develop generalized anxiety states. What are these etiological experiential factors and to what extent do they have parallels in the animal literature? Although there is probably less consensus about the etiology of generalized anxiety states in humans than there is regarding the etiology of phobias or obsessive-compulsive disorders, a variety of models have been proposed that have their roots in the animal literature.

Conditioning Models.   Wolpe (1958) argued that a simple classical conditioning model like that for phobias was also appropriate to explain the etiology of generalized anxiety states. This model proposed that fear/anxiety was conditioned to a multitude of environmental stimuli, thus accounting for the generalized nature of the situations in which these individuals experience anxiety. Although this model is appealing because of its simplicity, it has few adherents today, in large part for the same reasons that Wolpe's model for phobias has been considered to be inadequate (see above).

In the Russian literature a related account to that of Wolpe's has been offered by investigators who have studied interoceptive classical conditioning, i.e., conditioning where the CS and/or the US are interoceptive and largely unconscious in nature. (See Razran, 1961, for a review of the Russian literature on interoceptive conditioning.) In one experiment, for example, a dog underwent a conditioning procedure wherein mild stimulation of the colon was the CS, and electric shock was the US. Following conditioning, the dog showed intense signs of anxiety simply during natural passage of feces through the colon (which presumably mimicked the artificial stimulation of the colon—the CS—during conditioning). Such interoceptive conditioning is known to be highly stable and resistant to extinction when compared to exteroceptive conditioning. Furthermore, because such CSs (and USs) are a part of everyday living, although they may be quite unconscious, their opportunity for playing a role in generalized anxiety states is quite high. By this argument the anxiety appears to be generalized or free-floating simply because the CSs are interoceptive and largely unconscious. Given the high level of attention that has been paid to conditioning models of neurosis in the United States and Great Britain, it is somewhat surprising that more attention has not been paid to the interoceptive conditioning model. A large part of the problem has undoubtedly been the unavailability of most of the original experiments in translation. More research on this topic would appear to have considerable usefulness in understanding possible contributory factors to both generalized anxiety disorders and various psychosomatic disorders.

Several theorists have stayed within a conditioning framework but switched to instrumental rather than classical conditioning. According to this model, autonomic responses characteristic of anxiety are instrumentally conditioned, i.e., reinforced by their consequences which may be either of a positive or negative reinforcement variety. Such an argument began to be advanced following the demonstrations of DiCara and Miller (e.g., 1968a and b; Miller, 1969) showing instrumental conditioning of heart rate and other autonomic responses in rats using either rewarding brain stimulation or shock avoidance as the sources of reinforcement. Kimmel has done related work on instrumental conditioning of the galvanic skin response in humans and has argued that such conditioning may play a role in the origins of chronic anxiety states (see Kimmel, 1975, for a review). Brady has also proposed a role for instrumental conditioning in the etiology of anxiety states on the basis of his work on conditioning of high blood pressure in monkeys. In these experiments monkeys are trained to elevate their blood pressure to avoid electric shock, and after many months of such training it has been found that the elevations become chronic (Brady, 1980; Harris & Brady, 1977; see also Benson, Herd, Morse, & Kelleher, 1969). While of considerable interest and importance, upon close scrutiny none of these findings can plausibly be said to provide a reasonably complete model for the origins of most anxiety states. In most experiments on instrumental conditioning of autonomic responses the conditions of feedback and immediacy of reinforcement are far more tightly controlled than could ever be true in the real world. Yet the effects under such "ideal" conditions in the laboratory are often very small compared to the large effects that they are proposing to model and which would have to occur under much less ideal conditions of feedback and reinforcement. Furthermore, at most, such experiments could only provide a model for the autonomic symptoms of anxiety states, and they are silent on the relationship of these autonomic symptoms to other symptoms.

Unpredictability and Uncontrollability.   If simple classical and instrumental conditioning models are of limited usefulness, what other more prominent current theories of anxiety states deserve attention? In the past 15–20 years a variety of theories of anxiety have emerged that have one or both of the themes of uncertainty and uncontrollability playing a prominent role in the origins of anxiety-based disorders. For example, Mandler and Watson (1966; Mandler, 1972) have argued that arousal and anxiety occur when an integrated response sequence is interrupted and the individual has no perceived control over the interruption. If such a state of affairs continues, the anxiety may become generalized. Epstein (1972) has argued that anxiety states arise as a result of any one of three factors: primary overstimulation, cognitive incongruity, and response unavailability. By cognitive incongruity he means a violation of expectancies and/or the inability or failure to form a predictable pattern or model of the stimulation that is being experienced, leading to feelings of confusion, disorganization, and disorientation. By response unavailability he means the experience of an aroused response tendency that cannot be expressed, leading to feelings of helplessness. Similarly, Lazarus and Averill (1972; Lazarus, 1966) have argued that anxiety occurs when the person perceives a threat whose source is unknown or ambiguous, thus leaving no clear response or action tendency possible. Seligman (1975) has argued that feelings of unpredictability over important life events, especially negative ones, lead to symptoms of anxiety. (He has also argued that feelings of uncontrollability play a prominent role in certain kinds of depression.) As a final example, Garber, Miller, and Abramson (1980) have argued that anxiety occurs when a person perceives that a bad outcome may be impending (with a probability of greater than zero but less than one), and that he/she will be helpless to control it. Thus, both uncertainty and helplessness are suggested as playing important roles in the etiology of anxiety. It is obvious from this brief overview of recent theories of anxiety that many theorists believe that feelings of uncertainty and/or feelings of uncontrollability play an important causal role in the development of anxiety states.

Interestingly, over the same time period that these theories of human anxiety disorders have appeared, an enormous animal literature has also developed on the importance of predictability and controllability over important life events, especially aversive ones. In fact, the animal literature has had considerable impact on these theories of anxiety as evidenced by frequent references to the animal studies. To briefly summarize the animal literature, exposure to uncontrollable as opposed to controllable aversive events can be very stressful and can result in a wide range of behavioral deficits and physiological changes including impaired ability to learn control in subsequent tasks, passivity, lowered aggressiveness, alterations in levels of certain important neurotransmitters, ulcers, analgesia, cortisol increases, and many others (see Maier & Jackson, 1979; Maier & Seligman, 1976; Mineka & Kihlstrom, 1978; Mineka & Hendersen, in press; Overmier, Patterson, & Wielciwicz, 1980; Seligman, 1975; Weiss, 1977; for reviews). Exposure to unpredictable as opposed to predictable events can also be very stressful for the organism and lead to a wide range of behavioral and somatic changes including retardation of learning that subsequent events are predictable, ulcers, behavioral suppression, alterations in levels of certain important neurotransmitters, etc. (see Mackintosh, 1973; Mineka & Kihlstrom, 1978; Mineka & Hendersen, in press; Seligman, 1968; Seligman & Binik, 1977; Weiss, 1977). (However, there is also some evidence that predictability alone [i.e., without control] in some situations may be more stressful or aversive than lack of predictability, cf. Weinberg & Levine, 1980, for a review.) Of the two, control has probably been found to be an important variable more consistently, and it has been prominently implicated in a major theory of depression as well as anxiety (e.g., Abramson, Seligman, & Teasdale, 1978; Seligman, 1974, 1975). It should be noted, however, that it is very difficult to completely separate the effects of predictability and controllability because of their overlap, i.e., an organism with control over the termination of an aversive event also has predictability over when that event will terminate. (See Averill, 1973; Mineka & Kihlstrom, 1978; Mineka & Hendersen, in press; Weinberg & Levine, 1980, for reviews of the overlap.)

Although none of the investigators working on the topics of predictability or controllability have attempted to develop an animal model of generalized anxiety disorders, they have considered their work to be highly relevant to the general topic of "stress," which is frequently discussed in frameworks related to anxiety. At a theoretical level, one prominent theory of the effects of exposure to *uncontrollable* events is that it leads to an expectation of helplessness which, in turn, leads to cognitive, motivational and affective deficits (Seligman, 1975). These deficits include impaired ability to learn controlling or coping responses in new situations, reduced motivation to respond, and mood states of anxiety or depression. One prominent theory of the effects of exposure to *unpredictable* events is that it leads to feelings of chronic fear or anxiety, because in the absence of a signal for the aversive event, there is also no safety signal telling the organism when he/she can relax and feel safe (Seligman, 1968; Seligman & Binik, 1977). Although both of these theories have proved to be somewhat controversial, it is interesting to note the parallels between them and the themes discussed above, which have been prominent in so many theories of anxiety. The uncertainty theme in the anxiety literature seems to closely parallel the notion that without knowing what is going to happen, or when it is to happen, one remains in a constant state of vigilance or anxiety. The response unavailability theme in the anxiety literature also seems to closely parallel the theme of helplessness as discussed in the animal literature—in particular, the effects of helplessness on impairing the ability to learn new coping skills, on reducing motivation or incentive to try, and on inducing mood states of anxiety and/or depression.

In the section on symptomatology of anxiety disorders it was noted that the experimental neurosis literature probably contains the closest examples or analogues to generalized anxiety states in humans. Several years ago Mineka and Kihlstrom (1978) reviewed the classic studies of the experimental neurosis literature and concluded that the two most prominent themes in each case were the unpredictability and/or uncontrollability of important life events. None of the studies had been done with these concepts in mind, and in only a few instances were there appropriate control groups available to make the argument with any certainty. Nevertheless, Mineka and Kihlstrom observed that buried within each paradigm known to produce experimental neurosis one can consistently find evidence that environmental events of vital importance to the organism (e.g., food for a hungry animal, or shock for a restrained animal) become unpredictable, uncontrollable, or both. Thus, there appeared to be a common thread that ties together the experimental neurosis literature—the variables of unpredictability and uncontrollability. Furthermore, they suggested that the importance of this literature today derives from the fact that the apparent sources or causes of experimental neurosis seem highly similar or even identical to certain factors frequently considered to be important in anxiety states and depression. It is well known that anxiety and depression frequently appear in the same individual (e.g., Derogatis, Klerman, & Lipman, 1972; Garber et al., 1980; Mendels & Weinstein, 1972; Weissman, this volume). Therefore, the fact that depressive symptomatology also sometimes appeared in the experimental neurosis literature was not surprising, especially given that a sense of lack of control or helplessness has been implicated in one prominent theory of depression (Abramson et al., 1978; Seligman, 1975).

In sum, although there is no complete animal model for the etiology of generalized anxiety states, recent empirical and theoretical work on the effects of uncontrollable and/or unpredictable aversive events clearly has had an impact on theorizing in the area of human anxiety disorders. Given the strong parallels between some of the classic demonstrations of experimental neurosis and the symptoms of anxiety states, researchers interested in developing an animal model of anxiety states would do well to pay more than the minimal amount of lip service to it than has typically been done in recent years.

Therapy

In general, behavioral approaches to the treatment of generalized anxiety disorders have not been as successful as they have been in the treatment of phobias and obsessive-compulsive disorders, although relaxation training and biofeedback techniques occasionally have some success (see Foa & Kozak, this volume; Lader & Marks, 1971). Given that both systematic desensitization and flooding therapies derive most basically from a stimulus response framework, the failure of these techniques with generalized anxiety disorders is not too surprising. With both kinds of therapies an attempt is made to alter the inappropriate response to some stimulus (the phobic object or the obsessive thought and its associated anxiety), either through the practice of an alternative response as with systematic desensitization, or through extinction and/or the development of a competing response with flooding. Yet, the defining characteristic of generalized anxiety states is that there are no specifiable stimuli or events that reliably evoke the anxiety; it is there nearly all the time, in all situations. In the absence of any known stimulus or thought that clearly precipitates the anxiety, it is difficult to proceed with the basic elements of either systematic desensitization or flooding therapy, which, in each case, involves exposure to the real or imagined stimuli that elicit the anxiety.

It is also interesting to note from this perspective that behavioral approaches to generalized anxiety states might logically predict not only difficulty with these two kinds of behavior therapy, but also success with drug therapies. If there are no identifiable stimuli (or even if there are unidentifiable interoceptive ones) that elicit the nearly ubiquitous anxiety responses, then the best approach may simply be to suppress the responses directly through the use of antianxiety drugs. As is well known, drug therapies—especially the benzodiazepines—are widely and often effectively used in the management of generalized anxiety states (Gilman, Goodman, & Gilman, 1980; Klein, Rabkin, & Gorman, this volume; Lader & Marks, 1971). Such drugs are also known to reduce certain kinds of anxiety responses in animals, in particular the activity of the behavioral inhibition system which is activated by both conditioned fear and conditioned frustration (Gray, 1979; this volume).

One can also note that the widely used cognitive techniques for the treatment of anxiety disorders (e.g., Beck, 1976; Goldfried & Davison, 1976; Meichenbaum, 1977; Sarason, this volume) have at least an indirect connection to the animal literature. The work discussed above on the effects of unpredictability and uncontrollability has had a large impact on increasing the popularity of cognitive theories of animal learning (Mackintosh, 1974; Maier, Seligman, & Solomon, 1969; Seligman & Johnston, 1973). This has occurred, in large part, because work in this area has more than ever pointed up the inadequacies of traditional, noncognitive, purely S-R approaches to learning. Over the same time period that this increasingly cognitive approach to animal learning has occurred, we have seen the development of "cognitive" therapies for anxiety-based disorders as it became more and more apparent that purely behavioral approaches were not always wholly adequate. Moreover, some of the specific ideas contained in cognitive therapies derive out of the work discussed above on the importance of feelings of unpredictability and/or uncontrollability in causing anxiety states, e.g., Bandura's (1977) self-efficacy theory and its approach to therapy that has clear-cut connections to work on learned helplessness. (See also Delprato & McGlynn, in press, for a discussion of the status of cognitive-expectancy theories for the etiology and therapy of anxiety disorders.)

CONCLUSIONS

It is obvious from the above review that there are no full-fledged animal models for any of the three anxiety-based disorders, using the criterion approach of Seligman (1974, 1975), McKinney (1974), or Wolpe (1958). Yet it is also clear that in each case there is a great deal of animal research that has illuminated important features of these disorders and had a meaningful impact on theories of their origin and the variables that maintain them. It seems that the major reasons for dissatisfaction with conditioning models in the past have been that they have been too simplistic. As discussed above, none of the anxiety disorders can generally be thought to originate from a single or even a few trials of classical fear conditioning or avoidance learning occurring in a vacuum, as has often been proposed in the past. Instead, there appear to be a multitude of experiential variables that can occur prior to, during, or following a conditioning experience, that affect the amount of fear that is experienced, conditioned, and maintained over time. (See Mineka, in press, for a more complete discussion of this point.) For example, Mineka, Gunnar, and Champoux (submitted) showed that early experience with control and mastery can reduce the level of fear that is experienced in several different fear-provoking situations later in an infant monkey's life. Several investigators have also showed that control of, or feedback about, US offset during conditioning reduces the level of fear that gets conditioned to a neutral stimulus, thereby showing that the dynamics of fear conditioning are powerfully influenced by the controllability and predictability of the US (e.g., Desiderato & Newman, 1971; Mineka, Cook, & Miller, 1984). Furthermore, following conditioning, animals that are allowed to avoid the US (another form of control) show more rapid attenuation of fear than do animals that cannot avoid the US but receive equivalent amount of nonreinforced CS exposure (Cook, Mineka, & Trumble, in preparation; Starr & Mineka, 1977). Also a host of other factors occurring following conditioning, such as inflation (Hendersen & Blaccioniere, 1984; Rescorla, 1974) and forgetting of US specificity (Hendersen et al., 1980), can result in increases in fear or in the places in which fear is exhibited. Finally, it has also been shown that very intense and persistent fears can be learned through observational conditioning experiences alone in the absence of any overt traumatic US (Cook, Mineka, Wolkenstein, & Laitsch, submitted; Mineka, Davidson, Cook, & Keir, 1984). Thus, it is only with an acknowledgment of this kind of complexity and interaction of a wide range of experiential variables affecting conditioning that conditioning models will continue to prosper and maintain their usefulness in the future.

It is interesting to note that the review of the relevant literature on conditioning models was approximately twice as long for phobias as for obsessive-compulsive disorders, and approximately twice as long for obsessive-compulsive disorders as for generalized anxiety states. This in part reflects the overlap in the relevant literature on these topics. However, it also reflects the relative amount of attention that the three categories of disorders have received in the animal learning literature, and probably the relative amount of attention the human clinical literature on the three categories of disorders has paid to the animal learning literature. One possible reason for this state of affairs stems from the degree of overlap that may reasonably be expected between an animal syndrome and these three human anxiety-based disorders. Phobias (with the exception of agoraphobia) are relatively simple disorders without much prominent cognitive symptomatology; obsessive-compulsive disorders generally have both prominent cognitive symptoms (obsessive thoughts) and excessive behavioral rituals; generalized anxiety states have both prominent cognitive symptoms (worries, apprehensions, doubts, hyperattentiveness) and prominent behavioral and physiological symptoms (motor tension and autonomic hyperactivity). Given the difficulty in accessing the cognitions of animals, as well as the strong bias that existed for many years against even attempting to do so, it is not surprising that there has been more interchange between human and animal researchers on the topic of phobias than on the topics of obsessive-compulsive and generalized anxiety disorders. Nevertheless, given increasing trends toward psychiatric diagnosis by prototypes rather than by necessary defining features (e.g., Cantor et al., 1980; Cantor & Genero, in press; Horowitz, Wright, Lowenstein, & Parad, 1981), the usefulness of animal models that can resemble a prototype of the human disorder may increase. This may happen even if certain features are always missing or inaccessible in the animal model. (See Mineka, 1982, for a related argument.) Furthermore, it seems likely that as the animal conditioning literature becomes increasingly cognitive in its approach as has been the case since the early 1970s (e.g., Hulse, Fowler, & Honig, 1978; Mackintosh, 1974), the likelihood increases that there will be an impact of the conditioning literature on the cognitive features of these disorders as well.

ACKNOWLEDGMENTS

Preparation of this chapter was supported by grants from the University of Wisconsin Graduate School and by Grants BNS-8119041 and BNS-8216141 from the National Science Foundation to the author. The author would like to thank Robert Hendersen, Robert Hodes, John Kihlstrom, and the editors of this volume for their helpful comments on earlier versions of this chapter.

11 The Limitations of Animal Models in Understanding Anxiety

Frederick H. Kanfer, Ph.D.
University of Illinois

The use of laboratory animals for understanding human behavior can be traced back several centuries in the history of western thought. Despite the invaluable contributions of animal researchers to the biologial, behavioral and social sciences, several philosophical, theological, and methodological problems have not been sufficiently attended to.

Systematic investigations of biological structures and functions in animals and humans were not sanctioned for nearly a millenium during the era in which the cultural life in western Europe was dominated by theological doctrine. With the advent of the scientific revolution came a renewed interest in open investigation of the physical (biological) aspects of human functioning. During the early 17th century Descartes provided a clear philosophical conceptualization of the relationship between models of men and animals. He sharply set aside the human race as unique among all species in his doctrine of dualism. Paradoxically, his conception of the body as a machine set the stage for the study of physiological processes and body structures as the substratum of the human mind. Descartes' philosophy of interactionism of mind and body paved the way for the study of biological processes in behavior. It also focused attention on the nervous system as a locus of interaction between mind and body. The strong impetus for comparative psychology and for the later recourse to animal experiments as a basis for developing models of human behavior came in the middle of the 19th century with the publication of Darwin's *The Origin of Species*. The effects of this theory upon the development of psychology have persisted to our own time. Boring (1950) traces a rise of a modern animal psychology to Darwin. He states:

> When animals were automata and men had souls, there was not so much reason
> for scientific interest in the animal mind as there was when it became clear that

there is no break in continuity between man's mind (which by that time was being distinguished from his soul) and whatever it is that animals have for minds. So it comes about that we may properly regard Darwin as starting the modern era in animal psychology. (p. 472)

The trend of American Psychology at the beginning of the twentieth century toward functionalism and behaviorism strongly reinforced the broadening of the base of psychology by means of animal experimentation. The arguments against introspection as a data source and the emphasis on observable behaviors strengthened the attractiveness of the animal laboratory experiment as an analogue to human behaviors.

The study of the development and treatment of neurosis represents a particularly attractive area in which the animal analogue can be used. For both practical and ethical reasons, theories of etiology are difficult to test in humans. Once a generality of the laws of learning the across species is assumed, an extensive body of research on "'experimental neurosis'" in animals can serve as a blueprint for testing conceptualizations derived from clinical observations and for the development of new treatment methods. As described in Mineka's review of animal models of anxiety (chapter 10, this volume), research on learning in laboratory animals, ranging from rats and pigeons to cats and monkeys, have yielded paradigms of the genesis and dissipation of neurotic anxiety. In turn, these have served as a foundation for most current behavioral techniques used in the alleviation of behavior disorders that contain some anxiety component. The models have served a very useful purpose as heuristic guides for conceptualizing and treating anxiety disorders, with much greater success than earlier models of psychopathology. But, as the papers in this volume indicate, the animal models have not always been supported by clinical research. For example, Wolpe's widely used and very effective systematic desensitization treatment was based on the premise that anxiety reduction always requires the inhibition of anxiety by a competing response (Wolpe & Lazarus, 1966). Later work with flooding procedures and variants of the original desensitization method suggested the strong merit of the therapeutic approach, but also challenged the underlying theoretical rationale. Particularly, contributions of cognitive and symbolic variables that modify simple input-output relationships play a significant role in maintaining human anxiety. To date these cognitive factors have not yet been investigated, or perhaps are beyond reach, in the animal laboratory. Although laboratory research with animals has contributed much to the understanding of human anxiety, there are inherent limitations to the utility of animal models.

In this presentation I discuss some limitations of the animal paradigm as a basis for extrapolation to complex human behavior. The limiting factors fall into two interrelated classes. First, they are due to the difficulty in generalizing across species with differing CNS structures and functional capabilities. Second, they relate to the problem in extrapolating from any contrived laboratory situation to the complexities of free living organisms in their natural environment. These issues are considered in the context of the treatment of anxiety disorders. It is a further purpose of this paper to call attention to research areas, both at the human and animal levels, that may bring the laboratory setting closer to some human life situations and thereby direct refinement of current animal models of anxiety disorders. Although I attempt to describe limitations of the animal model under two major headings, there is considerable overlap between the issues raised under each.

Unlike basic research that aims primarily at developing conceptual models of human behavior or at discovering relationships between variables that affect human actions, animal research on anxiety at the very outset has had the implicit goal of contributing to the improvement of therapeutic interventions for clinical problems. In this sense the approach is characterized by the goals for science set by some as the contribution of knowledge to human welfare (Bevan, 1980). Other writers have questioned the *sine qua non* of ecological validity (Manicas & Secord, 1983; Mook, 1983). They suggest that preoccupation with external validity may confound the tasks of the scientist and clinician. Indeed, application of scientific principles nearly always requires utilization of knowledge beyond the observed scientific principles and is derived from sources other than experimental data or theoretical constructions (Kaminski, 1970). Moreover complexity and fluctuation of variables that enter into particular situations, and the effects of changes due to time alone, make it impossible to develop precise predictions from past research and theory. At best, scientific knowledge can provide heuristic guidelines to alert the professional to the sources of variation to which attention should be paid (Cronbach, 1975). Implementation of laboratory-derived procedures in natural settings also must take into account numerous factors that influence not only the course of an intervention or the effect of a variable, but even the likelihood that existing conditions will permit the application of known and empirically demonstrated therapeutic procedures (Reppucci & Saunders, 1974). Nevertheless, the clinician who wishes to practice in consonance with scientific knowledge needs empirically supported knowledge about the phenomena he or she encounters. Such data form a background for clinical formulations, decisions, and actions.

Theories of learning based on laboratory animals have provided one central organizing theme. Although this theme is a relatively general one, it approximates the belief or clinical inference that symptoms represent attempts to escape or avoid anxiety in situations in which other coping behaviors are not available or not appropriate. Learning theorists, like clinicians, differ in describing the specific conditions that initially produce neurotic anxiety and in postulating mechanisms that maintain or exacerbate the syndrome. However, there is general agreement that anticipation of severe pain or punishment, based on previous association with some aversive experience, characterizes this intense emotional state. Viewing this core model as a bare-boned skeleton, researchers and clinicians have attempted to investigate in the laboratory the variables that affect this process. They have also attempted to supplement this conceptual framework by additional complexity that embeds the animal model in the context of human life experiences.

ISSUES IN EXTROPOLATING FROM ANIMALS TO HUMANS

Among the many differences between human and nonhuman species only two are highlighted here because of their extraordinary relevance to the study of the anxiety disorders. First and foremost are considerations related to the capability of the human organism to use a sophisticated verbal-symbolic system in regulating its behavior. The second, not unrelated difference, concerns the social nature of the human animal and its development in a sociocultural environment that radically modifies the strictly biological nature of its action sequences. Animal research has been particularly deficient in evaluating the impact of the human capacity for verbal-symbolic behavior and the human sensitivity to social and cultural contextual factors in anxiety-related behaviors.

I have previously suggested that the analysis of the determinants of human behavior can be roughly organized around three sources of controlling influences (Kanfer, 1975). The first cluster describes variables originating in the external environment. We have described them as *alpha* variables. It is this source of influence that is commonly shared by animals and persons, and encompasses the range of inputs from the physical and social external environments. A second cluster of influences can be traced to the person's own psychological activities, both cognitive and overt, gradually modified by individual experiences but rooted in the socialization of the human animal. These self-generated cues, responses, and reinforcers can be jointly described as *beta* variables. They comprise the self-regulation system and enable the human being to act in relative independence of the external environment. It is a moot point whether such psychological self-regulation occurs in animals at a somewhat similar but nonverbal representational level. This self-regulatory system is not directly accessible in animals, and thereby makes it nearly impossible to directly assess its influence on animal behavior. While self-regulatory processes occur at various physiological levels, as described very early by Cannon's concept of homeostasis, any inference about such systems at the psychological level have come primarily from anthropomorphic inferences. A third source of control lies in the organism's biological system. I have used the term *gamma* variables as a generic for the stimuli and responses located in the biological system. This conceptualization has in common several features of Lang's model (this volume) of the three interacting response systems that need to be considered in understanding the full range of human activities.

In the context of research on anxiety disorders this model suggests that the human experience of anxiety involves not only biological components and reactions to external stimuli, but also the many cognitive events and self-regulatory psychological processes associated with the interpretation of external stimulation, the interaction of these cues with biological reactions and their integration into a complex event that has been called the "'subjective'" experience of distress. Further, *beta* variables can cause a person to alter environmental inputs, for example by avoiding or modifying external stimulation that is anxiety arousing. They can also influence *gamma* variables by enacting controlling responses over some biological functions. For example, the use of self-induced relaxation, biofeedback procedures, and cognitive events, such as imagery or self-talk to alter moods, all can affect the biological component of the anxiety syndrome. Indeed, numerous therapeutic intervention techniques have utilized self-regulatory processes in the service of anxiety reduction (Kanfer & Goldstein, 1980).

From this view of the human organism, a full description of the phenomena of anxiety requires (1) that events at all levels be considered in a total context, (2) that any single response must be seen as the product of the joint action of variables at all three levels, and (3) that each response, in turn, alters the organism's attention, conceptual organization and response patterns on subsequent occasions. Clearly, these alterations also include the trigger of moderating cognitive or self-regulatory events that can alter the observed output, even though the environmental inputs are kept constant.

Our conceptualization also suggests that a behavioral model must have a temporal quality that takes into account the continuous feedback and "'feedforward'" effects on the system in a recursive and dynamic manner. In the case of anxiety disorders, this conceptualization means that the environmental context combines with cognitive events and biological reactions to produce a behavioral pattern. When the person attempts to control, modify, tolerate, or disregard the environmental and biological inputs, these efforts in turn lead to changes in the situation. But the success or failure of these actions influences not only the response to current and subsequent situations. It also affects his or her judgments about the ability to cope with such situations and plans for meeting (or avoiding) them. Thus each repetition of a similar situation is met with a different cognitive, biological, and behavioral set at the outset.

The *episodic* or dynamic nature of behavior, which is described in the next section, is particularly relevant to the difficulty of replicating the natural environment with laboratory procedures using identical repeated trials. The episodic quality of behavior also implies that the complex that has been called "anxiety" represents a fluid constellation that changes with each successive experience and results in variations in input at each of the three levels. A person's chance exposure to an anxiety-arousing situation, feedback from others, self-generated attempts to cope with pain, subjective discomfort or fear components, and momentary biological conditions (such as fatigue or euphoria) change that current response. But they also alter the manner in which the person handles subsequent cues that signal a similar situation in the making. Unlike subhuman animals the human reaction to aversive stimulation includes a wide variety of ways to avoid, cope with, or tolerate anticipated repetitions. These adjustments may range from sweeping lifestyle changes in order to avoid all situations remotely associated with the anxiety-arousing cues, to deliberate efforts to expose oneself to the situation in an attempt to master it. Standards for personal conduct, derived from both individual experiences and social norms, can serve to set goals and provide motivation to tolerate pain or discomfort for the sake of long-term success or reward. Self-regulatory activities can direct behavioral patterns that either reduce or intensify the anxiety experience and responses to it, quite in contrast to the strong dependence of the animal on the immediate external environment and his genetic endowment.

It is not a coincidence that animal research on anxiety has grown out of learning theories that focus on motor behaviors. The theories underlying animal research paradigms deal with observable behaviors and all too often have excluded the mediating effects of human self-regulatory functions and, with few exceptions, the contributions of the information processing capabilities of the human.

The characteristics of the human as a social animal further requires supplementation of the animal model. For example, social norms provide both motivation and instrumental behaviors for coping with some anxiety reactions. Given a clear time limit, almost any phobic person can approach a feared object and tolerate anxiety for a while; any compulsive can deritualize for a limited time span. Strong social pressures can combine with self-generated incentives to help patients gain temporary control over the same behaviors that they had initially described as uncontrollable. Furthermore, in human situations the appropriateness of avoidance and escape responses and their social effectiveness are gauged against social norms and judged by both observer and subject in terms of these criteria. For example, phobic responses to small insects, to height, and to other conditions may represent socially accepted norms. Compulsive behaviors may be praised and encouraged in individuals if they follow the form prescribed by various religions and social institutions. In fact, in some cultural settings compulsive behaviors are encouraged by insistence that individuals practice, rehearse, and repeat magical thoughts in order to retain control over threatening events.

The social environment also attends to behaviors that a person executes in order to deal with perceived threat. Social demands and socially mediated standards for behaving fearlessly, or in a manner that confronts and masters an impending threat, may enhance coping efforts; sympathetic understanding and support for escape or avoidance behaviors may encourage adoption of evasive and avoidance patterns. Clinicians have frequently observed the salutary effect on the first anxiety reaction to a situation when other persons are exposed to the same threat. Anecdotal reports and clinical observations have described the salutary effects of strong social norms and prescribed standards of conduct for soldiers in combat or for individuals in emergency situations.

It is perhaps the countervailing effect of social support that tends to reduce the likelihood that a pathological anxiety disorder will develop after exposure to an intense life-threatening situation. In contrast, clinical folklore and experimental analysis of behavior in neurotic patients have illustrated the strong effects of such social reinforcers as excessive compassion, pity, or sympathy in maintaining pathological reactions to fear stimuli. All too often the neurotic response can become instrumental in procuring social reinforcers, thereby serving an important function in enhancing the patient's control over others.

The evaluative component of self-regulation surely plays a role in perception and assessment of the degree of current distress, and may thereby further affect the intensity of the resultant escape or avoidance response. Mineka (this volume) has noted the importance of interoceptive unconditioned stimuli as the basis for generalized anxiety. The role of such stimuli has probably been underestimated because of the methodological problems in experimentation. Research on the perception of physical symptoms (Pennebaker, 1982) and on the health belief model of the person might elucidate how variations in individual sensitivity to physical and psychological cues of similar levels of anxiety-related arousal may influence both the anxiety experience and the reactions to it. What may differentiate a patient from a nonpatient may not be only the degree of anxiety that has been aroused in various situations, but the self-reactions to such arousal in comparison to this individual's standards for well-being. The limited number of studies and theories on subjective happiness and well-being suggests that the intensity of significant life events influence biological function, that judgement of happiness and personal satisfaction may be influenced by social comparisons, and that mood is influenced by numerous factors, ranging from the weather to marital status and unemployment. Measurement of psychological well-being is in itself a difficult problem (Diener, submitted; Zautra & Goodhart, 1979). Such background factors as mood, personal judgments of well-being and social standards for happiness affect the ways in which an individual exposed to a fear-arousing situation will deal with it. These reactions, in turn, determine the likelihood that an enduring pathological anxiety reaction will be developed.

Cognitive and self-regulatory events have generally been part of the definition of human anxiety. The animal data, by necessity of methodology, have focused primarily on the change in escape and avoidance behaviors, acquired after exposure to intense fear-arousing situations. Both animal and human data suggest, however, a desynchrony between changes in observed distress and avoidance behaviors. Research on the utility of therapeutic intervention for reduction of phobic responses in humans has aimed mainly at reducing the avoidance behavior, assuming that the altered interaction with the environment subsequently results in a changed appraisal of the fear situation, thereby decreasing subjective discomfort. In contrast, earlier psychodynamic approaches to therapy have focused mainly on reducing subjective distress, presumably by altering the critical cues for avoidance. Early studies by Lang and his co-workers indicated the complex nature of the anxiety response (Lang, 1969; Lang & Lazovik, 1963; Lang, Lazovik, and Reynolds, 1965). During systematic desensitization in laboratory studies, changes in avoidance behavior preceded subjective reports of anxiety, although the subjective distress decreased later, as reported on follow-up interviews after termination of treatment.

A clear understanding of the processes by which cross effects between the cognitive and behavior systems occur in humans has not yet been offered. Different techniques may help an organism to learn to *act* differently or to *feel* differently in anxiety situations. The criterion for both development and alleviation of anxiety in most animals studies has been an observable operant response. In contrast, in clinical situations a patient's major complaint does not always focus on one or the other domain. Further, different social contexts may have different consequences for changing either a patient's behavior or subjective distress. For example, a soldier in combat might best learn to *act* differently for survival, even if he continues to be in distress. By contrast, a person to whom the survival consequences of an avoidance response are relatively trivial, such as avoidance of cats or spiders, reduction of subjective distress may be more important. The experiments on monkeys described by Mineka (this volume) illustrate this point. That monkeys in an avoidance paradigm changed their behavior but showed no change in disturbance might have been due to the fact that the experimental operations rewarded the animals primarily for an approach response to the snake, regardless of the coincidental consequences for their state distress or disturbance.

The Role of Worry

Another important limitation to studying the full range of sequences and components of human anxiety in the animal laboratory is highlighted by the role of worry in the sequence. Worry has been conceptualized as representing an attempt at "problem solving on an issue whose outcome is uncertain but contains the possibility of one or more negative outcomes. Consequently worry relates closely to fear process" (Borkovec, Robinson, Pruzinsky & DePree, 1983, p. 10; Borkovec, this volume). The mediational function of worry, in extending the impact of fear-generating situations beyond their actual physical presence, may not only maintain the exaggerated reaction to neutral stimuli. It may also produce a secondary reaction: anxiety about a person's inability to cope with anxiety-generating situations. This fear of fear phenomenon is noticeable particularly in generalized anxiety conditions. It has been proposed that fear of fear is not related to a specific situation, but may characterize an individual's "cognitive style." The only analogue to this phenomenon with which I am familiar in animal experiments is the repeated observation of experimenters that animals show both evidence of behavioral disturbance and spontaneous rehearsal of escape responses between exposure trials. An even more complex aspect of cognitive function is the paradox of anxiety associated with the fear of loss of control while exercising an effort to achieve control over emotional tension (Bernstein & Borkovec, 1973; Heide & Borkovec, 1983; Borkovec, this volume; Barlow, this volume). Indeed, relaxation-induced anxiety, as a side effect in treatment of anxiety reduction by systematic desensitization, presents a challenge to any animal experimenter in devising analogues to the human situation.

The Social Norm Context

The dependence of the human anxiety response on social norms is implied even in the common definition of anxiety as a response "'out of proportion'" to the demands of the situation. As noted earlier, control of evil forces by religious rituals or voodoo magic, or the training of meticulous routines for preventing evil by prescriptions for dress, body posture, or body orientation provide the cultural background for the development of coping techniques that in a different cultural context are viewed as pathological.

The strong dependence on sociocultural norms suggests a reexamination of Seligman's concept of prepared classical conditioning for possible extension to the sociocultural level. Just as biological predispositions prepare an organism for differential responding to various physical inputs, the acculturation process during childhood prepares persons to respond differentially to situations in which high anxiety tolerance is socially demanded or eschewed. In achievement-oriented western cultures, test taking, speech giving, social confrontations with others, sexual performance, and situations generally in which a person's social or physical competence and achievement must be demonstrated are recurrent themes in the complaints of patients with anxiety disorders. A catalogue of such social situations that may be "culturally prepared" might suggest preventive measures for coping with these specific situations during childhood training. Öhman's study on angry faces (Mineka, this volume) appears to be a transition from the concept of prepared classical conditioning to prepared cultural conditioning. Further research at the human level would be required to develop such an "'ecological map.'"

Research at the human level might help to resolve something that has puzzled me for quite a while. In our culture, persons seek experiences that produce the same physiological state of arousal as found in mild anxiety and require execution of the very same acts that are normally avoided. The attraction of roller coaster rides, high risk sports, challenges in mastering fear-inspiring tasks, and other thrill-seeking activities suggests that it is not simply the arousal state nor the uncertain or threatening information about the feared situation that triggers the anxiety response. Unpredictability and lack of control over an event have been viewed, both in animals and humans, as critical antecedents of anxiety. Yet to the thrill seeker they represent challenges rather than threats.

In contradiction to the drive reduction hypothesis, thrill-seeking situations appear to offer the delayed positive reinforcement of overcoming distress and risk, and achieving a goal that seems to be more powerful than the expected reaction to the immediate aversive elements of high arousal, danger, and threat. Anticipation of some discomfort is a hallmark of excitement in children's thrill-seeking activities. Initiation rites in primitive societies and in ceremonies of various groups in our society represent situations in which individuals clearly anticipate fear-related distress—yet they seek them for the ultimate social or personal rewards. Although the various elements of the situation differ among animals and humans, it would appear feasible to develop an animal analogue of the effects of training in high-risk situations and subsequent rewards, on later reactions in the conditioned emotional response paradigm. Would animals so trained show less response suppression and fewer behavioral disruptions than animals who are trained only to avoid such situations? The analogue may yield interesting possibilities for the hypothesis that early training in risk taking and anxiety tolerance, with clear and high positive outcomes, might be useful in the prevention of anxiety disorders.

In this section I have attempted to indicate some limitations of animal-based models for human anxiety, which are related primarily to two critical differences between human and animal functions. One difference lies in the role of self-regulatory processes in humans. The second difference is rooted in social learning, social norms, and other society-based information that moderates the input-output relationships that are generally the focus of animal research. In our own research on tolerance of aversive stimulation, we have shown that individuals can be trained to develop controlling responses that influence both behavioral and cognitive reactions to pain stimulation and fear stimuli (Avia & Kanfer, 1980; Grimm & Kanfer, 1976; Kanfer & Goldfoot, 1966; Kanfer, Karoly, & Newman, 1975; Kanfer & Seidner, 1973; Stevenson, Kanfer, & Higgins, in press). Expectations of one's capacity to cope and self-directed attention further modify behavior in anxiety-provoking situations (Bandura, 1977; Carver & Scheier, in press). In a revision (Kanfer & Hagerman, 1980) of our earlier self-regulation model (Kanfer, 1970), self-generated standards, attributions and beliefs in the controllability of an outcome are critical features in determining whether a situation will result in increased emotional arousal and detrimental self-preoccupation or in a resolution of the conflict situation. Current research also suggests that the interplay between affective and information processing components may have a considerable influence on a person's reaction to potentially anxiety-arousing situations. To date, systematic investigation of these factors in animal research has not yet been offered. Considering that the human self-regulatory system develops in a social context, utilizes verbal symbolic sequences, and affects self-generated motivation, both species differences and methodological problems may set clear limits to the extent to which a comprehensive model of human anxiety can be tested in the animal laboratory.

FROM THE LABORATORY TO THE NATURAL ENVIRONMENT

The richness, diversity, and adaptability of human behavior defy the orderly investigation and analysis of isolated causes and effects in a piecemeal approach. Laboratory experiments permit control of all but a specific target behavior, allow investigation of causal influences of single components, and reduce observer biases by rigorously fixed and replicable procedures. The effectiveness of the laboratory strategy has been well demonstrated by the progress of psychological science over the last century. The laboratory approach is particularly useful as a heuristic device in the development of theoretical formulations and for determining the consistency with which relatively powerful variables activate specific mechanisms in living organisms. Indeed, if psychological phenomena, such as anxiety, were caused by a single or very few factors, were invariant over time and unaffected by other parts of the human system, laboratory paradigms would be sufficient for application to all clinical situations.

The limitations of laboratory studies become apparent only when the investigator attempts to make predictions directly from the highly controlled environment to the multidetermined, complex situation encountered in the clinic. The contrived setting of the laboratory allows the experimenter to control the environment, so that stimuli and consequences are varied only as a function of a limited set of experimenter-determined contingencies. It is the experimenter who preselects the range of possible outcomes to be studied, and it is he or she who limits the response options of the subject for ease of observation. Despite such constraints, subjects do not respond only along the dimension selected for measurement. Specific outputs (responses) occur in a background of constantly fluctuating other behaviors, but the experimenter's attention is focused only on a single response, often selected for convenience in measurement.

Frequently these measured behaviors are not those that normally occur in the daily activities of humans or animals. For example, lever-pulling responses or jumping hurdles represent typically used, clean dependent variables for measuring the effect of specific inputs in animals. A measure of physical approach to a phobic object or a physiological response to a fear-arousing stimulus has often been selected as a convenient index of anxiety in humans. In fact, the selected response may not be one that is critical to the survival of the animal or the comfort of the person in a natural environment. Its "ecological validity" may be limited by the ingenuity of the experimenter to create approximations to natural situations that carefully balance richness and diversity with control, replicability, and ease of measurement. Further, stimuli that are selected in animal and human studies to elicit pain or arouse fear also are often quite foreign to the organism's natural habitat (e.g., shock). Such choices preclude the activation of natural (biological) adaptive responses and widen the gap between laboratory and everyday life. The arbitrary selection of subjects, target behaviors, assessment procedures, and treatment environments have been listed as common sources of errors in analogue studies of clinical phobias (Bernstein & Paul, 1971).

The decision to study specific input-output sequences in a static and isolated environment sacrifices first an appraisal of the complex interrelationships between various dependent variables that make up the rich texture of a response pattern. Secondly, it is a *tour de force* to adopt a static model of behavior, since it clouds the episodic and dynamic nature of human activities. Time, and changes associated with time, are central characteristic of human actions. In anxiety disorders, for example, the occurrence of many other life events, related or unrelated to an original traumatic experience, may alter its impact. In the laboratory neither the experimental task for the subject nor the environmental setting changes over time or as a function of the behavior of the subject.

In a recent paper Marks (1983) points out that duration of anxiety disorders often extends over many years, that there is frequent reacquisition and extinction, that the initial trauma is unknown (in contrast to the careful planning in the laboratory), and that the conditioned stimulus, unconditioned stimulus, conditioned response, and unconditioned response are all unknown, while they are stringently defined in the laboratory. Additionally, when research is conducted with animal organisms, environments and opportunities outside the experimental test situation are tightly controlled from birth to death. A unique history is provided for laboratory animals by control over their genetic inheritance, home cages, feeding, and other factors. This imposition of boundaries even makes questionable whether rats, cats, or monkeys reared in a natural environment would behave in a field situation, analogous to the laboratory test situation, in exactly the same way as laboratory-reared animals. In human anxiety the impact of an anxiety disorder on other humans is continuously modified and changes dynamically over time. A frequent result of this dynamic interaction is the well-known secondary gain phenomenon in patients. Secondary gain is characterized by a gradual and subtle change in the relationship between other persons and the patient over time in such a way that continuing reinforcement for the pathological behavior is maintained. In contrast to most case observations on individual patients, laboratory studies have failed to examine the pattern of changes in social interrelationships that may strongly influence the reduction or maintenance of an anxiety reaction.

Laboratory experiments represent a microanalysis of component processes, truncated in time, from which inferences are made both to natural settings and for events that develop over prolonged time periods. The limitations of laboratory research are not necessarily inevitable. For example, animal experiments can be carried out to approximate everyday conditions in a richer, quasi-social environment. Longitudinal studies could then yield observations of changes over time and in different contexts. A laboratory analogue could include not only test trials, but also observations of daily activities of test animals who are housed with other animals (not exposed to anxiety-arousing situations). Records of changes could then be made of other habitual responses occurring *outside* the test situation. Observations of changes in the interactional patterns with other animals could also document the broader effect of the anxiety-arousing experience. Such research would enlarge the utility of the laboratory model, by clarifying how an initially mild, circumscribed anxiety reaction spreads to apparently unrelated domains and contents, and how different reactions by conspecifics might affect these changes. Observation of such behavioral changes outside the test situation have been reported in anecdotal form by many experimenters since Pavlov's days; they have not been systematically explored.

In the development of human anxiety it is often not the behavior of the patient in a specific anxiety-arousing situation that matters. Many specific phobias or panic attacks narrowly define situations that can be avoided without significant social consequences. More frequently, it is the spread of the effects of an original anxiety-arousing situation, both on the stimulus and on the response side, that precipitates an incapacitating pathology. What may differentiate a patient from a nonpatient is not only the degree of anxiety that has been aroused in various situations and the specific consequences of the attempts to cope with that situation, but his or her evaluation of the arousal and coping effects in the context of overall life experiences. Do the pathogenic effects of objectively similar situations depend on the person's current mood, perceived control, level of life satisfactions, dominant concerns or other elements of the complex situation? The study of prevention of anxiety disorders would benefit from the extension of animal analogues toward greater human ecological validity and more extensive replication of natural situations. For instance, what effect would long-term pretraining in differential rates of reinforcements and social contacts have on reactions to exposure to fear-arousing test stimuli?

Mineka's data (this volume) on the acquisition of fear by observational learning in monkeys suggest the possibility of a reversed strategy for the treatment of anxiety. Observation of fearless behavior or gradual mastery of fears has been shown to reduce fear in children (Bandura, 1969). Perhaps such training, depending on the social context, the relationship of the model to the subject, and the breadth of the behaviors that are modeled, might yield a paradigm that suggests techniques for prevention rather than remediation of human phobias. Current emphasis on the importance of social networks in lowering high risks for pathology and in attenuating effects of treatment might be replicated in animal laboratory studies in which housing conditions rather than test parameters become critical independent variables.

Another critical factor that differentiates laboratory experiments from natural settings lies in the different incentive systems that prevail in laboratory research and in everyday settings. In animal work, experiments have been conducted mainly with procedures that use an intense but unidemensional biological base of motivation, such as food, shock, or loud noise. Both in animal and human situations real life motivations are much more complex and interrelated. It is indeed specious to argue that motivational conditions for a college student in a midwestern town who undergoes an experiment on snake phobia or even on test anxiety are sufficiently intense or complex for extrapolation to natural catastrophies, war situations or other life-threatening predicaments in which persons respond to a multiplicity of incentives and concerns. As we have already noted, and has been demonstrated (Bernstein 1973; Miller & Bernstein, 1972), social demand characteristics can influence most persons to tolerate temporary anxiety in a laboratory experiment. The effects of such brief and static interventions have neither been examined by follow-ups nor by examination of changes in covarying behaviors under a wide range of conditions.

In this chapter I have discussed a series of problems encountered when animal research or laboratory paradigms are used as a base for understanding human anxiety in a clinical context. My description of the limitations of laboratory research is not intended as criticism; on the contrary, laboratory research and animal paradigms have provided the best available approach to understanding human anxiety. The conditioning paradigm that served as a basis for most of the animal models of anxiety has its historical roots in the behaviorist movement that attempted to shift the focus of inquiry away from the search for inner determinants of behavior and speculative dualistic theories. This focus on observable behavior quite naturally resulted in some neglect in attending to cognitive, affective, and physiological components of the anxiety phenomenon and to its dynamic and complex nature in the context of daily experiences. It is quite possible, as Mineka has suggested, that animal laboratory research will provide only mini-theories that encompass selected segments of the total pattern of human anxieties. Nevertheless, recent advances in cognitive science, in the methodology of animal research, and greater attention to intra-individual variables and to episodic analysis of behaviors might increase the utility of animal and human laboratory research for better understanding of severe anxiety. Even with such further progress, we may still have to confront a critical issue posed at the beginning of this presentation. Laboratory research is a superb tool for testing hypotheses, developing theories, and suggesting heuristic procedures for application in human situations. Ultimately, our expectations of the utility of a scientific body of knowledge for immediate translation into clinical operations may be too high. The skill and perspicacity of clinicians in recognizing key variables in the situations that confront them, and relating these variables to the body of knowledge that psychological science makes available, may be critical factors in determining the success of the clinical enterprise. To this end, the information-processing skills of the clinician, the available body of knowledge, and the degree to which social, biological, and historical conditions are reversible may influence the ultimate success of the clinical intervention in an individual case (Kaminski, 1970; Kanfer, in press; Kanfer & Busemeyer, 1982).

12 Theoretical Models Relating Animal Experiments on Fear to Clinical Phenomena

Neal E. Miller
The Rockefeller University

As someone who started to work in this area 45 years ago but has been concentrating elsewhere more recently, I am enormously gratified at the great advances as exemplified by the excellent papers presented in this volume. As so often happens when more facts are acquired, the phenomena seem much more complicated. Because of the importance of fear for survival, the processes of natural selection that produced mammals may have operated on the principle of safety through redundancy, rather than on the principle of parsimony. On the other hand, it is possible that some of the complexities that confront the field arise from the clumsy way with which the phenomena are handled and perceived rather than from complexities inherent in them. Thus, there is an urgent need for a theory, or for a series of limited theories, that can make sense out of the many facts.

In these comments, I try to show how one of the older approaches, supported and amplified by experiments on animals, can deal with a considerable number, but certainly not all, of the clinical facts. I hope that the inevitable shortcomings of this approach will encourage others to formulate better ones. Since fear and anxiety (a term that is used when the source is obscure or ubiquitous) seem to have so much in common, I usually use the word "fear" to refer to both.

REDUCTION IN FEAR AS A REINFORCEMENT

Let us start with Mowrer's (1939) hypothesis that fear can be learned, that it can function as a drive, and that a sudden reduction in it can serve as a reward. One of the first experiments to provide rather convincing, but not perfect, evidence for this hypothesis may serve as an illustration (Miller, 1948a). Two

261

distinctive sides of an apparatus are separated by a guillotine door. Initially, rats exhibit no preference for either compartment. Then, with the door open, they are given a series of electric shocks in one compartment that they can escape by running through to the other one. After a series of trials, the shocks are turned off, but the animals continue to run. To demonstrate that a drive has been learned, the door is closed, but rotating a little squirrel-cage wheel above it will cause the door to drop open. On nonshock trials with the door closed, rats show signs of fear, such as urination and defecation. They scramble about, turn the wheel first by chance, cause the door to drop, and run through into the safe compartment. On subsequent trials, they eliminate unnecessary movements and learn to rotate the wheel promptly. If a different response, e.g., pressing a bar, drops the door so that the rat can escape the cues that induce the fear, it will learn this response. This learning shows that escaping to the safe compartment functions as a reward.

FEAR MOTIVATES ADAPTIVE AS WELL AS MALADAPTIVE BEHAVIOR

From the foregoing model, it is apparent that, depending on the environmental circumstances that allow escape from fear-inducing stimuli, the subject can be motivated by fear to learn any one of a considerable variety of responses. A student who has a strong fear of examinations may generalize this fear to the books that remind him of the examination. Then he may learn to avoid the books and go to the movies because such avoidance produces a prompt reduction in the strength of fear. Going to the theater is a maladaptive response, because it will make him more likely to get a poor grade and then to have increased fear of the next examination. Another student may reduce fear of examinations by studying hard. Thus, it is clear that fear can motivate adaptive as well as maladaptive behavior. Any insistence that investigations be confined to only those cases that come into the psychiatric clinic will result in a selected sample so that the picture of the functions of fear is likely to be distorted.

I can still vividly remember my first interview with a highly decorated U.S. war hero at the beginning of a study of fear and courage in combat (Dollard, 1943).[1] His initial statement was: "I think I did so well in combat because I was so used to intense fear in my everyday life." This man reacted to almost any

---

[1]At the time the book reporting this study was going to press the FBI was investigating the study because most of our interviewees were veterans of the Spanish Civil War (the only available veterans of recent fighting) and because the FBI had found a graduate assistant involved in the study to be a secret communist. I was an officer in the Psychological Research Program of the Army Air Force and had just seen someone inadvertently associated with communists ordered to an isolated camp in Montana where there was no way he could use his profession. Rather than risk this, I chose to have my name left off the book. Later the Army decided that they liked the study.

new situation with intense anxiety, but he tried to locate all of the possible sources of danger and then rehearsed ways of avoiding each of them. For example, in Officer Training School he was terrified by the prospect of being called upon to command troops marching on the parade ground. So he observed and thought about all the possible errors that one could make and rehearsed how he would avoid them. As a result, his performance was perfect. Later, I found that 50% of pilots reported they flew better when moderately afraid and 37% better when extremely afraid (Wickert, 1947 p. 131). For example, under fear-invoking conditions the pilots flew a tighter formation, which improved the defense of the formation's gunners against attack by fighter planes. From the point of view of performance, the important variable often may be not how strong the fear is, but rather the responses the person has learned to reduce that fear.

FEAR-REDUCING EFFECT OF AVOIDANCE

In the model experiment that we described, it was observed that as the rats learned to perform the wheel rotation response that allowed them to escape the feared compartment, they showed fewer behavioral signs of fear. The relaxation that occurred in the safe compartment appeared to move forward in the sequence of responses, as if the fear reduction had become conditioned to the succession of immediately preceding cues, including proprioceptive cues from anticipatory avoidance responses. These cues apparently had acquired the function of safety signals. The rats eventually performed in an extremely casual manner, but they continued to perform for hundreds of massed trials. This behavior was likened to *la belle indifférence* of the hysteric. But, if the avoidance response was interfered with by throwing a switch so that rotating the wheel no longer dropped the door, all the signs of fear promptly returned, indicating that the performance of the avoidance response was essential for its reduction. If a new response, pressing a bar, would cause the door to drop, the rats learned this response (Miller, 1948a).

Subsequently, studies of combat have noted an apparently similar phenomenon, the fear-reducing effect of learning what to do and of performing such a response (Dollard & Miller, 1950). Using physiological measures, such as the level of corticosteroids, in an avoidance situation, Sidman, Brady, Mason and Thach (1962) have made similar observations, as has Jay Weiss (1968) using level of plasma corticosterone, depletion of brain norepinephrine, and a measure of the extensiveness of stomach lesions. While this is exactly what one would expect from the theoretical analysis, it is possible that there are also some innate bases for uncontrollability to elicit fear and controllability to reduce it.

It should be noted, however, that the variable of controllability interacts with other factors. If the coping response is itself punished so that the subject is in an avoidance-avoidance conflict (Weiss, 1971b) or if it is too difficult (Tsuda

& Hirai, 1975), which itself elicits conflict, the results may be reversed. The subjects performing such a coping response may show more stomach lesions than their yoked partners exposed to exactly the same electric shocks without the opportunity of performing any avoidance responses.

The foregoing discussion provides ample reasons why Lang (this volume) should observe that there is a far from perfect correlation between the performance of an avoidance response and other indices of fear.

FEAR CAN MOTIVATE A COMPULSION

If one did not know the history of the rats in the model experiment I have described, one might find the persistent wheel turning to be puzzling, especially in comparison with rats with a different past history who had no tendency to do this. One could describe it as a compulsion. Indeed, for many cases, a subject who is prevented from performing a compulsive response will show definite signs of fear. But there are some cases in which fear may not be elicited, and a careful study of such cases may show that these compulsions have been rewarded in other ways. From the type of analysis we have been making, one might expect that an avoidance response learned in response to fear in one situation will generalize to a different situation if fear is aroused there either by stimulus generalization or by a conditioned or unconditioned stimulus that elicits fear. Mark May (1948) showed that this is the case. One would expect the same thing to occur with any compulsion that is motivated by fear and rewarded by a reduction in fear.

Yet other experiments show that a response learned to one drive, such as thirst, will tend to generalize to another one (e.g., hunger), and that a specific learned response may even generalize from hunger to fear (Miller, 1948b). This mechanism may be involved in the initiation of some compulsions, the origins of which are unclear.

From the foregoing analysis, one would expect there to be two ways of eliminating an avoidance response or a compulsion. One way would be to prevent the compulsion or avoiding behavior from being reinforced by the fact that it removes the subject from the cues eliciting the fear. This method was used in the experiment in which rotating a wheel no longer caused a door to drop allowing the rat to escape from a feared compartment into a safe one. One would expect this type of elimination of an avoidance response to be hastened if another response, such as pressing a bar, were made available to allow the escape from the fear-generating cues. From the point of view of therapy, it would be much more desirable if the second response was more adaptive (or less maladaptive) in the long run. Applying this analysis to a compulsion, it might be quite possible for the strength of the compulsive response to be reduced before the fear was fully extinguished. The second procedure for eliminating the response would be to reduce the fear motivating the compulsion or the phobic response by extinction, a drug, or strong enough reassuring stimuli.

INNATE RESPONSES TO FEAR

When a subject is exposed to a situation involving a specific pattern of cues and drives, some responses are more probable than others; the responses may be arranged in a hierarchy with the most probable one at the top. The array of responses innately elicited by such a situation has been called the *innate hierarchy* (Miller & Dollard, 1941); such responses are also called species-specific'behavior. It is obvious that the position of a response in this hierarchy will determine whether or not it needs to be acquired by learning and the ease of such learning. In addition to a hierarchy of probability of occurrence in a given situation (which can also be conceptualized as a hierarchy of strengths of response tendency), there is a hierarchy of belongingness (Thorndike, 1935), or in other words preparedness (Seligman & Hager, 1972), which also contributes to the ease or difficulty of learning specific responses in specific situations. Under stable conditions, natural selection will have produced innate hierarchies of responses that are likely to be adaptive. Thus, one can predict that it should be much easier to use the termination of a fear-inducing stimulus to train an infant monkey to run to its mother than to run away from her. We should not be surprised if the compulsion to pet every snake that one sees is an extremely rare one. Bolles (1970) has emphasized that because of the survival value of avoiding lethal dangers, innate responses are likely to play a large role in such avoidance. This does not mean, however, that learning cannot modify the details of such avoidance, especially in primates that have a large repertoire of available innate responses.

SKELETAL-VISCERAL PATTERNS

There are at least two general patterns of response to fear (Miller, 1951). One of these is the flight-fight response described by Cannon (1953). This behavior involves preparation for, and often performance of, vigorous muscular activity and vocalization, along with appropriate physiological responses (e.g., constriction of the blood vessels of the gut; dilation of the blood vessels in the skeletal muscles that produces an overall drop in peripheral resistance; an increase in heart rate and cardiac output great enough to produce an increase in blood pressure; antidiuresis; and the release of adrenalin and corticosteroids). The other pattern is one of freezing, of which death-feigning (or tonic immobility) may be an extreme form, or perhaps death-feigning could conceivably be somewhat different from freezing. The function of this other pattern is concealment; it consists of inhibition of vocalization and skeletal movement, an increase in peripheral resistance great enough to produce an increase in blood pressure in spite of no appreciable increase or even a decrease in heart rate and cardiac output, and little or no antidiuresis (Corson & Corson, 1976; Williams, in press). Which one of these two quite different patterns occurs can depend on a number of factors: the general nature of the stimulus situation, the strength of the fear, the administration of drugs, genetic factors, and which pattern has been reinforced (Miller & Weiss, 1969).

The foregoing description may well be oversimplified. The patterns of visceral reactions to fear may be much more complex, depending on the innate and learned responses to the demands of particular situations. Recent research has made it clear that the autonomic nervous system, even its sympathetic branch, has far more possibilities for specific action than has previously been realized (Smith, Galosy, & Weiss, 1982). Furthermore, responses to chronic fear may be different from those to acute fear. For example, although Cannon (1953) found that acute fear reduced the secretion of stomach acid, Mahl (1949, 1950, 1952) showed that chronic fear can increase stomach acidity.

The pattern of visceral activity can be altered by habituation. Ursin, Baade, and Levine (1978) found that as the parachute jumper becomes experienced, most of the visceral responses to the jump situation are reduced, but the accelerated heart rate remains.

Finally, there is evidence that at least some visceral responses can be modified by specific learning. A patient suffering from orthostatic hypotension can be trained to produce large increases in blood pressure. Initially, these usually are accompanied by sizable increases in heart rate, but with continued practice the increased heart rate, which is not essential to overcoming the fainting produced by the hypotension, often drops out. Extensive tests show that the increase in blood pressure is directly learned and not mediated by any skeletal response (Miller & Brucker, 1979). One sizable component of these patients' motivation for learning is fear of fainting, which can be fatal for a paralyzed patient, but other factors also are involved.

From the foregoing discussion it is clear that one should not expect the various visceral reactions to fear to comprise a functionally distinct, highly intercorrelated category of variables. It can also be seen that although the possibilities are complex, it is possible to make some theoretical sense out of them, especially when one considers the different physiological demands imposed by different types of responses to fear.

VERBAL RESPONSES

Verbal responses are another, albeit highly sophisticated, type of behavior; they are not a direct window to the emotions. Some people may not have been taught to label their emotions accurately; sometimes there is direct social pressure to punish people for saying that they are afraid and to reward them for saying that they are not. People exposed to a traumatic disaster are likely to give different reports of fear, depending on whether they are suing for compensation or applying for reemployment. When fear is extremely strong, putting fear-arousing images, thoughts, and statements out of one's mind is reinforced by a reduction in fear so that they are suppressed or, if the motivation is strong enough, they are repressed and cannot easily be recalled. Repression or suppression will be expected to reduce the effectiveness of using reasoning and other higher mental processes (now called cognitive) to deal with the danger (Dollard & Miller, 1950).

AROUSAL AND REDUCTION OF FEAR

Turning to the question of how fear may be aroused in a given situation, Seligman (1971) has stated that there have been no successful laboratory demonstrations in which animals have been trained to avoid the conditioned stimulus (CS); that all such demonstrations have involved avoiding the unconditioned stimulus (US). This does not happen to be accurate. In criticizing my original experiment on fear (Miller, 1948a) Brown and Jacobs (1949) correctly pointed out that the motivation might have come from blocking the previously learned escape response that was being performed in the absence of the US rather than from conditioned fear. Therefore, they performed an experiment in which fear was conditioned to a rapidly interrupted tone and light by following these cues with an unavoidable shock. After this training, during trials without shock, the rats were trained to climb over a little hurdle, an act that turned off the tone and light. Rats previously conditioned to fear the tone and light learned this response, whereas those not trained to fear these cues did not.

Later, to answer Brown's and other criticisms of my early experiment, Delgado, Roberts, and I (1954) placed cats alternately in two distinctive adjacent wire-mesh compartments. Using as the US electrical stimulation via a chronically implanted electrode in an area of the brain where such stimulation elicited a pain-fearlike response, we gave the cats alternate trials in compartments A and B. Half of the cats received the US only in compartment A and never in B; the other half only in B, and never in A. On subsequent trials without any electrical stimulation of the brain as a US, the animals continued to be placed alternately into the two compartments, but with a small hole near the ceiling now opened to provide them with a chance to climb from one to the other. In these trials without the US, the cats promptly learned to climb up and scramble through the hole into the safe compartment. No cat ever responded by going in the opposite direction. This experiment demonstrated learning to avoid a CS, with controls for the interruption of any learned avoidance response to the US and for any differences in the tendencies of the two compartments to arouse latent innate fear that was potentiated by exposure to the US (pseudoconditioning) rather than by association with it.

There also is convincing clinical evidence that fear sufficiently intense to motivate irrational avoidance can be conditioned to previously neutral cues. During World War II, as the first step of a study of fear in aerial combat, I interviewed a number of pilots who had just returned from extraordinarily harrowing air raids on the oil fields of Ploesti. Their planes had to fly far beyond the range of fighter support into territory that was heavily defended by antiaircraft guns and fighter planes. Only a small percentage of planes, most of them badly damaged, limped back to the Mediterranean where many of them were ditched. All of the aircrew that I interviewed had acquired a phobia of planes that was so strong that they made the irrational choice of returning to the United States by boat, which was both slower and more dangerous because although there were no fighters or antiaircraft to shoot at transport planes over the Atlantic, there were submarines to sink ships. It would be interesting to follow up these men to determine how long these phobias lasted in the face of higher pay and prestige for flight time.

The panic attacks that Kolb and Mutalipassi (1982) have found can still be elicited in some of the Vietnam veterans by sounds resembling those in battle appear to be fear conditioned to such sounds.

Some patients being treated for testicular cancer must suffer severe distress produced by radiation and chemotherapy. These patients often learn such overpowering fear of approaching the hospital that they choose to discontinue a therapy that will probably cure them, and knowingly face the prospect of imminent death. Perhaps the foregoing cases of classically conditioned irrational fears are rare but they obviously do occur.

Two experimentally demonstrated facts are highly relevant to the acquisition of fear. One is the possibility clearly raised by Thorndike (1935) and demonstrated by Öhman, Eriksson, and Olofsson (1975) that innate tendencies may make it much easier to condition (and harder to extinguish) fear to some stimuli than to others. The other is Mineka's (see chapter in this volume) seminal demonstration that fear can be learned by imitation. The imitative acquisition of fear does not expose the learner to lethal danger; it also can efficiently disseminate the lessons learned by the rare individuals who have encountered and escaped such dangers, for example, an animal wounded but not killed by a bullet or a trap. Therefore, imitative learning of fear considerably increases the usefulness of learned fears in the natural environment.

In combat situations that are dangerous only part of the time, as would be expected from principles of learning, the discrimination of what is dangerous and what is safe can greatly reduce the amount of chronic fear (Dollard, 1943, 1943; Wickert, 1947)—an observation that has been experimentally confirmed in my laboratory by Arlo Myers (1956) and by Jay Weiss (1970). There is also the possibility that unpredictability has some innate tendency to elicit fear, much as strangeness (Hebb, 1946) and stimulus overload (Fuller, 1967) do. And of course, there are many other types of situations that have an innate tendency to elicit fear (Gallup, 1974; Miller, 1951).

Conversely, there is evidence that certain situations, such as a child clinging to its mother, reassurance by an authority figure, presence of friends, and being in a thoroughly familiar environment, may have an innate tendency to reduce fear (Miller, 1951). From this fact, one would expect that if some circumstance, such as a highly traumatic experience or a biochemical change in the brain, produced a general increase in the level of fear, a person would be rewarded for approaching or remaining in one of these fear-reducing situations, a type of behavior that sometimes might be hard to discriminate from avoidance of other situations, in spite of the fact that no traumatic event had been associated specifically with them.

Finally, experimental evidence shows that subjects may be trained to persist in the face of pain and fear and that prior exposure to pain and fear can produce physiological changes that reduce the after-effects of such exposure on behavior (Miller, 1980).

SOMATIC CONSEQUENCES OF FEAR

In his excellent chapter in this book, Weiner has dealt with the clinical evidence for psychosomatic consequences of fear and other forms of emotional "stress." He has also pointed out a number of neural and humoral mechanisms that could be involved in the pathophysiology of such disorders.

While the causal factors in complex clinical situations are hard to prove, animal models provide clear evidence for a number of different adverse consequences on the physical health of the body due to purely psychological "stress" (often presumed to be fear). Henry and Stephens (1979) have shown that putting mice, reared in isolation after weaning, into a colony designed to produce a disorganized social system with many interrodent conflicts can cause the development of hypertension in a series of stages analogous to those involved in the development of human essential hypertension. Such conflict-inducing, rearing and living conditions cause mice to die prematurely from kidney failure, strokes, and other pathologies typical of human severe hypertension. The fact that mice reared in groups (so that they already have learned good forms of social coping) neither develop hypertension nor die prematurely when placed in the same colony proves the role of psychosocial factors.

Dahl, Heine, and Tassinari (1962) have shown that rats genetically selected to respond with hypertension to a high-salt diet will develop the disorder without saltloading when placed in a chronic approach-avoidance conflict situation. The importance of the genetic factor is shown by the fact that rats selected to be resistant to a high-salt diet are resistant also to the development of hypertension by exposure to conflict.

Both Lown's (Lown, Verrier, & Corbalan, 1973; Lown & Wolf, 1971) and Skinner's (Skinner, Lie, & Entman, 1975) groups have shown that fear can potentiate the tendency of a damaged heart to respond with a fatal arrhythmia.

Riley (1981) has shown that mild stresses can increase the susceptibility of mice to implanted and virus-induced tumors. Keller, Weiss, Schleifer, Miller and Stein (1983) have shown that exposure of rats to unpredictable, uncontrollable shocks can depress the response of T cells in the immune system to a mitogenic stimulus, even when changes in cortico-sterone and epinephrine have been eliminated by adrenalectomy. The effects on the immune system are complex; there are a few experiments that show an apparently opposite result. Some of these apparent discrepancies might be eliminated by suitable dose-response and time-response studies (Miller, 1980b, 1982a).

Jay Weiss (1968, 1970, 1971a, 1971b, 1971c; Weiss, Stone, & Harrell, 1970) has performed an analytical series of experiments demonstrating the effects of four different types of experimental treatment on five different types of experimental results. Figure 1 shows how the interrelationships among these types of independent and dependent variables may be summarized in terms of a single intervening variable, presumably fear (Miller, 1982b). The 17 effects predicted from this diagram that have been tested have yielded the expected results. Three of them have not yet been tested: the effect of 2 on C and the effects of 4 on C and on D. Experiments to test these predictions and some additional ones, such as the reinforcing effect of escaping from the experimental apparatus, would provide additional evidence on the usefulness of the formulation in terms of fear as an intervening variable.

FIG. 1 How the effects of the four treatments (at the left) in a series of experiments by Jay Weiss on the five measures he studied (at the right) can be summarized in terms of a single intervening variable, such as increased fear. (from Miller, 1982b)

To date, the rich potentialities of animal models of the types that have been described have not been fully utilized (Miller 1980a). In general, only one type of pathophysiology has been studied by each investigator—either hypertension, other cardiovascular damage, cardiac arrhythmias, or stomach lesions. What is needed are studies in which the effects of a number of independent variables are studied on a number of different types of pathology. Such studies will help determine whether the variables that increase one type of pathology will increase all others, or whether there are certain combinations of variables that predispose toward one type of pathology whereas others predispose toward a different type. Similarly, more use could be made of such models in analyzing specific neurohumoral mechanisms involved in the production of specific types of pathology.

LIMITATIONS OF CONCEPT OF FEAR AS A UNITARY ENTITY

Thus far, we have spoken of fear as an isolatable unitary entity. However, there appear to be certain similarities or common elements among different drives so that a habit learned under one drive will generalize to another (Miller, 1948b). For example, a habit learned under thirst has a tendency to be transferred to hunger, and a habit learned under the drive of hunger may predispose the type of an avoidance response that will be elicited by fear. Similarly, Fonberg (1956) has shown that a previously learned response of lifting a specific paw to avoid electric shock is more likely to be shown than other responses when a hungry dog is confronted with the task of making progressively more difficult discriminations between a cue reinforced by the food and a nonreinforced cue until an experimental neurosis is produced. There are a number of functional similarities between the effects of fear induced by electric shocks and the frustration induced by the removal of food as a reward in a situation in which it has repeatedly been given (Amsel, 1962; Daly, 1974; Wagner, 1966). For example, both are affected in the same way by alcohol and amobarbitol (Barry, Wagner, & Miller, 1962).

The foregoing results may help to explain certain clinical relationships such as those between anxiety and depression, but they also may indicate that new theoretical constructs are needed. Perhaps the situation will turn out to be like the following one. The concept of carbon as a single element is extremely useful for dealing with many of the phenomena of chemistry. On the other hand, the idea that carbon is not a single entity, but exists in a variety of isotopes, is necessary and valuable for applications such as radioimmune assays and radiocarbon dating. Perhaps the situation will be one that requires the radically different approach of dividing up the phenomena of fear and other motivations in completely new ways. Whatever the outcome, analytic studies guided by theoretical models are needed to continue the advances that I have witnessed over the past 4½ decades.

As Jeffrey Gray (this volume) suggests, advances in neurophysiology may provide significant answers to some of the foregoing questions. The pharmacological work that Costa (this volume) describes on benzodiazepine-GABA receptors is especially challenging. Perhaps the brain has certain cells that have benzodiazepine receptors and that also fire selectively to fear (Vertes & Miller, 1976) or to inhibition of fear. In view of the many stimulating studies and challenging ideas presented in this volume, further significant advances are virtually certain to continue to be made.

II CLINICAL RESEARCH APPROACHES TO ANXIETY

A. Epidemiology and Family Studies

13 The Epidemiology of Anxiety Disorders: Rates, Risks, and Familial Patterns

Myrna M. Weissman, Ph.D.
Yale University School of Medicine
Connecticut Mental Health Center

INTRODUCTION

While anxiety has been called by Klein (1981) a key word in psychiatry, it is also quite an ambiguous one. For the lay person, it means feeling uneasy, worried about what might be, not necessarily what has been. To the experimental psychologist it may be referred to as avoidance conditioning (Carey & Gottesman, 1981). For those who study personality, it may mean subject distress (as reported in self-rating scales) or changes in heart rate. Historically it has been referred to as nervous exhaustion, irritable heart, effort syndrome or neurocirculatory asthenia. For the modern psychopathologist anxiety is defined by a set of symptoms implying dysfunction and producing impairment, as described in the Research Diagnostic Criteria (RDC) (Spitzer, Endicott, & Robins, 1978) or the *Diagnostic and Statistical Manual of Mental Disorders*, Third Edition *(DSM-III)* (American Psychiatric Association, 1980).

The semantic ambiguity of anxiety disorders, the difficulty in separating trait from state conditions, and the heterogeneity of expression create an epidemiologic nightmare. Moreover, until the recent acceptance of Klein's notions about anxiety disorders, now incorporated in the *DSM-III*, the anxiety disorders usually had not been subdivided into different disorders such as phobia, panic, generalized anxiety disorders.

This paper reviews what we know about the epidemiology and familial patterns of anxiety disorders. Focus is on the current studies based on specified diagnostic criteria. Data are presented, when available, on the subclassifications of the anxiety disorders. Data from epidemiologic and family studies support the notion that anxiety disorders have a relatively high prevalence and are familial, that they are heterogeneous, and that some are related to depression. It also suggests

275

that panic disorder has the most severe consequence in terms of morbid risk to first-degree relatives, particularly risk to children, and that there may be a relationship between adult and childhood anxiety disorders.

WHAT IS EPIDEMIOLOGY?

Before presenting this review it may be useful to describe what is meant by epidemiology and to present some of the commonly used terms.

Epidemiology is the study of diseases in populations and the distribution and determinants of disease prevalence in man. It relates the distribution of disease (incidence and prevalence) to any conceivable factor (e.g., time, place, person) existing in or affecting that population. Epidemiology is a procedure for asking questions and getting answers that raise further questions or clues. It has been called the basic science of preventive medicine. By understanding the magnitude of a disorder (the rates) and the increased risks (the risk factors) for the occurrence of a disorder, clues as to what alterations might lead to nonoccurrence or prevention are estimated. Ultimately, the purpose of epidemiology is to abolish the clinical disorder.

Since, for many disorders, only a small fraction of ill persons seek medical treatment, study of populations independent of their treatment is essential for obtaining a true estimate of the disorder and for understanding the complete clinical picture. This is particularly true for the anxiety disorders since, as will be shown, only a fraction of persons diagnosed as having an anxiety disorder report seeking treatment. Those who seek treatment are usually not representative of the range of persons with the disorder.

Some basic epidemiologic terms include: *Point or period prevalence*—that proportion of the population that has the disorder being studied at a given point or period in time. *Morbid Risk*—the individual's lifetime risk of having a first episode. *Incidence*—the number of new cases of a disorder usually occurring in the population per year. *Risk Factor*—a condition that increases the likelihood of a person developing the disorder under study.

As will become apparent, there are no published data available on the incidence of anxiety disorders. The estimates of morbid risk are of the biological relatives of patients with anxiety disorders. Many studies are unclear as to the time period for prevalence rates, and are only of persons in treatment (treated prevalence). Most of the variability in rates between studies can probably be attributed to varying methods and case definitions.

In addition to the strictly epidemiologic data from population studies, data are also reviewed on family studies of probands with anxiety disorders. The family data are presented because they are currently a valuable source of information on one risk factor, the biologic family of origin. In general, information on risk factors is often, but not always, generated from case-control design studies and not from epidemiologic surveys of populations.

In studies of families the observation that certain disorders cluster in families raises the question as to what extent the familial recurrence is due to the repetition of specific gene combinations in families, and to what extent it is due to shared environmental factors. Since epidemiologists and population geneticists often use common methodologies and may deal with similar questions about familial patterns or resemblance, there has recently emerged a hybrid discipline called genetic epidemiology (Morton & Chung, 1978). While twin and cross-fostering studies provide the most powerful non-laboratory methods for detecting genetic etiology, genetic-epidemiologic family studies can provide a considerable amount of information about a variety of risk factors contributing to the development of a disorder. As will be shown, recent family studies of anxiety disorders are yielding new clues about the relationship between the anxiety disorders in adults and children, and the relationship between some anxiety disorders and depression.

EPIDEMIOLOGY: RATES AND RISKS IN ADULTS

Studies Prior to Specified Diagnostic Criteria

The epidemiology of anxiety states prior to the development of specified diagnostic criteria has been reviewed by Marks and Lader in 1973. Their review is described because it is usually referenced as the source of epidemiologic data on anxiety disorders. Although different diagnostic criteria and time periods between studies were used and the anxiety disorders were not separated out, Marks and Lader found surprising agreement among the five population studies conducted in the United States, the United Kingdom, and Sweden between 1943 and 1966 (Table 1). Anxiety states were fairly common (around 2.0 to 4.7/100

TABLE 1
Prevalence Rates/100 of Anxiety States
Based on Community Surveys[a]

		Prevalence Rates/100[b] *Anxiety States*
Britain	1966	3.6
Sweden	1966	4.6
Boston, MA, USA	1951	4.7
Britain	1948	2.0
Tennessee, USA	1943	2.0

[a]From Marks and Lader, 1973.
[b]Time period and diagnostic criteria between studies vary.

current prevalence) and were more prevalent in women, particularly younger women between 16 and 40 years of age.

We conducted a separate review of epidemiologic studies, as presented in Tables 2 and 3. Nine additional community studies of anxiety states were found. The time periods and diagnostic methods varied so that little can be said definitively. However, the additional studies show that the rates are higher in women than in men and are usually in the range reported by Marks and Lader (1973) regardless of the time period assessed. This latter finding is curious since one would expect that lifetime prevalence rates would be higher than 1-year rates. Not shown here, three of the nine studies (Bremer, 1951; Fremming, 1951; Hagnell, 1966) separated out from the anxiety states, neurasthenia, which was quite similar in description to panic attacks. It was described as an episodic event whose chief symptoms were fear, apprehension, inattention, palpitations, respiratory distress, dizziness, faintness, sweating, tremor, chest pains, and feeling of impending disaster. These occurred in the absence of other illness and existed independently of specific external situations. In between attacks the patient felt relieved but not completely well. The rates of these attacks were slightly lower than those of anxiety states and, again, were more common among women.

TABLE 2
Community Surveys of Anxiety States
Rates/100

Study Place (Year)	Sample Size	Period Prevalence	Male	Female	Total
Murphy, Canada (1952) [For reference see Murphy, 1980]	1010	Current	—	—	2.9
Brunetti,[+] France (1976)	101	1 Year	—	—	3.9
Brown et al.,[+] U.K. (1977)	612	1 Year	—	1.5	—
Angst & Dobler-Mikola Zurich, 1982	591	Current 1 Year	2.6 4.0	3.7 6.8	3.2 5.4
Bremer[+], Norway (1951)	All Members of Community	5 Years	.5	1.2	—
Fremming[+], Denmark (1951)	3467	Lifetime	.3	.1	—
Essen-Moller et al.[+], Sweden (1956)	2550	Lifetime	1.3	3.4	—
Hagnell[+], Sweden (1966)	2568	Lifetime	1.5	3.8	—
Väisänen[+], Finland (1976)	1000	Unspecified	—	—	.5

[+]From Carey, Gottesman, and Robins, 1980.

TABLE 3
Community Surveys of Phobias

Study Place (Year) Type of Phobia	Sample Size	RATES/100 Period Prevalence	Male	Female	TOTAL
Agras et al., Vermont (1969)	325	1 Year			
Agoraphobia			—	—	.63
Total Phobias			—	—	7.7
Severely Disabling Phobias			—	—	.22
Angst & Dobler-Mikola, Zurich (1982)	591				
All Phobias Including Agoraphobia		Current	0.6	4.9	2.6
		1 Year	1.2	4.9	3.0
Costello, Canada (1982)	449	1 Year			
All Phobias Including Agoraphobia			—	19.4	—
Severely Disabling Phobias			—	—	.70

Two studies (Agras, Sylvester, & Oliveau, 1969; Angst, Dobler-Mikola, & Scheidegger, 1982) reported community annual rates of mild phobias in the range of about 6-7/100 (Table 3). One study (Costello, 1982) reported very high annual rates of all types of phobias in women (19.4/100). However, when the criteria of severe impairment were added, these rates were markedly reduced, .22/100 (Agras et al., 1969) and .70/100 per year (Costello, 1982). The annual rates of agoraphobia were also considerably lower, .63/100.

Studies Using Specified Diagnostic Criteria

With the recent improvements in the reliability of psychiatric diagnoses, including use of structured diagnostic interviews and specified criteria, it was possible to obtain reliable information on the epidemiology of psychiatric disorders. Currently, data are available from three epidemiologic surveys conducted in the United States.

1975 Survey—New Haven. The first application of the new structured diagnostic interview techniques was incorporated in a pilot survey of persons living in the New Haven, Connecticut area in 1975–1976. Five hundred and eleven persons (a follow-up of a probability sample) were interviewed by clinically trained persons using the Schedule for Affective Disorders and Schizophrenia-Lifetime Version (SADS-L) which generated RDC. The details of the study are described elsewhere (Weissman, Myers, & Harding, 1978).

The current rate of any anxiety disorder (RDC) was 4.3/100 (Table 4). This was similar to the rate of major or minor depression (not shown here), also 4.3/100, and to the rates of anxiety states reviewed by Marks and Lader (1973). The current prevalence rates of the specific anxiety disorders were as follows: generalized anxiety (GAD) 2.5/100; phobic disorder 1.4/100; and panic disorder .4/100. No current cases of obsessive-compulsive disorder were found in this sample of 500. Since RDC were used, post-traumatic stress disorder (PTSD) was not assessed. Phobias were not categorized as to type in this study.

This study found an overlap within the anxiety disorders and between the anxiety disorders and major or minor depression. Over 80% of persons with GAD, 17% with panic disorder, and 19% with phobia had at least one of the other anxiety disorders in their lifetime. Thirty percent of persons with phobias had panic disorder at some time in their life. There was an overlap of the anxiety disorders with major depression: over 7% of persons with GAD, 2% with panic disorder, and 4% with phobia had major depression at some time in their life.

Sample sizes were too small to interpret rates by many sociodemographic or other risk factors. However, GAD was slightly more common in middle and younger aged women, nonwhites, persons not currently married, and those in the lower socioeconomic classes.

This study also pointed out the importance of population studies to determine the magnitude of the anxiety disorders. Only about a quarter of persons with any current anxiety disorder received treatment for an emotional disorder in the past year. Although they were not being treated for their anxiety disorder, they tended to be high utilizers of health facilities for nonpsychiatric reasons. Their use was higher than persons with any other psychiatric disorder or with no psychiatric disorder. Persons with panic disorder were the highest users of psychotropic drugs, especially the minor tranquilizers.

1979 National Survey of Psychotherapeutic Drug Use. From a symptom checklist administered by survey interviewers in a large-scale ($N = 3161$) survey

TABLE 4
Current Prevalence Rates/100 of RDC Diagnoses
New Haven Community Survey—1975[a]

	Current Prevalence Rates/100
Research Diagnostic Criteria	*(N = 511)*
Generalized Anxiety Disorder	2.5
Phobic Disorder	1.4
Panic Disorder	0.4
Any Anxiety Disorder	4.3

[a]Weissman, Myers, & Harding, 1978.

of psychotherapeutic drug use, some *DSM-III* diagnostic counterparts were identified (Uhlenhuth, Balter, Mellinger, Cisin, & Clinthorne, 1983). GAD was the most common disorder (6.4/100 1-year prevalence), followed by phobias other than agoraphobia (2.3/100) and agoraphobia/panic (1.2/100) (Table 5). The rates of all the anxiety disorders were higher in women than in men, showing a two-to-threefold difference. As reported in the 1975 New Haven survey, use of antianxiety agents was highest in the agoraphobia/panic group.

Because of the different diagnostic groupings between the 1975 and this 1979 survey, only direct comparisons with the GAD diagnosis are possible. The rates of GAD were higher in this 1979 survey (6.4%) as compared to the 1975 New Haven survey (2.5%). However, it should be noted that the former is a 1-year rate and the latter a current rate. The period difference and the somewhat different diagnostic classifications and sample sizes could account for the differences in rates. Both studies report higher rates in women in all the anxiety disorders studied.

1982 Epidemiologic Catchment Area Study Survey (ECA). Preliminary data on rates of some anxiety disorders (panic, obsessive-compulsive, and agoraphobia) based on the *DSM-III* are available from a large-scale United States community survey currently under way. This study may ultimately provide the most comprehensive epidemiologic data.

Because of the need for accurate epidemiologic information and because of the demonstration that the new methods were feasible in community studies and could be adapted for lay interviewers (Robins, Helzer, Croughan, & Ratcliffe, 1981), the National Institute of Mental Health, Division of Biometry and Epidemiology, initiated in 1980 an epidemiologic catchment area community study in the U.S.A. (Regier et al., 1984). Among the objectives of this multisite longitudinal study was to provide information on (1) the prevalence and incidence of specific psychiatric disorders in the community; and (2) for newly developed

TABLE 5
Annual Prevalence Rates from 1979 National Survey of
Psychotherapeutic Drug Use[a]

	RATES/100		
DSM-III Diagnoses Derived From Symptom Checklist	*Male*	*Female*	*Total*
Agoraphobia/Panic	0.5	1.8	1.2
Other Phobia	1.3	3.1	2.3
Generalized Anxiety	4.3	8.0	6.4

[a]Uhlenhuth, Balter, Mellinger, Cisin, & Clinthorne (1983).

mental disorders (i.e., incidence cases), the concomitant factors associated with or causative of the disorder.

Each catchment area had at least 200,000 inhabitants and boundaries that coincide with one or more contiguous comprehensive Community Mental Health Center (CMHC) catchment areas. Yale University in New Haven, Connecticut, received the first such grant, followed by Johns Hopkins in Baltimore, Maryland, and Washington University in St. Louis, Missouri, and subsequently by Duke University in Durham, North Carolina, and the University of California in Los Angeles. Data are currently available for the first wave at Yale, Johns Hopkins, and Washington University. Table 6 shows the sample characteristics of these three sites.

The information presented is preliminary and will be limited to *DSM-III* diagnoses of agoraphobia, obsessive-compulsive, and panic disorder for the first wave from the three sites. Data on GAD or PTSD are not yet available. Only community subjects are included. The details of the study including diagnostic methods, sampling, and design are described elsewhere (Myers et al., 1984; Robins et al., 1981).

Table 7 shows the 6-month prevalence rates of panic, obsessive-compulsive, and agoraphobia in the three sites. As can be seen, the rates of panic are similar in all three sites (.6 to 1.0/100). The rates are higher in women; there was no strong relationship with race or education, nor with age. Ages 25–44 were the highest period of risk, and the rates were generally lower in persons 65 and older.

The rates of obsessive-compulsive were also similar in the three sites (1.3 to 2.0/100) and were higher in women. There were no strong relationships with age.

The rates of agoraphobia have wider variations between sites (2.7 to 5.8/100) and are considerably higher than the other anxiety diagnoses and than the reports from earlier studies. The rates are two-to-fourfold higher in women than men, and twofold higher in less educated persons and nonwhites. There was no consistent

TABLE 6
ECA—Sample Characteristics[a]

	Yale	Hopkins	Washington U. St. Louis
Survey Date—Wave 1	1980–81	1981	1981–82
Sample Pop. Size (1980 census)	298,000	175,000	277,000
Sample Age Range	18 +	18 +	18 +
Completed Interviews—Household, Wave 1	5,035[b]	3,481	2,990
Completion Rate	75.3%	78%	79.1%

[a]From Regier et al., in press.
[b]Includes an oversampling of persons 65 + .

TABLE 7
Six-Month Prevalence of DIS/DSM-III Panic, Obsessive/Compulsive
Disorders and Agoraphobia by Sex and Age[a]

Diagnosis	Male	Female	Total
PANIC:			
New Haven	0.3	0.9	0.6
Baltimore	0.8	1.2	1.0
St. Louis	0.8	1.0	0.9
OBSESSIVE/COMPULSIVE:			
New Haven	0.9	1.7	1.4
Baltimore	1.9	2.2	2.0
St. Louis	0.9	1.7	1.3
AGORAPHOBIA:			
New Haven	1.1	4.2	2.8
Baltimore	3.4	7.9	5.8
St. Louis	0.9	4.3	2.7

[a]From Myers et al., in press.

age finding for agoraphobia overall. The lowest rates were in ages 65 and older. The higher rates in Baltimore are partly due to their large sample of black females. However, the source of this variability is under investigation. It may be due to differences between sites in interviewer instructions and wording. These methodologic differences between sites have been corrected for the subsequent interviewing waves. Rates of phobia are also sensitive to the criteria of impairment. Although many persons have phobias, a considerably smaller number have severe disabling impairments from their phobias.

EPIDEMIOLOGY: RATES AND RISKS IN CHILDREN

In general, there is a paucity of available data on the epidemiology of child psychiatric disorders based on studies of community samples. The situation is no less true for the anxiety disorders. After a review of the literature, Orvaschel and Weissman (in press) concluded that only data on the prevalence of anxiety symptoms were available. On the basis of seven community surveys (see Table 8) they concluded that anxiety symptoms of all types were quite prevalent for children of all ages and for both sexes. A determination of risk factors from the available data was premature, but there was some suggestive information reported. On the whole, anxiety symptoms were more prevalent in girls than boys, although there was considerable variation as a function of the type of anxiety and the age of the child. Anxiety symptoms show a general decline with age, although some types of phobias have onset in early adult or later adult life. There was also some indication that anxiety symptoms were more prevalent in black than white

TABLE 8
Studies Reporting Prevalence of Anxiety in Children[a]

Design	Lapouse & Monk (1958)	Agras et al. (1969)	Werry & Quay (1971)	Richman et al. (1975)	Earls (1980)	Kastrup (1976)	Abe & Masui (1981)
Location Sample Source	US Community	US Community	US School	UK Community	US Community	Denmark Community	Japan Community
Sample Size	482	325	1753	705	100	175	2500
Age of Sample	6–12 yrs.	Children & Adults	5–8 yrs.	3 yrs.	3 yrs.	5–6 yrs.	11–12 yrs.
Informants	Mother	Subject or Mother	Teacher	Mother	Mother	Parent	Subject
Results Fears and/or Worries	43%	7.7%	16.5%	12.8% (Fears) 2.6% (Worries)	14.0% (Fears) 8.0% (Worries)	4.0%	2%–43% (Fears) 4%–33% (Worries)
Separation Concerns	41%					13.7%	
Other Anxieties			18.0% (Tension) 18.0% (Nerves)			8.0% (Night-mares)	

[a]From Orvaschel & Weissman, in press.

children and more prevalent in lower than higher socioeconomic children. Finally, the significance of these childhood anxieties and the evidence regarding the relationship between anxiety symptoms and other indicators of child psychopathology was unclear. Even less was known about the long-term significance of anxiety symptoms of childhood.

FAMILIAL PATTERNS

The familial nature of anxiety disorders was noted over a century ago (Cohen, Badal, Kilpatrick, Reed, & White, 1951), and subsequent writers have frequently cited the occurrence of additional cases within a patient's family (Wood, 1941). Hence, the notion that anxiety disorders are familial is not new. Cohen et al. (1951) identified 19 separate reports published between 1869 and 1948 in which a familial predisposition to anxiety disorders was described. In addition, they reported on the results of a study in which the careful systematic collection of family history data revealed that two-thirds of the patients had at least one other affected relative. Despite these early findings, until recently anxiety disorders received little attention from investigators interested in the inheritance of psychiatric disorders.

Recent family studies of first-degree relatives of probands with anxiety neurosis have been reviewed by Carey and Gottesman (1981). Table 9 shows a similarity in rates (15/100) of anxiety neurosis among relatives. All of these rates were obtained from family history data (i.e., information collected only from the proband regarding his/her relatives).

Crowe, Pauls, Slyman, and Noyes (1980) presented the first and only comprehensive family study of probands with panic disorder alone, using specified (*DSM-III*, RDC) diagnostic criteria. In this study a majority of the relatives were interviewed. The rates of illness obtained were higher than reported in the family

TABLE 9
Frequency of Anxiety Neurosis Among First Degree Relatives of
Anxiety Neurotics

Family History Studies[a]	*Rate/100* *All First Degree* *Relatives*
McInnes	14.9
Brown	15.5
Cohen et al.	15.6
Noyes et al.[b]	18.4

[a]From Carey and Gottesman, 1982.
[b]Rates for Noyes et al. are age-corrected risks; all others are not.

history studies, but the patterns were the same. More females were affected, and the risk to siblings increased with the number of affected parents.

There have been attempts to explain the familial patterns observed with genetic models (Miner, 1973; Pauls, Noyes, & Crowe, 1979; Pauls, Bucher, Crowe, & Noyes, 1980; Slater & Shields, 1969). However, no genetic hypotheses have been conclusively rejected.

Family Study of Depression and Anxiety Disorders: Adults

Recent results from the Yale family-genetic study of probands with both affective and anxiety disorders provide additional information on familial patterns. Since these data are still in press they will be reported here in more detail. Data are available on both the probands' adult first-degree relatives and their offspring ages 6–17. The details of this study including the methodology are described fully (Leckman, Merikangas, Pauls, Prusoff, & Weissman, 1983; Leckman, Weissman, Merikangas, Pauls, & Prusoff, 1983; Weissman, Kidd, & Prusoff, 1982; Weissman, Gershon, Kidd, Prusoff, Leckman, Dibble, Hamovit, Thompson, Pauls, & Guroff, 1984; Weissman, Prusoff, Gammon, Merikangas, Leckman, & Kidd, 1984; Weissman, Leckman, Merikangas, Gammon, & Prusoff, 1984).

The study included 215 probands (82 normal controls drawn from a community sample and 133 probands with major depression), 1,331 of their adult first-degree relatives, and 194 of their children ages 6–17. Diagnoses were based on the RDC for all probands and adult first-degree relatives, and on the *DSM-III* for children ages 6–17.

Probands with major depression were divided into three groups: major depression with no anxiety disorder ($N = 52$); major depression with anxiety disorder only associated with the depression ($N = 51$); and with anxiety disorder only occurring separately from the major depression ($N = 30$). The rates of major depression and anxiety disorders in their first-degree relatives are shown in Table 10.

The first-degree relatives of individuals with major depression plus an anxiety disorder were at greater risk for major depression, as well as anxiety disorders, than were the relatives of individuals with major depression without an anxiety disorder (Leckman, Merikangas, Pauls, Prusoff, & Weissman, 1983). This increased risk appears to be present whether or not the anxiety disorder occurred solely in association with episodes of major depression or was temporally separate. These findings *did not* support the prevailing *DSM-III* and RDC nosologic convention in which episodes of anxiety disorder that are concomitant with episodes of major depression are not diagnosed. In subsequent analyses we diagnosed anxiety disorders regardless of their temporal sequence with depression.

For the next analysis we looked more closely at the specific anxiety disorders using a diagnostic hierarchy for probands with depression and anxiety disorders:

TABLE 10

Rates of Major Depression and Anxiety Disorders Among First Degree Relatives According to the Presence of Anxiety Disorders and Major Depression Among Relatives[a]

Proband Status	First Degree Relatives at Risk	Rates/100 of Relatives Affected With:		
		Major Depression[b]	Anxiety Disorders	
			Associated With Depression	Separate[c] From Depression
NORMAL (N = 82)	521	6	1	4
MAJOR DEPRESSION WITHOUT ANXIETY (N = 52)	308	10	1	8
MAJOR DEPRESSION WITH ANXIETY: Always associated with depressive episodes. (N = 51)	337	19	4	10
Separate from depressive episodes. (N = 30)	165	17	4	11

[a]From Leckman et al., 1983.
[b]Rate of major depression regardless of other diagnoses.
[c]Includes relatives with isolated anxiety disorders as well as relatives with depression plus a separate anxiety disorder.

agoraphobia > panic disorder > generalized anxiety disorder. Operationally, this meant that depressed probands with both agoraphobia and panic disorder would be classified as depressed with agoraphobia and so forth (Leckman, Weissman, Merikangas, Pauls, & Prusoff, 1983).

Table 11 presents the observed rate/100 among the first-degree relatives of major depression with or without anxiety disorders, anxiety disorder, alcoholism, and other psychiatric disorder. The probands with depression plus panic disorder or generalized anxiety disorder show a high rate of major depression among their first-degree relatives, with approximately 20/100 of relatives being affected. This compares with 11.5/100 of the relatives of depressed probands with agoraphobia, 10.7/100 of relatives of depressed probands without any anxiety disorder, and only 5.6/100 of the relatives of the normal controls.

In general, the first-degree relatives of probands with major depression and panic disorder had the highest rates of illness. They showed increased rates of major depression, anxiety disorders, and alcoholism when compared to the relatives of either the normal controls or the depressed probands without an anxiety disorder. These findings are independent of when the anxiety disorder occurred as well as independent of the presence of secondary alcohol abuse. Relatives of probands with major depression and generalized anxiety disorder show an increase of major depression compared to the relatives of either the normal controls or the depressed probands without an anxiety disorder.

Table 12 compares the rates of major depression (primary and secondary), anxiety, and alcohol abuse found in the Yale and Iowa studies among first-degree relatives of probands with depression and panic disorders, since similar diagnostic criteria were used in both studies. Although the rates are not age corrected, there is considerable similarity in the rates of depression among the relatives of the normal probands (about 6/100) and among the relatives of the probands with depression only and the probands with panic disorder only (10/100). There is considerably more anxiety among the relatives of probands with panic disorder only, and considerably more anxiety, major depression, and alcohol abuse in the probands with both panic disorder and depression. In presenting the Iowa data we included relatives with primary and secondary depression. In the original Iowa data, secondary depression was not included and they did not find familial aggregation of major depression in relatives of probands with panic disorder (Crowe, Noyes, Pauls, & Slymen, 1983; Shader, Goodman, and Gever, 1982). When the data were reexamined with both primary and secondary depression assessed, the elevated rates of major depression were found.

Family Study of Depression and Anxiety Disorders: Children

Finally, we looked at the rates for *DSM-III* diagnosis in 194 of the probands' children ages 6–17 (Table 13). The subgroups of probands were the same as those in Table 10 with the one exception (Weissman et al., 1984). Included in

TABLE 11
Rates of Diagnoses Among Relatives by Proband Groupings by Anxiety[a]

Proband Group[b]	N At Risk	DIAGNOSIS OF RELATIVES (RATES/100) (N = 1311)							
		Normal	Major Depression	Phobia	Panic	GAD	Total Anxiety	Alcohol Abuse	Other
Normal	521	75.2	5.6	1.2	0	4.0	5.2	7.9	9.7
Major Depression, No Anxiety	338	60.1	10.7	2.1	2.1	6.2	9.2	8.9	16.6
Major Depression Plus Agoraphobia	96	56.2	11.5	1.0	2.1	5.2	8.3	10.4	16.7
Major Depression Plus Panic Disorder	133	41.4	19.6	3.8	3.8	10.5	15.8	21.1	18.8
Major Depression Plus GAD	243	46.5	19.8	4.5	0.4	9.1	14.0	10.7	18.5

[a]From Leckman, Weissman, Merikangas, Pauls, & Prusoff (1983).
[b]With hierarchy applied to anxiety disorders as outcome measures.

TABLE 12
Rates/100 of Diagnoses Among Relatives by Proband Groups
(Yale/Iowa)[a]

Proband Group	N at Risk	Diagnosis of Relatives (Rates/100)		
		Major Depression[b]	Total Anxiety	Alcohol Abuse
Normal (Yale)	521	5.6	5.2	7.9
Normal (Iowa)	262	6.5	6.5	4.9
Depression Alone (Yale)	338	10.7	9.2	8.9
Panic Alone (Iowa)	278	10.1	25.2	9.0
Depression plus Panic (Yale)	133	19.6	15.8	21.1

[a]Presented by Leckman et al., American Psychiatric Association Annual Meeting, Toronto, Canada, 1982.
[b]Includes both primary and secondary depression.

TABLE 13
Rates of DSM-III Diagnoses Among Children[a]

Best Estimate DSM-III Diagnosis in Child		Rates/100 in Children Proband Group			
	Normal	Depression No Anxiety	Depression and Agoraphobia	Depression and Panic	Depression and GAD
Major Depression	0	10.5	22.2	26.3	3.1
Separation Anxiety	0	0	11.1	36.8	6.3
Panic Disorder	0	0	5.6	5.3	0
Agoraphobia	0	0	5.6	5.3	0
Social Phobia	1.2	0	11.1	5.3	0
Simple Phobia	0	0		5.3	0
Obsessive-Compulsive	1.2	0	5.6	0	0
Attention Deficit Disorder	1.2	13.2	11.1	5.3	9.4
Conduct Disorder	1.2	10.5	11.1	0	3.1
Substance Abuse	0	5.3	11.1	0	0
Developmental Reading	3.5	2.6	11.1	0	6.3
Other Diagnosis	0	2.6	16.7	10.5	0
Any Diagnosis	8.1	21.1	27.8	42.1	15.6**
One Diagnosis	8.1	7.9	0	10.5	6.3
Two or More Diagnoses	0	3.1	27.8	31.6	9.3

** $= p < .01$
[a]From Weissman, Leckman, Merikangas, & Gammon, 1984.

the depression and phobia group were those probands who had social and simple phobia as well as agoraphobia, since we were examining the outcome of the different phobias in children. As can be seen, the highest rates of illness were in the children of probands with both depression and panic disorder. The rates of major depression (26.3/100) and separation anxiety (36.8/100) were highest in their children. These findings give support to the association between childhood separation anxiety and panic disorder suggested by Klein and Gittelman-Klein (1978).

Summary of Yale Findings

Following are the findings of the Yale family-genetic study of adult relatives and children:

1. Major depression and anxiety disorders are probably heterogeneous diagnostic categories.

2. Probands with both major depression and panic disorder show markedly increased rates of major depression, anxiety disorders (phobia, panic disorder, and GAD), and alcoholism compared with the first-degree relatives of normal controls and depressed probands without an anxiety disorder. These findings were independent of when the anxiety disorder occurred *vis à vis* episodes of major depression (separated or concomitant) and also appear independent of the presence of secondary alcohol abuse.

3. These findings suggest that panic disorder and major depression may partially have a common underlying diathesis. This hypothesis should be tested prospectively in subsequent studies.

4. The first-degree relatives of probands with major depression and GAD also show a marked increase in rates of major depression compared to the first-degree relatives of normal controls and depressed probands without an anxiety disorder. Their relatives also had an increased rate of anxiety disorders compared to normal controls but not compared to depressed probands without an anxiety disorder.

5. The first-degree relatives of probands with major depression and agoraphobia also show increased rates of major depression compared with the relatives of normal controls, but not compared to relatives of major depression without an anxiety disorder.

6. The children (ages 6–17) of depressed probands as compared with the children of normal probands were at increased risk for major depression. Depression plus agoraphobia or panic disorder in the probands conferred an additional risk on the children. If the proband had both depression and panic disorder, the children were at the greatest risk for having a psychiatric disorder, particularly major depression and separation anxiety. More than one-third of the children of

probands with depression plus panic disorder had separation anxiety, and greater than one-fourth had major depression.

7. The risk to children for major depression or any psychiatric disorder increased linearly if two parents were ill. There was a similar, but nonsignificant, trend for anxiety disorders (Weissman, Prusoff, Gammon, Merikangas, Leckman, & Kidd, 1984).

8. The proband characteristics that did *not* increase risk of anxiety disorder or any psychiatric disorder in children were current age, sex, social class, marital status; number of other children; age of onset of depression, anxiety disorder, or any psychiatric disorder; childhood history of stuttering or sleepwalking; separation from parents during childhood. The child's age at exposure or years of exposure to parental illness also did not increase risk (Weissman et al., 1984).

9. The proband characteristics that significantly increased risk of anxiety to children were recurrent depressions, high familial loading of major depression or any anxiety disorder, and childhood history of enuresis (Weissman et al., 1984).

WHAT'S ON THE HORIZON?

Adults

In the next several years data from the ECA will provide information that is lacking on the prevalence and incidence and the risk factors for some of the anxiety disorders (phobias, panic, obsessive-compulsive disorder) based on the *DSM-III* in five U.S. sites. Information on the relationship between the anxiety disorders and other adult psychiatric disorders will also be available.

The ECA will have data on GAD from the second wave in several Centers and on PTSD from the second wave of the St. Louis Center. Efforts to understand the variability and possible unreliability of rates of phobias between Baltimore and the other sites are under way, but as yet unresolved.

While the ECA has included a number of demographic and social risk factors, it must be acknowledged that no biological risk factors (e.g., frequency of mitral valve prolapse, response to pharmacologic challenge) have been included. These might best be investigated in high-risk individuals using case-control designs comparable to, as well as included in, the family studies described.

Children and Adolescents

Study of the epidemiology of all psychiatric disorders and of the anxiety disorders in children is virgin territory. As the epidemiologic methodology for studies of children currently under development at the NIMH becomes available the ECA approach should be applied to surveys of children and adolescents. While the epidemiologic studies will provide information on rates and risks for the anxiety disorders, there are many key questions not answered. The following list, of course, is by no means exhaustive.

Do Adult Anxiety Disorders Transmit to Children?

While the Yale study suggested that some adult anxiety disorders transmitted anxiety and depression to children, to our knowledge there has been no systematic, blind, case-control study of the young children of adult probands with anxiety disorder or of the adult parents of children with anxiety disorder. Relevant data available from a few small studies suggest an association between adult and childhood anxiety disorders in families (Berg, Butler, & Pritchard, 1974; Berg, Marks, McGuire, & Lipsedge, 1974; Gittelman-Klein, 1975; Gittelman-Klein & Klein, 1980).

There have been several studies of the children of psychiatrically ill patients (Rutter, 1966) and the children of depressives (Beardslee, Bemporad, Keller, & Klerman, 1983; Orvaschel, 1983; Weissman, Prusoff, Gammon, Merikangas, Leckman, & Kidd, 1984). In general, these studies found that children of parents with a major affective disorder were at high risk for depression. Since most of the studies focused on depression in both the parents and the children, with few exceptions data on anxiety disorders in the children were not reported. Moreover, none of the studies included an assessment of any accompanying anxiety disorders in the depressed probands. If the convention of not diagnosing anxiety disorder when it occurs with depression were followed, then the anxiety disorders would have been missed in the depressed parent probands, further obscuring findings of anxiety in the children. Future studies should diagnose depression and anxiety disorders separately even if they co-occur.

Are Adult and Childhood Anxiety Disorders Similar?

The data suggest that the children of patients with agoraphobia or panic disorder are beginning to manifest similar disorders themselves, in particular, separation anxiety. A number of investigators have made similar *retrospective* observations about the onset of adult anxiety disorder in childhood or early adulthood (Agras et al., 1969; Berg, 1976; Berg, Marks, McGuire, & Lipsedge, 1974; Buglass, Clarke, Henderson, Krietman, & Presley, 1977; Klein, 1964; Roth, 1960; Tyrer & Tyrer, 1974). However, longitudinal studies of children or adolescents with anxiety disorders are needed to determine the degree to which childhood disorders are precursors of adult anxiety or of depressive states. These studies should include matched control groups of normal children and children with depressive disorders in order to determine the specificity of the childhood anxiety disorders, as well as to allow for calculations of relative risks.

Are the Anxiety Disorders Related?

While the Yale study of children found support for a distinction between GAD and panic or agoraphobia, this distinction was not found when adult relatives of probands were studied. Careful family studies are needed that select probands with GAD only, with panic disorder, with and without agoraphobia, as well as the range of phobias, and study adult relatives and minor children of these probands using the best current methodology. These studies should include control groups, blind diagnostic assessments, and best estimate of diagnosis from direct interviews with relatives and from multiple informants. Studies such as these will help determine if familial aggregation is similar between the anxiety disorders.

Longitudinal studies of adults with varying forms of anxiety disorders would also be useful to determine the relationship between the onset of the anxiety disorders, e.g.: Is one anxiety disorder the precursor of another? Does the presence of one anxiety disorder increase the risk of another?

Are Anxiety and Depression Related?

The current family studies of children and of adult relatives of probands with depression and anxiety disorders and of anxiety disorders alone (Crowe et al., 1983; Leckman et al., 1983; Weissman, Leckman et al., 1984) suggest a relationship between depression and anxiety disorders. This relationship is also suggested by the fact that patients with anxiety disorders respond to tricyclic and other antidepressant medications. Controlled family studies of children and of adult relatives of probands with panic disorder, with and without agoraphobia, with agoraphobia alone, or with secondary depression and primary anxiety disorders, in which careful attention is paid to the diagnosis of depression as well as the other disorders in relatives would be useful.

SUMMARY OF FINDINGS AND POSSIBLE FUTURE RESEARCH

Summary of Findings

This review of the epidemiology and familial factors of anxiety disorders showed that:

1. Anxiety disorders in adults are common, heterogeneous, and familial.
2. The rates and risks for the different anxiety disorders in adults vary; a rough estimate for all anxiety disorders is about 4–8/100 annual prevalence. The ECA data over the next few years will provide a more accurate estimate of

prevalence and incidence of all the anxiety disorders. Based on the two studies available using precise diagnostic techniques, there is some agreement that GAD is the most common and panic disorder the least common of the anxiety disorders; that the anxiety disorders are most common in women, younger populations (although this varies), and in the less educated (again, this varies). There are no epidemiologic data on PTSD (a recent article suggests that this diagnosis should be viewed with caution, Sparr & Pankratz, 1983), and only one of the two studies assessed obsessive-compulsive disorder.

3. There is an overlap within the anxiety disorders and between the anxiety disorders and depression. There is an increased probability that a person with one anxiety disorder will have another, or will have a major depression during his or her lifetime.

4. Only about a quarter of persons with anxiety disorders receive treatment for these problems. However, these persons are high users of health care facilities for reasons other than emotional problems. Persons with panic disorders have the highest use of psychotropic drugs.

5. There are no epidemiologic population studies of anxiety disorders in children. The studies available survey fears and anxiety symptoms and suggest that these are common in children, especially girls, and some decline with age in children.

6. Family studies support the familial nature of anxiety although the precise rates vary with the methods used. The earlier studies did not divide the anxiety disorders into subtype. The current studies show that first-degree relatives of probands with anxiety disorders have increased rates of anxiety disorder and of depression.

7. When anxiety disorders are examined in the context of depression in family studies, the results show that anxiety disorders are common in both the depressed probands and their first-degree relatives.

8. The first-degree relatives of depressed probands with secondary anxiety disorders had higher rates of depression and of anxiety disorder regardless of whether the proband's anxiety was associated with or occurred separately from the depression. The higher rates of depression, anxiety disorder, and alcoholism were highest in the relatives of probands with depression and panic disorder.

9. The children (ages 6–17) of probands with depression and panic disorder have very high rates of depression, separation anxiety, and other anxiety disorders.

10. The relationship between depression and anxiety is not clear. The family studies suggest that depression and anxiety may be part of a shared diathesis; that anxiety disorders are heterogeneous and separate disorders. Panic disorder may be the most severe form of the anxiety disorders, using familial transmission as the criteria for severity. The family data suggest that the risk of major depression and separation anxiety is markedly increased among the offspring (aged 6–17 years) of probands with depression and panic disorder.

Possible Future Research

Potentially useful areas of future research include:

(a) The assessment of biological risk factors (e.g., assessment of mitral valve prolapse, response to pharmacologic challenge) in future epidemiologic studies. These studies are more feasible if conducted in individuals at high risk for anxiety disorders using family case-control design studies, perhaps drawing the sample from community studies.

(b) Large-scale ECA type of study in children and adolescents to determine rates (prevalence and incidence) and risk factors.

(c) Well-designed case-control family studies of the adult and first-degree relatives and the young children of adults with varying types of anxiety disorders (e.g., agoraphobia with and without panic, obsessive-compulsive disorder, primary anxiety disorder and secondary depression) to learn more about the relationship among anxiety disorders and between anxiety disorders and depression; and to learn more about the relationship between the adult and childhood anxiety disorders.

(d) Longitudinal studies of children with anxiety disorders to learn about the course, pattern, and implications of these disorders in children and their relationship to the adult forms.

Although this is in contradiction to the current *DSM-III* convention, future research studies involving the anxiety disorders should diagnose anxiety disorders even if they occur solely in association with episodes of major depression. Taken together, there are many promising areas of epidemiologic and family study research for the anxiety disorders which can provide increasing information on nosology, magnitude, risks, course, and consequences of the anxiety disorders.

ACKNOWLEDGMENTS

This review was supported in part by Alcohol, Drug Abuse, and Mental Health Administration research grant MH 28274 from the Center for Epidemiologic Studies and the Center for Studies of Affective Disorders, and grant MH 36197 from the Center for Studies of Affective Disorders, National Institute of Mental Health, Rockville, Maryland, and by the Yale Mental Health Clinical Research Center (MHCRC), NIMH Grant MH 30929. Appreciation is expressed to Amy Rosen, B.A., for assistance in reviewing the epidemiologic studies.

14

Culture and Anxiety: Cross-Cultural Evidence for the Patterning of Anxiety Disorders

Byron J. Good
Arthur M. Kleinman
Harvard Medical School

INTRODUCTION

Recent advances in psychophysiology, psychological studies of affect, clinical and pharmacological research, and psychiatric epidemiology make it reasonable to postulate the existence of a discrete, heterogenous set of universal anxiety disorders that may vary across cultures in prevalence and form of expression, but not in essential structure. Research on several fronts raises the possibility of linking discrete physiological conditions to distinct combinations of symptom groups, which in turn may be represented by formal diagnostic criteria and identified through epidemiological instruments (see, for example, Klein & Rabkin, 1981; Sheehan, 1982; and Weissman & Klerman, 1978). Cross-cultural studies provide a critical opportunity to place this postulate in broader context. How are we to know whether the clinical syndromes identified in research in the United States and Europe are universal diseases, linked to discrete biological disorders, or culture-specific forms of illness behavior resulting from complex interactions among physiological, psychological, social and cultural variables? Are they universal behavioral syndromes that map onto underlying physiological patterns, representing "final common pathways" to be identified through studies of neurotransmitters and neuroendocrinology, or are they culture-specific syndromes, linked to underlying psychophysiological processes but produced as final common *ethno-behavioral* pathways (Carr, 1978)?[1]

---

[1] Our use of the term "ethno-behavioral" is drawn from the work of Carr (1978). He writes: "The notion that culture-bound syndromes share underlying common disease forms is rejected. Instead, the ethno-behavioral model postulates that culture-bound syndromes consist of culturally specific behavioral repertoires but with both behavior and norms acquired in accordance with basic principles of human learning universal to all cultures" (p. 269).

This chapter will not, of course, conclusively answer the question of the universality of particular anxiety disorders. Neither the empirical data nor theoretical conceptualizations currently allow such answers. Here we review what is known from cross-cultural studies that may indicate the dimensions and extent of cultural variation in anxiety disorders. In addition, recognizing that apparent universals may be artifacts of instruments and approaches employed, our aim is to provide a critical review of research methods used in cross-cultural research.

We are not suggesting a return to the debate over whether psychiatric disease is universal or culturally relative, characteristic of the culture and personality studies in the 1930s and the early writings of labeling theorists. Advances in biological research, genetic studies and cross-cultural psychiatry make those early accounts appear antiquated and clinically naive. At the same time, increasingly sophisticated studies of illness meanings and behavior in a variety of non-Western societies make many clinical and epidemiological accounts appear antiquated and culturally naive. Emerging "interactionist paradigms" suggest that interactions among physiological, psychological, social and cultural factors that produce and shape mental illness are far more complex than imagined in those early debates (see Hahn & Kleinman, 1983, for a review). It is critical to review cross-cultural data on anxiety disorders from the perspective of emerging theoretical frames.

The cross-cultural research reviewed below makes it abundantly clear that anxiety and disorders of anxiety are universally present in human societies. It makes equally clear that the phenomenology of such disorders, the meaningful forms through which distress is articulated and constituted as social reality, varies in quite significant ways across cultures. Although considerable research is needed if we wish to identify the full range of such variation, cultural differences in anxiety disorders appear to result in surprising variations in the "natural history" of the disorders in some societies — in the age of their onset, in their course, their social distribution, and their consequences for the lives of the sufferers. These findings, if borne out in future research, underline the importance of guarding against a "category fallacy" in anxiety research. In a cross-cultural context, a category fallacy is the reification of a nosological category developed for particular Western populations and the application of that category to the more than three quarters of the world's population who are non-Western, without establishing its validity within those populations. Having dispensed with indigenous illness categories because they are culture-specific, researchers too often go on to superimpose their own "scientific" categories on some sample of deviant behavior in another culture, as if their own disease categories were culture-free (Kleinman, 1977). Findings from cross-cultural research also suggest questions for the study of anxiety which can be answered only through meticulous cross-cultural research. What is the full range of anxiety disorders? What is the nature and the extent of their variation? Have our current diagnostic criteria and research instruments reified Western forms of the experience of anxiety; that is, have we produced nosologies of "illness" forms rather than of "diseases"? (In this paper "illness" refers to the culturally grounded perception and experience of sickness by individuals in social groups; "disease" refers to underlying patterns of physiological and psychological abnormality [see Kleinman, Eisenberg, & Good 1977].) Is the reliability of current psychological instruments used in cross-cultural settings matched by validity? What are the most significant phenomena to which research should be directed?

SELECTIVE LITERATURE REVIEW

The cross-cultural literature on anxiety is far less developed than that on depression or schizophrenia. Whereas Marsella (1980) was able to point to nine specific reviews of the cross-cultural literature on depression prior to 1975 (not including Marsella, 1978, 1980; and Bebbington, 1978), no comprehensive reviews of cross-cultural studies of anxiety disorders have appeared. Sharma (1977) has briefly reviewed the cross-cultural psychology literature on anxiety (in a publication of the East-West Center that is not widely available). Reviews of the cross-cultural psychiatry literature on anxiety disorders have appeared only as part of general reviews of psychopathology (Draguns, 1980), "culture-related specific psychiatric conditions" (Tseng & McDermott, 1981) or "minor psychological disturbances of everyday life" (Tseng & Hsu, 1980). The most comprehensive review of cross-cultural psychiatric epidemiology to appear to date, that of H.B.M. Murphy (1982), addresses anxiety disorders specifically only in a chapter on "neuroses and other minor disorders," in which Murphy reviews variations in the incidence and patterning of the war neuroses, phobic disorders, and forms of hysteria.

The general ambiguities in the field of anxiety studies—concerning the nature of the discontinuities of pathological and normal anxiety, the conceptual interrelationship of the emotion anxiety, anxiety as a symptom and anxiety disorders, and the relationship of various anxiety disorders to each other—compound the difficulties of studying psychopathology in societies radically different from those in which most psychiatric research is conducted. Despite these problems, a number of very important and suggestive conclusions may be drawn from a careful sifting of the cross-cultural literature.

Our review first examines the cross-cultural psychology literature, with its focus on anxiety states rather than discrete pathological forms. We then survey the most important cross-cultural epidemiological studies of anxiety disorders, including both those that have measured levels of anxiety symptoms in populations (using symptom checklist techniques) and those that have identified specific anxiety disorders (diagnostic entities) and measured their prevalence. Finally we review the literature that focuses on "emic" illness categories—categories held by members of a society itself, including the so-called culture-bound disorders—and address the issue of how these are related to Western diagnostic categories.

ANXIETY IN CROSS-CULTURAL PSYCHOLOGY

The cross-cultural psychological research on anxiety is most closely associated with the works of Cattell and Spielberger. This tradition of research has sought to measure anxiety both as a personality characteristic or trait and as a state of response to particular stressful situations. Cross-national researchers have hypothesized that various interrelated aspects of national culture—value systems, child-rearing patterns, forms of stress predominating during particular historical periods, institutionalized coping forms—produce variations along such personality dimensions as level of anxiety and extroversion. This work assumes a continuity between normal and pathological anxiety, and although the scales are often validated by contrasting scores of psychiatric outpatients and normal subjects, the scales were not in fact developed to measure levels of psychopathology. The literature seldom addresses the question of whether there are discrete anxiety disorders, and the instruments used are not designed to distinguish among various clinical syndromes.

The cross-cultural research generally follows the strategy of translating items from English language instruments into semantic equivalents in another language, administering the questionnaires to similar samples (most often students) in several national groups, then making both inter- and intra-cultural comparisons. The most common measures in current use are the IPAT Anxiety Scale of Cattell and Scheier (1961) and the State-Trait Anxiety Inventory (STAI) developed by Spielberger, Gorsuch and Lushene (1970). Both have been translated into many languages, with the STAI available in careful translations in Spanish, Hindi, French, Italian, Swedish and Turkish, and preliminary forms available in more than 15 other languages (Spielberger & Diaz-Guerrero, 1976). Several examples will illustrate the findings of cross-national research with these instruments. Tsujioka and Cattell (1965) and Cattell and Warburton (1961) compared students in the United States with Japanese and British students, respectively. It was found, for example, that Americans are less anxious and more extrovert than Japanese, and data suggested that damage to self-sentiment is more anxiety provoking for Japanese than Americans. Cattell and Scheier (1961) also studied six national groups, finding significant differences in anxiety levels among (ordered from most anxious to least) college students from Poland, India, France, Italy, Britain, and the United States. Cattell preferred to explain these in terms of standard of living and political freedom, rather than patterns of child rearing.

Similar studies have been conducted with other national groups. Using the Children's Manifest Anxiety Scale (CMAS), Iwawaki, Sumida, Okuno and Cohen

(1967) found that whereas adult Japanese have a higher level of anxiety than Americans, Japanese nine-year-olds have significantly lower levels of anxiety than the same age groups in France and the United States. Researchers have accounted for these findings in terms of changes in child rearing in Japanese families since World War II, social restrictions for particular age groups, and pressures for successful performance in Japanese university examinations (see Chiu, 1971, for a review of this issue). Chiu (1971) studied Taiwanese and American children in urban and small-town settings, using the CMAS. It was hypothesized that because of more severe child-rearing practices in Chinese families and a lower standard of living in Taiwan, Taiwanese students would score higher on the scale than Americans. In addition, it was predicted that small-town students (in both nations) would score higher than urban residents. These predictions were borne out.

In a more wide-ranging set of studies, Lynn (1982) has argued that differences in anxiety and extroversion account for a large amount of the variance in national rates of alcoholism, suicide, accidents, crime, divorce, illegitimacy, cigarette consumption, chronic psychosis, and coronary heart disease. Using data from 18 nations, he submitted the rates of these "anxiety equivalents" to factor analysis and argued that the resulting factors approximate anxiety and extroversion. He showed that anxiety increased in those nations that were suffering defeat and occupation during World War II, in contrast to the other nations, providing predictive validity for the factor. Findings for anxiety levels, using this method, were validated directly from findings from questionnaire data for several of the societies.

These studies raise obvious questions of validity. How do we know that the same thing, anxiety, is being measured in the various societies? Contributors to the Spielberger and Diaz-Guerrero collection went to great lengths to establish validity. They set very high standards for translation in order to ensure semantic equivalence. They administered the questionnaires in both English and native language to bilingual individuals, finding high correlations among individual items as well as scale scores. And they compared stressed subjects (usually students in examination settings) with nonstressed respondents, finding higher anxiety levels among the more stressed, as would be predicted.

Development of the research instruments described above indicated that anxiety may be derived as a single, underlying simple factor structure that can account for substantial variance in diverse introspective, behavioral, and physiological measures. The cross-cultural studies utilizing these instruments have shown that they measure some universal aspects of the psychobiological response to stress, and that to this extent they are valid. There are, however, serious limitations to what we can conclude from these studies about the universality of anxiety and its expression across cultures.

First, because of the strategy of simply translating items from an English instrument into semantically equivalent terms in another language in an effort to maintain comparability, no efforts were made to establish the full range of expressions of anxiety in the cultures studied and to sample items from these. Thus we do not know whether a factor analysis, based on measurement of distress expressed in culture-specific forms in a particular society, would have produced a factor equivalent to that constituted by translating from the American instrument into another language.

The claim that accurate translation of an instrument shown to have validity in one society is enough to establish its validity in another is tenable only if one makes several assumptions. It must be assumed that anxiety is a universal entity, that aspects of that psychobiological entity map directly onto experiences of symptoms and English language complaints, that the psychological instruments adequately sample from the full range of such complaints, and that accurate translation into another language will allow the researcher to measure the same underlying domain for members of another society. These assumptions essentially beg the question of validity (see Sharma, 1977, for a critical appraisal of these assumptions by a psychologist). In addition, the assumptions that anxiety is directly reflected in English language complaints and that semantically equivalent complaints in another language adequately represent the symptoms associated with anxiety (that is, that semantically equivalent items will necessarily map back onto the same entity, anxiety) are not borne out by research. Many studies (see below) indicate wide variation in the idiom of complaint across societies— in the specific symptoms brought to medical or mental health clinics, in the significance of particular body sensations, in the tendency to report or deny particular symptoms, and in the range of the expressions and interpretations of anxiety. In addition, quite different items correlate most highly with the overall scale scores on instruments administered in different societies, suggesting differences in "typical response modes" (Moerdyk & Spinks, 1979) and raising questions for the "centri-cultural" approach. A centri-cultural research strategy begins with research instruments developed exclusively in one culture and directly translates them into many languages for use in other cultures (Wober, 1969).

Second, because of their interest in comparing personality characteristics of entire populations, cross-cultural psychologists have left the issue of normative data remarkably ambiguous. On the one hand, intra-societal studies are represented as providing norms for members of that society. Cross-national studies have then used these studies to claim that anxiety levels are higher in some societies than others. Causes for these differences are then explained by differences in child-rearing patterns, standard of living, or political institutions. Such comparisons are highly dubious; they nonetheless remain common. (For a critique of this approach based on secondary analysis of a cross-national survey using the Cornell Medical Index, see Kalimo, Bice, & Novosel, 1970.) Both the cross-cultural and intra-cultural epidemiological research make it quite clear that norms vary not only by society but by social class and ethnic group as well. Whether these norms represent cultural differences in styles of presenting symptoms or differences in the level of anxiety of members of the society remains open to question.

Third, one can hardly refrain from noting the tendency to make global judgments about levels of anxiety in a culture based on responses of a sample of students in a university or a single primary school class. Significant differences in scores appear even when students of the same age but in different settings (e.g., small town vs. metropolitan area) are compared within the same society (Chiu, 1971). Moreover, the failure of many studies (including all those reported in the Spielberger and Diaz-Guerrero volume) to indicate socioeconomic status of the sample seems remarkable, given the well-known effects of social class found in nearly all epidemiological research. These sampling problems raise grave questions about what can be concluded from many of these studies.

Two suggestions follow from this critique of the cross-cultural psychology literature. First, if translations of psychological instruments developed in the United States are to be used in cross-cultural research, validity should be established using techniques as rigorous as those used to develop the instruments in the first place. That is, native language idioms of distress should be sampled and used to develop culture-specific instruments, and data should be submitted to factor analysis. Studies should then be undertaken to compare scores on such instruments with scores on instruments translated from American instruments. No less would be acceptable if one wished to establish the validity of a translation for American use of an instrument such as that developed by Ebigbo (1982— see below) for psychiatric screening among Ibos in Nigeria.

Second, because of the problems of the meaning of group specific norms, instruments should not be used for direct cross-cultural comparison. This does not imply that valid cross-cultural research may not be conducted using such instruments. Findings of covariation of anxiety with other variables (social class, social dislocation, etc.) within one society may usefully be compared with similar findings in another. The work of Chance, Rin, and Chu (1966) provides an excellent example. In separate studies, samples of Eskimos and Taiwanese were studied to investigate the effects of contact with modern society and value identity on mental health status (measured by the Cornell Medical Index). Similar covariation among comparable variables in the two societies suggested that "in rapidly changing societies, adequate knowledge of modern patterns of life together with a strong sense of one's own cultural identity provide in a people a psychic and cultural integration which promotes mental health. In contrast, . . . it appears that the removal of the center of one's own personal value system is a highly significant hazard to people undergoing rapid social and cultural change" (pp. 212-213). This study was able to test an important hypothesis in cross-cultural research by investigating relationship among comparable variables without dubious direct comparison of symptom level, as measured by a translated instrument, in two very different societies. This should provide one model for future cross-cultural and cross-national psychological studies of anxiety.

CROSS-CULTURAL EPIDEMIOLOGICAL STUDIES OF
ANXIETY DISORDERS

Cross-cultural studies of the prevalence of psychopathology have followed a course since World War II similar to that which Weissman and Klerman (1978) outline for post-war epidemiological studies in the United States. Recognizing the obvious inadequacy of comparing rates of institutionalization in developing countries as a basis for judging prevalence of psychiatric disorders, a number of researchers conducted population-based (or primary care-based) epidemiological studies in non-Western societies, several with the support of the World Health Organization (see Baasher, 1977, and Sartorius, 1980, for reviews). Researchers used various screening devices to identify potential cases and direct examination by research psychiatrists to determine diagnosis and level of impairment.

Critical comparisons of diagnostic practice of American and European psychiatrists revealed extraordinary problems with reliability. For psychiatrists working in non-Western cultures, difficulties of using Western diagnostic criteria in a reliable manner had long been recognized. In response, a number of researchers turned to utilization of symptom checklists, some of which incorporated a variety of culture-specific symptom forms. More recently, several efforts have been undertaken to adapt current diagnostic criteria and associated research instruments in a manner that is culturally sensitive and addresses questions of the relationship between culture and diagnostic entity.

At each stage of the development of new epidemiological methods, their adaptation for use in cross-cultural research has been especially difficult, both because of the inherent difficulties of diagnosis as one moves further from Western culture, and because logistical and financial resources have been limited. However, precisely because of the difficulty of applying Western research diagnostic criteria, findings emerging from such research may be particularly instructive. In this section we briefly review the cross-cultural epidemiological research on anxiety disorders.

Diagnostic Surveys Conducted by Research Psychiatrists

Population surveys have been conducted by research psychiatrists among Australian aborigines (Jones, 1972; Jones & Horne, 1972, 1973; Kidson & Jones, 1968), in urban and rural settings in Ethiopia (including both studies in primary care and population studies—Giel & Van Luijk, 1969, 1970), in both village and urban settings in Iran (Bash & Bash-Liechti, 1969, 1974), in a village in the Sudan (Baasher, 1961), in a variety of urban and rural settings in India (see Murphy, 1982, pp. 48–50 for a summary and references), in a small community in Norway (Bremer, 1951), as well as in other societies. In very few of these studies are anxiety disorders a focus of attention. In several of the studies, prevalence of anxiety cannot be separated from rates of neuroses in general; in others, the criteria for distinguishing anxiety, mixed neurotic forms, and various somatoform disorders are quite unclear. General findings, however, are that with the exception of the aborigines, anxiety disorders were diagnosed at a rate of 12 to 27 cases per thousand population. For example, the Iranian studies showed prevalence for all disorders of middle or high level of severity as 71 and 80/1000 for village and city, respectively; 27 and 8/1000 for anxiety disorders specifically; and 48 and 38/1000 for anxiety, hypochondriasis, and "polymorph forms." The Indian studies showed rates of 17.8, 20.5, and 12.0/1000 for anxiety neuroses, and the Norwegian study 11/1000 for anxiety neurosis, and 56/1000 for combined categories of neurasthenia, hypochondria, and "somatogenically acquired nervous states."

The studies of the aborigines provide the single sharp contrast to this pattern. Here, in population surveys of 2360 persons, only one case of "overt anxiety" was found, and this in the most Westernized individual in the group. Jones and Horne (1973) comment: "The term 'overt anxiety' has been used to describe the syndrome of persistent apprehension with restlessness, tremor and excessive sweating. Such a syndrome is seen when Aborigines are afraid, as they often are—of spirits, the dark, witchcraft, strangers and so on. This fear is short-lived and goes when the cause is removed. No intractable symptoms of 'overt anxiety' without a culturally appropriate cause were found. . . . hypochondriacal symptoms . . . certainly do exist and may be the Aborigine equivalent of anxiety" (p. 224). In addition, no phobic or obsessive-compulsive states were found among aborigines.

Research Using Standardized Symptom Rating Instruments

Given the disagreements about diagnostic categories and the unreliability of their application in research, utilization of a standardized household survey form administered by trained interviewers and rated by psychiatrists using specified criteria seemed an important advance and an opportunity for international and cross-cultural research. The Midtown Manhattan study provided a model, and Leighton and his colleagues exploited these methods in a series of cross-cultural studies. In the most complex of these studies, the Cornell-Aro Mental Health Project in Nigeria, a team of anthropologists and psychiatrists cooperated in all aspects of the research in an effort to overcome cultural biases (Leighton et al., 1966). We will not review that study in detail. It is worth noting, however, that in contrast to the findings of 1%-3% of the population having anxiety disorders in the studies reviewed above, the Cornell-Aro project reported 36% and 27% of town and village residents had symptoms of anxiety, and 19% and 16% of them were significantly impaired. By comparison, the Sterling County study had found far less anxiety symptoms (13% and 10%), but twice the rate of impairment (38% and 32% for town and country, respectively). Thus, although the Yoruba reported much greater subjective distress (in this and other symptom categories), their symptoms seemed to have less impact on their social functioning.

This discrepancy between subjective distress and social impairment, as estimated by interviewers and psychiatrist raters, suggests that these may be virtually independent cultural variables. On the other hand, it may reflect invalid ratings among populations having significantly different styles of communicating symptoms. Analysis of the Midtown Manhattan data raised the issue of the validity of this approach particularly acutely. This study, it may be recalled, did not specifically sample from an identified Puerto Rican stratum. When the small, naturally occurring Puerto Rican sample was analyzed separately, however, not one person was rated "well" and 52% were rated "impaired," a rating assigned to only 23% of other persons in the area (Srole, Langner, Michael, Opler, & Rennie, 1962, p. 291; cf. Murphy, 1982, p. 52). This suggested that not only diagnostic judgments but differences in level of impairment could also be influenced by cultural biases of the raters.

Symptom checklists were developed, in part, to remove the subjectivity of a rater. Although the cultural bias of the rater or diagnostician is removed by such a method, symptom checklists have their own sources of cultural bias. Brief review of one cross-national study will indicate one such problem that recent studies have sought to overcome. Inkeles' cross-national study of modernization (Inkeles, 1983) included a very brief symptom checklist, drawn from items common to various such instruments (see Murphy, 1982, pp. 55-56 for analysis of this study). The results, shown in Table 1, are instructive. Although the average percentage frequency with which symptoms were reported was quite similar in the four countries, leading one to believe the scale may have measured a common dimension in the four cultures, closer examination seems to indicate otherwise. The frequency of reporting particular symptoms varied greatly from country to country. If some of these symptoms had been omitted, and presumably

TABLE 1
Responses to Symptom Checklist in a Cross-National Study
(from Inkeles, 1983, pp. 262–263)

	India	Chile	Israel	Nigeria
Average percent of symptoms per country	24	29	22	28
Individual symptoms:				
Trouble sleeping	54	23	37	21
Nervousness	48	36	27	9
Heart beating	13	24	13	45
Shortness of breath	8	15	6	32
Disturbing dreams	21	22	35	48

if others had been added, quite different mean scores would have resulted. Thus, resort to quantitative "objectivity" does not ensure cross-cultural validity. In particular, this analysis indicates the importance of the selection of those symptoms included in the symptom checklist as a source of cultural bias.

Our comments on this last study simply illustrate a point that anthropologists and clinicians have made over and again. There is great variation across societies in the experience and expression of symptoms of anxiety, as there is in the experienced sources of anxiety. If anxiety is to be assessed in cross-cultural research—either in terms of levels of symptoms, or in terms of diagnoses based on symptoms—the variability of symptoms across societies must be recognized and accounted for.

Epidemiological Methods Using Culture-Specific Symptom Vocabularies

In the past decade, a number of research efforts have systematically studied the relationship between culture-specific forms of symptom expression, popular illness categories, and psychiatric disorder. Such research indicates some of the culture-specific forms of anxiety disorders and suggests new directions for investigating the validity of current diagnostic categories in non-Western societies.

First, the Nigerian literature—reports from the Cornell-Aro project, Collis's fine clinical descriptions (Collis, 1966), and reports from the University College Hospital at Ibadan (Anumonye, 1970; Jegede, 1978)—indicates that generalized anxiety disorders among the Yoruba are associated with three primary clusters of symptoms: worries, dreams, and bodily complaints. Each of these takes a form grounded in Yoruba culture. Collis (1966) found that villagers never expressed worries about "difficulty in applying oneself to work, difficulty in concentration, loss of interest and poor memory . . . though they were sometimes clearly present. . . . The predominant worry expressed by over two-thirds of these people was the culturally conditioned concern with the creation and maintenance of a large family. Under this wide heading may be included anxiety associated with sterility and impotence or with death of a child or spouse" (p. 12). Fertility is, of course, a major focus of discourse in Yoruba (and more generally African) religious and ritual life and central to the symbolism of affliction and healing (Janzen, 1978; Leighton et al., 1966; Turner, 1967). It should be no surprise that this prominent idiom should provide the language for expression of anxiety. Second, both Collis and the Cornell-Aro project found, as did Field (1958) in her research with the Ashanti in Ghana, that dreams were a major source of anxiety, mode of its experience, and reason for care seeking. Dream experiences provide primary evidence that one is being bewitched, and as Lambo (1962) notes, "morbid fear of bewitchment is the commonest cause of acute anxiety states in Africa" (p. 258). Third, a rich somatic discourse provides an essential vocabulary for anxiety symptoms. The 19 anxiety patients examined by Collis averaged 8.6 different bodily complaints, and many of these were in a form seldom heard in American clinics.

In a fascinating study of anxiety disorders and somatic idioms in Nigeria, Ebigbo (1982) has recently argued that "to have an effective diagnostic instrument for discriminating normals from abnormals and categorizing groups of abnormals among themselves in Nigeria, psychosomatic complaints must form the basis of such an instrument" (p. 30). Research is under way using a 65-item questionnaire consisting of common somatization complaints. (Table 2 shows a partial list of items from the symptom checklist, illustrating the form of a culture-specific symptom instrument.)

Analysis may indicate whether clusters or factors of these somatic symptoms are associated with diagnostic entities, or whether diagnoses are distinguished by a few distinct symptoms superimposed on a core of paraesthetic or psychosomatic symptoms. Ebigbo suggests the latter may be true: "If these core symptoms are accompanied by irrational talk, hallucination and delusion, the illness is labelled schizophrenia. If the symptom bearer is a student who cannot study because of the symptoms, his illness is called 'brain-fag' [Prince, 1960]. If the patient loses appetite and weight he is called a depressive, etc." (p. 30).

Several other studies have been completed in the past several years or are currently under way that have systematically used culture-specific vocabularies of symptoms in epidemiological instruments. Two studies completed in the

TABLE 2
Somatic Complaints in Nigerian Psychiatric Patients: Items from
Ebigbo's Psychiatric Screening Form (Ebigbo, 1982, pp. 34–36)

Occasionally I experience heat sensation in my head.
Sometimes it seems as if pepper were put into my head.
I have the feeling of something like water in my brain.
Things like ants keep on creeping in various parts of my brain.
I am convinced some types of worms are in my head.
If you look on my head exactly you can see it is sort of breathing.
I have very constantly severe headache.
By merely touching parts of my brain it hurts.
My shoulder is heavy, as if I were carrying a heavy load.
Intermittently I must breathe in fast otherwise I will be gone.
Clearly parts of my body are out of order.
Sometimes my heart suddenly wants to fly out (obi-ilo-miri).
You can hear the beating of my heart from a distance.
I feel that various parts of my body shiver.
I feel general weakness in all parts of my body.
While walking my feet cannot stand firm on the ground.
Very often I have continuous noise in my belly.
At the moment I get very weak erection.
Whenever the sun is shining I cannot walk far on foot, otherwise I am sure to collapse.

1970s—that of Beiser and his colleagues in Senegal (Beiser, Benfari, Collomb, & Ravel, 1976; Beiser, Ravel, Collomb, & Egelhoff, 1972; Benfari, Beiser, Leighton, & Mertens, 1972), and Carstairs and Kapur (1976) in India—developed interview schedules, beginning with clinical and anthropological findings concerning native illness lexicons as items for investigation. Beiser and his colleagues began with the Stirling County form, first used by Leighton and his colleagues in Nova Scotia, then revised symptom statements and added items based on interviews with native healers and discussions with persons identified by the members of the community as suffering from "illnesses of the spirit" (Beiser, Burr, Ravel, & Collomb, 1973). A factor analysis of symptoms revealed a "physiological anxiety" factor, similar to the symptom group in the Stirling County findings, that accounted for 24% of the variance (Benfari et al., 1972). Using the Present State Examination (PSE) as a model, Carstairs and Kapur went further in developing an instrument (the Indian Psychiatric Interview Schedule) based on local forms of symptom expression (Kapur, Kapur, & Carstairs, 1974). For example, they found that schedules developed in the West did not pay sufficient attention to "the psychiatric problems common in an Indian setting, such as the phenomenon of spirit-possession, preoccupation with symptoms of sexual inadequacy, and the frequency of vague somatic symptoms of psychological origin" (Carstairs & Kapur, 1976, p. 21). In addition, they made a serious effort to develop an instrument to measure social dysfunction based on criteria "derived from the norms of the group to which the person belonged and not from the aspirations and objectives of the investigator" (p. 22). While the Carstairs and Kapur study disavows diagnostic classification and they openly describe difficulties in developing a culture-specific social dysfunction scale, their detailed analysis of symptom level and care seeking (including resort to native healers) in a population allowed them to measure intra-societal differences in psychiatric distress in a manner assuring validity and reliability in the Indian setting. This enabled them both to test an important hypothesis about the mental health concomitants of legislated social change and to measure need for psychiatric services in a culturally sensitive manner.

Several other studies exemplify current efforts to utilize current diagnostic instruments in cross-cultural research. Orley and Wing (1979) translated the PSE into Luganda, tested the translation for comprehensibility and face validity with a group of Ugandan psychiatric patients, and administered the instrument to 206 adults in two Ugandan villages. They sought to translate "the concept behind each item rather than simply translating the questions in the English version" (p. 517). Results showed somewhat higher rates of anxiety states for the Ugandan villagers than for a sample of London women, but much higher rates of depression. In addition, Ugandans diagnosed as depressed showed much higher rates of pathological guilt, subjective anergia, and hypochondriasis, and lower rates of situational anxiety. Examination of their admirable description of the translation of specific items raises obvious questions about the cross-cultural comparability of particular symptoms. Should a positive response to the question "do you sometimes blame yourself for something that was a mistake?" be considered "pathological guilt"? Might not pathological guilt be more commonly expressed as self-accusation of witchcraft, as Field found for the Ashanti? Similar questions might be asked of the translation of situational anxiety. Although the study is an important one, it shares the problems of other instruments that begin with English symptom statements and seeks comparable statements, rather than beginning with the full range of native statements and selecting from these. (Okasha & Ashour, 1981, note this in their comments on the translation of the PSE into Arabic; they added several culture-specific items to the instrument.)

Because of its importance in cross-cultural psychiatric epidemiology, we might briefly mention here the World Health Organization's International Pilot Study of Schizophrenia (WHO, 1979). This study demonstrated that although there is a core schizophrenic disease across cultures, there is great variation in the symptomatology (e.g., almost all the cases of catatonia were in India) and course of the disorder. The finding of variation in the course of the disorder (better course in the developing societies, worse in the developed) shows the import of such cross-national and cross-cultural research, and also provides an important model for future research. The study indicates that social context and the meanings associated with a psychiatric disorder, even one that is usually believed to have relatively little "pathoplasticity," play an important role in amplifying and damping the symptoms and the social functioning of the sufferer. This suggests a key hypothesis, requiring new research strategies, for the cross-cultural study of anxiety disorders: longitudinal studies might be expected to reveal that not only may symptomatology and prevalence of anxiety disorders vary across cultures, but that variations in the course of the disorders and outcomes of treatment may be even more significant.

The most recent effort to bring together diagnostic instruments with assessment of native symptom forms and illness categories is currently under way in a study by Shore and Manson of depression in three Native American groups (see Manson, Shore, & Bloom, in press). They have translated and modified the Diagnostic Interview Schedule (DIS) (Robins, Holzer, Croughan & Ratcliff, 1981) to make it culturally appropriate, then linked it with a detailed questionnaire investigating a range of traditional symptoms and native diagnostic categories. That is, they created a separate instrument to assess indigenous categories of illness that overlap with Major Depressive Disorder as described in the *Diagnostic and Statistical Manual of Mental Disorders* (3rd ed.) *(DSM-III)* (American Psychiatric Association, 1980). This study provides an important model for research investigating both the validity of diagnostic criteria in cross-cultural settings and the specificity of native illness diagnoses. It is hoped such research will be encouraged in the study of anxiety disorders.

Summary

Several conclusions can be drawn from this section of the review. First, clinical reports, utilization of translated diagnostic instruments with normal and patient populations, and factor analyses of symptom checklists suggest generalized anxiety disorders exist in nearly all cultures. Only the Aborigine studies suggest the presence of anxiety but not of anxiety disorders. With the exception of occasional clinical reports (e.g., Hudson, 1981), there is little in the epidemiological literature to indicate the presence of agoraphobia or panic disorder. This should not be considered evidence that such disorders do not exist. Indeed, what evidence we have (Kleinman, 1982) suggests that panic disorder may be relatively prevalent in somatized form, and that studies of this disorder should focus on primary care settings as well as psychiatric outpatient clinics.

Second, the literature is quite clear that complaints associated with anxiety are articulated in culture-specific idioms. These findings raise important methodological issues and questions concerning diagnostic criteria that deserve further research. The preponderance of rich somatic idioms have produced difficulties for clinicians and researchers in distinguishing anxiety, depression, and various somatoform disorders (neurasthenia, hypochondriasis, psychophysiological reactions). (We will return to this issue.) The experience of anxiety and fears in relationship to fertility, dreams, magical aggression, and witchcraft raises culture-specific questions about the boundaries between normalcy and pathology and deserves further research.

Third, nearly all researchers indicate the difficulty of determining the basis of multiple somatic complaints in the context of prevalent parasitic, infectious, and nutritional disorders. With the exception of Collis's admirable study (1966), these issues have seldom been directly addressed in cross-cultural psychiatric research. Fourth, culture may play one of its most important roles in influencing the course of anxiety disorders and the evaluation and outcome of various therapeutics, including pharmaceutical treatments.

CULTURE SPECIFIC SYNDROMES AND ANXIETY DISORDERS

In addition to cross-cultural research that begins with diagnostic measures developed in Europe or America and translates these for use in non-Western cultures, an alternative and often complementary tradition has been research into disorders specifically identified and labeled by members of a society, especially those that appear unusual to Western-oriented clinicians. The so-called culture-bound disorders have aroused special interest over the years, in particular because they raise questions about the "naturalness" of the illness phenomena we see and the diagnostic criteria we use. Those who believe psychiatric disorders to be products of unique constellations of social, cultural, and personal forces have rested their case with these disorders. Those who claim universality of discrete and heterogenous disorders have sought to discover specific psychiatric diseases clothed in these strange forms. In the context of this review, we might ask whether there are culture-specific forms of anxiety disorders. Is there evidence that culture produces unique syndromes that overlap our diagnostic categories? How are we to approach the conceptual analysis of such syndromes? We briefly examine the various "fright disorders" described in the anthropological literature both to examine their potential relationship to anxiety disorders and to provide a model for investigating the nature of culture-specific illness categories. Second, we contrast the literature on *shinkeishitsu* in Japan with that on agoraphobia in the West. Third, we look briefly at research on neurasthenia in China.

Fright Disorders

Fright illnesses are culturally ubiquitous. *Latah* in Malay cultures, *susto* in Latin American cultures, *hak tsan* in Cantonese culture, fright illnesses in Middle Eastern cultures—all are disorders identified in folk cultures as caused by fear reactions or startling. It has been tempting to cross-cultural psychiatrists to read reports of such culture-specific disorders and look for the appropriate category in psychiatric nosology into which each can be made to fit. Kiev, with considerable naiveté, has sought to equate each of the cultural-bound disorders with a particular disease entity: anxiety states *(koro, susto,* bewitchment), obsessive-compulsive neurosis (frigophobia, *shinkeishitsu*), hysterical disorders *(latah),* phobic states (evil eye, voodoo death), and so forth (Kiev, 1972, pp. 78-108). Yap (1974, pp. 84-104), in a much more complex analysis, classifies all the fright illnesses as "fear reactions," belonging to a larger category of local-atypical psychogenic reactions, and analyzes each in relation to acute anxiety reactions and the universal-typical psychiatric disorders. Careful examination of recent research on several of these disorders reveals serious difficulties with this general approach.

   Latah is a socially stigmatized behavioral syndrome found in Malaysia and Indonesia. Those exhibiting the syndrome are characterized by exaggerated startle, often exclaiming obscenities in settings where it is very inappropriate and embarrassing for the individual and amusing for the other persons present. Individuals are purposely startled; they may exhibit echolalia or echopraxia or may obey a command of the startler. *Latah* has its usual onset in middle age, often following an acute life stress. Both men and women acquire the condition, though it is most common in post-menopausal women, especially widows and those of the lower social strata.

   The cross-cultural psychiatric literature has often interpreted this syndrome as a culture-specific psychiatric disorder, variously identifying it as a reactive psychosis, fright neurosis, or hysterical disorder. Anthropologists, on the other hand, have been fascinated by the social meanings of the disorder. *"Latah* is a very 'Javanese' way of expressing mental disorder," Geertz notes (1968), because it represents an inversion of the highly valued form of social etiquette through which status and refinement of self are expressed. This suggests a paradox, however, because very similar syndromes have been reported in Burma, Thailand, the Philippines, Siberia, and elsewhere. Simons (1980, 1983) recently declared resolution of the paradox. His research indicates that some individuals (in all societies) have particularly acute startle reflexes; when these persons experience heightened arousal or anxiety and are startled, the forms of behavior common to *latah* may be evoked. Hyperstartlers, he believes, are distributed in all societies. However, only in some societies is this behavioral form labeled, given meaning, socially stigmatized, and provoked in public situations. This explains why Indonesian *latah* sufferers are typically persons of marginal social status: only such persons are subject to public teasing or ridicule and made to personify the inversion of the normal valued symbolic order. Kenny (1978, 1983) has demonstrated how extensive the meanings of marginality associated with *latah* are in Malay culture, arguing even that interpretation of the phenomenon as a psychological disorder is inappropriate (see also Lee, 1981).

While these analyses make it clear that *latah* is not associated with an anxiety disorder, these recent studies suggest an important model for understanding culture-specific illness forms. A discrete neurophysiological and experiential abnormality that is distributed among individuals in all societies is in some societies left unmarked, though it may cause suffering for individuals (and even be treated as a member of some more general class of disorders). In other societies it acquires great symbolic significance, is responded to in a culturally specified manner, and is socially and culturally constructed into a major illness form. Does this model help us understand other fright disorders? Simons argues that it explains those other disorders that are essentially of the form of *latah*. However, many fright disorders seem to be of quite a different sort.

While working in Iran, Good and Good discovered that many persons suffered from illness they believed was caused by fright. There are quite specific popular beliefs about the symptoms, etiology, and pathophysiology associated with a fright illness, and a set of traditional religious rituals for its treatment (Good & Good, 1980, 1981, 1982). In addition, educated and upper-class Iranians, including Iranian immigrant patients we saw in an American psychiatric clinic, often describe their emotional illnesses as fright disorders. Are these disorders disease specific, we wondered? Are they constructed on some specific neurophysiological or psychopathological substrate—if not the startle reflex, then some other—in a manner suggested by the *latah* model? As we began to investigate cases, we discovered that quite a wide range of phenomena were explained as being caused by the individual having been startled or frightened. A child who developed conversion aphonia was believed to have a fright disorder, caused by a frightening dream of the death of her parents and a reaction to nearly being hit by a car, at a time when her parents were on the pilgrimage to Mecca. An Iranian university student in the United States who developed a psychotic manic episode following a kidney operation was believed by his family to have suffered a fright when told by a physician of the need for the operation. Others described their acute anxiety reactions or depressive episodes, as well as physical illnesses in adults or children, night terrors in children, or other acute disturbances, as being caused by fright. Clearly in Iranian popular culture fright is an "etiological" category, akin for example to "stress" in popular American culture, not a descriptive category as *latah* is in Malay culture (see Good & Good, 1982, for a full discussion). A network of important cultural meanings is associated with fright for Iranians. Individuals are more vulnerable to fright illness when they are constitutionally "sensitive" and are more likely to suffer illness from a fright when they are socially isolated, separated from their families and intimate social network. Diagnosis of the disorder focuses not on the emotional or behavioral characteristics of the illness, but on aspects of the social environment of the sufferer. And the attribution of fright as a cause of illness suggests the disorder should be acute and of relatively short duration, not ultimately impairing and stigmatizing. Persons whose mental illnesses are ascribed to fright are much less stigmatized than those believed to have a psychiatric illness, and the expectation is that they will quickly improve.

Fright illness in Iran contrasts not only with fright illness in Malay culture, but also with another popular illness category in Iran—"heart distress" *(narahatiye galb)* (Good, 1977; Good & Good, 1982). This category is descriptive; it labels individuals who experience particular sensations in their hearts, in particular palpitations, and places these in a rich framework of symbolic meanings. It is not yet clear what the relationship is between psychiatric diagnostic categories and this popular Iranian category. In our research, we saw cases of "heart distress" in which individuals suffered general anxiety disorders; others suffered minor depression; still others suffered symptoms much akin to what was once called "neurocirculatory asthenia" in the American medical literature (Wheeler, White, Reed, & Cohen, 1950). This suggests that rather than some aspect of the social environment being focused on in the popular labeling of an illness, as in the case of fright, for heart distress one particular symptom becomes the focus of the social and symbolic construction of an illness form. Because disturbing heart sensations may be symptoms associated with several diagnostic categories, particularly anxiety disorders and depression, Iranian culture appears to construct an illness form that cuts across several psychiatric diseases.

These studies provide us with the beginnings of a framework for a more complex analysis of the relationship between a psychiatric diagnostic category and a culture-specific form of illness. One final example of a fright disorder will illustrate the point further. *Susto* is a common popular illness form in Latin American, particularly Mexican, culture. It has at times been labeled an "anxiety state" (Kiev, 1972) or "fear reaction" (Yap, 1974). When one examines the recent anthropological reports carefully, it becomes clear that *susto* is an etiological category: When an individual falls ill, members of his or her family or a healer begin to search the sufferer's past for a frightening event that may have provoked the soul to flee the body (O'Nell, 1975; O'Nell & Rubel, 1976; Rubel, O'Nell, & Collada Ardon, 1984). Furthermore, research seems to indicate that the diagnosis is most commonly made for persons suffering certain forms of social dysfunction, rather than one particular category of psychiatric disorder, despite the typical descriptions of the symptoms associated with the disorder. Hence, what may appear to a psychiatrist or epidemiologist reading the literature as an anxiety disorder resulting from traumatic stress may actually be any one of a number of psychiatric disturbances, the reputed cause of which may be a "fright" imputed to the patient without clear evidence (to an outside observer) that the event was actually traumatic in the sufferer's experience.

This research indicates a complex relationship between culture-specific illness forms and psychiatric diagnostic entities. Three specific forms of relationship have been described. In the first, a particular neurophysiological propensity or a disease is symbolically labeled and exploited in the social construction of an illness. In the second, one particular symptom, present in several disorders, becomes the focus for elaboration of an illness. In the third, particular forms of social dysfunction are "diagnosed" and a particular etiological frame is used to construct an illness form that structures illness experience and dictates care-seeking processes. Research on the relation of anxiety disorders to culture-bound disorders thus must focus on the *interpretive processes* through which particular aspects of distress—whether based in disease, particular symptoms, or social dysfunction—are socially constituted as a culture-specific illness form (Good & Good, 1981, 1982).

The work on *shinkeishitsu* provides evidence for a fourth pattern, in which a particular psychiatric diagnostic group—anxiety disorders—are constructed in a culturally patterned fashion.

Shinkeishitsu ("Neurasthenia") and Taijin Kyofu ("Phobia of Interpersonal Relations") in Japan and Agoraphobia in the West: Culture Specific Forms of Anxiety Disorders?

In 1922 Shoma Morita published a treatise (in Japanese) entitled The Nature of *Shinkeishitsu* [Neurasthenia] and its Treatment. Morita was Professor of Psychiatry in Jikei University in Tokyo; he had trained under a student of Kraepelin. Morita developed his theory of the origin, nature, and treatment of neurosis in the Japanese personality in part in reaction to the neurologically oriented explanations of neurasthenia (as physiological nervous exhaustion) prevalent in that period, making a leap to "mentalistic" explanation parallel to that made by Freud

(Kondo, 1953; Reynolds, 1976). Morita focused his career on the analysis and treatment of persons suffering from a peculiarly Japanese anxiety disorder, producing in the process a following of Morita-oriented psychotherapists and clinics and a large professional and research literature. As a result, *shinkeishitsu* provides us with the most well-documented example of a culturally elaborated anxiety disorder.

Reynolds (1976, pp. 9-10) summarizes the clinical presentation of *shinkeishitsu*. From the perspective of the Morita therapist, the neurotic person has perfectionist tendencies and extreme self-consciousness. Some unpleasant event focuses the person's attention on a particular problem, such as blushing, headaches or constipation. The person increasingly worries about the problem and is "caught in a spiral of attention and sensitivity which produces a sort of obsessive self-consciousness" (p. 10). By the time the patient arrives for therapy, he is generally shy and sensitive, unable to function socially, and prefers to spend his life at home, withdrawn from the world outside. "He is immobilized by the storm of counterconflicts and pressures raging within his psyche" (p. 10).

Morita further classified *shinkeishitsu* neurosis into three clinical subcategories (Reynolds, 1976). Patients with "ordinary neurasthenic state" display strong hypochondriacal symptoms, poor concentration, and feelings of inferiority and shyness. Those with "obsessive-phobic state" have a strong fear of looking other people in the eye (Kasahara, 1976) and fear that some aspect of their personal presentation—blushing, unpleasant body odor, stuttering—will appear reprehensible to those with whom they come into contact. These are grouped together under the term *taijin kyofu-sho* or anthropophobia. A third group suffer from "anxiety state," a form usually beginning with "some sort of fit...such as palpitation attack, a dyspneic fit, or vomiting." The literature makes it unclear whether this "fit" might meet Western criteria for "panic attack."

A great deal has been written about how "Japanese culture shapes the basic neurotic character" (Reynolds, 1976), giving a special Japanese quality to the pattern of obsessive, phobic, and hypochondriacal symptoms. One cannot help but be struck by the similarities and differences between *shinkeishitsu* and the anxiety disorders described in the Western psychiatric literature. Although the subtypes of the disorder seem similar (though not identical), their distribution seems different. The obsessive/phobic form of *shinkeishitsu* appears to account for nearly 50% of the disorders, neurasthenic form 25%, and anxiety form 10% (adequate population studies are not available to determine whether this distribution is representative of the population or only of those who seek care). These percentages may be contrasted with the distribution of anxiety disorders in the United States, where generalized anxiety disorder (GAD) is most prevalent, followed by the phobias and then obsessive-compulsive disorder (OCD) (Weissman, this volume).

The disorders appear to be linked to first-order relatives for both Americans and the Japanese; Japanese studies have found that one or both parents of 15% to 30% of neurotic patients are also disturbed (Miura & Usa, 1970). Of particular interest is the similarity between agoraphobia or social phobia and the obsessive/phobic group of Japanese sufferers— both involving, as they do, fears associated with public places leading to great constriction of normal social activities. On the other hand, it is worth briefly outlining here some ways in which this subtype of *shinkeishitsu* contrasts with the Western pattern of agoraphobia and other anxiety disorders (Murphy, 1982; data for this comparison are drawn from Reynolds, 1976, and Kasahara, 1976). Agoraphobia is found predominantly in women; *shinkeishitsu* sufferers *who seek treatment* are predominantly men. (The ratio has shifted from 2:1 to 3:2 in the past two decades; it is unclear if this represents the population distribution of the disorder or is determined by the greater tendency in Japan for men to seek therapy.) Although the distribution by age category is clearly established for neither, there is some evidence that the Japanese disorder more often begins early (shortly after puberty, especially when adolescents are first leaving home) and is less likely to continue after age 40 (Murphy, 1982). The Japanese patients most often avoid contact with other persons (of these, they are least self-conscious among intimates or complete strangers, most among small groups of acquaintances). The Western patients are most commonly fearful of being alone in public. Of the phobic group in Japan, the great preponderance of symptoms are anthropophobic in character, in contrast with agoraphobic patients in the United States.

The Japanese material presents clear evidence of a culturally patterned set of anxiety disorders. The patterns of symptoms and their relationship to the neurotic character seem deeply cultural, related to differences in maternal-infant relationships (Caudill & Weinstein, 1969), norms of social interaction, and values embedded in Japanese symbolic life and ideals of personhood. The classification of anxiety disorders in Japanese psychiatry provides an important potential for further comparison with American diagnostic criteria and suggests the possibility of comparative epidemiological studies. In sum, the Japanese material does not answer the question of universality, but poses it more sharply. Are there constellations of anxiety symptoms peculiar to Japanese culture, represented by Japanese diagnostic criteria? Do American diagnostic criteria represent a reification and universalization of constellations of symptoms of anxiety peculiar to American or Western societies? These questions deserve further study.

Neurasthenia: The Chinese Example

Neurasthenia *(shenjing shuairuo*—literally "neurological weakness") is both a common popular illness form and a psychiatric diagnostic label in contemporary China and Taiwan (see Kleinman, 1980, 1982). A striking difference in the epidemiology of psychiatric disorders in China and the West is the very high prevalence of neurasthenia in the former and low prevalence in the latter. Although the term is relatively recent in Chinese culture, having been introduced from Western psychiatry, its popular conceptualization is grounded in an ancient tradition of Chinese medicine. As with *shinkeishitsu* in Japan, *shenjing shuairuo* is both a disease—a disorder diagnosed and clinically constructed by professional medicine—and an illness—a disorder popularly labeled and given meaning in lay experience and discourse. In the context of this review, *shenjing shuairuo* offers an important contrast to *shinkeishitsu* or neurasthenia in Japan and to American classification of depression, anxiety, and somatoform disorder. In addition, research on neurasthenia in China raises important methodological issues for the cross-cultural study of anxiety disorders.

Chinese neurasthenic patients present with a variety of complaints, predominantly somatic and somatopsychic in content: headaches, insomnia, dizziness, pain, memory problems, anxiety, weakness, loss of energy, feeling of swelling in head, neck or brain, irritability, disturbing dreams, palpitations, poor appetite, stomach complaints, tingling of head, poor concentration, and others. In addition, patients present with a number of culture-bound complaints: heaviness or pressure depressing into head or chest *(men)*, fear of excessive loss of semen with diminished vital energy, excess of hot inner energy, and fear of cold in the body. Virtually all neurasthenic patients in China are seen in primary care before being seen in a psychiatric setting.

Kleinman and his Chinese colleagues conducted a study of 100 consecutive patients diagnosed as neurasthenic in a psychiatric outpatient clinic at Hunan Medical College (see Kleinman, 1982, for a full report). All patients were interviewed concerning their explanatory model of their illness, their care-seeking patterns, and their associated psychosocial problems, and each was given a *DSM-III* diagnosis, based on administration of a Chinese translation of the Schedule of Affective Disorders and Schizophrenia (SADS). Of the 100 patients, 93 were diagnosed with depression (87 with major depressive disorder), 69 with anxiety states (35 with panic disorder, 13 with GAD, and 20 with phobic disorder), 25 with somatoform disorders, and 44 with chronic pain syndrome. A majority of the patients evidenced major depressive disorder along with anxiety disorder, chronic pain, and somatoform disorders.

Further interviews with patients revealed that neurasthenia provides individuals with a legitimated idiom through which to articulate and negotiate difficulties in the interpersonal and social arena. Of these patients, 75% were experiencing major work stress, 57% separation from family or home due to the location of work site, and others experienced financial, political, grief-related, school or family stresses. The somatic idiom associated with neurasthenia allows communication of personal distress and the opportunity to negotiate changes in interpersonal relations and work situations. Neurasthenia as illness is thus constituted in the social domain.

When those diagnosed with Major Depressive Disorder ($n = 71$) were treated with antidepressant drugs, 82% rated their symptoms as at least slightly improved, 65% as substantially improved. (Physician assessment of symptom outcome was considerably higher; 70% were rated as substantially improved [no significant current problems], and a total of 87% as at least somewhat improved.) By contrast, only 35% were less socially impaired, 34% showed no change, and 30% were more socially impaired on follow-up. Treatment of the primary associated disease problem (from a Western psychiatric perspective) did not produce resolution of the experience of illness for a majority of patients.

From the perspective of this review, several issues are important. First, neurasthenic patients display symptoms of both depressive disorder and anxiety states in a manner that often precludes clear differentiation. Given the similarity of the phenomenology of the disorder to classic descriptions in Western psychiatry, and given the distribution of similar "nerve" disorders across cultures (see, for example, Low, 1981; Ludwig, 1982), comparative studies of such disorders may well provide significant data for an area of confusion in Western psychiatric nosology. Second, neurasthenia focuses attention of those who would investigate anxiety disorders clearly on a problem common to Chinese, American, and other societies: chronic somatization, i.e, the presentation of bodily complaints in the absence of organic pathology or as an amplification of low level pathology owing to psychosocial problems (Katon, Kleinman, & Rosen, 1982; Kleinman & Kleinman, in press). The Chinese example demonstrates how a culturally salient form of chronic somatization, conceptualized as illness experience, can act as a final common behavioral pathway for several distinctive types of pathology, more than one of which may be suffered at the same time. Third, this study indicates that while comparison of diagnostic entities is an important task, failure to address illness as a social and cultural reality can only lead to misunderstanding. Neurasthenia has its prime locus in the social sphere, and investigations of its social meanings are critical for understanding its onset, its course, and its response to treatment. Neurasthenia continues to be an important diagnosis in the non-Western world because it maps a "real" phenomenon and is more culturally appropriate in those settings (even for psychiatrists) than the term "depression" or "anxiety."

Somatization is a style of illness behavior. While personality and situational variables as well as disease type all contribute to the style of somatization, and to its incidence, there is abundant evidence that culture is also a key contributor. Based on his field research with Chinese and on his reading of the cross-cultural literature, Kleinman (in press) has outlined a typology of somatization styles: (1) weakness-exhaustion style (e.g., neurasthenia); (2) pain preoccupation style (e.g., chronic pain syndrome); (3) illness preoccupation style (e.g., classical hypochondriasis, somatic delusions, or group preoccupation with symptoms allegedly caused by environmental toxins); (4) neurological loss or activation style (e.g., conversion symptoms of hysterical paralysis, blindness, or seizures);

(5) bowel preoccupation style (e.g., functional bowel disease, neurotic constipation, etc.); (6) semen loss (e.g., *shen kuei* syndrome in China, *dhat* syndrome in South Asia); (7) cosmetic preoccupation style (e.g., excessive concern with physical changes of aging, or with body weight, skin blemishes, sexual potency).

As we have already indicated, certain of these styles are more salient in some societies or among some subgroups in the same society than others, and they may also differ in frequency and distribution. Culture always particularizes; somatization styles are always integrated into particular local systems of meaning and social relationships, and thereby are shaped along culturally particular lines. At the same time, our reading of the literature indicates that somatization styles vary by culture areas. For example, East Asian societies share many of the same great traditions, including classical Chinese medicine, Confucianism and Buddhism, and these produce important similarities in somatic idioms in Chinese, Japanese, and Korean cultures. The same is true in Middle Eastern societies, sharing both the Galenic medical tradition, local traditions of popular Islam, and shared norms of family honor. South Asian and African culture areas may also have some distinctive characteristics of somatization style, though in these societies the interaction among various high traditions and elaborate, local indigenous traditions lead to great complexity. Cross-cultural research into these phenomena may significantly advance our understanding of somatization and its relationship to psychiatric disorders.

We also suggest that psychiatric disorders, which are among the well-known causes of somatization, vary in frequency and distribution across the different styles of somatization. For example, depression and anxiety disorders have been shown to have high frequency in the weakness-exhaustion style of somatization. It is our impression that careful clinical epidemiology of these illness behaviors will demonstrate that these two disorders also differ significantly in prevalence across other somatization styles. This is an important reason for epidemiology to focus on illness experience as well as disease entity. Hence a major issue for research is the investigation of interrelationships among type of anxiety disorder, type of culture, and type of somatization.

CONCLUSION

The contribution of anthropology to psychiatry is to raise fundamental questions and propose models for research that transcend parochial assumptions and observations. Suppose we were South Asian psychiatrists, deeply convinced that "semen loss" was a psychiatric disorder, who set out to conduct a scientific study of its prevalence world wide (Obeyesekere, in press, poses this example in a criticism of Western epidemiological studies of depression). Doubtless we would find cases with semen loss symptoms (e.g., drastic weight loss, weakness, sexual fantasies, hypochondriasis, night emission, urine discoloration) in virtually all societies. We could develop refined diagnostic criteria with inclusion and exclusion operationalized, draw up a relevant instrument translated into all the world's languages, back-translate it for semantic equivalence, validate it for differential distribution among normal and psychiatric patient populations, and derive prevalence rates for various societies. What would we have accomplished? If we claim this to be a universal psychiatric disorder, then this would be a stark illustration of the category fallacy. But would these methods differ from those employed by studies we have reviewed? A large number of them, regrettably, are of this type. Those that are not have attempted in various ways to negotiate between "local meanings" (Geertz, 1983) and scientific categories.

As we said at the beginning of this chapter, it is tempting to assume the existence of a universal set of discrete anxiety disorders, which are directly reflected in a discrete set of symptoms. Cross-cultural research would then be directed at studies of how culture influences the communication of symptoms and social responses to these disorders. Such studies would be analogous to anthropological studies of diseases such as measles. One may study how members of a society utilize cultural categories and explanatory forms to interpret the disease, but the interpretations are epiphenomenal, that is, they have no direct influence on the underlying disease entity. Although it may turn out that such a model will account for some important aspects of panic disorder, it is clearly a limited model to guide cross-cultural studies of most anxiety disorders. This is because *anxiety disorders are not merely the result of culturally influenced interpretations of an underlying disease; anxiety disorders are also disorders of the interpretive process.* It is precisely the dynamic interaction between the interpretation of particular experiences of distress and specific forms of psychophysiological disturbances of cognitive and interpretive processes that constitutes anxiety disorders. Psychophysiological processes not only produce disturbances calling forth responses; they also clearly influence the alterations in perception and cognition common to such disorders as phobias and generalized anxiety. At the same time, culture not only provides the categories, explanatory frames, and idioms for responding to physiological symptoms; it may also play a significant role in structuring pathologies of cognition and interpretation.

Figure 1 summarizes a model based on this perspective. In the limiting case, discrete psychophysiological disruptions may be reflected directly in illness forms, which are then responded to by medical professionals and popular care providers.

Most anxiety disorders, however, involve disorders of perception, cognition, and interpretation: Stressors in the social environment are perceived as threatening, eliciting peculiar social, psychological, and psychophysiological responses. Both popular illness meanings and professional diagnostic and therapeutic models feed into the individual's interpretations of the experience. Distress is articulated through culturally available idioms, producing expressions of illness responded to by professional and popular care-givers.

A model such as this focuses attention on the dynamic interrelations among cognitive and interpretive processes, psychophysiology, and systems of cultural

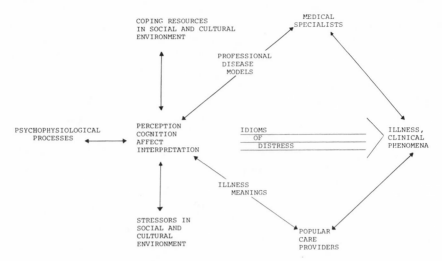

FIG. 1   A model for the cross-cultural study of anxiety disorder.

meanings, both scientific and popular, in the production of clinical phenomena. It implies that analyses of such phenomena as *shinkeishitsu*, Yoruba anxieties focusing on witchcraft, or agoraphobia in the United States require attention to such relationships. What are the cognitive forms specific to each? To what extent are they physiologically or psychologically constrained, to what extent are they influenced by culture-specific logics? How does each influence the perception of the social environment, and what are the typical coping responses? What are the idioms available for the articulation of distress, and what are the similarities and differences in the resulting clinical phenomena? How are we to translate between forms of distress expressed in religious or moral idioms and psychiatric categories? Given the diversity of the experience and articulation of anxiety worldwide, we believe such questions are central to the discipline. It is our contention that cross-cultural studies can contribute to the field not merely by indicating differences in prevalence or phenomenology of anxiety disorders, but by providing a much richer set of variations among variables usually assumed to be constants in research in the United States and Europe. Cross-cultural studies can contribute to more than epidemiological research, encouraging us to systematically and rigorously assess cultural bias implicit in our disease categories as well as in our social and psychological theories. A more discriminating cross-cultural understanding of anxiety disorders will emerge only from such an approach, one in which the very language and concepts we use are thoroughly biocultural, not reductionist or acultural.

We conclude by outlining a few of the salient questions that we see as basic issues for future research.

1. The epidemiological question: What is the frequency and distribution of anxiety disorders worldwide?

2. The biological question: Counter to the simplistic assumption that biological contributions to mental illness are manifested solely in universals, what are the cross-cultural differences (as well as universals) that biological and genetic processes contribute to differences in the anxiety phenomena (see Ernst Mayr, 1976, on biological diversity and geographic distribution in animals)?

3. The clinical descriptive question: What is the relationship of different anxiety disorders to different styles of illness behavior and idioms of distress among distinctive cultures, ethnic groups, and social classes?

4. The psychological question: Are there cross-cultural differences in the cognitive, affective and communicative processes that contribute to the development and expression of anxiety disorders? This question obviously includes a large number of subquestions regarding cross-cultural differences in the relevant processes of attention, perception, affective socialization, and the like.

5. The social question: Brown and Harris (1978) and Weissman and Paykel (1974) have disclosed particular constellations of social variables that place individuals at higher risk for depression. What are the social factors that increase risk for anxiety? Are they specific for anxiety or do they hold for all mental illness? How do they differ in societies that are very diverse?

6. The cultural questions: Can we assure ourselves that our contemporary cross-cultural understanding of anxiety disorders is not based on a category fallacy? Assuming that we can or with the appropriate research will be able to do so in the future, then how does culture contribute to disorders of anxiety and to the construction of its "illness behavior"? What are the interpretive processes through which illness forms specific to a society are generated, and how do they differ across societies? How do cultural meanings and social relationships interact with psychobiological processes to shape distinctive cultural forms of anxiety disorders? This final question emphasizes our view that future studies in this area require a problem framework integrating biology and culture.

ACKNOWLEDGMENTS

This paper was prepared with support from a grant from the Rockefeller Foundation. Special thanks to Anne Becker for assistance in searching the literature.

15 Epidemiology and Cross-Cultural Aspects of Anxiety Disorders: A Commentary.

Gregory Carey
Washington University
School of Medicine

The resurgent interest in anxiety disorders has been paralleled by a renewed effort to understand the distribution of these disorders in populations (epidemiology) and their transmission pattern in families (genetic epidemiology[1]). From Slater and Shields (1969) until Noyes, Clancy, Crowe, Hoenk, & Slymen (1978) and Carey (1978) there has been almost a 10-year lacuna for good empirical data on familial aspects of anxiety disorders. The situation has improved since 1978 with family studies at the University of Iowa and twin studies in Norway. The two chapters in this section point to the future directions in this field.

Good and Kleinman discuss differences among cultures in the distribution on anxiety, a formidable task given the variation in terminology and nosology in our own Western view of anxiety (see Jablonski, this volume). They focus on a search for what is universal, or common to different cultures, and what is culture-specific, noting that "biology as well as culture can account for cross-cultural differences." Their solution is to distinguish "disease" or psychophysiological lesion from "illness," the experience and communication of symptoms of a "disease."

---

[1]Some may regard the term "genetic epidemiology" with suspicion, implying as it does a focus on heredity. The term is actually something of a misnomer, but is used here in historical context to reflect a field of study that already has two textbooks *(Outline of Genetic Epidemiology* by Newton E. Morton, 1982 and *Methods in Genetic Epidemiology* by Morton, Rao, and Lalouel, 1983) and a journal *(The Journal of Genetic Epidemiology).* The aim of this field is to elucidate the distribution and transmission patterns of familial disorders and the risk factors associated with these disorders. Because familial transmission patterns include both genetic and cultural components, the field could also be termed "familial epidemiology." The success of genetic epidemiology in coronary heart disease (see Rao et al., 1983) is an excellent model for research on uncovering risk factors for anxiety disorders.

One may quibble with this terminology, but the conceptual differentiation between pathogenesis and the manner in which subsequent disturbance is experienced and communicated remains an important issue, not only for cross-cultural research but also for research within a culture. The implication is that two different populations may have a single etiological agent responsible for anxiety disorder, yet culture can modify the expression of this disorder. Hence, in one setting the panic attack may be expressed in psychological terms ("I get these attacks of nervousness and dread for no reason at all"), whereas in another, somatic manifestation may be accentuated ("I get these attacks where I can't catch my breath"). The two settings may be New York City and Nigeria or may reflect different socioeconomic strata within a single culture.

The difficulty with this approach is the lack of explicit criteria to distinguish "disease" from "illness" for anxiety disorders. To overgeneralize, most epidemiological and cross-cultural studies involve "dry laboratory" variables such as descriptive signs and symptoms, sex ratios, and prevalence as opposed to "wet lab" techniques involving, for example, benzodiazepine receptors or lactate infusions. The dangers of nosologizing from some "dry lab" variables are apparent to Good and Kleinman. Their example of the South Asian psychiatrist who could uncover "semen loss disorder" in Western cultures is a stark reminder. Their solution—"future studies in this area require a problem framework *integrating* biology and culture"—must be highlighted as a general principle, but I would like to make more specific recommendations.

One proposed criterion would be genetic and familial segregation. Huntington's disease illustrates this principle. This disorder is due to a single etiological agent (an autosomal dominant allele) and could be considered a single "disease" in Good and Kleinman's terminology. Yet there are two different forms for Huntington's which could loosely qualify as two "illnesses."

Table 1 summarizes the differences between these forms, although one must realize there is overlap. The more common form presents with arrhythmic semipurposive movements and with a variable age of onset, averaging somewhere between 35 and 40. There is an equal sex ratio for the adult onset form. A

TABLE 1

	Syndrome 1	Syndrome 2
Symptoms:	motor rigidity; hypokinesis, posturing	arrhythmic, semi-purposive movements
Prevalence:	3×10^{-6}	4×10^{-5} (USA) 3×10^{-6} (Japan)
Age Onset:	< 20	mean $= 35-40$
Sex ratio:	F:M $= 2:1$	F:M $= 1:1$
Transmission:	familial, paternal effect	familial, no paternal effect

second form of this illness, the Westphal variant, involves motor rigidity, hypo-kinesis, and posturing. It is associated with age of onset, seldom occurring in individuals over age 20, and the sex distribution approaches a 2:1 female to male ratio. There is familial aggregation of these cases. Given that an affected relative has had a Westphal form, the probability that a second relative in the pedigree will have that form is increased. Moreover, there may be a paternal effect; Bird, Caro, and Pilling (1974) report that the affected parent is more often the father than the mother. Although it may be tempting to note the differences in symptoms, prevalence, age of onset, sex ratio, and familial trans-mission as evidence for two separate syndromes, they fail to segregate inde-pendently among families. What may be occurring in Huntington's disease is that the single etiological agent can produce slightly different forms depending on the genetic background of the individual.

Given the abundant evidence for familial aggregation of anxiety disorders (Carey, 1982; Carey & Gottesman, 1981; see also Weissman, this volume), cross-cultural approaches could focus on pedigrees involving marriage between members of different cultures. For example, studies of the offspring of Cauca-sians with an anxiety disorder married to Japanese, and of Japanese with *shin-keishitsu* (see Good and Kleinman, this volume, for a definition) married to Caucasians, could help determine whether the two are culturally modified forms of a single pathogenic process. Such a design is feasible in, say, Hawaii, and it has proved useful in elucidating cultural differences in risk factors for coronary heart disease (Rao, et al., 1983). Of course, using intact nuclear families con-founds genetic with environmental transmission, but the techniques of genetic epidemiology (Morton, 1982) can be applied easily to nuclear family data.

Other criteria are equally apt. Would lactate infusion produce intense *shin-keishitsu*-like behavior or perhaps panic among Japanese suffering from this syndrome were one to hypothesize that this is merely a cultural manifestation of what would be termed a panic disorder in the United States? Or again, does the psychophysiological patterning of Galvanic Skin Response (GSR), alpha blockage, and so on, appear similar between individuals having these two dis-orders? Until such studies are done it will be difficult to determine whether *shinkeishitsu* and panic disorders represent two different etiologies and patho-physiological processes or a single "disease" with different cultural modifiers.

Weissman (this volume) and her colleagues present a thorough review of the literature on epidemiology and familial recurrence risks for anxiety disorder. They add a family study of their own, paying particular attention to the inter-relationship between anxiety disorders and depression and to the young children of anxiety-disordered probands. The chapter highlights future directions for genetic and family epidemiology of anxiety. In the past most research focused on a single disorder, reporting prevalence and familial aggregation. With the present review we move into the area of examining the familial interrelationship among psychiatric disorders, a topic that Gottesman and I suggested to be one of the most important for the anxiety disorders (Carey & Gottesman, 1981, p. 132). Here I would like to expand some of these thoughts, using the relationship between anxiety disorder and depression as presented by Weissman as a model.

It has long been known that the two disorders can be phenomenologically distinguished and have different correlates. The work of Martin Roth and his group at Newcastle (e.g., Roth, Gurney, Garside, & Kerr, 1972) pointed the way in this area. What Weissman's group at Yale has done is to focus this topic under a familial and epidemiological lens.

The Yale group should be congratulated for the nonhierarchical approach to this problem. Diagnostic hierarchies, while sometimes necessary, can involve a loss of information for research purposes. For example, the current rules in the *Diagnostic and Statistical Manual,* Third Revision (American Psychiatric Association, 1980) *(DSM-III)* imply a hierarchical association between major depression and the anxiety disorders, with the former precluding the latter. This type of rule would classify a patient with major depression and an associated panic disorder the same as a person with only major depression. A nonhierarchical approach is equivalent to the traditional multivariate analysis used for quantitative traits: Each diagnosis for which a person meets criteria is independently rated as present. One then lets the empirical data suggest what the hierarchy should be. (See Spitzer, this volume, on the proposed revisions in *DSM-III)* regarding diagnostic hierarchies in the anxiety disorders.)

Depression and anxiety disorders may be interrelated in a number of ways. They may share some common pathogenetic process, a view that cannot be lightly dismissed in face of the efficacy of tricyclic antidepressants and MAO inhibitors on panic disorders (see Klein, this volume). It is also possible that one may cause the other; specifically, individuals with severe panic disorder or agoraphobia may develop subsequent depressive episodes in face of the severe personal distress and social limitations caused by their disorders. Of course, there may be noticeable heterogeneity within both anxiety and depressive disorders.

At the same time, it is important for the researcher using this nonhierarchical approach to suggest mechanisms and/or hypotheses about the association among anxiety disorders and depression. To illustrate this, consider the data of Crowe, Noyes, Pauls and Slymen (1983) gathered at the University of Iowa.

Table 2 shows the hierarchical association between anxiety and depression when depression is divided according to the primary and secondary distinction originally espoused by Robins and Guze (1972). The top part of the table shows what happens when the diagnosis is used in a nonhierarchical fashion: there is an excess of depression among the first-degree relatives of anxiety disorder probands, 10.1% compared to 6.5% among the relatives of normal controls. The bottom half shows rates among these same relatives when depression is conditioned on anxiety. (That is, what is the rate of depression given that the relative has a diagnosis of panic disorder, and what is the rate of depression among relatives who have no other psychiatric disorder?) Notice now how similar the

TABLE 2
Effects of Hierarchical Classification on the Rates of Illness in First
Degree Relatives of Panic Disorder Probands and Controls.[a]

| | Percentage Affected in Relatives of: | |
Relatives Diagnosis	Probands	Controls
Non-Hierarchical:		
Any anxiety	24.5	5.0
Any depression	10.1	6.5
Hierarchical:		
Depression/Anxiety	19.1	23.1
Depression/no other diagnosis	4.0	4.6

[a]Data of Crowe et al. (1983)

rates of depression in the relatives of probands are to those of controls. Yet there is a large difference in rates of depression between those relatives who have panic disorder and those who do not.

To put this in different terms, relatives of panic disorder patients have a high rate of depression, but this is probably because they also have a high rate of panic disorder, and panic disorder itself is associated with depression. Once one controls for panic disorder among these relatives, their rates of depression become no different from those of control relatives. The Iowa data suggest that (1) there may be a hierarchical relationship between anxiety disorder and depression with panic disorder precluding a diagnosis of major depression, and/or (2) there is validity in the distinction between primary and secondary depression as applied to panic disorder, since Crowe used this distinction in making diagnoses.

The Yale data show a stronger association between major depression and anxiety disorders than do the Iowa data, but one could not make a strong argument that the two studies fundamentally disagree. The Iowa study started with probands with panic disorder, probably severe and clear-cut cases (see Carey, 1982, on this point). One might suspect that the Iowa group would have hesitated to include a potential proband where the diagnosis was unclear between panic disorder and depression. At New Haven, on the other hand, proband selection began with patients having major depression, irrespective of secondary or subsidiary diagnoses of anxiety disorders. Hence, the two proband groups are not comparable and recurrence risks in their respective groups of relatives will reflect these differences in selection criteria.

What is important for the future is the exploration of familial association *within* the anxiety disorders, including obsessive disorder. In this sense, we may have to take the multivariate and nonhierarchical approach so often used to test familial and genetic associations among quantitative traits like height and weight. The work of Harris, Noyes, Crowe, and Chaudhry (1983) on the families of agoraphobics and panic disorder probands and of Torgersen (1983) on twins with anxiety disorder point in the right direction. Both of these studies sample more than one group of probands with an anxiety disorder. Thus, the research is designed to report the prevalence of disorder X in the relatives of probands with disorder Y.

A particular problem is examining the relationship between anxiety disorders and depression is the issue of what I shall call confusability in diagnosis. Ordinarily we index diagnostic disagreements in terms of reliability, false positives, false negatives, or the analagous epidemiological concepts of sensitivity and specificity. All of these indices have in common—the assumption that the probability of diagnostic error is the same for all patients. Although this assumption makes interpretation of our statistical measures possible, it violates ordinary day-to-day clinical observation. It seems clear that some patients are easier to diagnose than others. To put it another way, it is easier to make diagnostic mistakes with some patients than with others.

What I have termed confusability is one aspect of these individual differences in "diagnostability." Roughly, confusability means that it is easy (or hard) to confuse diagnosis X with diagnosis Y. In more precise terms, it means that the probability of rater A independently diagnosing condition X given that rater B has independently diagnosed condition Y will be higher when condition X and Y are confusable. One might illustrate this by a hypothetical patient whose main symptoms are feeling worried all the time, restlessness, difficulty in concentration, insomnia, and periodic feelings of fatigue and lethargy. These symptoms were deliberately chosen to illustrate the overlap between a generalized anxiety disorder and major depressive disorder according to *DSM-III*. Given a large number of diagnosticians each independently diagnosing our hypothetical patient on the basis of the above information, one could probably see how confusion between Generalized Anxiety Disorder (GAD) and Depression might arise.

I have taken time to discuss this issue because the implications for the research of the Yale group are important. When the anxiety disorders become "confusable" with the depressive disorders, then there will be a forced positive correlation between the two disorders. Furthermore there will also be a familial association between anxiety and depression: Some probands who in fact suffer from anxiety disorders may be misclassified as depressives. Their relatives could also have depressive disorders correctly diagnosed, but they would all count as depressed relatives of anxiety probands.

Some precise mathematical treatment of confusability is definitely an important point for future research, as is a large data base to ascertain how much of a problem this may be for research. At present, we must simply be aware that it is an area of potential difficulty when looking for associations between anxiety disorders and depression.

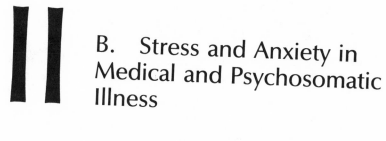

B. Stress and Anxiety in Medical and Psychosomatic Illness

16

The Psychobiology and Pathophysiology of Anxiety and Fear

Herbert Weiner, M.D.
School of Medicine
University of California

INTRODUCTION

Fear and anxiety play important roles in the everyday lives and in the survival of animals and humans. Despite their biological significance in human behavior, and in medicine, our knowledge of their physiology and pathophysiology remains limited. Why should that be so? The answer is that persistent problems in the precise identification of fear and anxiety remain with us and that the experimental study of anxiety, in particular, eludes us: Anxiety is a phenomenon that is difficult to induce, control, and measure experimentally. For that reason alone, the major emphasis in this essay is on objectively dangerous situations and the fear that they engender.

DEFINITION OF FEAR AND ANXIETY

Fear

All sentient creatures are alerted and respond in an integrated psychobiological manner to threats to their survival—to danger. Animals may also signal the presence of potential or actual danger to members of their own species—in particular their relatives. Behavioral measures are then taken to eliminate, avoid, or defend against the source of danger—to fight or to flee. Fear is a signal alerting the organism to external dangers.

We owe this statement to Darwin (1872) and to Cannon (1939). But they were only in part correct: The relationships of danger, fear, and avoidance behavior are more complex than they had envisioned. Avoidance behavior can accompany fear, or vary independently or inversely with it (Lang, 1967). Avoidance behavior may reduce fear, yet it may persist long after fear is no longer felt (Rachman & Hodgson, 1974). The persistence of defensive behavior may also outlast the original fear.

The relative independence of fear and avoidance behavior is confirmed by observations made on phobic or obsessional patients who were being treated by means of behavior therapy; very often a two-step process in the reduction of fear and avoidance behavior is seen. However, Gray (1971) believes that avoidance behavior is accompanied by safety signals, which are by themselves secondarily rewarding, and account for the persistence of avoidance maneuvers after fear has diminished. One would predict that blocking avoidance behavior would produce an upsurge of fear—a phenomenon that is observable only in some patients.

Abundant evidence exists that there is no close parallelism between measurable fear (or anxiety) and its autonomic or behavioral correlates (Lang, 1971; Leitenberg, Agras, Butz, & Wincze, 1971)—a fact that has confounded psychophysiology. Except under the most intense emotional arousal, the concordance between physiological measures is usually low (Hodgson & Rachman, 1974). Studies of this kind have suggested that fear is multidimensional: verbal-cognitive, behavioral, and physiological response systems are involved in fear; they may be coordinated under certain conditions but may be discordant under others—as the ensuing account tells.

Anxiety

We owe to Freud (1936) the insight that the source of the threat or the danger may be imaginary or unrecognized. Anxiety, in his view, is an internal signal anticipating such danger: It is experienced as an unpleasant sense of foreboding, alerting the person to defend against or avoid it.

The matter is not as simple as stated so far. Fear is not only generated by danger, it is also occasioned by ambiguous situations—a contingency that also applies to anxiety. Additionally, novel situations may be potent inducers of both (Lader, 1982; Mason, 1975).

Fear, Arousal, and Stress

Fear and anxiety alert and arouse the organism; they prepare it physiologically and stimulate it to act. But not all arousing stimuli and emotions are frightening or anxiety provoking—for example, a loud noise may startle, producing an orienting response; emotions such as joy, rage, sexual passion, and physical activity are also arousing. The claim that all emotional reactions should be conceived of in terms of a unidimensional concept of physiological arousal or activation is incorrect (Ursin, Baade, & Levine, 1978).

Duffy's (1962) original conceptualization of arousal was first brought into question by Lacey and Lacey (1974) who found that an experimental task such as mental arithmetic produced a heart rate increase and a fall in skin resistance. By contrast, the attentive observation of sensory input, which did not require any further processing, was accompanied by a decrease of heart rate and skin resistance. Heart rate, to use their term, was "directionally fractionated" (Lacey, 1967)—a result not predicted by arousal theory. The Laceys proposed instead that different patterns of physiological change occur in response to different environmental demands. Since that time the matter has become even more complex.

Other investigators subsume danger under the rubric of "stress"; yet immense and persistent difficulties remain with this concept. "Stress" is too general a category; furthermore, it is unclear whether danger, anxiety, or fear are necessarily stressful. Many situations are recognized as being stressful but are by no means dangerous. For heuristic, experimental, and clinical reasons the word "stress" should be eschewed when speaking of danger, fear, and anxiety.

PSYCHOBIOLOGICAL CORRELATES OF FEAR AND ANXIETY

Physical activity and emotional arousal are associated with a variety of integrated patterns of physiological change. Even the anticipation of, or the preparation for exercise, or the act of talking are accompanied by vasodilation, increased muscle blood flow, and by increases in heart rate and blood pressure (Rushmer, 1970; Weiner, Singer, & Reiser, 1962), and catecholamine secretion. However, attempts to define anxiety, fear, rage, and other emotions in terms of their associated or specific physiological responses have proved largely unsuccessful. Admittedly, increases in catecholamine excretion and turnover rates occur when subjects are frightened, but they are also seen when they are understimulated by the environment (Frankenhaeuser, Nordeheden, Myrsten, & Lundberg, 1971; Morrow & Labrum, 1978); they appear to be mobilized by any change in the level of stimulation.

The biological function of fear and anxiety is adaptive—to alert the organism to a threat to its survival, and make it take appropriate action. At peak levels these signals may be pathological—they may paralyze or disrupt behavior and prevent appropriate action. But at moderate or modest levels they may promote learning by acting as motives of behavior. Some human beings even court danger or find it exciting and have minimal physiological responses to it (Ursin, et al., 1978).

INDIVIDUAL DIFFERENCE IN INTEGRATED PSYCHOBIOLOGICAL RESPONSES TO DANGER

Clinical experience alone informs us that anxious patients differ in their bodily symptoms and signs: At least four groups are recognizable. Some patients experience marked increases in muscle tension in various regions of their bodies. A second group have mainly cardiorespiratory symptoms—changes in the rate and frequency of respiration, and/or the rate and force of the heart beat. They may become aware of their hearts pounding and beating more rapidly, or of an irregular heart beat. Another group of anxious persons tremble, ring their hands, have dry mouths, upper abdominal sensations ("butterflies"), or they vomit, have diarrhea, or an increased frequency of urination. A delay in the onset of sleep is observed in many anxious patients.

Combinations of any or all of these symptoms may occur. These "response stereotypes" are also seen in the laboratory. Lacey (1967) has pointed out that different stimuli and contingencies produce similar responses in the same—but not in another—person. Hence, one source of differences between persons is the relatively characteristic pattern of physiological responses of individuals, without regard to the manner in which they are incited.

Conversely, the same frightening context may produce highly individual behavioral and physiological responses across groups of subjects. Individual differences of this kind characterize the responses of groups of animals to danger; species differences are seen.

These generalizations do not exhaust the reasons for individual or group differences in the psychobiological responses to danger. They vary according to:

1. The novelty or the unpredictability of the situation.

2. The previous experiences the individual had with the danger.

3. The role assigned to and carried out by the person in the situation of danger; whether, for instance, he is the leader or the follower.

4. The demand characteristics of the situation. Miller and Bernstein (1972) showed that under situations of low demand, the intercorrelations between the length of time claustrophobic patients remained in a small chamber and subjective anxiety, heart and respiratory rate were -.42, -.56 and -.51, respectively; whereas under conditions of high demand there were no intercorrelations. Yet in other situations, high-demand characteristics produce positive correlations with hormonal measures and low-demand ones produce negative correlations with the same measures.

5. The quality of the performance: Does the person succeed or fail at it?

6. The manner in which the person copes with fear or defends himself against anxiety.

METHODOLOGICAL PROBLEMS IN STUDYING ANXIETY AND FEAR

The experimental study of anxiety has been fraught with a variety of serious problems. Problems of the induction, control, and measurement of anxiety in the laboratory largely remain unsolved with the result that we know little about the physiology of this emotion. In fact, most of the work to be reported here results from work on fear induced in naturalistic settings—a manner of gathering data that sets limits on physiologic measurement and control over variables.

Attempts to induce fear and anxiety in laboratory subjects have been made by the use of electrical shock or sparks of light, or contrived situations have been designed to make subjects fearful. These experiments have usually been unsuccessful because many subjects were not fooled by such feigned emergencies. Other experiments have attempted to simulate anxiety by injecting subjects with sympathomimetic drugs or lactic acid. Phobic subjects have been exposed to the feared object.

When the occurrence and degree of anxiety are assessed in subjects by psychological tests and physiologically by recording such measures as pupillary size, cerebral blood flow or metabolism, salivary flow, heart and respiratory rates, cardiac output, blood pressure, blood flow through muscle and skin, sweating, gastric motility, or various blood levels of catecholamines, hormones and free fatty acids, low correlations are obtained between the two sets of measures (Morrow & Labrum, 1978), and marked individual differences are obtained when subjects are compared with each other.

This conclusion is exemplified by studies on the central nervous system (CNS) correlates of fear and anxiety, some of which are contradictory. There is general agreement that the electroencephalogram (EEG) is desynchronized in anxious patients: An increase in low voltage fast activity (in the beta range) occurs and some theta waves (8–13 Hz) appear. The slow direct current potential, called contingent negative variation, which can be recorded over the frontal regions of the skull, is a measure of the subjects' expectancy or anticipation of a signal. In anxious patients its amplitude was diminished; the subject's expectancy of the occurrence of a signal was not maintained; that is, the subject was distracted from it (Lader, 1982), presumably by being anxious.

Various techniques for measuring cerebral circulation—blood flow and oxygen consumption—have been developed. Kety (1950) used the nitrous oxide technique and showed by its use that anxious subjects had a cerebral blood flow 21%, and a cerebral oxygen consumption 22% above calm subjects. The Xenon-inhalation technique is newer and is capable of measuring regional (mainly cortical) blood flow. Anxious subjects showed some reduction of cortical blood flow, particularly in the right prefrontal, left precentral, both parietal, and right posterior temporal areas (Mathew, Weinman, & Claghorn, 1982). Therefore, these two techniques (nitrous oxide and Xenon-inhalation) produce different results that are not easily reconciled.

Although the correlations between measures of anxiety and many physiological variables are low, and contradictory results have been reported in the literature, certain generalizations are possible: anxious subjects at rest tend to show:

1. Increased respiratory and heart rates, enhanced palmar sweating and forearm blood flow, and raised systolic blood pressure and pulse pressure.

2. Decreased ability to adapt and habituate: i.e., physiological activity—forearm blood flow, blood pressure (BP), skin conductance, muscle tension, and

pupil size—continues after stimulation has ceased. On subsequent stimulation these physiological responses do not extinguish (Lader, 1970).

More consistent data have been obtained by studying subjects in the field— in dangerous situations such as combat training or actual combat, examinations or frightening medical procedures. The drawbacks of this approach are that the situational and subject variables are difficult to isolate and control, and the data are of a correlative, not of an analytic, nature.

EXPERIMENTAL STUDIES IN CONTROLLED SETTINGS

The first question to be answered is, Are fear or anxiety, studied in the laboratory, associated with different patterns of physiological change than sadness, happiness or anger are? The answer to this question has only been obtained recently.

Schwartz and his co-workers (1981) used the technique of guided imagery to induce reminiscences and mental images associated with these four feelings in 32 subjects. These images were recreated during a second period when the subjects were also asked to imagine themselves walking up and down a step, followed by a control period. A third period ensued when they actually performed a step-test while again imagining the previous scenes and their associated feelings, followed by a neutral control condition when they just exercised.

The mean and diastolic BP increments were significantly greater with anger than with fear, but increases in systolic BP were the same for all four emotions. Heart rate rose in equal amounts with anger and fear, and was much greater than with images associated with feelings of happiness and sadness.

When anger was combined with exercise, the greatest increases in heart rate and systolic BP were achieved; these cardiovascular changes returned to baseline levels slower than with any other emotion.

In these experiments only anger was accompanied by distinctive cardiovascular changes. Fear produced no unique cardiovascular effects when compared with sadness and happiness.

Electromyography can be used to discriminate anger and fear. The former produces tonic, regular potential discharges and the latter phasic ones (Ax, 1953). These findings suggest that the potential changes in muscle prepare angry subjects for a single sustained movement (a blow), but that in fear, the muscle is ready for intermittent movements (running).

FEAR AND OTHER EMOTIONS AROUSED
BY VIEWING FILMS

Another experimental technique in a relatively controlled setting is to show subjects films of various emotional content (including a neutral one) in order to provoke fear with suspense films, boredom and fatigue with the control films, and erotic arousal with pornographic films. After the showing of each film the subject was asked to fill out a checklist designed to elicit his emotional responses to the film, and blood samples for hormonal measures were taken. In Brown and Heninger's study (1975) free fatty acid (FFAs) levels rose 250% in all eight male subjects 30 minutes after the fear accompanying the suspense film, and 300% 15 minutes after the erotic film. Cortisol levels increased from baseline levels from 4.0 to 15.1 µg/dl in four of eight subjects after the suspense film and from 4.2 to 8.1 µg/dl in three of eight subjects after the erotic film. All three films raised human growth hormone (hgH) levels in five of eight subjects— increments that were independent of the subjects' aroused feelings.

STUDIES OF PHOBIC PATIENTS

Autonomic Variables

A research strategy that has recently been developed is to confront phobic patients with the feared object or situation in order to induce phobic anxiety and follow its course with behavioral treatment while physiological measurements are made. Leitenberg, et al. (1971) used such a strategy while measuring heart rate under low-demand conditions. A variety of responses were seen—in some patients as phobic anxiety decreased the heart rate increased, in other patients the heart rate decreased, or it did not change at all. It is clear from this study that the heart rate correlates of phobic anxiety do not need to be inhibited before behavioral change occurs. This conclusion should be tentative, as only one cardiovascular measure was taken and gross motor activity was not controlled. These findings are also at variance with the finding that heart rate responses habituated to phobic and not to neutral stimuli (Grossberg & Wilson, 1968); that is, they do in some persons but not in others.

Hormonal Variables

Behavioral techniques for the treatment of phobias have also been adapted to study the correlated hormonal variables. The phobic subject was confronted with a feared object or situation in the third or fourth experimental session and responded initially with weeping, screaming, tremulousness, and chattering teeth. The subject rated his distress during two initial control sessions, two experimental sessions, and a final control session. In all instances distress ratings rose significantly in the experimental sessions. However, the intense fear induced by such "flooding" produced no change in prolactin levels (Nesse, Curtis, Brown, & Rubin, 1980). Changes in serum cortisol levels seemed unrelated to flooding whether measured at the crest (Curtis, Nesse, Buxton, & Lippman, 1978) or at the trough of the circadian cortisol cycle (Curtis, Buxton, Lippman, Nesse, & Wright, 1976). Cortisol levels progressively fell from 18–21 µ/dl to about 11 µg/dl during each of the five sessions. In half of the subjects, elevations occurred in the first and second (control) sessions, and in four subjects they rose during "flooding." Individual variability characterized the cortisol responses, which seemed mainly to occur in response to the novelty of the situation and the anticipation of "flooding."

Human growth hormone changes were also variable in 11 subjects. Main effects were obtained in 5 of these subjects: i.e., the highest levels occurred during the experimental sessions. In 4 of these subjects levels remained high even during the fifth session (Curtis, Nesse, Buxton, & Lippman, 1979).

One source of individual variability in hormonal responses has been identified, i.e., whether or not an anxious subject is involved in a relationship with the experimenter.

During cardiac catheterization, only the most overtly frightened patient had significant increases of serum cortisol—a traditional measure of "stress," unpredictability, novelty, pain, and danger in man. The frightened patients could be divided into two subgroups: Those who talked to the physicians about their concerns during the procedure showed no change in hGH levels; those who did not had significant increases in hGH levels and cortisol (Greene, Conron, Schalch, & Schreiner, 1970). Interestingly, both groups of patients maintained high levels of cortisol and FFAs from the beginning of the procedure.

A similar conclusion was arrived at by Brown and Heninger (1976). Using the same technique, only one-third of their patients showed hGH responses; no correlation was found between these and measures of anxiety. A measure of "non-involvement" (by the Mood Adjective Check List) did correlate with increases in hGH levels.

The results of these studies are surprisingly disappointing. They suggest again that in the laboratory physiological responses to the experimental induction of phobic anxiety are somehow modified. In addition, the literature on this topic is filled with contradictory data. Even when massive phobic anxiety is produced in subjects no hormonal changes may occur. Under other conditions (e.g., viewing films) the changes that occur do not discriminate fear from erotic arousal. Yet in situations of real danger more understandable results are obtained. However, they do not permit the control of many other variables—the effects of dietary intake, novelty, muscular movement, or exercise. Despite these drawbacks, consistent results have been obtained, and relevant behavioral variables affecting hormone patterns have been isolated in life-like situations of danger or challenge.

NATURALISTIC EXPERIMENTS: PHYSIOLOGICAL CORRELATES OF FEAR IN ANIMALS AND MAN

Confronting Animals with Predators

Hofer (1970) captured six species of wild desert rodents and exposed them to snakes and the silhouette of a hawk—their natural predators. Four of the six species—chipmunks, ground squirrels, wood rats and grasshopper mice—became tonically immobile. Immobility has obvious survival value because the prey is invisible to the predator whose retinal cells respond mainly to moving objects.

During the state of tonic immobility, their rate of breathing was increased fivefold. Although their heart rates showed little change, 56% of the animals had a variety of cardiac arrhythmias—sinus, different degrees of atrioventricular block, and ventricular ectopic beats. Individual and species differences in these variables were prominent. In the two other species—the deer mouse and kangaroo rat—the heart rose 33% to 100%, but no arrhythmias were recorded.

Wild rabbits, on the other hand, develop "fright" hyperthyroidism after initially being trapped by ferrets and again on being exposed to these predators or to dogs. Initially, they also became tonically immobile, tremulous, had marked increases in heart and respiratory rates, and developed exophthalmos. On reexposure to their predators the wild rabbits began to lose weight, showed increases in the update of radio-iodine and eventually died. Antithyroid drugs or thyroidectomy averted the weight loss and death (Kracht, 1954).

Studies in Man

Examinations. A number of reports have appeared in the literature on the physiological changes accompanying the taking of important tests—such as final, oral, medical-licensure examinations. These habitually caused fear and raised BP levels to clinically hypertensive levels (above 140/90 mm Hg) in young physicians. The BP levels began to rise even before the examination began, continued elevated in some candidates when the interrogation was over, and rose again on requestioning. Individual patterns were seen, but every student showed BP increases. von Uexküll and Wick (1962) call this phenomenon, "stress-hypertension," believing that this form of high blood pressure may presage essential hypertension.

Free fatty acid levels increased significantly, but only in the most anxious students taking examinations (Bogdonoff, Estes, Harlan, Trout, & Kirshner, 1960). Serum cholesterol levels increased by 10% to 25% in medical students taking a written examination, especially in those who performed poorly (Bloch & Brackenridge, 1972). Oral examinations seem to mobilize some hormone levels and not others more than written examinations. In 131 medical students (compared with 83 controls) a written exam raised hGH levels 33%, and an oral examination raised them 49%. (The highest mean levels of hGH occurred in women students.) Serum insulin levels rose 45% and 43%, respectively, without changing blood glucose levels. Plasma renin levels rose by 44% after a written examination and 27% following an oral examination. Significant increases in heart rate (44%) occurred during the oral examination (Sylvälahti, Lammintavsta, & Pekkarinen, 1976). However, the students were not used as their own controls; rather, their group means were compared with students not being examined. The variations in hormone levels after the examination were generally within the normal range, except for the changes in hGH levels.

Public Presentations.   Any young physician knows that one of the most fearsome experiences he must undergo in his early career is to present at Grand Rounds. With the development of reliable techniques for the estimation of epinephrine (E) and norepinephrine (NE) in serum, these catecholamines have been measured in physicians making presentations that demand peak performance (Dimsdale & Moss, 1980; Taggart, Carruthers, & Somerville, 1973).

Epinephrine levels rose sharply before and at the onset of the talk and then subsided during its course. Norepinephrine levels gradually increased and remained elevated throughout the period of the talk. Marked individual differences were observed in levels attained and in patterns. In some speakers the levels remained unchanged from the beginning to the end of the talk. The changes in catecholamine levels during the presentation differed from those seen during exercise when NE levels alone increased.

Dangerous Sports; the Effects of Driving a Racing Car.   Racing a car is generally acknowledged to be one of the most dangerous sports ever invented by man; yet it entails minimal physical effort. Taggart and Carruthers (1971) studied 16 drivers just before and during a 3-hour period of driving, and immediately following a race. Total catecholamine levels were raised at the time the race began and in the period immediately after it. Most of the increase (86%) was due to elevations of NE levels. Levels of FFAs rose 125% before the race, peaked at its start, remained high after the race, and returned to resting levels after 1 hour. Triglyceride levels began to increase when the starter dropped his flag and continued to rise after the race was over. One hour later they were 111% above baseline levels. Cholesterol levels remained unchanged throughout the race. A strong positive correlation ($r = .81$) was present between total catecholamine levels below 2µg/1 and FFA levels. When the catecholamine levels were greater than 2 µg/1 the Pearson correlation coefficient was a mere .31.

This study confirms the FFAs, which are readily measured in serum, are exquisitely sensitive to a wide variety of contingencies including dangerous and anxiety-provoking ones (Dimsdale & Herd, 1982). (Their relevance in clinical medicine is discussed later.) Free fatty acids seem to increase in anticipation of dangerous or anxiety-provoking situations, including cardiac catheterization.

Parachute Jumping: Cardiorespiratory Changes.   Training in the use of a parachute is a reliable way of inducing fear even in experienced jumpers. Fenz and Epstein (1967) compared 10 novice and 10 experienced jumpers while rating fear, heart rate, respiratory rate, and skin conductance before, during, and after a jump from 5,000 feet. The novices were frightened to the point of being disorganized in thought and behavior; most of them found the first jump terrifying, whereas some others found it thrilling.

In both experienced and novice jumpers, mounting, anticipatory fear manifested itself in the bus on the way to the airfield. But in the experienced jumpers, fear declined at the point of maximum danger—when jumping out of the aircraft. During the actual fall, they were relatively relaxed. The novices, on the other hand, continued to experience mounting fear until they had landed. Respiration rate was the first to increase, then heart rate rose and skin conductance fell in both groups. In experienced jumpers, the physiological changes peaked and then fell after they entered the aircraft, but in inexperienced ones they continued to increase in the expected manner with the actual jump. Precise correlations between the fear self-ratings and the physiological changes occurred in the novices. Among the experienced jumpers a dissociation between fear and the physiological changes took place while preparing for and engaging in the jump.

Even experienced jumpers performed differently when rated by two jumpmasters. Those who performed poorly had the greatest physiological changes. Their respiration rates rose sharply until the engines of the aircraft were warming up, and then they plateaued, but their heart rates continued to increase until the jump was completed. By contrast, in the good performers, respiration rates first increased and then fell, and heart rates plateaued.

The experienced men who performed poorly showed physiological patterns reminiscent of novice jumpers. It follows that the individual manner in which persons respond psychophysiologically to a frightening situation depends both on their experience, including a sense of control or mastery, and the quality of performance during this situation (Fenz & Jones, 1972).

Hormonal Responses.   Fourteen young soldiers had blood drawn for prolactin, thyrotropin, and hGH before and after their first military parachute jump. Baseline values for all three hormones were measured at 6:00 a.m., 13 days and 3 days before the jump. On the day of the jump, samples were obtained at 6:00 a.m. and 1:00 p.m. The jump was made from an altitude of 366 meters, and a final blood sample was obtained on landing. There were significant increases in the mean levels of all three hormones as follows:

Prolactin: From 10.4 ng/ml to 19.3 ± 3.1 ng/ml (Range: 6.5 to 40 ng/ml)
Thyrotropin: 2.9 ± 0.6 μU/ml to 4.1 ± 0.6 μU/ml (Range: 1.8-9 μU/ml)
hGH: 4.2 ± 1.2 ng/ml to 13.6 ± 3.5 ng/ml (Range: 1 to 42 ng/ml)

The authors of this report discounted the effects of cold, exertion, and altitude on the changes in hormone levels. This was a "one-trial" study. It did not attempt to examine the effects of repeated exposure to jumping nor account for individual differences in hormonal responses (Noel, Dimond, Earll, & Frantz, 1976). Ursin and his colleagues (1978) carried out a multiple measurement study on 44 young, novice soldiers undergoing parachute training. The patterns of fear displayed were similar to those seen in Fenz and his colleagues' studies (1967, 1972). But

Ursin et al. reported that 13 of the 44 soldiers quit training after the first jump, during which they had experienced great fear, very high levels of E and NE, and elevated blood glucose, FFAs, and testosterone levels. The remaining 31 soldiers performed variably. The good performers were relatively unafraid. They were impatient to try the jump again, which they found thrilling. Good performers had the highest FFAs and moderate E and NE increases during the jump. As they became increasingly adept, the acute increases in these measures became less with each successive jump. Throughout the series their cortisol levels were low. Those who performed poorly throughout and claimed to be unafraid had the largest rises in serum cortisol and hGH levels. Only minor increases in E, NE, and prolactin levels occurred. Soldiers who ultimately failed the course had a rise in prolactin and a fall in testosterone levels. These studies document that the novelty of a dangerous situation, the manner in which persons react psychologically to it, and the manner in which they perform in it determine the nature and the extent of the physiological responses.

Until the work by Ursin and his colleagues were reported, most studies were devoted to the examination of a single, isolated variable—cortisol, a catecholamine, or hgH. This single variable strategy has limited our understanding of the manner in which cardiovascular or hormonal patterns are generated during danger, fear, or anxiety. Only recently has it become apparent that different physiological patterns are generated in several different bodily systems, depending upon the specific type of frightening situation, the attitude with which it is faced, and the performance and experience of the participants. Each of these factors modifies an integrated pattern of hormonal response: "Any variable which can be described or measured independently is actually a component of several such patterns" (Hilton, 1975).

Training for or Actual Military Combat. Underwater demolition training is one of the most dangerous military procedures known. It consistently raised serum cortisol levels in men to three times normal levels (22 μg/dl). The introduction of novel procedures of unfamiliar equipment (e.g., scuba tanks and new masks) during training further increased serum cortisol levels. As soon as the new equipment was mastered these additional levels returned to steady high basal levels (Rubin, Rahe, Arthur, & Clark, 1969).

The landing of jet fighter planes on aircraft carriers produces a high death or accident rate in pilots and their crews. The successful completion of any landing is always in doubt. Even experienced pilots were fearful, although they rated themselves as less frightened than the crewmen who operated the plane's radar equipment. Yet the pilots showed a three fold increase in serum cortisol levels (from 4 to 13 μg/dl). The greatest increments occurred in the pilots during day landings, though landing at night was even more perilous. Even simulated landings were associated with a rise in cortisol levels in pilots. Therefore, the pilots, who perceived themselves as the responsible individuals, secreted more cortisol in this situation (Miller, Rubin, Clark, Poland, & Arthur, 1970).

3-Methoxy, 4-hydroxy phenylglycol (MHPG)—but not urine volume—rose significantly in the pilots and radar officers of U.S. Navy jet fighters making aircraft landings. The highest levels were obtained in pilots during actual night landings. Simulated landings produced no changes in MHPG levels (Rubin, Miller, Clark, Poland, & Arthur, 1970). (Norepinephrine is metabolized to MHPG. Twenty-five percent of all MHPG in urine is believed to derive from brain NE stores.)

The conclusion that the responsible person is more likely to secrete higher levels of corticosteroid than the subordinate one is borne out by the observations made by Bourne, Rose, and Mason (1967, 1968). They studied the experienced officers and men of a Green Beret combat unit in Viet Nam, while they were anticipating and undergoing a pre-announced Viet Cong attack. The highest increases in levels of 17-hydroxycorticosteroid excretion occurred in the two officers and in the radio operator. Actually, in the enlisted men the levels fell during the attack and then returned to baseline levels.

When other soldiers under fire were carrying out their customary duties and rituals with hope, or when resorting to prayer, seemingly oblivious of the threat of injury or death, they had lower urinary 17-hydroxycorticosteroid levels than predicted by their body weight (Bourne et al., 1967).

THE PATHOPHYSIOLOGICAL EFFECTS OF DANGER, FEAR, AND ANXIETY

The acute psychobiological effects of dangerous situations have been described; the consequences of persistent, or intermittent but long-term exposure to danger are largely unknown. By contrast, more is gradually being learned about the long-term psychological, physiological, and health consequences of forced unemployment (Farrow, 1983), and of separation or bereavement (Hofer, 1983; Weiner, 1983).

Furthermore, it is not known whether the acute cardiovascular or endocrine changes that accompany dangerous situations recur on each subsequent real-life exposure to them: Do physiological changes diminish over time—do adaptation or habituation occur? The evidence suggests that in anxious subjects they do not. Does improved performance during a dangerous frightening task reduce physiological change?

Because no firm answers exist to these questions one can only speculate about the roles played by cardiovascular and humoral responses to danger in disease onset. The question being asked here is whether the cardiovascular, endocrine (or immune) responses to danger act as mediators of fear and anxiety to produce functional or structural changes within the body.

Cortisol Cortisol has a potential role in a variety of pathological processes; in particular, it may play a significant role in atherogenesis by increasing serum lipids and damaging the endothelial cells of arterioles. It enhances atherosclerotic changes in dogs fed fat (atherogenic) diets (Henry, 1983).

In addition, multiple interactions between cortisol and catecholamine secretion and action are known. In the adrenal medulla, cortisol enhances catecholamine synthesis and retards their disposition (Kopin, 1980). Cortisol potentiates the vascular responses to alpha-adrenergic stimulation (Schmid, Eckstein, & Abboud, 1966), probably by inhibiting the breakdown of NE (Goldie, 1976). It reduces beta-receptor density on lymphocytes and increases it on granulocytes over the short term (Davies & Lefkowitz, 1980).

The only direct evidence that corticosteroids (in pharmacological doses) play a role in human atherogenesis is that their chronic administration to patients with rheumatoid arthritis accelerates arteriosclerosis (Kalbak, 1972). Cortisol also plays a permissive role in the production of FFAs by catecholamines.

Free Fatty Acids (FFAs)   The FFAs are rapidly mobilized in anticipation of danger. Excess FFAs may remain unoxidized and bind to acyl coenzyme A; the derivative of this reaction is cardiotoxic. The incidence of ventricular arrhythmias is proportional to levels of fatty acid acyl coenzyme A levels (Russel, 1983). The FFAs have also been implicated in coronary artery occlusion because they enhance the adhesiveness of blood platelets. On the other hand, other lipids— the triglycerides and cholesterol—are implicated in atheroma formation, as are hormones—cortisol, insulin, and androgens (Stout, 1982).

Catecholamines   A renewed role for the catecholamines has been found in the pathogenesis of one form of essential hypertension and in the pathophysiology of an autoimmune disease, Graves' disease (see below). Cortisol and the catecholamines may be involved in ischemia produced by coronary artery spasm (Raab, 1970), or they may produce a selective form of myocardial necrosis leading to sudden cardiac death (Baroldi, Falzi, & Mariani, 1979).

Other Hormones   A limited number of hormones have been assayed in studies on danger, fear, and anxiety. But the role played by elevations (when they occur) of prolactin, hGH, thyroid-stimulating hormone, testosterone, and other hormones in normal physiology and the eventual development of disease is by no means clear.

EFFECTS OF FEAR & ANXIETY ON ORGAN SYSTEMS

The Cardiovascular System

Many symptoms of heart disease—arrhythmias, pain, and dyspnea—are associated with anxiety and fear. Danger and the fear it generates may also play a role in the pathogenesis of essential hypertension. As we have already seen, examination fear is associated with "stress hypertension" which may eventuate in permanently raised blood pressures.

Evidence also exists that dangerous events or situations are associated with essential hypertension. Following the explosion of a munitions ship in Texas City a predominance of the population examined had elevated BP levels sustained for a period of 2 months (Ruskin, Beard, & Schaffer, 1948). Sustained military combat—in the North African desert and at Stalingrad—were associated with a disproportionate prevalence of high BP (Ehrstrom, 1945; Gelshteyn, 1943; Graham, 1945). Many factors must have played a role in this phenomenon—danger, malnutrition, cold (in Russia), heat (in North Africa), and exertion.

But the matter is even more complex. Although we have seen that piloting a Naval combat airplane is conducive to marked changes in hormone levels, studies of U.S. naval aviators over a 25-year period show that their BP levels do not increase with age—a most unusual circumstance in any population. Henry and Cassel (1969) ascribe this phenomenon to the fact that the subculture in which the pilots live is highly structured and stable with established rules and traditions. Conversely, ghetto black persons in the United States, who are frequently exposed to violence and police brutality, who live in crowded conditions in areas of social disorganization and economic deprivation, and whose personal and marital lives are disrupted, have higher levels of blood pressure than their black peers living in middle-class neighborhoods in which these conditions do not prevail (Harburg, et al., 1973).

Clearly danger and social disruption are not the only factors in essential hypertension—a disease that is heterogeneous in its etiology. A complex number of social, personal, genetic, nutritional, physiological and metabolic factors interact. It is recognized, however, that in the inception of one form of borderline (early) hypertension the sympathetic nervous system and catecholamine release may play major roles.

Not all patients with borderline essential hypertension go on to develop essential hypertension. Groups of patients with borderline hypertension tend to have some increase in cardiac output, increased cardiac contractility, and heart rate. The plasma catecholamine levels are likely to be higher, and the urinary excretion of catecholamines is excessive on standing. Stress produces exaggerated catecholamine and BP responses. Ganglionic blocking agents produce a fall in BP that closely correlates with a fall in plasma NE levels (DeQuattro & Miura, 1973; Julius & Esler, 1975; Kuchel, 1977).

Patients with borderline hypertension differ as a group (but not necessarily as individuals) from normotensive subjects. But the patients also differ from each other. Not all patients with borderline hypertension have an elevated cardiac output: in 30% the cardiac output is two standard deviations beyond the mean for normal, age-matched subjects. In this subgroup of patients, the total peripheral resistance is inappropriately normal at rest (it should be decreased when increased tissue perfusion is brought about by the increased cardiac output). In other patients with borderline hypertension, in whom a normal cardiac output and heart rate are found, the total peripheral resistance is increased at rest, possible owing to increased alpha-adrenergic vasoconstrictor tone. Blood volume is unevenly distributed in the circulation (mainly in the cardiopulmonary bed) in borderline hypertension in those patients with an increased cardiac output. In about 30% of all patients with borderline hypertension plasma, renin activity and NE concentration are elevated. Other patients increase their plasma renin activity excessively with postural changes. Yet the increased plasma renin activity does not seem to maintain the heightened blood pressure levels through its activity on angiotensin II and aldesterone production. The increased heart rate, cardiac output, and plasma renin activity can be reduced to normal levels with propranolol, but the plasma norepinephrine concentration and BP continue to remain elevated. Therefore, the enhanced plasma renin activity is believed to be a result of increased sympathetic activity, and is not the primary pathogenetic factor in raising the BP (Esler, et al., 1975; Julius & Esler, 1975). The obverse sequence is, however, thought to account for the malignant phase of hypertension when high plasma renin activity is found.

Nonetheless, many borderline hypertensive patients have normal and some have low plasma renin activity. Patients whose plasma renin activity is normal tend to be the ones with diminished stroke volume and cardiac index, normal pulse rate, but increased total peripheral resistance. Their plasma NE concentration is higher than normal, but lower than in patients with high plasma renin activity with borderline hypertension. The increased peripheral resistance and BP in patients with borderline hypertension with low or normal plasma renin activity is unaffected by the administration of alpha-adrenergic and beta-adrenergic blocking agents and atropine. The administration of these drugs causes a fall in BP and peripheral resistance in patients with high plasma renin activity, borderline hypertension (Esler, Julius, Randall, Ellis, & Kashima, 1977; Esler et al., 1975).

We do not know, however, whether the release of catecholamines in this group of patients is associated with exertion, danger, fear, or anxiety.

The Cardiorespiratory System

The claim made by Marks and Lader (1973) that anxiety states (anxiety neurosis) are indistinguishable from a syndrome variously known as Da Costa's or effort syndrome, cardiac neurosis, neurocirculatory asthenia, or the hyperventilation syndrome is not borne out by clinical observation (Magarian, 1982). Anxiety may antecede the hyperventilation syndrome, or it may be a consequence thereof. Both hysterical and depressed patients may hyperventilate, and different patterns of breathing are observable in these various clinical groups. For example, some hyperventilators increase the inspired air volume without an increase in respiratory rate. Others breathe rapidly and irregularly while taking shallow breaths. Still others complain of being unable to get satisfaction from breathing— their respirations are deep and sighing; such patients are often anxious. Hyperventilation can occur at rest; it fluctuates a great deal and it often occurs during social conversation or changes in the social field. It may occur before falling asleep or on awakening (Burns & Howell, 1969). Depressed patients often show increased resting respiratory rates and may occasionally complain of breathlessness (Damas Mora, Grant, Kenyon, Patal, & Jenner, 1976).

Marks and Lader (1973) also seem to be unaware of the pathophysiology of the hyperventilation syndrome. Having claimed that anxiety states and the hyperventilation syndrome are synonymous, they state that there are no characteristic electrocardiographic or hormonal abnormalities in the hyperventilation syndrome. They also state that infusions of sodium lactate produce anxiety in anxious patients. But endogenous increases in lactic acid induce an acidosis; when infused, an alkalosis ensues.

Anxiety may indeed antecede hyperventilation but not always. The hyperventilation syndrome also has a varied, interesting, and rich pathophysiology which is relevant to the pathophysiology of anxiety.

One may learn about the chronic, intermittent consequences of anxiety by studying the effects of hyperventilation in which the respiratory (ventilatory) effort exceeds the body's need for oxygen. As a result of hyperventilation the partial pressure of carbon dioxide ($PaCO_2$) falls, and respiratory alkalosis quickly ensues. The kidney attempts to compensate for the alkalosis by increased excretion of bicarbonate, sodium, and potassium ions, and by reducing the production of ammonia salts and acidic metabolites. When hyperventilation is persistent, about two-thirds of all patients will show a reduction of $PaCO_2$ (Lum, 1976).

If hyperventilation becomes continuous and persistent, as it does in some patients, a physiological adaptation occurs: The respiratory center becomes reset— it responds to persistently lower $PaCO_2$ levels in the face of a now-normalized blood pH (Gennari, Goldstein, & Schwartz, 1972). The net effect of this adaptation would be to sustain hyperventilation. Further reduction of the $PaCO_2$ would set off a new wave of the syndrome.

Other factors may trigger hyperventilation, and it is known that changes in respiratory patterns are produced with many kinds of emotions. Fear and anxiety, as we have seen, may produce beta-adrenergic discharge conducive to hyperventilation. Beta-adrenergic blocking agents reduce the increased ventilation due to beta-catecholamine release or to breathing carbon dioxide (Bosisio, Sergi, Sega, & Libretti, 1979; Heistad, Wheeler, Mark, Schmid, & Abboud, 1972).

One of the metabolic consequences of respiratory alkalosis is hypophosphatemia (Okel & Hurst, 1961). A reduction in inorganic phosphorus levels in serum occurs rapidly after the inception of hyperventilation and persists for its duration. It is apparently caused by the passage of phosphorus into cells (Brautbar, Leibovici,

Finlander, Campanese, Penia, & Massry, 1980). Hypophosphatemia can produce a variety of symptoms: disorientation, dizziness, diminished attention, malaise, and paresthesia (Kreisberg, 1978), common manifestations of the hyperventilation syndrome.

Hyperventilation, a reduced $PaCO_2$, and respiratory alkalosis have cardiovascular effects: initially vasodilation occurs, mean BP falls, cardiac output and heart rate increase. A few minutes later vasoconstriction occurs (Kontos, et al., 1972), and the rises in BP, cardiac output, and heart rate disappear.

One of the more common symptoms of the hyperventilation syndrome is chest pain. It can result from the increased respiratory effort and be muscular in origin, or it can be due to air swallowing. Yet very many patients with this syndrome are erroneously believed to have structural coronary artery disease. Hyperventilating patients may have sinus tachycardia at rest, sinus arrhythmias, ST segment elevations or depressions in the electrocardiogram (Tsivoni, Stein, Keren, & Stern, 1980). Both supraventricular and ventricular premature beats may be observed.

In the light of these changes physicians tend to assume that hyperventilating patients with chest pain, electrocardiogram changes, and arrhythmias must have ischemic heart disease. This assumption is not universally correct, although it does appear that hypocapnic alkalosis slows coronary blood flow (Neill & Hattenhauer, 1975), or produces coronary vasospasm in patients with Prinzmetal's variant angina (Mortensen, Vilhelmson, & Sande, 1981) or structural coronary artery disease.

Dizziness and fainting are common symptoms of the hyperventilation syndrome, although anxious patients rarely faint. Cerebral blood flow, both arterial and venous, is reduced during hyperventilation (Samuel, Grange, & Hawkins, 1968). (During states of anxiety cerebral blood flow is increased.) Hypocapnia reduces cerebral oxygen tension and flow (Raichle & Plum, 1972). In hyperventilating patients, the EEG is characterized by the rapid development of high voltage, paroxysmal or continuous slow wave activity in the delta range (Saltzman, Heyman, & Sieber, 1963), at which time the patient may lose consciousness.

Hyperventilation may also be anteceded by various drugs (e.g., salicylates), attaining an elevated altitude, exercise, alcohol withdrawal, brain lesions, depression, fears and anxieties (Pfeffer, 1978). Enough clinical evidence has been presented to suggest that it is an error to equate anxiety neurosis with the hyperventilation syndrome.

A necessary condition for the hyperventilation syndrome may be the tendency to thoracic breathing (Lum, 1976). Apprehension and fear may perpetuate the cycle (Lewis, 1954) in the face of a resetting of the set-point in the brain stem respiratory center. Normal respiratory patterns may only be reestablished when $PaCO_2$ levels return to normal. If this does not occur, a self-perpetuating cycle is set up (Folgerging & Colla, 1978), which is tripped off when the hyperventilator takes a deep breath or sighs. In this manner a vicious cycle is established.

Mitral Valve Prolapse, Anxiety and Hyperventilation

Many patients have asymptomatic mitral valve prolapse (MVP). Others become aware of this defect by developing supraventricular premature beats, which may cause them to become fearful. The postulate that panic or anxiety attacks are solely the result of MVP is not proven.

As often happens, the matter is more complex. Only a small proportion of patients with MVP show elevations or depression of their ST wave segments on hyperventilation (Gardin, Isner, Roman, & Fox, 1980). These particular subgroup patients may be predisposed to respond to hyperventilation by these electrocardiogram changes, and the response may be averted by administration of the beta-blocking agent, propranolol (Furberg & Tengblad, 1966). In such patients epinephrine infusions reproduce these electrocardiogram changes (Yu, Yim, & Stanfield, 1959). In this particular subset of MVP patients, reduced vagal and increased alpha-sympathetic responses occur (Gaffney, Karlsson, & Campbell, 1979). The anxiety that induces hyperventilation may, therefore, produce especial cardiac symptoms in a small group of patients with mitral valve prolapse.

Bronchial Asthma

This complex, recurrent and chronic, multidimensional disease occurs in an allergic (extrinsic) and a nonallergic (intrinsic) form. In both forms, a predisposition (bronchial hyperreactivity) to a large variety of stimuli occurs, which interacts with a number of inciting factors—allergens, pulmonary infections, dusts, cold air, odors, fumes, local irritation of the upper airways, exercise, and emotional arousal.

The extrinsic form of bronchial asthma is characterized by immune mechanisms that are necessary but not sufficient to incite asthmatic attacks. Antigens elicit the production of immunoglobulin-E antibodies, which attach themselves to mast cells and basophils located in the bronchial tree. The antigen-antibody reaction releases a series of chemical mediators that directly or reflexly produce bronchospasm in an already overreactive bronchial tree. In most instances, the allergic mechanisms interact with infectious and psychological factors.

It is now recognized that many aroused emotions (laughter, weeping, anger, fear, and sexual excitement) may precipitate asthmatic attacks in predisposed persons. Together they alter breathing patterns. Anxiety in asthmatic patients is often occasioned either by separation, or by interpersonal closeness or intimacy.

Viruses and certain stimuli, such as ozone, lower the threshold of parasympathetic receptors of the lung to produce rapid, shallow breathing patterns. Hyperventilation due to and following exercise may induce bronchospasm (Deal, McFadden, Ingram, Breslin, & Jaeger, 1980). Cold and dry air stimulate parasympathetic bronchial receptors.

A common mechanism mediating all the precipitants of the asthmatic attack has been identified recently; it interacts with altered patterns of breathing, and with stimulation of afferent vagal receptors in the lung. In bronchial asthma, the vagus reflexly induces bronchial hyperreactivity. A defect in the postganglionic muscarinic vagal synapse in the lung of asthmatic patients is responsible. This defect consists of either an increased presynaptic release or an enhanced binding affinity of the postsynaptic receptor for acetylcholine (Boushey, 1981).

The Endocrine System

Knowledge about the role of anxiety in the endocrinopathies is limited. The hormone most readily available to researchers studying danger, fear, and anxiety is cortisol, which is especially responsive to novelty, unpredictable situations, danger, pain, anticipation, psychological disruption, and depression. Whether exposure to chronic danger or the persistence of anxiety ever produce sustained hypercortisolism is unknown. Nor is a role known for cortisol in Cushing's disease or syndrome.

However, danger and fear may be associated with the onset of Graves' disease, especially in its acute form. Many of such patients are already programmed to respond to danger because they have a fear of dying. In the largest series of thyrotoxic patients ever published, 13% of 3343 patients with Graves' disease had been involved in accidents, were otherwise injured, had found themselves in situations of imminent danger, and an additional 7% developed the disease following surgery (Bram, 1927).

Thyrotoxicosis, a generic name for a hypermetabolic state, of which Graves' disease is one example, often increases in incidence during wartime, as long as nutrition is adequate. Major increases in thyrotoxicosis incidence and prevalence occurred in Denmark and Norway during the German occupation of World War II (Iversen, 1948, 1949). In countries not invaded, or in those in which the German invaders starved the population (e.g., Holland and Belgium), no such increases occurred.

Danger may play either an inciting or permissive role in Graves' disease. The most common symptom of Graves' disease is nervousness, which has been considered by some as the response to life-threatening danger. Other students of the disease interpret it as a consequence of the hypermetabolic state. In fact, there is a remarkable similarity between the symptoms of anxiety and hypermetabolic states. (However, about one-half of all patients with clinical Graves' disease are also significantly depressed.)

We have no idea how danger and the fear it generates interact with the autoimmune antibody against the thyroid-stimulating hormone receptor to set into motion the complicated alterations in thyroid physiology that characterizes Graves' disease. Suffice it to say that once the disease begins, complex synergisms exist between the thyroid hormones and catecholamines (for review see

Weiner, 1977), some of which may account for the symptomatology of Graves' disease. In fact, the extreme form of the disease—thyroid storm— is best treated by the beta-adrenergic blocking agent, propranolol, which also reduces the nervousness, tremor, excessive sweating and palpitations of uncomplicated Graves' disease. Although there is no evidence of excessive catecholomine secretion in the disease, thyroid hormones in excess increase the number of catecholamine receptors.

Gastrointestinal Disease

Diarrhea is cited to be a feature of 14% of patients with anxiety states (Wheeler, White, Reed, & Cohen, 1950). Conversely, the so-called "functional" gastrointestinal disorders account for 50%-60% of the gastrointestinal complaints seen by physicians. The most prevalent "functional" disorder is the irritable bowel syndrome, which consists of alternating diarrhea and constipation, abdominal pain (cramps), mucus in the bowel movement, or diarrhea alone. Seventy-two percent of such patients had a clinically diagnosable psychiatric disorder. Patients whose irritable bowel syndrome was characterized mainly by diarrhea could be classified independently as suffering from an anxiety neurosis or somatization disorder. When constipation and pain predominated, they were either depressed or suffering from a somatization disorder. In two-thirds of the patients, psychiatric symptoms anteceded the bowel symptoms. Patients with other chronic bowel diseases had an 18% incidence of psychiatric disorders (Alpers, 1981, 1983).

One may conclude that a chronic anxiety neurosis or state is responsible for one form of irritable bowel syndrome.

CONCLUSION

The psychobiology of fear and anxiety is as muddled as is the clinical literature. On the basis of this review very few generalizations are possible.

This chapter has emphasized the fact that data on fear and anxiety are contradictory and altogether anti-intuitive—one example is the almost total lack of ("stress") hormonal responses to "flooding" in the face of behavioral manifestations that one would clinically diagnose as panic. Experimental data have, however, yielded the useful insight clinicians frequently overlook: that fear, anxiety, and avoidance behavior can be dissociated; and there is clinical evidence for this dissociation in the anxiety states.

The inconsistent results obtained in the laboratory and the low order of the correlations between physiological responses and measures of anxiety are usually ascribed to "individual differences" not further identified. Clearly, there are nonlinear relationships at work.

Emphasis has been placed in this review on "real-life" experiences in dangerous situations and occupations. In this light, the source of "individual differences" in response measures begins to emerge. What is dangerous to one person is a thrill to another. Novelty, ambiguity, and inexperience are more likely to mobilize physiological responses, especially heart rate, catecholamine, FFAs, and cortisol responses. Oral examinations are more likely to raise blood pressure levels than written ones. Good performance is more habitually associated with a decline in physiological responses during the task than is poor performance. The demand characteristics of a situation, in part, determine physiological responses. Leaders are more responsive physiologically than followers in situations of danger. (Reliance on others seems to dampen physiological responses?) Note, however, that almost all the data on the physiological responses to danger are done in acute situations and with male subjects.

The long-term physiological effects of danger, fear, and anxiety are unknown, and the empirical link of fear and anxiety to bodily disease states is at best tenuous. The physiological consequences of hyperventilation are examples of the complexity of the relationships to be found.

Throughout this chapter, an attempt has been made to underline the fact that fear and anxiety are basic biological—not only clinical—phenomena. They play a central role in alerting the organism to danger. Without them, animals would not survive predation and bodily harm, and their species would be selected out of existence. Recent studies on separation in animals indicate that the mother-infant interaction is vital to survival and to maturation and development of the brain, behavioral systems, and bodily function. Separation uncovers the manner in which the mother regulates the psychobiological function of the infant through various input channels. Separation of 14-day-old rats permanently alters the cardiac, gastric, and immune systems and places them at risk for future disease when challenged (Hofer, 1983; Weiner, 1983). Later as the organism develops behavioral programs for fending on its own, new (or more refined) dangers appear to which it must be alerted; it responds in species-specific (not only individual) ways. The organism's performance in such situations, including its physiological responses, will determine whether it survives or not.

17 A Psychosomatic Perspective on Anxiety Disorders

Joel E. Dimsdale, M.D.
Massachusetts General Hospital
Harvard Medical School

Anxiety has long been of interest to psychosomatic medicine and yet its definition and conceptualization are somewhat different from that used by investigators who study anxiety disorders per se. It is the thesis of this brief paper that these differing perspectives are valuable for increasing our understanding of anxiety and the anxiety disorders. There are five characteristics that define the psychosomatic approach:

1. Rather than focus on pathologies of behavior, the psychosomatic approach focuses on normal behaviors and normal physiological responses to stressors. This is not to say that the psychosomatic perspective denies the reality of clearly demarcated illnesses, but rather that it focuses primarily on the impact of stressors on the basic underlying physiological responses common to all healthy persons.

2. Because anxiety is difficult to induce, control, and measure experimentally, the psychosomatic approach focuses on the stressors and the physiological responses that such stressors engender. Less emphasis is placed on subjective states, such as anxiety. The focus on stimulus and response has provided a strong tool for investigation. On the other hand, treating anxiety as an intervening variable has meant that anxiety, arousal, excitement, and a host of other subjective states have been defined by antecedent events and indirect measures, but not directly observed.

3. The psychosomatic approach has difficulty teasing out the exact boundaries between subjective, behavioral, and physiological responses. In general, the field has remained rather atheoretical about which conditions precede the others. There is a decided reluctance to focus on one response domain to the exclusion of others.

4. Psychosomatic researchers see a different pool of anxious patients. The patients are either those with both anxiety and a physical illness or anxiety-free

patients who complain of physical symptoms without demonstrated pathophys-iological abnormalities. For the first group the focus is on explicating the phys-iological links between emotional upset and ongoing medical illness. For the latter group, the physical symptoms are inferred to be an alternative mode of expressing emotional distress. For both groups the observed or inferred emotion is frequently anxiety or anxiety alloyed with anger or depression.

5. Finally, there is a profound skepticism about dividing illnesses into psy-chosomatic versus nonpsychosomatic. Most studies, for instance, find that fol-lowing major traumatic stressors, all illnesses are increased, not just classical psychosomatic illnesses (Eitinger, 1980).

DIFFERENT MODELS OF ANXIETY

Observed or inferred anxiety underlies a number of psychiatric and medical disorders. Psychosomatic researchers would point to a fundamental problem in defining which form of "anxiety" one is studying. Running through all of the anxiety disorder literature is a pervasive confusion between *at least* three different forms of anxiety (Fig. 1). The borders between these three forms of anxiety are ill-defined.

At one extreme there is the acute anxiety triggered by exposure to an alarming or exciting stimulus. This is the type of anxiety that is most widely studied in psychosomatic medicine. Since everyone is prone to the insults and assaults of the environment, the focus on acute arousal is usually examined in normals. Although the distinction between anxiety, excitement, and arousal is muddled, there are clear, transient physiological consequences of such acute states. These

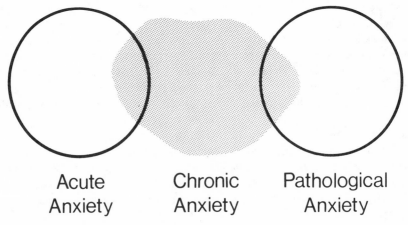

| Acute | Chronic | Pathological |
| Anxiety | Anxiety | Anxiety |

FIG. 1   Conceptual models for the anxieties.

consequences (e.g., increased arrhythmias and increased blood pressure) presumably reflect the activity of the sympathetic and adrenomedullary systems. In a person free from psychiatric disorder but with an underlying physiological vulnerability, these usually benign effects of acute anxiety may become life threatening (Dimsdale, 1977).

At the opposite extreme is a form of anxiety not found in normals, which may be called "pathological" corresponding to *Diagnostic and Statistical Manual (DSM-III)* categories of panic disorder or agoraphobia. With some exceptions (Curtis, Nesse, Buxton, & Lippman, 1978), this form of anxiety is less commonly investigated by psychosomatic researchers. What are the physical health consequences of the pathological anxieties? Unfortunately, this area has been understudied. The flurry of interest in mitral valve prolapse as associated with various anxiety disorders is a refreshing exception, but there has been little agreement about the nature of that relationship (Coryell & Noyes, & Clancy, 1982). Researchers studying anxiety disorders have been interested more in refining the diagnosis and treatment of the disorder per se as opposed to examining some of its other health consequences. Since psychosomatic researchers concentrate on medical illness or on normal responses to anxiety, they less commonly study patients with formal anxiety disorders.

In between these two poles is a large, vague category referred to by psychosomatic investigators as chronic anxiety and by anxiety disorder researchers as generalized anxiety disorder (GAD). This is a common disorder in the general population, and in primary care and psychosomatic practices (Barrett, 1981). It may have pronounced health consequences particularly for coronary artery disease, hypertension, thyrotoxicosis, and irritable bowel syndrome with diarrhea (Elliott & Eisdorfer, 1982; Weiner, this volume). As portrayed in Fig. 1, there are ragged boundaries between these disorders and normal arousal and pathological anxiety. Furthermore, the chronic anxiety disorders border on other psychiatric disorders, shading into somatoform disorders, hypochondriasis, and post-traumatic stress disorder.

It is short-sighted to focus exclusively on one category of anxiety disorder and yet there has been a de facto split in the research community. Investigators studying anxiety disorders will generally select pathological anxiety for study, and yet investigators interested in the broader medical health consequences of anxiety will focus more attention on acute arousal and chronic anxiety.

DIFFERENT SITES FOR STUDYING ANXIETY

Psychosomatic researchers focus on detecting the peripheral physiological signals resulting from exposure to stressors, usually *acute* stressors. There is a difference of opinion about where to best study such states of anxiety—in the laboratory or in the field. The laboratory is advantageous because of the ease of experimental arrangements, design, and control. The major disadvantage to laboratory studies is an ethical one, the difficulty in imposing truly anxiety-provoking stimuli in the laboratory. Attention to criteria of informed consent decreases the likelihood of being able to observe the physiological response of subjects to genuine anxiety. As a result, what laboratory investigators label "anxiety" may bear only a pale resemblance to what patients or anxiety researchers label anxiety. The dysphoric affect triggered in laboratory studies may be more a measure of vigilance and subtle anger than anxiety. This low amount of laboratory-kindled anxiety may account for the low correlation between emotional distress ratings and physiological measures found in most psychosomatic studies (Weiner, this volume).

The laboratory has not formed an ideal setting for studying physiological measures that discriminate between subjectively different emotional states. For instance, viewing either a suspense or an erotic film leads to similar increase in free fatty acids and cortisol, yet the emotional states are obviously quite different (Dimsdale & Herd, 1982). One wonders whether the physiological findings might be different in the field under truly suspenseful or erotic conditions.

One advantage of examining peripheral physiological signals of acute arousal under laboratory conditions is the potential to observe interactions of personality traits with particular behavioral stressors. Experience tells us that responses to stressful stimuli vary considerably according to the individual's interpretation of the event and his underlying motivations (Dimsdale, 1982). During hurricanes with their destructive surfs, there are to be found surf riders who gratefully regard the hurricane as the font of the most glorious waves possible. Thus the stimulus—the huge wave—is the same, but the individual's perception and interpretation of the event markedly determines the degree of anxiety that he experiences. This sort of interaction of personality with a given stressful stimulus has been effectively studied in the laboratory. For instance, recent studies have found that the plasma catecholamine levels of individuals with Type A behavior are indistinguishable at rest from those with Type B behavior. However, when subjects are put in a competitively stimulating circumstance, the Type A's respond with significantly higher elevations of norepinephrine and epinephrine than do the Type B's (Williams et al., 1982).

Field studies offer an opportunity for observing physiological responses to significant life stressors. In general, field studies have been held back by the lack of technological devices, an impediment that has diminished in recent years. One can easily observe heart rhythm, heart rate, and blood pressure in the field, and even obtain ambulatory blood samples through indwelling catheters and portable blood withdrawal pumps (Dimsdale & Moss, 1980a). The disadvantages to field studies are clear; there is poor experimental control. However, the field studies find a powerful association between emotion and endocrine measures, an association that is not observed well in the laboratory (Weiner, this volume).

Examination of the plasma epinephrine levels reported in a number of recent studies reveals that the levels of epinephrine observed in response to field stressors are much higher than the levels found in response to laboratory stressors (Dimsdale, 1983). This finding is further support for the contention that the laboratory has some disadvantages to studying physiological responses to anxiety.

One of the natural field sources for anxiety is performance anxiety in subjects who are presenting formal speeches or lectures in the early days of their academic careers. Using portable blood withdrawal pumps and nonthrombogenic catheters, Dimsdale and Moss found that although both norepinephrine and epinephrine increased in the course of public speaking, the pattern for epinephrine was much more pulsatile (Dimsdale & Moss, 1980b). Epinephrine tripled or quadrupled in the initial 3 minutes of public speaking, but, as Fig. 2 shows, by the time the speaker had spoken for 15 minutes, his epinephrine level was returning to baseline (see Fig. 2).

TRACKING THE PERIPHERAL SIGNS OF ANXIETY

A number of studies have recently observed a dissociation in panic and phobic disorder patients between cortisol and adrenomedullary responses to panic (Appleby, Klein, Sacher, & Levitt, 1981; Curtis, et al., 1978). Contrary to expectations, the laboratory panic, induced either by lactate or by exposure to a dreaded phobic object, was not associated with increases in cortisol; however there were increases in plasma epinephrine levels. This is vital information; for too long we have treated stress responses as if they were a totally homogeneous, consistent entity. Psychosomatic researchers have been focusing carefully on this area for years in an effort to delineate response profiles under different circumstances (Mason, 1975). To speak in terms of "a sympathetic nervous system response" is not technically accurate, for the sympathetic nervous system and adrenomedullary system can be dissociated. The sympathetic nervous system is more responsive to circumstances of exercise and postural change, whereas the adrenomedullary system is more sensitive to anxiety and the energy needs of the organism (LeBlanc, Cote, Jobin, & Labrie, 1979).

I discussed earlier the importance of considering the interpretation of the stressful stimulus. This was recently examined in some depth in another field-based psychosomatic study, the Air Traffic Controller study. Using an ecological analysis of the density of job pressures (e.g., number of planes landing), subjective report of pressure, and cortisol samples obtained on the job, the investigators found that cortisol was unrelated to the ecological indices of job stress unless the subjective interpretation of job satisfaction was also considered (Rose, Jenkins, & Hurst, 1978). Thus, consideration of the way the subject views the stressor is vital for understanding the trail of its physiological responses.

Psychosomatic medicine has also been concerned with physiological concomitants of chronic tension. The clinical course of many illnesses has been considered a marker for chronic anxiety in the same way that epinephrine has been

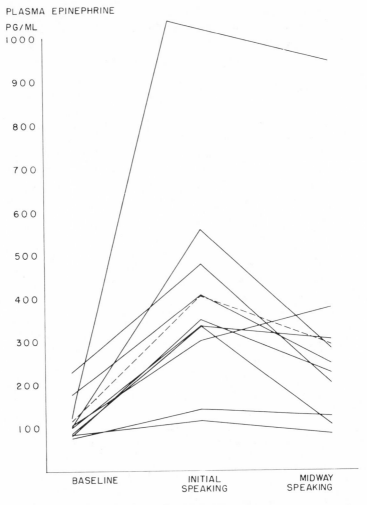

Legend: Each line represents one subject; the dotted line represents the mean response. Reprinted with permission from *Psychosomatic Medicine* 42, 496, 1980.
FIG. 2   Time course of epinephrine during public speaking.

a marker for acute anxiety. Indeed, the classical specificity theory developed by Alexander and his group suggested that there was a point-to-point correspondence between specific illnesses and chronic tension over specific conflict areas (Alexander, 1939). Although the specificity hypothesis has not been widely supported, it is clear that given chronic tension, some individuals will habitually respond to stressors with muscular, cardiorespiratory, or gastrointestinal symptoms (Weiner, this volume).

In the world according to *DSM-III*, psychosomatic disorders stand apart from other psychiatric disorders, and, if space allocated to discussion is any indicator, they are not recognized as being very important (they are the most briefly described disorder in the manual). Psychosomatic disorders are not viewed in the context of anxiety disorders but are shunted aside to "psychological factors affecting physical condition." The fact that there are such clear health consequences of this behaviorally mediated condition suggests that psychosomatic disorders merit more careful attention in the future. The most likely berth for them would be in some reconceptualized view of anxiety disorder.

CONCLUSION

The psychosomatic approach clearly delineates differences between an acute anxiety response common to all individuals, a response to chronic tension, and a response to "pathological" anxiety. In this sense we are in agreement with the *DSM-III* approach of labeling the various forms of pathological anxiety as different from a normal anxiety response. I would like to close this chapter with a brief anecdote that highlights this distinction between acute normal and pathological anxiety, and suggests the importance of studying both forms.

> Mr. Adams is a 40-year-old divorced white man whom I had been treating because of a four-month history of panic attacks. He described his attacks as of sudden onset and accompanied by fears of dying and many unpleasant somatic sensations. In addition to his panic attacks, he mentioned that all his life he had suffered from a fear of drowning. Mr. Adams lived on the sea shore and, in an unusual twist of fate, came to therapy one day recounting how a fisherman's corpse had washed ashore next to his house that morning. When I asked him how he reacted to this and how it compared with the anxiety he felt during his panic attacks, he responded "Doc, of course I was anxious about the corpse but the attacks are very different. I can't put it into words other than to say that it's an entirely different kettle of fish."

Because of its different perspective, a psychosomatic approach may be helpful in clarifying the nature of anxiety disorders. Although our end points are somewhat different from researchers whose interest is on anxiety disorders per se, our conclusions are overlapping—that careful attention to the phenomenology of the anxiety is crucial lest unrelated illnesses be lumped together.

ACKNOWLEDGMENTS

This work was supported by a Clinician Scientist Award from the American Heart Association with funds contributed in part by the Massachusetts Heart Affiliate and by grant #HL 31574 from the National Heart, Lung, and Blood Institute.

18 Stress, Panic, and the Cardiovascular System

W. Stewart Agras
Stanford University

As Weiner notes in his excellent review (this volume), "The psychobiology of fear and anxiety is as muddled as is the clinical literature." The causes of the muddle are, first, the remarkable interindividual variation in physiological responding to similar situations and, second, the lack of consistency between different response systems within individuals. These phenomena are seen not only in normal individuals, but also in those suffering from anxiety disorders.

The between-person variation is shown by recent work in our laboratory where the physiologic responding of agoraphobic individuals and age-matched non-anxious controls was measured before and after treatment in a standard laboratory situation. As might be expected, the mean heart rate of the agoraphobics was significantly higher than that of the control subjects both before and after treatment. However, there was a substantial overlap in the distributions of heart rate between the two groups: fully one third of the agoraphobics had heart rates indistinguishable from those of the control subjects.

Other workers have noted the lack of correspondence between verbal report of physiological symptoms, physiological measures, and avoidance behavior in phobic individuals (Barlow, Mavissakalian, & Schofield, 1980; Lang, 1964; Leitenberg, Agras, Butz, & Wincze, 1971; Sartory, Rachman, & Grey, 1982). This phenomenon has been termed desynchrony (Rachman & Hodgson, 1974). Such desynchrony is evident both before and after treatment, and to a different degree in different individuals.

In one study where heart rate was measured during the course of exposure therapy, not only was desynchrony observed in a number of patients, but an inverse relationship was found in some instances between heart rate and behavioral improvement (Leitenberg et al., 1971). Thus, a patient with separation anxiety was enclosed in a small room and required to press a foot level an unknown number of times to obtain release (a perfect replication of the phobic situation according to the patient). As the rate of requests for release diminished, the patient's heart rate, instead of diminishing, actually increased. Yet the patient felt that her phobia was in complete remission, and a one-year follow-up visit confirmed this observation.

A fuller understanding of the processes underlying these inter- and intra-individual variations is obviously important from both a theoretical and a clinical viewpoint. Does lack of correspondence among measures have prognostic implications? Does the continuing elevation in heart rate in a phobic situation constitute a nucleus for relapse? Or does the noncorrespondence disappear over time?

Weiner (this volume) points out that research into real life fear-provoking situations provides some leads as to the reasons for the between-person variation in physiological responding. This class of responses is evoked and modified by novel and ambiguous situations, by the adequacy of coping behavior in the face of stress, and by the role of the subject. These considerations highlight some of the problems encountered in the laboratory investigation of phobia. For phobics, experimental situations are both novel and ambiguous. When fear is evoked they will not be able to cope well, since their usual strategy is to avoid such situations. Laboratory situations of this type are, then, liable to be perceived very differently by each phobic individual. Agoraphobics asked to sit in a sound-attenuated booth for physiologic recordings react very differently. Some agoraphobics have no obvious problem, others want the door left open, and still others want someone to be in the room with them. Three different responses to the same situation, and the experiment has not even begun!

These not so subtle influences, combined with overt and covert instructions in the experimental situation, are presumably one source of the between-individual variation in physiological responding, but they could not account for the lack of correspondence between response systems within individuals. Here Lang's (this volume) suggestions are cogent. He proposes that the psychophysiology of emotion is represented in associative memory as an action tendency, and that the degree of associative coherence determines the correspondence between response systems. Research suggests that the simple phobic has a tight "linkage" between arousing responses and affect networks, whereas the agoraphobic does not. The extreme case of associative fluidity of affective response structures is the generalized anxiety disorder, in which many environmental, visceral, motor, and cognitive cues may provoke anxiety. Such a situation is very different from that of the snake phobic, where a more limited set of cues provokes the action tendency. Lang also suggests that response to treatment varies along the same continuum, with the simple phobic showing the best response, and generalized anxiety disorder the worst.

PHOBIA AND THE CARDIOVASCULAR SYSTEM

As noted earlier, the majority of evidence suggests that the agoraphobic shows increased cardiovascular response to stressful situations as compared with simple phobics or normal controls (Lader & Wing, 1966). This increased responding is reminiscent of the Type A individual who also shows greater cardiovascular response to stressors of various types than does the Type B individual (Dembroski, MacDougall, & Shields, 1977). Moreover, Type A behavioral characteristics appear to be a risk factor for coronary heart disease (Rosenman et al., 1964), perhaps due to excessive adrenergic arousal (Friedman, St. George, Byers, & Rosenman, 1960). Is there any evidence that the agoraphobia-panic disorders constitute a risk factor for coronary heart disease?

Unfortunately, much less attention has been paid to agoraphobia as a risk factor for cardiovascular disease than to Type A behavior. Psychiatric disease in general appears to be associated with higher death rates; however, the reasons for the excess mortality vary according to the disorder, and some disorders, for example hysteria, do not appear to be associated with excess mortality (Coryell, 1981). In one study, 113 former inpatients with agoraphobia-panic disorder were located some 35 years after admission, and their mortality rates were compared with the expected death rates for persons in their location (Coryell, Noyes, & Clancy, 1982). A significantly higher rate of cardiovascular death was found for the panic disorder patients than for the general population, but no differences were observed in death rates due to cancer. Interestingly, the death rates due to suicide were also elevated for the panic disorder patients. Although this study was relatively small scale and not prospective in its design, the findings provide preliminary evidence that the cardiovascular arousal associated with the agoraphobia-panic disorder may be a risk factor for cardiovascular disease.

A further possible linkage between cardiovascular disease and panic disorder is the apparently higher incidence of mitral valve prolapse in panic disorder patients than in the general population. While methodologic problems plague this area, both in the accurate diagnosis of anxiety disorder and of mitral valve prolapse, if the existing studies are pooled then 43 of 106 panic disorder patients have mitral valve prolapse (40%) as compared with 4 of 43 nonanxious controls (9.3%), a significant difference ($p < .001$) using a chi-square comparison (Gorman, Fyer, & Glicklich, 1981; Grunhaus, Golgen, & Rein, 1982; Kantor, Zitrin, & Zeldis, 1980; Venkatesh, Pauls, & Crowe, 1980). It should be noted, however, that most of the existing studies, perhaps because of their small sample sizes, do not show significant differences between the groups.

If real, what could these mitral valve prolapse and cardiovascular death differences mean? One possibility is that there is a genetic linkage between mitral valve prolapse and the agoraphobia-panic disorders. A second possibility is that continued adrenergic arousal may lead to the valvular defect. Third, since procedures that increase anxiety seem to increase both the signs of, and the likelihood of, diagnosing mitral valve prolapse, the association may simply be an artifact of a highly anxious state, with phobic patients responding with more anxiety than normals to cardiovascular examination. Since an examination of the heart is stressful to most individuals, and more stressful to the agoraphobic-panic patients because of their hypochondriacal preoccupations, this provides another example of the problem of between-individual variation in physiological responding to a stressor. Nonetheless, complications from mitral valve prolapse such as progressive mitral regurgitation and cardiac failure, infective endocarditis, and stroke are relatively rare, and thus could not entirely explain the excess cardiovascular mortality observed by Coryell et al. (1982).

WHAT KIND OF ANXIETY IS THE BASIS FOR AGORAPHOBIA-PANIC?

Given that anxiety characterizes the agoraphobia-panic syndrome, some speculation concerning the specific type of response tendency characterizing agoraphobia may be in order. One recurrent theme in recent research is the relationship between depression and the agoraphobia-panic syndrome. The family studies reported by Weissman (this volume) suggest that depression and panic disorder may share a common underlying diathesis. Clinical observation also reveals many depressive symptoms in the agoraphobic-panic disorders (Roth, Gurney, Garside, & Kerr, 1972). This connection between depression and panic disorder is further strengthened by the possible linkage between separation anxiety in childhood and agoraphobia-panic, as illustrated in papers by Gittelman (this volume) and by Klein, Rabkin, & Gorman (this volume). The phenomenology of separation anxiety, like homesickness, includes both sadness, as manifested by crying, and anxiety (Eisenberg, 1958).

Affective states can be conceived of, either in terms of a general arousal continuum, or as a specific action tendency. Could it be that in the agoraphobia-panic disorders we are dealing with a specific action tendency that is characterized by both depression and anxiety, and persisting from childhood? If so, then this affective state might best be regarded as separation anxiety. The question then becomes, what is the action of both imipramine and exposure therapy in the treatment of these disorders, since both apparently lead to reductions in panic, phobic, and depressive symptomatology (Foa & Kozak, this volume; Klein et al., this volume)?

Klein et al. (this volume) make an interesting case for an effect of imipramine in blocking the signs of separation anxiety in mammals, perhaps similar to the effect of imipramine in the school phobic child. Klein's (1981) description of the help-seeking behavior of inpatients following a panic attack could be regarded as an aspect of separation anxiety. "Patients ran to the nursing station . . . the nurses would hold the patient's hands, reassure them, and sit with them for about 20 minutes. The patients would finally walk away, their acute overwhelming stress somewhat alleviated" (p. 238). Surely this could be construed as dealing with separation anxiety by seeking the presence of a comforting "safe" person. Could panic be simply an aspect of a broader class of behavior, namely separation anxiety? Certainly, many agoraphobic-panic disorders are precipitated by separation experiences (Thorpe & Burns, 1983), and in my own experience at least, some panic attacks are not at all spontaneous, but are precipitated by separation threats. Thus, in one patient undergoing continuous physiological monitoring on an outpatient basis, a panic attack exhibited by both rapid and sustained elevation of heart rate in the absence of increased activity, as well as by self-report, was triggered by a telephone call. During the call the patient was told that a close relative had suddenly died. This was an event particularly threatening to the patient, since she had developed her first panic attack at the same age, and in similar circumstances to the heart attack that killed her father. The steep cardiac acceleration began during the phone call, yet the patient simply reported a "spontaneous" panic attack.

Given the possible central importance of separation anxiety in the agoraphobia-panic disorders, it is curious that no attempt has been made to measure such anxiety. Measurements are usually restricted to anticipatory anxiety and panic on the one hand, and to phobic avoidance on the other. Recently, Rachman (in press) has focused upon the other side of separation anxiety, namely factors such as the presence of a trusted person or a talisman which function to reduce anxiety. He has also suggested the possibility of measuring the effects of such safety signals in reducing anxiety, a measure that may better tap the dimensions of separation anxiety than existing instruments. Here is an area of assessment beyond the traditional measures of anxiety (Finney, this volume) that is in urgent need of development.

A recently concluded study in our laboratory supports the notion that reduction of panic may not be central to the mechanism of action of imipramine. In this study (Telch, Agras, Taylor, Roth, & Gallen, in preparation), 37 agoraphobic individuals with panic were randomly allocated to three groups: imipramine with instructions not to expose themselves to their feared situation; imipramine plus in vivo exposure; and placebo plus in vivo exposure. The aim of this study was to remove the confound existing in previous reports between the effects of imipramine and of exposure. After 8 weeks of treatment there were no significant differences in the number of panic attacks between the groups. However, the group receiving both exposure and imipramine showed a significant reduction in the number of panic attacks from pretreatment to posttreatment. The same trend was more obvious at 6 months follow-up. Clearly, the combination treatment was the most effective across all the measures, but the failure of imipramine to reduce panic in the absence of exposure suggests that the drug does not specifically block panic.

Several alternative theories have been advanced to explain the mechanism of action of imipramine. These include the possibility that imipramine exerts its beneficial effect by means of its antidepressant effect, although no conclusive evidence exists to support this position (Marks et al., 1983). Another possibility is that imipramine works not by reducing depression per se, but by enhancing the work of exposure by reducing dysphoria, i.e., an interaction between the beneficial effects of imipramine and exposure. Another possibility, in line with the arguments put forward here, is that the effect of imipramine is primarily to reduce separation anxiety, making it easier for phobics to forgo safety signals and hence to expose themselves to the feared situation.

To sum up then, these considerations suggest that the agoraphobia-panic disorders may be characterized by a specific affective state based upon a developmental disorder in which excessive separation anxiety is experienced in childhood. It is possible that imipramine specifically blocks separation anxiety, which in turn may be the central core of the agoraphobia-panic syndrome rather than panic.

If this is so, then we must begin to wonder what factors predispose an individual to develop this syndrome in adult life. One possibility is that such individuals are biologically programmed to form too close a relationship with significant others, hence separation promotes more than the usual anxiety. Other possibilities include social learning experiences leading to exaggerated separation anxiety, or specific traumatic incidents that later promote excessive separation anxiety. For the moment, of course, these possibilities must remain as speculations. Nonetheless, such speculations may serve as pointers to neglected areas in the psychopathological investigation of these all too prevalent disorders.

19

Children's Reactions to Medical Stressors: An Ecological Approach to the Study of Anxiety

Barbara G. Melamed
University of Florida

Lawrence J. Siegel
University of Texas Medical Branch

INTRODUCTION

This chapter advances the position that the study of how children cope with medical stress can be of considerable value in understanding the ontology of fear and anxiety. Almost all children are exposed to medical and dental procedures. These experiences, including hospitalization for surgery, outpatient diagnostic procedures, and restorative dental treatment, are often highly stressful. The pain and discomfort that occur when the child is exposed to noxious stimuli in an unfamiliar environment prompt avoidance, loss of control, and heightened arousal. Furthermore, these reactions are enhanced if separation or inadequate support from parents occurs. Such events may predispose an individual to the formation of maladaptive anxiety responses. In some children, these responses are of sufficient duration and intensity to interfere with their future adjustment to the medical and dental situation. In addition, these maladaptive anxiety responses may generalize to other settings and people. Some research suggests that over one third of all hospitalized children have long-term behavioral adjustment problems related to brief hospital experience (Vernon, Foley, & Schulman, 1967).

This paper argues for the importance of investigating specific anxiety responses to stressful medical and dental settings irrespective of the co-occurrence of these responses with other constellations of symptoms as specified in the *Diagnostic and Statistical Manual of Mental Disorders* (*DSM-III*) (1980). Many of these anxiety responses are sufficiently problematic to warrant intervention whether or not they are associated with multiple symptomatic behaviors. Of at least equal

369

value is the potential relevance of this domain of study for the understanding of aversive emotions in children and the assessment of theories of affective pathology.

First, these settings permit an investigation of normal anxiety in children in response to naturally occurring stressors. The nature and mechanisms underlying the manifestation of anxiety in children have received little empirical investigation. For example, there are very few data regarding the expression of anxiety responses in children across the three primary modalities of verbal, physiological, and motor components (Johnson & Melamed, 1979). Furthermore, there are few developmental data available to establish the baseline of normative stress responses of children of different sexes and ages. Therefore, it is difficult to determine what is pathological.

Second, different theoretical perspectives regarding the development of fear in children can be examined by the reaction of children in the medical situation. Psychodynamic models view anxiety as a derivative of instinct, but their definitions of instinct are very different (Michels, Frances & Shear, this volume). The specific nature of the fear may be, in part, related to so-called unconscious factors, but symptoms often emerge in the context of real trauma. Whereas the psychodynamic model emphasizes the importance of innate constitutional tendencies, the learning model places greater emphasis on environmental events that elicit or maintain the conditional emotional response. The conditioning model would view the medical situation as an unconditioned stimulus. Noxious events occur repeatedly over a brief period of time, in the absence of an escape or avoidance response. Aversive emotional responses conditioned in this context may generalize to similar stimuli or persons. The social learning approach focuses on the interaction between parents and their children, on the potential roles of the parent as a stress reducer, or in directly reinforcing fear responses, or in providing models of anxiety expression. The biological theories view the individual differences in temperament as they affect the vulnerability of children for maladaptive anxiety responses.

Finally, the vulnerability of children toward development of adult psychopathology is not necessarily predicted by behaviors that mimic adult disorders. In a recent review on developmental psychopathology, it was noted that "the strongest predictors of later pathology are not likely to be early replicas of the behavioral indicators of adult pathology. The strongest predictors likely will be adaptational failures, defined in age-appropriate terms" (Sroufe & Rutter, 1984, p. 24). The literature suggests that there are a number of factors that predispose a child to maladaptive anxiety responses during stressful experiences. Among these factors are biological and/or temperament factors, the extent to which the situation permits control over the stressor, the nature of mother-child attachments, and their previous experience with the stressor. These factors are each briefly addressed as they operate within the medical setting and are identified as components of specific theories of anxiety development.

An ecological framework, which views the child interacting in the naturalistic medical setting, can advance the integration of the theories of stressful experience within a developmental perspective. This position postulates the importance of considering cognitive abilities of children to deal with externally precipitated stressors at a given age and the nature of the mother-child attachment during the experience as predictive of adjustment.

RESPONSE TO MEDICAL STRESSORS: A PROTOTYPE FOR ANXIETY MANAGEMENT

Each year 5 million children undergo numerous medical and dental procedures. Over 45% of all children have had a hospital experience by age 7 (Davies, Butler, & Goldstein, 1972). An ecological approach to the study of childhood fears in medical and dental settings is possible because of the natural occurrence of aversive experiences. The child is confronted with experiences that allow for minimal control, unfamiliar adults, and often separation from parents. In the hospital, children are often restricted in movement, isolated from their peer group, and lack the information or ability to control their situation. Although the severity of the illness or physical dysfunction can enhance the stress with its concomitant pain, at least some portion of children's reactions can be attributed to the aversive properties of the setting itself (Traughber & Cataldo, 1982). These situations provide relatively controlled environments in which stressful stimuli that elicit anxiety-related behaviors are easily identifed. Children typically have repeated contact with medical and dental procedures; thus the opportunity to study the effects of repeated experience and long-term adaptability are present.

Those individuals facing hospitalization or outpatient medical treatment ordinarily function adequately, but may become anxious to the point where emotional equilibrium is disrupted and normal coping behaviors are rendered ineffective. Following a hospital stay, approximately 32% of all children develop severe, long-term disturbances such as soiling, bedwetting, increased dependency, aggressiveness, excessive fear, sleeping or eating disturbances. For some children, hospitalization may have a beneficial effect, since 25% were rated as improved in behavior after a hospital stay (Vernon et al., 1967). Little information exists on factors that predict coping versus maladaptive behavior among children following hospitalization.

There are several other findings that suggest that medical settings are useful for investigating the formation of maladaptive anxiety disorders. For instance, those children with early traumatic dental or medical experiences have been found to show a greater incidence of somatic disturbances and neurotic tendencies (Cuthbert & Melamed, 1982; Sermet, 1974; Shaw, 1975). Evidence based on retrospective reports in the adult dental literature indicates that dental fears may be learned in childhood (Kleinknecht, Klepac, & Alexander, 1973).

The fear of injections, choking, and the sound of drilling are the three most common fears associated with visits to dentists reported consistently by children from 4 to 14. Several studies demonstrate that children who had early negative experience with doctors or surgery later have increased dental anxiety (Martin, Shaw, & Taylor, 1977). Children may become increasingly sensitized to repeated dental or medical visits (Katz, Kellerman, & Siegel, 1981; Venham, Bengston, & Cipes, 1977).

Finally, the nature and quality of the mother-child relationship prior to a hospital experience have been related to the child's in-hospital adjustment (Brown, 1979). Studies of emotional contagion (Escalona, 1953) consistently document that anxious mothers have children who are also anxious in the face of hospitalization or medical procedures. The literature on preparation of parents and their children for hospitalization and stressful medical and dental procedures was based on the assumption that reducing maternal anxiety would reduce their children's stress (Melamed & Bush, in press). However, the mechanism of change was never well specified. Interventions consisted of general psychological packages of coping skills such as relaxation or cognitive distractions. The data on mothers' absence or presence as it influences children's maladaptive behavior in face of invasive medical procedures have been much less consistent. Few studies actually observed what the mothers or fathers did in facilitating their children's coping, even though lip service has been given to the importance of assessing the quality of the parenting. In fact, two recent studies suggested that parent presence in the doctor's treatment room during the venipuncture procedure led to more intense and longer lasting crying in children than when the parent was not present, particularly with those children under the age of five (Gross, Stern, Levin, Dale, & Wojnilower, 1983; Shaw & Routh, 1982). Although the younger children exhibited more aggression, resistance, and crying whether the mothers were present or absent, older children with mothers present also cried immediately prior to the initiation of the blood test. This behavior has been interpreted as a form of protest, since the children believe that the parent will emit comforting responses at the signal of distress. Identifying those interactive patterns that enhance emotional distress during outpatient treatment or hospitalization may pinpoint those families with members who are at high risk for the development of emotional patterns indicative of anxiety disorders or somatoform disorders.

DEFINITION OF MALADAPTIVE ANXIETY RESPONSES

Expressions of fear are most often normal adaptive responses to distressing or threatening events. Whether the anxiety-related behaviors are considered maladaptive depends on a number of factors including the duration and severity of the problem and the degree to which it is disruptive to the child's life (Barrios, Hartmann, & Shigetomi, 1981; Morris & Kratochwill, 1983; Richards & Siegel, 1978). Incidence rates of phobias in the child population are dramatically lower than are incidence rates of normal fears. Reports consistently indicate that 0.5% to 2% of children have specific clinical fears (Agras, Sylvester, & Oliveau, 1969;

Kennedy, 1965; Miller, Barrett, & Hampe, 1974; Rutter, Tizard, & Whitmore, 1970). Therefore, the evaluation of normal children's varied reactions during an intense stress, such as hospitalization, can be useful in understanding adaptive functioning and providing age-appropriate norms by which the children who fail to cope and show long-term behavioral disturbances can be identified. Prospective longitudinal research may identify continuities in maladaptive functioning in face of other stressors.

Although fears are a common problem of normal childhood, they are often quite transient and tend to dissipate with age (McFarlane, Allen, & Honzik, 1954). Miller et al. (1974) provided a useful set of criteria for judging the dysfunctional nature of the anxiety response. They suggested that anxiety states warrant treatment when they (1) are out of proportion to the demands of the situation, (2) cannot be explained or reasoned away, (3) are beyond voluntary control, (4) lead to avoidance of the feared situation, (5) persist over an extended period of time, (6) are maladaptive, and (7) are not age or stage specific. Richards and Siegel (1978) have noted that the diagnosis of any Anxiety Disorder rests on points similar to the Miller et al. (1974) criteria for defining a phobia. Use of the label "behavior disorder," then, requires more than documentation of the fear-related behavior. It requires a judgment that the behavior exceeds certain limits of severity and disruptiveness characteristic of normal fears. Knowledge regarding age-appropriate reactions to specific stressful experiences would provide a normative baseline against which to judge the maladaptive behavior. Developmental theory must, therefore, guide the assessment process as specified in the seventh of Miller et al.'s (1974) criteria for a phobia: "Is not age or stage specific" (p. 90). Cognitive and emotional development are reciprocal processes and so the content and incidence of children's fears vary at differing stages of development. Fear results from understanding the significance of stimuli; consequently, the types of fear-eliciting stimuli change from infancy through adolescence.

Factor analytic studies have identified content categories of children's fears, based on parent ratings of children's fear. Miller, Barrett, Hampe, and Noble (1972) identified three factors in a factor analytic study using the Louisville Fear Survey Schedule: (1) fears of physical injury or personal loss (e.g., having an operation, being kidnapped, parental divorce); (2) fears of natural and supernatural dangers (e.g., fear of the dark, storms, monsters, and ghosts); and (3) fears reflecting "psychic stress" related most often to interpersonal relationships (e.g., school attendance, fears of making mistakes). Miller (1983) cites a more recent factor analysis of the same instrument by Staley and O'Donnell, who found five similar factors for ages 6 to 16. These were fears of (1) physical injury, (2) animals, (3) school, (4) night, and (5) public places.

The range of fear-eliciting stimuli broadens with increasing age (Morris & Kratochwill, 1983). Infants show fear reactions to excessive or unexpected sensory stimuli and strangers; separation anxiety is evident around the first year (Miller, 1983). Preschoolers' fears tend to focus on animals, the dark, and imaginary creatures (Bauer, 1976; Jersild & Homes, 1935; Miller, 1983). Coinciding with both school entrance and the development of concrete operational thought, school and social fears, and fears of injury predominate (Lapouse & Monk, 1959; Miller, 1983), whereas fears of animals, the dark, and imaginary creatures decline (Jersild & Holmes, 1935; Lapouse & Monk, 1959; Morris & Kratochwill, 1983). Social fears become more complex during adolescence, including anxieties concerning social alienation and the macabre (Miller, 1983).

In distinguishing between a normal and a clinical fear in children, the developmental appropriateness of the fear content needs to be assessed. Treatment for age-appropriate fears is most often not indicated, as developmental data suggest the fear may spontaneously decrease with age. However, a single symptomatic behavior reflecting anxiety response to a stressful experience such as a medical procedure may be an appropriate focus of treatment because it is maladaptive based on the criteria noted earlier. A symptom may be dysfunctional whether or not it appears as part of a syndrome or constellation of symptoms which might meet the criteria for the diagnosis of Anxiety Disorder as specified in *DSM-III*. For example, among the *DSM-III* guidelines for the diagnosis of a Separation Anxiety Disorder are the presence of three of nine possible symptoms. One of these symptoms, "a persistent reluctance or refusal to go to sleep without being next to a major attachment figure or to go to sleep away from home" (p. 53), is a problem that may be manifested by children who are hospitalized for medical treatment. This symptom may sufficiently interfere with their adaptive functioning within this setting and warrant intervention irrespective of its association with other problems exhibited by the child.

The two critical reviews of the literature on children's fears (Harris & Ferrari, 1983; Winer, 1982) have revealed a tremendous gap in the understanding of the development of fears in children. Although there are many treatments available (Morris & Kratochwill, 1983), there is no research that evaluates the effective therapeutic ingredients or that takes the children's level of development into account. Melamed, Robbins, and Graves (1982) critically reviewed the treatment studies and pinpointed the need to take into account developmental factors including age, cognitive style, previous experience, as well as the quality of parenting, prior to selecting a therapeutic strategy for preparation.

LEARNING THEORY APPROACHES TO FEAR DEVELOPMENT

Learning theory provides a useful framework for investigating the etiology and maintenance of anxiety and fear in children. Learning approaches lend themselves to an operationalization of the constructs posited by the theories and, thereby, permit an adequate empirical test of the constructs.

A conceptualization of anxiety disorders that emphasizes learning has at least four separate sources that are of theoretical value. Therefore, there is no single theoretical statement regarding the development of anxiety disorders. The strength of the learning conceptualization lies, perhaps, in the successful intervention it offers, rather than in etiological explanations of the phenomenon. The success of these interventions derives from careful analysis of the current influences that maintain behavior.

Trauma is one obvious causal variable in the development of children's excessive fears. A respondent-conditioning paradigm explains the fear as a conditioned response elicited by a conditioned stimulus, a neutral stimulus that was present when the original trauma involving fear (an unconditioned response to an unconditioned stimulus) occurred. For example, a child undergoing treatment for cancer is typically exposed to a number of painful and frightening medical procedures. After several experiences with these procedures, the child may develop an anxiety response (i.e., vomiting) to the hospital setting and medical personnel that have become associated with stressful procedures. A precipitating traumatic event cannot, however, be identified in many clinical cases of children's fear (Solyom, Beck, Solyom, & Hugel, 1974). Seligman and Johnston (1973) have noted that avoidance behavior is not always mediated by fear. Classical conditioning alone, therefore, cannot account for children's fears.

Operant conditioning may often be a causal process in the acquisition of fearful behavior and is usually a critical component of its maintenance. Fearful behavior is developed and/or supported by reinforcing environmental consequences. The child may be rewarded for exhibiting fearful behavior, for example, by receiving solicitous attention from others. Avoidance behaviors, such as throwing a tantrum when the doctor enters the room, may be reinforced by postponing or avoiding the procedure.

Modeling may be a process involved in the acquisition of children's fears. A fear may be vicariously conditioned by observing a model undergo a fearful experience, or by observing a model reinforced for fearful behavior (Bandura & Rosenthal, 1966). Parental fearful behavior and anxiety appear to be an especially potent factor in the acquisition and maintenance of children's fears (e.g., Bandura & Menlove, 1968; Bush, 1982; Shaw, 1975; Solyom et al., 1974). Thus, through observing a parent respond in a fearful manner to specific events or objects, a child may develop similar avoidance behaviors.

Respondent or operant conditioning, either directly or by modeling, thus represents learning conceptualizations of children's anxiety reactions. In addition, influential explanations of children's fears have been offered by Mowrer (two-factor learning theory, 1960) and Wolpe (1958) which explain the fear acquisition via classical conditioning, and the subsequent maintenance of the avoidance response by instrumental or operant conditioning. Although intuitively satisfying, empirical data have not supported this position. In addition to the criticisms of the classical conditioning explanation which were previously noted, one problem with the two-factor theory is the resistance of avoidance responses to extinction (Marks, 1969).

It is most likely that etiology differs across cases of children's fearful and anxious behavior. Classical or operant processes, modeled or direct, may be contributors to varying degrees and in varying combinations among children in the acquisition of the behavior. Certainly, learning processes help to sustain fearful behavior and are useful in its modification.

Predisposing Influences

Hereditary factors may possibly predispose some children to the development of an anxiety disorder. As noted by Johnson and Melamed (1979), individual differences in arousal and habituation to stimulation may be related to children's acquisiton of fears. Individual differences in temperament have been demonstrated in infancy (e.g., Thomas, Chess, Birch, Hertzig, & Korn, 1963), and infants' ability to regulate their physiological states is considered an important index of their adaptability and developmental status. Thus, from birth, children vary in their reactivity and ability to adjust to environmental stimulation. In addition, some researchers have reported that psychiatric problems are more common in the families of patients with anxiety disorders (Solyom et al., 1974).

Certain stimuli appear more likely to elicit fear in humans than others (for example, fear of animals are more common than fear of objects), suggesting a genetic basis for increased reactivity to some stimuli. As previously discussed, the content of children's fears changes over the developmental course, suggesting that sensitivity to stimuli varies developmentally as well.

Rachman and Hodgson (1974) have postulated that fears can be innate and maturational, such as fear of the dark, sudden noises, and the presence of strangers. Similarly, Seligman (1971) has proposed an evolutionary approach which focuses on human fears and phobias as a form of "prepared classical conditioning." He believes that there is a selective process in the development of fear-related behaviors that have an evolutionary basis. Fears or phobias may be conceptualized along a dimension of preparedness. On the one extreme of the preparedness dimension are fear responses that occur instinctively, followed by responses that occur after only a few pairings. Next are responses that occur after many pairings (unprepared responses). Responses on the other extreme of the continuum are what Seligman (1971) refers to as contraprepared (i.e., responses that occur only after a large number of pairings). Although there is some support for this model of fear-related behaviors in adults (Hugdahl, Fredrikson, & Ohman, 1977; McNally & Reiss, 1983; Ohman, Eriksson, & Olofsson, 1975), there has been no research conducted on the preparedness of children's fears or phobias.

The following two sections illustrate how the medical situation is a useful environment in which to evaluate the manifestation of children's anxiety and fears and the processing by which these responses are acquired and maintained.

THE STUDY OF MATERNAL-CHILD ATTACHMENT IN THE MEDICAL SETTING

The medical situation is an ideal environment to study maternal-child attachment. Separation from parents is frequently cited as a source of stress for hospitalized children (Nasera, 1978). The dental or medical situation often evokes anxiety because of separation from mothers during aversive procedures. Even when the parents are present, aversive procedures are often carried out by unfamiliar adults. This situation may be analagous to anxiety elicited by stranger approach. Some important implications from the maternal deprivation studies following Bowlby (1973) and Spitz (1950), and Bretherton and Ainsworth's (1974) stranger approach situations, relate to the degree of bonding of the parent and child (Michels et al., this volume).

Growing out of the psychoanalytic position, Bowlby (1973) recognizes the existence of constitutional factors in susceptibility to fear and includes both cognitive considerations and evolutionary notions in his theories. However, the most distinctive feature of his views resides in his arguments that a person's tendency to respond with fear is determined in large part by the perceived availability of attachment figures. In this way, most fears are considered as derivatives of separation anxiety, with the persistence of fear mainly due to the individual having developed anxious insecure attachments in early childhood as a result of disturbed family interaction.

The work of Ainsworth (1982) and Sroufe (1979) has done much to emphasize the importance of variations in the quality of attachments—with particular emphasis on the differences between secure and insecure attachments, as judged by responses during the strange situation procedures. Securely attached infants explore their environment freely when with their mothers, but following a brief separation they tend to seek closeness and comfort. Anxiously attached infants appear less secure in their mothers' presence and are acutely distressed during brief separations, but they are angry, as well as seeking closeness, on reunion. Avoidant infants, in contrast, appear undisturbed during separations, but avoid their mothers on reunion. The insecurity of their attachment is inferred from the infant's aggressive behavior toward the mother in other situations. The secure attachments constitute an adaptive norm, with insecure attachments likely to lead to maladaptive outcomes. The quality of the dyadic relationship has been shown to be an important predictor of the infant's later social development (Lewis, Feiring, McGuffey, & Jaskir, 1984; Sroufe, Fox, & Pancake, 1983); it is not regarded as something within the child or part of the child's makeup. The nature of the parenting in strange situations, such as medical visits where noxious events co-occur, may provide a prototype for the development of fear.

Few investigators have applied this notion to children above 3 years of age (Rutter, 1981). In dealing with medical emergencies, where the threat of illness exists, many mothers respond by overprotecting their children. This is seen in their encouraging dependent behavior by consistently assisting the child or displaying excessive concern when the child becomes upset or stressed. Longitudinal studies suggest that maternal overprotectiveness may be related to excessive dependency in older children (Kagan & Moss, 1962; Levy, 1943). Martin (1975) has explained the mechanism by which overly protective mothers foster the development of dependent behaviors in their children as follows:

> Separate tendencies on the part of the child may be experienced as aversive by the mother, and her attempts to restore the closeness may be reinforced by the reduction of (her) distress. The child, at the same time, may also experience forced separation as aversive, and returning to the mother may be reinforced by the reduction of his distress . . . When (this) system becomes especially strong and the negative affect associated with separation behavior becomes intense, . . . phenomena such as school phobia may appear. (p. 487)

Lewis and Michalson (1981) studied very young children from 3 months to 3 years who were rated on five affective states: fear, anger, happiness, competence, and attachment/dependency. The children were observed across a wide range of situations including competence in meeting the task demands of a day-care program. Fearful behavior was found to be positively related to attachment/dependence and negatively to competence.

Kagan and Moss (1962) investigated the long-term effects of maternal overprotectiveness in 54 adults who had been observed in the home, school, and summer camp between the ages of 3 and 10 years. As children, the subjects were observed in terms of behavioral dimensions such as passivity, seeking nurturance, and seeking reassurance. In addition, the mothers were observed interacting with their children and were interviewed regarding their attitudes toward their children and child rearing. As adults, the subjects were interviewed regarding their dependent behaviors such as seeking support and nurturance from significant others. Kagan and Moss (1962) found that girls who had been highly protective as children tended to withdraw from stressful or challenging situations as adults. For boys, maternal protectiveness was positively related with the boys' passivity and dependence throughout childhood. Maccoby and Masters (1970) have written about the means by which parental restrictiveness is associated with a child's emotional dependency: "restrictiveness will prevent the child from acquiring autonomous skills for coping with his needs, and will therefore be associated with continued high dependency on parents and other adults" (p. 143).

Research has been undertaken in our laboratory to identify dysfunctional patterns of interaction between mothers and their children during medical stressors by developing a Dyadic Prestressor Interaction Scale (DPIS), guided by theoretical positions involving emotional contagion (Escalona, 1953; Vanderveer, 1949), crisis parenting (Kaplan, Smith, Grobstein, & Fischman, 1973;

Melamed & Bush, in press), and work on attachment behavior and stranger approach (Bretherton & Ainsworth, 1974).

The emotional contagion hypothesis states that parental anxiety is communicated to the child by nonverbal as well as verbal means and that this, in turn, increases the child's anxiety level. The hypothesis is nonspecific as to exactly how or why the parental anxiety elicits child anxiety. It does have empirical support in studies correlating parental and child state anxiety in medical situations (Bailey, Talbot, & Taylor, 1973; Sides, 1977).

The crisis parenting model is more specific and emphasizes the increased importance of parenting when children face stressors. Vernon et al. (1967) found that maternal presence had a calming effect on children's (2 to 6 years old) distress during anesthesia induction but made little difference during a nonstressful procedure such as admission to the hospital. High parental anxiety at such times is thought to lead to impaired parental functioning (Duffy, 1972; Skipper, Leonard, & Rhymes, 1968) and consequently to less adequate support for the child's coping efforts. Supportive of this hypothesis, Robinson (1968) found that more fearful mothers of hospitalized children were likely to spend less time visiting, less frequently entered into conversations with the child's surgeon, and were less likely to complain or criticize aspects of their children's hospitalizations.

There are many correlational studies demonstrating that parental anxiety has a negative effect on children's adjustment to medical/dental procedures (Becker, 1972). However, this relationship is stronger in preschoolers than in older children. Many of these correlations were found for a first dental visit, but not during repeated visits (Koenigsberg & Johnson, 1972). The relationship between Children's Manifest Anxiety Scale scores correlated positively with mothers' Taylor Manifest Anxiety Scale scores for 9- to 10-year-olds, but not for 11- to 12-year-olds (Bailey et al., 1973).

The mother-child relationship prior to hospitalization was also important to consider. Brown (1979) found that children 3 to 6 years of age, who had closer relationships with their mothers, were likely to show more distress and withdrawal during a short hospital stay than were those with poorer quality relationships. Mothers who were themselves anxious and highly accepting of the hospital authorities tended to have children who were distressed and withdrawn.

The crisis parenting hypothesis takes a closer look at the specific parenting strategies in effect during the crisis. Parental anxiety at such times may have a disorganizing influence on effective parenting behaviors. In our research program, we have undertaken an ecological approach to defining dyadic interactions.

The DPIS presented as Table 1 was devised out of the theoretical work on children in a stranger approach situation in order to operationalize the interactions (Melamed & Bush, in press). Categories of children's behavior in this situation were elaborated from the four categories used: Distress, Attachment, Exploration,

TABLE 1

Dyadic Prestressor Interaction Scale: Functional Definitions

CHILD BEHAVIOR CATEGORIES

Attachment

Look at Parent: Child looking at parent

Approach Parent: Child motorically approaching parent

Touch Parent: Child physically touching parent

Verbal Concern: Child verbalizing concern with the parent's continuing presence throughout the procedures

Distress

Crying: Child's eyes watering and/or (s)he is making crying sounds

Diffuse Motor: Child running around, pacing, flailing arms, kicking, arching, engaging in repetitive fine motor activity, etc.

Verbal Unease: Child verbalizing fear, distress, anger, anxiety, etc.

Withdrawal: Child silent and immobile, no eye contact with parent, in curled-up position

Exploration

Motoric Exploration: Child locomoting around room, visually examining

Physical Manipulation: Child handling objects in room

Questions Parent: Child asking parent a question related to doctors, hospitals, etc.

Interaction with Observer: Child attempting to engage in verbal or other interaction with observer

Social-Affiliative

Looking at Book: Child is quietly reading a book or magazine unrelated to medicine or looking at its pictures

Other Verbal Interaction: Child is verbally interacting with parent on topic unrelated to medicine

Other Play: Child playing with parent, not involving medical objects or topics

Solitary Play: Child playing alone with object brought into room, unrelated to medicine

PARENT BEHAVIOR CATEGORIES

Ignoring

Eyes Shut: Parent sleeping or has eyes shut

Reads to Self: Parent reading quietly

Sitting Quietly: Parent sitting quietly, not making eye contact with child

Other Noninteractive: Parent engaging in other medically-unrelated solitary activity

Reassurance

Verbal Reassurance: Parent telling child not to worry, that (s)he can tolerate the procedures, that it will not be so bad, etc.

Verbal Empathy: Parent telling child (s)he understands his/her feelings, thoughts, situation; questions child for feelings

Verbal Praise: Parent telling child (s)he is mature, strong, brave, capable, doing fine, etc.

Physical Stroking: Parent petting, stroking, rubbing, hugging, kissing child

Distraction

Nonrelated Conversation: Parent engaging in conversation with child on unrelated topic

Nonrelated Play: Parent engaging in play interaction with child unrelated to medicine

Visual Redirection: Parent attempting to attract child's attention away from medically related object(s) in the room

Verbal Exhortation: Parent telling child not to think about or pay attention to medically related concerns or objects

TABLE 1 (continued)

Restraint
   Physical Pulling: Parent physically pulling child away from an object in the room
   Verbal Order: Parent verbally ordering child to change his/her current activity
   Reprimand, Glare, Swat: Parent verbally chastising, glaring at, and/or physically striking child
   Physically Holds: Parent physically holding child in place, despite resistance
Agitation
   Gross Motor: Parent pacing, flailing arms, pounding fists, stomping feet, etc.
   Fine Motor: Parent drumming fingers, tapping foot, chewing fingers, etc.
   Verbal Anger: Parent verbally expressing anger, dismay, fear, unease, etc.
   Crying: Parent's eyes watering, verbal whimpering, sobbing, wailing
Informing
   Answers Questions: Parent attempting to answer child's medically relevant/situationally relevant questions
   Joint Exploration: Parent joining with child in exploring the room
   Gives Information: Parent attempting to impart information, unsolicited by child, relevant to medicine/the current situation, to the child
   Prescribes Behavior: Parent attempting to describe to the child appropriate behaviors for the examination session

---

and Social-Affiliative behaviors. Functional definitions were derived that would be suitable across a wide range of ages—4 to 12 years. Another six categories of parenting behaviors were derived from the parenting literature with a specific focus on the surgery preparation literature: Agitation, Ignoring, Reassurance, Information Provision, Distraction, and Restraint. All the categories except Restraint met acceptable reliability. In order to investigate combinations of parenting behavior and their relationship to the children's distress and attachment, canonical correlations were undertaken. It was found that observations about the mother's behavior accounted for 49% of the observed child categories. Knowledge about the children's behaviors accounted for 36% of the variance of the parenting behaviors. All four canonicals were significant beyond the .05 level. Age, sex, type, and severity of the diagnosis did not correlate with the categories on this Dyadic Prestressor Interaction Scale.

The investigation of the mother-child interaction patterns revealed that the same strategies of information provision or distraction used by the mothers could lead to different patterns of children's behaviors depending upon other indices of maternal affect, i.e., agitation, reassurance, and ignoring. Mothers who were calm and interactive with their children, providing them with information about what to expect, were more likely to have less distressed children than mothers employing the same strategies, who were seen to be agitated or to ignore their children. Mothers who had reported higher state anxiety on the Spielberger State Trait Anxiety Inventory Test were more likely to ignore their children ($r = .35$, $p < .01$). Ignoring the child had a more detrimental effect on 4- to 6-year-old children than on 7- to 10-year-olds.

The effects of maternal reassurance also depend upon whether or not the mother is using any other parenting strategies to help her child cope with the medical visit. When reassurance is used in the absence of other strategies, children exhibit a high degree of all behaviors, including distress, attachment, exploring, and social-affiliative behaviors. Again, younger children were more likely to exhibit attachment behavior in this condition. If, on the other hand, mothers of these young children provided them with information and were not overly reassuring, their youngsters showed more interest in exploring the examination room.

Thus, in terms of the emotional contagion theory (Escalona, 1953), it was found that agitated mothers were likely to have distressed children who were showing inhibition of attachment behaviors. These findings are similar to those reported by Bretherton and Ainsworth (1974) with younger children in the stranger approach situation. The results, furthermore, are consistent with crisis parenting, in that the behaviors of mothers who are agitated tended to be dysfunctional in the time of stress. Agitated mothers provided their children with less information relevant to the medical situation and tended to ignore them more. Mothers who used informing without agitation had children who explored the medical environment.

It is interesting that the ratings of mothers' anxiety by physicians also tended to influence how much information mothers received. Anxious mothers were given more information and were rated as less helpful in achieving their children's cooperation with medical procedures. Based on the preliminary findings from this study, a sequential analysis of the patterns of mother-child interactions will be used to help pinpoint the direction of influence in addressing the children's ability to cope with medical examinations.

INTERACTION BETWEEN TEMPERAMENT, COPING STYLES, AND ENVIRONMENTAL DEMANDS

Another factor that may mediate the child's response to the hospitalization is individual temperamental traits or behavioral styles. Temperament is defined as the child's behavioral style or emotional reactivity as he or she interacts with the environment (Willis, Swanson, & Walker, 1983). There is some evidence that these temperamental characteristics are innate and identifiable at the time of birth (Thomas & Chess, 1977).

The longitudinal research by Thomas, Chess, and Birch (1968) has demonstrated that a child's temperament is an important variable that relates to later adjustment. They identified nine dimensions of temperament including (1) level and extent of motor activity; (2) rhythmicity or degree of regularity of functions (i.e., sleep-wake cycle, hunger); (3) approach or withdrawal in response to new

stimuli; (4) adaptability to new or altered situations; (5) threshold or responsiveness to stimulation; (6) intensity of reactions; (7) quality of mood; (8) distractibility; and (9) length of attention span and persistence. Five of these
dimensions were found to cluster together to determine three general classes of
temperament. "Difficult" children are described as displaying irregularity in
biological functions, negative withdrawal responses to new stimuli, slow adaptability to change, and intense mood expressions that are generally negative.
"Easy" children, on the other hand, are characterized by regularity in biological
functions, positive approach responses to new stimuli, high adaptability to change,
and mild or moderately intense moods that are usually positive in nature. The
"slow-to-warm-up" child displays a combination of negative responses of mild
intensity to new stimuli with slow adaptability after repeated contact. Furthermore, this child shows a mild intensity of reactions, whether positive or negative,
and less tendency to exhibit irregularity of biological functions. Thomas et al.
(1968) found that 70% of the children classified as "difficult" developed a variety
of behavior problems at some later point, whereas only 18% of those children
identified as "easy" developed such problems. The individual differences in
children's adjustment to a hospital experience as prompted by temperament
factors has yet to be investigated.

The hospital environment presents the child with many experiences over which
the child has little or no control. The relationship between control over an aversive
event and the amount of anxiety that it produces is a complex but critical question
(Thompson, 1981). The research generated has not been tied to a single theoretical framework, although each perspective has some notion that a lack of
control is basic to enhancing the anxiety state. The difficulties of finding convergence in the research literature are further increased by a confounding between
the operational definitions of controllability and predictability. Although animal
research (see Mineka in this volume) allows for the most careful separation of
these factors, such key cognitive variables as perceived controllability, self-
efficacy, desirability of outcomes, and availability of coping resources clearly
demand research on humans. Unfortunately, the ethics of presenting aversive
stimulation has limited research designs to brief presentation of controlled noxious stimuli such as loud tones, ischemic pressure, cold pressor task, and electric
shock. Self-administration rather than experimenter administration of the noxious
event has been evaluated by Staub, Tursky, & Schwartz (1971). These laboratory
studies often do not take into account the process of receiving an aversive event
from the anticipatory period. The legitimacy of generalizing data from laboratory
studies to real-life situations has not been demonstrated, thus limiting their
theoretical relevance. In fact, the diversity of presenting the aversive event and
the variety of ways of measuring the anxiety reaction impede cross-study comparison. There are fewer controlled studies in which naturally occurring aversive
events such as surgery and dental work have been employed. Using children
who are experiencing these situations over repeated examinations places the

investigator in an excellent position to study the developmental changes that occur with repeated experience at different ages.

The degree to which a medical experience is perceived as controllable by the child may be a function of the child's coping or behavioral style. Research evidence suggests that individual differences exist in information-seeking preferences. Although there has been considerable research on coping styles utilized by adults in stressful situations (e.g., Auerbach, 1977; Miller, 1983; Shipley, Butt, & Horwitz, 1978), there has been limited research in this area with children.

In one of the few studies with children, Burstein and Meichenbaum (1979) found that children who tended to avoid playing with hospital-related toys one week before surgery were more anxious about hospitalization than those who chose to play with such toys. Unger (1982) found that children who tended to deny worry actually obtained less information from videotaped models prior to impending dental procedures, and they showed more behavioral disruption than those who were low on denial. This indicates that anxiety in the face of stressors may affect information processing. Knight et al. (1979) found lower cortisol production in children who wanted to know about the upcoming hospital experience and used flexible defenses of intellectualization and isolation. The children who used denial, denial with isolation, displacement, or projection regarding the upcoming hospital experience showed maladaptive stress physiology reflected in increased cortisol production rates on the day after hospital admission.

Finally, a child's previous experience can provide information about the controllability or lack of controllability in a stressful situation and may affect the child's expectations regarding his or her ability to cope with the experience. There is, in fact, some evidence that exposure to information about medical or dental treatment in children with previous experience in these settings can reinvoke anxiety responses that had previously been conditioned to situations similar to those about which the child receives preparatory information (Faust & Melamed, 1984; Melamed, Dearborn, & Hermecz, 1983; Siegel & Harkavy, in review). These conditioned emotional responses can later inferfere with the child's adaptive functioning in the medical or dental setting.

FUTURE DIRECTIONS FOR RESEARCH ON CHILDHOOD FEARS

The medical/dental prototype offers a naturalistic setting in which the principles underlying the different theoretical positions can be addressed. The data reported in this chapter suggest that one must consider transactions between the individual, with his or her biological, temperamental, and behavioral coping styles, and the particular set of stressors. The relevance of attachment figures may be important only during certain developmental phases as they may reduce or enhance the child's emotional responding.

A number of issues remain to be explored within child developmental theory that are prerequisite to the study of children's fear. What is the relationship between cognition and emotion? This review has pinpointed some research which suggests that a child's understanding and interpretation of the stressors can influence whether an emotional response, including physiological arousal and avoidance behaviors, will necessarily be prompted by a medical experience. There is little in the developmental literature regarding the preschool and older child that relates cognitive ability and emotional development, especially as fear is expressed. Lang's (this volume) bioinformational theory provides a conceptual framework for understanding the cognitive events in emotion. Viewing the problem from this perspective, Hermecz and Melamed (1984) found that reinforcement of verbal reports of physiological change and descriptions of overt behavior in dental phobic children allowed for the accessing of the fear memory. This greater emotional processing was evidenced in measured physiological change. Furthermore, this procedure enhanced the congruence between semantic and physiological components of the imagery experience with therapeutic implications as an anxiety reduction procedure with children.

How does arousal level affect children's capacity to learn to cope with stress? Level of arousal has been demonstrated to influence the amount of information a child acquires from a psychological preparation procedure in the face of an impending stressor such as medical and dental treatment. Yet few studies have consistently measured the retention of information under varying levels of arousal; an understanding of the relationship would have implications for the manner in which one would teach a child to cope with a stressful event. For example, if a child is excessively aroused while being taught to cope, the child may fail to acquire the information required to effect change in his or her fear responses. Attentional factors need to be examined within this paradigm.

What are reliable indices of children's anxiety-related responses? Although the adult literature on phobias and fear has adopted a three-systems approach, the use of multidimensional assessment is still a rarity with children. In addition, the process of adaptation across the different time phases (i.e., anticipation of a medical stressor, actual procedural impact, post-medical stressor) needs to be looked at in terms of desynchronies across response systems. Differences in patterns of these responses may help operationalize such concepts as maladaptive versus adaptive anxiety. For instance, if in the face of an impending invasive procedure the child is concordant in physiological arousal and self-reported anticipatory concerns but is low on avoidance behavior and also shows adaptation across events, these conditions might predict effective coping. On the other hand, a child showing an invariant pattern across these phases may be more vulnerable to the development of maladaptive anxiety-related behaviors.

Several research strategies that have not thus far been applied could be most useful in answering these questions. By undertaking prospective longitudinal approaches to studying children's behavior in the face of medical stress, we can evaluate predisposition for vulnerability to dysfunctional anxiety responses. The strategy taken by developmental psychopathologists as described by Sroufe & Rutter (1984) could profitably be adapted to some of these problems. For example, if normative data were collected across individuals coping with invasive medical procedures that are repeated during different phases of development, then the interaction between biological predisposition, parenting behaviors, and responses to other nonmedical stress situations can be evaluated. In addition, the subsample of children who do not develop maladaptive behaviors can also be studied to identify those factors that make them less vulnerable to stress.

ACKNOWLEDGMENTS

The first author received support to attend the National Institute of Mental Health Anxiety and Anxiety Disorders conference through National Institute of Dental Research Grant DE-05305-04. Both authors acknowledge the writing effort was supported through NIDR 5T32DE07133-02. Peter Lang and Paul Greenbaum are thanked for helpful recommendations on the organization of this chapter.

II

C. Developmental Aspects of Anxiety

20 Childhood Separation Anxiety and Adult Agoraphobia

Rachel Gittelman, Ph.D.
Donald F. Klein, M.D.
New York State Psychiatric Institute
Columbia University, College of Physicians and Surgeons

Children's distress at separation from a caretaker is a well-established developmental phenomenon. Attesting to the importance attached to separation anxiety is the fact that there is no personality theory, or theory of child development, that has not postulated a framework to account for it. Separation anxiety is typically conceptualized as one aspect of the complex behavioral repertoire that is involved in the establishment of attachment and bonding between the child and other individuals. Rajecki, Lamb, and Obsmacher (1978) have summarized most of the theories of human attachment and response to separation, including models of reinforcement, social learning, instrumental and classical conditioning, contiguity, ethology, and others.

Those who have conducted observations of infants' response to separation from the mother in humans, lower primates, and other animals, have consistently reported a great deal of variability in the intensity of the offspring's responses to separation and loss of the mother. This observation has generated concern regarding the significance of early strong reactions to normal separation experiences. However, in studies of monkeys, early behavioral characteristics have not been found to be good predictors of the intensity of reactions to separation from the mother (Reite, Short, Seiler, & Pauley, 1981). Prospective systematic developmental studies of reactions to separation from a parenting figure have not been conducted in humans. There are obvious ethical and practical impediments to longitudinal studies in humans, especially because of their very long period of immaturity. So far, factors identified as contributing to children's responses to loss of mother have been retrospective reconstructions conducted after naturalistic separations.

The relevance of children's responses to separation for later personality development and psychopathology is unknown. Most of the investigations regarding the impact of separation on children have dealt with reactions to major life-disrupting events, such as total removal of the child, or the parent, from home. In animal studies as well, experimentally induced separation of offspring and parent typically has consisted of marked alterations of the mother-child relationship. In such cases it is difficult to relate the reaction of the youngster to the parent's absence exclusively, without regard for the contribution of other factors, such as greatly modified life circumstances or social deprivation, might make to the observed behavioral changes in the child.

We are also ignorant of the nature of the relationship between normal separation anxiety and its clinical forms. We have suggested that both the timing and severity of the child's response define the presence of pathology (Gittelman-Klein & Klein, 1980). However, we do not know whether the disorder is a severe expression of the normal behavior or a distinct condition. (The issue of dimensional constructs versus categorical classifications of anxiety is well discussed in the chapter by Achenbach.)

Studies of the relationship between childhood and adult anxiety would be helpful in clarifying the significance of anxiety states in children. If such a relationship were found, it would also provide important clinical information regarding the evolution of adult anxiety disorders. The implementation of this goal is limited by the fact that the evaluation of anxiety disorders has not followed a consistent pattern, so that even when information about "anxious" children is available, it is difficult to identify the nature of the anxiety in question. Furthermore, no long-term prospective studies of the psychiatric status of children with anxiety disorders have been reported.

Several adult anxiety disorders are known to have an onset in childhood or adolescence. Such instances are simple phobias and social phobias. In such cases, the early or late clinical manifestations are not clearly distinguishable.

Only one of the childhood anxiety disorders, separation anxiety disorder, has been postulated to have a relationship to another adult anxiety syndrome, agoraphobia. In 1962, Klein (Klein & Fink, 1962) first suggested that the panic attacks commonly observed in agoraphobic patients seem to be a variant of childhood separation anxiety.

This chapter reviews the evidence bearing on a possible relationship between early separation anxiety and adult agoraphobia.

DEFINITION OF SEPARATION ANXIETY

We have described separation anxiety as taking three overlapping forms: The most obvious form consists of overt distress and misery, sometimes panic, when separation occurs. Second is the child's mental content, consisting of morbid preoccupations and worries concerning harm befalling either the child himself or, more commonly, someone he cares about. Third is homesickness, manifested by a yearning to return home. In symptomatic children, all these occur to a degree that leads to impairment, either in the children's manifest behavior or their subjective well-being.

The central concern of children with separation anxiety is easy access to the mother or home. The situations that are viewed as interfering with reaching the mother differ in type and in intensity from child to child, and the specific behavioral consequences of pathological separation anxiety vary with age.

Some clinicians judge that separation anxiety is not present unless the child refuses to be separated from the parents, and no attention is given to the child's mental content. This clinical practice is felt to be misguided, because some children will separate from home or their parents, but experience considerable anxiety while doing so. Many feel ashamed of what they perceive as childish and irrational concerns; therefore, they may avoid separation with excuses that camouflage their ego-dystonic anxious feelings. They may blame other children, their teachers, or report illness, and so on, in order to remain close to home or parents. In such children, the presence of significant separation will be missed if the definition of separation anxiety does not take into account the child's thought processes and associated affective state.

Though separation anxiety in children has been well described, as exemplified by Freud's report on Little Hans, a classical example of separation anxiety (Freud, 1950), it is only with *DSM-III* that it has become established as a clinical entity. Studies anteceding *DSM-III* did not select children with separation anxiety per se. However, a number of reports on children with school phobia have appeared and it is generally accepted that separation anxiety symptoms are salient among school phobic youngsters. In our experience, the vast majority of school phobic children (about 80%), regardless of age, have clinically significant levels of separation anxiety (Gittelman-Klein & Klein, 1980). Because investigators have used different clinical standards for establishing the presence of separation anxiety, reported rates among school phobics have varied from 30% to 90%.

For purposes of this review, the studies of school phobic children will be used as representative of separation anxiety. This is done with the understanding that an unknown degree of diagnostic error is bound to be present.

However, in examining the relationship between childhood separation anxiety and adult agoraphobia, diagnostic imprecision in either condition should weaken their association. Thus, the clinical inaccuracy that is introduced by equating school phobia with separation anxiety should lower correlations obtained between childhood separation anxiety and any other variable. (We are aware of the fact that not all school phobias reflect separation anxiety. However, school phobia is associated with separation anxiety often enough to justify the present exercise, if only for heuristic purposes. No claim is advanced that the presence of separation anxiety disorder is well established in all the studies reported.)

TYPES OF RELATIONSHIPS BETWEEN SEPARATION ANXIETY AND AGORAPHOBIA

Very little systematic research has appeared that helps answer the question whether childhood separation anxiety and agoraphobia are related clinical conditions. In spite of this scarcity of data, some information is available regarding several aspects of both conditions, namely, their treatment, their familial concordance, and the occurrence of separation anxiety in the childhood histories of agoraphobic adults.

Tricyclic Treatment of Separation Anxiety

The positive effect of imipramine in agoraphobia and panic disorders is well established. A similarly favorable outcome in children with separation anxiety should be expected were the two conditions to represent variants of similar pathology.

Only two placebo-controlled studies of tricyclic antidepressant (TCA) compounds in children with school phobia have been reported. The first (Gittelman-Klein & Klein, 1973; Gittelman-Klein & Klein, 1980) was a 6-week trial of imipramine in doses up to 200 mg/d (mean daily dose at termination, 159 mg/d) in 45 youngsters who had been refractory to vigorous but brief efforts to force them back to school. Marked amelioration of separation anxiety was obtained among the children on imipramine; 90% of the drug-treated children reported feeling much better, compared with 24% of those on placebo.

Compared with the placebo, imipramine treatment also had a positive effect on the physical complaints that occurred on school days prior to the children going to school. Furthermore, imipramine significantly reduced the children's response to separation as reported by the mothers.

The second placebo-controlled study, by Berney et al. (1981), consisted of a 12-week trial of clomipramine (CLO) in doses of 40 to 75 mg in school phobic children. The mean daily dose is not indicated. No difference between the medication and placebo was found.

TABLE 1
School Phobic Children's Self-Ratings of Feeling Better
($N = 44$)

	No Change or Slightly Better	Much Improved
Placebo ($N = 25$)	76%	24%
Imipramine ($N = 19$)	10%	90%

$\chi^2 = 18.55, p = .000.$

When drug-placebo differences are not obtained, two possible patterns of change are possible. In one, the patients may have improved regardless of treatment; in the other, little change is obtained with either treatment. The latter outcome is apparent in this study. There was much room for further improvement in both the placebo- and CLO-treated children at the end of the study. At the end of the 12-week CLO or placebo trial, 40% of the children were not attending school on their own, and 75% still had significant levels of separation anxiety. These results are very similar to those obtained by Gittelman-Klein and Klein (1980) among children treated with placebo for 6 weeks; 53% were still not attending school independently, and 80% were still suffering from separation anxiety at the end of treatment.

Unfortunately, the CLO doses used by Berney et al. were very low. In our original report on imipramine, we noted that no child had improved on doses below 75 mg/d. Since CLP and imipramine have similar potency, it would be surprising if doses of CLO between 40 and 75 mg sufficed. Clinical considerations other than dosage, such as patient characteristics, or the type of psychotherapy used, do not appear to have contributed to the difference in results between the two studies since the placebo effects in the investigations were almost identical. Therefore, we conclude that this CLO study suffered from inadequate dosage.

To summarize the treatment data, the imipramine study supports the expectation that childhood separation anxiety responds to tricyclic medication. However, further investigation is necessary for confirmation of this effect in childhood, since another study with low tricyclic dosage was negative.

FAMILY CONCORDANCE FOR SEPARATION ANXIETY AND AGORAPHOBIA

The hypothesized relationship between childhood separation anxiety and adult agoraphobia leads to the expectation that an increase of the childhood condition should be present in the children of agoraphobic parents, as compared to children whose parents are not agoraphobes. Conversely, the parents of children with separation anxiety disorder should display greater frequency of panic disorder or agoraphobia than parents of other children.

Separation Anxiety in Children of Agoraphobic Parents

Berg has published the only study of the children of agoraphobes (Berg, 1976). A questionnaire sent to a nationwide sample of English agoraphobic women inquired about the presence of school refusal and difficulties with separation in their children.

There was a 7% overall prevalence of school phobia in the children between 7 and 11 years of age. In older children, those between 11 and 15, the prevalence of school phobia was 14%. Girls were somewhat more frequently affected than boys.

The study did not include a comparison group of normal women. However, as the author notes, school phobia is a rare childhood condition, and the prevalence found in this sample far exceeds expected population rates. Nevertheless, one cannot conclude that separation anxiety in children is associated specifically with agoraphobic mothers, since it may also be prevalent in the offspring of parents with other psychiatric illnesses.

A recent study by Weissman, Leckman, Merinkangas, and Gammon (1984) examined the prevalence of separation anxiety in the 6- to 18-year-old-children of depressed and normal adults, identified in community surveys. This study had the marked methodological advantage of using formal diagnostic criteria (Spitzer & Endicott, 1979) and relying on reports from direct structured clinical interviews for the formulation of diagnoses. The depressed patients were classified into four separate clinical groups, those (1) without any anxiety disorder, (2) with agoraphobia, (3) with panic disorder, and (4) with generalized anxiety disorder, at any time in their adult life.

The number of children is small in each clinical group (from 32 to 38), but the results are provocative. Separation anxiety disorders were diagnosed in 24% of the children whose parents had a diagnosis of both depression *and* agoraphobia or panic. In contrast, the children of adults with pure depressions and the children of normals had no (0%) separation anxiety. The adults diagnosed as having both depression and generalized anxiety disorder had children with a 6% rate of diagnosable separation anxiety. They fell between the rates found in children of pure depressed patients and those with depression and panic disorder (24% and 0%). The pattern of results suggests that parental psychopathology, in general,

TABLE 2
Frequency of Separation Anxiety in the Offspring of Depressed
and Normal Adults

| | Separation Anxiety in Offspring | | | | |
| | Present | | Absent | | Total |
Parents' Diagnosis	N	(%)	N	(%)	N
1. Normal	0	(0)	87	(100)	87
2. Depression Only	0	(0)	38	(100)	38
3. Depression with Agoraphobia/Panic	9	(24)	28	(76)	37
4. Depression with GAD[a]	2	(6)	30	(94)	32

[a]Generalized Anxiety Disorder
2 vs. 3, $\chi^2 = 10.50$, $p < .001$
2 vs. 4, $\chi^2 = 2.44$, n.s.
3 vs. 4, $\chi^2 = 4.18$, $p < .05$, two-tailed tests
From Weissman et al., 1982.

is not associated with separation anxiety in the offspring. Rather, the latter seems linked to parental panic anxiety.

The adult patients in the Weissman et al. study were all diagnosed as depressed; none had anxiety disorders exclusively. Therefore, it is not possible to generalize, with confidence, to other patient groups. We cannot assume that the children of adults with pure panic disorders are also at much greater risk for separation anxiety than children of patients without anxiety disorders. However, the evidence is strongly suggestive and certainly encouraging of further investigation.

The questionnaire study of adult agoraphobes by Berg (1976) bears further on the possible importance of separation anxiety in the adult condition. The study includes a comparison between the agoraphobic mothers who had children with separation anxiety and those whose children had no evidence of separation anxiety. Patients with anxious children differed significantly from the others with regard to childhood history of fears and current fears. The agoraphobic mothers who had a school phobic child reported their childhood as characterized by more school phobia and fear of school, more fear of the dark, and more fear of separation from parents. Their current clinical picture was also marked by a greater number of fears. From this report, it would appear that agoraphobic women with early separation anxiety are more likely to have children with separation anxiety than agoraphobics who do not report childhood separation anxiety.

In summary, the two investigations of offspring of adults with agoraphobia and panic disorder are consistent in suggesting that their children are more likely to have separation anxiety than other children.

Agoraphobia in Parents of Children With Separation Anxiety Disorder

Berg, Butler and Pritchard (1974) surveyed the physicians of mothers of 100 hospitalized school phobic adolescents and 100 controls. No differences in rate of psychiatric problems were found between the two groups of mothers. The authors do not report the standards applied to determine the presence of psychiatric illness, or whether the judges were blind to the children's diagnoses. The results are unclear since illness was classified as affective if the symptoms consisted of depression, or anxiety and phobias. Therefore, there was no opportunity to assess the differential frequency of anxiety disorders in the mothers of school phobic and normal children independently from other psychopathology.

A further report of the psychiatric characteristics of families of children with separation anxiety (Gittelman-Klein, 1975) used relatives of children treated for hyperkinesis as controls. In this small study of 45 school phobic children, almost all of whom had documented separation anxiety, no parent was found to suffer from agoraphobia (or panic disorder). The only finding of note was that the rate of separation anxiety in the parents and siblings of probands was significantly higher than among the relatives of controls (19% vs. 2%, $\chi^2 = 12.4, p < .001$). One might argue that the parents of the separation-anxious youngsters present with a higher rate of anxiety, regardless of its type. This was not the case. The rate of specific or simple fears did not differ significantly between the parents of separation-anxious and hyperkinetic children (21% and 14%, $\chi^2 = 1.55, ns.$).

This study suffers from a lack of diagnostic criteria for establishing the presence of psychiatric illness in the parents and from the fact that interviewers were aware of the children's diagnoses. However, the individuals who conducted the interviews were not aware of the theoretical issues involved in the assessments.

The rate of depression in parents of the anxious and hyperkinetic children did not differ (8.3% and 9.5%, respectively). The lack of relationship between parental depression and childhood separation anxiety is consistent with the finding of Weissman and colleagues who found no increase of separation anxiety in the children of depressives (Weissman et al., 1984).

The familial studies that have examined offsprings of identified adults with agoraphobia and panic disorder have yielded results consistent with the hypothesis linking separation anxiety to the adult anxiety syndromes. However, the

TABLE 3
History of Separation Anxiety among Parents of School Phobic
and Hyperkinetic Children

| | Separation Anxiety | | | | |
| | Present | | Absent | | |
Parents of	N	(%)	N	(%)	N
School Phobic Children	16	(19)	67	(81)	83
Hyperkinetic Children	2	(2)	82	(98)	84

$\chi^2 = 12.4, p < .001$, two-tailed.

TABLE 4
History of Specific Fears among Parents of School Phobic and
Hyperkinetic Children

| | Specific Fears | | | | |
| | Present | | Absent | | |
Parents of	N	(%)	N	(%)	N
Phobic Children	18	(22)	65	(78)	83
Hyperkinetic Children	12	(14)	72	(86)	84

$\chi^2 = 1.55$, n.s.

single study of parents of separation-anxious children, though positive for separation anxiety, was negative for agoraphobia. This is not totally unexpected. From a selection of ill children, it would require an unusually high rate of concordance between separation anxiety in the probands and agoraphobia in the parents to enable the successful identification of affected parents.

In sum, family data are only suggestive of increases in rates of separation anxiety among adults with panic disorder and agoraphobia, and among their offspring.

HISTORY OF CHILDHOOD SEPARATION ANXIETY IN AGORAPHOBIC ADULTS

If separation anxiety in childhood is a precursor of adult panic disorder and agoraphobia, separation anxiety should be a more common feature of the early histories of adults with panic or agoraphobic disorders than in those of other patients. In the original observations by Klein (1964) of 32 inpatients with agoraphobia, half reported marked separation anxiety in childhood. Klein noted that this developmental pattern was specific to this patient group and was not found in other inpatients, such as patients with schizophrenia, affective, or character disorders. These patients were all severely ill. Since hospitalization is infrequent in the treatment of panic and agoraphobic disorders, the patients in Klein's study were unusual. Therefore, the results reported in 1964 may have been biased as a result of the atypical severity of the patient sample. Perhaps different results would emerge from a comparison between agoraphobic disorders and other psychiatric disorders with less morbidity.

There have been two investigations of early separation anxiety in outpatient agoraphobic adults. Berg, Marks, McGuire, & Lipsedge (1974) examined the frequency of reported previous school phobia among the English nationwide sample of nearly 800 agoraphobic women compared to a group of 57 neurotic outpatients. Both groups reported a very high frequency of school phobia (22%). The authors conclude that childhood school phobia is a precursor of later neurotic illness, but not of agoraphobia specifically. This report would have benefited from a more detailed description of the neurotic group. The authors do not indicate that the presence of panic or agoraphobia was ruled out in the neurotic group.

Klein and his co-workers (Klein, Zitrin, Woerner, & Ross, 1983; Zitrin, Klein, Woerner, & Ross, 1983) recently reported a treatment study of imipramine and behavioral treatment in outpatient agoraphobic and simple phobic patients. Details regarding the diagnostic and other characteristics of the patients are provided in the previously published reports (Klein et al., 1983; Zitrin et al., 1983). The remainder of this section, including Tables 20.5, 20.6, 20.7, and 20.8, presents data collected by Drs. D. F. Klein and C. M. Zitrin, who were co-principal investigators on NIMH grant #MH23007. A manuscript now in preparation by C. M. Zitrin, M.G. Woerner, D. Ross, and D. F. Klein (in preparation), entitled, "Predisposition in Phobias," will present these data more completely.

Summaries of clinical interviews done during the diagnostic process were reviewed and each patient was rated for the presence of separation anxiety by a senior psychologist. Assessments of childhood and adolescent separation anxiety were obtained for 66 of 77 agoraphobic, and 66 of 81 simple phobic, patients. There were instances where histories were unratable for separation anxiety, because the family had been unusually closeknit and no separation had occurred, except for unavoidable situations such as work and school attendance. Thus, these families never sent the children to camp, the children and parents did not socialize outside the immediate family circle, the patient had not stayed at other people's homes or gone on trips without the family, and had had little if any independent social activities.

This familial pattern is suggestive of tight attachment bonds or of avoidance of separation among the family members. Since separation anxiety is viewed as a mechanism that maximizes bonding, Zitrin et al. (in preparation) examined the prevalence of separation anxiety, as well as the relative absence of family separations, in the childhoods of agoraphobic and other anxiety patients.

The number of patients who had not been separated from their parents was sizable. A total of 15 were rated as never separated in childhood, 32 in adolescence.

Table 5 presents the rate of separation anxiety and the rate of never-separated families in the childhoods of male and female anxiety disorders. Table 6 presents similar data for the adolescent period.

In both childhood and adolescence, agoraphobic patients had significantly more separation anxiety than patients with simple phobia. However, this group difference appears entirely due to the high prevalence of separation anxiety in female agoraphobes. Thus, a history of separation anxiety disorder does not

TABLE 5
Type of Separation History in Childhood by Diagnosis and Sex
(N = 132)

	Diagnosis										
	Agoraphobia						Simple Phobia				
	Men		Women				Men		Women		
Separation Anxiety	N	(%)	N	(%)	N	(%)	N	(%)	N	(%)	N	(%)
Absent	13	(65)	17	(37)	29	(44)	9	(53)	34	(69)	43	(65)
Present	6	(30)	22	(48)	29	(44)	6	(35)	10	(20)	16	(24)
Never Separated	1	(5)	7	(15)	8	(12)	2	(12)	5	(10)	7	(11)
Total	20	(100)	46	(100)	66	(100)	17	(100)	49	(100)	66	(100)

Separation Anxiety × Diagnosis, χ^2 = 5.84, 2 df, p = .054
Separation Anxiety × Gender, χ^2 = .81, 2 df, ns
Separation Anxiety × Diagnosis × Gender, χ^2 = 5.62, 2 df, p = .06
p values are two-tailed.

TABLE 6
Type of Separation History in Adolescence by Diagnosis and Sex
(N = 132)

	Diagnosis										
	Agoraphobia						Simple Phobia				
	Men		Women				Men		Women		
Separation Anxiety	N	(%)	N	(%)	N	(%)	N	(%)	N	(%)	N	(%)
Absent	16	(80)	19	(41.3)	35	(53)	12	(71)	40	(82)	52	(79)
Present	3	(15)	7	(15.2)	10	(15)	1	(6)	2	(4)	3	(4)
Never Separated	1	(5)	20	(43.5)	21	(32)	4	(23)	7	(14)	11	(17)
Total	20	(100)	46	(100)	66	(100)	17	(100)	49	(100)	66	(100)

Separation Anxiety × Diagnosis, $\chi^2 = 11.10$, 1 df, $p < .004$
Separation Anxiety × Gender, $\chi^2 = 4.12$, 2 df, ns
Separation Anxiety × Diagnosis × Gender, $\chi^2 = 9.22$, 2 df, $p = .01$
p values are two-tailed.

TABLE 7
Separation Anxiety in Childhood in Women Patients
(N = 95)

| | Diagnosis | | | |
| | Agoraphobia | | Simple Phobia | |
Separation Anxiety	N	(%)	N	(%)
Absent	17	(37)	34	(69)
Present	22	(48)	10	(20)
Never Separated	7	(15)	5	(10)
Total	46	(100)	49	(100)

$\chi^2 = 10.42$, 2 df, $p < .01$, two-tailed.

appear to be related to agoraphobia in the men, but it seems to be in the women. In order to facilitate an examination of the results in the women patients, they are presented separately in Tables 7 and 8.

Not only is the rate of separation anxiety greater in agoraphobic women than in other anxious patients but, during adolescence, a significantly larger proportion (43.5% vs. 14%) had not separated from their families (never separated women vs. all other women, $\chi^2 = 9.4$, 1df $p = .002$).

OUTCOME OF CHILDREN WITH SEPARATION ANXIETY

An association between childhood separation anxiety and adult panic disorders would suggest that affected children are at greater risk for the adult disorder. The follow-up literature is scant. It fails to clarify the issue, since children have

TABLE 8
Separation Anxiety in Adolescence in Women Patients
($N = 95$)

	Diagnosis			
	Agoraphobia		Simple Phobia	
Separation Anxiety	N	(%)	N	(%)
Absent	19	(41.3)	40	(82)
Present	7	(15.2)	2	(4)
Never Separated	20	(43.5)	7	(14)
Total	46	(100)	49	(100)

$\chi^2 = 16.43$, 2 df, $p < .001$, two-tailed.

not been followed into adulthood, and no attempt has been made to elicit the presence of panic disorder or agoraphobia among those studied (Berg, 1970; Coolidge, Brodie, & Feeney, 1964; Roberts, 1975; Rodriguez, Rodriguez, & Eisenberg, 1959; Weiss & Burke, 1970). Typically, the outcome indices are overall adjustment, work and school return.

CLINICAL FEATURES ASSOCIATED WITH SEPARATION ANXIETY IN AGORAPHOBIA

It is legitimate to question whether the presence of separation anxiety in the histories of agoraphobic patients has any consequence with regard to other clinical events. In the small sample of inpatient agoraphobes, Klein (1964) reported that those with separation anxiety had an earlier age of onset. This observation was replicated in a large series of nonhospitalized agoraphobes (Berg et al., 1974). In both samples, the onset of patients with a history of separation anxiety anteceded the onset of the other patients by 10 years. In addition, in Berg et al.'s study (1974) the patients with a childhood history of separation anxiety rated themselves as more fearful and as being more impaired as adults.

In the large outpatient sample studied by Klein and co-workers (1983), significant correlations were not obtained between a history of separation anxiety in childhood and clinical ratings of severity of illness at the time of treatment initiation. Therefore, the evidence is equivocal with regard to the relationship between early separation anxiety and severity of adult agoraphobia.

COMMENT

The possible link between separation anxiety, early during development, and a specific adult anxiety disorder is an important clinical hypothesis. If supported, it would provide yet another source of data to indicate that agoraphobia is distinct from other adult anxiety disorders and that it may, in some cases, have specific childhood prodromal signs. A relationship between a childhood behavior pattern and later psychiatric disorder would not be unique to the anxiety disorders. Early asocial, schizoid, adjustment in nonpsychotic children seems associated with the development of schizophrenia (Wolff & Chick, 1980). In turn, schizophrenia associated with early asocial adjustment seems to differ from the other forms of schizophrenia with regard to level of intellectual functioning, neurological status (Quitkin & Klein, 1969; Quitkin, Rifkin, & Klein, 1976; Weinberger, Cannon-Spoor, Potkin, & Wyatt, 1980), and long-term outcome (Gittelman-Klein & Klein, 1969). This clinical pattern indicates that developmental characteristics may influence a number of clinical outcomes.

A clear statement regarding the strength of the relationship between separation anxiety and agoraphobia is limited by the methodological shortcomings that pervade all investigations in this area. No uniform criteria for separation anxiety yet exist. Ratings of separation anxiety have not been independent of clinical status, and methods are vague. It would be difficult to replicate exactly any one of the published reports. Yet, in spite of the measurement variance across studies, several investigational approaches give empirical support to a positive relationship between separation anxiety and agoraphobia.

From the literature, it appears that both conditions may respond to TCA treatment, that they coexist in family members, and that both conditions occur in the same patients more frequently than would be expected by chance alone. An association between separation anxiety and adult agoraphobia seems to occur in women, but not in men. This finding, if replicated, would suggest that agoraphobia may have different causal antecedents in men and women patients. Some reservation concerning this possibility is in order since distinct etiologies have never been reported for each gender, and it may be that men do not report separation anxiety as readily as women do. If the relationship between childhood separation anxiety and adult agoraphobia were supported, there might be scientific merit in separating agoraphobic patients with positive histories of separation anxiety from those without such histories for study purposes.

If only for heuristic purposes, it seems potentially fruitful to identify the presence of separation anxiety in adult agoraphobes. It is possible that by doing so, more homogeneous subgroups of adult patients will be generated.

It is self-evident to suggest that prospective longitudinal studies would be most helpful to elucidate the ultimate clinical significance of childhood anxiety. By studying children with various levels of manifest anxiety, we could clarify the ever present controversy whether a dimensional or a taxonomic model provides the best explanation of the clinical phenomena. For instance, if mild to moderate degrees of separation anxiety had no significant sequelae, but the disorder did, it would argue for discontinuity across different anxiety levels. In contrast, if the severity of early status predicted the severity of risk later on, then no qualitative distinctions could be suggested.

What seems needed at present is a systematic assessment of separation anxiety, with demonstrable reliability. A recent version of the Schedule for Affective Disorders and Schizophrenia—Lifetime version (SADS—L) (Spitzer & Endicott, 1979) includes an inverview section designed to elicit a history of separation anxiety. However, it has not been put to the test and its validity is not established. In view of the possible importance of separation anxiety in the study of agoraphobia, the development of reliable and valid measures of early and current status seems highly desirable.

ACKNOWLEDGMENTS

This paper was supported, in part, by grants MH 23007, and MHRC 30906.

21

Discussion of Chapters by Gittelman and Klein and Achenbach: A Clinician's Perspective

E. James Anthony
Washington University, St. Louis

Gittelman and Klein's contribution in this volume is scientifically elegant: well crafted, lucidly exposed and closely argued with full respect for the supportive, the suggestive, and the negating evidence. The authors convincingly build a connection between separation anxiety in the child and agoraphobia in the adult. They make this connection by trying to establish concordance in the therapeutic response of the two conditions to tricyclics; in the occurrence of separation anxiety in children and agoraphobia in their parents when both the parents and the children present symptomatically; in the finding of childhood separation anxiety in agoraphobic adults; and in the finding of agoraphobia among adults who as children suffered from separation anxiety.

The research strategy that seeks to demonstrate the link between the two conditions is therefore a comprehensive one: the childhood anxiety is searched for in the adult, although manifested differently; adult anxiety is followed back, retrospectively, to childhood anxiety; cross-sectionally, anxiety in the parent (i.e., mother) directs the inquiry to the possibility of anxiety in the child, and vice versa; and the anxiety in the child is treated pharmacologically in the same way as anxiety in the adult. These converging operations are a powerful strategy in studies where the purpose is to show meaningful connections across the human life cycle, but the area of investigation is so complex that such endeavors can hardly be expected to progress beyond "mere empiricism" unless there is some guarantee that the measurement of fundamental units meets acceptable criteria of reliability and validity. Gittelman and Klein rightly point to the methodological shortcomings that render replication so very difficult, but they comfort themselves on the ground that several studies offer some degree of support for the existence of the relationship. Nevertheless, the very factor contributing to the neatness of their design generates doubt in the clinician who might feel that multiple hypotheses are needed for investigating such complicated, multidetermined phenomena. At best, their study could be said to offer a strong inference, and at worst, the approach is too simplistic. It is, however, possible to argue the reverse proposition: that what looks deceptively complex may be relatively simple, and that it is the clinician's bane to suspect that all psychological phenomena, in the tradition of Freud, are heavily overdetermined. Are we, in fact, in this study taking a scientific look at such well-worn truisms as anxious children become anxious adults, anxious adults have been anxious children, and anxious parents have anxious children? All these statements have been taken for granted in the literature, but an important function of science is to offer rigorously collected evidence for what has been intuitively believed on the basis of unsystematic and uncontrolled clinical observations.

What is missing from the set of converging operations is the longitudinal perspective that would help to cement the connection between the child and adult anxiety states. Gittelman and Klein call attention to this fact several times in their presentation. Prospective investigations offer the most convincing evidence in favor of an evolving psychopathology. Although difficult to carry out because of the time factor, the use of a short-term longitudinal design permits us to capture at least some of the advantages inherent in such prospective-predictive investigations. Longitudinal studies also enable the researcher to follow the course of anxiety, to study its "natural history" and inherent variations, to observe changes in the manifestations of anxiety at different developmental stages with perhaps a concomitant increase in frequency and intensity, and to note symptomatic transformations in the making (e.g., separation anxiety into agoraphobia). With the possibility of a longitudinal type of investigation excluded, the result is inevitably a limited study that is certainly more than the usual drug study but less than what the problem demands.

When one considers the label "separation anxiety" in the context of the diagnostic label "agoraphobia," one makes a mysterious leap from one diagnostic category to another, but if one simply thinks of both labels as manifestations of anxiety, the transition from one to the other appears much more explicable. Both may be separation anxiety, since in agoraphobia there is often inability to separate from the "agoraphobic companion." Gittelman and Klein have worked toward the idea of agoraphobia being a specific condition different from other anxiety manifestations along the anxiety spectrum, and they offer some support for their view. Perhaps the response to the unfamiliar might be the common denominator with separation anxiety in the child and stranger anxieties in the adult.

A prospective study by the "follow along" design could bring into more detailed focus such perplexing transformations as that from normal to clinical, from diffuse to focal (as in phobias), from external to internal, and from the nonverbal somatically expressed to verbally communicated mental content. The general trend would be from the simple to the complex. School refusals in nursery school, kindergarten, and first grade are very different clinically from the school refusals of early adolescence with their schizoid characteristics and worsening prognosis. Coolidge has provided the closest approximation to a longitudinal study of school phobias, and could have been profitably cited in this chapter, especially with regard to developmental changes (Coolidge & Brody, 1974; Coolidge, Brody, & Fenney, 1964; Coolidge, Tessman, Waldofogel, & Willer, 1962). The longitudinal perspective can be an invaluable corrective experience for the researcher, as Bleuler points out (1978), not only highlighting the vicissitudes in the course of a particular disorder, but also challenging long-held notions of prognosis. In this respect, a single cross-sectional assessment can be quite misleading. An important issue implicit in Gittelman and Klein's chapter is that of anxiety-proneness or the inherent tendency to overreact to unexpected and unfamiliar exposures. Although the authors mention one piece of negating evidence, there has been an impressive amount of suggestive support for the presence of low thresholds for reactivity coupled with high ratings for sensitivity in about 10% of infants. A study of nursery school children by Walker (1962, 1963) found that a significant relationship existed between physique components and specific behavior items. The most interesting and the most consistent of these findings was the linkage between ectomorphy and nervousness, fearfulness and anxiety that seemed to dispose such children to the development of internalizing syndromes. Other studies have offered relatively frail evidence for increased anxieties in children who have sustained obstetrical complications, and there has also been work apparently supporting the lifelong continuation of an anxious dispositional character. However, the evidence, in general, has been based more on clinical inquiry than on carefully controlled evidence.

The connection between anxiety and depression has had affirmation as well as refutation. There are clinicians who have postulated two separate lines of development for anxiety and depression, classifying them as the two basic affects with an inherent individual proneness toward one or the other expression. Other clinicians have regarded them as closely associated emotional states, overlapping with each other within the spectrum of affective disorders that were generally anxiety-depression syndromes. Clinicians have pointed, for example, to the increased rate of maternal depression (and treatment with electroconvulsive therapy) in children with school phobia. Any tendency to compartmentalize the affects treads on highly controversial ground and is likely to provoke skepticism even in the face of significant group differences. Clinicians who view the course of the child's development in the context of gradual separation from the mother have called attention to both anxiety and depression as concomitants of the process and have been inclined to assume that the clinical manifestations of separation would be likely to show both components. This fact would also hold true in the transmissions across generations.

Those implacable scientific furies—reliability and validity—that forever pursue transgressing researchers create several questions for any therapeutic testing: First whether children and adults react similarly to medication, since the child's reaction with some drugs is paradoxically at variance with that of the adult; whether one can justifiably conclude (if the child and adult react in the same direction to medication) that the conditions being treated are similar; and whether one can reach such a conclusion based on testing when it is not followed up repeatedly over time. I am somewhat biased in this respect, and tend to feel that the only convincing evidence is serial evidence covering a duration of time that spans the different developmental stages. Gittelman and Klein call attention to the absence of such prospective pharmacological investigations, and one would hope that with their many research skills in hand, they will undertake a study of this kind. In addition, one would also hope that other teams of investigators would independently research the same issues in the same way, since replication is never as convincing when conducted by the same investigator. It is interesting to note that the one other independent study examining the effect of clomipramine (CLO) in school phobic children found no differences between medication and placebo, but Gittelman and Klein dismiss this result as being due to inadequate dosage based on their own experience of a similar lack of response.

Scientifically impeccable studies like this one provide an unfortunately truncated review of the complex field of anxiety reactions, even though they constitute a genuine contribution to difficult nosological problems. Speaking as a clinician rather than a clinical investigator, future studies should emphasize an epigenetic understanding that covers the developmental point of view, the setting within a family and its other children, the socio-economic and cultural environment from which the target child emerges with his anxieties, a child's eye view of his or her own dynamic and phenomenological experience of the anxiety-provoking situation, and the differential risks, vulnerabilities, and resiliences that distinguish the children in a particular family. These emphases would offer a comprehensive developmental psychopathology and allow the construction of some helpful "grounded" theory as an additional, if not essential, bonus. Gittelman and Klein have provided some important converging operations to illuminate the field, and I am suggesting further convergences that might afford some answer to the perplexing problem of the genesis of anxiety. We might, like Professor Kingsfield in *The Paper Chase* be compelled to admit that we may *never* "find the ultimate, correct and final answer," but the world "never" is not one that the good researcher should consider (except as a null hypothesis).

The strength of the null hypothesis lies in its ability to detect slight but important effects that would otherwise be obscured by large individual differences and other sources of error to which I have already alluded in discussing the Gittelman-Klein "experiments." It permits the researcher, as Doherty, Tweney, and Mynett (1981) have pointed out, to detect even weak signals "in a sea of noise." Its rejection can be regarded as highly informative and reflective of powerful research and good theory. We can stand here on relatively safe ground. With the factor analytic approach to clinical problems, there remains a degree of uncertainty as to its capacity to answer the kind of clinical question posed, for instance, by the operations of anxiety. Clinicians, in particular, find it hard to accept conclusions that suggest a superficial recording of data without the emergence of new knowledge. They tend to feel that the method does little more than dress up their hunches, stemming from protracted experiences, in a mathematical garb. This type of reasoning probably reflects the clinician's bias toward the qualitative over the quantitative.

As long ago as 1966, Achenbach not only furnished a good review of the various factor analytic approaches to classification, but he also tried to elucidate the relationship between the general symptom clusters found, for example, in some child nosological studies and the specific functional syndromes employed in adult psychiatry. His aims, almost 20 years ago, were to obtain a more differentiated empirical classification of child psychiatric cases, and to discover whether the classifications deriving from the factor analysis of symptoms bore a significant relationship to biographical variables. At that time, five principal-factor analyses were performed on the symptoms and biographical data from the case histories of 300 male and 300 female child psychiatric patients. The symptoms were intercorrelated and factor analyzed, separately for each sex, by the principal-factor method and the factors were rotated to the verimax, quartimax and oblimin criteria for simple structure. The first principal factor for both sexes was bipolar, with antisocial behavior ("externalizing") at one end and neurotic symptoms ("internalizing") at the other end. For the boys alone, his analysis revealed a factor labeled sexual problems. For the girls alone, factors labeled depressive symptoms, anxiety symptoms, neurotic and delinquent behavior, obesity, enuresis, and other immaturities were found. The parents of externalizers were found to have significantly more overt social problems and were rated as less concerned with their child's difficulty than the parents of internalizers. The obesity factor classified only girls aged 10 to 14. The neurotic and delinquent behavior factor, found between the ages of 12 and 15, suggested that these were phenomena belonging to a specific developmental stage and should not be expected in patients from other age groups. It thus appeared that the internalizing-externalizing dichotomy could be used readily for classifying case histories and live patients dimensionally, taking as a criterion point 60% or more diagnostic items belonging to one or other category. If more subtle differences were being investigated, a more rigorous criterion (75% or more) could be put to use.

Achenbach's earlier work highlights his consistent and systematic development as a nosologist, and it at once raises what Gittelman and Klein refer to as "the ever present controversy" whether a dimensional or taxonomic model provides the best explanation for clinical phenomena. Psychiatric clinicians have tended to veer away from the factor analytic approach, preferring, apparently, the less rigorous method of consensus among reputable clinicians.

My own experience of researching the children of psychotic parents has led me to take a close look at the catastrophic levels of anxiety shown by the children when the parent becomes suddenly and unexpectantly acutely psychotic. The initial response by the child suggests a traumatic stress disorder with anxiety as the nuclear component. First there is a numbness and an absence of manifest anxiety, but this rapidly passes off and the subjects become diffusely anxious, haunted by the traumatic experience, and plagued by anxiety dreams. There is also considerable separation anxiety (accompanied by some guilty relief) when the parent is hospitalized. Of particular importance is the dysphoric condition that takes the place of acute anxiety as the earlier state subsides. This dysphoric condition is made up of anxiety as a central ingredient, but includes fear of being attacked by the sick parent, angry resentment at having one's life style radically altered, guilt over the notion that the child is responsible for driving the parent crazy, depression provoked by the loss of the normal parent and normal parenting activities, and great concern about the possibility of becoming similarily crazy. Here we have a cluster of affects, the extent and intensity of which varies with the vulnerability of the child. The anxiety factor appears, disappears, and reappears, often in close relationship to the course of the parental psychosis. Some children show a decided resilience to the anxiety process but, as Manfred Bleuler has remarked, anxiety is never very far away in the lives of children who perpetually walk in the shadow of psychosis.

The Achenbach dimensions have helped researchers see their risk cases within a more intelligible and shareable framework. At one pole, there is a subgroup of internalizers who handle anxiety inwardly through neurotic developments and somatizations, and at the other pole a subgroup of externalizers in whom anxiety appears to be conspicuously absent. The latter cases habituate rapidly to the parental psychotic episodes and dissipate their feelings in antisocial and delinquent activities. In my own sample, I was not able to predict which subjects would use an internal or external mode of outlet but once the differences arose, they were clearly demarcated. In between these subgroups, mixed clinical pictures are present.

Achenbach's approach is consonant with my view (Anthony, 1970) that the quintessence of childhood stems from the fact that it is an open system in the process of continuously becoming, changing, and reshaping itself, both normally and clinically. MacFarlane, Allan, and Hozik (1954) have chronicled the waxing and waning of anxiety signs and symptoms from infancy to adulthood in the Berkeley studies, and the idea of a rigid static label is at complete variance with this longitudinal perspective.

Clinical research is becoming more and more a feature of children's psychiatric clinics throughout the country, and Achenbach's assessment procedure is being incorporated into the traditional focus on guidance and treatment schedule of many of these clinics. It had its antecedent in Eysenck's factor analytic noso-logical approach, and in his dichotomous dimensions of introversion-extraver-sion. It is also of interest that both Gittelman and Achenbach cite Freud's pioneer work on childhood anxiety in the case of Little Hans. Freud (1909/1955) described an orderly sequence of transformation from diffuse anxiety to the formation of a phobia. Little Hans's anxiety starts without an object, and then finds one—a horse. This development might seem foolish, said Freud, but added that "a neurosis never said foolish things." Achenbach does a succinct review of the early work on anxiety as well as the early observational measures of anxiety. His grasp of conceptual issues is equally well done as he contrasts a variety of theoretical orientations.

Achenbach's approach, in general, represents an important contribution to the taxonomy and taxometry of anxiety, and a number of his implicit and explicit postulates are on target. For example, he approaches anxiety disorders within a framework of broad and narrow dimensional bands that match the clinician's experience. He sees them within a developmental context so that early school phobias can be differentiated from later ones, a distinction overlooked by Git-telman and Klein but readily recognized by clinicians. And finally, he brings the anxiety disorders together with concomitant developing events and problems and with the interplay between differences belonging to the individual and those accruing from changes brought about by ongoing development. What appeals to the clinicians especially is the fact that he derives his data, as does the clinician, from a multiplicity of sources, and is open to obtaining the "best" information possible, which may be sometimes from the parent and sometimes from the child.

I also resonated sympathetically to his statement that "it would not be fruitful to study anxiety disorders as encapsulated entities independent of the develop-ment of other problems and competences." In this sense, I leaned more favorably to his point of view than to Gittelman's, even though there are decided limitations to the factor analytic approach to such clinical problems.

I would also agree with Achenbach that there is little "hard" evidence on casual connections between early anxieties and later psychiatric problems of any sort. However, my own experience of infant and toddler development does not lead me to share the opinion that he quotes of Thomas, Chess, and Birch (1968) that anxiety was *not* an initial factor in the development of symptoms. I have observed anxiety in the infant in a diffuse form, and have seen it become crystalized and clustered into symptom formations in the course of time. The view of Thomas and his co-workers is that anxiety, inner conflict, and defense are secondary to the child's response to an initial maladaptation; once they appear a new dimension is added to the picture. Anxiety is then such a striking symptom that it dominates the clinical picture. For these investigators it is not surprising that anxiety is regarded as primary and that subsequent syndromes are seen to originate from it. Once again the familiar chicken and egg problem arises and my own clinical experience takes an opposite view.

Achenbach's approach does make sense out of widely disparate and confusing data, and it seems to generate a great deal of productive research. There is no doubt that clinics need an assessment procedure similar to his to bring order into their lengthy, redundant case studies. Still open to question is whether or not factor analysis brings additional insights to the clinical understanding of individual cases and to the mechanism of symptom formation. The clustering effects are interesting, but it is not clear why certain clusters occur. Cluster analytic techniques obviously tap some commonality, but what this is, is not at all evident. Although Achenbach espouses the developmental approach and although he has carried out some relatively short-term longitudinal research, he is really a cross-sectional developmentalist. He recognizes that children are different at ages 5, 10, and 15, but he seems unconcerned about how they become different. His focus, as that of other cross-sectionists, is on the state of being, rather than the state of becoming, which is a fundamental definition of childhood. (Piaget, it will be remembered, criticized Freud for not being a developmental psychologist. In fact, Freud was a retrospective developmentalist, that is, he approached development backwards.)

And what happens when anxiety enters the very fabric of the personality and becomes part and parcel of the child's response to life. Cimbal (quoted by Kanner, 1957) referred to certain immature children who manifested a permanent attitude of apprehensiveness and overreacted to almost every unexpected environmental stimulus. This combination of a lowered stimulus threshold, a tendency to generalize responses, and a protracted lability of affect causing the child to react for long periods after a disturbing experience, produces a clinical picture of a timid, undecided, fearful, withdrawing child, who through the course of development has been overwhelmed by separation anxieties, stranger reactions, animal fears, dread of going to school, and general social anxiety. There are no specific phobias of any kind, nor do the anxieties confine themselves to any particular object or situation. Darkness, being alone, people, storms, insects, and noises are all included in the apprehensions of the child who is sometimes so afraid that he cannot talk above a whisper (Anthony, 1975). Cimbal referred to this reaction as *lebensfeigheit*, meaning cowardliness with regard to living. Nightmares are frequent, enuresis is common, and anxious preoccupation with bodily functioning is often the rule. The child tends to be delicate and finicky about food to the constant concern of his equally nervous mother.

Here we have another variation of the anxieties, a more chronic type, that makes working with precise and carefully demarcated labels even harder. One is reminded of Darwin (1881/1958) visiting the zoo and noticing something he could incorporate into his thinking about variation: "George the lion is extraordinarily cowardly.—The other one nothing will frighten—hence variation in character in different animals of same species." Had he not been thinking about variation, he might have noticed something else, but it is also true that perhaps he was thinking about variation in this way because the world was full of such individual differences. Individual differences are of special interest to the clinician; less so to the clinical investigator of group differences. The difference in perspective becomes the source of different orientations, different theorizing and even different observations, as illustrated by Darwin.

22

Early Development and Opportunities for Research on Anxiety

Robert N. Emde, M.D.
School of Medicine
University of Colorado

In contributing to the discussion of basic psychological processes and anxiety, I have decided to touch on early developmental research. A theme is that longitudinal research provides particular opportunities for understanding predisposition to anxiety and its disorders.

A number of assumptions enter into my discussion. Among them are the following: that anxiety is a universal experience; that there is a functional or reactive anxiety as well as a maladaptive or disordered anxiety; that forms of anxiety and its disorders change with development; and finally, that the psychobiology of early development is patterned and organized in a way that has implications for understanding anxiety predispositions.

DEVELOPMENTAL CONTINUITIES AND THE NATURE OF EARLY EXPERIENCE

The past two decades have witnessed an intensive concentration of research in early development, much of it fueled by a search for continuities from early experience to later periods of development. From a mental health standpoint, the thinking was that if continuities could be documented, early identification of problems and the institution of ameliorative efforts could take place. Indeed, many health care professionals believed that significant amounts of adult psychopathology (maladaptive anxiety included) had its origins in early experience. But the findings from longitudinal studies were unexpected. Researchers encountered disappointment in finding little predictability from infancy to later ages. This was true for behavior related to cognition, as well as behavior presumed related to temperament (Kagan, in press; McCall, 1979; Plomin, 1983). Correspondingly, clinicians were repeatedly surprised by well-documented instances of childhood "resiliency" following major infantile deficit or trauma (for review see Clarke & Clarke, 1976; Emde, 1981; Kagan, Kearsley, & Zelaso, 1978).

It is important to realize, however, that this developmental research was not simply negative. Much was learned about early developmental processes and, related to this, new strategies have now emerged for investigating meaningful continuities. I return to the new strategies in my conclusion; for now, let me review some principles about early developmental processes as they bear on the question of predisposition to anxiety.

A first principle has to do with developmental discontinuities or transformations. It is clear that early development does not take place in a straightforward, linear fashion; there are nodal times of qualitative change when behavior is reorganized and when new modes of activity emerge. Since these involve widespread changes in state development, in perception, in cognition, in motor and in affective development, there is reason to speculate that these times reflect normative central nervous system regulatory shifts. In a pioneering theoretical work, Spitz (1959) referred to these times as those of new "psychic organizers"; in a longitudinal study, we referred to them as times of "biobehavioral shift" (Emde, Gaensbauer, & Harmon, 1976). Others have referred to them as times of developmental discontinuity or as times of stage boundaries in cognitive development (McCall, 1979; Uzgiris, 1976). Research observations converge on the normative times of these infancy transformations. They are observed at 2 months, at 7–9 months, at 12–13 months, and at 18–21 months. It seems that a question for anxiety research is the following: Do these times of transformation also represent times of increased vulnerability for anxiety predisposition? Can environmental disruptions at these times predispose to a failure of affective and cognitive regulation later on?

Another principle that has been emphasized by recent longitudinal research concerns self-righting tendencies. From a biological viewpoint, development is goal oriented, and for species-important developmental functions there is a strong tendency to get back on a developmental pathway after deficit or perturbation (Sameroff & Chandler, 1976; Waddington, 1962). Observations of developmental resiliency—severe retardation due to deprivation which is corrected by later environmental change—are illustrations of this tendency (see Clarke & Clarke, 1976). Also related to this principle is the fact that there are multiple ways of reaching biologically important developmental goals (Bertalanffy, 1968). Thus, it has been documented that children who are congenitally blind (Fraiberg, 1977), congenitally deaf (Freedman, Cannady, & Robinson, 1971), without limbs (DeCarie, 1969), or have cerebral palsy (Sameroff, personal communication) go through infancy with different sensory motor experiences, but typically develop object permanence, representational intelligence and self-awareness in early childhood. The question for anxiety research is as follows: With deflection from a usual developmental pathway, with early perturbation or deficit, and with resiliency, is there any added propensity for anxiety?

A third early developmental principle has to do with environmental trans-actions. It has been shown that developmental outcomes are a joint function of mutual influences between the child and his or her caregiving environment. This is especially dramatic when considering the outcomes of perinatal trauma or of an infant considered to have a "difficult" temperament; a favorable caregiving environment can be described in terms of cycles of positive, mutual influence and, as is well known, the opposite also occurs (Sameroff & Chandler, 1976). The subfield of temperament research, having found few developmental contin-uities in infant temperament, is now appreciating continuities and changes in the "match" or "mismatch" between the infant and caregiving environment (Plomin, 1983; Thomas & Chess, 1977; Thomas & Chess, 1984). Questions for anxiety research include the following: To what extent will transactional processes with an anxious caregiver predispose to later anxiety disorder? Will certain infants and young children, such as those with a "difficult" temperament (irregular sleep and eating, fussy), generate anxious interactions from particular caregivers and predispose to later anxiety? Are there particular times in early development when transactional processes can go awry, disrupt regulatory systems, and generate tension between caregiver and child, thus predisposing to anxiety?

It should be pointed out that the questions for anxiety research generated by these three principles of early development require a commitment to prospective longitudinal research. The questions highlight the importance of variations in the dynamics of development and require an individual differences approach, one that takes account of patterns within individuals and their circumstances over time.

EMOTIONAL ORGANIZATION

In the previous section we considered the biological patterning of developmental processes; the presumption was that variations of early experience might influence these processes and predispose to later anxiety disorders. In this section we consider an area even closer to the topic of predisposition to anxiety, namely the early patterning of basic emotions.

Although cognitive approaches have dominated modern developmental psy-chology, there is now a resurgence of research in emotional development. This has been due, in part, to a change in thinking. Emotions were previously regarded as primarily reactive, intermittent, and disruptive states; they are now increas-ingly appreciated as active, ongoing, and adaptive processes (see Izard & Blum-berg, this volume). Emotions serve evaluation, and they provide incentives for new plans and actions. At any given time they allow us to monitor ourselves and our states of being and engagement with the world; in addition, they allow us to monitor others, their intentions, needs, and states of well-being. Furthermore, it has become apparent that emotions are biologically patterned with a similar organization throughout the life span. Thus, emotions may provide with a core of continuity for our self-experience throughout development: Since we can get in touch with our own consistent feelings, we know we are the same in spite of the many ways we change. An "affective self" (Emde, 1983), because of its basis in a species-wide biological patterning of emotions, may also allow us to get in touch with the feelings of others and be empathic.

Recent infancy research has contributed in a major way to this picture. There is a highly patterned emotional signaling system between infant and caregiver, and emotional availability of both is essential for development.

Our Colorado infancy studies have shown a striking consistency concerning the organization of infant facial expression of emotions (Emde, 1980; Emde, Kligman, Reich, & Wade, 1978). Using a multidimensional scaling approach for analyzing adult judgments, photographs of infant facial expressions were sampled. It was found that after 3 months, three-dimensional scaling solutions are typical, with hedonic tone (unpleasant to pleasant) consistently predominant, with activation the second most prominent dimension, and with an internally oriented/externally oriented dimension third and least prominent. These results show striking consistency with research on adult emotional expression, going back to the psychologist-philosophers of the last century and including experimental investigations in the 1950s, 1960s, and 1970s (for example, see Abelson & Sermat, 1962; Frijda, 1970; Frijda & Phillipszoon, 1963; Gladstone, 1962; Osgood, 1966; Woodworth & Schlosberg, 1954). Recently, a similar organization has been found in a series of studies of school children from grades 3 through 7 (Russell & Ridgeway, 1983). (For a review of these studies see Ekman, Friesen, & Ellsworth, 1972; also see discussion in Lang, this volume.) It should be pointed out that the third dimension in this organizational structure often accounts for little variance in scaling studies and is variously labeled in other ways, such as "control," or "acceptance-rejection"; it seems that this dimension is a less central aspect of emotional organization and may represent a related subsystem of mental functioning.

Other evidence for affective continuity comes from cross-cultural findings of agreement about facial expressions of discrete emotions (Ekman, Friesen, & Ellsworth, 1972; Izard, 1971). Agreement was found among adults in non-Western as well as Western cultures, and in nonliterate as well as literate cultures. Agreement was found for the emotions of joy, surprise, anger, fear, sadness, disgust and, to a lesser extent, for interest. The agreements seem to imply a universal human basis, not only for the expression of particular emotions, but for their recognition. Specific facial movements involved in each of these patterns of emotion has subsequently become specified (see Ekman, 1982; Izard, 1982). Among other directions of research, the cross-cultural findings have stimulated research in infancy to look for preadapted readiness for expressing and recognizing these patterned emotions. Although research is ongoing, there are already consistent conclusions. Infant facial expressions of emotions can be judged reliably by those who know nothing about eliciting circumstances or context, and the expressions fit the patterning suggested from the research on adult discrete emotions. So far this can be said for happiness, fear, sadness, surprise, anger, disgust and pain (Emde, Kligman, Reich, & Wade, 1978; Hiatt, Campos, & Emde, 1979; Izard, Huebner, Risser, McGinnis, & Dougherty, 1980; Stenberg, 1982; Stenberg, Campos, & Emde, 1983).

Another line of evidence for this biologically patterned emotional organization concerns its use in caregiving and early development. Not only do parents rely on emotional expressions to guide caregiving (emotions are often considered the "language of infancy"), but infants seek out and make use of emotional signals of caregivers. One form of this is an object of our current program of research. "Social referencing" is an aspect of emotional signaling which begins toward the end of the first year of life and continues to have major importance during the second year. The infant may seek out emotional information in order to make sense of an event which is otherwise ambiguous, and then uses that emotional information to regulate his or her behavior (Campos & Stenberg, 1981; Feinman & Lewis, 1981; Klinnert, Campos, Sorce, Emde, & Svejda, 1982; Sorce, Emde, Campos & Klinnert, in press). Social referencing may be especially prominent at the dawn of self-awareness, during the second year, when it is assumed that infants regularly experience more uncertainty about the impact of environmental events in terms of their own safety or in terms of the consequences of their own actions. Related to emotional signaling is the importance of emotional availability. The importance of the emotional availability of the caregiver in infancy has been noted by several researchers, including Bowlby (1973) and Mahler and her colleagues (Mahler, Pine, & Bergman, 1975). In a recent experimental study of 15-month-olds, we found effects of mother's emotional availability on infant exploration and play, effects that depended upon whether mother was reading a newspaper or not (Sorce & Emde, 1981).

If it is the case that there is such a strong biological patterning to early emotional organization, what are the consequences of individual differences in this organization? Are there individual variations that can be seen as predisposing to later anxiety disorders? Are there specific consequences of emotional unavailability of a caregiver for later forms of anxiety? If fear is to be considered the central emotional component of anxiety (Izard & Blumberg, this volume), will excessive fear expressions in infancy prove to be an antecedent, or marker, for later excessive anxiety? Again, these questions call for a longitudinal research strategy.

TRANSITION FROM INFANCY TO EARLY CHILDHOOD

At what age can we consider anxiety to have its developmental onset? The answer to this question will, of course, depend upon one's definition of anxiety. Certainly the capacity for tension and generalized conditioned avoidance with evidence of fearfulness and distress is present during the first year. For many investigators, however, anxiety would require the acquisition of self-awareness, which is now known to occur normally during the age period bracketed by 15 to 20 months (Amsterdam, 1972; Kagan, 1981; Lewis & Brooks-Gunn, 1979; Mahler, Pine, & Bergman, 1975; Schulman & Kaplowitz, 1977). Indeed, this period and the broader period from 1 to 3 years of age is one that is now coming under intense research scrutiny. It is a period when there are many developmental acquisitions which have not been well studied, but which are of major importance. These include not only the emergence of self-awareness and of self-consciousness, but of core gender identity, the acquisition of language, and symbolic play. They also include advanced cognitive capacities, such as the attribution of causality and the beginning awareness of social rules. Socially, the toddler becomes acutely sensitive to being included or "left out," and there is an increasing sense of autonomy with the acquisition of a sense of personal space and possession. As Kagan (1981) has pointed out, coincident with the child's greater representational capacities, signs of anxiety can be seen in anticipation of task failure and, correspondingly, pride can be seen following success obtained with effort. In addition, evidence suggests that more complex emotions based on new cognitive capacities appear. These include shame and what may be early forms of guilt (an awareness of social rules and an elementary sense of right and wrong). Emotional expressions begin to be used instrumentally, wherein particular expressions, such as smiling, sounding angry, or looking sad, are used to influence adults for a purpose. Correspondingly, certain expressions become socialized so that they are sometimes inhibited or "masked" (especially anger and sadness expressions).

Indications are that this is a period when behavioral continuities become apparent, such that some of the variation observed in 3-year-olds is preserved through school entrance. It seems plausible to assume that during the second year children begin to relate their experiences to an inner executive and to evaluate themselves, in some sense, as competent or incompetent or as "good" or as "bad" (see Bandura, 1981). It may be that this is a time when reliable patterns of reaction to conflict, potential failure, violation of adult standards, social skills, and dominance by other children may emerge. Perhaps investigation will reveal why some children are more resilient to conflict or anxiety than others.

In a recent longitudinal study, Klinnert, Sorce, Emde, Stenberg, and Gaensbauer (1984) found that mothers begin to hold their infants accountable for emotional expressions such as anger around 12 months of age; in a current family-oriented study of emotional development through the toddler period, Ann

Easterbrooks and I are finding remarkable individual differences in parental beliefs and socialization practices with respect to emotional expression. Some parents believe that anger and sadness should be expressed in front of the child as a natural part of life. Others feel just as strongly that the child needs to be protected in a secure environment and should not be a part of such expressions. Similarly, there are differences in attitudes about allowing emotional expressions in one's children. There is every indication that the second and third years are when emotions become socialized, or displayed according to convention. There is also evidence that this is the time when internal feeling states become increasingly organized, and when emotional connections are made with internalized social "objects." It is likely that patterned feeling states become connected in clusters that are linked to memories of events, and thus are used in anticipation; in other words, an increasingly complex form of internal affect signaling develops (Engel, 1962; Freud, 1926). Clustered signal affects of anxiety, shame, depression, and forerunners of guilt may begin during this time.

Another acquisition during this period is the capacity for empathy. Research has shown that prosocial behaviors, and by inference empathic processes, begin during the second year (Zahn-Waxler & Radke-Yarrow, 1982). Much needs to be understood about the acquisition of empathy, with the response to the pain of another; perhaps this emerges with other complex capacities that link cognition and emotion. Do variations in the capacity for empathy and in its socialization within families relate to the predisposition to anxiety? Again, there are major opportunities here for research with a longitudinal approach.

STRATEGIES OF PROMISE

In conclusion, I believe there is major promise for learning about the predisposition to anxiety from early developmental research. Longitudinal study is a core strategy, especially with populations at risk for the later development of anxiety disorders. Risk can be defined by genetic studies, by psychosocial stress factors and, hopefully in the near future, by biological markers. This will provide the opportunity to observe crucial developmental transformations in the path from predisposition to manifest pathological anxiety in such a way that we can understand ameliorating and harmful factors in individual experience. Newer methods in longitudinal research will add to this promise. These include methods that look for developmental continuities and change within an individual, instead of relying on correlative approaches that depend upon rank ordering within an arbitrary group distribution over time. Methods (such as the "Q sort," developed by Block, 1971) can trace meaningful constant relationships among intraindividual variables of behavioral organization as an individual passes through developmental transformations, such as occur frequently in early development. Another method has to do with the appreciation of subgrouping, not just according to gender and age, but according to other characteristics. A recent promising set of findings using this strategy may be relevant to anxiety predisposition. Two longitudinal studies from infancy into the preschool years, one conducted in the United States by Kagan and associates (Kagan, Reznick, Clarke, Snidman, & Coll, in press) and another in Japan by Miyake and associates (personal communication), have found a subgroup of behaviorally inhibited infants who remain that way in early childhood, showing continuity in their behavior in social situations. This subgrouping is based on infants who are considered shy by their parents and who have a physiological pattern of high unvarying heart rate when processing information during a cognitive task. Although this work is ongoing and incomplete, there are other indications of high sympathetic tone with a continuity across development manifesting itself from this kind of subgrouping. Indeed, this work introduces another strategy in longitudinal study, namely that of using extreme groups for study and comparison; very sociable children are compared with markedly behaviorally inhibited children. Aside from efficiency in studying targeted subgroups, findings could be lost in a study of a large population if variables of interest are not normally distributed within that population.

Other longitudinal strategies of promise were alluded to in the previous discussion of developmental continuities. Since researchers are no longer merely interested in the stability of behavior over time, but are interested in antecedent-consequent relations across times of developmental transformation, newer strategies take this into account. In particular, there is careful attention to sampling enough behavior at any given point in time to allow for a meaningful test of such dynamic relationships. Furthermore, in light of our appreciation of infant transactions in early development, methods are being developed for searching for continuities in the relationship of the developing infant with the environment and in "matching," as has been noted in the field of temperament research.

It is important in multidisciplinary work to search for predispositions to anxiety by paying attention to context and meaning. In doing this, data must be understood at several levels: at the level of individual meaning (including awareness of worries, internalized conflict, and transformations of experienced anxiety); at the level of emotional signaling and communication processes (including binds and double binds, and deviant socialization patterns in families); at the level of parental contributions (including attributions and role conflicts); and finally at the level of feelings. It is especially important to include feelings in our data. The study of feelings has been out of fashion recently; however, feelings are not only important in the development of the child's empathy, but also the observer's empathy in relation to anxiety. One line of fascinating research focuses on "intersubjectivity," or the matching of affective states between caregiver and infant (Stern, 1984). It seems likely that this kind of matching is a form of emotional availability that is blocked in the caregiver. Indeed, from the point of view of empathy a whole new set of productive questions for developmental psychopathology may soon be upon us.

D. Behavioral Treatment of Anxiety: Implications for Psychopathology

23

Treatment of Anxiety Disorders: Implications for Psychopathology

Edna B. Foa
Michael J. Kozak
Temple University

Phobias, characterized by intense anxiety to circumscribed stimuli and a strong tendency to their avoidance, have been conceptualized by learning theorists as involving both classical and operant conditioning processes (Mowrer, 1960). If phobias are thought to involve conditioned responses, then therapeutic procedures should resemble extinction paradigms. Behavior therapists have, indeed, tried to emulate experimental paradigms in developing clinical procedures. Despite the shortcomings of the two-factor theory of fear acquisition (e.g., Bolles, 1970; Herrnstein, 1969; Rachman, 1976), behavior therapy has been so successful with neurotic fears that it was termed by Marks (1978) "the behavioral revolution."

Procedures such as desensitization and flooding have been developed to dissociate fear responses from the stimuli that evoke them by exposing the patient to these stimuli under "therapeutic" conditions. Social skills enhancement and assertion training were developed for individuals who suffer from social fears or inadequacies. Although they focus on competency in environmental interactions, these techniques also invariably include exposure to feared situations. Cognitive therapies directed at reducing fear by modifying thought habits usually encourage patients to expose themselves to feared situations using the new cognitive skills acquired in therapy.

The last two decades have brought remarkable development in the treatment of anxiety disorders. Psychopathological conditions that were formerly untreatable (e.g., obsessive-compulsive disorder, agoraphobia) have become amenable to therapy as more effective techniques have replaced their less effective predecessors. Unfortunately, the advances in treating anxiety have been unparalleled by corresponding advances in understanding the mechanisms of treatment. This is perhaps because their theoretical exploration has been pursued less vigorously than the research on outcome variables. Nor have we advanced much in our understanding of anxiety development and maintenance. The genesis of anxiety disorders remains largely enigmatic.

The development of an effective therapy for a particular problem may have little to teach us about its development. Just as amelioration of depression by tricyclic antidepressants sheds little light on its genesis, the reduction of anxiety by deliberate exposure itself implies little about the origin of phobias. However, the assessment of responses during treatment, guided by a theoretical concept of anxiety, can lead to explication of the mechanisms involved in its reduction. The identification of such mechanisms may illuminate the nature of impairments specific to particular anxiety disorders and may lead to hypotheses about their development. These hypotheses can then be examined independently of treatment outcome.

In the present paper we briefly consider the classification of anxiety disorders, and provide an overview of the literature on the relative efficacy of behavioral and cognitive treatments for the various disorders (for thorough reviews see Barlow & Beck, in press; Emmelkamp, 1982; Marks, 1978). We then suggest mechanisms of fear reduction. Finally, we attempt to develop hypotheses about the nature of the psychological deficits that are involved in anxiety disorders.

CLASSIFICATION OF ANXIETY DISORDERS

The seven anxiety disorders listed in *DSM-III* (American Psychiatric Association, 1980) seem to be divided into three major categories: (1) phobic disorders, which include agoraphobia, social phobia, and simple phobia (e.g. acrophobia), (2) anxiety states, including panic disorder, generalized anxiety disorders and obsessive-compulsive disorder, and (3) post-traumatic stress disorder, which is characterized by the presence of excessive anxiety and distress following a traumatic event. Unlike *DSM-II*, this classification emphasizes descriptive aspects of the disorders. Agoraphobia is fear and avoidance of being alone or in public places without help or ability to escape. Simple phobia is irrational fear and avoidance of a situation or object other than social situations and public places. Social phobia is persistent fear of and desire to avoid social situations in which the individual is afraid of scrutiny and embarrassment. Common to phobias is some identified external source of anxiety (e.g., social situation, supermarket, snake) and its avoidance. In addition, descriptions of both social phobia and agoraphobia include fear of anticipated loss or catastrophe. The agoraphobic anticipates incapacitation (e.g., heart failure, fainting) and avoids situations from which escape is impossible or help is unavailable. The social phobic avoids public humiliation and embarrassment. On the other hand, occupation with future harm is not a diagnostic requirement for simple phobia.

The second class of anxiety disorders, anxiety states, is distinguished in *DSM-III* by the absence of avoidance behavior as a diagnostic requirement. Panic disorder and generalized anxiety disorder are characterized by heightened physiological responding and the absence of a circumscribed source of anxiety. Criteria for obsessive-compulsive disorder are recurring unwanted thoughts or repetitive stereotypical behaviors that are recognized as senseless. Evoked reexperiences of the stress of an identifiable traumatic event, and numbness or withdrawal from the external world following such an event, are the hallmarks of post-traumatic stress disorders.

While providing clear descriptions for the identification of anxiety disorders, *DSM-III* offers no theoretical dimensions on which these disorders can be defined. Several axes were proposed by Foa, Steketee, and Young (1984). These include the presence or absence of *avoidance behaviors,* the presence or absence of *external fear cues,* and presence or absence of *anticipated harm.* Given that nonexternal cues for fear (e.g., thoughts, physiological responses, impulses) occur in every anxiety problem, eight categories emerge from the listing of all possible combinations of these three dimensions, each representing a different type of fear structure. In Figure 1, the categories proposed here are mapped against the *DSM-III* anxiety disorders. It is apparent that some anxiety disorders are more homogeneous with respect to their fear structures than others. Agoraphobics for example are quite homogeneous: Most fear their own physiological responses since they signal potential harm. To protect themselves from harm agoraphobics avoid arousing situations. All three types of fear cues compose the agoraphobic fear structure. Obsessive-compulsive disorder, in contrast to agoraphobia, is highly heterogeneous. Some obsessive-compulsives are similar to agoraphobics in that their fear contains all three components (e.g., fear of contamination that will lead to illness). Ruminators are more similar to patients with generalized anxiety disorder. Both are concerned with nonexternal feared events.

The validity of any theoretical classification of psychopathology depends on its usefulness in relation to treatment procedures and etiology. An advantage of a theoretically based classification is guidance in forming hypotheses about etiology and treatment. A relationship between treatment procedures and fear structures has already been proposed for phobias (Chambless, Foa, Groves, & Goldstein, 1979) and for obsessive-compulsives (Foa, Steketee, & Ozarow, 1983). Here, we try to relate hypothesized fear structures to the outcomes of treatments for various disorders and to hypothesized deficits specific to these disorders.

TREATMENT OF ANXIETY DISORDERS

Early conceptualizations of neurotic anxiety in the terms of learning theory emphasized external fear cues and overt avoidance while nonexternal fear cues, including anticipated harm, were largely ignored. Even in the case of generalized

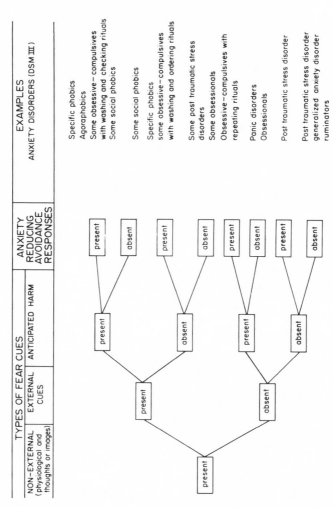

FIG. 1.   Functional analysis of anxiety disorders.

anxiety disorders, where identified external cues are absent, Wolpe (1958) suggested that such cues do exist but are less well defined because of the intensity of the original conditioning and/or the lack of distinct external stimuli at the time of conditioning. This focus on external fear cues might explain why behaviorists have concentrated on treatments for phobics and obsessive-compulsives, for whom such stimuli are readily identified, rather than on treatments for panic disorder and generalized anxiety. More recently (Beck, 1976; Meichenbaum, 1977) the emphasis has shifted to nonexternal fear cues (e.g., autonomic arousal, thoughts of impending catastrophes) with the resultant development of cognitive techniques.

Exposure-Based Treatment of Anxiety

Exposure treatment is a set of techniques whose common denominator is confronting patients with their feared cues. These techniques can be divided according to the medium of exposure (imaginal vs. in vivo), the length of exposure (short vs. long), and level of arousal (low vs. high). If the various exposure procedures are ordered along these dimensions, then systematic desensitization, where exposure is imaginal, brief, and minimally arousing, occupies an extreme position on each dimension. In direct contrast is in vivo flooding where exposure is to actual life events, prolonged, and designed to elicit high levels of anxiety.

Imaginal Techniques.   Many studies have demonstrated the efficacy of systematic desensitization with simple phobics (e.g., Cooper, Gelder, & Marks, 1965; Marks & Gelder, 1965). When compared with other therapeutic procedures (including hospitalization, insight, groups, and individual psychotherapy), systematic desensitization was superior (Gelder, Marks, & Wolff, 1967). Moreover, phobics who failed to benefit from traditional psychotherapy later improved when treated with systematic desensitization (Gelder & Marks, 1968).

The effects of systematic desensitization with agoraphobics are less impressive: They tend to be poor responders to this procedure (Gelder & Marks, 1966; Gelder et al., 1967; Yorkston, Sergeant, & Rachman, 1968). In reviewing the behavioral treatment of agoraphobia, Jansson and Ost (1982) concluded that "of the five studies which hitherto have evaluated systematic desensitization, four found the method ineffective and one study found it more effective than a control condition" (p. 325).

In comparing the responsiveness of simple phobics and agoraphobics to systematic desensitization and imaginal flooding, Marks, Boulougouris and Marset (1971) found the former to profit equally from the two techniques whereas the latter improved with flooding but not with desensitization. In a replication and extension of this study, Gelder, Bancroft, Gath, Johnston, Matthews, & Shaw (1973) concluded that both desensitization and flooding were superior to placebo control treatment, and were equally effective for both disorders. Inspection of the results, however, suggests that for the behavior-test measure, flooding was superior to desensitization for agoraphobics. Crowe, Marks, Agras, & Leitenberg (1972) compared in vivo practice with imaginal flooding and desensitization. In vivo practice was best, followed by flooding and desensitization which did not differ from one another. Since most of their subjects were simple phobics, the results further indicate that simple phobias are equally amenable to treatment by either desensitization or flooding.

Chambles, Foa, Groves, and Goldstein (1979) found flooding in conjunction with intravenously administered barbiturate less effective than flooding alone. Since the drug led to lower anxiety during flooding, its detraction from improvement suggests that the experiencing of anxiety may be an important component of therapy for agoraphobics. Some support for this notion comes from Watson and Marks' (1971) finding that agoraphobics profited from anxiety-evoking images even when irrelevant to their phobias.

No controlled prospective studies have been conducted to evaluate the effects of desensitization with obsessive-compulsives. The available case reports, however, suggest its ineffectiveness with these patients. Cooper et al. (1965) reported that only 3 of 10 patients improved with this technique; Beech & Vaughan (1978) reported that only 4 of 10 cases improved. Better results were found when desensitization was conducted in vivo: 7 of 11 evidenced gain.

Several variants of prolonged imaginal exposure (implosion, satiation) have been employed with obsessionals who did not have overt rituals. Emmelkamp and Kwee (1977) found disappointing results for imaginal flooding, as did Stern (1978) for satiation. In a series of case studies, however, Boulougouris & Bassiakos (1973) and Stampfl (1967) found it to be effective with ritualizers.

Investigations of exposure-based treatments with socially anxious patients have been surprisingly limited. In contrast to volunteer subjects, for whom desensitization has consistently been found effective, socially anxious patients do not seem to benefit from this procedure. Marzillier, Lambert and Kellet (1976) compared desensitization with social skills training and a waiting list control. Social functioning improved following both treatments, but at follow-up the desensitization group lost its gains. Neither treatment, however, produced reduction in self-reported anxiety. Conversely, Trower, Yardley, Bryant, and Shaw (1978) found self-reported anxiety reduced following both desensitization and social skills training, but social functioning improved only after skills training. Shaw (1979) described a flooding group that improved as much as did the desensitization and skills training groups in the Trower et al. (1978) study. Ost, Jerremalm, and Johansson (1981) examined the effectiveness of social skills training versus relaxation during role playing for "physiologically reactive" and "behaviorally reactive" socially anxious outpatients. Although both treatments were generally effective, skills training worked better for behaviorally reactive patients, and relaxation for physiologically reactive patients. Emmelkamp (1982) concluded that "desensitization is of limited value with socially anxious patients [and that] social skills training seems to be of more value in the treatment of social anxiety" (p. 135).

Post-traumatic-stress disorder is particularly suitable for treatment by imaginal exposure, because a past event that cannot be readily recreated in reality underlies this disorder. Behavior therapy for this disorder resembles the treatment by abreaction employed with war neuroses, which involved evocation of traumatic memories (Grinker & Spiegel, 1943). Cases in which imaginal flooding was used with veterans who reported flashbacks, nightmares, or intrusive thoughts have been described (Fairbank & Keane, 1982; Keane & Kaloupeck, 1982). Flooding involved imagining the material of the flashbacks and nightmares. Improvement following this treatment was reported in all cases after relatively few sessions. Systematic desensitization has also been found highly effective (Kipper, 1977; Schinder, 1980).

In summary, imaginal flooding and systematic desensitization are both effective with simple phobics. For agoraphobics, most evidence indicates the superiority of flooding over desensitization, and flooding is more effective when not accompanied by pharmacological agents that usually suppress physiology. Obsessive-compulsives, like agoraphobics, are largely unaffected by desensitization but benefit somewhat from flooding. Systematic desensitization appears quite successful in many studies with socially anxious volunteers, but marginally effective compared to social skills training in the few studies of socially anxious patients. For post-traumatic-stress disorders, flooding and desensitization have both been found useful.

In vivo Exposure.   In recent years imaginal procedures have fallen out of favor as evidence favoring in vivo exposure has accumulated. As mentioned earlier, Crowe et al. (1972) found reinforced practice (in vivo graded exposure) superior to systematic desensitization and imaginal flooding. Despite Wolpe's assertion (1973) that generalization from imaginal to real stimuli is direct and immediate, Barlow, Leitenberg, Agras, & Wincze (1969) noted that such transfer occurred only 50% of the time. In the same vein, Watson, Gaind, and Marks (1972) found that fear, as measured by heart rate, was higher during in vivo exposure to feared situations although patients had previously habituated to them during imaginal exposure. In all the above studies, subjects were simple phobics. As noted by Mathews (1978) "the available evidence suggests that direct exposure is always superior with simple phobics" (p. 399). There also seems to be an agreement about the superiority of real-life procedures for analogue population of specific phobics (e.g., Bandura, Blanchard, & Ritter, 1969; Barlow, Agras, Leitenberg, & Wincze, 1970).

With agoraphobics, it has been demonstrated that variants of in vivo confrontation are equivalent to one another (Emmelkamp, 1974; Emmelkamp & Ultee, 1974; Everaerd, Rijken, & Emmelkamp, 1973) and that imaginal flooding was inferior to in vivo exposure on some measures (Emmelkamp & Wessels,

1975; Stern & Marks, 1973). Also with agoraphobics, Mathews et al. (1976) found these two forms of exposure to yield equivalent results, as did Rabavilas, Boulougouris, & Stefanis (1976) with obsessive-compulsives (with the exception of one measure on which in vivo exposure was superior). The addition of imaginal exposure to in vivo confrontation was found to enhance maintenance of treatment gains (Foa, Steketee, Turner, & Fischer, 1980; Steketee, Foa, & Grayson, 1982). Comparison of imaginal and in vivo exposure is difficult because in most studies some in vivo exposure was introduced during the course of imaginal treatment either as formal in vivo sessions or homework assignments.

An apparent contradiction emerges between Emmelkamp and Wessel's finding that in vivo exposure was superior to imaginal and Mathews et al.'s finding of their equivalence. Johnston, Lancashire, Mathews, Munby, Shaw, and Gelder (1976) pointed out procedural differences between the two studies that could account for the discrepancy. They suggested that in the Mathews et al. study greater emphasis on in vivo exposure homework assignments and longer inter-session intervals, which allowed more home practice, increased the effects of treatment. The authors concluded that imaginal exposure is effective only to the extent that it promotes in vivo confrontation with the feared stimuli.

Most of the clinical studies on the efficacy of in vivo exposure involved agoraphobics and obsessive-compulsives. From parametric studies it has been learned that prolonged exposure is better than short exposure (Rabavillas et al., 1976; Stern & Marks, 1973) that massed sessions are better than spaced sessions (Foa, Jammison, Turner, & Payne, 1980) and that self-exposure is better than modeled exposure (Roper, Rachman, & Marks, 1975). Graded exposure was equivalent to abrupt exposure (Boersma, den Hengst, Dekker, & Emmelkamp, 1976; Hodgson, Rachman, & Marks, 1972) and group exposure, to individual exposure (Emmelkamp & Emmelkamp-Benner, 1975; Hafner & Marks, 1976). The presence of a therapist during exposure seems unnecessary (Emmelkamp, 1974; Emmelkamp & Kraanen, 1977; Mathews, Gelder, & Johnston, 1981). Neither did spouse-assisted exposure enhance treatment efficacy (Emmelkamp, 1982; Mathews, Jannoun, & Gelder, 1979).

The efficacy of in vivo exposure with agoraphobics was evidenced in several studies. Emmelkamp & Kuipers (1979) found that at one year follow-up, 75% of 70 agoraphobics improved with an average of 18 sessions. Improvement was defined as a 2-point reduction on a 0–8 scale. Overall group improvement was found by McPherson, Brougham, & McLaren (1980) and by Munby and Johnston (1980), but the number of patients who improved was not reported in these studies.

The application of in vivo exposure to obsessive-compulsives is complicated by the nature of their fears. For an obsessive-compulsive the physical removal of a feared object or situation does not necessarily constitute escape. The patient who had touched a contaminated object continues to feel contaminated for a long period after touching the contaminant, often until ritualistic washing is performed. Likewise a "checker" worries for hours after leaving the door that it may be unlocked. In contrast, for simple phobics and agoraphobics removal from the feared situation constitutes escape.

In 1966, Victor Meyer described treatment program for obsessive-compulsives that included (1) exposure, i.e., contact with discomfort-evoking stimuli; (2) response prevention, the blocking of ritualistic behavior. Through the use of these two procedures exposure was prolonged and avoidance or escape blocked. Treatment involved graded exposure to feared situations and 24-hour supervision to prevent the patient from ritualizing. At follow-up, 80% of 15 patients thus treated were improved (Meyer, Levy, & Schnurer, 1974). Exposure combined with instructions to refrain from ritualizing was also found effective (Rachman, Marks, & Hodgson, 1973): at a 2-year follow-up, 75% of the patients remained improved (Marks, Hodgson, & Rachman, 1975). A slightly better outcome, 85% improvement, was reported by Foa & Goldstein (1978) who combined imaginal and in vivo exposure with response prevention. At present, hundreds of obsessive-compulsives were treated in programs that included variants of in vivo exposure and response prevention, with improvement ranging from 60% to 85% (for review see Foa, Steketee, & Ozarow, 1984).

In an attempt to identify the relative contributions of exposure and response prevention to treatment outcome, Foa and her colleagues conducted several studies (Foa, Steketee, & Milby, 1980; Steketee, Foa, & Grayson, 1982). In general, in vivo exposure mainly affected anxiety to contaminants whereas response prevention influenced ritualistic behavior. A combination of the two procedures was superior both at post-treatment and follow-up.

The effects of in vivo exposure on social phobics have not been systematically explored. However, social skills training, which can be construed as in vivo exposure to contrived social situations, generally yielded more satisfactory results than did imaginal procedures. For the most part, in vivo exposure is impractical for post-traumatic stress disorder, although tales about "curing" soldiers by sending them back to the battle are quite common.

In summary, in vivo exposure is the treatment of choice for simple phobics and possibly also for agoraphobics. In combination with response prevention it is highly effective with many obsessive-compulsives.

What do exposure-based techniques offer for generalized anxiety disorder? When interventions for pervasive anxiety were developed, the focus shifted from external stimuli to anxiety responses themselves. Goldfried (1971), for example, extended systematic desensitization to encompass all anxiety-arousing situations. Rather than perceiving desensitization as a technique to dissociate conditioned stimuli from anxiety responses, Goldfried viewed it as a method of teaching the skill of coping with anxiety. Suinn and Richardson (1971) developed a technique called Anxiety Management Training, which consists of exposure to any anxiety-evoking situations primarily to allow rehearsal of anxiety management skills. Common to both approaches, as well as to Meichenbaum and Turk's (1976) stress inoculation training, is an assumption that generalized anxiety disorders reflect deficits in the management of anxiety rather than simply abnormally strong fear reactions to a particular set of cues. According to a rationale analogous to that for social skills training, patients are exposed to an anxiety-evoking situation not for anxiety to diminish in that situation, but rather for skills to be learned. On the other hand, Borkovec (1983) seems to suggest that these patients fear somatic cues that portend loss of control and social rejection. Treatment based on this view should involve exposure to situations involving loss of control and social rejection so that anxiety aroused by these circumstances would decrease.

Cognitive Therapies

Theoretical Considerations. An evaluation of what cognitive therapies can offer for our understanding of anxiety disorders must first come to grips with some conceptual issues surrounding these approaches. What is a cognitive therapy and what are its active elements? Cognitive psychotherapy is founded in assumptions of a causal role of thoughts and beliefs for emotion and behavior. Although this emphasis on private events primarily involves conscious processes, there are also attempts to identify unconscious or automatic processes that are said to contribute to pathology. Assessment of these private events is primarily via self-report of the patient. The interventions represent attempts to modify automatic thoughts, belief systems, irrational ideas, and so on, and are for the most part interpersonal and linguistic: The therapist tries to produce cognitive changes in the patient by what is verbally communicated in therapy.

While this is a general description of what is common to cognitive psycho-therapies, it belies the diversity of the various approaches and excludes techniques that might properly be called "cognitive." For example, systematic desensitization, which usually relies on modifying verbally evoked images (private events) of feared situations, is nevertheless not considered cognitive therapy. Conversely, many cognitive therapists include behavioral rehearsal, self-monitoring, and exposure as part of their program.

Cognitive therapy is a composite of different techniques. Therefore, when its efficacy and the mechanism by which it produces change are examined, one should delineate the specific technique under consideration. Compared to what is available about exposure, information about the efficacy of specific cognitive techniques is somewhat scarce. Therefore, several prevalent cognitive approaches are examined for what techniques are claimed to be effective. Some speculations about the mechanisms of their presumed effects can then be offered. This discussion includes Ellis' rational-emotive therapy, Beck's cognitive therapy, and what is generally known as cognitive-behavior therapy (Lazarus, 1976; Mahoney, 1979; Meichenbaum, 1979).

According to Ellis (1980) emotional disturbance is caused by a specific set of cognitive structures involving mistaken ideas about how one sees others and the conditions of life in general. Rational Emotive Therapy (RET) espouses a philosophy of life for adoption by clients that includes atheistic humanism, scientific thinking, risk taking, acceptance of uncertainty, self-direction, and tolerance of self and others. By vigorously disputing clients' competing ideas, the therapist promotes their adoption and thereby facilitates the formation of new cognitive structures. Although a variety of techniques, such as imagery, relaxation, thought stopping, and so forth, are employed, many are considered palliative methods of only temporary usefulness. Notably, while RET favors belief change through verbal persuasion, it recognizes the potency of behavior changes for producing cognitive changes (Ellis, 1968). Accordingly, "RET favors in vivo desensitization and flooding homework assignments, and hypothesizes that they will result in more profound and lasting philosophic changes than will, say, imaginal and/or gradual desensitization" (Ellis, 1980, p. 332). Overall, RET is extremely eclectic in techniques used, because interventions as apparently divergent as marathon encounters (Ellis, 1977a) and assertion training (Ellis, 1977b) are interpreted as producing similar belief changes.

Cognitive-behavior therapy, as derived from what Mahoney (1979) calls the "cognitive-social-learning-perspective," acknowledges biological, psychological, and environmental causes of behavior. Although this perspective is an extension of behavioral models, learning is explained in terms of changes in "rules" or "cognitive blueprints" for action rather than as simple conditioning. Although its primary emphasis is on social learning processes, the cognitive-social-learning approach posits that the sources of maladaptive behavior can vary across individuals and situations and are not always best explained by constructs about ideas or beliefs. Nevertheless, interventions are usually directed toward skills deficits or cognitive distortions that are attributed to maladaptive learning. Thus, this approach is not distinguished so much by specific techniques, but rather by the ways in which obtained changes are explained. Techniques such as modeling, assertion training, self-monitoring, imaginal and in vivo exposure are targeted at specific areas of dysfunction and are expected to produce cognitive changes.

Beck's cognitive therapy was developed primarily for the treatment of depression. More recently, however, Beck (1976) has begun to extend this work to the treatment of anxiety. As noted in Dryden's (in press) comparison of RET and cognitive therapy, Beck maintains that a wide variety of beliefs, including errors of inference, rather than only finite clusters of irrational ideals, can underlie emotional problems. Cognitive therapists argue that cognitive schemata are used in faulty information processing to distort and nullify the effects of information that might otherwise disconfirm erroneous assumptions (Beck, Rush, Shaw, & Emery, 1979). Cognitive therapy "consists of a particular therapeutic style, as well as a set of techniques" (Young & Beck, 1982). The style is collaboration with the patient in considering evidence relevant to erroneous beliefs. The techniques are standardized and involve the identification of automatic dysfunctional thoughts via daily self-monitoring, their disconfirmation by active hypothesis testing (including homework exposure to relevant situations), and the patient's independent application of this strategy to novel situations.

This brief overview of cognitive approaches reveals that although some techniques are specific to a given approach, all include an exposure component for treating anxiety. Indeed Ledwidge's (1978) attempt to distinguish cognitive, behavioral, and cognitive-behavior therapies has prompted much controversy and little satisfaction (Ledwidge, 1978; Locke, 1979; Mahoney & Kazdin, 1979; Meichenbaum, 1979).

A consideration of cognitive therapy raises at least two issues. First, what is the evidence that techniques derived specifically from cognitive hypotheses contribute to anxiety reduction? Second, how strongly does this evidence support the idea that these techniques are effective because they influence cognitive processes such as beliefs, evaluations, inferences. Out strategy of examining the outcome of these techniques begs the question of whether the efficacy of a variety of other techniques is best explained by "cognitive" mechanisms. It allows us, however, to focus on techniques that are labeled "cognitive."

Outcome of Therapy. In an earlier exploration of the contributions of cognitive techniques, Ledwidge (1978) examined 13 controlled studies comparing behavior therapy and what he called cognitive behavior modification, i.e., therapies that "attempt to change behavior by influencing the client's pattern of thought and rely chiefly on speech as the instrument of change" (p. 356). All involved nonpatient volunteers; 10 addressed various simple fears. The reviewer noted that of 6 studies using RET or cognitive restructuring to discover and correct irrational self-statements, 1 found rational emotive therapy superior on a verbal measure, 1 found behavior therapy superior on a behavioral measure, 3 produced mixed results depending on the measure, and 1 revealed no differences on any of the measures used. Of 3 studies using self-instruction training, which involves rehearsal of adaptive self-statements, 1 found this superior to systematic desensitization, 1 found desensitization and anxiety relief superior, and a third found no differences between treatment groups. The study of anxiety management training, involving the use of coping imagery and self-statements in addition to relaxation, revealed no differences from systematic desensitization.

Ledwidge's conclusion of "no difference" between cognitive and behavioral techniques was criticized by Meichenbaum (1979) on the basis of the selection and interpretation of the studies reviewed. Nevertheless, there was no disputing the conclusion that the relative efficacy of cognitive techniques remains unclear and that pertinent data were lacking with clinical populations. With volunteers, the finding of "no difference" among techniques (including placebo) is quite common (e.g., Kazdin & Wilcoxon, 1976; Marks, 1978). The results of a few more recent studies, several involving clinical populations, begin to address the question of the efficacy of particular techniques for particular disorders.

One of the few controlled clinical trials was performed by Emmelkamp, Kuipers, & Eggeraat (1978) with agoraphobics. They found of in vivo exposure superior to cognitive restructuring on a variety of measures. De Voge, Minor, & Karoly (1981) reported a single case study comparing relaxation, self-instruction, cognitive restructuring, and interpersonal feedback techniques with an agoraphobic patient. Clinical improvement was noted but no differences among the techniques emerged on a variety of behavioral measures. These results are difficult to interpret, however, because effects of sequential presentation of these treatments are confounded with cumulative effects of in vivo exposure and Valium intake.

In a study of 28 agoraphobic women, Jannoun, Munby, Catalan, & Gelder (1980) compared a home-based self-exposure program to a cognitively oriented strategy emphasizing identification of life stresses and problem solving for their reduction. Outcome measures included a behavior test, assessor ratings, and a variety of self-report instruments, with follow-up assessments at 3 and 6 months post-treatment. The programmed exposure was found superior on a variety of measures immediately post-treatment, although follow-up improvement in the problem-solving group diminished the treatment differences on some of the measures. The authors concluded that although the exposure treatment was superior, the unexpectedly large effects of the cognitive approach suggest that systematic in vivo exposure is not essential for the treatment of agoraphobia.

In vivo exposure, cognitive restructuring, and exposure preceded by self-instructional training were examined by Emmelkamp and Mersch (1982) with 27 agoraphobic patients. Behavioral and questionnaire measures were taken before and after treatment, and at 1-month follow-up. At post-treatment, exposure and the combined treatment were superior to cognitive restructuring on rated anxiety and avoidance, but these differences diminished at 1-month follow-up because of continuing improvement in the cognitive group and some relapse in the other groups. The combination of self-instructional training with in vivo exposure did not enhance the effect of exposure. Cognitive treatment alone, however, was found superior on questionnaire measures of depression, locus-of-control, and self-assertion. The authors concluded that although exposure was superior on some measures, cognitive restructuring did lead to clinically meaningful improvements. It should be noted that the cognitive techniques employed with the combined-treatment group were different from those used with the cognitive restructuring group; only the latter included analysis of irrational beliefs.

Studying 15 obsessive-compulsive patients, Emmelkamp, van der Helm, van Zanten, and Plocha (1980) compared graded exposure in vivo with exposure preceded by self-instructional training. Treatment produced significant improvement in both groups on therapist and patient ratings of anxiety, avoidance, depression, and a questionnaire measure of obsessions. No differences between the conditions were found at post-treatment or at 1- and 6-month follow-ups

434 FOA AND KOZAK

(with the exception of assessor-rated avoidance at post-treatment, where exposure alone was superior). The authors concluded that the cognitive technique did not enhance the efficacy of exposure.

Of the many studies that examined cognitive techniques with fearful volunteers, two that assessed fear responses not only by verbal report but also by behavioral observation and physiological monitoring may shed light on the contributions of cognitive techniques. Via newspaper advertisements, Biran and Wilson (1981) recruited 22 volunteer phobics of heights, elevators, and darkness who failed a series of behavior tests and reported fears severe enough to restrict daily activities. Guided exposure and cognitive restructuring were compared. Measures included approach behavior, self-reported anxiety and self-efficacy, and physiological reactivity during imagery of fearful situations. Exposure was found superior in enhancing approach behavior and in reducing self-reported fear and physiological reactivity.

Cognitive and behavioral interventions for musical performance anxiety were examined in another study in which self-report, behavioral, and physiological data were collected (Kendrick, Craig, Lawson, & Davidson, 1982). Fifty-three pianists, identified by their music teachers as highly performance-anxious, and meeting a criterion on a self-report scale for disruptive anxiety during musical performance, received either cognitive-behavioral therapy emphasizing self-instruction and attention-focusing techniques during rehearsal, behavioral rehearsal alone, or no treatment. No significant differences among the groups emerged immediately post-treatment. At follow-up, the two therapy groups were superior on a self-report of performance anxiety scale and on quality-of-playing ratings, but did not differ from one another on these measures. Only for self-efficacy expectations at follow-up was the cognitive treatment superior to behavioral rehearsal.

Cognitive interventions with 12 free-floating anxiety patients were studied by Ramm, Marks, Yuksel, & Stern (1983), who compared the effectiveness of positive and negative self-statements, combined with self-exposure, on subjective anxiety and reported frequency of panic attacks. Overall anxiety reductions on the various measures were small, and disappeared by 1-month follow-up. A marginal tendency for positive self-instruction to be more effective in reducing post-treatment frequency of panic attacks also became nonsignificant at 1-month follow-up. Woodward and Jones (1980) studied 27 generalized anxiety patients, comparing the effectiveness of cognitive restructuring, systematic desensitization, and their combination, on subjective anxiety, behavior self-ratings, and self-recorded thoughts. Desensitization and the combined treatment were generally superior to cognitive restructuring alone, which was found ineffective on all the measures. The combined treatment was superior to desensitization only on change in Fear Survey Schedule scores.

The effects of cognitive and relaxation treatment on general anxiety level and panic episodes were examined for three panic disorder patients by Waddell,

Barlow, and O'Brien (in press). In a multiple-baseline design, cognitive therapy (self-statement training, analysis of faulty logic, and attention focusing) was compared to a combined cognitive-plus-relaxation treatment. Self-reported negative thoughts and frequency of panic attacks seemed to decrease during the cognitive phase, and these improvements were maintained during the combined treatment phase. Self-report measures of "background" anxiety seemed less affected by either of the treatments. The available physiological data was not interpretable with respect to treatment differences. Although the authors suggested that the cognitive procedures are superior to relaxation, they recognized that their data did not really clarify this issue.

The foregoing studies indicate that some techniques are particularly effective with certain disorders, and others less effective. For example, systematic desensitization compares well to imaginal flooding for simple phobics but not for agoraphobics. Moreover, some techniques appear generally more powerful than others: In vivo exposure is better than imaginal techniques, particularly for simple phobias, and cognitive techniques seem generally impotent with patient populations. Understanding these outcomes in terms of the mechanisms of fear reduction can shed light on psychopathological differences among the disorders. Toward this end, we attempt to explain anxiety reduction in terms of processing new information about fear. A more complete consideration of this approach can be found in Foa & Kozak (1984).

ANXIETY AND ITS MODIFICATION: VARIABLES AFFECTING ANXIETY REDUCTION

Lang's (1979) bioinformational conceptualization of the structure of affect seems to provide a useful theoretical framework within which to examine the mechanisms of anxiety reduction. According to Lang, fear exists as an information structure (prototype) in memory that includes information about feared *stimuli*, about fear *responses*, and about their *meanings*. This information structure is conceived of as a program for fear behavior itself, which occurs when the affective memory is accessed or activated.

We propose that regardless of the type of therapeutic intervention selected, two conditions are required for the reduction of fear. First, a person must attend to fear-relevant information in a manner that will activate his/her own fear memory (Lang, 1977). Indeed, if the information remains unaccessed (i.e., the fear is not experienced), as would be the case for a successful avoider, the fear structure could not be modified. Second, the information that evoked the fear must contain elements that are incompatible with some of the elements that exist in the patient's fear structure so that a new (non-fear) structure can be formed. The new information, about fear ideation and fear responses, must be perceived and integrated into the existing fear structure for an emotional change to occur.

This hypothesized change might be what Rachman (1980) has called emotional processing. One way such change can occur is through exposure to an event that contains elements that are sufficiently compatible (similar to) with an existing fear structure to activate it, and at the same time contains elements that are incompatible enough to change it.

A set of responses that have been observed in patients who improve with treatment may be useful indicators of emotional processing. First, these patients show physiological responses and self-reports of fear that evidence activation of anxiety. Second, their reactions decrease *gradually* while they are being confronted with fear-relevant information, e.g., feared objects or situations. Third, initial reactions to the fear at each exposure session decrease across successive activations. Support for the validity of these indicators comes from clinical outcome studies and experimental manipulations that affect both the indicators and treatment outcome (for review see Foa & Kozak, 1984). The activation of anxiety, its reduction during sessions, and its decrease across sessions appear positively related to treatment outcome, denoting modification of fear during therapy. Conversely, deviations from this pattern may signify that the fear structure has been unavailable for modification or that new information has not replaced components of the preexisting fear memory. Within this framework, the differential success of different therapies can be attributed to differences either in their effectiveness in accessing fear or in providing information that will modify (correct) the fear structure.

Accessing Fear

Information Medium.   Experimental evidence for the effectiveness of different media in activating emotion comes from a variety of paradigms (e.g., Barber & Hahn, 1964; Craig, 1968; Kozak, 1982; McLean, 1981). However, the media may differ in their relative efficacy in activating a fear memory. For example, Watson, Gaind, & Marks (1972) found that the average initial heart rate response of simple phobics during fearful images was much smaller than that during in vivo exposure. Perhaps in vivo exposure conveyed more information and was therefore more effective in evoking fear. On the other hand, more information can increase the likelihood for a mismatch with the patient's fear memory, and may thereby interfere with accessing. It is not uncommon for a social phobic who is exposed to contrived social criticism to be unable to experience fear because the situation lacks "reality" for him.

In general, while an affective memory can be accessed by information delivered through a variety of media, a medium that enables the relevant fear information to be accurately and completely presented will better evoke that fear. Discussions about anxiety may or may not access the affect even though some aspects of the fear information are present, whereas confrontation with the feared situation usually evokes anxiety. It is commonly recognized that talking about fear is not tantamount to being afraid.

Content of the Fear Situation. In studying variables that influence the accessing of fear, Lang and his associates found that the inclusion of fear responses (e.g., sweating, heart racing) in descriptions of fear images resulted in heightened fear activation during those images when subjects had been trained to focus on these responses. (Lang, Kozak, Miller, Levin, & McLean, 1980; Lang, Levin, Miller, & Kozak, 1983). Training to focus on responses may have helped subjects to attend to response elements in the scripts, thus enhancing the match between this information and that stored in memory and thereby calling up the structure more fully. Thus, flooding, in which patients are explicitly encouraged to experience fear, would be expected to evoke larger responses than systematic desensitization in which relaxation is emphasized. Cognitive therapies in which patients are not enjoined to experience fear would be expected to evoke little anxiety.

Individual Differences. Individuals differ in their capacity to attend to fear-relevant information and to use that information to activate fear. For example, only good imagers benefited from the training to attend to information about responses (Miller, Levin, Kozak, Cook, McLean, Carroll, & Lang, 1981). Phobic good imagers showed better ability to access fear even when not trained (Levin, 1982; Levin, Cook, & Lang, 1982). Thus, for individuals who are poor imagers, in vivo techniques might be more profitable.

In the clinical setting, inattention to fear-evoking information is sometimes labeled cognitive avoidance or the absence of "functional" exposure (Borkovec & Grayson, 1980). This is exemplified in distraction strategies such as pretending to be somewhere else, distorting a fearful image, and concentrating on non-feared elements of a situation. Paradoxically, discussing anxiety can be a way to avoid accessing. This may explain the relative ineffectiveness of traditional psychotherapy and cognitive procedures with phobias. When fear information is presented, cognitive avoidance is evidenced by the absence of fear responses. A repeated pattern of large initial fear responses followed by their premature reduction can signify escape via cognitive defenses.

Modifying Anxiety

Once a fear structure is accessed, two phenomena have been suggested to indicate emotional processing: short-term (within-sessions) and long-term (between-sessions) habituation. Given the validity of these indicators, conditions that enhance habituation should improve treatment outcome and vice versa.

Degree of Attention.   Investigating the process of desensitization, Borkovec & Sides (1978) found that relaxed speech phobics benefited more from treatment than did nonrelaxed ones. The relaxed group also reported greater imagery vividness, showed greater initial heart rate responses during imagery, and evidenced greater habituation over both identical and hierarchical presentations. The authors suggested that these seemingly diverse effects are quite coherent if relaxation is hypothesized to enhance attention to fear-relevant information. If a relaxed subject is indeed more attentive, he would be expected to access his fear memory more fully; this fear can then be processed and habituation to the fear content can take place.

Grayson, Foa, & Steketee (1982) investigated patterns of habituation during exposure under attention focusing and distraction conditions. Gradual within-sessions decreases in self-reported anxiety and in heart rate were found in both attention and distraction conditions. However, patients who were encouraged to focus attention on the feared situations maintained their gains, whereas those who were distracted showed a return of fear. Thus, attention facilitated between-sessions, but not within-sessions habituation. Similar results were found by Sartory, Rachman, and Gray (1982) who also found increased attention to influence long-term, but not short-term habituation.

Duration of Exposure.   Physiological activity during imagined exposure generally follows a quadratic trend for heart rate (Mathews & Shaw, 1973; Ornstein & Carr, 1975) and for skin conductance (Mathews & Shaw, 1973; McCutcheon & Adams, 1975). Responses gradually increase, then plateau, and gradually decrease again. During long imaginal and in vivo exposure similar patterns of self-reported fear have also been observed (Chaplin & Levine, 1980; Foa & Chambless, 1978). In contrast, during shorter exposures, reported anxiety increased continuously and long exposures appeared to produce more between-sessions reduction of reported speech anxiety (Chaplin & Levine, 1980). Similar results for both heart rate and self-reported fear were observed with agoraphobics by Stern & Marks (1973). If prolonged exposure promotes habituation which indicates more complete emotional processing, it should yield superior therapy outcomes to those achieved with short exposure. This was, indeed, found in a large number of experiments with animals, human volunteers, and patients, including those of Chaplin & Levine (1980), and Stern and Marks (1973) (see Marks, 1978, for review).

Notably, the length of exposure required for habituation differed across disorders, being shorter for specific phobics (Watson, Gaind, & Marks, 1972), and longer for agoraphobics (Foa & Chambless, 1978; Stern & Marks, 1973) and obsessive-compulsives (Foa & Chambless, 1978). It is reasonable to view the fears of agoraphobics and obsessive-compulsives as more pervasive and intense than those of simple phobics. Thus, it appears that the more intense the fear is, the more exposure time is required for habituation within sessions and some change in the prototype to take place.

Information Medium and the Content of Exposure.   It has been suggested earlier that in vivo exposure to actual feared situations may access fear better than do imaginal procedures. It follows that in vivo treatment should better facilitate emotional processing and thereby lead to superior clinical outcomes. Indeed, the available data converge to evidence the superiority of in vivo exposure at least for simple phobics, if not for agoraphobics and obsessives. Matthews (1978) suggested that in vivo exposure would be superior to imaginal techniques when specific skills are needed in the fear situation. He proposed that simple phobics have such skills deficits and thus would profit more from in vivo exposure, whereas agoraphobics lack such deficits and therefore would benefit equally from imaginal and in vivo techniques. Although some simple phobias clearly involve a skills deficit (e.g., hydrophobia), it is not generally the case (e.g., bug phobia, claustrophobia). Nevertheless, fears that do involve deficits in motor coordination would probably be best treated with in vivo methods that entail actual rehearsal of motor acts.

The superiority of in vivo exposure to other media might reflect either better accessing of the fear memory, or better delivery of incompatible information. If an in vivo situation is poorly matched to the patient's fear, the fear memory will be poorly accessed and its processing will be impeded. Conversely, imaginal situations with content that matches the fear will better access it and consequently facilitate its processing.

Arousal.   High tonic arousal seems to impede the short-term habituation that indicates emotional processing. Lader & Wing (1966) reported that complex phobics (agoraphobics, social phobics, anxiety neurotics, etc.) showed greater activity level and less habituation of skin conductance responses to neutral stimuli than did simple phobics. The latter, in turn, were more aroused and habituated more slowly to tones than did normals. Interestingly, Lader, Gelder, & Marks (1967) found that patients who habituated to tones benefited more from systematic desensitization than did nonhabituators. These results led Lader and Matthews (1968) to hypothesize a critical level of arousal above which responses to a repetitive stimulus would not habituate.

Unlike arousal, high initial responsiveness was found to be positively related to cardiac decreases during imaginal desensitization of snake phobics (Lang, Melamed, & Hart, 1970). In contrast, with obsessive-compulsives, Foa, Steketee, Grayson, & Doppelt (1983) reported a negative, albeit small, correlation between initial verbal report of anxiety during in vivo exposure and decreases in these ratings. The observation that high intensity stimuli hinder habituation in animals (Davis & Wagner, 1969; Groves & Thompson, 1970) as well as in humans (Grayson, 1979; O'Gorman & Jamieson, 1975) appear consistent with the Foa et al. findings. Perhaps it is *moderate* responding that signifies that an affective structure has been accessed. In contrast, excessive responding, like high arousal, may hinder emotional processing because it hinders complex learning. It is more likely that interference from excessive activity would occur during in vivo exposure than during fantasies and with obsessive-compulsives than with snake phobics. The hypothesis that moderate activity is optimal for emotional processing may explain the apparently inconsistent findings about the relationship between responsiveness and habituation.

Investigators have attempted to manipulate arousal level with relaxation (e.g., Benjamin, Marks, Huson, 1972) and with psychotropic drugs (see Marks, 1978 for review). The picture emerging from these studies is unclear: Some indicated the enhancement of treatment outcome by high arousal, others by medium arousal, still others by low arousal. Moreover, some studies found arousal level unrelated to treatment outcome. Interpretation of these findings is difficult because homework exposure assignments were uncontrolled with respect to arousal level, and because information allowing comparison of arousal levels during treatment across studies is unavailable. Furthermore, the role of arousal level may vary for different disorders. If a particular disorder involves a fear of arousal itself (e.g., agoraphobia), then the presence of arousal during exposure would be required to activate the fear structure sufficiently for emotional processing. Indeed, Chambless et al. (1979) found brevitol-assisted imaginal flooding inferior to flooding without the arousal-reducing drug.

MECHANISMS FOR FEAR REDUCTION

Successful treatment, we suggest, activates fear and provides information to modify it. In this section we discuss what kinds of information are needed for fear reduction.

Dissociation of Responses to Stimulus Situations

Habituation in the fear context (within sessions) provides the information that physiological responses associated with fear decrease in the fear situation. This new information about the absence of arousal supplants some of the response structure of the fear memory. Systematic desensitization is a deliberate attempt to provide such information via associating relaxation with the feared situation. In flooding, exposure is prolonged to allow response decrements and the dissociation of fear responses from the feared situation.

Given this hypothesized role of habituation, one might expect that biofeedback-assisted relaxation during exposure would enhance its therapeutic effects. The literature on biofeedback and anxiety reduction is inconclusive because (1) only few controlled studies compared exposure and exposure-plus-feedback, and (2) the results of the available comparisons yield a mixed picture of the contribution of biofeedback (for review see Rice & Blanchard, 1982). Several hypotheses may account for the ambiguous results about biofeedback and fear reduction. If exposure alone is generally effective in producing habituation, additional response decreases derived from biofeedback training may be therapeutically insignificant except for the exceptional nonhabituating patient. Alternatively, the biofeedback task could be viewed as a distractor that would reduce accessing of fear during exposure and impede emotional processing. A third hypothesis is that response decreases during biofeedback-assisted exposure will be perceived by patients as peculiar to the biofeedback situation, and thus as not generalizable to other fear contexts.

Evaluation of Threat

As we noted in discussing the classification of anxiety disorders, anticipated threat constitutes a particular focus in some of the categories. Accordingly, interpretive evaluations of both stimuli and responses may require modification. Several types of evaluations can characterize the fear structures of those who manifest anxiety disorders. First, there is a reluctance to engage in fear-provoking experiences because of one's evaluation that anxiety will persist until escape is realized. Second, the fear stimuli and/or the fear responses are estimated to have an unrealistically high potential for causing either psychological (e.g., going crazy, losing control) or physical (e.g., dying, being ill) harm. Third, the anticipated consequences have a relatively high negative valence, i.e., are extremely aversive for the individual. The first evaluation is corrected via short-term habituation in the feared situation. Correction of patients' inaccurate estimates of eventual harm often requires repeated exposures; such changes are reflected in long-term habituation. Valence changes through habituation and through exposure to values that involve low negative valence.

Individuals, as well as disorders, may differ with respect to the recalcitrance of their deviant evaluations. Several factors may account for resistance to change. First, the nature of a belief may preclude its ready disconfirmation during the course of therapy, e.g., "visiting a hospital will result in cancer development sometime within the next several years." Second, the patient's theory of potential harm may be so prolific with qualifications (like so many "epicycles"!) that any disconfirming information is readily accomodated, and thus, an incompatible information set is difficult to provide. Another problem with elaborate prototypes may be difficulty in accessing the fear because it is difficult to generate the elaborate evocative situation in therapy.

In proposing that fear reduction occurs through changes in stimulus-response associations and related evaluations, we do not imply that all this information would be available to introspection. As noted by Nisbett and Wilson (1977), cognitive processes are not always amenable to accurate assessment via self-report. Rimm, Janda, Lancaster, Nahl, & Dittman (1977), for example, found that only in a minority of instances were reported thoughts catastrophic in nature during imagery of feared situations. Neither do we imply that modification of evaluations is necessarily accomplishable via their discussion with the patient. In fact, a technique that relied heavily on self-reports of cognitive processes might have limited effectiveness with anxiety.

Beliefs and Attitudes

Emotional processing of anxiety might be conveniently viewed as a hierarchical set of changes in an information structure of which only certain elements may be available to introspection. Unconscious changes, such as stimulus-response dissociations, may influence beliefs and attitudes that are more readily related to overt actions. For example, habituation of autonomic nervous system responses in the presence of a feared stimulus may lead to reduced estimates about the persistence of anxiety, and in turn, to a change in the attitude that "anxiety should be avoided at all cost." This could lead to more general changes in perception of self-efficacy and to accompanying behavioral changes.

Once a fear memory has been evoked by information that sufficiently matches an individual's fear prototype, several mechanisms come into play. The information that short-term physiological habituation has occurred leads to dissociation of response elements from stimulus elements of the fear memory structure. The lowered arousal consequent to habituation enhances capacity to process evaluative information (relevant to feared stimuli and responses) that is incompatible with preexisting unrealistic evaluations. Indeed, high levels of arousal are known to interfere with information processing (Yerkes & Dodson, 1908). Reduced estimates of anticipated harm, as well as decreases in the negative valence associated with it, obviate the disposition to avoid the feared situation, thus further reducing the associated physiological preparatory activity. Between-sessions habituation is then observed. Longer-term decreases in anxiety constitute additional information which accumulates to modify more general beliefs and attitudes about one's ability to cope with feared situations in general.

DEFICITS AND IMPAIRMENTS IN ANXIETY DISORDERS

After reviewing literature on treatment outcome for anxiety disorders, we have conceptualized therapy as the modification of specific fear structures. Accordingly, therapy provides information pertinent to stimuli and/or response elements of the fear structure, and also to its evaluative elements. Once fear is evoked, the underlying information structure is modified by certain information provided during therapy. In this section, we explore what these therapies suggest about deficits and impairments in specific anxiety disorders.

Exposure-based therapies were developed on the assumption that certain associations between stimuli and responses constitute the fundamental pathology of anxiety disorders in which otherwise neutral stimuli evoke the anxiety responses. This associative model implies a fear structure of disordered stimulus/response links. Both desensitization and flooding are designed to break pathological associations. On the other hand, cognitive therapies are based on the assumption that anxiety disorders are caused by erroneous interpretations of various situations, so that the fundamental pathology of anxiety disorders lies in the evaluations of stimuli and responses. Cognitive therapy is aimed at correcting beliefs or thinking habits, via their discussion and rehearsal of new thinking habits as well as via reality testing. Thus, exposure-based therapies assume that disordered associations among stimuli and anxiety responses constitute the pathology, whereas cognitive therapies focus on faulty evaluations. We propose that the deficits lie in *both* stimulus-response associations and their evaluations. Successful treatment changes stimulus-response associations through habituation. It also changes estimates of threat and valence.

Phobics' fear structures are noted for their persistence, coherence, *and* irrationality. This view entails that either the phobic structure itself differs from a non-neurotic fear structure and/or that anxiety-disordered individuals are impaired in the mechanisms by which fear is usually modified. With regard to their fear structures, we propose that *both* normal and neurotic fears involve stimulus and response elements as well as evaluations or beliefs about them. Neurotic anxiety, however, is characterized by unusually high negative valences associated with the fear structure. For some disordered individuals, the "badness" of an event is simply much greater than for other individuals. Only sometimes, however, is valence related to an erroneous evaluation about the consequences of the event. In addition, high negative valence in a fear structure can derive from erroneously high estimates of the probability of occurrence of an event. Thus, one individual may fear making a social faux pas because the embarrassment feels terrible; another may be convinced that a single faux pas will bring his job dismissal; a third may believe he will almost *surely* make a faux pas *at any social occasion*. As discussed earlier, erroneous estimates of harm may persist because of the belief structure itself, i.e., the belief by its very nature defies disconfirmation.

Anxiety disorders are also characterized by large fear responses. For example, phobias are defined in *DSM-III* as including excessive avoidance responses, and generalized anxiety disorders must include autonomic or somatic muscle hyperactivity. The excessive responses may reflect a more elaborate fear structure; perhaps more stimulus and response elements are present in the network. Another possibility is that the associations in the disordered fear structure are more strongly formed. In either case, the fear structure would be more readily evoked.

Of course it is also possible that magnitude information is coded into the response structure, and that some individuals are predisposed to larger responses (Lader & Wing, 1966).

It is clear, then, that neurotic fears do differ structurally from normal fears. Although examination of treatment outcome cannot tell us how neurotic structures developed, their identification may lead to hypotheses about the development of anxiety disorders and to treatment strategies directed at correcting the impaired features. The presence of structural problems is a necessary, but itself insufficient, condition for anxiety disorders. *DSM-III* specifies *persistence* as a major criterion for these disorders. Indeed, most fears disappear spontaneously (Agras, Chapin, & Oliveau, 1972). The persistence of pathological anxiety implies some deficit or impairment in the mechanisms by which a fear structure is usually modified. The literature on treatment outcome may help to identify the nature of this impairment for particular disorders.

If exposure treatment reduces anxiety, it is plausible to hypothesize that either anxiety-disordered individuals receive less than normal spontaneous contact with their feared situations or they require more exposure for fear reduction than is normally encountered. Reduced exposure can stem simply from active avoidance and escape that may be caused by high negative valence for anticipated harm. The anticipated level of discomfort from a dog bite, for example, differs from one individual to another and is extremely high for the dog phobic. The high negative valence for anxiety itself, which often characterizes individuals with anxiety disorders, will also result in increased avoidance behavior. This negative valence for anxiety may reflect a more general attitude about discomfort. One of the factors that may be involved in the development of at least certain anxiety disorders is relative intolerance of discomfort and the belief that stress should be avoided (see Carr, 1974).

Deliberate avoidance may not fully account for insufficient exposure. Some fears are composed of a collection of structures that must be addressed independently through exposure to a wide variety of situations. For example, a patient who feared contact with cancer also feared bald people and items connected to the state of Delaware where her fears first developed. Although they had been strongly related, the separate structures became more loosely linked. To modify such a complex fear, exposure to a plethora of situations is required. Accidental contacts with a small subset of these situations would be insufficient.

Insufficient exposure need not stem from lack of contact: "Functional" exposure may not occur upon confrontation with the feared situation. Since phobics are not particularly poor in ability to access fear by attending to feared material (Burgess, Jones, Robertson, Radcliffe, & Emerson, 1981; Lang, Levin, Miller, & Kozak, 1983), a lack of functional exposure might be attributable to active cognitive defenses such as distraction and distortion. Cognitive defenses may not only hinder fear activation, but also fear modification, by reducing the impact of corrective information.

Another factor that may hinder spontaneous fear reduction in the face of contact with the feared situation is excessive arousal and an associated deficit in habituation capacity (Lader & Wing, 1966). One would expect that routine confrontations with feared situations, which would be sufficient for fear reduction in normals, would be ineffective for people with excessive arousal. If fear activation persists during contact, its reduction via escape is more likely, and stimulus-response dissociation would not occur in the fear-context. Consequently erroneous evaluations about the relentless persistence of anxiety and the ensuing harm remain uncontradicted. High arousal may also hinder change in the face of disconfirming evidence. As noted earlier, excessive physiological activity can interfere with attention. This interference may result in incomplete processing of the information embedded in the exposure situation: If the information that some anticipated harm had not occurred is not incorporated, the structure will not be corrected.

Contact with the feared situation may fail to reduce fear because the information provided during exposure is misinterpreted. Cognitive theorists posit that anxiety-disordered individuals use mistaken premises for evaluating information. It seems that for Ellis the core of pathology is mistaken values which affect the valence of stimuli and responses: The belief that "everybody should love me" increases the negative valence of being rejected. Beck, on the other hand, focuses on distorted interpretations that result in overestimation of negative outcome: The interpretation of a stern face as a personal rejection leads to overestimates of personal rejection.

The persistence of erroneous evaluations and interpretations in the face of corrective information might also be mediated by impairments in rules of inference. Basic epistemological errors such as affirmation of entities simply because their existence has not been *dis*proven and failure to make inductive leaps from specific situations could mitigate the effects of fear-relevant evidence. For example, for a germ phobic the absence of evidence that leukemia is contagious is not grounds for comfort. Rather, it is supportive of the hypothesis of contagion. For many phobics, multiple encounters with a feared situation fail to constitute inductive evidence for future safety. This failure to generalize from a disconfirming situation could also stem from theories of harm of the sort mentioned earlier in which elaborate qualifications prevent a person from perceiving two situations as alike.

The assumption that impairments in mechanisms of information processing underlie anxiety disorders is reflected in attempts to ameliorate them by the use of cognitive techniques. The existing techniques seem directed mainly at faulty premises. Impaired rules of information processing have received little emphasis. Although the relative impotence of available cognitive techniques with anxiety disorders offers little support for the hypothesized cognitive deficits, it can hardly be considered conclusive. Perhaps these techniques are either ill-formed or mistargeted.

Our hypothesis that fear reduction requires fear evocation might be questioned in the light of de Silva and Rachman's (1982) observations that fear is sometimes reduced following verbal persuasion, cognitive therapy, traditional psychotherapy, or administration of placebo. It is difficult to interpret the extent to which these techniques may succeed because they sometimes access pathological fear networks, or, alternatively, succeed only in reducing "normal" fears which may not need to be activated for modification. We have already suggested that neurotic fear structures include excessive response elements that are strongly associated with the network. Perhaps fear activation during therapy simply implies that fear memories have been accessed: Because of the special coherence of pathological fear, fear activation would be elicited by any information pertinent to the network, while this would not necessarily be so for less coherent "normal" fears. In addition, the correction of the especially strong response associations of pathological fears may require the information provided by physiological habituation.

In summary, neurotic fear structures are distinguished by the presence of erroneous estimates of threat, high negative valence for the threatening event, and excessive response elements (e.g., physiological, avoidance). In addition, neurotic fear structures are characterized by their resistance to modification. As we hypothesized earlier, change requires fear evocation and evocation requires some sort of exposure. The persistence of fear may reflect failure to access the fear prototype either because of active avoidance or because the content of the fear structure precludes spontaneous encounters with evocative situations in everyday life. Alternatively, fear may persist in the face of exposure because of some impairment in the mechanism of change. Cognitive defenses, excessive arousal with failure to habituate, faulty premises, and erroneous rules of inference are all impairments that would hinder processing of information necessary for changing the fear structure.

Individual anxiety disorders will now be examined with respect to distinguishing characteristics of their hypothesized structures and with respect to possible impairments in the mechanisms of fear reduction. The outcomes of behavioral and cognitive therapies for specific disorders will be interpreted in view of our hypotheses about the pathology of each disorder.

As previously noted, the seven anxiety disorders listed in the *DSM-III* can be divided according to the presence or absence of clear avoidance behavior, which in the main corresponds to the presence or absence of identifiable external stimuli. Four of them, simple phobia, social phobia, agoraphobia, and obsessive-compulsive disorder are characterized by overt patterns of avoidance. Avoidance seems to be absent in panic disorder and generalized anxiety disorder. Post-traumatic stress disorder occupies an intermediate position, since avoidance behavior often occurs but it is not an essential diagnostic criterion. The relationship between the presence of avoidance and the efficacy of certain treatments (e.g., Barlow & Beck, in press; Foa, Steketee, & Ozarow, 1984) leads to hypotheses about specific deficits underlying the various disorders.

Simple Phobia

The fear structure of simple phobias consists of stimulus-response associations and erroneous evaluations of the stimulus situations, i.e., of the estimated probabilities of associated harm. For example, the dog phobic experiences anxiety about dogs and supposes them to be ferocious. This mistaken evaluation inspires avoidance which precludes structural change via corrective information. Any therapy that will both access the structure and at the same time include elements inconsistent with its problematic components should be effective. Thus, procedures that promote association between the stimulus and nonanxiety responses, and at the same time provide information that disconfirms the mistaken beliefs about the stimulus, will result in positive outcome.

The outcome literature on simple phobias indicates, indeed, that all variants of exposure treatment are effective. Systematic desensitization and flooding seem roughly equivalent, although in vivo confrontation yields results superior to imaginal procedures. Cognitive therapy by itself is generally ineffective. Both systematic desensitization and imaginal flooding modify stimulus-response associations. In vivo techniques may be superior because, as we noted earlier, they better access the fear structure. Perhaps in vivo techniques also better disconfirm erroneous expectations of harm. Cognitive therapies, on the other hand, do not much activate the fear structure and thus do not provide conditions to dissociate response from stimulus elements. In addition, disconfirming information that they provide is less likely to be incorporated (see Bower, 1981 on mood-state dependent learning).

Social Phobias

Social fears are characterized by unusually high negative valence for social scrutiny and criticism as well by overestimation of their likelihood. Social phobics often believe this high likelihood to stem from their own deficits in social performance, which, in turn, are exacerbated by anxiety. In addition, these patients think that responses that exemplify anxiety are subject to social opprobrium. Thus, the social fear structure includes associations about social situations and anxiety responses, evaluation of social encounters as threatening (e.g., criticism) and evaluation of anxiety responses as portending criticism and therefore as being harmful themselves. The disruptive effect of anxiety is compounded by the high tonic arousal and slow habituation that has been found in social phobics.

The limited outcome literature with socially anxious patients favors social skills training even for patients without identified social skills deficits. Systematic desensitization is generally less effective. If social skills training is construed as a form of in vivo exposure with an additional important component, then its superiority to desensitization may be explained by the specific nature of the social fear structure. In addition to promoting habituation and the resultant dissociation of fear responses from social situations as does desensitization, social skills training also corrects beliefs about social inadequacy, either by teaching those skills or rehearsing them. When a simple phobia involves either actual or perceived performance deficits (e.g., swimming), skills training is expected to be superior for the same reason.

Agoraphobia

Although the presence of a relationship between certain situations and fear responses in agoraphobics indicates a disordered link among stimulus and response elements of their underlying fear structure, it appears that erroneous evaluations of the fear *responses* distinguish the structure of agoraphobia from that of simple phobia. Agoraphobics commonly perceive anxiety itself to be dangerous, the risks being of either physical harm (e.g., heart attacks) or psychological harm (e.g., going crazy, being embarrassed). Stimulus elements (e.g., supermarkets) are not evaluated as intrinsically threatening: The danger is perceived to lie in the anxiety which they evoke. In contrast, in simple phobias the potential harm does stem from the stimulus situation itself (e.g., snakes, wasps, dogs).

The differential efficacy of therapies for simple phobia and agoraphobia is interpretable as supporting our hypotheses about differences in their fear structures. Accordingly, the relative inefficacy of systematic desensitization (compared to flooding) with agoraphobics would stem from its focus on minimizing anxiety during exposure. Flooding procedures promote large anxiety responses that continue over a long period before decreasing, thus disconfirming patients' erroneous beliefs about the dangers of anxiety itself. Additional support for our hypothesis that the major impairment in agoraphobia involves faulty response evaluations is found in the mitigating effects of brevitol on fear reduction via flooding. The reduction of anxiety during flooding with brevitol allows little opportunity for direct disconfirmation of evaluations about the anxiety. We have previously suggested that the maintenance of certain disorders is mediated by a general attitude that arousal should be avoided. If agoraphobics generally avoid arousal, the effort to minimize anxiety in systematic desensitization would reinforce this attitude. On the other hand, flooding, in which high arousal is prompted, would contradict this attitude.

The effect of cognitive therapy on agoraphobia is somewhat unclear. The addition of cognitive procedures to in vivo exposure did not enhance treatment efficacy. This may derive from the sufficiency of exposure alone to change the relevant structural elements. Alternatively, the available cognitive techniques do not address themselves to the reevaluation of anxiety responses. When cognitive therapy alone was examined no immediate effects were found; at follow-up, however, some improvement was noted. It is possible that this therapy produced change in the general attitude of avoidance, thus promoting exposure during follow-up, which in turn resulted in evocation of the fear structure and its modification. Another cognitive technique, directed at solving problems of general stress, seems more promising. Perhaps, then, agoraphobics are deficient in their ability to solve problems when stressed.

Two additional findings outside of the outcome psychotherapy literature bear on impairments characteristic of agoraphobia: high tonic arousal and slow habituation. While the extensive avoidance behavior of the agoraphobic suggests that the maintenance of the fear is due to lack of fear evocation, these two impairments may account for the failure of occasional accidental confrontations with feared situations to promote change.

Obsessive-Compulsives

Several forms of fear structure occur in obsessive-compulsives. The patient who fears contracting VD from public bathrooms and exhibits washing rituals has a fear structure that includes disordered associations among stimulus and response elements and mistaken evaluations about the harm from the stimulus situation. This fear structure resembles that of simple phobia. The woman who feels contaminated by her mother and avoids even the most indirect contact with her for fear that the anxiety generated by such contamination would make her crazy is similar in her fear structure to an agoraphobic. For other obsessive-compulsives, fear responses are associated with evaluative elements rather than with a particular stimulus set. For example, patients who are disturbed by perceived asymmetry and reduce anxiety by rearranging objects do not fear the objects themselves, nor do they anticipate disaster from the asymmetry. This last form does not resemble those of any of the phobias previously discussed.

It appears from the examples cited that no one form of fear structure is common to obsessive-compulsives. One unifying variable, however, is an impairment in the interpretive rules for making inferences about harm. Typically, obsessive-compulsives base their beliefs about danger on the *absence* of disconfirming evidence and often fail to make inductive leaps about general safety from specific disconfirmations regarding danger. Consequently, although rituals are performed to reduce the likelihood of harm, they can never really provide safety and therefore must be repeated. In observing obsessive-compulsive checkers, one is impressed by what seems to be a memory deficit for their own actions vis à vis danger situations. However, a patient's doubt about the status of the just-checked gas burners may reflect impairment in evidential rules for inferring danger. The epistemological idiosyncrasies of obsessive-compulsives foster the resistance of fear structures to modification.

Because obsessive-compulsive disorder has often been construed as a type of phobia, treatment has focused on fear reduction (modifying the fear structure) rather than on correcting information processing impairments. Systematic desensitization is generally ineffective for this disorder, and imaginal flooding seems to fare little better. Treatment of choice is in vivo exposure with response prevention; exposure alone affects physiological and reported fear whereas response prevention influences rituals. The two treatment components interact to produce greater change than the sum of their separate effects. Exposure to feared situations without its ritualistic undoing is necessary to allow disconfirmation of anticipated harm. The relative inefficacy of treatment programs that use imaginal methods may be rooted partly in their omission of response prevention and partly in the failure of imaginal methods to provide for exposure beyond that of the session. Imaginal exposure to one's feared harm when added to in vivo confrontation was found to assist maintenance of treatment gains for some individuals, perhaps because imaginal realization of the disaster scenario allows response habituation and decreases in associated negative valence.

Since an impairment in the rules for processing information about harm seems central to obsessive-compulsive disorder, one might expect that cognitive techniques would be beneficial. However, the addition of cognitive techniques to exposure has not been found to enhance treatment efficacy. Perhaps for most patients exposure in vivo is sufficient to modify the targeted fear structure, including erroneous evaluations of harm. Disordered information processing rules may also be unlearned during in vivo exposure for patients who succeed with this treatment. Cognitive techniques specifically directed at information processing impairments, however, might increase the likelihood of their correction. The available cognitive techniques have not been adapted to these impairments.

Generalized Anxiety Disorder and Panic Disorder

These two disorders are distinguished by the absence of specific stimulus elements in their fear structures and the absence of corresponding avoidance. The structure of panic disorder includes response propositions and their evaluation. Like the agoraphobics, these patients construe anxiety responses as dangerous. Unlike agoraphobics, they do not seem to develop spurious stimulus-response associations. In the absence of a ready explanation for this difference, it is reasonable to examine possible differences in rules of processing information about harm, or in risk-taking attitude.

Generalized anxiety disorder seems to be characterized by high tonic arousal with associated negative valence which becomes temporarily linked to various negatively valent stimulus structures. Unlike the other anxiety disorders, this pathology is not one of stable disordered associations. Neither can its maintenance be explained by avoidance of fear. Efforts to reduce the negative valence associated with high arousal and to prevent accidental associations would follow from this conceptualization. The preliminary nature of the available research with cognitive therapy for general anxiety disorder severely limits the inferences that can be made from it. Investigation of alternative hypotheses involving fear of loss of control and resultant social scrutiny is also in its very early stages.

Post-Traumatic-Stress Disorders

Among the various anxiety disorders, post-traumatic stress is the only one that is defined in part by a precipitating event. Stimulus and response associations regarding that event form the basic fear structure for this disorder. Since precipitating events are of the sort that would be stressful for almost anyone, the *persistence* of the fear structure, rather than simply the formation of these associations, distinguishes the disorder from normal reactions, i.e., there is an impairment in the process of extinction.

The handful of reported instances of behavioral treatments with these disorders indicates the effectiveness of both systematic desensitization and imaginal flooding. These findings coincide with earlier reports of the effectiveness of sodium pentothal-assisted abreaction with war neuroses. The success of a variety of exposure therapies suggests that, as with simple phobics, the persistence of fear reflects avoidance. Perhaps traumatic-stress disorder victims differ from non-victims in having a greater general attitude of anxiety avoidance. The *DSM-III* description of "numbness" to the environment, constricted affect, and estrangement from others might be interpreted as support for the hypothesis of a general tendency to avoid affect in these individuals. In apparent contradiction to the avoidance hypothesis are the spontaneous fear episodes that characterize post-traumatic stress disorders. These episodes, however, are of short duration and long interval. Brief interrupted exposures are known to be ineffective for fear reduction, probably because they are insufficient for habituation to occur.

The fear structures of post-traumatic-stress disorders resemble those of simple phobias in that both have identifiable stimulus elements, associated response elements, and their evaluations. Furthermore, as with simple phobias this fear seems to persist, because of insufficient exposure, and is reduced equally well with systematic desensitization and imaginal flooding. This apparent structural similarity suggests that, as has been found for simple phobias, post-traumatic-stress disorders might be reduced more effectively with in vivo techniques, were not the precipitating stress situations impractical to reproduce.

SUMMARY

In this chapter we have examined the literature on cognitive and behavioral treatments and advanced hypotheses about the etiology of anxiety disorders. Strong conclusions about the *development* of psychopathology cannot be derived from knowledge of treatment outcome. On the other hand, therapy can tell us about *deficits* or *impairments* that underlie disordered behaviors and emotions, and these were the foci of our etiological hypotheses. Specifically, we have identified two kinds of impairments: disordered fear structures and disordered extinction processes. We have deliberately refrained from offering hypotheses about the acquisition of these impairments. Findings from areas outside the treatment-outcome literature, such as epidemiology or abnormal personality, may lead to specific developmental hypotheses.

Many of the hypotheses we have offered remain speculative. They are nevertheless amenable to experimental testing. Available methodology can accomodate some of these hypotheses; the investigation of others will require new assessment procedures. Once a specific impairment is identified, treatment strategies aimed at its correction can be devised. In addition, impairments identified for a particular disorder can lead to hypotheses about its development.

ACKNOWLEDGMENTS

The presentation of this paper was supported in part by NIMH grant 31634 awarded to the first author.

The authors wish to thank Dick Hallam, Isaac Marks, Richard McNally, Jacquelin Persons, Jack Rachman, and Gail Steketee for their helpful comments.

24 The Treatment of Anxiety Disorders: A Critique of the Implications for Psychopathology

S. Rachman
University of British Columbia

The ambitious and wide-ranging chapter by Foa and Kozak (this volume) raises many matters of significance. As it is not possible, nor would it be desirable, to attempt to deal with all of the points raised, this discussion deals mainly with their attempt to connect Lang's (this volume) concept of "fear structures" to the concept of emotional processing. This main discussion is supplemented by reference to a selection of specific questions relating to the nature and treatment of excessive anxiety, including the role of exposure, and the nature of agoraphobia.

The attempt by Foa and Kozak to connect the concept of "fear structure" to that of emotional processing certainly shows promise and appears at its most successful when the authors apply it to the analysis of simple phobias and to post-traumatic stress. Additionally, their discussion of why some fears fail to disappear spontaneously is particularly clear. Their analysis also leads them to pose a penetrating (but unanswered) question regarding panic disorders: "Unlike agoraphobics, they do not seem to develop spurious stimulus-response associations." Before leaving these introductory remarks, it should be said that their attempt to deal simultaneously with panic disorders and generalized anxiety disorders, under the same terms, is perhaps mistaken. For the present at least, there is a good case for regarding them as separate problems (see Klein, Rabkin, & Gorman, this volume). Generalized anxiety disorders are characterized by persisting, raised levels of general anxiety, whereas panic disorders are marked by sudden eruptions of extremely high anxiety. Also, the psychopharmacological characteristics that form the basis for Klein's analysis of panic disorders are not found in generalized anxiety disorders.

PHOBIA AND TRAUMA

These successful applications (to phobias and traumatic stress) justify their attempt to link the two concepts, but they encounter difficulties when attempting to cope with the full complexities of obsessional-compulsive disorders. Similarly, and partly for the reason just stated, their analysis of panic disorders and of general anxiety is not satisfactory. As far as general anxiety is concerned, at this juncture it might be best to follow the clear recommendations made by Mineka (this volume). The two main themes in the literature on experimental neuroses are unpredictability/uncontrollability of important life events (Mineka and Kihlstrom, 1978). Exposure to these conditions is followed by a wide range of persisting behavioral and somatic changes. Mineka argues persuasively that these findings provide a sound basis for constructing a model of generalized anxiety disorders.

Foa and Kozak's identification of some similarities between post-traumatic stress and phobias is plausible, and the ensuing analysis is useful. There is little to add to it except perhaps to suggest that here, as in all other parts of their argument connecting fear structure and emotional processing, it would be illuminating and beneficial to introduce the concept of desynchrony. The three main response systems in fear (behavioral, verbal, psychophysiological) are imperfectly coupled, and can change at varying speeds, i.e., desynchronously. Some of the implications of this concept were drawn out by Rachman and Hodgson (1974) and specific predictions were put forward (see also Grey, Sartory, & Rachman, 1979). For example, a discordance between excessively high heart rate responding and verbal reports of fear can be predictive of a return of fear (Grey, Sartory, & Rachman, 1979). Rachman and Hodgson (1974) and Lang (this volume) have postulated that discordances may prove to be predictive of poor therapeutic outcomes, and recent data go some way to supporting this hypothesis (Vermilyea, Boice, & Barlow, 1984).

The analysis of agoraphobia is not as productive, but within Foa and Kozak's discussion a potentially important distinction is made between this disorder and other types of phobia. In the case of most phobias, it is the object (e.g., animal or insect) that is feared for the harm or discomfort that it may cause. In agoraphobia, however, the person does not fear the stimulus as such (open spaces and supermarkets are not of themselves threatening), but rather the person fears what might happen to him in the situation. "Agoraphobics commonly perceive anxiety itself to be dangerous, the risks being either physical harm or psychological harm. Stimulus elements are not evaluated as intrinsically threatening: the danger is perceived to lie in the anxiety which they evoke. In contrast, in simple phobias the potential harm does stem from the stimulus situation itself" Foa & Kozak, this volume). This analysis is helpful as far as it goes, but could be expanded by relating it to Lang's (this volume) discovery of differences in the fear structure of agoraphobics and focal phobias. So, for example, Lang has found that the fear structures of "focal phobics" are far more coherent and stable than those of "social phobics"; they are also more easily accessed and in all probability, more easily modifiable—presumably because of their coherence and accessibility.

AGORAPHOBIA

Foa and Kozak's distinction provides a useful jumping-off point for alternative approaches to the treatment of agoraphobia. It is an easy step from their distinction to the introduction of what has been called the "safety perspective" into the study of agoraphobia. The underlying argument here is that the fears described by agoraphobics can be appreciated better when account is taken of their striving for safety in those very situations that provoke the fear (for a full account, see Rachman, 1983, 1984). Agoraphobia can be seen as constituting a balance between fear (e.g., of collapsing or losing control) and access to safety. The fluctuations in agoraphobia usually can be traced to changes in safety factors (e.g., presence of spouse) rather than to changes in the physical environment, i.e., fear factors. The availability of safety signals or procedures moderates the fear. Furthermore, the person's apprehension about what might happen to him/her in the situation can be reconstrued in terms of the predictability and controllability of the situation, a subject that has been thoroughly and fruitfully developed by Mineka (this volume).

If further encouragement were needed, the recent report by Michelson, Mavissakalian, and Meminger (1983) might provide it. They found that external locus of control scores were strongly associated with improvement in a group of 50 agoraphobic patients. Patients who attributed their difficulties to internal sources were less likely to show improvement.

EXPOSURE AND FEAR-REDUCTION

Although it contains some useful elements, the therapeutic implications of the distinction between agoraphobia and other phobias, as set out by Foa and Kozak, may encounter difficulty. Their therapeutic argument depends on the pivotal assumption that the relevant anxiety has to be experienced before it can be overcome. However, there are good reasons for supposing that these and other sorts of fears can be significantly reduced without any exposure experience (de Silva & Rachman, 1981). The occurrence of significant fear reduction even in the absence of exposure to the fearful stimulus (see below) will limit the explanatory value of their formulation.

As the problem of the reduction of fear without exposure crops up at several points in the Foa and Kozak paper, a few words of explanation are necessary.

De Silva and Rachman argued that even though exposure to the fear-provoking stimulus is a prominent feature of most of the effective procedures, "there is no good reason for supposing that such exposure is a necessary condition for fear reduction" (1981, p. 227). While pointing out that no attempt had been made systematically to collect the evidence pertinent to the argument, and that the available evidence is incomplete and not satisfactory, they nevertheless pursued the argument and pointed out that the positive assertion had never been satisfactorily proven, i.e., no one had shown that exposure is indeed a necessary condition for fear reduction. The list of examples they set forth in support of the argument that fear reduction can occur even without exposure included the following: The provision of corrective information about the harmlessness of stimuli can lead to a reduction of fear; in some instances, cognitive therapy is followed by fear reduction; spontaneous remissions of anxiety reactions occur in some patients; fear reduction has been observed after the administration of placebos; experimental tests show reductions in fear after nonexposure types of therapy; improvements sometimes are seen in fears other than the one being treated (usually after some reduction in the target fear), fears can be reduced by drug treatments (Klein, Rabkin, & Gorman, this volume; Telch, Tearnan and Taylor, 1983). The role of exposure remains to be clarified and opposing views have been expressed (Boyd & Levis, 1983; de Silva & Rachman, 1983).

At several points in their paper, Foa and Kozak argue that the experience of anxiety is or may be an important component of procedures for reducing fear. The evidence for this assertion is weak and incomplete. In the study by Watson and Marks (1971), it was reported that agoraphobics benefited from anxiety-evoking images even when these images were not relevant to their phobias. However, the earlier study on this subject, carried out with subjects who had intense but circumscribed fears, produced a different result. In their attempt to test out some of the assumptions of implosion therapy, Hodgson and Rachman (1970) compared the effects on fear of high arousal evoked by irrelevant fearful material and high arousal provoked by relevant fear material. The subjects who were aroused by irrelevant fear material showed no signs of significant fear reduction, and the finding reported by Watson and Marks would benefit from a replication (and the inclusion of appropriate control conditions).

In the treatment of agoraphobic patients, as indeed in the treatment of obsessional-compulsive patients, it is possible in many cases to achieve substantial reductions in fear by a graded and gradual procedure in which the patient experiences minimal anxiety throughout (Rachman & Hodgson, 1980). It simply is not the case that significant anxiety has to be experienced before fear reduction can be achieved. Nor is it necessary for the person to experience strong physiological reactions. In the laboratory study by Grey, Sartory, and Rachman (1979), fearful subjects with high heart rate responses were compared with those who showed low heart rate responses; the subjects in both groups showed comparable improvements. In the same experiment, some subjects who reported comparatively low subjective levels of fear also made significant progress.

Returning to the question of the treatment of agoraphobia, Foa and Kozak's analysis would lead them to say that because agoraphobics fear what might happen to them in the situation (i.e., they might have an attack of anxiety) the exposure should be to the experience of anxiety rather than to the stimulus elements as such (e.g., supermarkets). Exposure should consist of experiencing anxiety in the relevant situations. This certainly is a plausible line of argument, and echoes of it can be found in the clinical applications known as anxiety management training. Nevertheless, we have to consider how to account for improvements in those agoraphobics who do not experience anxiety or panic attacks during the course of the treatment. Might the answer be that these patients learn that the anxiety attacks or panics are not likely to occur and/or that they are not likely to act in a socially unacceptable manner? In other words, they acquire corrective information, but it is not dependent upon "exposure" in the sense in which Foa and Kozak argue the case. Rather one can incorporate all of the information by saying that what is being disconfirmed in the successful treatment of these patients is that anxiety attacks or panics are likely to occur, and if they do, the anxiety is intolerable.

The question of whether or not fear can be reduced without direct exposures to the fear-provoking stimulus is of wide significance and certainly extends beyond agoraphobia. Nonexposure reductions of fear present no difficulty for the model of emotional processing (Rachman, 1980), but can Lang's (this volume) bio-informational theory accommodate the phenomenon?

Incidentally, a recognition of nonexposure reductions in fear will open new doors. For example, it enables one to think constructively about means for preventing fear. It also enables one to think of constructive alternatives when an anxiety patient fails to respond to exposure treatment (see Rachman, 1983, for examples). Third, it helps one to avoid an embarrassed silence when presented with evidence of drug-induced reductions in fear—in the absence of exposure treatment.

Foa and Kozak repeatedly assert that fear *must* be evoked before it can be modified. "Indeed, if the information remains unaccessed (i.e., the fear is not experienced), as would be the case for a successful avoider, the fear structure could not be modified." To quote again, they say that "change requires fear evocation, and evocation requires some sort of exposure." Each of these statements, and their interconnection, can be doubted.

As mentioned earlier, there are plausible examples of fear changing, indeed reducing, without evocation. Second, it is possible to evoke fear without exposure; threatening information will do it, and so will the withdrawal of safety signals (Rachman, 1978, 1984).

The question remains, is it possible to change fear by the mere provision of corrective information (or by other nonexposure methods)? If the answer is yes, can such changes be incorporated into Lang's bio-informational theory? My own view is that as a bio-*informational* theory, there should be no objection to allowing the possibility that *various* forms of information are capable of changing fear structures. There seems to be no fundamental reason for insisting that fear must be evoked in order for the fear structure to be changed. Given that information of various kinds, coming in through various channels, is capable of changing the fear structure, one can attempt to account for reports such as that by Kleinknecht (1982). In his fascinating study of a group of tarantula enthusiasts, Kleinknecht found that of those who had previously been fearful of these creatures but who had overcome their fears, no less than 70% attributed the reduction in their fears to acquired knowledge of tarantulas and spiders. Forty percent attributed the fear reduction, at least in part, to observation and a further 27% attributed part of the change to direct contact. Before leaving this matter, I cannot refrain from mentioning a case illustration. An agoraphobic patient whose fears arose out of a deep concern (not entirely baseless) about her health received an excellent X-ray report and reassuring information from her physician; her anxiety diminished and her agoraphobic avoidance became less pronounced.

There is another reason for urging that the bio-informational theory be expanded. So far, the problem of whether or not fear structures can be reduced without evocation has been addressed. The argument that fear structures can indeed be changed without the evocation of anxiety is, I believe, strengthened by drawing attention to fear increases as well as fear reduction. Elsewhere, it has been suggested (Rachman, 1981) that there is an asymmetry in the relations between information and fear, such that provision of information is a weak means of reducing fear but can be a powerful means of inducing or increasing fears. If it is conceded that fear can be induced (or increased) by the provision of information, then the claim that fear structures "require fear evocation" (Foa & Kozak this volume) before they can be changed is left in need of modification. Exclusive concentration on fear *reductions* may lead to this point being overlooked.

PERSISTING FEAR

Another outstanding problem, bearing on fear and its relation to avoidance, plays a smaller part in Foa and Kozak's presentation, but it is of considerable significance and is addressed in part by Gray (1971) and in greater detail by Mineka (this volume). It concerns the persistence of excessive fear, or more correctly in a number of cases, the persistence of excessive avoidance behavior. This excessive persistence of avoidance is, of course, an old and difficult question that remains to be resolved. Most psychologists now acknowledge that the Miller-Mowrer two-stage theory of fear and avoidance (Mowrer, 1960) is capable of coping with much of the available information but that it has significant limitations. It was argued that fear is both a response and a drive. The arousal of fear acts as a drive that promotes escape or avoidance. The successful reduction of fear that follows escape or avoidance behavior serves to reinforce such actions. Fear-motivated avoidance behavior is strengthened by its success in reducing fear. Some of the weaknesses of the Miller-Mowrer theory were set out by Gray

(1971), Seligman and Johnston (1973), and Rachman (1976) and therefore will not be considered in full. The difficulties include the following. Even if fear is a necessary cause of avoidance behavior (itself questionable), there are grounds for concluding that it is not necessary for the continuance of avoidance behavior. Furthermore, as Mineka (this volume) remarks, "It seems clear that fear extinction is rarely, if ever, necessary as a precursor of avoidance response extinction." The two-stage theory assumes that all fears are acquired by conditioning and that neutral stimuli are all equally prone to be turned into fear signals. Both of these assumptions have been challenged (Rachman, 1978; Seligman & Johnston, 1973). It has also been observed that the theory exaggerates the motivating role of fear in human behavior, and it was implied in this criticism that avoidance behavior can be motivated and maintained in other ways (Rachman, 1978). There are other difficulties, but perhaps the most important one is that the two-stage theory postulated a synchronous causal relationship between fear arousal and subsequent avoidance behavior. Variations on this pattern have, however, been observed (Rachman & Hodgson, 1974).

In pursuit of the argument that the undue persistence of avoidance behavior cannot be accounted for adequately by the two-stage theory, de Silva and Rachman (1983) carried out a pilot study on three small groups of agoraphobic patients. Two groups were treated with one or other form of exposure therapy, and the third group acted as a waiting control. Patients in the first group stayed in the target situation until their self-rated anxiety dropped by half (the endurance condition). The patients in the second group were required to leave the fear situation when their anxiety reached a high pre-set level without waiting for the anxiety to drop (escape condition). Both groups of patients improved, in contrast to those in the waiting list control group. (It is interesting to note, however, that a third of the patients in the escape condition showed no change, and only one in six of the endurance group failed to improve.) Contrary to prediction from the two-stage theory on fear and avoidance, the patients who were told to escape when they were still fearful did not show signs of increased avoidance behavior. In light of this result and a number of other considerations, it now seems worthwhile to incorporate the role of safety signals in attempts to explain the persistence of agoraphobic avoidance behavior (see Gray, 1971; Rachman, 1984). These other considerations include the fact that agoraphobic reactions are not stimulus-bound, tend to fluctuate, can change without exposure, and are strongly influenced by safety factors, especially the presence of a trusted companion.

OBSESSIONS

Foa and Kozak's analysis of obsessional-compulsive disorders is partly confounded by the complexity of this disorder, which has at least two major elements, i.e., obsessions and compulsions (see Rachman & Hodgson, 1980). These two elements usually occur in association but do not always do so, and in many instances the disorder can be characterized as being mainly obsessional or mainly compulsive. In any event, it has been found necessary to attempt related but separate explanations to account for these two problems—indeed, it was even found necessary to add a third element of "obsessional slowness" (Rachman & Hodgson, 1980). The attempt by Foa and Kozak to encompass both of the main elements, obsessions and compulsions, in the same explanation presents problems, and their explanations (that there is an impairment in inferential ability regarding harm) would gain in plausibility if they concentrated on that element of obsessional-compulsive disorders which comes closest to resembling anxiety—i.e., the compulsive element, and especially the cleaning compulsions in which fear often is prominent. They have, in fact, left this option open by conceding that "no one form of fear structure is common" to these disorders, and by noting the differences between types of obsessional problems.

One final point, not central to Foa and Kozak's argument, is worth mentioning. In their introductory discussion, it is clear that they regard anxiety disorders as a form of illness, perhaps even as a form of mental illness, following the *DSM-III* classification. It has often been remarked that anxiety can instead be construed as a psychological variation along a continuum, rather than as being qualitiatively different from "not anxiety." The claim that phobias or anxiety disorders are more irrational or more persistent than other types of fears is difficult to sustain. For example, a common and intense fear that is regarded by most people as "normal" is a fear of spiders. Nevertheless, this fear has a large irrational element in it, can be extremely intense, and is exceedingly persistent—more persistent than most agoraphobia problems (Marks, 1969). Moreover, in agoraphobia, which commonly is regarded as an illness, there is a great deal of rational prediction of discomfort or distress. Agoraphobic patients are not being irrational when they say they expect to feel considerable discomfort in specific public places, and they are not being irrational when they say that they are likely to feel faint and that they may even collapse. These expectations are more rational than those of the spider-phobic undergraduate. That a great deal of constructive explication and development of these subjects is possible without construing them as forms of illness is convincingly demonstrated by the stimulating and constructive paper of Foa and Kozak (this volume) which, after the introductory remarks, has little more to say about anxiety as illness and a great deal more to say about anxiety as a psychological phenomenon.

CONCLUSIONS

To sum up, Foa and Kozak have made a most promising start in the worthy enterprise of connecting Lang's bio-informational theory of fear structures to the concept of emotional processing. Most progress is seen in their analyses of phobias and post-traumatic stress. It is suggested that further advances are impeded by their retention of two doubtful assumptions, both of which can be dropped without loss. Exposure methods are a powerful means of reducing fears, but do not constitute a necessary condition for change. Information (and experiences) of various forms are capable of changing fears—and I can see no obstacle to incorporating this liberalized interpretation into Lang's bio-*informational* theory; it already is incorporated in the concept of emotional processing. Similarly, there is little to be gained by insisting that fear *must* be evoked in order to be changed; again, this is often observed, but the case for setting it down as necessary condition is weak. A simplified version is preferable; various forms of information (including the exposure methods) can change fear, and fear evocation may facilitate change but is not a precondition for such change.

25 The Role of Cognitive and Somatic Cues in Anxiety and Anxiety Disorders: Worry and Relaxation-Induced Anxiety

T.D. Borkovec
The Pennsylvania State University

Basing its conceptualization of human anxiety on simple conditioning models, behavior therapy has developed several effective treatment procedures in the last two decades. Exposure techniques such as systematic desensitization, flooding, and participant modeling have been demonstrated to have significant therapeutic impact on simple phobias, agoraphobia, post-traumatic stress disorder, and obsessive-compulsive disorder (see Foa & Kozak, this volume). In each case, success has been associated with the identifiability of environmental stimuli that elicit the anxiety response. If a client can indicate precisely the cues that trigger his/her anxiety, then systematic exposure to those cues will ordinarily be therapeutic. Conversely, those neurotic disorders for which we do not have demonstrably effective psychological interventions share the opposite characteristic. Environmental triggers are either absent or quite diffuse, e.g., generalized anxiety disorder, social phobia, panic disorder, and pure obsessions. Under such circumstances, exposure becomes a less viable intervention, in both a theoretical and a practical sense.

Faced with this problem, some behavioral researchers have turned their attention to the possible role of internal cues. For example, the concepts of fear of fear and fear of loss of control in agoraphobia (Chambless & Goldstein, 1980) and the importance of response propositions in fear imagery (Lang, 1977) have highlighted the relevance of cognitive and somatic cues in the elicitation of anxiety.

Our research group has focused on two phenomena related to the role of internal anxiety cues: worry and relaxation-induced anxiety. Most humans are well acquainted with worry, but little scientific information on the topic exists. We were drawn to the construct on the basis of several years of insomnia research (see Borkovec, 1979). Psychologically based insomnias were found to be associated with uncontrollable cognitive intrusions at bedtime, and successful relaxation treatment was related to significant decreases in the frequency of those intrusions. Interest in relaxation-induced anxiety emerged from clinical experience with individuals who experienced increasing anxiety under relaxing conditions. Despite frequent observation of the phenomenon by relaxation therapists, little was known about this event as well. Our expectation is that the experimental elucidation of these two constructs will contribute significantly to our understanding of the origins and maintenance of human anxiety, particularly those anxiety disorders for which environmental elicitors are less clearly identifiable.

COGNITION, WORRY, AND ANXIETY

The Role of Cognition in Anxiety

Among the many cognitive capabilities of human beings, the ability to create mental representations of past events or of infinitely variable, anticipated future events has great significance. Planning and problem solving based on this representational process have provided us with tremendously adaptive skills. At the same time, however, that we can present to ourselves internal stimuli representing past or anticipated aversive events indicates that we also have great potential for creating anxiety in the absence of any existing threat. Animals can certainly be conditioned to show fear behavior to anticipatory stimuli and to engage in avoidance behavior in response to such stimuli. Such is the essence of avoidance conditioning. Given their animal heritage, humans no doubt are susceptible to the same simple conditioning principles, and the success of exposure therapies based on such principles reflects their relevance to human anxiety process. However, the ability of humans to generate anxiety cues mentally provides a basis for understanding why anxiety may become a more frequent experience in relatively benign environments and why anxiety may occur in the absence of clearly identifiable environmental cues. It is quite likely that the summed frequency and intensity of the fear responses of any given individual to clear and imminent physical or psychological threat (e.g., being rejected by a friend, a near-miss of an automobile accident, having a heart attack) would lag far behind the summed amount of fear in response to the anticipation of such events and the myriad of anxious "What if…" mental representations of possible future events that are common in daily life. The ability to represent those anxiety triggers in thought and image, to associate those triggers with even more remote and anticipatory thoughts, and to construct images that represent future possible traumatic events regardless of their actual likelihood, greatly expands the human capacity for anxious experience. Thus, although classical aversive conditioning and avoidance learning may provide a useful model for the etiology and maintenance of fear (see Mineka, this volume), the evolution of long-lasting human anxiety disorders may well depend upon certain cognitive events.

Cognitive Contributions to Anxiety Maintenance

What might be the nature and process of such cognitive activity? At least three possibilities have a firm empirical foundation. The first two derive from an extension of Mowrer's (1947) two-stage theory of fear to human cognition. Classical aversive conditioning, from Mowrer's point of view, resulted in the establishment of previously neutral cues as eliciting stimuli (CS) for fear reactions. In stage two, the drive properties of the CS motivated instrumental escape and avoidance behavior in response to the discriminative CS complex. That CS complex included both associated environmental cues and the response-produced stimuli of the conditioned fear response itself. One learned to fear (conditioned response, CR) events that were associated with trauma (unconditioned stimuli, UCS), and one ultimately learned to avoid those events because fear was not a pleasant experience. The "neurotic paradox" was explained by Mowrer in terms of a preservation of the CS-CR relationship due to the preclusion of extinction by the efficient and rapid avoidance of conditioned environmental stimuli.

If Mowrer's model is generalized to human cognitive activity, then attentional avoidance and imaginal avoidance represent two reactions to environmental anxiety cues, in addition to overt avoidance, that may maintain a conditioned anxiety response despite repeated exposure. If an individual shifts attention away from fear cues as soon as they are confronted, very little CS exposure takes place and little information is processed to allow for change, whether those cues are physically present or imaginally induced. The results of the Grayson, Foa, and Steketee (1982) study nicely demonstrated that instructed distraction during fear stimulus exposure mitigated between-session anxiety reduction in the long term. Instructions increasing attention to fear cues facilitated fear reduction in both this study and one by Sartory, Rachman, and Gray (1982). Motivated, attentional avoidance may thus serve the same function as overt avoidance in maintaining fear.

Even if functional exposure takes place in the sense that the person does attend to the fear cues for some period of time, fear reduction may not occur if the person engages in imaginal avoidance activity after the exposure. Empirical evidence for this cognitive/imaginal extension of two-stage theory exists. In one study (Borkovec, 1974), phobic subjects imagined a hierarchy of fear scenes. Immediately after each scene, one group focused their attention on deep relaxation sensations (desensitization), one group imagined lengthy horrific images (implosive therapy), and one group imagined avoiding the situation depicted by the scene (avoidance response placebo). The first two conditions showed equivalent and significant reductions in heart rate throughout the four sessions of treatment. The imaginal avoidance group maintained its heart rate level, significantly higher than the two therapy groups.

A third cognitive process that may maintain anxiety became apparent in the next study. Grayson and Borkovec (1978) provided a conceptual replication of the avoidance response placebo condition and found similar effects on subjective fear reactions to a hierarchy of disturbing scenes. Moreover, an additional condition wherein catastrophic outcomes were imagined in response to the phobic scene produced even greater increases in fear over repeated exposures. Mineka's review (this volume) indicates that the administration of unrelated, traumatic UCSs can lead to the recovery of previously extinguished fear responses; catastrophizing thoughts may well represent the human, cognitive analogue of this empirical observation.

Despite fear-cue exposure then, attentional avoidance may preclude extinction, imaginal avoidance may negate it, and imagining negative outcomes can lead to fear maintenance or increment. One implication of this view is that the large body of research on personality and cognitive coping styles can be seen as elaborations of how people differ in their immediate and subsequent reactions to the same stressful event and how those differences in response to stress predict change or absence of change, the development of neurotic disorder or the learning of adaptive methods for coping with life's stresses. A second implication is that the success of exposure therapies may be based on their ability to establish therapeutic conditions that motivate the client to fully process the feared material (see Lang, this volume), instead of engaging in customary attentional avoidance, imaginal escape, or catastrophizing. Evidence exists to suggest that this may be precisely the function served by both relaxation and therapeutic expectancy in desensitization technique (Borkovec & Sides, 1979).

Empirical outcomes like those described above naturally led us to conclude that persistence or change in "fear structure" will be a function of what the person does not only in immediate but also in subsequent reaction to the feared stimulus. Anxiety reduction will occur to the extent that full attention is devoted to the feared stimulus, such that Foa and Kozak's (this volume) and Lang's requirement of eliciting the entire fear structure is fulfilled. Any avoidance (overt, attentional, or imaginal) of processing fear-related information will mitigate change, and contiguous association of further catastrophizing images and thoughts may strengthen the fear structure.

The Process and Effects of Worry

Our conceptualization of the effects of worry draws heavily from the above context. With the possible exception of attentional avoidance, worry for us refers in its most general sense to all of the anxiety-related cognitive events discussed above; it subsumes what is called the cognitive aspects of anxiety. Our working definition specifies that worry involves a chain of negatively affect-laden, relatively uncontrollable thoughts and images, elicited by fear-associated stimuli and reflecting attempts to engage in mental problem solving on an issue whose outcome is uncertain but contains one or more negative outcome possibilities (Borkovec, Robinson, Pruzinsky, & DePree, 1983). We hypothesize that the process includes two of the three earlier described cognitive events that can maintain anxiety. First, worry involves thoughts and images regarding antici- pated, traumatic events, best exemplified by the "What if..." verbal statements of anxious clients and chronic worriers. As such, worry contains anxiety-pro- voking internal cues that may be sufficient to maintain anxiety in the absence of imminent environmental threat. Second, a basic function of worry is to avoid or ward off anticipated traumatic events; it is the prototype of cognitive avoid- ance. Once future catastrophy is imagined, cognitive avoidance in response to the fear elicited by such thoughts is a reasonable response, understandable from the account provided by Mowrer's two-stage theory. If one learns frequently to imagine possible traumatic events, one available coping response is to develop, in imagination, possible ways of avoiding or preparing for such events. When humans are faced with a problem, then cognitive problem-solving strategies may be highly adaptive methods of mental experimentation. When the problem is an imagined, and often improbable or unrealistic, aversive event in the future, and when numerous possible problematic events are imagined, problem solving can become an unending process that contains anxiety-provoking material and rarely allows for testing any solutions reached. Moreover, on the basis of clinical interviews with chronic worriers, our research group has concluded tentatively that the actual problem solving involved in worry is brief and ineffective in reaching rational solutions, and virtually never results in any decision regarding actions that might be taken for eliminating the threat or providing a means of coping with its possible occurrence.

On the basis of the above reasoning, worry can play an important, perhaps essential, role in the etiology and maintenance of human anxiety. Simple classical aversive conditioning may provide a foundation for unrealistic fear responses, but how the individual mentally reacts after the establishment of a conditioned fear response will determine whether it rapidly extinguishes or develops into a persistent neurotic condition. Thus, worrisome, catastrophizing thoughts, in strengthening fear structure by contiguous association, can contribute to anxiety maintenance. Moreover, the extent to which an individual develops a worrisome cognitive style may influence either the ease with which aversive events create new conditioned fear responses or the extent to which the daily world is seen as a potentially dangerous place. In the latter case, worry may well provide the initial basis for the development of new fear structures.

Empirical Investigations of Worry

Of course, the above discussion is a highly speculative account of a private event that is difficult to study. Much of this conceptualization derives from clinical experience, the extant literature on worry, extrapolations from existing learning theories of anxiety, and the thinking and writings of several contributors to this volume, in particular, Barlow, Foa, Lang, Rachman, and Sarason. Empirical evidence was required for the testing and further development of these ideas. In an effort to provide initial empirical foundations for the construct, our laboratory program has taken three directons: the description of the characteristics of worries and worrisome thoughts, the search for tasks that might reflect the mechanisms and cognitive processes of worry, and the manipulation of worry in its long-term outcome and acute form.

Characteristics of Worriers.   Early work (Borkovec, Robinson, Pruzinsky, & DePree, 1983) involved the comparison of self-labeled worriers and non-worriers on a variety of questionnaire materials. We needed to validate the relationship of worry to anxiety process. Worry and general tension reports were found to correlate at a level (.68) normally reported for the cognitive and somatic components of anxiety in the text anxiety literature (Deffenbacher, 1980). How-ever, worry had a higher correlation than tension with trait anxiety, depression, and most fear survey schedule items. Among those items, social-evaluative fears were the most strongly related to worry: feeling self-conscious, making mistakes, meeting someone for the first time, failing tests, being criticized, being a leader. Subjective experiences most highly associated with worry were, in order, anxiety, tension, apprehension, frustration, nervousness, distraction, and insecurity. Per-haps most discriminating between our sample of worriers and nonworriers were the subjects' responses to the rated degree of controllability of worries once initiated; worriers reported great difficulty in shutting off worry activity, whereas nonworriers could do so with relative ease.

Our subjects have also completed the Autonomic Perception Questionnaire (Mandler, Mandler, & Uviller, 1958), rating various somatic signs for their frequency during worry episodes. Awareness of somatic cues was not as extensive during worry as it was during depressed or anxious states. The most highly rated symptoms were, in order, muscle tension, upset stomach, and sinking or heaving feelings in the stomach. In a separate study (Hatfield, Doyle, & Borkovec, 1981), subjects imagined scenes designed to elicit various emotions, including worry, and completed the autonomic questionnaire after each scene. Spearman rank correlations of the somatic symptoms in these states indicated that worry and fear profiles were more highly similar (.859) than worry relationships with depres-sion (.756), frustration (.667), and elation (.158). Correlation of worry profiles from the Borkovec, Robinson, Pruzinsky, and DePree (1983) and Hatfield et al. (1981) studies indicated that worry pattern is fairly robust (.804).

Worry, Cognitive Intrusion, and Incubation.   While the above questionnaire data provided some information characterizing the experience of worry, we wanted an assessment task that would be sensitive to interference by the worry process. Moreover, to strengthen our assumption that worry is related to anxiety, we needed to test specific deductions from anxiety theory when applied to worry. Because our definition of worry contained reference to fear-eliciting thoughts and images, we hoped to demonstrate that under some conditions, worry would show signs of extinction whereas, under other conditons, maintenance of worry would occur. Our first experimental study (Borkovec, Robinson, Pruzinsky, & DePree, 1983) had these three goals in mind. Worriers and nonworriers were exposed to a pretest task wherein they were to focus attention exclusively on their breathing for a 5-minute period. The experimenter contacted the subject every 60 seconds during that task and asked whether attention at the moment of contact was focused on breathing or distracted by negative thought intrusions, positive thought intrusions, or by "other" stimuli. Subsequently, the subjects were exposed to 0, 15, or 30 minutes of worry, and the breathing task was then readministered to assess the interfering effects of the preceding worry on attentional concentration. Subjects in the zero-minute worry condition simply allowed their minds to wander for 30 minutes; those in the 15-minute worry condition let their minds wander for 15 minutes, followed by 15 minutes of worry; subjects in the 30-minute worry condition worried for the entire period. Worry instructions simply asked subjects to choose a topic about which they were currently concerned and to worry about it in their typical fashion. The decision to use this particular manipulation was based on Eysenck's (1979) theory of fear incubation, born of observations in the animal (Rohrbaugh & Riccio, 1970) and human (Miller & Levis, 1971; Stone & Borkovec, 1975) fear literatures suggesting that brief exposures to feared stimuli could lead to paradoxical increases in fear when compared to lengthy exposure and nonexposure.

As expected, worriers reported significantly more negative thought intrusions than nonworriers during the pretest. Also as predicted, the 15-minute worry condition resulted in an increase in the number of negative thought intrusions during the post-worry task, significantly greater than the declines observed in the other two conditions. This was true regardless of worry group status. Analysis of continuously monitored heart rate data revealed no differences due to worry status, treatment condition, or their interaction during tasks or worry periods. The incubation demonstration had important implications. Worry behaves like fear. Brief periods of worry can lead to increases in negative thought intrusions, whereas lengthy exposures can produce an extinction-like effect. Because worrying is typically done sporadically throughout the day and only for brief time intervals due to distracting environmental demands, the typical worry episode may have incubating effects on its fear-eliciting components. The experiment also provided a basis for the claim that worry involves uncontrollable, negatively toned cognitive activity. Uncontrollability was demonstrated by reports of distraction, despite task demands to focus exclusively on breathing, among worriers at pretest and among both worriers and nonworriers after an incubating worry period. The content of those distractions was reported to be negative in affective tone.

Cognitive Content of Worry. A separate investigation (Pruzinsky & Borkovec, 1983) focused on a more direct attempt to access the cognitive content of worriers and to assess whether instructed fear imagery would have the same effect as an incubating worry period. The study included an anagram test in an effort to identify performance measures sensitive to the interfering effects of worry. Worriers and nonworriers engaged in a pretest assessment procedure that included attending to their breathing, an anagram test, and a thought-sampling procedure during a 5-minute relaxed wakefulness period. During the thought-sampling procedure, subjects were asked simply to let their minds wander and to report the content of their thoughts and images each time the experimenter contacted them over an intercom. Subjects were then exposed to 3 minutes of either pleasant imagery or fear imagery, followed by posttesting with the breathing task and the anagram test. A variety of affect and imagery questionnaires were administered during the course of the experiment.

As we have routinely found in several of our studies, worriers were significantly more depressed and anxious than the nonworriers on general affect questionnaires. They also showed significantly more negative imagery and more difficulty with attentional control on the Imaginal Process Inventory (Singer & Antrobus, 1972), greater incidence of obsessional symptoms, but not of obsessional traits, on the Sandler and Hazari (1960) obsessionality scale, and more public self-consciousness and social anxiety on Fenigsten, Scheir, and Buss (1975) self-consciousness scale.

We failed to find any differences due to imagery conditions, nor did worriers and nonworriers differ on anagram performance. Brief, structured fear imagery does not seem to induce the same functional state produced by instructed worry, and being a chronic worrier does not always result in performance decrements. However, worriers retrospectively reported significantly greater worry, emotionality, and task-generated interference during the anagram tasks. Moreover, replicating the earlier experiment, worriers reported significantly more negative thought intrusions during both the pre-test and posttest breathing tasks, and objective raters of the thought samples taken from the relaxed wakefulness period judged the worriers' mental content to be significantly more negative and ambivalent in emotional valence. We did accidentally discover one behavioral discriminator of the two groups: Worriers arrived for their scheduled sessions significantly earlier than did the nonworriers. The above study provided correlational ties between worriers and obsessional symptoms, poor control of attention, and social anxiety. Moreover, the content of the mental activity of worriers in a neutral task was found to be negative in emotional tone. On the other hand, fear imagery may not be a sufficient condition to elicit worrisome activity. The content of the imagery may not have been relevant to current worries for our subjects, its duration may not have been sufficiently long to engage worry process, or we are simply wrong in assuming that fear stimuli play a necessary role in the elicitation of worry.

Worry and Information Processing. In pursuit of cognitive tasks that might reflect worry mechanisms, a collaborating research group has discovered an information-processing task sensitive to the effects of worry. Three studies using simple and choice reaction time paradigms were conducted by Metzger, Miller, Sofka, Cohen, and Pennock (1983) at The Pennsylvania State University. In the first study, worriers and nonworriers simply responded as fast as they could to a series of tone and light presentations, and they were forewarned about the type of stimulus to be presented. Subsequently, choice reaction times were obtained to the two randomly presented types of stimuli without forewarning. The resulting absence of any worry group differences allowed ruling out the relevance of general arousal, initial detection abilities, and selection and responding mechanisms in worry process. In the second study, a new sample of worriers and nonworriers were trained to identify a tachistoscopically presented geometric shape, the "Lubnick." Random presentations of the Lubnick, Lubnicks that varied in increasing degrees from the training Lubnick, and a completely different shape were then presented, and the subjects were instructed to indicate by choice buttons whether the stimulus was or was not a Lubnick. The two groups did not differ in accuracy of categorization choice. No reaction time differences appeared between the two groups in response to Lubnicks, first-degree variations of Lubnick, or completely different shapes. As Lubnick variation increased to second and third degree of variation, however, worriers showed significantly longer reaction times. Discrepancy or stimulus ambiguity thus resulted in longer decision times for worriers.

The final study in this series attempted to demonstrate the incubation effect on this performance task. Worriers and nonworriers either relaxed for 15 minutes or were instructed to engage in 15 minutes of worry. The brief, preceding relaxation period was expected to reduce intrusive worry effects among worriers on the subsequent Lubnick task, whereas preceding worry among nonworriers was predicted to produce increased reaction times as ambiguity of the stimulus in the Lubnick task increased. A manipulation check indicated successful reduction in negative thought intrusions for the 15-minute relaxed groups and increment in intrusions for the 15-minute worry groups, although overall the worriers reported the customary higher levels of negative cognitions. Again, no differences were found in categorization accuracy. The 15-minute worry condition resulted in increased reaction times as stimulus ambiguity increased for both worriers and nonworriers, whereas 15-minute relaxed condition produced reaction times for both groups that were constant over stimulus ambiguity levels and faster than those in the worry condition.

The above outcomes begin to shed some light on the information-processing effects of worry. In a neutral task involving simple matching of stimuli, worry results in a lengthening of decision time as the ambiguity of the match increases. Extrapolating from these results, our speculation is that worry produces increasing indecision and a decrement in ability to match current environmental events to preexisting cognitive categories established by past experience. For the anxious worrier, this may imply indecision about the significance of an event (e.g., "Is this a threatening situation?") regardless of past innocuous experiences with the event.

The Treatment of Worry.   Given how little we knew about worry, attempts to develop therapy procedures were perhaps premature. However, early stimulus control applications to the problem had been clinically successful. Stimulus control procedures adopted from operant research have long been employed in behavior modification programs to restrict the conditions under which a maladaptive behavior, especially habit disorders, occurs and thereby to reduce the frequency of its occurrence. Bootzin (1972) applied such a program to the treatment of insomnia, and several controlled outcome investigations have documented its efficacy with even chronic, severe insomniacs.

The procedure basically involves a set of instructions designed to reduce the occurrence of sleep-incompatible behaviors in the presence of bed-related stimuli and to increase the frequency of sleep-compatible activity. Insomniacs are told to refrain from being in the bedroom unless they are retiring for sleep, to go to bed only when sleepy, to avoid naps, and to leave the bedroom if sleep has not occurred within about 10 minutes, repeatedly if necessary. Recent theorizing about the mechanisms by which the procedure produces its therapeutic influence emphasizes the reduction of performance anxiety and the breaking up of stimulus-response worry chains (VanOot, Lane, & Borkovec, 1984). Worry, from our model of uncontrollable learned cognitive events, can be viewed as a cognitive habit disorder, initiated by fear images in response to fear-related stimuli. Because of its internal nature and incubating effects, worry activity can occur under a wide variety of environmental conditions, resulting in the contiguous association of the process with many environmental stimuli and thus creating a history of poor discriminative control for its occurrence.

Several years ago, I applied a simple stimulus control program to worry and found significant clinical benefits from its application to a number of anxious, psychiatric patients. Like Bootzin's procedure, the client is given a set of instructions designed to develop more restricted conditions for the activity: (a) Establish a half-hour worry period which will occur the same time each day and will take place in the same location. (b) Self-monitor worry behavior, learning to identify its occurrence increasingly rapidly. (c) Postpone worry until the worry period, as soon as it is identified. (d) Replace worry, when identified during the day, with present moment experience, e.g., attend to environmental events, objects, or tasks. (e) Make use of the half-hour worry period to worry intensely about today's concerns.

If worry involves contiguously associated chains (fear trigger → feared images → habitual worrisome cognitive activity), then breaking that chain during the day and allowing its occurrence only under limited conditions should reduce its frequency. If daily worry, as customarily performed in brief fashion, incubates fear, then a 30-minute period of worry should engage extinction processes, as we found in the earlier incubation study. We have conducted three group outcome studies using this procedure, and each provided initial support for its efficacy in reducing daily reports of worry frequency. In the first two experiments (Borkovec, Wilkinson, Folensbee, & Lerman, 1983), college students with chronic worry problems were selected for the treatment trial. After one week of baseline recording of daily worry levels, they were randomly assigned to treatment or waiting-list, no-treatment conditions. Treated subjects met with group leaders at the end of the baseline week, were given a written copy of the above instructions, and discussed their application. They were then asked to employ the program for 4 consecutive weeks, the first 3 of which were under counterdemand instructions. The latter device, used to reduce the impact of demand, expectancy, and placebo effects on self-report data, involved instructing the subjects not to expect improvement until the fourth week of application and practice (O'Leary & Borkovec, 1978). Critical statistical comparisons were then conducted on data obtained from the daily monitoring of worry levels during the third week.

In both experiments, the stimulus control package led to significantly greater improvement than no-treatment on subject reports of the percentage of the day spent worrying. Average reduction in worry from baseline to end of the treatment trial was 35%. Generally parallel results occurred on daily ratings of tension levels. Apparently, self-monitoring, postponement of worries to restricted conditions, and substitution of present moment awareness were separately or in combination effective in providing some degree of reported control over the occurrrence of intrusive cognitive activity.

Despite these encouraging data and the use of counterdemand instructions, placebo remained a viable rival explanation for treatment efficacy. Moreover, dependence on college student samples limited the generalizability of our conclusions. Folensbee (1984) conducted an investigation to overcome these deficiencies. The stimulus control package was compared to a placebo condition, using volunteer clients from the community who were experiencing chronic worry. Given our insomnia findings that progressive relaxation techniques can reduce the frequency of cognitive intrusions at bedtime, we expect a well-learned and well-applied relaxation response to be an active therapy procedure for worry. If, however, only a brief trial of the technique is administered and if clients are instructed merely to practice twice a day without the provision of instructions for effective application of the procedure to the daily occurrence of worry, then this treatment should theoretically have minimal impact on the target problem. Progressive relaxation training under these conditions thus served as the placebo treatment. A third condition was also developed: The basic stimulus control package was administered, but instead of using the half-hour worry period to worry intensively, subjects applied problem-solving and decision-making strategies to their concerns.

Daily worry percentage reports declined from baseline to weeks 3 and 4 to a significantly greater degree for the two stimulus control treatments when compared to progressive relaxation placebo; the two stimulus control approaches did not differ from each other. Thus, we are in a position to conclude that the phenomenological experience of the frequency of daily worry can be reduced via the stimulus control procedure among self-referred, volunteer chronic worriers, and that such improvement cannot be attributed solely to demand or placebo effects.

The data from these outcome studies do not provide direct support for the notion that contiguous association of worry with diffuse environmental situations can lead to a generalization of the activity. Other rival hypotheses can explain the worry reduction (e.g., the practicing of a coping response incompatible with worry activity). If the hypothesis of worry generalization is valid, however, then a potential basis exists for understanding the insidious development of chronic tension, general anxiety, and a worrisome lifestyle.

The above studies suggest that worry has a close relationship to fear process, that it can interfere with task performance via attention-distracting effects and/ or retardation of decision-making processes, and that it may be characterized as an uncontrollable cognitive habit that can be reduced by stimulus control techniques. At the conceptual level, worry appears to involve affectively negative thoughts and images that incubate fear during brief exposures, becomes associated with diffuse environmental stimuli, and may represent cognitive avoidance responses to anticipated threats. Like some obsessive-compulsive individuals, the chronic worrier may fear what will happen if he/she stops worrying and ceases to watch out for and prepare for possible disaster. The possibility exists that such a process is fundamental to the maintenance, and perhaps the origins, of many conditions. As an example of uncontrollable, negative cognitive activity, its mechanisms may lie at the base of the automatic, habitual thought styles cited by cognitive behavior therapists as being involved in depression (Beck, 1976) and anxiety (Dow & Craighead, 1982) disorders. More broadly, the process may cut across a variety of categories found in the *Diagnostic and Statistical Manual (DSM-III)* (American Psychiatric Association, 1980) as the following descriptions reveal:

(a) Generalized anxiety disorder: worry, ruminations;
(b) Obsessive-compulsive disorder: recurrent, persistent ideas, thoughts, or impulses; not voluntarily produced;
(c) Schizophrenia: obsessions sometimes occur transiently during prodromal phase;
(d) Major depressive episode: brooding; excessive concern with physical health; recurrent thoughts of death;
(e) Compulsive personality disorder: preoccupation; rumination; indecisiveness;

(f) Manic episode: flight of ideas or subjective experience that thoughts are racing;

(g) Agoraphobia: frequent presence of rumination.

Of course, the various labels for the unusual cognitive phenomena listed above may not reflect the same process. Yet, if overlap in mechanisms does exist, the study of normal worry would be a useful means of acquiring information of relevance and value for understanding several psychological disorders. In the only extant study relevant to this question, Rachman and DeSilva (1978) found that qualitative differences in obsessional content and process were virtually nonexistent between normals and obsessive-compulsive neurotics, although the groups did differ in intensity, duration, and frequency of obsessional activity.

At a broader level, the study of uncontrollable cognition represented by worry should tell us something about human cognition in general. Our mental life is composed of many subjective experiences, including relatively uncontrolled thoughts and images flowing continuously and effortlessly. One only needs to focus on a specific stimulus (e.g., a candle flame or one's breathing) to appreciate the extent to which that stream occurs and the difficulty that is encountered if one attempts to shut it off. The extent to which its content is epiphenomenal, indirectly reflective of important individual differences, or causally linked to affective, perceptual, and behavioral reactions is an interesting and important question.

RELAXATION-INDUCED ANXIETY

Although worry appears to be a predominantly cognitive process, relaxation-induced anxiety is a phenomenon primarily related to the role of internal somatic events in the development of anxiety. The event has been mentioned anecdotally in numerous literatures, including those of biofeedback (Budzynski, Stoyva, & Peffer, 1980), transcendental meditation (Carrington, 1977), autogenic relaxation (Luthe, 1970), and progressive muscular relaxation (Bernstein & Borkovec, 1973). What has been intriguing to us is that most of these reports cite the preponderance of the event among chronically anxious individuals. If the absence of environmental fear cues in generalized anxiety disorder implies the existence of crucial internal cues, then the study of relaxation-induced anxiety may provide clues to the nature and process of those inner triggers and, thus, may lay a theoretical foundation for developing theory and therapy for the diffuse anxiety conditions. We have devoted less attention to this phenomenon than to worry, but what is known so far suggests an important place for it in anxiety theory.

Besides clinical experience with this phenomenon, our first serious reckoning with relaxation-induced anxiety occurred in the context of an outcome investigation of the effects of progressive relaxation on general tension. We found to our surprise that progressive relaxation, involving systematic tension release of various muscle groups and focus of attention on the resulting physiological sensations, to be no more effective than no treatment. However, a tension-release condition that substituted pleasant imagery for physiological attention focusing was significantly superior to the other two conditions in reducing general tension (Borkovec & Hennings, 1978).

Close to the time of this study, Denny (1976) published a summary of his research findings demonstrating that incipient relaxation sensations in rats could be established as conditioned fear cues. From these data, he extrapolated a learning-based model of generalized anxiety disorder. The sufficient historical conditions for etiology resided in the repeated occurrence of traumatic, environmental events contiguously associated with feelings of relaxation. If internal relaxation sensations become a trigger for an anxiety response, then the only way to avoid relaxation and its consequential anxiety is to maintain a greater than normal level of tension. This animal conditioning model provided an explanation of our earlier, unexpected results and led us to discover the extensive anecdotal literature cited above.

Heide (Heide & Borkovec, 1983) subsequently conducted a controlled investigation of relaxation-induced anxiety in an effort to document its occurrence and to begin the search for its mechanisms. Chronically anxious subjects from the community were exposed to one session of progressive relaxation and one session of meditative (Benson, 1975) relaxation, counterbalanced across subjects, while extensive physiological and subjective report measures were obtained. Progressive relaxation produced significantly greater reductions in tension and arousal when compared to meditation. Both conditions produced evidence of relaxation-induced anxiety in some subjects, with a greater frequency of the event under meditative conditions. Indeed, 1 of the 14 clients experienced a panic attack while 4 others required a temporary cessation of the session due to anxiety-related experiences, and therapist intervention before training could resume.

Particularly interesting was the nature of some of the pretreatment self-report variables predicting paradoxical increases in tension and anxiety: belief in effortful or controlling strategies in life, fear of inactivity, and fear of losing control. Our conclusion from these correlations is that inability to relax and the occurrence of relaxation-induced anxiety come from a psychological style of excessive effort to control oneself and the environment. On what basis does excessive control emerge? Denny's theory indicates that classical aversive conditioning can establish relaxation as a danger signal; controlling one's level of tension at high levels serves to avoid that danger. However, another learning-based theory may provide a more reasonable explanation. Mineka (this volume) has concluded that anxiety can originate within the context of frustrative nonreward experiences. Moreover, Gray (this volume) and Becker and Flaherty (1983) have provided evidence indicating that anxiolytics reduce the effects of frustrative nonreward and negative contrast, respectively. The development of early behavioral interventions for anxiety depended so heavily upon classical aversive conditioning accounts for their conceptual base that other potentially useful models were relatively ignored. Chronic tension and inability to relax can be widely observed among highly achievement-oriented individuals. The "workaholic" is a classic example. Indeed, in our own professional lives, the existence of deadlines and the massive amount of work that often faces us frequently result in high levels of activity and, more relevantly, growing feelings of tension and anxiety. Under these circumstances where high rate activity is necessary in order to obtain desired rewards, inactivity and relaxation are danger signals indicating lack of progress toward goals, or anticipated frustrative nonreward. Seligman (1975) has offered similar comments on the aversive consequences of feeling out of control. Motor tension, autonomic hyperactivity, apprehensive expectation, vigilance, and scanning would seem to be reasonable by-products of such conditions.

The possibility of relaxation becoming an internal anxiety cue does provide a reasonable basis for the development of generalized anxiety conditions. Obviously, it will be necessary to document how relaxation acquires such a function in the developmental histories of chronically anxious individuals. Demonstrating Denny's conditions of contiguity between relaxation and traumatic events would be difficult. Identifying the paramount goals that an anxious client has in his/her life, documenting the frustrations encountered in their pursuit, and assessing changes in anxiety symptoms as a function of achievement of those goals through therapeutic intervention may be a more manageable research enterprise. The work of Chambless and Goldstein (1980) with agoraphobics is instructive in this regard. Successful treatment of the condition is often contingent on the resolution of interpersonal problems in the marriage of the patient. Certainly marital problems may be seen as a source of stress and background anxiety, but the distinction may be important between the anxiety caused by arguments and conflict and the anxiety caused by lack of progress toward that satisfying, pleasurable, and intimate human relationship depicted idealistically by poets and song writers.

CONCLUDING OBSERVATIONS

As Lang implies in his chapter, evolution appears to build upon previous response organizations in the development of new, more adaptive systems. Learning within the developmental progression of a single organism reflects the same process. While some degree of uniqueness is associated with higher levels of organization, evidence of their evolutionary or developmental traces often remains. Our own theorizing clearly emphasizes the continuity of principles governing stimulus-response and cognitive processes. It is not surprising to us that laws of contiguity and laws of effect observed for decades in behavioristically oriented animal and human laboratories should find some expression in the developing laws of cognitive activity.

Given that attitude, one notion was particularly intriguing to me during the conference upon which this book was based. The topic of anxiety is being studied by researchers with various points of view and at numerous levels of analysis: behavioral, psychoanalytic, cognitive, developmental, psychopharmacological, neuropsychological, psychophysiological, neurochemical, and anthropological. These represent different perspectives of the same ultimate phenomenon. Is it possible that unifying theory, somewhere in the vague future, will state principles that, in retrospect, will have captured the threads of valid conclusion within each of these approaches and will show them to be reflections of one another? The activity of the neurochemical substrate of anxiety may be governed by laws analogous to those of environmental/response relationship, and vice versa, while the same patterns of relationship may be seen on a larger scale from an anthropological analysis. That this is true at some level of abstraction must be the case. Whether this is true at a more practical, theory-guiding level remains to be seen. It does occur to me, however, that whenever different levels of analysis appear to generate similar conclusions, then that area of overlap is undoubtedly of heuristic value. Relationships between stimulus-response theory and cognitive theory exemplify this conclusion, and encourage us to continue to look for common threads in process, patterns, or laws across the various disciplines addressing the areas of anxiety and anxiety disorders.

ACKNOWLEDGMENTS

The author wishes to thank the current members of the research group for their invaluable contributions to the ideas and research reported in this chapter: Vivian Andrews, Xyna Bell, Deborah Block, Andrew Kelly, Paul McCarthy, Thomas Pruzinsky, Janet Stavosky, and Peter VanOot.

26 The Dimensions of Anxiety Disorders

David H. Barlow
State University of New York at Albany

Recent research suggests a variety of different dimensions of emotion in general and anxiety specifically that are important. These dimensions are relevant not only for clinical treatment considerations, but also for theoretical formulations as to the nature of anxiety. Although ideas about some of these dimensions have emerged from treatment studies, the notion that the process and outcome of treatment can tell something about the nature of anxiety is logically falacious. Foa and Kozak (this volume) also point out that the successful treatment of a specific anxiety disorder, by whatever means, does not imply either an etiology or a set of maintaining factors, whether biological or psychological. But careful assessment of different dimensions of anxiety during treatment for an anxiety disorder, particularly if guided by theory, can suggest important questions for research into the nature of anxiety. These observations can also lead to more specific hypotheses on important maintaining factors as well as etiology.

Before one can speculate on critical dimensions that might be common to all anxiety disorders and to anxiety in general, it is necessary to elaborate the various anxiety-related phenomena that are sufficiently disruptive to require a visit to a clinician. This is an appropriate place to start, since the initial level of analysis of critical features of anxiety must be phenomenological or clinical. Classification is the heart of the process with its attendant issues of reliability and validity. *The Diagnostic and Statistical Manual (DSM-III),* of course, is the latest development in systems of classification (American Psychiatric Association, 1980) and data now exist on the reliability of the various categories of anxiety disorders.

THE RELIABILITY OF
DSM-III ANXIETY DISORDERS CATEGORIES

The heterogeneity of behavioral, somatic, and experiential aspects of anxiety disorders is well known and oft noted by both clinicians and researchers (cf. Barlow & Beck, 1984). In all likelihood this heterogeneity was responsible for the rather poor reliability of previous attempts to classify anxiety disorders. Yet, anyone embarking on a clinical research project on the anxiety disorders must be able to identify and describe in as clear a fashion as possible the group of patients under study. The *DSM-III,* with its descriptive and in some cases empirically derived categories, represents a major advance in diagnosis and classification for those involved in treatment assessment research as well as others.

But the need for studies of reliability was undiminished by the promise of *DSM-III.* In our Center for Stress and Anxiety Disorders in Albany, it was important to determine if patients entering various clinical trials in the areas of agoraphobia, panic disorder, generalized anxiety disorder, and social phobia could not only be identified reliably, but could be differentiated from one another. As in other disorders, the increasing specificity and complexity of diagnostic criteria evident in *DSM-III* seemed to require a standardized interview protocol. This structured interview is necessary to test the reliability of these categories as well as to sample the broad range of phenomenology present even in the most discrete categories such as simple phobia. This goal has been accomplished in the area of schizophrenia and affective disorders with the construction of the Schedule for Affective Disorders and Schizophrenia (SADS) interview (Endicott & Spitzer, 1978, 1979). For this purpose, within the anxiety disorders, we have developed the Anxiety Disorders Interview Schedule (ADIS) (DiNardo, O'Brien, Barlow, Waddell, & Blanchard, 1982). The ADIS was designed to permit not only differential diagnoses among the *DSM-III* anxiety disorder categories, but also to provide data beyond the basic information required for establishing the diagnostic criteria. To this end, information such as history of the problem, situational and cognitive factors influencing anxiety, and detailed symptom ratings provide a data base for investigation of the clinical characteristics of the various categories. Data on some of these issues are presented below. Since depression is often associated with anxiety, a fairly detailed examination of depressive symptoms as well as their relationship to symptoms of anxiety disorders was included in the interview. In addition, the Hamilton Anxiety and Depression Scales were administered.

In order to provide as much detailed information as possible, for purposes of later descriptive studies, we did not adhere to the *DSM-III* hierarchical organization. There were very few cut-off questions where, for example, if one ascertained the presence of a major affective disorder, then any evidence of panic disorder would be subsumed under the affective disorder category. This break with the manual's rules turned out to be an important step in describing as fully as possible the phenomenology of patients presenting with one or another of the anxiety disorders. Our strategy also allowed the collection of data on co-morbidity of the anxiety disorders, once again without regard to presumed hierarchical organizations. Disorders were often ranked as primary or secondary, but only on the basis of degree of interference with functioning or severity.

With these revised guidelines in mind, an extremely stringent test of reliability was conducted. In a preliminary study, each of 60 consecutive admissions to the Phobia and Anxiety Disorders Clinic (within the Center for Stress and Anxiety Disorders) was administered the ADIS at a different time by a different and independent interviewer. The second interviewer was blind to the results of the first interview. Furthermore, diagnostic agreement was defined as an exact match of the two clinicians' primary diagnosis. For example, in our sample there were several cases in which the interviewers arrived at the same two anxiety disorders, but did not agree on which of the two was the primary diagnosis. In calculating Kappa coefficients, these cases were scored as disagreements. When disagreements occurred, a consensus diagnosis was arrived at after a detailed discussion of the case at a staff meeting. At this meeting the apparent reasons for the disagreement were also identified. Preliminary reliability data on 60 patients can be found in DiNardo, O'Brien, Barlow, Waddell, and Blanchard (1983). Table 26.1 presents up-dated Kappas calculated on the first 125 consecutive admissions. The sample size enabled the calculation of a Kappa on a reasonable number of cases in each of the *DSM-III* anxiety disorders with the exception of Post-Traumatic Stress Disorder (PTSD).

Ignoring simple phobia for a moment, one can see that the lowest Kappas are in the categories of Panic Disorder (PD) and Generalized Anxiety Disorder (GAD). There are few behavioral referents in PD and GAD and the clinician must rely on evidence, mostly self-reports, of somatic or cognitive phenomena. On the other hand, the Kappa for Agoraphobia is quite high and represents about as good an agreement as one could expect in a study of diagnostic reliability. Similarly, the Kappa for Obsessive-Compulsive Disorder (OCD) is high despite the fact that we have fewer cases in this category than any other. The low number

TABLE 26.1
Kappa Coefficients for Specific Diagnostic Categories After 125
Consecutive Admissions

Diagnosis	*N*	*Kappa*
Agoraphobia with panic	41	.854
Social phobia	19	.905
Simple phobia	7	.558
Panic disorder	17	.651
Generalized anxiety disorder	12	.571
Obsessive-compulsive disorder	6	.825

of cases reflects the relative rarity of this disorder vis-à-vis other anxiety disorders, but the high Kappa highlights the fact that, at least in its severe form, it presents as a distinctive, recognizable entity. With this in mind, the rather low Kappa for Simple Phobia would seem somewhat surprising. Difficulties and disagreements were not due to inability to recognize the simple phobia, but rather to the fact that almost all of our simple phobics also present with other anxiety disorders, making the clinical weighting of the primary and secondary disorder somewhat difficult. In other words, if one presented with both a simple phobia and panic disorder, both interviewers might recognize the simple phobia, but one would rate it primary and the other secondary, resulting in a disagreement.

In summary, it appears that the *DSM-III* provides very good descriptions of the phenomenology presenting the clinicians in the anxiety disorders, with the possible exception of simple phobia and Generalized Anxiety Disorder. Work is continuing in order to generate sufficient numbers of cases in all categories, but it would seem that when disagreements on simple phobia and GAD occur, the problem occurs in determining the importance of features of other anxiety disorders also present that are less severe or subclinical. This issue is relevant to the question of ascertaining the distinguishing dimensions across all anxiety disorders and is discussed once again below.

CO-MORBIDITY STUDIES

Another method of examining the phenomenology of anxiety disorders and specifying particular dimensions of anxiety as they present to clinicians is to examine co-morbidity or the distribution of additional diagnoses among the anxiety disorders (Barlow, DiNardo, Vermilyea, & Vermilyea, submitted). Table 26.2 presents the number and percentage of anxiety disorder cases in which additional, but secondary, anxiety diagnoses were assigned.

As one can see, one or more additional diagnoses were assigned in a substantial number of cases, and the frequency of additional diagnoses appears related to the primary diagnosis. In approximately half of the cases of social phobia and agoraphobia no additional diagnoses were assigned. However, there were relatively few cases of PD, GAD, and obsessive-compulsive disorder in which no additional diagnoses were assigned. For example, only 12% of the PD cases and 17% of the cases of GAD did not receive an additional diagnosis. None of the cases of OCD went without an additional diagnosis, although there are only six cases presently in this category.

Table 26.3 shows the distribution of specific additional diagnoses among the anxiety disorder cases. The first number of each entry indicates the total number of cases in which the particular additional diagnosis was assigned by either or both raters. The parenthetical figure indicates the number of those cases in which

TABLE 26.2
Number of Anxiety Disorder Cases in Which Additional Diagnoses
Were Assigned

Additional Diagnoses	Primary Diagnosis						
	Agoraphobia	Social Phobia	Simple Phobia	Panic Disorder	GAD	Obsessive Compulsive	Major Affective
None	20 (49%)	10 (53%)	3 (43%)	2 (12%)	2 (17%)	0	0
One	8 (20%)	7 (37%)	2 (29%)	11 (65%)	5 (42%)	3 (50%)	3 (50%)
Two	9 (22%)	2 (11%)	2 (29%)	3 (18%)	3 (25%)	3 (50%)	2 (33%)
Three or More	4 (1%)	0	0	1 (6%)	2 (16%)	0	1 (17%)

the diagnosis was independently assigned by both raters or by consensus of the staff.

Generalized Anxiety Disorder is infrequently assigned as an additional diagnosis despite the fact that phenomenologically the four criteria for GAD are commonly found in other anxiety disorders (see Table 26.5). This is because the four features of GAD are almost always an associated feature of another anxiety disorder rather than an independent co-existing complication (Barlow, Di Nardo, et al., submitted). For example, anticipatory anxiety is really generalized anxiety in which apprehensive expectation is focused on an upcoming phobic event. Occasionally, however, GAD exists as an independent co-existing complication and requires a separate diagnosis. Of particular interest in this table is the frequency with which a depressive diagnosis (either major affective disorder or dysthymic disorder) appears as an additional diagnosis among the anxiety disorders. If a diagnosis is counted by either clinician as a depressive disorder, then this diagnosis occurs in 16, or 39%, of the 41 cases of agoraphobia; 6, or 35%, of the 17 cases of PD; 4, or 21%, of the 19 cases of social phobia; and 2, or 17%, of the 12 cases of Generalized Anxiety Disorder. Four out of 6 cases of OCD received a depressive diagnosis, and in all 4 cases each interviewer agreed that this was a major affective disorder. On the other hand, none of the simple phobics was found to be depressed. The prevalence of depression in these categories also parallels clinicians' ratings of severity of the anxiety disorders. The potential importance of determining the coexistence of anxiety and depression has been demonstrated recently by Leckman, Merikangas, Pauls, Prusoff, and Weissman (1983). They found an increased risk for a variety of problems in families of depressed patients with panic in contrast to families of depressed patients without panic, where the risk for other problems was less.

TABLE 26.3
Additional Diagnoses Among Anxiety Disorder Cases

Additional Diagnoses	Primary Diagnosis						
	Agoraphobia	Social Phobia	Simple Phobia	Panic Disorder	GAD	Obsessive Compulsive	Major Affective
Agoraphobia	—	0	1(1)*	0	2(2)	1(1)	2(0)
Social Phobia	7(5)	—	2(2)	6(4)	4(2)	0	0
Simple Phobia	7(4)	1(1)	—	5(4)	5(3)	1(1)	3(3)
Panic Disorder	0	0	1(1)	—	0	1(0)	1(0)
GAD	1(0)	1(1)	0	—	1	1(1)	1(0)
Obsessive Compulsive	3(1)	2(2)	0	1(1)	0	—	1(1)
Major Affective Disorder	6(4)	1(1)	0	1(2)	0	4(4)	—
Dysthymic Disorder	10(3)	3(2)	0	4(1)	2(0)	0	0
Somatization Disorder	0	0	0	1(1)	0	0	0
Axis III	2(2)	1(1)	1(1)	0	4(1)	0	1(1)
Alcohol Abuse	0	1(1)	0	0	0	0	1(1)
Conversion	0	0	0	0	0	1(1)	0
Cyclothymic	0	1(1)	0	0	0	0	0
Axis 2	2(1)	0	1(1)	0	0	0	0

*Additional diagnoses assigned independently by both raters or by staff consensus appear in parentheses.

It seems clear from the above data that a number of distinct anxiety disorders varying in severity may occur at the same time in any one individual. These additional diagnoses also seem to have important treatment implications for many cases. For example, an agoraphobic in one of our groups also presented with a distinct blood and injury phobia, which would be categorized as a simple phobia. This complicated treatment by graduated exposure. When confronted with a specifically phobic object, such as a dead squirrel in the road, during practice sessions that patient experienced the brachycardia and hypotension that is paradoxically characteristic of a blood and injury phobic (Connolly, Hallam, & Marks, 1976; Yule & Fernando, 1980). Occasionally the patient would faint, something agoraphobics, of course, almost never do. In this case, the specific phobia had to be treated before substantial progress could be made with the agoraphobia.

COMMON DIMENSIONS OF ANXIETY DISORDERS

Data reviewed above confirm heterogeneity in the presentation of anxiety disorders. The fact that at least six different anxiety disorders can be differentiated from one another in a reliable fashion attests to the variety of cognitive, behavioral, and somatic phenomena that can combine in different ways to form what appears to be any one of a number of relatively cohesive syndromes. Another perspective involves examining what is common to anxiety disorders specifically and anxiety in general. Other chapters in this book have also taken this perspective. For example, Good and Kleinman (this volume) from an anthropological point of view describe commonality across cultures in the presentation of anxiety.

To determine the essential features of anxiety, many researchers are returning to more basic investigation of the psychological structure of emotion. In an important theoretical account of the basic nature of anxiety and emotion, Lang (this volume) points to dimensions that may be common to all emotions. Lang suggests, after reviewing the literature (e.g., Mehrabian & Russell, 1974; Russell, 1979), that emotion in general and anxiety in particular are composed of three dimensional predispositions. The first is an arousal dimension, the second is a particular valence on a continuum from pleasurable to unpleasurable, and the third is a dimension of control extending roughly on a continuum from helplessness or lack of control to control. Tellegen (e.g., Zevon & Tellegen, 1982; Tellegen, this volume) in an original course of basic research comes up with a slightly different structure of mood or emotion based on his own research. In his view, all mood change can be categorized within two broad dimensions, positive and negative affect. These dimensions are not on a continuum as is the positive-negative valence dimension described by Lang, but rather are unipolar. Both positive and negative affect may be high or low; when high these affective states are accompanied by arousal. High negative affect would encompass anxiety, although high positive affect would not necessarily be absent. The dimensions of pleasurable and unpleasurable valence or positive and negative affect along with a dimension of arousal have much in common. These conceptions differ somewhat from multiple mood categories (e.g., joy, guilt, fear, and fatigue), also derived from multifactorial analyses (Izard, 1972; this volume). But a derivation of multiple mood categories from these analyses is not nearly as consistent across individuals as the positive-negative affect structure mentioned above (Zevon & Tellegen, 1982). We further consider these concepts below.

Returning to our more clinical perspective once again, at least two broad-based phenomena, shared to some extent by all the anxiety disorders, appear to be emerging from clinical and phenomenological studies. The first is the phenomenon of panic, the second is more chronic, generalized anxiety. Referring back to the co-morbidity data, it is already obvious that panic and generalized anxiety seldom occur alone and most often are a component of all anxiety disorders. Let us turn to an examination of the phenomenology of panic and generalized anxiety.

THE PHENOMENOLOGY OF PANIC

One of the most important developments in the study of anxiety disorders during the past several years, in addition to the appearance of the *DSM-III* itself, has been the focus on panic as a qualitatively different anxiety phenomenon. Credit for this is due to Klein (1981) and his colleagues who have demonstrated in their initial work the differential response to pharmacological treatment of panic versus anticipatory anxiety within the agoraphobia syndrome (Zitrin, 1981; Zitrin, Klein, & Woerner, 1980; Zitrin, Klein, Woerner, & Ross, 1983). In addition, the preliminary observation that lactate infusion produces panic only in those with panic disorders and not normals lends further support to the importance of the phenomenon of panic (Klein, 1981).

In a preliminary experiment evaluating the effects of psychosocial treatments on intense anxiety, which included but was not limited to panic episodes, we also found that a combination of relaxation and cognitive restructuring procedures affected intense anxiety but not background anxiety, lending further support to Klein's pharmacological dissection work (Waddell, Barlow, & O'Brien, 1984). In this experiment, three panic-disordered patients were treated with cognitive therapy followed by a combined cognitive therapy and relaxation training phase in a multiple baseline across subjects design. These patients recorded both number and duration of episodes of "heightened or intense" anxiety, defined as "4" or higher on a 0–8 rating scale, using detailed self-monitoring forms devised for this purpose. In addition, they recorded ratings of background anxiety, not necessarily associated with periods of intense anxiety, four times a day. Data are presented in Figs. 26.1 and 26.2. Despite some missing data, these preliminary results indicate that all subjects demonstrated a marked decrease in the number and duration of episodes of heightened or intense anxiety, an improvement that was maintained at a 3-month follow-up (see Fig. 26.1). However, Subjects 1 and 3 evidenced an increase in background anxiety simultaneous with this decrease in intense anxiety during the combined treatment phase. Subject 2, on the other hand, also demonstrated decreases in background anxiety (see Fig. 26.2). These

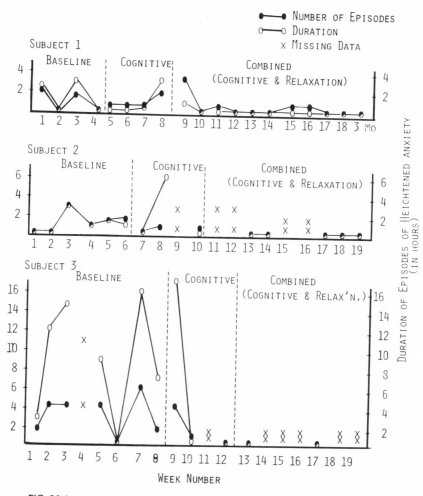

FIG. 26.1.   Total number of episodes of heightened anxiety per week and duration of episodes. (Redrawn from: Waddell, M. T., Barlow, D. H., & O'Brien, G. T. (1984). A preliminary investigation of cognitive and relaxation treatment of panic disorder: Effects on intense anxiety versus "background" anxiety. *Behavior Research and Therapy.*

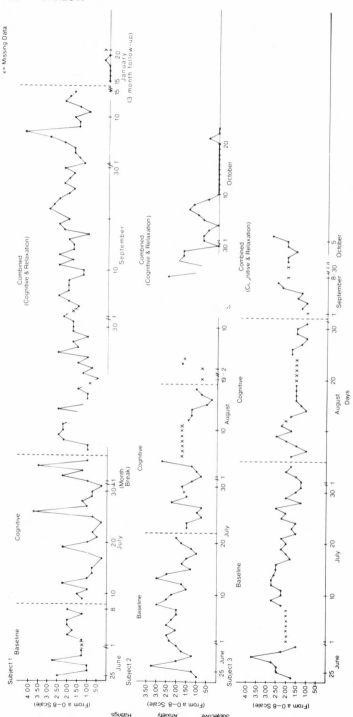

FIG. 26.2   Average of daily time-sampled ratings of anxiety. (Based on a 0 to 8 anxiety scale. Ratings were recorded four times daily. X = missing data.) (Redrawn from: Waddell, M. T., Barlow, D. H., & O'Brien, G. T. (1984). A preliminary investigation of cognitive and relaxation treatment of panic disorder: Effects on intense anxiety versus "background" anxiety. *Behaviour Research and Therapy*.

data suggest that panic and generalized anxiety may be qualitatively different, although it is also possible that they are simply quantitatively different but respond differentially to certain treatments.

There is also preliminary evidence of different developmental antecedents of panic and GAD (Raskin, Peeke, Dickman, & Pinkster, 1982), and one cannot ignore the fact that patients report these types of anxiety to be qualitatively different. On the other hand, some investigators have found panic and GAD to appear very much alike on the whole (Hoehn-Saric, 1981), whereas others suppose the panic and GAD are at different points on a dimension of severity (see Barlow & Maser, in press).

Another important step in the validation process includes ascertaining the prevalence and phenomenology of panic across various diagnostic categories, and we have completed a preliminary analysis with 108 of our initial patients (Barlow, Vermilyea, Blanchard, Vermilyea, DiNardo, & Cerny, in press). The *DSM-III*, of course, lists 12 symptoms that may contribute to the identification of panic, along with the sudden occurrence of discrete periods of apprehension and impending doom. The presence of any four or more symptoms are necessary to label the event a true panic. In addition to detailed questions on specific diagnostic criteria for panic, the ADIS requires that the clinician review and rate each of the 12 symptoms on a 0–4 scale where zero indicates the absence of the symptom and 4 indicates that the symptom is very severe and grossly disabling. Table 26.4 presents some data from this analysis.

If one looks at the percentage of the 12 symptoms experienced by each of the anxiety disorder categories as well as the category of major depression, it is evident that all categories, including GAD, have at least 50% (or 6 of these symptoms). While some statistically significant differences emerge, PD or agoraphobia with panic do not differ significantly from OCD or even major depression on a number of these panic-like symptoms. In fact, looking at the last column in the table, there are no differences among patient reports of panic attacks among the diagnostic categories. Even if frequency of panics in the past 3 weeks is examined, one can find little to choose at the present time. The exception is major depression, where several patients reported experiencing numerous panics, thereby inflating this category. Finally, if one looks just at the data from the ADIS and averages the responses across two raters, which gives a slightly different picture than the final consensus diagnosis, it can be seen that a substantial percentage of most anxiety disorder categories would meet criteria for the diagnosis of panic disorder, the only exceptions being GAD and simple phobia. But even here approximately 30% would qualify. If the criteria of three panics in a 3-week period of time is ignored, then almost everyone in each category would otherwise qualify for the diagnosis of panic.

If these data hold up, one might speculate that the occurrence of panic is a dimension differing only in reported frequency across some of the disorders. These panics would not indicate the existence of a panic disorder as we now conceive it in each of these categories, since the diagnosis of PD requires that

TABLE 26.4
Incidence of Panic Across Diagnostic Categories

	Agoraphobia with Panic	Social Phobia	Simple Phobia	Panic Disorder	GAD	Obsessive-Compulsive Disorder	Major Depressive Disorder	
Percent of Symptoms	85.6^b	61.3^a	68.0^{ab}	83.3^b	58.3^a	90.2^b	61.6^a	$F_{(6, 91)} = 6.21, p < .001$
Panic Frequency	10.47^a	4.68^a	2.28^a	6.00^a	4.33^a	19.67^a	67.67^b	$F_{(6, 70)} = 7.37, p < .001$
Diagnosis on DSM-III Panic Criteria	74%	50%	33%	82%	29%	100%	100%	$x^2(6) = 14.67, p < .03$
Diagnosis met except for Panic Frequency	98%	84%	85%	100%	75%	83%	83%	$x^2(6) = 9.50$, NS
Reports of Panic	98%	89%	100%	100%	83%	83%	83%	$x^2(6) = 7.27$, NS

a, b indicate significant Duncan groupings

it be "unpredictable," according to *DSM-III*. Within the category of simple phobia on the other hand, the cues are clear both to the patient and to the therapist, and therefore, the panics that occur are predictable (e.g., when the patient enters the specific phobic situation). Within the category of major depression, there are also good examples of cases for whom cues for panic exist. Making any decision, however small, resulted in panic in one recent case, but these cues were not clear to the patient initially and only became clear upon examination. One major difference between biological and psychological conceptions of panic lies in assumptions concerning the presence of cues in patients for whom panic is otherwise occasionally unpredictable.

While most investigators agree that cues for or antecedents to panic exist in most anxiety disorder categories, diagnoses such as PD and agoraphobia with panic, as noted above, often seem characterized by a lack of clear antecedents to panic, accounting for patients' reports of the unpredictable nature of these events. Searches for either biological determinants of panic or the presence of psychological (or physiological) antecedents is ongoing in a number of laboratories and may well influence our notions on the classification of panic in the years to come. My clinical impression is that cues for panic in our agoraphobics are usually associated with mild exercise, sexual relations, sudden temperature change, stress, or other situations associated with altered physiological functioning in some discernible way, albeit out of the patient's awareness.

An interesting trend emerges from consideration of the sex distribution of patients with GAD and PD. While females outnumber males in receiving the diagnosis of PD in our sample by almost two to one, we find the reverse distribution for Generalized Anxiety Disorder.

THE PHENOMENOLOGY OF GENERAL ANXIETY

General anxiety, as distinct from panic, also seems a variable feature in the anxiety disorders. Within *DSM-III*, GAD is currently considered a residual category, only to be diagnosed if the specific symptoms of phobic disorders, PD, or OCD are not present. Administration of the ADIS to the same 108 individuals presenting to the Phobia and Anxiety Disorders Clinic allowed a determination of which individuals in the various diagnostic categories met the GAD inclusion criteria. Table 26.5 lists the average severity ratings of the four symptoms associated with GAD in *DSM-III* for each diagnostic group. Also presented are answers to questions of whether patients believe they can identify sources of their anxious feelings and whether they feel anxious in particular situations or in multiple situations.

Patients with GAD have arithmetically higher severity ratings for three of the four symptom clusters; in no instance do differences in the symptom severity ratings across groups reach statistical significance. Interestingly, on the most subjective of the symptoms (and the one most characteristic of the traditional

TABLE 26.5
Generalized Anxiety Disorder Symptoms Across Diagnostic Categories

Item	Agoraphobia with Panic	Social Phobia	Simple Phobia	Panic Disorder	GAD	Obsessive Compulsive	Major Depressive Episode	Statistical Comparison
Muscle Tension (0–4)	$1.45_{n=37}$	$1.53_{n=17}$	$1.08_{n=6}$	$1.56_{n=17}$	$2.18_{n=11}$	$1.38_{n=4}$	$2.10_{n=5}$	$F_{(6,90)} = 1.34$, NS
Autonomic Hyperactivity (0–4)	$1.95_{n=38}$	$1.62_{n=17}$	$1.00_{n=6}$	$2.04_{n=17}$	$2.18_{n=11}$	$2.13_{n=4}$	$1.70_{n=5}$	$F_{(6,91)} = 1.92$, NS
Vigilance and Scanning (0–4)	$1.81_{n=39}$	$1.85_{n=17}$	$1.25_{n=6}$	$1.78_{n=17}$	$1.81_{n=11}$	$2.50_{n=4}$	$2.40_{n=5}$	$F_{(6.92)} = 1.36$, NS
Apprehensive Expectation (0–4)	$2.22_{n=39}$	$2.12_{n=17}$	$1.58_{n=6}$	$2.25_{n=17}$	$1.77_{n=11}$	$2.63_{n=4}$	$2.40_{n=5}$	$F_{(6.92)} = 1.13$, NS
Percent able to identify sources of anxiety	$62\%_{n=32}$	$94\%_{n=18}$	$80\%_{n=5}$	$65\%_{n=17}$	$75\%_{n=12}$	$100\%_{n=5}$	$83\%_{n=6}$	
Percent able to identify situations that lead to anxiety	$90\%_{n=31}$	$100\%_{n=15}$	$100\%_{n=4}$	$100\%_{n=16}$	$92\%_{n=12}$	$74\%_{n=5}$	$100\%_{n=6}$	

Severity Ratings
0 = None
1 = Mild
2 = Moderate
3 = Severe
4 = Very Severe

view of general anxiety, apprehensive expectation), the patients with GAD have the next to lowest severity. When one looks at the percentage of patients in each diagnostic category who meet the inclusion criteria for GAD, one finds that 84% of the agoraphobics, 79% of those with panic disorder, and 100% of obsessive compulsives would meet these inclusion criteria. Somewhat lower are the other phobic disorders, with only 55% of the social phobics also meeting GAD criteria, and 40% of the simple phobics. Another interesting difference between panic disorder and GAD does occur, however, when one calculates the percentage of the patient's life that he or she had experienced anxiety and tension. Patients with PD had experienced anxiety problems for 16% of their life span, whereas the percentage for GAD is 56%, a highly statistically significant difference.

It seems clear that generalized anxiety, much like panic, is present across the anxiety disorders, although it is more frequent in some disorders than in others. On the other hand, only in OCD do all of the patients we have interviewed also present with general anxiety, but this may be a function of the currently rather small number of people ($N = 6$) in this category. It may be that general anxiety is another important dimension of anxiety that stands alone, and thus will have important treatment and prognostic implications. Alternatively, since GAD is a residual diagnostic category, many of those patients falling into the category of GAD or a primary diagnosis may simply be "sub-threshold" for other anxiety disorders. In this case, generalized anxiety may be irrelevant and simply a variable feature of all anxiety disorders.

THE STRUCTURE OF ANXIETY

Another perspective on possible dimensions of anxiety revolves around methods of assessing anxiety. Whether one is dealing with the variety of phenomena connected with the anxiety disorders as represented in the descriptive diagnostic categories or the dimensions that simply run through all of the anxiety disorders, measures of anxiety are collected in one of three response systems (Lang, 1968; Mavissakalian & Barlow, 1981). These response systems, now well known to most anxiety researchers, include verbal report of distress, overt behavioral responses, and physiological or visceral responses. As noted above, overt behavioral features are most present in phobic and obsessive-compulsive disorders, but are more subtle in the anxiety states (PD and GAD). But all anxiety disorder patients present with a verbal report of distress and heightened physiological responding, at least under certain circumstances.

Unfortunately, methods of assessing emotionally related phenomena such as anxiety, which must occur in these three response systems, seem to have become confused with three more basic dimensions of generalized anxiety or panic. These dimensions could best be described as (1) the cognitive process dimension, (2) a somatic dimension, and (3) a dimension of avoidance. These three dimensions comprise the structure of anxiety (eg., Lang, this volume). In fact, both panic and general anxiety would seem to possess each of these dimensions to some extent, although the relative balance will differ, particularly as one moves from one identifiable anxiety disorder to another. Furthermore, each of these dimensions can be assessed theoretically in each of the three response systems. This will become clear by referring to Table 26.6 and from descriptions provided below. Finally, a wide range of cues, both internal and external, are associated to varying degrees with specific anxiety phenomena. Internal cues could include subtle biological changes as well as cognitive processes. External cues could be pervasive or very focused.

Returning to the broad-based clinical dimensions reviewed above, both panic and GAD have prominent cognitive and somatic components, although recent evidence indicates that panic is weighted toward the somatic dimension (Barlow, Cohen, Waddell, Vermilyea, Klosko, Blanchard, DiNardo, in press). Descriptions of these cognitive phenomena, common in anxiety disorders, can be found in other chapters throughout this book (e.g., Foa & Kozak, Lang, and Sarason). Generally, cognitive processes can be characterized by erroneous estimates of threat or faulty interpretations of events (e.g., Beck, Laude, & Bohnert, 1974). Feelings of control, also hypothesized to be a critical dimension of emotion (Borkovec, this volume; Lang, this volume), may be represented within the cognitive processes of anxiety along a continuum from helplessness to control. Helplessness may be particularly salient during episodes of panic. Naturally, these cognitions are associated with negative affect or a high negative valence, as well as a basic dimension of arousal common to all emotions.

These cognitive processes could be assessed theoretically in all three response systems. For example, overestimation of threat or a highly negative interpretation of a situation will produce not only reports of subjective distress but also physiological changes (e.g., increases in heart rate or skin conductance) (Mavissakalian & Barlow, 1981) and behavioral changes such as interference with ongoing behavior due to shifts in attention.

Somatic manifestations are common in most anxiety disorders, but perhaps more ubiquitous in panic disorder and its close relatives (e.g., agoraphobia) than in social or simple phobia. Somatic manifestations, with origins perhaps at a biochemical level, include the high resting state of arousal found in some, but not all, anxiety disorders (e.g., Holden & Barlow, submitted; Lader & Wing, 1966) as well as systemic changes. Somatic manifestations will also produce subjective reports of distress and behavioral changes, most notably agitation, as well as marked changes in autonomic responding evident from psychophysiological recording.

Avoidance, on the other hand, is most prominent in the phobic and obsessive-compulsive disorders and less prominent in the anxiety states. Avoidance can be either behavioral or cognitive. Cognitive avoidance is observed most frequently in cognitive rituals, often found in obsessional checkers and perhaps in the "numbing" response found in PTSD. Avoidance also has distinctive self-report, behavioral, and physiological characteristics. For example, avoidance,

TABLE 27.6
Internal (Biological or Cognitive) or External Cues

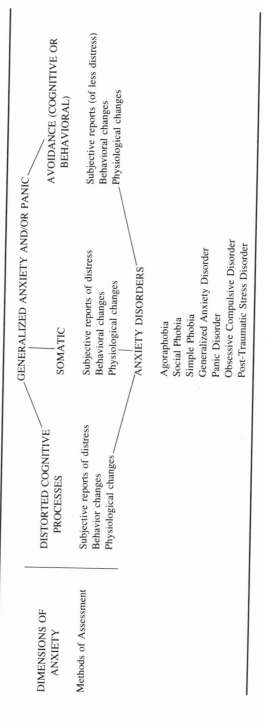

whether behavioral or cognitive, often decreases physiological responding and self-reports of distress in OCD (Steketee & Foa, in press). If one is going to measure change in the anxiety disorders or in their major components, one must do so in as many of these dimensions and response systems within the dimensions as possible. To reiterate, panic and general anxiety may be qualitatively separate processes with differential biological underpinnings. However, both have cognitive as well as somatic and avoidance dimensions, although seemingly in a somewhat different "balance." The difference in "balance" determines the specific anxiety disorder with which a patient presents.

Thus, the specific anxiety disorder will depend on the specific cues, the relative balance between panic and general anxiety, and the relative balance of the three major dimensions within the anxiety structure. For example, GAD is characterized by relatively less panic, and a highly distorted cognitive process, but only mild disturbance on somatic and avoidance dimensions. Agoraphobics, on the other hand, display marked difficulties in all three dimensions with high resting autonomic lability compared to normals (Holden & Barlow, submitted; Vermilyea, Boice, & Barlow, in press), cognitive and behavioral avoidance, and distorted cognitive processes. Simple phobics would be characterized by panic and problems with all three dimensions, but very narrow cues allowing for successful avoidance. Of course, as Lang points out (this volume), since the "affective network" of the anxiety disorder, including cues as well as the anxiety structure, is located in memory, then all dimensions, including behavioral and somatic, are really cognitive.

There is some evidence that the relative balance of these dimensions or the relative strength of the response systems comprising the dimensions have treatment implications. In a landmark study, Ost, Jerremalm, and Johansson (1981) assessed social phobics in a specific phobic situation prior to treatment. Based upon this assessment, patients were classified as "behavioral reactors" or "physiological reactors," depending upon which response pattern was prominent in a specific test situation. Two treatment approaches were applied, social skills training and applied relaxation. Among behavioral reactors, social skills training produced maximal results, whereas relaxation was superior with physiological reactors. The Ost et al., data suggest that clinically meaningful results can be obtained with these two treatment approaches given careful patient-to-treatment matching. This study further points out the importance of collecting data across various dimensions in all three response systems where possible or in as many dimensions and response systems as are represented in the particular anxiety disorder. Certainly establishment of the predictive validity of the various combinations of dimensions comprising anxiety for treatment planning purposes is a significant step. These data also have important implications for basic research on the nature of anxiety.

From a somewhat different perspective, other investigators have begun to assess dimensional change in all three response systems during treatment of phobic disorders, and they have noticed a phenomenon originally termed by Rachman and Hodgson (1974) as "desynchrony." Desynchrony refers to a low degree of covariance in change among the various response systems. Preliminary data suggest that desynchrony (or lack of positive generalization among response systems) following treatment may indicate high potential for relapse (e.g., Barlow, Mavissakalian, & Schofield, 1980; Grey, Rachman, & Sartory, 1981). Someone with reduced anxiety in subjective and behavioral response systems during a specific test following treatment (e.g., fewer reports of distress and less behavioral agitation or avoidance) but continued high autonomic responding, might be a greater risk for relapse than a patient showing "synchronous" decrease in all three response systems.

Most recently, Vermilyea et al. (in press) assessed all three response systems during a treatment program for 28 agoraphobics. Heart rate as well as subjective distress were assessed in a specific situation as each agoraphobic attempted a walk along a course that began at the Clinic and ran for one mile into an increasingly crowded, and therefore more frightening, section of the city. Each agoraphobic attempted this walk three times at pre-, mid-, and post-treatment. Outcome at post-test on a composite measure of change was examined as a function of synchronous or desynchronous changes in subjective distress and heart rate during treatment. The results are presented in Table 26.7. Synchrony or desynchrony did not predict response to treatment. But the critical question will be the relationship of desynchrony to follow-up in order to determine if desynchrony predicts relapse. A determination of outcome at a follow-up period of at least 6 months, and preferably 1 year, would be necessary. This follow-up is currently in progress.

In yet another indication of the potential importance of arousal or physiological responsiveness in predicting outcome, our analyses indicated that patients who began with highest levels of physiological responsiveness on the behavioral walk were most likely to evidence improvement on the composite measure of change. In Table 26.8, data are presented on agoraphobics who either responded or did not respond to treatment as a function of heart rate being higher or lower than it was in a group of non-agoraphobic subjects who also underwent this assessment procedure (the walk). This difference was statistically significant. Potential

TABLE 26.7
Degree of Synchrony by Response to Treatment

	Synchronous Subjects	Desynchronous Subjects
Treatment Responders	11	11
Treatment Non-Responders	3	3

TABLE 26.8
Relative Heart Rate Level at Pre-Treatment by Response to
Treatment

	Mean Heart Rate Above "Normal"	Mean Heart Rate Below "Normal"
Treatment Responders	17	5
Treatment Non-Responders	1	5

explanations for this phenomenon, more relevant to the basic nature of anxiety, are outlined by Lang (this volume), and Foa and Kozak (this volume). Specifically, the particular assessment, and perhaps treatment conditions, employed in our program may have more sucessfully tapped the "affective network" representing the nucleus of the agoraphobia in our responders, thereby allowing an "emotional processing" of this affective network during treatment. Emotional processing is a process theorized by Lang to underlie the reduction of fear (Lang, this volume). Once again, process studies of treatment procedures may have implications for understanding the nature of anxiety.

The studies reviewed above have, for the most part, examined the relationship of various response systems during a specific test without evaluating the three dimensions comprising the structure of anxiety (see Table 26.6). As noted above, these have often been confused or intermingled. Part of the difficulty lies in conceptualizing physiological changes. Many, but not all, anxiety disorders have high resting arousal and marked systemic changes characteristic of chronic stress (Holden & Barlow, submitted; Lader & Wing, 1966). On the other hand, autonomic reactivity to a specific anxiety-producing situation is most often what is assessed in the physiological response system. Clearer definition will be necessary to understand the relationship of these phenomena.

Social phobia is essentially a fear of scrutiny or evaluation. It is possible that the cognitive dimensions may play a critical role in the performance anxiety that is so often a part of social phobia, and that this will have treatment implications. In a detailed examination of test anxiety, which is a variant of social phobia, Sarason (1982; this volume) found that reports of the somatic dimensions of anxiety (e.g., increased heart rate, perspiration, rapid breathing) did not interfere with performance, but cognitive distortions (e.g., "I'm going to fail. What will my parent think? What will I do?") were responsible for decrements in performance. The area of sexual dysfunction, in fact, also seems to be a variant of social phobia with fear of performance or subsequent evaluation as prominent features.

Increasing somatic or physiological aspects of anxiety in normals by threat of shock concurrent with viewing an erotic stimulus, actually facilitated sexual arousal (Barlow, Sakheim, & Beck, 1983). Specifically, subjects trained to anticipate a painful electric shock signaled by light, demonstrated increased sexual arousal during viewing of an erotic film compared to a condition in which they viewed similar films without expecting an electric shock (without the signal light on). In yet a third condition, shock threat was also present but subjects were instructed to expect it only if they did not achieve an erection of a certain size. Subjects were never actually shocked during the experiment. The results of this experiment are presented in Fig. 26.3. Presumably, subjects attributed their increased autonomic arousal to the sexual context in a "transfer of emotion" fashion, commonly seen in the laboratories of social psychology (e.g., Schachter, 1966; Zillmann, 1983). Other researchers have demonstrated that task-irrelevant cognitive distractions reliably lower sexual arousal (Farkas, Sine, & Evans, 1979; Geer & Fuhr, 1976; also see Beck & Barlow, in press). More attention to cognitive factors and the possible implementation of cognitive focusing strategies

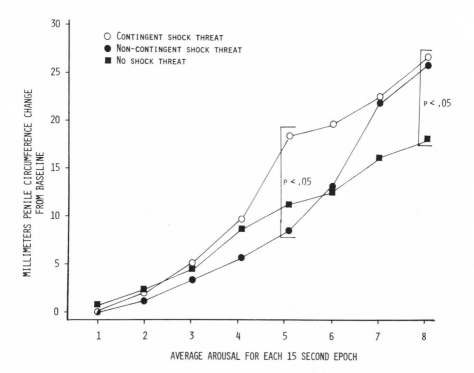

FIG. 26.3   Average penile circumference change for each 15-sec epoch during each of three conditions: no-shock threat (NS), noncontingent-shock threat (NCS), and contingent-shock threat (CS). (Reprinted from Barlow, D. H., Sakheim, D. K., & Beck, J. G. (1983). Anxiety increases sexual arousal. *Journal of Abnormal Psychology, 92,* 49-54.

in the treatment of fear of social evaluation may contribute to our knowledge of this particular anxiety disorder (Beck, Barlow, & Sakheim, 1983).

CONCLUSIONS

We have reviewed a number of suggested dimensions of anxiety from various levels of analysis. We have presented data on the core clinical dimensions that seem to run across the anxiety disorders, specifically the broad-based phenomena of panic, general anxiety, and the avoidance, cognitive, and somatic dimensions that characterize, in greater or lesser degree, the various anxiety disorders. Further investigation of these dimensions may have profound implications for treatment and the investigation of the nature of anxiety and anxiety disorders. Of course, other views on the interrelationship among the core dimensions of clinical anxiety exist. For example, Foa and Kozak (this volume) describe a somewhat different ordering of cues and avoidance. Finally, investigators who are working on the theoretical nature of emotion in general and anxiety specifically, have elucidated other basic factors such as positive or negative affect (valence), arousal, and perhaps the dimension of control. Anxiety is characterized by relatively negative valence and lack of perceived control (helplessness) accompanied by high arousal. Similarly, Zevon and Tellegen (1982) write of negative affect and high arousal.

These varying dimensions come from different levels of analysis of emotion and anxiety and therefore need not necessarily be contradictory. As Lang points out, that measuring the various dimensions of anxiety in the three response systems (behavioral, verbal, and physiological) often produces discrepant results where response systems correlate poorly with each other may represent something basic about the nature of anxiety rather than a measurement artifact. He proposes that the particular affective networks associated with each anxiety disorder may be quite different and more or less coherent, depending on the disorder. These internally coherent but different affective networks account for divergences in the response system making up the basic data of anxiety. In this view, the affective network underlying a simple phobia would be much more coherent, and one could expect more concordance and synchrony among response systems than in such disorders as agoraphobia, which are much more pervasive. This speculation needs to be confirmed.

Delineating similarities and differences in the phenomenology of the anxiety disorders and determining in a more precise way the core dimensions of the anxiety disorders and the relationship of these dimensions to basic emotional processes will be difficult. But advances in our thinking during the last 5 years suggest that this will be a fruitful inquiry.

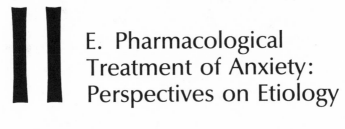

E. Pharmacological Treatment of Anxiety: Perspectives on Etiology

27 Etiological and Pathophysiological Inferences from the Pharmacological Treatment of Anxiety

Donald F. Klein, M.D.
Judith Godwin Rabkin, Ph.D., M.P.H.
Jack M. Gorman, M.D.
New York State Psychiatric Institute and
College of Physicians and Surgeons, Columbia University

Our review addresses the possibility of deriving etiological insights from the pharmacological treatment of anxiety. We pursue three aspects of this topic: specific drug-psychopathology interactions, receptorology, and the psychopharmacology of the infant separation reaction. Clearly, there is no immediate leap to be taken from the success or failure of any form of treatment to an understanding of etiology. Headaches are not caused by a lack of aspirin. Nonetheless, successful treatment should allow inferences concerning possible components of the pathophysiological derangement.

It seems overwhelmingly likely that the behaviorally defined categories of human psychopathology are heterogeneous. Just as measles and typhus both cause rashes, quite distinct pathophysiological chains may engender behavioral resemblances. Accordingly, searching for etiological commonalities in heterogeneous groups may well be fruitless. A more effective strategy for detection of specific etiologies would seem to be reduction of heterogeneity within groups. To this end, one could aggregate those patients who share some important defining characteristic, such as common heredity, illness course, or reactions to specific medications (Klein, 1973).

The utility of psychopharmacological efficacy, as a tool to delineate relatively homogeneous subgroups from heterogeneous behavioral categories, has long been recognized in the study of schizophrenia and affective disorders. Can anything be eked out from the literature on anxiety disorders that would help us recognize medication-relevant subgroups who may be relatively etiologically uniform? We review this material in the first part of our chapter.

501

Are there other aspects of psychopharmacological treatment that may have etiological implications? If it were shown that apparently diverse medications were uniformly beneficial for some illnesses and also that they had similar effects on some aspect of neural functioning, it could help us theorize about underlying pathophysiological derangements. In recent years, receptorology has come to the forefront, particularly in the area of affective disorder. However, since many drugs useful for affective disorders are also useful for anxiety disorders, a review of the relationship between receptor changes and clinical benefits may prove illuminating for the anxiety area.

One major problem in the experimental study of psychopathology is the absence of appropriate animal models. This is particularly clear when it is realized that the antidepressants, lithium, and antipsychotics have singularly little effect upon the normal human being. Their benefits probably occur by ameliorative interaction with some deranged control mechanism, perhaps along cybernetic lines (Klein, Gittelman, Quitkin, & Rifkin, 1980).

The generally poor showing of animal screening for antidepressant and antipsychotic drugs is well known, but punished-response disinhibition techniques for the detection of the benzodiazepine-like drugs are clearly useful. These drugs have effects upon normal human beings that are on a continuum with their psychoactive benefits. They can be conceptualized as rheostat-like drugs, rather than cybernetic in their effects.

One possible animal model for human psychopathology is the apparently "prewired" protest reactions that occur in the infants of many species upon separation. Reports of particular efficacy of antidepressant drugs in this area may help us to delineate further the peculiar relationship between panic disorder and depressive states (Klein, 1981). Therefore, we review what is currently known about the psychopharmacology of animal separation reactions. Parallels between the infant separation model and the clinical treatment of human anxiety disorders would suggest one etiological possibility.[1]

DRUG EFFICACY AND ETIOLOGICAL IMPLICATIONS: A REVIEW OF THE LITERATURE ON CONTROLLED TRIALS

Obsessive Compulsive Disorder: OCD (see Table 27.1)

Relatively few psychopharmacological studies have been conducted with obsessive-compulsive disorder (OCD). Unlike studies of patients with "anxiety neuroses" published before the introduction of *DSM-III* where specific diagnostic

---

[1] Drug Names and Abbreviations used in this chapter: clomipramine (CLO); imipramine (IMI); phenelzine (PZ); monoamine oxidase inhibitor (MAOI); chlordiazepoxide (CDZ); chlorpromzine (CPZ); haloperidol (HAL); diphenylhydantoin (DPH).

criteria were largely absent, the earlier studies of OCD continue to be useful since the essential features of the syndrome were delineated in *DSM-II*.

Several factors have contributed to the dearth of psychopharmacological research with OCD: the low prevalence of the disorder, difficulties in measuring change and improvement, and the frequent unwillingness of OCD patients to tolerate research participation in general and drug side effects in particular, given the often hypochondriacal nature of their obsessional preoccupations. Other difficulties include the diagnostic challenge of sorting out essential OCD features from paranoid ideation, anxiety attacks, and depressive symptoms.

Although OCD is usually described as a chronic, nonepisodic disorder, symptoms may vary from week to week. Rituals may alternate with obsessional thoughts or periods of augmented anxiety, and high placebo response rates have been reported (Insel & Murphy, 1982).

In assessment of clinical change, this multidimensional configuration must be taken into account. Also a distinction should be made regarding improvement in associated features (e.g., depresses mood) versus central features (e.g., number and duration of specific rituals).

Because we were able to find very few studies comparing two active drugs with OCD samples, our review was broadened to include trials of one active drug and placebo, as well as case reports related to issues raised in the comparative trials. Most drug studies of OCD used antidepressant medications. The available evidence concerning anxiolytics and neuroleptics is also considered.

Antidepressants.   Clomipramine (CLO) is by far the most widely studied antidepressant in the treatment of OCD. All of the comparative drug trials with OCD patients that we were able to locate include CLO as one of the active drug conditions. The first of these (Waxman, 1977) compared the relative efficacy of CLO and diazepam. The others compared CLO with either amitriptyline, nortriptyline, or clorgyline (see Table 27.1)

Waxman (1977) contrasted the effects of diazepam and CLO on 41 patients with "phobias and obsessional disorders" not further described, with depression often presenting as the primary symptom. Although Waxman concluded that CLO has "specific value" in treatment of phobic and obsessional illness, its advantage is not completely clear from the data presented. More apparent is the toxicity of CLO in this patient group: of 12 patients who discontinued treatment because of side effects, 11 were taking clomipramine.

Thoren, Asberg, Cronholm, Jornestedt, & Traskman (1980) were referred patients from all over Sweden who had OCD of at least 1 year and who had been treatment failures at least once. Diagnosis was based on occurrence of pronounced compulsive rituals and thoughts. All cases met Research Diagnostic Criteria (RDC) for obsessive-compulsive disorder. The investigators assigned 24 inpatients to CLO, nortriptyline (NOR), or placebo for 5 weeks. The Comprehensive Psychiatric Rating Scale and Leyton Obsessional Inventory were the

TABLE 27.1
Obsessive Compulsive Disorder

Authors	Sample (Dx; Criteria; N)	Drug Conditions	Placebo	Trial Duration	Outcome: Evidence Re: Differential Drug Effects
ANTIDEPRESSANTS, COMPARATIVE TRIALS					
Waxman, 1977	obsessional disorders and phobias, often with depression as primary symptom, N=41	diazepam clomipramine	—	6 weeks	no clearcut advantage for either drug; clinical effects unclear
Thoren et al., 1980	primary OCD inpatients, N=24	clomipramine nortriptyline	yes	5 weeks	CLO superior to placebo; no difference between CLO & NOR
Rapoport et al., 1980	inpatients at NIMH severe OCD for 1 + yr, N=8	clomipramine desmethylimipramine	yes	5 weeks each, cross-over design	no differences between drugs and placebo
Ananth et al., 1981	primary OCD refractory to therapy, N=17	clomipramine amitriptyline	—		CLO > AMI in change from baseline for obsessional symptoms, anxiety + depression, CLO superiority at endpoint for anxiety and depression only
Insel et al., 1983	primary OCD DSM-III; N=13	clomipramine clorgyline	yes	6 weeks each; cross-over design	CLO > clorgyline on obsessional symptoms, anxiety and depression
ANTIDEPRESSANTS, OPEN TRIALS, PLACEBOS TRIALS AND CASE REPORTS					
Ananth, 1977	OCD N=18	clomipramine	no	4 week open study	obsessional symptoms, severity and depression and phobia scores improved over baseline
Karabanow, 1977	primary depression with OCD traits	clomipramine	yes	6 weeks	CLO > placebo for scores on obsessional symptoms, phobias, depression

Study	Sample	Drug		Duration	Outcome
Singh & Saxena, 1977	chronic OCD, N=17	clomipramine	—	4 weeks	assessments of obsessive symptoms, anxiety, depression and phobias reportedly showed improvement after 2 weeks
Solyom, Sookman, 1977	obsessive symptoms, N=6	clomipramine; behavior therapy	—	6 weeks	CLO useful in reducing anxiety and phobic symptoms; behavior therapy > compulsive symptoms
Marks et al., 1980	chronic OCD, N=40	clomipramine	yes	8 months	CLO > placebo on depression measures and anxiety measures, with greatest effect for those most depressed at baseline
Yaryura Tobias, 1977	OCD, N=7	L-tryptophan + pyridoxine + nicotinic acid	—	4 weeks	treatment considered successful for OCD symptoms
Isberg, 1981	OCD without depression, DSM III; N=1 history of panic	imipramine phenelzine	—	6 weeks 1 year	IMI reduced frequency but not intensity of OCD symptoms; PZ induced remission
Jenike, 1981	OCD without depression, N=2	tranylcypromine	—	8 days 16 months	in both cases, OCD symptoms remitted. In #1, switch to mania → discontinuation.

OTHER PSYCHOTROPIC DRUGS

Rivers-Bulkeley, 1982	OCD without depression, N=1	loxapine	—	4 months	symptom abatement
Burrell et al., 1974	obsessional symptoms, N=220	bromazepam	—	open treatment	authors report 40% = marked improvement; 40% = moderate improvement.

change measures. On the former, percentage improved by drug condition was 0% for placebo patients, 21% for NOR, and 42% for CLO. In view of the small sample sizes, only CLO effects differed significantly from placebo outcome, with no differences found between the two active drugs. The authors report "a favorable response was seen in many patients who did not have secondary depression," but this finding includes clinical results from open treatment after study completion. Of the eight patients treated with CLO in the 5-week trial, three were classified as having secondary depression; all were responders. Of the five nondepressed patients, only one was called a responder in the study. The authors concluded that CLO has a specific antiobsessive effect, but Marks, Stern, Mawson, Cobb, & McDonald (1981) and Emmelkamp (1982) attribute the observed improvement to CLO's antidepressant effects.

Rapoport and colleagues (Rapoport, Elkins, & Mikkelsen, 1980) published a brief report of a 16-week trial of desmethylimipramine, CLO, and placebo, using a randomized crossover design with 5-week trial of each condition. The patients were nine severely ill children, hospitalized at the NIMH, whose daily functioning was gravely disrupted by rituals and/or repetitive thoughts of at least 1 year's duration. Although the children showed gradual improvement over the course of the trial, this change was not associated with any one drug condition, but rather to "support and removal from home." The "apparent lack of effect of CLO on obsessional symptoms" was perhaps due, the authors suggested, to the brevity of the trial.

Ananth and colleagues (Ananth, Pecknold, van den Steen, & Engelsman, 1981) compared the efficacy of amitriptyline (AMI) and CLO in a 4-week randomized double-blind trial of 20 patients, 17 of whom completed the trial. The Psychiatric Questionnaire for Obsessive Compulsive Disorder, which generates scores for obsessive symptoms, anxiety, and depression, and the Clinical Global Impression (CGI) Severity Scale were used as outcome measures. Between baseline and end of the study, the CLO but not the AMI patients showed significant decreases in both number and severity of obsessional symptoms, although the authors noted that there were no significant differences between the overall performances of the two drug groups on either measure. In contrast, there was a clear superiority of CLO over AMI on measures of depression and anxiety both at end of study and in terms of change over time. CGI global severity ratings also show an advantage for clomipramine.

Although the authors suggested that the observed improvement in depression and anxiety on CLO may have been contingent upon the amelioration of obsessive symptoms, their data do not demonstrate this point. Further, despite their report of no relation between improvement of depression and decrease in obsessional symptoms, the data they present suggest the presence at baseline of considerable depression in both treatment groups. Accordingly, in this sample they cannot assess the impact of CLO in the absence of depressive symptomatology except statistically, which was not described in this report.

The most recently published study is also the most persuasive regarding the efficacy of CLO as an antiobsessive agent. Insel and colleagues (1983) at NIMH conducted a double-blind randomized crossover study of CLO and clorgyline, a selective MAO inhibitor, with 13 OCD patients, 10 of whom completed the entire crossover sequence. An initial 4-week single-blind placebo trial produced no significant improvement, nor was a 6-week course of clorgyline effective for the sample as a whole. In contrast, CLO was associated with significant improvement on measures of obsessions, anxiety, and depression.

These authors made a concerted effort to develop a battery of differentiated outcome measures for assessing change in OCD, since there exists for this syndrome no standard instrument equivalent to the Hamilton or Raskin scales for depression. They also placed emphasis on identifying changes in OCD symptomatology independent of alterations in depressive symptoms. In this context, they identified the three most and three least depressed patients at baseline, compared the amount of change on OCD measures, and found greater OCD change in the least depressed patients.

Insel et al. (1983) concluded that a broad spectrum of OCD patients may benefit from CLO. The effects, however, are not dramatic, at least in a 6-week period. Obsessional measures averaged a 30% improvement, consisting primarily of decreased intensity of symptoms. There were no complete remissions during this time, but "clomipramine's therapeutic effects seem more subtle than the efficacy of many drugs in other anxiety and affective disorders" (p. 611).

Several other investigators have reported promising results with CLO for OCD patients in placebo-controlled trials (Karabanow, 1977), comparison with behavioral treatment (Marks et al., 1980; Solyom & Sookman, 1977), and in open studies (Ananth, 1977; Singh & Saxena, 1977). Karabanow's sample consisted of patients with primary depression accompanied by obsessional traits. His finding that obsessional symptoms resolved on active drug when the depression was alleviated does not demonstrate a specific antiobsessive effect, nor does it rule it out. Both Solyom and Sookman (1977) and Marks and colleagues (1980) found CLO effective in reducing phobic anxiety and depressive mood. Marks et al. found that CLO caused a reduction in rituals, but only for patients who were initially depressed.

Singh and Saxena (1977) and Ananth (1977) conducted open CLO trials in which patient scores on obsessive symptoms, depression, and phobias all improved. Again, whether the improvement was due to a primary antiobsessive effect or was secondary to amelioration of anxiety or depression is uncertain. Ananth did find that scores on obsessional severity improved before mood changes were observed, which does suggest independence of effects. Additional case reports and open studies of CLO with OCD patients, reviewed by Emmelkamp (1982), Salzman and Thaler (1981), and Insel and Murphy (1981) provide further evidence that CLO is useful for obsessional patients with depressed mood.

We found no controlled studies of other antidepressants with OCD samples. Observations based on single cases suggest that tranylcypromine (Jenike, 1981) and phenelzine (Isberg, 1981) can ameliorate OCD symptoms. Since the patients treated in these reports each had features of panic disorder, the observed improvement may be due largely to the amelioration of the panic, as elsewhere reported for depressed patients with panic attacks (Liebowitz, Quitkin, & Stewart, 1983). Treatment with L-tryptophan supplemented by pyridoxine and nicotinic acid was also found helpful for an OCD patient (Yaryura-Tobias & Bhagavan, 1977).

Overall, the available evidence suggests that CLO, a tricyclic antidepressant (TCA), is useful in the treatment of obsessive symptoms in depressed patients, and monoamine oxidase inhibitors (MAOIs) may ameliorate obsessive symptoms in patients with panic attacks. Only three studies so far have been reported to document any specific antiobsessive effects of antidepressant drugs in the absence of depressive symptoms or anxiety attacks. These studies together suggest that CLO is somewhat effective in modifying the intensity and functionally disabling aspects of OCD symptoms. The total number in these studies who were treated with CLO and who completed the protocols was only 27, so that considerably more research remains to be done before firm conclusions can be drawn.

Critical viewers of this literature excluding the Insel study have reached different conclusions. Emmelkamp (1982) concluded that antidepressants in general and CLO in particular are "of little or no value for undepressed patients" with OCD (p.244), while Salzman and Thaler call for additional research, and Insel and Murphy (1981) suggest cautiously that CLO may have antiobsessive effects. They propose further testing of the hypothesis that OCD is related to serotonin deficiency by conducting trials of more selective serotonin uptake inhibitors such as fluoxetine "or by future studies of other drugs with serotonin system effects including tryptophan, 5 hydroxytryptophan, fenfluramine, amphetamine and clorgyline" (p.309). Their own study of clorgyline, however, showed no evidence of efficacy in a 6-week trial, arguing against the serotonin hypothesis.

Anxiolytics.   The only comparative drug trial of anxiolytics in OCD we were able to locate was conducted by Waxman (1977) and compared diazepam with CLO. The author reported better response to the latter, although as noted above these data are not clearly presented. In contrast, Burrell, Culpan, Newton, Ogg, & Short (1974) found bromazepam useful in the open treatment of 220 patients with obsessional symptoms, often accompanied by other psychopathology. Other reports of open trials, as summarized by Ananth (1976), have been mixed regarding the utility of anxiolytics for obsessive compulsive disorder.

As noted by Insel and Murphy (1981) in their review of the literature on psychopharmacological treatment of OCD, further clinical trials with anxiolytics are indicated. Although their effectiveness is not established, too few studies have been conducted to dismiss them as useless primary or ancillary treatment for OCD patients. Further studies may also illuminate more clearly the role of anxiety in OCD. Insel and Murphy (1981) point out that higher anxiety levels may accompany either increases or decreases in compulsive behavior: "reducing anxiety may paradoxically lead to greater difficulty for the patient with self-doubt and checking rituals for whom the slightest impairment of vigilance leads to greater uncertainty and more checking" (p.309). The sedative effects of many anxiolytics are in this context also potentially distressing.

In summary, anxiolytics do not appear to be a treatment of major promise for OCD, but the available data are limited. Controlled comparative trials including anxiolytics would be useful for the generation of both clinical and etiological insights.

Antipsychotics. We found no reports of controlled clinical trials of antipsychotics in the treatment of OCD. Anecdotal evidence for their efficacy has been reported. For example, Rivers-Bulkeley (Rivers-Bulkeley & Hollender, 1982) found loxapine effective in the abatement of obsessional thoughts, avoidant behavior, and compulsive acts of a patient convinced that he was being poisoned. This patient was close to the border of paranoid schizophrenia, which may account for his good response to a neuroleptic. Mixed results have been reported for haloperidol (Ananth, 1976), which was selected for trial with OCD patients because of its efficacy in Tourette's Disorder. This disorder is thought possibly associated with OCD because of the shared subjective experience of irresistible impulse preceding the expression of pathological behavior. For patients with pure OCD, there is no research evidence to support the efficacy of antipsychotics.

Summary. As several commentators regretfully have observed, there is no known antiobsessive drug or other treatment of established efficacy in the management of OCD. Of all drugs studied, clomipramine emerges as most promising, although additional comparative trials are necessary to clarify its efficacy for nondepressed OCD patients.

Etiological Implications. Several investigators have formulated explanations of observed drug effects in neurochemical terms. The most widely endorsed hypothesis is that OCD is related to serotonin deficiency (Insel & Murphy, 1981) but this seems unsupported by the clorgyline data. Others have suggested that a hyperdopaminergic state may exist in OCD (Ananth, 1976) but antipsychotics are ineffective, or that the limbic system is implicated (Burrell et al., 1974) but this seems an undefined hypothesis.

Agoraphobia-Panic Disorder (see Table 27.2)

The hallmark of panic and agoraphobia disorders is not the occurrence of discrete episodes of acute anxiety, which virtually everyone experiences in acutely stressful situations. Rather, as Sheehan (1982) puts it, "the suddenness of the surge of symptoms and their occurrence without warning and in the absence of any clear-cut precipitant" are its distinguishing characteristics. Traditionally considered in psychological terms as the manifestation of neurotic disorder, it is only in the past 20 years that pharmacological and behavioral treatments have been applied. In view of the demonstrated efficacy of at least two classes of antidepressant drugs, the exclusively psychodynamic model formerly used to understand this disorder is in competition with a medical-illness model that suggests a biochemical abnormality in the nervous system (Sheehan, 1982).

This syndrome has two illness components: the panic attack itself, which is a sudden discrete episode accompanied by various symptoms of autonomic arousal as well as a subjective sense of impending doom, and a low-grade chronic anticipatory anxiety that develops secondarily as the person begins to anticipate future panic attacks. This distinction between panic and anticipatory anxiety is supported by the finding that different drug classes differentially ameliorate one or the other.

Klein and colleagues have described behavioral concomitants of each of these illness components. They observed that panic attacks lead to help appeals, but anticipatory anxiety eventually culminates in avoidant behavior. Klein (Klein, 1981) described help-seeking behavior as follows: "Patients ran to the nursing station three times a day, every day, proclaiming that they were about to die and neded instant succor. The nurses would hold the patients' hands, reassure them, and sit with them for about 20 minutes. The patients would finally walk away, their acute, overwhelming distress somewhat alleviated" (Klein, 1981, p. 238). In the presence of clinical response to medication, this behavior fades away. Similarly, avoidant behavior associated with anticipatory anxiety is modified when the anticipatory anxiety is alleviated, although this is more often a direct product of in vivo exposure than a primary drug effect.

Anxiolytics.   Despite their widespread use in clinical practice for panic attacks, no studies have demonstrated that any of the benzodiazepines are effective treatment agents, although they often alleviate the associated anticipatory anxiety. The only comparative trial we were able to locate is a 10-week trial of imipramine (IMI) and chlordiazepoxide with 26 agoraphobic patients (McNair & Kahn, 1981).

Multiple measures of anxiety and depression as well as global clinical improvement showed an overall superiority of IMI as well as greater efficacy for panic attacks. The authors note that there is a correlation of .5 between severity ratings at baseline of anxiety and depression, which makes it impossible to study their separate responses to drug conditions in small groups. They also note that few outcome differences appeared before the eighth week, and caution that other studies of shorter duration are unlikely to constitute adequate trials.

The assessment of anxiolytics for panic disorder has not been pursued because

TABLE 27.2

Agoraphobia/Panic Disorder

Authors	Sample (Dx; Criteria; N)	Drug Conditions	Placebo	Trial Duration	Outcome: Evidence Re: Differential Drug Effects
ANXIOLYTICS					
McNair & Kahn, 1980	agoraphobia; RDC N = 26	imipramine; chlordiazepox- ide (CDZ)	—	10 weeks	IMI>CDZ
ANTIDEPRESSANTS					
Klein, 1964	phobic anxiety reaction	imipramine; chlorpromazine (CPZ)	Yes	6 weeks	IMI > placebo > chlorpromazine
Zitrin et al, 1983	agoraphobics, mixed phobics, simple phobics, DSM-III; N = 218	imipramine (plus behavior or supportive therapy)	Yes	26 weeks	IMI>placebo for spontaneous panic attacks
Sheehan, 1980	agoraphobia with panic attacks, DSM-III; N = 57	imipramine; phenelzine	Yes	12 weeks	IMI = PZ Both IMI + PZ > placebo inde- pendent of baseline depression scores.
Gittelman-Klein & Klein, 1971	school phobias, N = 35	imipramine	Yes	6 weeks	IMI > placebo
Berney et al, 1981	school phobias N = 46	clomipramine (plus suppor- tive psychotherapy)	Yes	12 weeks	CLO = placebo. Both groups improved significantly

511

it is now generally recognized that these drugs are not effective. The large majority of patients with panic disorder who are treated with other drugs report a history of benzodiazpines. Sheehan (1982) reported that 98% of the patients seen in his unit for spontaneous panic attacks had already received anxiolytics, sometimes for many years. Our experience has been similar.

Antidepressants.   It is curious that antidepressants and not anxiolytics have turned out to be the treatment of choice in this core subtype of anxiety disorder. Beginning with the work of Klein and Fink in 1962, imipramine (IMI) and later phenelzine (PZ) have been shown to prevent panic attacks, although they do not eliminate the associated anticipatory anxiety (see Klein et al., 1980). Klein conducted a comparative trial of placebo, IMI, and chlorpromazine with phobic-anxious patients experiencing sudden panic attacks. IMI stopped the panic attacks but chlorpromazine exacerbated the disorder (Klein et al., 1980, p. 549).

A subsequent study of agoraphobic, simple phobic, and mixed phobic (having both circumscribed phobias and spontaneous panic attacks) patients was initiated by Klein and colleagues in 1972 (see Klein et al., 1980). Patients were randomly assigned to IMI or placebo, and in addition all received either behavior therapy or supportive therapy. Results for 171 patients who completed the study support the hypothesis that IMI would prove effective for the agoraphobics and mixed phobics but not simple phobics. Since these patients were not depressed, the beneficial effects of the medication cannot be attributed to a nonspecific anti-depressant response (Zitrin et al., 1978, 1980, 1983). IMI was significantly better than a placebo in blocking recurrence of panic attacks. The addition of either form of psychotherapy to IMI significantly reduced the patients' avoidance behavior associated with anticipation of panic attacks.

Based primarily on these studies, IMI has come to be recognized as an effective treatment for panic attacks. Other treatments may be needed for management of associated anticipatory anxiety and avoidant behavior patterns characteristically found in patients with panic disorder or agoraphobia, (Davis, Suhayl, Spira, & Vogel, 1981; Grunhaus, Sloger, & Weisstub, 1981; Sheehan, 1982).

In analyzing treatment response for disorder of such complexity, cross-sectional studies using global outcome ratings have limited utility. Additional information is needed from process time-series longitudinal studies that include fine-grained measures of physiological parameters as well as subjective reports and behavioral observations.

Klein and colleagues (1980) reviewed seven uncontrolled clinical reports concerning the use of oral or intravenous CLO in patients with phobic anxiety. These studies, including approximately 200 patients, all concluded that CLO was an effective treatment. Unfortunately, results are not reported in terms of specific effect on panic attacks, anticipatory anxiety, or avoidant behavior. It remains to be determined whether CLO differs from IMI in the treatment of panic disorder.

Monoamine Oxidase Inhibitors.   We found one study, conducted by Sheehan and colleagues (Sheehan, Ballenger, & Jacobson, 1980, 1981), in which IMI and the MAOI PZ were compared with a placebo in the treatment of agoraphobic patients with panic attacks. Fifty-seven patients received either IMI, PZ, or placebo and all received supportive psychotherapy. Despite rather low doses (maximum of 150 mg/day of IMI, or 45 mg/day of PZ), both IMI and PZ produced greater mean improvement scores than placebo on a variety of outcome measures, including clinical ratings. Patients with high and low baseline depression scores were found to have similar response rates.

Several controlled trials of MAOI and placebo support the finding of MAOI efficacy in treating agoraphobia with panic attacks (reviewed in Klein et al., 1980, pp. 553-557). Their cumulative results demonstrate a statistical superiority of MAOI over placebo in alleviating anxiety. This may derive entirely from a primary effect on spontaneous panic with secondary extinction effects on anticipatory anxiety. Since no comparative trial has measured discrete outcome components, firm conclusions are not warranted at this time.

Tricyclic Antidepressants versus Monoamine Oxidase Inhibitors.   At present, there is no evidence to demonstrate that one is superior to the other, or that they have different effects on illness components. Sheehan's (Sheehan et al., 1981) data led him to suggest that more PZ patients than IMI patients may improve "markedly," although average group changes were equivalent.

Variants of Agoraphobia

School phobia

Klein (Klein et al., 1980) observed that a large proportion of adult agoraphobic patients had a childhood history of severe separation anxiety and that their response to initial panic was clinging behavior. It was reasoned that imipramine, found effective for adult agoraphobia, would be effective for children with pathological levels of separation anxiety. This reasoning led first to open treatment with imipramine, and then a placebo-controlled trial with school-phobic children (Gittelman-Klein & Klein, 1971). The children, who did not respond to a vigorous 2-week effort to encourage school attendance, were randomly assigned to imipramine or placebo. Using return to school as an index of improvement, 81% of the IMI group and 47% of the placebo group improved. All IMI-treated children and 21% of the placebo-treated children felt that they had improved.

A more recent study of school-phobic children conducted by Berney and colleagues (1981) compared CLO and placebo in a 12-week trial. They failed to find any difference between groups, perhaps because they used far lower doses of clomipramine. In the first study of 6- to 14-year-old children, the maximum dose was 200 mg/day imipramine, whereas Berney and colleagues prescribed a maximum of 40 to 75 mg/day of CLO, depending on the age of the child. In view of this enormous discrepancy in dose, which in the youngest age group may have been fivefold, it is not surprising that the two studies found different results.

Simple and social phobias (see Table 27.3)

The majority of people with only simple or social phobias are not severely impaired in terms of daily functioning and consequently seldom seek psychiatric treatment. While simple phobias are the most common type of phobia in the general population, they constitute a negligible proportion of psychiatric patients.

Very few pharmacologic studies have been conducted with simple phobic patients, although there have been many analog studies of behavioral treatments. Apart from the Klein, Zitrin studies of IMI and placebo for simple, mixed, and agoraphobic patients described above, where IMI was not helpful for simple phobias, we found only one other drug study with carefully diagnosed simple phobics, and these are symptomatic volunteers rather than people seeking treatment on their own. Bernadt, Silverstone, & Singleton (1980) solicited the cooperation of 22 volunteers with snake or spider phobias, and conducted three exposure sessions at weekly intervals. Before exposure to the feared object, the subject was given a single dose of either tolamolol (a beta adrenergic blocker), diazepam (a benzodiazepine) or placebo. Outcome measures included participants' ratings of fear and anxiety, a behavioral measure of how close the person could get to the snake or spider, and an electrocardiogram. Stress-induced tachycardia was abolished only by tolamolol, whereas behavioral effects (proximity to snake/spider) were influenced only by diazepam. Subjective fear ratings were influenced more by order effects than drug condition. The authors conclude that, since their effects on somatic symptoms do not generalize to subjective components of phobic response, beta blockers are not likely to be useful in the clinical treatment of simple phobias. Phobias include both a specific fear (e.g., of getting killed by a snake) and somatic symptoms triggered by actual or anticipated exposure to the feared object (e.g., tachycardia). A third component, avoidant behavior, is secondary to the anticipatory fear. In Bernadt et al.'s study (1980), diazepam decreased the anticipatory anxiety and the associated avoidant behavior, while the beta blocker influenced only the somatic symptoms.

Numerous clinical reports have been published testifying to the efficacy of acute doses of beta blockers in the treatment of social phobias (e.g., public speaking, performance anxiety). As observed by Bernadt, these drugs were found to suppress physiological symptoms of distress, such as palpitations and tremor (Noyes, 1982), which may serve as distress-enhancing cues.

In summary, no psychotropic drug has been demonstrated to be effective in the treatment of simple phobias. Acute doses of beta blockers may be useful in managing the somatic symptoms of social phobias, although controlled studies are lacking. To date, in vivo exposure is the treatment of choice: If anxiolytics

TABLE 27.3
Simple and Social Phobias

Authors	Sample (Dx; Criteria; N)	Drug Conditions	Placebo	Trial Duration	Outcome: Evidence Re: Differential Drug Effects
Bernadt et al, 1980	simple phobics N = 22	tolamolol diazepam	Yes	acute dose, cross-over design, 3 occasions	stress-induced tachycardia abolished by tolamolol only; avoidance behavior reduced by diazepam only
Zitrin et al, 1983	simple phobics, DSM-III; N = 62	imipramine (plus behavior or supportive therapy)	Yes	26 weeks	IMI = Placebo

reduce anticipatory anxiety and so facilitate entry into the fear situation, or if beta blockers interfere with a positive feedback loop of anxiety-causing tremor and tachycardia which then increases anxiety, their use may be advantageous.

Generalized Anxiety Disorder (GAD) (See Table 27.4)

This diagnostic category includes patients with nonspecific, persistent nonepisodic anxiety. It is a residual category in the sense that patients with panic disorder, OCD, agoraphobia and simple or social phobias are not included here. It seems likely that many patients classified simply as anxiety neuroses or chronic anxiety disorders in studies conducted before publication of *DSM-III* fall into this category.

Five comparative clinical trials have been published in which the patients were selected to fulfill *DSM-III* criteria for Generalized Anxiety Disorder. Rickels (1981) found alprazolam and diazepam equal in efficacy in terms of anxiety ratings and global clinical improvement after 4 weeks; both were superior to placebo. In a replication with 151 GAD patients, the same results were obtained (Rickels et al., 1983). In the latter report it is noted that both drugs produced greater improvement than placebo after the first week of treatment.

Three comparative studies of buspirone (a nonbenzodiazepine anxiolytic), diazepam, and placebo including nearly 400 patients consistently found equivalent efficacy for both drugs, which were significantly better than placebo on measures of anxiety, mood, and global clinical ratings. Goldberg and Finnerty (1982) reported that, according to self-report, more buspirone than diazepam patients felt improved. Feighner and colleagues (Feighner, Meredith, & Hendrickson, 1982) concluded that buspirone led to greater improvement than diazepam for impaired cognition (Hopkins Symptom Check List items) and confusion (Profile of Mood States), but these measures are weak. Rickels et al. (1982) suggested that diazepam is slightly better for somatic symptoms, and buspirone is better for cognitive and interpersonal problems, again using data from the Profile of Mood States and the Hopkins Symptom Check List.

An additional 36 studies were located in which the investigators compared the efficacy of two active drugs, some of which also had placebo groups. In none of these studies were the diagnostic characteristics of the sample described in detail: they were usually called "anxiety neurosis," "patients with anxiety," or simply patients with scores above a specified level on the Hamilton Anxiety Scale or another rating instrument. The presence or primacy of additional symptoms was not noted in most, although some studies reported concomitant depression.

These 36 studies comparing two active drugs fall into three groups based on drug class: comparisons of two different types of anxiolytics; anxiolytic and neuroleptic; anxiolytic and antidepressant. They are reviewed in turn.

TABLE 27.4
Generalized Anxiety Disorder (GAD)

Authors	Sample (Dx; Criteria; N)	Drug Conditions	Placebo	Trial Duration	Outcome: Evidence Re: Differential Drug Effects
COMPARATIVE TRIALS					
Rickels, 1981	GAD, DSM-III, N = 164	alprazolam, diazepam	Yes	4 weeks	both drugs > placebo, alprazolam = diazepam
Rickels et al, 1983	anxiety disorders, N = 151	alprazolan, diazepam	Yes	4 weeks	both drugs > placebo, Alprazolam = diazepam.
Feighner et al, 1982	GAD, DSM-III, N = 100	buspirone, diazepam	—	4 weeks	buspirone = diazepam
Goldberg & Finnerty, 1982	GAD, DSM-II, N = 54	buspirone, diazepam	Yes	4 weeks	both drugs > placebo; buspirone = diazepam
Rickels et al, 1982	GAD, DSM-III, N = 240	buspirone, diazepam	Yes	4 weeks	both drugs > placebo; buspirone = diazepam

TABLE 27.5
Anxiety Reactions

Authors	Sample (Dx; Criteria; N)	Drug Conditions	Placebo	Trial Duration	Outcome: Evidence Re: Differential Drug Effects
COMPARISONS OF ANXIOLYTICS					
Aden & Thien, 1980	moderately or severely anxious out-patients, N = 235	alprazolam diazepam	Yes	4 weeks	both drugs > placebo; alprazolam = diazepam
Allin, 1982	neurotic, anxious general practice patients, N = 44	chlormezanone diazepam	No	4 weeks	equal efficacy
Goldberg & Finnerty, 1982	moderate anxiety N = 129	buspirone, chlorazepate	No	4 weeks	equal efficacy
Maletzsky, 1980	moderate to severe anxiety, N = 86	alprazolam, diazepam	Yes	4 weeks	alprazolam > placebo diazepam = placebo alprazolam > diazepam
Rickels et al, 1974	anxious neurotic outpatients, N = 154	chlormezanone, chlordiazepoxide	Yes	6 weeks	both drugs > placebo; chlormezanone = chlordiazepoxide
Wheatley, 1982	anxious outpatients N = 131	buspirone diazepam	Yes	3 weeks	both drugs > placebo; buspirone = diazepam

TABLE 27.6
Anxiety Reactions: Anxiolytics vs. Neuroleptics

Authors	Sample (Dx; Criteria; N)	Drug Conditions	Placebo	Trial Duration	Outcome: Evidence Re: Differential Drug Effects
LOXAPINE					
Brauzer, 1974	mild to moderate anxiety, N = 96	loxapine chlordiazepoxide (CDZ)	Yes	4 weeks	loxapine = CDZ both drugs > placebo
Claghorn, 1973	anxiety neuroses, N = 171	loxapine chlordiazepoxide	Yes	4 weeks	LOX = CDZ = placebo
Mahal et al, 1976	anxious outpatients, N = 42	loxapine chlordiazepoxide	No	4 weeks	equal efficacy
Rickels et al, 1978	anxious neurotic outpatients, N = 135	loxapine chlordiazepoxide	Yes	6 weeks	loxapine = placebo CDZ > loxapine or placebo
Versiani et al, 1976, 1977	neurosis with anxiety, N = 52	loxapine chlordiazepoxide	No	4 weeks	equal efficacy
HALOPERIDOL					
Budden, 1979	anxiety neuroses, N = 48	haloperidol (HAL) diazepam	No	6 weeks	HAL > diazepam
Fyro et al, 1974	anxious neurotic outpatients, N = 51	haloperidol, diazepam	Yes	1 week trials, cross-over design	both drugs > placebo Diazepam > HAL only for patients with illness precipitant
Lord, Kidd, 1973	inpatients with anxiety, N = 45	haloperidol, diazepam	No	2 week trials, cross-over design	equal efficacy
Stevenson et al, 1976	outpatients with anxiety as primary complaint, N = 40	haloperidol, diazepam	No	3 weeks	equal efficacy

519

TABLE 27.6 (continued)

Authors	Sample (Dx; Criteria; N)	Drug Conditions	Placebo	Trial Duration	Outcome: Evidence Re: Differential Drug Effects
HALOPERIDOL (continued)					
Donald, 1969	anxiety as primary complaint, N = 31	haloperidol chlordiazepoxide	—	2 week trials, crossover design	HAL > CDZ
PIMOZIDE					
Doongaji et al, 1976	anxiety neuroses, N = 18	pimozide chlordiazepoxide	—	4 weeks	equal efficacy
Doongaji et al, 1981	anxiety neuroses, N = 47	pimozide, chlordiazepoxide	—	4 weeks	equal efficacy
Kenway, 1973	anxiety symptoms, N = 70	pimozide haloperidol	—	4 weeks	equal efficacy
Poldinger, 1976	anxiety neurosis or psychovegetative syndrome, N = 50	pimozide diazepam	—	2 weeks	equal efficacy
OTHER NEUROLEPTICS					
Lofft, Demars (1974)	anxiety or depressive neuroses, N = 26	thioridazine diazepam	—	4 weeks	equal efficacy
Rosenthal, Bowden, 1973	mixed anxiety-depressive neuroses, N = 47	thioridazine diazepam	—	4 weeks	equal efficacy
Wadzisz, 1972	anxiety neuroses, N = 40	oxypertine diazepam	—	4 weeks	equal efficacy
Yamamoto, 1973	anxiety-tension, N = 40	chlorpromazine chlordiazepoxide & antiparkinsonian or hypnotic drugs	—	4 weeks	equal efficacy

TABLE 27.7
Anxiety Reactions: Anxiolytics vs. Antidepressants

Authors	Sample (Dx; Criteria; N)	Drug Conditions	Placebo	Trial Duration	Outcome: Evidence Re: Differential Drug Effects
Bianchi, 1974	anxiety neuroses, Also, 26% had nonendogenous depressive symptoms, N = 50	doxepin diazepam	—	3 weeks	anxiety: doxepin = diazepam, depression: doxepin > diazepam
Goldberg, Finnerty, 1972	anxiety neuroses with depression, N = 52	doxepin	yes	4 weeks	anxiety: doxepin > placebo
Henry et al, 1971	primarily depressed and other; N = 240	tricyclics benzodiazepines	—	4 weeks	equal efficacy
Kleber, 1979	predominating symptons of depression and anxiety, N = 53	desmethylimipramine diazepam	—	4 weeks	DMI superior on both global rating and HAM-D and HAM-A factor scores
Johnstone et al, 1980	mixed depressive-anxious neurotic outpatients, N = 240	amitriptyline; diazepam; amitriptyline + diazepam	Yes	4 weeks	AMI most effective for both anxiety and depression; all 4 groups improved greatly
Magnus, Schiff, 1977	mixed anxious-depressed outpatients; N = 40	amitriptyline; nortriptyline plus fluphenazine	—	4 weeks	depression: equal efficacy. anxiety: NOR + FLU > AMI
Conti, Pinder, 1979	outpatients with primary anxiety, N = 40	mianserin, diazepam	—	2 weeks	anxiety: equal efficacy; global illness severity: mianserin > DZ
Bjertnaes et al, 1982	primary anxiety	mianserin chlordiazepoxide	Yes	6 weeks	mians. = DZC = placebo. All groups improved

521

Anxiolytics. Two comparative trials of alprazolam, diazepam, and placebo were conducted. Aden (1980) found equal efficacy for the active drugs, which were significantly more effective than placebo. In contrast, Maletzky (1980) fround alprazolam superior to both diazepam and placebo. He observed that diazepam patients showed some improvement in the first 2 weeks but not thereafter, whereas alprazolam patients improved steadily throughout the 4-week trial. No specific differences in effect were reported. (See Table 27.5).

Two comparative trials of chlormezanone were conducted. Allin (1982) compared it with diazepam and found both drugs ameliorated but did not eliminate anxious mood and tension, according to both doctor and patient ratings. Note was made that patients taking chlormezanone reported improved quality of sleep but in view of the multiple variables studied, this finding may be due to chance. Rickels et al. (1974) compared chlormezanone, chlordiazepoxide, and placebo and found both drugs superior to placebo from week 3 on. For both drugs, the largest treatment effect was on measures of somatic symptomatology. No significant differences between drugs were observed, either with respect to predictor variables or outcome.

The last two studies in this group entailed comparison of buspirone with clorazepate or diazepam and placebo. Goldberg and Finnerty (1982) found equal efficacy for buspirone and chlorazepate, with no differences in effect reported. Wheatley (1982) found equal efficacy between buspirone and diazepam, both of which were more effective than placebo after the second week.

Overall, no pronounced differences emerge between anxiolytics in terms of who responds or the nature of their improvement.

Anxiolytics vs. Neuroleptics. Five investigators compared loxapine and chlordiin CDZ; three of these had placebo controls. Brauzer (Brauzer, Goldstein, Steinbook, & Jacobson, 1974) found both active drugs significantly better than placebo. Rickels (Rickels, Weisse, Feldman, Fee, & Wiswesser, 1978) found only chlordiazepoxide CDZ better than placebo, and Claghorn (1973) found neither active drug effective. Both Rickels and Claghorn concluded that loxapine was not an effective anxiolytic and Claghorn went so far as to say that "loxapine. . . will drift into a tranquil obscurity, the only tranquility that can be expected from this compound." In view of these mixed findings, the two studies finding no difference in effect between loxapine and CDZ are not informative in the absence of placebo controls, since it is possible that the two drugs were equally ineffective. Neither author reported percentage improved or recovered. The cumulative results do not provide evidence for the efficacy of loxapine as an anxiolytic. (See Table 27.6)

In five studies, haloperidol was compared to an anxiolytic; one study had a placebo control group (Fyro, Beck-Friis, & Sjostrand, 1974), but this was a 1-week crossover design at low doses with undefined diagnostic groups and no standardized outcome measures. Accordingly, the authors' report that both active drugs reduced symptoms more than placebo, and that haloperidol has anxiolytic properties, is of limited utility. Budden (1979) found that haloperidol was more effective than diazepam, whereas Lord and Kidd (1973) and Stevenson (Stevenson, Burrows, & Chiu, 1976) reported equal efficacy. Lord et al. correctly observed that they could not detect a true difference in drug effect with their small sample size. Donald (1969) compared haloperidol and CDZ in a 2-week crossover design and found that, almost invariably, the first drug produced much greater improvement than the second. In these 2-week trials, haloperidol tended to have an advantage in terms of overall improvement, according to Donald.

Four nonplacebo-controlled studies of pimozide were conducted. The comparison drug in two studies (Doongaji, Sheth, Teste, & Ravindranath, 1976; Doongaji et al,., 1981) was chlordiazepoxide, and in the others (Kenway, 1973; Poldinger, 1976), haloperidol and diazepam. All investigators reported equal efficacy for the two drugs studied. The extent of improvement was reported by Doongaji et al. (1976) as 2/3 in each group. He noted earlier onset of action of chlordiazepoxide, which also seemed more effective for somatic symptoms including sleep disturbance. As noted above, the small samples and weak outcome measures in each study would permit identification of outcome differences between drugs only if the differences were of considerable magnitude, which evidently was not the case.

Thioridazine was compared to diazepam in two studies. Rosenthal and Bowden (1973) found significant improvement on all measures for both drugs. Thioridazine seemed better for changes in depression and demoralization as measured by the Hopkins Symptom Check List and Hamilton Depression Scale items; and diazepam for psychic anxiety. Lofft (Lofft & Demars, 1974) found that each drug showed an advantage for about half the outcome measures. They suggested that behavioral symptoms may be more responsive to thioridazine, and diazepam more effectively relieves subjective feelings. These post hoc interpretations must be regarded as tentative given the small samples, imprecise measures, and multiple variables studied.

Anxiolytic vs. Antidepressants.   Eight studies entailed comparison of a TCA or mianserin with an anxiolytic (or, in one case, combined antidepressant and antipsychotic) (see Table 27.7). All eight studies reported effects for depressive symptoms. With respect to anxiety symptoms, three studies reported equal efficacy for the antidepressant and anxiolytic; four reported superiority of the antidepressant, and one found the addition of fluphenazine to a TCA better than a TCA alone. In the five studies regarding effects on depression, tricyclics were more effective than anxiolytics in three and equally effective in two. Overall, no obvious superiority of either anxiolytics or antidepressants emerges in these studies of diagnostically heterogeneous patients; since antidepressants are sometimes more and never less effective, they are probably the more active drug, but differential prescription is not possible on the basis of these data.

Other Comparative Trials. The remaining four studies each compared an anxiolytic to another drug class, as shown on Table 27.8. No consistent patterns emerge.

Comment

In view of the large number of drug trials comparing two active drugs in the treatment of patients with anxiety disorders, remarkably few positive conclusions can be drawn. No single drug class emerges as consistently superior to any other in the treatment of any subtype of anxiety disorder with the exception of panic disorder, where antidepressants are clearly the treatment of choice. In general, antidepressants seem to have an advantage over anxiolytics, although the relative predominance of anxiety or depression in these diagnostically heterogeneous patients was seldom delineated, nor have there been substantial findings with regard to specific differential predictors of drug efficacy.

ANIMAL SEPARATION ANXIETY

There are several reasons to believe that the psychopharmacology of infant animal separation reactions is relevant to human anxiety disorder. Much of our clinical interest stems from the earlier mentioned reports that IMI is an effective treatment of separation-anxious, school-phobic children (Gittelman-Klein & Klein, 1971), and the high incidence of histories of childhood pathological separation anxiety in adults with agoraphobia (Klein, 1981). As noted, agoraphobia is also a condition highly responsive to pharmacotherapy. If medications that effectively cure human anxiety states also have a specific positive impact on separation distress in infant animals, a bona fide animal model would be available for one form of pathological human anxiety.

At the risk of being teleological, it is impossible to avoid noting how well designed is the mechanism of separation protest for maximizing the protection of young animals. Infants from mammalian and avian species such as higher primates, ungulates, and porpoises protest vigorously when removed from the mother. In small rodents, the protest takes the form of ultrasonic calls generally known as distress vocalizations (DVs).

According to Noirot (1972), these distress vocalizations (DVs) can be experimentally produced by two separate forms of noxious stimuli, cold and tactile stimuli. Each provokes a distinct form of distress vocalization. Rat pups do not emit DVs in response to lowering of the ambient temperature during the first days of life. As they become increasingly able to regulate body temperature, cold stress leads to more and louder DVs. At the point where temperature regulation becomes fully developed, DVs in response to cold stops. The type

TABLE 27.8
Anxiety Reactions: Other Drugs

AUTHORS Authors	SAMPLE Dx; Criteria; N) Sample (Dx; Criteria; N)	DRUG CONDITIONS Drug Conditions	PLACEBO Placebo	TRIAL DURATION Trial Duration	OUTCOME: EVIDENCE RE: DIFFERENTIAL DRUG EFFECTS Outcome: Evidence Re: Differential Drug Effects
Uhlenhuth et al, 1972	psychoneurotic patients excluding severe depression, N = 80	diphenylhydatoin (DPH) phenobarbitol	—	8 weeks	equal efficacy
Tyrer, Lader, 1974	anxiety state, N = 12	propanolol diazepam	Yes	1 week each, cross-over design	diazepam > propanolol. For 6 patients in subgroup with somatic anxiety, propanolol > placebo. For total group, propanolol = placebo.
Wheatley, 1969	anxiety neuroses; N = 105	propanolol, chlordiazepoxide	—	6 weeks	equal efficacy; both reduced symptoms
Vinar et al, 1979	anxiety and personality disorders, N = 108	natrium oxybutyrate oxazepam	—	1 week	no effects from any drug condition

525

of DV elicited by cold attracts the attention of the mother, who rapidly locates the infant and retrieves it. This retrieval behavior seems immune to extinction. The second type of DV, elicited by unusual tactile stimulation of the young rodent, is loudest and at the highest rate in the first days of life, when an animal is otherwise most defenseless. It declines progressively thereafter. This type of DV inhibits the mother from handling the infant.

Panksepp and his group have demonstrated repeatedly that morphine inhibits DVs provoked by social isolation whereas naloxone stimulates them. To summarize their findings:

1. Morphine sulphate reduces DVs in puppies at doses as low as 125 micrograms/kg. Beta endorphin works as well as morphine (Panksepp, Herman, Vilberg, Bishop, & DeEskinazi, 1980).
2. This is also true for young guinea pigs (Herman & Panksepp, 1978) and chicks (Panksepp, Vilberg, Bean, Coy, & Kostin, 1978).
3. In the morphine experiments, the doses are low and the animals do not appear sedated. Panksepp et al. take great pains to demonstrate that the decrease in DVs is not due to a sedative effect of morphine on the animals.
4. Naloxone, in doses of 1 mg/kg, increased DVs significantly in chicks (Panksepp, Meeker, & Bean, 1980) and in guinea pigs (Panksepp et al., 1978).
5. This group also examined the effects of a great number of other drugs on separation distress in chicks, including d-amphetamine, 1-amphetamine, apomorphine, haloperidol, propanolol, IMI, chlordiazepoxide, and chlorpromazine. Of all the nonopiate drugs tested "only clonidine was as effective as morphine in reducing isolation induced distress vocalization" (Panksepp, Meeker, & Bean, 1980, p. 442).

Thus, for chicks and guinea pigs, DVs provoked in an infant by separation from the mother are inhibited by morphine, endorphin, and clonidine. Naloxone increases them. The implication is that in these species, the endogenous opiate system might control separation distress behavior. Baby rodents may be "addicted" to their mother the way human addicts are to heroin.

Although morphine, endorphin, and clonidine are the most potent DV suppressors, other drugs are also effective. Specifically, blockade of the serotonin system with methysergide increases DVs whereas the serotonin agonist quipazine reduces DVs (Panksepp, Meeker, & Bean, 1980). Evidence also suggests that cholinergic receptor agonists (e.g., carbachol and nicotine) reduce DVs and scopolamine (a cholinergic antagonist) increases them (Sahley, Panksepp, & Zolovick, 1981). Unfortunately, we have very little knowledge about the effects of purely serotonergic and cholinergic drugs on human anxiety states.

The finding that clonidine is capable of blocking separation distress in animals is of particular interest. In humans, clonidine appears to block the symptoms of opiate withdrawal (Gold, Redmond, & Kleber, 1979) by means of the drug's ability to curtail firing of the locus ceruleus and decrease central noradrenergic firing. Furthermore, clonidine has been shown to have at least a transient antipanic effect in patients with panic disorder (Liebowitz, Fyer, McGrath, & Klein, 1981).

On the other hand, IMI appears to have surprisingly little effect on protest behavior in young rodents and chicks, limiting the usefulness of separation anxiety in these species as a model of anxiety reactions in higher mammals. As we move higher phylogenetically, an IMI effect does emerge, but the literature in this area is meager.

Scott (1974) administered a host of drugs to puppies separated from their mothers and studied the effect on reducing separation distress. Drugs with no effect were chlorpromazine, reserpine, meprobamate, diazepam, sodium pentobarbital, and alcohol. D-amphetamine may have increased distress vocalizations. In the beagle, but not in the telomian dog breed, 8 mg/kg of IMI virtually eliminated DVs without producing side effects.

An acknowledged limitation of Scott's study is that all drugs were given only acutely. In humans, medications must often be administered on a chronic basis before there is a substantial antianxiety effect. Also, drugs like morphine and clonidine that seem to reduce DVs in more primitive species and may control certain forms of anxiety in humans were not tried against IMI in the dogs.

Suomi, Seaman, Lewis, DeLizio, and McKinney (1978) treated separated rhesus monkeys with IMI using a well-conceived design. These monkeys were raised with peers instead of the mother, a technique apparently felt valid for studying separation anxiety by experts in the field. The peer-raised monkeys were divided into a placebo group and an IMI group (10 mg/kg) and were separated from their peers for 19 days, beginning at 90 days of age. They were reunited for 9 days, separated for 19 more days, reunited for another 9 days, and further separated for 19 days. Treatment with IMI began on the eighth day of the second separation and continued through the final day of the third reunion. Imipramine clearly reduced separation distress compared to placebo, an effect that diminished when the drug was discontinued. The effect became more pronounced with longer IMI treatment. Of course, no one knows if this is an effect specific to IMI or might occur with other medications as well.

The findings of Scott and of Suomi's group are nevertheless stimulating, indicating that the effects of IMI on protest anxiety in infant animals may resemble the drug's effects on school-phobic children and agoraphobic adults. Further investigation on higher mammals seems clearly warranted.

RECEPTOROLOGY

For several reasons belief in the monoamine hypothesis of affective disorders—that depression, for example, is the result of a relative deficiency of central neurotransmitters—has begun to wane in recent years. In its place are hypotheses that relate antidepressant drug activity to effects on central nervous system receptors, giving rise to the new field of receptorology. Many of the medications used for anxiety disorders—especially panic disorder, agoraphobia with panic attacks, and obsessive compulsive disorder—are also antidepressants. Consequently, we wonder whether patterns of antidepressant drug-induced receptor changes would yield a clue to the etiology or pathophysiology of anxiety disorder.

We are indebted to an article by Charney, Menkes, and Heninger (1981), which painstakingly lays out what is known about the central receptor effects of antidepressant drugs. Our purpose, in serially addressing the alpha-2 (presynaptic), alpha-1 (postsynaptic), beta, serotonergic, histaminic, gamma aminobutyric acid (GABA) and cholinergic receptors, as do Charney et al., is to see if any of the known receptor effects described can be related to anxiety.

Alpha-2 Receptor

The alpha-2 or presynaptic receptor, when stimulated, provokes a net reduction of neural transmission via an inhibitory loop and provokes a net increase in transmission when blocked. Clonidine is the prototypic alpha-2 receptor agonist, used primarily as an antihypertensive agent in humans. As already discussed, the drug quiets the locus ceruleus and decreases noradrenergic turnover in brain cells. This may explain its ability to block the symptoms of opiate withdrawal, although clonidine probably has other effects since it also ameliorates the rhinorrhea and lacrimation of opiate withdrawal, which are not noradrenergically mediated. We have alluded to work indicating that clonidine is at least transiently effective in blocking the spontaneous panic attacks of patients with panic disorder. Hence, we might expect that other drugs that stimulated the alpha-2 receptor could be anxiolytic, perhaps by reducing locus ceruleus discharge.

Huang (1979) has shown that chronic desipramine administration to rats does inhibit norepinephrine-containing cells in the locus ceruleus. These cells inhibit firing of hippocampal cells, so the net effect of chronic treatment is to facilitate hippocampal activity.

Desipramine and possibly imipramine, both perfectly respectable antipanic drugs, seem to affect the alpha-2 receptor. A number of studies have reported a reduction in sensitivity of the alpha-2 receptor after long-term treatment with these drugs (Svennson & Usdin, 1978). It might be expected that this effect should actually cause anxiety, since decreased alpha-2 receptor function theoretically should increase locus ceruleus discharge. However, the exact relationship between tricyclic desensitization of alpha-2 auto-receptors and locus ceruleus activity is as yet not well understood. Many compensatory mechanisms can be theorized that would override the effects of alpha-2 receptor subsensitivity on locus ceruleus firing rate. Whether decreases in locus ceruleus discharge caused by chronic tricyclic administration are truly mediated by changes in alpha-2 receptor sensitivity is thus still unclear.

Looking at the effect of other drugs on the alpha-2 receptor makes the picture even more confusing. Amitriptyline and CLO do not appear to have any effect on this receptor, even though they are probably also good antipanic drugs and CLO is well known to be effective in obsessive-compulsive disorder (Thoren, Asberg, Cronholm, Jornestedt, & Traskman, 1980).

Acute administration of mianserin blocks the alpha-2 receptor, the opposite effect from clonidine. However, there are no reports of mianserin causing panic attacks or exacerbating panic disorder as would be expected if the alpha-2 receptor is involved in anxiety. We have seen one panic disorder patient benefit from mianserin. Chronic mianserin administration may not antagonize the alpha-2 receptor (Charney, Heninger, & Sternberg, in press).

Finally, benzodiazepines have no known alpha receptor effects and the possible role of MAOIs is unknown. One study found an increase in alpha-2 receptor density in rat brain after 7 days of treatment with the MAOI nialamide (Asakura, Tsukamoto, & Hasegawa, 1982). There is not a necessary relationship, however, between receptor number and sensitivity. The same report describes chronic administration of tricyclics as increasing alpha-2 density even though others report they decrease alpha-2 sensitivity. From this, it is difficult to conclude that a specific defect in alpha-2 receptor sensitivity is a factor in anxiety disorder.

Alpha-1 Receptor

The postsynaptic alpha receptor is less well studied than the presynaptic, making it difficult to reach firm conclusions. Almost all TCAs, according to Charney et al. (1981), produce supersensitivity of the alpha-1 receptor when given on a chronic basis. Chlorpromazine, which has little antianxiety effect except in psychotic patients, does not have this effect. Neither, however, does fluoxetine, an experimental antidepressant that we have been studying, which may have antipanic effects in patients with panic disorder. Finally, as is the case with the alpha-2 receptor, it is not known whether MAOIs have any effect on the alpha-1 receptor.

Before any firm conclusion can be made, we would like to know for certain whether fluoxetine is an antipanic drug. It would also be important to know whether MAOIs as well as alpha-1 blockers such as prazosine have antipanic effects.

Beta Receptor

The beta adrenergic receptor is blocked by propranolol and stimulated by isoproterenol. Although propanolol has been cited as an antianxiety agent, the evidence is conflicting (Cole, Altesman, & Weingarten, 1980). Evidence that propranolol causes depression (Petrie, Mafucci, & Woolsky, 1982) is also inconsistent. It is possible, however, that although blockade of beta receptors reduces anxiety, it also causes depression. While it is well known that chronic treatment with all TCAs, MAOIs, and trazodone leads to reduced sensitivity ("down regulation") of central beta receptors, this effect, which is not seen with mianserin, may be related to antidepressant activity. It is also our experience that while traditional benzodiazepines—which have no consistent antipanic effects—do not down-regulate beta receptors, the new benzodiazepine analogue alprazolam is antipanic and it does affect the beta receptor (Sethy & Hodges, 1982). Like desipramine, and unlike diazepam, alprazolam blocked the reserpine-induced increase in the number of rat brain beta receptors. Alprazolam did not, however, reduce sensitivity of beta receptors the way TCAs do.

There are good reasons to be skeptical that reducing the sensitivity of beta receptors is responsible for antidepressant activity. Nemeroff and Evans (1983) described a patient with depression treated with maprotiline at the same time he received propranolol for a tremor. The patient's depression responded to maprotiline, which down-regulates beta receptors, despite his also being on propanolol, which leads to an increased number of beta receptors when given chronically. Theoretically, propranolol should block the effect of tricyclics and tetracyclics if the true mode of their antidepressant action is beta receptor down-regulation. Hence, conflicting evidence again makes it impossible to confirm a receptor etiologically in the production of pathological anxiety.

Serotonergic Receptor

Chronic treatment with most known TCAs produces enhanced sensitivity of postsynaptic serotonin receptors. However, zimelidine and CLO appear not to affect the serotonin receptor, whereas the MAOI clorgyline may have a blunting effect on the receptor.

Cholinergic, Dopaminergic, and Histaminic Receptors

No consistent effects on either cholinergic, dopaminergic, or histaminic receptors by the antidepressant drugs have been found.

Gamma-Aminobutyric Acid (GABA)

The effect of benzodiazepines to enhance GABA transmission via the benzodiazepine receptor is discussed elsewhere in this volume. Interestingly, long-term TCA administration does not affect GABA receptors. However, isoniazid, an MAOI precursor, may increase central GABA levels (Manyam, More, & Katz, 1980).

More knowledge increases the chance of validating (or disproving) a hypothesis: The notion that some defect in central receptor sensitivity, which is corrected by drug action, actually causes pathological anxiety conceivably could be proven if more were known about this action of various drugs on these receptors. Thus, one cannot escape the disappointing observation that there is always at least one clinically effective drug that violates the pattern set by other drugs for a specific receptor action.

CONCLUSIONS

Our search for inferences derived from pharmacological treatment concerning the etiology of anxiety has been largely unrewarding, and should stir reflection upon the paucity of our findings.

With regard to psychopharmacological treatment studies, a major difficulty in conducting proper pharmacological dissections seems to lie in the small-scale, efficacy-oriented approach of most studies in this area. These studies are really dedicated to showing that the drug has some discernible superiority to placebo and are only secondarily, if at all, concerned with the issue of the specific indications for specific drug actions. Since it is by pursuing the issue of specific indications (whether psychological, biological, or behavioral) that the existence of homogeneous subgroups may be inferred, the kind of drug projects reviewed here simply do not afford a data base of the requisite magnitude or complexity.

Statistical power considerations make it evident that even if there were some subgroup of the anxiety states that manifest a distinctive pattern of drug reactions, the attempt to detect such a discrete pattern of response on a post hoc basis requires very large sample sizes. Sample sizes of this magnitude cannot be met by the usual investigator or by the usual funding mechanisms. Attempts to deal with this issue by multicenter studies have run afoul of the problem of large attrition rates and problems in calibration of behavioral measures across centers. It is noteworthy that statistical attempts to define the right drug for the right patient have usually failed replication. If the strategy of pharmacological dissection is to work, it depends either upon the development of specific hypotheses, as in the area of panic disorder and atypical depression, or in the development of large clinical programmatic research centers (Klein, 1970).

Attempts to develop fruitful biological hypotheses with regard to etiology and pathophysiology have been greatly stimulated by our psychopharmacological therapeutic success. However, it is clear that our theories with regard to pathophysiological processes and the ameliorative effects of psychotropic agents are still primitive. Conceptualization in this area still depends largely upon a rheostat model of pathology and drug effects. Klein and Davis (1969) pointed to the striking fact that the powerful psychotropic agents have remarkably little effect upon normal functioning. Antidepressants do not make normals more cheerful, an indication that their benefits come from normalizing a deranged regulatory mechanism. That drugs such as the phenothiazines benefit both excited and retarded schizophrenia, and that lithium is prophylactic for both manic and depressive states, are further evidence that a rheostat model may be inappropriate. The shift in focus from the early biogenic amine theories, which emphasized excessive or insufficient amounts of synaptic neurotransmitter, to receptor theory remains framed in rheostat terms. Rather than having too little neurotransmitter, the receptor hypothesis refers to a down-regulated receptor. However, receptor theory is more easily compatible with concerns about negative feedback circuits, possible pathogenic positive feedback circuits, and drug benefit via alterations in timing and amplitude of neural transmission.

Clearly, if there were an adequate animal model for human psychopathology, experimental approaches would be tremendously enhanced. The utility of the punished response-disinhibition model makes considerable sense with regard to benzodiazepines' effect in anticipatory anxiety, but seems less relevant for the apparently spontaneous panic attack. Hypotheses relating the spontaneous panic attack to a deranged protest mechanism find some support in the studies concerning antidepressant effects on separation-induced distress. Nonetheless, it is clear that considerably more work is necessary before these hypotheses are confirmed or rejected.

Of great promise is the possibility held out by behavioral genetics. Conceivably, one could breed animals for separation anxiety and by sufficient inbreeding provide a pathologically anxious strain. Such animals might provide clinically realistic experimental models. The most powerful arguments for biological etiology have come from studies on the genetics of mental illness. We believe it is time to apply those insights to animal experimentation and psychobiological analysis.

ACKNOWLEDGMENTS

This work was supported in part by grants (MH 30906, MH 33422) to Donald F. Klein, and Research Scientist Development Award (MH 00416) to Jack M. Gorman.

28

Neurochemical Basis for Anxiety and Anxiety Disorders: Evidence from Drugs Which Decrease Human Fear or Anxiety

D.E. Redmond, Jr.
Yale University School of Medicine

The effects of drugs that alter the emotions of fear and anxiety in human subjects may provide useful information about the brain structures, neural circuitry, and biochemistry of these emotions. This chapter reviews the biochemical effects of anxiolytic drugs to determine whether significant common mechanisms can be found. Understanding these drug effects might provide a basis for understanding the excessive anxiety, fear, or panic that disables some individuals and contributes to other psychiatric and psychosomatic conditions.

As a preface to this review, it is important to mention some limits of our knowledge and some areas of controversy. Since anxiety and fear can be observed and/or experienced on a number of dimensions of cognition, behavior, physiology, and feeling, these dimensions largely determine how the emotions are defined. Darwin (1872), Freud (1936), Kierkegaard (1944), May (1950), Gray (1976, 1982, this volume), Sarason (this volume), and Costa (this volume), to cite a few examples, all seem to mean something slightly different by "anxiety." Most people agree that in the anticipation of pain, bodily injury, or death, nearly everyone experiences a particular type of subjective discomfort, accompanied by physiological manifestations that are distinguishable from other emotional states. Little empirical data exist to distinguish fear from anxiety, although this distinction is usually made based on the internal and external origin of the stimuli that elicit these emotions, or on the duration or chronicity of the emotions, without showing that either the subjective or physiological phenomenology of the two differ.

There is disagreement whether clinical anxiety "disorders" constitute discrete entities with pathophysiological mechanisms. Alternatively, these disorders may represent continuous variations in the activity of one or more normal neurobiological systems, which are responding or over-responding to internal or external stimuli that would not be threatening to others. This review assumes that both interpretations may be correct—that there are biological substrates for the normal emotion or emotions fear/anxiety and that these substrates may underlie pathological fear, anxiety, and panic that may also have specific biological pathophysiologies in some individuals. The specific question posed by this review is whether reasonable inferences about the biological mechanisms of human anxiety or fear can be drawn, based on what is known about the neurochemistry and neurophysiology of drugs with anti-fear or anxiolytic effects, even though we cannot precisely define the nature of the emotions or the disorders.

A PHARMACOLOGICAL APPROACH TO ANXIETY

In addition to the long-known opiates, Cannabis, Rauwolfia, and ethanol, this century has added new "tranquilizers" of various classes from the phenothiazines to the benzodiazepines. Although these drugs have been enormously successful and widely used, they have not yet provided the keys to understanding the biochemistry of anxiety even though much is known about their effects in the brain. The pharmacological approach to studying the nature of fear can be traced to Walter Cannon's work (1915) on the nature of anxiety, fear, and rage, which was followed by numerous attempts to induce fear in human subjects by the infusion of epinephrine (Basowitz, Korchin, & Oken, 1956; Cantril & Hunt, 1932; Jersild & Thomas, 1931; Koppanyl, 1928; Landis & Hunt, 1932; Marañon, 1920, 1924; Peabody, Sturgis, & Tompkins, 1921; Pollin & Goldin, 1961; Schacter & Singer, 1962, 1966; Wearn & Sturgis, 1919), norepinephrine (Chessick, Bassan & Shattan, 1966; King, Sokoloff, & Wechsler, 1952; Vlachakis, DeGuia, Mendlowitz, Antram, & Wolf, 1974), and lactate (Pitts, 1969, 1971; Pitts & McClure, 1967).

An important milestone in the development of pharmacological inferences about anxiety disorders was the observation that benzodiazepines were not effective in the treatment of sudden and spontaneous panic attacks, whereas tricyclic "antidepressants" (TCAs) were (Klein, 1964; Klein & Fink, 1962). This led Klein to postulate two types of anxiety in these subjects, "anticipatory" anxiety and panic, and to note that the benzodiazepines decreased anticipatory anxiety and TCAs diminished panic attacks differentially. These differences in pharmacological effects also suggested that subjects who experienced panic attacks might be biologically different from those who experienced more generalized anxiety, with different biological mechanisms altered by chemically distinct classes of drugs. Recent understanding of the mechanisms through which these and other drugs interact with neurons provides new evidence for actions the various anxiolytic drugs might have in common. The congruence of these actions at specific systems in the brain also supports the possibility that the areas of common actions identify neural substrates for anxiety or panic (see Fig. 28.1).

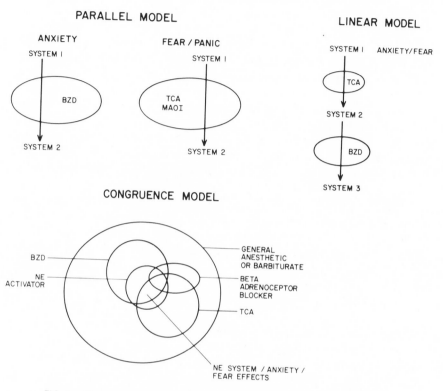

FIG. 1. Three models showing (1) the hypothesis of separate biological systems and pharmacologic agents affecting separate "parallel" systems for anxiety and for fear/panic; (2) a "congruence" model where overlapping and common effects of various drugs point to a particular neurochemical system which might be involved in both anxiety and fear; and (3) a linear model in which a single effector system was involved in anxiety and fear, but where different anxiolytic drugs acted at different points. The drugs or actions identified are illustrative examples only. In the first parallel model benzodiazepines (BZD), tricylic antidepressants (TCAs), & monoamine oxidase inhibitors (MAOIs) act on separate mechanisms or systems. In the second model, mechanisms of general anesthetics or barbiturates, benzodiazepines, TCAs, and beta-adrenoceptor blockers are shown to converge on a single noradrenergic effector system for anxiety/fear. A norepinephrine activator (such as yohimbine) is shown that produces opposite effects on the same system. In the linear model a TCA is illustrated as acting on one system, with a BZD acting on another system. Combinations of the above models also seem likely to be necessary to explain the actions of all anxiolytic compounds, with localizations having to be determined both at anatomically and biochemically specific sites.

Models for the cellular actions of drugs include active sites where the drugs bind to neuronal membranes and where "receptor" activation is translated by second messengers into alterations in membrane potentials (see Cooper, Bloom, & Roth, 1983). These changes serve to increase or decrease the threshold for (and therefore usually the rates of) neuronal firing and neurotransmitter release. Neurotransmitter concentrations can be changed by alterations in synthesis, synaptic storage, and intraneuronal metabolism. Presynaptic effects increase or decrease neurotransmitter release into the synapse, and re-uptake and metabolic blockades serve to enhance "available" synaptic neurotransmitter concentrations with measurable effects on metabolic and biochemical processes. Finally, effects on postsynaptic receptor affinity, density, and conformation, and on associated second messengers in the target neurons can be seen as a result of direct or indirect drug actions. In addition, these actions take place in a variety of neurons that have somewhat distinctive biochemical properties, anatomic localizations, and interconnections, as well as multiple receptors and neurotransmitter regulatory inputs. This neuronal model is highly dynamic, with multiple homeostatic regulatory mechanisms and numerous regulatory inputs from other neurotransmitter systems. The "pharmacological congruence" of action of two drugs can be demonstrated and illustrated at the receptor level. Two compounds bind stereospecifically to the same receptor, and blockade by a specific receptor antagonist blocks electrophysiologic effects of both as measured on the same neuron. Another compound with the same physiologic effects that did not bind to that receptor and could not be blocked by the receptor antagonist would require an explanation at a higher level of complexity. Such an explanation might be an action at a parallel receptor that also regulated the same class of neurons. Both of these examples illustrate congruences of action, the first on a specific receptor type and the second on the same type of neuron.

The existence of congruences of anxiolytic drug actions on central noradrenergic neurons will be described as an example of the "congruence of action" approach. Other evidence in addition to these congruences also suggests that the action of these norepinephrine (NE) releasing or noradrenergic neurons might be relevant broadly to an "alarm" or "warning" function that includes aspects of attentiveness, but may also underline anxiety, fear, terror, or panic at high levels of activation. This schematic paradigm should be judged not by its completeness, for it is most certainly incomplete and partially wrong, but by its ability to generate testable hypotheses and to explain data parsimoniously.

Before proceeding further, several limitations of pharmacological inferences and experimental methods should also be acknowledged: (1) that all drugs have many actions in the brain and the body that are probably irrelevant to a particular therapeutic effect; (2) that the demonstration of a particular effect does not necessarily imply a deficit or disorder in the affected system; (3) that differences in actions between drugs may reveal differences between the drugs rather than about the system with which they interact; (4) since there is so little agreement regarding the nature of anxiety or the more practical problem of how to recognize and rate it, a pharmacological approach has serious problems with both reliability and validity of what is identified as anxiety; (5) that the individuals who have been studied in most of the available literature are very likely to have heterogenous anxiety disorders, if indeed such classifications are valid, and much speculation is derived from studies of animal "models" or cognitive studies in "normal" human subjects who rate themselves as "slightly" anxious, and (6) that many studies are too small to determine differences between drugs and do not study placebos as well as "reference" compounds. Of these limitations, the most serious is *the variability of the identification and quantitation of anxiety present,* underscoring one of the major obstacles to progress in the field. At the present time the data are based essentially on people saying that they are anxious or afraid, with all of the apparent problems for validity and reliability that this involves. Physiological changes, behavioral avoidance of stimuli, or termination of help seeking are no more reliable, although they have also sometimes been used as criteria for anxiety reduction. After recognizing the limitations of the data and some of the pitfalls of interpretation, I want to address three broad classes of drug actions—first, the various drugs that reduce anxiety or fear, and second, some major drug classes that do not seem to alter anxiety and may, therefore, be important for ruling out the involvement of some important neurochemical systems. Third, in order to improve the probability that a particular biochemical effect of an anxiolytic drug is essential to the brain mechanism(s) of anxiety, brief mention will be made of drugs which have been reported to produce or increase anxiety and would be expected to produce opposite changes during the experimental production of anxiety.

COMMON BIOCHEMICAL EFFECTS OF ANXIOLYTIC DRUGS

The drugs and drug classes that have been reported to have anti-fear or anti-anxiety properties are the benzodiazepines, barbiturates, alcohol, propanediols, neuroleptics, opiates, tricyclic and monoamine oxidase inhibitor (MAOI) antidepressants, beta-adrenoceptor antagonists, alpha-2 adrenoceptor agonists, cannabinols, antihistamines, and Rauwolfia alkaloids. In this review each class is described briefly with references to further sources for a description of the range of biochemical effects of each.

Benzodiazepines (BZD)

Certainly the benzodiazepines enjoy the most popularity as anxiolytic agents, and enormous amounts are both legally prescribed and illicitly used (see Costa & Greengard, 1975). These compounds are now thought to initiate their actions at specific benzodiazepine receptors (Braestrup & Squires, 1977; Mohler &

Okada, 1977a, 1977b; Squires & Braestrup, 1977) which interact with receptors for GABA (Costa & Guidotti, 1979; Costa, Guidotti, & Mao, 1975; Haefely et al., 1975). These receptors are widely distributed throughout the brain and are believed to mediate the principal anxiolytic, sedative, muscle relaxant, and anticonvulsant properties of this class of drugs (Iversen & Schon, 1973; Tallman, Paul, Skolnick, & Gallager, 1980). Evidence suggesting the existence of endogenous benzodiazepine-like compounds has been published, but further work is needed to clarify their existence and role (Clow, Glover, Armando, & Sandler, 1983; Costa, this volume; Glover, Armando, Clow, & Sandler, 1983; Glover, Bhattacharya, Sandler, & File, 1981; Guidotti, Toffano, & Costa, 1978; Petursson, Bhattacharya, Glover, Sandler, & Lader, 1982). As might be expected from the extremely broad range of actions of the BZD's, they have been found to have activity in a number of major neurotransmitter/neuroanatomical systems. It seems likely, based on this very wide neuroanatomic distribution, that these compounds act on neural substrates for anxiety at multiple sites.

The benzodiazepines have remarkably wide margins between the therapeutically effective and toxic doses, particularly with regard to sedative effects and the depression of vital functions, in contrast to the barbiturates and propanediols, which have more general cell depressant properties (Greenblatt & Shader, 1974). Also remarkable is the fact that benzodiazepines have little effect on severe fear in doses that are tolerated by ambulatory individuals. This may, however, contribute to the safety of their use generally, since benzodiazepine-treated individuals are able to respond to genuine crises in an appropriate manner.

In certain types of anxiety recent studies (McNair & Kahn, 1981) confirm the superiority of imipramine over chlordiazepoxide in a direct comparison, supporting the ideas that anxiety and fear have different neural substrates, and secondarily that generalized anxiety disorder (GAD) and panic disorder have different biological abnormalities (Klein, 1964) (see Fig. 28.1, Model 3). Opposed to this idea that fear and anxiety are qualitatively as well as quantitatively different is the fact that high doses (100 mg) of diazepam are effectively used against iatrogenic fear (for example, pre-operative medication, Edmondson, Roscoe, & Vickers, 1972; Ellison, 1979; Foreman, 1974; Hall & Edmondson, 1983; Litchfield, 1972; Weiner, 1979; and for cardiac catheterization, Cote, Campeau, & Bourassa, 1976; Markiewicz, Hunt, Harrison, & Alderman, 1976; Wood, Robertson, Robertson, Wilkinson, & Wood, 1980). Also, a recent study shows some reduction in the number of panic attacks in panic disorder subjects in a blind cross-over study of lower diazepam doses (Noyes et al., 1984). Further, a triazolobenzodiazepine (alprazolam) appears to be efficacious for panic attacks (Chouinard, Annable, Fontaine, & Solyom, 1982) as well as for generalized anxiety (Anden & Thein, 1980; Chouinard et al., 1982; Fabre & McLendon, 1979; Maletzky, 1980; Rickels et al., 1983). So far, it is not clear whether these pharmacological properties of alprazopam are due to very high potency at benzodiazepine receptors (10 times the potency of diazepam) combined with diminished sedative side effects, which allows the greater potency to be tolerated clinically. Alternatively, unusual pharmacological properties may be due to the triazolo ring (Rudzik et al., 1973).

Benzodiazepines (BZD) appear to interact with many neurotransmitter systems. The closest interactions, as noted above, are with the neurotransmitter gamma amino butyric acid (GABA), and can be demonstrated in a variety of ways (Costa & Guidotti, 1979). Interactions with cholinergic, serotonergic, dopaminergic and noradrenergic systems are usually thought of as secondary to primary effects on GABA/BZD receptors (Tallman et al., 1980). Benzodiazepines decrease NE turnover in rat brain after high doses (Taylor & Laverty, 1969), an activity that has been attributed to locus coeruleus-cortical pathways by Corrodi, Fuxe, Lidbrink, & Olson (1971). High doses of diazepam (5 mg/kg) antagonize the effects of piperoxane or yohimbine (two alpha-2 adrenoceptor antagonists which increase NE activity) on cortical NE turnover in the rat (Fuxe et al., 1975). Similar physiological effects of chlordiazepoxide, norepinephrine synthesis inhibitors, or lesions of the dorsal noradrenergic bundle (Gray, 1982) occur in the septo-hippocampal system. The high doses required to produce these effects and the tolerance to the changes in norepinephrine turnover, which occurs while anxiety-reducing activity increases (Cook & Sepinwall, 1975; Stein, Wise & Belluzi, 1975), might suggest that these decreases in NE function are not essential. In monkeys, however, doses of diazepam in the "clinical" range (0.15 mg/kg) decrease fear-like behavioral effects of electrical field stimulation of the noradrenergic nucleus locus coeruleus (Redmond, 1977). This finding is consistent with the decrease in single unit activity in the locus coeruleus after intravenous (Grant, Huang, & Redmond, 1980) and microiontophoretic (Strahlendorf & Strahlendorf, 1981) administration of benzodiazepines. This effect is most pronounced in rats that are awake and restrained. The decreased locus coeruleus activity is very likely to result, as in other areas, from benzodiazepine receptor interactions with GABA receptors, which are located on locus coeruleus and central NE neurons (Iverson & Schon, 1973) where GABA also inhibits neuronal activity (Cedarbaum & Aghajanian, 1977; Guyenet & Aghajanian, 1979).

With the exception of a benzodiazepine-GABA receptor complex, there is no compelling evidence that any of the neurotransmitter systems affected by benzodiazepines, including norepinephrine, are responsible for anxiolytic actions of these drugs. The actions of this drug class are far too broad to eliminate many possibilities. It is only as more specific research drugs are analyzed and their effects considered that particular neurotransmitter systems might be ruled out.

Barbiturates, Alcohol, and Propanediols

These longer-known anxiolytic compounds are even less specific than the benzodiazepines (Nicoll, 1978). Barbiturates, alcohol, and propanediols are no longer widely used in psychiatric or medical practice for their anxiolytic properties, although perhaps the social and recreational use of alcohol and barbiturates results partially as a consequence of social disinhibition secondary to a reduction in anxiety. Augmentation by barbiturates of inhibitory effects of GABA (Haefely & Polc, 1983; MacDonald & Barker, 1979; Olsen, Leeb-Lundberg, Snowman, Stephenson, 1982; Study & Barker, 1981), or the reduction of unit activity in the locus coeruleus (Olpe & Jones, 1983) provide pathways to explain effects on noradrenergic function as well as effects on many other neural systems. Again, like the benzodiazepines, the biochemical effects of these compounds are so general that specific neurotransmitter systems cannot be ruled in or out based on their effects.

Phenothiazine/Butyrophenones and other Antipsychotics

These compounds were thought initially to be "major tranquilizers," and indeed produce highly specific improvement in the psychotic symptoms of schizophrenia and other psychotic disorders, as well as a sedative/calming effect in animal models. These observations led to the hope that the neuroleptic drugs would also have therapeutic effects on patients with anxiety disorders and anxiety-related conditions. These hopes have not been fulfilled, although some compounds in these classes have been shown to have anxiolytic properties compared with placebo or in some cases appear superior to the benzodiazepines. A major action of these drugs (and the one most often cited as responsible for antipsychotic effects) is a blockade of dopamine, although the major compounds have slightly different profiles of receptor binding and agonist/antagonist properties at other receptors in addition to dopamine.

Chlorpromazine has been consistently less effective than benzodiazepines against nonpsychotic anxiety in controlled double blind cross-over studies and it exacerbates panic (Klein, Gittelman, Quitkin, & Rifkin, 1980, p. 549). Haloperidol, pimozide, thioridazine, and loxapine are equally effective as a reference benzodiazepine (Brauzer, Goldstein, Steinbook, Jacobson, 1974; Doongaji, Sheth, Teste, Ravindranath, 1976; Doongaji et al., 1981; Lofft & Demars, 1974; Lord & Kidd, 1973; Poldinger, 1976; Reyntjens & van Mierlo, 1972; Rosenthal & Bowden, 1973; Stevenson, Burrow, & Chiu, 1976; Versiani et al., 1976) or superior to benzodiazepines (Budden, 1979; Donald, 1969) against generalized and "neurotic" anxiety (see Klein et al., this volume, for detailed discussion of these and other comparisons). Two studies found loxepine no better than placebo (Claghorn, 1973; Rickels, Weisse, Feldman, Fee, & Wiswesser, 1978); diazepam was better than haloperidol in a subgroup of anxious "neurotic" out-patients in one study (Fyro, Beck-Friis, & Sjostrand, 1974). Since all of these compounds share potent dopamine antagonist properties and antipsychotic potency (Carlsson, 1978), anti-dopamine effects seem unlikely to explain the different anxiolytic potencies of these drugs. Further, since many compounds with potent anti-dopamine effects do not seem to have anxiolytic effects, the fact that some anxiolytics and some animal models of stress do alter dopamine turnover (Fuxe et al., 1975) may not be relevant to anxiety mechanisms.

The differences in the effects of individual compounds suggest, therefore, that the explanation for anxiolytic properties might lie in differential effects on other systems. The neuroleptics may have different effects on subpopulations of dopamine receptors (such as "auto-receptors" or receptors that respond to the principal neurotransmitter of the neuron), alpha-1 and alpha-2 adrenoceptors (Peroutka, U'Prichard, Greenberg, & Snyder, 1977), opiate receptors (Creese, Finberg, & Snyder, 1976), and muscarinic acetylcholine receptors (Yamamura, Manian, & Snyder, 1976). The neuroleptics also have antihistaminic and anti-cholinergic effects. The ratio of potency at presynaptic versus postsynaptic receptors of different types coexisting on the same neurons would therefore determine the net effect of these compounds both on noradrenergic activity and on anxiety reduction (Redmond, 1979), and some data exist showing alterations in NE function resulting from neuroleptic treatment (Graham & Aghajanian, 1971). There is no correlation between anxiolytic and sedative effects of these compounds, but sedative effects do correlate with alpha-1 adrenoceptor postsynaptic blockade (Peroutka et al., 1977).

In summary, the effects of these drugs seem to provide more definite information suggesting that the blockade of dopamine receptors is not responsible for anxiolytic actions. Effects at opioid or other peptide receptors, alpha-2 adrenoceptors, and muscarinic acetylcholine receptors provide alternative mechanisms for those compounds that are effective anxiolytics, and these might be responsible for secondary alterations in noradrenergic function consistent with a noradrenergic congruence model. But because of multiple actions at different receptors, it is more difficult to assess their net effect on noradrenergic activity. For example, simultaneous effects on alpha-2 presynaptic and alpha-1 postsynaptic receptors might be additive, or they might cancel each other out.

Opiates

The effects of opiates on anxiety and fear have long been noted and utilized in medical practice (Jaffe & Martin, 1980). Morphine is used before surgery and to treat myocardial infarction as much for its fear-reducing properties as for its analgesia, yet this property is not well demonstrated in animal models (Geller, Bachman, & Seifter, 1963; Gray, this volume). One human study found that the most consistent behavioral/emotional effect of heroin is anxiolytic (Mirin, Meyer, & McNamee, 1976). There are no controlled studies on the use of opiates as treatment for anxiety disorders or on their effects on naturally occurring panic in patients with panic disorders. However, based on the potency of some opiates for reducing iatrogenic fear, and anecdotal and epidemiological reports of heroin use by soldiers in combat (Robins, 1974), some opiate receptors appear to exert powerful anti-fear effects. This property, like most other effects of opiates, shows rapid tolerance (Meyer & Mirin, 1979) which, combined with the associated addiction, makes the opiates of little utility in the treatment of anxiety disorders. Furthermore, the addiction liability and consequent ethical considerations have precluded the careful and systematic studies in opiate-naive individuals that are necessary to establish anxiolytic properties of the opiates according to stringent scientific criteria. In the opposite direction, the evidence is quite clear that the experimental (or spontaneous) induction of the classical morphine withdrawal syndrome is remarkably similar to natural fear and panic, and includes, in addition to almost identical physiological changes, subjective anxiety ranging from mild discomfort to fear of impending doom and death (Redmond, 1981, p. 153).

Opiates act through several receptors for endogenous peptide neurotransmitters, such as endorphin, enkephalin, and dynorphin (Jaffe & Martin, 1980). These receptors are widely distributed in the brain and the body, entirely consistent with the evidence that opiates affect and interact with numerous other neurotransmitters. There is also evidence of functional interaction of opiates with noradrenergic neurons. For example, morphine and the alpha-2 adrenoceptor agonist clonidine have the same effect on neuronal firing rates, but the effects are mediated by independent receptor sites (Aghajanian, 1978), sharing common intracellular mechanisms (Aghajanian & Andrade, 1984; Aghajanian & VanderMaelen, 1982; Pepper & Henderson, 1980). Considerable evidence links the opiates with the reduction of central noradrenergic neuronal activity acutely. With chronic intake of opiates, postsynaptic mechanisms may compensate to normalize NE function and to produce functional hyperactivity during withdrawal (see Redmond & Krystal, 1984). The pharmacological actions of the opiates, and those of endogenous peptides with similar properties, suggest an adaptive evolutionary role for one or more of these peptides in the suppression of fear as well as pain, after pain has resulted from injury. Under these "fight or flight" circumstances, the behaviorally inhibitory effects of fear may be detrimental. Such functional interactions between pain and fear/anxiety have been described, and anatomical connections between known pain pathways and noradrenergic systems have been noted in support of the teleologic speculation that anxiety/ fear as an emotion developed as an "early warning" system to prevent injury by invoking many of the same emotional and physiological warnings associated with pain. Morphine prevents the fear-like behavioral effects of locus coeruleus stimulation or piperoxane administration in monkeys, and clonidine blocks the effects, including anxiety, of precipitated morphine withdrawal (Charney, Riordan, Kleber et al., 1982; Redmond, 1977; Redmond & Huang, 1979; Redmond, Huang, Snyder, & Maas, 1976b). Although opiates have been considered primarily as analgesics because of their clinical uses for this purpose, the noradrenergic system also appears to mediate some analgesic properties, indicating a different type of possible interaction between opioid systems and NE neurons (Margalit & Segal, 1979). "Stress-induced analgesia" is not suppressed by opiate antagonists but by the alpha-2 antagonist, yohimbine (Chance, 1980; Chance & Rosecrans, 1979; Chance & Schechter, 1979). In the opposite direction, clonidine has a higher dose-potency as an analgesic than morphine (Aceto & Harris, 1981; Fielding et al., 1978).

To summarize the present situation with regard to anxiety or fear-relevant biochemical effects of opiates, the same problem of multiple actions that was noted with the benzodiazepines makes it difficult to determine which other neurochemical systems are involved in the many subjective and physiological effects. As far as a noradrenergic system model is concerned, however, the opiates have very potent and clear effects in reducing noradrenergic activity acutely. Resolving the question about opiate-receptor mediated anti-fear, anti-anxiety, and anti-panic effects in human subjects seems to be of some import, since other theories (a specific benzodiazepine-receptor anxiety linkage) must then take these properties into account. These properties would also challenge the often assumed equivalency between effects in many animal screening tests for anxiolytic activity and the actual effects in humans, as has been previously noted (Redmond & Huang, 1979).

Tricyclic Compounds and Monoamine Oxidase Inhibitors (MAOIs)

The observation that these drugs were effective treatment agents for panic attacks was remarkable in the context of what was known about their actions at the time (Klein & Fink, 1962). The tricyclics were known to block monoamine reuptake mechanisms and the MAOIs to block the enzymatic degradation of the monoamine neurotransmitters to increase neurotransmitter availability in the synapse, consistent with (and partially giving rise to) a catecholamine hypothesis that depression was due to deficiency of available norephinephrine (Bunney & Davis, 1965; Schildkraut, 1965, 1978). These compounds do not bind to opiate or benzodiazepine receptors, but appear instead to have complex effects at alpha-1, alpha-2, and beta adrenoceptors which are secondary to their primary effects on reuptake or enzymatic degradation. Early reports suggested that drugs from both classes were effective in patients with "mixed" anxiety and depression (Klein, 1964; Klein & Fink, 1962; Ravaris et al., 1976; Robinson, Nies, Ravaris, & Lamborn, 1973). Moreover, there was a suspicion based on the firm identification of the compounds as "antidepressants" that any therapeutic effects were due to the amelioration of "underlying" depression in the patients who improved. The unique responses in patients who experienced panic attacks were identified later (Klein, Zitrin, & Woerner, 1978; Sheehan, Ballenger, & Jacobsen, 1980; Zitrin, Klein, & Woerner, 1978). The presumed alleviation of depression was carefully evaluated and rejected by studies that showed that these compounds act by specifically preventing the panic attacks, but have little effect on the reduction of generalized or "anticipatory" anxiety (Zitrin et al., 1978, 1980). Overall improvement which occurred later was seen by these investigators as secondary to the elimination of the threat of having a panic attack. Recent data, however, continue to suggest the coexistence of depression and anxiety in otherwise "pure" diagnostic groups. The distinct classification of the traditional "antidepressants" is confounded by the observations that anxiolytic effects are the earliest and most reliable behavioral effect detectable in groups of depressed subjects (Katz, Robins, Croughan, Secunda, & Swann, 1982), and that these compounds have anxiolytic properties in some anxious patients with "anxiety neuroses" (and undetermined incidence of panic attacks) (Bianchi & Phillips, 1972; Henry, Overall, & Markette, 1971; Kleber, 1979; Johnstone et al., 1980). These interactions further suggest, as many others have noted, that the emotions of anxiety/fear and depression share underlying neuronal mechanisms.

Biochemically these compounds have antihistaminic and anticholinergic effects. They also affect serotonin, dopamine, and NE systems, but not in the simple fashion previously supposed (Kessler, 1978; Koslow et al., 1983; Murphy, Campbell, & Costa, 1978). If these drugs actually increase NE function, as postulated by the catecholamine hypothesis of the affective disorders (Schildkraut, 1978), this would be exactly opposite to the effects of the other classes of anxiolytics reviewed so far and would necessitate either dismissing the reduction of noradrenergic hyperactivity as a common effect of most anxiolytics or accepting the idea that panic and anxiety were qualitatively as well as quantitatively different. In such a multisystem model, different drugs would act at different sites on anxiety or panic (see Fig. 28.1, Model 1). However, a number of models for assessment show that both the tricylics and the MAOIs reduce noradrenergic function both acutely and chronically. Acutely, desmethylimipramine and imipramine effects on noradrenergic function result from blockade of the reuptake of NE at two sites with theoretically opposite effects. A somatodendritic site increases the inhibitory actions of NE at alpha-2 adrenoceptors which decrease neuronal firing (Nyback, Walters, & Aghajanian, 1975; Svensson & Usdin, 1978). The other simultaneous blockade of neurotransmitter reuptake at the synapse would have an opposite facilitatory effect, as previously hypothesized. It is, therefore, impossible to know whether a net functional decrease would occur from decreased neuronal firing rates and neurotransmitter release or whether the synaptic facilitation of released neurotransmitter would predominate. When these multiple effects are tested from the perspective of postsynaptic neurochemical effects (Vetulani & Sulser, 1975; Sulser, Vetulani, & Mobley, 1978) or electrophysiological effects on the beta-adrenoceptors to which NE cells partly project, the inhibitory effects of tricyclics predominate both acutely (Huang, 1979) and chronically (Huang, Maas, & Hu, 1980; McMillen, Warnack, German, & Shore, 1980). The net effects at the alpha-1 projections appear to be different, with a net facilitatory effect, making a consistent interpretation impossible at this time (Charney, Menkes, and Heninger, 1981; Menkes, Aghajanian,

& McCall, 1980). One MAOI, tranylcypromine, reduces the firing rate of locus coeruleus neurons (Scuvee-Moreau & Dresse, 1979), but its effects on projection areas and after chronic treatment have not been studied. Combined with studies that have shown evidence for decreases in post synaptic receptor mechanisms during chronic treatment, these data have led many investigators either to abandon the old catecholamine hypothesis for depression, or at least to adopt an inverse hypothesis in which depression is associated with elevated NE system function (Koslow et al., 1983).

The newer interpretation of the functional effects of tricyclics and MAOIs is completely compatible with the reduction of NE function by all other classes of anxiolytics, at least with regard to the beta-adrenergic projections. Differences in the onset of anxiolytic action and potency of these compounds compared with each other and with the benzodiazepines are entirely consistent with known characteristics of their mechanisms of action to reduce net noradrenergic neuronal function, as is described in more detail later.

These recent data, therefore, have supported a parsimonious biochemical theory for anxiety, fear, and panic. These emotions exist on a continuum of function that, at the lowest levels, involves selective attention and increases from detectable anxiety to panic and terror. The central noradrenergic system appears to be responsive to the behavioral and experiential processes that influence the occurrence or suppression of anxiety. All of the emotions in the continuum can be diminished or suppressed by benzodiazepines and by the MAOI and tricyclic "antidepressants" in a dose/mechanism dependent fashion. This fact suggests that a common noradrenergic physiological system, involved in effects of all three classes of drugs, should be scrutinized for pathophysiological and genetic-biochemical defects associated with possible discrete disorders.

Atypical Compounds

New compounds are patentable by virtue of being novel and many, therefore, cannot be fully evaluated by impartial scientists for some time. The "atypical" antidepressants, mianserin, iprindole, and fluoxetine, for example, cannot yet be accommodated by the traditional categories in spite of their efficacy as anti-depressants. Some compounds, such as buspirone, appear to have both anxiolytic and antidepressant properties (Goldberg & Finnerty, 1979; Rickels et al., 1983; Wheatley, 1982), but are unrelated to the benzodiazepines and are only very weakly neuroleptic. Buspirone does not decrease neuronal activity in the locus coeruleus (Sanghera, McMillen, & German, 1983), although the net effect on noradrenergic function cannot be predicted based on acute effects on neuronal firing rates alone. These compounds are useful, however, for pursuing biochem-ical mechanisms, but a particular mechanism should not be ruled in or out until it has been studied carefully by a number of methods.

In order to improve the precision of a biochemical model, it is worth considering compounds that have much higher degrees of specificity for particular neurotransmitter systems to determine whether their effects on anxiety or fear are consistent with the involvement of that system. For example, a compound that clearly reduces net NE neuronal function would argue strongly against the essential involvement of NE systems if it had no anxiolytic properties.

Beta-Adrenoceptor Antagonists

These compounds were tested originally because of data suggesting that some groups of patients (Frolich, Dustan, & Page, 1966; Frolich, Tarag, & Dustan, 1969) had beta-adrenergic hypersensitivity. Propranolol, a beta-antagonist, was found consistently to block physical symptoms of anxiety (Gottschalk, Stone, & Gleser, 1974; Granville-Grossman & Turner, 1966; Kielholz, 1977; Stone, Gleser, & Gottschalk, 1973; Turner, Granville-Grossman, & Smart, 1965; Wheatley, 1969), with some evidence for effects on subjective anxiety as well (Kellner, Collins, Shulman & Pathak, 1974; Suzman, 1976; Tyrer & Lader, 1974). These same results have been found for other beta-blockers, such as oxprenolol (Gosling, 1977), sotalol (Lader & Tyrer, 1972), and practolol (Bonn, Turner, & Hicks, 1972). The fact that similar beneficial effects occur with practolol, which does not cross the blood-brain-barrier, has been used to support a peripheral mode of action for these compounds, without eliminating the possibility of central effects in those compounds that do penetrate the central nervous system. Some studies find them inferior to diazepam (Greenblatt & Shader, 1978; Tyrer & Lader, 1974), especially in patients with more exclusively subjective anxiety. One study showed a persistence of fear in phobic subjects exposed to a phobic stimulus, in spite of a reduction in heart rate following tolamolol administration (Bernadt, Silverstone, & Singleton, 1980).

The relative biochemical specificity of action of these compounds makes these effects of theoretical interest. With regard to a noradrenergic hyperactivity model, it should be noted that the central NE systems have postsynaptic projections to alpha-1 as well as beta-1 adrenoceptors, and possibly postsynaptic projections to alpha-2 adrenoceptors. These "selective" beta-1 antagonists would be expected, at best, to block only a portion of the projections from these neurons. It is possible also that effects at other projections might even increase under these conditions (see Grant & Redmond, 1982).

Alpha-2 Agonists

The alpha-2 agonists, best represented by clonidine, have highly specific effects on noradrenergic activity. In low doses they acutely decrease net NE neuronal function by simulating the effects of the neurotransmitters NE or epinephrine at alpha-2 mediated somatodendritic autoreceptors to decrease neuronal firing and at presynaptic sites to decrease NE release (Cedarbaum & Aghajanian, 1976; Svensson, Bunney, & Aghajanian, 1975). Clonidine alters receptor sensitivity and density after chronic treatment, as confirmed by neurophysiological measures (Engberg, Elam, & Svensson, 1982) and produces a withdrawal syndrome probably by way of several mechanisms. Clonidine, and other similar alpha-2 agonists, so clearly reduce NE function in low doses that the absence of anti-anxiety or anti-fear properties of these compounds would be incompatible with an NE hyperactivity hypothesis for anxiety. This test of the NE hyperactivity hypothesis was published prior to any specific clinical studies of the anxiolytic potential of clonidine (Redmond, 1977) and in spite of the absence of any confirming data from the widespread use of clonidine as an antihypertensive in patients whose anxiety was undetermined (see Redmond, 1982).

Since then, several specific clinical reports have appeared. Leckman, Maas, Redmond, & Heninger (1980) reported that three subjects without medical or psychiatric illness showed no change in self-rated anxiety after doses of 1, 2, or 5 micrograms/kg clonidine, in spite of statistically significant decreases in plasma concentration of the NE metabolite 3-methoxy 4-hydroxy phenylethylene glycol (MHPG), suggesting that adequate clonidine was administered. None of these subjects was anxious before clonidine, so rated effects appeared to represent merely sedation at the highest dose level. No data were available in these non-anxious subjects to compare with the effects of "standard" anxiolytic drugs. (Benzodiazepines have been reported even to increase anxiety in normal subjects with "low" anxiety, DiMascio & Barrett, 1965; Zuardi, Shirakawa, Finkelfarb, & Karniol, 1982).

The finding by Leckman et al. was replicated in a report by Uhde and his co-workers at the NIMH, who showed no effect of clonidine in 12 normal volunteers rated with the Spielberger State-Trait Anxiety Inventory, but suggested that a change in a measure of pain insensitivity might be due to diminished anxiety (Uhde, Post, Siever, & Buchsbaum, 1980, Udhe et al., 1981). These subjects also had low anxiety ratings before clonidine. Svensson, Persson, Wallin, & Walinder (1978) reported that 150-225 micrograms/day clonidine treatment improved 6 of 13 hospitalized patients who were incapacitated by severe anxiety. Four subjects did not complete the 2-week trial, and 4 others did not improve. Unfortunately, diagnostic criteria and specific rating information were not published, and the study was open and uncontrolled. Uhde et al. (1981) also reported that 13 depressed patients with high anxiety ratings before clonidine showed statistically significant reductions on the Spielberger State-Trait Anxiety Scale after clonidine (in contrast to previous findings in normals). Although, in this study, the question that this finding perhaps represented a sedative effect was also raised, the anti-anxiety and sedative effects were uncorrelated.

Liebowitz, Ryer, McGrath, & Klein (1981) reported that 4 of 11 phobic-anxious subjects showed good responses to clonidine up to the end of a 6-week trial; four showed initial responses and then became worse or had significant side effects; and 3 showed no response or could not tolerate doses greater than two micrograms/kg/day. It was not clear in this study whether or not poor response was due to inadequate dampening of brain noradrenergic activity secondary to very low clonidine doses and unacceptable side effects. However, a number of subjects who were clonidine treatment failures subsequently responded to treatment with the usual tricyclic antidepressants.

Another study by Hoehn-Saric, Merchant, Keyser, & Smith (1981) reported that clonidine was superior to placebo in the majority of 23 patients (9 with GAD and 14 with panic disorders). There was no difference in response between the two diagnostic groups, but 4 subjects became worse on clonidine. There were more side effects on clonidine than on placebo, and other treatments were felt to be superior for all but 4 subjects who chose to remain on clonidine after the study. The formal double-blind cross-over comparison of therapeutic and side effects with standard drugs was not done, however. Also, since there was no independent assessment of the suppression of noradrenergic activity by clonidine, it is impossible to know whether the clonidine doses administered were sufficient to decrease noradrenergic activity and thereby to test the hypothesis of the involvement of that system. It does seem likely, from the previous two studies, that the side effects of LC suppressant doses of clonidine are less well tolerated by patients with anxiety disorders than by subjects undergoing opiate withdrawal, who receive up to 30 micrograms/kg/day (Charney, Sternberg, Kleber, Heninger, & Redmond, 1981).

A small double-blind cross-over study of 5 micrograms/kg clonidine daily versus 100 mg imipramine by Ko et al. (1983) suggests that clonidine and imipramine both reduce panic attacks and block panic symptoms in the presence of the phobic stimuli that previously elicited panic attacks. Plasma MHPG concentrations were reduced to a greater degree in four subjects who responded to clonidine than in two who did not. Cross-over to imipramine treatment for a comparable 4-week period was not superior in any subject with the same four subjects showing favorable responses. During baseline, or after exposure to phobic stimuli, plasma MHPG correlated with patient-rated anxiety during the drug, clonidine, and imipramine treatment periods. A recent report suggested that clonidine also has some effectiveness in the treatment of post-traumatic-stress syndrome (Kolb, Burris, & Griffiths, 1983).

These clinical results were predicted based on a theoretical model for anxiety. Since there is fairly rapid tolerance to some effects of clonidine, and since effects of clonidine on NE neurons do not increase with increasing intensity of the stimuli, the probability that clonidine's effects might not be of long duration was also predicted. These actions of clonidine, as well as effects of the tricyclics, MAOIs and BZDs, are consistent with the functional effects of each class of compounds on central NE neurons. The tricyclics and MAOIs would have the most potent effects because the inhibition of NE firing is not directly dependent upon the drug concentration but upon how much neurotransmitter is released at alpha-2 auto-receptors. Therefore, the greater the stimulus and hence larger release of NE, the stronger is the subsequent inhibitory effect of these compounds. Prior to a fear or anxiety stimulus, these compounds would have little effect or might produce anxiety by increasing postsynaptic NE, depending upon a number of factors. The benzodiazepines, in contrast, would be entirely dependent upon their concentrations at the benzodiazepine/GABA receptor complex. Stimuli at the other regulatory receptors could overcome the resulting inhibition. This is consistent with the anxiolytic efficacy of the benzodiazepines against low-intensity anxiety, but would predict that greatly increased doses would be necessary to counteract the effects of strong fear or phobic/panic stimuli. Clonidine has a mode of action in between the tricyclics/MAOIs and benzodiazepines. Its effects in normal subjects are more like those of the tricyclics than the benzodiazepines. Since clonidine acts on NE function at one of the same receptors as the tricyclics, it would have a profile of activity more like them; but the neuronal inhibition could be overcome by strong stimuli. However, higher doses of clonidine would also block fear or panic, as would higher doses of benzodiazepines or more potent benzodiazepine compounds.

Clonidine has a number of other biochemical effects that might be responsible for some of its physiological effects. For this reason, the fact that clonidine has anti-anxiety properties is less convincing evidence in favor of a noradrenergic mechanism than the absence of such properties would have been against this theory. Nonetheless, further studies with other alpha-2 adrenergic agonists with dissimilar profiles at other receptors (such as histamine) would help to clarify which effects are most relevant to anxiety.

Other Older Compounds

So far I have omitted several groups of compounds that have been postulated to have anxiolytic properties based on clinical impressions or on animal studies. *Cannabis sativa* is widely utilized for its psychotropic effects consisting of increased sense of well-being or euphoria, relaxation, and sleepiness (Jaffe, 1980). The possibility that cannabinoids contained in marihuana might have anxiolytic or tranquilizing effects has been considered (Hollister, 1971; Weil, Zinberg, & Nelsen, 1968), and several compounds have been studied in normal subjects. The data from these clinical studies, however, have produced conflicting results, with studies suggesting such an effect (Lemberger, 1976), and others even suggesting increased anxiety with some experimental compounds, especially delta-9-tetrahydrocannabinol (Jones, 1978; Meyer, 1978; Pillard, McNair, & Fisher, 1974; Zuardi et al., 1982). The biochemical actions of these compounds are also not yet clear, with evidence supporting interactions with a number of systems, including acetylcholine, NE, dopamine, and serotonin (5-hydroxytryptamine, 5-HT) (Harris, Dewey, & Razdan, 1977). Another class of compounds that has been implicated in anxiety reduction is believed to interact with the neurotransmitter adenosine (Daly, Bruns, Snyder, 1981). Many "tranquilizers" also have antihistaminic properties, and some compounds that are mainly antihistaminics have been also used to treat anxious patients. How these compounds fit into any of the above mechanisms is not clear, although it does appear that there are antihistaminics that are not useful anxiolytics. The Rauwolfia alkaloids have been used for centuries in India for their calming and tranquilizing properties. Reserpine, the best known compound of this class, is thought to act by depletion of norepinephrine storage granules leading to functional deficits (Weiner, 1980). With the exception of endorphins and enkephalins, the effects of peptide hormones which interact with alterations of neurotransmitters in experimental animal models (Wendlandt & File, 1979) have been omitted in this review. Some evidence suggests that some of these, for example corticotropin-releasing factor (CRF), will be important for future research in humans (Valentino, Foote, & Aston-Jones, 1983).

CAN ANXIETY BE EXPERIMENTALLY INDUCED BIOCHEMICALLY IN HUMANS?

Administration of Drugs

Studies of "adrenin" or "adrenalin" in the early part of this century (Elliot, 1905) attempted to characterize the role of the adrenals in physiology and behavior. Infusion of purified epinephrine and norepinephrine led to mixed and inconclusive results (Basowitz et al., 1956; Cantril & Hunt, 1932; Chessick et al., 1966; Jersild & Thomas, 1931; King et al., 1952; Koppanyl, 1928; Landis & Hunt, 1932; Marañon, 1920, 1924; Peabody, Sturgis, & Tompkins, 1921; Pollin & Goldin, 1961; Schacter & Singer, 1962, 1966; Wearn & Sturgis, 1919; Vlachakis et al., 1974). These results are more understandable in view of what we now know about how norepinephrine and epinephrine are distributed in the body. Although neither was thought to cross the blood-brain barrier to any substantial degree (Rothballer, 1959), recent electrophysiological studies in rats show that intravenously infused NE decreases neuronal function in the locus coeruleus (Elam, Yao, Svensson, & Thoren, 1984), most likely via alpha-2 adrenergic autoreceptors (Cedarbaum & Aghajanian, 1976, 1977). Consistent with a central noradrenergic hypothesis for anxiety, these findings might explain the striking quality of the subjective effects in many subjects who reported that they felt "as if" they were anxious (peripheral manifestations) but were not, or were even strangely calm, after infusions of NE or epinephrine. The beta-adrenoceptor agonist, isoproterenol, simulates the beta-adrenoceptor effects of NE and locus coeruleus stimulation in some brain areas (see Grant & Redmond, 1981, for review). It has some effects in patients with increased awareness of cardiac activity and subjective anxiety (Frolich et al., 1966, 1969). Recently the alpha-2 adrenoceptor antagonist, yohimbine, has been reported to increase anxiety in normal subjects (Charney, Heninger, & Redmond, 1983), and to a greater extent in patients with anxiety disorders or depression (Charney, et al., 1983), consistent with earlier dramatic effects reported (Holmberg & Gershon, 1961). High doses of amphetamine are also reported to induce anxiety, panic, and dysphoria in some subjects (Weiner, 1980). Acutely increased (>25 - 30%) CO_2 concentrations in inspired air result in changes in arterial pCO_2 and have been reported to produce anxiety in human subjects (Smith, Cooperman, Wollman, 1980; Waeber, Adler, Schwank, & Galeazzi, 1982). These behavioral and subjective effects are consistent with the striking effect of increases in pCO_2 concentrations on locus coeruleus activity in the rat (Elam, Yao, Thoren, & Svensson, 1981). If the resulting increases in noradrenergic activity are, in fact, relevant to anxiety, either direct physiological effects or learned/conditioned effects of this interaction may be relevant to the pervasive hyperventilation seen in association with anxiety (Lum, 1981) and other psychosomatic syndromes. "Carbon dioxide therapy" as a treatment for anxiety (Greiz & van den Hout, 1983; Haslam, 1974; Leake, 1973; van den Hout & Griez, 1982) might work because of the mild increases in NE activity and anxiety which could be "mastered." All of the compounds or procedures noted in the preceding discussion alter NE function as noted. Of these, increasing the pCO_2 and yohimbine increase the function of the entire NE system more completely and more "physiologically" than other compounds that have been tested in humans.

Other compounds also reported to increase anxiety act, at least initially, at non-adrenergic receptors and sites. The GABA antagonist, pentylenetetrazol (Metrazol), induces a severe anxiety syndrome at doses slightly below the convulsant ones (Rodin, 1958). The benzodiazepine "inverse agonists," the beta-carbolines, have been reported to produce severe fear and threat of annihilation in a few individuals (Dorow, Horowski, Paschelke, & Amin, 1983). In addition, high doses of alkylxanthines, such as caffeine and theophylline, produce anxiety-like effects in humans (Greden, 1974; Udhe, Boulenger, & Post, 1983); and the regular amounts of caffeine consumed correlate with state- and trait-anxiety measures in normals and psychiatric patients (Boulenger & Uhde, 1982; Gilliland & Andress, 1981; Greden, Fontaine, Lubetsky, & Chamberlin, 1978; Winstead, 1976). Finally, lactate infusion has been reported to precipitate panic attacks in subjects with previous attacks, but does not do so in normal individuals (Gorman et al., 1983; Pitts, 1969, 1971; Pitts & McClure, 1967). Many of these compounds also can be related to effects that increase noradrenergic functional activity, exactly opposite from the model described for the effects of anxiolytics. GABA antagonists and methylxanthines increase locus coeruleus activity (Grant, Huang, & Redmond, 1980; Grant & Redmond, 1982a). Locus coeruleus activity and behavioral effects of methylxanthines are reversed by clonidine (Grant & Redmond, 1982b). Behavioral effects of the 3-beta-carbolines in monkeys are reversed by clonidine (Crawley et al., 1983). All of these anxiety-producing compounds have a variety of other primary effects that might also be implicated in the mechanisms of anxiety induction. It is of particular interest, therefore, that clonidine antagonizes the effects of the beta-carboline (inverse benzodiazepine agonist). It would also be of interest to characterize whether specific receptor blockers or specific inhibitors of particular systems will interfere with the anxiety-producing effects of other compounds. For example, does clonidine antagonize the anxiety-producing effects of Metrazol or lactate in humans? Or does yohimbine antagonize effects of diazepam? Further review of the literature regarding elicitation of anxiety by chemical agents appears elsewhere (Charney & Redmond, 1983).

By Drug Withdrawal

The major groups of anxiolytic drugs produce some tolerance and are associated with increased anxiety or spontaneous panic attacks after prolonged drug treatment and withdrawal. This specifically includes the benzodiazepines (Greenblatt & Shader, 1974; Kramer, Klein, & Fink, 1961), the tricyclic antidepressants (see Charney, Heninger, Sternberg, & Landis, 1982, for review), opiates (Charney, Sternberg, Kleber, Heninger, & Redmond, 1981; Gold, Redmond, & Kleber, 1978a, 1978b; Jaffe, 1980), and clonidine (see Svensson & Strombom, 1977). All of these withdrawal syndromes produce noradrenergic hyperactivity, which has been postulated to be responsible for the behavioral and physiological effects. This area has been recently reviewed and new data published elsewhere (Redmond & Krystal, 1984). Some of these withdrawal syndromes have been noted to be very close approximations to natural anxiety or fear. Severe opiate withdrawal, as previously noted, produces a behavioral and subjective state that includes most of the physiology associated with fear, as well as the subjective feeling states of anxiety, restlessness, fear, terror, and fear of annihilation or impending doom (Redmond, 1981). The benzodiazepine withdrawal syndrome is also so similar to natural anxiety that the very existence of a true withdrawal syndrome was controversial until recently.

SYSTEMS NOT ASSOCIATED WITH ANXIETY

Several compounds that produce highly specific effects on particular neuronal systems have not been associated with fear or with anxiolytic effects. The absence of such effects is perhaps more important than many of the drug-effect correlations just reviewed. The dopamine antagonists, per se, do not appear to have useful anxiolytic or anti-fear activity (see Klein, Rabkin, & Gorman, this volume). The dopamine agonist, apomorphine, also does not appear to have anxiolytic or anxiogenic properties. The same is true for cholinergics and anticholinergics. Likewise, there is no evidence that alpha-1 adrenoceptor antagonists have anxiolytic activity. Although many psychoactive compounds have antihistaminic properties, the pure antihistaminics do not have anxiolytic potency, although the emerging evidence of multiple specific histamine receptors raises the possibility that some particular receptor type (e.g., histamine-2 receptors) might be the starting point for anxiolytics that are also antihistaminics.

Each of these negative findings is important for suggesting that other compounds with multiple biochemical and receptor effects are unlikely to produce anxiolytic effects by virtue of their actions on that system. The systems that cannot be ruled out, or that are clearly implicated in anxiety or fear are various endogenous opioid peptide systems, benzodiazepines, serotonin, adenosine, norepinephrine, and epinephrine.

CONSISTENCY WITH A NEUROPHYSIOLOGIC SCHEMA FOR CENTRAL NE FUNCTIONS

The pharmacological model for common effects of the major class of anxiolytics on noradrenergic system function is consistent with a large body of data from animal studies. These animal studies have the advantage that much more direct and powerful interventions can be made, and the disadvantage that there is no certainty that the behavioral effects in animals correspond to human anxiety. Studies of the nucleus locus coeruleus in animals contributed to the idea that NE systems were involved in anxiety as suggested in this review. This notion was also arrived at by Lader (1974) and Gray (1976, 1982) based on other evidence. Behavioral data resulting from electrical stimulation and lesions of the locus coeruleus in monkeys and the effects of many of the drugs reviewed here might also support noradrenergic involvement in fear. Stimulation produces fear-like behaviors, which are indistinguishable from spontaneous or conditioned fear, and are diminished or blocked by locus coeruleus lesions and by specific anti-noradrenergic drugs and by many anxiolytics (Redmond, 1977; Redmond & Huang, 1979; Redmond, Huang, Snyder, & Maas, 1976; Redmond, Huang, Snyder, Maas, & Baulu, 1976). The model is also consistent with specific functions of neuroanatomical connections of the LC, which suggests that this nucleus might serve as a relay center for a "warning" or "alarm" system, which includes "normal" and "pathological" fear or anxiety during higher levels of activation. On the afferent side, the locus coeruleus receives innervation directly from pain pathways in the spinal cord and cranial nerve nuclei. Physiologically, the locus coeruleus shows sustained responses to repeated presentations of "noxious" stimuli originating from these afferents even in anesthetized animals (Cedarbaum & Aghajanian, 1978). In the awake monkey there is rapid "habituation" of locus coeruleus activity to novel non-noxious stimuli as well as a consistent association of spontaneous LC activity with the level of "vigilance" and arousal (Foote, Aston-Jones, Bloom, 1980; Foote, Bloom, & Aston-Jones, 1983), and clear activation in response to fear-associated stimuli (Grant & Redmond, in press). The efferent pathways from the locus coeruleus include most of the areas responsible for the physiological responses to pain and fear (see Grant & Redmond, 1981; Redmond, 1981), including increased blood pressure, heart rate, tremor, changes in fatty acid mobilization, and clotting tendency in the blood (of those which have been studied). In addition, pathways to and from the cerebral cortex provide the necessary feedback loops to explain the apparent influence which the "meaning," "relevance," or conditioning of a stimulus may exercise on the response, as well as to provide access to areas that may underlie the cognitive experience of the emotional state (or states) (Redmond, 1977). This circuitry, therefore, provides an outline of how the locus coeruleus (very likely in concert with other central noradrenergic nuclei) may function as a part of an alarm-relay system that modulates the disagreeable and emotional side of the response to pain, as well as participating in the control of some of its physiology. Such a system is the logical one to have provided the evolutionary mechanism for elaboration of the anticipation of possible pain, into the emotions generally called fear or anxiety, as theorized in different ways by Pavlov (1927) and Freud (1936). The picture of locus coeruleus function that emerges experimentally across the spectrum of its activity, from locus coeruleus lesions in the nonhuman primate to "high" intensity electrical field stimulation, is that of an "alarm" system, which filters and discriminates potentially noxious from irrelevant stimuli. High intensity activation produces effects on nearly every major brain and autonomic function that is activated by fear, with profound effects on behavior (Redmond, 1979). At moderate levels, locus coeruleus activity is correlated with attentiveness and vigilance to physiologically relevant stimuli (Foote et al., 1980). Progressive subnormal functioning of this system in the primate is best characterized by inattentiveness, impulsivity, carelessness, recklessness, and fearlessness (Redmond, 1979).

IMPLICATIONS FOR THE ANXIETY "DISORDERS"

In conclusion, this neurophysiologic and biochemical model is consistent with much that is known about human fear or anxiety. It is supportive of a physiological role for the central noradrenergic systems which is far broader than that of an "anxiety or fear center." Instead, it seems to be more of a warning or "alarm" system that gets direct and interpreted nociceptive information to which it responds by progressive activation of the structures known to mediate the "fight or flight" response. It is an automatic system generally, but "rings" a further warning if it is activated too strongly or for too long a time. "Normal" anxiety or fear is our perception of this ringing, along with the accompanying physiologic, cognitive, and behavioral expressions that occur at higher intensities of activation of this system.

Pathological anxiety might be the result of aberrations in the operation of this system at a number of points. Genetically influenced differences in catecholamine related enzymes (Nies, Robinson, Lamborn, & Lampert, 1973; Ross, Wetterberg, & Myrhed, 1973; Weinshilboum, Raymond, Elveback, & Weidman, 1973), receptor function, and neurotransmitter release mechanisms may be relevant to how active this system is in a particular individual. Changes in these same mechanisms due to environmental exposure to strong, threatening stimuli or to chronic anxiety itself may lead to further increases in function; e.g., induction of synthetic enzyme activity or non-homeostatic increases in receptor sensitivity or density. The further cognitive effects of learning and experience on subsequent responses may also contribute to dysfunction in some individuals who may or may not have additional biological vulnerabilities. Velley, Cardo, & Bockaert (1981) have noted that electrical stimulation of the locus coeruleus in rats is followed even 4 weeks later by increased receptor binding of both alpha-1 and alpha-2 agonists and by increased behavioral effects in a "rebound" after clonidine administration. If these neurons and receptors have something to do with anxiety, the results described above might suggest that exposure to anxiety could have the paradoxical effect of sensitizing the individual to repeated exposures.

The identification of neural substrates for anxiety in normal individuals would have implications for treatment, not only because it would provide a rational basis for designing more effective and more specific drugs, but because it would also allow for the characterization of any biochemical pathophysiology of anxiety, if it exists in particular groups of subjects. We would therefore have a rational basis for deciding under what circumstances and with which patients anxiolytic drugs might be helpful.

ACKNOWLEDGMENTS

This manuscript was prepared on a contract from N.I.M.H. Research cited from my laboratory was supported in part by U.S.P.H.S. Grants DA02321, MH31176, MH25642, MH30929, Research Scientist Career Development Award DA-00075, the Harry Frank Guggenheim Foundation, the St. Kitts Biomedical Research Foundation, and the State of Connecticut.

29 Phenomenology and Neurobiology of Panic Disorder

Thomas W. Uhde
*Chief, Unit on Anxiety
and Affective Disorders,
Biological Psychiatry Branch,
National Institute of Mental
Health*

Peter P. Roy-Byrne,
*Senior Staff Fellow, Unit on
Anxiety and Affective
Disorders,
Biological Psychiatry Branch,
NIMH*

Bernard J. Vittone
*Senior Staff Fellow, Unit on Anxi-
ety and Affective Disorders,
Biological Psychiatry Branch,
NIMH*

Jean-Philippe Boulenger,
*Visiting Associate, Unit on
Anxiety and Affective
Disorders,
Biological Psychiatry Branch,
NIMH*

R.M. Post
*Chief, Biological Psychiatry
Branch,
National Institute of Mental
Health*

INTRODUCTION

Compared to depression, pathological anxiety is an emotional state that has received little attention in the field of psychiatric research, despite its more frequent occurrence (Sartorius, 1980). Recent evidence has suggested that several kinds of pathological anxiety may be described in terms of clinical symptoms, evolution, and response to psycho-pharmacological agents (Klein, 1980; Zitrin, Woerner, & Klein, 1981). This has permitted current investigators to abandon the use of vague labels such as "anxious" or "neurotic" and employ more well-defined diagnostic criteria to clarify types of anxiety, i.e., panic attacks as distinct

557

from phobic anxiety. Whether the resultant *Diagnostic and Statistical Manual, 3rd Edition (DSM-III)* diagnoses (i.e., panic disorder versus agoraphobia with and without panic attacks) (American Psychiatric Assoc., 1980) represent distinct illnesses in relation to pathogenesis, natural course and treatment is unclear. Even the association between primary anxiety disorders, particularly panic disorder, and other medical and psychiatric conditions, remains controversial.

The purpose of this chapter is to summarize our attempts, based on several different research strategies, to characterize the clinical and biological nature of panic disorder. First, new data regarding the phenomenological and longitudinal features of the disorder are presented. Second, biological and psychophysiologic correlates of anxiety are reviewed in relation to research from our laboratory investigating the sleep architecture, pain perception, glucose metabolism and platelet receptor function in patients with panic disorder. Finally, data from our pharmacologic challenges in humans with clonidine, yohimbine, and caffeine are discussed within the context of current biological theories of anxiety.

PHENOMENOLOGY AND LONGITUDINAL COURSE OF PANIC DISORDER

Psychosensory Phenomena

The overlap of symptoms in patients with temporal lobe epilepsy and panic disorder have been observed by several investigators (Roth & Harper, 1962; Uhde, Boulenger, Roy-Byrne et al., 1984). Although fear occurs following stimulation of limbic portions of the temporal lobe (Gloor, Olivier, Quesney, Andermann, & Horowitz, 1982), it is not typically associated with neocortical discharge. Thus, one might speculate some regional brain specificity for the neurobiology of fear and related human emotions. It is noteworthy in this regard that agoraphobia has developed in patients with complex partial seizures (Roth, 1960), suggesting, perhaps, that avoidance behaviors may develop as a secondary consequence following repeated "inexplicable" bouts of fear or panic. In an attempt to systematically assess the prevalence of psychosensory-psychomotor phenomena in patients with panic disorder, we administered a structured interview designed by Silberman and Post to elicit those symptoms associated with complex partial seizures. As reported previously (Boulenger & Uhde, 1983; Roth, 1960; Roth & Harper, 1962; Uhde, Boulenger, Roy-Byrne et al., in press) and illustrated in Table I, multiple psychosensory disturbances frequently contribute to the symptomatic profile of nonepileptic patients with panic disorder. It is noteworthy that these symptoms are not prominent during well intervals, and also occur during episodes, but not well intervals, in affectively ill patients (Silberman, Post, Nurnberger, Theodore, & Boulenger, in press). Furthermore,

TABLE 29.1
Most Frequent Psychosensory Symptoms Reported by Patients
with Panic Disorder While Symptomatic (*N* = 43)

DISTORTION OF LIGHT INTENSITY	59%
DISTORTION OF SOUND INTENSITY	46%
DEREALIZATION	46%
STRANGE RISING FEELING IN STOMACH	41%
DEPERSONALIZATION	37%
SENSATION OF FLOATING, TURNING, MOVING	32%
SPEEDING UP OF THOUGHTS	22%
SLOWING DOWN OF THOUGHTS	20%
"JAMAIS VU" SENSATION	17%

several manifestations of complex partial seizures such as automatisms, stereotyped repetitive movements, and gustatory or tactile hallucinations were extremely rare or nonexistent in our panic patients, even during the severe phases of illness.

Longitudinal Course

All patients participating in research studies carried out by the NIMH intramural Program on Anxiety and Affective Disorders have the longitudinal course of their illness retrospectively characterized and graphically represented on a timeline (Uhde, Boulenger, Roy-Byrne et al., in press). In an attempt to obtain accurate information, rigid and restrictive criteria for panic attacks and depressive symptoms are employed and information is, in most cases, confirmed by interviews with family members, hospital records, or personal diaries. Patients who are unable to recall in detail the exact time, place, situation, and characteristics of their first panic attack are considered atypical and excluded from the study. Agoraphobia is rated on the basis of four levels of functional impairment, as indicated by degree of avoidance behavior. Panic attacks are defined according to *DSM-III* criteria. Anxiety that fails to meet criteria for panic attacks or specific phobic anxiety is rated under the overall rubric of generalized anxiety. Duration requirements for depression and agoraphobia, as specified in *DSM-III,* are eliminated to allow an improved understanding of temporal rhythms. Finally, very restrictive criteria for depression are used, which do not utilize symptoms of initial insomnia, psychomotor agitation, and hyperphagia, since these are often common in anxiety disorders.

Thus far, data gathered on 38 patients (28 female and 10 male) (Uhde, Boulenger, Roy-Byrne et al., in press) show great variation in the frequency and distribution of panic attacks within and across individuals. Panic attacks sometimes occurred in waves, but this was extremely unusual. Instead, they tended to occur in random patterns with intervals between episodes ranging from hours to months or years. The lack of any discernible rhythm (i.e., no regular cycling or circadian-related panic attacks) is of interest given the regular alterations in mood that have been observed in affectively ill patients. Furthermore, these findings are consistent with reports that panic attacks seem to come "out of the blue." The lack of predictability is also of theoretical interest in the development of generalized anxiety and avoidant behavior, since normal coping mechanisms may be rendered ineffective and variable interval schedules of reinforcement have been shown to produce behaviors that are slower to extinguish (Ferster & Perrott, 1968).

Moderate to severe agoraphobia and moderate to severe generalized anxiety were associated symptoms in 84% of our patients with panic attacks. Patients without these associated symptoms were all men and had relatively infrequent episodes of panic over weeks to months followed by longer periods of remission. Because our contact with this subgroup of patients was through family physicians (none had made contact with a mental health professional), it is possible that there is a substantial proportion of such patients with only panic attacks who never come to psychiatric attention and never become involved in research studies. Conclusions that are based on studies whose subjects come only from psychiatric treatment facilities, therefore, should be interpreted with caution.

The majority of our patients developed both pathological degrees of anxiety (99%) and avoidant behavior (97%) after, rather than before, their first panic attacks. These data certainly argue against the notion that panic attacks simply represent a marked exacerbation of generalized anxiety and are partially consistent with Klein and Fink's (1962) original theoretical notion that agoraphobia develops in most patients as a "secondary" consequence of repeated panic attacks. It is noteworthy, however, that all of our patients who developed agoraphobia after the onset of panic attacks did so within 6 months. In fact, many patients developed agoraphobia within 1 month of their first panic attack, perhaps suggesting an overlap in the biological substrate of panic anxiety and agoraphobia.

Fifty percent of patients had a lifetime incidence of depression. Although the symptoms were quite severe, only 24% of all patients in our sample had depressive episodes lasting greater than the 2 weeks' duration required by DSM-III for major depression. As illustrated in Fig. 29.1, patients who experienced depressions of greater than 2 weeks' duration developed their first depressive episode either before or within 12 months after the initial onset of panic attacks. In contrast, patients with transient depressions (< 2 weeks) typically had their initial depressive episode many months (> 12 months) or years after the onset of their first panic attack. Except for this distinction in duration, the two groups did not differ in symptomatology. Depressions were endogenomorphic in nature with the notable absence of psychomotor retardation and suicidal ideation (Table 29.2).

As noted by others (Roth, 1959), our preliminary data indicate that approximately 80% of patients with panic disorder reported one or more stressful life

PANIC ATTACKS WITH MAJOR DEPRESSIVE SYMPTOMS   PT. 1019

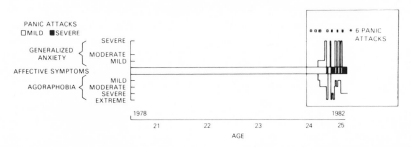

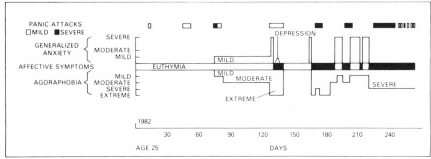

FIG. 29.1. Symptoms of depression emerge in this 24-year-old woman approximately 4 months after the onset of her first panic attack (Uhde et al., in press).

events within 6 months of their initial panic attacks. Our initial studies using a structured interview technique (Brown, Sklair, & Harris, 1973), are now being replicated using more controlled methodologies (i.e., the PERI-M life events scale). Preliminary analysis of these data is consistent with our impression that an important association between life events and the onset of panic attacks may occur in many patients. A more detailed discussion of our findings on the phenomenology and longitudinal course of panic disorder is the subject of a separate report (Uhde, Boulenger, Roy-Byrne et al., in press).

AGORAPHOBIA AND DEPRESSION:
THEORETICAL ISSUES AND BIOLOGICAL MARKERS

Agoraphobia with panic attacks is an anxiety syndrome complicated frequently by the presence of depression. As previously discussed, we found a lifetime prevalence of melancholic depression in 50% of our patients, although illness duration was limited to depressive periods of less than 2 weeks in many patients. Our findings are consistent with several previous studies demonstrating a history of depression in 33%—91% of patients with primary anxiety disorders (Bowen

TABLE 29.2
Depression Types in Patients with Major Depression and Panic
Disorder

	MAJOR DEPRESSION	PANIC DISORDER
BLUE	PRESENT	PRESENT
SAD	PRESENT	PRESENT
ANXIETY	PRESENT	PRESENT
PANIC ATTACKS	PRESENT	PRESENT
EMA	PRESENT	PRESENT
△ APPETITE	PRESENT	PRESENT
△ LIBIDO	PRESENT	[UNKNOWN]
PSYCHOSENSORY DISTURBANCES	PRESENT	PRESENT
PSYCHOMOTOR AGITATION	PRESENT	PRESENT
PSYCHOMOTOR RETARDATION	PRESENT	[ABSENT]
SUICIDAL IDEATION	PRESENT	[ABSENT]

FROM: UHDE ET AL., 1984, PROGRESS IN NEURO-PSYCHOPHARMACOLOGY AND
        BIOLOGICAL PSYCHIATRY

& Kohout, 1979; Buglass, Clarke, Henderson, Kreitman & Presley, 1977; Dealy, Ishiki, Avery, Wilson & Dunner, 1981; Munjack & Moss, 1981). In patients with major affective illness, anxiety is almost always a prominent symptom. In fact, the anxiety measure of the Hamilton Depression Scale was found to be significantly higher in patients with major depression compared to either panic or obsessive-compulsive patients (see Insel, this volume). This overlap of symptoms has led some writers to view anxiety and depression as phenomenologically indistinguishable (Lewis, 1966).

As reviewed in this volume (see Klein & Redmond, this volume), tricyclic and MAO inhibitor antidepressants are effective in the treatment of patients with panic disorder and agoraphobia with panic attacks. These observations have led some investigators to conclude that panic disorder, with or without agoraphobia, and major depressive illness, simply represent different expressions of the same underlying biological disturbance. Other investigators emphasize the differences between anxiety and depression and hold the position that panic disorder and major depressive disorder represent separate disorders with different psychobiologic abnormalities. To address this controversy, our laboratory studied, in nondepressed panic disorder patients, several biological indices known to be altered in patients with endogenous depression. In collaboration with Marian Kafka and Wade Berrettini, we investigated ^{3}H-imipramine and ^{3}H-dihydroergocryptine binding to the human platelet, respectively. In addition, our laboratory has investigated the growth hormone response to clonidine. This latter research was conducted in collaboration with Dr. Larry Siever.

There was no significant difference in the number of ^{3}H-imipramine binding sites in the patients with panic disorder compared to age- and sex-matched normal controls. Samples from both groups were obtained within the same week to control for the influence of seasonal variation on this measure. Our negative finding in panic patients stands in contrast to affectively ill patients in whom reductions in ^{3}H-imipramine binding may be related to severity, e.g., the "state" of depressive symptoms (Asarch, Shih & Kulcsay, 1981; Berrettini, Nurnberger, Post, & Gershon, 1982; Briley et al., 1980). These data suggest that nondepressed panic patients do not share with actively ill depressed patients a disturbance in ^{3}H-imipramine binding. It would be of interest, however, to determine whether panic disorder patients have alterations in ^{3}H-imipramine binding during "superimposed" episodes of depression. A comparison of ^{3}H-imipramine binding in nondepressed and depressed panic patients is indicated, since a number of biological markers are reported to be disturbed in "primary-endogenous," but not "secondary-reactive," depressions—the latter type of depression being felt by some authors to characterize the nature of dysphoria seen in patients with panic disorder.

^{3}H-dihydroergocryptine binding was significantly increased ($p < .05$), whereas prostaglandin E_1 (PGE_1)-stimulated cyclic AMP (cAMP) production was decreased ($p < .05$) in patients with panic disorder compared to controls. The percent inhibition by norepinephrine of PGE_1-stimulated cyclic AMP was lower in patients than controls ($p < .05$). Similar alterations in alpha-adrenergic platelet receptor function have been found in patients with major depressive illness (Kafka, et al., 1981), suggesting that alterations in nonadrenergic function may be common to both mood and anxiety disorders. Consistent with this notion is the emerging body of data suggesting a blunted growth hormone response to clonidine in patients with major depressive (Charney, Heninger, Sternberg, Hafstead et al, 1982; Checkley, Slade, & Shur, 1981; Matussek et al., 1980; Siever & Uhde, 1984), obsessive-compulsive (Siever, et al., 1983), and panic disorders (Table 29.3). As reviewed elsewhere (Siever & Uhde, 1984; Uhde, Siever, & Post, 1984), the growth hormone response to clonidine may provide a selective index of postsynaptic alpha-2 adrenergic receptor responsiveness.

As indicated in Table 29.3, both obsessive-compulsive and panic-anxious patients have significantly blunted growth hormone, an abnormality which has been consistently reported in depressed patients by four independent research teams. This disturbance, however, does not occur in schizophrenia or in patients with reactive depression, suggesting that the blunted growth hormone response is not simply a consequence of chronic stress. Overall, our findings of increased ³H-dihydroergocryptine binding and blunted growth hormone responses to clonidine in patients with panic disorder corroborate and expand previous research suggesting an important role for noradrenergic function in both mood and anxiety disorders.

TABLE 29.3
Blunted Growth Hormone Response to Clonidine in Patients with
Obsessive-Compulsive Illness and Panic Disorder

	Baseline Levels of Growth Hormone	Average Post-Clonidine Growth Hormone Peak (ng/ml)
PANIC DISORDER ($N = 10$)	1.5 ± 0.8	1.8 ± 1.3
OBSESSIVE COMPULSIVE DISORDER ($N = 9$)	4.5 ± 8.4	8.5 ± 18.4
NORMAL CONTROLS ($N = 9$)	2.5 ± 1.5	11.2 ± 9.5

Growth hormone determinations were performed in all subjects using a double antibody radioimmunoassay (BIO-RIA). Data for obsessive-compulsive patients derived from Siever et al., 1983.

PHYSIOLOGY

A recent review of psychophysiologic studies on anxiety markers (Lader, 1980) suggests that the bulk of research using autonomic and somatic measures (galvanic skin response, electromyography, pulse rate, blood pressure and blood flow studies) and electroencephalography points to a nonspecific heightening of general activity that can be interpreted as "overarousal." Early studies in patients suffering from "neurocirculatory asthenia," the forerunner of panic disorder, showed that such patients were hyper-responsive to thermal, auditory, and visual stimuli and had more symptoms of fatigue and dyspnea after muscular work compared to normal controls (Cohen & White, 1951). Other studies noted that they were more sensitive than controls to the ischemic pain produced by a tight sphygmomenometer cuff as measured by an increased respiratory rate (Jones, 1948) and that they often failed on several autonomic measures to habituate to repeated psychophysiological stimuli (for review, Boulenger & Uhde, 1982a).

Pain Perception

Using threshold pain and signal detection measures, our group undertook an investigation of pain sensitivity in panic patients. This method was employed in order to permit separate identification of the effects of anxiety on subjects' response bias and their ability to discriminate varying intensities of stimuli, presumably a function of sensory perceptual variables. Although recent reports indicate that such procedures may not achieve a clearcut separation of cognitive and sensory variables (Coppola & Gracely, 1983), several studies have shown that only the discriminability measure (pain insensitivity) is related to analgesia in humans (Buchsbaum & Davis, 1979; Davis, Buchsbaum, van Kammen, & Bunney, 1979). Data on a subset of normal controls have been previously published by our group (Uhde, Boulenger, Siever, DuPont, & Post, 1982) and showed an inverse relationship between state anxiety as measured by the Spielberger Anxiety Scale (Spielberger, Gorsuch, & Luschene, 1970) and pain sensitivity (i.e., the more anxious, the worse the ability to discriminate varying intensities of stimuli).

In a separate study (Roy-Byrne, Uhde, Post, King, & Buchsbaum, in press), an index of pain insensitivity (Buchsbaum & Davis, 1979) was obtained in 18 patients with panic disorder and age- and sex-matched normal volunteers. Subjects received three shocks at each milliamperage increment from 1 to 31 for a total of 93 randomly presented shocks. Subjects judged each shock as noticeable, distinct, unpleasant, or very unpleasant. This index is derived from the subjects' ability to distinguish between distinct and unpleasant sensations. Increases in this measure have been associated with morphine and aspirin analgesia (Buchsbaum & Davis, 1979) and decreases with naltrexone-induced hyperalgesia in schizophrenics (Davis et al., 1979). In addition, the milliamperage level that best separates the "distinct" and "unpleasant" judgments was computed (e.g., the stimulus intensity for which the least overlap between judgments occurred) and termed "response criterion." The "response criterion" is a measure of the patients' propensity to call stimuli painful. Finally, threshold pain measures were computed. The number of responses out of the total of 93 judged "unpleasant" or "very unpleasant" were counted and termed "pain counts." Also, the mean milliamperage intensity for stimuli termed "unpleasant" or "very unpleasant" was also computed as a rough approximation of "pain threshold." Ten patients and 12 normal controls filled out a Spielberger State Anxiety inventory between 8 and 9 on the morning of the testing.

Surprisingly, patients with panic disorder were not different from age- and sex-matched controls (Fig. 29.2) on any of the four measures of pain sensitivity. Comparison of the slopes of the best fit lines to the bivariate plot of anxiety and insensitivity index in normals (m = 0.65) and patients (m = -0.74) revealed that the slopes were significantly different (t = -2.93, p < .01). Comparison of the correlation coefficients between anxiety and insensitivity index in normals

NORMAL PAIN SENSITIVITY
IN PATIENTS WITH PANIC DISORDER

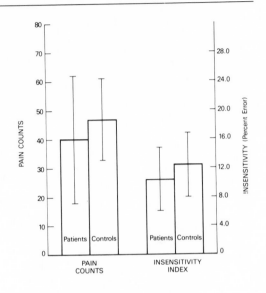

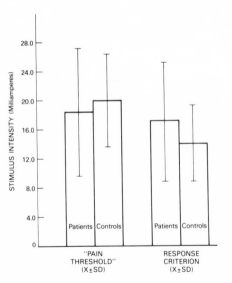

FIG. 29.2 Panic patients (*n* = 18) are similar to age- and sex-matched normal controls on four measures of pain sensitivity.

(r = .62) and patients (r = -.31) also yielded a significant difference (z = 2.2, p < .03). (Fig 29.3). The number of panic attacks in the month prior to testing was unrelated to any measure of pain sensitivity.

Together, these data suggest that panic patients are not more sensitive than controls to experimentally induced phasic pain stimuli. Our data further suggest that panic patients are not simply more reactive to all nonspecific "distress" signals. Despite the lack of difference between panic patients and normal controls on four measures of pain perception, these data are not inconsistent with our original hypothesis (Uhde, Siever, & Post, 1984; Uhde, Siever et al., 1982) which predicted that anxiety and pain may be related in a non-linear or inverted U fashion.

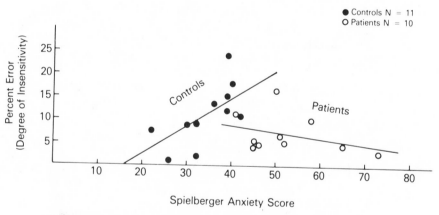

Opposite Relationship Between Anxiety and Pain Sensitivity in Panic–Anxious Patients and Normal Controls

FIG. 29.3 The relationship between anxiety and pain sensitivity is significantly different in patients with panic disorder and normal controls. While controls show increased insensitivity with higher levels of anxiety, patients show decreased insensitivity with higher levels of anxiety.

Sleep

Anecdotal reports of disturbed sleep in panic patients are ubiquitous. The EEG sleep of depressed patients has been extensively studied and certain characteristic abnormalities have been replicated by a variety of investigators. These include shortened REM latency and increased REM activity and density. Although some investigators have studied the EEG sleep of patients with generalized anxiety disorder (GAD) (Reynolds, Shaw, Newton, Coble, & Kupfer, 1983) and of mixed patient groups containing some with generalized anxiety and some with panic disorder (Akiskal & Lemmi, 1983; Akiskal et al., in press), no laboratory has investigated the EEG sleep of patients with pure panic disorder. As part of an ongoing study, we report preliminary data on the EEG sleep of nine patients with panic disorder compared to age- and sex-matched normal subjects studied previously in the same laboratory (Uhde, Roy-Byrne et al., 1984).

Despite patients' reports of restless and broken sleep, their mean total time awake, sleep latency, and sleep efficiency were not different from normals. This lack of difference between the two groups on these objective measures might suggest that patients with panic disorder overreact to relatively minor disturbances in sleep performance. However, patients with the highest ratings of anxiety and most frequent panic attacks did have the shortest total sleep and least delta sleep, respectively. As illustrated in Fig. 29.4, the patients showed significantly increased movement time, suggesting that anxious patients who typically have high levels of arousal and psychomotor activity during the day might have similar increases in motor activity during the night. Thus, reports of insomnia in panic patients may be related, in part, to a state of chronic physiologic hyperarousal, including marked increases in motor activity throughout the sleep-wake cycle.

Although our patients had shortened REM latency compared to normals (Fig. 29.4), the values were considerably greater than those seen in depressed patients in other studies (Gillin et al., 1984; Kupfer & Thase, 1983). Furthermore, our

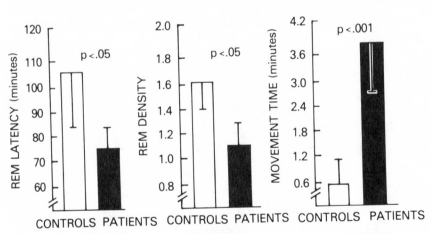

ALTERED SLEEP VARIABLES IN PANIC DISORDER
PATIENTS COMPARED TO NORMAL CONTROLS

FIG. 29.4. Although the panic patients ($n = 9$) had a shortened REM latency compared to age- and sex-matched normal controls, the REM latency is approximately two times greater than that reported in patients with endogenous depression. Panic patients have significantly less REM density but greater movement time than controls (Uhde et al., 1984).

patients had a significantly lower REM density associated with their shorter REM latency, whereas depressed patients may have a higher or equal REM density compared to normals (Gillin et al., 1984). Finally, our patients demonstrated a significant increase in REM length with each successive REM period, a pattern that may be blunted or absent in unipolar depressed patients (for review see Gillin et al., 1984).

Overall, our preliminary findings suggest that compared to controls the sleep architecture of nondepressed panic patients shows a different pattern of abnormality compared to endogenously depressed patients. Even the apparent shortened REM latency in our patients cannot be attributed to concurrent symptoms of depression, since the patients had no depressive symptoms (mean 2.7; range 1–15) on the Bunney-Hamburg Global Depression Scale, and since there was even a trend ($p = .06$) for depression ratings to be correlated with *increased,* rather than *decreased,* REM latency. In view of these findings, it would be of particular interest to use this methodology in the study of panic-anxious patients with and without concurrent symptoms of major depression, two groups that may have common and/or disparate biological substrates (Leckman, Merikangas, Pauls, Prusoff, & Weissman, 1983; Uhde, Boulenger, Roy-Byrne et al., in press).

Hypoglycemia

Symptoms associated with hypoglycemia bear a close resemblance to panic attacks. Some investigators have suggested that panic attacks may often be caused by hypoglycemia (Edwards & Lummus, 1955; Greene, 1944; Salzer, 1966), while others contend that this is rarely the case (Cahill & Soeldner, 1974). It has also been suggested that anxiety may directly influence glucose metabolism (Diethelm, 1936). Our laboratory has preliminary data addressing these issues.

Nine consecutive patients with panic disorder have received standard oral glucose tolerance testing following an oral challenge with glucose. Eight of these patients reported a marked exacerbation of their anxiety, and seven reported somatic complaints characteristic of hypoglycemia (Uhde, Vittone, & Post, 1984). Four patients completed analogue self-ratings that demonstrated a significant increase ($p < .01$) in generalized anxiety 3 hours after glucose ingestion. Baseline anxiety, as measured on the Zung scale, was correlated at a trend level with the glucose nadir ($r = 0.65$; $p < .06$). Eight of nine patients developed plasma glucose nadirs falling within the hypoglycemic range (< 60 mg/dl). Seven of nine demonstrated a hypoglycemic index (HI) of greater than 1.0. A hypoglycemia index, a measure of the rate of fall of glucose relative to the nadir, with a value above 1.0 is often associated with hypoglycemic symptoms (Hadjigeorgopoulos, Schmidt, Margolis, & Kowalski, 1980). It is noteworthy that none of the nine patients reported having a panic attack.

These preliminary data are of interest from several perspectives. First, these data suggest that as a group, patients with panic disorder may have abnormal glucose metabolism as indicated by low glucose nadirs and high rates of fall during a 90-minute period prior to the glucose nadirs. Second, generalized anxiety and somatic symptoms consistent with symptomatic hypoglycemia developed in a high percentage (79%) of our patients with panic disorder. Finally, that no patient experienced a panic attack despite the above two factors suggests that panic attacks in patients with panic disorder are not, in most cases, likely to be directly linked to episodes of hypoglycemia. Despite the lack of connection between hypoglycemia in our patients and panic attacks, the high percentage of patients who experienced symptomatic hypoglycemia, i.e., tremors, hunger, sweating, and generalized anxiety, remains impressive. Since most of our patients had been ill for many years (X = 9.8 ± 10), one might entertain the hypothesis that chronic stress leads to disturbed glucose metabolism, a causal relationship different from the usual assumption that hypoglycemia is a direct cause of anxiety. Of course, the most parsimonious explanation is that the biological substrates of stress, anxiety, and glucose metabolism may involve an overlapping network of related neuroendocrine pathways. Further placebo-controlled research might include both a glucose test and insulin challenge test to more directly investigate the relationships among these variables and to determine whether or not some subjects might be unusually sensitive to glucose itself (as distinct from the resultant hypoglycemia of a glucose challenge) or insulin, or both. The lack of induction of panic attacks in these vulnerable individuals following reactive hypoglycemia further supports the relative selectivity, if not specificity, of other paradigms discussed below that have been associated with panic attacks.

NORADRENERGIC SYSTEM

Several lines of evidence suggest an important role for noradrenergic function in the neurobiology of fear, anxiety, alarm, and arousal (for review, Uhde, Boulenger et al., 1982; Uhde, Boulenger, Vittone & Post, 1984; Uhde, Siever & Post, 1984; Uhde, Boulenger, Post et al., 1984). Redmond and Huang (1979) demonstrated that electrical and pharmacological activation of the noradrenergic nucleus locus coeruleus (LC) in the monkey produced fear behaviors similar to those occurring during exposure to natural threat in the wild. These behavioral changes were accompanied by increased levels of noradrenaline and its metabolite, 3-methoxy-4-hydroxyphenyl-ethylene glycol (MHPG), in the brain, CSF and plasma (Redmond, 1977; Redmond & Huang, 1979; Redmond et al., 1976, 1977; see Redmond, this volume). In humans, increases in noradrenergic function have been associated with state anxiety measures in depressed patients (Post, Ballenger, & Goodwin, 1980) and with measures of anxiety (MHPG) in normal volunteers (Ballenger et al., 1981; Ballenger, Post, Jimerson, Lake, & Zuckerman, 1984). In addition, plasma MHPG and state anxiety are positively correlated during anxiety-provoking situations in both normal volunteers (Uhde, Siever, et al., 1982) and panic patients (Ko et al., Elsworth, 1983). Finally, drugs that are capable of decreasing LC activity in animal models, including ethanol (Pohorecky & Brick, 1977), benzodiazepines (Redmond, 1977), and tricyclic antidepressants (Nyback, Walters, Aghajanian, & Roth, 1975), have been shown to have anxiolytic effects in humans.

Clonidine

Since clonidine, an alpha-2 agonist, is also a potent inhibitor of LC activity in animal preparations (Aghajanian, 1978), our group tested the hypothesis that clonidine might have antianxiety properties in humans. As an additional probe of the noradrenergic system, we also initiated studies with yohimbine, an alpha-2 antagonist which, in contrast to clonidine, increases LC activity (see Redmond, this volume).

Intravenous clonidine (2 ug/kg) was given to 18 anxious depressed, 11 agoraphobic patients with panic attacks, and 19 normal controls to assess the effect of this drug on state anxiety (Uhde, Boulenger et al., 1982; Uhde, Siever, & Post, 1984; Uhde, Boulenger, Vittone et al., 1984; Siever & Uhde, 1984). Clonidine had robust antianxiety effects as indicated by changes on the Spielberger State Anxiety Scale (Spielberger et al., 1970) in both patient groups ($p < .006$), although both the placebo response and anxiolytic effects of clonidine appeared to be more robust in the patients with panic disorder (Fig. 29.5). Although the panic patients tended to improve following placebo, clonidine's placebo-corrected effects remained highly significant ($p = .01$). There also was no relationship between the degree of placebo-response and clonidine's anxiolytic effects in the panic patients. Euthymic normal controls had no antianxiety response to clonidine, a finding also reported by Leckman, Maas, & Redmond (1980). However, the apparent lack of anti-anxiety response in normals might be related to low baseline ratings of anxiety. Although clonidine produced noteworthy drowsiness, there was no correlation between the anxiolytic and sedative properties of clonidine in anxious or depressed patients. In the combined group of depressed patients and normal controls, those subjects with the highest baseline levels of plasma MHPG had the most robust decrement in measures of anxiety after clonidine ($r = -.41$, $p < .03$) (Siever & Uhde, 1984; Uhde, Siever, & Post, 1984). Whether the extent of anxiety reduction following acute clonidine infusion or baseline adrenergic indices predict longer term response to oral clonidine is currently unclear.

Yohimbine

In order to confirm findings of previous investigators that yohimbine, an alpha-2 antagonist, is capable of producing anxiety-like symptoms in humans (Garfield, Gershon, Sletten, Sunland, & Ballou, 1967; Charney, Heninger, & Sternberg, 1982; Charney, Heninger, & Redmond, 1983), we administered low dose oral

Acute Anxiolytic Effects of Clonidine in Depressed and Panic Anxious Patients

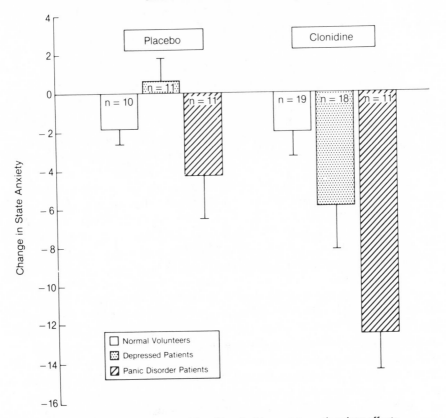

FIG. 29.5. Intravenous clonidine (2 ug/kg) has acute antianxiety effects in panic anxious and depressed patients (Siever & Uhde, 1984, and Uhde, Boulenger, Vittone, & Post, 1984).

yohimbine (20 mg) to agoraphobic patients with panic attacks. Nine of the first 11 patients studied to date had profound anxiety, including several patients who had panic attacks, after yohimbine, whereas none had anxiety to this degree or panic attacks while receiving placebo ($p = .003$). This significant increase in ratings of state anxiety on the Spielberger Scale following low dose yohimbine (20 mg) in panic patients was not observed in five normals challenged with the same dose of yohimbine. Thus, our findings are consistent with the observations of Charney et al. (1983), and suggestive of altered noradrenergic function or receptor sensitivity in patients with panic disorder.

Because recent studies (Charney et al., 1983) have established that diazepam can antagonize yohimbine-induced anxiety without blocking increases in MHPG, further studies manipulating noradrenergic and benzodiazepine systems are indicated to clarify the biological similarities and differences among different anxiety disorders and mechanisms by which anxiolytic agents mediate their therapeutic effects.

CAFFEINE

Several studies have reported a statistically significant positive association between caffeine consumption and scores of self-rated anxiety and/or depression in both college students (Gilliland & Andress, 1981; Primavera, Simon, & Camiza, 1975) and psychiatric inpatients (Greden, Fontaine, Lubetsky, & Chamberlin, 1978; Winstead, 1976). Consumption of caffeine above 600 mg/day also has been reported to induce symptoms of "caffeinism," a syndrome characterized by anxiety, nervousness, sleep disturbances and psychophysiological complaints that may be indistinguishable from anxiety neurosis (Greden, 1974).

The possible anxiogenic effects of caffeine in humans and its influence on various systems that may be involved in the regulation of anxiety-like behaviors in animals (Marangos, et al., 1979; Olpe, Jones, & Steinman, 1983) led us to undertake a survey studying caffeine consumption and its effects in 30 patients with panic disorder, 23 patients with major depressive disorder, and comparable numbers of age- and sex-matched normal controls (Boulenger & Uhde, 1982b; Boulenger, Uhde, Wolff, & Post, 1984). Twenty-three of the 29 panic patients and 7 of the 23 depressed patients were medication free. The average daily caffeine consumption (DCC) before admission to NIMH was calculated according to the quantities of caffeine suggested by Gilbert (1976) for different beverages. In addition, the Spielberger State-Trait Anxiety Inventory (STAI), the Beck Depression Inventory, and the Hopkins Symptom Checklist (SCL-90) were given to all subjects. Subjects also recorded the effects of various amounts of coffee on a 5-item scale measuring alertness, mood, anxiety and sleep.

In panic patients, 11 of 16 psychopathological measures were significantly positively correlated with the DCC, including a high correlation between DCC and both state ($r = .50$, $p = .006$) and trait ($r = .50$, $p = .006$) (Fig. 29.6) anxiety, as well as depression ($r = .56$, $p = .02$). As illustrated with trait anxiety in Fig. 29.7, these relationships were not observed in either the affectively ill patients or control groups. In addition, the consumption of one cup of coffee was associated with significantly more intense ratings of anxiety, alertness, and insomnia in the patients with panic disorder. The patients with affective disorders did not report an increased sensitivity to one cup of coffee in a significantly different way than their controls, despite having high levels of state and trait anxiety similar to panic patients. Finally, a significantly greater percentage of panic anxious patients than controls reported having given up coffee (67% versus 20%). These findings suggest an increased sensitivity to caffeine in panic patients

DAILY CAFFEINE CONSUMPTION AND TRAIT-ANXIETY IN PATIENTS WITH PANIC DISORDERS AND THEIR CONTROLS

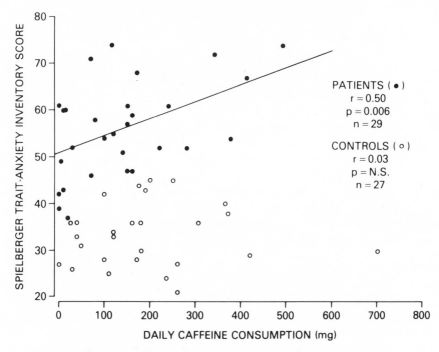

FIG. 29.6. Daily caffeine consumption is correlated with measures of trait anxiety in patients with panic disorder but not normal controls (Boulenger & Uhde, 1982).

and are consistent with previously cited reports of the anxiogenic effects of caffeine in humans.

To further explore these relationships, our group initiated studies of the effects of orally administered caffeine in panic disorder patients and normal controls (Uhde, Boulenger, Jimerson, & Post, 1984; Uhde, Boulenger, Vittone, in press). Thus far, three separate single-dose caffeine (240, 480, and 720 mg p.o.) challenges compared to placebo have been administered to eight normal subjects and two panic patients. In the combined group of subjects, there was a significant dose-related anxiogenic effect of caffeine (ANOVA, $p < .04$). Although the panic patients appeared more sensitive to caffeine, two normal subjects developed unequivocal panic attacks after receiving caffeine at 720 mg. These caffeine-related panic attacks were characterized in both normal controls by an acute fear of imminent death. Dose-related increases in cortisol were observed. Moreover, the two normals who panicked had a greater than fivefold increase in mean

DAILY CAFFEINE CONSUMPTION AND TRAIT-ANXIETY IN PATIENTS WITH MAJOR DEPRESSIVE DISORDERS AND THEIR CONTROLS

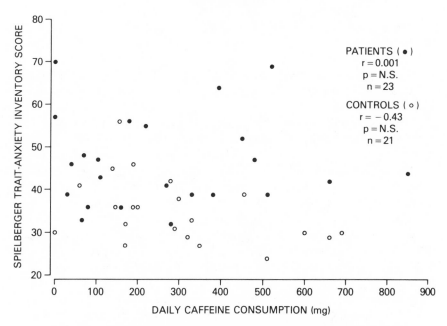

FIG. 29.7   Although patients with major depressive disorders have high measures of trait-anxiety, there is no relationship between daily caffeine consumption and measures of trait anxiety.

cortisol after 720 mg compared to the increase in cortisol in the six normals who did not experience panic attacks. There was no significant increase in MHPG at any dose. Further exploration of other adrenergic indices as they relate to caffeine-induced anxiety are clearly indicated. In addition to the possible effects of caffeine on the noradrenergic system, effects on benzodiazepine-GABA and adenosine function also may be implicated in the neurobiology of both normal and pathological anxiety (Boulenger, Patel, & Marangos, 1982; Boulenger, Patel, Post, Parma, & Marangos, 1983) and should be systematically pursued as well.

CONCLUSIONS

Findings have been presented from a number of ongoing projects at NIMH investigating the neurobiology of panic disorder. Our systematic data on the longitudinal course of panic disorder are generally consistent with the clinical impressions of many investigators that panic attacks, when present in agoraphobic patients, almost always precede the onset of pathological degrees of generalized anxiety, and agoraphobia. These observations argue against the traditional concept that panic attacks simply represent marked exacerbations of generalized anxiety. If they did, it would seem more reasonable to expect a pattern of increasingly more severe generalized anxiety culminating in time with a panic attack. While these data are suggestive that panic attacks are distinct from generalized anxiety, they are not conclusive and should be viewed with caution. Clearly, the prospective study of patients at risk for anxiety disorders is indicated to improve our understanding of the pathogenesis and treatment of panic and related anxiety disorder.

Preliminary data from our sleep laboratory suggest that panic patients may have increased motor activity during sleep. While this increased activity during sleep is consistent with an "overarousal" theory of anxiety, we failed to demonstrate an increased sensitivity to pain in panic patients. Thus, panic patients would not appear, as suggested by some authors, to be unequivocally more sensitive and "overreactive" to all nonspecific stimuli or situations of novelty. Given this perspective, it is noteworthy that panic patients appear more sensitive to yohimbine and caffeine, two agents that increase noradrenergic function, although caffeine influences several other neurotransmitter systems implicated in the neurobiology of anxiety. Clonidine, an alpha-2 agonist that in low doses decreases noradrenergic function, had rather robust antianxiety effects in our panic anxious and anxiously depressed patients. Although these results generally support previous theories implicating the noradrenergic system in arousal, alterations in benzodiazepine-GABA and adenosine function may be equally critical in the neurobiology of alarm, fear and anxiety (see Costa, this volume).

30 Obsessive-Compulsive Disorder: An Anxiety Disorder?

Thomas R. Insel,
Clinical Neuropharmacology Branch
National Institute of Mental Health

Theodore Zahn,
Laboratory of Psychology and Psychopathology
National Institute of Mental Health

Dennis L. Murphy
Clinical Neuropharmacology Branch
National Institute of Mental Health

Those who classify psychiatric syndromes have never been able to agree on the proper category for obsessive-compulsive disorder (OCD). More than a century ago, Westphal (1878), focusing on the bizarre behavior and intrusive thoughts of obsessional patients, described the syndrome as "abortive insanity," a pale form of schizophrenia. Maudsley (1895), an English contemporary, connected the syndrome to a disturbance of affect, and included it with nonpsychotic depressions as "simple melancholy." Following a French tradition, Janet (1903) considered obsessional phenomena, along with phobias, under the broad rubric of "psychasthenia." And Freud (1909/1959), for entirely different reasons, linked obsessive-compulsive neurosis and hysteria together as the two forms of transference neurosis.

Over the past 50 years, in spite of considerable strides in classifying the types and subtypes of other psychiatric syndromes, there is still no consensus regarding obsessive-compulsive disorder. *The Diagnostic and Statistical Manual (3rd Revision) (DSM-III)*, breaking with an earlier neurosis-psychosis distinction, classifies it as an anxiety disorder (American Psychiatric Association, 1980). By contrast, most European diagnostic schemes recognize an overlap with both anxiety and affective disorders (see Jablensky, this volume). For instance, the most recent International Classification of Diseases (World Health Organization, 1978), which combines OCD with neurotic depression and depersonalization syndrome under the rubric of neurotic disorders, recognizes anxiety as a contributing feature to these disorders, whereas phobias and panic disorder are viewed as neurotic disorders for which anxiety is a major defining feature.

What does the *DSM-III* classification of OCD as an anxiety disorder imply? In addition to sharing cardinal clinical features, one would presume that anxiety disorders, as a group, share either a common pathophysiology, a common response to treatment, or a common genetic predisposition. In the present chapter, evidence for each of these features is reviewed. In addition, we summarize the evidence for each feature linking obsessional disorder to depression. Finally, some recommendations for a new look at obsessive-compulsive disorder are made.

CLINICAL SYMPTOMS

Obsessive-compulsive disorder, in terms of symptoms, is a heterogeneous syndrome. Each of the forms of the disorder involves intrusive thoughts or impulses that are experienced as internal, ego-alien, and reprehensible. These thoughts, along with associated behavioral or cognitive rituals, are resisted (the patient struggles against them) and they interfere with functioning. Despite this common ground, one may be more struck by the differences rather than the similarities among patients who meet *DSM-III* criteria for obsessive-compulsive disorder.

With respect to anxiety, obsessionals can be divided into three categories. First, there is a small subgroup who manifest little or no anxiety. Most such patients are in the group that Rachman (1974) described as having primary obsessional slowness, a form of OCD in which the patient may require an hour to brush his teeth or shave. The patient's slowness may be related to a compulsion to repeat, but fear or anxiety of the consequences of not repeating or not finishing are minor. While slowness may be a feature of many obsessionals, those for whom it is the primary difficulty probably comprise less than 10% of most samples with an OCD diagnosis.

A second group of patients complains of anxiety regarding something that could happen, e.g., fears of making a mistake, saying something obscene, or doing something awful. These patients may suffer with pathologic doubt, and they often develop checking rituals to resolve doubts about what they might do or might have just done. One such patient was afraid to leave his apartment because he feared that his water faucet would leak, his sink would overflow, and the water would flood the apartment beneath him where an elderly tenant might slip and hurt herself, all from his negligence. This patient became a "shut-in," but he was not truly agoraphobic. His anxiety was related more to a fantasy than to an external cue, as one would expect with a phobic patient. Unlike the phobic who can avoid the external fear stimulus, this patient's staying at home did not allow him any respite from his anxiety about the potential water faucet leak.

A third group of obsessional patients have anxiety-related complaints that more closely resemble those of phobics. These obsessionals are afraid of "contamination," they have classic avoidance (e.g., of public restrooms, money, doorknobs, or newspapers), and they wash compulsively. While Straus (1948) once described their reaction as disgust rather than anxiety, for many, anxiety seems an appropriate term. Can this anxiety be distinguished from phobic anxiety? Nemiah (1975) stressed that phobics are more afraid of being hurt, while obsessionals are more afraid of hurting others. This distinction may hold for those with obsessional doubt, but does not seem valid for compulsive washers (Insel, 1984). Perhaps the most useful distinction between these obsessionals who fear "contamination" and true phobics is the internal and inescapable nature of their fear. Most often, obsessionals are afraid of something that is microscopic (e.g., "germs") or an unavoidable natural product (e.g., urine, feces, sweat, vaginal secretions). For obsessionals, avoidant behavior can never be entirely successful.

One additional, distinctive feature of the anxiety found in obsessive-compulsive patients is its dysphoric quality. Obsessions are accompanied by tears, feelings of guilt, and helplessness, as well as anxiety (Insel, 1984). One patient, for instance, would have the intrusive thought (which to him was both irrational and exceedingly painful), "I am a homosexual." He would lock himself in his bedroom, check and recheck his bureau drawers (his words), while tearfully attempting to rearrange his thoughts. For another patient, the repetitive thought that she had molested her young daughter was precipitated by the thought, "I have done something bad," which in turn was preceded by an original feeling of worthlessness. Although these patients often appeared depressed, the profile of symptoms on the Hamilton Depression Rating Scale resembled panic disorder patients more than depressives (Fig. 30.1).

It appears then that anxiety as a symptom in OCD is (a) not always present, and (b) when present, differs phenomenologically from anxiety as it exists in other anxiety disorders. An exception may be found in some cases of compulsive washing, where obsessions with contamination appear to overlap with phobias.

A related question regarding the clinical picture of OCD is whether it aggregates epidemiologically with other anxiety disorders. In a population survey, Weissman, Myers, and Harding (1978) found considerable overlap between other forms of anxiety disorder, yet, perhaps due to the low prevalence of the syndrome, failed to find a single case of OCD. Follow-up studies of obsessional patients (Black, 1974; Kringlen, 1965; Lo, 1967) suggest a considerable number with phobic symptoms. However, a close examination of the inclusion criteria in these studies suggests that many of these patients would have met the *DSM-III* criteria for phobia and not OCD. Most studies of syndromes that are associated with OCD note a high incidence of depression, but do not tabulate panic attacks or nonobsessional phobias (Goodwin, Guze, & Robins, 1969). In our own investigation of 30 adults meeting *DSM-III* criteria for OCD, we found

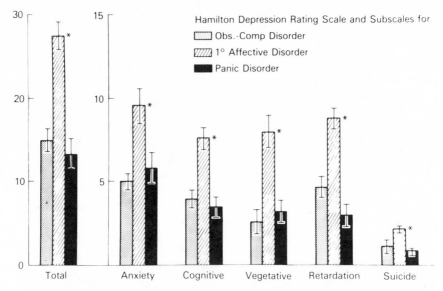

FIG.30.1. Mean ± S.E.M. scores of age and sex-matched patients with obsessive compulsive disorder ($n = 10$), primary 1° affective disorder ($n = 10$), and panic disorder ($n = 10$) on Hamilton Depression Rating Scale. Subscales for anxiety (items 10, 11, 12, 13, 15, 17), cognitive (items 2, 3, 9, 19, 20), vegetative (items 4, 16 A&B, 18, 5, 6), retardation (items 1, 7, 8, 14), and suicide (item 3) show significant (* denotes $p < .05$) differences for t tests between depressed and other groups, but no difference between obsessive-compulsive and panic patients. Item 21 (obsessive-compulsive symptoms) was omitted.

many who met criteria for the diagnosis of an associated anxiety disorder with a structured interview, such as the Schedule for Affective Disorders and Schizophrenia - Life Time Version (SADS-L). However, as may be seen in Table 30.1, with few exceptions, these anxiety disorders were complications of the primary diagnosis. For instance, social phobia, in all but one case, was found to be fear of public restrooms due to obsessions with contamination. Similarly, agoraphobia in these obsessionals was really "staying at home" behavior resulting from fears of a catastrophe happening at home when the patient was out or occasionally, worrying about doing something reprehensible in public.

PSYCHOPHYSIOLOGY

A number of physiologic alterations are associated with the anxiety disorders, the most carefully studied being electrodermal measures. In several studies, increased palmar sweat gland activity (i.e., increased skin conductance level,

Table 30.1
Incidence (%) of Anxiety Disorder in 30 Patients
with Obsessive-Compulsive Disorder

	Generalized Anxiety Disorder	Panic Disorder	Simple Phobia	Social Phobia	Agoraphobia
Preceding obsessive-compulsive disorder	10	0	16	10	0
Secondary to obsessive-compulsive disorder	40	0	57	20	20

SCL), increased frequency of spontaneous skin conductance fluctuations (SSCR), or slower habituation of the orienting response has been reported in anxious patients compared to normal controls (reviewed by Horvath, 1980; Lader, 1980).

Other physiological abnormalities have also been noted. Kelly (1980) has shown that increased forearm blood flow is a powerful correlate of anxiety, and heart rate has been reported increased in some but all studies (Monti, Altier, & Prandro, 1975). Among anxiety disorders, there appears to be some diagnostic specificity. In particular, simple phobics do not show the physiologic abnormalities reported in patients with generalized anxiety disorder (GAD) (Kelly, 1980; Lader, 1967). However, these physiologic measures that reflect heightened arousal are not limited to the anxiety disorders, as agitated depressives have been shown to be abnormal on precisely the same measures. (This issue is discussed at length in Kelly, 1980.)

Although several studies of obsessional patients have used electrodermal or cardiovascular measures as correlates of treatment response (Boulougouris, 1977; Kelly, 1980; Zahn, Insel, & Murphy, in press), only two have investigated obsessionals prior to treatment in relation to controls. Boulougouris (1977) found no physiologic differences between eight obsessionals and eight controls during baseline conditions. However, under conditions of shock anticipation or psychological threat, the obsessionals showed greater changes in heart rate and skin conductance, and they showed slower habituation across trials. In contrast, Kelly (1980), using cardiovascular measures in a large group of patients with various diagnoses, found significantly higher resting heart rate and diastolic blood pressure and trends for greater forearm blood flow and systolic blood pressure in obsessionals ($n = 40$) than in controls ($n = 60$). Patients with diagnoses of chronic anxiety and agitated depression were even more extreme on these measures, and those labeled nonagitated depressives had more modest elevations on all variables (except forearm blood flow, for which nonagitated depressives were lower than normals). Also unlike the Boulougouris study, the obsessionals, like the other diagnostic groups, had attenuated reactions to stress (mental arithmetic) on most of the variables.

We are investigating SCL, SSCR, and habituation of the orienting response and heart rate in adults with *DSM-III* diagnosed obsessive-compulsive disorder. The sample thus far consists of 18 patients, of whom 10 are male and 8 are female. Their mean age is 30.7 ± 10.1 years, and they have been ill for at least one year and drug-free for at least 4 weeks prior to participating in the study. Controls are 17 nonpatient paid volunteers (7 male, 10 female, mean age 40.4 ± 14.2 yrs). The procedure includes a 5-minute rest period, followed by presentation of 10 85 dB, 1000Hz tones of 1.5 seconds duration at 30–50 second intervals through headphones. This is followed by a 2-minute mental arithmetic task in which subjects are given a series of challenging, but solvable, multiplication problems under time pressure.

Results shown in Table 30.2 reveal that under resting baseline conditions, OCD patients are higher than controls on all three indices of arousal.

However, habituation of the orienting response to the auditory tones does not differentiate the two groups. During the stressful arithmetic task only SCL remained higher in the OCD group. Analysis of the stress-rest difference scores shows that the increase in heart rate is greater in the controls ($t = 2.76$, $p < .01$), reflecting the higher baseline value in the obsessionals. The magnitude of the stress-related increases in the electrodermal indices does not differ significantly

TABLE 30.2
Means for Skin Conductance (SC) and Heart Rate Indices
of Autonomic Arousal

	Obsessive-compulsives (n = 18)		Controls (n = 17)		
Baseline	Mean	SD	Mean	SD	t
Spontaneous SC Responses (number/minute)	2.70	2.13	1.35	1.57	2.30*
SC Level (℠mho)	4.90	2.56	2.60	2.11	2.92**
Heart Rate (BPM)	81.2	13.6	72.6	9.9	2.15*
Auditory Tones					
Number of SC Orienting Responses	5.00	2.75	4.88	3.46	< 1
Amplitude of SC Orienting Responses (℠mho)	0.20	0.25	0.21	0.21	< 1
Mental Arithmetic Task					
Spontaneous SC Responses (number/minute)	9.63	4.28	9.22	3.24	< 1
SC Level (℠mho)	6.72	2.58	4.53	2.35	2.63**
Heart Rate (BPM)	83.7	13.1	83.1	12.0	< 1

*$p < .05$
**$p < .02$
***$p < .01$

between the two groups. Male and female subgroups show the same effects within each diagnostic group. The difference in age between the groups is significant ($t = 2.30$, $p < .05$), and this may render the results more ambiguous than we would prefer.

The results of higher heart rate at baseline and a smaller reaction to stress in OCD patients compared to controls is a direct confirmation of Kelly's (1980) results described above. It is important to note that both cardiovascular and electrodermal indices of arousal have been found to be elevated in agitated depressives (Kelly, 1980; Lader & Wing, 1969) and are not unique to the anxiety disorders. In what is presumed to be a baseline or resting state, physiologic arousal is present in a wide range of psychiatric disorders; and, as shown by our data (see table 30.2), roughly equivalent levels of arousal are present in normal individuals with a mild psychological stress.

The failure to find retarded habituation in OCD patients is surprising in view of the positive findings on this measure in both anxiety states (Horvath & Meares, 1979, Lader, 1975; Raskin, 1975) and agitated depressives (Lader & Wing, 1969). In addition, changes in habituation to auditory tones appear to correlate with improvement in obsessional symptoms during treatment with clomipramine (Zahn et al., in press). Slow habituation has also been suggested as an explanation for the efficacy of prolonged exposure in behavioral treatments of obsessional ritualizers. The absence of a difference in habituation between obsessionals and controls in this study may reflect the incomplete matching for age and gender. As additional subjects are added to this sample, a more accurate comparison should be forthcoming.

GENETICS

Do obsessionals have a family history of other anxiety disorders? Again, the literature is sparse, but an early study by Brown (1942) deserves close attention. In the course of 500 interviews, Brown obtained information on more than 2000 first- and second-degree relatives of out-patients with various anxiety disorders. Although his study pre-dates any diagnostic research criteria, he includes a description for each diagnosis. In Table 30.3, we have taken the liberty of replacing Brown's original labels with the DSM-III diagnosis when the descriptions coincide. Anxiety state is specified only as "amounting to social or work incapacity at some time"; anxious personality includes "excessive worrying, phobias not amounting to definite psychoneurosis, obsessional personality, . . . and depressive personality." As is apparent in Table 30.3, Brown diagnosed major depression ("manic-depressive psychosis, with suicides, mental hospital admissions, depressive stupor . . . includes involutional . . . and puerperal depressions") slightly more often than anxiety state in the first-degree

TABLE 30.3
Psychiatric Disorders in First Degree Relatives
of Obsessive-Compulsive Disorder Patients (Percent Affected)*

Proband Diagnosis (n)	Total n	No Psych Diagnosis	Anxiety States	OCD	Major Dep Disorders	Anxious Personality
Anxiety State (63)	365	57.0	15.1	0.5	2.5	16.7
Obs-Comp Disorder (20)	101	59.4	3.0	6.9	4.4	24.8
Non-psychiatric control (31)	189	86.8	0.	0	0	10.1

*Adapted from Brown (1942)

relatives of obsessional probands. Furthermore, of the 40 parents of the obsessionals, none had a history of anxiety state, 7.5% had obsessive-compulsive disorder, 7.5% major depression, and 32.5% "anxious personality." By contrast, 21% of the parents of the anxious probands were labeled anxiety state and none were obsessional.

A slightly different picture was reported by Rosenberg (1967) from a review of the histories of 547 first-degree relatives of 144 patients hospitalized for OCD. Rosenberg found only two relatives (0.4%) treated for OCD, 14 (2.5%) treated for anxiety states, and 14 (2.5%) treated for depression. As with Brown's data for first-degree relatives, there is a relatively similar rate of anxiety states and depression. Unfortunately, since Rosenberg did not include a control group, it is not clear if the 2.5% prevalence of anxiety disorders he reports represents an increased rate.

Recently Flament and Rapoport (1984) administered the SADS-L to 54 parents and the Diagnostic Interview for Children and Adolescents (Herjanic & Campbell, 1977) to 58 siblings of 27 children with OCD diagnosed by *DSM III* criteria. Anxiety disorder of any type was found in only one parent; major depression was noted in two (4%). Among the siblings there were three cases of generalized anxiety and two cases of panic disorder, presumably a high incidence, although the authors mention that all of these cases were represented within a single family.

Thus far, the data suggest that anxiety disorders are not particularly common (compared to the rate of depression, for instance) in the parents of obsessionals, and may be less common than in the parents of patients with other anxiety disorders. Because of the low prevalence of OCD, its absence in the relatives of patients with other anxiety disorders is difficult to interpret.

One other approach to demonstrate a common genetic substrate for OCD and other anxiety syndromes is to look for concordance in twins in which one co-twin has either disorder. Although there have been several series of obsessional twins reported (Carey & Gottesman, 1981; Inouye, 1965), only one report directly examines the concordance of obsessional disorder with other anxiety syndromes. Torgerson (1983) presented three monozygotic and nine dizygotic pairs in which the proband met *DSM-III* criteria for OCD. Using assessment by a structured interview, one of the monozygotic co-twins met criteria for agoraphobia without panic and one of the dizygotic co-twins met criteria for GAD. Three other co-twins, all dizygotic, had another (i.e., non-anxiety) unspecified psychiatric diagnosis. Although the numbers are too small for a rigorous comparison, Torgerson also reports concordance rates for twins with other anxiety disorders. For 29 probands with either panic disorder or agoraphobia with panic, 10 co-twins had anxiety disorders (non OCD) and only two had other (unspecified) psychiatric diagnoses. It appears that, at least compared with panic-related syndromes, OCD may have less concordance with the anxiety disorders and more with other psychiatric diagnoses.

TREATMENT

Obsessive-compulsive disorder has been noted to be refractory to most traditional psychological treatments (Salzman & Thaler, 1981). Behavioral treatments such as desensitization, which are effective in phobic states, have not been as clearly useful for obsessionals (Foa & Steketee, 1984). A different strategy, which includes prolonged exposure to the stimulus that evokes obsessions paired with prevention of rituals, has been developed for compulsive ritualizers (reviewed by Marks, 1981).

Pharmacologic treatment of OCD is also quite different from most of the other anxiety disorders. In studies of GAD, for instance, as many as 30%–50% of all subjects respond to placebo and 50%–70% respond to a benzodiazepine (Klein, Gittleman, Quitkin, & Rifkin, 1980; Rickels, 1978). Placebo response in obsessionals is considerably lower (Montgomery, 1980; Thoren, Asberg, Cronholm, & Jorenstedt, 1980); in our own studies placebo response occurs in less than 10% of the subjects. In addition, anxious patients with high scores on the obsessive-compulsive subscale of the Hopkins Symptom Checklist (including items for difficulty concentrating, slowness, trouble remembering, worries about carelessness, checking, mind going blank) appear less responsive to benzodiazepines than those with low scores on this subscale (Rickels, 1978). There is insufficient evidence to determine if anxiolytics are useful for patients with obsessive-compulsive disorder. Rao (1964), Orvin (1967), Burrell, Culpan, and Newton (1974) claimed that benzodiazepines were more effective than placebo for obsessionals, but these early reports provide insufficient details of the method of assessment. An additional study (Waxman, 1977) compared clomipramine to diazepam. Again, the data are not entirely clear. Although clomipramine appears more effective than diazepam on most measures, the effects on obsessions are not specified.

In contrast to anxiolytics, which have not been adequately investigated as either primary or adjunct treatments for obsessionals, there are several carefully controlled studies of the tricyclic antidepressant (TCA) clomipramine (Ananth, Pecknold, van der Steen, & Englesman, 1981; Insel, Murphy et al., 1983; Marks, Stern, Mawson, Cobb, Cobb, & McDonald, 1980; Montgomery, 1980; Thoren, Asberg, Cronholm, Jornestedt, Traskman, 1980). Each of these studies documents a significant drug effect, although Marks et al. (1980) found that this effect was limited to patients with secondary depressions.

Tricyclic antidepressants have also been demonstrated as effective treatments for panic disorder with agoraphobia and GAD (see Klein, Rabkin,& Gorman, this volume), so these results with clomipramine do not really distinguish OCD from other anxiety disorders. Curiously however, other TCA's that have been effective for agoraphobia or panic disorder, do not appear to be useful for OCD. For instance, desipramine (Insel & Mueller, 1984), amitryptiline (Ananth et al., 1981), and nortriptyline (Thoren et al., 1980) have not been found effective for obsessionals. Although it is not yet clear that clomipramine is the only effective TCA, preliminary results do suggest some advantage for this compound over other antidepressants in the treatment of obsessionals, a difference that has not emerged in treatment studies of other anxiety disorders or affective disorders.

There is one additional distinction to be mentioned with obsessive-compulsive disorder. The use of intravenous sodium lactate has been proposed by several investigators as a potential diagnostic test for patients with panic disorder (Gorman, Fyer, Gliklich, King, Klein, 1981; Kelly, Mitchell-Heggs, & Sherman, 1971; Pitts & McLure, 1967). Klein recently described eight obsessional patients who received sodium lactate, none of whom panicked, suggesting that the syndromes may be quite distinct biologically (personal communication, 1983).

In summary, OCD appears pharmacologically different from other anxiety disorders by its low frequency of placebo response, poor response to some antidepressants (although good response to clomipramine), and in a preliminary report, absence of response to intravenous sodium lactate.

RELATIONSHIP OF OBSESSIVE-COMPULSIVE DISORDER TO OTHER PSYCHIATRIC SYNDROMES

Just as anxiety as a symptom occurs across the spectrum of psychiatric disorders, obsessions and compulsions are common in several *DSM-III* syndromes. Patients with anorexia nervosa, for instance, may have classic obsessions and rituals (Welner, Reich, Robins, Fishman, Van Doren, 1976), and adult OCD patients frequently give a history of anorexia during adolescence (Insel, 1984). Similarly, there is a conspicuous overlap in the symptoms (Cohen, Detlor, Young, &

Freedman, 1980), clinical course (Nee, Caine, & Polinsky, 1979), and family history (Montgomery, Clayton, & Friedhoff, 1982) of Tourette Syndrome and obsessive-compulsive disorder.

But perhaps the most complex intertwining of obsessional symptoms, pathophysiology, genetics, and treatment response is with affective illness (see Table 30.4). Symptoms common to both depression and OCD include guilt, low self-esteem, indecision, anxiety, exhaustion, and sleep disturbance. In a chart review of 150 cases of obsessional behavior, Welner et al. (1976) found only 30 cases without significant depression. Goodwin et al. (1969), reviewing a series of outcome studies, concluded that depression was the most common complication of obsessive-compulsive disorder. On the other hand, studies of patients with primary depression have reported about 30% to have obsessions (Gittleson, 1966). Videbech (1975) and Vaughan (1976) have reported obsessions to be especially common in patients with agitated as opposed to retarded depressions. Whether viewed from the perspective of patients with depression who subsequently develop obsessions or patients who develop obsessions first and depression later, the literature consistently demonstrates a blurred boundary for which

Table 30.4
Links Between Obsessive-Compulsive and Affective Disorders

Obsessive-Compulsive Disorder	Both Syndromes	Depression
	Symptoms	
Ritualistic washing or checking	Guilt, Exhaustion, Low Self-Esteem, Indecision, Anxiety, Sleep Obsessions, Rumination	Loss of libido Diurnal variation Anorexia Anhedonia
	Clinical Course	
Usually chronic Childhood onset (50%)		Usually episodic Adult onset
	Biologic Markers	
	DST Sleep EEG-REM Latency Clonidine Response	
	Treatment Response	
Exposure and responsive prevention	Clomipramine	ECT Tricyclic antidepressants MAO-inhibitors

the "primary" symptoms are chronologically first but may be secondary in importance. For instance, some patients with chronic OCD may only present for
treatment when depressed.

Several physiologic abnormalities previously reported to be specific to major
depression have recently been reported in patients with obsessive-compulsive
disorder. These include nonsuppression on the dexamethasone suppression test
in 25%–40% of primary obsessionals (Insel, Kalin, Guttmacher, Cohen, & Murphy, 1982; Asberg, Thoren, & Bertilsson, 1982; Insel, Mueller, Gillin, Siever
& Murphy, in press). Sleep electroencephalographic (EEG) findings in obsessionals resemble those of depressives, including shortened latency to rapid eye
movement (REM) sleep and diminished stage 4 sleep (Insel, Gillin et al., 1982).
These findings were not limited to obsessionals with secondary depressions. In
addition, the growth hormone response to intravenous clonidine, which is blunted
in primary depressives, is also abnormally reduced in patients with obsessive-
compulsive disorder (Siever, et al., 1983).

The genetic links between obsessional and affective disorder can be surmised
from data already presented. In our own series, 11% of obsessional patients had
a mother hospitalized for depression and an equal number had a father treated
for alcoholism (Insel, Hoover, & Murphy, 1983). An increased incidence of
depression was not, however, reported in a chart review study (Coryell, 1981).

Finally, the response of many obsessional patients to clomipramine raises the
possibility of a neurochemical abnormality shared with depression. As summarized above, however, the response of obsessionals to antidepressants may
be selective. At least some compounds that are effective for reducing depressive
symptoms in patients with primary affective illness do not reduce either the
obsessional or depressive symptoms of patients with primary obsessive compulsive disorder.

CONCLUSION

Although OCD frequently involves anxiety as a symptom, the classification of
this complex syndrome as an anxiety disorder may be misleading. For many
obsessional patients, the primary symptoms may be an intrusive thought, guilt,
or dysphoria, and not anxiety. Depression may be a more likely concomitant of
obsessional disorder than agoraphobia or generalized anxiety. The parents of
obsessionals, in the few studies that have been published, appear either as likely
or more likely to have had a history of depression rather than an anxiety disorder.
Pharmacologic response in obsessionals also points more to the antidepressant
rather than anxiolytic compounds, although data on both counts are inconclusive.
There is too little information with which to discount anxiolytics, and the response
of obsessionals to antidepressants appears somewhat different than the response
of primary depressives. Although preliminary endocrine evidence and sleep EEG

data suggest a link with depression, there are significant differences between the age of onset, the clinical course, and possibly the genetic backgrounds of the two disorders. On one variable, psychophysiologic measures of arousal, obsessionals do resemble patients with generalized anxiety, but this abnormality is also common in agitated depressives.

Perhaps the most heuristic approach at the current stage is to view OCD as an independent entity that overlaps with a number of other psychiatric syndromes. The original description of this syndrome by Westphal (1878, not previously translated) deserves note:

> Compulsive ideas are not caused by an emotional or affect-like state. Actually, the person afflicted often is in a completely peaceful and indifferent mood condition when the compulsive idea first arises, and is not under the influence of any mood or affect—and I lay special importance on this fact with respect to the concept of this disease and its position vis-a-vis other diseases. Nevertheless, the patients in the course of the disease often complain of a feeling of anxiety. . . . Just by closer analysis . . . I have always found that these feelings of anxiety were secondary, produced by the pathologic compulsion in thinking (p. 738).

This original conception of obsessive-compulsive disorder as a primary disorder in thinking complicated by secondary anxiety and depression deserves a renewed emphasis.

31

Some Observations on the Problem of Anxiety

Richard I. Shader
Tufts University
New England Medical Center

The contributions from Klein and co-workers and Redmond in this volume are important overview statements of the state of the art in contemporary thinking about anxiety disorders. By reviewing responses, both specific and nonspecific, to psychopharmacologic agents, Klein and colleagues have done much to clarify the phenomenology of anxiety and to dissect out certain treatment-responsive subtypes that transcend such earlier concepts as trait versus state anxiety or signal anxiety versus anxiety-neurosis. Similarly, by reviewing pharmacologic perturbations of the locus coeruleus, Redmond has offered a potential model for the underlying pathophysiology of anxiety states, emphasizing the pathogenic role of norepinephrine. My own thinking has been focused upon how to relate their observations to the ubiquitous nature of anxiety as it appears in everday life, and as it is seen by psychiatrists and other clinicians alert to the anxiety present in their patients. The model of Klein and colleagues, which appropriately urges us to view the panic attack as the key antecedent to the pathology of the agoraphobic who is also tortured by panic and anticipatory anxiety, restates with even greater clarity an early view of Freud.

In his 1895 paper on obsessions and phobias, Freud argued "In the case of agoraphobia, etc., we often find the recollection of a state of *panic;* and what the patient actually fears is a repetition of such an attack under those special conditions in which he believes he cannot escape it . . . . The fear of this emotional state, which underlies all phobias, is not derived from any memory whatever; we must ask what the source of this overpowering nervous state can be" (Freud, 1895/1959). Unfortunately, Freud in this same essay answered his own question and concluded without sufficient data that sexual conflict was the origin of the nervous condition underlying panic states. "Its specific cause is the

591

accumulation of sexual tension, produced by abstinence or by frustrated sexual excitation . . . . It is under such conditions . . . especially among women, that anxiety-neurosis develops; phobias are a psychical manifestation of it."

Although Redmond has amassed considerable data to support his hypothesis that the locus coeruleus plays a central mediating role in anxiety states, it seems premature to accept this blue site as the seat of Freud's blue notions—and it has no connection at all to blue panic, a robust type of glabrous leafy perennial grass so common to the southeastern states. I wish it did, however, because it would be an apt way to capture a notion I have been speculating about during this past year or so—that the panic attack for some individuals may be a response to an ultrasensitive or subliminal perception of hypoxia. So many patients who are about to panic feel the need to get air. (One patient of mine describes the moments before the panic becomes uncontrollable as, "It is as if all the air was sucked right out of the room"). Many get panic attacks in closed spaces or from high places. And then there are the iatrogenic panic attacks produced by carbon dioxide, sodium lactate, and marijuana. I do not wish to be any more speculative than Freud, and I shall leave my blue (hypoxic) panic notions to future testing.

Anxiety is a common symptom physicians encounter in consultations to pulmonary services of general hospitals—more so than depression. The fear of suffocating or drowning must be an adaptive response built into us when we evolved from the primordial swamps. What else could stir up a more primitive anxiety response than the fear of not being able to get your breath? Particularly when it cannot be overcome by our usual fight or flight perspectives. In other words, panic attacks might not come "out of the blue" but could be triggered, for example, by a direct cause of hypoxia in some, a supersensitivity or lower threshold to hypoxia in others, or as a learned or conditioned response linked to prior experiences in still others. Redmond curiously has found that hypoxia is a profound stimulus to locus coeruleus firing. Perhaps I am getting too speculative. I would add only one further finding, which in this instance is contrary to Redmond's ideas about the locus coeruleus—buspirone, a relatively new and apparently effective anxiolytic, increases rather than decreases locus coeruleus noradrenergic neuronal activity (Hjorth & Carlsson, 1982; Sanghera, McKillen, & German, 1983). Buspirone also has probable presynaptic dopaminergic effects and serotonin effects, reminding us that a focus on any single substrate is probably too limiting.

AN INTERACTIVE MODEL

One way of thinking about the relationship between anxiety and panic that may help clarify the relationship between overall anxiety levels and the frequency of panic attacks is an interactive model. The greater the background level of anxiety, whether related to acute or chronic situational anxiety or to life stress or marked anticipatory anxiety, the greater the frequency of panic attacks. This model is consistent with interactions that occur with certain epilepsies. For example, Fydor Dostoevsky, who so richly described at least five types of epileptic patterns in his writings, was himself a probable victim of grand mal and temporal lobe seizures (Shader, in press). When stressed, his seizures came as frequently as twice a month. When freer from excitement, seizure-free intervals from 4 to 5.5 months were recorded by the author in this autobiographical account in his diaries and notebooks (Alajouanine, 1983; Clark, 1915; Proffer, 1973, 1975, 1976). It is sometimes suggested that Dostoevsky's first seizure occurred in 1860 while being punished in Semipalatinsk Prison for socialist activities, as his exile in Siberia was coming to an end; he is said to have reported to friends that his first attack occurred following an excited argument over religion with an atheistic friend who visited him after a period of social isolation. One of his biographers, however, indicates that his first attack occurred almost 30 years earlier at age 7 during an upsetting event in his parents' lives—the nature of which has never been divulged (Alajouanine, 1983). In commenting on Dostoevsky, Freud unfortunately again states his views as fact and not as hypothesis or opinion. Freud (1928/1959) labels him an "instinctual character," emphasizing Dostoevsky's extraordinarily intense emotional life, his "perverse instinctual predisposition, which inevitably marked him out to be a sado-masochist or a criminal, and his unanalyzable artistic endowment..." and concludes, with only a slight note of caution, that his "so called epilepsy was only a symptom of his neurosis and must accordingly be classified as hystero-epilepsy, that is, as severe hysteria."

I feel that Freud missed an opportunity to help us see how life experiences and levels of stress or anxiety may interact with genetically determined or acquired predispositions or organic vulnerabilities. If we transpose these thoughts about epileptic events to panic attacks, could we not speculate that kindling-like processes, associated, for example, with anticipatory anxiety or social phobias, increase paroxysmal firing from the locus coeruleus? Perhaps the successful agoraphobe reduces tension levels to the degree that the firing rate decreases to preanticipatory anxiety levels—panic attacks then may become so mild or so infrequent that they go unrecognized. May this not explain how behavior therapy works?

It seems reasonable to postulate that paroxysmal activity can be suppressed, or reduced in frequency, by behaviors, tasks, or approaches that distract or focus attention. Support for the connections between anxiety and stress and the frequency of seizure activity can be found in the studies of Feldman and Paul on the emotional triggers of electroencephalograph (EEG) documented seizure activity (Feldman & Paul, 1976), and in the observations of Gottschalk (1953) that psychodynamically oriented psychotherapy markedly reduced EEG documented seizure frequency in children whose seizures were not adequately controlled by medication.

A possible direct linkage between epilepsy and agoraphobia is also worthy of emphasis. Pinto (1972) has described a 31-year-old man with no family history of epilepsy, but with a positive family history for mild phobias. Following a head injury at age 7, this patient developed seizures precipitated by startle responses or sudden movements. He could have from 6 to 50 attacks per day, the frequency depending on the stresses in his life. About age 16, he began to be agoraphobic, fearing at first that his epileptic attacks would be observed. Later, he was afraid to go out of his house without his wife, and he avoided crowded shops and cinemas. Anticonvulsant medications were without consistent benefit. Still later, at age 31, when he was having about one attack per week, he was treated with a flooding technique. This approach utilized audiotapes describing him having seizures in embarrassing situations, and subsequent actual practice sessions in the imagined places or situations. Following 10 such sessions and their associated practice during a 3-week treatment course, he was able to travel widely and to enter crowded places. He was seizure free during a 16-week follow-up, in comparison to the longest pre-treatment seizure-free interval of 2 weeks. Could this patient have had both epilepsy and panic disorder? Although this is possible, no anxiety attacks were described. It seems possible that dependent, help-seeking behaviors in both panic disorders can become linked to anticipatory anxiety and/ or phobic avoidance (agoraphobia), and that in both disorders, reduced fear or anxiety could lower attack or seizure frequency.

I would like to conclude with a final speculation. The views that I have expressed suggest at least two possible pharmacologic approaches to anxiety and panic disorders. Some drugs may actually block anxiety (e.g., by blocking the paroxysmal or chronic firing of structures such as the locus coeruleus), while other drugs (or therapies) may reduce anxiety and work more indirectly by reducing the frequency or threshold for paroxysmal or chronic discharges from the locus coeruleus or similar or interrelated structures.

ACKNOWLEDGMENTS

Preparation of this chapter has been supported in part by USPHS grant MH-34223.

II

F. Psychodynamic Perspectives on Anxiety

32 Psychodynamic Models of Anxiety

Robert Michels, M.D.
Allen Frances, M.D.
M. Katherine Shear, M.D.
The New York Hospital—Cornell Medical Center

INTRODUCTION

Psychoanalysis has regarded anxiety as (1) an affect, (2) a psychological construct central to the psychoanalytic model of intrapsychic conflict and its resolution, and (3) a symptom common to many psychopathologic syndromes and the central feature of several of them.

Psychoanalysis developed a coherent theory of affect much later than theories of drive, motivation, or defense. This probably reflected the clinical emphasis on symbols, language, and communication in early psychoanalytic work and the central role of instinctual drives in early psychoanalytic theories of behavior. Affects were viewed as discharge byproducts, derivatives or epiphenomena of the drives, and were therefore not the central focus of theoretical inquiry. The relatively unimportant role of affects in early analytic theory contrasts sharply with their obvious central role in the phenomena of psychopathology and in the psychotherapeutic process.

Among the affects, anxiety was the only one to be discussed extensively in early psychoanalytic writings and it has continued to hold a special and central place in psychoanalytic theory. In recent years, however, a more comprehensive and systematic psychoanalytic theory of affects has evolved (Basch, 1976) and other specific affects, particularly depression, have been integrated into a modern psychoanalytic model of dysphoric emotions.

Freud developed several partly complementary and at times contradictory models of anxiety. His original *neurophysiological* model regarded anxiety as the result of the transformation and discharge of excessive central nervous system

(CNS) excitation that had accumulated because of inadequate sexual discharge and/or because of traumatic stimulation from without. It is ironic that although this model has been largely discarded by most modern psychoanalysts, it is similar in some regards to popular contemporary, nonpsychoanalytic neurophysiologic models. Freud's *psychological* or psychodynamic model, in which anxiety is the reaction to and signal of unconscious memories of real or imagined dangers that are often associated with infantile wishes, is fundamental to contemporary psychoanalysis. Freud's *evolutionary* model of anxiety emphasizes its adaptive value and attributes its origin and form to the phylogenetic transmission of sensations related to experiences of birth, copulation, and dangerous situations during the prehistory of the species. Freud's *learning theory model* traces the emergence of a hierarchy of childhood danger situations whose anxiety-eliciting properties are enhanced through learned association with earlier traumatic experiences. In this model anxiety reduction is a secondary drive important in symptom formation.

Freud's intuition that any complete theory of anxiety would necessarily contain psychological, neurobiological, evolutionary, and learning components has been confirmed by subsequent developments and is reflected in the organization of this conference. Because he was limited by the biology of his time, it is no great surprise that many of Freud's specific biologic hypotheses seem outdated by modern standards. His theories do remind us, however, that a modern theory of anxiety must integrate psychodynamic with neurobiological, ethological, and learning theory models. This chapter discusses some of the theoretical, clinical, and research strategies that might promote such integrations as well as some of the remaining obstacles.

The remainder of the chapter is divided into three sections: (1) a more detailed discussion of the origins of the psychoanalytic model of anxiety; (2) a review of later developments in that model; and (3) a discussion of the implications of a current psychodynamic model for classification and research.

THE ORIGINS OF THE PSYCHOANALYTIC MODEL

The topic of anxiety was central in Freud's thinking from his earliest psychoanalytic writings to the end of his career. Although consistency and tidiness were not usually Freud's highest priority in theory building, his model of anxiety does hold together remarkably well. We outline the neurophysiological, psychological, ethological, and learning theory components of Freud's model and discuss how they were integrated. Readers who are interested in the details of the historical evolution of Freud's writings on anxiety are referred to Freud himself and to Compton's (1972a, 1972b) reviews. From a modern perspective, Freud's psychological and learning theory models retain substantial explanatory power, while his ethological and neurophysiologic models are primarily of historic interest.

Neurophysiologic Model

Freud's first fully formulated theory of anxiety was embedded in a neurophysiologic model that would either be rejected or seen as nonpsychoanalytic by most modern psychoanalysts. In this model, anxiety resulted from the transformation of an accumulation of undischarged sexual tension or libido. He said that this relationship could not be proven by any clinico-psychological analysis since it was not of a psychical nature but physical processes with psychical consequences (1894a, p. 53).

Freud's neurophysiological model of anxiety was based on the assumption that a major regulatory principle of CNS function is the tendency to reduce excitation. According to this so-called "economic" hypothesis, undischarged neural excitations were presumed to arise and accumulate from internal sources (named instincts) and/or from excessive and traumatic stimulation from without ("without" means outside of the mental apparatus, and would include for Freud somatic excitement, e.g., cardiorespiratory, as it registers in the CNS). He used the term libido to describe the psychic energy of sexual excitation, and said that anxiety represented a transformation of libido that occurs when its direct discharge in sexual activity is prevented. The notion that disturbance in the discharge of the sexual instinct plays a significant role in neurotic symptom formation would be broadened and elaborated in Freud's later psychological model, but the shift from neurophysiological to psychological mechanisms would mean that the origins of anxiety would be explained in a radically different way.

At this stage of his thinking, Freud had observed and carefully described the clinical syndrome of anxiety neurosis. He explained the syndrome as an "actual" neurosis, which he differentiated from the psychoneuroses (hysterical and obsessive-compulsive). The term "actual" was based on the German "aktual" meaning "current" or "present day." He hypothesized that current sexual practices (abstinence, excitation without climax, or coitus interruptus) interfered with libidinal discharge. He introduced this concept to emphasize that anxiety neurosis is a state not a trait, and that it has a biological not a psychological basis, with the accompanying psychological phenomena understood as the product rather than the cause of the anxiety. This reflected the clinical observation that there is no consistent conscious mental content associated with episodes of anxiety. Later psychological models and the theory of repression would explain this observation in terms of unconscious mental processes. Presumably the cure for anxiety neurosis would involve a biological intervention; in this case, the discharge of libido through the channels of sexual activity. Although his later work emphasized a psychological explanation for anxiety, Freud never totally abandoned biological thinking. Even late in his career, when he had developed a highly sophisticated psychodynamic model of anxiety, Freud continued to adhere to the biological notion that the energy for signal anxiety was derived from dammed-up libido. He saw no inherent incompatibility between his early biological and later more psychological models of anxiety, just as modern psychoanalysts see no inherent incompatibility between psychoanalytic understanding and neurophysiological conceptions. However, today most analysts restrict their interest and attention to psychodynamic considerations.

Psychological Model

Freud's second major theory of anxiety was psychological rather than physiological. It was the central theme of his 1926 monograph on *Inhibitions, Symptoms and Anxiety*. In the interval since the formulation of his first model, psychoanalytic theory had changed considerably. The earlier focus on drives and their derivative wishes as determinants of behavior had expanded to include other components of psychic conflict. Psychologic forces that conflict with drives had been identified and traced to unconscious fantasies of imagined dangers that stem from early childhood. Freud had introduced the idea of a psychologic structure that results from the internalization of parental authority, the superego. In addition, he was increasingly interested in the importance of the various patterns of conflict resolution and regulation represented by the mechanisms of defense and the psychologic structure called the ego. Psychoanalytic theory had grown more complex, and the explanation of symptoms now included consideration of fears and defenses as well as wishes.

The new psychoanalytic model of anxiety conceptualized it as a psychological event, the mental reaction to the anticipation of danger. Importantly, the generation of anxiety occurred unconsciously, outside of the individual's awareness. The dangers that trigger anxiety were fantasized situations that evolved originally in the mental life of the child: separation, loss of love, castration, and guilt. These were perceived as real threats by the young child, who saw himself as helpless in the face of them. They are often linked to unconscious wishes, and in the adult anything that activates those wishes or otherwise stimultes the fantasies of danger (as, for example, a real danger that is symbolically or associatively linked to them) triggers the mental state called anxiety. Anxiety may or may not be experienced consciously as a feeling state. In either case it acts as a signal eliciting a defensive response. Defenses act to reduce anxiety, often by regulating or inhibiting the wishes related to the fantasized dangers.

Two central features of this psychodynamic model directly contradict the earlier neurophysiologic one. First, anxiety always has ideational mental content, although this content is unconscious (Brenner, 1983; Fenichel, 1945; Lewin, 1965; and others).[1] The modern psychoanalytic theory of anxiety is largely a

---

[1] Some psychoanalysts have suggested that certain pathologic conditions (e.g., primitive regressive states, "actual" neuroses, frightening dreams, night terrors, or traumatic states) might have "blank" anxiety without ideational content, possibly reflecting presymbolic developmental experiences, but even these would represent a form of mental content.

theory of the unconscious ideational components of anxiety. In many ways the ideational aspect of mental life is really a defining methodologic assumption rather than an empiric finding of modern psychoanalysis. The method is one of discovering and inferring hidden meanings that may be distorted or concealed from the subject and unavailable to casual inquiry.

Second, the model argues that in spite of its apparent immediate situational cause, neurotic anxiety is always related to unconscious fantasies that stem from childhood and therefore reflects a predisposing trait as well as a current state. The immediate situation may be a precipitant because it activates a wish linked to that fantasy, or because of its direct association to the fantasized danger, but the understanding and psychodynamic treatment of the anxiety requires attention to the fantasy. Psychoanalytic theory distinguishes anxiety from fear. Fear is based on current real dangers, whereas anxiety is based on unconscious fantasies of imagined dangers that stem from childhood. Nevertheless, fear and anxiety are often associated. For example, a realistic fear such as finding oneself facing major surgery may be enhanced by castration anxiety triggered in this situation. Realistic fears may also be exaggerated or manufactured and used defensively to displace, symbolize, disguise, and rationalize neurotic anxiety, a mechanism most easily observed in phobias.

Freud discussed inhibitions, symptoms, and anxiety within one book because these phenomena are closely related in his psychological model. Neurotic inhibitions were understood to be restrictions of instinctual expression in order to avoid the anxiety occasioned by the associated unconscious imagined dangers. (Note that the avoiding of real dangers because of realistic fears is not neurotic inhibition but rather reflects simple good sense.) Neurotic symptoms are understood to be compromises that allow partial and often symbolic gratification of instinctual drives, but avoid the anxiety that would have been occasioned by the imagined danger if there were the direct, undisguised expression of the drive. The symptom of anxiety occurs when anxiety increases in intensity beyond the level of signal and becomes a conscious affect. Anxiety feelings may also represent a partial symbolic expression of the feared danger and/or punishment, or even of the excitement associated with the instinctual wish. When defense mechanisms fail to provide an adequate solution to intrapsychic conflict anxiety is intensified. The particular form taken by the various neurotic syndromes (e.g., anxiety, hysteric, obsessive-compulsive, and phobic) reflect the particular characteristics of the individual's defense mechanisms.

Evolutionary Model

Freud's evolutionary hypotheses were influenced by both Darwin and Lamarck. Darwin suggested that behavioral patterns (including emotions) were subject to the same forces of evolution and natural selection that had shaped the physical attributes of animals and men. Freud adopted Darwin's notion that currently experienced affects consist of sensations that originally had a meaning and served a purpose in the prehistory of the species (Freud, 1915–1917). Employing the Lamarckian model of the inheritance of acquired characteristics, Freud attempted to explain the specific physiologic symptoms of anxiety (especially the shortness of breath and palpitations) as the result of phylogenetic inheritance of the physiological manifestations first of copulation (Freud, 1905) and later of birth (Freud, 1926). He also used an evolutionary model when he argued that the fear of castration in each individual does not depend only on direct experience of castration threats, but is augmented by phylogenetic transmission from a prehistoric era when actual violence was rife (Freud, 1918).

Freud was interested in the adaptive value of anxiety. While Darwin discussed the use of affects as signals between or among individuals, Freud emphasized the usefulness of internal signals in facilitating communication among the various structures of the mental apparatus. He noted (1926) that the physiological concomitants of anxiety (associated with the feeling state) may be appropriate and expedient in the face of real danger situations and become inexpedient only when they occur anachronistically in response to "memories" of an ontogenetic or phylogenetic past. Freud was particularly interested in the social value of anxiety during infancy when behavioral manifestations of the distressed child facilitate adaptation to his external world by attracting the ministrations of the mother. Freud also noted that in the genesis of phobias "available anxiety is simply employed to reinforce aversions which are instinctively implanted in everyone" (1894b, p. 96). This is similar to modern ethological notions of prepotency (Marks, 1969) and preparedness (Seligman & Hager, 1972) that innate tendencies to adaptive avoidance may serve both as a template and a precursor for simple phobias.

Learning/Developmental Theory

Freud discussed, in terms that retain their freshness and clinical relevance, the epigenetic unfolding of danger situations that generate anxiety. The steps he describes in order of ascending chronological age and maturation of the individual are (1) a fear of being overwhelmed by traumatic excitation which may be infringing from without or generated from within, (2) a fear of the loss of the object of primary care and attachment (e.g., mother), (3) a fear of the loss of the object's love (Freud believed this to be especially prominent in girls), (4) a fear of castration or other bodily punishment or hurt (Freud believed this to be especially common in boys), and (5) a fear of the superego or of conscience.

Several quotations from Freud clearly express his views on the impact of learning on the perception of danger.

> When the infant has found out by experience that an external, perceptible object can put an end to the dangerous situation which is reminiscent of birth, the content of the danger it fears is displaced from the situation [i.e. the overstimulation] on

to the condition which determined that situation, viz., the loss of object. It is the absence of the mother that is now the danger; and as soon as that danger arises the infant gives the signal of anxiety, before the dreaded situation has set in. This change constitutes a first great step forward in the provision made by the infant for its self-preservation, and at the same time represents a transition from the automatic and involuntary fresh appearance of anxiety to the intentional repro-duction of anxiety as a signal of danger (1926, pp. 137-138). The progress which the child makes in its development—its growing independence, the sharper division of its mental apparatus into several agencies, the advent of new needs—cannot fail to exert an influence upon the content of the danger situation (1926, p. 139). The significance of the loss of object as a determinant of anxiety extends considerably further. For the next transformation of anxiety, viz. the castration anxiety belonging to the phallic phase, is also a fear of separation and is thus attached to the same determinant (1926, pp. 138-139). The next change is caused by the power of the super-ego. With the depersonalization of the parental agency from which castration was feared, the danger becomes less defined. Castration anxiety develops into moral anxiety (1926, p. 139).

In each transformation, Freud believed that the later appearing danger situation emerges from the earlier one by a process that involves associational learning.

Summary of Freud's Integrated Model

Anxiety is a signal of the unconscious fantasies of imagined danger situations that are provoked by instinctual wishes or by external perceptions. The affect of anxiety receives its psychic energy from and is created by a transformation of excessive CNS stimulation, often derived from instincts, particularly the sexual instinct. Humans have inherited their capacity for anxiety because of its adaptive value. Its particular physiologic manifestations reflect the phylogenetic trans-mission of reactions to stimulating or dangerous experiences (e.g., copulation, birth, and/or physical violence). The specific fantasies of danger that trigger anxiety are determined by a developmental progression that is influenced both by the maturation (especially psychosexual) of the individual, and by associa-tional learning. The avoidance of anxiety is a powerful secondary drive or motivator and shapes much that is normal and neurotic in human behavior. The individual configuration of the various mental mechanisms of defense determine the specific behaviors that result.

LATER DEVELOPMENTS

Biological Model

Freud's hypothesis (that anxiety results from the transformation of dammed-up sexual excitation) was consistent with and limited by the neurophysiological knowledge of his time. The role of the neuron as the functional unit in the CNS had just been accepted. (Freud, the neurobiologist, had participated in this discovery.) Freud's "economic" model of psychic libidinal energy pressing for discharge has received no confirmation from outside of psychoanalysis and has had little heuristic value in the development of either modern neurobiology or modern psychoanalysis. Holt (1965) and Emde (1980) have summarized a number of currently accepted biological facts unknown to Freud, all of which refute his reflexive discharge model of the psychic apparatus. The "power engineering" constructs Freud borrowed from Brucke, Meynert, and Exner do not apply to the central nervous system. This is a system better characterized by "information engineering" as in the signal anxiety hypothesis.

Within psychoanalysis, the economic or energy theory has been the subject of heated controversy and vigorous attack. Many analysts (Holt, 1965; Rosenblatt & Thickstun, 1977; Stewart, 1967) argue that Freud's assumptions about psychic energy are untestable, are descriptive rather than explanatory, and run counter to evidence that the CNS is an open rather than a closed system. In addition, many analysts believe that Freud's neurophysiologic speculations are not really necessary to his psychological theories and can be abandoned without loss. If psychoanalytic observations are to be related to neurophysiology, they clearly require integration with modern neurophysiological findings, rather than with speculations that were current at the turn of the century.

Psychological Theory

The psychological model elaborated by Freud in *Inhibitions, Symptoms, and Anxiety* (1926) has proven to be remarkably robust and influential. Later psychoanalysts have confirmed the usefulness of Freud's hypotheses with a great weight of anecdotal clinical experience. Although there have also been numerous theoretical contributions, they were primarily elaborations on Freud's model and have changed its emphasis without adding a great deal that is new.

Freud's consideration of the relation of instinctual drive to anxiety focused almost exclusively on the transformations and dangers evoked by the sexual instinct. Later writers (Deutsch, 1929; Flescher, 1955; Klein, 1952; Zetzel, 1955) have emphasized the importance of aggression in the generation of anxiety, and Melanie Klein (1952) in particular has traced anxiety to the child's response to destructive rage, both within himself and as projected onto the mother. Freud had noted the importance of loss of object as the first step in his hierarchy of psychologically mediated fears, but tended in his clinical discussions to emphasize the central importance of castration fear related to forbidden genital sexual impulses. More recent thinking has viewed separation anxiety from the perspective of ego development rather than the oral phase of libidinal development and has placed greater emphasis on pre-oedipal factors in many forms of anxiety, including even anxiety about genital integrity. This view is more compatible with modern ethological notions elaborated by Bowlby and described in more detail below.

Sullivan (1953) and the interpersonal theorists also traced anxiety back to the early mother-child relationship, but they placed greatest emphasis on the social transmission of anxiety from mother to infant and regarded anxiety more as a learned response than as an expression of instinct. Anxiety in the adult was seen as a function of the relationship of the individual to significant other persons in his or her social world.

There has been something of a shift away from early psychoanalytic formulations of agoraphobia that emphasized the projected libidinal temptations with their associated dangers symbolized by the feared territory. In this formulation the symptoms were seen as an expression of unconscious conflicts over sexual fantasies—often of prostitution in women, homosexuality in men (Fenichel, 1944). A parallel and historically later literature places less emphasis on the frightening outside territory and instead focuses attention on the safety of the home and the companion without whom the patient is fearful. Deutsch (1929) stressed the hostile identification with this companion. She regarded the symptom as the patient's magical attempt to protect the companion from murderous impulses. Bowlby (1973), Frances and Dunn (1975), Mahler (1968), and Rhead (1969) have elaborated Freud's suggestion that the basic original psychological fear is loss of the object, or in more current terminology, separation anxiety. They suggest that those situations are avoided that symbolize or threaten separation from the object. This may help explain the importance of object loss as a precipitant to agoraphobia and the alleviation of agoraphobic symptoms in the presence of a companion.

Freud's stages of danger situation development have also been expanded and detailed by others. Several types of "narcissistic catastrophe" (A. Freud, 1946) have been proposed—e.g., fear of fusion, fear of ego disintegration in the face of excessively strong drives, fear of humiliation, fear of loss of self-esteem. There have also been detailed discussions (Brenner, 1953; Schur, 1953) of the ego functions that constitute the anxiety response, and of the other affects that can function as signals analogously to anxiety (Brenner, 1983).

Learning Theory

The recent, and unfortunate, stridency in the debate between psychodynamic and behavioral therapists should not obscure the long history of collaboration and dialogue between theorists of both schools. The many fruitful efforts at integration (see especially Dollard & Miller, 1950; Kubie, 1941; Marmor & Woods, 1980; Mowrer, 1960) have resulted in a general realization that the two approaches share many assumptions and implications. Both models conceive of anxiety as an important secondary motivation. The relief of anxiety is a reinforcer for a wide array of avoidant and symptomatic behaviors. It would seem that the concept of "signal anxiety" is more or less equivalent in many of its usages to the "conditioned anxiety response." The differences between the psychodynamic and the learning theory model are nonetheless important. In the psychodynamic model (1) the origin of anxiety is attributed to unconscious fears; (2) there is greater emphasis on symbolization and displacement as opposed to simple conditioning; (3) defense mechanisms are included as mediating variables between anxiety and symptom formation; and (4) the importance of innate constitutional tendencies is recognized.

Evolutionary Model

Freud's evolutionary ideas were based on the biological theories of his day and were limited by the lack of available ethological data.

John Bowlby (1973) has been especially influential in integrating modern ethological concepts with data from child observation and with psychoanalytic theory. He has stressed the importance of a primary instinct for attachment and regards anxiety as an innately programmed component of the response to separation. In Bowlby's definition, instincts are behavior patterns that are similar in almost all members of a species, are adaptive (i.e., enhance survival and reproductive success), and develop in the absence of opportunity for learning. Causal factors (called "releasers") that activate or terminate these behavioral systems are often "extra psychological," i.e., hormonal changes, autonomic nervous activity, proprioceptive or environmental stimuli.

Bowlby (1973) observed that fears are commonly and strongly aroused in situations that are not very likely, in themselves, to cause damage, i.e., the dark, being alone or being with strangers, and sudden loud noises. Freud's psychological model explains fear in those situations largely as a symbolic displacement of unconscious conflict, while Bowlby claims these are "natural fears" and represent situations which could presage danger (especially during the prehistoric eras to which our species is preadapted). He suggests that pathology occurs if these natural fears are either too easily aroused or are totally absent.

Bowlby frames his ideas in systems theory terms: Every individual develops a set of working models of the world that color his perceptions, guide his forecasts of the future, and influence his plans. Bowlby agrees that psychoanalytic observations provide evidence that individuals develop multiple models of self and others and that influential working models may be unconscious (i.e., there is a dynamic unconscious). He also agrees that in psychoanalytic treatment the perceptions and forecasts about the analyst (transference) provide a particularly valuable source of information about the individual's dominant model.

Anxiety is considered by Bowlby to be one component of a more general reaction that he labels "fear." Fear is defined behaviorally and consists of withdrawal, avoidance and escape or clinging to an object of attachment. Using a military analogy, he suggests that threats "at the front" produce an "alarm" reaction characterized by avoidance. Threats "to the base" lead to "anxiety" that is characterized by attempts to cling to safety (attachment figures). Fearful behavior is triggered by cues of danger. Infants react to "natural" cues (being alone, being in the dark, strangers, heights, and sudden noises); in adults, assessment of danger continues to be based on these natural cues, but this is modulated by cultural and learned cues. Fear is enhanced when cues are present in combination and is diminished in the presence of an attachment figure.

Bowlby views simple phobia to be a disorder of the alarm reaction to natural cues. Symbolic thinking has little or no role in the genesis of a phobia. In anxiety disorders and "pseudophobia" (his term for "agoraphobia") what is feared is the absence of an attachment figure, a secure base. Bowlby suggests that agoraphobia is almost always associated with diffuse personality disturbance and is better conceptualized as a separation anxiety disturbance than as a phobia. In general, psychoanalytic writers have emphasized the characterologic, as well as the symptomatic components of the agoraphobic syndrome.

Bowlby's notion of separation or neurotic anxiety (also called overdependence) is that it results from the real life experience of unavailable or unresponsive caretakers. Disciplinary threats to abandon a child and/or frequent parental quarrels are seen as common antecedents to insecure attachment. This would suggest research strategies designed to study the relationship between parental patterns of child rearing and subsequent susceptibility to anxiety. Many traditional psychoanalysts criticize Bowlby's emphasis on the external reality of the child's experience to the exclusion of the internal representations constructed by the child. Similarly, the importance of the child's constitutionally determined responses in shaping parental behavior is relatively neglected.

Child Development

One of the major contributions of psychoanalysis has been its stimulation of interest in the developmental psychology of infants and young children. Psychoanalytic developmental theory has suggested hypotheses to be tested and has resulted in research strategies based on observation of infants and children, alone and in interaction with important caretakers. Freud's first developmental hypotheses focused on the epigenesis of the psychosexual stages. His next developmental model, described in detail above, focused on the sequence of danger situations, and it is this later model that is especially pertinent to the study of anxiety disorders.

A number of researchers (Ainsworth & Bell, 1970; Benjamin, 1961, 1963, 1965; Bowlby, 1973; Emde, 1980; Lewis & Brooks, 1974; Scarr & Salapetek, 1970; Shapiro & Stern, 1980; Spitz, 1950; Sroufe, 1977; Stern, 1974) have provided a fairly comprehensive description of the evolution of infantile and childhood fears, their chronology and content. As researchers have focused specific attention on infant behavior, they have found that complex interactions of maturational, social, and emotional systems influence human development. The capacity for fearfulness is dependent on the capacity to appraise a provocative stimulus, as well as specific cognitive skills including recognition memory and the evaluation of discrepancies between past and present. The onset of fearfulness occurs in the context of simultaneous development of other behavioral systems including attachment, exploratory, and affiliative behaviors and interacts with these. The appraisal of a potential fear stimulus depends in part on the state of these behavioral systems as well as others. For example, the degree of stranger wariness depends on whether the mother is present, on the infant's mood, the familiarity of the setting, the stranger's degree of intrusiveness, and the limitations of the infant's options.

Although studies of preverbal children have been pioneered by psychoanalytically trained observers, they have also been criticized by other psychoanalysts, who claim that such observational methods are inherently incapable of determining the infant's subjective mental experience. In addition, little is known of the later vicissitudes of early fearful behavior, especially as these relate to the development of adult anxiety disorders. Gittelman (this volume) reviews the evidence for a relationship between childhood separation disorder and adult agoraphobia. She, too, stresses the need for longitudinal studies. The available evidence suggests that the fate of fearfulness depends upon constitutional factors in interaction with the infant's other developing biological and behavioral systems and the environment. There is hope that we may ultimately be able to tease apart the variables and interactions that predispose to adult pathology. Perhaps the greatest value of infant fear studies is that they serve as a model for conceptualization of the dynamic interaction among various psychological, maturational, and environmental factors which may codetermine the later vulnerability to anxiety disorders. Psychoanalytic understanding of the developmental origins of anxiety argues for the value of a developmental psychodynamic approach in studying the anxiety disorders.

Klein's Critique

We will discuss briefly Klein's (1981) critique of the psychodynamic and learning theory models of anxiety. Klein regards psychodynamic and learning theories as variants on a similar theme, "in their common emphasis on the importance of contiguity conditioning, which leads to anxiety as a signal of anticipated traumatic states" (p. 244). Klein's major criticism of both theories is their inability to explain the distinction he has proposed between panic and general anxiety disorders. He believes that this distinction is better explained on neurophysiological and ethologic grounds and suggests that panic disorder results from dysfunction in the CNS regulation of separation anxiety, a widely distributed trait of obvious survival value.

Klein's argument suffers from an unnecessary biological reductionism. In his model, the panic attack first occurs "spontaneously"[2] and then becomes the

---

*In reply to this section of Chapter 32, Dr. Klein stated that "Webster defines spontaneous as proceeding from natural feeling or native tendency without external constraint'. Spontaneous does not mean acausal." Also he fails to see where he has "underestimated the possibility of psychological predisposition. This certainly would be inconsistent with my data on antecedent separation anxiety.

conditioned stimulus for the development of anticipatory anxiety. It is not at all clear why Klein insists on calling the original attack "spontaneous" or why he underestimates the possibility of psychological predisposition to the disorder. His own data reveal that "50% of patients showed distinct evidence of separation anxiety in childhood, occurring well before the onset of agoraphobia" and "the initial panic episode has often been preceded by significant object loss" (1981, p. 245). Raskin, Pecks, Dickman, and Pinsker (1982) report similar findings in an independent sample of panic and generalized anxiety disorder patients. It seems plausible that real or symbolic experiences of separation anxiety might serve as triggers of panic attacks. There is an inconsistency in Klein's assumptions that (1) separation anxiety regulation is dysfunctional in panic disorder patients, but that (2) attacks are spontaneous and more or less independent of psychological triggers. It seems far more likely that psychologically mediated concerns about separation precede and increase vulnerability to panic attacks, at least in some patients. Furthermore, the postulation of a "spontaneous" behavioral response is inconsistent with the proximal releasing stimuli that are consistently uncovered in ethological studies.

It seems clear that the modifying term "spontaneous" for describing panic attacks is a cause for confusion in this regard and is best dropped in favor of the term "unpredictable" or perhaps "intermittent." By "spontaneous," Klein meant to distinguish panic disorder from the panic attacks occasioned by stereotyped repetitive triggers in the simple and social phobias. Unfortunately one possible connotation of "spontaneous" has been that these attacks are free of psychological influence.

In the clinical experience of most dynamic psychiatrists it is usually possible to find specific psychologic antecedents to a panic attack if one questions the patient carefully and associatively. In an interesting exchange with Nemiah (1981), Klein correctly points out that the specific psychological hypotheses about etiology that are developed by the patient and/or therapist may in fact be rationalizations concocted after the fact. This is no doubt sometimes true of conscious mental explanations, but hardly sufficient grounds for ignoring all subjective data. The question is not answered on the basis of current evidence and must be kept open pending further (admittedly difficult) research. Psychodynamic and learning theory hypotheses complement Klein's neurophysiological and ethological speculations in ways that seem quite natural and plausible. It is no surprise that biological answers are most effective in answering Klein's basic question ("Why do antidepressants work for panic disorder and not for other forms of anxiety?"), since the question itself arises from a biological finding. Nonetheless, man is a symbol-making and symbol-responding animal whose

---

The authors have misunderstood "spontaneous" as denying possible psychologically manifest antecedents."

temptations and fears are often experienced on an unconscious level. Psycho-dynamically oriented therapists regularly find that their panic disorder patients associate to fears of separation, punishment, and guilt in a way that suggests that these fears help to precipitate episodes. One is not compelled to accept this uncontrolled clinical observation but one should also be cautious in discarding it, especially when there is no contradictory evidence.

Summary: A Modern Psychoanalytic View

A modern psychodynamic theory of anxiety recognizes that the physiology of the emotional state is part of the biologic capacity of the organism and not amenable to psychoanalytic inquiry. Freud explained anxiety in terms of over-stimulation; Bowlby as an innate response to the disruption of attachment behavior, and psychoanalysts today await its further elucidation with eager interest, but they do not anticipate that psychoanalytic data will shed more light on the issue. Anxiety appears throughout the life cycle, originally as a diffuse and at times overwhelming response to situations which, seen from an adult perspective, involve threats to the safety and comfort of the child as well as disruptions of the biologically expectable environment essential for survival and growth (including the availability of the caretaker). This kind of global panic generally disappears early in development, to be replaced by more focused and specific responses to various situations that can be explained as learned derivatives of the earlier, innate triggers.

Separation, castration, and parental disapproval are important themes of these more specific responses, but there are undoubtedly others, and they reflect social, cultural, and accidental variation as well as species-wide themes. The boundary between innate and learned stimuli is unclear, but the relative prominence of the latter increases rapidly with development. As a result, anxiety in the adult is virtually always linked to mental imagery of frightening situations, usually unconscious but nonetheless powerful in shaping behavior. This anxiety can serve as a signal triggering one of a number of patterns of response, all of which involve strategies for anxiety reduction by diminishing the power of the frightening, unconscious fantasy. When this fantasy is activated by an unconscious wish, the strategy also involves arranging some partial or symbolic gratification of the wish. The behaviors that result include a variety of symptoms and personality traits, some of which may themselves include diffuse or episodic anxiety as a component. This symptomatic (as opposed to signal) anxiety often has the same psychodynamic structure as other symptoms; that is, the anxiety can be understood not only as the subjective awareness of an emotional state, but also as a symbolic representation of both a forbidden unconscious wish and a related unconscious fantasy of danger. The psychoanalytic exploration of symptomatic anxiety thus involves identifying the danger, the wish, the pattern of defense used in constructing the symptom, and the developmental history of each of these. These are frequently not apparent in the manifest conscious phenomenology of anxiety, just as the unconscious themes in dreams, or in conversion of obsessional symptoms may be difficult to discover. The defensive response to signal anxiety can involve the formation of almost any psychiatric symptom, but there is a special link between anxiety and phobic syndromes because of the prominence of symptomatic anxiety in phobias.

In one sense, all pathologic anxiety involves the persistence or reactivation of infantile modes of psychological functioning, in which anxiety is disruptive or even paralyzing, and functions adaptively only if it elicits help from others or contributes to avoidance of real dangers. (This is in contrast to the more mature signal function of anxiety, which may be inferred as a component of almost any psychopathology, but is not itself pathologic and from the point of view of descriptive phenomenologic psychiatry is not even anxiety.) The interpersonal help eliciting aspect of pathologic neurotic anxiety is an important theme in the therapeutic transference relationships of patients with anxiety disorders, and they are often desirous of (and therefore open to) psychotherapeutic interventions as a result. In fact, this theme of their character structure is frequently more prominent than the symptomatic anxiety itself in the course of their treatment.

IMPLICATIONS FOR CLASSIFICATION

During his career as a clinical and research neurologist, Freud had been very interested in classification, particularly of cerebral palsy and the aphasias. Soon after he turned his attention to psychiatry, he suggested a sweeping change in the psychiatric nosology of the day—that "neurasthenia" be subdivided into a number of different syndromes (1894b). For one of these he suggested the term "anxiety neurosis" and set out to demonstrate that "the symptoms of this syndrome are clinically much more closely related to one another than to those of genuine neurasthenia (that is, they frequently appear together and they replace one another in the course of the illness); and both the aetiology and the mechanism of this neurosis are fundamentally different from the aetiology and mechanism of genuine neurasthenia" (p. 91).

Freud's description of anxiety neurosis is elegant, complete, and quite modern. One part of the syndrome is the anxiety attack (Freud includes in his description 10 of the 12 symptoms listed in the *DSM-III* diagnostic criteria for panic disorder). Freud also included within the syndrome of anxiety neurosis all of the diagnostic criteria for generalized anxiety disorder now listed in *DSM-III*, and he made a point of differentiating between simple phobias and agoraphobia. He stated (1894b) that "we frequently find that this phobia is based on an attack of vertigo that has preceded it; but I do not think that one can postulate such an attack in every case" (p. 96). Freud also discussed the relation of anxiety to obsessional neurosis.

Thus we see that Freud's earliest effort at psychiatric classification was the attempt to differentiate between "actual" neuroses (i.e., anxiety, neurasthenia) caused by a direct biological (sexual) etiology and psychoneuroses (hysterical, compulsive) caused by a psychological (although also sexual) etiology. He partially abandoned this distinction as have most contemporary analysts (Brenner, 1953; Stewart, 1967) who now regard all neuroses as having a psychological (although perhaps also biological) etiology.

There is no inherent reason within the psychodynamic conception of anxiety to expect a qualitative differentiation to exist between panic and generalized anxiety disorders, a distinction asserted by *DSM-III*. Most analysts have assumed that panic and anxiety are on a severity continuum. If the recently proposed differentiation of the two disorders is confirmed by additional research, it will be interesting to determine the extent to which it is based primarily on biological vulnerabilities or whether psychological variables are also involved. Recent studies (Hoehn-Saric, 1981, 1982) have suggested that anxiety and panic disorder patients are equivalent in measures of the psychic symptoms of anxiety, personality, social adjustment, and childhood history and that some patients who were first diagnosed as meeting criteria for one disorder later crossed over to the other and vice versa. The only measures that distinguished the two patient groups were the somatic symptoms of anxiety, specifically the cardiovascular and respiratory symptoms. This suggests that the presence or absence of panic attacks in anxious patients might occur more on the basis of predisposing autonomic lability rather than because of a particular psychological configuration. In Raskin et al. (1982), the only developmental variables that were present significantly more often in patients meeting criteria for panic disorders than in those with general anxiety disorders were a grossly disturbed childhood environment and a proneness for depression. The available studies are too few in number and too primitive in their psychological instrumentation to yield firm conclusions differentiating the psychological background of patients with panic and generalized anxiety disorder.

The Anxiety Disorder section of *DSM-III* comprises nine diagnostic categories. The introduction to the section suggests that the criteria used in selecting this group of syndromes as anxiety disorders (and presumably in excluding others) were that anxiety be the predominant symptom or that it be experienced if the individual attempts to master another symptom (as by confronting a phobic situation or resisting a compulsion). It is clear, however, that this definition is so broad that it might logically cover a variety of closely related disorders now listed in *DSM-III* in the Somatoform, Dissociative, Psychosexual, Impulse, Substance Abuse, and Personality sections. *DSM-III* differs from *DSM-II* specifically in its placement of conversion, dissociative, and hypochondriacal disorders under categories separate from the anxiety disorders and generally in its tendency to split rather than lump.

Given our current lack of knowledge about underlying mechanisms, differences in preference between "lumpers" and "splitters" probably reflect individual cognitive style and cannot yet be settled by scientific data. It should be noted, however, that the psychodynamic model does offer what is probably the simplest and most appealing explanation of the relationship between anxiety disorder and each of its close cousins—the phobic, compulsive, conversion, and (perhaps) dissociative disorders. In the psychodynamic model, phobias, compulsions, and conversions are understood to result from the different unconscious defensive operations that respond to signal anxiety. Direct experience of conscious anxiety is thereby avoided. This is in contrast to the learning theory model, which explains the development of the anxiety-ameliorating symptoms (phobias, compulsions, and conversions) on the basis of contiguity conditioning. The psychodynamic model differs from the one based on learning theory in postulating a separate developmental line of defenses importantly based on the maturation of constitutional predispositions. There is as yet no convincing biological explanation of the close relationship between anxiety and possibly related syndromes. We are hard put to understand how "stepping on a crack" and there "breaking mother's back" might cause anxiety without invoking psychological models. The psychodynamic model of anxiety as a signal triggering various defenses that become manifest in symptom formation is still the most comprehensive and parsimonious of the hypotheses about the generation of anxiety-related symptoms and is complementary, not competitive, with available learning, biological, and ethological models.

Among the conditions listed in the Anxiety Disorder section of *DSM-III*, post-traumatic stress disorder (PTSD) best fits Freud's early model of anxiety as a discharge of excessive excitations experienced in a traumatic situation. The *DSM-III* definition of PTSD requires that it follow a "psychologically traumatic event that is generally outside the range of usual human experience" with a stressor that "would evoke significant symptoms of distress in most people" (1980, p. 236). The symptom pattern of intrusive thoughts, emotional numbing, and anxiety is quite distinctive and, in fact, premorbid differences among patients often seemed dwarfed by the overwhelming impact of the traumatic event. Some analysts (Furst, 1967) have regarded traumatic neurosis as a prototype and proof of Freud's economic hypothesis about traumatic stimulation and the resulting collapse of the stimulus barrier. More recently, however, the economic theory has found less favor among psychoanalysts even in regard to this disorder, and the focus of inquiry has shifted to the psychological meaning to the individual of the traumatic event (Brenner, 1953; Grinker & Spiegel, 1945; Horowitz, 1976).

The differential therapeutic response to various classes of psychotropic medication has been suggested as a method of teasing apart different diagnostic categories of anxiety disorders (Klein, 1981). Theoretically, at least, the differential response to various classes of psychotherapeutic treatment (e.g., psychodynamic versus behavioral) might be used in a similar way to sharpen diagnostic categories. For example, differential response to treatment might be used to discriminate between developmentally determined castration anxiety and situational performance anxiety in cases of impotence. Differential results could occur only if the various treatments have sufficiently strong specific and different effects. Available research indicates that psychotherapy is significantly more effective than no treatment, but there are no convincing data that support specific and differential effect of different psychotherapies on specific disorders (Sloane, Staples, Cristol, Yorkston, & Whipple 1975; Smith, Glass, & Miller, 1980). It is not clear whether the inability to demonstrate specific effects reflects the shortcomings of available methodologies or the greater power of nonspecific interpersonal effects shared by all psychotherapies. This fundamental question must be resolved before differential response to different psychotherapies will be useful as a tool of diagnostic dissection.

RESEARCH IMPLICATIONS

There is voluminous literature discussing the question of whether psychoanalysis is a science and/or amenable to systematic investigation by behavioral science methods, and there are frequent suggestions that psychoanalytic hypotheses be operationalized in ways that can be more easily tested. Over the years a fairly large body of systematic studies testing very specific, and often not very interesting, psychodynamic hypotheses has accumulated. Much of this work consists of dissertations performed by psychology doctoral candidates using dream or Rorschach material gathered from college student volunteers. The most popular topics for clinical investigation in psychoanalysis have been the process and outcome of treatment, personality disorders, homosexuality, paranoia, and schizophrenia, but there has been a surprising dearth of studies on anxiety disorders.

The difficulties in performing research testing psychodynamic hypotheses are well known (Fisher & Greenberg, 1977; Hook, 1959; Wallerstein & Sampson, 1971) and include:

1. Instrument problems resulting from the difficulty encountered in operationalizing concepts about subtle and inferential unconscious mental functioning; these often involve a series of hypothesized intervening transformations before becoming manifest in overt behavior:
2. The large number of interacting variables that confound the measurement of the impact of any one variable in isolation;
3. The very nature of the variables, which are difficult or impossible to control;
4. The importance of specific fantasies in individual patients and the consequent difficulty in aggregating data across patients;

5. The profession of psychoanalysis has developed outside of the academic tradition; most psychoanalysts neither have acquired nor value the methodologic skills esential for research advance.

Freud's method of scientific investigation was naturalistic and inductive. He formulated hypotheses that were derived from clinical observation and then validated them with further observations. His arguments rested on the weight of the evidence rather than on experimental data gathered under carefully controlled conditions. The epistemological weaknesses of this approach are well known. However, we should not altogether ignore the importance of clinical observations even if they are uncontrolled. The concept of anxiety as a signal of unconscious dangers stimulated by the press of unconscious wishes has informed much of the clinical work with neurotic patients in this century. Its clinical value has been confirmed over and over again and by now it has achieved the status of generally accepted common sense, not only for psychiatrists but also for the man on the street. This does not necessarily mean that the psychodynamic model of anxiety is valid and this form of confirmation does not replace more systematically gathered empirical evidence, but the model cannot be discounted lightly without major efforts at validating it.

There are several reasons for optimism that the testing of psychodynamic hypotheses will soon make a much greater contribution than has heretofore been the case. First we must realize that behavioral science research of all types has made giant strides in just the past two decades. Although psychoanalysis has not been in the forefront of this movement, a 20-year lag is excusable in view of the complexity of its problems. The current availability of increasingly powerful multivariate statistical methods and computers potentially render complicated questions more amenable to study. Moreover advances in other disciplines help to clarify which psychodynamic questions are most important.

Summary of Psychoanalytic Research

There have been numerous psychodynamic studies relating anxiety to oral, anal, and genital levels of psychosexual development and their associated personality types. Specific mothering styles have been associated with the development of individuals with the oral personality traits of anxiety and separation difficulties (Finney, 1961; Goldman-Eisler, 1951; Whiting & Child, 1953). In a longitudinal study, Kagan and Moss (1960) demonstrated that oral traits (dependency, passivity, and separation anxiety) correlate with one another and persist from birth to adulthood, especially in females. In attempts to distinguish oral and anal anxiety, Rapaport (1963) and Sarnoff and Zimbardo (1961) found that oral characters chose to affiliate when faced with an oral stress and that anal characters chose to be alone when faced with a situation stressful to an anal character. Rosenwald (1972) found that the degree to which individuals expressed anxiety about anal matters predicted their obstinacy and need to arrange piles of magazines. Many other studies have confirmed intercorrelations of aspects of the oral and anal personality and that predictions about behavior can be made based on this level of diagnosis (Lazare, Klerman, & Armor, 1966).

Castration anxiety has been investigated in a number of studies measuring whether men are more fearful of bodily injury than are women (Blum, 1949; Gottschalk, Gleser, & Springer, 1963; Pitcher & Prelinger, 1963; and many others). Findings have been consistently in the expected direction in studies of different age groups and using different methods of measurement (including projective tests, manifest content of dreams, and verbal samples). Moreover, several other studies (Sarnoff & Corwin, 1959) indicate that castration anxiety in males is increased in response to sexually exciting stimulation. Other studies have confirmed Freud's view that anxiety about loss of love is more common in females (Bradford, 1968; Gleser, Gottschalk, & Springer, 1961; Manosevitz & Lanyon, 1965). There is also evidence that castration anxiety is especially prominent in homosexual males (Bieber et al., 1962; Schwartz, 1955).

The literature on oral, anal, and genital fears and character traits has been reviewed most thoroughly by Fisher and Greenberg (1978). Although they found that many of Freud's hypotheses have yet to be tested adequately, and that some results contradict his view of the oedipal situation, most of the available experimental and observational evidence confirms Freud's observations about psychosexual stages of development and their associated fears and demonstrates the internal consistency of the model. Although the specific results of the available studies have contributed little to our understanding of anxiety, they do demonstrate the potential of the research strategy and the feasibility of operationalizing and testing psychodynamic hypotheses and their relationship to clinical phenomena.

Unfortunately, very little systematic research has been performed relating psychodynamic theory to manifestations of the psychopathology of anxiety disorders and their treatment. A notable exception is the psychodynamically informed work of Horowitz (1976) on the stress response syndromes. Additional investigation of the other anxiety syndromes is in order. We will discuss some areas in which improvements in psychodynamic research methodology may contribute to the study of anxiety disorders.

Prospects for Psychodynamic Research

Operationally defining psychodynamic terms and demonstrating their reliable use is a prerequisite to psychodynamic contributions to research on anxiety. Unfortunately, very few psychodynamic instruments are available. The revolution in psychometric technology achieved during the past two decades has had a minimal impact on psychodynamic research methods. There are now many instruments to rate the symptoms, thoughts, and behaviors of anxiety, but none to assess whether and which unconscious conflicts are involved in its generation.

Nonetheless, there is cause for optimism. The advances in our research methodology in the assessment of the psychotherapy process and outcome demonstrate the possibility of developing reliable instruments. An exciting development is the creation of rating scales for psychodynamic change by Malan (1963, 1976) and by Kaltreider, Dewitt, Weiss and Horowitz (1981). Moreover, Luborsky's "Core Conflictual Relationship Theme" (1977) method of scoring psychotherapy sessions is a very promising, if largely untested way of systematically identifying and measuring recurrent conflictual themes (including unconscious dangers). High reliability has been achieved by psychodynamic raters assessing the conflictual meaning of patient productions in several situations (e.g., a psychotherapy session or Rorschach test). These methods have not yet been used for patients with anxiety disorders, but potentially could be.

It is also important to determine whether psychodynamically meaningful information can be gathered with the much more convenient and structured method of patient self-report. There is still controversy regarding the validity of self-report measures. Many analysts would deny this possibility out of hand and some would go so far as to argue that uncontaminated unconscious material can be generated only in the setting of a full-fledged psychoanalysis (Schafer, 1973). They would assume that conscious self-report is so greatly influenced by defense and disguise that it is an invalid gauge of unconscious process. In this model, the highly specialized tools of the psychoanalytic method of observation are essential in order to discover the unconscious themes that form the substrate of the patient's self-report.

A more recent trend of opinion within psychoanalysis encourages greater optimism about the use of self-report as a source of data about unconscious process. Ego psychology and structural theory have shifted attention from exclusive focus on the deepest unconscious derivatives of infantile drives to much more available, although still unconscious, aspects of ego functioning. As Fisher and Greenberg (1977) conclude, "There is probably a continuum of degrees to which an individual's direct reports about himself in a questionnaire or brief interview situation are relevant to Freud's constructs. There may be a great deal more pertinent information in presumably 'surface' material than has been suspected or acknowledged. . . . The exploration of this matter should have priority" (p. 399). Empirical study of this question should not be difficult. Responses to self-report instruments can be correlated with data that have been obtained in unstructured situations and rated for unconscious content by psychodynamic experts. Success of this method would also depend on establishing reliability among the raters.

A second methodological question arises in relation to psychotherapy outcome studies: Should measures of psychodynamic conflict be based on individualized goal assessment (as in Malan's work, 1963, 1976) or should they follow the more traditional method of universal measures that are generalized across patients (as in Kaltreider, et al., 1981)?

Personality functioning is an additional area of instrument development that has great importance for anxiety research. Available studies of anxiety disorders have focused almost exclusively on the Axis I diagnoses and have tended to ignore the patient's underlying personality functioning. This omission may limit understanding of the etiology of anxiety disorders, of their effect on personality functioning, and of the variability of treatment responses. Unfortunately, there are no satisfactory measures of personality functioning in our current repertoire of instruments. Personality instruments are difficult to develop and tend to be contaminated greatly by the patient's current state. However, personality diagnosis is important and work must be continued despite its difficulties. Certainly the relationship between Axis I and Axis II has been much better studied for affective than for anxiety disorders, although it is likely to be equally important in both conditions. The current active work at the interface between Axis I and II for depression may serve as a model for similar efforts with the anxiety disorders.

Methdological Issues

The availability of psychodynamically informed instruments of the kind discussed above would allow for greater comprehensiveness of patient characterization than is currently possible. This, in turn, could increase the specificity of selection and homogeneity of patient samples and also permit comparative treatment studies of great power. The population of patients who satisfy the set of criteria for any given *DSM-III* anxiety disorder are heterogeneous in regard to other variables that are not included within that criteria set, and these variables may be important in determining treatment response. Attention to psychodynamic measures may thus improve both the specificity of classification of anxiety disorders and the analysis of variability in treatment outcome. The aim is eventually to predict which patients are most likely to respond to pharmacological, behavioral, or psychodynamic interventions or to their sequential or concurrent combinations. As mentioned above, response to specific psychotherapeutic treatment interventions may also be useful in dissecting differences in patient characteristics.

Psychodynamic research must become more clinically relevant and clinically based than heretofore has been the case. Studies of the internal consistency of psychoanalytic theory are of continued interest but will not greatly increase our understanding of the etiology, pathogenesis, classification, and treatment of anxiety disorders. A possible strategy emerges from the realization that psychoanalysis is valuable as a psychological theory but is incomplete in its biological, learning theory, and ethological underpinnings. Studies of anxiety disorder should seek to define the boundaries and exploit the interactions among psychological, biological, learning, and ethological approaches.

Several avenues for the study of the interface between the psychology and biology of anxiety disorders have been opened by the availability of new and convenient methods of monitoring the physiologic correlates of anxiety. Ambulatory ECG/BP monitors allow for more or less continuous 24-hour recordings so that one can study the physiological events that precede and comprise the panic attack. Correlations may then be made with psychological experiences as recorded in concurrent diaries. This may help to answer the question of whether panic attacks are "spontaneous" or whether they have predictable psychological and/or physiological precipitants. It should also be possible to develop psychological stress tests specific to different types of unconscious danger situations and to determine a given patient's pattern of psychological and physiological response following psychodynamic stressors. It will also be interesting to learn if psychological treatments are able to reverse the vulnerability to lactate infusion in panic disorder patients in a manner comparable to that achieved by antipanic medication.

The interaction between psychodynamic and learning conceptions has received considerable attention but little systematic research. Perhaps the most interesting lead for future investigation is the use of behavior therapy methods to desensitize fears of unconscious danger situations assessed with psychodynamic methods (Feather & Rhoads, 1972). In this regard, Kamil (1970) found that snake phobics had significantly decreased castration anxiety as measured by projective tests after undergoing systematic desensitization.

The interface between psychodynamics and infant and child observation has already been particularly enriching in both directions. Any comprehensive program of research into anxiety disorders must include the study of precursors in infancy and childhood. One strategy would be to compare infants and children at high risk for anxiety disorders with normal controls to determine the onset of abnormalities in fear behaviors. Only through longitudinal study will it be possible to correlate the experiences of danger situations in children with anxiety disorders in adults. One possible design would be to determine the differential effects of major surgery performed on children at high versus low risk for castration anxiety when the surgery occurs during the oedipal versus latency periods. The prediction would be that high-risk castration anxiety patients would be particularly prone to anxiety disorders if their surgery occurs during the oedipal period rather than later during latency. Similarly it might be possible to test the impact of separation at different ages on high- and low-risk populations.

It remains to be seen whether the vicissitudes of danger situations experienced early in life powerfully predict the later occurrence of anxiety disorders. However, even if the incidence of anxiety disorder turns out to be independent of such precursors, it is still conceivable that the mental content of the anxiety disorder will be shaped by the particular coloring of that individual's profile of greatest dreads.

We have offered the above examples of possible research approaches not because of any great confidence that any one or all of them will provide the best avenue for study, but rather to illustrate the possibility of developing scientifically sound and interesting research strategies that are sensitive to psychodynamic concepts and that can enrich our understanding of anxiety and its related clinical syndromes. Psychodynamic concepts may be difficult to formulate and study, but any research effort that ignores them is likely to be incomplete.

CONCLUSION

As a science matures and becomes increasingly differentiated, earlier efforts at explanation often seem excessively broad in scope and superficial in depth. Freud made an ambitious attempt to develop a comprehensive model of anxiety and he allowed himself wide latitude in biological, psychological, evolutionary, and developmental-learning theory speculation in order to do so. This style of multipurpose theory building was very much in the tradition of central European science at the turn of the century, but it seems somewhat out of place today.

The methods of observation associated with psychoanalysis provide little opportunity for generating or testing neurobiological hypotheses and have only a limited role in generating new models in ethology or learning theory. Psychodynamic methods of observation do provide a remarkably rich opportunity for studying the world of subjective experience: thoughts, feelings, motivations, and their various relationships. This opportunity has not yet been fully exploited and there are many methodologic obstacles that have not been resolved. Nonetheless, mental experience is central to the phenomena of anxiety and related states, and the psychological aspects of psychoanalytic thinking have a unique contribution to make to their scientific study.

Two conclusions emerge: (1) No single model (biologic, psychologic, evolutionary, or learning theory) is likely to explain everything about anxiety disorders. A complete theory will require contributions from each. (2) Psychoanalysis does not provide a general psychological theory or a total model of anxiety. It does provide a model for understanding and a strategy for investigating the thoughts and feelings that are associated with various types of anxiety, their developmental origins, their impact on adaptive functioning, and in some situations psychological intervention that can be effective in treatment.

33 Anxious States of Mind Induced by Stress

Mardi J. Horowitz, M.D.
University of California

This paper has two intents: (1) to provide this volume with a perspective on how traumatic life events may play a role in causing anxious states of mind and (2) to examine unconscious thinking as an intervening variable that may contribute to the formation of anxiety symptoms. It is a theoretical essay that follows only a single thread, and does not examine the whole fabric. That thread begins at the surface by viewing anxiety symptoms as embedded in states of mind and ends by considering multiple self-concepts of the individual as important unconscious determinants of such states. The history of psychoanalytic theories of anxiety has been reviewed by Michels, Frances, and Shear (this volume). While this essay in contemporary information processing language articulates to that history, specific references will not be repeated.

ANXIOUS AND FEARFUL STATES OF MIND

Anxiety symptoms include conceptualized threats such as expectant dread of suddenly dying, of finding oneself alone and fatally vulnerable, of crazily acting out of control in the company of others. Anxiety symptoms also consist of sensed physiological changes such as respiratory smothering sensations, racing heart, dizziness, sweating, or faintness. Other specific but less severe symptoms are: acting jittery, having startle reactions, and being abrupt with others. A single symptom such as tension may be found to cohere with other symptoms and experiences. This coherence in time of onset and offset could be called a state of mind. The defining characteristics of the Anxiety Disorders in the 3rd revision of the Diagnostic and Statistical Manual (APA, 1980) DSM–III are not only

619

symptoms but states of mind in relation to volitional control, duration, and external events or environmental contexts.

If descriptions of the external environment and events are omitted, as well as how these events are rationally or irrationally interpreted by the subject of an experience, one finds that anxiety and fear states have similar descriptions. This has long been noted by clinicians. Table 33.1 provides a list of some anxious and fearful states of mind commonly observed in clinical practice. The distinction between fear and anxiety is, in clinical practice, the difference found in an analysis of the articulation of the experience and behavior of a person to current external events and environmental conditions. Unlike present or anticipatory fear, anxiety appears to be a false alarm. When one includes internal conscious events and unconscious propositions as part of the internal environment then anxious states of mind are like anticipatory or emergency alarms that are not necessarily "false," although they may be based upon irrational beliefs.

REPERTOIRES OF STATES

Each individual has a repertoire of states of mind that he has experienced before and that are coded into some type of memory. Schemata for these states of mind are derived from repertoires of self-concepts, object concepts, and beliefs about relationships that can be activated. It will be easier for a person to repeat a state of mind experienced previously than to experience a novel state of mind for the first time because it is easier to reactivate schemata in a symbolic complex than it is to form them for the first time.

Suppose an individual has experienced a panic-stricken state of mind earlier in developmental history as a consequence of a powerful threat of loss or injury. New events that also threaten loss or injury are likely to lead to a panic state similar to that experienced in the past. Once this person has had a panic state caused by a traumatic experience, he will be rendered more vulnerable to a repetition of a panic state when exposed to similar trauma (Freud, 1926). All things being equal, this person is more likely to experience a panic state when minimally or moderately exposed to threat than one who had not had that experience in the past.

Many individuals enter adulthood with a firm belief in their personal exemption from threats of harm, illness or death. Their first major trauma may be when they are exposed to death, separation, assault, rape, accident, experience in combat, or some catastrophic event. Recognition of the personal reality of such events may evoke a novel fear state. This comparatively new state of fear is then likely to be repeated in the presence of cues of which neither the patient nor therapist may be aware.

The prior experience of anxious states of mind is not always a one way affair: the more you are anxious, the more anxious you get. There are also coping

TABLE 33.1
Some Anxious or Fearful States of Mind

State Labels	State Descriptions
1. Distraught panic	Bodily feeling of weak knees, lump in throat, dry mouth, sweaty, heart pounding or palpitating, flutters or tingles, feeling like collapsing, faintness, unable to focus eyes, with ideas of immediately impending harm to self or others, and feelings of terror or dread.
2. Excited disorganized	Feeling worried about having made or being about to make wrong decisions, trouble concentrating, jumbled images, restless body.
3. Apprehensive vigilance	Racing thoughts, tense, too alert to outside stimuli, unable to relax, ties or twitches, sense of urgency or impatience, pressured.
4. Worried mood	Preoccupation with possible misfortunes, inability to put aside cares, fretting, nervous, pressured, tense muscles, "butterflies" in the stomach.
5. Irritable mood	Feeling others are unsympathetic, feeling unsympathetic to others, brusque, prone to be sarcastic, whiney, or rude, easily hurt by others, grudging or sullenly tense.
6. Benumbed mood	Feeling insulated, avoiding threatening ideas or actions, wanting to withdraw from people, work, or pressing concerns, rigid intellectualization, focus on peripheral details.
7. Queasy mood	Pallor or greening of complexion, slowing of heart rate, feeling nauseous and weak.

capacities developed from adversity: better the distress we know we can handle than some novel form of terror. What Lazarus (1966) calls "secondary appraisal" of personal coping capacity is an important component in the reaction to a subjective experience. A person who has been accustomed to fear states may be less surprised and worried by entry into a panic state than a person who has such emotionally intense experiences for the first time.

STRESS INDUCED ANXIETY: EVENTS AND REPETITIVE MEMORIES OF EVENTS

Stressful life events may lead to fearful and anxious states of mind. An instructive prototype for theoretical analysis of this proposition is one in which the external event starts suddenly and then is abruptly over. The internalized event does not subside rapidly. One form of repetition of anxious or fearful states of mind occurs during the intrusive phase of psychological response to stressful life events (Horowitz, 1976; Horowitz, Wilner, & Alvarez, 1979; Horowitz, Wilner, Kaltreider, & Alvarez, 1980; Zilberg, Weiss, & Horowitz, 1982). With repetition, and perhaps also by single "trial" learning, a very stressful situation can lead to a symbol structure for a new state of mind. As already mentioned, this symbol structure is then more readily reactivated than created de novo.

A traumatic event remains recorded in an active memory storage, active because it tends toward repeated representation (Broadbent, 1971, Horowitz, 1976). This memory consists of external stimuli as transformed in the process of perception and immediate appraisal (Neisser, 1967; Lazarus, 1966; Janis, 1969). Continued information processing, and the passage of time, leads to both reorganization and decay of the original active memory, and transformation of it into various systems of long term memory such as schematizations of self and the external world.

The process of transformation takes time and, until it is relatively completed, recollections of the internal and external events will tend to occur, accompanied by the emotions of these recollections. Fearful states of mind may recur as a part of directly recalling the event. Recall at different times, in different situations, and with varied internal attitudes will alter emotional responses to event-related themes. Because the external event is over, the external environment looks safe to an observer and these lingering emotional states of mind may now be labeled as anxious rather than fearful.

Trigger stimuli in the external environment promote recall of the memory of the event and so may instantiate fearful or anxious states of mind. Objects become triggers to fear because of the establishment during and after the trauma of conditioned associations of stimuli with threat. New conceptualizations also occur at the time that the trigger object or situational reminder again instigates an anxious or fearful state of mind. These new thoughts become part of a now revised thematic complex.

Clinical observations, field studies, and laboratory experiments indicate that intrusive repetitions of traumatic memories occur without external trigger stimuli as well as with them (Horowitz, 1975, 1982). These episodes require explanation in terms of *internal* trigger stimuli such as thoughts and emotions. A traumatic event may establish conditioned associations between external stimuli and internal alarm reactions (Pavlov, 1927). New associations with internal triggers may also be established. In addition to establishing conditioned associations, traumatic events effect higher order conceptual processes, ones that often gain conscious representation. That is, traumas set in motion trains of ideational and emotional responses which are not completed until the active memory of the event decays with the sheer passage of time or until the new realities are modeled as acceptable mental schemata. Until such completion of processing and revision of mental structures of meaning there is a tendency to review the memory, its internal thematic enlargement, and its implications. Because the event has serious personal implications, each contemplation is likely to arouse high emotional response and to threaten the person with a repeated entry into a fearful or anxious state of mind. Entry into such states is a source of secondary fear or anxiety, because of concerns about the intensity of displeasure, loss of volitional control, and loss of a sense of self-efficacy (Bandura, 1982; Seligman, 1975).

Anticipation of emotionally intense, negatively toned, and uncontrolled states of mind leads to anxiety or fear. This has been called "signal anxiety" (Freud, 1926). Because of such anticipations, regulatory processes are increased after the trauma in order to control excitation. These regulatory processes may lead to conditions that observers might judge to be coping, defensive, or defensive failures. These terms may be operationally defined as follows:

1. "coping" is when the person assimilates the traumatic memory and revises schemata in a tolerable manner; this may be done by assimilation and accommodation in small, one-dose-at-a-time increments.
2. "defensive" is when the person so avoids or deflects processing that perseveration of a now unrealistic self or world view interferes with adaptive functioning.
3. "defensive failure" is when, in spite of inhibitory efforts, the person is flooded and overwhelmed by memories of, fantasies about, or other reactions to the traumatic event.

Psychologically motivated defenses may fail when the neurological substrates of regulation are altered. High activity in certain neural nets may heighten impulse toward expression in relation to defensive inhibitions. Lowered activity in the higher cortical functions, presumably those necessary for differentiated psychological defenses, may lower defensive capacity and lead to higher frequency of regulatory failure. Toxins, malnutrition, or fatigue from prolonged arousal could all lead to more regulatory failures during or after highly stressful periods.

PSYCHOLOGICALLY INDUCED ANXIETY

Traumatic events may end, yet be followed by anxious states of mind. These states contain expectations of repetitions of the personal effects of the trauma. Expectation of dreaded states of mind may lead to anxious states of mind without the necessary presence of terrible external events. The fearful expectation of entering a dreaded state of mind is the condition that Freud labeled as a process called "signal anxiety" (Freud, 1926).

While unpleasant, the fearful or anxious state of mind nonetheless serves a defensive purpose in helping to prevent a yet more dreaded state of mind. For example, if a man dreads entering a rage he may reduce anger by flooding himself with fear. This is accomplished by anticipating dreadful consequences of rage or by shifting topics to a memory that evokes fear. The point is that entry into an anxious or fearful state of mind is not necessarily a regulatory failure or just a defensive failure. Such entries into anxious or fearful states may sometimes be a consequence of unconscious thought processes aimed at calling out a warning that some more threatening situation or more dreaded state of mind might occur if avoidances are not instituted. Jones (1929) indicated how fear, guilt, and hate are especially common as various reciprocally inhibiting state qualities, and used in any combination to defend one against the other. By becoming anxious one may dampen or avoid rage or guilt.

A typical trauma is an external and violent event that intrudes suddenly upon the undefended individual. The event may be as literal as an intruder into the home, bent on robbery, rape, or assault. Recognition of the presence of the intruder sets off an alarm reaction. These extremely anxious states may recur later, after the intruder is gone. Intrusive images, ideas, and feelings may also come, or threaten to come, from within. An extreme instance would be a hallucination or illusion of a "violent intruder." A less dramatic, but more frequent, psychological cause of entry into an anxious state of mind would be the intrusion of an unwanted emotional proposition.

What are threatening internal propositions? Passionate wishes reaching the level of intentions, and morbid fears reaching the level of expectancy would be prominent examples. Their contents such as the lust to possess or kill, the fear of castration, loss of love, or loss of volition control are reviewed in the chapter by Michels, Frances, and Shear (this volume). What may be added to these unconscious factors is some explanation of the threat imposed by the expectation of a regressive shift in self-organization (Jacobson, 1964, Kohut, 1971, Kernberg, 1975, Horowitz & Zilberg, 1983; Horowitz, Marmar, Krupnick et al., 1984). To continue the alarming intruder metaphor, the intruder may not be external but internal, may not be the "I" of the present moment of the subject but another "I," one usually dormant in the repertoire of the individual and threatening to emerge and take over the organization of intentions and experiences.

The "I" or "me" of this moment, as related to significant others, may be appraised as able to ward off or cope with a given untenable but passionate impulse. This conflictual, passionate impulse might not be warded off as well in states of mind organized by a different schemata such as alternate self-concepts, other role-relationship models, and different scripts and views. Suppose a passionate impulse contains the intention to do harm to someone, but it is checked by counter intentions to protect the same person from malice. The balancing of these contradictory plans may not pose a threat in one state of mind, yet the subject of such a psychic conflict may fear that he will enter another state of mind that is organized by a self-concept that will release the harmful plans into action. An anxiety state, an alarm reaction, might be aroused in anticipating that danger.

In another example, the theme might be dread of personal vulnerability to submitting to the will or authority of another. Organization of thought with a self-concept strong enough to resist submission to anyone blunts the threat. A shift in self-concept from strong to weak threatens to change the situation to a context in which the subject is helplessly and dangerously submissive. Anticipation of such a shift in self-concept would lead to an alarm reaction which, when prolonged, is experienced as an anxious state of mind.

The exit from anxious states may follow a model similar to the last example. The self-concept may shift from weak to strong leading to a restoration of calm. Self-concepts are coherent structures of psychological meaning. They are supported or undermined in terms of priority as an organizing schemata by situations, especially social supports, and by the current stability or instability of neural networks. This general systems view of transitions from anxious to calm states of mind is diagrammed in Figure 33.1 in a manner that contains psychological, neural, and social levels.

CONCEPTUAL CONTENTS IN ANXIOUS STATES OF MIND

A distinguishing characteristic of particularly "anxious" rather than "fearful" states of mind has long been regarded as the absence of sufficient conceptual basis for the sense of ominous foreboding that is consciously experienced. Yet Beck, Laude, and Bohnert (1974) reported another not uncommon clinical observation: if one inquires systematically and thoroughly there are usually consciously experienced conceptual contents of anxious states of mind. These cognitions concern incipient "traumas," such as images of an immediately impending earthquake or devastatingly shameful social gaffes.

FIG. 33.1 A model of completing a thought cycle initiated by anxiety.

Level of Theoretical Constructs	Transition Pattern	
	Fearful or Anxious State	→ Calm State
Organization of thought:		
Self-Concept:	Vulnerable and weak	Safe and strong
Concept of "it":	Dangerous and strong	Safe
Proposition:	Because it may harm me, I need help fast (e.g., assistance, real action plan or a fantasy riddance of threat)	I am ready to take on my next purpose
Organization of neural networks:	Alerts, alarms, and interrupt mechanisms "on"	Alerts, alarms, and interrupt mechanisms "off"
Social organization:	Attachments are deranged or insecure: signal for help	Attachments stable and secure: explore for opportunities

In earlier paragraphs we considered intruding stressor events in the form of external shocks and alarming internal propositions. The alarm system itself may go off falsely, in a psychological sense, because of pathogenic electrochemical triggers or anatomical dispositions. These conditions may occur with pheochromocytomas and aberrations yet to be adumbrated, such as those that might involve noradrenergic brain pathways. The results are intrusive physical sensations unmatched by objective events in the external environment.

To explain these inner sensations, higher order conceptualizations may be elaborated as causal "stories." These causal stories may be in error, as suggested by Klein (1981). That is, an individual may explain felt physiological alarm responses to himself as being due to preexistent acts or "bad thoughts" in those instances when the physiological sensations were due to neural or metabolic triggers alone. This conceptual "error" may then enter into the causal matrix because the concepts become part of the state of mind and reactions to the perceived reality. An enlarged symbol structure includes the story of explanation which, while "incorrect," now has a psychological reality in that it has become part of a complex causal matrix. The erroneous belief might have to be challenged at some point, as in a psychotherapeutic dialogue, in order to deactivate its power.

In many instances, the themes, as consciously represented during anxious states of mind, are incomplete. Additional components, such as untenable self-concepts and role-relationship models, are warded off from conscious representation. These components may be consciously represented in other states of mind. The evidence for these statements consists, in part, of consensually validated recognitions of defensive operations in subjects who have not *consciously* decided to inhibit or distort information processing on a given theme.

A CLINICAL EXAMPLE

We have provided detailed expositions of this type of evidence through intensive case-studies by multiple clinicians, working independently using the configurational analysis method for case formulations (Horowitz, 1979; Horowitz, Marmar, Krupnick, et al., 1984). From the latter reference, a tiny fragment from the case discussed in detail in Chapter 6 can provide an illustration.

Ann, a young woman in her twenties, sought psychotherapy because of a pathological grief reaction following the death of her father after a long, painful illness. Her symptoms included periods of intense anxiety with intrusive thoughts about and pining for her father, pangs of dispair for herself and impaired work functioning. In addition, she occasionally had brief periods of explosive rage and intrusive thoughts indicative of searing guilt. From this complex syndrome of anxiety, depression, and other affective symptoms it is worthwhile to examine first how she experienced "anxiety" in three states of mind, varying from under-controlled to overcontrolled.

In a relatively undercontrolled state, colored by feelings of severe anxiety and loss of connection, Ann felt a frightened yearning bordering on panic. We used this everyday terminology, *frightened yearning*, to label the state. During it she had waves of shame, weakness, pining for her father, intrusive thoughts of being too alone as well as bodily sensations of fear. Her ideas did not clearly indicate the basis for all these emotions, although they clearly connected the affective experiences to issues related to her father's death. Some ideational components were "missing."

In a more controlled state of mind, labeled as *vulnerable working*, Ann experienced her ideas as more constant with her emotional sensations. She felt tense, worried, and anxious but also felt more in command of these feelings and could more freely communicate them, although she spoke of them in a nervous, abrupt manner with a tight inflection. Ann also spoke of her anxiety after her father's death in a third, overcontrolled state of mind. In this state Ann described her symptoms as if she were talking about some absent third party. Her strong reactions to the topic of her father's death were not felt in this state, instead she spoke in a contrived, overmodulated manner.

We called this a state of *artificial engagement*. Anxiety, thus, was "expressed" in uncontrolled, controlled, and overcontrolled ways in these three states of mind. During all three of these states of mind Ann spoke of anxiety and was to various degrees not aware of some trains of thought and feeling connected thematically to her father's death. In the course of psychotherapy these warded off ideas and feelings become more clearly articulated. Even before the psycho-therapy, however, there were states of mind in which she experienced elements of the warded off ideas and the feelings related to them. In one of these states, which we labeled as *explosive rage*, Ann felt dangerously impulsive and was anxious that she might be going "crazy." She was concerned with ideas that she had been a dangerous assailant to her father, hurting him in revenge for his being a willful abandoner and failed caretaker of her. In another of these out of control, and warded off states of mind, she felt *searing guilt*, saw herself as a person who had wrongfully and perhaps devastatingly failed her father. Instead of being an adequate caretaker she had failed to prevent his death or to smooth out his terminal illness with her continued presence. She had spent time pursuing her career and now faced the punishment that she imagined she deserved for her attitude and behavior.

These themes of failed caretaking, aggression, victimization, guilt, and pun-ishment had been present before her father's death, during the terminal illness, and in the earlier developmental history of the relationship. Her father had sometimes been a beloved figure, and sometimes an inadequate caretaker. She was ambivalent: lovingly yearning yet containing a smoldering resentment at him for not always fulfilling an idealized father's role. During his long illness he had not only sometimes acted in a very self-centered way, but also had accused her for following her own career path and not attending more to him. At the same time, during his illness, she had tended at times to deny its severity, or to avoid opportunities to visit with him because of the turbulent and upsetting emotions that would result were she to acknowledge his impending death or face him in that context.

After his death there was a tendency towards trains of thought in which she would remember that she had continued her work rather than visiting him as he died, would think that she had been selfish, and would compare this memory and current self attitude with an enduring value attitude that "one ought to take care of another even at the deprivation of oneself." This theme would be conscious in the searing guilt state of mind during which there was activation of self-concepts as a failed caretaker, and a role-relationship model in which a righteously angry assailant attacked her for being an insufficiently caring, self-centered daughter. When not in the searing guilt state of mind these self-concept and role-relationship models were not principle organizers of conscious interpersonal perceptions, thought and memory.

In the rage theme she would tend to remember her father's many absences or episodes of self-centered behavior, to feel reactively that her father had deprived her, and to compare this with the enduring attitude that she as a child deserved much more from a parent. The roles of the guilt state were reversed in the explosive rage state. She viewed herself as a person seeking a justifiable redress for neglect. In this thematic framework her father's death was appraised as if it were purposive, on the grounds that parents can do whatever they want (are omnipotent).

This brief vignette illustrates the complexity of an anxious state of mind following a stressful life event: Ann's frightened yearning state, which constituted part of her chief complaints in seeking professional help. During that frightened yearning state Ann was not as fully conscious of the rage and guilt themes as she was of themes of pining and worry for the future. She warded off self-concepts as an assailant. Dwelling on the anxious and sad topic of the severed connection from her father, during the frightened yearning state, was both dealing with real concerns that required reflective working-through (as part of her grief) and defensively avoiding other dreaded themes from the negative side of her ambivalence towards her father. During the frightened yearning state, Ann tended to organize her experiences according to a positive role-relationship model in which the good father was lost to the good, loving, and now alone daughter. Stabilizing these self- and object concepts served as well to prevent entry into more dreaded states of mind, explosive rage and searing guilt, which tended to contain ideas and feelings organized according to negative views of the relationship: either the aggressive self and harmed father roles, or the failed caretaker-father and harmed self views. These latter self-concepts as damaged by or as damaging to her father were a part of the anxiety during the *frightened yearning* state just as were the more conscious lost caretaker and vulnerable self views. The emotion of anxiety in the frightened yearning state had both expressive and defensive functions. Feeling anxiety tended to reduce feeling enraged or guilty. Ann at other times also tended to undo rage inspiring ideas with guilt inspiring ones, and vice versa, in an undoing defensive maneuver. Looking only at the expressed ideas and emotions of the frightened yearning state of mind would lead to the impression that Ann suffered from sorrow plus separation anxiety. Looking at the larger picture one gathers more of an interplay between conscious and unconscious thematic contents as activated by a mourning process and regulated by unconscious inhibitions and facilitations. The felt anxiety is related to feeling alone, separated, and also related to fear of contemplation of the rage and guilt themes. For a more extended analysis of this case, in its larger complexity, the reader is referred to the previously cited reference.

SITUATIONAL TRIGGERS TO WARDED OFF THEMES

Social opportunities as well as social or physical injuries may contribute to the formation of anxious states of mind; the proximity of an attractive other person may activate sexual fantasies. If these aims lead to intentions that conflict with taboos, the "opportunity" may lead to an increased threat of an action that would then lead to severe self-reproach, social ostracism, or biological danger (physical attack by rivals or contact with infectious agents). A new social condition might create an opportunity to take a long cherished revenge. As hostile wishes reach the threshold of intentionality, the threat of regulatory failure increases, and so does the risk of guilt or shame over an attack that would be disapproved of by both the self and others. These social opportunities for release of passions are not stressors in the ordinary sense, since observers see nothing to fear. However, the opportunities may stir up dormant conflicts within the individual, and the arousal of conflict acts like an internal stressor event. That is, the intentional arousal leads to alarm, anticipatory anxiety or chronic tension depending on time factors as well as on other neural, social, and psychological features of the individual.

Those who work with animal models of what they call "anxiety" regard anxiety as an organismic error in relation to the real external environment, and assume this error, or false alarm reaction, is due to some aberration of the neurobiological substrate of fear, an alarm system (e.g., Kandel, 1983). The psychodynamic position recognizes the potential importance of such aberrations, and asserts that arousal of alarm systems may also occur as a product of assessment of threat at a higher order but nonetheless functionally unconscious level of information processing. Those who present conditioned response and social learning explanations of anxious states of mind (e.g., Foa, this volume) will find open receptivity in those who take a dynamic point of view, as long as a "both/and" explanatory model is not rejected: one that contains both lower order associative linkages and higher order, conceptualized, unconscious thinking as possible causal components.

CONCLUSION

From a psychoanalytic point of view there is, with one exception, no argument with prevailing theories that see the causation of anxious states of mind as the possible result of neural dispositions, current neural or metabolic aberrations, conditioned associations, or social shaping of response patterns. The exception is any statement that higher order thoughts and emotions, at conscious and unconscious levels, are epiphenomenal rather than part of a transactive causal matrix. This paper has described some ways in which conceptual level or "higher order," yet unconsciously proceeding thoughts and anticipated emotions may play a role in determining the onset, quality, and continuation of anxious states of mind. A stress model emphasizing both intrusive and unconscious thinking was used in order to consider as analogous both external and internal sources of threat as triggers to alarm reactions and anxious anticipations.

ACKNOWLEDGEMENTS

This paper was prepared while the author was a Fellow at the Center for Advanced Study in the Behavioral Sciences. I am grateful for financial support provided to that fellowship year by the John D. and Catherine T. MacArthur Foundation.

34 Psychoanalysis, Anxiety, and the Anxiety Disorders

Marshall Edelson
Yale University School of Medicine

Thirty or forty years ago, it would have been inconceivable for a group on the frontier of investigations of anxiety and the anxiety disorders to report their ideas and findings, as has been done here, largely without any reference to—without feeling any need even to refute—the ideas and findings of psychoanalysis, and indeed allocating a very limited amount of space to a presentation and discussion of psychodynamic theory and research. Has psychoanalysis then lost not only any intellectual commitment it may once have enjoyed but, now in competition with numerous apparent rivals, its claim as well even to the attention of the present generation of scientists? How has this happened? Have psychoanalytic hypotheses about anxiety disorders been rejected in empirical studies as less credible than rival hypotheses? Such studies are not cited here. We witness rather, I believe, the consequences, not only of sociological and cultural changes since World War II, but of a failure of the psychoanalytic community to fulfill an earlier promise. This failure is largely the result, not of an increase in the strength of putative irrational forces opposed to psychoanalysis, or of the unavailability of adequate procedures for measurement, but rather of certain attitudes toward scientific work that are representative of the psychoanalytic community. In this chapter, I spell out what I mean by this assessment, although it is possible, of course, that the diagnosis comes too late to help revive the patient.

I shall develop the following thesis. Differences in the conclusions of psychoanalysis and other disciplines (e.g., neurobiology or neuropsychology) often reflect differences in what is meant by the term "anxiety"—differences in domains chosen by each discipline for study.

The thesis can be elaborated in this way. One set of psychological events includes activities subserved or supported by cortical systems. These activities contribute to determining or processing meanings and are carried out in (1)

633

identifying or representing states of affairs, including anticipated states of affairs; (2) evaluatively assessing the meanings or significances of states of affairs, including assessing an anticipated state of affairs as dangerous (here is where psychoanalysis uses the term "anxiety"); and (3) operating upon mental representations (as defenses do) to prevent actualization of a dangerous state of affairs.

A second set of psychological events includes responses to stress that are subserved or supported by subcortical systems. Such responses to stress—involving, for example, arousal, or mobilization of physiological resources preparatory to fight or flight—may or may not occur following the processing of meanings of either anticipated or actual states of affairs. Indeed, as a final common pathway, such a stress response can be precipitated or "triggered off" by a wide variety of internal stimuli, external stimuli, and experimental probes. When an investigator studying such stress responses refers to his model of anxiety, he uses the term "anxiety" differently than does the psychoanalyst; and this difference, of course, raises questions concerning the extent to which animal models of anxiety actually model what is referred to as anxiety by psychoanalysis.

These two approaches seem complementary rather than competitive. My thesis, therefore, leads somewhat naturally to a call for a clarification of just what questions about anxiety and anxiety disorders belong in the province of psychoanalysis and what questions, perhaps suggested by psychoanalytic propositions, belong in the province of some other discipline.

Finally, I discuss the problems of carrying out research on anxiety and anxiety disorders in psychoanalysis, and conclude by making some proposals for dealing with these problems. I emphasize those proposals that are based on the importance for psychoanalysis of conceptual and methodological developments in single-subject research.

DIFFERENT MEANINGS OF "ANXIETY"

Some differences between psychoanalytic and other views about anxiety and anxiety disorders do not seem to involve the kind of competition between rival hypotheses formulated within the same frame of reference with which we are familiar in science. Instead, these differences seem to reflect different definitions of what is to be designated by the term "anxiety."

What is at issue, then, cannot be decided by simple reference to empirical facts. At issue are choices among different domains of study, different entities and different properties of these entities, different ways of cutting the phenomenal world at its joints, different conceptual proposals or inventions—in other words, different concepts of anxiety. I have considered elsewhere questions about the choice of domain, in the context of an examination of the relation between neural science and psychoanalysis (Edelson, 1984, pp. 109-120).

A psychoanalyst here will not say, "I disagree with what you say about anxiety disorders" but rather, "You are not talking about what I mean about 'anxiety' at all." Redmond, a neurobiologist, has a good sense of how problems of definition may play a role in discussions of anxiety and the anxiety disorders. A "paradigm should be judged . . . by its ability to generate testable hypotheses and to explain a large amount of data parsimoniously" (Redmond, this volume, p. 536).

Decisions about the domain to be investigated are ultimately evaluated by (1) the extent to which such decisions enhance a scientist's capacity to generate interesting and testable hypotheses; (2) the explanatory power of these hypotheses; and (3) the scientific credibility such hypotheses ultimately achieve through empirical tests of them. It is with this third criterion that psychoanalysis has had particular difficulty (Edelson, 1984).

According to psychoanalysis, anxiety is a subject's appraisal of a state of affairs as dangerous. The state of affairs is anticipated by the subject; it does not actually exist. Thus, it is imagined, not perceived, by the subject. The subject believes (not necessarily as the result of generalizing from causal connections or space-time contiguities encountered in experience) that this imagined state of affairs will become an actual state of affairs if he acts upon some impulse of his own. Further, although the subject is under internal pressure to act on this impulse, it is nevertheless possible for him to delay such action indefinitely and still survive.

Like other affects, anxiety has both a cognitive component (a subject's mental representation of a state of affairs) and an evaluative component (an appraisal of the significance by the subject of this state of affairs as, for example, threatening, thwarting, or gratifying). (An elaboration of this concept of affects may be found in Edelson, 1984, pp. 88-90.) The cognitive component is the mental representation of an anticipated (not an existent) state of affairs, which is imagined (not perceived). The evaluative component is an appraisal of the anticipated, imagined state of affairs as dangerous.

Psychoanalysis distinguishes anxiety from fear, for example, by locating the source of danger (i.e., the subject's impulse) in the intrapersonal realm. Therefore, it is impossible for the subject to avoid the danger through physical movements in the service of fight or flight—and that this is impossible is a defining characteristic of anxiety. This formulation is congruent with the theory of affects just mentioned, in which a particular affect is defined, in part, in terms of the type of state of affairs evaluated by the subject.

In the most distinctive psychoanalytic account, it is expression of an aggressive or sexual impulse (or, secondarily, expression of certain affects) the subject has come to believe will produce in actuality a dangerous state of affairs. (These are impulses that can be indefinitely deferred, unlike the impulses to alleviate hunger, pain, or thirst that so often figure in animal models.) That an aggressive or sexual impulse is active is indicated by the presence of a fantasy of a state of affairs in which the impulse is gratified in action. That state of affairs is imagined and appraised as pleasurable. The fantasy is associated with a pressure to realize in actuality what is so imagined. Another state of affairs, which the realization of the impulse in action is expected to produce, is also imagined; anxiety is the appraisal of that state of affairs as dangerous.

Anxiety then, according to psychoanalysis, is always bound up with an ideational content. The activation of a subcortical physiological system ("arousal") or of a behavioral system ("fight or flight") may or may not occur following anxiety. If such activation does occur, it may occur on some occasions and not others or with different degrees of duration or strength in different subjects. In any event, such activation is certainly not identical with anxiety, which is essentially an evaluative assessment (subserved or supported by cortical systems), a "signal" that an imagined state of affairs is both dangerous and highly likely to become an actual state of affairs.

THE PATH TO ANXIETY DISORDERS

Psychoanalytic hypotheses about anxiety, unlike definitions of anxiety, make empirical claims that certain vicissitudes of anxiety are stages on the path to anxiety disorders. Five such stages are described below.

1. Anxiety results in either rational problem solving or defense. Problem solving includes a conscious recognition and assessment of the likelihood of actualization of the anticipated dangerous state of affairs (secondary process thinking, reality testing) and may result, for example, in a utilitarian decision to inhibit impulse-gratifying behavior, in order to avoid pain. (Such an inhibition of impulse-gratifying behavior, or the mobilization of physiological processes leading to or subserving such inhibition, are not, of course, identical with the anxiety that motivates them.)

Because the act of imagining or fantasizing gratification of a sexual or aggressive impulse is associated with a pressure to act upon the impulse, fantasizing may itself come to be appraised as dangerous. This may happen, even though the fantasied state of affairs itself is appraised as pleasurable (the subject has "mixed feelings"). The subject may resort then, among many possible defenses, to repression; that is, a fantasy of gratification of an impulse is denied access to consciousness in order to deny the impulse access to the motor apparatus.

Defenses, in general, are mental operations. They are directed to and alter processes of forming and maintaining mental representations or the content of such representations. Defenses determine how perceptions of external reality are interpreted (e.g., what motives are attributed to others). They also determine what objects become objects of identification, and the fate of such identifications.

If conscious problem solving or successful repression occurs, anxiety disorders do not develop. Factors in the external world are negative causal factors with respect to the development of anxiety disorders (or positive causal factors with respect to the mitigation of anxiety disorders) only insofar as they promote problem solving (including access to consciousness) over repression and primary process, weaken impulses relative to defenses, or strengthen defenses relative to impulses.

Primary processes accord primacy to the aim of achieving immediate gratification without regard to recognition of or accommodation to external reality. Mental representations that are produced by or are part of a primary process are used in imagining wishes as fulfilled without regard to obstacles or opportunities in external reality. Such mental representations are subject to or are the product of such operations as condensation, displacement, and the substitution of iconic symbols or images for linguistic signs to represent concepts. Alteration of the balance between defense and impulse by situational factors may not be caused directly by intrinsic features of the external world; usually, rather, the impact of features of the external world is mediated by or depends on the subject's interpretation of them. Such interpretation is often determined by linkages between these features and the subject's unconscious fantasies of wish-fulfillment and danger, linkages that have been forged by primary process operations.

2. If a first act of defense (repression) subsequently fails, if derivatives of unconscious (repressed) contents become increasingly explicit and peremptory, a subject is motivated by anxiety to resort to other defenses. For example, a subject may transform a dangerous internal impulse into a danger from without (an object in external reality is seen as expressing the dangerous impulse or tempting the subject to express it, or as ready to attack or attacking the subject for harboring or expressing the dangerous impulse). (Such transformations are based upon personal-symbolic linkages forged by primary process operations.) Now that the danger is an external one, the subject can resort to fight or flight and may mobilize physiological resources preparatory to such action.

A subject may also subsequently internalize such an attacking object in external reality, identifying with it; here, especially, affects of rage and depression may be generated in response to imagined attacks upon the subject, or imagined interferences with the pleasure seeking of the subject, by the internalized object. This account constitutes one possible explanation of the oft-made observation in the pages of this volume—that anxiety and depression seem frequently to co-occur.

Factors in the external world are positive causal factors with respect to the development of anxiety disorders only insofar as they undercut secondary process thinking and reality testing, intensify impulses relative to defenses, or weaken defenses relative to impulses. Again, that these causal factors have such effects may not be due to intrinsic features of the external world, but rather to the subject's interpretation of them, and such interpretation, as has been pointed out, is often determined by linkages between these features and the subject's unconscious fantasies of wish-fulfillment and danger, linkages that have been forged by primary process operations.

3. If defensive operations continue to fail, more anxiety is generated.

4. The experience of anxiety, or the manifestations of physiological arousal in preparation for fight or flight, may themselves come to be linked by primary process operations to unconscious fantasies and interpreted as a particular kind of substitute gratification, or as a particular kind of danger. They may be exploited as well (complicating the clinical picture) to obtain gratification or punishment in interactions with others—by patients, for example, suffering from hysteria (an illness that largely goes unrecognized today, certainly by nearly all contributors to this volume).

5. Different anxiety disorders are characterized by the occurrence of the dysfunctional consequences of a more or less continuous or intermittently recurring failure of defense; or by the occurrence of the dysfunctional consequences associated with the particular type of defense(s) the subject uses.

ANIMAL MODELS

Various experimental procedures involving animal subjects purport to provide a so-called animal model of human anxiety or anxiety disorders. Conclusions about human anxiety or anxiety disorders are then drawn from observations of the effects of various kinds of interventions (e.g., the introduction of pharmacologic agents). As interesting and suggestive as such accounts are (see, e.g., Costa's discussion of behavioral models of anxiety, this volume, Gray's discussion of a behavioral inhibition system, this volume, and Mineka's discussion of the usefulness and limitations of animal models, this volume), in considering generalizations based upon work with them it is appropriate to ask: Does this animal model in fact model what psychoanalysts mean when they speak of anxiety or anxiety disorders?

In general, an animal model will fail to model what psychoanalysis terms "anxiety" if one or more of the following statements is true of it.

1. The responses of the animal that are of interest are those subserved or supported by subcortical rather than cortical systems. That is, what is of interest in the investigator's observations are the manifestations or effects of subcortical rather than cortical activity.

2. The animal responds automatically, physiologically or motorically, to cope with an existent threatening or thwarting state of affairs; an actual frustration of or attack upon the animal occurs. The state of affairs is existent and perceived rather than anticipated or imagined. The activation of a physiological or motoric-behavioral system (as part of the animal's response to that state of affairs) is

considered equivalent to anxiety. The investigator is unable to distinguish anxiety from fear, rage, or hopelessness. The investigator tends to regard evaluative assessments of state of affairs (affects) and mobilization of resources for physical action as equivalent.

3. The animal acts to satisfy drives that do not tolerate indefinite deferral of gratification, such as hunger or thirst; in so acting, the animal meets and attempts to overcome an actual obstacle.

4. The obstacle to gratification is arbitrarily imposed by the investigator—and therefore is made up of features of the external situation (external stimuli) that are inescapable and coercive. The connection between the animal's drive-reducing actions (drinking) and external stimuli that cause the animal pain (electric shocks) is determined by space-time contiguity, or physical causal laws.

5. The animal's utilitarian solution of the problem posed by its recognition that attack upon it is instigated by its own drive-reducing actions (for example, that it is shocked when it drinks) and the activation of the physiological or motoric-behavioral system involved in effecting that solution (avoidance of drinking) are considered to be equivalent to anxiety.

QUESTIONS FOR PSYCHOANALYSIS

A number of problems are raised when variables such as unconscious fantasies of wish-fulfillment or danger, whose measurement is expressed in values such as "is present" or "is not present," are used in a theory.

1. How does psychoanalysis obtain measures of variables which refer to the presence or absence of hypothetical or inferred dispositions or propensities? These dispositions may or may not be realized on any particular occasion the subject is observed, and such variables cannot merely indicate the presence or absence of some particular kind of observable action. A particular set of data may provide no evidence of a fantasy of wish-fulfillment or a fantasy of danger, or even of a fleeting occurrence of anxiety. It may only provide evidence of the presence of operations of defense.

2. What limits to hypothesis testing are set by the present inability of psychoanalysis to quantify these variables? A crude dichotomous scale (is present/ is not present), or at the most an ordinal scale (more/less), are all that is available now, resulting in hypothesis testing that is less precise and rigorous than one might wish.

3. Demonstrating the presence of unconscious fantasies of wish-fulfillment or danger depends upon reference to their hypothetical causal links to observable phenomena other than, and ideally independent of, those manifestations of anxiety and defense that their presence supposedly explains. How does psychoanalysis establish the credibility of such hypothetical causal links, which are often complex if not downright tortuous?

4. What is relevant to observe in establishing the credibility of these hypotheses? For example, the relation between inferred unconscious fantasies and observable states of affairs (i.e., bodily or environmental states of affairs) in the situation of the person-as-a-psychological-system is, according to psychoanalytic theory, a complicated one. It is not the case that presence or absence of features of a situation are causes, and fantasies are their effects. But what, then, is the relation between fantasy and reality? On the one hand, an inferred unconscious fantasy is the expression of an impulse, which provides a constant, not a momentary, pressure, presumably quasi-independent of situational vicissitudes that might be directly observed. On the other hand, the intensity of an unconscious impulse or wish may vary in response to situational vicissitudes; states of affairs perceived to be opportunities (or incentives or inducements) to gratify such a wish, as well as certain bodily changes, may intensify the wish. How can psychoanalysis deal methodologically with the complications introduced by the phrase "perceived to be"—the complications that follow from postulating the importance of the interpretation a person makes of an observable state of affairs compared to the importance of the intrinsic features of that state of affairs.

So it is, also, with fantasies of danger. Clearly, dread of being overwhelmed by the torment of unsatisfied need is not in any simple way caused by intrinsic features of a situation; nor are fantasies of castration, or of loss of love, or of visitations of shame or guilt, or even of loss of a loved object. But is is just intrinsic features of a situation that investigators are likely to regard as accessible to observation.

5. Finally, how is psychoanalysis to capture empirically the occurrence of anxiety itself? The signal of anxiety, to the extent it acts effectively as a signal, is itself fleeting and often so efficiently followed by defense that it is lost to awareness. Its occurrence must often be inferred rather than observed—even under the special conditions created in the psychoanalytic treatment situation. Here, in this unique situation, the whole process is made to occur in slow motion, as it were, so that—now I mix metaphors—the complete process can sometimes be observed microscopically, with every fine detail in bold relief.

These are all questions for psychoanalytic psychology.

QUESTIONS FOR OTHER DISCIPLINES

There are also questions about anxiety that are simply outside the province of psychoanalytic psychology. It is to their credit that Michels, Frances, and Shear (this volume), in considering such questions, do not espouse a vapid integration of multiple frames of reference and of investigations of vastly different domains. They do make it clear that the psychoanalytic theory of anxiety neither should nor could answer every question of interest about anxiety; and they do start to specify which questions are in the domain of psychoanalytic psychology and which questions it cannot—with its concepts and methods—profitably pursue. We tend to be on our guard lest political or intellectual interest in "integration" prevent recognition that two hypotheses are indeed rival propositions about the same domain, and that both cannot survive. If the chapters in this volume also show that some differences are differences in the complementary, but not necessarily competing, questions that investigators of different domains are capable of addressing, we shall have done well.

The First Question.   What brings about or causes the linkage between an unconscious fantasy of wish-fulfillment and an unconscious fantasy of danger? Another way to ask this question is: What causes a person to believe, or to respond as if he believes, that gratification of a wish will lead to a dangerous state of affairs? Is this linkage—or this belief—due to contiguity in experience of expression or gratification of the wish and a dangerous state of affairs?

Psychoanalytic psychology, on the whole, answers this last question no. David Rapaport (1960) rejected the notion that a theory of learning can help explain the linkage between wish and danger, if that theory depends on mechanisms of conditioning or reinforcement, which give a place of prominence to the role of situational stimuli acting as indices. But a more complex theory of learning, which, for example, makes use of the distinction between indices (whose meaning is grounded in existential connections), on the one hand, and icons and symbols, on the other hand, or a theory that builds on postulated central and innate mechanisms, might indeed help to explain this linkage (Edelson, 1984, pp. 91-92). Since the effects of early childhood experiences can be investigated, and also are accessible to influence, by psychological means, current psychoanalytic psychology itself may have a bias against a theory of learning emphasizing central and innate mechanisms. That would certainly not have been Freud's bias.

The Second Question.   How can one differentiate the affective appraisal associated with unconscious fantasies of danger and the physiological and behavioral responses to such appraisal? One may observe a fleeting purposeful anticipatory premonitory "watch out!" buzz, a transient state of tension or readiness, a continuing diffuse unregulated state of arousal, or an overwhelming incapacitating panic. Why this variability? Developmental psychologists and biologists in studies of the maturation of psychological capacities, and biological investigations of such phenomena as inborn differences in autonomic lability, can help answer this kind of question.

The Third Question.   What is the fate of the defensive operation? To what extent does it serve adaptation? If it does serve adaptation, to what extent is its survival, in the life of an individual and in the species, independent of the vicissitudes of intrapsychic conflict? Michels et al. (this volume) suggest that ethology and evolutionary theory have something to contribute here.

The Fourth Question.   What innate or constitutional factors determine the strength and choice of defense; the tenacity of desire; and propensities to fixation, regression, and conflict? Clearly, Freud always regarded such constitutional factors as important, but just as clearly he did not expect the investigation of such factors to be carried out primarily in the psychoanalytic situation or even necessarily by psychoanalysts.

IMPEDIMENTS TO RESEARCH IN PSYCHOANALYSIS

I turn now to suggestions for a research strategy that might be adopted by psychoanalytic investigators in testing their hypotheses. The suggestions offered by Michels et al. (this volume) seem to me to be good ones, given the impediments to research they have identified. The impediments of which I am most aware, however, are conceptual and attitudinal rather than matters of methods and instruments (Edelson, 1984).

One impediment is the lack of a skeptical or critical attitude in the psychoanalytic community toward its own conjectures. (I write as a member of that community.) On the whole, we seem inclined to give priority to the search for confirmations of hypotheses, rather than to the policy of subjecting hypotheses to a risk of falsification. Positive instances of a hypothesis are overvalued, without regard to whether or not all such positive instances are relevant in establishing the scientific credibility of that hypothesis. In other words, psychoanalysts tend to overvalue demonstrations of the explanatory power of a hypothesis over attempts to establish its scientific credibility through empirical tests. David Rapaport in 1959, regretting this community's continued reliance on its wealth of clinical observations, warned psychoanalysts that while "the evidence [for psychoanalytic hypotheses] . . . seems massive and imposing, the lack of clarification as to what constitutes a valid clinical [that is, nonexperimental] research method leaves undetermined the positive evidential weight of the confirming clinical material." Because the required "canon of clinical investigation is lacking, much of the evidence for the theory remains phenomenological and anecdotal, even if its obviousness and bulk tend to lend to it a semblance of objective validity" (Rapaport, 1959, p. 111). More than 80 years have elapsed since the appearance of Freud's *Interpretation of Dreams.* Surely that is time enough to move on to undertaking the task Rapaport calls on psychoanalysis to achieve.

A second impediment involves a related conceptual failure. Members of this community frequently neglect the strategy of formulating rival hypotheses within the psychoanalytic frame of reference, then seeking evidence, even in case studies, that will support one hypothesis and eliminate another rival hypothesis (or that at least will provide one hypothesis with much more support than another). Here, J. Platt's explication of strong inference (1964), which details this strategy and shows how advance in science depends upon it, and Ian Hacking's explication of his premise of comparative support (1965), which shows how evidence may provide one hypothesis more support than another (though that evidence is consistent with both hypotheses), are important contributions—apparently unknown to most psychoanalysts.

The final impediment I shall mention is that in establishing the credibility of a hypothesis the psychoanalytic literature, on the whole, does not demonstrate much appreciation for the necessity of presenting an argument, even a weak argument, that one's own hypothesis explains one's finding much better than do plausible alternative hypotheses (plausible, in the light of background knowledge). Freud, who struggled throughout his writings with the question of whether suggestion might not explain the outcome of psychoanalytic treatment, is, on the whole, an exception to this judgment.

PROPOSALS

These conceptual and attitudinal deficiencies can be corrected to some extent even in the clinical case study or in investigations carried out with data obtained from the psychoanalytic situation itself. One does not, for example, have to consider every known plausible alternative explanation of one's findings. Eliminating even one or two alternative explanations is better than making no attempt to eliminate any alternative explanation (Campbell & Stanley, 1963). As Cook and Campbell have pointed out in their book on quasi-experimental and naturalistic field studies (1979), one does not have to rely on experimental design methods alone in attempting to eliminate at least some plausible alternative explanations of one's findings; nondesign arguments can also be useful. Luborsky's symptom-context method (Luborsky, 1967, 1973; Luborsky, Bachrach, Graff, Pulver, & Christoph, 1979; Luborsky & Mintz, 1974) though it is naturalistic and nonexperimental, and makes use of data from the psychoanalytic situation, involves a design that is capable of eliminating some alternative explanations of an obtained outcome, and, therefore, of testing hypotheses of interest to psychoanalysis. So, also, the philosopher of science Clark Glymour (1980) has shown that Freud (1909) in the case of the Rat Man study followed the same procedure in testing his hypotheses that Kepler and Newton used in testing theirs.

Psychoanalysis, especially, should not be derided for pursuing intensive studies of single subjects, but instead should be encouraged to turn its attention to and assimilate for its own purposes conceptual and methodological developments in single-subject research (e.g., Campbell & Stanley, 1963; Chassan, 1979; Hersen & Barlow, 1976; Kazdin, 1981, 1982; Shapiro, 1961, 1963, 1966; Sidman, 1960). It should consider the use of (1) individualized ipsative measurements, which can objectify and quantify subjective data; (2) baseline observations, which make systematic comparisons (based on multiple measures of a subject under different conditions) possible; (3) direct and systematic replication, which can deal with problems respectively of internal validity and of external validity or generalization in single-subject research; and (4) probabilistic or statistical reasoning about the relation between hypothesis and evidence. Then (and this is just one possibility) psychoanalysts, following Luborsky's methodological leads, might test psychoanalytic hypotheses about the anxiety disorders by studying and comparing those contexts in the protocol of a single psychoanalysis in which anxiety is reported or is exacerbated and the otherwise similar contexts in which is it not. These proposals are elaborated at much greater length, with additional references, in *Hypothesis and Evidence in Psychoanalysis* (Edelson, 1984).

II

G. Assessment of Anxiety

35

Anxiety: Its Measurement by Objective Personality Tests and Self-Report

Joseph C. Finney, M.D., Ph.D.

This chapter first discusses the tests that have been commonly used for anxiety, and some of the findings related to those tests. Then we turn to some of the issues, problems, and needs for future research. The Minnesota Multiphasic Personality Inventory (MMPI), the Cattell tests, and Spielberger's State-Trait Anxiety Index (STAI) have been the main tests used.

MMPI DERIVED ANXIETY MEASURES

The MMPI was developed in an extensive series of research studies that began about 1940, by Starke R. Hathaway and J. Charnly McKinley in the psychiatry department of the University of Minnesota (see Hathaway & McKinley, 1942). It consists of a number of statements or items (in the final form, 550 plus 16 repeats) to be marked true or false. Nine "clinical" scales were developed by finding items that correlated with psychiatric diagnoses as made in 1940–1942 at the University of Minnesota Hospital. The scale developed for male homosexuality (then considered a disorder) was later renamed Masculinity-Femininity. As it became apparent that the scale scores had meanings beyond their disease-names, and had some usefulness beyond psychopathology, perhaps even as general personality measures, the names were replaced by letter designations and then by numbers (Table 35.1).

Three scales of "validity" or test-taking attitude (L, F, K) were added. Paul H. Meehl, in his doctoral dissertation, developed the K scale and K-correction system, to improve the validity of clinical classification, and its use has become routine with five clinical scales. Many other researchers at Minnesota and elsewhere have developed scales from the MMPI, and the number of scales now far

645

TABLE 35.1
The Classical Clinical Scales of the MMPI

Name	Designation	Number
Hypochondriasis	Hs	1
Depression	D	2
Hysteria	Hy	3
Psychopathic Deviate	Pd	4
Masculinity-Feminity	Mf	5
Paranoia	Pa	6
Psychasthenia	Pt	7
Schizophrenia	Sc	8
Mania (or Hypomania)	Ma	9

outnumbers the 550 items, though only one of the later scales has been included by the publishers on the printed graph.

At first the MMPI scales were scored and interpreted by hand and that method is still in use. However, by the mid-1960s three systems had been developed for computer interpretation of the MMPI by Pearson and Swenson (1967), by Fowler (1968), and by Finney, Smith, Skeeters, and Auvenshine (1970). Early versions of these three papers were presented in a symposium at the 1965 annual meeting of the American Psychological Association. Others have been developed since.

TAYLOR SCALE

The anxiety measure derived from the MMPI that is best known and that has been most widely used is the Taylor Scale of Manifest Anxiety (MAS). It was developed by Janet A. Taylor (now Janet T. Spence) as part of her doctoral dissertation in psychology at the University of Iowa under the direction of Kenneth W. Spence. Spence and Taylor were studying conditioned responses in human beings, and asking how the conditioning process is affected both by characteristics of the subjects and by external conditions. In general, they found confirmation of their hypothesis that a high level of drive and motivation (including anxiety, but not limited to it) would interfere with learning in the early stages, especially in difficult or unfamiliar tasks; learning of familiar tasks was facilitated.

The Taylor scale consists of 50 MMPI items: 37 scored true and 13 scored false. Its items are listed in Volume 2 of *An MMPI Handbook* by Dahlstrom, Welsh, and Dahlstrom (1972, 1975) in an Appendix which also lists the items of 454 other scales. The Taylor items were chosen by agreement of raters, based on the content of the items. It therefore stands on the shaky foundation of face validity, the bane of all tests of the questionnaire type. Nevertheless, it correlates significantly with other variables in many studies; and the MAS has been shown repeatedly to load around .90 or more on the first principal axis or Thurstone factor (unrotated). Taylor's MAS also correlates around .90 or better with other anxiety scales that were later derived more elegantly from the MMPI.

The full MMPI takes an hour and a half to administer. Perhaps for that reason, Taylor gave her scale without the full MMPI, and she changed the wording of some of the items. The Taylor scale came to be used rather widely, for a time, in human experimental psychology, not only in conditioning-learning experiments, but also in experimental social psychology and other research.

Clinical psychologists, who typically give the complete MMPI, could easily score the Taylor scale, but seldom do. Instead, they tend to score routinely the Welsh Anxiety scale. Thus, psychologists may be said to divide into two traditional groups, each using its own MMPI-derived anxiety measure, each group oblivious of the other.

Some interesting results from the use of the Taylor scale are as follows: Taylor scores rise when post-addicts are given LSD-25 (Belleville, 1956); long-term administration of phenobarbital (but not chlorpromazine or placebo) decreased the Taylor scores for 6 weeks in 700 nonpsychiatric VA Hospital patients (Gordon, 1958); subtotal gastrectomy lowered the scores on Taylor's anxiety scale as well as on scales 1, 2, 3, and F of the MMPI (Weiner, 1956). In group psychotherapy of alcoholics, self-descriptions improve and scores fall on Taylor anxiety as well as scales 2 and 7 (Ends & Page, 1957a, 1957b). Among post-hospitalized schizophrenics, those who failed to stay out of the hospital for 1 year were those who had high scores on scales 6, 8, and Taylor anxiety (Glasscock, 1954). Students seeking help from a university student counseling service had higher Taylor MAS scores than students in general (Terwilliger & Fiedler, 1958). Boys with high-anxiety scores had greater discrepancies between their own personality descriptions and their mothers' ideals for them on a Q-sort (Stewart, 1958). Students with personalities like their parents had lower anxiety scores (Lazowick, 1955).

Hodges and Spielberger (1966) used the Taylor scale to investigate the effects of stress on changes in heart rate in undergraduate males who were high or low in trait anxiety. The stress condition showed an immediate rise of 15 heart beats per minute in the anxiety group, whereas control subjects showed none. Contrary to what was expected, persons grouped as high and low in trait anxiety by the Taylor scale did not differ in their heart rate response to stress, but those who had reported great fear of shock increased by 23 beats per minute. Those subjects who had reported little or no fear of shock rose only 11 beats. This study points up the fact that response to stress depends on the degree of threat perceived by the individual. The anticipation of shock was perceived as less threatening by some than by others.

Rappaport and Katkin (1972) obtained MAS scores on 48 undergraduate males and measured their galvanic skin responses (GSR). They then were exposed to mild stress or nonstress conditions. Among those exposed only to the nonstress condition, Taylor anxiety did not predict GSR change; under stress, those high on the MAS showed a greater increase in GSR than those scoring low.

Parkinson & Gillis (1977) used the Taylor Anxiety scale among others in finding that schizophrenic patients receiving intermediate doses of antipsychotic medicines had less anxiety and depression than those getting high or low doses of the medicines.

WELSH SCALE

The next best known MMPI scale on anxiety is the Welsh A scale. George S. Welsh early became interested in the fundamental dimensions underlying the MMPI scale scores, and to that end developed an Anxiety Index as follows (Welsh, 1952):

$$AI = 1.33 D + 1.00 Pt - .66 Hy$$

Today that index has only historical interest, being regarded as a forerunner of the Welsh Anxiety scale. It still turns up occasionally in research papers but almost never is found in clinical use.

Welsh's A scale (Welsh, 1956) was developed after a number of authors, including Welsh, had done factor analyses on the MMPI scale. Before the development of sophisticated computers and programs, factor analysis was a difficult and laborious task. Nevertheless, from the beginning years to the present day, the same first two or three factors have shown up in analysis of the MMPI, when the Thurstone centroid method or its successor, the Principal Axis Factor Analysis, is used. This latter method, without rotation, puts as much of the variance as possible into the first factor, and as much of the remaining variance as possible into the second. The factors turn out alike, even though some research- ers have used the standard 12 or 13 MMPI scales, some (mainly Welsh) have used "purified" scales eliminating items common to two or more scales, and others, such as Finney (1961), have used a longer and broader list of scales. Nearly all workers in this area have entered T scores ($\overline{X}$ = 50, σ = 10), not raw scores, as the data. The amount of the total variance attributable to the first factor varies inversely with the number of scales entered; in the author's 1961 study it was 45%.

The second Principal Axis factor, found repeatedly, runs from assertiveness at one end (Boldness, Factor B) to inhibition (Welsh calls it Repression, Factor R) at the other. Welsh and Pearson, quoted by Welsh, (1956) have proposed to describe personality efficiently by the simultaneous coordinates of scores on the first and second factors (A and B or R). They used Welsh's A and R scales. Today, however, factor scores, not Welsh's A and R scales, which approximate them, would be used to describe personality. Psychiatric outpatients score high on the Anxiety Factor (A factor) and at the inhibited end of the second factor.

Criminals and delinquents are also high on the anxiety factor, but they score at the assertive end of the second factor. Alcoholics tend to score between those two groups.

Welsh has noted that a number of researchers, including Brackbill and Little (1954), Ends and Page (1957b), and Eriksen and Davids (1955) found correlations around .92 between Taylor's scale and scale 7, Pt (without K correction). Welsh complains, "With correlations as high as these values, there would appear to be little advantage to the introduction of the (Taylor) scale over and above the use of the Pt scale that is routinely included in the MMPI profiles as scale 7" (Welsh, in Dahlstrom & Welsh, 1960, p. 294). What Welsh evidently means is that the Taylor scale is superfluous because of the Welsh scale, as he adds "for most purposes the Welsh A scale appears to be the most satisfactory single measure of anxiety in the MMPI" (p. 295).

FINNEY SCALES

Generally, the method of scale derivation that is most acceptable among psychologists is to select items that make the scale correlate highly with an external criterion. Among MMPI measures of anxiety, the only one derived in this manner is the Finney anxiety scale, one of 45 MMPI scales based on research done in Champaign-Urbana (Finney, 1965) and incorporated into the University of Kentucky MMPI computer system (Finney, 1966b). This empirically based scale was published 20 years ago, but essentially nobody has done further research with it, not even the author. A computer, unlike a human scorer, can calculate a factor score almost instantaneously and cheaply; many people regard each anxiety scale as an approximation of the factor on which it loads more than .90; so why not use the more accurate factor score itself in research and in making clinical decisions?

Anxiety can also be differentiated by content. In developing the new set of 45 empirical scales, Finney included not only a general anxiety scale, but also four kinds of anxiety by content: guilt, embarrassment, fear/phobia, and obsessive worry (Finney, 1965). Later, in organizing the University of Kentucky computer system, he included for each of these four qualities not only the empirical scale but also a rational scale based on items chosen for their manifest content (Finney, 1965). Table 35.2 shows the number and letter designation of the eight scales.

For many who have worked with the MMPI for years, it is bewildering to find people searching for measures of anxiety. If by "anxiety" we mean what is found in the first Principal Axis factor, the MMPI suffers from having too much of it. We have mentioned at least four scales that load above .90 on anxiety (Taylor's, Welsh's, Finney's anxiety scales, and the Pt scale without correction) and there are others shown in Table 35.3. People keep deriving new scales, but

TABLE 35.2
Finney MMPI Scales Measuring Specific Types of Anxiety

Quality Measured	Empirical Scale	Rational Scale
Guilt	29 GF	90 GU
Embarassment	27 CWO	89 EM
(Concern with what others think)		
Fear, Phobia	43 PAF	83 PH
Worry	44 WaO	110 OB
(and obsession)	(also Pt?)	

most of them are so highly loaded on the First Factor ("Anxiety") that they duplicate existing scales and provide little or no new information. The problem is not how to measure the First Factor, but how to get rid of it so that something else can be measured. Various solutions have been attempted, as for example, Meehl's K scale, which is substantially loaded negatively on A (McKinley, Hathaway, & Meehl, 1948).

It is not only in questionnaire tests that anxiety is so pervasive a contaminant that we look for ways of keeping it out. In the work that was this author's doctoral dissertation (1961a), children's personality and character were rated by clinicians, so that their qualities could be correlated with behavior of their parents. Four of the main qualities rated in the children were dependency, anxiety, pessimism, and passive resentment or covert hostility. These four qualities, as rated, turned out to correlate positively with one another so greatly that we looked for ways of rating dependency that would not correlate so highly with anxiety.

It is still not clear that "anxiety" is the best description of what is measured by the First Factor. As we have seen, the First Factor is loaded with scales of anxiety, dependency, self-pity, disappointment, delinquency, and various neuroses and psychoses. Many observers have preferred to consider it a dimension of "General Maladjustment."

A few papers dealing mostly with asthma have appeared using something called the panic-fear scale of the MMPI (Dirks, Kleiger, & Evans, 1978; Dirks, Schraa, Brown, & Kinsman, 1980). What is not needed in the MMPI is another duplicating scale measuring anxiety: duplication has happened over and over again with the MMPI. Somebody researching a specific field (in this case, asthma), without much experience with the MMPI, decides to create a new scale for his purpose. Excitement builds when the investigator finds that his new scale correlates with other measures. That is not surprising, since the MMPI First Factor correlates with many things. Generally, the new scale turns out to correlate .9 or more with the Welsh scale, the Taylor scale, and the Finney scale, and to load .9 or more on the MMPI First Factor (the anxiety factor). There is, in fact, a heavy presumption that a new MMPI anxiety scale will do so. It should be obvious that a very limited value can be ascribed to a new scale that merely

TABLE 35.3

Intercorrelations of MMPI anxiety scales and their loadings on the first Principal Axis. The upper figures for Anxiety Factor Loading, and the figures for intercorrelations of scales, are from Finney's study (unpublished) of 100 soldiers at Fort Knox. The lower figures for Anxiety Factor Loadings for each scale are from the Finney-NIMH MMPI restandardization sample of 1024 men and 1024 women. These previously unpublished data were produced at the University of Kentucky under Research Grant RD 2465-P. The scales are numbered by the University of Kentucky system.

	Anxiety Factor Loadings (two samples)	Finney Anxiety	Embarrassment concern with what people think (27)	Guilt (29)	Feeling sorry for self (33)	Fear, phobia (42)	Worry (44)	Pt (without K) (63)	Welsh A (70)	Phobia content (83)	Embarrassment content (89)	Guilt content (90)	Obsessive worry content (110)
(7)	.882 / .890	1.000											
(27)	.338 / .248	.376	1.000										
(29)	.848 / .841	.839	.428	1.000									
(33)	.922 / .917	.882	.397	.848	1.000								
(42)	.888 / .897	.923	.357	.827	.884	1.000							
(44)	.892 / .877	.894	.423	.856	.916	.966	1.000						
(63)	.898 / .889	.884	.331	.867	.888	.882	.883	1.000					
(70)	.927 / .931	.878	.305	.828	.914	.870	.892	.906	1.000				
(83)	.651 / .573	.528	.264	.524	.509	.535	.503	.562	.535	1.000			
(89)	.542 / .501	.473	.298	.538	.464	.439	.475	.552	.527	.401	1.000		
(90)	.692 / .708	.618	.216	.591	.684	.632	.628	.666	.710	.452	.370	1.000	
(110)	— / .793	.778	.310	.705	.803	.763	.801	.793	.820	.504	.404	.596	1.000

duplicates older measures. Yet the new scale may become a fad among workers who know much about the other field (such as asthma) and little about the MMPI. Anybody who proposes a new anxiety scale from the MMPI has an obligation to correlate it with all the existing MMPI anxiety scales and to determine its loading in the first Principal Axis. The author of the new scale bears a heavy burden of proof to show that the new scale differs from the old ones.

Dirks et al. (1978), in the *Journal of Asthma Research,* reported that the MMPI panic-fear scale measures a basic personality characteristic, and the categories of the Asthma Symptom Checklist (ASC) measure situation-specific anxiety. He would have reached the same conclusion had he used the Welsh, Finney, or Taylor Anxiety scales. Dirks et al. (1980) showed that among asthma patients, high rates of hospitalization were found in those having either extremely high or extremely low scores on the panic-fear scale. These are interesting results, but it would be wiser to score first one or more of the established MMPI anxiety measures and examine the results. Only then should one try a new MMPI anxiety scale. It is unlikely that the results obtained with the new scale differ from those with the established scale. The burden is on Dirks and his collaborators to show that the Taylor, Welsh, and Finney anxiety scales would not give the same results. (Even before that, one should correlate the new scale with established MMPI scales for anxiety.) Without these precautions, researchers who are interested in a specific application and unfamiliar with the MMPI may be misled into thinking that the new scale is unique in its relation to their field.

Kinsman, Dirks, Dahlem, and Heller (1980) studied 140 asthmatic patients with the MMPI and the ASC, which includes a panic-fear symptom scale. MMPI panic-fear scale scores correlated highly with Taylor MAS scores, and both were classed as trait anxiety measures. They continued to correlate highly even after checklist panic-fear scores were partialed out. In contrast, panic-fear symptomatology had a lower relation to Taylor scores and was independent of them after MMPI panic-fear scores were partialed out. Checklist panic fear symptom reports were concluded to measure an illness-specific state anxiety that is not, in itself, a measure of trait anxiety.

CATTELL ANXIETY TESTS

Another major movement in personality testing by questionnaire is that founded and led by Raymond B. Cattell, an Englishman who spent most of his professional life at the University of Illinois in Urbana. Although Cattell had some clinical training, including early work in a Child Guidance Clinic in England, his overriding interest has been in the scientific determination of the structure of personality. His main tool was factor analysis (the determination of Eigenvectors). When Cattell and I were colleagues in the Psychology Department of the University during 1956–1960, my main occupation was running the Champaign

County Mental Health Center, and Cattell's was running factor analyses on the Illiac computer. The department at that time also included O. Hobart Mowrer, Joseph McV. Hunt, Charles Osgood, and Lee Cronbach, forming an intellectually impressive group to investigate personality.

As we have noted, the approach most accepted among psychologists was to begin by deriving scales empirically from correlation of item responses with some external criterion applied to the test-takers. That approach was pioneered by E. K. Strong for vocational interests, and later by Hathaway for the MMPI. Cattell chose to begin by searching dictionaries and compiling lists of adjectives that describe personality or character. After eliminating clear synonyms, he asked people to rate one another on the reduced list of 171 trait names. By factor analysis of the results, Cattell eventually settled on a test of 16 qualities, each of which could be called a factor. One of the 16 was intelligence, not usually considered a "personality" trait. Cattell's test is published as the Sixteen Personality Factors (16 PF).

When there is a plethora of variables, psychologists often do a factor analysis, or what mathematicians call a determination of eigenvectors and eigenvalues. This procedure is an establishment of dimensions. An advantage is that establishing a small number of dimensions or factors enables the researcher to understand a greater number of variables. Another advantage is that individuals can be described more economically by a small number of factor scores, rather than by a great number of overlapping variables. A correlation coefficient is the cosine of the angle between two vectors in multidimensional space, as shown in Fig. 35.1.

If one of the vectors is an empirical measure and the other a calculated vector (a factor, a dimension), the cosine is called a loading. The square of the correlation coefficient (or loading) gives the portion of the variance in one variable that is accounted for by another variable (or factor). If the factorial dimensions

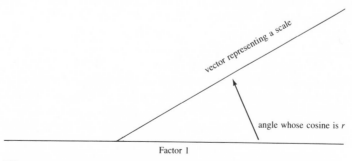

FIG. 35.1 Geometry showing the angle whose cosine is *r*, where *r* is the loading of a scale on Factor 1, or the correlation of the scale with another scale coinciding with the position of Factor 1.

are orthogonal (independent, at right angles to one another) their variance portions can be added to show how much of the variance of the mass of data is accounted for by, say, the first three, or four, or n factors. These last two propositions are true because they are corollaries of the Pythagorean theorem as extended to more than two dimensions.

Among Cattell's firm beliefs are the following: (1) The mathematical process of factor analysis is the key to finding the true structure of human personality; (2) true structure does not abide in Principal Axis factors such as Welsh's A factor, but is found only on rotation to simple structure; and (3) true simple structure cannot be achieved by orthogonal rotations, such as Henry Kaiser's Varimax, but only in oblique rotation. All three of Cattell's postulates are reasonable and, I find, hard to refute.

Oblique factor scores can themselves be entered into a matrix and factor analyzed, yielding second-order factors. Since "anxiety" is a Principal Axis factor before rotation, it is not surprising to see it reappear as a second-order factor, even when the second-order analysis is itself oblique.

The early 16 PF had some drawbacks, consistent with the fact that its author was stronger as a mathematician and theoretician than as a clinician. What the 16 scales measured that was valuable in diagnosis or treatment was not clear. The items were not well worded initially, and the items and scales had some of the drawbacks of the old Bell Adjustment Inventory and Bernreuter test (Bernreuter, 1933), in which self-ratings were taken as valid. Yet Cattell and his students worked persistently, improving the items and scales, finding empirical correlates for them, and developing multiple regression equations, to predict or measure a number of qualities and outcomes. In the mid-1960s Herbert Eber developed a computer interpretation of the Cattell 16 PF. He presented this along with the three groups who were pioneering in MMPI computer interpretation at the 1965 American Psychological Association Convention. The 16 PF came into some use in personnel and industrial testing. At last, in order to meet the needs of psychiatric diagnosis and treatment, Cattell and others developed the Clinical Analysis Questionnaire (CAQ). It includes a modified version of the 16 Personality Factors, plus seven factors of depression and five other factors intended, as Krug (1980) says, "to measure factor-analytically identified traits that were discovered in the MMPI item pool."

The MMPI has gone unrevised for nearly 40 years. But Cattell has repeatedly performed factor analyses on new data and rewritten scale items. For years the 16 PF came in three forms: A, B, and C. Now the CAQ includes new forms of the 16 normal factors (scales based mostly on Form A) plus the 12 new clinical factor scales; and its manual comments that many clinicians use the old 16 PF for the first 16 factors, and add part 2 of the CAQ for the 12 new ones.

The CAQ Manual quotes (from Krug & Laughlin, 1977) the latest pattern for the second-order Anxiety factor from the simple factor scales:

TABLE 35.4

Name of Factor Scale		Loading on Second-Order Anxiety Factor	
		(Males)	(Females)
C	Emotionally Stable	−.57	−.56
L	Suspicious	+.59	+.47
O	Worried	+.39	+.44
Q_3	Controlled	−.48	−.53
Q_4	Tense	+.63	+.74
D_6	Guilt and Resentment	+.33	+.35
Pa	Paranoia	+.30	n.s.
As	Psychasthenia	+.42	+.34
D_5	Low Energy	n.s.	+.31

Curiously, neither D_3, agitated Depression, nor D_4, Anxious Depression, loaded on the second-order Anxiety factor. Among second-order factors, Anxiety correlated with Depression (+.52, +.50) and somewhat negatively with factors deemed Extraversion and Independence.

Cattell and his associates at the Institute of Personality and Ability Testing (IPAT) developed an Objective-Analytic (O-A) Anxiety Battery (Cattell & Scheier, 1960), and several of its subtests were then included in the IPAT 8-Parallel form Anxiety Battery (8-PF) by Scheier and Cattell (1960), intended as a test for State Anxiety. Spielberger (1972a) has complained that more of the subtests measure Trait than State Anxiety. He notes (1976) that the IPAT Anxiety scale has repeatedly correlated between .80 and .90 with the Taylor scale.

Spielberger (1972a) has well summarized the anxiety work of the Cattell group as follows:

Cattell and Scheier (1961) have pioneered in the application of multivariate techniques to the definition and measurement of anxiety. In their research, both phenomenological and physiological variables presumed to be related to anxiety have been studied with factor analytic procedures, notably; such methods as P-technique, dR (differential R) technique, and chain-P technique (Cattell, 1966). In this multivariate approach, which permits investigation of the covariation of a number of different measures over time, "state" and "trait" anxiety have consistently emerged as principal personality factors. Many of the variables that load Cattell and Scheier's state-anxiety factor also have high loadings on their trait anxiety factor. Since the pattern of these loadings is quite different, Cattell hypothesizes that it should be possible to assess both state and trait anxiety from a single personality questionnaire by applying different weights to each scale item according to its unique contribution to the state and trait factors.

In a rigorous study, Munjack, Kanno, and Oziel (1978) gave the MMPI, the IPAT (Cattell) Anxiety scale, and other tests to 35 males seeking help for premature or retarded ejaculation, and 91 controls. Excluded were patients with co-existing arousal problems and those whose symptoms were secondary to psychoses, medications and drugs of abuse, or medical illnesses. Both premature and retarded ejaculators were more anxious and depressed, and had more general psychopathology than the controls. The only significant difference between retarded and premature ejaculators was the higher Mf scores in the retarded ejaculators.

TYPES OF ANXIETY SCALES

Before discussing the Spielberger State-Trait Anxiety Index (STAI), consider what is meant by a state and a trait. A state is a condition that holds true now, or at a specified time, but may not hold true for the individual at other times. A trait is a condition that is permanent, or at least long-lasting, and changes rather slowly, if at all. We can speak of a person as having a trait of anxiety, or ranking high on a trait of anxiety. Over the years, such a person is anxious much of the time; he becomes anxious to a greater degree than most people would in the same circumstances; or is made anxious by a greater variety of circumstances than other people. All of these statements are ways of saying that the person has greater readiness or susceptibility to anxiety than others have.

Similarly, we can say that a person has a trait of depression, but may not be depressed at any given moment. A person has schizophrenia, a psychosis, but is not psychotic at the moment: he is in remission. A person has tuberculosis, and will never be considered cured, though his disease has been inactive for years. A person has diabetes, but it is under control now. Alcoholics Anonymous considers that once a person is an alcoholic, he is always an alcoholic, even through he has not had a drink in 10 years. If he denies that dictum and tries to drink socially again, he is likely to relapse. It is more usual to speak of intelligence as a trait, or vivaciousness as a trait, than to call diabetes or schizophrenia or tuberculosis a trait, but the concept in terms of duration over time is much the same.

The MMPI is neither clearly a state nor clearly a trait instrument. Its scale scores change with time, but many of the scores tend to stay fairly constant in their absolute or relative values. It is commonly noted that when applying for psychiatric services people show generally elevated scores in the clinically significant range, and when completing treatment show lower, more normal, healthier scores. Hathaway has called this the "hello-goodbye" effect (1948). His implication, with which most clinicians agree, is that the changes are not in traits (not a deep, long-lasting change), but are in states (hence, superficial change, not likely to be permanent change). The changes are mostly in the anxiety factor (also called the General Maladjustment factor) and observed in the MMPI clinical scales most loaded on it, scales 2 and 7. No rigorous systematic studies have been done on this matter. Patients are seldom tested at the close of treatment, partly because few outpatients give advance notice of termination. (Also because patients and insurers are less willing to pay for testing at the time of recovery.)

We do know that people can and do change their MMPI scores sharply, even from one hour to the next, when they are instructed, for example, to take the test first straight as per the manual, then as if trying to make a good impression in a job application, and then to exaggerate their troubles in seeking help or in claiming to be not guilty by reason of insanity. That sort of experiment has been done several times by psychologists developing scales to measure social desirability or test-taking attitude. Scales measuring anxiety are among those whose scores are most sharply altered by such instructions. Nevertheless, the MMPI measures of anxiety are generally classified as trait measures, not state measures. In many of the MMPI items, the wording does not make the time frame clear. Often patients will ask, "Shall I answer the questions the way I feel now, or the way I normally feel?" And they may make some compromise. This ambiguity is one reason for the development of separate measures of state and trait anxiety.

The Finney scales (1965) for four specific kinds of anxiety (guilt, embarrassment, fear/phobia and worry) have already been mentioned. This systematically classified set of anxiety scales is ideal for use in research on anxiety. Others have gone even farther, and have developed tests that are far more specific in the content of the anxiety that they measure. Fear of snakes, fear of tests, and fear of death are some of the specific content areas for which tests have been written. Mellstrom, Cicala, and Zuckerman (1976) found that fear of snakes (in a real situation) was predicted better by a paper-and-pencil test specifically dealing with fear of snakes, than by general anxiety tests, but that finding was only slightly true for fear of heights and for fear of darkness. With this background, let us examine the Spielberger scales.

SPIELBERGER'S STATE-TRAIT ANXIETY INDEX

Cattell was perhaps the first researcher to become systematically interested in the variation of test scores over time. In the context of factor analysis Cattell and Scheier (1961) first proposed the concepts of state anxiety and trait anxiety. Spielberger discussed these concepts in a 1966 book, and progressively developed the State-Trait Anxiety Inventory (STAI) with the aid of his students and associates. The STAI Manual (Spielberger, Gorsuch, & Lushene, 1970) defined State Anxiety (A-State) as a transitory emotional state or condition characterized by subjective feelings of tension and apprehension, and by activation of the autonomic nervous system (ANS). States fluctuate over time as a function of the ANS and various stressors impinging on the individual. Trait Anxiety (A-Trait) refers to relatively stable individual differences in proneness to anxiety state.

The STAI consists of two sets of 20 items each, both sets frankly worded as self-reports. The state items ask about feelings at the moment, and the trait items ask about how the person generally feels. Both scales show a high degree of homogeneity in terms of inter-item correlations, but only the A-Trait scale has high test-retest reliability (.73 to .86, compared with .16 to .54 for A-State). (The reader is also referred to Spielberger's chapter in this volume for further discussion of the STAI.)

In 1972a, Spielberger discussed at length the concept of anxiety and its measurement in the STAI. He postulates that childhood experiences are the reason one person is more readily aroused to anxiety (i.e., is higher on A-Trait) than another. Spielberger takes note of such earlier scales to measure feeling states as Hildreth's Feeling and Attitude Battery (1946), Wessman, Ricks and Tyl's Personal Feeling Scales (1960), Nowlis and Green's Mood Adjective Check List (1964) and Zuckerman's (1960) Affect Adjective Checklist (AACL, later MAACL, Zuckerman & Lubin, 1965).

Spielberger remarked, "The stronger a particular personality trait, the more probable it is that an individual will experience the emotional state that corresponds to this trait, and the greater the probability that behaviors associated with the trait will be manifested in a variety of situations." Spielberger (1972a) agrees that the evidence is impressive for the validity of Zuckerman's "Today" version of Zuckerman's Affect Adjective Check List. He complains, however, that the General Form of the AACL as a measure of Trait Anxiety correlates less with other measures of the trait (MAS and IPAT Anxiety Scales) than they correlate with one another.

In developing the STAI, Spielberger thought at first that the same items could be used with different instructions, to answer "today" for the State, and to answer "usually" for Trait. But he found that this approach did not work. Some statements, such as "I feel upset" work well for State but not for Trait, even with trait-oriented instruction. He eventually developed separate sets of items, each to be answered on a 4-point scale. (For example, for the Trait items, Almost Never, Sometimes, Often, Almost Always; for the State items, Not at All, Somewhat, Moderately, Very Much So.) From the pool of items tried, items for A-Trait were chosen if they correlated with Taylor's MAS and with IPAT Anxiety, were stable over time, and were not much affected by situational stress. Items for A-state were chosen to change with situational stress.

Spielberger (1972b) noted that persons with the high A-Trait would not be expected to make high A-state responses to all stressors, but only to those seen as threatening by the person. Most people with high A-Trait are especially threatened not by physical dangers but by social dangers; they have self-deprecating attitudes.

Newmark (1972) tested nearly 200 undergraduates four times within 10 months and found, as expected, that the trait anxiety scores were rather stable, while the state anxiety scores varied greatly from one occasion to another. This result validated the STAI in showing that what should stay the same did, and what should not, did not. In another sense, Newmark's study did not attempt to validate the test, as there was no independent measure to show that what was being measured was anxiety.

Spielberger (1973) showed that A-State was raised before surgery, but A-Trait was not (nor were Mini-Mult scores). (The Mini-Mult is one of several abbreviated versions of the MMPI.) Tennyson and Boutwell (1973) used STAI State, with Taylor MAS as a Trait measure, on 75 students weekly for 3 weeks and just before and after a task. They found that State measure at the time of the task predicted performance better than State measures at other times, or the MAS at any time. Newmark, Hetzel, and Frerking (1974) found that State and not Trait Anxiety rises after administration of the Thematic Apperception Test or Rorschach Inkblot Test, but there is no change from being given an MMPI. Martuza and Kallstrom (1974) in a multi-trait, multi-measure study obtained results supporting the State-Trait distinction. Gaudry, Vagg, and Spielberger (1975) did an interesting study, giving the STAI and other tests to 345 tenth-grade girls. The State Anxiety was given under one nonstress and two stress conditions. Factor Analysis showed six factors: trait anxiety, three state anxiety factors corresponding to the three administrations, and two other factors. Any study of state and trait variables should involve repeated administrations of the tests. The Gaudry et al. (1975) study suffered from not having the trait anxiety measure repeated, and it was less than convincing because the number of factors scarcely exceeded the number and kind of variables. Table 35.5 summarizes some of the major factor analytic studies of the STAI.

Davidson (1976) classified people into four groups by the extent to which they had practiced meditation, and found that A-Trait was progressively lowered by extent of meditation; State Anxiety was not measured. That study is important not only for showing the effect of meditation, but also for showing that A-Trait can change over time. Newmark, Faschingbauer, Finch and Kendall (1975) gave the STAI and the MMPI to 311 psychiatry inpatients (13% psychotics) and factor-analyzed the results. They found four factors, (adjustment, passivity, somatic concern, and anxiety proneness) and concluded that Welsh's A is a measure of chronic anxiety. Endler, Magnusson, Ekehammar, and Okada (1976) tested 159 university students in Sweden with the STAI and two other tests (one for state and one for trait). Separate factor analyses of the state and trait scales showed that both sets were multidimensional, and that the correlations between the State and Trait measures were higher than between the two state measures. Factor analysis of all the scales failed to yield separate state and trait measures, results that call into question the State-Trait distinction. It must be remembered that studies confirming the distinction have usually involved multiple administrations of the tests over an extended period of time.

Spielberger, O'Neil, and Hansen (1972) found that students with high A-State scores made more errors on the difficult tasks and fewer errors on the easy

TABLE 35.5
Results of Some Factor Studies
on Spielberger's STAI

Author	Trait Anxiety Factors	State Anxiety Factors
Barker, Barker & Wadsworth (1977)	Trait absent Trait present	State
Gaudry & Poole (1975)	Six 1st-order factors One 2nd-order factor	Four 1st-order factors One 2nd-order factor
Gaudry et al. (1975)	Trait	One state factor for each of 3 occasions, plus one state-absent factor
Kendall, Finch, Auerbach, Hook, & Mekulka (1976)	Trait	State absent State present
Spielberger, Vagg, Barker, Donham, & Westberry (1980) Form X (1980)	Male: Female Trait present State present Trait absent (Both present)	Male: Female: State Trait present (both present)
Vagg, Speilberger, & O'Hearn (1980) Form Y	Trait present Trait present	State present State absent

tasks than did student low in A-State scores. Spielberger (1976) noted that in a number of studies, stress raised both the State Anxiety scores and physiological measures, notably heart rate and blood pressure.

Beginning with the work of Mandler and Sarason (1952), considerable research has been done on test anxiety, i.e., anxiety connected with taking examinations in school or university. Much of this extensive work is peripheral to the concern of this review, but Spielberger, Anton, and Bedell (1976) have described test anxiety as a situation-specific trait anxiety. Spielberger's colleagues (King & Heinrich, 1976) found that A-Trait may have a direct influence on achievement in addition to influencing it through A-State. Their study included three administrations of the STAI just prior to an academic examination.

Spielberger (1977) notes a number of studies showing that changes in State Anxiety are related to general measures of trait anxiety (such as STAI Trait Scale and Taylor MAS) under conditions of psychological stress, but not stress of physical dangers. He comments that these general A-Trait scales measure individual differences in proneness to anxiety in situations of being evaluated by people (with self-esteem at stake). In that sense, even A-Trait is situation specific. Wadsworth, Barker, and Barker (1976) studied 54 graduate students with the STAI. The State but not the Trait measure rose at examination time. But factor analysis found only one Principal Axis factor, leaving Wadsworth et al. to discount the notion that the State and Trait scores measure anything different.

Blankstein (1976) found that Trait Anxiety correlated with the social anxiety scale of the Activity Preference Questionnaire (APQ), but not with APQ physical anxiety. Lykken's APQ is unpublished, but the manual can be obtained from the Department of Psychiatry, University of Minnesota. Martens & Simon (1976) attempted to predict anxiety in female athletes before high school basketball games. Their criterion was the State Anxiety score, and their three predictors were the Sport Competition Anxiety Test (SCAT), which did best; coaches' ratings (which did worst); and the A-Trait score. But in all studies limited to correlations among test scales, it is necessary to question why one scale deserves to be the criterion.

Magarey, Todd, and Blizard (1977) used the STAI with the MMPI D scale and other measures in women about to undergo biopsy of breast lumps. Evidence tended to show that women who had delayed seeking medical attention were deniers, low in anxiety shown verbally, high in anxiety shown nonverbally, and high in depression shown verbally.

Lira, White, and Finch (1977) gave the STAI for Children (STAIC) and the Profile of Mood States (POMS) to 41 youth offenders. A-State correlated with the vigor-activity and the anger-hostility portions of the POMS and also with the total mood disturbance index. A-Trait correlated with depression-dejection, tension-anxiety, and fatigue-inertia parts of the POMS, and with the total mood disturbance index. So, if the STAI is the criterion, the POMS, surprisingly, turns out to measure trait at least as much as state anxiety.

Redfering and Jones (1978) tested 105 Naval Aviation cadets and 105 male university seniors with the STAI and two MMPI scales: Barrons's ego strength (Es) and Meehl's K scale "as measures of psychological defensiveness." He summarized disparagingly, "In contrast to the impressive accumulation of research showing that the State-Trait Anxiety Inventory can discriminate between state and trait anxiety in a contrived situation, this study showed that the inventory did not differentiate between the two dimensions when tested in vivo." But that conclusion rests on Redfering and Jones's unproven assumption that the Navy cadets were, in fact, in a temporary state of anxiety, and the university seniors were not. Redfering and Jones also complain that, contrary to their hypothesis, "increased defensiveness" (Es and K scores) correlated negatively with reported anxiety levels. In fact, both the Es and K scales are known to correlate negatively with anxiety measures, so one can only be amazed at Redfering and Jones's amazement. They seem to have been misled by their own use of the ambiguous term "defensiveness." Things called by the same name are not necessarily the same. I have reviewed this paper mainly to warn the reader that Redfering and Jones's conclusions do not follow from their data.

Banahan (1979) screened employees in five industries for high blood pressure, and gave the STAI to all 279 hypertensives found, as well as to a sample of the essentially normal employees. Hypertension correlated strongly with scores on A-State, and only weakly with scores on A-Trait. Multiple regression identified obesity and A-State as the most important modifiable risk factors to include in a preventive program.

OTHER OBJECTIVE PSYCHOLOGICAL TESTS FOR ANXIETY

The California Psychological Inventory (CPI) is a true-false test of the same format as the MMPI (Gough, 1957). Indeed, the 480 items of the CPI have about 200 in common with the 566 items of the MMPI. I say "about" because the CPI author, Harrison Gough, reworded some of the MMPI items and it is questionable whether to call them the same item or not. In general, many of the highly pathological items of the MMPI are eliminated, and other items having to do with one's values and with variations in normal lifestyle are added.

Alan M. Leventhal (1966) developed an anxiety scale for the CPI by taking the records of 110 students who had sought help at the University of Maryland Counseling Center for social or emotional problems rated by the counselors as moderate or extreme in severity. For controls he used four times as many students (with the same sex distribution) who had not sought help. For both criterion and control groups he used CPI protocols taken a year earlier as part of freshman orientation. Leventhal divided the sample in half, derived items from one half, and cross-validated them on the other half. The cross-validation reduced the number of items only slightly, from 24 to 22. A new sample showed no sex differences in scores and the criterion and control groups did not differ much on the standard CPI scales. Later Leventhal (1968) showed that his anxiety scale correlated positively with MMPI F, D, Pt, and Si, and with the Taylor, Welsh, and IPAT anxiety scales, though not as highly as those scales correlated among themselves. He found that high scorers on his Anxiety scale stayed longer in counseling and improved more slowly. Although it was well derived, the Leventhal scale has been used very little in clinical practice or in research.

Theodore Millon (1977) has developed the Millon Multiaxial Clinical Inventory, which he later renamed the Millon Clinical Multiaxial Inventory (MCMI) to lessen the confusion with the MMPI. Millon was a psychologist involved in developing the *DSM-III* (American Psychiatric Association, 1980), and he oriented his theory-based test with the intention of relating it to *DSM-III* categories. His test includes a scale for Anxiety Disorder, though not for specific diagnoses within that broad category. The test has not yet been used enough to draw firm conclusions about its validity or reliability.[1]

In preparing this chapter, I wrote to Janet Taylor (Spence), Welsh, Cattell, Spielberger, and Millon, asking for any information they have on the use of their anxiety scales either to diagnose Anxiety Disorder in general, or to differentiate among specific diagnoses within Anxiety Disorder. Cattell and Spielberger

---

[1]There are, however, both reliability and validity data in the manual, as well as a number of papers (e.g., Green, 1982, *Journal of Personality Assessment*).

sent me pertinent materials. Taylor (Spence) and Welsh separately wrote me saying that they had lost interest in measuring anxiety. In the past 15 years, neither had done anything in the field, nor had they kept up with what others have done in measuring anxiety, nor even with what others have done using the scales that they developed. Welsh wrote, "Though it is true that I developed the MMPI A scale (and I must agree with your use of the term 'elegant' for its derivation) I am by no means an 'expert' on anxiety. In fact, I have not followed the use of my scale and all I know about it is what Grant and Leona (Dahlstrom) put in the revision of the MMPI *Handbook*. In fact, I have very little interest in the MMPI and the assessment of pathology. My only MMPI paper recently is the one that appears in their updated *Readings*." Theodore Millon has commented (personal communication), "I wish I could aid you in your efforts to locate studies on the anxiety disorders via the MCMI. We have no papers specific to that topic. However, the manual does discuss how the MCMI scales were developed and cross-validated, including the anxiety disorders scale. Our research group has not sought to validate the anxiety scale *itself*, that is, independent of its relationship to other scales, notably those on the personality disorders. That the scale correlates with other instruments measuring anxiety does not strike me as of particular value, even though data exists to suggest reasonably high *rs* (.55 to .60)."

DISCUSSION, SUMMARY AND RECOMMENDATIONS

One way to classify anxiety measures is in terms of generality: scales can measure anxiety in general; anxiety at a middle level of generality; or anxiety with a specific content. The anxiety scales of Taylor, Welsh, Finney (University of Kentucky Scale 7, see Table 35.3), Cattell, and Spielberger are all measures of anxiety in general, and, as we have noted, they correlate highly with one another. The same appears to be true of Millon's Anxiety Disorder Scale (the r's above).

At an intermediate level are the Finney (1965) MMPI scales for types of anxiety: guilt (scale 29)[2], embarrassment, concern with what people think (scale 27), fear or phobia (scale 42) and worry (scale 44). At one time psychological anthropologists liked to classify cultures as guilt cultures and shame cultures. People in guilt cultures are anxious if they fail to meet their own internalized standards of right and wrong; people in shame cultures are anxious (embarrassed) if they look bad to other people. I once did field work in Tuvalu, formerly the Ellice Islands, which turned out to be a so-called shame culture. I frequently heard somebody say "Aku e maa!" (I am embarrassed!). They had been taught to translate *maa* as "ashamed," but "embarrassed" was a more accurate rendering. The system of social control on that island consisted mainly of ridicule, which

---

[2]The scale numbers here refer to the systems of numbering used at the University of Kentucky.

embarrassed the offender, and people's self-restraints were motivated by the fear of being embarrassed and exposed to ridicule. I did not give them MMPI's because the test has never been translated into Tuvalu, but one could expect the Tuvalu people to rank high on scale 27.

At the most specific level are tests of specific fears, called phobias. *DSM-III* distinguishes between simple phobia, social phobia, and agoraphobia (with or without panic attacks), as well as panic disorder, obsessive-compulsive disorder, acute and chronic post-traumatic stress disorder, generalized anxiety disorder, and atypical anxiety disorder. People who fear snakes do not necessarily fear knives, height, darkness, being on stage, or meeting strangers at a party. It is no surprise to find that questions about fear of snakes are better than a general anxiety scale for predicting who will turn out to run from a snake—at least in a situation where there is no incentive to fake positive or negative on the test.

The topic for this chapter is phrased both as Self-Report Tests and as Objective Personality Tests. Both terms refer to paper-and-pencil tests of the questionnaire type consisting of statements with which a person is asked to agree or disagree. In some cases the respondent is asked to show the degree of his agreement or disagreement, or a neutral reply may be allowed. Some of the same tests have been called by both terms (self-report tests and objective personality tests), but the connotations of the terms differ, and the implications for validity differ. The term "self-report" stresses the weaknesses of the tests, and the latter term emphasizes their strengths. The developers of the MMPI were especially offended when anyone spoke of the MMPI as a self-report test, for the term "self-report" implies certain weakness which the developers of the MMPI diligently avoided. Two earlier attempts to develop personality tests, the Bell and the Bernreuter, were indeed self-report tests, and had all the weakness that the term implies. The Strong Vocational Interest Blank (which may or may not be called a personality test) was more clearly an objective test, and the strength of the MMPI flows from the fact that its developers followed the Strong model and not the Bell-Bernreuter model.

Spielberger (1972b) has said, "Moreover, subjective reports about emotional states came to be viewed with extreme suspicion because they were unverifiable and easily falsified. This distrust of verbal reports was further intensified by psychoanalytic formulations which emphasized the distortion in mood and thought that may be produced by unconscious mental processes....Self-report measures such as the STAI may be criticized on many grounds. It may be argued, for example, that the items are ambiguous and mean different things to different people, or that people do not know themselves well enough to give truthful answers, or that many people are unwilling to admit negative things about themselves."

Here are three criteria for distinguishing a self-report test from an objective test. The first criterion is that right out in the open and without disguise or subtlety, some items ask a person to rate himself or report on himself. An example is, "I feel scared"; another example, only slightly less obvious in its self-focus, is "Thunderstorms terrify me." Those are clearly self-report items. In contrast is an item such as "Politicians are usually honest." On the surface, that item is not a self-report statement; it does not ask about the responder; it asks about politicians. When the item is viewed critically, however, it does ask, by implication, about the responding individual. The statement about politicians is embedded in a framework, a higher order clause that is not expressed. The thought is, "I think that politicians are usually honest" or "I believe that politicians are usually honest." Would people answer the statement differently if "I think" were placed at the beginning?

Some MMPI items have this phrase and others do not. I am unaware of any studies that have tested alternate forms with or without the "I think." It is known that making some information explicit can make it salient and can affect the answers that people give. For example, if people's attitudes on birth control are surveyed, and if the survey begins by asking people their religion, some Catholics may feel that they are representing their religion in answering the questions, and may give different answers than they would otherwise give. Still, it seems likely that with a non-self-referent item, such as "Politicians are usually honest," some respondents may, when it is given as part of a personality test, respond to it as such, and where applicable, respond to it in terms of the impression they try to give about their personality, rather than as in an opinion survey.

In terms of manifest content, the MMPI is a mixture of items that are openly self-referent and others that are not; the Spielberger STAI consists entirely of frankly self-referent items; and the Cattell tests consist very heavily of self-referent items. On the face of it, the STAI is much more a self-report test than the Cattell, and the Cattell much more a self-report test than the MMPI.

The second criterion for distinguishing a self-report from an objective test is the crucial one: *in tests more properly called self-report, the content of the items determines their scoring.* In most cases, this means that we must assume the respondent perceives accurately the facts about himself, and that he is willing and motivated to tell truthfully the facts about himself as he perceives them. The weakness of the Bell and Bernreuter tests was the naive assumption that what people say about themselves is true. For the classical MMPI scales, and for most MMPI scales developed since, the items were selected purely on the basis of their correlation with an external criterion, without regard to their content.

Consider this multiple choice: Suppose on the MMPI that a person answers "true" to the item, "My mother was a good woman." This will be scored (a) as showing that his mother was a good woman; (b) as showing that he thinks his mother was a good woman; (c) as showing that he wishes us to think that he thinks his mother was a good woman; or (d) in accordance with its mathematical relation to a criterion. The answers from (a) to (d) are progressively more sophisticated, but only the (d) answer is correct. Basically the STAI items are interpreted as in (a), and to do so seems naive. The MMPI items selected by an external criterion (often, ratings of the person by others) may have content related to the criterion (and hence to the conclusion we reach from the test score), or may have content unrelated to the criterion and the conclusion that is interpreted. The former are called obvious items, and the latter, subtle items. A potential weakness of the STAI is that all its items are obvious, and therefore answers are easier to falsify. On the other hand, with some criteria, such as violence, the obvious items predict better than the subtle ones (presumably because people who do not have enough social judgment to falsify successfully are more likely to do violence).

The third criterion of self-report as distinguished from objective test is the consequence that flows from the first two criteria: *a score that is affected by conscious or unconscious falsification can hardly be called an objective test.* This third criterion is a product of the first two, but it is appropriately listed as a third criterion because it refers to something that is itself independently meas-urable; the degree of falsification or distortion is at least potentially measurable.

Of the anxiety scales, the only ones derived by external criteria are Leventhal's (1966) CPI scale and Finney's five MMPI scales (for general anxiety and for guilt, embarrassment, fear/phobia and obsessive worry). Welsh's A has a some-what weaker foundation, being derived from an internal criterion (factor analysis without rotation) based on scale scores that, in turn, had been derived from external criteria. Cattell's anxiety scales are on a still weaker foundation, being derived from factor analysis of scales that were in no way empirically based. The STAI scales have the shakiest foundation of all, as the items were written purely on face validity.

It must be recognized that even when external criteria were not used in derivation of the scale, such criteria can be correlated with the scale scores in later research, and the deficiency can, to a great extent, be repaired. Even the much-maligned Bell had substantial external criterion validity added to it by later research, and the same is true of such face-validity scales as the Taylor MAS and the Spielberger STAI. Among the MMPI anxiety scales, the Taylor, Welsh, and Finney scales (varying from no external criterion to a firm one) all correlated very highly among themselves and with the MMPI (K uncorrected) Pt scale, which has its own unique idiosyncratic history.

The clinical criterion for the Pt scale was psychiatric diagnoses of obsessive-compulsive neurosis, or, as it was then called, psychasthenia. Some items were derived properly from that criterion. A second set of items was derived by tetrachoric correlation with the first set of items, and the two sets were combined. Hathaway and McKinley never told which items were the ones properly derived from the criterion, and which items were the one improperly added. In fact, from what we know now, the second set of items fit the definition of a suppressor variable and therefore they should have been not added but subtracted, i.e., added in with reversed scoring. Nobody at the University of Minnesota has any record to indicate which items were which, and so it is impossible to reconstruct the primary, valid scale for Pt. Later it became clear that the Pt scale (without K correction) is a nearly pure measure of the first, or A, factor; and the K-corrected Pt scale is a rather good measure of neurosis, but not specifically obsessive-compulsive neurosis. High K-corrected scores are found in the (rather uncommon) cases of obsessive-compulsive neurosis, in the (far commoner) cases of phobia, and in individuals diagnosed under *DSM-II* criteria as depressive neurosis (many of whom were, in fact, histrionic personalities with depressed mood).

Meehl, in an interesting personal communication (1983), has thrown light on the idiosyncratic development of the Pt scale. It seems that when the Pt scale was being developed, Hathaway's research assistant working on it was William Estes, and Estes, who believed in internal consistency methods of scale development, persuaded Hathaway to let him use that method. The result was a hybrid scale, not comparable to the other "clinical" scales of the MMPI. To quote this personal communication:

An interesting historical point about Pt that does not become clear in reading the published article, is that the chief reason for using an internal consistency criterion for item choice was that during the time the Pt scale was being developed, Hathaway's research assistant was, of all people, William K. Estes. I dare say the great majority of psychologists don't think of Estes as ever having had anything to do with the MMPI even though he was a Minnesota Ph.D. He got tired of being a TA in the department and he had been a pre-med with an interest in psychiatry, so working with Hathaway as a research assistant, was more appealing to Bill. Skinner didn't care one way or the other, so he got his degree running rats in Skinner boxes while he was earning his hamburgers building the Pt scale! Now Estes was more mathematically inclined than Starke and he had ideas about factorial purity and such like, which as you know Starke never believed in very much. So when they had some of these items that didn't act quite right, combined with the fact (I can't find a sentence in the article about this but I thought there was one) that the number of cases available was somewhat smaller than had been true of some of the other scales, Estes was able to twist Starke's arm to include internal consistency as a criterion. So what you have is a research assistant with a different psychometrical orientation from his boss, being able to use some other arguments than statistical purity to persuade the boss to do it.

This had some effect upon my own thesis work and our later developments from that. It turned out that the K-factor—whose nature we obviously didn't understand very well when we first published on it—kept popping up with big correlations with Pt, and I am now inclined to believe that is largely attributable to the fact that the Pt scale was in part derived by internal consistency.

It is a curious fact, however, that the MMPI anxiety scale that was derived without any empirical foundation (Taylor's) correlates very highly with the anxiety scale derived empirically from an external criterion (Finney's), and with the anxiety scale derived only from an internal criterion (Welsh's). So, in the end, one is no better or worse than another, or only minimally so. How can that be? I suggest that there are two reasons. First, all of the anxiety items are obvious items. Even the empirically derived scale can easily be distorted by conscious or unconscious attempts to make one impression or another. Second, in research studies, all the scales work as valid measures of anxiety and correlate with what they are supposed to, because the subjects had minimal or no motivation to give a false impression. The validity of the measurement might not be so good when research is done retrospectively on patients who took the test clinically (and there was some material advantage in being "sick" or "healthy").

The excellent validity shown for the STAI, the beautiful correlation with other variables, takes place in research settings where there is no motivation to dissemble. The STAI is seldom given in a psychiatric diagnostic evaluation. If administered in the clinical setting, the "obvious" nature of its items assures that it would be found subject to heavy response-set effects, at least as much as the MMPI anxiety measures, and possibly more so.

Twenty years ago, clinicians used the Welsh anxiety scale and researchers used the Taylor. Today, researchers use the STAI, but clinicians continue to use the Welsh anxiety scale, if they use any. As noted, some excellent research has been done using the STAI and other anxiety scales, and all indications are that anxiety is being validly measured, at least in research projects in which there is no motivation to appear more or less anxious.

SYMPTOM CHECKLISTS

Symptom checklists have been used by public health physicians, but have not found much favor among psychometricians. Checklists consist of items whose meanings are not subtle, but transparent, open, and obvious. The Cornell Medical Index is the traditional checklist and was used in some mental health population studies, including Leighton's in Digby County, Nova Scotia. More recently the Hopkins Symptom Checklist (HSCL) has been used.

The problem with symptom checklists, as with all self-report tests, is that they are so transparent. Their purpose is open and undisguised, and they are, therefore, easily faked. That problem is acceptable if the people being tested are taking part in a research study, and they know that their answers will not affect their future. In such a case, people will usually tell what they really believe of themselves (which is not always the same as what is objectively true of them). But clinical testing is normally done in a situation where the results can affect the person's welfare, and some people are motivated to deny their troubles, whereas others exaggerate or dramatize them. A person completing the HSCL as a hurdle to acceptance into employment can easily fake the answers to deny every symptom. A person taking the HSCL as part of an examination for disability payments can easily fake the answers to claim every symptom. That is the basic weakness of such instruments.

The major psychometric instruments for anxiety have been discussed earlier, but there are many that were not discussed. Among these, the Profile of Mood States (POMS) measures (as its name implies) mood states, and is transparent; in both regards it resembles the STAI. The Haertzen group at the U.S. Public Health Service Addiction Research Center (since moved from Lexington, Kentucky, to Baltimore, Maryland) developed a number of short scales to measure transient emotional states in addicts.

ANXIETY AND HYSTERIA

Since an aim of much of this book is toward improved diagnosis and classification, I have a final point to make, ultimately relating back to measurement. A key issue that has not been sufficiently discussed is the relation of anxiety and anxiety disorders to hysteria. Klein, however, has published elsewhere on "hysteroid" dysphoria (Klein & Davis, 1968; Liebowitz & Klein, 1979). The statement often heard, that hysteria has disappeared, is, I believe, false. Three good books about hysteria have appeared in recent years (Horowitz, 1977; Krohn, 1978; Roy, 1982). Sigmund Freud once commented that the findings of psychoanalysis are so disconcerting that each generation will be in danger of losing the knowledge. People forget or deny information that threatens them. Similarly, the historian Santayana said that people who forget their history are condemned to repeat it. That is true, as Santayana meant it, in the context of world history. It is also true in psychopathology, of the history of an individual's life.

We need to keep our awareness of the processes that Freud discovered—even while disapproving of the way in which some of his followers enshrine his writings as a quasi-religious orthodoxy. Freud was a brilliant and creative thinker who made shrewd and skillful observations of psychopathology.

Hysteria was a major focus, 50 to 100 years ago, of the great psychopathologists, Charcot, Freud, Janet, Jung, and Prince. Some of the major conclusions I draw from Freud and other are as follows:

1. There is a major syndrome, dubbed hysteria, consisting of a fluctuating selective attention and inattention. The processes called repression and dissociation allow some information to be blocked from awareness.

2. As part of this syndrome of hysteria, emotional reactions are exaggerated and dramatized, including anger, depression, discouragement, anxiety, and panic. The individual has episodes of behavior that differ sharply from the same person's normal and usual behavior, and so the person will say, "I can't understand why I did that; that's not like me."

3. This syndrome, hysteria, occurs very commonly, and is one of the major categories of psychopathology.

4. Some anxiety and some panic disorders are a form of the hysteria syndrome. Freud divided hysteria into anxiety hysteria and conversion hysteria. Many of the cases that Freud called anxiety hysteria are currently called phobia.

5. The symptoms, including behaviors, are motivated and directed toward achieving goals, and can be called purposive, though the goals and purposes are not in awareness ("unconscious"), and the individual cannot verbalize or admit these goals to himself, much less to other people.

6. The goals are typically directed toward influencing and affecting the behavior of other people toward the individual.

These principles are valid today, and it is disappointing and disquieting that so little recognition has been given them by experts in the anxiety disorder field. Many of the recent discoveries in the anxiety field have been biochemical and pharmacological, and although these are important, we should not lose sight of the forest while observing the trees. Reassertion of the hysteria syndrome is not a contradiction of biochemistry. It may turn out that the hysteria syndrome itself has its basis in biochemistry and genetics. Freud predicted that eventually hysteria and other psychiatric illnesses would be found to have a biological basis, even while he explored the ways in which psychopathological syndromes are learned by early experience in the individual's lifetime. A recent study suggests that among atypical depressives, the "hysteroid" dysphorics respond better to phenelzine than to tricyclics (Liebowitz et al., 1984).

My doctoral dissertation (1961a) (under Robert R. Sears) investigated the influences of mothers on the developing personality of their children. Hysteria turned out to be one of the features for which a high portion of the variance was not accounted for by maternal attitudes and behaviors. General anxiety in children was rather well correlated with maternal features, but hysteria was not.

In 30 years of practicing psychiatry and clinical psychology, nearly every one of the patients and clients I have seen can be assigned to one of three or four categories: hysteria, schizophrenia, and affective disorder. (The fourth category can be organic brain syndrome, antisocial personality, or marital maladjustment, in normal persons, depending on the setting.) Certain other categories, such as true obsessive-compulsive neurosis, which are featured prominently in textbooks, are rarely seen. I have seen true obsessive-compulsive neurotics, but only three or four in my professional life. Hysterical neuroses are far more common. When I worked in a mental health clinic in the Southern Appalachian mountains, hysterical neuroses were seen daily, and hysterical personalities are seen nearly every day in most practitioners' offices. Compulsive personalities are equally common, but they do not often seek treatment. Hysterical personalities not only are common in the general population, but also make up a disproportionate share of persons who come to the attention of psychologists, physicians, counselors, social caseworkers, clergymen, lawyers, police officers, judges, and correctional officers. They have a talent for getting into problems of all kinds, and for making problems for other people. They do so with a naive and innocent air.

Hysterical personality has been renamed Histrionic personality in *DSM-III*. The syndrome defined in *DSM-III* attempts to concern itself only with disorders, including personality disorders, but not including variations of normality. The line, however, is not always clear between a disorder and a variant of the normal. Perhaps the main consideration of the *DSM-III* committee was to list the conditions whose "treatment" should be compensable under health insurance. (Someone has called this an unkind dig, but not so: to set standards of compensability is a legitimate task.)

In my experience, hysterical personalities are best described as naive, idealistic, and dissociating. There is a discrepancy between their behavior and their ideals, but the hysteric is unaware of it. These people communicate indirectly, nonverbally. They do not say what they mean; they imply it: they do not tell you what they mean; they show you what they mean.

In the first year of practice beyond my residency, I interviewed a young woman in Champaign County who sought mental health services. When I asked her about her father, she said (pausing between utterances), "My father was the most wonderful man I have ever known. (pause) He never used to beat mother and us kids. (pause) Except when he was drunk." This is a classical hysterical personality's way of saying one thing consciously, in words, while managing to convey the opposite meaning. It was clear that she hated her father. The effect of her utterance was to give me a very bad impression of her father, and perhaps to motivate me to rescue her. But when I said, "You seem to hate your father; you bear him a lot of resentment," she answered, "Oh no! Just the opposite! Didn't you hear what I said? I said that my father is the most wonderful man I've ever known."

Haertzen, Hill, and Monroe (1968) empirically developed an MMPI scale of items on which narcotic addicts gave cynical answers and alcoholics gave idealistic answers to expressing opinions on parents, God, and patriotism. These differential responses show that the alcoholics had more of a hysterical personality than did the addicts. I went on to develop (as part of a computer MMPI interpretation) an index of hysterical personality that agrees well with my clinical diagnoses of hysterical personality. So the concept of hysterical personality is indeed measurable.

Hysterical personalities are, par excellence, those who play "games" in Eric Berne's sense. I believe that they can do so because it is easier to engage in vicious conduct if you do not have to recognize such behavior for what it is. Hysterics often show rapid or sudden changes in mood and behavior, including outbursts of anger, spells of depressed mood, suicide attempts (often misdiagnosed as endogenous depression), and periods of anxiety or panic.

From clinical observation, I hypothesize that patients who present themselves with anxiety symptoms have a far higher share of hysterical personality than does the general population, as measured on the MMPI by the Finney hysterical personality index. This measure should be helpful in distinguishing among various diagnostic categories of anxiety, and in selection of different treatment procedures for different kinds of patients. Clinical researchers engaged in anxiety research could test these hypotheses.

The most unfortunate feature of *DSM-III* is that it abolishes the unitary concept of hysterical neurosis and scatters the hysterical neuroses among three major headings: Dissociative Disorders, Somatoform Disorders, and Anxiety Disorders (and among three subheadings of Anxiety Disorders). Under each heading, some hysterical neuroses are lumped together with conditions that are not hysterical neuroses, such as obsessive-compulsive neurosis under the anxiety disorders, and hypochondriasis under Somatoform Disorders. This is a serious error, because it groups illnesses that do not belong together, and separates those that do belong together. *DSM-III* creates this situation by over-weighting some superficialities while ignoring true similarities.

As a result, some clear cases of hysterical neurosis fall between the cracks and cannot be properly diagnosed under *DSM-III* categories. Patients in the Southern Appalachians often have somatic conversions. Headache, vomiting, backache, pain in the chest, or shortness of breath (a popular preoccupation because of the real prevalence of miners' lung disease) are not uncommon. Mild anxieties or phobias ("Doc, I feel nervous!"), and perhaps some dissociation of hysterical acting-out may be seen, but not enough of any one category to reach a *DSM-III* diagnosis. The Manual allows clinicians to add various bodily symptoms to reach a diagnosis of somatization disorder (Briquet syndrome or "St. Louis hysteria"), but because of its fragmentation, clinicians may not add anxiety symptoms or dissociation symptoms to somatoform manifestations. As a result, many patients having symptoms of hysterical neurosis are misdiagnosed or undiagnosed.

FUTURE OUTLOOK

Which of the objective measures of anxiety should be used in the future? Each of the various scales has good points to recommend it.

From a research standpoint, the Cattell scales offer an advantage. There are seven scales measuring anxiety in different aspects and rather independently. (Nine scales, counting one that relates to anxiety only in males, and another that relates to it only in females.) A research project on the diagnosis or treatment of anxiety can score all seven, or eight, or nine scales, as well as compute the score on the second-order anxiety factor. It is possible that one combination of anxiety scale scores measures one type of anxiety disorder, whereas another combination of scores measures another type. It is also possible that one combination of scores predicts successful treatment by one method, and another combination of scores predicts successful treatment by another method.

One could also look for differential diagnosis by differing combinations of scales from the MMPI. A problem is that MMPI anxiety scales are highly correlated with one another; especially the general anxiety trait scales of Taylor, Welsh, and Finney. One way to deal with that problem is first to calculate scores on the general anxiety factor, and then calculate revised scores on the several scales by mathematically removing the anxiety factor from them by the Finney formula:

$$T = \frac{S - r\,A}{\sqrt{a - r^2}}$$

T is the true score after correction; S is the measured score; A is the variable to be partialed out (such as the general Anxiety factor); and r is the correlation of S and A. (The formula requires modification if S and A are not expressed in z scores.) This procedure yields corrected scale scores that are orthogonal to (i.e., uncorrelated with) the A factor. The University of Kentucky computer system routinely calculates such corrected scores on all scales. Other scales should be included in the study: all of the old clinical scales of the 1942 MMPI (of which D, Pt, and Sc are most loaded on the A factor), without K correction; and some of the writer's empirical scales related to aspects of anxiety, such as scale 29 (guilt), scale 42 (phobia and fear), and scale 42 (worry and obsession).

If one were to design a major research project on the anxiety disorders, a wide variety of anxiety measures from the MMPI, the Cattell CAQ, and the STAI should be included as the bare minimum. The project should also include physiological measures of anxiety, such as GSR and heart rate. The project should include a sufficient sampling of patients with all the different kinds of anxiety disorders recognized in *DSM-III*, and carefully diagnosed by a reliable system, using a standardized interview, such as the Diagnostic Interview Schedule (DIS). Finally, all tests should be repeated a number of times under conditions that include several kinds of anxiety-provoking stressors, and a variety of treatments designed to reduce anxiety, including several psychotherapeutic or behavioral treatments, and several pharmacological treatments. Then we can determine which diagnostic measures can predict outcome for specific methods of treatment.

It is only when projects of this scope have been carried out that clinicians will be able to say that they understand how anxiety works, and use this knowledge to benefit patients and clients.

What is exciting about the future is the prospect that objective psychological test measures may be combined with physiological measures. In the past, Cattell was the major researcher who combined the two types of measures, and he did so mainly for the purpose of factor analysis. Future studies should use objective psychological test measures in combination with physiological measures in all lines of research on diagnosis and treatment.

36 The Measurement of Anxiety: Reply to Finney

E. H. Uhlenhuth, M.D.
The University of Chicago

Dr. Finney provides us with a charming historical review of the development of questionnaire measures of anxiety, laced as it is with personal anecdotes and references to his interactions with other major workers in this area. He focuses on the Minnesota Multiphasic Personality Inventory (MMPI) and its derivatives, such as the Taylor Manifest Anxiety Scale (TMAS), the Welch Anxiety Scale, and Finney's own anxiety scales; Cattell and Scheier's Sixteen Personality Factors, Clinical Analysis Questionnaire, and Institute of Personality and Ability Testing Objective-Analytic Anxiety Battery and 8-Parallel Form Anxiety Battery; Spielberger's State-Trait Anxiety Inventory (STAI); and Harrison Gough's California Psychological Inventory (CPI). Using these as his raw materials, Finney discusses a number of significant issues raised by such instruments.

He points out that all of these different measures tap very much the same area, as indicated by their high intercorrelations, whether they were derived by assembling items that have face validity, by factoring a pool of items, or by selecting items, regardless of content, that correlate with an external criterion. Thus, he suggests, there is little need at this time for additional scales to measure anxiety. The development of improved measures certainly is limited both by technical problems and by the conceptual state of the field. The unidimensional view of anxiety implied by Finney's discussion may limit further instrument refinement. However, if one accepts the notion of discontinuity between normal and pathological anxiety, then improved measures to discriminate and quantify these types, along the lines of Klein's agoraphobia and panic attack scales (personal communication), would be most welcome.

Measures that more effectively discriminate anxiety from depression also would represent a definite step forward. The behavioral and cognitive (in the sense of Beck, 1976) aspects of anxiety in patients also represent neglected areas of measurement. To what extent such measures would correlate with the more traditional measures of anxiety is an interesting question for investigation.

Finney also discusses the relationship of state and trait anxiety, particularly with respect to the STAI. He notes that measures of these two aspects are often correlated, and suggests that specification of the time frame for the subject to consider in responding may be crucial. It seems unlikely that pure measures of these aspects of anxiety can be constructed, since high trait is defined as a high probability of high state. In this framework, the possibility arises of assessing a trait by averaging across repeated measures of the corresponding state. In a recent study, measures employing this strategy correlated with preferential drug-taking behavior in normal subjects where more traditional assessments of traits failed to do so (Uhlenhuth, Johanson, Kilgore, & Kobasa, 1981).

Finney points out that self-report tests differ from objective tests in that scores on the former depend upon the manifest content of the test items. Self-report tests, therefore, are subject to distortion on the basis of conscious dissembling or defenses such as denial. The ambiguous meanings of language also can introduce variability. To these problems may be added respondents' tendencies to develop idiosyncratic theories about themselves which they support with biased data and other reporting strategies that are not congruent with the objectives of the investigator. We shall return to this point. The important issue here is that most of these opportunities for "error" seem equally likely to affect any type of questionnaire response.

In this connection, Robert Kellner's very practical approaches to making technical improvements in questionnaire design and administration are quite interesting. His work suggests, for example, that positively oriented items may be more sensitive than negatively oriented symptom items in detecting drug effects (Kellner, Rada, Andersen, & Pathak, 1979). Also, contrary to psychometric lore, he finds that simple, dichotomous response alternatives provide more reliable information than scales with finer gradations, at least in work with samples consisting of patients. These results suggest that efforts to further refine self-report measures may be worthwhile.

Finally, Finney emphasizes the importance of external criteria in constructing, or at least in validating, questionnaire instruments. In a practical sense, he seems to be referring primarily to diagnosis by skilled clinicians as a suitable external criterion. He also mentions physiological variables, however.

There is a striking lack of congruence between the measures on which Finney bases his discussion and those most commonly employed by clinical psychopharmacologists in their research. Most of these investigations rely heavily on scaled ratings made by skilled clinicians or other trained observers. These observations are used for two major purposes. One group of instruments is designed basically to detect clinically significant anxiety, i.e., for diagnosis. This group includes the Schedule for Affective Disorders and Schizophrenia (Endicott & Spitzer, 1978), the Diagnostic Interview Schedule (Robins, Helzer, Croughan,

& Ratcliff, 1981), and the Structured Clinical Interview for *DSM-III* (Spitzer & Williams, 1983). Another group of observer-rated instruments is designed primarily to quantify levels of pathology in diagnosed patients. This group includes the Hamilton Anxiety Scale (Hamilton, 1959) and the Covi Anxiety Scale (Lipman, 1982), as well as simple global scales for rating the clinical concept of anxiety (Lipman, Cole, Park, & Rickels, 1965).

Even in the realm of self-reports, however, clinical psychopharmacologists tend to use instruments hardly touched upon by Finney in his review. These include the General Health Questionnaire (Goldberg & Hillier, 1979), the Hopkins Symptom Checklist or HSCL-90 (Lipman, Covi, & Shapiro, 1979), and the Profile of Mood States (McNair, Lorr, & Droppleman, 1971). In the remainder of this discussion, we reexamine some of the issues raised by Finney in light of data from some of these additional measures.

It is easy to agree with Finney in principle about the importance of external criteria in the construction of measures. Often, however, reliable, valid, and theoretically significant external criteria are themselves not readily available. Psychopharmacologists are particularly fortunate in this regard. Since drug treatment is precisely specifiable, both qualitatively and quantitatively, the response to drug provides a solidly anchored criterion for validating measures.

The Profile of Mood States (POMS), for example, is finding increasing application in studies of the subjective effects of psychotropic drugs. The current augmented version (Cole, Pope, LaBrie, & Ionescu-Pioggia, 1978) consists of 72 adjectives or brief phrases describing aspects of mood. Subjects report the presence of each item, usually within a "right now" time frame, on a five-point scale ranging from "not at all" to "extremely." Scores are generated on eight mood dimensions, empirically derived by factor analysis: anxiety, vigor, confusion, fatigue, anger, friendliness, depression, and elation. The anxiety scale is quite sensitive to the therapeutic effects of the benzodiazepines (Uhlenhuth, unpublished data), although a clear dose/response relationship cannot always be demonstrated. The vigor, fatigue, and confusion scales are sensitive to the sedative effects of benzodiazepines (Johanson & Uhlenhuth, 1982).

In our laboratory, four of the POMS factors have been combined in simple linear fashion: anxiety plus vigor minus fatigue minus confusion. We call this composite arousal, as it seems to reflect that major mood dimension, described elsewhere in this volume by Lang. Arousal scores are normally distributed, and they respond in close relationship to the dose of a benzodiazepine (Johanson & Uhlenhuth, 1982).

Certain measures of psychomotor performance also are closely correlated with arousal scores. Figure 36.1, for example, shows a scatter plot of finger-tapping rates and POMS arousal scores from one subject who took single doses of diazepam or placebo prior to testing on different days separated by several rest days. Note that performance was related more closely to the arousal score than to the dose of diazepam. This same relationship held within five other subjects

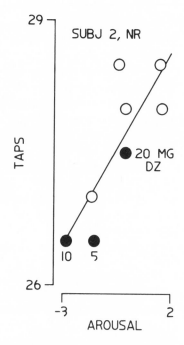

FIG. 36.1 Scattergram of finger-tapping rate (without reinforcement for speed) versus POMS arousal scores on eight occasions for one subject. Open circles represent performance after placebo; filled circles represent performance after diazepam, with doses as indicated.

who participated in this experiment, whether or not they were reinforced for speed. Furthermore, subjects with high mean tapping speed across sessions were those with high mean arousal scores across sessions. Thus, there was a high correlation between tapping speed and arousal scores both within and between subjects.

Let us turn now to the performance of the Hamilton Anxiety Scale (HAS), rated by a skilled observer, and the Hopkins Symptom Checklist (HSCL), a self-report measure, against the benzodiazepine response criterion. We examined a substantial number of clinical studies that used both of these scales to compare the effects of a benzodiazepine and placebo in anxious patients (Glass, Uhlenhuth, & Kellner, 1982). In the overwhelming majority of these studies, the HAS was more sensitive than the HSCL in discriminating benzodiazepine-treated from placebo-treated patients. There were no distinctions in sensitivity between the total score of the HAS and its psychic and somatic subscale scores or between the total score of the HSCL and its anxiety and somatic subscale scores.

One might suspect that the apparent sensitivity of the HAS was due to clinical raters picking up sedative side effects in benzodiazepine-treated patients (breaking the double blind), rather than due to superior sensitivity to the specific antianxiety effects of the drug. If this were true, then one would expect the HAS to be most sensitive in studies where patients taking the benzodiazepine reported sedative side effects more frequently than patients taking placebo. This turned out not to be the case: the HAS was, if anything, slightly (nonsignificantly) more sensitive in discriminating drug-treated from placebo-treated patients in those studies where patients in both treatment groups reported sedation with about equal frequency.

When the sensitivity of the HSCL was examined in a parallel way, an interesting finding emerged. The HSCL was about as sensitive as the HAS in discriminating drug-treated from placebo-treated patients in studies where patients in the two treatment groups reported sedation with about equal (low) frequency. However, in studies where benzodiazepine-treated patients reported sedation more frequently than placebo-treated patients, the HSCL failed to discriminate the two treatment groups. Sedation appeared to interfere with the patients' self-reports of anxiety on the HSCL. One may suspect that the patients' rating strategy differed from that of the clinical observers. Perhaps patients employed an overall cost/benefit analysis in making their ratings, rather than attempting to discriminate antianxiety effects specifically. Here, then, may be an example of the divergent interests of patients and investigators differentially affecting their rating strategies, as mentioned earlier.

The foregoing discussion has placed heavy emphasis on detection of the response to benzodiazepines as a criterion for validating measures of anxiety. This position clearly has heuristic value for investigators concerned with the psychopharmacology of anxiety. This viewpoint may be too narrow, however, to accommodate research on other aspects of anxiety. In this connection, it is particularly interesting when measures derived from one realm of data (factored self-descriptions of subjective experience) display a close relationship to a quite independent realm of data (the effect of a specific chemical substance), as in the examples above. Until the relationships among various aspects of anxiety (see Lang, this volume) are clearer, it seems prudent to use multiple external criteria, perhaps including the effects of several different classes of drugs, in validating measures of anxiety.

37

Structures of Mood and Personality and Their Relevance to Assessing Anxiety, With an Emphasis on Self-Report

Auke Tellegen
University of Minnesota

METHODOLOGICAL AND CONCEPTUAL ISSUES

The Role of Self-Report

The manifestations of anxiety are varied, and verbal report is one of its many indicators. Since much of this chapter will be about self-report, it may be useful first to consider generally the role of this medium.

Psychological tests, including self-report scales, are often treated as tools for predicting rather remote nontest behaviors, i.e., behaviors very different from the test behavior itself. In the case of personality tests this stance is not unreasonable insofar as assessment studies have demonstrated important biographical and mental health correlates of these measures (Block, 1965, 1971; Dahlstrom, Welsh, & Dahlstrom, 1972, 1975).

Nonetheless, even the most positive findings, which include correlations exceeding .50 and even .60 between self-ratings and peer-ratings (Ashton & Goldberg, 1973; McCrae, 1982; Norman, 1969), do not warrant viewing self-report measures as almost interchangeable with related non-self-report observations. Skeptics of cross-domain consistencies have been moved to claim that the glass that seemed partially filled to some is in reality nearly empty (Mischel, 1968; Peterson, 1968). These critics have in turn been challenged by others who continue to emphasize the threads of consistency that run through surface inconstancy (Block, 1977; Epstein, 1979; Hogan, DeSoto, & Solano, 1977).

The consistency issue arises in part from a difference in descriptive preference. Behaviorally oriented psychologists have tended to target specific behaviors in specific situations, while psychometrically and trait-oriented psychologists have been interested in more encompassing classes of situations and responses such as those represented by personality tests. Significantly, correlations among specific measures or items are often low, whereas for good psychometric reasons correlations among aggregates, combining a variety of specific indicators, can be substantial (Epstein, 1979). One of the often-cited studies by Hartshorne and May (1928) concerning the consistency of honesty in school children provides a striking example of this aggregation effect. The children were observed in 23 different situations, each of which afforded an opportunity for an act of dishonesty such as lying, cheating, and stealing. The average correlation among the 23 single behavioral items was .23, and this result is often mentioned, and rightly so, as an example of behavioral specificity. But an aggregate formed by combining seven of the measures had a reliability of about .80 (Jackson & Paunonen, 1980). In other words, averaged over a range of situations a child's honesty was quite predictable although behavior in specific situations was not. Theoretically and practically, the former finding represents an important kind of orderliness. Aggregation may reveal greater consistencies not only within a given data domain, but also between domains. Thayer (1970) has made this point specifically with respect to relationships between questionnaire measures of arousal and indices of psychophysiological reactivity. The same data, then, are interpretable on different levels of aggregation, but they may show low intercorrelations on a low level of aggregation and high ones on a higher level.

Weak convergence between indicators from different data domains, but presumably measuring the same construct, has also been explained in part as the work of "method factors." The term refers to distortions or biases peculiar to a given data source or method. Inasmuch as method factors are nuisance variables that attenuate correlations between measures of the same thing, efforts have been made to minimize their contribution (Jackson, 1971; Norman, 1963, 1969). Concern over method variance is certainly warranted. Inadequate response formats, unclear wording, intrusiveness of the questions asked, can all increase unwanted variance or reduce desired variance. For example, responses to self-report adjective checklists (also used to assess affect) are distorted by individual differences in the tendency to make check marks (Bentler, 1969), best avoided by having respondents mark every item either "true" or "false." Other unwanted response variations are more difficult to control but they can be measured. Response inconsistencies such as those that result from incorrectly marked answer sheets, poor comprehension, carelessness, and stereotypic true or false responding can be detected through appropriate scales (Tellegen, 1982). Although inconsistency measures of this kind are clearly useful for identifying invalid records, they are not yet widely used.

Some problems of method variance have proven to be more refractory and controversial. A great deal of controversy has surrounded the often high correlations between measures of presumably distinctive forms of psychopathology or maladjustment, for instance, between different scales of the Minnesota Multiphasic Personality Inventory (MMPI). Does this covariation pattern reflect individual differences in a generalized desirable-response set, which contribute unwanted method variance and need to be minimized (Jackson, 1971), or does it represent a substantively important personality factor (Block, 1965)? The answer to both these questions is undoubtedly affirmative. There can be no doubt that manipulative self-representation, or "impression management," does occur. One approach to this problem has been to construct so-called validity scales to detect and even correct for these tendencies. The MMPI validity scales are a well-known example. How well do these scales work? The answer, I believe, is that the success has not been spectacular. Although it appears to be possible to construct a scale that will detect deliberate faking in a specific setting by particular respondents, its usefulness may be strictly limited to that setting (Norman, 1963). I am unaware of any scales measuring validity-impairing impression management that are highly effective over a wide range of situations. Scores on such general-purpose scales are usually equivocal unless interpreted in conjunction with other data about the setting and the respondent. Another proposed solution to the problem of impression management is the use of "subtle" rather than "obvious" items. The evidence, however, has not favored subtle items. In the case of the MMPI, the more obvious items appear to be the more discriminating ones (Duff, 1965; Koss & Butcher, 1973). Obvious items can be expected to work only when respondents are candid. The implication is that more important than indirection and detection efforts are attempts to establish a relationship of trust and functional collaboration with the respondent. This would preferably include some useful feedback of test results.

The concern with eliminating or reducing invalid method variance and with enhancing connections between different domains through aggregation needs to be balanced by a recognition that some discrepancies between different data sources are unavoidable. The point made in the beginning of this section stands: self-report scales tend to be no more than moderately correlated with important variables from other domains. This point is also true for the anxiety area; different data systems are said to be only loosely coupled (cf. Lang, this volume; Rachman & Hodgson, 1974).

Discrepancies can be psychologically informative, however. In the case of self-report the point is nearly self-evident. Some individuals may respond to a given stressful situation with both verbal denial and physiological arousal suggesting fear. Such occurrences reduce the predictability of one type of indicator from the other, but the discrepancy can still reflect an interpretable coping pattern. This also means that a self-report measure can provide us more information when combined with other measures, including additional verbal indicators (as is illustrated in the last section of this chapter). As a given data source is incorporated into an increasingly multichannel assessment program, there is an increase in its distinctive contribution, in conjunction with other verbal and nonverbal measures, as an indicator of the particular psychological processes that govern it. A self-report scale in that role could be treated as a probabilistic indicator not only of certain relatively remote nontest variables, but also of the appraisals (perceptions, feelings, thoughts) and any other factors that can be inferred as its proximal antecedents. Among these inferences could be statements about a respondent's impression management or candor, and her or his self-deception or self-awareness. Only if self-report is exploited in these various ways will its use be optimal. In each case the investigator attempts to zero in on a target construct through multiple measures, a process that has been described as "convergent operationism" or "methodological triangulation" (Campbell & Fiske, 1959; Cronbach & Meehl, 1955; Garner, Hake, & Eriksen, 1956).

States and Traits

Anxiety has been said to occur both as a state and as a trait. The distinction is embodied in Spielberger's well-known State-Trait Anxiety Inventory (STAI) (Spielberger, Gorsuch, & Lushene, 1970).

Traditionally, states are viewed as comparatively short-lived processes (e.g., a momentary surprise, a flash of anger, a brief scare), manifested as short-term intra-individual fluctuations. Defined in this way, states can be sharply distinguished from traits, which are generally defined as durable dispositions (response tendencies) that reflect individual differences. When applicable, these clear-cut distinctions between states and traits can lead to elegant and powerful analyses (e.g., Nesselroade, 1983). For the study of psychopathology, however, more complex constructs are needed to accommodate the actual phenomena.

As a case in point, anxiety and depression are viewed as states that are changeable but can be of long duration and can have dispositional properties. For example, the *Diagnostic and Statistical Manual (DSM-III)* Generalized Anxiety Disorder (GAD) is characterized by a state of anxious mood that has been "continuous" for at least a month, as well as by fatigability, irritability, and other dispositional features (American Psychiatric Association, 1980). Similarly, among the *DSM-III* criteria of Major Depressive Episode with Melancholia are a state of depressive mood lasting for at least 2 weeks and a "lack of reactivity to usually pleasurable stimuli" (the latter being a dispositional feature even though the disposition is one of unresponsiveness). These temporary but extended episodes, then, can be classified unequivocally as "states" only if a broader state construct is adopted. Such a construct would have to encompass features that are relatively persistent (without ruling out superimposed short-term fluctuations) and clearly dispositional (although the dispositions would not outlast the episode).

Given clinically more appropriate state constructs that allow for dispositional components and extended durations, certain "trait" meaures of anxiety, neuroticism, and so forth could be interpreted as state-related. Indeed, experience with such scales indicates that they are sensitive to major clinical affective changes, as clinical users of the MMPI know. At the same time, some of these measures show relatively high test-retest stabilities, and even evidence a substantial genetic component (Eaves & Young, 1981; Lykken, 1982). In other words, these same scales also behave as indicators of "real traits."

These measures, as well as other state or trait scales, cannot be linked in a simple one-to-one manner to clinically relevant state or trait constructs, but must be assumed to reflect to some extent both construed states and traits. Whether inferences are to be made about an individual's characterological, temperamental, or state-related attributes, self-report "state" and "trait" measures cannot be interpreted simplistically but should be used in combination with other evidence. This rule also applies to the self-report measures that are considered in more detail below.

Options in Scale Construction

In this volume Finney has pointed out that many different anxiety scales are in existence and that they have been constructed in a variety of ways. What are the main options for constructing a scale and what purposes do they serve? The classification of test construction techniques that Hase and Goldberg (1967) have used is a good starting point for this discussion. Their classification distinguishes between approaches whose predictive effectiveness has been compared in a number of empirical studies. Three basic options for constructing personality and psychopathology inventory scales are recognized: "intuitive," "internal," and "external."

The distinguishing feature of the intuitive or "deductive" (Burisch, 1984) approach is that scale construction requires the adoption of a set of constructs from which the items can be "derived." The test constructor begins by defining and describing the trait or clinical syndrome he or she wishes to measure (for example, "dominance," "achievement motivation," "anxiety," "depression"). Someone must then either choose or create items that fit the definition. This approach, the least technical and most nearly commonsensical of the three, was used in the construction of the earliest inventories.

The internal or "inductive" (Burisch, 1984) approach is to construct scales on the basis of correlations among the test items themselves. Factor analysis is the method most commonly used. With this approach, construct definitions and number of constructs (dimensions) are not defined ahead of time but are based on the analyses, hence the "inductive" label. "Neuroticism," "extraversion," and "ego-strength" are among the dimensions that have come out of factor-analytic research.

The external approach bypasses considerations of multivariate internal structure in favor of a single-minded bivariate search for items that correlate with a chosen criterion. Among externally developed clinical self-report instruments the MMPI, whose construction was based on psychiatric diagnostic criteria, is still the exemplar. Implementation of the external approach requires of course that the target constructs be chosen and operationalized before test construction begins. Prior commitment to a particular set of constructs is an important feature that the external and deductive approaches have in common. The important difference is that the external approach selects construct-relevant items on the basis of empirical correlations, "blindly," rather than on the basis of psychological insight.

Burisch's (1984) provocative paper presents a review and evaluation of the findings on the comparative merits of the three approaches. First, reaffirming the conclusion Goldberg reached on the basis of his pioneering study (Goldberg, 1972; Hase & Goldberg, 1967), Burisch observes that scales produced by the three approaches do not differ dramatically in their correlations with relevant nontest variables. Second, he points out that of the three methods, the deductive approach requires appreciably less test-construction effort, tends to get by on shorter scales, and is apt to produce instruments whose meaning is more easily communicated. In fact, he finds that the most economical and straightforward deductive measures, direct self-ratings, tend to do better than multi-item scales. However, Burisch acknowledges that the advantage of global self-ratings may be limited to research settings in which respondents remain anonymous. On the basis of his review Burisch recommends that the deductive approach be adopted wherever there is a real choice, and that commonsensical approaches generally be given (more of) a chance.

It is important, however, to keep in mind the conditions under which these conclusions apply. Burisch's analysis describes what tends to happen when different types of scales are used to predict defined criteria, in itself an interesting issue. What if a researcher is interested not only in implementing the measurement of an already delineated construct, but in discovering, amplifying, and delineating new constructs? Burisch's conclusions have little relevance for someone with these aspirations.

 It is obvious, then, that at least in a research context the first important assessment question to be answered is whether scale construction should serve as an exploration for new or changed constructs or as the implementation of already formulated ones. If a researcher is not satisfied with available concepts and wishes to deal with description in a discovery-oriented way, then a test-construction approach is indicated that for obvious reasons we can call "exploratory." If the objective is to measure an already delineated concept, then a different approach is called for, which we may label "structured."

If the approach is exploratory, constructs are formulated and elaborated largely as part of the test construction process itself. In the case of a self-report instrument a diverse item pool is assembled. The pool can sample a natural domain of descriptors (for example, mood adjectives) or it can represent a number of psychologically interesting but as yet unsettled constructs, each in a number of alternative versions (Loevinger, 1957). If factor analysis is the adopted psychometric model, its application to the data is frequently exploratory. The data are permitted to "choose" the particular set of converging descriptors that characterize an emerging construct. Because of the composition of the pool, the analysis is expected to yield more than one major dimension. A multifactorial solution contributes to the discriminant characterization of each construct since the descriptors associated with a given construct define features that do not characterize the other constructs.

The exploratory approach resembles the inductive method described earlier, but construct clarification does not stop after a single round of collecting and analyzing data. The exploratory beginning is only one part of the iterative inductive-hypothetico-deductive cycle of research of which Cattell (1966) has spoken. Only if used as a tool in a program of progressive and self-corrective construct clarification and corresponding repeated revisions of the item pool can a computational procedure like factor analysis be expected to aid and consolidate new insights. Its potential value in this role is not to derive better predictor scales once a construct is defined, but to help in the formulation and clarification of the constructs themselves. Unfortunately, since exploratory projects require a sustained iterative effort, they are sometimes brought to a premature conclusion. Consequently, some factor-analytically derived instruments feature murky constructs and dubious structures.

A structured approach proceeds very differently. The constructs are defined or anchored before test construction begins. Test construction can have the strictly applied purpose of measuring an auxiliary construct that is not itself at stake, or it can operationalize a construct that is going to be subjected to an empirical test.

One of the structured methods is the convenient and effective deductive approach described earlier. Adoption of the deductive approach can eliminate the need for the item pool to encompass different tentative versions of the same construct. In the extreme deductive case the scale is simply constructed according to construct specifications, and there it ends. A less highly structured approach allows the initial item pool to include some minor variations on the general construct theme, with final item selection to be made on the basis of data, for example, item-total correlations. Measurement of several constructs allows the discriminant properties of the scales to be enhanced through elimination of items that correlate too highly with the wrong scales.

An alternative structured method is the external approach. It is considered structured here because scale items are selected on the basis of a predetermined criterion variable and because the construct represented by the criterion is not subject to change within the purview of the scale-construction project. Externally developed scales tend to be heterogeneous in content and can have low internal consistencies. The meaning of scores on external scales is less easily communicated than those on deductive scales or well-constructed internally developed tests, but some externally developed scales have considerable relevance to real life.

In the studies referred to earlier, exploratory and structured approaches have been cast in the role of contestants. The perspective stressed here is that they serve the differing purposes of discovery and implementation, respectively.

Selecting Subjects

Exploratory and structured approaches to test construction have their counterparts in relatively unrestrictive versus highly restrictive approaches to subject selection. In studies of psychopathology a restrictive approach seems more widely favored. The use of Research Diagnostic Criteria (RDC) is often recommended, resulting in the selection of narrowly defined samples. A restrictive selection can be desirable for testing specific and theoretically focused research hypotheses. But a different situation obtains when natural clusters of variables and natural dimensions are themselves objects of systematic exploration. Given such an objective, a restrictive selection of discrete nosological groups and other narrowly defined groups can be counterproductive. Covariation patterns emerging from a mixture of distinct subgroups could merely reflect the initial selection and the concepts guiding it. For exploratory descriptive purposes, then, the less restrictiveness the better. An unrestrictive policy could involve the use of epidemiological samples, or samples from other nonpsychopathologically defined populations.

THE STRUCTURE OF MOOD AND ITS RELATION TO MEASURES OF ANXIETY AND DEPRESSION

Whether used in a descriptive or explanatory sense, anxiety has remained an elusive concept. In this volume three authors stress this point. Izard describes anxiety as a generic term that refers to a variable blend of emotions; Jablensky documents continuing disagreements in European psychiatry concerning the boundaries and subdivisions of the anxiety disorder domain; and Good and Kleinman call attention to the protean manifestations of anxiety across cultures. These comments could be seen as implying that (in terms used earlier) an exploratory rather than a structured approach should be adopted in the development of anxiety measures. Systematically gathered data, as opposed to preexisting ideas, would then play a dominant role in shaping constructs and instruments.

So far, however, clinical measures of anxiety have been developed through highly structured test-construction methods. An example is the Zung Anxiety Status Inventory (ASI) (Zung, 1971). The items of this scale (which comes in two forms, self- and clinician-administered) were selected to represent consensual diagnostic criteria, clearly a structured approach. Some observers, including Zung (1979), believe that the better way of progressing in an area of uncertainty is just this kind of structured translation of consensus into measurement-operational terms. Efforts to construct reliable assessment procedures based on *DSM-III* are in the same spirit.

Although structured methods can be appropriate (see previous section of this chapter), exploratory approaches should not be excluded. In this volume Detre has expressed concern that future studies not be constrained by premature resolutions of dimensional and classificatory ambiguities, and he recommends freer exploration. In the following I will describe results obtained when the structure of mood is approached in exploratory ways.

The Structure of Mood

Mood self-ratings have been widely used to assess the effects of drugs and psychological treatments. Over the years several instruments have been developed for that purpose, including the Mood Adjective Checklist by Nowlis and Nowlis (1956), the Clyde Mood Scale (Clyde, 1963), the Multiple Affect Adjective Checklist (MAACL) (Zuckerman & Lubin, 1965), the Profile of Mood States (POMS) by McNair, Lorr, and Droppleman (1971), Lorr and McNair's more recent bipolar version of the POMS, the POMS-BI (Lorr & McNair, 1982), and Curran and Cattell's 8-State Questionnaire (Institute for Personality and Ability Testing, 1976).

In addition to these clinical inventories, several instruments have been constructed primarily for research purposes (e.g., Izard, 1972, 1977; Meddis, 1972; Schulterbrandt, Raskin, & Reatig, 1974; Thayer, 1967; Zevon & Tellegen, 1982). Spielberger's STAI (Spielberger et al., 1970) occupies a special place among these scales because of its focus on both state and trait assessment.

The dimensional structure of most of these instruments has been explored factor-analytically, and 10 or so replicable mood dimensions have been identified. Izard's work has been particularly systematic in its focus on the identification of fundamental discrete emotions, of which he recognizes ten: interest, joy, surprise, distress/sadness, anger, disgust, contempt, fear, shame, and guilt, each of which is represented in his Differential Emotions Scale (see Izard & Blumberg, this volume).

Our own work with mood scales was motivated differently. We were interested in finding relationships between major dimensions of reported mood and personality, hoping to clarify the organization of both domains. Data were collected with representative current-mood self-rating inventories using 120-item and 60-item versions. Our multifactorial solutions essentially replicated the primary factors found by Izard and others. In addition, our data clearly showed that the item intercorrelations were dominated by two large dimensions, Positive Affect and Negative Affect (they are described more fully later). These two simple-structure factors emerged equally clearly from cross-sectional studies of groups of individuals tested on one occasion and from longitudinal studies of single individuals who completed ratings over a 3-month period (Watson, Clark, & Tellegen, 1984; Zevon & Tellegen, 1982). Positive Affect and Negative Affect were not only evident as dominant primary factors but were equally well recovered as higher-order dimensions. This is conceptually more satisfactory since it shows that the two can be viewed and measured as "aggregates" (see earlier discussion) that capture the more general aspects of mood variation and complement rather than contradict the more fine-grained multifactorial solutions.

One salient feature of our two-dimensional structure is that the arrangement of descriptors is roughly circular. Circumplicity of emotional stimuli has also been found in other kinds of data (e.g., facial expressions) and through different techniques (e.g., multidimensional scaling). Russell in particular has advocated a general circumplex model of emotion (e.g., Russell, 1980). Although the circular patterns from different data sets are similar, there are also distinct differences. For us the structure of mood self-ratings was of particular interest. Most of the previous mood studies, however, were concerned with identifying primary mood factors rather than with the broader dimensions. David Watson and I therefore reanalyzed available data from several of these studies for evidence of the same two dimensions we had encountered. The results were quite clear: dominant Positive and Negative Affect factors were found repeatedly, and the configuration of descriptors in two-space was so similar across studies that we were able to derive a consensual circumplex (Watson & Tellegen, 1984). The circumplex was constructed by dividing each of the two-spaces into octants and identifying descriptors that consistently appeared in the same octant across studies.

Figure 37.1 is based on this analysis. Each of the eight lines that project from the midpoint of Fig. 37.1 bisects one of the eight octants. The adjectives placed on each line are representative of all those descriptors that predominantly occurred in the corresponding octant. Figure 37.1 is only a schematic representation, of course, and it does not show that most of the descriptors tend to cluster in a few areas: the High Positive Affect and Pleasantness zone and the High Negative affect and Unpleasantness zone. This clustering pattern explains, incidentally, why rotation to simple structure, which tends to align factors with dense regions, has consistently resulted in Positive Affect and Negative Affect dimensions.

Taking a closer look at Fig. 37.1 (and remembering that it represents ratings) we see that high Positive Affect is characterized by high ratings on such descriptors as "elated," "active," "enthusiastic," and low ratings for "drowsy," "sleepy," "sluggish." This observation suggests that high Positive Affect is a state of positive or pleasurable "engagement." Its reverse, low Positive Affect (low ratings for "elated," etc., high ratings for "drowsy," etc.), can be seen as the absence of pleasurable engagement, or a state of nonpleasurable disengagement. High Negative Affect (i.e., high ratings for such adjectives as "distressed," "fearful," "hostile," and low ratings for "relaxed," "calm," "placid") is obviously a state of unpleasurable engagement. Finally, low Negative Affect (low ratings for "distressed," etc., high ratings for "relaxed," etc.) by the same token represents nonunpleasurable disengagement. The "engagement" terminology is used here in some preference over "arousal" language to convey that these descriptors refer not only to activation but to characteristic cognitive modes and relationships with the environment, a point that is taken up again in the final section of this chapter. Although all four poles of these dimensions represent feeling states,

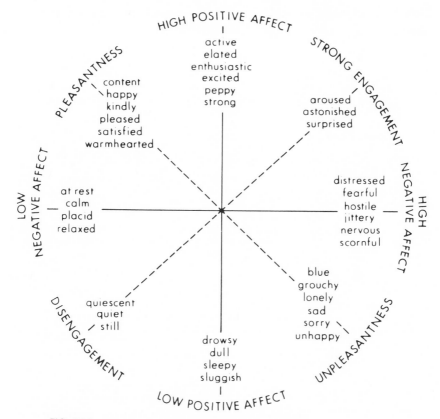

FIG. 37.1. The two-factor structure of self-rated mood.

only the high poles can be properly called "emotional" in the sense of engaged or aroused. The two dimensions are therefore seen as descriptively bipolar but emotionally unipolar (Zevon & Tellegen, 1982).

A 45° rotation of Positive Affect and Negative Affect results, respectively, in the Strong Engagement (or "arousal") versus Disengagement, and Pleasantness versus Unpleasantness axes of Fig. 37.1. The latter two dimensions provide a familiar alternative characterization of mood space, the one adopted, for example, by Lang (this volume) in his discussion of affective dimensions. Although any rotation accounts equally well for observed relationships, we prefer the Positive Affect and Negative Affect pair as reference axes. First, they conform more closely to the natural configuration of common descriptors, as mentioned earlier. Second, Positive Affect and Negative Affect correspond more directly to major personality factors. Third, they seem to identify those features that most clearly distinguish measures of anxiety from measures of depression. The psychometric aspects of this clinical issue is considered in the next section.

Differentiating Anxiety Ratings from Depression Ratings

As noted earlier, one problem in the study of anxiety is the delineation of its boundaries. Thus the differentiation between anxiety and depression as diagnostic categories has been a matter of controversy (Foa & Foa, 1982), and even their distinctness as disorders has been disputed. Short of that, syndromes of anxiety and depression are often considered to have substantially overlapping features. If consensual diagnostic indicators overlap, then the content of corresponding deductive diagnostic scales will be similarly entangled. This is the case with the Hamilton Anxiety and Depression scales (Hamilton, 1959, 1967). Methodologically this overlap is not a virtue since it makes the correlations between the two scales partially artifactual (Foa & Foa, 1982).

Apart from nosological issues, anxious and depressive mood states are viewed as typically distinct, the former often being characterized as fear, the latter as sadness. In factor analyses of self-rated mood, fear and sadness/distress have also emerged as different dimensions, provided enough factors are extracted. Qualitative distinctions notwithstanding, self-report measures of anxiety and depression turn out to be highly correlated, however (e.g., Foa et al., 1983; Gotlib, 1984). It is generally the case that correlations between measures of emotional adjustment tend to be substantial, giving rise to a large—sometimes very large—general demoralization or subjective discomfort factor in such inventories as the MMPI and SCL-90. As Finney (this volume) points out, one challenge in developing new self-report scales is to find ways of *not* measuring this general factor. The problem may be that the item pools for typical adjustment scales or inventories are saturated with generally dysphoric content to begin with, possibly reflecting traditional clinical inquiry. Consequently, the possibilities for developing scales that are distinct and relatively independent are limited.

The gross structure of representative mood ratings, on the other hand, is decidedly not one- but two-dimensional. It might be instructive to place a pair of representative anxiety and depression scales in this more roomy two-space. One could then visualize how these scales might be transformed into comparable but more differentiated measures to capture more nearly the "essence" of what differentiates anxious and depressive mood states. The analysis I did along these lines is straightforward.

First, the following five scales were assembled using our 120-item current-mood inventory:

1. Negative Affect (17 items). This scale consists only of clearly high and clearly (reversed) low Negative Affect markers such as those shown in Fig. 37.1.
2. Anxiety (21 items). Included in this scale were any items of the MAACL Anxiety scale and adjectival descriptors in Spielberger's State Anxiety scale that had been included in our inventory.

3. Pleasant versus Unpleasant Mood (14 items). The items in this scale represent the descriptors (appropriately keyed) shown in the Pleasantness and Unpleasantness octants of Fig. 37.1.
4. Depression (21 items). This scale consists of any items in the MAACL Depression scale, and any adjectival descriptors in Beck's Depression scale (Beck, 1972) that were included in our questionnaire.
5. Positive Affect (17 items). Included in this scale were high and (reversed) low Positive Affect markers such as the ones displayed in Fig. 37.1.

Correlations among the five scales were computed from ratings completed by a sample of 284 college students (50% females) and factor-analyzed. Two factors, accounting for 89% of the total variance, were rotated to simple structure. The result is the configuration shown in Fig. 37.2. The Pleasantness-Unpleasantness and Positive Affect scales have been reflected in the figure so that they now represent "Unpleasant Mood" and "Low Positive Affect," respectively, and thus occur in the same quadrant as the other three scales.

Figure 37.2 shows that the (reversed) Positive Affect and Negative Affect scales are, as expected, largely independent ($r = .30$). In contrast, the Anxiety and Depression scales are highly correlated ($r = .83$), and are both close neighbors of the general Unpleasant-versus-Pleasant Mood scale ($r = .89$ and .93,

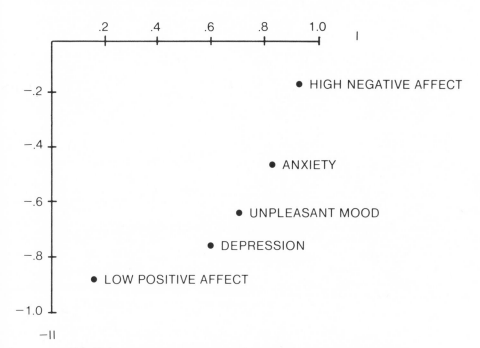

FIG. 37.2. Two-factor structure of five mood scales. "I" identifies the positive pole of Negative Affect; "-II" identifies the negative pole of Positive Affect.

respectively). A sample of individuals scoring high on the Anxiety scale would substantially overlap with a group scoring high on the Depression scale.

To the extent that the Anxiety and Depression scales are not interchangeable, what is it that distinguishes the two, and how might their mutually distinctive features be enhanced? Figure 37.2 suggests an answer: turn the Anxiety scale into more nearly a measure of Negative Affect and the Depression scale into more nearly a measure of (reversed) Positive Affect. As was mentioned earlier, the two Affect dimensions seem to represent major differentiating features of mood measures of anxiety and depression. One can also turn this around, and define Positive Affect and Negative Affect as that pair of orthogonal dimensions that are closest to being mood measures of depression and anxiety.

A more complete description of anxious and depressive mood is possible by taking primary factors as well as higher-order dimensions into consideration. Anxious mood can then be characterized as heightened Negative Affect (or unpleasurable engagement) with a particularly salient fear component. Depressed mood can be described as lowered Positive Affect (or nonpleasurable disengagement), often with salient features of sadness and fatigue. The latter description is consistent with the "loss of interest and pleasure" specified by *DSM-III* as the one invariably required criterion for major depressive episode.

RELATIONSHIPS BETWEEN DIMENSIONS OF MOOD AND PERSONALITY

The large number of personality inventories in existence today reflects a variety of theoretical orientations. The names of Cattell, Comrey, Eysenck, Gough, Guilford, Hathaway, Hogan, and Jackson, to name a few, are all associated with distinctive instruments. Although these inventories differ with respect to guiding conceptions, areas of content most emphasized, and method of construction, a small number of broad self-appraisal dimensions stubbornly recur in each, either as higher-order factors or embodied in single scales. The meaning of some of these pervasive sources of variance has been a matter of controversy (Block, 1965). One broad factor has been variously labeled Neuroticism, (low) Ego Resiliency, (low) Social Desirability, and Anxiety, and a second one Extraversion, (low) Ego Control, Acquiescence, and (low) Repression.

These differences motivated me some years ago to seek more clarity by undertaking a project of exploratory scale construction. Consistent with the earlier description, the process was iterative and cyclic, and involved progressive construct clarifications as well as repeated item pool revisions. Out of these procedures evolved the Multidimensional Personality Questionnaire (MPQ) (Tellegen, 1982).[1] Each of the 11 primary MPQ scales consists of items that sample a

---

[1] The MPQ was formerly referred to as the Differential Personality Questionnaire (DPQ).

distinctive family of interrelated statements about the self. A score on any given scale can be viewed as reflecting the importance or salience of the statement-family represented by that scale in the respondent's self-description. Although the correlations among the primary scales are on the whole quite low, they still exhibit a pattern that is consistent with the presence of three higher-order factors that resemble those found in other inventories. In the following paragraphs these three broad self-descriptive trait dimensions are described and interpreted in the light of the pattern of relationships within the MPQ shown in Table 37.1 and the correlations obtained with current-mood measures of Positive Affect and Negative Affect. Observed relationships with major dimensions of several other inventories are also characterized.

Table 37.1 shows that higher-order Factor I, called Positive Emotionality, is primarily associated with the MPQ Well-being, Social Potency, and Achievement scales. This trait factor is also positively correlated (between .40 and .50) with current-mood Positive Affect and is essentially uncorrelated with Negative Affect. The content of the scales associated with this first trait dimension and its mood correlate indicate that a high score on this factor reflects a generalized sense of well-being, an appraisal of oneself as pleasurably and effectively engaged inter-personally and through achievement, as active and generally self-efficacious in Bandura's sense (Bandura, 1977). The high Positive Emotionality person, then, presents herself or himself as perceiving, thinking, and acting in ways that would be conducive to positive emotional experiences. A low Positive Emotionality score suggests a weak sense of well-being, an appraisal of oneself as not plea-surably engaged, as not self-efficacious. It portrays a person who does not

TABLE 37.1
Factor Analyses of MPQ Scales

| | Higher-Order MPQ Factors | | | | | |
| | College Females (N = 600) | | | College Males (N = 600) | | |
	I	II	III	I	II	III
1. Well-being	*61*	−20	−06	*61*	−13	−05
2. Social Potency	*49*	−02	−24	*54*	20	−09
3. Achievement	*47*	−05	12	*51*	07	20
4. Social Closeness	20	−26	14	*33*	−21	00
5. Stress Reaction	−13	*59*	02	−21	*62*	−05
6. Alienation	−07	*55*	04	01	*58*	08
7. Aggression	00	*39*	−29	10	*51*	−19
8. Control	−01	−15	*54*	02	−14	*53*
9. Harm Avoidance	−19	−05	*45*	−17	−15	*40*
10. Traditionalism	05	04	*44*	12	12	*38*
11. Absorption	40	*43*	−20	29	*34*	−20

Note—Decimals omitted. Highest loading of each variable italicized. I: Positive Emotionality, II: Negative Emotionality; III: Constraint.

function in ways that facilitate positive emotional experiences and whose outlook may have a depressive quality.

Higher-order Factor II, called Negative Emotionality, is mostly associated with the MPQ Stress Reaction, Alienation, and Aggression scales, and is positively correlated (about .50) with current-mood Negative Affect and essentially uncorrelated with Positive Affect. A high score on this trait factor suggests an appraisal of oneself as unpleasurably engaged, as stressed by one's own and others' actions and attitudes. It describes a tendency to worry, to be anxious, to feel victimized and resentful, and to appraise generally in ways that foster negative emotional experiences. A low score describes someone who does not experience life as stressful and disturbing, does not tend to feel put upon and harassed, and recovers quickly when upsets occur.

Higher-order Factor III is labeled Constraint. This trait dimension is characterized by salient loadings on the Control-versus-Impulsiveness, Harm Avoidance-versus-Danger Seeking, and Traditionalism scales, and is basically uncorrelated with state measures of Positive Affect and Negative Affect. A high Constraint score indicates a description of oneself as cautious, restrained, as refraining from risky adventures, and as accepting the strictures of conventional morality. High Constraint persons, in other words, tend to consider relatively larger areas of action and living as off-limits, dangerous, out-of-line. A high score may be associated with avoidant, timid, anancastic (obsessive-compulsive-phobic) patterns. A low Constraint score reflects appraisals of oneself as relatively impulsive, adventurous, and inclined to reject conventional restrictions on behavior.

A clear and consistent pattern of correlations has been found between these broad MPQ dimensions and major factors in other well-known instruments, such as the California Psychological Inventory (CPI) (Gough, 1975), the Eysenck Personality Questionnaire (EPQ) (Eysenck & Eysenck, 1975), the Personality Research Form (PRF) (Jackson, 1974), and the 16-PF (Cattell, Eber, & Tatsuoka, 1970). For example, the MPQ Positive Emotionality, Negative Emotionality, and Constraint factor scores are substantially correlated in a convergent-discriminant pattern with Eysenck's EPQ Extraversion-versus-Introversion, Neuroticism, and (reversed) Psychoticism scales, respectively, and similarly with Cattell's second-order 16-PF Extraversion ("Exvia"), Anxiety, and Superego Strength factor scores. The content of the second-order and some first-order MPQ dimensions is also similar to the five or so factors that have been found repeatedly in analyses of peer-ratings (Digman & Takemoto-Chock, 1981) and for which corresponding self-report factors have also been identified (Goldberg, 1981; McCrae & Costa, in press; Norman, 1969), including extraversion and neuroticism factors.

While these patterns of overlap are helpful, I submit that among the different conceptions proposed for the larger self-statement trait dimensions, the MPQ constructs are especially descriptive and plausible. The interpretation of the first two higher-orders as Positive Emotionality and Negative Emotionality allows one to view these "big two" (Wiggins, 1968) as nonarbitrary in number and in directionality and as both distinctive and complementary. Although Constraint, the third higher-order factor, is not directly correlated with mood, it too may be an affect-relevant indicator of a person's "preparedness" to respond to a range of emotion-related circumstances (impulse, physical danger, adventure, authority, taboos) with either caution, timidity, and respect or with recklessness, boldness, and defiance. These three second-order self-descriptive trait factors are a suitable vehicle for the present discussion, but the reader is reminded that they account for only a portion of the total primary scale variance.

In the next section I speculate about links between the three broad and recurring self-descriptive trait dimensions just described and basic constructs of two affect-centered psychological theories: Gray's psychobiological model and the Freudian model. The hope is that connections of this sort will encourage further interchanges among researchers in the field of psychological measurement and those who develop models of personality and psychopathology.

PSYCHOBIOLOGICAL AND PSYCHODYNAMIC VIEWS ON POSITIVE AND NEGATIVE EMOTIONALITY

A Psychobiological View

Among modern personality conceptions, Gray's emotion-based psychobiological model is one of the most comprehensive (e.g., Gray, 1970, 1973, 1981, this volume). Marshaling data and adapting concepts from the areas of learning, psychopharmacology, and neurophysiology, Gray argues that the major dimensions of temperament and major psychiatric syndromes reflect basic individual differences in emotional functioning. In discussing Gray's ideas, I will focus on topics that relate most directly to our own psychometric findings.

Gray proposes three fundamental emotional systems, each with its own behavioral functions and neural substrate: (1) the Behavioral Activation System (BAS; Fowles, 1980) which is subserved by Olds' reward system; (2) the Behavioral Inhibition System (BIS) whose neural substrate is the septo-hippocampal "stop" system; and (3) the Fight/Flight system which has an amygdalo-hypothalamo-midbrain substrate. Of these three systems, the BAS is said to control active approach and avoidance behavior in response to signals of reward (which includes "relieving" nonpunishment). The BIS regulates extinction and passive avoidance in response to signals of punishment (which includes frustrative nonreward). The Fight/Flight System mediates escape and defensive aggressive behavior in response to unconditioned (rather than conditioned signals of) punishment and nonreward. Gray believes that each system gives rise to a major personality dimension. The BAS is linked to individual differences in sensitivity to reward signals; the BIS to differences in "anxiety" or sensitivity to signals of punishment; and the Fight/Flight System to differences in responsiveness to unconditioned punishment.

In the present context it is especially interesting that Gray has attempted to clarify relations between his three emotional responsiveness dimensions and Eysenck's three factors of Extraversion versus Introversion (E versus I), Neuroticism (N), and Psychoticism (P). Beginning with the "big two," Gray assumed that E and N account for the same phenomena and therefore define the same factor space as his two signal-sensitivity dimensions; but he also concluded that the two pairs of orthogonal dimensions represent different rotations. E was interpreted as a dimension of greater sensitivity to signals of reward *versus* greater sensitivity to signals of punishment, and N was construed as greater sensitivity to signals of *both* reward and punishment. Given these interpretations Gray could readily show that his two dimensions can be obtained quite simply by a 45° rotation of E and N (e.g., Gray, 1973, p. 434, Fig. 11). Of these two pairs Gray naturally viewed the two signal sensitivity dimensions specified by his model as representing the actually operating causal influences.

It is possible to link these ideas to our mood analyses. First, note that Gray's N concept is actually close to Eysenck's own view that N is a general emotionality trait. This interpretation, linking the N trait to a state of general emotional arousal, is conceptually (and visually) helpful by implying that, given the structure of mood shown in Fig. 37.1, the state dimension corresponding to the N trait is the diagonal axis of strong Engagement versus Disengagement (or high versus low arousal). If we are to maintain orthogonality then this interpretation identifies Pleasantness versus Unpleasantness as the state counterpart of E. Next we note that a 45° rotation of the Pleasantness and Engagement pair of axes produces the Positive-Affect and Negative-Affect axes. It is therefore consistent with Gray's interpretation of his own dimensions as a 45° rotation of Eysenck's, to treat Positive Affect and Negative Affect as the *state* dimensions that correspond to his reward signal-sensitivity and punishment-signal sensitivity *trait* dimensions. The implied state correlates of reward-signal sensitivity and punishment-signal sensitivity are the same as the observed state correlates of Positive Emotionality and Negative Emotionality. This means that rather than Eysenck's E and N, Gray's reward- and punishment-signal sensitivity are the constructs and correspond best to our "big two" self-descriptive trait factors of Positive Emotionality and Negative Emotionality, respectively.

The E and N scales (as distinct from the constructs) are a different matter. The reader may remember that they behaved in our analyses as markers of Positive Emotionality and Negative Emotionality. Others have obtained comparable results (Warr, Barter, & Brownbridge, 1983). It appears that our two Emotionality trait concepts and Gray's two signal-sensitivity constructs fit the E and N scales better than do Eysenck's own E and N constructs (as interpreted by Gray).

Another potential issue of fit involves one of Gray's constructs, reward-signal sensitivity, which he has also labeled "impulsivity." The latter term may have been chosen because the mediating emotional system is the Behavioral Activation System, whose behavioral expression, as the term implies, is active rather than inhibitory. Although the idea of active coping is congruent with the Positive Emotionality construct and its associated sense of effectance and achievement, this kind of action-readiness will at some point have to be distinguished from "impulsivity." Perhaps the impulsivity view of reward-signal sensitivity reflects Eysenck's long-held view that Extraversion is a mixture of impulsivity and sociability (Eysenck & Eysenck, 1969). This view has been roundly criticized (Guilford, 1975) because of the absence of correlation between these two components. The lack of relationship is consistent with the fact that impulsivity is a marker of low Constraint, whereas sociability is associated with Positive Emotionality. The impulsiveness component of Eysenck's old Eysenck Personality Inventory *E* scale has not been retained in the more recent EPQ *E* scale (it has in effect been moved to the EPQ *P* scale, which can be considered a low-Constraint marker). The current *E* scale is consequently a more valid Positive Emotionality marker than was its predecessor (Warr et al., 1983). It would be helpful if the psychometric separation of impulsiveness and sociability were more commonly recognized conceptually, as is the case for the Positive Emotionality and Constraint concepts. This recognition could benefit the further development of reward-signal sensitivity as an individual-differences concept.

As for the third dimension, Gray, for a number of reasons, has equated his parameter of responsiveness to unconditioned punishment, which is regulated by the Fight/Flight System, with Eysenck's *P*. Among these reasons are the aggressive content and correlates of the *P* scale. As with *E* and *N*, the issue concerning *P* involves the construct rather than the scale which behaves, as mentioned earlier, as a low-Constraint marker, consistent with its impulsive and antisocial content. Hirschfeld made that point succinctly when suggesting that the *P*-scale be used as a measure of antisocial personality, not psychoticism (Hirschfeld, 1978). If one were to interpret unconditioned punishment responsiveness in terms of the *P*-scale content and not the ill-fitting *P*-construct, then an alignment between Gray's dimension and (reversed) Constraint seems more plausible.

Returning to the issues that concern us most here, Gray has proposed three major dimensions of emotional responsiveness. He has mapped these onto Eysenck's three-space, and so onto the self-descriptive domain. Within that domain his two signal-sensitivity constructs, reward-signal sensitivity and punishment-signal sensitivity, appear to be quite consistent with, respectively, the higher-order Positive-Emotionality and Negative-Emotionality dimensions.

More recently Gray has considered arrangements of explanatory vectors other than the ones described above. One reason apparently is his assumption that in Eysenck's current three-space (obtained by adding the *P* dimension to the earlier

E-plus-*N* space) locating one pole of a dimension is not sufficient to specify its opposite pole. Thus he believes that the anxiety dimension could have any number of opposite poles, mentioning primary psychopathy and psychotic depression as possibilities. Actually, locating one pole of a dimension fully defines it regardless of number of dimensions, since any dimension runs through the origin and therefore is defined as soon as one more point, for example, one pole, has been defined. (On the other hand, while fixing the location of one dimension, say, *N*, in two-space also fixes that of the second, doing the same in three-space only fixes the plane of the remaining two dimensions and not their location in that plane. In this plane, then, which is orthogonal to *N*, alternative solutions are available while no such flexibility exists when *N* is located in two-space. This may be what Gray had in mind. Thus the welcome change, discussed earlier, from the old Eysenck Personality Inventory *E* scale to the new EPQ *E* scale can be seen as a rotation of *E* in the plane orthogonal to *N*).

Note on the Two Signal Systems of Psychoanalysis

Michels, Frances, and Shear point out in this volume that psychoanalytic conceptions of affect have focused primarily on the role of anxiety. In Freud's final two-process formulation, drive arousal and external circumstances activate images of danger related to separation and loss. The anxiety-provoking images provide signals and negative goal representations that mobilize and direct protective avoidance responses. Operating in this manner the anxiety process is believed to play a central role in a broad range of psychopathology.

This orientation has undoubtedly heightened psychoanalytic *sensitivity* to the subtle signs and workings of anxiety. However, *specificity*, in the sense of not invoking anxiety as a major factor when its role is only secondary or incidental, is also important, especially if one of the descriptive and explanatory tasks is to circumscribe the anxiety domain. In dealing with troubled and distressed people, greater specificity with respect to anxiety is aided by greater sensitivity to other equally basic affective phenomena.

Meehl has expressed views relating to this issue (Meehl, 1975). He begins by declaring that many clinicians, influenced by psychoanalysis, adhere to the "impedance doctrine" of psychological malfunctioning. By that Meehl means that the psychological difficulties and suffering of patients are typically attributed to the impeding influence of negative affects, particularly anxiety. Meehl does not deny that differential susceptibility to anxiety makes an important contribution to the difference between those who fall victim to emotional disorder and those who do not. On the other hand, he stresses that significant individual differences also exist in the basic capacity for experiencing pleasure (or hedonic capacity). These variations have equally important clinical consequences. Among existing psychometric personality constructs, Meehl singles out Cattell's "surgency" dimension as a good candidate for representing individual differences in hedonic capacity. Surgency is in fact the most important marker of Cattell's higher-order 16-PF Extraversion ("Exvia") factor, which I found to be the counterpart of the MPQ Positive Emotionality dimension. Meehl also attaches significance to the fact that reward responsiveness and punishment responsiveness are subserved by distinct brain structures, a view elaborated by Gray in a signal-sensitivity framework.

Although the psychoanalytic tradition may have overextended the use of anxiety as an explanatory construct, it is worth noting that from its onset the broader theory has attached basic significance to both experiences of satisfaction and pain (Freud, 1895). Furthermore, Freud's ideas about the primary and secondary process, formulated early in his career as a psychologist (Freud, 1900), remain central to psychoanalytic theory (Brenner, 1973; Holzman, 1970). Although not elaborated in specifically positive-affective terms, these ideas are concerned with the management of pleasurable experiences.

In brief outline, when the more primitive primary process is regnant, internal needs and external perceptions activate pleasurable images that vividly and wish-fulfillingly recapture past experiences of satisfaction. When the later developing secondary process operates, satisfaction is no longer attained through immediate wish fulfillment but through a two-step sequence. Images of satisfaction continue to be elicited by drive arousal and external stimuli, but only to provide signals and positive goal representations that energize and guide instrumental responses geared to produce realistic satisfaction. Passive wish fulfillment has been superseded by active and realistic wanting and striving.

The parallels between the models of satisfaction and anxiety are remarkably close, even though they were promulgated at widely separated points in Freud's career. The two-process anxiety theory postulates (1) an anxiety-signal system activated by external and drive-related internal stimuli, that (2) controls avoidance of distress. The two-process theory of the secondary process correspondingly involves (1) a hope-signal system, also activated by external and drive-related stimulation, that (2) controls the procurement of satisfaction. For an early two-stage formulation of the secondary process (using Pavlovian terms but describing a kind of two-process learning model) the interested reader is referred to French (1933).

My purpose is to suggest boldly or foolishly that in spite of the prominence traditionally accorded to signal anxiety, the real psychoanalytic model incorporates not one but two basic affect-signal systems.

The Different Models Compared

There are some obvious parallels between the hope-signal and anxiety-signal systems of the latent (and less one-sidedly impedance-oriented) psychoanalytic model and Gray's two emotional systems of reward-signal sensitivity and punishment-signal sensitivity. Both these twofold signal systems can be linked to the Positive and Negative Emotionality dimensions of self-descriptive inventories. Although the similarities among these bi-two-process models and the trait-descriptive two-Emotionality scheme are skeletal, and the domains, methods, and concept elaborations vastly different, they all stress or imply: (1) the pervasively affective organization of personality and psychopathology, (2) the basic distinctiveness of positive-affective variations and negative-affective variations as expressions of different systems, and (3) the prominent role of these variations in shaping inter-individual trait differences (in temperament, character, life-style) as well as intra-individual state differences. One obvious implication is that greater readiness to distinguish between variations in positive emotionality and negative emotionality would mean better psychometric description and clinical interpretation of normal and clinical emotional phenomena.

EXTENDING THE ASSESSMENT OF AFFECTIVE PHENOMENA

The notions about affect just outlined are simple and quite general. To be useful in the face of known complexity, including loose couplings and unusual uncouplings, they require multiple measures and convergent operations. In the following, the role of multiple measures in the assessment of affect and some complications associated with verbal report are illustrated through a few examples of actual or possible research.

One potentially complicating factor with verbal report is of course its varying accuracy. Problems of impression management and the need to establish a cooperative relationship with respondents have already been mentioned. Even when respondents are cooperative, accuracy can still be surprisingly low because of the limitations of humans as data processors, a theme much stressed by cognitive psychologists (e.g., Nisbett & Ross, 1980). Among available assessment methods, self-monitoring techniques are designed to enhance accuracy by taking these processing limitations into account. Although most frequently used in cognitive-behavioral intervention programs, self-monitoring techniques can also be adapted to research purposes (Hollon & Kendall, 1981). These techniques require the subject to record *in situ* designated target events soon after they occur in daily life. Sampling procedures can be used as well and require subjects to carry a random-signal device that will tell them when to record ongoing thoughts and actions (Hurlburt, 1979; Klinger, 1978). Although self-monitoring is not without problems because of the necessary reliance on the subject's own observations, it can eliminate or greatly reduce the forgetting and distortions that with passage of time impair reports of specific events.

Deliberate variation of accuracy conditions can also be informative, however. Evans and Hollon, in a study cited by Hollon and Kendall (1981), obtained results that highlight affect-related differences between immediate and delayed reports. They found that delayed mood ratings of depressed college students showed more dysphoria than those completed immediately and more than ratings of either type completed by nondepressed individuals. While these results suggest, as expected, greater accuracy of immediate reports, the interaction illustrates that a verbal account can be informative in more than one way: as a descriptive *report* or simply as a significant *response,* to use Natsoulas' terminology (Natsoulas, 1967). Immediacy appeared to improve substantially the ratings as reports of current mood state, but delay enhanced their informativeness as responses, namely as indicators of a depressive condition. The intentional variation of reporting condition produced a meaningful verbal behavior pattern. It would be worth knowing how anxious patients would respond. One could not expect large differences between "depressed" and "anxious" individuals, however, unless the measures of anxiety and depression were relatively independent along Negative- and Positive-Affective lines, respectively, as discussed previously.

Sometimes even immediacy seemingly does not produce an accurate report, and all one can do is try to understand it as a response only. This is the problem Zevon and Tellegen encountered in the earlier mentioned study of mood change (Zevon & Tellegen, 1982). The problem is particularly interesting here because it seems to be specific to the reporting of affective states. For the most part our findings showed a recurring orderly pattern, but some startling exceptions complicated the picture. They appeared to invalidate any generalizations and in the end forced us to collect additional responses.

In the study 23 subjects each completed mood self-ratings over a 90-day period. The 23 individual data sets were factor analyzed separately. In 21 of the cases the mood fluctuations revealed the anticipated two-Affect pattern, but in the two remaining cases the analyses drew a blank. Not only did the two familiar affect dimensions fail to materialize, but results obtained with a variety of alternative solutions and different item sets were equally uninterpretable. We were quite puzzled because these two subjects had been fully as cooperative and interested, and were as verbally competent and grossly normal as the others. We wondered at this point whether the problem might not be specifically related to their affective semantics. Did the way they used the emotion words perhaps involve unusual links or gaps between words and private events? The concept "alexithymia" ("no words for moods") was introduced a few years ago (Sifneos, 1972) to describe individuals who have great difficulty verbalizing their emotions. Some interpretations attribute alexthymia to an encoding deficit in assessing affect, i.e., unavailability of adequate language for describing emotional experiences (Lesser, 1981). Were our two subjects in some sense alexithymic?

We tried to get closer an answer by asking 15 subjects who could still be reached to sort the 60 mood terms used in the main study into subsets of terms that had similar meanings. A quantitative index of consensuality was then computed for each individual's sort on the basis of its congruence with an aggregate sort based on all the individual sortings. A comparison of the individual congruences confirmed that the two subjects whose mood self-descriptions had eluded us now also produced the least consensual sorts. Unfortunately, these were all the data we could collect. Our tentative generalization based on this incomplete assessment was that changes in self-monitored mood are indeed broadly two-dimensional, provided respondents are able to report emotional experiences in accordance with consensual semantic rules. Problems of affective semantics appear amenable to analysis through multiple measures and would be well worth intensive study.

Self-monitoring is a flexible technique, but its potential for studying anxiety and other emotional disorders has not been exploited. Emotional experiences could be sampled, along with surrounding events and behaviors, in ways designed to capture the respondents' characteristic ways of reacting emotionally and of managing emotions. Analyses could focus specifically on low-positive, high-positive, low-negative, and high-negative affective events.

The importance of distinguishing positive from negative variables has already been stressed by Kendall and Hollon (1981), who observed that in a number of studies positive and negative self-statements do not have the same correlates. They found, specifically, a negative relationship between adjustment and the frequency of negative self-statements, but no relationship with positive self-statements. Interestingly, "adjustment" in the reviewed studies was measured by indicators of anxiety and stress, in other words, negative affect. One would anticipate a complementary picture, a positive relationship with positive self-statements, and no or a weaker relationship with negative self-statements, if adjustment was assessed using indicators of high Positive Affect as well as (reversed) indicators of depression-like low Positive Affect.

Positive- and negative-affective thought processes do not differ only in hedonic tone and content. Different feeling states also appear to be characterized by thoughts differing in form or mode. Cognitive mode should be amenable to assessment. Affectively engaged states are often cognitively unsettled and future-oriented, with elements of surprise, interest, and expectancy mixed with uncertainty, indicating a scanning, wondering, *orienting* mode. In the case of positive affective arousal, the engaged state is one of happy and hopeful excitement and anticipation. In the case of negative affect, particularly anxiety, to be engaged means to scan the environment and wonder fearfully about the future. In this volume Sarason defines "cognitive anxiety" as worry-proneness, and he has shown that especially under stress, worries interfere with task performance (Sarason, 1984). Affectively disengaged states are cognitively more settled and past-centered, and reflect a perceiving, "knowing," *oriented* mode. Thus low positive affect, particularly a depressive disengagement from pleasurable experiences, can be seen as a state of hopelessness in the sense of "knowing" that the future is without joy. It is often characterized by dwelling on the past. To experience lowered negative affect, particularly nonanxiousness, is to feel secure (literally, free from care), which again is a form of "knowing" (just as "sure" is a contraction of "secure").

The notion that distinctive cognitive forms are connected with distinctive emotional states may derive some plausibility from associations that appear to exist between certain emotional conditions and particular cognitive treatment methods. For example, one distinctive characteristic of Beck's collaborative empiricism in the treatment of depression is to test the validity of the patient's beliefs through the gathering of data, with the Popperian aim of refuting and thus eliminating those convictions that are invalid (e.g., Beck, Rush, Shaw, & Emery, 1979, pp. 54–57). This approach (which in effect uses what is known in formal logic as the _modus tollens_, the "eradicating" mode) would seem tailor-made for disposing of false depressive "knowing." In contrast, when the problem is not to refute wrong answers but to put an end to poor questions, particularly the "what-if" questions of anxious people, then a different approach may be necessary. Ellis's rational-emotive therapy is designed to eliminate "negative thinking" in a number of ways, some of which appear to be particularly apt for dealing with problems of excessive orienting. One approach could be described as an effort to minimize and trivialize patients' worries and questions not so much by empirically refuting false beliefs as by persuasively disputing dys-functional values and imperatives underlying their anxieties, by emphasizing that people can make choices in these matters and by advocating new stances (e.g., Ellis, 1977). The successfully treated patient asks questions that are task-oriented rather than debilitating (Sarason, 1984, this volume).

The assessment of distinctive cognitive modes that are associated with dis-tinctive feeling states could be carried out in a number of ways, including self-monitoring. The focus would be on recording whether thoughts occur in the form of questions, wonderings, guesses, or of conclusions and assertions. The pattern emerging from these variables could be expected to show affective con-sistencies, as well as some deviating patterns calling for additional measures.

SUMMARY

In the more method-oriented part of this chapter potentials and limitations of self-report are discussed generally and in reference to measuring states and traits. Self-reports can have informative nontest correlates, but as in the case of other psychological measures, they can be used to much greater advantage in com-bination with other indicators. Discrepancies as well as congruencies between different measures can then be observed and interpreted. Used in this way self-report scales become uniquely useful as a way of structuring respondents' self-descriptions. Those who wish to construct a self-report instrument will have to make a choice between "exploratory" and "structured" approaches. It was argued that for research in the area of anxiety an exploratory approach holds special promise. This is also seen as implying the desirability of a nonrestrictive approach to the selection of subjects.

In the more content-oriented sections of the chapter the structure of mood is discussed and results are reported indicating the existence of two higher-order state dimensions, Positive Affect and Negative Affect. The relevance of these two dimensions of current mood to the study of anxiety is suggested by data showing that typical self-rating measures of anxiety and depression appear distinctive to the extent that they measure Negative and (low) Positive Affect. Mood scales measuring the two affect factors are also systematically related to self-descriptive personality trait measures representing general dimensions of Positive Emotionality and Negative Emotionality. These dimensions are speculatively linked to basic affective parameters of a psychobiological and a psychodynamic model of personality and psychopathology. Jointly these descriptive and conceptual schemes stress a view of personality and psychopathology as reflecting the influence of distinctive and pervasive positive and negative affective systems that give rise to both intra-individual variations in emotional state and inter-individual differences in emotionality. This view, even if stated in this general way, may have heuristic value. It may sensitize observers to characteristic expressions of the two affect (state) dimensions and the two emotionality (trait) dimensions that might otherwise be overlooked or discounted, and it may lead to indicators that provide fuller descriptions and sharper differentiations than are now available in the study of anxiety and other emotional disorders. Some of the examples used in this chapter (including the analyses of anxiety and depression scales in a two-affect framework, just mentioned), if not substantiating this point, illustrate it.

38 Assessment of Anxiety in Children

Thomas M. Achenbach, Ph.D.
University of Vermont

Early in this century, anxiety in children was of great concern from at least two theoretical perspectives on psychopathology: Assigning anxiety a key role in the psychoanalytic theory of psychopathology, Sigmund Freud illustrated his theory of neurosis with the lengthy case history of a phobic child, Little Hans (Freud, 1909). As the developmental aspects of anxiety became increasingly crucial to Freud's theory, he later reinterpreted Little Hans's phobia to illustrate his revised theory of neurosis (Freud, 1926). Rather than portraying anxiety as a by-product of blocked libido or of conflicts between the ego and the superego, Freud now argued that defense mechanisms and neurotic symptoms were triggered by anxiety responses having their prototypes in the birth trauma.

Meanwhile, in a very different arena, John B. Watson, the father of American behaviorism, blamed adult abnormalities on fears learned in childhood. Like Freud, Watson and his colleagues illustrated their theory with case histories of children's fears. In the case of Albert, for example, Watson and Rayner (1920) demonstrated the conditioning of fears to innocuous stimuli, whereas in the case of Peter, Jones (1924) demonstrated the deconditioning of fear.

Fears were also of considerable interest to students of normal child development, such as Jersild and Holmes, whose 1935 survey of children's fears became a classic of the child development literature. When efforts were made to combine psychoanalytic and learning theories in the 1940s and 1950s, the hypothesized childhood roots of neurotic anxiety retained a major role. Dollard and Miller (1950), for example, viewed anxiety as fear whose source is vague or obscured by repression. Such anxiety occurs when the victim lacks appropriate verbal labels, either because a fear began before language skills were advanced enough to provide labels or because repression separated verbal labels from the source of the fear.

With the rise of interest in personality traits, children's versions of adult anxiety tests were developed. The Children's Manifest Anxiety scale (CMAS; Castaneda, McCandless, & Palermo, 1956), for example, is a downward extension of the Taylor (1951) Manifest Anxiety Scale for adults. (A revision of the CMAS has since been published by Reynolds and Richmond, 1978, with the title "What I Think and Feel.") Dating from the same era as the original CMAS is the General Anxiety Scale for Children (GASC; Sarason, Davidson, Lighthall, Waite, & Ruebush, 1960). A specialized version of the GASC, the Test Anxiety Scale for Children (TASC), was designed to identify children whose anxiety about testing may interfere with their school performance (Sarason et al., 1960). A more elaborate measure derived from adult tests is the State-Trait Anxiety Inventory for Children (STAIC; Spielberger, 1973), which has separate scales for the child's current anxiety *state,* as well as a more enduring anxiety *trait.* The Personality Inventory for Children (PIC; Wirt, Lachar, Klinedinst, & Seat, 1977), a multidimensional personality inventory completed by parents and modeled on the Minnesota Multiphasic Personality Inventory (MMPI), also contains an anxiety scale.

The revival of behavioral therapies in the 1960s rekindled interest in the direct observation and conditioning of fears. Behavioral treatments were illustrated in numerous case studies of adult fears, as well as in some child clinical cases and in experiments with children having subclinical fears. Rejecting "traditional" clinical assessment in favor of "behavioral" assessment, behavior modifiers devised their own procedures for documenting fearful behavior. These included behavioral avoidance tests in which the child is asked to perform a graded series of approach behaviors toward the phobic object (e.g., Bandura & Menlove, 1968; Kornhaber & Schroeder, 1975). Observational schedules have also been developed to assess signs of anxiety, such as crying, trembling, stuttering, and talking about fears (e.g., Glennon & Weisz, 1978; Melamed & Siegel, 1975). A behaviorally oriented self-report measure, the Fear Survey Schedule for Children (Scherer & Nakamura, 1968), has been developed as a childhood version of Wolpe and Lang's (1964) Fear Survey Schedule for adults.

Applying psychometric methods to behavioral ratings by informants such as parents and teachers, factor analyses of behavior checklists have identified syndromes of behaviors indicative of anxiety in a variety of clinical samples (see Achenbach & Edelbrock, 1978; Quay, 1979). Some of the factor analytic results have been used to construct and norm scales for assessing children's deviance in terms of these syndromes as compared to their deviance in terms of other factorially derived syndromes (Achenbach & Edelbrock, 1983; Miller, 1977).

Children's fear inventories and self-report anxiety scales have also been factor analyzed. Scherer and Nakamura (1968), for example, obtained eight factors from normal children's self-reported fears on the Fear Survey Schedule for Children. Miller, Barrett, Hampe, and Noble (1972) obtained three factors from fears reported on the Louisville Fear Survey for Children by parents of normal and phobic children. Despite differences in the numbers of factors attributable to different rotational procedures, Miller et al. considered their findings similar to those of Scherer and Nakamura: Three Scherer-Nakamura factors were represented by a factor that Miller et al. designated as *physical injury and personal loss;* two Scherer-Nakamura factors were represented by a factor that Miller et al. designated as *psychic stress,* with highest loading on items such as taking tests, making mistakes, being criticized, and social events; another Scherer-Nakamura factor was represented by Miller et al.'s *natural and supernatural dangers* factor, with highest loadings on items such as lightning, thunder, the dark, and ghosts. Comparisons with studies of adult fears suggested that the dimension representing fears of natural and supernatural events tended to disappear with age, but that dimensions representing fear of small animals and sexual and moral fears tended to emerge in adulthood.

Factor analyses of the CMAS (Finch, Kendall, & Montgomery, 1974) and the Revised Children's Manifest Anxiety Scale have yielded dimensions designated as *physiological, worry/oversensitivity,* and *concentration* (Reynolds & Paget, 1981). Reflecting the experiential content of the CMAS, these factors are defined by aspects of the child's self-reported *subjective experiences,* rather than by classes of *fear-evoking stimuli,* such as those that define the factors of the Fear Survey Schedule and the Louisville Fear Survey.

Beside the host of paper-and-pencil and observational measures of anxiety, physiological measures have occasionally been used with children, although they have been confined largely to research contexts. Skin conductance, changes in heart rate, and palmar sweat prints have been used in several studies, but correlations with other measures are generally low, and such measures are seldom practical for routine clinical assessment. Their child value may be in assessing physiological responsiveness to situational stresses such as dental procedures, surgery, and various experimental manipulations, rather than in assessing clinical anxiety states or traits (see Johnson & Melamed, 1979).

CONCEPTUAL ISSUES

As outlined above, childhood anxiety has been a central variable in major theories of psychopathology. Assessment of childhood anxiety has generally involved extrapolation of adult measures of children, and Gittelman (this volume) discusses some possible relations between child and adult anxiety phenomena. In considering the current status of assessment of anxiety in children, however, it is important to note the following conceptual issues that arise from contrasting theoretical orientations and from the origins of most assessment methods in the study of adults.

Contrasting Theoretical Orientations

In psychodynamic theory, anxiety is a hypothetical construct whose meaning depends on a chain of inferences about inner states, other hypothetical personality variables, and the interpretation of various signs and symptoms. (See Edelson; Horowitz; Michels, Frances & Shear; this volume.) Specific fears are viewed more as symptoms of underlying pathology than as objects of assessment in their own right. Accordingly, psychodynamic assessment is directed at inner states and affects, of which anxiety is an especially important one. Projective tests and unstructured clinical interviews have been mainstays of this approach to assessment. They have not, however, yielded much formal research on clinical anxiety in children as a separate independent or dependent variable, apart from including it in idiographic diagnostic formulations.

The personality trait approach to assessment has been the source of most of the self-report and parent-report scales modeled on adult meaures, such as the CMAS, GASC, STAIC, and Personality Inventory for Children. Like the psychodynamic approach, the trait approach aims to assess a hypothetical construct of anxiety, although it is usually viewed as a more persisting dispositional characteristic than is the psychodynamic construct of anxiety. An exception among trait measures is the STAIC, which has separate scales for anxiety as a trait and as a state, but even the STAIC's state construct represents a relatively isolated variable, rather than a facet of inferred psychodynamics.

In contrast to the psychodynamic and trait approaches, behavioral assessment focuses on specific fears and the accompanying avoidance behavior. Most behavioral studies of children's fears deal with a very specific fear, such as fear of dogs. When a child has multiple fears, behavior modifiers usually try to pinpoint the one that is primary or to group the fears into separately treatable hierarchies. While acknowledging the possible relevance of self-reports and cognitions, behavior modifiers seldom invoke hypothetical constructs of anxiety per se.

The psychodynamic, trait, and behavioral approaches to assessment of anxiety in children can be viewed along a conceptual continuum: At one extreme, the psychodynamic approach embeds anxiety in a complex network of personality variables inferred from interviews, projective techniques, and overt signs and symptoms. Occupying an intermediate position, the trait approach treats anxiety as a more circumscribed construct that can be psychometrically assessed in isolation from other facets of personality. Finally, the behavioral approach eschews anxiety as a general construct, focusing instead on direct assessment of fears and avoidant behaviors. Related to this continuum of theoretical orientations is a continuum of target problems ranging from fears and phobias to anxiety and "internalizing" disorders that I shall consider before turning to other issues.

Fears and Phobias

The different theoretical orientations have tended to focus on different classes of problems related to fears and anxiety. In accord with the behavioral emphasis on the similarity between subclinical behavior problems of everyday life and more severe disorders, many behavioral studies have used school, college, and other general population samples rather than clinical samples. The criteria for inclusion typically involve volunteering for participation in the research, self-reported fear of the specific type under study, and evidence of fearful and avoidant behavior under standardized assessment conditions. A major advantage of this approach is that relatively large samples of subjects can be obtained for study of well-defined behaviors under well-controlled conditions, uncomplicated by the need to deal with other psychopathology. A possible disadvantage is that the subjects are not representative of people who are disabled enough to obtain clinical services under ordinary conditions. Although many behavioral studies might be dismissed from clinical consideration on the grounds that the disorders are benign, techniques and findings developed with nonclinical samples have later been applied to more severely disabled children, some of whom suffer multiple problems in addition to a specific fear. Furthermore, numerous behavioral studies and clinical applications have emerged outside the mental health fields, especially in helping children adapt to dental and medical procedures (see Johnson & Melamed, 1979; Melamed, this volume).

Dental and Medical Fears. Although most children's fears of dental and medical procedures would not be considered anxiety disorders per se, the accumulating knowledge base, assessment technology, and clinical experience are worth noting. A recent review of research on children's fearful behavior in dental settings, for example, reports the widespread use of convenient, reliable scales for rating cooperative behavior and anxiety (Winer, 1982). Self-report measures, physiological techniques, and projective techniques have also been used in numerous studies. Although relations among the measures are often weak or untested, several studies have shown significant correlations between heart rate and behavioral measures of anxiety in preschool-aged dental patients. This led Winer (1982) to suggest that correlations between measures may be highest at early ages but then decrease as children's emotions and anxiety behaviors become more differentiated, a developmental hypothesis that deserves further testing.

As for developmental trends in the overt expression of fears, there is a steady diminution of problems in dental settings during the preschool years and relatively low rates of overtly disruptive behavior through about the age of six. Data on older children present a more mixed picture, however, with some evidence for increased rates of fearful behavior at later ages, but a need for more careful study of developmental changes. Assessment of other variables in relation to dental fears indicates less fear in children from well-structured home environments than those from more permissive homes, but variables such as sex and social class show no clear associations with dental fears. The rapidly expanding literature on children's fears of medical procedures is far more complex, because fear is often confounded with the pain and physical debilitation accompanying illness (e.g., Katz, Kellerman, & Siegel, 1981; Shacham & Daut, 1981).

Specific Phobias. Whereas most dental and medical fears may be realistically justified by the risk of pain under clearly defined conditions, *phobias* consist of persistent, debilitating fears that are unjustified by actual risks. This section deals with phobias of specific objects, such as animals; the next section deals with phobias involving more complex conditions, such as separation and school. Despite the ostensible simplicity of phobias of specific objects, however, it has been found that such phobias "are often variable responses to multiple stimuli and that assessment of phobia is a complex problem" (Miller, Barrett, & Hampe, 1974, p. 96). A child may fear the dark only when left alone, for example, or may fear small energetic dogs but not large lethargic ones.

Although epidemiological and longitudinal studies show that most children have fears at some time (Achenbach & Edelbrock, 1981; MacFarlane, Allen, & Honzik, 1954), children are seldom brought for professional help unless the fears interfere significantly with their development or with the lives of other people, such as family members, peers, and teachers. Even then, phobias to specific objects are seldom the sole reason for seeking mental health services. In a review of literature published from 1924 to 1978, Graziano and DeGiovanni (1979) found 40 case studies involving fears in a total of 130 children. Of these, 112 were school phobics, whereas all other phobias accounted for only 18 cases. A survey of behavior therapists showed that only 6.8% of recent child referrals had been for any kind of phobia (Graziano & DeGiovanni, 1979). Only 3 to 4% of referrals to child psychiatrists are reported to be for fears (see Johnson & Melamed, 1979).

In a general population survey, Rutter, Tizard, and Whitmore (1970) found handicapping phobias in only 16 of 2,199 children, for a rate of about 7 per 1000. A comparison of parents' reports on clinically referred children and demographically matched nonreferred children yielded prevalence rates for specific fears declining from about 50% in 4- and 5-year-olds down to about 10% in 16-year-olds, as shown in Fig. 38.1 (Achenbach & Edelbrock, 1981). Clinically referred children had significantly higher scores than nonreferred children only at ages 6 through 9 for boys and 8 through 11 for girls. The magnitude of these significant differences between referred and nonreferred children in reported fears was considerably smaller than for many other behavior problems.

A 5-year follow-up of untreated phobics identified in an epidemiological survey showed that all the children and adolescents (i.e., below age 20 years) had improved or recovered, compared to only 43% of the adult phobics. Among

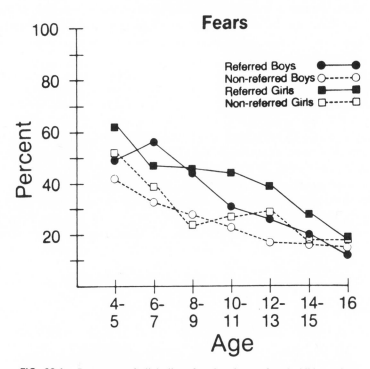

FIG. 38.1.   Percentage of clinically referred and nonreferred children whose parents endorsed the CBCL item *Fears certain animals, situations, or places, other than school.* Parents rated the item on a 3-step scale including *not true, somewhat or sometimes true,* and *very true or often true.* The top two steps are included in the percentage reporting fears as present. Total N = 2600. (From Achenbach & Edelbrock, 1981.)

the unimproved adults, 20% were unchanged, while 33% were worse (Agras, Chapin, & Oliveau, 1972). Hampe, Noble, Miller, & Barrett (1973) also found a high rate of improvement in the treated phobias of 6- to 16-year-olds, with only 7% still having severe phobias 2 years after outpatient treatment. It thus appears that most childhood fears of specific objects are not associated with significant psychopathology and do not cause long-term debilitation.

Separation Anxiety and School Phobia.   Separation anxiety and school phobia differ markedly from most other childhood phobias, in that the focus is on social relationships, rather than danger of physical harm. Both are also more specific to childhood than other phobias. Separation anxiety is inferred from the distress most children show during the first year of life when separating from familiar caretakers, especially parents. The degree and type of separation distress have been used as indices of children's attachment to their mothers (Lieberman,

1977). Many children continue to show at least some separation anxiety throughout the preschool period, intensified on occasions such as the start of nursery school and regular school. Later school phobias are also widely interpreted as reflecting separation anxiety more than fear of school per se.

School phobia is a much more common cause of clinical referral than other phobias and often occurs in children who do not show other major problems (Graziano et al., 1979; Miller et al., 1974). Unlike other phobias of childhood, it does not decline steadily with age, as shown in Fig. 38.2 (Achenbach & Edelbrock, 1981). There may, however, be developmental trends in the type and prognosis of school phobias. Miller et al. (1974) have listed criteria for two types of school phobias, as shown in Table 38.1. They consider six of the nine criteria for each type to be sufficient for differential diagnosis.

Kennedy (1965) included age as a criterion for differentiating between the two types, with Type I being more prevalent in the lower grades and Type II in the upper grades. Miller et al. omit age as a criterion, however, because they view age as a crucial variable in its own right, aside from any association with

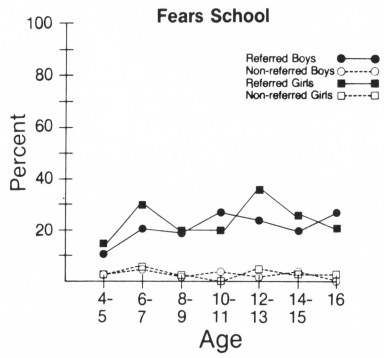

FIG. 38.2.   Percentage of clinically referred and nonreferred children whose parents endorsed the CBCL item *Fears going to school*. (From Achenbach & Edelbrock, 1981.)

Table 38.1
Characteristics of Type I and II School Phobias

Type I	*Type II*
1. The present illness is the first episode.	1. Second, third, or fourth episode.
2. Monday onset, following an illness the previous Thursday or Friday.	2. Monday onset following minor illness not a prevalent antecedent.
3. An acute onset.	3. Insidious onset.
4. Expressed concern about death.	4. Death theme not present.
5. Mother's physical health in question; actually ill or child thinks so.	5. Health of mother not an issue.
6. Good communication between parents.	6. Poor communication between parents.
7. Mother and father well adjusted in most areas.	7. Mother shows neurotic behavior; father, a character disorder.
8. Father competitive with mother in household management.	8. Father shows little interest in household or children.
9. Parents achieve understanding of dynamics easily.	9. Parents very difficult to work with.

Adapted from Miller et al., 1974.

the type of school phobia. There are insufficient data on the actual relation between age of onset and type of phobia, but Miller et al. cite outcome data showing that school phobias occurring below the age of 10 have a much better prognosis than those occurring above the age of 11. Yet, age is inevitably confounded with Miller's criteria for differentiating between Type I and Type II school phobias: A criterion for Type I school phobia is that it be the first episode, whereas a criterion for Type II is that it be the second, third, or fourth episode. On the average, first episodes would have to occur at younger ages than later episodes. Furthermore, confirmation of the good prognosis ascribed to young school phobics requires longitudinal studies across the children's entire school careers to track recurrences and/or changes from Type I to Type II patterns.

Despite the potential confounding of age, type of school phobia, and prognosis, the following conclusions seem justified:

1. Type I school phobia resembles normal forms of separation anxiety.
2. This type tends to occur during the elementary school period.
3. Most children probably experience it at some time in some degree, especially after absence from school because of illness.
4. Firm management and a healthy family situation can quickly overcome it.

Type II school phobia is more problematic and may be more similar to adult anxiety disorders and agoraphobias, which have not been well documented in children. In their criteria for Type II school phobia, both Kennedy (1965) and Miller et al. (1974) include multiple episodes, parental psychopathology, lack of communication between parents, lack of paternal involvement, and difficulty working with parents. These factors suggest individual and family pathology, of which school phobia is just one manifestation. The phobic aspect of the pathology may also reflect generalized anxiety about association with others, especially peers, perhaps owing to fears of adolescent developmental challenges.

There is little firm evidence on the developmental relations between this type of school phobia and adult disorders, however. Although difficulties in childhood school attendance are reported more often by adult psychiatric patients than nonpsychiatric control subjects (e.g., Tyrer & Tyrer, 1974), such retrospective data are vulnerable to pathological biases and other systematic errors. For example, adults who had difficulties in school attendance but no subsequent psychiatric problems may be less likely to recall attendance difficulties than are adults for whom they were part of an important psychiatric sequence. Furthermore, retrospective reports of attendance difficulties are a flimsy basis for determining the type of school phobia, and adults diagnosed as suffering from phobic neuroses, anxiety states, or depressive illnesses have not differed significantly in the proportion who recall attendance difficulties (Tyrer & Tyrer, 1974). Long term follow-up studies of school phobic children suggest elevated rates of problems in later life, but the studies are handicapped by a lack of standardized initial assessment, failure to analyze the type and age of onset of the phobia, and other methodological weaknesses (e.g., Coolidge, Brodie, & Feeney, 1964; Waldron, 1976). It is difficult to draw conclusions about relations between childhood school phobias and adult disorders without better data, preferably prospective longitudinal studies that include standardized assessment of children's disorders and of subsequent functioning in adolescence and adulthood.

Anxiety and Internalizing Disorders

Moving now from fears having a specific focus to more generalized patterns of problem behavior, we find that multivariate analyses have repeatedly identified a broad-band grouping of problems comprised of fearfulness, anxiety, withdrawal, unhappiness, and somatic complaints (for reviews, see Achenbach & Edelbrock, 1978, and Quay, 1979). This grouping has been given various labels, such as Personality Problem (Peterson, 1961), Internalizing (Achenbach, 1966, 1978), Inhibition (Miller, 1967), Overcontrolled (Achenbach & Edelbrock, 1978), and Anxiety-Withdrawal (Quay, 1979). In his review of multivariate studies, Quay (1979) concluded that a problem he summarized as "anxious, fearful, tense" was found in more versions of the Anxiety-Withdrawal grouping than any other problem. In our comparison of clinically referred and nonreferred children, we found that the item "Too fearful or anxious" discriminated much better than reports of specific fears, as shown in Fig. 38.3 (Achenbach & Edelbrock, 1981).

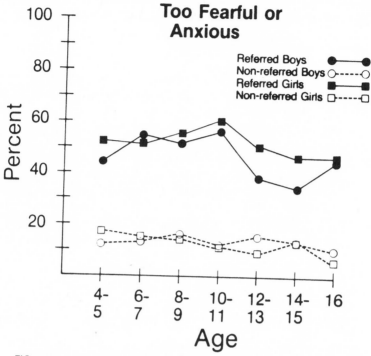

FIG. 38.3. Percentage of clinically referred and nonreferred children whose parents endorsed the CBCL item *Too fearful or anxious*. (From Achenbach & Edelbrock, 1981.)

Virtually all multivariate studies that have identified a broad-band Internalizing or Anxiety grouping have also identified a broad-band grouping of behavior problems variously labeled as Conduct Problem (Peterson, 1961), Externalizing (Achenbach, 1966, 1978), Aggression (Miller, 1967), and Undercontrolled (Achenbach & Edelbrock, 1978).

Narrow-Band Syndromes and the Broad-Band Groupings.   Hierarchical multivariate analyses, such as second-order factor analyses, have shown that the two broad-band groupings are comprised of several narrower-band syndromes which are more like traditional diagnostic categories. The Internalizing grouping includes certain narrow-band syndromes comprised mainly of anxious behaviors, but also a syndrome comprised mainly of somatic complaints and other syndromes comprised of depression, withdrawal, obsessions and compulsions, and deviant behaviors suggestive of a schizoid condition. Because these narrow-band syndromes are sufficiently intercorrelated to form a higher order grouping, and anxious behaviors seem to be one of the strongest common links, the narrow-band syndromes might be viewed as a family of anxiety disorders. The syndromes of the Externalizing grouping, by contrast, are characterized mainly by aggressive, hyperactive, and delinquent behaviors, perhaps indicating a *lack* of appropriate anxiety.

The two higher order groupings can be thought of as representing a dimension analogous to introversion-extroversion, which is fundamental to Eysenck's (1973) theory of psychopathology. However, unlike the bipolar introversion-extroversion dimension found in personality research, the behavior problems of the two broad-band groupings may not always be negatively correlated. Whereas the forced-choice formats of personality measures can lead to negative correlations between introversion and extroversion, empirically based assessment of children's behavior problems involves a tabulation of all the problems reported for a child, rather than forced choices between pairs of problems thought to be of opposing types. When multivariate analyses are applied to behavior problems assessed in samples of disturbed children, the results often resemble multivariate analyses of cognitive ability tests. Rather than the bipolar dimension that emerges from tests of introversion-extroversion, there is often a general factor on which nearly all behavior problems have positive loadings. Smaller, more specific factors are more like separate syndromes, and rotations to simple structure produce an array of narrow-band syndromes. The Internalizing and Externalizing groupings can be derived from second-order analyses of the narrow-band syndromes.

The narrow-band syndromes are in some respects like the subtests of an omnibus measure of cognitive ability, such as the Wechsler intelligence tests: They measure different facets of a general or g dimension, but are all positively correlated with each other across heterogeneous samples of individuals. Similarly, the broad-band groupings of behavior problems, like the Verbal and Performance IQ scales of the Wechsler tests, are positively correlated with each other across heterogeneous samples of individuals. This is because most individuals who are exceptionally high on one constituent of the g dimension are at least above average on other constituents of the g dimension, as well. Nevertheless, individuals can be found who show clinically significant disparities between scores in the different areas. A much higher Verbal than Performance IQ, for example, may indicate right hemisphere brain damage. Analogously, a great excess of Internalizing over Externalizing problems may implicate anxiety, whereas an excess of Externalizing problems may suggest an anxiety deficit. For the children who fall between these extremes, anxiety may not be such a crucial variable.

Summary.   To summarize, fears of specific objects and situations are common among children. Most of these fears are not associated with major psychopathology. They can be successfully treated by a variety of procedures, many remit without treatment, and the overall prevalence rate declines steadily with age. School phobias, however, do not decline steadily with age, although there are developmental changes in their nature and prognosis. Those occurring in the elementary school years appear to reflect the separation anxiety that most children show during their early years. Such school phobias usually have a good prognosis, if the family situation is healthy and the child is returned to school firmly and quickly. School phobias occurring in the later school years are harder to treat and may reflect more general psychopathology in the child and family.

Although clear-cut anxiety disorders are relatively rare in children, multivariate analyses have identified a broad-band grouping of "internalizing" syndromes characterized by anxiety problems. This broad-band grouping contrasts with a second broad-band grouping of "externalizing" syndromes that may reflect an absence of appropriate anxiety. The multivariate findings represent a taxonomic approach differing from nosological approaches such as that embodied in the *Diagnostic and Statistical Manual of Mental Disorders (DSM-III)* (American Psychiatric Association, 1980). The different taxonomic approaches have contrasting implications for the conceptualization of disorders involving anxiety in children, as discussed next.

TAXONOMIC ISSUES

The multivariate studies that have identified a broad-band internalizing grouping were originally inspired by dissatisfaction with the neglect of children's disorders by psychiatric nosologies. The edition of the *Diagnostic and Statistical Manual (DSM-I)* used from 1952 until 1968, for example, included only two categories of childhood disorders. These were *Adjustment Reaction of Childhood* and *Schizophrenic Reaction, Childhood Type.* Although adult diagnoses could also be applied to children, most children seen for mental health services were either diagnosed as having adjustment reactions or were left undiagnosed (Achenbach, 1966; Rosen, Bahn, & Kramer, 1964). As interest in child psychopathology grew, it became clear that more meaningful differentiation among disorders was required for research purposes, as well as for clinical communication and decisions about treatment.

Most disorders of childhood differ in the following ways from the diseaselike entities of Kraepelinian nosology that are the basis for the taxonomy of adult disorders:

1. Children's disorders usually involve behaviors that most children show at some time, rather than behavior that is intrinsically pathognomic.

2. Children do not seek mental health services for themselves, but are referred because their behavior or failure to develop distresses somebody else, especially parents or teachers.

3. Children cannot provide much of the historical and self-report data on which diagnoses of adults depend. Instead, most of the data must be obtained from significant others in the children's lives, such as parents and teachers.

4. Most adults have reached plateaus with respect to biological, cognitive, educational, and social development that provide a basis for judging deviant behavior. Most children, by contrast, are continually changing. Their problem behaviors must be judged not only in relation to their past developmental history and present level of attainment, but also in relation to norms for their age and needs for futher development along multiple dimensions.

To determine what syndromes actually exist, researchers turned to multivariate analyses of children's behavior problems. Early studies by Richard Jenkins and his colleagues (Hewitt & Jenkins, 1946; Jenkins & Boyer, 1968) identified some syndromes that were incorporated into the 1968 edition of the *DSM* (American Psychiatric Association, 1968). However, *DSM-II* incorporated the syndromes in the form of narrative descriptions of the clinical concepts suggested by the statistical findings, rather than operational definitions derived directly from the findings.

The 1960s and 1970s saw numerous multivariate analyses of children's behavior problems. Despite differences in subject samples, rating instruments, and analytic methods, there has been considerable convergence on a fairly large number of narrow-band syndromes in addition to the broad-band internalizing and externalizing syndromes discussed earlier (see Achenbach, 1982; Achenbach & Edelbrock, 1978). These findings are not very evident in the childhood disorders included in *DSM-III,* however. Although *DSM-III* offers far more categories of childhood disorders than its predecessors, the disorders are defined by lists of fixed decision rules stipulated by the *DSM* committee, rather than by research-based operations for obtaining and aggregating data. As Spitzer and Cantwell (1980) put it, the general *DSM-III* approach

starts with a clinical concept for which there is some degree of face validity. Face validity is the extent to which the description of a particular category seems on the face of it to describe accurately the characteristic features of persons with a particular disorder. It is the result of clinicians agreeing on the identification of a particular syndrome or pattern of clinical features as a mental disorder. Initial criteria are generally developed by asking the clinicians to describe what they consider to be the most characteristic features of the disorder. (p.369)

This procedure of starting with a clinical concept and then negotiating a set of fixed decision rules differs in the following ways from the empirical derivation of syndromes through multivariate analyses:

1. Its main basis for a disorder is agreement that the disorder exists, rather than empirical data.

2. Once there is agreement on the existence of a disorder, the criteria for diagnosing the disorder are formulated by a process of negotiation, rather than by systematic derivation from empirical data.

Multivariate approaches, of course, require decisions as to what type of data to seek, how to obtain the data, on what subjects, and what analyses to perform. It is also necessary to compare the results of various analyses and to decide how to apply the results in the actual assessment of individual children for research, clinical, or epidemiological purposes. Yet, most multivariate research of the 1960s and 1970s failed to take this step—it was as if the finding of statistical associations among the items analyzed was the ultimate goal. When research went only this far, perhaps the *DSM-II's* translation of the findings into narrative descriptions of clinical concepts was all that could be expected.

If the logic of multivariate research is extended, however, it implies a taxonomic approach differing in another interesting way from that of categorical nosologies, where each criterial attribute must be judged as present or absent and the absence of any criterial attribute precludes the disorder. Unlike disorders that are defined categorically, quantitative syndromes derived through multivariate analyses preserve information about gradations of intensity in the expression of particular problems and in the number of different problems evident. When a factor analysis reveals covariation among a group of anxiety items, for example, individual children can be scored according to the intensity with which they manifest each item. If desired, the items can be weighted according to their loadings on the factor, which reflect the strength of their covariation with the factor or syndrome as a whole. The result is a metrical index of the degree to which individuals manifest the components of a syndrome, rather than a yes-or-no judgment as to whether they have it, based on a series of yes-or-no judgments of each constituent criterion. In the early stages of identifying disorders, as we are with respect to most childhood disorders, and where there is no litmus test for the positive diagnosis of disorders, this metrification of quantitatively derived criteria preserves important gradations better than categorical rule systems can. Categorical cutoff points can, nevertheless, be established on quantitative distributions of scores, if desired.

Categorical and Quantitative Aspects of DSM-III

Most of *DSM-III's* childhood disorders are defined in terms of four types of criteria. One type of criterion is an age requirement. For example, a diagnosis of Avoidant Disorder of Childhood or Adolescence requires an age of at least 2½.

A second type of criterion specifies a duration. For both the Avoidant Disorder and the Overanxious Disorder, the requisite duration is 6 months, whereas for the Separation Anxiety Disorder, the duration is 2 weeks.

A third type of criterion involves preemption of one diagnosis by others. This is usually stated in terms of a disturbance being "due to" a *DSM-III* disorder other than the one under consideration. Separation Anxiety Disorder, for example, can be diagnosed only if the problems are "Not due to a Pervasive Developmental Disorder, Schizophrenia, or any other psychotic disorder" (American Psychiatric Association, 1980, p. 53).

These three kinds of criteria involve arbitrary judgments. The duration criteria are necessarily arbitrary, because the onset of disorders cannot be precisely documented and there is little data on their typical duration. The same is true for the age criterion, although good developmental data might help to improve guidelines for age and duration criteria.

A different issue is raised by the exclusionary criterion for preempting certain diagnoses with others. If the *DSM-III* is intended as a descriptive taxonomy, then why should a child meeting all the other criteria for separation anxiety be excluded from that diagnosis merely because he or she also meets the criteria for schizophrenia as well? We would, of course, want to avoid making multiple diagnoses for exactly the same problem, but there is little basis for determining when one *DSM-III* childhood disorder is "due to" another. The logic becomes especially dubious as the number of preemptory diagnoses increases. One criterion for Overanxious Disorder, for example, is that "the disturbance is not due to another mental disorder, such as Separation Anxiety Disorder, Avoidant Disorder of Childhood or Adolescence, Phobic Disorder, Obsessive Compulsive Disorder, Depressive Disorder, Schizophrenia, or a Pervasive Developmental Disorder" (American Psychiatric Association, 1980, p. 57). Might some of these disorders be manifestations of an Overanxious Disorder instead of the other way round?

The preceding problems do not necessarily argue for multivariate approaches. However, the fourth type of criterion used to define *DSM-III* childhood disorders is where multivariate approaches can be most helpful. This is the *description* of the disorders themselves. For most DSM-III childhood disorders, the descriptions consist of lists of behaviors, some or all of which must be judged present to qualify a child for a particular diagnosis. Overanxious Disorder, for example, requires at least four of the following seven items to be judged present:

1. unrealistic worry about future events;
2. preoccupation with the appropriateness of the individual's behavior in the past;
3. overconcern about competence in a variety of areas, e.g., academic, athletic, social;
4. excessive need for reassurance about a variety of worries;
5. somatic complaints, such as headaches or stomachaches, for which no physical basis can be established;

6. marked self-consciousness or susceptibility to embarrassment or humiliation;
7. marked feeling of tension or inability to relax.

Note that most of these imply quantitative judgments: For item 1, for example, we must decide how extreme a child's worry must be to be judged unrealistic. For item 2, most children may show some concern for the appropriateness of past behavior, but how much concern constitutes "preoccupation"? In items 4, 6, and 7, the words "excessive" and "marked" imply quantitative judgments. Item 5, regarding somatic complaints, does not include a quasi-quantitative term, but would we judge the criterion to be met by *every* complaint of a headache or stomachache for which "no physical basis can be established"?

The symptomatic criteria for other childhood disorders include terms such as "persistent," "excessive," "repeated," "severe," "pervasive," "frequently," "has difficulty," "a lot," "often," and "easily." Despite the implied quantitative variation in the criterial behavior, each one must be judged as present or absent. Furthermore, all children having the requisite number of yes judgments are concluded to have the disorder, while all children not having the requisite number are concluded to be free of the disorder. This places children into two arbitrary categories that mask variations in the diversity, density, and intensity of their anxiety problems.

What is more, if a child meets the criteria for the disorder, this may imply that his or her anxiety is to be understood as a specific illness, apart from all the other problems the child may have. If the child fails to meet the criteria, it suggests that anxiety is not a problem for that child. How can we make better use of potentially important quantitative variations in the assessment of children's disorders?

Taxometric Approaches

The term *taxometrics* has been applied to the construction of taxonomies via cluster analysis. Paul Meehl has also used it in reference to formalizing the diagnosis of schizophrenia through psychometric methods (Meehl & Golden, 1982). Beyond these specific usages, however, the general concept of taxometrics implies a shift from a *nominal* to a *metrical* framework for assessment and taxonomy. Metrification is of obvious relevance to constructs like anxiety, which are conceived in quantitative terms. Most efforts to assess anxiety specify the *degree* of anxiety, whether in terms of responses to questionnaire items, ratings from interviews, physiological measures, behavioral avoidance tests, or behavioral ratings. When conducting research on anxiety or clinically assessing individuals, we would be foolish indeed to judge anxiety merely as present or absent.

Because disorders defined only by anxiety seem rare in childhood, but broad groupings of disorders seem linked by exceptionally high or exceptionally low levels of anxiety, it is especially important to extend the process of metrification from assessment to the taxonomic phase of defining disorders. The *DSM-III's* listing of behaviors in quasi-quantitative terms is conceptually consistent with this notion, but more formal metrical procedures are needed to capitalize on quantitative variations in the phenomena used to identify syndromes, assess individuals, and group individuals into "types."

Illustration of a Taxometric Approach.   To illustrate, a program of taxometric research is briefly outlined. The focus is mainly on results derived from parents' ratings of the behavior of their disturbed children, but we also employ behavioral ratings by teachers, direct observers, clinical interviewers, and children themselves, where feasible. The basic data are obtained from parents' responses to the Child Behavior Checklist, which consists of 20 social competence items and 118 behavior problem items (Achenbach & Edelbrock, 1983). The parents score the behavior problems *0* if an item is *not true* of their child; *1* if it is *somewhat* or *sometimes true;* and *2* if it is *very true* or *often true.* To reflect sex and age differences in the patterning and prevalence of behavior problems, we factor analyzed parents' ratings of disturbed children, separately for each sex at ages 4 to 5, 6 to 11, and 12 to 16. For each group, we found either eight or nine syndromes that were robust with respect to variations in criteria for rotation of the factors to simple structure. Some of the syndromes are similar to those identified by nosological approaches to taxonomy, whereas others are not. Some syndromes are similar across the sex and age groups, whereas others are peculiar to one sex or a particular age group.

To apply the factorial findings to the assessment and taxonomy of children's disorders, we constructed scales consisting of the high loading items on each factor. To quantify children's standing on a syndrome, we sum the parents' ratings on all the items of the scale corresponding to that syndrome. To reflect a child's standing compared to normative groups of age-mates, we then transform these raw scores to standard scores derived from checklist data obtained from parents of randomly selected children not referred for mental health services. Rather than viewing each set of behavior problems in absolute terms, we can thus view them relative to the problems reported for other children and can determine the areas in which a child is most and least deviant. Because the taxometric approach highlights quantitative variations in syndromes, we display the syndromes for each age group of each sex in a profile format, called the Child Behavior Profile. Figure 38.4 illustrates a profile scored for a 9-year-old boy. The headings "Internalizing" and "Externalizing" across the top of the profile indicate the groupings of syndromes formed by second-order factor analyses, as mentioned earlier.

The syndrome at the left, called *Schizoid or Anxious* for 6- to 11-year-old boys consists of several anxiety items, plus "Hears things" and "Sees things that aren't there." Because it is somewhat similar to a syndrome found for other groups that included "Hears things," "Sees things," "Strange behavior," and "Strange ideas," we originally named it Schizoid. However, as pointed out by Rachel Gittelman and others, the anxiety items are numerous enough to generate a deviant score in the absence of the more schizoid items. For boys aged 6–11, we now acknowledge this ambiguity by calling the syndrome *Schizoid or Anxious*. (In other age/sex groups, the lack of association between schizoid and anxious items has persuaded us to retain the label "schizoid" alone.)

The items forming each scale of the profile represent a level of analysis analogous to the syndromes listed by *DSM-III* for most childhood disorders. On our scales, however, each item is judged in quantitative gradations on a 3-step scale, rather than being judged as present versus absent. Furthermore, a child's standing on each syndrome as a whole is not decided in a present-versus-absent fashion, but is scored on a continuous scale that can be used either in raw score form or converted to standard scores for comparison with normative samples.

The overall pattern formed by scores across all the syndromes of the profile provides a much more comprehensive basis for a taxonomy of disorders than does categorization according to individual syndromes. For example, two children who qualify for a *DSM-III* diagnosis of Separation Anxiety may obtain identical scores on our profile scale most like the list of *DSM* items. Yet their overall profile pattern shows that they differ markedly in other areas. The profile in Fig. 38.4 shows the presence of all the items needed to qualify for a *DSM-III* diagnosis of separation anxiety disorder. The profile in Fig. 38.5 includes exactly the same scores for items needed to qualify for *DSM's* Separation Anxiety Disorder, but includes other items indicative of even greater deviance in social withdrawal.

Taxonomy of Profile Types.   By cluster analyzing profiles, we have identified groups of clinically referred children who have each of the two types illustrated in Figs. 38.4 and 38.5 (Achenbach & Edelbrock, 1983; Edelbrock & Achenbach, 1980). Although *DSM-III* would classify both of these boys as having Separation Anxiety Disorders, a taxometric approach utilizing behavior problem profiles shows that they resemble two different groups, one of which manifests considerably more withdrawn behavior than do most clinically referred 6- to 11-year-old boys.

Not only can a taxometric approach provide a more comprehensive basis for a typology of behavior problem patterns, but it can also be used to construct hierarchies of patterns. Whereas second-order factor analysis forms broad-band groupings of *syndromes,* hierarchical cluster analyses can show how differentiated behavior problem patterns, such as those just illustrated, form more global groupings of *individuals* whose profiles share certain common elements. Figure

REVISED CHILD BEHAVIOR PROFILE
Behavior Problems—Boys Aged 6-11

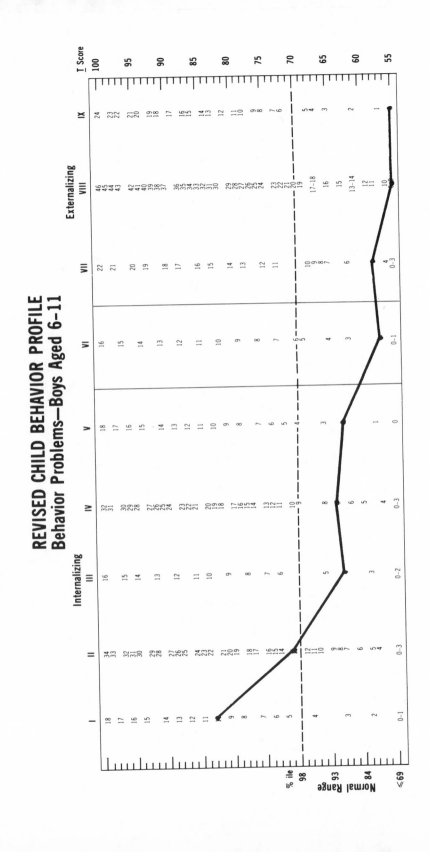

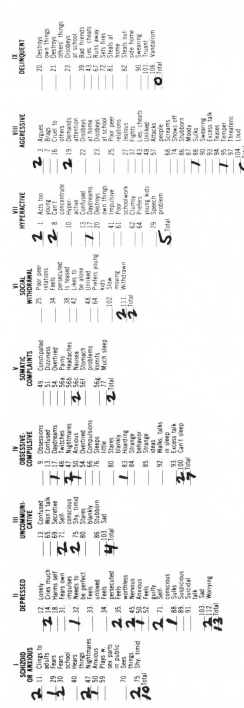

FIG. 38.4. Child Behavior Profile of a 9-year-old boy who meets *DSM-III* criteria for Separation Anxiety and whose parent's ratings show no deviance in other areas.

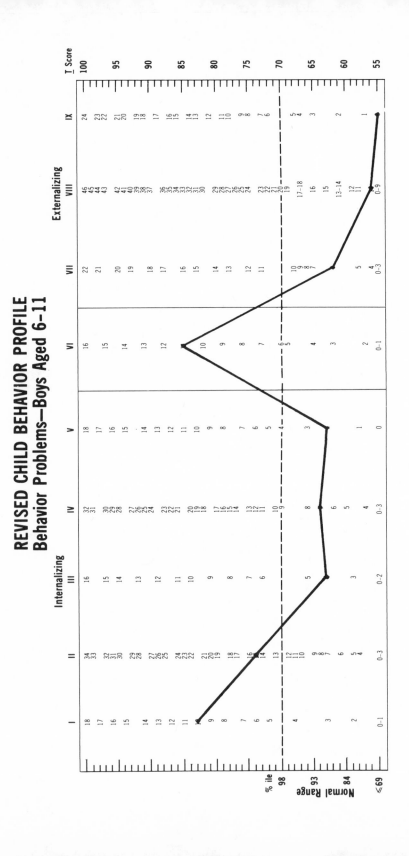

REVISED CHILD BEHAVIOR PROFILE
Behavior Problems—Boys Aged 6-11

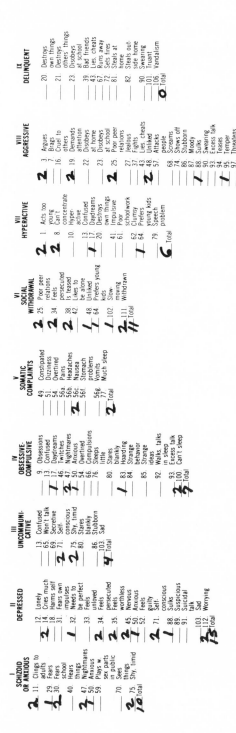

FIG. 38.5.   Child Behavior Profile of a 9-year-old boy who meets *DSM-III* criteria for Separation Anxiety and whose parent's ratings show equal deviance in social withdrawal.

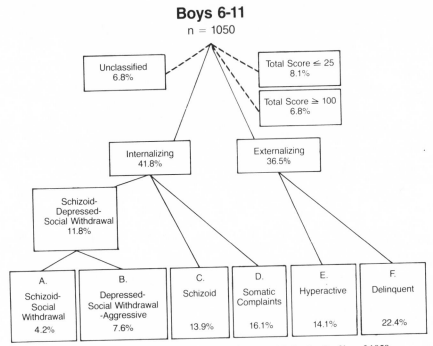

Boys 6-11
n = 1050

Unclassified
6.8%

Total Score ≤ 25
8.1%

Total Score ≥ 100
6.8%

Internalizing
41.8%

Externalizing
36.5%

Schizoid-
Depressed-
Social Withdrawal
11.8%

A.
Schizoid-
Social
Withdrawal
4.2%

B.
Depressed-
Social Withdrawal
-Aggressive
7.6%

C.
Schizoid

13.9%

D.
Somatic
Complaints

16.1%

E.
Hyperactive

14.1%

F.
Delinquent

22.4%

FIG. 38.6.   Results of hierarchical clustering of Child Behavior Profiles of 1050
6- to 11-year-old boys. (From Edelbrock & Achenbach, 1980.)

38.6 illustrates the results of a hierarchical clustering of the profile types we have identified for clinically referred boys. Both the profile types having high elevations on the Schizoid-Anxious syndrome ultimately merge into the global Internalizing grouping, but before they do, the Schizoid-Social Withdrawal type joins the Depressed-Social Withdrawal-Aggressive type. We have some evidence that this group has a worse prognosis than the other Internalizing groups.

Assigning Individuals to Types.   One last point regarding the taxometric approach: With the centroid method of cluster analysis we have used, the operational definition of each profile type is the *centroid* of the cluster—that is, a profile pattern formed by averaging the profiles of all the members of the cluster identified in the initial cluster analysis. Once the centroid has been formed, the degree to which a child's profile resembles each type can be quantitatively assessed by computing an intraclass correlation between the child's profile and the centroids of each type identified for that child's age and sex. Because the intraclass correlation provides a quantitative basis for judging the child's membership in each group, we are not forced into rigid categorical judgments. Instead, research and clinical decisions can be based on explicit gradations of resemblance to various criterion groups. To create very pure groups, it can be stipulated that all members must have a high correlation with the centroid that operationally defines a group. To classify larger proportions of children at the cost of less pure groups, we can use a lower correlation as a cutoff point.

DEVELOPMENTAL CONSIDERATIONS

As outlined in relation to taxonomic issues, most disorders of childhood differ in important ways from the disease-like entities of Kraepelinian nosology. In this section, I expand on these points and explore some additional developmental implications.

Children's disorders usually involve behavior that is not intrinsically abnormal, but is deviant in its intensity, frequency, pervasiveness, or developmental parameters. Separation anxiety, for example, is normal and expected during the first 2 years of life. Yet, extremely intense or disruptive separation behavior during this period might be considered deviant, even though milder degrees are normal. A total lack of separation anxiety might also be considered abnormal, although this would seldom be a reason for clinical referral unless a child also had other problems of concern to parents or pediatricians.

In addition to extreme forms of behavior occurring during developmental periods when moderate forms are normal, certain behaviors are normal if they occur in one developmental period but abnormal if they occur in another. Marked separation anxiety during middle childhood, for example, would be considered abnormal, even though the same degree of separation anxiety would be normal at younger ages. Not only the persistence of behavior beyond its normal developmental period, but also behavior occurring at an earlier than normal age can evoke concern. Anxieties about relations with the opposite sex or ruminations about one's personal identity, for example, are expected in adolescence but not at earlier ages.

Beside developmental variations in the intensity and appropriateness of various anxieties, there are important developmental variations in how anxiety is manifested. Infants show their distress in obvious ways, although it may be difficult to distinguish distress due to anxiety from that due to other psychological variables or physical discomfort. The expression of anxiety in preschoolers becomes more complex, as it may involve ritualistic behavior, fantasy, aggression, withdrawal, clinging, and other behaviors shaped by a host of factors beside anxiety. By adolescence, of course, the range of behavior potentially associated with anxiety becomes enormous. In fact, it may be difficult to determine whether anxiety is involved in a particular problem behavior at all. The broad-band internalizing versus externalizing distinction that I discussed earlier implies the presence versus absence of anxiety but might also be construed in other ways. For example, it might reflect a general reaction to stress by turning inward versus outward, or by flight versus fight. It might also reflect cognitive and other coping mechanisms that show developmental differences, as well as individual differences that persist across developmental periods.

The interplay between individual differences and developmental differences is an especially difficult but fascinating aspect of psychopathology during the period of rapid development from birth to maturity. This interplay precludes assessment of disorders as static disease entities in a uniform fashion at all ages. Instead, it requires assessment procedures that are standardized and normed for each developmental period, and that take account of the implications of particular behaviors for long-term adaptation. Behaviors that are troublesome at one developmental period, for example, may herald important developmental advances. On the other hand, an appearance of exceptional well-being at one period may not predict competence at later periods. We are all familiar, for example, with the high school athletic hero who is unable to assume adult roles.

The interplay between individual and developmental differences greatly complicates the assessment of children's disorders. Whereas adult patients provide most of the assessment data about their own problems, children's self-reports vary greatly in their nature and value. At all ages from birth through adolescence, at least some assessment data must be obtained from children's primary caregivers, usually parents. During middle childhood, teachers become an important source of assessment data for many but not all children. The value of teachers' and parents' reports is much more variable for adolescents, whose problem behaviors may be less open to observation or complicated more by conflicts with the informants. Whereas adolescents' cognitive ability should make them better able to communicate problems as adult patients do, the emotional complications and alienation of adolescence often interfere. Some very young children may communicate their problems more effectively than most adolescents.

Because we cannot count on obtaining definitive assessment data from most children, it is necessary to obtain data from as many sources as possible, including parents, teachers, direct observers, and clinicians, as well as the children themselves. Because each informant sees the child from different perspectives and in different situations, disagreements among them are to be expected. These disagreements do not necessarily indicate unreliability. For example, 10-year-old children may be the best informants about their own inner experience of anxiety, but their parents may be better informants about the range and nature of its overt manifestations, while teachers are better informants about its role in the children's school functioning.

A final point concerns the possible significance of anxiety at various developmental periods for the onset and outcome of psychopathology. As mentioned earlier, psychoanalytic and learning theories have both invoked childhood anxiety to explain later psychopathology. Yet, there is little hard evidence for predictive or causal relations between specific anxiety phenomena at specific developmental periods and later problems of any sort, anxiety or otherwise. Based on their longitudinal study of children's behavior disorders, Thomas, Chess, and Birch (1968) concluded that anxiety was not an initial factor in the development of symptoms. Instead, when it did appear, it was usually

> . . . a secondary phenomenon, a consequence rather than a cause of symptom development . . . . once anxiety, intrapsychic conflict, and psychodynamic mechanisms appear, they add new dimensions to the dynamics of the child's functioning . . . . The painfulness of severe anxiety makes it a striking symptom which may dominate our perceptions of the clinical picture . . . . It is, therefore, not surprising that in retrospective studies that begin when the child already presents with an elaborated psychological disturbance, the prominent phenomena of anxiety and psychodynamic defenses dominate clinical thinking and come to be labeled primary, rather than as secondary, influences in the genesis of behavior disturbance. (pp. 188-189)

This suggests that we cannot study anxiety disorders in children as encapsulated illnesses, apart from other aspects of functioning, independent of developmental level and course. Instead, assessment of anxiety problems must include assessment of a broad range of other problems and competencies, across multiple developmental periods.

SUMMARY

Early psychoanalytic and behavioral theories blamed later psychopathology on early childhood anxiety and used child case histories to illustrate hypothesized pathological mechanisms. Clinical assessment of anxiety in children has been modeled largely after adult assessment, including projective techniques, self-report questionnaires for trait and state anxiety, fear inventories, physiological measures, and behavioral avoidance tests. The various approaches to assessment reflect a continuum of theoretical orientations ranging from psychodynamic to personality trait and state constructs to behavioral.

Related to the continuum of theoretical orientations is a continuum of target problems ranging from fears and phobias to anxiety and internalizing disorders. Most children's fears and phobias are not symptoms of major psychopathology and can be effectively treated by a variety of procedures. Certain school phobias, however, may be associated with significant psychopathology, especially in older children and their families. Other forms of anxiety, such as separation anxiety, are normal developmental phenomena that may warrant concern when they are deviant in degree, pervasiveness, or developmental timing.

Multivariate studies of children's behavior problems have repeatedly identified two broad-band groupings of syndromes. One consists largely of overcontrolled, "internalizing" behaviors that seem linked by anxiety problems. The second consists largely of undercontrolled, "externalizing" behaviors that reflect a lack of appropriate anxiety. These broad-band groupings subsume narrower band syndromes analogous to some of the syndromes of standard psychiatric nosology.

At this stage in the study of childhood anxiety disorders, taxometric approaches offer many advantages for quantifying and aggregating data for both clinical and research purposes. The study of the developmental course of anxiety disorders and the interplay between developmental and individual differences could especially benefit from quantification and standardization of assessment procedures in a taxometric fashion. However, it would be less fruitful to view anxiety disorders in children as encapsulated entities, independent of the development of other problems and competencies.

II

H. Diagnosis and Classification

39

Approaches to the Definition and Classification of Anxiety and Related Disorders in European Psychiatry

A. Jablensky, M.D., D.M.Sc.
World Health Organization, Geneva

Few terms in psychopathology and clinical psychiatry give rise to more ambiguity of interpretation than the terms "anxiety," "phobia," and "panic," although the symptoms and conditions which these words denote are neither rarities nor phenomena too refractory to clinical analysis. The prevalence of anxiety and phobic states in the general population in European countries may be as high as 2% to 3% according to a review of the epidemiological evidence by Sartorius (1980). The frequency of anxiety symptoms occurring in the context of other psychiatric and medical conditions is likely to be much higher. That the classification of anxiety disorders is still a matter of controversy and significant disagreement is, however, only one aspect of the generally unsatisfactory state of the nosology of nonpsychotic disorders, an area that "has still to attract its Kraepelin" (Shepherd, 1982).

HISTORY AND EVOLUTION OF THE CONCEPTS AND TERMS RELATED TO ANXIETY

Some of the sources of the present nosological ambiguities surrounding the concepts of anxiety and phobia can be traced back to their uneven evolution and remarkably ramified pedigree. The term "phobia" was used by Celsus and known to medical writers from the 5th century onwards (Errera, 1962; Lewis, 1976). Apparently, its connotations have always been similar to the present-day meaning of the term: referring to "irrational" or disproportionate fears (*phobos* = "terror") attached to particular objects or situations. Snaith (1968) has drawn attention to an alleged description of agoraphobia in Richard Burton's "Anatomy of Melancholy," published in 1621.

References to morbid anxiety and phobia in the medical and psychiatric classifications are rare (but not entirely missing, as it is sometimes claimed) until the second half of the 19th century.[1] Morel (1809–1873) was perhaps the first builder of a classification system in psychiatry who identified "phobia and other neuroses" under the heading *délire émotif,* the class of neurotic illnesses, which he made into a major component of his system.

However, it was in 19th-century philosophy and theology that the concept of anxiety (or "dread") first found a detailed phenomenological analysis, as part of a significant chapter in European thought, associated with the name of the Danish theologian Sören Kierkegaard (1813–1855). In describing the pervasive psychological experience of anxiety, Kierkegaard ascribed to it an exclusive ontological status in the sense of its being one of the basic attributes of man and a philosophical category necessary for the interpretation of human existence. Anxiety, according to Kierkegaard, is the unavoidable companion of reflective consciousness in man; it arises from the recognition, by the reflective human intellect, that a negation of being or a state of nothingness is both thinkable and possible: "With every increase in the degree of consciousness, and in proportion to the increase, the intensity of despair increases: the more conscious, the more intense the despair" (Kierkegaard, 1849).

The conceptualization of anxiety as an imminent feature of the human condition was a distinctive theme of that stream in European philosophy that became popularly known as "existentialism" and that transposed into the 20th century some of the principal ideas of Kierkegaard. Thus, to Martin Heidegger (1889–1976) being-in-the-world "is in anxiety" and anxiety itself is intrinsically linked to human freedom. This is because only the acceptance of the "terminality" of existence and the experience of *Angst* (anxiety, dread) makes that freedom possible. Karl Jaspers (1883–1969), one of the eminent figures of European psychiatry and philosophy, remarked that "large numbers, particularly of modern people, seem to live fearlessly because they lack imagination...the freedom from anxiety is but the other side of a deeper loss of freedom" (Jaspers, 1963).

Under the influence of existential philosophy, the study of anxiety became one of the central concerns of existential psychiatry *(Daseinsanalyse)* and psychotherapy. This school of thought, which attempted to link analytical psychotherapy

---

[1]Pinel (1803), in his *Nosographie philosophique,* gave a special place to "spontaneous hydrophobia" and its distinction from "hydrophobia communicated by contagion" (rabies). By all appearances, the former was an acute anxiety state. In the same treatise, Pinel described in considerable detail a number of syndromes consisting chiefly in bodily complaints accompanied by *une certaine anxiété:* for example "cardialgia" or "gastrodinia."

to philosophical concepts, sought to emphasize those positive aspects of anxiety which enhance the sense of being: "we are as doubtful whether we really want a life without anxiety as we are certain that we want a life without fear" (von Gebsattel, 1938). Morbid anxiety was thought to be "cued off by a threat to some value the individual holds essential to his existence as a personality" (May, 1950). The subtle phenomenological analysis of what today might be called the cognitive aspect of the anxiety experience was undoubtedly a significant contribution of existential psychiatry to the general body of psychopathology.

Apart from the above-mentioned reference to phobias in the classificatory system of Morel (1860), the interest in delineating clinical syndromes of anxiety and related states developed in European psychiatry only in the second half of the 19th century. Since clinical psychiatry was almost entirely hospital- or asylum-based, it is not surprising that for a long time anxiety states and phobias were subsumed under the classificatory rubrics for the severe mental disorders that came to the attention of the "alienists." In the 1870s Benedikt (1870) and Westphal (1872) described under the names of *Platzschwindel* (dizziness occurring in open spaces) and *Platzangst* (fear of open spaces), or "agoraphobia," the syndrome as we know it today. Anxiety as a morbid response to severe stress was described by Oppenheim (1892) under the heading "traumatic neurosis," a concept that Kraepelin incorporated in his description of *Schreckneurose* (fright neurosis) in the 1896 edition of his textbook. The *Schreckneurose* was seen by Kraepelin as a separate clinical entity which "is composed of multiple nervous and psychic phenomena arising as a result of severe emotional upheaval or sudden fright which build up great anxiety; it can therefore be observed after serious accidents and injuries, particularly fires, railway derailments or collisions, etc." (Kraepelin, 1896). The clinical picture included, notably, agoraphobia as one of the possible symptoms, along with depressive mood, obsessive ideas, rumination, and hypochondriacal complaints.

Around the same time, Wernicke (1984) described a "fear psychosis" (*Angstpsychose*), a condition that was perhaps the prototype of the "fear-happiness psychosis" *(Angst-Glück Psychose)* that was later to be classified among the cycloid psychoses identified by the Kleist-Leonhard school (Leonhard, 1957).

An entirely different line of clinical observation and investigation, unrelated to psychiatric research, was pursued since the middle of the 19th century by European and North American cardiologists and general physicians who described the cardiac manifestations of anxiety under a bewildering variety of diagnostic labels: "nervous palpitation," "irritable heart" (Da Costa, 1871), "soldier's heart," "aviator's syndrome," "hyperventilation syndrome," or "hyperaesthesia of the cardiac nerve centers." In a recent review, Skerritt (1983) made the observation that new diagnostic categories for the cardiac and other somatic "neuroses" have tended to emerge after each major war, with the "effort syndrome" (T. Lewis, 1917) and "neuro-circulatory asthenia" (Oppenheimer et al., 1918) following

World War I, and "effort phobia" or "anxiety state" following World War II. Today, the same clinical syndrome is likely to be labeled "beta-hyperresponsiveness" or "mitral valve prolapse syndrome." Skerritt concluded that "authors still tend to see the whole of anxiety neurosis from the viewpoint of the symptoms presenting to their own specialty."

The credit for the description of anxiety neurosis as a clinical entity and for its separation from the ubiquitous "neurasthenia" belongs to Freud (1895). Freud clearly distinguished three components of anxiety as an affective state: (1) a subjective feeling of a "specific unpleasurable quality"; (2) physical sensations due to "efferent or discharge phenomena"; and (3) "the perception of these."

Over a period of three decades, he developed two different and, as he himself thought, contrasting theories of anxiety (known in the psychoanalytical literature as the "first" and "second" theory). The first theory (1895) led to the separation of the *Angstneurose* from neurasthenia. At that point Freud regarded anxiety as one of the "actual" neuroses, i.e., more or less as a somatic (possibly toxic) process, devoid of symbolic value. Anxiety was seen as the "automatic" product or transformation of dammed-up libidinal energy; such a transformation could occur whenever "sexual excitation is inhibited, frustrated or diverted in the course of its discharge in gratification." The later, or "metapsychological," theory (1926) reversed this view by affirming that the ego was "the real locus of anxiety" and that the emergence of anxiety within the ego system caused the repression of "dangerous" contents from consciousness, rather than vice versa. In this version of the theory, Freud attributed to anxiety an affective signal function with regard to danger coming from within, thus minimizing the difference between anxiety and the "reality fear normally manifested by the ego in situations of danger." Anxiety could assume two forms: normal anxiety and neurotic anxiety. Both had as their prototypes the separation and castration anxieties of the early childhood; however, the latter always resulted in symptoms tending to reproduce in adult life infantile or childhood ways of dealing with the unpleasurable tension of signal anxiety. From the point of view of the phenomenology and nosology of anxiety states it is important to emphasize that in addition to the diagnostic entity, we also owe to Freud some basic descriptive distinctions, e.g., those between generalized diffuse anxiety, anxiety attacks, and phobias.

Any overview of the evolution of concepts related to the classification of anxiety would be incomplete without a reference to the work of I.P. Pavlov (1849–1936), whose observations on experimental neuroses in laboratory animals and later extrapolations of some of the physiological constructs to the clinical interpretation and classification of neuroses in man were influential in preparing the ground for the behavioral approaches to the treatment of neuroses. Pavlov regarded fear as the result of an environmental activation of the inborn passive-defensive unconditioned reflex, manifesting itself either in a behavioral inhibition or in a hyperkinetic excitement. A pathological hyperactivation of this reflex

could occur in any subject in response to exceptional stimuli, but more important
was the constitutional predilection of certain "types of higher nervous activity"
to react with fear and inhibition to stimuli that would not evoke the same reaction
in other types of higher nervous activity organization. Pavlov and several of his
collaborators, working on the induction and treatment of experimental neuroses
in dogs, recorded a number of observations that supported the constitutional
point of view on neurosis. A good deal of this support was owed to an accidental
event: the disastrous flood in Leningrad in 1924.

The "natural experiment" of the flood, during which laboratory dogs that had
been experimentally studied for years had to be evacuated to safety, suggested
some new conditioning procedures which resulted in the modeling of phobias.
Later, in extrapolating the conclusions of his experimental work with animals
to human neuroses, Pavlov proposed that it was the "weak inhibitory" or "melancholic" type of higher nervous activity that was predisposed to pathological
anxiety. Pavlov, however, did not separate anxiety neurosis as an entity. In his
classification there were three human neuroses: neurasthenia, psychasthenia
(obsessive neurosis), and hysteria, each of which could include among its manifestations anxiety and phobias. This point of view is influential in Soviet psychiatry until the present day and is reflected, for example, in the latest *USSR
Handbook of Psychiatry* (edited by Snezhnevsky, 1983).

Even a brief look at the history of the concept suggests that the study of
morbid anxiety and related phenomena was to a large extent hampered by the
protean nature of their manifestations and the extremely varied kinds of settings
in which anxiety disorders presented themselves with a frequency and severity
sufficient to call for scientific investigation. As long as the mainstream of clinical
psychiatry remained hospital-oriented, it was mostly the psychotic manifestations
of anxiety and the severe forms of "traumatic neuroses" that attracted diagnostic
and classificatory interest. The common neurotic disorders, such as generalized
anxiety states and phobic disorders, were mainly seen and treated by psychotherapists who had little contact with either the hospital or the university psychiatrists. Still farther away were the cardiologists, neurologists, and other medical
specialists who each focused on a particular aspect of the neurovegetative and
somatic components of the anxiety response. It is not surprising that the explanatory theories, diagnostic concepts, and classifications of anxiety developed by
these three main categories of professionals were radically different, offering
practically no chance of a unified point of view. Much of the confusion undoubtedly persists until today.

In the period 1968–1973 the World Health Organization (WHO) carried out
an international program on the standardization of psychiatric diagnosis, classification, and statistics (known also as "Programme A"), with the participation
of leading psychiatrists from some 30 countries. These experts were asked to
make diagnoses after being presented with excerpts of clinical notes and films

or videotapes of interviews of a number of patients, selected to illustrate all the principal areas of psychopathology and psychiatric classification. Although some types of disorders (e.g., functional psychoses) commanded a relatively high degree of diagnostic agreement, the concurrence of the experts was remarkably low in the instances of the neuroses (WHO, 1970). In a case that would probably meet fully both the ICD-9 (International Classification of Diseases—9th Revision) description of an anxiety state and the *DSM-III (Diagnostic and Statistical Manual*—3rd Edition) criteria of "generalized anxiety disorder," only 9 out of 21 experts made a diagnosis of "anxiety neurosis." The remaining diagnostic opinions were split among other neuroses, personality disorder, and "cardiac neurosis." It is likely that the results of a similar experiment today would not be very different, in spite of the fact that the ICD classification of mental disorders has been adopted by all European countries.

Description and Classification of Anxiety Symptoms and Syndromes

There is agreement in the European psychiatric literature: (1) that anxiety is an affective state or response; (2) that it is one of the most common manifestations in a host of mental and psychophysiological disorders; (3) that there is a quantitative distinction and, at the same time, a basic qualitative continuity between normal and pathological anxiety; and (4) that it is diagnostically important to distinguish between anxiety as a personality trait and anxiety as a pathological state (Lader, 1972). However, by and large, the similarities between the different schools of thought end there, and a number of differences persist regarding the specific content and scope of the concept and its delimitation from other affective states and responses.

Semantic Difficulties.   At rock bottom, it appears that some of the differences of interpretation and emphasis are related to a purely semantic problem. As Lewis (1970) pointed out, in most of the European languages there are a great many words and idiomatic expressions describing intrapsychic and bodily states that are different facets of the anxiety experience. Thus, any discussion of the phenomenology and classification of anxiety is likely to be colored, to some extent, by the lexicology of the language in which it is conducted.

The English word "anxiety" (from the Latin *anxietas*) does not cover the same semantic space as the French *anxiété* or the Spanish *ansiedad,* although they all derive from a common root. In both the French and Spanish languages, a closely related word, *angoisse* and *angustia* respectively, is often used as a near-synonym, but it is claimed (e.g., Porot, 1981) that the connotation of the French *angoisse* emphasizes more strongly the physical sensations (e.g., of constriction or oppression) accompanying the experience and, as such, it should be closer to the English "anguish" rather than to "anxiety." In the German language, *Angst* is more general than "anxiety" and encompasses an element of fear as well. The distinctions between "free-floating" *(freiflottierende)* and "object-related" *(objektbezogene) Angst* have been elaborated in great phenomenological detail by Jaspers (1963). Kraepelin (1896) felt that a single term such as *Angst* was insufficient to denote the variety of psychopathological experience, and introduced in his description of clinical anxiety two further terms: *Aengstlichkeit* ("anxiousness," a habitual anxious response) and *ängstliche Spannung* ("anxious tension"). In the Russian language the two words usually used to describe clinical anxiety are страх (read "strakh") and тревога (read "trevoga"). The first, however, has a strong connotation of fear and the latter has the connotation of *alarm*. In the recent Soviet psychiatric literature there are also attempts to introduce the term *anksioznost*, a direct borrowing from the English usage.

In the face of such diversity of meaning of the everyday, colloquial words and expressions available for the description of anxiety in the major European languages, glossaries and other definitions of the relevant scientific terms assume particular importance.

Definitions of Anxiety. Most European authors would probably agree with Lader (1981) that it is useful to distinguish four dimensions of the phenomenon of anxiety: (1) the subjective, (2) the cognitive, (3) the behavioral, and (4) the physiological. According to Lader, "the ineffable feeling of foreboding is the core of anxiety," both as a normal emotion and as a clinical phenomenon. Other definitions (e.g., Piotrowski, 1957) articulate at least five components of the subjective experience: awareness of one's own powerlessness in the face of threat; a feeling of impending danger; a state of tense alertness; apprehensive self-absorption; and doubts as to the effectiveness of action to counter the threat. Jaspers (1963) described free-floating anxiety as "a primary psychic state, all-pervasive and dominating...and involving existence as a whole. There is every degree from contentless, powerful anxiety that leads to a clouding of consciousness and ruthless acts of violence against oneself or others, down to a slight, anxious tension where the anxiety is experienced as alien to the self and inexplicable."

The behavioral manifestations range from extreme excitement or hyperkinesis (a "fright-flight" reaction according to Cannon, or a "motility storm" according to Kretschmer) to stuporous inhibition ("feigned-death reflex"), with most of the common clinical manifestations falling in between these two extremes. The physiological accompaniments (Tyrer, 1976) comprise signs of both sympathetic and parasympathetic overactivity and general overarousal. The former include an increased heart rate, palpitations, raised arterial blood pressure, increased perspiration, palm sweating, dilatation of the pupils, dryness of the mouth. The parasympathetic responses include increased bowel movements, nausea, vomiting, and increased frequency of urination. None of these physiological manifestations are specific to anxiety (nor can they distinguish normal from pathological anxiety); many of them occur also in other emotional states, e.g., rage or intense, ecstatic excitement. The German literature puts a special emphasis on the vital or bodily aspects of anxiety that may arise either as primary phenomena in anxiety disorders or are secondary to a physical disease or physiological dysfunction causing an anxious mental state.[2]

One of the first steps toward the standardization of the assessment of anxiety states by using a clinical rating scale was made by Hamilton (1959). Subsequently, operational distinctions between free-floating and situational anxiety have been proposed and incorporated in the glossary accompanying the 9th edition of the Present State Examination (PSE) (Wing, Cooper, & Sartorius, 1974). The PSE is a structured psychiatric interview which has found wide applications in psychiatric research, both within and outside Europe. According to this glossary, the essential requirement for a rating of the symptom of free-floating autonomic anxiety is the presence of "clear-cut automatic reactions such as palpitations, difficulty getting breath, etc. accompanied by an affect of fear or apprehension. . . . The autonomic anxiety should be free-floating, that is, not exclusively tied to some particular situation." The rating of free-floating anxiety presupposes the exclusion of "realistic" fears and anxieties, as well as of anxiety due to delusions in psychotic states. In the PSE, a distinction is made between this type of free-floating autonomic anxiety and the "anxious foreboding with autonomic accompaniments" which is considered a separate symptom: "The

---

[2]Anxiety as a symptom of physical or cerebral disease (thyrotoxicosis, pheochromocytoma, angina pectoris, asthma, Vitamin B deficiency, and temporal lobe epilepsy) has received surprisingly little attention in the psychiatric literature. Greer, Ramsay, and Bagley (1973), who compared neurotic and thyrotoxic anxiety on a number of variables, failed to identify indicators that could reliably distinguish between the two. In view of the fact that various manifestations of anxiety come to the fore in the descriptions and definitions proposed by different authors and schools, it is desirable to achieve agreement on a "core" definition that would bring the different strands of the concept together. Such an attempt has been made in the recently published "Lexicon of Psychiatric and Mental Health Terms" (prepared in the context of the joint WHO/ADAMHA project on diagnosis and classification). The definition proposed there is as follows:

In its morbid connotation, anxiety is a subjectively unpleasant emotional state of fear or apprehension directed towards the future, either in the absence of any recognizable threat or danger or when such factors are clearly out of keeping with the reaction. Subjective bodily discomfort and manifest voluntary and autonomic bodily dysfunction may accompany the anxiety. Anxiety may be situational or specific, i.e. tied up to some particular situation or object, or "free-floating", when no such link to an external triggering factor is apparent. (WHO document MNH 83.9, p. 9)

subject feels anxious but this is due to a feeling that something terrible is going to happen (death, disaster, ruination). It may occur in particularly concentrated form first thing in the morning, when the subject feels that he is unable to face the day ahead and experiences autonomic symptoms as he thinks about it."

Panic. The PSE glossary defines panic attacks as "discrete episodes of autonomic anxiety...which the subject tries to terminate by taking some drastic avoiding action." It is worth mentioning however, that, with the exception of English-language psychiatry, the term "panic" is hardly ever used in Europe. Although the phenomenon of acute attacks or exacerbations of anxiety "out of the blue" is recognized (e.g., as an "attack-like anxiety syndrome"—Langen, 1971), it has received far less attention in non-English speaking psychiatry and certainly has not been regarded as a phenomenon presenting any special problems for classification. For example, the manual to the AMDP[3] System (1982), a widely used methodology for the standardized recording of clinical information, does not contain a reference to panic. A rare example of explicit interest in the nosology of panic attacks is a recent paper by van den Hout and Griez (1983) who elaborated on the concept of "phobophobia" and proposed that "the patient suffering from an anxiety neurosis with panic attacks is merely phobophobic. He panics because he fears to do so." These two authors consider panic to be an anxiety state provoked by interoceptive stimuli.

Phobias. The definition and classification of phobic symptoms and syndromes has probably given rise to the greatest number of inconsistencies, disagreements, and other obstacles to communication. Lewis (1976) has noted that "the term phobia is used so loosely that one is uncertain if it refers to a symptom, a symptom complex or an anomaly of personality...the introduction of the diagnostic term led to the erroneous idea of a unitary disease, whereas phobic manifestations appear in many different kinds of clinical disorder." Indeed, since the 18th century the term "phobia" has been applied to a great variety of subjective experience and to objectively observable behavior which had as a common feature a specific apprehension or fear that appeared to the observer as unrealistic or bizarre; the subject usually had insight into the unreasonableness of his fears or apprehensions. The usual way of classifying phobias in the 19th century (but also in quite a few present-day textbooks) was by their object or situation attachment. This soon resulted in a self-expanding list of Latin nouns that could be practically infinite, e.g.:

---

[3]*Arbeitsgruppe für Methodik und Dokumentation in der Psychiatrie* – "Working Group on Methods and Documentation in Psychiatry."

Nosophobias

cancerophobia (fear of cancer)
cardiopathophobia (fear of heart disease)
epistaxiophobia (fear of nasal bleeding)

luiphobia (fear of syphilis)
lyssophobia (fear of rabies)
tuberculophobia (fear of tuberculosis)
venerophobia (fear of venereal disease)

Situational and "nature" phobias

agoraphobia (fear of open spaces)
aichmophobia (fear of pointed objects)
bathyphobia (fear of depths)
claustrophobia (fear of enclosed spaces)
dromophobia (fear of streets)
ereuthophobia (fear of red, e.g., blood)

keraunophobia (fear of lightning)
monophobia (fear of being alone)
nyctophobia (fear of darkness)
phobophobia (fear of fearing)
topophobia (fear of place)

Zoophobias

ophidiophobia (fear of snakes)

suriphobia (fear of mice)

More recent approaches to classifying phobias have relied on factor analysis. For example, Torgersen (1979) identified five factors: (1) separation fears (including agoraphobia), (2) animal fears, (3) mutilation fears, (4) social fears, and (5) nature fears.

The unsatisfactory character of classifications proceeding from the contents of phobias should be obvious; they lump together at least five groups of different psychopathological phenomena:

1. free-floating, or generalized, anxiety which secondarily becomes localized in a vital organ ("cardiopathophobia");
2. hypochondriacal preoccupations or beliefs, often but not always associated with anxiety, and usually arising within a particular personality structure (Ryle, 1948);
3. obsessive fears, mostly lacking the autonomic component of anxiety, and experienced as an inner compulsion which must be resisted; anxiety may be a secondary phenomenon;
4. circumscribed, discrete or specific phobias (phobias proper), characterized by a strong autonomic anxiety reaction and avoidance behavior in the presence (real or imagined) of specific external cues;
5. agoraphobia, a situational phobia which is not linked to specific cues and therefore occupies an intermediate position between the discrete phobias and generalized anxiety.

Of particular importance is that in many schools and national traditions in European psychiatry a clear-cut distinction between phobias and obsessions is not attempted; all or most of the phobias may be subsumed under the obsessive-compulsive phenomena. Thus, following Pitress and Régis (1902), the French nosographic tradition regards the phobias and obsessions as different degrees of the same condition, which can be distinguished from one another only on the ✳ basis of the relative predominance of the emotional and the ideational elements. The assimilation of phobias and obsessions, however, was not limited to French psychiatry: E. Bleuler (1920) in his influential textbook listed all the phobias under the heading of obsessional neurosis and used the terms "obsessional fears" and "phobias" as synonyms. In Sweden, phobias were also often regarded as a component of the "anancastic syndrome" (Forssman, 1963). In contrast to such views, Schipkowenski (1960) insisted that all phobias should be regarded as metamorphoses of a thanatophobia (fear of dying), and classified under the heading of anxiety neurosis.

The systematic delimitation of phobias as specific forms of morbid anxiety from other psychiatric disorders is largely a contribution of British psychiatric research during and after World War II. This research was based to some extent on epidemiological evidence, but its main empirical support came from the systematic study of the clinical features and treatment responses of a large number of patients with phobic symptoms. In his review of the classification of phobic disorders, Marks (1970) pointed out that although these disorders could occur in any situation and could be found in association with any other disorder (e.g., depression, obsessive neurosis, diffuse anxiety states, personality disorders, schizophrenia), they appeared as the only or as the dominant symptom in at least 3% of the psychiatric out-patients. Within the group of phobias there are relatively discrete subgroups. In spite of the presence of common characteristics, the phobias cannot be arranged along a single continuum. Both Snaith (1968) and Hallam (1978), in agreement with Marks (1970), who regards phobias as a series of related disorders with overlapping features, stressed the differences between the symptom-complex of agoraphobia and the specific phobias. Agoraphobia is not linked to specific causes, such as those triggering off the discrete phobias, and can best be described as "staying-at-home-behavior," rather than as avoidance of a specific situation. Further support for the relatively independent position of the agoraphobic syndrome is provided by follow-up studies. For example, Emmelkamp and Kuipers (1979), who followed up 70 agoraphobics for 4 years after behavioral treatment, found that no other neurotic features had emerged in the follow-up period. Sustained improvement was reported in 75% of the cases. Clinical, epidemiological, treatment response, and psychophysiological observations led Marks to the differentiation of two classes of phobic disorders:

Class I: Phobias of External Stimuli
1. Agoraphobia (about 60% of the phobic cases presenting for treatment; onset between ages 15 and 35; tendency to generalization; abnormal skin resistance response)
2. Social phobias (characteristics intermediate between 1 and 3)
3. Animal phobias (onset early in life, little generalization)

4. Miscellaneous specific phobias (usually normal physiological responses)

Class II: Phobias of Internal Stimuli
5. Illness phobias
6. Obsessive phobias (e.g., fear of harming people, of contamination.)

A brief mention should be made here of the phobic disorders specific to childhood (excluding those phobias that have an onset in childhood and continue into adulthood). School phobia (a term introduced by Johnson, Falsteen, Szursk, & Svendsen, 1941) appears to be a relatively frequent problem in the European context. A classification of school phobias has been proposed by Berg, Nichols, and Pritchard (1969). The features of the disorder include severe emotional upset in attending school, frequent and prolonged absences, and a tendency to stay at home, usually with the knowledge of the parents. Asocial behavior and delinquent truancy do not develop in children with school phobia (Baker & Wills, 1978). Follow-up studies indicate that adult agoraphobia is the outcome in only a small proportion of the cases of school phobia. Berg et al. (1974) concluded that both school phobia and agoraphobia reflect a "lasting tendency to neurotic illness," but do not represent different phases of the same disorder.

To sum up, there is little agreement within European psychiatry on the scope and boundaries of the several interrelated concepts that refer to the different forms and aspects of anxiety. Although many psychiatrists agree on the general description of the syndrome of anxiety (including its subjective and physiological components) and on the distinction between generalized (free-floating) and object-related anxiety, there is still a great diversity of views on the nature of situational or phobic anxiety. To many schools of thought (e.g., the French, Russian, and partly German) phobias are not a separate class of psychopathological disorders akin to anxiety, but manifestations of other neurotic disorders; mostly obsessional ones. It is mainly British investigations (Marks & Lader, 1973) who have insisted on the separate status of phobic neuroses (or disorders), and they have advanced considerable clinical, epidemiological, and experimental evidence in support of this view.

The Nosological Status of Anxiety Disorders

The lack of good agreement on the delimitation and nature of the anxiety and phobic syndromes in the different schools and traditions of European psychiatry is reflected in uncertainties and divergent views on how to classify these disorders among the other psychiatric syndromes and diseases with which they often appear in association.

The most frequent association is that with depressive disorders. A recent WHO multicenter study in which the symptomatology of 572 depressive patients in Canada, Iran, Japan, and Switzerland was compared (Jablensky, Sartorius, Gulbinat, & Ernberg, 1981; Sartorius et al., 1983) demonstrated that anxiety and tension were among the most frequent symptoms in such patients in each one of these very different settings, occurring at the height of a depressive episode in 76%–100% of the cases.

A number of influential European psychiatrists have placed anxiety and phobia syndromes mainly under the heading of affective illnesses. Thus, Lewis (1966), who generally held a "unitary" view of the nosology of affective disorders, nevertheless distinguished three subgroups of manic-depressive states, each exhibiting a "major" and a "minor" form. Subgroup 3 in his typology contained agitated depression as a major form and anxiety neurosis as its minor form of manifestation. Kelly and Walter (1969) compared the clinical features and phys-iological measurements in a group of patients with anxiety states, a group of patients with depressive illnesses, and a group of normal controls. They found marked differences between the patients and the control subjects, but relatively few differences between the patients with anxiety states and patients with depressions.

The differentiation of phobic anxiety from obsessive-compulsive neurosis is equally difficult. Stern and Cobb (1978) reported that "avoiding" rituals, often associated with marked anxiety, were among the most common manifestations in a series of 45 obsessive patients.

Hypochondriacal states present yet another difficult problem of differential diagnosis. Agras, Sylvester, & Oliveau (1969) found that as many as 77% of the patients with a diagnosis of a hypochondriacal state also had illness phobias, and Kenyon (1976) observed that the physiological manifestations of anxiety, such as tachycardia, palpitations or tremor, may easily become the focus of hypochondriacal preoccupation.

Notwithstanding such problems of differential diagnosis, the balance of the currently available evidence favors the view that anxiety disorders (including phobias) represent a nosological group *sui generis,* which can be distinguished from other disorders in terms of its clinical features, course and outcome, response to specific treatments, and, to a certain degree, physiological measures.

The Newcastle Studies. A significant step in the differentiation of anxiety disorders from depressive illnesses was made in the 1960s by Roth and his collaborators in Newcastle (Gurney, Roth, Garside, Kerr, & Shapira, 1972; Kerr, Roth, & Shapira, 1974; Roth, Gurney, Garside, & Kerr, 1972; Shapira, Roth, Kerr, & Gurney, 1972). These investigators studied prospectively 145 patients admitted with a diagnosis of either "depressive illness" or "anxiety state," and using a structured interview and various scales, examined the presenting symp-toms of the two series, their family history, premorbid personality characteristics, mode and timing of onset, and outcome at a mean of 3.8 years after the initial assessment.

Although the two groups of patients showed a number of overlapping features, there were significant differences in the frequency of certain symptoms. Thus, panic attacks, vasomotor signs, emotional lability, dizzy attacks, agoraphobic experiences, depersonalization, and derealization occurred with a much higher frequency in the patients with anxiety states. Symptoms like depression worse in the morning, depressive mood reactive to change, early waking, suicidal acts, and psychomotor retardation were significantly more frequent in the depressive group than in the anxiety patients. Depressive mood and tension appeared to be equally frequent in both diagnostic groups. However, when these two symptoms were rated so as to separate a "persistent" from an "episodic" form, it appeared that the combination of persistent depression and episodic tension was more frequent among patients with depressive illnesses, and the combination of episodic depression and persistent tension was characteristic of the patients with anxiety disorders.

The symptoms of the two diagnostic groups were further separated by principal component analysis, which produced a bipolar component with depression and anxiety as two contrasting poles, and by a discriminant function which yielded a bimodal distribution. On the basis of the discriminant function analysis, a diagnostic index for anxiety states was derived, which was composed of 13 weighted items. Nine of these items were positively correlated with anxiety and 4 were negatively correlated.

It should be noted that among these diagnostic items, panic attacks had the largest single contribution (34%) to explaining the variance in the data. With regard to other nosologically important variables investigated in the Newcastle study, mention should be made of the family history. The occurrence of both neurotic illnesses and personality disorders was significantly more frequent in the parents and siblings of patients with anxiety states than in the families of depressive patients. As regards premorbid personality, the patients with anxiety states had shown more social anxiety and social maladjustment than their depressive counterparts.

Of decisive importance for the validation of the syndromes, however, was the follow-up of 126 cases, which was carried out by investigators who were blind to the original diagnoses. All aspects of course and outcome considered, the patients with an initial diagnosis of depressive illness had a better prognosis than the patients with diagnoses of anxiety states. Many of the anxiety patients were found on follow-up to have persisting symptoms that were similar or identical to the symptoms they had exhibited at the initial examination. Symptomatological "cross-over" between the depressive group and the anxious group did not occur, or occurred only in exceptional cases, and the predictors of outcome in the two groups of conditions were different. On the whole, the patients in both groups retained the original qualitative characteristics of their symptomatology. On the basis of these studies, Roth and his collaborators concluded that the nosological distinction between anxiety states and depressive illnesses is both valid and useful.

In a second study at Newcastle (Roth & Mountjoy, 1982) a structured interview and seven rating scales were used in an investigation of 117 patients with "depressive anxiety" and phobias. Endogenous depressions were excluded from the sample. Multivariate statistical analyses produced results that, by and large, confirmed the conclusions of the earlier study: anxiety and depression could be clearly differentiated. A similar conclusion was made by Marks (1971) on the basis of a 4-year prospective follow-up of 65 phobic patients. Although more than one-half of the patients improved after behavior therapy, those who remained symptomatic exhibited phobic symptoms and did not develop other forms of neurotic disturbances.

Further evidence supporting the notion of a separate nosological status for the anxiety disorder has been put forward as a result of several types of investigations.

Genetic Studies. A "neurotic constitution" (Slater, 1943) has been postulated for the anxiety and phobic disorders. Some partial support for this view has been provided by twin studies. Levitt (1968) examined 17 MZ and DZ twin pairs and established that the intraclass correlation coefficient for free-floating anxiety was .56 for MZ pairs and .12 for DZ pairs. For phobic anxiety the correlation coefficients were .60 and .12 respectively. Torgersen (1979) concluded on the basis of an investigation of 99 same-sex twin pairs (50 MZ and 49 DZ) in Norway that phobic fears (but not agoraphobia) were "influenced by genetic factors." In contrast to this, another study (Schepanck, 1974) of 50 twin pairs (21 MZ and 29 DZ) in the Federal Republic of Germany failed to establish a hereditary factor for the phobic syndrome, although it did establish such a factor in other neurotic (e.g., depression) and personality (sociopathic) disorders. The finding of an increased frequency of anxiety syndromes in first-degree relatives of index cases of anxiety or phobic disorders (including the higher risk for "school phobias" in the children of female agoraphobics, Berg, 1976) does not necessarily support a genetic contribution, and adoption studies have not yet thrown any light on the inheritance of anxiety. The question of the heritability of the anxiety disorders, important as it is for their nosology, has not been answered in a conclusive manner up to date.

Physiological Measurements. Forearm blood flow, skin resistance, heart rate, eyeblink conditioning procedures, and a variety of other techniques have been employed to provide objective measures of anxiety that could be used to discriminate anxiety states from depression (e.g., Kelly & Walter, 1969), or to validate the distinctions between separate syndromes within the group of anxiety disorders (Marks, 1970). The results seem to support the distinction between anxiety and other neurotic states, although none of the measures is specific. Even less clear is the criterion value of the sodium lactate infusion technique (Pitts & McClure, 1967), which has been replicated in Europe (Kelly, Mitchell-Heggs, & Sherman, 1971). The infusion evokes episodes of acute anxiety in volunteers suffering from phobic disorders. It has been pointed out, however, that the endogenous lactate formed in the body as a result of muscle activity leads to a metabolic acidosis, whereas the infusion of sodium lactate causes an alcalosis, an inconsistency that makes it difficult to propose a specific mechanism for the experimental induction of acute anxiety. (Also, see Klein, Rabkin, & Forman, this volume).

Treatment Response.   There is now an impressive body of evidence on the effectiveness of behavioral psychotherapy (desensitization, exposure techniques) in phobic disorders (Marks, 1981), obsessive-compulsive disorders, social skill problems, and sexual dysfunctions, but not in other nonpsychotic conditions. The volume of the literature on the response to anxiolytic pharmacological agents is exceedingly large. Evidence has also been accumulated on the therapeutic effects of antidepressants including inhibitors of the monoamine oxidase (Kelly, Guirguis, Frommes, Mitchell-Heggs, & Sargant, 1970; Pollitt & Young, 1971) and beta-adrenergic blockers (Bernadt, Silverstone, & Singleton, 1980).[4]

Subdivisions Within the Group of Anxiety Disorders

A clinical classification of affective illnesses that has been proposed recently by Roth and Mountjoy (1982) includes the following entities:

1. *Neurotic depression* (depressive illness without "endogenous" features).
2. *Anxious depression* (depression and simple anxiety are both present, but neither has a clear predominance).
3. *Simple anxiety neurosis* (the main features are psychic tension, anxious thoughts and ruminations, somatic anxiety, hypochondriasis, and mild or variable phobic symptoms).
4. *Agoraphobia* (inability to leave the home or to stay alone, fear of losing control, etc; a range of situations may provoke anxiety; feelings of unreality; social phobic symptoms; depressive symptoms).
5. *Social phobic neurosis* (anxiety, blushing, tremor, etc. in social situations).
6. *Primary depersonalization syndrome* (depersonalization/derealization experiences dominate the picture; anxiety is secondary and variable).
7. *Anxiety psychosis* (a rare acute psychotic condition, usually preceded by a psychic trauma).

Most European classifications that subdivide the anxiety disorders use at least two criteria of differentiation: the degree of generalization of anxiety and the

---

[4]Beta-adrenergic blockers seem capable of abolishing some of the physiological accompaniments of anxiety (e.g., stress-induced tachycardia) without reducing the subjectively experienced anxiety affect. In contrast, diazepam, which has no significant effect on the heart rate, has a strong effect on the subjective component of anxiety.

temporal aspect of the syndrome (acute or chronic, "state" or "trait"). It is not feasible, however, to describe or even list all classifications that have been proposed. As an example of a classification that is likely to be acceptable to many European clinicians, the scheme proposed by Langen (1971) in the Federal Republic of Germany is summarized below.

I. DIFFUSE ANXIETY SYNDROMES

1. *Acute diffuse anxiety syndrome.* This is described as a condition occurring typically after acute stress (e.g., a traffic accident) and is characterized by severe autonomic manifestations of anxiety.

2. *Chronic diffuse anxiety development.* Anxiety is often triggered off by a traumatic event, but it tends to persist after the traumatizing factor or situation is removed. A tendency to anxiety responses can be detected in the pre-morbid history of such patients.

3. *Attack-like anxiety syndrome.* The syndrome consists of "elementary" attacks of anxiety occurring "out of the blue." The clinical picture is often dominated by fear of the next attack. Depressive mood is a frequent accompaniment of this syndrome. In a proportion of cases manifesting attack-like anxiety the aetiology can be linked to a physical disorder.

II. PHOBIC SYNDROMES

1. *Phobic responses.* This is the mildest form of phobic disorder which borders on normal behavior. It is manifested in exaggerated anxiety responses to everyday situations and events, lack of self-confidence, and a feeling of uncertainty.

2. *Psychasthenic phobic syndrome.* The combination of psychasthenic features (uncertainty, self-observation, doubt, a feeling of weakness, or lack of energy) and phobic anxiety is a characteristic of the syndrome. Typical presenting complaints are sexual dysfunctions or social phobias.

3. *Phobic syndromes occurring during biological crises.* These are syndromes that may appear in association with the post partum period, climacterium, or puberty. They have a transient character and tend to remit with the termination of the biological "crisis."

4. *Phobic syndromes associated with neurotic development or phobic neuroses proper.* The premorbid personality shows a peculiar mixture of an active, energetic attitude and a tendency to anxiety. Hysterical features are also common. When phobic disturbances appear, the patient often reacts with denial or repression to the anxiety experience.

5. *Phobic abnormal personalities*. The family history often contains phobic disorders or cyclothymia. The patients exhibit multiple phobic features, as well as a tendency to hypochondriasis. The course shows fluctuations but no increase in severity.

6. *Chronic progredient anxiety syndromes, malignant anxiety, or anxiety disease*. This group of patients shows a marked tendency to a chronic or phasic course that resembles affective psychosis. Diffuse anxious agitation plus specific phobias are the main features of the disorder. The incidence is higher in females. The condition is often misdiagnosed as hysteria or as agitated depression.

An example of an aetiologically oriented classification of anxiety states has been proposed by Kielholz (1971). The classification has two axes, one corresponding to the "somatogenic" aetiological factors and the other corresponding to "psychogenic" causation. Most anxiety states arise as result of the combined action of both kinds of aetiological factors, but one or the other of the two aetiologies may play a dominant role:

Predominantly Somatogenic:

1. Organic anxiety states (vital anxiety)—e.g., associated with myocardial infarction, angina, thyrotoxicosis, pheochromocytoma.
2. Toxic anxiety states, e.g, pharmacogenic (Lysergic acid diethylamid, LSD, amphetamines), in withdrawal syndromes, or in other exogenous reaction types.

Mixed aetiology (both somatogenic and psychogenic factors):
3. Anxiety states in endogenous depression
4. Anxiety states in schizophrenia

Predominantly psychogenic:
5. Anxiety neuroses
6. Anxiety personality development
7. Anxiety reactions

Environmental
8. Realistic (normal) anxiety

A very different approach to the classification of anxiety in relation to other psychiatric syndromes was proposed by Foulds and Bedford (1976) as part of a more general classificatory theory. Psychiatric disorders are seen in that theory as forming several hierarchical levels that involve different degrees of personality disorganization. Each hierarchical level also contains, in addition to the symptoms and syndromes that define it, symptoms from levels that lie lower in the hierarchy (the reverse, however, is not true). Since anxiety (but not phobias), together with other "dysthymic" states like depression and elation, is empirically known to occur in association with practically any psychiatric syndrome, its place in the hierarchical taxonomy should be on one of the bottom levels. In the classification, reproduced below, anxiety is placed one level lower than phobic disorders which are in a class with other specific neurotic disorders:

Class 4: Delusions of disintegration
Class 3: Integrated delusions (contrition, grandeur, persecution)
Class 2: Neurotic symptoms (conversion, dissociative, phobic, compulsive and ruminative)
Class 1: Dysthymic states (anxiety, depression, elation)
Class 0: Symptom-free.

ANXIETY IN THE INTERNATIONAL CLASSIFICATION OF DISEASES (ICD)

The International Classification of Diseases (ICD) is a statistical classification of diseases; complications of pregnancy, childbirth and the puerperium; congenital anomalies; causes of perinatal morbidity and mortality; accidents, poisonings, and violence; and symptoms, signs and ill-defined conditions. Its principal use is in the statistical recording and reporting of morbidity and mortality; however, it has been partially adapted to serve as a nomenclature of diseases. It differs from a true nomenclature in that it has a limited number of categories, which must encompass the entire range of diseases and morbid conditions (Kramer, Sartorius, Jablensky, & Gulbinat, 1979). The ICD is not a diagnostic manual; it is a systematic ordering of diagnoses. Although the mental disorders chapter (Chapter 5) now contains, in addition to the list of diagnoses, a glossary, the definitions given there are designed to serve as clarification notes on the coding of different clinical diagnoses, rather than as operational rules for making such diagnoses.

By its nature, the classification of mental disorders in the ICD represents a compromise among different approaches and schools of thought. European psychiatry has, of course, a major input, but so has United States psychiatry. It should be noted that the differences between ICD-8 and *DSM-II* were relatively minor in comparison to the divergences that have emerged between ICD-9 and *DSM-III.*

Anxiety appeared in ICD for the first time in the 7th revision (1955) as "anxiety reaction without mention of somatic symptoms" under the heading of "psychoneurotic disorders." In the subsequent 8th and 9th revisions the provisions for classifying psychiatric disorders that encompass anxiety as either a major or a secondary component have been increased very substantially. As Table 39.1 shows, there are now altogether 18 ICD rubrics in which either anxiety, or

TABLE 39.1
The Classification of Anxiety (including states of anxiety, fear, dread,
panic, phobias, apprehension and worry) in ICD-9

I. *Categories for which anxiety is a major defining feature*
   300.0 *Anxiety states* (include panic attacks, disorder, or state)
   300.2 *Phobic state* (includes agoraphobia, animal phobias, anxiety hysteria, claustrophobia,
   phobia NOS)
   308.0 *Acute reaction to stress, with predominant disturbance of emotions*
   309.2 *Adjustment reaction, with predominant disturbance of other emotions* (includes abnormal
   separation anxiety, culture shock)
   312.3 *Mixed disturbance of conduct and emotions*

II. *Categories in which anxiety is a contributory defining feature*
    291.0 *Delirium tremens*
    291.3 *Other alcoholic hallucinosis*
    292.0 *Drug withdrawal syndrome*
    296.1 *Manic-depressive psychosis, depressed type*
    300.3 *Obsessive-compulsive disorders*
    300.4 *Neurotic depression*
    300.6 *Depersonalization syndrome*
    300.7 *Hypochondriasis*
    301.1 *Affective personality disorder*
    302.7 *Frigidity and impotence*
    310.2 *Postconcussional syndrome*
    316.0 *Psychic factors associated with diseases classified elsewhere*

III. *Categories in which anxiety is a defining feature by implication (though not specifically mentioned
     in glossary)*
     306.0 *Physiological malfunction arising from mental factors*
     307.4 *Specific disorders of sleep*

TABLE 39.2
Items Positively and Negatively Correlated with a Diagnosis of
Anxiety State (Kerr, Roth, & Shapira, 1974)

Positively correlated	Negatively correlated
Panic attacks	Depressed mood
Anxiety symptoms	Early waking
Neuroticism	Suicidal tendencies
Neurotic traits in childhood	Retardation
Dependence	
Physical stress	
Agoraphobia	
Derealization	
Compulsive phenomena	

closely related symptoms like fear, worry, dread, panic, or apprehension, are mentioned in the rubric description.

Of these 18 rubrics, at least 6 can be regarded as being reserved for anxiety disorders proper: anxiety states, phobic state, acute reaction to stress with predominant disturbance of emotions, adjustment reaction with predominant disturbance of other emotions, mixed disturbance of conduct and emotions, and disturbance of emotions specific to childhood and adolescence, with anxiety and fearfulness. Anxiety states are defined in the ICD as "various combinations of physical and medical manifestations of anxiety, not attributable to real danger and occurring either in attacks or as a persisting state. The anxiety is usually diffuse and may extend to panic. Other neurotic features such as obsessional or hysterical symptoms may be present but do not dominate the clinical picture."

This definition is clear enough (considering the classificatory confusion that still characterizes the international scene), but it lacks the specificity that "operational" diagnostic algorithms offer. For example, Tyrer (1982) has drawn attention to the fact that the ICD definition does not specify whether physical and mental manifestations of anxiety have *both* to be present for making the diagnosis.

Panic states are subsumed under the anxiety states in the ICD, and are not regarded as a disorder that should be specifically differentiated. It has been pointed out, however, that very little research has been done so far in Europe on panic states and the problem of their nosology cannot be resolved satisfactorily at the present time (Editorial, Lancet, 1983).

In addition to these 6 rubrics, the ICD contains a number of other categories, ranging from neurotic depression to the postconcussional syndrome, or from frigidity and impotence to delirium tremens, where anxiety appears as a secondary symptom significant enough to be specifically mentioned in the glossary description of the category.

Special problems of classification are posed by those conditions in which psychological factors (including, in particular, anxiety) appear in combination with various physical symptoms or complaints. The provision of the ICD in that respect is that code 316 (psychic factors associated with diseases classified elsewhere) should be used, and then the nature of the physical symptom or syndrome indicated by the corresponding code contained in another chapter of the classification, for example, 242 (thyrotoxicosis). This biaxial method of information recording, however, is unlikely to be applied consistently, unless the coder (or the diagnostician) believes that the psychologic concomitant of a given physical disorder is important enough to be recorded. This is rarely the case in busy general hospitals and out-patient departments, and it is unrealistic to expect that the perfectly logical rule of biaxial recording would be followed in practice.

Another "conflict of interest" within the framework of the present ICD-9 may arise with regard to category 306, "Physiological malfunction arising from mental factors." This rubric, designed to accommodate the so-called "psychosomatic" disorders without tissue damage, is neatly subdivided into 4-digit categories corresponding to anatomical or physiological systems, e.g., musculoskeletal and respiratory. A "cardiac neurosis" or a syndrome of "neurocirculatory asthenia," which to many investigators and clinicians is one of the most frequent forms of presentation of anxiety neurosis, should, according to the present rules, be classified under category 306.2 (cardiovascular malfunction), rather than under category 300.0 (anxiety states) for which the glossary definition mentions in a general way the "various physical manifestations" of anxiety.

CONCLUSIONS

The brief review of the various European points of view on the nature and classification of anxiety, panic and phobic phenomena—mental, behavioral and somatic—inevitably leads to the conclusion that these disorders represent an area of psychopathology and clinical psychiatry in which the divergencies between different "schools" are most pronounced. If these different points of view could be arranged along a simple continuum, then at one extreme of the continuum we could place those classifications that regard the anxiety disorders as nothing more than nonspecific symptoms that occur in a great variety of psychiatric disorders: depressive illnesses, obsessive-compulsive neurosis, and so forth. The other end of the continuum would be occupied by notions attributing an independent nosological status to symptom complexes such as agoraphobia, social phobias, other specific phobias, and generalized anxiety. The 9th revision of the International Classification of Diseases (ICD) takes an intermediate position, by allocating two separate codes to the anxiety states and phobic states, but also reserving an ample number of classificatory options for those conditions that do not fit into the main categories.

What can explain the uncertainties and the tenuous status of anxiety disorders in contemporary European psychiatry? We can propose, tentatively, three reasons for the present state of affairs.

The first, and perhaps, least influential one, has to do with the differing semantic "spaces" of the words and terms that denote phenomena of anxiety, fear, and similar terms in the different European languages (e.g., the English "anxiety" does not equal the German *Angst*).

The second reason is linked to the fact that the past "grand masters" of European psychiatry, who shaped the concepts and the thinking of generations of psychiatrists, were predominantly academic or hospital-based clinicians. As such they simply did not see large enough numbers of anxious or phobic patients, in order to give these conditions more than a secondary place in the classification of neurotic illnesses and abnormal reactions of the personality. The diagnosis and practical management of the anxiety disorders was mainly a task for psychotherapists (mostly of an analytical orientation) and general medical practitioners. Neither of these categories had much influence over the development of psychiatric taxonomy.

The third reason is that until recently the treatment and management of anxiety disorders was rather nonspecific and did not call for fine diagnostic and classificatory distinctions as prerequisites for a rational choice of therapeutic modalities. Only with the advent of the benzodiazepines, the coinage of the new term "anxiolytic," and the discovery of a putative benzodiazepine receptor in the brain did anxiety disorders reemerge on the psychiatric *avant-scene*. The epidemic of over-prescription and over-use of anxiolytics gave psychiatrists, for the first time, an inkling of the true epidemiological dimensions of the problem of anxiety in the community.

In the period after World War II, a disproportionate share of the research into anxiety syndromes has been carried out in Britain. One can only guess at the origins of this phenomenon. One thing, however, is extremely likely: British psychiatrists see a greater number of anxious and phobic patients than their counterparts in other European countries. It is very unlikely that this could be due to a higher incidence and prevalence of these syndromes on the British Isles. More plausible is an explanation taking into account the probability that a greater proportion of the patients suffering from anxiety and phobic disorders come forward for treatment in Britain than elsewhere in Europe. It is impossible to say whether this may be an effect of a greater cultural acceptability of a "sick role" for a person admitting to irrational fears, or whether the special attention to the clinical aspects of anxiety, dating back to the wartime experience has resulted in a greater readiness of the average doctor to make a diagnosis of anxiety. Whatever the ultimate explanation, the attention given to the problem of anxiety in British psychiatry has stimulated clinical, epidemiological, and pathophysiological research which supports the hypothesis of a separate nosological status of the anxiety disorders among other psychiatric conditions, as well as the proposed internal subdivisions within the anxiety disorders group.

These conclusions inevitably lead to questions concerning the various comparisons possible between European points of view and the classification of anxiety in the current *DSM-III*. Although an analysis of the similarities between European classifications and *DSM-III* is not among the aims of this review, it is not possible to entirely circumvent the issue. It appears that the main differences between European concepts and *DSM-III* can be found on several levels:

On a general level, European classifications are more obviously influenced by theoretical issues than *DSM-III*, which allegedly takes an "atheoretical position." Thus, most European classifications, as well as ICD-9, prefer to retain the theoretically "loaded" terms "neurosis" and "psychosis," although these terms increasingly shed their confusing aetiological and pathogenetic connotations and become mainly descriptive labels. In contrast, *DSM-III* has dispensed with the notion of neurosis, without replacing it, even descriptively, with anything else. This has resulted in new groupings of disorders in *DSM-III* which might appear to the European psychiatrist as arbitrary and lacking an underlying classificatory principle. For example, it would not be clear to a European clinician why obsessive-compulsive disorder is placed under the rubric of anxiety disorders, and why hypochondriasis is not.

On a more specific level, current European classification does not imply such hard-and-fast dividing lines between individual disorders, as *DSM-III* seems to require. It would be difficult, for example, for a European psychiatrist to understand the need for giving a separate nosological status to each of two varieties of agoraphobia, generalized anxiety disorder, and panic disorder, although the existence of relative syndromological differences between these conditions would raise no questions. Do these attributions of separate status imply that a generalized anxiety disorder and a panic disorder are mutually exclusive entities?

These comparisons, their implications, and the questions they raise do not necessarily favor one kind of classification over another. On the contrary, the emergence of a novel approach to the classification of psychiatric disorders, such as the one embodied in *DSM-III*, should play the role of a stimulus for a critical reexamination of the rather unsatisfactory current state of classification of anxiety disorders, and for finding acceptable solutions to the outstanding problems, and for developing a common language for scientific communication in the mental health field.

40

Proposed Revisions in the DSM-III Classification of Anxiety Disorders Based on Research and Clinical Experience

Robert L. Spitzer, M.D.
Janet B. W. Williams, D.S.W.
Columbia University
New York State Psychiatric Institute

INTRODUCTION

Mental disorders with some form of anxiety as the predominant feature have been recognized since antiquity, although the approach of grouping them together into a single diagnostic class called Anxiety Disorders was first taken only a few years ago in the third edition of the American Psychiatric Association's *Diagnostic and Statistical Manual of Mental Disorders (DSM-III)* (1980). In this chapter we review the background to the *DSM-III* classification of Anxiety Disorders for adults and discuss problems with the diagnostic criteria that have recently become apparent, as well as possible solutions to these problems. A reexamination of how these important categories are defined is timely, since in May, 1983, a Work Group to Revise *DSM-III* was appointed by the American Psychiatric Association. This Work Group will consider modifications in the criteria for the various disorders and is scheduled to complete the revision, *DSM-III-R*, by December, 1985.

BACKGROUND

As is well known, the developers of *DSM-III* decided to base the classification on shared descriptive features when etiology was unknown, rather than on presumed etiologies. The consequence of this approach was abandoning the traditional diagnostic class of neuroses, which according to *DSM-II* included categories that shared a common cause: unconscious conflict arousing anxiety and leading to the maladaptive use of defense mechanisms that results in symptom formation.

In *DSM-III* the individual *DSM-II* neuroses were reclassified with other diagnostic categories that shared their essential descriptive features. Depressive Neurosis (renamed Dysthymic Disorder) joined the Affective Disorders, the two types of Hysterical Neuroses were subsumed under Somatoform and Dissociative Disorders, Hypochondriacal Neurosis joined Somatoform Disorders, and Depersonalization Neurosis joined Dissociative Disorders. The low energy of Neurasthenic Neurosis apparently led to its demise. The remaining Neuroses, Anxiety Neurosis, Phobic Neurosis, and Obsessive Compulsive Neurosis are all characterized by anxiety being either the predominant symptom, or experienced if the individual attempts to master the symptoms. These last three *DSM-II* categories, two of which were further subdivided in *DSM-III*, were joined by the new category of Post-traumatic Stress Disorder, which also always involves symptoms of anxiety, to constitute the *DSM-III* diagnostic class of Anxiety Disorders.

The elimination of Neurosis as a diagnostic class from the *DSM-III* classification was extremely controversial. However, since the publication of *DSM-III*, with only a few exceptions (Frances & Cooper, 1981; Lopez-Ibor & Lopez-Ibor, 1983), researchers and clinicians seem to have accepted the basic utility of the concept of Anxiety Disorders as a diagnostic class.

Examples of this acceptance include the large number of recent studies in which investigators have used the *DSM-III* criteria for describing samples of patients with Anxiety Disorders (Barlow & Beck, 1984; Klein & Rabkin, 1981), the proliferation of specialized clinical services organized to treat these disorders, the convening of two major conferences on the subject (Anxiety Disorders, Panic Attacks, and Phobias, sponsored by The Upjohn Company 1982; Anxiety and the Anxiety Disorders, sponsored by NIMH, 1983) and the decision of the 1984 Scientific Program Committee of the American Psychiatric Association to have a major section of its Annual Review program devoted to the subject of Anxiety Disorders. In addition, the *DSM-III* classification of Anxiety Disorders has stimulated and generated new research questions and issues.

OVERVIEW OF THE DSM-III ANXIETY DISORDERS

Table 40.1 lists the eight specific *DSM-III* Anxiety Disorders, plus the residual undefined category of Atypical Anxiety Disorder. To facilitate understanding of the historical origins of these disorders, they are discussed in four groups.

TABLE 40.1
DSM-III Classification of Anxiety Disorders

Phobic disorders (or Phobic neuroses)
   Agoraphobia with panic attacks
   Agoraphobia without panic attacks
   Social phobia
   Simple phobia
Anxiety states (or Anxiety neuroses)
   Panic disorder
   Generalized anxiety disorder
   Obsessive compulsive disorder (or Obsessive compulsive neurosis)
Post-traumatic stress disorder
   acute
   chronic or delayed
Atypical anxiety disorder

Phobic Disorders

The essential feature of each phobic disorder is persistent and irrational fear of a specific object, activity, or situation that results in a compelling desire to avoid the dreaded object, activity, or situation (the phobic stimulus). The fear is recognized by the individual as excessive or unreasonable.

In partial accordance with the classification of phobias proposed by Marks (1970), *DSM-III* subdivided the Phobic Disorders into three types based on differing symptomatology, age at onset, sex ratio, and treatment response: Agoraphobia (marked fear of being alone or being in public places from which escape might be difficult or help not available in case of sudden incapacitation), Social Phobia (fear of situations in which the individual may be exposed to scrutiny by others), and Simple Phobia (fear of situations other than those subsumed by Agoraphobia and Social Phobia, such as fears of animals and heights).

Based on Klein's observation that most cases of Agoraphobia begin following the development of what he calls "spontaneous panic attacks" (Klein, 1981), the typical form of the disorder was called Agoraphobia with Panic Attacks. In order to provide a category for cases of Agoraphobia in which there was no history of panic attacks (although it was not clear if such cases existed) another subtype was added, Agoraphobia without Panic Attacks.

Anxiety States

The syndrome of recurrent panic attacks has been recognized as a separate disorder as far back as 1871 when Da Costa described the "irritable heart" (1871) and later in 1894 when Freud (1962) first applied the name Anxiety Neurosis to the syndrome, separating it from the category of Neurasthenia. However, in *DSM-II*, Anxiety Neurosis was applied to individuals who experienced generalized anxiety, whether or not it also occurred in discrete attacks of panic that were assumed to be merely symptomatic of the more severe form of the same disorder. This same conceptualization is expressed in the Ninth Revision of the International Classification of Diseases (ICD-9) in which the category Anxiety States includes "Various combinations of physical and mental manifestations of anxiety, not attributable to real danger and occurring either in attacks or as persisting state" (World Health Organization, 1978, p. 35).

Because in the early 1960s Klein had demonstrated that imipramine blocks recurrent panic attacks (Klein 1964), and later showed that imipramine has no apparent effect on phobic anxiety that is not associated with panic attacks (Zitrin, Klein, Woerner, 1978), it was decided that there should be a separate category in *DSM-III* for conditions characterized by recurrent panic attacks. Therefore, the *DSM-II* category of Anxiety Neurosis was divided into two categories. The first category, Panic Disorder, requires recurrent panic attacks (in the absence of Agoraphobia), and corresponds to Freud's "Anxiety Neurosis." The diagnostic criteria for Panic Disorder in *DSM-III* were based on the Feighner criteria for Anxiety Neurosis (Feighner et al., 1972). The second category was newly created for those cases that would have been given the diagnosis of Anxiety Neurosis using *DSM-II,* yet did not have recurrent panic attacks. This category is called Generalized Anxiety Disorder (GAD) in *DSM-III* and is for conditions in which there is generalized, persistent anxiety of at least one month's duration, without the specific symptoms of any of the other Anxiety Disorders. When this residual Anxiety Disorder category was created, no one was quite sure how prevalent such a condition was and whether it would have a differential treatment response from Panic Disorder.

Obsessive Compulsive Disorder

The developers of the *DSM-III* classification initially were unsure under what diagnostic rubric to put the time-honored category of Obsessive Compulsive Disorder. Eventually it was subsumed under the Anxiety Disorders with the rationale that even though the predominant symptoms are obsessions or compulsions rather than anxiety itself, anxiety is almost invariably experienced if the individual attempts to resist the obsessions or compulsions. In addition, most patients with the disorder also experience anxiety apart from the obsessions and compulsions.

Post-traumatic Stress Disorder (PTSD)

This category was first referred to as Traumatic Neurosis (Keiser, 1968), and was included in *DSM-I* as Gross Stress Reaction. However, it had no direct counterpart in *DSM-II* despite experience with delayed forms of the disorder resulting from concentration camp experiences during the second World War. The criteria for the *DSM-III* category were developed with the help of clinicians who were involved in treating Vietnam War veterans. According to clinicians who study patients experiencing trauma associated with civilian life, such as the trauma of rape or physical assault, the essential clinical features of the disorder are apparently the same regardless of the trauma.

PROBLEMS AND PROPOSED SOLUTIONS FOR DEFINING THE DISORDERS

Despite extensive field testing of the *DSM-III* criteria prior to their official adoption, experience with them since their publication in 1980 has revealed, as expected, many instances in which the criteria are not entirely satisfactory and need to be revised. The following is a discussion of problems that have been identified by investigators, including ourselves, in the application of the Anxiety Disorders diagnostic criteria. Case examples are presented to illustrate the points discussed, frequently the very cases that directed attention to a particular problem.

Hierarchic Structure of the Classification

A case example is Ms. G., a 48-year-old mother of three children, admitted to the hospital for her third episode of severe depression, which met the *DSM-III* criteria for Major Depression with Melancholia. She reported that at the onset of each depression, she began to have terrifying panic attacks, which she believed were triggered by the thought that she would never recover. She claimed that she has never had a panic attack when she has been in a nondepressed state. Her description of individual panic attacks fulfilled the inclusion criteria for Panic Disorder.

In *DSM-III* the diagnostic classes are hierarchically organized on the assumption that a disorder high in the hierarchy may have symptoms found in disorders lower in the hierarchy, but not the reverse. The hierarchic structure of the classification is operationalized by exclusion criteria so that a diagnosis (in this case the "excluded diagnosis") is not given if its inclusion symptoms are considered to be a symptom of a more pervasive disorder (the "dominant disorder").

Do the panic attacks of Ms. G. have any diagnostic significance? According to the *DSM-III* criteria for Panic Disorder, this diagnosis is not given if the panic attacks occur only in the course of—that is, are judged "due to"—an episode of Major Depression. According to *DSM-III*, and perhaps usual clinical practice, the panic attacks would be regarded as merely associated symptoms of the Affective Disorder and of no diagnostic significance.

Data from the NIMH sponsored Epidemiologic Catchment Area Program (ECA) (Regier et al., 1982) have called into question the fundamental assumptions that form the basis of many of the *DSM-III* hierarchies, and particularly those for the Anxiety Disorders. Boyd et al. (in press) using data from this project found that the presence of a dominant disorder (e.g., Major Depression) greatly increased the likelihood of the presence of a related excluded syndrome (e.g., panic attacks), as would be predicted by the *DSM-III* hierarchies. However, there was also a tendency for the presence of any *DSM-III* syndrome to increase the likelihood of the presence of almost any other *DSM-III* syndrome.

Other research has also challenged the validity of the *DSM-III* hierarchic principle that gives Affective Disorders precedence over Anxiety Disorders. Leckman, Weissman, Merikangas, Pauls and Prusoff (1983), in a large case-control family study of depression found that the presence of a history of panic attacks in the probands, whether associated with a major depressive episode or occurring at other times, increased the family prevalence of depression, alcoholism, and other anxiety disorders. These data suggest that research, and perhaps clinical practice as well, might be improved by eliminating some of the *DSM-III* diagnostic hierarchies that prevent the joint diagnosis of different syndromes when they occur together in one episode of illness.

There are other problems with some of the hierarchic principles embodied in the exclusion criteria for the Anxiety Disorders. Some exclusion principles are not applied consistently. For example, a psychotic disorder in *DSM-III*, such as Schizophrenia, explicitly takes precedence over all of the Anxiety Disorders except Social Phobia and Post-traumatic Stress Disorder. Yet it is not at all clear why Schizophrenia should preempt a diagnosis of Agoraphobia or Panic Disorder but not of Social Phobia. In addition, some of the exclusion criteria confuse differential diagnostic issues with hierarchic issues. Thus, the *DSM-III* exclusion criteria for Agoraphobia list Obsessive Compulsive Disorder and Paranoid Personality Disorder. These two diagnoses are noted because it was recognized that individuals with Obsessive Compulsive Disorder and Paranoid Personality Disorder are sometimes afraid to go out of their houses alone. The need for a differential diagnosis of the symptom of fear of going out of the house should not be confused with a hierarchic principle, since the fear of leaving the house because of a fear of sudden incapacitation (the hallmark of Agoraphobia) is not a symptom of Obsessive Compulsive Disorder or Paranoid Personality Disorder.

We have agonized long and hard over the problem of the *DSM-III* hierarchies, attempting to identify general principles for diagnostic hierarchy that will avoid many of the problems previously noted, yet will not reduce the classification of mental disorders to a list of symptom complexes or syndromes. We propose (and the Work Group to Revise *DSM-III* will consider) that the following principles for diagnostic hierarchy be consistently applied to all of the *DSM-III* categories:

Principle #1.   When a syndrome has a known organic etiology, the diagnosis of an organic mental disorder takes precedence over the diagnosis of that syndrome outside of the class of organic mental disorders. For example, a manic syndrome that is judged to be due to the use of amphetamines would be diagnosed as an Amphetamine Induced Organic Mental Disorder rather than as an Affective Disorder; a persecutory delusional syndrome judged to be due to a brain tumor would be diagnosed on Axis I as an Organic Delusional Syndrome (with the brain tumor noted on Axis III) rather than as a Paranoid Disorder. This hierarchic principle is fundamental to virtually all classifications of mental disorder.

Principle #2. A symptomatically more pervasive disorder preempts the diagnosis of a less pervasive disorder that is based on a symptom that is part of the essential features of the more pervasive disorder. According to this principle, a patient with Schizophrenia who has persecutory delusions and hallucinations would not also be diagnosed as having a Paranoid Disorder. Similarly, a patient with both manic episodes and major depressive episodes would not be given diagnoses of both Bipolar Disorder and Major Depression.

Principle #3. A diagnosis is not given if its essential features are typically associated features of another disorder whose essential features are also present. According to this principle, chronic dysphoric mood is such a typical associated feature of such chronic disorders as Alcohol Dependence, Agoraphobia and Obsessive Compulsive Disorder that an additional diagnosis of Dysthymic Disorder would not be given. Another example would be the presence of generalized anxiety during an acute psychotic episode; Generalized Anxiety Disorder would not be diagnosed in addition to the psychotic disorder. This is the most problematic principle because it requires knowledge about the relative frequency of associated features in any given diagnosis.

The following shows the *DSM-III* exclusion criteria for Anxiety Disorders and our proposed revisions based on the above principles.

Agoraphobia

DSM-III: Not due to a major depressive episode, Obsessive Compulsive Disorder, Paranoid Personality Disorder, or Schizophrenia

Revised: No exclusions

Social Phobia

DSM-III: Not due to another mental disorder, such as Major Depression or Avoidant Personality Disorder

Revised: Unrelated to the fear of having a panic attack or to engaging in a compulsion in a social situation.

Simple Phobia

DSM-III: Not due to another mental disorder, such as Schizophrenia or Obsessive Compulsive Disorder

Revised: Unrelated to the content of the obsessions of Obsessive Compulsive Disorder

Panic Disorder

DSM-III: Not due to a physical disorder or another mental disorder, such as Major Depression, Somatization Disorder, or Schizophrenia

Revised: Not due to a specific organic factor (e.g., Amphetamine Intoxication, Hyperthyroidism)

Obsessive Compulsive Disorder

DSM-III: Not due to another mental disorder, such as Tourette's Disorder, Schizophrenia, Major Depression, or Organic Mental Disorder

Revised: No exclusions

Post-traumatic Stress Disorder

DSM-III: No exclusions

Revised: No exclusions

Generalized Anxiety Disorder

DSM-III: Not due to another mental disorder, such as a Depressive Disorder or Schizophrenia

Revised: Not due to a specific organic factor (e.g., Hyperthyroidism, Caffeine Intoxication); has not occurred only during the course of an active phase of a psychotic disorder, or another Anxiety Disorder in which generalized anxiety is usually present, i.e., Panic Disorder, Agoraphobia, Obsessive Compulsive Disorder, or Post-traumatic Stress Disorder

As can be seen, the revised exclusion criteria are unambiguous, and with the exception of the residual category of Generalized Anxiety Disorder, far simpler than the *DSM-III* criteria. Furthermore, the revised criteria remove the hierarchical principle of a major depressive episode excluding a diagnosis of an anxiety disorder, a principle that the ECA data have called into question. As a consequence, many of the previously excluded diagnoses would, with the revised criteria, be regarded as complications of the dominant diagnosis.

One important consequence of the application of these principles would be that Affective Disorders would no longer preempt a concurrent diagnosis of an Anxiety Disorder. As applied to Ms. G., this would mean that both Major Depression and Panic Disorder, which in her case could be thought of as a complication of each major depressive episode, would be diagnosed.

The application of these principles would also mean that Generalized Anxiety Disorder could be given as an additional diagnosis to an individual who concurrently has a depressive disorder. This would respond to the criticism of Shader and Greenblatt (1981) that *DSM-III* does not recognize the validity of mixed anxiety-depressive disorders. It is also in accord with the findings of a recent study by Finlay-Jones and Brown (1981) in which it was found that individuals who had experienced both severe loss and severe danger developed mixed depression/anxiety states. The application of the traditional diagnostic hierarchy to these cases would have obscured the mixed nature of the disorder.

What would happen to the combination category of Agoraphobia with Panic Attacks with the adoption of the proposed hierarchic principles? We believe that there is sufficient clinical evidence that Agoraphobia is usually a complication of recurrent panic attacks to justify the following revision in the *DSM-III* classification of Agoraphobia and Panic Disorder: The category of Agoraphobia without panic attacks would be unchanged but the diagnoses of Panic Disorder and Agoraphobia with Panic Attacks would be combined into a single category of Panic Disorder that would have three subtypes:

Panic Disorder, Uncomplicated
Panic Disorder, with Limited Phobic Avoidance
Panic Disorder, with Agoraphobia (extensive phobic avoidance)

This revision would acknowledge the central role of panic attacks in the typical development of Agoraphobia. It would also provide a subtype of Panic Disorder for cases in which the individual avoids one or more activities because of a fear of having panic attacks (e.g., going into restaurants) yet the phobic avoidance is not as extensive as would be the case with Agoraphobia. There is no satisfactory way to diagnose such cases according to *DSM-III*.

Another case example is a 42-year-old housewife with a history of panic attacks and agoraphobia who was unable to leave her home unless accompanied by her husband or a friend, even though she had not actually had a panic attack for several years.

A current problem with the *DSM-III* classification of Agoraphobia with Panic Attacks is that there is no way to indicate the common clinical condition in which, with psychopharmacologic treatment (or with time), panic attacks have remitted but phobic avoidance behavior of the Agoraphobia persists. A new convention could be adopted that would allow for indicating any disorder in remission, so that with the new principles such cases would be diagnosed as Panic Disorder with Agoraphobia (panic attacks in remission).

Problems Defining the Individual Disorders

Agoraphobia. The problems of defining agoraphobia may be seen in the following case example. A 37-year-old former teacher complained of panic attacks of 11 years' duration, which made it impossible for him to work outside of the home. During the last few years he had accommodated himself to his illness by organizing his life so that he rarely had to leave his house. He had assumed responsibility for taking care of his children while his wife was away at work, he prepared the family meals, and spent several hours each day lifting weights.

According to *DSM-III*, in order to give a diagnosis of Agoraphobia there must be "increasing constriction of normal activities until the fears (of being alone or in public places) or avoidance behavior dominate the individual's life." Clinically, there seems little doubt that Mr. M. has Agoraphobia. However, since he has made a new life for himself inside his home, it is not clear whether, strictly speaking, the fears or avoidance behavior now "dominate" his life. The ambiguity inherent in the word "dominate" has led to the following proposed rephrasing: "numerous important activities are avoided or endured with dread." With this proposed revision, Mr. M's illness clearly meets the criteria for Agoraphobia.

Agoraphobia without Panic Attacks.   This category requires further study and we are only aware of two papers that have commented specifically on it. In a reliability study of 60 consecutive outpatients at an Anxiety Disorders clinic, there were 23 cases of Agoraphobia with Panic Attacks but not a single case of Agoraphobia without Panic Attacks (Di Nardo, O'Brien, Barlow, Waddell, & Blanchard, 1983), raising the issue of the validity of the category. On the other hand, according to Klein (in press), Agoraphobia without Panic Attacks is regularly associated with episodic autonomic symptoms, primarily light-headedness and gastrointestinal distress. If Klein's observation is confirmed, the issue is whether these autonomic symptoms are fundamentally different from panic attacks or are merely minor forms of panic attacks that do not justify a separate diagnostic category.

Social Phobia.   Another case example is Mr. S., a 43-year-old construction manager and father of two, who sought treatment because "I seem to be afraid of everything and I have been this way since I was a kid." Two months ago his symptoms intensified when he began a new job that required him to have more interaction with other employees. On detailed questioning it turned out that his fears all involved situations in which he believed that others might think him incompetent or might be angry with him. For example, he was afraid to change the oil in his car because a new neighbor next door might see him and think that he did not know what he was doing. He was afraid that while driving his car he might stop at an intersection and another driver would be annoyed with him for stopping. When he first was introduced to someone he would be so anxious that he could hardly talk. He also complained of numerous physical manifestations of anxiety, such as muscle tension, palpitations, and trouble concentrating.

In *DSM-III* a Social Phobia is defined as a persistent, irrational fear of, and compelling desire to avoid, a situation in which the individual is exposed to possible scrutiny by others and fears that he or she may act in a way that will be humiliating or embarrassing. According to this definition, Mr. S. would seem to have many Social Phobias, yet the text states that "generally an individual has only one Social Phobia." This statement was added to the text because the descriptions of prototypical cases usually involved isolated phobias, such as fear of eating in public or of writing in the presence of others. However, the category is apparently commonly applied to patients who, like Mr. S., have multiple social situations that they fear and avoid (Amies, Gelder, & Shaw, 1983; Falloon, Lloyd, & Harpin, 1981). There seems to be no valid reason to exclude such cases from the diagnosis, provided that the basic fear is of humiliation or embarrassment rather than, for example, fear of being harmed, as might be seen in cases of Paranoid Personality Disorder. Therefore, in the proposed revision, the criteria state that the diagnosis is appropriate even when the phobic situations are numerous and pervasive.

A further case example is Mr. T., a fourth-year medical student, who came to the Student Health Service complaining of intense anxiety whenever he had to present a patient to his attending physicians. For days before a presentation he would ruminate about the possibility that he would be unable to speak coherently and that his anxiety would be obvious to everyone. Recognizing that it would hurt his career if he attempted to avoid case presentations, he always forced himself to go through with them, usually finding that he was not as anxious as he expected to be.

Does Mr. T. have a Social Phobia? According to *DSM-III* there has to be a "compelling desire to avoid" the phobic situation. This leaves unclear the issue of whether the diagnosis can or should be given to individuals who dread entering the phobic situation, but force themselves to do so nevertheless. We propose changing this criterion (which is also in Simple and Agoraphobia) to the requirement that "the activity is avoided or endured with dread."

Mr. T.'s public speaking phobia raises the issue of whether or not public speaking phobia should be classified separately from the other Social Phobias. Almost all individuals experience anxiety when speaking before a large group of people or to a small group if their performance is being evaluated. Thus, anxiety about public speaking is extremely common and "normal" anxiety about public speaking is on a continuum with phobic anxiety and in this way differs from the other Social Phobias (e.g., of eating and writing in public) which tend to be extremely rare and discontinuous with normal experience. In addition, individuals with public speaking phobia usually show little evidence of other psychopathology, whereas clinical experience indicates that individuals with other Social Phobias usually have considerable associated personality pathology.

Simple Phobia.   A case example is Ms. B., a 55-year-old woman in good physical health, who admitted during a community survey that she avoided crossing any streets that were more than two lanes wide because "I might fall down and be hit by a car." For many years she had avoided such streets and had changed her shopping and visiting habits so that she could avoid wide streets.

She acknowledged that her fear of falling was unreasonable, but denied that this fear and the resulting avoidance activity caused her any distress.

According to *DSM-III* an individual with Simple Phobia (and Social Phobia) must have "significant distress because of the disturbance." Yet it is clinically well known that some individuals, such as Ms. B., with phobic avoidance of an important activity, may deny any distress because they have altered their lives to adjust to their incapacity. In the proposed change, this criterion would state that "the (feared) activity is important in the context of the individual's life circumstances, or the fear of the activity causes significant distress." According to this revised criterion, the diagnosis of Simple Phobia would clearly apply to Ms. B.'s case.

Panic Disorder.   A case example is Ms. F., a 50-year-old woman who was presented to a case conference. She complained of panic attacks that almost always occurred, according to her, only when she was either in crowds or in enclosed places, such as on buses, cars, or elevators—situations that, whenever possible, she avoided. Typically she would start to feel uneasy in anticipation of entering one of these situations. Once in the situation, after a few minutes to up to an hour, a panic attack would begin, or it might not occur at all. She denied ever having an attack while at home. The staff was divided as to the diagnosis. Some argued that her panic attacks were not "spontaneous" since they occurred only in certain situations, and therefore the diagnosis was Simple Phobia. Others argued for a diagnosis of Panic Disorder.

We agree with the diagnosis of Panic Disorder. The basis for this confusion is the statement in *DSM-III* that in Panic Disorder the panic attacks are "not precipitated only by exposure to a circumscribed phobic stimulus." The purpose of this statement is to exclude from the diagnosis of Panic Disorder panic reactions that inevitably occur in response to a specific phobic stimulus, such as the panic reaction that an individual with a morbid fear of heights experiences in such a situation. Ms. F. is predisposed to having a panic attack in certain situations, but unlike an individual with a true Simple or Social Phobia, she does not always have an attack in the feared situations. Furthermore, when she does have an attack, it does not occur immediately upon exposure to the phobic stimulus, but rather after a variable period of time. In the revised criterion for Panic Disorder the differential diagnosis with a panic reaction to a circumscribed phobic stimulus is clarified by the statement that the attack must occur at "times other than...immediately before or upon exposure to a situation that always causes anxiety or avoidance."

In our experience, in interviewing patients with a chief complaint of anxiety, there is rarely difficulty in distinguishing true panic attacks from periods of intense anxiety. When there is difficulty, examination of the temporal course of the anxiety experience usually clarifies the situation. In true panic attacks the peak intensity of the experience is always reached within a few minutes. Therefore, in the revised criteria we have added a statement that "the peak intensity of the experience (must be) reached within ten minutes from its onset." This requires that clinicians ask, if the patient has not described the temporal course of the onset of the attack, "How long does it take from when it begins to when it is the worst?"

Generalized Anxiety Disorder (GAD). As already noted, GAD is a new category in *DSM-III*, with a description not based on systematic studies. According to *DSM-III*, it is possible to meet the criteria for the disorder with only relatively transient (1 month) complaints of anxiety. The duration requirement of only 1 month makes it difficult to distinguish this category from relatively transient stress reactions, and investigators who have studied this category have generally limited their sample selection to individuals who have had the symptoms of the disorder for much longer periods of time (Cloninger, Martin, Clayton, & Guze, 1981; Raskin, Peeke, Dickman, & Pinsker, 1982). We propose that the duration requirement be changed to 6 months, during which time the individual has experienced either "nervousness or anxiety," "worry," or "inability to relax." We recognize that our proposal to change the duration requirement to 6 months is based on clinical judgment only and its validation needs research confirmation.

Another problem with the *DSM-III* criteria is that by only requiring a single anxiety symptom from each of three out of four areas, an individual who only has "jumpiness," "feeling on edge," and "worry" satisfies the symptom criteria. In order to better define a syndrome, the new criteria require the presence of at least 6 of an 18-item index of commonly associated symptoms taken from those currently listed in the *DSM-III* criteria.

Finally, as discussed previously, we propose that GAD no longer be considered residual to all other specific Anxiety Disorders. It is recognized that individuals with circumscribed anxiety syndromes, such as Social or Simple Phobia frequently do not have generalized anxiety. When they do, recognition of an associated GAD might have important treatment implications. Therefore, we propose that GAD only be excluded by those Anxiety Disorders in which persistent anxiety is usually present, i.e., Agoraphobia, Obsessive Compulsive Disorder, and Post-traumatic Stress Disorder.

Obsessive Compulsive Disorder. During the development of *DSM-III*, there was a proposal to subdivide this category according to the presence of obsessions alone, or obsessions and compulsions. As Insel (1982) has noted in a provocative article, the heterogeneity of the disorder was recognized by Sir Aubrey Lewis (1936) who described "obsessionals" as distinct from "compulsives." However, the proposal for two separate categories in *DSM-III* was not accepted, since at that time there did not seem to be a compelling reason for making this subtype distinction. More recently, Barlow's review of psychosocial treatments of Anxiety Disorders (Barlow & Beck, 1984) indicates that whereas behavioral treatments are often effective when both obsessions and compulsions are present, this is not the case when only obsessions are present. This suggests the value of sub-typing the disorder.

Post-traumatic Stress Disorder (PTSD). This category has been the focus of much recent research, particularly as the category applies to Vietnam veterans (Atkinson, Henderson, Sparr, & Deale, 1982; Frye & Stockton, 1982). Based on their experience with Vietnam veterans, Hough and Gongla (1982) have suggested that the *DSM-III* criteria can be improved by including symptoms of the disorder that are listed in *DSM-III* as associated features, such as rage, explosions of aggressive behavior, fear of aggressive behavior, and impulsive behavior, in the diagnostic criteria themselves.

Horowitz, Wilner, Kaltreider, & Alvarez (1980) have reported a study of PTSD in individuals experiencing the death of someone close to them and individuals who had sustained personal injuries by violence, accidents, or illnesses. In this study, completed prior to the publication of *DSM-III*, individuals were apparently included even if the stress was not outside the range of normal experience (e.g., bereavement). Apparently the same distinctive syndrome of reexperiencing the trauma is often present even when the traumatic event is not outside the range of normal experience. This raises the question of whether *DSM-III* is correct in stating that the essential feature is "the development of characteristic symptoms following a psychologically traumatic event that is generally outside the range of usual human experience...such as simple bereavement (or) chronic illness." Perhaps the criteria for PTSD should be modified to allow the inclusion of cases in which the characteristic symptoms follow a trauma, such as bereavement, that is within the range of usual human experience.

Anxiety Syndromes Due to Known Organic Factors

In *DSM-III*, the discussions of the differential diagnoses of Panic Disorder and GAD note the need to consider organic etiologies for these syndromes, such as the taking of stimulants (e.g., amphetamine or caffeine). Yet in the *DSM-III* classification there is no category for anxiety syndromes caused by such organic factors. Mackenzie and Popkin (1983) have suggested the addition of a category of Organic Anxiety Syndrome, with text and criteria that are parallel to the category of Organic Affective Syndrome.

CONCLUSION

The *DSM-III* concept of Anxiety Disorders has been widely accepted and the diagnostic criteria for the separate disorders have facilitated much needed research in this area. Problems in the definition of the disorders and their hierarchical interrelationships have been discussed.

There are many other diagnostic issues relevant to Anxiety Disorders that have not been discussed here. One issue that has plagued nosologists and clinicians for many decades is the relationship between anxiety and depressive states (Foa & Foa, 1982; Gurney, Roth, Garside, Kerr, & Schapira, 1972; Klerman, 1980). The Anxiety Disorders tend to be chronic and patients often develop depressive symptoms in reaction to the chronic incapacity caused by the Anxiety Disorders. In such patients it is unclear to what extent these depressive symptoms constitute true superimposed depressive illness or merely reactive demoralization. Similarly, patients with episodic or chronic depressive illness often have anxiety symptoms. Does this represent a superimposed Anxiety Disorder or merely reactive anxiety symptoms? Prospective follow-up and family studies are necessary to resolve these issues.

In future research on Anxiety Disorders, diagnostic reliability will be facilitated by the availability of two new standardized diagnostic interview schedules that can be used for diagnosing all of the *DSM-III* Anxiety Disorders: the Anxiety Disorders Interview Schedule (ADIS) (Di Nardo et al., 1983) and the Structured Clinical Interview for *DSM-III* (SCID) (Spitzer & Williams, 1983b).

41

Controversies in Research on Psychopathology of Anxiety and Anxiety Disorders

Gerald L. Klerman, M.D.
Harvard Medical School
Massachusetts General Hospital

INTRODUCTION

At the Research Conference on Anxiety Disorders, Panic Attacks, and Phobias, held in Key Biscayne, Florida, December 1982, Daniel X. Freedman remarked that we are entering a new age of anxiety research. He noted that the 1980s are a period of growing interest in anxiety disorders. There is intense research activity in the epidemiology, genetics, neurobiology, learning theory, and therapeutics of anxiety states and anxiety disorders. Also, he noted that, as often happens in the history of science, excellent ideas lie dormant.

This historical trend seems to be the case with anxiety research. The basic clinical phenomena of the anxiety disorders were described in the 19th century (Jablensky, this volume; Roth, 1984) Westphal, (1871), Freud (1894), and Kraepelin (1919) had described many of the basic clinical syndromes and Mandel Cohen (1951) reported on familial aggregation in the early 1950s. However, only recently have issues of diagnosis and psychopathology become active.

Determinants outside the scientific field, such as the decisions of governmental agencies or pharmaceutical firms, may have had influence, since they decided where to invest research and development funds. Whatever the historical reasons, the "Sleeping Beauty" of anxiety research has been awakened and is again an active field.

This volume, therefore, comes at a propitious time and has captured much of the current excitement and controversy in the field of anxiety research.

The most salient and controversial issues emerging recently are those related to psychopathology, especially issues of diagnosis and classification. The specific psychopathological issue this chapter focuses upon relates to the proposal to separate panic states and agoraphobia from other anxiety disorders and group them together. This proposal, parts of which are embodied in the *Diagnostic and Statistical Manual (DSM-III)* classification (APA, 1980) of anxiety disorders, represents a departure from the consensus about anxiety and anxiety disorders that characterized the field since the end of World War I. That consensus viewed anxiety, phobias and anxiety states on a continuum with normal anxiety and fear at one end and various anxiety symptoms, anxiety neurosis, and phobic states at the other end. The various clinical states aligned themselves on this continuum and the gradations between them were seen as ones of intensity of distress and degree of social impairment.

In the mid-1970s, this continuum paradigm was challenged by a number of researchers, particularly Donald Klein (1980), who emphasized the crucial role of the panic attack in the pathogenesis of agoraphobia. Further evidence derived from the differential response to pharmacologic agents. A new paradigm emphasizing discontinuity emerged, which proposed that panic disorders and agoraphobia were related to each other, but separate from normal fear, anxiety, and anxiety neurosis.

This new discontinuity paradigm was partially incorporated in the *DSM-III* classification of anxiety disorders, a decision that has led to considerable controversy within the United States and between American investigators and those in Europe, particularly those who follow ICD-9. The divergence between American and European traditions is described in detail in the chapter by Jablensky (this volume). These differences involve more than just matters of nosology. They represent a basic shift in scientific thinking about anxiety, a shift that is best explained by Kuhn's theory of the role of the paradigm in the history of science.

KUHN'S THEORY OF SCIENTIFIC CHANGE: THE ROLE OF PARADIGMS

There is no single American school of psychiatry. The multiple schools of American psychiatry and psychology differ markedly in their concepts of mental illness and in their concern with the reliability, validity, and utility of diagnosis. Attitude toward diagnosis among the schools encompass moral and ethical judgments; some schools, for example, regard diagnostic efforts as depersonalizing, antitherapeutic, and politically repressive. The differences between schools of thought are often intense, approaching proportions of ideology rather than science. These ideological forces have often influenced efforts at revision of diagnostic nomenclatures, as manifested in some of the debates and controversies attendant upon the creation and promulgation of *DSM-III*.

Given the ideological character of the current American mental health scene, how can its structure and dynamics be understood? Theories of Thomas Kuhn (1970) on the nature of change and progress in science are especially relevant and applicable to changes in this focus of anxiety research.

Kuhn has proposed that the history of a science is punctuated by "revolutions," the essence of a scientific revolution being the emergence of a new paradigm that provides a significant restructuring of the ways in which the particular science defines its problems and orders its ways of looking at them. In the revised second edition of *The Structure of Scientific Revolutions* (1970), Kuhn describes two components of a "paradigm"—the cognitive and the communal. The cognitive component refers to the theories, concepts, and ideas by which a science is delineated and the rules it employs in conducting research and evaluating evidence. The communal component refers to the collectivity of scientists (or practitioners) who share the ideas and values and who affirm the particular form of scientific "truth."

Kuhn's theory has been the subject of much discussion among scholars and scientists. His theories have been criticized for using the physical sciences as the basis for assessing other sciences, for identifying substantive issues too closely with vicissitudes in the social composition of scientific communities, and for overstating the emotional allegiance of scientists to a specific paradigm. Nonetheless, Kuhn's theory presents a coherent framework for understanding change within a science, particularly one as diverse as psychiatry and psychology, for which no one school has yet provided a dominant and unifying paradigm.

Kuhn suggests that when a single paradigm emerges as dominant within a science, the status of that science becomes defined and disputes are resolved. Within this framework, two assessments of the scientific status of the current American psychiatric scene are possible. First, each separate school could be regarded as paradigmatic. According to this assessment, the current American psychiatric scene would be regarded as an arena for multiple, competing, scientific paradigms, each with its own cognitive structure (theories and research methodologies) and its own community of investigators and practitioners. The numerous paradigms compete with each other for scientific dominance, for intellectual status and prestige, and for the allegiance of mental health practitioners, including psychiatrists, psychologists, social workers, and nurses. Second, an alternative view would be that since no school has yet emerged as dominant, psychiatry should be described as a "preparadigmatic" science. Seen from this perspective, psychiatry and psychology are still prescientific since a single, dominant paradigm does not exist.

The attitudes of the various schools toward diagnosis and classification vary; but among the different schools, the biological school, with its historical roots in classic medical thinking, has been the most consistent advocate of the concept of multiple diagnostic classes and the importance of diagnosis and classification for research and for selection of appropriate therapies for clinical care. In the 1970s, as *DSM-III* was being formulated, a number of new ideas emerged, some of which have the characteristics of a new paradigm that has revitalized interest in diagnosis and classification and provided the scientific basis for many of the innovations. Some of these ideas are discussed in the following section. The activity that led to the formulation of *DSM-III* involved a reorientation toward psychiatric diagnosis and a consistent attention toward psychiatric diagnosis and a consistent attention to psychopathology based on descriptive symptomatology. In previous writings, I have called this the neo-Kraepelinian group. Whether or not it constitutes a distinct paradigm is not certain. The crucial event that stimulated the neo-Kraepelinian paradigm was the problem of reliability. The reliability problem was in principle solved by the use of operational criteria and structured interviews, which dealt respectively with information variance and criterion variance. The development of the structured interviews and operational criteria codified, for example, in the SADS and the RDC, allowed a systematic research program on various aspects of psychiatric illness. Initially, this was applied with vigor to affective illness and to schizophrenia. Only recently has it been applied to anxiety disorders.

THE CONTINUUM PARADIGMS IN ANXIETY RESEARCH

As Jablensky (this volume) and Roth (1984) have pointed out, attention to the clinical states which today are called Anxiety Disorders, did not emerge until the second half of the 19th century. Psychiatry as a medical specialty began in the late 18th century with medical responsibilities in the asylums and mental hospitals. Given that historical context, it is understandable that the initial efforts in scientific psychopathology would focus on "insanity" and "lunacy," which were regarded as "psychotic." In the last decades of the 19th century, physicians in major cities of Western Europe and North America began to focus on a visible group of noninstitutionalized patients, who though not psychotic suffered from distressing bodily symptoms and irrational thoughts and behaviors. Prominent symptoms among these patients were fearfulness, distress, bodily complaints, sweating, and palpitations.

Various terms were applied to these phenomena, particularly neurasthenia, hypochondriasis, and hysteria. Clinical descriptions by Westphal (1871) were incorporated by Kraepelin into his concept of "Schenkenneurosie." Beard (1880), in the United States, had described "neurasthenia" and called it the American disease of civilization because of his speculation that the increased frequency of this disorder was due to the pace of civilized living, particularly in urbanized and industrialized countries. The term "anxiety" did not come into general intellectual and clinical use until the latter part of the 19th century, and its adoption was heavily influenced by the philosophical ideas of Kierkegaard.

Freud's influential psychoanalytic theories were applied to psychoneurosis. In 1894, he proposed separating anxiety neurosis from neurasthenia. A number of psychoanalysts have reconstructed Freud's thinking about the clinical phenomenology of the anxiety state (Michels, Frances, Shear et al., this volume). They note that Freud's early papers contain excellent clinical descriptions of phenomena that would now be considered panic attacks. He also described the role of panic in initiating phobic behavior. In many ways, Freud was the Kraepelin of the psychoneuroses, having described disorders such as obsessive/compulsive states and phobia, and having related these clinical states to normal fear and anxiety. In an attempt to develop a comprehensive theory, in 1923 Freud formulated his signal theory of anxiety, whereby he postulated that anxiety arose in the ego and served as a signal to mobilize the defenses against internal drives (in the psychoneuroses) and against external threats (in normal fear).

Based upon these clinical writings, as well as the theoretical implications of the work of Pavlov and Cannon, the consensus emerged that there was a continuity of anxiety disorders.

SEPARATING PANIC DISORDERS AND AGORAPHOBIA FROM THE OTHER ANXIETY DISORDERS

Applying Kuhn's model of scientific change to anxiety research, the question arises, "what was the puzzle that has prompted the "Sleeping Beauty" to reawaken?" I think there were three "puzzles."

1. The terms used failed to convey precise meaning. David Sheehan has identified 37 different nosologic terms that overlap with anxiety (Sheehan & Sheehan, 1982).

2. Two classes of drugs—the MAO inhibitors and the tricyclics which by conventional psychopharmacological logic are called "antidepressants"—were shown to be effective for anxiety disorders. On phenomenologic grounds, these disorders were different from depression.

3. Certain forms of anxiety disorder, particularly agoraphobia, did not respond to neuroleptics or benzodiazepines, the prototypic antianxiety drugs. This was paradoxical. Why should the most intensive anxiety states not respond even to powerful neuroleptic drugs?

In response to these puzzles, a new paradigm emerged in the early 1970s. This paradigm proposed bringing panic disorder and agoraphobia together, and separating these two conditions from the other anxiety states. This implied a new paradigm, which emphasized the discontinuity of panic and agoraphobia for other anxiety states.

The central feature of this paradigm was that panic attack was a unique psychic experience and not a more intense form of normal fear and anxiety. Panic attack occurs as the sudden onset of intense fear and anxiety with a sense of dread and foreboding and fear of being trapped. These cognitive elements were combined with awareness of physiologic change, particularly autonomic arousal manifested by sweating, palpitations, feeling of light-headedness, and so forth.

The initial panic attack and the onset of the episode occur spontaneously without apparent environmental precipitant. The repeated episodes of spontaneous panic attack postulated to drive phobic avoidance behavior are not based on a classic Pavlovian conditioning model. In contrast to behavior therapies, the panic attack is regarded as the initiator of the avoidant behavior.

Sources of Evidence

The evidence in support of this paradigm derives from a number of sources.

1. The most important evidence is the clinical observation of the phenomenology of psychopathology of the disorder, and a careful dissection of the sequence of symptoms and behavior in the chronology of individual patient conditions.

2. The second source of evidence is response to pharmacological therapy. Panic states and agoraphobia do not respond to benzoidiazepines, the prototypic antianxiety drugs, but were found serendipitously to respond to monoamine oxidase inhibitors and to TCAs, which are antidepressants (Klein, 1980). This differential drug response lent powerful evidence to the discontinuity paradigm.

3. Family and twin studies indicate that anxiety and depression aggregate in the same families, and that the presence of phobic avoidance is often associated with childhood episodes of separation anxiety (Crowe, Noyes, Pauls, & Slymen, 1983; Crowe, Pauls, Slymen, & Noyes, 1980; Leckman, Weissman, Merikangas, Pauls, & Prusoff, 1983). Recent twin studies have substantiated the separation of panic and agoraphobia from other anxiety disorders (Surman, Sheehan, Fuller, & Gallo, 1983).

4. Psychophysiologic studies use lactate infusion as the experimental mode of induction of episodes similar to those occurring in panic (Ackerman & Sachar, 1974; Fink, Taylor, & Volavka, 1970; Laprirre, Knott, Gray, 1984).

These lines of evidence support the new paradigm. There is a psychopathologic cluster composed of panic attacks, agoraphobia, and extensive phobic avoidance. This cluster constitutes a separate psychopathologic entity, different from other forms of phobia, generalized anxiety, and obsessive/compulsive disorders.

All forms of anxiety disorders share some similarities, particularly the symptoms of anxiety, dread, and foreboding. But the complex of panic disorder, agoraphobia and phobic disorder, is considered different from other disorders; its unique feature is the panic attack. The panic attack is not only the "sine qua non" for diagnosis, but is considered the "driving force" in the pathogenesis of the phobic and avoidance behavior. Phobic avoidant behavior, anticipatory anxiety, and help-seeking behavior are important features of the syndrome but are seen as responses of the individual to the aversive experience of the panic attack.

CONCLUSIONS

The chapters in this book highlight the controversies and differences between the old and new paradigms. Understanding the scientific issues has unfortunately been confounded because of professional and theoretical background. The psychoanalytically oriented theorists and behavior therapists accept the continuum paradigm, but the position of biologists has been divided. Many biologists, particularly those involved in benzodiazepine research and the new GABA-benzodiazepine receptor research have accepted implicitly the continuum model of anxiety, seeking continuities between normal anxiety and clinical states.

In contrast, the proponents of the new paradigm, which emphasizes the discontinuity between panic/agoraphobia and other clinical conditions, tend to be psychiatrists strongly influenced by the descriptive-phenomenologic view and even by the neo-Kraepelinian view. They tend to emphasize the biological pathogenesis of the panic attack and the unique role of central nervous system physiology, particularly as elucidated by the studies of lactate infusion. In this model, genetic factors predispose to panic attack. The panic attack is the driving force for anticipatory anxiety and phobic avoidance, and psychological mechanisms such as conditioning, avoidance, and mental representations take on a secondary role. In therapeutics, the emphasis is on treatment with drugs such as MAO inhibitors, tricyclic antidepressants and the new triazo-benzodiazepines, particularly alprazolam. Pharmacologic therapy is regarded as the most powerful therapy, and behavior therapy and other forms of psychological management are relegated to a secondary and ancillary role.

These new ideas represent a typical controversy in scientific discourse. Competing ideas require further investigation, and controversy is likely to continue until one paradigm or another emerges dominant.

42 Is the Grouping of Anxiety Disorders in *DSM-III* Based on Shared Beliefs or Data?

Thomas Detre
University of Pittsburgh

This discussion will begin by focusing on two papers published in this volume which, when considered together, suggested to me certain strategies that might be used to refine the nosology of pathologic anxiety. Both papers, the first by Jablensky and the second by Spitzer and Williams, contain a wealth of information and should be read by everyone interested in psychiatric nosology. However, it is what I perceive to be the limitations of even the most current concepts that has led me to formulate several approaches for clarifying whether the present *DSM-III* grouping of anxiety disorders is a clinically viable one.

The views espoused by my European (Jablensky) and American (Spitzer and Williams) colleagues also offer a fascinating cultural perspective on different approaches to problem solving. In Europe the task of creating order out of diagnostic chaos, in the absence of hard data, is the responsibility of prominent academicians, each of whom commands loyalty only in his or her own geographic area. Since the customary outcome is an invigorating but seemingly endless intellectual duel, we in the United States believe that consensus conferences aimed at resolving diagnostic controversies are a more efficient method of coping with our ignorance. Although we claim that the product emerging from such encounters is nothing more than a series of testable hypotheses, quite mysteriously our deliberations soon are viewed as the "official position," and what was intended to serve as a catalyst to some extent becomes our catechism. Those who complain about the process or the outcome are politely told that order is nearly always preferable to uncertainty because it tends to stimulate scientific productivity. For example, it has been repeatedly stated that rising interest in anxiety and phobias is attributable to the enthusiastic acceptance of the various conditions now grouped together in the third edition of the *Diagnostic and Statistical Manual of Mental Disorders (DSM-III)*, even though it is well known

783

that rigorous research on anxiety actually began during World War II, long before *DSM-III* was conceived.

It is also known that the base of investigative activity increased in the late fifties when behaviorally oriented psychotherapies were introduced both because their effectiveness in the treatment of phobias could be shown in controlled clinical trials and because these resulting studies provided convincing evidence that complex problems can be examined by relying on what is directly observable. This "return to the conscious" also characterizes *DSM-III,* and I agree unequivocally with the descriptive-phenomenologic approach to classification adopted by the *DSM-III* Task Force. I do feel, however, that the conceptual strategy used to carve out this new class now called anxiety disorders and the introduction of so-called decision rules will lead to premature reification of the system and kindle naive fantasies that what were intended to be reasonable collections of seemingly associated symptoms have come to represent "biological entities."

Let me cite several examples of this premature quest for certainty. Jablensky, in his paper, points out that separating hypochondriacal states from phobias by assigning them to somatoform disorders is of doubtful value since many such patients have both illness phobias and somatic symptoms. Others wonder why the decision was made to group obsessive-compulsive neurosis with anxiety disorders and what the justification is for neatly separating phobic from obsessive states. Still others are deeply puzzled as to why depersonalization and derealization were exiled to the camp of dissociative disorders, particularly since such symptoms occur with reasonable frequency in patients suffering from anxiety.

I also find the newly created category of organic anxiety troublesome, as the term implies that all other types of anxiety symptoms or disorders are nonorganic. Moreover, while it is true that anxiety symptoms can be precipitated by a biologic insult, they are not present in all or even most patients who have suffered the same insult. If our experience with affective disorders has taught us anything, it should be that the removal of the cause, as for instance the correction of metabolic problems in hypothyroidism, does not necessarily lead to the cessation of symptoms or to a different long-term outcome.

For several reasons, I also share the doubts of my European colleagues about the existence of panic as an independent disorder. I am prepared to entertain the *possibility* that symptoms of panic are qualitatively different or that panic represents a distinct nosologic entity, but I have misgivings about the method by which the conclusion was reached.

This category, as Spitzer and Williams state in their paper, was created for conditions characterized by recurrent panic attacks on the basis of the observation that imipramine blocked the recurrence of panic attacks but had no effect on anticipatory anxiety. Unquestionably, treatment response can be used as a probe to differentiate between groups of disorders, but skepticism is in order when it is used as the sole proof. Most clinical researchers would hesitate to regard the proven effectiveness of an anticonvulsant, Dilantin, in the management of ventricular ectopic rhythms either as a clarion call for the reclassification of cardiac arrhythmias or for regarding arrhythmia as an epilepsy equivalent.

Other evidence marshaled in favor of the current grouping based on case-controlled studies or the alleged relationship between separation anxiety, school phobia, and adult anxiety—particularly agoraphobia—is not yet on firm ground. What data have been reported thus far are at least as consistent with the overlap of depression and anxiety as they are with the familiar aggregation of symptom complexes constituting the *DSM-III* category of anxiety disorders. Even if future studies could confirm that first-degree relatives of probands with panic disorder and depression are at higher risk for both major depression and anxiety than are relatives of probands with agoraphobia plus depression, the most parsimonious interpretation is that the presence of symptoms characteristic of panic represents a different order of severity. That panic may and often does complicate the clinical picture in patients whose symptoms appear circumscribed lends further support to the view that this collection of symptoms is nothing more than an index of severity. With regard to the relationship of separation anxiety and agoraphobia, Achenbach (this volume) points out quite rightly that retrospective data thus far available are vulnerable because adults who had difficulty in school attendance but no subsequent psychiatric problems are less likely to report such difficulties than are adults for whom the occurrence of school phobia was but one important landmark in the development of a chronic or recurrent psychiatric disorder which has plagued them throughout their lives.

Anxiety research has made remarkable advances over the past decades, but it is mandatory that the field pause briefly and think through its strategy before proceeding. We have already embarked on large-scale epidemiologic, family, and genetic studies on anxiety (see Weissman and also Carey, this volume), but the validity of these investigations may be seriously compromised precisely because of an excessively narrow definition of the clinical picture and an attendant loss of important data.

At this point, it is even difficult to differentiate shy, dependent, socially awkward, and slightly withdrawn individuals from those who have generalized anxiety. Criteria for considering these personality characteristics as primary or secondary to generalized anxiety are not clearly spelled out. The interaction between symptoms of anxiety and symptoms of "low-grade" depression observed in dysthymia and cyclothymia of predominantly depressive type is equally unexplored. It does deserve our attention, however, as depression—whether mild or severe—tends to be preceded by (and is often concomitant with) symptoms of anxiety.

Jablensky reminds us that the term *anxiety* is a source of semantic confusion because it encompasses different meanings in different languages. It is equally possible, however, that the various descriptions of anxiety (such as a feeling of foreboding, awareness of one's powerlessness in the face of a threat, or a state of tense alertness) represent qualitatively different affective responses of potential diagnostic significance. To complicate matters further, none of the nosologic systems now in vogue looks at symptoms and behavior from a developmental perspective. Consequently, age-related changes—even though these are known to occur throughout life, not just in the course of the first and second decades—are ignored. For both of these reasons it would be desirable that all future assessment instruments include an exhaustive list of symptoms and behaviors.

Another weakness or omission mentioned in both Lang's and Akiskal's papers (this volume) is our failure to separate the type of data that is verifiable by direct observation or by other means from the type of data provided by the patient's self-description. Although we do not as yet have biologic markers, a few examples of potentially valuable data that should be collected in future studies include changes in neurovegetative functions, the spectrum of autonomic manifestations, hyperventilation, diurnal variations in the severity of symptoms, adaptation to novel environments (as, for instance, the studies of adaptation to the sleep laboratory by Akiskal et al., 1984 and Reynolds et al., 1983), and disorders of attention observable in stressful situations.

Accordingly, until we have a better idea of what would constitute an adequate data base, it would be counterproductive to screen patients using *DSM-III* criteria only, although it may be desirable to insist that all nosologic investigations collect information necessary to make a *DSM-III*-based diagnosis. Unless we have epidemiologic data to prove that the collection of symptoms listed in the various subcategories of anxiety disorders does indeed appear in sufficiently pure form to be regarded as a syndrome, we may end up with artifacts rather than syndromes. For the same reasons, the decision made by Spitzer and his collaborators to abolish one of the hierarchical rules dealing with depression and panic disorders is a step in the right direction; but it would be advisable, for the time being at least, to abandon all decision rules that are based on intuition rather than information.

43

Anxiety: Definition, Relationship to Depression, and Proposal for an Integrative Model

Hagop Souren Akiskal
University of Tennessee Center for the Health Sciences

In this volume, Assen Jablensky has probed nosologic aspects of the anxiety disorders with phenomenologic sophistication, providing a scholarly review of anxiety states in the empirical European tradition. By contrast, in his attempt to bring biometric precision to this area, Robert Spitzer (this volume) often finds it necessary to break with this tradition. In discussing the contributions of these authors, I focus primarily on definitional issues and on the relationship of anxiety to depressive states, and then present some of our data—including recent sleep electroencephalographic (EEG) findings that bear on these issues. Finally, I raise some general questions about etiologic models, and present a heuristic attempt to integrate various approaches to anxiety.

DEFINITIONAL ISSUES

Clinical Setting and Mode of Presentation

When psychiatry was hospital-based and preoccupied with severe mental disorders, neurotic misery was largely the domain of neurologists and internists. Freud's pioneering work on anxiety neurosis came from his neurologic practice and perhaps, as Sheehan and Sheehan (1983) suggest, from his personal acquaintance with the illness. Although Freud influenced the thinking of many psychiatrists, the systematic study of anxiety, until recently, was undertaken almost exclusively by academic clinical psychologists who had access to (minimally symptomatic) outpatients as well as volunteer subjects. To this day, relatively few biologically oriented psychiatrists seem interested in anxiety states. Jablensky's description of these diverse settings is à propos to this discussion, because the observations coming from each reflect the limitations that the setting may impose on clinical research. Recent unpublished data from our program have shown that patient presentations of anxiety states differ considerably from one setting to another. For instance, somatic presentations with cardiovascular, musculoskeletal, and gastrointestinal symptoms predominate in primary care settings. Insomnia is common to primary care settings and sleep disorders centers. In addition, a small number of patients referred to our sleep disorders center to rule out sleep apnea seem to suffer from a special form of anxiety disorder. These patients—in whom we have excluded the diagnosis of sleep apnea by appropriate polysomonography—complain of the fear that they will die in their sleep, are unable to sleep lying down in their beds, and obtain some (but still insufficient) sleep in a sitting position. Finally, in our mental health center, anxious patients commonly present with depression as their predominant complaint; a small number are referred because of "unusual" thought content such as agoraphobics' "fear of disappearing into space" when forced to walk across a bridge. In view of these differences in clinical presentation, it is desirable to conduct research on anxiety states on samples representing these diverse clinical settings.

The Distinction between Normal and Clinical Anxiety

In addressing the dimensional aspects of anxiety, Jablensky discusses the adaptive value of the emotion and its existential ramifications. The issue is raised at what point anxiety should be considered pathological, a question left unanswered by Spitzer. I suggest that the threshold for clinical anxiety is reached when:

1. the emotion is recurrent or persistent;
2. it is out of proportion to the situation eliciting it, or occurs in the absence of any ostensible danger;
3. the individual is paralyzed with a sense of helplessness, or unable to take appropriate action to terminate the anxiety-provoking situations; and
4. psychosocial or physiologic functioning is impaired.

State Versus Trait Anxiety

A threshold, such as the one proposed, may be more appropriate for clinical anxiety than for anxiety as a personality trait. The latter concept, sometimes referred to as "anxiousness," is perhaps better expressed on a rating scale than in a clinical diagnosis. Actually, it has no nosological equivalent at the present time, unless the rubric of generalized anxiety disorder (GAD) in the third edition of the *Diagnostic and Statistical Manual* of the American Psychiatric Association (*DSM-III*, 1980) were to cover a prolonged period of time, i.e. 2 or more years.

Spitzer's suggestion to "tighten up" the GAD criteria by incorporating a greater number of panic symptoms will bring GAD closer to panic disorder. In such a modification, GAD may emerge as a *forme fruste* of panic disorder. This would be similar to the concept of "subpanic attacks" as a prodromal phase of panic disorder, antedating it by months to years (Sheehan & Sheehan, 1983). The idea that some GAD cases represent attenuated forms of panic disorder is an interesting hypothesis that could be tested with such strategies as family interview, lactate infusion, and imipramine response.

The *DSM-III* definition of GAD is inadequate in that it combines subjective, physiological, and behavioral manifestations in confusing admixtures. Instead, I would propose a modification of Lang's approach to defining emotions (1978). His tripartite description at verbal, behavioral, and physiological levels can be expanded as follows:

1. *Subjective experience*—an ineffable and unpleasant feeling of foreboding (Lader & Marks, 1971)
2. *Cognition*—worrying; rumination about groundless feelings of insecurity about the future, ill health, or misfortune to family (Roth & Mountjoy, 1982).
3. *Arousal and vigilance*—most commonly, feeling "on edge," difficulty concentrating, and insomnia.
4. *Autonomic nervous system hyperactivity*—tension, headaches, palpitations, hyperventilation, dry mouth, clammy hands, urinary and bowel urgency.
5. *Observable behavior*—fidgeting, tremulousness, twitching of eyelids, and irritability.

It would be necessary to specify age of onset (most likely childhood or teens), duration (at least 2 years), and course (waxing and waning).

In the modification proposed here, GAD emerges as a lifelong trait. The question is whether such a condition should be classed as "anxious personality" and coded on Axis II of the *DSM*. GAD may exist as a "pure" disorder, or be complicated by superimposed panic attacks, phobic avoidance with agoraphobic coloring, and either minor or major depressive episodes. It may also form the substrate for substance use disorders, peptic ulcer, hypertension, and coronary artery disease. Research on GAD should be of high priority during the remainder of this century in view of its theoretical and public health relevance.

The Necessity of Defining Anxiety in Terms of Physiologic, Experiential, and Behavioral Components

Spitzer raises the question of whether an individual who dreads entering a given situation, yet forces himself to do so, should be considered phobic. This is a good example of self-initiated exposure, and of an individual (hopefully) on the road to recovery. It illustrates how subjective experience (fear) and behavior (avoidance) can be dissociated from one another in anxiety disorders (Barlow & Mavissakalian, 1981).

According to the James-Lange theory of emotion (reviewed by Lang, 1978), physiology (e.g., cardiac acceleration) precedes experience (fear). This is embodied in Klein's concept of "spontaneous panic attacks," where the experience of fear is a correlate of the unexplained and sudden upsurge of autonomic nervous system activity (Klein, 1982). In such a model, the occurrence of avoidance (which, in the extreme, may manifest as agoraphobia) can be considered as a complication. However, discordance between the three systems of expressing anxiety is common and, therefore, not all patients need exhibit all three components of anxiety. Viewed from this perspective, Spitzer's vignette ("Mr. T.," p. 769), this volume) illustrates pathologic anxiety without the behavioral component, and underscores the necessity of defining anxiety in three component systems—physiologic, experiential, behavioral.

It is a sad commentary on the practice of psychotherapy that clinicians typically do not evaluate the manifestations of anxiety in terms of these three components. In particular, attention is often focused on one system, e.g., subjective report by psychodynamic clinicians, and observable behavior by behavioristic practitioners. Physiologic measures, which have proved valuable assessment tools in behavior therapy, are, unfortunately, used rarely in office practice. Psychotherapeutic practice would greatly benefit from including the physiologic concomitants of anxiety in the assessment of treatment and outcome.

A Spectrum of Anxiety Disorders, or Discrete Categories?

Unlike the *DSM-III* categorization of discrete anxiety disorders, European thinking, as exemplified here by Jablensky, favors a spectrum concept. This approach is characteristic not only of Freudian thinking, but of neo-Kraepelinian psychiatry. Lewis (1938) has suggested a nosologic model that ranges from the affective psychoses at one extreme to the anxiety states at the other. Roth and Mountjoy (1982) have conceptualized a spectrum of "affective neuroses" that includes neurotic depression, anxious depression, anxiety neurosis, social phobia, and agoraphobia; however, these conditions are sharply demarcated from endogenous depressions.

 Sheehan and Sheehan (1983) have recently proposed a spectrum concept in which anxiety progresses through subpanic, panic, somatization, hypochondriacal, agoraphobic, and depressive phases. Although this viewpoint may seem unorthodox to the architects of *DSM-III*, it has much to commend it from a heuristic standpoint. Indeed, Spitzer's proposal to combine panic and agoraphobic categories is, in part, in line with the Sheehan schema. Spitzer's recognition of a three-stage phenomenon that ranges from uncomplicated panic, through

panic with limited phobic avoidance, to panic with agoraphobia is a tacit acknowledgment that agoraphobia represents a complication of panic disorder.

It is conceivable that some of the heterogeneity in the area of anxiety disorders
stems from personality differences. For instance, panic disorder patients with
histrionic-sociopathic traits may be different from those with obsessional traits.
Therefore, it would be desirable in future research on anxiety disorders to make
use of Axis II distinctions.

RELATIONSHIP BETWEEN ANXIETY AND DEPRESSION

Symptom Overlap

While not all psychiatrists in Great Britain subscribe to a spectrum concept such
as that proposed by Lewis (1938), it is interesting that the term "affective disorder" is used in that country not only for depression and mania but for anxiety
states as well. This usage underscores some of the clinical problems in differentiating between anxiety and depressive states, which together constitute the
most common psychiatric disorders seen in outpatient practice. Depression is a
frequent complication of anxiety disorders, and anxiety symptoms are common
in primary depressive illness. To complicate matters, Watts (1966) has described
patients seen in primary care settings who present with severe anxiety states in
middle age, in the absence of pre-morbid neuroticism. He suggests that such
patients are actually suffering from a primary depressive illness, as judged from
course of illness and response to electroconvulsive therapy. These patients may
represent atypical forms of agitated depression which, in Meyer's apt terminology
(1948), are best described as "anxiety psychosis."

The results of our own study (VanValkenburg, Akiskal, Puzantian, & Rosenthal, 1984) of patients with primary panic, panic complicated by depression,
depression complicated by panic, or primary depression highlight the difficulties
of distinguishing clinically between anxiety and depressive states (Table 43.1).
On most phenomenologic, familial, treatment-response and outcome parameters,
the four groups appeared to form a spectrum, with primary panic and primary
depression representing the extreme poles of a continuum joined by two intermediate groups of anxious depressions.

Clinical and pharmacological treatment response studies, using various rating
scales, have failed to provide unequivocal evidence for differentiation between
anxiety and depressive states (reviewed in Foa & Foa, 1982, and Lipman, 1982).
Widlöcher, Lecrubier, and Le Goc (1983) have recently argued that this failure
to distinguish anxiety from depressive states may be due to the fact that anxiety
and agitation are typically measured on rating scales, whereas retardation is

TABLE 43.1
Comparisons of four groups of patients with various admixtures of
anxiety and depression given in percentages unless otherwise
specified*

	Panic Disorder	Panic Disorder + II° Depression	Depression + II° Panic Attacks	I° Depression
General				
N	18	31	23	42
Age (mean)	46.9	37.3	45.3	42.3
Sex	F = M	F = M	F > M	F > M
Age, onset panic attacks				
(mean)†	19.9	20.8	37.1	—
Age, onset depression (mean)	—	27.2	29.1	32.9
Psychiatric hospitalization				
(mean)†	.17	1.8	2.3	1.3
Complications				
Alcohol abuse	47	40	30	19
Sedative-hypnotic abuse†	33	42	35	7
Amphetamine abuse†	0	6	26	2
Agoraphobia†	65	35	35	0
Chronic depression†	—	71	83	24
Divorce and separation	0	22	18	21
Symptomatology				
Retardation†	0	6	22	29
Agitation†	55	94	100	67
Suicide attempts	0	23	30	21
Delusions†	0	6	30	19
Hypochondriasis†	55	65	65	21
Depersonalization/derealization†	56	39	26	5
Obsessionalism	50	61	90	29
Histrionic-sociopathic traits	18	26	26	20

*Summarized from VanValkenburg et al., 1984.
†Overall 4-group differences, $p < .05$

derived from global assessments. Using the Salpêtrière retardation scale (Wid-löcher, 1983), they have demonstrated that differentiation between the two affec-tive states is possible on the ideic, subjective and cognitive subscales of retardation. Lader's (1975) findings on electrodermal activity and habituation have also sep-arated retarded depressives from agitated depressive and anxious subjects. It is likely that anxiety and depression coexist in a subtype of nonretarded affective disorder which is qualitatively different from retarded (typically endogenous and often bipolar) conditions.

To understand the frequent coexistence of anxiety and depressive states, it would be necessary to briefly consider the evolutionary background of the two emotions. Anxiety may be the first line of adaptation in the primate's attempt to survive after separation from members of the group (Akiskal & McKinney, 1973). Indeed, the protest stage of separation in monkeys has all the behavioral, biochemical, and physiological markers of an acute anxiety state. Although in many cases it forms the prelude to the despair or "depression" stage, not all monkeys make this transition. So it is with humans as well. The transition from grief to melancholia is uncommon (Clayton, 1979), and an anxiety state is not always followed or complicated by depression. Furthermore, retardation is almost never seen in the depression of bereaved subjects (Clayton, Herjanic, Murphy, & Woodruff, 1974), providing further support for the proposed distinction between anxiety-depression and (retarded) depression.

Familial-Genetic Aspects

Although Leckman, Weissman, Merikangas, Pauls and Prusoff (1983) have reported considerable familial overlap between anxiety and depressive condi-tions, other data from family studies (Cloninger, Martin, Clayton, & Guze, 1981; Crowe, Noyes, Pauls, & Slymen, 1983) and genetic findings from identical twins (Torgersen, 1983) are more supportive of the hypothesis that the two affective states are distinct.

Sleep Electroencephalographic (EEG) Differentiation

Recent sleep electroencephalographic data from our laboratory also support the distinctness of anxiety and depressive states (Akiskal et al., 1984). Anxiety states (with or without depression) were found to be clearly distinguishable from pri-mary depressive states. Because our anxious depressives had a chronic history, the depressive comparison group was also chosen for chronicity (Table 43.2). Psychometric data indicate that the two groups had similar Beck Depression Inventory scores, and that chronic primary depressives were more "neurotic" (higher psychasthenia scores) than the anxious depressives. These features further confound diagnostic issues at the symptomatic level and, therefore, the ability of sleep EEG measures to distinguish between the two groups should be evaluated

TABLE 43.2
Demographic, Clinical, Psychometric, and Sleep EEG Comparisons
Between Anxious Depressive and Chronic Primary Depressive Groups.*

	Anxious Depression (N = 22)	Primary Dysthymia* (N = 20)	Significance
General			
Age (mean)	43	36	ns
Female %	41	65	ns
Insomnia %	82	40	< .05
Beck scores (mean)	15	17	ns
Relevant MMPI Scores†			
Hypochondriasis	68 ± 12	71 ± 11	ns
Depression	72 ± 16	81 ± 13	ns
Hysteria	68 ± 18	69 ± 16	ns
Psychasthenia	72 ± 9	82 ± 10	< .02
Night 2—Sleep continuity measures			
Total time in bed (min)	444 ± 48	448 ± 112	ns
Sleep latency (min)	15 ± 10	21 ± 26	ns
Sleep efficiency %	89 ± 7	90 ± 11	ns
Awakenings	3.6 ± 2.1	1.9 ± 2.2	< .05
Body movements	42 ± 24	45 ± 19	ns
Stage shifts	38 ± 8	31 ± 10	≤ .05
Delta sleep %	20 ± 8	19 ± 8	ns
Night 2—REM measures			
REM latency (min)	99 ± 45	53 ± 21	< .01
REM %	21 ± 6	26 ± 5	< .01
REM density %	18 ± 14	16 ± 8	ns
Night 1 minus Night 2			
Sleep latency (min)	10.7	− 4.6	< .05
Sleep efficiency	− 9.8	− .2	< .001
Awakenings	3.4	.3	< .01
Delta %	2.4	3.9	< .05
REM latency (min)	23.8	9.4	ns
REM %	− 5.1	− 3.7	ns

*As defined by Akiskal et al. (1984) from which data is summarized.
†Analysis based on 13 dysthymics and 16 anxious depressives who completed the MMPI.

against this background. The sleep EEG findings from the second night of recording summarized in the table clearly indicate that there is a biologic drive to produce Rapid Eye Movement (REM) sleep earlier in depression, but not in anxiety. By contrast, anxiety is characterized by a higher arousal level, as measured by multiple awakenings and sleep stage shifts. Comparisons across nights indicate that the environmental challenge of the first night in the sleep laboratory was very potent in disturbing the sleep of patients with anxiety disorders, especially with respect to sleep continuity measures. The adaptation night had little impact on depressed patients.

Taken together, these findings suggest that anxiety—even when complicated by depression—is psychophysiologically a distinct disorder from primary depression. Furthermore, these data support the anxiety-depression versus retarded depression distinction in that my definition of primary (or subaffective) dysthymia refers to hypersomnic-retarded chronic depressives with bipolar family history (Akiskal, 1983b).

Our data are generally consistent with those of Reynolds, Shaw, Newton, Coble and Kupfer (1983) with respect to REM latency findings and those of Uhde and colleagues at NIMH (personal communication, January, 1984) with respect to greater arousal in anxiety states. In related attempts at sleep EEG differentiation between depressive and anxiety states, a report from the Lafayette Clinic (Sitaram, personal communication, January, 1984) indicates that arecoline REM induction is fastest in endogenous major depressions without anxiety; nonendogenous depressives with or without anxiety are indistinguishable from nondepressed anxiety disorder and normal controls; and that modest REM-induction is also seen in endogenous major depressives with anxiety.

These sleep EEG and pharmacologic challenge findings suggest that when anxiety and nonendogenous depression coexist, the more appropriate diagnosis is anxiety. This position is the opposite of that in *DSM-III*, which designates depression as the primary diagnosis and tends to disregard the anxiety disorder. Indeed, Weissman (this volume) has suggested that when major depression and panic attacks coexist, both conditions should be diagnosed. It is my contention that depression coexisting with anxiety is a complication of a primary anxiety disorder. However, as argued elsewhere (Akiskal, 1983a) the presence of endogenous depressive features—irrespective of "neurotic" and "characterologic" pathology—should give precedence to the diagnosis of primary depressive disorder.

The sleep EEG data described above can also be interpreted as demonstrating greater psychophysiological lability and environmental reactivity in anxiety disorders, and greater autonomy from the environment in depressions. These findings provide biologic support for the position of Klein (1982), Roth and Mountjoy (1982) and others who distinguish between anxiety and depressive disorders. They also explain, in part, why autonomous depressions tend not to respond to placebo or to nonspecific environmental manipulation, and why anxiety states may show dramatic *initial* response to placebo, social support, and brief psychotherapeutic interventions, but tend to relapse; psychophysiologic lability, which probably reflects a trait disturbance in anxiety disorders, is unaffected by such procedures.

In summary, our data are in line with those of Lader (1975) showing that anxiety (and agitated depression) increases psychophysiologic activity, whereas retarded depression decreases it. Future studies of the psychophysiologic lability in anxiety disorders may provide evidence germane to the very etiology of these disorders.

TOWARD A CONCEPTUAL INTEGRATION

Anxiety appears to be a distinct emotion that has evolved over millions of years. It refers to a universal primate experience and behavior that have important adaptive functions (Gray, 1971). Some individuals experience anxiety repeatedly and with such intensity that it becomes maladaptive, a disordered function. This disorder can be understood as the interaction of various factors:

1. There is a built-in neurophysiological substrate which prepares the individual to cope with danger.
2. Evolution has affected this substrate in such a way that certain stimuli which are especially threatening to survival are avoided selectively.
3. Certain individuals appear to be born with a central autonomic nervous system that is overly sensitive to stimuli that are generally innocuous.
4. Childhood and adult learning experiences may ultimately determine the extent, severity, and nature of the situations that will evoke anxiety.
5. Chronic inability to cope with dangerous situations adaptively, especially if rooted in unresolved separation anxiety, could maintain the high propensity to respond with fear.
6. The symbolic cognitive functions of man might permit the maintenance of fear reactions by obsessive ruminations, such that the mere anticipation of aversive situations can provoke anxiety.
7. An individual so burdened would perhaps be more vulnerable to existential insecurities, especially if intelligent and introspectively inclined.

Such a formulation accommodates data generated from ethological, neurophysiologic, genetic, behavioral, social-learning, cognitive, psychodynamic, and existential perspectives. Although each perspective is reductionistic in its attempt to analyze variables within a given area, a true understanding of anxiety states would ultimately require integration of data from all perspectives. Such an integrative approach should help to resist certain current temptations inherent in reductionism.

First, we must not forget that the emotion of anxiety cannot be fully defined unless physiologic, experiential, and behavioral aspects are included.

Second, the term "organic anxiety disorder" (Spitzer, this volume) is problematic, as it implies that other anxiety states are less biologic. Furthermore, it assumes that biologic factors provide a sufficient etiological basis for the occurrence of an anxiety disorder. It would be preferable to limit *DSM-III* Axis I diagnoses to descriptive aspects, noting relevant contributions from somatic disease on Axis III, very much like the current recommendation of noting relevant psychosocial contributions on Axis IV.

Third, antidepressant and exposure therapies are not necessarily antagonistic. Indeed, I submit that they may share a common biochemical mode of action. For instance, by preventing the re-uptake of norepinephrine, imipramine-type drugs may initially somewhat worsen the anxiety state, but ultimately lead to postsynaptic subsensitivity (Sulser, 1980) and decreased autonomic nervous system hyperactivity mediated through the locus coeruleus (Redmond & Huang, 1979). Likewise, exposure therapies are distinctly unpleasant when first introduced, yet in "bombarding" the noraderenergic system they may ultimately lead to better synaptic homeostasis by lowering postsynaptic sensitivity, and thereby dampening the impact of previously panicogenic stimuli on the noradrenergic system. This can be inferred from what is known about the neurochemical impact of stress on synaptic function (Anisman & Zacharko, 1982).

The challenge for future research efforts in the area of anxiety and anxiety disorders is to bridge biologic and psychologic concepts at the level of measurement, etiologic conceptualization, and therapy.

List of Abbreviations and Their Meanings

Abbreviation	Meaning
5-HT	5-hydroxytryptophan, serotonin
8 SQ	Eight State Questionnaire (IPAT)
8 PF	8 Parallel Form Anxiety Battery (Sheier & Cattell)
16 PF	16 Personality Factor Questionnaire (Cattell, Eber & Tatsuoka)
17-OHCS	17-hydroxycorticosteroid
μg/dl	micrograms per deciliter

A

AACL	Affect Adjective Checklist (Zuckerman)
ACTH	adrenocorticotrophic hormone
ADAMHA	Alcohol, Drug Abuse, and Mental Health Administration
ADIS	Anxiety Disorders Interview Schedule (DiNardo, O'Brien, Barlow, Waddell, & Blanchard)
AMDP	Arbeitsgruppe für Methoeik und Dokumentation in der Psychologie (Working Group for Methodology and Documentation in Psychiatry)
AMI	Amitriptyline
ANOVA	Analysis of variance
ANS	Automonic nervous system
APQ	Activity Preference Questionnaire (Lykken)
ASC	Asthma Symptom Checklist
ASI	Anxiety Status Inventory (Zung)

B

BAS	Behavioral activiation system
BIS	Behavioral inhibition system
BP	Blood pressure

Abbreviation	*Meaning*
BPM	Beats per minute
BZD	Benzodiazepine

C

CA	Cornu ammonis of the hippocampus
Ca	Calcium
cAMP	cyclic-Adenosine monophosphate
CAQ	Clinical Analysis Questionnaire (Cattell)
CBCL	Child Behavior Checklist (Achenbach & Edelbrock)
beta-CCE	Ethyl-beta-carboline-3-carboxylate
beta-CCM	Methyl-beta-carboline-3-carboxylate
beta-CCMA	Beta-carboline-3-carboxylate methylamide
CDI	Children's Depression Inventory (Kovacs & Beck)
CDZ	Chlordiazepoxide
CGI	Clinical Global Impressions
CGS 8216	2 phenyl pyrazolo (4, 3, -c) quinolin-3-(5 Hone)
cGMP	cyclic-Guanyl Monophosphate
CIQ	Cognitive Interference Questionnaire (Sarason)
Cl$^-$	Chloride ion
CLO	Clomipramine
CMAS	Children's Manifest Anxiety Scale (Castaneda, McCandless, & Palermo)
CMHC	Community mental health center
CNS	Central nervous system
CO$_2$	Carbon dioxide
CPI	California Psychological Inventory (Gough)
CPZ	Chlorpromazine
CR	Conditioned response
CRF	Corticotropin releasing factor
CS	Conditioned stimulus
CS$^+$, CS$^-$	In a discriminative conditioned paradigm, the CS$^+$ signals the UCS and the CS$^-$ signals the absence of the UCS
CSF	Cerebrospinal fluid.

D

DBI	Diazepam binding inhibitor
DCC	Daily caffeine consumption
DES-IV	Differential Emotions Scale—4th Revision (Izard, Dougherty, Bloxom, & Kotsch)
DIS	Diagnostic Interview Schedule (sometimes seen as NIMH-DIS)
DMCM	Methyl-4-ethyl-6, 7-dihydroxy-beta-carboline-3-carboxylate
l-Dopa	*levo*-Dopamine
DPH	Diphenylhydantoin
DPIS	Dyadic Prestressor Interaction Scale (Melamed)
DPQ	Differential Personality Questionnaire (Tellegen) (see MPQ)
DPT	Diphtheria, pertussis, typhus inoculation
DRL	Differential reinforcement of low rates of responding
DS	Dizygotic twins
DSM-III	Diagnostic and Statistical Manual of Mental Disorders (third revision)
DST	Dexamethasone suppression test

Abbreviation	*Meaning*
DV	Distress vocalization
DZ	Diazepam (Klein, Rabkin & Gorman's chapter only)
DZ	Dizygotic twins

E

E	Epinephrine
E	Extraversion
EBI	Emotions—Behavior Inventory (Lelwica, Izard, & Blumberg)
ECA	Epidemiologic catchment area
ECT	Electroconvulsive therapy
EEG	Electroencephalograph
EMG	Electromyograph
EPQ	Eysenck Personality Questionnaire
Es	Ego Strength Scale (Barrons)

F

F	Fahrenheit
FBI	Federal Bureau of Investigation
FFA	Free fatty acid
FG 7142	beta-carboline-3 carboxylic acid ethylester methyl amide
FLU	Fluphenazine
FSS-FC	Fear Survey Schedule—For Children (Scherer & Nakamura)
FSH	Follicle stimulating hormone

G

GABA	Gamma aminobutyric acid
GABA-ergic	A neuron or synapse that "works with" GABA
GAD	Generalized anxiety disorder
GASC	General Anxiety Scale for Children (Sarason, Davidson, Lighthall, Waite, & Ruebush)
GH	Growth hormone
GHRF	Growth hormone releasing factor
GM	GABA modulin
GSR	Galvanic skin response

H

HAL	Haloperidol
HAM	Hamilton Depression or Hamilton Anxiety Scales
HAS	Hamiliton Anxiety Scale
hgH	Human growth hormone
HI	Hypoglycemic index
HPLC	High pressure liquid chromatography
HSCL-90	Hopkins Symptom Checklist—90 items; Also, SCL (Derogatis, Lipman, & Covi)
HYPAC	Hypothalamic-pituitary-adrenocortical system

Abbreviation	*Meaning*
	I
I	Introversion
I_R	Reactive Inhibition
IC_{50}	Inhibition concentration, 50%
ICD-9	International Classification of Diseases (9th Revision)
IMI	Imipramine
IPAT	Institute for Personality and Ability Testing
I.Q.	Intelligence quotient
IV	Intravenous
	L
LC	Locus coeruleus
LH	Luteinizing hormone
LOX	Loxapine
LSD, LSD-25	Lysergic acid diethylamide
	M
MAACL	Multiple Affect Adjective Checklist (Zuckerman & Lubin)
MAO	Monamine oxidase
MAOI	Monomine oxidase inhibitor
MAS	see TMAS
MCMI	Millon Clinical Multaxial Inventory (T. Millon)
MHPG	3-methoxy, 4-hydroxy phenethylene glycol
MMPI	Minnesota Multiphasic Personality Inventory (Hathaway & McKinley)
MPQ	Multidimensional Personality Questionnaire (Tellegen)
MVP	Mitral valve prolapse
MZ	Monozygotic twins
	N
N	Number of subjects
N	Neuroticism
NE	Norepinephrine, noradrenalin or noradrenergic
NIMH	National Institute of Mental Health
NOR	Nortriptyline
NOS	Not otherwise specified (i.e., unspecified)
	O
O-A	Objective-Analytic Anxiety Battery (Cattell & Scheier)
OCD	Obsessive-compulsive disorder
	P
P	Psychoticism
PALR	Photoaffinity labeling ratio

Abbreviation	*Meaning*
pCO_2, $PaCO^2$	Partial pressure of carbon dioxide
PD	Panic disorder
PERI-M	Psychiatric Epidemiologic Research Interview—Modified Life Events Scale (Hirschfeld, Schless, Endicott, Lichtenstaedter, & Clayton)
PGE_1	Prostaglandin E_1
PIC	Personality Inventory for Children (Wirt, Lachar, Klinedinst, & Seat)
PK	Protein kinase
POMS	Profile of Mood States (McNair, Lorr, & Droppleman)
POMS-BI	Profile of Mood States-Bipolar Version (Lorr & McNair)
PRF	Personality Research Form (Jackson)
PSE	Present State Examination (Wing)
PTSD	Post-traumatic stress disorder
PZ	Phenelzine

R

r	Pearson product moment correlation coefficient
RDC	Research diagnostic criteria
REM	Rapid eye movement
RET	Rational emotive therapy
RIA	Radioimmunoassay
RO 5-4864	4'-Chlordiazepam
RO 15-1788	Imidobenzodiazepine
RTT	Reactions to Tests (Sarason)

S

SADS	Schedule for Affective Disorders and Schizophrenia (-L, Lifetime version; -C, Change version) (Spitzer & Endicott)
SAM	Self-assessment manikin
SAM	Sympatho-adreno-medullary axis
SCAT	Sport Competition Anxiety Test (Martens & Simon)
SCID	Structured Clinical Interview for DSM-III (Spitzer & Williams)
SCL	See HSCL-90
SCL	Skin conductance level
S^D	Discriminative stimulus
SMBP	Small molecular weight myelin basic protein
S—R	Stimulus-response
S—S	Stimulus—stimulus
SSCR	Spontaneous skin conductance fluctuations
STAI	State-Trait Anxiety Inventory (or Index) (Spielberger, Gorsuch, & Lushene)
STAIC	State-Trait Anxiety Inventory for Children (Spielberger, Edwards, Lushene, Montuori, & Platzek)

T

TAS	Test Anxiety Scale (Sarason)
TASC	Test Anxiety Scale for Children (Sarason)
TCA	Tricyclic antidepressant

Abbreviation	*Meaning*
delta-9-THC	delta-9-Tetrahydrocannabanol
TMAS	Taylor Manifest Anxiety Scale
TOQ	Thought Occurrence Questionnaire (Sarason)
TRH	Thryoid releasing hormone
TSH	Thyroid stimulating hormone

U

UCS	Unconditioned stimulus
UR	Unconditioned response

W

WAIS	Wechsler Adult Intelligence Scale
WISC	Wechsler Intelligence Scale for Children
WHO	World Health Organization

List of Phobias[1]

The terms that follow are no longer a part of the official psychiatric nomenclature. They are presented here for historical reasons. The Editors have found widespread interest in the terms, even though only a few are currently accepted. Except in a historical context, the Editors do not endorse the use of these labels. The Greek and Latin terms used to label phobic disorders (and their English equivalents) are listed below.

A

acarophobia	insects, mites
acerophobia	sourness
achluophobia	darkness, night
acousticophobia	sounds
acrophobia	heights
aerophobia	air currents, drafts, wind
agoraphobia	open spaces
agyiophobia	crossing the street
aichmophobia	sharp, pointed objects, knives being touched by a finger
ailurophobia	cats
algophobia	pain
amathophobia	dust
amychophobia	laceration. being clawed, scratched

[1]Compiled by Jack D. Maser

805

androphobia	men (and, sex with men)
anemophobia	air currents, wind, drafts
anginophobia	angina pectoris
anthropophobia	human society
antlophobia	floods
apeirophobia	infinity
aphenphobia	physical contact, being touched
apiphobia	bees, bee stings
asthenophobia	weakness
astraphobia	thunderstorms, lightening
ataxiophobia	disorder
atephobia	ruin
auroraphobia	northern lights
automysophobia	personal filth
autophobia	being alone, solitude, oneself, of being egotistical

B

bacillophobia	bacilli
bacteriophobia	bacteria, microorganisms
ballistophobia	missiles, projectiles
barophobia	gravity
basiphobia	walking, standing upright
bathophobia	depth, deep places
batophobia	high objects
batrachophobia	frogs
belonephobia	pins, needles, sharp objects
bibliophobia	books
bromidrosiphobia	personal odor
brontophobia	thunder

C

cainophobia	novelty, newness
cancerophobia	cancer
cardiophobia	heart disease
catagelophobia	ridicule
cenophobia	empty rooms, open places
ceraunophobia	thunder
cheimaphobia	cold
cherophobia	gaiety, happiness
chionophobia	snow
cholerophobia	cholera
chrematophobia	money

chromatophobia	certain odors
chromophobia	certain odors
chronophobia	time
cibophobia	food
claustrophobia	enclosed, confined spaces
cleithrophobia	being locked in an enclosed place
cleptophobia	stealing
climacophobia	staircases, climbing
coitophobia	coitus
cometophobia	comets
coprophobia	defecation
cremnophobia	cliffs, steep places, precipice
crystallophobia	glass
cynophobia	dogs, rabies
cypridophobia	venereal disease

D

demonia	demons
demonomania	demons, devils
demonophobia	demons, devils
demophobia	crowds
dermatopathophobia, dermatosiophobia	skin disease
dermatophobia	skin lesion
dextrophobia	objects on the right side, right side of body
diabetophobia	becoming diabetic
dikephobia	justice
dipsophobia	drinking
domatophobia	being in a house
doraphobia	touching fur or animal's skins
dromophobia	crossing streets, wandering about
dysmorphophobia	deformity

E

ecophobia	home surroundings
eisoptrophobia	mirrors
electrophobia	electricity
emetophobia	vomiting
entheomania	demons
entomophobia	insects
eosophobia	dawn
epistaxiophobia	nose bleeding

eremophobia	solitude, stillness, desolate places
ereuthophobia	blushing; red, e.g., blood
ergasiophobia	functioning, work
ergophobia	functioning, work
erotophobia	sexual love
erythrophobia	red colors
esophobia	dawn
eurotrophobia	female genitals
examination phobia	examinations

F

febriphobia	fever

G

galeophobia	cats
gamophobia	marriage
gatophobia	cats
genophobia	sex
gephyrophobia	crossing bridges
geumaphobia	taste
graphophobia	writing
gymnophobia	naked bodies, nakedness, left sides of naked bodies
gynephobia	women

H

hadephobia	hell
hamartophobia	sin, error
haphephobia	being touched, touching
harpaxophobia	robbers
hedonophobia	travel
heliophobia	sunlight, the sun
hellenologophobia	pseudoscientific terms
helminthophobia	worms, infestation with
hematophobia (hemophobia)	blood, bleeding
hierophobia	sacred things, religious objects
hodophobia	travel
homichlophobia	fog
homilophobia	sermons
hormephobia	shock
horror feminae	women
hydrargyrophobia	mercurial medicines
hydrophobia	water

hydrophobophobia	hydrophobia
hyelophobia (hyalophobia)	glass
hygrophobia	moisture
hylephobia	materialism
hylophobia	forests, woods
hypengyophobia	responsibility
hypnophobia	sleep
hypsophobia	heights

I

ichthyophobia	fish
ideophobia	ideas
iophobia	poisons, rust

K

kainophobia (kainotophobia)	novelty, change
kakorrhaphiophobia	failure
kathisophobia	sitting down
kenophobia	void, emptiness, large empty spaces
keraunophobia	lightening, thunder
kinesophobia	motion, movement
kleptophobia	becoming a kleptomanic, robbers
kopophobia	fatigue, weariness, exhaustion

L

laliophobia	talking, speaking, stuttering
leprophobia	leprosy
levophobia	objects on the left, left side of body
linonophobia	string
luiphobia	syphilis
lyssophobia	rabies, becoming insane, becoming hydrophobic

M

maieusiophobia	childbirth, pregnancy
maniaphobia	insanity
mastigophobia	flogging
mechanophobia	machinery
megalophobia	large objects
melissophobia	bees, bee stings, stinging insects
meningitophobia	meningitis
merinthophobia	being bound or tied up
metallophobia	touching metals, metal objects

meterophobia	meteors
microbiophobia	microbes
microphobia	small objects, germs, microorganisms
molysmophobia	contamination, infection
monopathophobia	definite disease
monophobia	being alone, being lonely, desolate places
musophobia	mice
mysophobia	contamination, dirt, filth
mythophobia	lying, myths, stories

N

necrophobia	dead bodies, cadavers, death
negrophobia	negroes
neophobia	novelty, innovation, change
noctiphobia	night
nomatophobia	names
nosophobia	disease
nostophobia	returning home
nyctophobia	darkness, night

O

ochlophobia	crowds
odonophobia	teeth
odynesphobia	pain
odynophobia	pain
oikophobia	home surroundings
olfactophobia	odors
ombrophobia	rain
ommatophobia	eyes
onomatophobia	certain names, hearing certain words
ophidiophobia	snakes, reptiles
opthalmophobia	being stared at
ornithophobia	birds
osmophobia	smells
osphreisiophobia	body odors

P

panphobia (panophobia)	everything
pantophobia	everything
paraliphobia	neglect of duty
parasitophobia	parasites
parthenophobia	girls, virgins

pathophobia	disease
patriophobia	heredity
pavor sceleris	bad men
peccatiphobia	sinning
pediculophobia	lice
pediophobia	dolls, children, infants
peniaphobia	poverty
phagophobia	eating
pharmacophobia	drugs, taking medicine
phasmophobia	ghosts
phengophobia	daylight
phobia	an abnormal, unreasonable fear
phobophobia	fear of developing a phobia
phonophobia	speaking aloud, noise, one's own voice
photoaugiaphobia	glare
photophobia	light
phronemophobia	thinking
phthiriophobia	lice
phthisiophobia	tuberculosis
pnigerophobia	smothering, choking
poinephobia	punishment
polyphobia	many things
ponophobia	work, fatigue
potamophobia	rivers, sheets of water
protophobia	rectum, rectal disease
psychophobia	mind
psychrophobia	cold
pteronophobia	feathers
pyrexiophobia	fever
pyrophobia	fire

R

rhabdophobia	being beaten, sticks
rhypophobia	filth, dirt
rupophobia	filth, dirt

S

satanophobia	devils
scabiophobia	scabies, itch
scelerophobia	bad men, burglars
school phobia	school
scopophobia	being stared at
scotophobia	darkness

selaphobia	flashing light
siderodromophobia	railroad travel, trains
siderophobia	stars
sitophobia	eating, food
spectrophobia	mirrors
spermatophobia	loss of semen
stasibasiphobia	standing upright, walking
stasiphobia	standing upright
stigiophobia	hell
suriphobia	mice
symbolophobia	symbolism
syphilophobia	syphillis

T

tabophobia	tabes dorsalis
taeniophobia	tapeworms
taphephobia	being buried alive, tombs
teratophobia	bearing a monster, of deformed people
tetanophobia	lockjaw, tetanus
thaasophobia	sitting
thalassophobia	sea, ocean
thanatophobia	death, dying
theophobia	God
thermophobia	heat
tocophobia	childbirth
tonitrophobia	thunder
topophobia	certain places
toxicophobia	poison, being poisoned
traumatophobia	injury
tremophobia	trembling
trichinophobia	trichinosis
trichopathophobia	hair
trichophobia	hair
triskaidekaphobia	the number 13
tuberculophobia	tuberculosis

U

uranophobia	heaven

V

vaccinophobia	vaccination
venereophobia	venereal disease
vermiphobia	worms

X

xenophobia   strangers

Z

zelophobia   jealousy
zoophobia   animals

References and Author Index

Abboud, F.M., **346, 349**

Abe, K., & Masui, T. Age-sex trends of phobic and anxiety symptoms. *British Journal of Psychiatry*, 1981, *138*, 197-302. **284**

Abelson, R.P., & Sermat, V. Multidimensional facial expressions. *Journal of Experimental Psychology*, 1962, *63*, 54. **416**

Abplanalp, J.M., Livingston, L., Rose, R.M., & Sandwisch, D. Cortisol and growth hormone responses to psychological stress during the menstrual cycle. *Psychosomatic Medicine*, 1977, *39*, 158-177. **74**

Abraham, K. Notes on the psychoanalytic investigation and treatment of manic-depressive insanity and allied conditions. In W. Gaylin (Ed.), *The meaning of despair*. New York: Science House, 1968. **125**

Abramson, L.Y., **238, 240**

Abramson, L.Y., & Seligman, M.E.P. Modeling psychopathology in the laboratory: History and rationale. In J.D. Maser & M.E.P. Seligman (Eds.), *Psychopathology: Experimental models*. San Francisco: Freeman, 1977, pp. 1-26. **203**

Abramson, L.Y., Seligman, M.E.P., & Teasdale, J.D. Learned helplessness in humans: Critique and reformulation. *Journal of Abnormal Psychology*, 1978, *87*, 32-48. **121, 239, 240**

Aceto, M.D., & Harris, L.S. Antinociceptive mechanism and acute and chronic behavioral effects of clonidine. In H. Lal & S. Fielding (Eds.), *The psychopharmacology of clonidine*. New York: Alan R. Liss, Inc., 1981. **543**

Achenbach, T.M., **725, 730, 785**

Achenbach, T.M. The classification of children's psychiatric symptoms: A factor-analytic study. *Psychological Monographs*, 1966, *80* (Whole No. 615). **407, 408, 409, 411, 716, 717, 719**

Achenbach, T.M. The child behavior profile: I. Boys aged 6-11. *Journal of Consulting and Clinical Psychology*, 1978, *46*, 478-488. **716, 717**

Achenbach, T.M. *Developmental psychopathology (2nd ed.)*. New York: Wiley, 1982. **720**

Achenbach, T.M., & Edelbrock, C.S. The classification of child psychopathology: A review and analysis of empirical efforts. *Psychological Bulletin*, 1978, *85*, 1275-1301. **708, 716, 717, 720**

Achenbach, T.M., & Edelbrock, C.S. Behavioral problems and competencies reported by parents of normal and disturbed children aged 4 through 15. *Monographs of the Society for Research in Child Development*, 1981, *46* (Serial No. 188). **712, 713, 714, 716, 717**

Achenbach, T.M., & Edelbrock, C.S. *Manual for the child behavior checklist and revised child behavior profile*. Burlington, VT: Department of Psychiatry, University of Vermont, 1983. **xxiii, 708, 724, 725**

Ackenheil, M., **563**

Ackerman, S., & Sachar, E. The lactate theory of anxiety: A review and re-evaluation. *Psychosomatic Medicine*, 1974, *36*, 69-81. **780**

Adams, D.B. Brain mechanisms for offense, defense, and submission. *Behavioral & Brain Science*, 1979, *2*, 201-241. **115**

Adams, H.E., **438**

Aden, G.C., & Thein, S.G. Alprazolam compared to diazepam and placebo in the treatment of anxiety. *Journal of Clinical Psychiatry*, 1980, *41*, 245-248. **518, 522, 538**

Ader, R., & Friedman, S.B. Plasma corticosterone response to environmental stimulation: Effects of duration of stimulation and the 24-hour adrenocortical rhythm. *Neuroendocrinology*, 1968, *3*, 378-386. **65**

Adler, R.H., **551**

Aghajanian, G.K., **539, 541, 544, 545, 547, 550, 553, 571**

Aghajanian, G.K. Tolerance of locus coeruleus neurons to morphine and suppression of withdrawal response by clonidine. *Nature (London)*, 1978, *176*, 186-188. **542, 571**

Aghajanian, G.K., & Andrade, R. Locus coeruleus activity *in vitro*: Intrinsic regulation by a calcium-dependent potassium conductance but not alpha-2 adrenoceptors. *Journal of Neuroscience*, 1984, *4*, 161-170. **542**

Aghajanian, G.K., & VanderMaelen, C.P. Alpha$_2$-adrenoceptor-mediated hyperpolarization of locus coeruleus neurons: Intracellular studies in vivo. *Science*, 1982, *215*, 1394-1396. **542**

Agnati, L.F., **539, 540**

Agras, W.S., **132, 233, 234, 334, 339, 363, 364, 367, 426, 427**

Agras, W.S., Chapin, H.N., & Oliveau, D.C. The natural history of phobia: Course and prognosis. *Archives of General Psychiatry*, 1972, *26*, 315-317. **444, 713**

Agras, W.S., Sylvester, D., & Oliveau, D. The epidemiology of common fears and phobias. *Comprehensive Psychiatry*, 1969, *10*, 151-156. **165, 279, 284, 293, 372, 747**

Ainsworth, M.D., **377, 379, 382**

Ainsworth, M.D., & Bell, S.M. Attachment, exploratory behavior and separation: Illustrated by the behavior of one-year-olds in a strange situation. *Child Development*, 1970, *41*, 49-67. **605**

Ainsworth, M.D.S. Attachment: Retrospect and prospect. In C.M. Parkes & J. Stevenson-Hinde (Eds.), *The place of attachment in human behavior*. London: Tavistock Press, 1982. **377**

Akiskal, H.S., **791**

Akiskal, H.S. Diagnosis and classification of affective disorders: New insights from clinical and laboratory approaches. *Psychiatric Developments*, 1983a, *2*, 123-160. **795**

Akiskal, H.S. Dysthymic disorder: Psychopathology of proposed chronic depressive subtypes. *American Journal of Psychiatry*, 1983b, *140*, 11-20. **795**

Akiskal, H.S., & Lemmi, H. Sleep EEG in anxiety and dysthymic disorders. Paper presented at 136th annual meeting, American Psychiatric Association, New York, May 3, 1983. **568**

Akiskal, H.S., Lemmi, H., Dickson, H., King, D., Yerevanian, B., & Van Valkenburg, C. Chronic depressions: Part 2. Sleep EEG differentiation of primary dysthymic disorders from anxious depressives. *Journal of Affective Disorders*, 1984, *6*, 287-295. **568, 786, 793, 794**

Akiskal, H.S., & McKinney, W.T., Jr. Depressive disorders: Toward a unified hypothesis. *Science*, 1973, *182*, 20-28. **793**

Akiskal, H.S., & McKinney, W.T., Jr. Overview of recent research in depression. *Archives of General Psychiatry*, 1975, *32*, 285-305. **xxi, 200**

Alajouanine, T. Dostoiewski's epilepsy. *Brain*, 1983, *86* (part 2), 209-218. **593**

Albala, A.A., **66, 67**

Albertson, T.E., Petersen, S.C., Stark, C.G., Lakin, M.L., & Winters, V.P. The anticonvulsant properties of melatonin or kindled seizures in rats. *Neuropharmacology*, 1981, *20*, 61-66. **49**

Alderman, E.L., **538**

Alexander, F. Emotional factors in essential hypertension. *Psychosomatic Medicine*, 1939, *1*, 173. **360**

Alexander, L., **371**

Allen, L., **373, 408, 411, 712**

Allen, R.E., **81**

Allin, D.M. Successful treatment of anxiety with a single night-time dose of chlormezanone: Double-blind comparison with diazepam. *Current Medical Research & Opinion*, 1981, *8*, 33-8. **518, 522**

Allport, F.H. *Social Psychology*. Cambridge, MA: Houghton Mifflin, 1924. **111**

Aloi, J., **563, 564, 588**

Alpers, D.H. Irritable bowel syndrome—still more questions than answers. *Gastroenterology*, 1981, *80*, 1068. **353**

Alterman, I., **586**

Altersman, R.I., **529**

Altier, H., **581**

Altman, F., **120**

Alvarez, W., **622, 772**

Ambrose, M.J., **17, 18, 19, 20**

American Psychiatric Association. *Diagnostic and statistical manual of mental disorders (DSM-III)*. Washington D.C.: American Psychiatric Association, 1980. **82, 133, 201, 275, 310, 328, 369, 422, 479, 558, 577, 619, 719, 720, 722, 759, 776, 788**

Amin, M., **34, 35, 36, 551**

Amsel, A., **19, 20**

Amsel, A. Frustration, persistence and regression. In H. Kimmel (Ed.), *Experimental psychopathology: Recent research and theory*. New York: Academic Press, 1971, pp. 51-69. **213, 229, 230**

Amsel, A., & Rashotte, M.G. Transfer of experimenter-imposed slow-response patterns to the extinction of a continuously rewarded response. *Journal of Comparative and Physiological Psychology*, 1969, *69*, 185-189. **230**

Amsterdam, B.K. Mirror self-image reactions before age 2. *Developmental Psychology*, 1972, *5*, 297-305. **418**

Ananth, J. Treatment of obsessive compulsive neurosis: Pharmacological approach. *Psychosomatics*, 1976, *17*, 180-183. **508, 509**

Ananth, J. Treatment of obsessive compulsive neurosis with clomipramine (Anafranil). *Journal of International Medical Research*, 1977, *5*, Suppl. 5, 38-41. **504, 507**

Ananth, J., Pecknold, J., van den Steen, N., & Engelsman, F. Double-blind comparative study of clomipramine and amitriptyline in obsessive neurosis. *Progress in Neuropsychopharmacology*, 1981, *5*, 257-262. **504, 506, 586**

Andermann, F., **558**

Andersen, T., **676**

Anderson, D.J., **538, 682**

Anderson, J.R. *Language, memory, and thought*. Hillsdale, NJ: Lawrence Erlbaum Associates: 1976. **158**

Anderson, J.R., & Bower, G.H. A propositional theory of recognition memory. *Memory & Cognition*, 1974, *2*, No. 3, 406-412. **158**

Andrade, R., **542**

Andress, D., **551, 573**

Angst, J., Dobler-Mikola, A., & Scheidegger, P. *A panel study of anxiety states, panic attacks, and phobia among young adults*. Paper presented at the Research Conference on Anxiety Disorders, Panic Attacks and Phobia, Key Biscayne (FL), December 9, 1982. **279**

Anisman, H., & Zacharko, R.M. Depression: The predisposing influence on stress. *Behavioral and Brain Sciences*, 1982, *5*, 89-137. **797**

Annable, L., **538**

Annau, Z., & Kamin, L.J. The conditioned emotional response as a function of intensity of the US. *Journal of Comparative and Physiological Psychology*, 1961, *54*, 428-432. **203**

Anthony, E.J. Behavior disorders. In P.H. Musser (Ed.), *Manual of child psychology* (Vol. 2, 3rd ed.). New York: Wiley, 1970. **408, 411**

Anthony, E.J. Neurotic disorders. In A.M. Freedman, H.I. Kaplan, & B.J. Sadock (Eds.), *Comprehensive textbook of psychiatry* (Vol. 2). Baltimore: Williams & Wilkins, 1975. **410, 411**

Anthony, J., **282, 283**

Anton, W.D., **660**

Antram, S., **82, 534, 550**

Antrobus, J.S., **470**

Anumonye, A. Outpatient psychiatry in a Nigerian University General Hospital 1958-63. *Social Psychiatry*, 1970, *5*, 96-99. **307**

Appel, M.A., **95**

Appleby, I.L., **551**

Appleby, I.L., Klein, D.F., Sachar, E.J., & Levitt, M. Biochemical indices of lactate-induced panic: A preliminary report. In D.F. Klein & J. Rabkin (Eds.), *Anxiety: New research and changing concepts.* New York: Raven Press, 1981. **83, 359**

Apte, J.S., **523, 540**

Arieti, S. Cognition in psychoanalysis. *Journal of The American Academy of Psychoanalysis*, 1980, *8*, 3-23. **103**

Arkin, R.M., Detchon, C.S., & Maruyama, G.M. Roles of attribution, affect, and cognitive interference in test anxiety. *Journal of Personality and Social Psychology*, 1982, *43*, 1111-1124. **121**

Armando, I., **538**

Armor, D.J., **613**

Arnold, M.B. *Emotion and personality, Vol. I: Psychological aspects.* New York: Columbia University Press, 1960. **110, 112, 114**

Aron, C., Simon, P., Larousse, C., & Boissier, J.R. Evaluation of a rapid technique for detecting minor tranquilizers. *Neuropharmacology*, 1971, *10*, 459-469. **31**

Arthur, R.J., **344, 345**

Asakura, M., Tsukamoto, T., & Hasegawa, K. Modulation of rat brain alpha-2- and beta-adrenergic receptor sensitivity following long-term treatment with antidepressants. *Brain Research*, 1982, *2*, 235, 192-197. **529**

Asarch, B., Shih, J., & Kulcsar, A. Decreased ^{3}H-imipramine binding in depressed males and females. *Communications in Psychopharmacology*, 1981, *4*, 425-432. **563**

Asberg, M., **503, 504, 529, 585, 586**

Asberg, M., Thoren, P., & Bertilsson, L. Clomipramine treatment of obsessive disorder-biochemical and clinical aspects. *Psychopharmacology Bulletin*, 1982, *18*, 13-21. **588**

Ascough, J.C., **159**

Ashour, A., **310**

Ashton, S.G., & Goldberg, L.R. In response to Jackson's challenge: The comparative validity of personality scales constructed by the external (empirical) strategy and scales developed intuitively by experts, novices, and laymen. *Journal of Research in Personality*, 1973, *7*, 1-20. **681**

Aston-Jones, G., **550, 554**

Atkins, A., **62, 384**

Auerbach, S.M., **177, 660**

Auerbach, S.M. Surgery-induced stress. In R.H. Woody (Ed.), *Encyclopedia of clinical assessment* (Vol. II). San Francisco-Josey-Bass, 1977. **384**

Auvenshine, C.D., **646**

Averill, J.R., **112, 119, 119-20, 238**

Averill, J.R. Personal control over aversive stimuli and its relationship to stress. *Psychological Bulletin*, 1973, *80*, 286-303. **239**

Avery, D.H., **562**

Avia, M.D., & Kanfer, F.H. Coping with aversive stimulation: The effects of training in a self-management context. *Cognitive Therapy and Research*, 1980, *4*, 73-81. **254**

Ax, A.F. The physiological differentiation between fear and anger in humans. *Psychosomatic Medicine*, 1953, *15*, 433-442. **113, 137, 138, 338**

Ax, A.F. Psychophysiological methodology for the study of schizophrenia. In R. Roessler & N.S. Greenfield (Eds.), *Physiological correlates of psychological disorders*. Madison: University of Wisconsin Press, 1962. **137**

Baade, E., **266, 334, 335, 343, 344**

Baasher, T.A. Survey of mental illness in Wadi Halfa. *World Mental Health*, 1961, *13*, 181-185. **304**

Baasher, T.A. Epidemiological surveys in developing countries. *Acta Psychiatrica Scandinavica Supplementum 296*, 1977, *65*, 45-51. **304**

Bachman, E., **14, 541**

Bachrach, H., **643**

Badal, D.W., **285**

Baer,L., **67**

Bagley, Ch., **742**

Bahn, A.K., **719**

Bailey, P.M., Talbot, A., & Taylor, P.P. A comparison of maternal anxiety levels with anxiety levels manifested in the child dental patient. *Journal of Dentistry for Children*, 1973, *40*, 277-284. **379**

Bailey, W.H., **17, 18, 19, 20**

Baird, A., **68**

Baker, H., & Wills, U. School phobia: classification and treatment. *British Journal of Psychiatry*, 1978, *132*, 492-499. **746**

Ballenger, J.C., **513, 543, 570**

Ballenger, J.C., Post, R.M., Jimerson, D.C., Lake, C.R., Lerner, P., Bunney, W.E., Jr., & Goodwin, F.K. Cerebrospinal fluid (CSF) noradrenergic correlations with anxiety in normals. *Scientific Proceedings, American Psychiatric Association*, 1981, *134*, 235. (Abstract #96). **570**

Ballenger, J.C., Post, R.M., Jimerson, D.C., Lake, C.R., & Zuckerman, M. Neurobiological correlates of depression and anxiety in normal individuals. In R.M. Post & J.C. Ballenger (Eds.), *Neurobiology of mood disorders*. Baltimore, Williams & Wilkins, 1984. **570**

Ballou, S., **571**

Balter, M.B., **281**

Banahan, B.F. Hypertension and stress: A preventive approach. *Journal of Psychosomatic Research*, 1979, *23* (1), 69-75. **661**

Bancroft, J.H.J., **220, 425**

Bandura, A. *Principles of behavior modification*. New York: Holt, Rinehart, & Winston, 1969. **214, 257**

Bandura, A. Self-efficacy: Toward a unifying theory of behavioral change. *Psychological Review*, 1977, *84*, 191-215. **169, 242, 254, 695**

Bandura, A. Reflections on self-efficacy. *Advances in Behavior Research and Therapy*, 1978, *1*, 237-269. **101**

Bandura, A. Self-referent thought: A developmental analysis of self-efficacy. In J.H. Flavell & L. Ross (Eds.) *Social cognitive development: Frontiers and possible futures*. Cambridge: Cambridge University Press, 1981. **418**

Bandura, A. Self-efficacy mechanism in human agency. *American Psychologist*, 1982, *37*, 122-147. **101, 623**

Bandura, A., Blanchard, E.B., & Ritter, B. Relative efficacy of desensitization and modeling approaches for inducing behavioral, affective, and attitudinal changes. *Journal of Personality and Social Psychology*, 1969, *13*, 173-199. **427**

Bandura, A., & Menlove, F.L. Factors determining vicarious extinction of avoidance behavior through symbolic modeling. *Journal of Personality and Social Psychology*, 1968, *8*, 99-108. **375, 708**

Bandura, A., & Rosenthal, T. Vicarious classical conditioning as a function of arousal level. *Journal of Personality and Social Psychology*, 1966, *3*, 54-62. **375**

Baraldi, M., **11**

Baraldi, M., Grandison, L., & Guidotti, A. Distribution and metabolism of muscimol in the brain and other tissues of the rat. *Neuropharmacology*, 1979, *18*, 57-62. **11**

Baraldi, M., Guidotti, A., Schwartz, J.P., & Costa, E. GABA receptors in clonal cell lines: A model to study benzodiazepine action at the molecular level. *Science*, 1979, *205*, 821-823. **43**

Barber, T.X., & Hahn, K.W. Experimental studies in "hypnotic" behavior: Physiologic and subjective effects of imagined pain. *Journal of Nervous and Mental Disease*, 1964, *139*, 416-425. **436**

Barchus, J.D., **118**

Bardach, E., & Weerts, T.C. *Assessment of controllability and vividness of visual imagery in two types of phobia*. Unpublished manuscript, University of Iowa. **164**

Barker, B.M., Barker, H.R., Jr., & Wadsworth, A.P. Factor analysis of the state-trait anxiety inventory. *Journal of Clinical Psychology*, 1977, *32*, 450-455. **660**

Barker, H.R., Jr., **660**

Barker, J.L., **28, 40, 540**

Barker, J.L., & Ransom, B.R. Pentobarbitone pharmacology of mammalian central neurones grown in tissue culture. *Journal of Physiology* (London), 1978, *280*, 355-372. **7, 11, 12**

Barker, M., **660**

Barlow, D.H., **xxiv, 233, 234, 253, 386, 434-35, 454, 480, 481, 486, 487, 488, 493, 494, 496, 497, 498, 499, 500, 643, 768, 773**

Barlow, D.H., Agras, W.S., Leitenberg, H., & Wincze, J.P. An experimental analysis of the effectiveness of "shaping" in reducing maladaptive avoidance behavior: An analogue study. *Behaviour Research and Therapy*, 1970, *8*, 165-173. **427**

✳ Barlow, D.H., & Beck, J.G. The psychosocial treatment of anxiety disorders: Current status, future directions. In J.B.W. Williams & R.L. Spitzer (Eds.), *Psychotherapy research: Where are we and where should we go?* New York: Guilford Press, 1984. **187, 195, 422, 446, 480, 760, 771**

✳ Barlow, D.H., Vermilyea, J.A., Blanchard, E.B., Vermilyea, B.B., DiNardo, P.A. & Cerny, *The phenomenon of panic*. in press. **489**

Barlow, D.H., Cohen, A.S., Waddell, M.T., Vermilyea, B.B., Klosko, J.S., Blanchard, E.B., & DiNardo, P.A. Panic and generalized anxiety disorders: Nature and treatment. *Behavioral Therapy*, in press. **494**

Barlow, D.H., DiNardo, P.A., Vermilyea, B.B., Vermilyea, J.A., & Blanchard, E.B. *Co-morbidity within the anxiety disorders*. Manuscript submitted for publication. **482, 483**

Barlow, D.H., Leitenberg, H., Agras, W.S., & Wincze, J.P. The transfer gap in systematic desensitization: An analogue study. *Behaviour Research and Therapy*, 1969, *7*, 191-196. **427**

✳ Barlow, D.H., & Maser, J.D. Psychopathology in anxiety disorders. *Journal of Behavioral Assessment*, in press. **489**

Barlow, D.H., & Mavissakalian, M. Directions in the assessment and treatment of phobia. In M. Mavissakalian & D.H. Barlow (Eds.), *Phobia: Psychological and pharmacological treatment*. New York: Guilford Press, 1981, pp. 199-245. **790**

Barlow, D.H., Mavissakalian, M., & Schofield, L. Patterns of desynchrony in agoraphobia: A preliminary report. *Behaviour Research and Therapy*, 1980, *18*, 441-448. **132, 165, 363, 497**

Barlow, D.H., Sakheim, D.K., & Beck, J.G. Anxiety increases sexual arousal. *Journal of Abnormal Psychology*, 1983, *92*, 49-54. **150, 499**

Barlow, D.H., & Wolfe, B. Behavioral approaches to anxiety disorders: A report on the NIMH-SUNY research conference. *Journal of Consulting and Clinical Psychology*, 1981, *49*, 448-454. **99**

Barnet, S.A. Physiological effects of "social stress" in wild rats: I. The adrenal cortex. *Journal of Psychosomatic Research*, 1958, *3*, 1-11. **55**

Barnett, J. Interpersonal processes, cognition, and the analysis of character. *Contemporary Psychoanalysis*, 1980, *39*, 4, 291-301. **103, 104**

Baroldi, G., Falzi, G., & Mariani, F. Sudden coronary death. A postmortem study in 208 selected cases compared to 97 "control" subjects. *American Heart Journal*, 1979, *98*, 20-31. **346**

Barrett, C.L., **373, 708, 709, 712, 713, 714, 715**

Barrett, J., **547**

Barrett, J. Psychiatric diagnosis (research diagnostic criterion) in symptomatic volunteers. *Archives of General Psychiatry*, 1981, *38*, 153-157. **357**

Barrett, K.C., **123**

Barrios, B.A., Hartmann, D.P., & Shigetomi, C. Fears and anxiety in children. In E.J. Mash & L.G. Terdal (Eds.), *Behavioral assessment of childhood disorders*. New York: Guilford Press, 1981. **372**

Barta, S.G., **92**

Barter, J., **698, 699**

Bartholomay, A., **59**

Bartlett, E.S., & Izard, C.E. A dimensional and discrete emotions investigation of the subjective experience of emotion. In C.E. Izard (Ed.), *Patterns of emotions: A new analysis of anxiety and depression*. New York: Academic Press, 1972. **124**

Bartlett, J.C., & Santrock, J.W. Affect-dependent episodic memory in young children. *Child Development*, 1979, *50*, 513-518. **149**

Basch, M.F. The concept of affect: A re-examination. *Journal of the American Psychoanalytic Association*, 1976, *24*, 759-777. **595**

Bash, K.W., & Bash-Liechti, J. Studies on the epidemiology of neuropsychiatric disorders among the rural population of the province of Khuzestan, Iran. *Social Psychiatry*, 1969, *4*, 137-143. **304**

Bash, K.W., & Bash-Liechti, J. Studies on the epidemiology of neuropsychiatric disorders among the population of the city of Shiraz, Iran. *Social Psychiatry*, 1974, *9*, 163-171. **304**

Basham, R.B., **94**

Bash-Liechti, J., **304**

Basowitz, H., **60, 65**

Basowitz, H., Korchin, S.J., & Oken, D. Anxiety and performance changes with a minimal dose of epinephrine. *Archives of Neurology and Psychiatry*, 1956, *27*, 98-106. **534, 550**

Bassan, M., **534, 550**

Bassiakos, L., **426**

Bauer, D. An exploratory study of developmental changes in children's fears. *Journal of Child Psychology and Psychiatry*, 1976, *17*, 69-74. **374**

Baulu, J., **553**

Baum, M. Extinction of avoidance responding through response prevention (flooding). *Psychological Bulletin*, 1970, *74*, 276-284. **205, 221, 233**

Baysinger, C.M., **236**

Beard, G.. *A practical treatise on nervous exhaustion (neurasthenia)*. New York: William Wood, 1880. **778**

Beard, O.W., **347**

Beardslee, W.R., Bemporad, J., Keller, M.B., & Klerman, G.L. Children of parents with major affective disorder: A review. *American Journal of Psychiatry*, 1983, *140*, 825-832. **293**

Beaton, R., **94**

Bebbington, P.E. The epidemiology of depressive disorder. *Culture, Medicine and Psychiatry*, 1978, *2*, 297-341. **299**

Beck, A.T., **126, 144, 431**

Beck, A.T. Thinking and depression. *Archives of General Psychiatry*, 1963, *9*, 324-333. **192, 193**

Beck, A.T. Role of fantasies in psychotherapy and psychopathology. *Journal of Nervous and Mental Disease*, 1970, *150*, 3-17. **194**

Beck, A.T. *Depression: Causes and treatment*. Philadelphia: University of Pennsylvania Press, 1972. **693**

Beck, A.T. *Cognitive therapy and the emotional disorders*. New York: International Universities Press, Inc., 1976. **185, 241, 425, 431, 474, 675**

Beck, A.T., Laude, R., & Bohnert, M. Ideational components of anxiety neurosis. *Archives of General Psychiatry*, 1974, *31*, 319-325. **194, 494, 625**

Beck, A.T., Rush, A.J., Shaw, B.F., & Emery, G. *Cognitive therapy of depression*. New York: Guilford Press, 1979. **431, 705**

Beck, J.C., **58**

Beck, J.G., **150, 187, 195, 422, 446, 480, 499, 760, 771**

Beck, J.G., & Barlow, D.H. Current conceptualizations of sexual dysfunction: A review and an alternative perspective. *Clinical Psychology Review*, in press. **499**

Beck, J.G., Barlow, D.H., & Sakheim, D.K. The effects of attentional focus and partner arousal on sexual responding in functional and dysfunctional men. *Behaviour Research and Therapy*, 1983, *21*, 1-8. **500**

Beck, P., **375, 376**

Becker, H.C., & Flaherty, C.F. Chlordiazepoxide and ethanol additively reduce gustatory negative contrast. *Psychopharmacology*, 1983, *80*, 35-37. **476**

Becker, R.D. Therapeutic approaches to psychopathological reactions to hospitalization. *International Journal of Child Psychotherapy*, 1972, *1* (2), 64-97. **379**

Beck-Friis, J., **519, 522, 540**

Bedell, J., **660**

Bedford, A., **752**

Beech, H.R., & Perigault, F. Toward a theory of obsessional disorder. In H.R. Beech (Ed.), *Obsessional states*. London: Methuen & Co., Ltd., 1974, pp. 113-141. **231**

Beech, H.R., & Vaughan, M. *Behavioral treatment of obsessional states.* New York: Wiley, 1978. **426**

Beer, B., **12, 32, 34, 37, 50**

Beiser, M., **309**

Beiser, M., Benfari, R.C., Collomb, H., & Ravel, J. Measuring psychoneurotic behavior in cross-cultural surveys. *Journal of Nervous and Mental Disease,* 1976, *163,* 10-23. **309**

Beiser, M., Burr, W.A., Ravel, J., & Collomb, H. Illnesses of the spirit among the Serer of Senegal. *American Journal of Psychiatry,* 1973, *130,* 881-886. **309**

Beiser, M., Ravel, J., Collomb, H., & Egelhoff, C. Assessing psychiatric disorder among the Serer of Senegal. *Journal of Nervous and Mental Disease,* 1972, *154,* 141-151. **309**

Bell, S.M., **605**

Bellack, **xxiv**

Belleville, R.E. MMPI score changes induced by lysergic acid diethylamide (LSD-25). *Journal of Clinical Psychology,* 1956, *12,* 279-282. **647**

Belluzzi, J.D., **35, 36, 539**

Bemporad, J., **293**

Benedikt, P. Uber Platzchwindel. *Allgemeine Wiener medizinische Zeitung,* 1870, *15,* 488. **737**

Benfari, R.C., **309**

Benfari, R.C., Beiser, M., Leighton, A.H., & Merteus, C. Some dimensions of psychoneurotic behavior in an urban sample. *Journal of Nervous and Mental Disease,* 1972, *155,* 77-90. **309**

Bengston, D., **372**

Benjamin, J.D. Some developmental observations relating to the theory of anxiety. *Journal of the American Psychoanalytic Association,* 1961, *9,* 652-668. **605**

Benjamin, J.D. Further comments on some developmental aspects of anxiety. In H.S. Gaskill (Ed.), *Counterpoint: Libidinal object and subject.* New York: International Universities Press, 1963. **605**

Benjamin, J.D. Developmental biology and psychoanalysis. In N.S. Greenfield & W.C. Lewis (Eds.), *Psychoanalysis and current biological thought.* Madison: University of Wisconsin Press, 1965. **605**

Benjamin, S., Marks, I.M., & Huson, J. Active muscular relaxation in desensitization of phobic patients. *Psychological Medicine,* 1972, *2,* 381-390. **440**

Bennett, C.D., **39, 50**

Benson, D.I., **12**

Benson, H. *The relaxation response.* New York: Morrow & Company, 1975. **476**

Benson, H., Herd, J.A., Morse, W.H., & Kelleher, R.T. Behavioral induction of arterial hypertension and its reversal. *American Journal of Physiology,* 1969, *217,* 30-34. **238**

Bentler, P.M. Semantic space is (approximately) bipolar. *Journal of Psychology*, 1969, *71*, 33-40. **682**

Berens, S.C., **74, 75**

Berg, I. A follow-up study of school phobic adolescents admitted to an in-patient unit. *Journal of Child Psychology and Psychiatry*, 1970, *11*, 37-47. **399**

Berg, I. School phobia in the children of agoraphobic women. *British Journal of Psychiatry*, 1976, *128*, 86-89. **293, 393, 395, 749**

Berg, I., Butler, A., & Pritchard, J. Psychiatric illness in the mothers of school phobic adolescents. *British Journal of Psychiatry*, 1974, *125*, 466-467. **293, 395, 400**

Berg, I., Marks, I., McGuire, R., & Lipsedge, M. School phobia and agoraphobia. *Psychological Medicine*, 1974, *4*, 428-434. **293, 397**

Berg, I., Nichols, K., & Pritchard, C. School phobia, its classification and relationship to dependency. *Journal of Child Psychology and Psychiatry*, 1969, *10*, 123-141. **746**

Bergen, J.R., **8, 58, 149-154**

Bergen, K., **34**

Bergman, A., **417, 418**

Bergman, M.D., **40**

Berkowitz, L. Whatever happened to the frustration-aggression hypothesis? *American Behavioral Scientist*, 1978, *21*, 691-708. **140**

Berkowitz, L. Aversively stimulated aggression: Some parallels and differences in research with animals and humans. *American Psychologist*, 1983, *38*, 1135-1144. **156, 157**

Berman, J.S., **102**

Berman, J.S., & Katzev, R.D. Factors involved in the rapid elimination of avoidance behavior. *Behaviour Research and Therapy*, 1972, *10*, 247-256. **234**

Bernadt, M.W., Silverstone, T., & Singleton, W. Behavioural and subjective effects of beta-adrenergic blockage in phobic subjects. *British Journal of Psychiatry*, 1980, *137*, 452-457. **514, 515, 546, 750**

Bernard, P., Bergen, K., Sobisky, R., & Robson, R.D. CGS 8216 (2-phenylpyrazol [4,3c]quinolin-3-(5H)-one)—an orally active benzodiazepine antagonist. *Pharmacologist*, 1981, *23*, 150. **34**

Berney, T., Kolvin, I., Bhate, S.R., Garside, R.F., Jeans, J., Kay, B., & Scarth, L. School phobia: A therapeutic trial with clomipramine and short-term outcome. *British Journal of Psychiatry*, 1981, *138*, 110-118. **392, 393, 511, 513**

Bernreuter, R.G. The theory and construction of the personality inventory. *Journal of Social Psychology*, 1933, *4*, 387-405. **654**

Bernstein, D.A., **258, 336**

Bernstein, D.A. Situational factors in behavioral fear assessment: A progress report. *Behavior Therapy*, 1973, *4*, 41-48. **258**

Bernstein, D., & Borkovec, T.D. *Progressive relaxation training*. Champaign, IL: Research Press, 1973. **253, 475**

Bernstein, D.A., & Paul, G.L. Some comments on therapy analogue research with small animal "phobias". *Journal of Behavior Therapy & Experimental Psychiatry*, 1971, *2*, 225-237. **256**

Berrettini, W.H., **563**

Berrettini, W.H., Nurnberger, J.R., Post, R.M., & Gershon, E.S. Platelet ³H-imipramine binding in euthymic bipolar patients. *Psychiatry Research*, 1982, *7*, 215-219. **563**

Berry, J.C., & Martin, B. GSR reactivity as a function of anxiety, instructions, and sex. *Journal of Abnormal and Social Psychology*, 1957, *54*, 9-12. **120**

Bersh, P.J. Eysenck's theory of incubation: A critical analysis. *Behaviour Research and Therapy*, 1980, *18*, 11-17. **210**

Bertalanffy, L., von. *General system theory, foundations, development, applications*. New York: George Braziller, 1968. **414**

Bertilsson, L., **588**

Bevan, W. On getting in bed with a lion. *American Psychologist*, 1980, *35*, 779-789. **247**

Bhagavan, H., **394, 395, 508**

Bharucha, M., **523, 540**

Bhate, S.R., **392, 393, 511, 513**

Bhattacharya, S.K., **538**

Bianchi, G.N., & Phillips, J. A comparative trial of doxepin and diazepam in anxiety states. *Psychopharmacologia*, 1972, *25*, 86-95. **544**

Bice, T., **302**

Bieber, I. *Cognitive Psychoanalysis*. New York: J. Aronson, 1980. **103**

Bieber, I., Dain, H.J., Dince, P.R., Drellich, M.G., Grand, H.G., Gundlach, R.H., Kremer, M.W., Rifkin, A.H., Wilbur, C., & Bieber, T.B. *Homosexuality: A psychoanalytic study of male homosexuals*. New York: Basic Books, 1962. **614**

Bieber, T.B., **614**

Biersner, R.J., **135**

Biggio, G., **36**

Billingsley, M.L., & Kubena, R.K. The effects of naloxone and picrotoxin on the sedative and anti-conflict effects of benzodiazepines. *Life Sciences*, 1978, *22*, 897-906. **11**

Binik, Y., **239, 240**

Biran, M., & Wilson, G.T. Treatment of phobic disorders using cognitive and exposure methods: A self-efficacy analysis. *Journal of Consulting and Clinical Psychology*, 1981, *49*, 886-899. **99, 434**

Birch, H.G., **376, 382, 383, 409, 411, 733**

Bird, E.D., Caro, A.J., & Pilling, J.B. A sex-related factor in the inheritance of Huntington's Chorea. *Annals of Human Genetics*, 1974, *37*, 255-260. **327**

Bishop, P., **526**

Blaccioniere, M., **211, 243**

Black, A. The natural history of obsessional neurosis. In H.R. Beech (Ed.), *Obsessional states*. London: Methuen & Company, 1974. **579**

Black, A.H., **205**

Blaker, W.D., **32, 34**

Blanchard, E.B., **427, 441, 480, 481, 482, 483, 489, 494, 768, 773**

Blankstein, K.R. Relationships between Spielberger trait anxiety and Lykken social and physical trait anxiety. *Journal of Clinical Psychology*, 1976, *32* (4), 781-782. **661**

Blazer, D.G., **281, 282**

Bleuler, E. *Lehrbuch der Psychiatrie*, 3. Auflage. Berlin: Springer, 1920. **745**

Bleuler, M. *The schizophrenic disorders*. New Haven: Yale University Press, 1978. **405, 408, 411**

Bliss, E.L., Migeon, C.J., Branch, C.H., & Samuels, L.T. Reaction of the adrenal cortex to emotional stress. *Psychosomatic Medicine*, 1956, *18*, 56-76. **56, 58, 59**

Blizard, P.J., **661**

Bloch, E., *8*, 58, 149-154

Bloch, S., & Brackenridge, C. Psychological performance and biochemical factors in medical students under examination stress. *Journal of Psychosomatic Research*, 1972, *16*, 25-33. **341**

Block, J. *The challenge of response sets*. New York: Appleton-Century-Crofts, 1965. **681, 683, 694**

Block, J. *Lives through time*. Berkeley, CA: Bancroft Books, 1971. **419, 681**

Block, J. Advancing the psychology of personality: Paradigmatic shift or improving the quality of research. In D. Magnusson & N.S. Endler (Eds.), *Personality at the crossroads: Current issues in interactional psychology*. Hillsdale, NJ: Erlbaum, 1977. **681**

Bloom, F.E., **536, 554**

Bloom, J., **310**

Bloxom, B.M., **126**

Blum, G.S. A study of the psychoanalytic theory of psychosexual development. *Genetic Psychology Monographs*, 1949, *39*, 3-99. **613**

Blumberg, S.H., **415, 417, 689**

Blumberg, S.H., & Izard, C.E. *Emotions and cognition in depressed and non-depressed ten year old children*. Unpublished masters thesis, University of Delaware, 1983. **125, 126**

Boarder, M.R., **20**

Bockaert, J., **555**

Boersma, K., den Hengst, S., Dekker, J., & Emmelkamp, P.M.G. Exposure and response prevention in the natural environment: A comparison with obsessive-compulsive patients. *Behaviour Research and Therapy*, 1976, *14*, 19-24. **428**

Bogdonoff, M.D., Estes, E.H., Harlan, W.R., Trout, D.L., & Kirsher, N. Metabolic and cardiovascular changes during a state of acute central nervous system arousal. *Journal of Clinical Endocrinology and Metabolism*, 1960, *20*, 1333-1340. **341**

Bohnert, M., **194, 494, 625**

Boice, R., **454, 496, 497**

Boissier, J.R., **31**

Bolles, R.C., **210**

Bolles, R.C. Species-specific defense reactions and avoidance learning. *Psychological Review*, 1970, *77*, 32-48. **227, 265, 421**

Bolme, P., **539, 540**

Bond, A., & Lader, M. Benzodiazepines and aggression. In M. Sandler (Ed.), *Psychopharmacology of aggression*. New York: Raven Press, 1979. **81**

Bonetti, E.P., **29, 33, 34, 35**

Bonn, J.A., Turner, P., & Hicks, D.C. Beta-adrenergic receptor blockage with practolol in treatment of anxiety. *Lancet*, 1972, *1*, 814-815. **546**

Bootzin, R.R. Stimulus control treatment for insomnia. *Proceedings of the 80th annual convention of the American Psychological Association*, 1972, *7*, 395-396. **472**

Borenstern, M., **66**

Boring, E.G. *A history of experimental psychology* (2nd ed.). New York: Appleton-Century-Crofts, 1950. **245**

Borkovec, T.D., **253, 466, 468, 469, 470, 472, 473, 475, 476**

Borkovec, T.D. Heart-rate process during systematic desensitization and implosive therapy for analogue anxiety. *Behavior Therapy*, 1974, *5*, 636-641. **465**

Borkovec, T.D. Pseudo (experiential)-insomnia and idiopathic (objective) insomnia: Theoretical and therapeutic issues. In H.J. Eysenck & S. Rachman (Eds.), *Advances in behaviour research and therapy* (Vol. 2). London: Pergamon Press, 1979, pp. 27-55. **463**

Borkovec, T.D. Unpublished manuscript, 1983. **253, 430, 494**

Borkovec, T.D., & Grayson, J.B. Consequences of increasing the functional impact of internal emotional stimuli. In K. Blankstein, P. Pliner, & L.H. Polivey (Eds.), *Advances in the study of communication and affects* (Vol. 3). New York: Plenum Press, 1980. **437**

Borkovec, T.D., & Hennings, B.L. The role of physiological attention-focusing in the relaxation treatment of sleep disturbance, general tension, and specific stress reaction. *Behaviour Research and Therapy*, 1978, *16*, 7-19. **476**

Borkovec, T.D., Robinson, E., Pruzinsky, T., & DePree, J.A. Preliminary exploration of worry: Some characteristics and processes. *Behaviour Research and Therapy*, 1983, *21*, 9-16. **95, 252, 467, 468, 469**

Borkovec, T.D., & Sides, J.K. The contribution of relaxation and expectancy to fear reduction via graded, imaginal exposure to feared stimuli. *Behaviour Research and Therapy*, 1979, *17*, 529-540. **438, 466**

Borkovec, T.D., Wilkinson, L., Folensbee, R., & Lerman, C. Stimulus control applications to the treatment of worry. *Behaviour Research and Therapy*, 1983, *21*, 247-251. **473**

Bosisio, E., Sergi, J., Sega, R., & Libretti, A. Respiratory response to carbon dioxide after propranolol in normal subjects. *Respiration*, 1979, *37*, 197-202. **349**

Boulenger, J.-P., **551, 558-59, 561, 562, 565, 567, 568, 569, 570, 571, 572, 574, 795**

Boulenger, J.-P., Patel, J., & Marangos, P.J. Effects of caffeine and theophylline on adenosine and benzodiazepine receptors in human brain. *Neuroscience Letters*, 1982, *30*, 161-166. **575**

Boulenger, J.-P., Patel, J., Post, R.M., Parma, A., & Marangos, P.J. Chronic caffeine consumption increases the number of brain adenosine receptors. *Life Science*, 1983, *2*, 1135-1142. **575**

Boulenger, J.-P., & Uhde, T.W. Caffeine consumption and anxiety: Preliminary results of a survey comparing patients with anxiety disorders and normal controls. *Psychopharmacology Bulletin*, 1982b, *18*, 53-57. **551, 564, 573, 574**

Boulenger, J.-P., & Uhde, T.W. Le traitement des attaques de panique. *Encephale*, 1983. **558**

Boulenger, J.-P., Uhde, T.W., Wolff, E.A., & Post, R.M. Increased sensitivity to caffeine in patients with panic disorders: Preliminary evidence. *Archives of General Psychiatry*, 1984. **573**

Boulougouris, J.C., **220, 425, 428**

Boulougouris, J.C. Variables affecting the behavior modification of obsessive-compulsive patients treated by flooding. In J.C. Boulougouris & A.D. Rabavilas (Eds.), *The treatment of phobic and obsessive-compulsive disorders*. Oxford: Pergamon Press, 1977. **581**

Boulougouris, J.C., & Bassiakos, L. Prolonged flooding in cases with obsessive-compulsive neurosis. *Behaviour Research and Therapy*, 1973, *11*, 227-231. **426**

Bourassa, M.G., **538**

Bourne, P.G., Rose, R.M., & Mason, J.W. Urinary 17-OCHS levels. Data on seven helicopter ambulance medics in combat. *Archives of General Psychiatry*, 1967, *17*, 104-110. **59, 345**

Bourne, P.G., Rose, R.M., & Mason, J.W. 17-OCHS levels in combat. Special forces "A" team under threat of attack. *Archives of General Psychiatry*, 1968, *19*, 135-140. **345, 61, 63**

Boushey, H.A. Neural mechanisms in bronchial asthma. In H. Weiner, M.A. Hofer & A.J. Stunkard (Eds.), *Brain, behavior and bodily disease*. New York: Raven Press, 1981. **352**

Bouton, M.E., & Bolles, R.C. Role of conditioned contextual stimuli in reinstatement of extinguished fear. *Journal of Experimental Psychology: Animal Behavior Processes*, 1979, *5*, 368-378. **210**

Boutwell, R.C., **659**

Bowden, C.L., **67, 520, 523, 540, 544, 545**

Bowen, R.C., & Kohout, J. The relationship between agoraphobia and primary affective disorders. *Canadian Journal of Psychiatry*, 1979, *24*, 317-322. **561-62**

Bower, G.H., **144, 158**

Bower, G.H. Mood & memory. *American Psychologist*, 1981, *36* (2), 129-148. **142, 143, 144, 145, 146, 157, 447**

Bower, G.H., & Cohen, P.R. Emotional influences in memory and thinking: Data and theory. In S. Fiske & M. Clark (Eds.), *Affect and social cognition.* Hillsdale, NJ: Erlbaum Assoc., 1982. **142**

Bowers, K., & Meichenbaum, D. (Eds.). *The unconscious reconsidered.* New York: John Wiley, in press. **106**

Bowery, N.G., Hill, D.R., Hudson, A.L., Dauble, A., Middlemiss, D.N., Shaw, J., & Turnbull, M.J. (-)Baclofen decreases neurotransmitter release in the mammalian CNS by an action at the novel GABA receptor. *Nature*, 1980, *283*, 92-94. **13, 15, 40**

Bowlby, J. *Attachment and loss, Vol. 2: Separation: Anxiety and anger.* New York: Basic Books, 1973. **114, 236, 377, 417, 602, 603, 605, 608**

Bowlby, J. *Loss: Sadness and depression.* New York: Basic Books, 1980. **236**

Boyd, J.H., **282, 283**

Boyd, T.L., **211, 218, 226**

Boyd, T.L., & Levis, D.J. The effects of single component extinction of a three-component serial CS on the resistance to extinction of the conditioned avoidance response. *Learning & Motivation*, 1976, *7*, 517-531. **226**

Boyd, T.L., & Levis, D.J. Exposure in a necessary condition for fear reduction. *Behaviour Research and Therapy*, 1983, *21*, 143-150. **456**

Boyd, J.H., Burke, J.D., Jr., Gruenberg, E., Holzer, C.E. III, Rae, D.S., George, L.K., Karno, M., Stoltzman, R., McEvoy, L., & Nestadt, G. Exclusion criteria of DSM-III: A study of co-occurrence of hierarchy-free syndromes. *Archives of General Psychiatry*, 1984, *41* (10), 983-989. **xxx**

Boyer, A., **720**

Brackbill, G., & Little, K.B. MMPI correlates of the Taylor scale of manifest anxiety. *Journal of Consulting Psychology*, 1954, *18*, 433-436. **649**

Brackenridge, C., **341**

Bradford, J.L. *Sex differences in anxiety.* Unpublished doctoral dissertation, University of Minnesota, 1968. **614**

Brady, J.P., & Levitt, E.E. Hypnotically induced visual hallucinations. *Psychosomatic Medicine*, 1966, *28*, 351-353. **159**

Brady, J.V., **55, 238**

Brady, J.V. Emotion: Some conceptual problems and psychophysiological experiments. In M.B. Arnold (Ed.), *Feelings and emotions: The Loyola Symposium.* New York: Academic Press, 1970. **115**

Brady, J.V. Experimental studies of stress and anxiety. In I. Kutash & L. Schlesinger (Eds.), *Handbook on stress and anxiety*, 1980, pp. 207-236. **238**

Braestrup, C., **34, 35, 36, 538, 551**

Braestrup, C., Honore, T., Nielsen, M., Petersen, E.N., & Jensen, L. H. Benzodiazepine receptor ligands with negative efficacy: Chloride channel coupling. *Advances in Biochemistry and Psychopharmacology*, 1983, *38*, 249-254. **30, 41, 42**

Braestrup, C., & Nielsen, M. Benzodiazepine receptors. *Arzneimittelforschung*, 1980, *30*, 852-857. **7, 13**

Braestrup, C., & Nielsen, M. ^{3}H-Propyl-β-carboline-3-carboxylate as a selective radioligand for the BZ^1, benzodiazepine receptor subclass. *Journal of Neurochemistry*, 1981, *37*, 333-341. **34, 50**

Braestrup, C., Schmiechen, R., Neef, G., Nielsen, M., & Petersen, E.N. Interactions of convulsive ligands with benzodiazepine receptors. *Science*, 1982, *216*, 1241-1243. **32, 34**

Braestrup, C., & Squires, R.F. Specific benzodiazepine receptors in rat brain characterized by high affinity ^{3}H-diazepam binding. *Proceedings of the National Academy of Sciences, U.S.A.*, 1977, *74*, 3805-3809. **28, 537**

Braestrup, C., & Squires, R.F. Brain specific benzodiazepine receptors. *British Journal of Psychiatry*, 1978, *133*, 249-260. **28**

Bram, I. Psychic trauma in the pathogenesis of exopthalmic goiter. *Endocrinology*, 1927, *11*, 106-121. **352**

Branch, C.H., **56, 58, 59**

Brautbar, N., Leibovici, H., Finlander, P., Campanese, V., Penia, C., & Massry, S.G. Mechanism of hypophosphatemia during acute hyperventilation. *Clinical Research*, 1980, *28*, 377A. **350**

Brauzer, B., Goldstein, B., Steinbook, R., & Jacobson, A. The treatment of mixed anxiety and depression with loxapine: A controlled comparative study. *Journal of Clinical Pharmacology*, 1974, *14*, 455-463. **519, 522, 540**

Braverman, P., **542**

Bregman, E. An attempt to modify the emotional attitudes of infants by the conditioned response technique. *Journal of Genetic Psychology*, 1934, *45*, 169-198. **208**

Brehm, S.S., **95**

Bremer, J. A social psychiatric investigation of a small community in Northern Norway. *Acta Psychiatrica Scandinavica Supplementum 62*, 1951, 1-62. **278, 304**

Brennan, J.F., & Riccio, D.C. Stimulus generalization of suppression in rats following aversively motivated instrumental or Pavlovian training. *Journal of Comparative and Physiological Psychology*, 1975, *88*, 570-579. **212**

Brenner, C. An addendum to Freud's theory of anxiety. *International Journal of Psycho-Analysis*, 1953, *34*, 18-24. **603, 609-10, 611**

Brenner, C. *An elementary textbook of psychoanalysis* (2nd ed.). New York: International Universities Press, 1973. **701**

Brenner, C. *The mind in conflict*. New York: International Universities Press, 1983. **598, 603**

Brenner, R., **66**

Bretherton, I., & Ainsworth, M. Responses of 1-year-olds to a stranger in a strange situation. In M. Lewis & L.A. Rosenblum (Eds.), *The origins of fear*. New York: Wiley, 1974. **377, 379, 382**

Breznitz, S. A study of worrying. *British Journal of Social and Clinical Psychology*, 1971, *10*, 271-279. **94**

Brick, J., **571**

Bridges, P.K., Jones, M.T., & Leak, D.A. A comparative study of four physiological concomitants of anxiety. *Archives of General Psychiatry*, 1968, *19*, 141-145. **61**

Briley, M.S., Raisman, R., Sechter, D., Zarifian, E., & Langer, S.Z. [^{3}H]-Imipramine binding in human platelets: A new biochemical parameter in depression. *Neuropharmacology*, 1980, *19*, 1209-1210. **563**

Brimer, C.J., **205**

Brisson, G., **71**

Broadbent, D. *Decision and stress*. New York: Academic Press, 1971. **622**

Broadhurst, P.L. Abnormal animal behavior. In H.J. Eysenck (Ed.), *Handbook of abnormal psychology*. New York: Basic Books, 1960, pp. 726-763. **235**

Broadhurst, P.L. Animal studies bearing on abnormal behavior. In H.J. Eysenck (Ed.), *Handbook of abnormal psychology* (2nd ed.). New York: Basic Books, 1973, pp. 721-754. **235**

Brody, R.D., **400, 405, 411, 716**

Bronson, F.H., & Eleftheriou, B.E. Adrenal responses to crowding in peromysus and C5 BL/105 mice. *Physiological Zoology*, 1963, *36*, 161-166. **55**

Bronson, F.H., & Eleftheriou, B.E. Chronic physiological effect of fighting in mice. *Journal of General and Comparative Endocrinology*, 1964, *4*, 9-14. **55**

Bronson, F.H., & Eleftheriou, B.E. Chronic physiological effects of fighting mice. Separation of physical and psychobiological causes. *Science*, 1965, *147*, 627-628. **55**

Bronson, W.C. Stable patterns of behaviors: The significance of enduring orientations for personality development. In J.P. Hill (Ed.), *Minnesota symposia on child psychology* (Vol. 2). Minneapolis: University of Minnesota, 1968. **113**

Brookes, S., **21**

Brooks, J., **605**

Brooks-Gunn, J., **418**

Brougham, L., **428**

Brown, A., **516, 517, 538, 545**

Brown, B. Beyond separation. In D. Hall & M. Stacey (Eds.), *Beyond separation*. London: Routledge and Kegan Paul, 1979. **372, 379**

Brown, B.B. Visual recall ability and eye movements. *Psychophysiology*, 1968, *4*, 300-306. **159**

Brown, E.L., **650, 652**

Brown, F. Heredity in the psychoneuroses. *Proceedings of the Royal Society of Medicine*, 1942, *35*, 785-790. **583, 584**

Brown, G., & Harris, T. *Social origins of depression*. New York: Free Press, 1978. **323**

Brown, G.M., **71, 339**

Brown, G.M. & Reichlin, S. Psychologic and neural regulation of growth hormone secretion. *Psychosomatic Medicine*, 1972, *34*, 45-61. **67**

Brown, G.W., **194, 766**

Brown, G.W., Davidson, S., Harris, T., Maclean, U., Pollock, S., & Prudo, R. Psychiatric disorder in London and North Uist. *Social Science and Medicine*, 1977, *11*, 367-377. **278**

Brown, G.W., Sklair, F., & Harris, T.O. Life events and psychiatric disorders: I. Some methodological issues. *Psychologic Medicine*, 1973, *3*, 74-87. **561**

Brown, J.S. Factors influencing self-punitive locomotor behavior. In B.A. Campbell & R.M. Church (Eds.), *Punishment and aversive behavior*. New York: Appleton-Century-Crofts, 1969, pp. 467-514. **228**

Brown, R.T., & Wagner, A.R. Resistance to punishment and extinction following training with shock or non-reinforcement. *Journal of Experimental Psychology*, 1964, *68*, 503-507. **20, 213**

Brown, S.L., **138**

Brown, W.A., & Heninger, G. Cortisol, growth hormone, free fatty acids, and experimentally evoked affective arousal. *American Journal of Psychiatry*, 1975, *132*, 1172-1176. **339**

Brown, W.A., & Heninger, G.R. Stress-induced growth hormone release: Psychologic and physiologic correlates. *Psychosomatic Medicine*, 1976, *38*, 145-147. **67, 68, 340**

Brownbridge, G., **698, 699**

Brunetti, P.M. Rural vaucluse: Two surveys on the prevalence of mental disorders. In T. Andersen, C. Astrup, & A. Forsdahl (Eds.), Social, somatic and psychiatric studies of geographically defined populations. *Acta Psychiatrica Scandinavica*, 1976, Supplement 263. **278**

Bruns, R.F., **550**

Bryant, B.M., **426**

Bryant, J., **149**

Bucher, K.D., **286**

Buchsbaum, M.S., **547, 565, 567, 570**

Buchsbaum, M.S., & Davis, G.C. Application of somatosensory event-related potentials to experimental pain and the pharmacology of analgesia. In D. Lehmann & E. Collaway (Eds.), *Human evoked potentials: Applications and problems*. New York: Plenum Press, 1979. **565**

Buckland, C., **8, 11, 12, 13, 15**

Budden, M.G. A comparative study of haloperidol and diazepam in the treatment of anxiety. *Current Medial Research & Opinion*, 1979, *5*, 759-765. **519, 523, 540**

Budzynski, T.H., Stoyva, J.M., & Peffer, K.E. Biofeedback techniques in psychosomatic disorders. In A. Goldstein & E.B. Foa (Eds.), *Handbook of behavioral interventions*. New York: Wiley & Sons, 1980. **475**

Buechler, S., & Izard, C.E. Anxiety in childhood and adolescence. In I.L. Kutash, L.B. Schlesinger & Associates (Eds.), *Handbook on stress and anxiety*. San Francisco: Jossey-Bass, Inc., 1980. **122, 123**

Bueno, J., **519, 540**

Buglass, D., Clarke, J., Henderson, A.S., Krietman, N., & Presley, A.S. A study of agoraphobic housewives. *Psychological Medicine*, 1977, *7*, 73-86. **293, 562**

Bunney, B.S., **547**

Bunney, W.E., Jr., **547, 568, 569, 570**

Bunney, W.E., Jr., & Davis, J.M. Norepinephrine in depressive reactions. *Archives of General Psychiatry*, 1965, *13*, 483-494. **543**

Burchfield, S., Sarason, I.G., Sarason, B.R., & Beaton, R. *Test anxiety and physiological responding*. Unpublished study, 1982. **94**

Burgess, I.S., Jones, L.M., Robertson, S.A., Radcliffe, W.N., & Emerson, E. The degree of control exerted by phobic and non-phobic verbal stimuli over the recognition behaviour of phobic and non-phobic subjects. *Behaviour Research and Therapy*, 1981, *19*, 233-243. **444**

Burisch, M. Approaches to personality inventory construction. *American Psychologist*, 1984, *39*, 214-227. **685, 686**

Burkard, W.P., **29, 33, 34, 35**

Burke, G., **400**

Burke, J.D., **xxx, 282, 283**

Burno, B.H., & Howell, J.B.L. Disproportionately severe breathlessness in chronic bronchitis. *Quarterly Journal of Medicine*, 1969, *38*, 277-285. **349**

Burns, S., **367**

Burr, W.A., **309**

Burrell, R.H., Culpan, R., Newton, K., Ogg, G., & Short, J. Use of bromazepam in obsessional, phobic and related states. *Current Medical Research & Opinion*, 1974, *2*, 430-436. **505, 508, 509, 585**

Burris, B.C., **548**

Burrows, G., **519, 523, 540**

Burstein, S., & Meichenbaum, D. The work of worrying in children undergoing surgery. *Journal of Abnormal Child Psychology*, 1979, *7*(2), 121-132. **384**

Burton, R., **736**

Busemeyer, J.P., **259**

Bush, J.P., **372, 379**

Bush, J.P. *An observational measure of parent-child interactions in the pediatric medical clinic: Relationship with anxiety and coping style.* Unpublished doctoral dissertation proposal, University of Virginia, Charlottesville, 1982. **375**

Buss, A.H., **470**

Buss, A.H. Critique and notes: Two anxiety factors in psychiatric patients. *Journal and Social Psychology*, 1962, *65*, 426-427. **131, 132, 167**

Butcher, J.N., **683**

Butler, A., **293, 395, 400**

Butler, G., & Mathews, A. Cognitive processes in anxiety. *Advances in Behavior Research and Therapy*, 1983, *5*, 51-62. **167, 194**

Butler, N., **371**

Butt, J.H., **384**

Butz, R., **132, 334, 339, 363, 364**

Buxton, M., **63-64, 64, 65, 66, 67, 72, 339, 340, 357, 359**

Byers, S.O., **365**

Cahill, G.F., & Soeldner, J.S. A non-editorial on non-hypoglycemia. *New England Journal of Medicine.*, 1974, *291*, 905-906. **569**

Caine, E.D., **587**

Cameron, O.G., **66**

Camiza, J., **573**

Campanese, V., **350**

Campbell, D., **643**

Campbell, D., Sanderson, R., & Laverty, S.G. Characteristics of a conditioned response in human subjects during extinction trials following a single traumatic conditioning trial. *Journal of Abnormal and Social Psychology*, 1964, *68*, 627-639. **206**

Campbell, D., & Stanley, J. *Experimental and Quasi-Experimental Designs for Research.* Chicago: Rand McNally, 1963. **643**

Campbell, D.T., & Fiske, D.W. Convergent and discriminant validation by the multitrait-multimethod matrix. *Psychological Bulletin*, 1959, *56*, 81-105. **684**

Campbell, I., **544**

Campbell, W., **351, 584**

Campeau, L., **538**

Campos, J., **125, 417**

Campos, J., & Stenberg, C. Perception, appraisal, and emotion. In M. Lamb & L.R. Sherrod (Eds.), *Infant social cognition.* Hillsdale, NJ: Lawrence Erlbaum Associates, 1981. **114, 417**

Campos, J.J., & Barrett, K.C. A new understanding of biological and cognitive influences on emotional development. In C.E. Izard, J. Kagan & R.D. Zajonc (Eds.), *Emotions, cognitions, and behaviors.* New York: Cambridge University Press, in press. **123**

Cananzi, A.R., Costa, E., & Guidotti, A. Potentiation by intraventricular muscimol of the anticonflict effect of benzodiazepines. *Brain Research*, 1980, *196*, 447-453. **35**

Candland, D.K. The persistent problems of emotion. In D.K. Candland, J.P. Fell, E. Keen, A.I. Leshner, R. Plutchik, & R.M. Tarpy (Eds.), *Emotion*. California: Wadsworth Publishing Co., 1977. **110**

Cannady, C., **414**

Cannon, W.B., **779**

Cannon, W.B. New evidence for sympathetic control of some internal secretions. *American Journal of Psychiatry*, 1922, *2*, 15-30. **55, 56**

Cannon, W.B. The James-Lange theory of emotions: A critical examination of an alternative theory. *American Journal of Psychology*, 1927, *39*, 106-124. **138**

Cannon, W.B. *Bodily changes in pain, hunger, fear and rage: An account of recent researchers into the function of emotional excitement* (2nd ed.). New York: Appleton-Century-Crofts, 1929. **111, 173, 189, 265, 266, 534**

Cannon, W.B. *The wisdom of the body* (2nd ed.). New York: Norton, 1939. **138, 333**

Cannon, W.B., & DeLaPaz, D. Emotional stimulation of adrenal secretion. *American Journal of Physiology*, 1911, *12*, 64-70. **55, 56**

Cannon-Spoor, H.E., **401**

Cantor, J.R., Zillmann, D., & Bryant, J. Enhancement of experienced sexual arousal in response to erotic stimuli through misattribution of unrelated residual excitation. *Journal of Personality and Social Psychology*, 1975, *32*, 69-75. **149**

Cantor, N., & Genero, N. Psychiatric diagnosis and natural categorization: A close analogy. In T. Millon & G. Klerman (Eds.), *Contemporary issues in psychopathology*. New York: Guilford, in press. **243**

Cantor, N., Smith, E., & French, R., & Mezzich, J. Psychiatric diagnosis as prototype categorization. *Journal of Abnormal Psychology*, 1980, *89*, 181-193. **235, 243**

Cantril, H., & Hunt, W.A. Emotional effects produced by the injection of adrenalin. *American Journal of Psychology*, 1932, *44*, 300-307. **534, 550**

Cantwell, D.P., **125, 126, 720**

Cardo, B., **555**

Carey, G. *A clinical genetic twin study of obsessional and phobic states*. Unpublished doctoral dissertation, University of Minnesota, 1978. **325, 785**

Carey, G. Genetic influences on anxiety neurosis and agoraphobia. In R.J. Mathew (Ed.), *The biology of anxiety*. New York: Brunner/Mazel, Inc., 1982, pp. 37-50. **327, 329**

Carey, G., & Gottesman, I.I. Twin and family studies of anxiety, phobic, and obsessive disorders. In D.K. Klein & J. Rabkin (Eds.), *Anxiety: New research and changing concepts*. New York: Raven Press, 1981. **275, 285, 327, 328, 585**

Carey, G., Gottesman, I.I., & Robins, E. Prevalence rates for the neuroses: Pitfalls in the evaluation of familiality. *Psychological Medicine*, 1980, *10*, 437-443. **278**

Carlson, G.A., **125, 126**

Carlson, G.A., & Cantwell, D.P. A survey of depressive symptoms, syndromes and disorder in a child psychiatric population. *Journal of Child Psychology and Psychiatry*, 1980, *21*, 19-25. **125**

Carlsson, A., **592**

Carlsson, A. Mechanisms of action of neuroleptic drugs. In M.A. Lipton, A. DiMascio, & K.F. Killam (Eds.), *Psychopharmacology: A generation of progress*. New York: Raven Press, 1978. **540**

Caro, A.J., **327**

Carr, A.T. Compulsive neurosis: A review of the literature. *Psychological Bulletin*, 1974, *81*, 311-318. **230, 444**

Carr, J.E., **438**

Carr, J.E. Ethno-behaviorism and the culture-bound syndromes: The case of amok. *Culture, Medicine and Psychiatry*, 1978, *2*, 269-293. **297**

Carrington, P. *Freedom in meditation*. New York: Doubleday-Anchor, 1977. **475**

Carroll, B.J. Control of plasma cortisol levels in depression: Studies with the dexamethasone suppression test. In B. Davis, B.J. Carroll, & R.M. Mowbray (Eds.), *Depressive illness: Some research studies*. Springfield, IL: Charles C. Thomas, Publishers, 1972, pp. 23-201. **60**

Carroll, B.J., Feinberg, M., Greden, J.F., Tarika, J., Albala, A.A., Haskett, R.F., James, N.McI., Kronfol, Z., Lohr, N., Steiner, M., DeVigne, J.P., & Young, E. A specific laboratory test for the diagnosis of melancholia. *Archives of General Psychiatry*, 1981, *38*, 15-24. **66, 67**

Carroll, J., **437**

Carruthers, M., **342**

Carstairs, G.M., **309**

Carstairs, G.M., & Kapur, R.L. *The great universe of Kota: Stress, change and mental disorder in an Indian village*. Berkeley, CA: University of California Press, 1976. **309**

Carter, C., **325, 327**

Carver, C.S., & Scheier, M.F. Functional and dysfunctional responses to anxiety: The interaction between expectancies and self-focused attention. In R. Schwarzer (Ed.), *Self-related cognitions in anxiety and motivation*. Hillsdale, NJ: Lawrence Erlbaum Associates, in press. **177, 254**

Case, W., **518, 522**

Casper, R., **58**

Cassel, J.C., **347**

Castaneda, A., McCandless, B.R., & Palermo, D.S. The children's form of the Manifest Anxiety Scale. *Child Development*, 1956, *27*, 317-326. **708**

Catalan, J., **433**

Cataldo, M., **371**

Cattell, R.B., **300, 652-53, 654, 655, 662, 665, 666, 673, 675, 700, 701**

Cattell, R.B. The scree test for the number of factors. *Multivariate Behavioral Research*, 1966, *1*, 245-276. **687**

Cattell, R.B., Eber, H.W., & Tatsuoka, M.M. *The handbook for the sixteen personality factor questionnaire.* Champaign, IL: Institute for Personality and Ability Testing, 1970. **696**

Cattell, R.B., & Scheier, I.H. The nature of anxiety: A review of thirteen multi-variate analyses comprising 814 variables. *Psychological Reports*, 1958, *4*, 351-388. **177**

Cattell, R.B., & Scheier, I.H. *Handbook for the objective-analytic anxiety battery.* Champaign, IL: IPAT, 1960. **655**

Cattell, R.B., & Scheier, I.H. *The meaning and measurement of neuroticism and anxiety.* New York: Ronald Press, 1961. **177, 300, 657**

Cattell, R.B., & Warburton, F.W. A cross-cultural comparison of patterns of extraversion and anxiety. *British Journal of Psychology*, 1961, *52*, 3-15. **300**

Caudill, W., & Weinstein, H. Maternal and infant behavior in Japan and America. In T.K. Lebra & W.P. Lebra (Eds.), *Japanese culture and behavior.* Honolulu: University Press of Hawaii, 1969, pp. 225-276. **317**

Cedarbaum, J.M., & Aghajanian, G.K. Noradrenergic neurons of the locus coeruleus: Inhibition by epinephrine and activation by the alpha-antagonist piperoxane. *Brain Research*, 1976, *112*, 413-419. **547, 550**

Cedarbaum, J.M., & Aghajanian, G.K. Catecholamine receptors on locus coeruleus neurons: Pharmacological characterization. *European Journal of Pharmacology*, 1977, *44*, 375-385. **539**

Cedarbaum, J.M., & Aghajanian, G.K. Activation of locus coeruleus neurons by peripheral stimuli: Modulation by a collateral inhibitory mechanism. *Life Sciences*, 1978, *23*, 1383-1392. **553**

Cerny, **489**

Chamberlin, K., **551, 573**

Chambless, D.L., **438**

Chambless, D.L., Foa, E.B., Groves, G.A., & Goldstein, A.J. Flooding with brevital in the treatment of agoraphobia: Countereffective? *Behaviour Research and Therapy*, 1979, *17*, 243-251. **423, 426, 440**

Chambless, D.L., & Goldstein, A.J. Clinical treatment of agoraphobia. In M.R. Mavissakalian & D.H. Barlow (Eds.), *Phobia: Psychological and pharmacological treatment.* New York: Guilford Press, 1980. **463, 477**

Champoux, M., **212, 242**

Chance, N.A., Rin, H., & Chu, H. Modernization, value and identification and mental health: A cross-cultural study. *Anthropologica*, 1966, *8*, 197-216. **303**

Chance, W.T. Autoanalgesia: Opiate and non-opiate mechanisms. *Neurosciences Biobehavioral Reviews*, 1980, *4*, 55-67. **543**

Chance, W.T., & Rosecrans, J.A. Lack of effect of naloxone on autoanalgesia. *Pharmacology, Biochemistry, and Behavior*, 1979, *11*, 643-646. **543**

Chance, W.T., & Schechter, M.D. Autoanalgesia: Blockade by yohimbine. *European Journal of Pharmacology*, 1979, *58*, 89-90. **543**

Chandler, M., **414, 415**

Chape, C., **347**

Chapin, H.N., **444, 713**

Chaplin, E.W., & Levine, B.A. The effects of total exposure duration and interrupted versus continuous exposure in flooding. Paper presented at the annual convention of the Association for the Advancement of Behavior Therapy, New York, November 1980. **438**

Charney, D.S., Heninger, G.R., & Redmond, D.E., Jr. Yohimbine induced anxiety and increased noradrenergic function in humans: Effects of diazepam and clonidine. *Life Science*, 1983, *33*, 19-29. **551, 571, 572**

Charney, D.S., Heninger, G.R., & Sternberg, D.E. Assessment of alpha-2 adrenergic autoreceptor function in humans: Effects of oral yohimbine. *Life Science*, 1982, *30*, 2033-2041. **571**

Charney, D.S., Heninger, G.R., Sternberg, D.E., Hafstad, K.M., Griddings, S., & Landis, D.H. Adrenergic receptor sensitivity in depressive illness. *Archives of General Psychiatry*, 1982, *39*, 290-294. **563**

Charney, D.S., Heninger, G.R., & Sternberg, D.E. The effect of mianserin on alpha-2 adrenergic receptor function in depressed patients. *British Journal of Psychiatry*, in press. **529**

Charney, D.S., Heninger, G.R., Sternberg, D.E., & Landis, H. Abrupt discontinuation of tricyclic antidepressant drugs: Evidence for noradrenergic hyperactivity. *British Journal of Psychiatry*, 1982, *141*, 377-386. **552**

Charney, D.S., Menkes, D.B., & Heninger, G.R. Receptor sensitivity and the mechanism of action of anti-depressant treatment. *Archives of General Psychiatry*, 1981, *38*, 1160-1180. **528, 544**

Charney, D.S., & Redmond, D.E., Jr. Neurobiological mechanisms in human anxiety. *Neuropharmacology*, 1983, *22*, 1531-1536. **552**

Charney, D.S., Riordan, C.E., Kleber, H.D., Murburg, M., Braverman, P., Sternberg, D.E., Heninger, G.R., & Redmond, D.E., Jr. Clonidine and naltrexone: A safe, effective, and rapid treatment of abrupt withdrawal from methadone. *Archives of General Psychiatry*, 1982, *39*, 1327-1332. **542**

Charney, D.S., Sternberg, D.E., Kleber, H.D., Heninger, G.R., & Redmond, D.E., Jr. The clinical use of clonidine in abrupt withdrawal from methadone: Effects on blood pressure and specific signs and symptoms. *Archives of General Psychiatry*, 1981, *38*, 1273-1277. **529, 548, 552**

Charry, J.M., **17, 18, 19, 20**

Chase, W.G., Graham, F.K., & Graham, D.T. Components of HR response in anticipation of reaction times and exercise tasks. *Journal of Experimental Psychology*, 1968, *76*, 642-648. **152**

Chassan, J. *Research Design in Clinical Psychology and Psychiatry* (2nd ed. enl.). New York: Irvington, 1979. **643**

Chaudhry, D.R., **329**

Checkley, S.A., Slade, A.P., & Shur, E. Growth hormone and other responses to clonidine in patients with endogenous depression. *British Journal of Psychiatry*, 1981, *138*, 51-55. **563**

Chen, J.S., & Amsel, A. Prolonged, unsignalled, inescapable shocks increase persistence in subsequent appetitive instrumental learning. *Animal Learning and Behavior*, 1977, *4*, 377-385. **19, 20**

Chess, S., **376, 382, 383, 409, 411, 415, 733**

Chessick, R.D., Bassan, M., & Shattan, S. A comparison of the effect of infused catecholamines and certain affect states. *American Journal of Psychiatry*, 1966, *123*, 156-165. **534, 550**

Chevalier, J.A., **60, 65**

Chick, J., **401**

Child, I.L., **613**

Chiu, E., **519, 523, 540**

Chiu, L.H. Manifested anxiety in Chinese and American children. *Journal of Psychology*, 1971, *79*, 273-284. **301, 303**

Chouinard, G., Annable, L., Fontaine, R., & Solyom, L. Alprazolam in the treatment of generalized anxiety and panic disorders: A double-blind placebo-controlled study. *Psychopharmacology*, 1982, *77*, 229-233. **538**

Christian, J.J. Effects of population size on adrenal glands and reproductive organs of male mice in populations of fixed size. *American Journal of Physiology*, 1955, *182*, 292-300. **55**

Christian, J.J., & Davis, D.E. The relationship between adrenal weight and populations status of urban Norway rats. *Journal of Mammalogy*, 1956, *37*, 475. **55**

Christie, J.E., **65**

Christoph, P., **643**

Chrousus, G.P., **552**

Chu, H., **303**

Chuang, D.M., **40**

Chung, C.S., **277**

Ciba Foundation. *Functions of the sept-hippocampal system* (Ciba Foundation Symposium New Series No. 58). Amsterdam: Elsevier, 1978. **8**

Cicala, G.A., **657**

Cipes, M., **372**

Cisin, I.H., **281**

Claghorn, J. A comparative study of loxapine succinate, librium and placebo in neurotic outpatients. *Current Therapeutic Research*, 1973, *15*, 8-12. **519, 522, 540**

Claghorn, J.L., **337**

Clancy, J., **325, 357, 365, 366, 538, 682**

Clark, B.R., **344, 345**

Clark, L.A., **689**

Clark, L.P. A study of the epilepsy of Dostojewsky. *Boston Medical Surgical Journal*, 1915, *172*, 46-51. **593**

Clark, M.S., **143**

Clark, M.S., Milberg, S., & Ross, J. Arousal cues, arousal-related material in memory: Implications for understanding effect of mood on memory. *Journal of Verbal Learning and Verbal Behavior*, 1983, *22*, 633-649. **147, 148, 149**

Clarke, A.D.B., **414**

Clarke, A.M., & Clarke, A.D.B. *Early experience: Myth and evidence*. London: Open Books, 1976. **414**

Clarke, C., **420**

Clarke, J., **293, 562**

Clarke, M., & Fiske, S. *Affect and cognition*. Hillsdale, NJ: Lawrence Erlbaum Associates, 1982. **123**

Claycomb, J.B., **67**

Clayton, P.J., , **587, 771, 793**

Clayton, P.J., Herjanic, M., Murphy, G.E., & Woodruff, R. Mourning and depression: Their similarities and differences. *Journal of the Canadian Psychiatric Association*, 1974, *19*, 309-312. **793**

Clayton, P.J. The sequelae and nonsequelae of conjugal bereavement. *American Journal of Psychiatry*, 1979, *136*, 1530-1534. **793**

Clemens, T.L., **137**

Clifton, R.K., **153, 156**

Clinthorne, J., **281**

Clody, D.E., **32, 34, 37, 50**

*⁎ Cloninger, C.R., Martin, R.L., Clayton, P., & Guze, S.B. A blind follow-up and family study of anxiety neurosis: Preliminary analysis of the St. Louis 500. In D.F. Klein & J.G. Rabkin (Eds.), *Anxiety: New research and changing concepts*. New York: Raven Press, 1981, pp. 137-154. **771, 793**

Clow, A., **538**

Clow, A., Glover, V., Armando, I., & Sandler, M. New endogenous benzodiazepine receptor ligand in human urine: Identity with endogenous monoamine oxidase inhibitor. *Life Sciences*, 1983, *33*, 735-741. **538**

Clyde, D.J. *Manual for the Clyde Mood Scale*. Miami, FL: Clyde Computing Service, 1963. **689**

Cobb, J.P., **506, 507, 586, 747**

Coble, P.A., **567, 786, 795**

Coccaro, E., **66**

Coe, C., & Levine, S. Normal responses to mother-infant separation in non-human primates. In D. Klein & J. Rabkin (Eds.), *Anxiety: New research and changing concepts*. New York: Raven, 1981, pp. 155-177. **236**

Cohen, A.S., **494**

Cohen, D.J., **368**

Cohen, D.J., Detlor, J., Young, J., & Freedman, D. Clonidine ameliorates.

Conti, L., & Pinder, R.M. A controlled comparative trial of mianserin and diazepam in the treatment of anxiety states in psychiatric outpatients. *Journal of International Medical Research*, 1979, *7*, 285-289. **521**

Cook, E. *Human classical conditioning and the preparedness hypothesis.* Unpublished doctoral dissertation, University of Wisconsin-Madison, 1983. **207**

Cook, E.W., III, **136, 153, 154, 155, 162, 163, 208, 437**

Cook, J.M., **38, 39**

Cook, L., & Sepinwall, J. Behavioral analysis of the effects and mechanisms of action of benzodiazepines. In E. Costa & P. Greegard (Eds.), *The mechanism of action of benzodiazepines.* New York: Raven Press, 1975. **539**

Cook, M., **212, 215, 216, 227, 234, 242, 243**

Cook, M., Mineka, S., & Trumble, D. The role of control and feedback in the attenuation of fear over the course of avoidance learning. *Journal of Experimental Psychology: Animal Behavior Processes.* **205, 227**

Cook, M., Mineka, S., & Trumble, D. *Observational conditioning of snake fear in unrelated rhesus monkeys.* In preparation. **216, 243**

Cook, T., & Campbell, D. *Quasi-experimentation.* Boston: Houghton-Mifflin, 1979. **643**

Coolidge, J.C., & Brody, R.D. Observations of mothers of forty-nine school phobic children: evaluated in a 10-year follow-up study. *Journal of the American Academy of Child Psychiatry*, 1974, *13*, 275-285. **405, 411**

Coolidge, J.C., Brody, R.D., & Feeney, B. A ten-year follow-up study of 66 school phobic children. *American Journal of Orthopsychiatry*, 1964, *34*, 675-684. **400, 405, 411, 716**

Coolidge, J.C., Tessman, E., Waldofogel, S., & Willer, M.L. Patterns of aggression and school phobia. *Psychoanalytic study of the child*, 1962, *17*, 319-333. **405, 411**

Cooper, J.E., **742**

Cooper, J.E., Gelder, M.G., & Marks, I.M. Results of behaviour therapy in 77 psychiatric patients. *British Medical Journal*, 1965, *1*, 1222-1225. **425, 426**

Cooper, J.R., Bloom, F.E., & Roth, R.H. *The biochemical basis of neuropharmacology* (5th ed.). New York, London, Toronto: Oxford University Press, 1983. **536**

Cooperman, L.H., **551**

Coppola, R., & Gracely, R.H. Where is the noise in SDT pain assessment? *Pain*, 1983, *17*, 257-266. **565**

Corda, M.G., **36, 39, 41, 43, 44, 45, 50**

Corda, M.G., Blaker, W.D., Mendelson, W.B., Guidotti, A., & Costa, E. β-Carbolines enhance shock-induced suppression of drinking in rats. *Proceedings of the National Academy of Sciences, U.S.A.*, 1983, *80*, 2072-2076. **32, 34**

Corda, M.G., Costa, E., & Guidotti, A. Specific preconvulsant action of an imidobenzodiazepine (RO 15-1788) on isoniazid convulsions. *Neuropharmacology*, 1982, *21*, 91-94. **33, 37**

Corrodi, H., **7, 15**

Corrodi, H., Fuxe, K., Lidbrink, P., & Olson, L. Minor tranquilizers, stress, and central catecholamine neurons. *Brain Research*, 1971, *29*, 1-16. **539**

Corwin, S.M., **614**

Coryell, W.H., Noyes, R., Jr., & Clancy, J. Excess mortality in panic disorder: A comparison with primary unipolar depression. *Archives of General Psychiatry*, 1982, *39*, 701-703. **357, 365, 366**

Cosenza-Murphy, D., **39**

Costa, E., **7, 11, 28, 32, 33, 34, 35, 36, 37, 38, 39, 40, 41, 43, 44, 45, 49, 50, 538**

Costa, E. Coexistence of putative neuromodulators in the same axon: Pharmacological consequences on receptors. In C.C. Cuello (Ed.), *Cotransmission*. London: The Macmillan Press, Ltd., 1982. **28, 29, 48**

Costa, E. Are benzodiazepine recognition sites functional entities for the action of endogenous effectors or merely drug receptors? *Advances in Biochemistry and Psychopharmacology*, 1983, *38*, 249-259. **28, 29, 77, 78, 114, 116, 272, 533, 538, 576, 638**

Costa, E., & Greengard, P. (Eds.). *Mechanism of action of benzodiazepines*. New York: Raven Press, 1975. **27, 537**

Costa, E., & Guidotti, A. Molecular mechanisms in the receptor action of benzodiazepines. In G.R. Okun & A.K. Cho (Eds.), *Annual Review of Pharmacology and Toxicology* (Vol. 19). Palo Alto, CA: Annual Review Inc., 1979, pp. 531-545. **28, 33, 39, 45, 538, 539**

Costa, E., Guidotti, A., & Mao, C.C. Evidence for involvement of GABA in the action of benzodiazepines: Studies on rat cerebellum. In E. Costa & P. Greengard (Eds.), *Mechanism of action of benzodiazepines*. New York: Raven Press, 1975. **28, 35, 538**

Costa, E., Guidotti, A., Mao, C.C., & Suria, A. New concepts on the mechanism of action of benzodiazepines. *Life Sciences*, 1975, *17*, 167-186. **28, 33, 35**

Costa, E., Guidotti, A., & Toffano, G. Molecular mechanisms mediating the action of benzodiazepines on GABA receptors. *British Journal of Psychiatry*, 1978, *133*, 239-248. **28**

Costa, J.L., **544**

Costa, P.T., **696**

Costello, C.G. Dissimilarities between conditioned avoidance responses and phobias. *Psychological Review*, 1970, *77*, 250-254. **203, 209**

Costello, C.G. Fears and phobias in women: A community study. *Journal of Abnormal Psychology*, 1982, *91*, 280-286. **279**

Cote, P., Campeau, L., & Bourassa, M.G. Therapeutic implications of diazepam in patients with elevated left ventricular filling pressure. *American Heart Journal*, 1976, *91*, 747-751. **538**

Coulter, X., Riccio, D.C., & Page, H.A. Effects of blocking an instrumental avoidance response: Facilitated extinction but persistence of "fear". *Journal of Comparative and Physiological Psychology*, 1969, *68*, 377-381. **221**

Covi, L., **525, 677**

Cowen, E., **300-01**

Cowen, P.J., Green, A.R., Nutt, D.J., & Martin, I.L. Ethyl β-carboline carboxylate lowers seizure threshold and antagonizes flurazepam-induced sedation in rats. *Nature*, 1981, *290*, 54-55. **34**

Cox, D.N., **24**

Craig, K.C. Physiological arousal as a function of imagined, vicarious, and direct stress experiences. *Journal of Abnormal Psychology*, 1968, *73*, 513-520. **436**

Craig, K.D., **434**

Craighead, W.E., **474**

Crawley, J.N., Marangos, P.J., Paul, S.M., Skolnick, P., & Goodwin, F.K. Interaction between purine and penzodiazepine: Inosine reverses diazepam-induced stimulation of mouse exploratory behavior. *Science*, 1981, *211*, 725-727. **31**

Crawley, J.N., Ninan, P.T., Pickar, D., Linnolla, M., Chrousis, G.P., Skolnick, P., & Paul, S.M. Behavioral and physiological responses to benzodiazepine receptor antagonists. *American College of Psychopharmacology Abstracts*, 1983, 26. **552**

Creese, I., Finberg, A.P., Snyder, S.H. Butyrophenone influences on the opiate receptor. *European Journal of Pharmacology*, 1976, *36*, 231-235. **541**

Cristol, A.H., **612**

Cronbach, L.J., **653**

Cronbach, L.J. Beyond the two disciplines of scientific psychology. *American Psychologist*, 1975, *30*, 116-127. **247**

Cronbach, L.J., & Meehl, P.E. Construct validity in psychological tests. *Psychological Bulletin*, 1955, *52*, 281-302. **684**

Cronholm, B., **503, 504, 529, 585, 586**

Croughan, J., **65, 281, 282, 310, 544, 677**

Crow, M.J., Marks, I.M., Agras, W.S., & Leitenberg, H. Time-limited desensitization implosion and shaping for phobic patients: A cross-over study. *Behaviour Research and Therapy*, 1972, *10*, 319-328. **426, 427**

Crowe, R.R., **286, 325, 329, 365, 538, 682**

Crowe, R.R., Noyes, R., Jr., Pauls, D.L., & Slyman, D. A family study of panic disorder. *Archives of General Psychiatry*, 1983, *40*, 1065-1069. **288, 294, 328, 329, 780, 793**

Crowe, R.R., Pauls, D.L., Slyman, D.J., & Noyes, R., Jr. A family study of anxiety neurosis. *Archives of General Psychiatry*, 1980, *37*, 77-79. **285, 780**

Cuello, A.C. (Ed.). *Co-transmission*. London: The Macmillan Press, Ltd., 1982. **28**

Culpan, R., **505, 508, 509, 585**

Cumin, R., **28, 29, 33, 34, 35**

Curtis, G.C., **71, 339**

Curtis, G.C., Buxton, M., Lippman, D., Nesse, R.M., & Wright, J. "Flooding in vivo" during the circadian phase of minimal cortisol secretion: Anxiety and therapeutic success without adrenal cortical activation. *Biological Psychiatry*, 1976, *11*, 101-107. **63-64, 65, 339**

Curtis, G.C., Cameron, O.G., & Nesse, R.M. The dexamethasone suppression test in panic disorder and agoraphobia. *American Journal of Psychiatry*, 1982, *139*, 1043-1046. **66**

Curtis, G.C., Nesse, R.M., Buxton, M., & Lippman, D. Anxiety and plasma cortisol at the crest of the circadian cycle: Reappraisal of a classical hypothesis. *Psychosomatic Medicine*, 1978, *40*, 368-378. **64, 65, 66, 339, 357, 359**

Curtis, G.C., Nesse, R.M., Buxton, M., & Lippman, D. Plasma growth hormone: Effect of anxiety during flooding in vivo. *American Journal of Psychiatry*, 1979, *136*, 410-414. **65, 67, 72, 340**

Cuthbert, B.N., **159, 165, 166**

Cuthbert, M., & Melamed, B.G. A screening device: Children at risk for dental fears and management problems. *Journal of Dentistry for Children*, 1982, *49*, 432-436. **371**

Czeisler, C.A., Moore Ede, M.C., Regestein, Q.E., Kisch, E.S., Fang, V.S., & Ehrlich, E.N. Episodic 24 hour cortisol secretory patterns in patients awaiting elective cardiac surgery. *Journal of Clinical Endocrinology and Metabolism*, 1976, *42*, 273-283. **61**

Da Costa, J.M. On irritable heart: A clinical study of a functional cardiac disorder and its consequences. *American Journal of Medical Science*, 1871, *61*, 17-52. **737, 761**

Dahlem, N.W., **652**

Dahlstrom, L.E., **646, 681**

Dahlstrom, W.G., & Welsh, G.S. *An MMPI handbook*. Minneapolis, MN: University of Minnesota Press, 1960. **649**

Dahlstrom, W.G., Welsh, G.S., & Dahlstrom, L.E. *An MMPI handbook, Volume I: Clinical interpretation*. Minneapolis: University of Minnesota Press, 1972. **646, 681**

Dain, H.J., **614**

Dale, J., **372**

Daly, J.W., Bruns, R.F., & Snyder, S.H. Adenosine receptors in the central nervous system: Relationship to the central actions of methylxanthines. *Life Sciences*, 1981, *28*, 2083-97. **550**

Damas Mora, J., Grant, K., Kenyon, P., Patal, M.K., & Jenner, F.A. Respiratory ventilation and carbon dioxide levels in syndromes of depression. *British Journal of Psychiatry*, 1976, *129*, 457-461. **349**

Danton, J., **516, 519, 538, 545**

Darsie, M.L., **137**

Darwin, C., **xxii**

Darwin, C. (1872). *The expression of the emotions in man and animals*. Chicago: University of Chicago Press, 1965. **111, 116, 118, 172, 173, 174, 199, 245, 333, 410, 411, 533, 599, 600**

Da Silva, J.A.R., **519, 540**
Dauble, A., **13, 15, 40**
Davidian, H., **519**
Davids, A., **649**
Davidson, J.M. The physiology of meditation and mystical states of consciousness. *Perspectives in Biology and Medicine*, 1976, *19*(3), 345-379. **659**
Davidson, K.S., **708**
Davidson, M., **215, 216, 243**
Davidson, P.O., **434**
Davidson, S., **278**
Davies, A.O., & Lefkowitz, R.J. Corticosteroid-induced differential regulation of adrenergic receptors in circulating human lymphonuclear leukocytes and mononuclear leukocytes. *Journal of Clinical Endocrinology and Metabolism*, 1980, *51*, 599-605. **346**
Davies, S.O., **551**
Davis, D.E., **55**
Davis, G.C., Buchsbaum, M.S., van Kammen, D.P., & Bunney, W.E., Jr. Analgesia to pain stimuli in schizophrenics and its reversal by naltrexone. *Psychiatry Research*, 1979, *1*, 61-69. **565**
Davis, J., **67, 74, 75, 118, 531, 543, 544, 545, 669**
Davis, J. Theories of biological etiology of affective disorders. *International Review of Neurobiology*, 1970, *12*, 145-175. **115**
Davis, J., Suhayl, N., Spira, N., & Vogel, C. Anxiety: Differential diagnosis and treatment from a biological perspective. *Journal of Clinical Psychiatry*, 1981, *42*, (11, sec. 2), 4-14. **512**
Davis, M., **95**
Davis, M., & Wagner, A.R. Habituation of the startle response under incremental sequence of stimulus intensities. *Journal of Comparative and Physiological Psychology*, 1969, *67*, 486-492. **439**
Davis, N., Brookes, S., Gray, J.A., & Rawlins, J.N.P. Chlordiazepoxide and resistance to punishment. *Quarterly Journal of Experimental Psychology*, 1981, *33b*, 227-239. **21**
Davison, G.C., **220, 241**
Deakin, J.F.W., **24**
Deal, E.C., Jr., McFadden, E.R., Jr., Ingram, R.H., Jr., & Jaeger, J.J. Airway response to cold air and hyperpnea in normal subjects and in those with hay fever and asthma. *Annual Review of Respiratory Diseases*, 1980, *121*, 621-632. **351**
Dealey, R.S., Ishiki, D.M., Avery, D.H., Wilson, L.G., & Dunner, D.L. Secondary depression in anxiety disorders. *Comprehensive Psychiatry*, 1981, *22*, 612-618. **562**
Dearborn, M., **384**
DeCarie, T.G. A study of the mental and emotional development of the thalidomide child. In B.M. Foss (Ed.), *Determinants of infant behavior* (Vol. 4). London: Methuen, 1969. **414**

Deckert, G.H. Pursuit eye movements in the absence of moving visual stimulus. *Science*, 1964, *143*, 1192-1193. **159**

DeEskinazi, F.G., **526**

Deffenbacher, J.L. Worry and emotionality. In I.G. Sarason (Ed.), *Test anxiety: Theory, research, and applications.* Hillsdale, NJ: Lawrence Erlbaum Associates, 1980. **468**

DeGiovanni, I.S., **712, 714**

De Guia, D., **82, 534, 550**

Dekker, J., **428**

De La, Mora, M.P., **539, 540**

DeLa Paz, D., **55, 56**

DeLeon-Jones, F., **75**

Delgado, J.M.R. *Physical control of the mind: Toward a psychocivilized society.* New York: Harper and Row, 1971. **115, 118**

Delizio, R.D., **224, 236, 527**

DeLongis, A., **110, 119**

Delprato, D. Hereditary determinants of fears and phobias. *Behavior Therapy*, 1980, *11*, 79-103. **208**

Delprato, D., & McGlynn, F.D. Behavioral theories of anxiety disorders. In S.M. Turner (Ed.), *Behavioral treatment of anxiety disorders.* New York: Plenum Press, in press. **227, 242**

Demars, J.P., **520, 523, 540**

Dembroski, T.M., MacDougall, J.M., & Shields, J.M. Physiologic reactions to social challenge in persons evidencing the Type A coronary prone behavior pattern. *Journal of Human Stress*, 1977, *3*, 2-10. **365**

Den Hengst, S., **428**

Dennenberg, V.H., **62**

Dennenberg, V.H. Critical periods; stimulus input, and emotional reactivity. *Psychological Review*, 1964, *71*, 335-351. **139**

Denny, M.R. Post-aversive relief and relaxation and their implications for behavior therapy. *Journal of Behavior Therapy and Experimental Psychiatry*, 1976, *7*, 315-322. **476, 477**

Denny, R. Relaxation theory and experiments. In F.R. Brush (Ed.), *Aversive conditioning and learning.* New York: Academic Press, 1971. **227**

Depree, J.A., **95, 252, 467, 468, 469**

DeQuattro, V., **348**

DeQuattro, V., & Miura, Y. Neurogenic factors in human hypertension: Mechanism or myth. *American Journal of Medicine*, 1973, *55*, 362-369. **347**

Derogatis, L.R., Klerman, G.L., & Lipman, R.S. Anxiety states and depressive neuroses: Issues in nosological discrimination. *Journal of Nervous and Mental Disease*, 1972, *155*, 392-403. **240**

Descartes, R., **xxii, 245**

Desiderato, O., & Newman, A. Conditioned suppression produced in rats by tones paired with escapable or inescapable shock. *Journal of Comparative and Physiological Psychology*, 1971, *77*, 427-431. **212, 242** de Silva, P., **475**

de Silva, P., & Rachman, S. Is exposure a necessary condition for fear-reduction? *Behaviour Research and Therapy*, 1981, *19*, 227-232. **455, 456**

de Silva, P., & Rachman, S. Exposure and fear reduction. *Behaviour Research and Therapy*, 1983, *21*, 151-152. **446**

de Silva, P., & Rachman, S. Does escape behaviour strengthen agoraphobic avoidance? A preliminary study. *Behaviour Research and Therapy*, 1984, *22*, 87-92. **456, 459**

de Silva, P., Rachman, S., & Seligman, M.E.P. Prepared phobias and obsessions: Therapeutic outcomes. *Behaviour Research and Therapy*, 1977, *15*, 65-78. **209, 231-32**

DeSoto, C.B., **681**

Detchon, C.S., **121**

Detlor, J., **587**

Deutsch, H. The genesis of agoraphobia. *International Journal of Psychoanalysis*, 1929, *10*, 51-69. **602, 603**

DeVigne, J.P., **66, 67**

De Voge, J.T., Minor, T., & Karoly, P. Effects of behavioral intervention and interpersonal feedback on fear and avoidance components of severe agoraphobia A case analysis. *Psychological Reports*, 1981, *49*, 595-605. **433**

De Wit, H., **21**

Dewitt, K.N., **614, 615**

Diamond, R.C., **69, 70, 343**

Diaz-Guerrero, R., **300, 303**

Dibble, E., **286**

Dicara, L.V., & Miller, N.E. Long term retention of instrumentally learned heart-rate changes in the curarized rat. *Communications in Behavioral Biology, Part A*, 1968, *2*, 19-23. **237**

Dick, H., **65**

Dickman, W., **489, 607, 610, 771**

Dickson, H., **568, 786, 793, 794**

Diener, E. *Subjective well-being*. Manuscript submitted for publication, 1983. **251**

Dienstbier, R.A. Emotion-attribution theory: Establishing roots and exploring future perspectives. In R.A. Dienstbier (Ed.), *Nebraska symposium on motivation*. Lincoln: University of Nebraska Press, 1979. **118**

Diethelm, O. Influence of emotion on dextrose tolerance. *Archives of Neurology and Psychiatry*, 1936, *36*, 342-361. **569**

Digman, J.M., & Takemoto-Chock, N.K. Factors in the natural language of personality: Re-analysis, comparison, and interpretation of six major studies. *Multivariate Behavioral Research*, 1981, *16*, 149-170. **696**

Dillon, D.J., **551**

Dim, B., **525**

DiMascio, A., & Barrett, J. Comparative effects of oxazepam in "high" and "low" anxious student volunteers. *Psychosomatics*, 1965, *6*, 298-302. **547**

Dimberg, U., **208, 216**

Dimsdale, J. Emotional causes of sudden death. *American Journal of Psychiatry*, 1977, *134*, 1361-1366. **357**

Dimsdale, J. Helping patients cope. *Consultant*, 1982b, *22*(7), 171-180. **358**

Dimsdale, J. Wet holter monitoring: Techniques for studying plasma responses to stress in ambulatory subjects. In T. Dembroski, T. Schmidt, & G. Blumchen (Eds.), *Biobehavioral bases of coronary heart disease*. Basel: Karger Publishers, 1983. **359**

Dimsdale, J., & Herd, J.A. Variability of plasma lipids in response to emotional arousal. *Psychosomatic Medicine*, 1982a, *44*, 413-430. **342, 358**

Dimsdale, J., & Moss, J. Short-term catecholamine response to psychological stress. *Psychosomatic Medicine*, 1980b, *42*, 493-497. **342, 358, 359**

DiNardo, P.A., **482, 483, 489, 494**

DiNardo, P.A., O'Brien, G.T., Barlow, D.H., Waddell, M.T., & Blanchard, E.B. *Anxiety disorders interview schedule (ADIS)*, 1982. Available from Phobia and Anxiety Disorders Clinic, Draper 107, 135 Western Avenue, Albany, NY 12222. **480**

DiNardo, P.A., O'Brien, G.T., Barlow, D.H., Waddell, M.T., & Blanchard, E.B. Reliability of DSM-III anxiety disorder categories using a new structured interview. *Archives of General Psychiatry*, 1983, *40*, 1070-1075. **481, 768, 773**

Dince, P.R., **614**

Dirks, J.F., **652**

Dirks, J.F., Kleiger, J.H., & Evans, N.W. ASC panic-fear and length of hospitalization in asthma. *Journal of Asthma Research*, 1978, *15*(2), 95-97. **650, 652**

Dirks, J.F., Schraa, J.C., Brown, E.L., & Kinsman, R.A. Psychomaintenance in asthma: Hospitalization rates and financial impact. *British Journal of Medical Psychology*, 1980, *53*(4), 349-354. **650, 652**

Dittman, K., **213, 442**

Dobler-Mikola, A., **279**

Doctor, R.M., & Altman, F. Worry and emotionality as components of test anxiety: Replication and further data. *Psychological Reports*, 1969, *24*, 563-568. **120**

Dodson, J.D., **442**

Doherty, M.E., **406, 411**

Dollard, J., & Miller, N.E. *Personality and psychotherapy*. New York: McGraw-Hill, 1950. **100, 203, 214, 224, 225, 263, 267, 603, 707**

Donald, J.F. A study of a recognized antipsychotic agent as a tranquilizer in general practice. *Practitioner*, 1969, *203*, 684-687. **520, 523, 540**

Donham, G.W., **660**

Donnerstein, E., **149**

Donnerstein, E., & Hallam, J. Facilitating effects of erotica on aggression against women. *Journal of Personality and Social Psychology*, 1978, *36*, 1270-1277. **149**

Doongaji, D.R., Sheth, A., Apte, J.S., Bharucha, M., Mindra, V., & Ramesh, S. Pimozide versus chlordiazepoxide in anxiety neurosis. *Acta Psychiatrica Belgica*, 1981, *81*, 416-423. **520, 523, 540**

Doongaji, D.R., Sheth, A., Teste, D.V., & Ravindranath, P. A double blind study of pimozide versus chlordiazepoxide in anxiety neuroses. *Acta Psychiatrica Belgica*, 1976, *76*, 632-643. **520, 523, 540**

Doppelt, H.G., **106, 439, 692**

Dorow, R., Horowski, R., Paschelke, G., Amin, M., & Braestrup, C. Severe anxiety induced by FG 7142, a β-carboline ligand for benzodiazepine receptors. *Lancet*, 1983, *2*, 98-99. **34, 35, 36, 551**

Dostalova, J., **525**

Dostoevsky, F., **593**

Dougherty, F.E., **126**

Dougherty, L.M., **114, 417**

Dow, M.G., & Craighead, W.E. Cognition and social inadequacy: Relevance in clinical populations. In P. Trower (Ed.), *Cognitive perspectives in social skills training*. Oxford: Pergamon Press, 1982. **474**

Dowie, C., **521, 544**

Downey, K., **62, 63**

Downing, R.W., **79**

Doyle, L.A., **468**

Draguns, J.G. Psychological Disorders of Clinical Severity. In H. Trindis & J. Draguns (Eds.), *Handbook of cross-cultural psychology: Psychopathology* (Vol. 6). Boston: Allyn and Bacon, 1980, pp. 1-60. **299**

Drellich, M.G., **614**

Dresse, A.E., **545**

Droppleman, L.F., **135, 677, 689**

Dryden, W. Rational-emotive therapy and cognitive therapy: A critical comparison. In M.J. Mahoney & M. Reda (Eds.), *Cognitive psychotherapies: Recent developments in theory, research, and practice*. New York: Ballinger, in press. **431**

Duff, F.L. Item subtlety in personality inventory scales. *Journal of Consulting Psychology*, 1965, *29*, 565-570. **683**

Duffy, E. An explanation of "emotional" phenomena without the use of the concept "emotion". *Journal of General Psychology*, 1941, *25*, 283-293. **138, 139**

Duffy, E. *Activation and behavior*. New York: Wiley, 1962. **138, 334**

Duffy, E. Activation. In N.S. Greenfield & R.A. Sternbach (Eds.), *Handbook of psychophysiology*. New York: Holt, Rinehart, & Winston, 1972. **139, 140, 379**

Duffy, J.C., **58**

Duncan, W., **568, 569**

Dunlap, K., & Fischbach, G.D. Neurotransmitters decrease the calcium conductance activated by depolarization of embryonic chick sensory neurones. *Journal of Physiology*, 1981, *317*, 519-535. **13**

Dunn, J., Scheving, L., & Millet, P. Circadian variation in stress-evoked increases in plasma corticosterone. *American Journal of Physiology*, 1972, *223*, 402-406. **65**

Dunn, P., **603**

Dunn, T.M., **177**

Dunner, D.L., **562**

DuPont, R.L., **565, 570, 571**

Dustan, H.P., **82, 546, 551**

Dyrenfurth, I., **58**

Eagle, C., **62, 384**

Earll, J.M., **69, 70, 343**

Earls, F. The prevalence of behavior problems in three-year-old children. *Archives of General Psychiatry*, 1980, *37*, 1153-1157. **284**

Eaton, W.W., **281, 282**

Eaves, L., & Young, P.A. Genetical theory and personality differences. In R. Lynn (Ed.), *Dimensions of personality. Papers in honour of H.J. Eysenck*. New York: Pergamon Press, 1981. **685**

Eber, H.W., **654, 696**

Ebigbo, P.O. Development of a culture specific (Nigeria) screening scale of somatic complaints indicating psychiatric disturbance. *Culture, Medicine and Psychiatry*, 1982, *6*, 29-43. **303, 308**

Ebstein, B., **41, 43, 44, 45**

Eckstein, J.W., **346**

Edelbrock, C.S., **xxiii, 708, 712, 713, 714, 716, 717, 720, 724, 725**

Edelbrock, C.S., & Achenbach, T.M. A typology of child behavior profile patterns: Distribution and correlates for disturbed children aged 6-16. *Journal of Abnormal Child Psychology*, 1980, *8*, 441-70. **725, 730**

Edelson, M. *Hypothesis and Evidence in Psychoanalysis*. Chicago: University of Chicago Press, 1984. **634, 635, 641, 642, 644**

Edelson, R.J., **710**

Edmondson, E.D., Roscoe, B., & Vickers, M.D. Biochemical evidence of anxiety in dental patients. *British Medical Journal*, 1972, *4*, 7-9. **538**

Edmondson, H.D., **538**

Edwards, C.D., **126**

Edwards, W.L., & Lummus, W.F. Functional hypoglycemia and the hyperventilation syndrome: A clinical study. *Archives of Internal Medicine*, 1955, *42*, 1031-1040. **569**

Egelhoff, C., **309**

Eggeraat, J.B., **433**

Ehrlich, E.N., **61**

Ehrstrom, M.D. Psychogene blutdrucksteigerung in Kriegshypertonien. *Acta Medica Scandinavica*, 1945, *122*, 546-561. **347**

Eibl-Eibesfeldt, I. Similarity and differences between cultures in expressive movements. In R.A. Hinde (Ed.), *Nonverbal communication*. Cambridge, MA: Cambridge University Press, 1972, pp. 20-33. **116**

Eidelson, R.J., & Epstein, N. Cognition and relationship maladjustment: Development of a measure of dysfunctional relationship beliefs. *Journal of Consulting and Clinical Psychology*, 1982, *50*, 715-720. **93**

Eisdorfer, C., **357**

Eisenberg, L., **299, 400**

Eisenberg, L. School phobia: A study in the communication of anxiety. *American Journal of Psychiatry*, 1958, *114*, 712-718. **366**

Eitinger, L. The concentration camp syndrome and its late sequelae. In J. Dimsdale (Ed.), *Survivors, victims, and perpetrators*. Washington, D.C.: Hemisphere Publishing, 1980. **356**

Ek, J.I., **58**

Ekehammar, Bo., **659**

Ekman, P. Cross-cultural studies of facial expression. In P. Ekman (Ed.), *Darwin and facial expression*. New York: Academic Press, 1973. **135, 138**

Ekman, P. (Ed.). *Emotion in the human face* (2nd ed). Cambridge: Cambridge University Press, 1982. **417**

Ekman, P. Emotion differences in automatic nervous system activity. *Science*, 1983, *221*, 1208-1210. **135, 138**

Ekman, P., & Friesen, W.V. *The facial action coding system (FACS)*. California: Consulting Psychologists Press, 1978. **116**

Ekman, P., Friesen, W.V., & Ellsworth, P. *Emotion in the human face: Guidelines for research and an integration of findings*. New York: Pergamon Press, 1972. **112, 115, 116, 416**

Ekman, P., Levenson, R., & Friesen, W. Autonomic nervous system activity distinguishes among emotions. *Science*, 1983, *221*, 1208-1210. **113, 116**

Elam, M., **547**

Elam, M., Yao, T., Svensson, T.H., & Thoren, P. Regulation of locus coeruleus neurons and splanchnic, sympathetic nerves by cardiovascular afferents. *Brain Research*, 1984, *290*, 281-287. **550**

Elam, M., Yao, T., Thoren, P., & Svensson, T.H. Hypercapnia and hypoxia: Chemoreceptor-mediated control of locus coeruleus neurons and splanchnic, sympathetic nerves. *Brain Research*, 1981, *222*, 373-381. **551**

Eleftheriou, B.E., **55**

Elkins, R., **504, 506**

Elliot, T.R. The action of adrenalin. *Journal of Physiology*, 1905, *32*, 401-467. **550**

Elliott, G., & Eisdorfer, C. (Eds.). *Stress and human health*. New York: Springer Publishing, 1982. **357**

Ellis, A. What really causes a therapeutic change? *Voices*, 1968, *4*, 90-97. **431**

Ellis, A. *The essence of rational psychotherapy: A comprehensive approach to treatment.* New York: Institute for Rational Living, 1970. **102**

Ellis, A. Emotional education in the classroom: The living school. *Journal of Clinical Child Psychology*, 1971, *1*, 19-22. **167, 169**

Ellis, A. The basic clinical theory of rational-emotive therapy. In A. Ellis & R. Grieger (Eds.), *Handbook of Rational-Emotive Therapy.* New York: Springer, 1977. **431, 705**

Ellis, A. Skill training in counseling and psychotherapy. *Canadian Counsellor*, 1977b, *12*, 30-35. **431**

Ellis, A. Rational-emotive therapy and cognitive behavior therapy: Similarities and differences. *Cognitive Therapy and Research*, 1980, *4*, 325-340. **430**

Ellis, C.N., **348**

Ellis, J.P., Jr., **58**

Ellison, R.L. Pharmacologic control of anxiety, apprehension, and tension in dental practice. *General Dentistry*, 1979, *27*, 23-27. **538**

Ellsworth, P., **112, 115, 116, 416**

Elmadjian, F., **8**, 58, 149-154

Elmadjian, F. Adrenocortical function in combat infantrymen in Korea. *Ciba Foundation Colloquium on Endocrinology*, 1955, *8*, 627-653. **55**

Elmadjian, F., & Pincus, G. The adrenal cortex and the lymphocytopenia of stress. *Endocrinology*, 1945, *37*, 47-49. **55**

Elmadjian, F., & Pincus, G. A study of the diurnal variations in circulating lymphocytes in normal and psychotic subjects. *Journal of Clinical Endocrinology and Metabolism*, 1946, *6*, 281-294. **55**

Elston, R.C., **325, 327**

Elsworth, J.D., **548, 570**

Elveback, L.R., **555**

Emde, R.N., **125, 417, 418**

Emde, R.N. Levels of meaning for infant emotions: A biosocial view. In W.A. Collins (Ed.), *Minnesota symposia on child psychology, (Vol. 13): Development of cognition, affect and social relations.* Hillsdale, NJ: Lawrence Erlbaum Associates, 1980, pp. 1-37. **140, 416, 602, 605**

Emde, R.N. Changing models of infancy and the nature of early development. *Journal of the American Psychoanalytic Association*, 1981, *29*, 179-219. **414**

Emde, R.N. The prerepresentational self and its affective core. *The psychoanalytic study of the child* (Vol. 38). New Haven: Yale University Press, 1983, pp. 165-192. **416**

Emde, R.N., Gaensbauer, T.J., & Harmon, R.J. Emotional expression in infancy: A biobehavioral study. *Psychological Issues*, 1976, *10*(1), *Monograph 37*. New York: International Universities Press. **114, 414**

Emde, R.N., Kligman, D.H., Reich, J.H., & Wade, T.D. Emotional expression in infancy: Initial studies of social signaling and an emergent model. In M. Lewis & L. Rosenblum (Eds.), *The development of affect.* New York: Plenum Publishing Corp., 1978. **416, 417**

Emerson, E., **444**

Emery, G., **431, 705**

Emlen, J., **201, 215**

Emmelkamp, P.M.G., **427, 428**

Emmelkamp, P.M.G. Self-observation vs. flooding in the treatment of agoraphobia. *Behaviour Research and Therapy*, 1974, *12*, 229-237. **427, 428**

Emmelkamp, P.M.G. Cognition and exposure *in vivo* in the treatment of agoraphobia. Short term and delayed effects. *Cognitive Therapy and Research*, 1982, *6*, 77-88. **428**

Emmelkamp, P.M.G. *Phobic and obsessive compulsive disorders.* New York: Plenum, 1982. **422, 426, 506, 507, 508**

Emmelkamp, P.M.G., & Emmelkamp-Benner, A. Effects of historically portrayed modeling and group treatment on self-observation: A comparison with agoraphobics. *Behaviour Research and Therapy*, 1975, *13*, 135-139. **428**

Emmelkamp, P.M.G., & Kraanen, J. Therapist controlled exposure *in vivo* versus self-controlled exposure *in vivo*: A comparison with obsessive-compulsive patients. *Behaviour Research and Therapy*, 1977, *15*, 491-495. **428**

Emmelkamp, P.M.G., Kuipers, A.C., & Eggeraat, J.B. Cognitive modification versus prolonged exposure *in vivo*: A comparison with agoraphobics as subjects. *Behaviour Research and Therapy*, 1978, *16*, 33-41. **433**

Emmelkamp, P.M.G., & Kuipers, A.C.M. Agoraphobia: A follow-up study four years after treatment. *British Journal of Psychiatry*, 1979, *134*, 352-355. **428, 745**

Emmelkamp, P.M.G., & Kwee, K.G. Obsessional ruminations: A comparison between thought-stopping and prolonged exposure in imagination. *Behaviour Research and Therapy*, 1977, *15*, 441-444. **426**

Emmelkamp, P.M.G., & Mersch, P. Cognition and exposure *in vivo* in the treatment of agoraphobia. Short term and delayed effects. *Cognitive Therapy and Research*, 1982, *6*, 77-88. **433**

Emmelkamp, P.M.G., & Ultee, K.A. A comparison of successive approximation and self-observation in the treatment of agoraphobia. *Behavior Therapy*, 1974, *5*, 605-613. **427**

Emmelkamp, P.M.G., van de Helm, H., van Zanten, B., & Plochg, I. Contributions of self-instructional training to the effectiveness of exposure *in vivo*: A comparison with obsessive-compulsive patients. *Behaviour Research and Therapy*, 1980, *18*, 61-66. **433**

Emmelkamp, P.M.G., & Wessels, H. Flooding in imagination vs. flooding *in vivo*. A comparison with agoraphobics. *Behaviour Research and Therapy*, 1975, *13*, 7-16. **427-28**

Emmelkamp-Benner, A., **428**

Endicott, J., **60, 275, 394, 402**

Endicott, J., & Spitzer, R.L. A diagnostic interview: The schedule for affective disorders and schizophrenia. *Archives of General Psychiatry*, 1978, *35*, 837-844. **480, 676**

Endicott, J., & Spitzer, R.L. Use of the research diagnostic criteria and the schedule for affective disorders and schizophrenia to study affective disorders. *American Journal of Psychiatry*, 1979, *136*, 52/56. **480**

Endler, N.S., Magnusson, D., Ekehammar, Bo., & Okada, M. The multidimensionality of state and trait anxiety. *Scandinavian Journal of Psychology*, 1976, *17*(2), 81-96. **659**

Ends, E.J., & Page, C.W. Functional relationships among measures of anxiety, ego strength and adjustment. *Journal of Clinical Psychology*, 1957, *13*, 148-150. **647**

Ends, E.J., & Page, C.W. A study of three types of group psychotherapy with hospitalized male inebriates. *Quarterly Journal of Studies of Alcohol*, 1957, *18*, 263-277. **647**

Engberg, G., Elam, M., & Svensson, T.H. Clonidine withdrawal: Activation of brain noradrenergic neurons with specifically reduced alpha 2-receptor sensitivity. *Life Sciences*, 1982, *30*, 235-243. **547**

Engel, B.T., **137**

Engel, G. Anxiety and depression-withdrawal: The primary affects of unpleasure. *International Journal of Psycho-Analysis*, 1962, *43*, 89-97. **419**

Engelsman, F. , **504, 506, 586**

Epstein, N., **93**

Epstein, S., **132, 342, 343-44**

Epstein, S. The nature of anxiety with emphasis upon its relationship to expectancy. In C.M. Spielberger (Ed.), *Anxiety: Current trends in theory and research*. New York: Academic Press, 1972, pp. 291-337. **238**

Epstein, S. The stability of behavior: I. On predicting most of the people much of the time. *Journal of Personality and Social Psychology*, 1979, *37*, 1097-1126. **681, 682**

Erfurt, J.C., **347**

Ericksson, A., **207, 209, 268, 376**

Eriksen, C.W., **684**

Eriksen, C.W., & Davids, A. The meaning and clinical validity of the Taylor anxiety scale and the hysteria-psychasthenia scales from the MMPI. *Journal of Abnormal Social Psychology*, 1955, *50*, 135-137. **649**

Ernberg, G., **746**

Errera, P. Some historical aspects of the concept of phobia. *Psychiatric Quarterly*, 1962, *36*, 325-336. **735**

Esaki, M., **67, 68**

Escalona, S. Emotional development in the first year of life. In M.J. Senn (Ed.), *Problems of infancy and childhood*. New Jersey: Foundation Press, 1953. **372, 378, 382**

Esler, M.D., **347, 348**

Esler, M.D., Julius, S., Randall, O.S., Ellis, C.N., & Kashima, T. Relation of renin status to neurogenic vascular resistance in borderline hypertension. *American Journal of Cardiology*, 1977, *36*, 708-715. **348**

Esler, M.D., Julius, S., Zweifler, A., Randall, O.S., Harburg, E., Gardiner,

H., & DeQuattro, V. Mild high-renin essential hypertension. *New England Journal of Medicine*, 1975, *296*, 405-409. **348**

Essen-Moller, E., Larsson, H., Uddenberg, C.E., & White, G. Individual traits and morbidity in a Swedish rural population. *Acta Psychiatrica et Neurologica Scandinavica*, 1965, Supplement 100. **702**

Estes, E.H., **341**

Estess, F.M., **137**

Estis, W.C. A factor and comparative study of the state trait anxiety inventory. *Dissertation Abstracts International*, 1978, *39* (4-A), 2063. **667**

Evans, D.L., **530**

Evans, I.M., **499**

Evans, N.W., **62, 384, 650, 652**

Everaerd, W.T.A.M., Rijken, H.M., & Emmelkamp, P.M.G. A comparison of "flooding" and "successive approximation" in the treatment of agoraphobia. *Behaviour Research and Therapy*, 1973, *11*, 105-117. **427**

Eysenck, H.J., **408, 698**

Eysenck, H.J. *The handbook of abnormal psychology*. Basic Books: New York, 1961. **131, 135, 168**

Eysenck, H.J. *The biological basis of personality*. Springfield, IL: Thomas, 1967. **23, 25**

Eysenck, H.J. A theory of the incubation of anxiety/fear response. *Behaviour Research and Therapy*, 1968, *6*, 309-321. **210**

Eysenck, H.J. *Eysenck on extraversion*. New York: Wiley, 1973. **718**

Eysenck, H.J. The learning theory model of neurosis—a new approach. *Behaviour Research and Therapy*, 1976, *14*, 251-267. **210**

Eysenck, H.J. The conditioning model of neurosis. *The Behavioral and rain Sciences*, 1979, *2*, 155-199. **210, 469**

Eysenck, H.J., & Eysenck, S.B.G. *Personality structure and measurement*. London: Routledge & Kegan Paul, 1969. **699**

Eysenck, H.J., & Eysenck, S.B.G. *Manual of the Eysenck personality questionnaire*. London: Hodder & Stoughton, 1975. **696**

Eysenck, H.J., & Eysenck, S.B.G. *Psychoticism as a dimension of personality*. London: Hodder & Stoughton, 1976. **24**

Eysenck, H.J., & Rachman, S. *Causes and cures of neurosis*. London: Routledge & Kegan Paul, 1965. **203, 220**

Eysenck, S.B.G., **24, 696, 699**

Fabre, L.F., & McLendon, D.M. A double-blind study comparing the efficacy and safety of alprazolam with diazepam and placebo in anxious out-patients. *Current Therapeutic Research*, 1979, *25*, 519-526. **538**

Fair, P.L., **114, 116**

Fairbank, J.A., & Keane, T.M. Flooding for combat-related stress disorders: Assessment of anxiety reduction across traumatic memories. *Behavior Therapy*, 1982, *13*, 499-510. **427**

Falstein, E.L., **746**

Falzi, G., **346**

Fanelli, C., **68**

Fang, V.S., **61**

Farkas, G.M., Sine, L.F., & Evans, I.M. The effects of distraction, performance demand, stimulus explicitness and personality on objective and subjective measures of male sexual arousal. *Behaviour Research and Therapy*, 1979, *17*, 25-32. **499**

Farmer, B.B., **82**

Faschingbauer, T.R., **659**

Faust, J., & Melamed, B.G. The influence of arousal, previous experience, and age on surgery preparation of same day of surgery and in-hospital pediatric patients. *Journal of Consulting and Clinical Psychology*, 1984, *52*, 359-365. **384**

Feather, B.W., & Rhoads, J.M. Psychodynamic behavior therapy. I. Theory and rationale. *Archives of General Psychiatry*, 1972, *26*, 496-502. **617**

Fee, E.M., **519, 522, 540**

Feeney, B., **400, 405, 411, 716**

Feighner, J., Merideth, C., & Hendrickson, G. A double blind comparison of buspirone and diazepam in outpatients with generalized anxiety disorder. *Journal of Clinical Psychiatry*, 43, (*12*, section 2), 103-107, 1982. **516, 517**

Feighner, J.P., Robins, E., Guze, S.B., Woodruff, R.A., Winokur, G., & Munoz, R. Diagnostic criteria for use in psychiatric research. *Archives of General Psychiatry*, 1972, *26*, 57-63. **60, 762**

Feinberg, M., **66, 67**

Feinleib, N., **325, 327**

Feinman, S., & Lewis, M. *Social referencing and second order effects in ten-month old infants.* Paper presented at the Society for Research in Child Development, Boston, 1981. **417**

Feiring, C., **377**

Feldman, H., **519, 522, 540**

Feldman, R., & Paul, N. Identity of emotional triggers in epilepsy. *Journal of Nervous and Mental Disease*, 1976, *162*, 345-353. **593**

Feldon, J., **14, 20**

Feldon, J., & Gray, J.A. The partial reinforcement extinction effect after treatment with chlordiazepoxide. *Psychopharmacology*, 1981, *73*, 269-275. **21**

Feldon, J., Guillamon, A., Gray, J.A., De Wit, H., & McNaughton, N. Sodium amylobarbitone and responses to nonreward. *Quarterly Journal of Experimental Psychology*, 1979, *31*, 19-50. **21**

Felling, J.P., **177**

Fenichel, O. Remarks on the common phobias. *Psychoanalytic Quarterly*, 1944, *13*, 313-326. **603**

Fenichel, O. *The psychoanalytic theory of neurosis.* New York: W.W. Norton, 1945. **598**

Fenigsten, A., Scheir, M.F., & Buss, A.H. Public and private self-consciousness: Assessment and theory. *Journal of Consulting and Clinical Psychology*, 1975, *43*, 522-527. **470**

Fenton, F.R., **746**

Fenz, W.D. Specificity in somatic responses to anxiety. *Perceptual and Motor Skills*, 1967, *24*, 1183-1190. **132**

Fenz, W.D., & Epstein, S. Manifest anxiety: Unifactorial or multifactorial composition? *Perceptual and Motor Skills*, 1965, *20*, 773-780. **132**

Fenz, W.D., & Epstein, S. Gradients of physiological arousal of experienced and novice parachutists as a function of an approaching jump. *Psychosomatic Medicine*, 1967, *29*, 33-51. **342, 343-44**

Fenz, W.D., & Jones, G.B. Individual differences in physiological arousal and performance in sport parachutists. *Psychosomatic Medicine*, 1972, *34*, 1-18. **343**

Fernando, P., **485**

Ferrari, M., **374**

Ferster, C.B., & Perrott, M.C. *Behavior Principles*. New York: Appleton-Century-Crofts, 1968. **560**

Fiedler, F.E., **647**

Field, M.J. Mental disorder in rural Ghana. *Journal of Mental Science*, 1958, *104*, 1043-1051. **307**

Fielding, S., Wilker, J., Hynes, M., Szewczak, M., Novick, W.J., Jr., & Lal, H. A comparison of clonidine with morphine for antinociceptive and anti-withdrawal actions. *Journal of Pharmacology & Experimental Therapeutics*, 1978, *207*, 899-905. **543**

File, S.E., **538, 550**

File, S.E. Effects of benzodiazepines and naloxone on food intake and food preference in the rat. *Appetite*, 1980, *1*, 215-224(a). **31**

File, S.E. The use of social interactions as a method for detecting anxiolytic activity of chlordione epoxide-like drugs. *Journal of Neuroscience Methods*, 1980, *2*, 219-238(b). **31**

Fillenz, M., **8, 11, 12, 13, 15, 20**

Finberg, A.P., **541**

Finch, A.J., Jr., **659, 660, 661**

Finch, A.J., Jr., Kendall, P.C., & Montgomery, L.E. Multidimensionality of anxiety in children: Factor structure of the children's Manifest Anxiety Scale. *Journal of Abnormal Child Psychology*, 1974, *2*, 331-336. **709**

Findlander, P., **350**

Finesinger, J.E., **82**

Fink, G., **65**

Fink, M., **390, 512, 534, 543, 552, 560**

Fink, M., Taylor, M., & Volavka, J. Anxiety precipitated by lactate. *New England Journal of Medicine*, 1969, *281*, 1429. **82, 780**

Finkelfarb, E., **547, 549**

Finklestein, J.W., **62, 384**
Finlay-Jones, R.A., & Brown, G.W. Types of stressful life-events and the onset of anxiety depressive disorders. *Psychological Medicine*, 1981, *11*, 803-815. **194, 766**
Finnerty, R.J., **516, 517, 518, 521, 522, 545**
Finney, J.C., **367, 666, 667, 675, 676, 677, 685, 692**
Finney, J.C. The MMPI as a measure of character structure as revealed by factor analysis. *Journal of Consulting Psychology*, 1961, *25*, 327-336. **650, 670**
Finney, J.C. Some maternal influences on children's personality and character. *Genetic Psychology Monographs*, 1961, *63*, 199-278. **613, 648**
Finney, J.C. Development of a new set of MMPI scales. *Psychological Reports*, 1965, *17*, 707-713. **649, 657, 663**
Finney, J.C. Programmed interpretation of MMPI and CPI. *Archives of General Psychiatry*, 1966, *15*, 75-81. **649**
Finney, J.C., Smith, D.F., Skeeters, D.E., & Auvenshine, C.D. *Validation of computer diagnosis in psychiatry*. Unpublished paper, 1970. **646**
Fischbach, G.D., **13**
Fischer, S.C., **428**
Fischman, S.E., **378**
Fisher, S., **549**
Fisher, S., & Greenberg, R.P. (Eds.). *The scientific evaluation of Freud's theories and therapy*. New York: Basic Books, 1978. **612, 614, 615**
Fishman, J.R., **58, 61**
Fishman, R., **586, 587**
Fiske, D.W., **684**
Fiske, S., **123**
Flaherty, C.F., **476**
Flament, M., & Rapoport, J.L. Childhood obsessive compulsive disorder. In T.R. Insel (Ed.), *New findings in obsessive compulsive disorder*. Washington, D.C.: American Psychiatric Association Press, 1984. **584**
Flescher, J. A dualistic viewpoint on anxiety. *Journal of the American Psychoanalytic Association*, 1955, *3*, 415-446. **602**
Fletcher, H., **201, 215**
Flynn, J.P. The neural basis of aggression in cats. In D.C. Glass (Ed.), *Neurophysiology and emotion*. New York: Rockefeller University Press, 1967. **115**
Foa, E.B., **98, 423, 426, 428, 429, 438, 440, 465, 496**
Foa, E.B., & Chambless, D.L. Habituation of subjective anxiety during flooding in imagery. *Behaviour Research and Therapy*, 1978, *16*, 391-399. **438**
Foa, E.B., & Foa, U.G. Differentiating depression and anxiety: Is it possible? Is it useful? *Psychopharmacology Bulletin*, 1982, *18*, 62-68. **60, 692, 773, 791** ✳
Foa, E.B., & Goldstein, A. Continuous exposure and complete response-prevention in the treatment of obsessive-compulsive neurosis. *Behavior Therapy*, 1978, *9*, 821-829. **233, 429**

Foa, E.B., Grayson, J.B., & Steketee, G.S. Depression, habituation, and treatment outcome in obsessive-compulsives. In J.C. Boulougouris (Ed.), *Learning theory approaches to Psychiatry*. New York: Wiley & Sons, 1982. **144**

Foa, E.B., Grayson, J.B., Steketee, G.S., & Doppelt, H.G. Treatment of obsessive-compulsives: When do we fail? In E.B. Foa & Emmelkamp (Eds.), *Failures in behavior therapy*. New York: Wiley, 1983. **439**

Foa, E.B., Grayson, J.B., Steketee, G.S., Doppelt, H.G., Turner, R.H., & Latimer, P.R. Success and failure in the behavioral treatment of obsessive-compulsives. *Journal of Consulting and Clinical Psychology*, 1983, *51*, 287-297. **106, 692**

Foa, E.B., Jameson, J.S., Turner, R.M., & Payne, L.L. Massed vs. spaced exposure sessions in the treatment of agoraphobia. *Behaviour Research and Therapy*, 1980, *18*, 333-338. **428**

Foa, E.B., & Kozak, M.J. *Emotional processing of fear: Exposure to corrective information*. Unpublished manuscript, 1984. **xxxv, 218, 219, 220, 233, 241, 366, 435, 436, 453, 454, 455, 457, 458, 460, 463, 466, 479, 494, 498, 500**

Foa, E.B., & Steketee, G. Behavioral treatment of obsessive-compulsive ritualizers. In T.R. Insel (Ed.), *New findings in obsessive compulsive disorder*. Washington, D.C.: American Psychiatric Association Press, 1984. **585**

Foa, E.B., Steketee, G.S., & Milby, J.B. Differential effects of exposure and response prevention in obsessive-compulsive checkers. *Behaviour Research and Therapy*, 1980, *18*, 449-455. **429**

Foa, E.B., Steketee, G.S., & Ozarow, B.J. Behavior therapy with obsessive-compulsives: From theory to treatment. In M. Mavissakalian (Ed.), *Obsessive-compulsive disorder: Psychological and pharmacological treatment*. New York: Plenum Press, 1983. **423, 429, 446**

Foa, E.B., Steketee, G.S., Turner, R.M., & Fischer, S.C. Effect of imaginal exposure to feared disasters in obsessive-compulsive checkers. *Behaviour Research and Therapy*, 1980, *18*, 449-445. **428**

Foa, E.B., Steketee, G.S., & Young, M. *Agoraphobia: Phenomenological aspects*. Unpublished manuscript, 1984. **423**

Foa, U.G., **60, 692, 773, 791**

Fogarty, S.J., **143**

Folensbee, R., **473**

Folensbee, R. *The effects of stimulus control procedures on chronic worry*. Unpublished manuscript, Pennsylvania State University, 1983. **473**

Foley, J., **369, 371, 379**

Folgering, H., & Colla, P. Some anomalies in the control of $PaCo_2$ in patients with a hyperventilation syndrome. *Bulletin of the European Physiopathology of Respiration*, 1978, *14*, 503-509. **350**

Folkman, S., **112, 114, 119**

Fonberg, E. On the manifestation of conditioned defensive reactions in stress. Bulletin of the Society of Science and Letters of Fodz. Class III. *Science, Mathematics, and Nature*, 1956, *7*, 1. **148, 229, 271**

Fontaine, P., **551, 573**

Fontaine, R., **538**

Foote, F., **213, 214**

Foote, S.L., **550**

Foote, S.L., Aston-Jones, G., & Bloom, F. Impulse activity of locus coeruleus neurons in awake rats and monkeys is a function of sensory stimulation and arousal. *Proceedings of the National Academy of Sciences, U.S.A.*, 1980, *77*, 3033-3037. **554**

Foote, S.L., Bloom, F.E., & Aston-Jones, G. Nucleus locus coeruleus: New evidence of anatomical and physiological specificity. *Physiological Reviews*, 1983, *63*, 844-914. **554**

Forchetti, C.M., **39, 50**

Foreman, P.A. Control of the anxiety-pain complex in dentistry. Intravenous psychosedation with techniques using diazepam. *Oral Surgery*, 1974, *37*, 337-349. **538**

Forsman, L., **57**

Forssman, H. The anancastic syndrome. *Acta Psychiatrica Scandinavica*, 1963, *39*, 208-217. **745**

Foulds, G.A., & Bedford, A. The relationship between anxiety-depression and the neuroses. *British Journal of Psychiatry*, 1976, *128*, 166-168. **752**

Fowler, H., **243-44**

Fowler, R.D. MMPI computer interpretation for college counseling. *Journal of Psychology*, 1968, *69*, 201-207. **646**

Fowles, D.C. The three arousal model: Implications of Gray's two-factor learning theory for heart rate, electrodermal activity, and psychopathy. *Psychophysiology*, 1980, *17*, 87-104. **697**

Fox, C.F., **15**

Fox, H.M., Murausku, B., Bartholomay, A., & Giffords, S. Adrenal steroid excretion patterns in healthy subjects: Tentative correlations with personality structure. *Psychosomatic Medicine*, 1961, *23*, 33-40. **59**

Fox, N., **377**

Fox, S.M., **351**

Fraiberg, S. *Insights from the blind*. New York: Basic Books, 1977. **414**

Frances, A., **370, 377, 619, 641, 642, 700**

Frances, A., & Dunn, P. The attachment-autonomy conflict in agoraphobia. *International Journal of Psycho-Analysis*, 1975, *56*, 435-439. **603**

Frankenhaeuser, M. Behavior and circulating catecholamines. *Brain Research*, 1971, *31*, 241-262. **137**

Frankenhaeuser, M. Sympathetic adrenomedullary activity, behavior and the psychosocial environment. In P.H. Venables & M.J. Christie (Eds.), *Research in psychophysiology*. London: Wiley, 1975, pp. 71-94. **57**

Frankenhaeuser, M. Psychoneuroendocrine approaches to the study of emotion as related to stress and coping. *Nebraska Symposium on Motivation*, 1978, *26*, 123-161. **56, 57**

Frankenhaeuser, M. Psychoneuroendocrine approaches to the study of emotion as related to stress and copying. In R.A. Dienstbier (Ed.), *Nebraska symposium on motivation*. Lincoln: University of Nebraska Press, 1979. **115**

Frankenhaeuser, M. Psychobiological aspects of life stress. In S. Levine & H. Ursin (Eds.), *Coping and health*. New York: Plenum, 1980, pp. 203-223. **56**

Frankenhaeuser, M., Lundberg, U., & Forsman, L. Note on arousing type A persons by depriving them of work. *Journal of Psychosomatic Research*, 1980, *24*, 45-47. **57**

Frankenhaeuser, M., Nordheden, B., Myrsten, A.L., & Post, B. Psychophysiological reactions to understimulation and overstimulation. *Acta Psychologica*, 1971, *35*, 298-308. **335**

Frankenhaeuser, M., Rauste von Wright, M., Collins, A., von Wright, J.M., Sedvall, G., & Swahn, C.G. Sex differences in psychoneuroendocrine reactions to examination stress. *Psychosomatic Medicine*, 1978, *40*, 334-343. **66**

Frankenhaeuser, M., & Rissler, A. Catecholamine output during relaxation and anticipation. *Perceptual and Motor Skills*, 1970, *30*, 745-746. **57**

Fransson, C., & Gemzell, C.A. Adrenocortical activity in the preoperative period. *Journal of Clinical Endocrinology* (Kobenhavn), 1955, *15*, 1069-1072. **56, 58**

Frantz, A.G., **69, 70, 343**

Fredrikson, M., **207, 209, 376**

Freedman, D.A., **587, 775**

Freedman, D.A., Cannady, C., & Robinson, J.S. Speech and psychic structure. *Journal of the American Psychoanalytic Association*, 1971, *19*, 765-779. **414**

Freedman, M., **116**

Fremming, K.H. The expectation of mental infirmity in a sample of the danish population. *Occasional Papers on Eugenics, No. 7.*, London: Cassell, 1951. **278**

French, R., **235, 243**

French, T.M. Interrelations between psychoanalysis and the experimental work of Pavlov. *American Journal of Psychiatry*, 1933, *12*, 1165-1203. **701**

Frerking, R.A., **659**

Freud, A. *The ego and the mechanisms of defence*. New York: International Universities Press, 1946. **603**

Freud, S., **77, 105, 174, 175, 176, 180, 194, 409, 410, 591, 592, 596, 597, 599, 601, 602, 608, 609, 611, 612, 614, 615, 642, 669, 670, 700, 701, 779, 787**

Freud, S. *Collected papers* (Vol. I). London: Hogarth Press, 1924. **173**

Freud, S. *New introductory lectures in psychoanalysis*. New York: W.W. Norton, 1933. **173**

Freud, S. *The problem of anxiety* (translated by H.A. Bunker from "Hemmung, Symptom und Angst"). New York: The Psychoanalytic Quarterly Press & W.W. Norton, 1936. **173, 177, 334, 533, 554**

Freud, S. Analysis of a phobia in a five-year-old boy (1909). In *Standard edition of the complete works of Sigmund Freud* (Vol. 7). London: Hogarth Press, 1953. **707**

Freud, S. The interpretation of dreams (1900). In *Standard edition of the complete psychological works of Sigmund Freud* (Vols. 4 & 5). London: Hogarth Press, 1953. **701**

Freud, S. The analysis of a phobia in a 5-year-old boy. *Standard edition of the complete psychological works of Sigmund Freud* (Vol. 10). London. Hogarth Press, 1955, pp. 26-27. **408**

Freud, S. From the history of an infantile neurosis (1918). In *Standard edition of the complete psychological works of Sigmund Freud* (Vol. 17). London: Hogarth Press, 1955. **411, 600, 707**

Freud, S. Notes upon a case of obsessional neurosis (1909). *Standard edition of the complete works of Sigmund Freud* (Vol. 10). London: Hogarth Press, 1955, pp. 153-318. **577, 643**

Freud, S. Dostoevsky and parricide. In *Sigmund Freud collected papers* (Vol. 5). (J. Riviere, translator). New York: Basic Books, 1959, pp. 224-225. **593**

Freud, S. Inhibition, symptoms, and anxiety (1926a). In *Standard edition of the complete psychological works of Sigmund Freud* (Vol. 20). London: Hogarth Press, 1959. **120, 419, 598, 600, 601, 602, 620, 623, 624, 700, 707, 738**

Freud, S. Obsessions and phobias; their psychical mechanisms and their aetiology (1895). In *Sigmund Freud collected papers* (Vol. 1). (J. Riviere, translator). New York: Basic Books, 1959, pp. 136-137. **120**

Freud, S. Introductory lectures on psycho-analysis (1915-1916). In *Standard edition of the complete psychological works of Sigmund Freud* (Vol. 15). London: Hogarth Press, 1961. **600**

Freud, S. The neuro-psychoses of defence (1894a). In *Standard edition of the complete psychological works of Sigmund Freud* (Vol. 3). London: Hogarth Press, 1962. **597, 761, 775**

Freud, S. On the grounds for detaching a particular syndrome for neurasthenia under the description "anxiety neurosis" (1894b). In *Standard edition of the complete psychological works of Sigmund Freud* (Vol. 3). London: Hogarth Press, 1962. **600, 609**

Freud, S. Project for a scientific psychology (1895). In *Standard edition of the complete psychological works of Sigmund Freud: Vol. 1*. London: Hogarth Press, 1966. **591, 738**

Freyberger, H., **167**

Fridlund, A.J., & Schwartz, G.E. Facial muscle patterning and emotion: I. Implementation of multivariate pattern-classification strategies. Paper presented at the 19th annual meeting of the Society for Psychophysiological Research, Cincinnati, October 1979. **114**

Friedhoff, A.J., **587**

Friedman, M.S., **365**

Friedman, M.S., & Rosenman, R.H. Type A behavior pattern: Its association with coronary heart disease. *Annals of Clinical Research*, 1971, *3*, 300-312. **68**

Friedman, M.S., St. George, S., Byers, S.O., & Rosenman, R.H. Excretion of catecholamines, 17-ketosteroids, 17-hydroxy-corticoids, and 5-hydroxyindole in men exhibiting a particular behavior pattern (A) associated with high incidences of clinical coronary artery disease. *Journal of Clinical Investigation*, 1960, *39*, 758-764. **365**

Friedman, S.B., **59, 65**

Friend, R., **120**

Friesen, W.V., **112, 113, 115, 116, 416**

Frieze, L., **121**

Friis, W., **539**

Frijda, N., & Phillipszoon, E. Dimensions of recognition of expression. *Journal of Abnormal Social Psychology*, 1963, *66*, 45-51. **416**

Frith, C., **521, 544**

Frohlich, E.D., Dustan, H.P., & Page, I.H. Hyperdynamic beta-adrenergic circulatory state. *Archives of Internal Medicine*, 1966, *117*, 614-619. **82, 546, 551**

Frohlich, E.D., Tarazi, R.C., & Dustan, H.P. Hyperdynamic beta-adrenergic circulatory state. Increased beta-receptor responsiveness. *Archives of Internal Medicine*, 1969, *123*, 1-7. **82, 546, 551**

Frommer, E., **750**

Fuhr, R., **499**

Fujii, I., **746**

Fukushima, D., **62, 65, 384**

Fulker, D.W. The genetic and environmental architecture of psychoticism, extraversion, and neuroticism. In H.J. Eysenck (Ed.), *A model for personality*. Berlin: Springer, 1981. **23, 236**

Fuller, T.C., **780**

Fung, S.C., **8, 11, 12, 13, 15**

Funkenstein, D.H. The physiology of fear and anger. *Scientific American*, 1955, *192*, 74-80. **113**

Funkenstein, D.H., Greenblatt, M., & Solomon, H.C. Nor-epinephrine-like and epinephrine-like substances in psychotic and psychoneurotic patients. *American Journal of Psychiatry*, 1952, *108*, 652-661. **137**

Furberg, C., & Tengblad, C.F. Adrenergic beta-receptor blockade and the effect of hyperventilation on the electrocardiogram. *Scandinavian Journal of Clinical and Laboratory Investigation*, 1966, *18*, 467-472. **351**

Furst, S.S. *Psychic trauma*. New York: Basic Books, 1967. **611**

Fuxe, K., **7, 15, 539**

Fuxe, K., Agnati, L.F., Bolme, P., Hokfelt, T.I., Lidbrink, P., Ljungdahl, A., de la Mora, M.P., & Ogren, S.-O. The possible involvement of GABA mechanisms in the action of benzodiazepines on central catecholamine neurons. In E. Costa & P. Greengard (Eds.), *The mechanism of action of benzodiazepines*. New York: Plenum Press, 1975. **539, 540**

Fyer, A.F., **365, 586**

Fyer, A.J., **527, 547**

Fyrò, B., Beck-Friis, J., & Sjostrand, I.-G. A comparison between diazepam and haloperidol in anxiety states. *Acta Psychiatric Scandinavica*, 1974, *50*, 586-595. **519, 522, 540**

Gaensbauer, T.J., **114, 414, 418**
Gaensbauer, T.J., Emde, R.N., & Campos, J.J. Stranger distress: Confirmation of a developmental shift in a longitudinal sample. *Perceptual and Motor Skills*, 1976, *43*, 99-106. **125**
Gaffney, F.A., Karlsson, E.S., & Campbell, W. Autonomic dysfunction in women with mitral valve prolapse syndrome. *Circulation*, 1979, *59*, 894-891. **351**
Gaind, R., **427, 436, 438**
Galeazzi, R.L., **551**
Gallager, D.W., **33, 538, 539**
Gallager, D.W., Mallorga, P., Oertel, W., Henneberry, R., & Tallman, J.F. [^{3}H] Diazepam binding in mammalian central nervous system: A pharmacological characterization. *Journal of Neuroscience*, 1981, *1*, 218-225. **40**
Gallagher, T.E., **62**
Gallagher, T.F., **65**
Gallen, C.C., **367**
Gallo, J., **780**
Gammon, G.D., **40, 286, 288, 290, 292, 293, 294, 394, 396**
Gantt, H., **xxi**
Gantt, H. Principles of nervous breakdown in schizokinesis and autokinesis. In E.J. Kempf (Ed.), Comparative conditioned neuroses. *Annals of the New York Academy of Science*, 1953, *56*, 141-169. **222**
Ganzer, V.J., **180**
Garattini, S., **30**
Garber, J., Miller, S., & Abramson, L. On the distinction between anxiety and depression: Perceived control, certainty and probability of goal attainment. In J. Garber & M. Seligman (Eds.), *Human helplessness: Theory and applications*. New York: Academic Press, 1980, pp. 131-171. **238, 240**
Garcia, K.A., **714**
Gardin, J.M., Isner, J.M., Ronana, J.A., & Fox, S.M. Pseudoischemia "false positive" S-T segment changes induced by hyperventilation in patients with mitral prolapse. *American Journal of Cardiology*, 1980, *45*, 952-957. **351**
Gardiner, H., **348**
Garfield, S., Gershon, S., Sletten, I., Sunland, D.M., & Ballou, S. Chemically induced anxiety. *International Journal of Neuropsychiatry*, 1967, *3*, 426-433. **571**
Garfield, S.L., **195**
Garner, W.R., Hake, H.W., & Eriksen, C.W. Operationism and the concept of perception. *Psychological Review*, 1956, *63*, 149-159. **684**
Garside, R.F., **328, 366, 392, 393, 511, 513, 747, 773**

Gasonov, G.G. Emotions, visceral functions, and limbic system. In G.G. Gasonov (Ed.), *Emotions and visceral functions*. Moscow: Elm Press, 1974. **115**

Gasonov, G.G. Self-control and predictability: Their effects on reactions to aversive stimulation. *Journal of Personality and Social Psychology*, 1971, *18*, 157-162. **115**

Gastpar, M., **746**

Gath, D.H., **220, 425**

Gaudry, E., & Poole, C. A further validation of the state-trait distinction in anxiety research. *Australian Journal of Psychology*, 1975, *27*, 119-125. **660**

Gaudry, E., Vagg, P., & Spielberger, C.D. Validation of the state-trait distinction in anxiety research. *Multivariate Behavioral Research*, 1975, *10* (3), 331-341. **649**

Geer, J., & Fuhr, R. Cognitive factors in sexual arousal: The role of distraction. *Journal of Consulting and Clinical Psychology*, 1976, *44*, 238-243. **499**

Geer, J., Morokoff, P., & Greenwood, P. Sexual arousal in women: The development of a measurement device for vaginal blood volume. *Archives of Sexual Behavior*, 1974, *3*, 559-564. **140**

Geertz, C. *Local knowledge: Further essays in interpretive anthropology*. New York: Basic Books, 1983. **321**

Geertz, H. Latah in Java: A theoretical paradox. *Indonesia*, 1968, *3*, 93-104. **313**

Gelder, M.G., **216, 217, 218, 425, 426, 428, 433, 439**

Gelder, M.G., Bancroft, J.H.J., Gath, D.H., Johnston, D.W., Mathews, A.M., & Shaw, P.M. Specific and non-specific factors in behaviour therapy. *British Journal of Psychiatry*, 1973, *123*, 445-462. **220, 425**

Gelder, M.G., & Marks, I.M. Severe agoraphobia: A controlled prospective trail of behaviour therapy. *British Journal of Psychiatry*, 1966, *112*, 309-319. **64, 425**

Gelder, M.G., & Marks, I.M. Desensitization and phobias: A crossover study. *British Journal of Psychiatry*, 1968, *114*, 323-328. **425**

Gelder, M.G., Marks, I.M., & Wolff, H.H. Desensitization and psychotherapy in the treatment of phobic states: A controlled enquiry. *British Journal of Psychiatry*, 1967, *113*, 53-73. **425**

Gelhorn, E. Prolegomena to a theory of the emotions. *Perspectives in Biology and Medicine*, 1961, *4*, 403-436. **115, 118**

Gelhorn, E. Motion and emotion: The role of proprioception in the physiology and pathology of the emotions. *Psychological Review*, 1964, *71* (6), 457-472. **115, 138**

Gelhorn, E. The neurophysiological basis of anxiety: A hypothesis. *Perspectives in Biology and Medicine*, 1965, *8*, 488-515. **115**

Geller, I., Bachman, E., & Seifter, J. Effects of reserpine and morphine on behavior suppressed by punishment. *Life Sciences*, 1963, *4*, 226-231. **14, 541**

Geller, J., & Seifter, J. The effects of meprobamate, barbiturate, diamphetamine and promazine on experimentally induced conflict in the rat. *Psychopharmacologia*, 1960, *1*, 482-492. **32**

Gelles, L., **67**

Gelshteyn, E.M. Clinical characteristics of hypertensive disease under wartime conditions. *Klinika Medicina (Moskova)*, 1943, *21*, 10-15. **347**

Gemzell, C.A., **56, 58**

Genero, N., **243**

Gennari, F.J., Goldstein, M.B., & Schwartz, W.B. The nature of the renal adaptation to chronic hypocapnia. *Journal of Clinical Investigation*, 1972, *51*, 1722-1727. **349**

Gentil, M.L.F., & Lader, M. Dream content and daytime attitudes in anxious and calm women. *Psychological Medicine*, 1978, *8*, 297-304. **167, 194**

George, L.K., **xxx**

Geraci, M.F., **558, 559, 561, 569**

German, D.C., **544, 545, 592**

Gershon, E.S., **286, 563**

Gershon, S., **551, 571**

Gever, J., **288**

Ghoneim, M.M., **538, 682**

Gibree, N.R., **8**, 58, 149-154

Giel, R., & Van Luijk, J.N. Psychiatric morbidity in a rural village in South-Western Ethiopia. *International Journal of Social Psychiatry*, 1970, *16*, 63-71. **304**

Giencke, L., **234, 236**

Giffords, S., **59**

Gilbert, R.M. Caffeine as a drug of abuse. In Gibbins, R.J. et al. (Eds.), *Research advances in alcohol and drug problems* (Vol. 3). New York: John Wiley & Sons, 1976. **573**

Gilligan, S.G., & Bower, G.H. Cognitive consequences of emotional arousal. In C. Izard, J. Kagan, & R. Zajonc (Eds.), *Emotion, cognition, and behavior*. New York: Cambridge University Press, 1984. **144**

Gilliland, K., & Andress, D. Ad lib caffeine consumption, symptoms of caffeinism and academic performance. *American Journal of Psychiatry*, 1981, *138*, 512-514. **551, 573**

Gillin, J.C., **568, 588**

Gillin, J.C., Sitaram, N., Wehr, T., Duncan, W., Post, R.M., Murphy, D.L., Mendelson, W.B., Wyatt, R.M., & Bunney, W.E., Jr. Sleep and affective illness. In R.M. Post & J.C. Balenger, (Eds.), *Neurobiology of mood disorders*. Baltimore: Williams & Wilkins, 1984. **568, 569**

Gillis, J.S., **648**

Gilman, A., **241**

Gilman, A.G., Goodman, L.S., & Gilman, A. *Goodman and Gilman's The Pharmacological Basis Therapeutics* (6th ed.) New York: MacMillan, 1980. **241**

Gilmore, J.B., **106**

Gino, A., **205, 221, 234, 236**

Gittelman, R., **366, 403, 404, 406, 407, 408, 409, 502, 512, 513, 540, 585, 606, 709, 725**

Gittelman-Klein, R., **291**

Gittelman-Klein, R. Psychiatric characteristics of the relatives of school phobic children. In D.V. Siva-Sankar (Ed.), *Mental health in children* (Vol. 1). New York: PJD Publications, Inc., 1975. **293, 395**

Gittelman-Klein, R., & Klein, D.F. The relationship between promorbid asocial adjustment and prognosis in schizophrenia. *Journal of Psychiatric Research*, 1969, *7*, 35-53. **401**

Gittelman-Klein, R., & Klein, D.F. Controlled imipramine treatment of school phobia. *Archives of General Psychiatry*, 1971, *25*, 204-207. **511, 513, 524**

Gittelman-Klein, R., & Klein, D.F. School phobia: Diagnostic considerations in the light of imipramine effects. *Journal of Nervous and Mental Diseases*, 1973, *156*, 199-215. **392**

Gittelman-Klein, R., & Klein, D.F. Separation anxiety in school refusal and its treatment with drugs. In L. Hersov, & I. Berg (Eds.), *Out of school*. New York: John Wiley & Sons, 1980. **293, 390, 391, 393**

Gittelson, N. The fate of obsessions in depressive psychosis. *British Journal of Psychiatry*, 1966, *112*, 705-708. **587**

Gladstone, W.H. A multidimensional study of facial expressions of emotion. *Australian Journal of Psychology*, 1962, *14*, 95-100. **417**

Glass, G.V., **612**

Glass, R., Uhlenhuth, E.H., & Kellner, R. *The value of self-report assessment in studies of anxiety disorders*. Presented at a research conference on Anxiety Disorders, Panic Attacks, and Phobias, Key Biscayne, Florida, December 10, 1982. **678**

Glasscock, E.M. *An investigation of the value of the MMPI as a prognostic instrument*. Unpublished doctoral dissertation, Washington University, 1954. **647**

Glazer, H.I., **17, 18, 19, 20, 25**

Gleitman, H., Nachmias, H., & Neisser, U. The S-R reinforcement theory of extinction. *Psychological Review*, 1954, *61*, 23-33. **203**

Glennon, B., & Weisz, J.R. An observational approach to the assessment of anxiety in young children. *Journal of Consulting and Clinical Psychology*, 1978, *46*, 1246-1257. **708**

Gleser, G.C., **546, 614**

Gleser, G.C., Gottschalk, L.A., & Springer, K.J. an anxiety scale applicable to verbal samples. *Archives of General Psychiatry*, 1961, *5*, 593-605. **614**

Glick, S.M., **68**

Glicklich, J., **365, 586**

Gloger, S., **512**

Gloor, P., Olivier, A., Quesney, L.F., Andermann, F., & Horowitz, S. The role of the limbic system in experiential phenomena of temporal lobe epilepsy. *Annals of Neurology*, 1982, *12*, 129-144. **558**

Glover, V., **538**

Glover, V., Armando, I., Clow, A., & Sandler, M. Endogenous urinary monoamine oxidase inhibitor: The benzodiazepine connection. *Modern Problems of Pharmacopsychiatry*, 1983, *19*, 118-125. **538**

Glover, V., Bhattacharya, S.K., Sandler, M., & File, S.E. Benzodiazepines reduce stress-augmented increase in rat urine monoamine oxidase inhibitor. *Nature*, 1981, *292*, 347-349. **538**

Glymour, C. *Theory and evidence*. Princeton, NJ: Princeton University Press, 1980. **643**

Goddwin, F.K., **49**

Goetz, F.C., **55**

Gold, A., **521, 544**

Gold, M.S., & Fox, C.F. Antianxiety and opiates. *Behavioral and Brain Sciences*, 1982, *5*, 486-487. **15**

Gold, M.S., Pottash, A.L.C., Sweeney, D.R., & Kleber, H.D. Clonidine detoxification: A fourteen day protocol for rapid opiate withdrawal. In *Problems of drug dependence*, NIDA Research Monograph Vol. 27. Rockville: U.S. Department of Health, Education and Welfare, 1979. **15**

Gold, M.S., Redmond, D.E., Jr., & Kleber, H.D. Clonidine blocks acute opiate-withdrawal symptoms. *Lancet*, 1978, *2* (8090), 599-602. (a). **552**

Gold, M.S., Redmond, D.E., Jr., & Kleber, H.D. Clonidine in opiate withdrawal. *Lancet*, 1978, *1* (8070), 929-930. (b). **552**

Gold, M.S., Redmond, D.E., Jr., & Kleber, H.D. Noradrenergic hyperactivity in opiate withdrawal supported by clonidine reversal of opiate withdrawal. *American Journal of Psychiatry*, 1979, *136*, 100-102. **526**

Goldberg, D.P., & Hillier, V.F. A scaled version of the general health questionnaire. *Psychological Medicine*, 1979, *9*, 139-145. **677**

Goldberg, H.L., & Finnerty, R. The use of doxepin in the treatment of symptoms of anxiety neurosis and accompanying depression: A collaborative controlled study. *American Journal of Psychiatry*, 1972, *129*, 74-77. **521**

Goldberg, H.L., & Finnerty, R.J. The comparative efficacy of buspirone and diazepam in the treatment of anxiety. *American Journal of Psychiatry*, 1979, *136*, 1184-1187. **545**

Goldberg, H.L., & Finnerty, R. Comparison of buspirone in two separate studies. *Journal of Clinical Psychiatry*, 1982, *43*, (12, section 2) 87-91. **516, 517, 518, 522**

Goldberg, L.R., **681, 685, 686**

Goldberg, L.R. Parameters of personality inventory construction and utilization: A comparison of prediction strategies and tactics. *Multivariate Behavioral Research Monographs*, 1972, *72* (2). **686**

Goldberg, L.R. Language and individual differences: The search for universals in personality lexicons. In L. Wheeler (Ed.), *Review of personality and social psychology* (Vol. 2). Beverly Hills, CA: Sage, 1981. **696**

Golden, R.R., **723**

Goldfoot, D.A., **254**

Goldfried, M.R. Systematic desensitization as training in self-control. *Journal of Consulting and Clinical Psychology*, 1971, *37*, 228-234. **429**

Goldfried, M.R. The use of relaxation and cognitive relabeling as coping skills. In R.B. Stuart (Ed.), *Behavioral self management*. New York: Brunner/ Mazel, 1977. **102**

Goldfried, M.R. (Ed.) *Converging themes in psychotherapy: Trends in psychodynamic, humanistic, and behavioral practice*. New York: Springer, 1982. **103, 106**

Goldfried, M.R., & Davison, G.C. *Clinical behavior therapy*. New York: Holt, Rinehart, & Winston, 1976. **241**

Goldie, R.G. The effects of hydrocortisone on responses to and extraneuronal uptake of (-) isoprenaline in cat and gut atria. *Clinical and Experimental Pharmacology and Physiology*, 1976, *3*, 225-233. **346**

Goldin, S., **534, 550**

Goldman-Eisler, F. The problem of "orality" and of its origins in early childhood. *Journal of Mental Science*, 1951, *97*, 765-782. **613**

Goldstein, A.J., **233, 423, 426, 429, 440, 463, 477**

Goldstein, A.P., **249**

Goldstein, B., **519, 522, 540**

Goldstein, H., **371**

Goldstein, M.B., **349**

Golgen, S., **365**

Good, B., **299, 325, 326, 327, 485, 688**

Good, B. The heart of what's the matter: The semantics of illness in Iran. *Culture, Medicine and Psychiatry*, 1977, *1*, 25-58. **314**

Good, B., & Good, M. The meaning of symptoms: A cultural hermeneutic model for clinical practice. In L. Eisenberg & A. Kleinman (Eds.), *The relevance of social science for medicine*. Dordrecht, Holland: Reidel, 1980. pp. 165-196. **313**

Good, B., & Good, M. The semantics of medical discourse. In E. Mendelsohn & Y. Elkana (Eds.), *Sciences and cultures: Sociology of the sciences* (Vol. 5). Dordrecht, Holland: Reidel, 1981. pp. 177-212. **313, 315**

Good, B., & Good, M. Toward a meaning-Centered Analysis of Popular illness categories: "Fright illness" and "heart distress" in Iran. In A.J. Marsella & G.M. White (Eds.), *Cultural conceptions of mental health and therapy*. Dordrecht, Holland: Reidel, 1982. pp. 141-166. **313, 314**

Good, M., **313, 314, 315**

Goodhart, D., **251**

Goodman, L., **241**

Goodman, M., **288**

Goodman, P.A., **17, 18, 19, 20**

Goodwin, D., Guze, S., & Robins, E. Follow-up studies in obsessional neurosis. *Archives of General Psychiatry*, 1969, *20*, 182-187. **579, 587**

Goodwin, F.K., **28, 31, 48, 570, 573**

Gordon, M.H. *Analysis of project one.* Research conference, Veterans Administration Hospital, Downey, Illinois, June 1958. **647**

Gorman, J.M., **xxxiii, 241, 328, 366, 453, 456, 540, 552, 586, 591**

Gorman, J.M., Fyer, A.F., & Glicklich, J. Mitral valve prolapse and panic disorders: Effect of imipramine. In D.F. Klein & J. Rabkin, (Eds.), *Anxiety: New research and changing concepts.* New York: Raven Press, 1981. **365**

Gorman, J.M., Fyer, A.F., Glicklich, J., King, D., & Klein, D.F. Effects of sodium lactate on patients with panic disorder and mitral valve prolapse. *American Journal of Psychiatry*, 1981, *138*, 247-249. **586**

Gorman, J.M., Levy, G.F., Liebowitz, M.R., McGrath, P., Appleby, I.L., Dillon, D.J., Davies, S.O., & Klein, D.F. Effect of acute beta-adrenergic blockade on lactate-induced panic. *Archives of General Psychiatry*, 1983, *40*, 1079-1082. **551**

Gorsuch, R.L., **300, 565, 571, 657, 684, 689**

Gosling, R.H. Clinical experience with oxprenolol in treatment of anxiety in the United Kingdom. In P. Kielholz (Ed.), *Beta-blockers and the central nervous system* Baltimore: University Park Press, 1977. **546**

Gotlib, I.H. Depression and general psychopathology in university students. *Journal of Abnormal Psychology*, 1984, *93*, 19-30. **692**

Gottesman, I.I., **275, 278, 285, 327, 328, 585**

Gottschalk, L.A., **546, 614**

Gottschalk, L.A., Gleser, G.C., & Springer, K.J. Three hostility scales applicable to verbal samples. *Archives of General Psychiatry*, 1963, *9*, 254-279. **614 614**

Gottschalk, L.A., Stone, W.N., & Gleser, G.C. Peripheral versus central mechanisms accounting for antianxiety effects of propranolol. *Psychosomatic Medicine*, 1974, *36*, 47-56. **546**

Gough, H.G. *The California psychological inventory manual.* Palo alto, CA: Consulting Psychologists Press, 1957. **662**

Gough, H.G. *Manual for the California psychological inventory.* Palo Alto, CA: Consulting Psychologists Press, 1975. **696**

Grace, W.J., **58**

Gracely, R.H., **565**

Graff, H., **643**

Graham, A.W., & Aghajanian, G.K. Effects of amphetamine on single cell activity in a catecholamine nucleus, the locus coeruleus. *Nature* (London), 1971, *234*, 100-102. **541**

Graham, D.T., **152**

Graham, D.T. Psychosomatic Medicine. In N.S. Greenfield & R.A. Sternbach (Eds.), *Handbook of psychophysiology.* New York: Holt, Rinehart, & Winston, 1972. **137**

Graham, D.T., Kabler, J.D., & Graham, F.K. Physiological responses to the suggestion of attitudes specific for hives and hypertension. *Psychosomatic Medicine*, 1962, *24*, 159-169. **137**

Graham, F.K., **137, 152**

Graham, F.K., & Clifton, R.K. Heart rate change as a component of the orienting response. *Psychological Bulletin*, 1966, *65*, 305-320. **153, 156**

Graham, J.D.P. High blood pressure after battle. *Lancet*, 1945, *1*, 239-240. **347**

Graham, P.J., **284**

Graham, S., **121**

Grand, H.G., **614**

Grandison, L., **11**

Grange, R.A., **350**

Grant, K., **349**

Grant, S.J., Huang, Y.H., & Redmond, D.E., Jr. Benzodiazepines attenuate single unit activity in the locus coeruleus. *Life Sciences*, 1980, *27*, 2231-2237. **539, 551**

Grant, S.J., & Redmond, D.E., Jr. The neuroanatomy and pharmacology of the nucleus locus coeruleus. In H. Lal & S. Fielding (Eds.), *The psychopharmacology of clonidine*. New York: Alan R. Liss, Inc., 1981. **550, 554**

Grant, S.J., & Redmond, D.E., Jr. Methylxanthine activation of noradrenergic unit activity and reversal by clonidine. *European Journal of Pharmacology*, 1982, *85*, 105-109 (a). **551**

Grant, S.J., & Redmond, D.E., Jr. Clonidine suppresses methylxanthine induced quasi-morphine withdrawal syndrome. *Journal of Pharmacology, Biochemistry, and Behavior*, 1982, *17*, 655-658 (b). **546, 551**

Grant, S.J., & Redmond, D.E., Jr. Neuronal activity of the locus coeruleus in awake *Macaca arctoides*. *Experimental Neurology*, 1984, *84*, 701-708. **554**

Granville-Grossman, K.L., **546**

Granville-Grossman, K.L., & Turner, P. The effect of propranolol on anxiety. *Lancet*, 1966, *1*, 788-790. **546**

Graves, S., **374**

Gray, J.A., **12, 14, 20, 21, 22, 23, 25, 78, 114, 116, 118, 139, 272, 541, 638, 699, 700, 701**

Gray, J.A. Sodium amobarbital, the hippocampal theta rhythm and the partial reinforcement extinction effect. *Psychological Review*, 1970, *77*, 465-480. **23, 697**

Gray, J.A. *The psychology of fear and stress*. New York: McGraw-Hill, 1971. **59, 114, 236, 334, 458-459, 796**

Gray, J.A. Causal theories of personality and how to test them. In J.R. Royce (Ed.), *Multivariate analysis and psychological theory*. New York: Academic Press, 1973. **697**

Gray, J.A. The neuropsychology of anxiety. In I.G. Sarason & C.D. Spielberger, (Eds.), *Stress and anxiety*. Washington, D.C.: Hemisphere Publishing, 1976. **533, 553**

Gray, J.A. Drug effects on fear and frustration: Possible limbic site of action of minor tranquilizers. In L.L. Iversen, S.D. Iversen & S.H. Snyder (Eds.), *Handbook of psychopharmacology 8: Drugs, neurotransmitters and behaviour*. New York: Plenum Press, 1977. **5, 6, 12, 14, 21**

Gray, J.A. Anxiety and the brain: not by neurochemistry alone. *Psychological Medicine*, 1979, 9, 605-609. **7**   ⚹

Gray, J.A. A neuropsychology of anxiety. In C. Izard (Ed.), *Emotions in personality and psychopathology*. New York: Plenum, 1979, pp. 303-335. **7, 11, 213, 241**

Gray, J.A. A critique of Eysenck's theory of personality. In H.J. Eysenck (Ed.), *A model for personality*. Berlin: Springer, 1981. **23, 24, 697**

Gray, J.A. *The neuropsychology of anxiety: An enquiry into the functions of the septo-hippocampal system*. Oxford: Oxford University Press, 1982a. **5, 7, 8, 10, 14, 15, 16, 17, 18, 19, 20, 21, 24, 25, 539**   ⚹

Gray, J.A. Precis of 'The Neuropsychology of anxiety: An Enquiry into the functions of the septo-hippocampal system'. *Behavioral and Brain Sciences*, 1982b, 5 469-534. **5, 8, 10, 14, 15, 16, 20, 25, 553**

Gray, J.A. On mapping anxiety. *Behavioral and Brain Sciences*, 1982c, 5, 506-525. **10**   ⚹

Gray, J.A. Where should we search for biologically based dimensions of personality? *Zeitschrift fur Differentiellee und Diagnostische Psychologie*, 1983, 4, 165-176. **24, 25, 109, 118**

Gray, J.A., Feldon, J., Rawlins, J.N.P., Owen, S., & McNaughton, N. The role of septo-hippocampal system and its noradrenergic afferents in behavioural responses to nonreward. In K. Elliott & J. Whelan (Eds.), *Functions of the septo-hippocampal system* (Ciba Foundation Symposium No. 58, New Series). Amsterdam: Elsevier, 1978. **14**

Gray, J.A., McNaughton, N., Holt, L., Tsaltas, E., Feldon, J., & Shemer, A. The effects of anti-anxiety drugs on tolerance for stress. In A. Levy & M.Y. Spiegelstein (Eds.), *Behavioral models and the analysis of drug action*. Amsterdam: Elsevier, 1982. **20**

Gray, J.A., Quintero, S., & Mellanby, J. Gamma-aminobutyrate, the benzodiazepines and the septo-hippocampal system. In M. Trimble (Ed.), *Benzodiazepines divided*. Chichester: Wiley, 1983. **7, 11, 12, 13**

Gray, J.A., Quintero, S., Mellanby, J., Buckland, C., Fillenz, M., & Fung, S.C. Some biochemical, behavioural and electrophysiological tests of the GABA hypothesis of anti-anxiety drug action. In N.G. Bowery (Ed.), *Actions and interactions of GABA and benzodiazepines*. New York: Raven Press, 1984. **8, 11, 12, 13, 15**

Gray, R., **780**

Gray, S.J., **368**

Grayson, J.B., **106, 144, 428, 429, 437, 439, 692**

Grayson, J.B. *The elicitation and habituation of orienting and defensive re-*

sponses to phobic imagery and the incremental stimulus intensity effect. Paper presented at the annual convention of the Association for the Advancement of Behavior Therapy, San Francisco, 1979. **440**

Grayson, J.B., & Borkovec, T.D. The effects of expectancy and imagined response to phobic stimuli on fear reduction. *Cognitive Therapy and Research*, 1978, *20*, 323-328. **466**

Grayson, J.B., Foa, E.B., & Steketee, G. Habituation during exposure treatment: Distraction vs. attention-focusing. *Behaviour Research and Therapy*, 1982, *20*, 323-328. **98, 438, 465**

Graziano, A.M., & DeGiovanni, I.S. The clinical significance of childhood phobias: A note on the proportion of child-clinical referrals for the treatment of children's fears. *Behavior Research and Therapy*, 1979, *17*, 161-162. **712**

Graziano, A.M., DeGiovanni, I.S., & Garcia, K.A. Behavioral treatment of children's fears: A review. *Psychological Bulletin*, 1979, *86*, 804-830. **714**

Greden, J.F., **66, 67**

Greden, J.F. Anxiety of caffeinism: A diagnostic dilemma. *American Journal of Psychiatry*, 1974, *131*, 1089-1092. **551, 573**

Greden, J.F., Fontaine, P., Lubetsky, M., & Chamberlin, K. Anxiety and depression associated with caffeinism among psychiatric inpatients. *American Journal of Psychiatry*, 1978, *135*, 963-966. **551, 573**

Green, A.R., **34**

Green, A.R., & Deakin, J.F.W. Brain noradrenaline depletion prevents ECS-induces enhancement of serotonin- and dopamine-mediated behaviour. *Nature (London)*, 1980, *285*, 232-233. **24**

Green, R.F., **658**

Green, S., **12, 14**

Greenberg, D.A., **541**

Greenberg, P.S., **116**

Greenberg, R.P., **612, 614, 615**

Greenblatt, D.J., & Shader, R.I. *Benzodiazepines in clinical practice.* New York: Raven Press, 1974. **538, 552**

Greenblatt, D.J., & Shader, R.I. Pharmacotherapy of anxiety with benzodiazepines and B-adrenergic blockers. In M.A. Lipton, A. DiMascio & A.F. Killam (Eds.), *Psychopharmacology: A generation of progress.* New York: Raven Press, 1978. **79, 546**

Greenblatt, M., **137**

Greene, R. Cardiac neurosis as a manifestation of hypoglycemia. *Lancet*, 1944, *2*, 307-308. **569**

Greene, W.A., Conron, S., Schalch, D.S., & Schreiner, B.F. Psychologic correlates of growth hormone and adrenal secretory responses of patients undergoing cardiac catheterization. *Psychosomatic Medicine*, 1970, *32*, 599-614. **67, 68, 340**

Greengard, P., **27, 537**

Greenlee, D.V., **40**

Greenwood, P., **140**

Greer, S., Ramsay, I., & Bagley, Ch. Neurotic and thyrotoxic anxiety: clinical, psychological and physiological measurements. *British Journal of Psychiatry*, 1973, *122*, 549-554. **742**

Grey, S.J., **132, 363, 438, 465**

Grey, S.J., Rachman, S., & Sartory, G. Return of fear: The role of inhibition. *Behaviour Research and Therapy*, 1981, *19*, 135-144. **497**

Grey, S.J., Sartory, G., & Rachman, S. Synchronous and desynchronous changes during fear reduction. *Behaviour Research and Therapy*, 1979, *17*, 137-148. **454, 456**

Griddings, S., **563**

Griez, E., **551**

Griez, E., & van den Hout, M.A. Treatment of phobophobia by exposure to CO_2-induced anxiety symptoms. *Journal of Nervous and Mental Disease*, 1983, *171*, 506-508. **551**

Griffiths, S., **548**

Grimm, L., & Kanfer, F.H. Tolerance of aversive stimulation. *Behavior Therapy*, 1976, *7*, 593-601. **254**

Grinker, R.R., **60, 65**

Grinker, R.R., & Spiegel, J.P. *War neurosis in North Africa, the Tunisian Campaign, January to May 1943*. New York: Josiah Macy Foundation, 1943. **427**

Grinker, R.R., & Spiegel, J.P. *Men under stress*. Philadelphia: Blakiston, 1945. **611**

Grobstein, R., **378**

Gross, A.M., Stern, R.M., Levin, R.B., Dale, J., & Wojnilower, D.A. The effect of mother-child separation on the behavior of children experiencing a diagnostic medical procedure. *Journal of Consulting and Clinical Psychology*, 1983, *51*, 783-785. **372**

Grossberg, J.M., & Wilson, H.K. Physiological changes accompanying the visualization of fear and neutral situation. *Journal of Personality and Social Psychology*, 1968, *10*, 124-133. **339**

Grossman, S.P., **31**

Grosz, H.J., **58**

Grosz, H.J. The relation of serum ascorbic acid level to adrenocortical secretion during experimentally induced emotional stress in human subjects. *Journal of Psychosomatic Research*, 1961, *5*, 253-262. **58**

Grosz, H.J., & Farmer, B.B. Blood lactate in the development of anxiety symptoms. A critical examination of Pitts & McClure's hypothesis and experimental study. *Archives of General Psychiatry*, 1969, *21*, 611-619. **82**

Groves, G.A., **423, 426, 440**

Groves, P.M., & Thompson, R.F. Habituation: A dual-process theory. *Psychological Review*, 1970, *77*, 419-450. **439**

Gruenberg, E., **xxx**

Grunhaus, L., Gloger, S., & Weisstub, E. Panic attacks: A review of treatments and pathogenesis. *Journal of Nervous and Mental Disease*, 1981, *169*, 608-613. **512**

Grunhaus, L., Golgen, S., & Rein, A. Mitral valve prolapse and panic attacks. *Journal of Medical Science*, 1982, *18*, 221-223. **365**

Guaitani, A., Marcucci, R., & Garattini, S. Increased aggression and toxicity in grouped male mice treated with tranquilizing benzodiazepines. *Psychopharmacologia*, 1971, *19*, 241-245. **30**

Guidotti, A., **11, 28, 32, 33, 34, 35, 37, 38, 39, 41, 43, 44, 45, 49, 538, 539**

Guidotti, A. Synaptic mechanisms in the action of benzodiazepines. In M.A. Lipton, A. DiMascio & K.F. Killam (Eds.), *Psychopharmacology: A generation of progress*. New York: Raven Press, 1978. **27**

Guidotti, A., Baraldi, M., Leon, A., & Costa, E. Benzodiazepines: a tool to explore the biochemical and neurophysiological basis of anxiety. *Federation Proceedings*, 1980, *39*, 3039-3042. **11**

Guidotti, A., Corda, M.G., Wise, B.C., Vaccarino, F., & Costa, E. GABAergic synapses: supramolecular organization and biochemical regulation. *Neuropharmacology*, 1983, *22*, 1471-1479. **36**

Guidotti, A., Forchetti, C.M., Corda, M.G., Konkel, D., Bennett, C.D., & Costa, E. Isolation, characterization, and purification to homogeneity of an endogenous polypeptide with agonistic action on benzodiazepine receptors. *Proceedings of the National Academy of Sciences, U.S.A.*, 1983, *80*, 3531-3535. **39, 50**

Guidotti, A., Konkel, D.R., Ebstein, B., Corda, M.G., Wise, B.C., Krutzsch, H., Meek, J.L., & Costa, E. Isolation, characterization and purification to homogeneity of a rat brain protein (GABA-modulin). *Proceedings of the National Academy of Sciences, U.S.A.*, 1982, *79*, 6084-6088. **41, 43, 44, 45**

Guidotti, A., Toffano, G., & Costa, E. An endogenous protein modulates the affinity of GABA and benzodiazepine receptors in rat brain. *Nature (London)*, 1978, *275*, 553-555. **7, 28, 538**

Guilford, J.P. Factors and factors of personality. *Psychological Bulletin*, 1975, *82*, 802-814. **699**

Guillamon, A., **21**

Guirguis, W., **750**

Gulbinat, W., **746, 753**

Gundlach, R.H., **614**

Gunnar, M., **212, 242**

Gurney, C., **328, 366, 747**

Gurney, C., Roth, M., Garside, R.F., Kerr, T.A., & Shapira, K. Studies in the classification of affective disorders. The relationship between anxiety states and depressive illnesses - II. *British Journal of Psychiatry*, 1972, *121*, 162-166. **747, 773**

Guroff, J.J., **286**

Guthrie, E.R. *The psychology of learning*. New York: Harper, 1935. **218**

Gutman, Y., **38**
Guttmacher, L.B., **588**
Guze, S.B., **60, 328, 579, 587, 762, 771, 793**

Hacking, I. *Logic of statistical inference*. Cambridge: Cambridge University Press, 1965. **642-43**
Hadji-georgopoulos, A., Schmidt, M.I., Margolis, S., & Kowalski, A.A. Elevated hypoglycemic index and late hyperinsulinism in symptomatic postprandial hypoglycemia. *Journal of Clinical Endocrinology and Metabolism*, 1980, *50*, 371-376. **569**
Haefely, W. Antagonists of benzodiazepines: Functional aspects. *Advances in Biochemistry and Psychopharmacology*, 1983, *38*, 73-96. **29**
Haefely, W., Bonetti, E.P., Burkard, W.P., Cumin, R., Laurent, J.-P., Mohler, H., Pieri, L., Polc, P., Richards, J.G., Schaffner, R., & Scherschlicht, R. Benzodiazepine antagonists. In E. Costa (Ed.), *The benzodiazepines: From molecular biology to clinical practice*. New York: Raven Press, 1983. **29, 33, 34, 35**
Haefely, W., Kulcsar, A., Mohler, H., Pieri, L., Polc, P., & Schaffner, R. Possible involvement of GABA in the central action of benzodiazepines. In E. Costa & P. Greengard (Eds.), *Mechanism of action of benzodiazepines*. New York: Raven Press, 1975. **28, 538**
Haefely, W., Pieri, L., Polc, P., & Schaffner, R. General pharmacology and neuropharmacology of benzodiazepine derivatives. In F. Hoffmeister & G. Stille (Eds.), *Handbook of experimental psychology* (Vol. 55/II). Berlin: Springer-Verlag, 1981. **11, 14**
Haefely, W., & Polc, P. Electrophysiological studies on the interaction of anxiolytic drugs with GABAergic mechanisms. In J.B. Malick, S.J. Enna, & H.I. Yamamura (Eds.), *Anxiolytics: Neurochemical, behavioral, and clinical perspectives*. New York: Raven Press, 1983. **540**
Haefely, W., Polc, P., Pieri, L., Schaffner, R., & Laurent, J.-P. Neuropharmacology of benzodiazepines: Synaptic mechanisms and neuronal basis of action. In E. Costa (Ed.), *The benzodiazepines: From molecular biology to clinical practice*. New York: Raven Press, 1983. **13, 28, 29, 32, 38**
Haertzen, C.A., Hill, H.E., & Monroe, J.J. MMPI scales for differentiating and predicting relapse in alcoholics, opiate addicts, and criminals. *International Journal of the Addictions*, 1968, *3*, 91-106. **671**
Hafner, R.J., & Marks, I.M. Exposure *in vivo* of agoraphobics: Contributions of diazepam, group exposure, and anxiety evocation. *Psychological Medicine*, 1976, *6*, 71-88. **428**
Hafstad, K.M., **563**
Hager, J., **114, 206, 265, 600**
Hagerman, S., **254**
Hagnell, O. *A prospective study of the incidence of mental disorder*. Norstedts: Svenska Bolfolaget, 1966. **278**

Hahn, K.W., **436**

Hahn, R., & Kleinman, A. Biomedical practice and anthropological theory: Frameworks and directions. *Annual Review of Anthropology*, 1983, *12*, 305-333. **298**

Hahn, W., **365**

Hake, H.W., **684**

Halal, M., **146-47, 169**

Hale, H.B., Duffy, J.C., Ellis, J.P., Jr., & Williams, E.W. Flying stress in relation to flying proficiency. *US Air Force School of Aerospace Medicine*, 1964, *1-8*. **58**

Hall, J., **220**

Hall, N., & Edmondson, H.D. The aetiology and psychology of dental fear. A five-year study of the use of intravenous diazepam in its management. *British Dental Journal*, 1983, *154*, 247-252. **538**

Hallam, J., **149**

Hallam, R.S., **485**

Hallam, R.S. Agoraphobia: A critical review of the concept. *British Journal of Psychiatry*, 1978, *133*, 314-319. **745**

Haltmeyer, G.C., **62**

Hamburg, B.A., **118**

Hamburg, D.A., **58, 60, 61, 65**

Hamburg, D.A. Emotions in the perspective of human evolution. In P.H. Knapp (Ed.), *Expression of emotions in man*. New York: International Universities Press, 1963. **118**

Hamburg, D.A., Hamburg, B.A., & Barchus, J.D. Anger and depression in perspective of behavioral biology. In L. Levi (Ed.), *Emotions—Their parameters and measurement*. New York: Raven Press, 1975. **118**

Hamilton, M. The assessment of anxiety states by rating. *British Journal of Medical Psychology*, 1959, *32*, 50-55. **80, 131, 167, 677, 692, 742**

Hammen, C., **92**

Hamovit, J., **286**

Hampe, E., **373, 708, 709, 712, 714, 715**

Hampe, E., Noble, H., Miller, L.C., & Barrett, C.L. Phobic children one and two years posttreatment. *Journal of Abnormal Psychology*, 1973, *82*, 446-453. **713**

Handlon, J.H., **58, 61**

Handlon, J.H., Wadeson, R.W., Fishman, J.R., Sachar, E.J., Hamburg, D.A., & Mason, J.W. Psychological factors lowering plasma 17-hydroxycorticosteroid concentration. *Psychosomatic Medicine*, 1962, *24*, 535-542. **58**

Hanin, I., **67, 544, 545**

Hansen, D.N., **659**

Harburg, E., **348**

Harburg, E., Erfurt, J.C., Hauenstein, L.S., Chape, C., Schull, W.J., &

Schork, M.A. Socio-ecological stress, suppressed hostility, skin color, and black-white male blood pressure: Detroit. *Psychosomatic Medicine*, 1973, *35*, 276-296. **347**

Harding, P.S., **279, 280, 579**

Hare, R.D., & Cox, D.N. Clinical and empirical conceptions of psychopathy, and the selection of subjects for research. In R.D. Hare & D. Schalling (Eds.), *Psychopathic behaviour: Approaches to research*. Chichester: Wiley, 1978. **24**

Harkavy, J., **384**

Harlan, W.R., **341**

Harlow, H.F., **xxi, 200**

Harmon, R.J., **114, 414**

Harper, M., **558**

Harris, A.H., & Brady, J.V. Long term studies of cardiovascular control in primates. In G.E. Schwartz & J. Beatty (Eds.), *Biofeedback: Theory and research*. New York: Academic Press, 1977. **238**

Harris, E.L., Noyes, R., Jr., Crowe, R.R., & Chaudhry, D.R. Family study of agoraphobia: Report of a pilot study. *Archives of General Psychiatry*, 1983, *40*, 1061-1064. **329**

Harris, L.S., **543**

Harris, S.L., & Ferrari, M. Developmental factors in child behavior therapy. *Behavior Therapy*, 1983, *14*, 54-72. **374**

Harris, T.O., **278, 323, 561**

Harrison, D.C., **538**

Harrison, W., **670**

Hart, J.D., **162, 164, 219, 439**

Hart, J.D. Physiological responses of anxious and normal subjects to simple signal and non-signal auditory stimuli. *Psychophysiology*, 1974, *11*, 443-451. **167**

Hart, R., **79**

Hartley, L.H., **71**

Hartmann, D.P., **372**

Hartshorne, H., & May, M.A. *Studies in the nature of character, Vol. 1: Studies in deceit*. New York: Macmillan, 1928. **682**

Harwood, C.T., **55, 65**

Hase, H.D., & Goldberg, L.R. Comparative validity of different strategies of constructing personality inventory scales. *Psychological Bulletin*, 1967, *67*, 231-248. **685, 686**

Hasegawa, K., **529**

Haselrud, G. The effect of movement of stimulus objects upon avoidance reactions in chimpanzees. *Journal of Comparative Psychology*, 1938, *25*, 507-528. **201**

Haskett, R.F., **66, 67**

Haslam, M.T. The relationship between the effect of lactate infusion on anxiety states, and their amelioration by carbon dioxide inhalation. *British Journal of Psychiatry*, 1974, *125*, 88-90. **551**

Hastrup, J.L., **116**

Hatfield, B.D., Doyle, L.A., & Borkovec, T.D. A validation of the automatic perception questionnaire with implications for sports anxiety management. *National association for the study of the psychology of sport and physical activity*, Monterey, CA., June, 1981. **468**

Hathaway, S.R., **650**

Hathaway, S.R. Some consideration relative to nondirective counseling as therapy. *Journal of Clinical Psychology*, 1948, *4*, 226-241. **656**

Hathaway, S.R., & McKinley, J.C. *The Minnesota multiphasic personality schedule*. Minneapolis: University of Minnesota Press, 1942; rev. ed. 1943. **645, 666**

Hattenhauer, M., **350**

Hauenstein, L.S., **347**

Havlik, R., **325, 327**

Hawkins, T.D., **350**

Haynes, S.N., **98**

Hazari, A., **470**

Hebb, D.O. On the nature of fear. *Psychological Review*, 1946, *53*, 259-276. **112, 139, 201, 208, 268**

Hebb, D.O. *The organization of behavior*. New York: John Wiley, 1949. **112, 139, 156**

Heide, F., & Borkovec, T.D. Relaxation-induced anxiety: Paradoxical anxiety enhancement due to relaxation training. *Journal of Consulting and Clinical Psychology*, 1983, *51*, 171-182. **253, 476**

Heidegger, M., **736**

Heinrich, D.L., **660**

Heistad, D.D., Wheeler, R.C., Mark, A.L., Schmid, R.G., & Abboud, F.M. Effects of adrenergic stimulation on ventilation in man. *Journal of Clinical Investigation*, 1972, *51*, 1469-1473. **349**

Heller, A.S., **652**

Hellman, L., **62, 65**

Helzer, J.E., **281, 282, 310, 677**

Hembree, E.A., **114**

Hendersen, R., & Blaccioniere, M. Long term retention of conditioned fear. Submitted to *Journal of Experimental Psychology: Animal Behavior Processes*, 1984. **211, 243**

Hendersen, R.W. Forgetting of conditioned fear inhibition. *Learning and Motivation*, 1978, *8*, 16-30. **211, 227**

Hendersen, R.W., Patterson, J.M., & Jackson, R.L. Acquisition and retention of control of instrumental behavior by a cue-signaling airblast: How specific are conditioned anticipations? *Learning and Motivation*, 1980, *11*, 407-426. **211, 243**

Henderson, A.S., **293, 562**

Henderson, G., **542**

Hendrickson, G., **516, 517**

Heninger, G.R., **67, 68, 339, 340, 528, 529, 542, 544, 547, 548, 551, 552, 563, 571, 572**

Henneberry, R., **40**

Hennings, B.L., **476**

Henry, B.W., Overall, J.E., & Markette, J. Comparison of major drug therapies for alleviation of anxiety and depression. *Diseases of the Nervous System*, 1971, *32*, 655-667. **521, 544**

Henry, J.P. Coronary heart disease and arousal of the adrenal cortical axis. In T.M. Dembroski & T. Schmidt (Eds.), *Biobehavioral bases of coronary heart disease*. Basel: Karger, 1983. **346**

Henry, J.P., & Cassel, J.C. Psychosocial factors in essential hypertension. Recent epidemiologic and animal experimental evidence. *American Journal of Epidemiology*, 1969, *90*, 171-193. **347**

Herd, J.A., **238, 342, 358**

Herjanic, B., **793**

Herjanic, B., & Campbell, W. Differentiating psychiatrically disturbed children on the basis of a structured interview. *Journal of Abnormal Child Psychology*, 1977, *5*, 127-135. **584**

Herman, B.M., **526**

Hermecz, D.A., **384**

Hermecz, D.A., & Melamed, B.G. The assessment of emotional imagery training in fearful children. *Behavior Therapy*, 1984, *15*, 156-172. **385**

Herrington, L.P., & Nelbach, J.H. Relation of gland weights to growth and aging processes in rats exposed to certain environmental conditions. *Endocrinology*, 1942, *30*, 375-386. **55**

Herrnstein, R.J. Method and theory in the study of avoidance. *Psychological Review*, 1969, *76*, 49-69. **228, 421**

Hersen, M., **xxiv**

Hersen, M., & Barlow, D.H. *Single-case experimental designs*. New York: Pergamon Press, 1976. **643**

Hershberg, S.G., Carlson, G.A., Cantwell, D.P., & Strober, M. Anxiety and depressive disorders in psychiatrically disturbed children. *Journal of Clinical Psychiatry*, 1982, *43*, 358-361. **125, 126**

Hertzel, B.S., Schotistaedt, W.W., Grace, W.J., & Wolff, H.G. Changes in urinary 17-hydroxycorticosteroid excretion during stressful life experiences in man. *Journal of Clinical Endocrinology*, 1955, *15*, 1057-1068. **58**

Hertzig, M., **376**

Hesster, J.B., **539**

Heth, C.D., **210**

Hetzel, W., **659**

Hewitt, L.E., & Jenkins, R.L. *Fundamental patterns of maladjustment: The dynamics of their origin.* Springfield, IL: State of Illinois, 1946. **720**

Heyman, A., **350**

Hiatt, A.S., Campos, J.J., & Emde, R.N. Facial patterning and infant emotional expression: Happiness, surprise, and fear. *Child Development*, 1979, *50*, 1020-1035. **417**

Hibbert, G.N. Ideational components of anxiety: Their origin and content. *British Journal of Psychiatry*, in press. **194**

Hicks, D.C., **546**

Higgins, J.M., **254**

Hildreth, H.M. A battery of feeling and attitude scales for clinical use. *Journal of Clinical Psychology*, 1946, *2*, 214-221. **658**

Hill, D.R., **13, 15, 40**

Hill, H.E., **671**

Hill, R., **368**

Hillier, V.F., **677**

Hilton, S.W. Ways of reviewing the central nervous control of the circulation—old and new. *Brain Research*, 1975, *87*, 213-219. **344**

Hinrichs, J.V., **538, 682**

Hippius, H., **563**

Hirata, F., **49**

Hiroyuki, A., **67, 68**

Hirsch, J.D. Photolabeling of benzodiazepine receptors spares [^{3}H]propyl β-carboline binding. *Pharmacol. Biochem. Behav.*, 1982, *16*, 245-248. **33**

Hirschfeld, R.M.A. Review of psychoticism as a dimension of personality by H.J. Eysenck and S.B.G. Eysenck. *Psychiatry*, 1978, *41*, 411-412. **699**

Hjorth, S., & Carlsson, A. Buspirone: effects on central monoaminergic transmission—possible relevance to animal experimental and clinical findings. *European Journal of Pharmacology*, 1982, *83*, 299-303. **592**

Hoagland, H., **55**

Hoagland, H., Bergen, J.R., Bloch, E., Elmadjian, F., & Gibree, N.R. Adrenal stress responses in normal men. *Journal of Applied Physiology*, 1955, *8*. 149-154. **58**

Hodes, R., **204**

Hodes, R. *A psychophysiological investigation of the classical conditioning model of fears and phobias.* Unpublished doctoral dissertation, University of Wisconsin, 1981. **207**

Hodes, R., Cook, E.W., III, & Lang, P.J. *Individual differences in autonomic reaction: Conditioned association or conditioned fear.* In preparation. **153, 154, 155**

Hodes, R., Cook, E.W., III, Ohman, A., & Lang, P.J. *"Ontogenetic"* and *"phylogenetic"* *fear-relevance of the conditioned stimulus in electrodermal and heart-rate conditioning.* In preparation. **208**

Hodges, D.H., **530**

Hodges, H.M., & Green, S. Evidence for the involvement of brain GABA and serotonin systems in the anti-conflict effects of chlordiazepoxide in rats. *Behavioral and Neural Biology*, 1984, in press. **12, 14**

Hodges, J.R., Jones, M.T., & Stockham, M.A. Effect of emotion on blood corticotrophin and cortisol concentrations in man. *Nature*, 1962, *193*, 1187-1188. **58**

Hodges, W.F., & Felling, J.P. Types of stressful situations and their relation to trait anxiety and sex. *Journal of Consulting and Clinical Psychology*, 1970, *34*, 333-337. **177**

Hodges, W.F., & Spielberger, C.D. The effects of threat of shock on heart rate for subjects who differ in manifest anxiety and fear of shock. *Psychophysiology*, 1966, *2*, 287-294. **177, 647**

Hodgson, R.J., **xxiv, 10, 89, 133, 144, 201, 204, 223, 225, 226, 227, 230-34, 334, 363, 376, 429, 454, 456, 459, 460, 497, 505, 507, 683**

Hodgson, R.J., & Rachman, S. An experimental investigation of the implosion technique. *Behaviour Research and Therapy*, 1970, *8*, 21-28. **456**

Hodgson, R.J., & Rachman, S. The effects of contamination and washing in obsessional patients. *Behaviour Research and Therapy*, 1972, *10*, 111-117. **225**

Hodgson, R.J., & Rachman, S. Desynchrony in measures of fear. *Behaviour Research and Therapy*, 1974, *12*, 319-326. **201, 222, 334**

Hodgson, R.J., Rachman, S., & Marks, I.M. The treatment of chronic obsessive-compulsive neurosis: Follow-up and further findings. *Behaviour Research and Therapy*, 1972, *10*, 181-189. **428**

Hoehn-Saric, E. Characteristics of chronic anxiety patients. In D.F. Klein & J. Rabkin (Eds.), *Anxiety: New research and changing concepts.* New York: Raven Press, 1981. pp. 399-409. **489, 610**

Hoehn-Saric, R. Comparison of generalized anxiety disorder with panic disorder patients. *Psychopharmacology Bulletin*, 1982, *18*, 104-108. **610**

Hoehn-Saric, R., Merchant, A.F., Keyser, M.L., & Smith, V.K. Effects of clonidine on anxiety disorders. *Archives of General Psychiatry*, 1981, *38*, 1278-1282. **548**

Hoenk, P.R., **325**

Hofer, M.A., **59**

Hofer, M.A. Cardiac and respiratory function during sudden prolonged immobility in young rodents. *Psychosomatic Medicine*, 1970, *32*, 633-647. **340**

Hofer, M.A. Presidential address. Relationships as regulators: A psychobiological perspective on bereavement. *Psychosomatic Medicine*, 1983, *45*, in press. **345, 354**

Hofer, M.A., Wolff, C.T., Friedman, S.B., & Mason, J.W. A psychoendocrine study of bereavement. Part I: 17-hydroxycorticosteroids excretion rates of patients following deaths of their children from leukemia. *Psychosomatic Medicine*, 1972a, *34*, 481-491. **59**

Hofer, M.A., Wolff, C.T., Friedman, S.B., & Mason, J.W. A psychoendocrine study of bereavement. Part II: Observations on the process of mourning in relation to adrenocortical function. *Psychosomatic Medicine*, 1972b, *34*, 492-504. **59**

Hoffman, H.S., **156**

Hoffman, L.J., **17, 18, 19, 20**

Hoffman, M.L. The measurement of empathy. In C.E. Izard (Ed.), *Measuring emotions in infants and children*. New York: Cambridge University Press, 1982. **116**

Hogan, R., DeSoto, C.B., & Solano, C. Traits, tests, and personality research. *American Psychologist*, 1977, *32*, 255-264. **681**

Hokfelt, T.E., **539, 540**

Holden, A.E., & Barlow, D.H. Heart rate and heart rate variability recorded in vivo in agoraphobics and non-phobics. Manuscript submitted for publication. **494, 496, 498**

Holland, H.C. Displacement activity as a form of abnormal behaviour in animals. In H.R. Beech (Ed.), *Obsessional States*. London: Metheun & Co., Ltd., 1974, pp. 161-173. **224**

Hollender, M., **509**

Hollister, L.E. Marihuana in man: Three years later. *Science*, 1971, *172*, 21-29. **549**

Hollon, S.D., **704**

Hollon, S.D., & Kendall, P.C. *In vivo* assessment techniques for cognitive-behavioral processes. In P.C. Kendall & S.D. Hollon (Eds.), *Assessment strategies for cognitive-behavioral interventions*. New York: Academic Press, 1981. **702**

Holmberg, G., & Gershon, S. Autonomic and psychiatric effects of yohimbine hydrochloride. *Psychopharmacologia*, 1961, *2*, 93-106. **551**

Holmes, D.S. Investigations of repression: Differential recall of material experimentally or naturally associated with ego threat. *Psychological Bulletin*, 1974, *81*, (10), 632-653. **142**

Holmes, F.B., **374, 707**

Holmgren, A., & Strom, G. Blood lactate concentrations in relation to absolute and relative work load in normal men, and in mitral stenosis, atrial septal defect, and vasoregulatory asthenia. *Acta Medica Scandinavica*, 1959, *163*, 185-193. **82**

Holroyd, K.A., & Appel, M.A. Test anxiety and physiological responding. In I.G. Sarason (Ed.), *Test anxiety: Theory, research, and applications*. Hillsdale, NJ: Lawrence Erlbaum, 1980. **95**

Holt, L., **12, 20**

Holt, L. *Proactive behavioural effects of septal stimulation in the rat.* Unpublished doctoral dissertation, Oxford University, 1982. **23, 25**

Holt, L., & Gray, J.A. Septal driving of the hippocampal theta rhythm produces a long-term, proactive and non-associative increase in resistance to extinction. *Quarterly Journal of Experimental Psychology*, 1983, *35B*, 97-118. **23, 25**

Holt, R.H. A review of some of Freud's biological assumptions and their influence on his theories. In N.S. Greenfield & W.C. Lewis (Eds.), *Psychoanalysis and current biological thought.* Madison: University of Wisconsin Press, 1965. **602**

Holzer, C.E., **xxx, 282, 283**

Holzman, P.S. *Psychoanalysis and psychopathology.* New York: McGraw-Hill, 1970. **701**

Honig, W.K., **243-44**

Honore, T., **30, 41, 42**

Honzik, M.P., **373, 408, 411, 712**

Hood, S. (Ed.). *Psychoanalysis, scientific method, and philosophy.* New York: New York University Press, 1959. **612**

Hooke, J.F., **660**

Hoon, E., **149-50**

Hoon, P., Wincze, J.P., & Hoon, E. A test of reciprocal inhibition: Are anxiety and sexual arousal in women mutually inhibitory? *Journal of Abnormal Psychology*, 1977, *86*, 65-74. **149-50**

Hoover, C., **504, 507, 588**

Horne, D.J., **304, 305**

Horowitz, L.M., Wright, J.C., Lowenstein, E., & Parad, H.W. The prototype as a construct in abnormal psychology: I. A method for deriving prototypes. *Journal of Abnormal Psychology*, 1981, *90*, 568-574. **243**

Horowitz, M.J., **614, 615, 622, 710**

Horowitz, M.J. Intrusive and repetitive thought after experimental stress: A summary. *Archives of General Psychiatry*, 1975, *32*, 1457-1463. **623**

Horowitz, M.J. *Stress response syndromes.* New York: Jason Aronson, 1976. **611, 614, 622**

Horowitz, M.J. *Hysterical personality.* New York: Jason Aronson, 1977. **669**

Horowitz, M.J. *States of mind.* New York: Plenum, 1979. **627**

Horowitz, M.J. Stress response syndromes and their treatment. In L. Goldberger & S. Breznitz. *Handbook of stress: Theoretical and clinical aspects.* New York: The Free Press, 1982. **623**

Horowitz, M.J., Marmar, C., Krupnick, J., Wilner, N., Kaltreider, N., & Wallerstein, R. *Personality styles and brief psychotherapy.* New York: Basic Books, 1984. **624, 627**

Horowitz, M.J., Wilner, N., & Alvarez, W. The impact of event scale: A measure of subjective stress. *Psychosomatic Medicine*, 1979, *41*, 209-218. **622**

Horowitz, M.J., Wilner, N., Kaltreider, N., & Alvarez, W. The signs and symptoms of post-traumatic stress disorders. *Archives of General Psychiatry*, 1980, *37*, 85-92. **622, 772**

Horowitz, M.J., & Zilberg, N. Regressive alteration in the self-concept. *American Journal of Psychiatry*, 1983, *140*, 289-290. **624**

Horowitz, S., **558**

Horowski, R., **34, 35, 36, 551**

Horvath, T.B. Arousal and anxiety. In D.G. Burrows & B. Davies (Eds.), *Handbook of studies on anxiety*. New York: Elsevier, 1980. **581**

Horvath, T.B., & Meares, R.A. The sensory filter in schizophrenia: A study of habituation, arousal, and the dopamine hypothesis. *British Journal of Psychiatry*, 1979, *134*, 39-45. **583**

Horwitz, B.A., **384**

Hough, R.L., **281, 282**

Howell, J.B.L., **349**

Hsu, F., **299**

Hu, G.H., **544**

Huang, Y.H., **539, 542, 543, 551, 553, 570, 797**

Huang, Y.H. Net effect of acute administration of desimipramine on the locus coeruleus-hippocampal system. *Life Sciences*, 1979, *25*, 739-746. **528, 544**

Huang, Y.H., Maas, J.W., & Hu, G.H. The time course of noradrenergic pre- and postsynaptic activity during chronic desipramine treatment. *European Journal of Pharmacology*, 1980, *68*, 41-47. **544**

Hudson, A.L., **13, 15, 40**

Hudson, C.J. Agoraphobia in Alaskan Eskimo. *New York State Journal of Medicine*, 1981, *81*, 224-225. **311**

Huebner, R., **417**

Hugdahl, K., **207, 209, 213, 217**

Hugdahl, K., Fredrikson, M., & Öhman, A. "Preparedness" and "arousability" as determinants of electrodermal conditioning. *Behaviour Research and Therapy*, 1977, *15*, 345-353. **376**

Hugdahl, K., & Kàrker, A. Biological vs experiential factors in phobic conditioning. *Behaviour Research and Therapy*, 1981, *19*, 109-116. **208**

Hugel, R., **375, 376**

Hughes, C.A., **305, 307**

Hull, C.L. *Hypnosis and suggestibility: An experimental approach*. New York: Appleton-Century-Crofts, 1933. **138**

Hulse, S.H., Fowler, H., & Honig, W.K. (Eds.). *Cognitive Processes in Animal Behavior*. Hillsdale, NJ: Lawrence Erlbaum Associates, 1978. **243-44**

Hunt, J. McV. Intrinsic motivation and its role in development. In D. Levine (Ed.), *Nebraska symposium on motivation*. Lincoln: University of Nebraska Press, 1965, pp. 189-282. **112**

Hunt, J.M., **653**

Hunt, S., **538**

Hunt, W.A., **534, 550**
Hurlburt, R.T. Random sampling of cognitions and behavior. *Journal of Research in Personality*, 1979, *13*, 103-111. **702**
Hurst, J.W., **349**
Hurst, M.W., **62, 63, 65, 68, 359**
Huson, J., **440**
Hutchings, C.H., **95**
Hynes, M., **543**

Ingram, R.E., **95**
Ingram, R.H., Jr., **351**
Inkeles, A. *Exploring individual modernity*. New York: Columbia University Press, 1983. **306**
Inouye, E. Similar and dissimilar manifestations of obsessive-compulsive neurosis in monozygotic twins. *American Journal of Psychiatry*, 1965, *121*, 1171-1175. **585**
Insel, T.R., **38, 39, 562, 563, 564, 581, 583, 588**
Insel, T.R. Obsessive compulsive disorder: The clinical picture. In T.R. Insel (Ed.), *New findings in obsessive compulsive disorder*. Washington, D.C.: American Psychiatric Association Press, 1984. **579, 586**
Insel, T.R., Gillin, J.C., Moore, A., Mendelson, W.B., Loewenstein, R.J., & Murphy, D.L. Sleep in obsessive-compulsive disorder. *Archives of General Psychiatry*, 1982, *39*, 1372-1377. **588, 771**
Insel, T.R., Hoover, C., & Murphy, D.L. Parents of patients with obsessive compulsive disorder. *Psychological Medicine*, 1983, *13*, 807-811. **504, 507, 588**
Insel, T.R., Kalin, N.H., Guttmacher, L.B., Cohen, R.M., & Murphy, D.L. The dexamethaxsone suppression test in patients with primary obsessive-compulsive disorder. *Psychiatry Research*, 1982, *6*, 153-160. **588**
Insel, T.R., Mueller, E.A., Gillin, J.C., Siever, L.J., Murphy, D.L. Biological markers in obsessive compulsive and affective disorders. *Journal of Psychiatric Research*, in press. **588**
Insel, T.R., & Murphy, D.L. The psychopharmacological treatment of obsessive-compulsive disorder: A review. *Journal of Clinical Psychopharmacology*, 1981, *1*, 304-311. **503, 507, 508, 509**
Insel, T.R., Murphy, D.L., Cohen, R.M., Alterman, I., Kilts, C., & Linnoila, M. Obsessive-compulsive disorder: A double-blind treatment of clomipramine and clorgyline. *Archives of General Psychiatry*, 1983, *40*, 605-612. **586**
Ionescu-Pioggia, M., **677**
Isaacson, R.L. *The limbic system*. New York: Plenum Press, 1974. **115**
Isberg, R. A comparison of phenelzine and imipramine in an obsessive-compulsive patient. *American Journal of Psychiatry*, 1981, *138*, 1250-1251. **505, 508**
Isen, A.M., Means, B., Patrick, R., & Nowicki, G. Some factors influencing

decision-making strategy and risk taking. In M.S. Clark & S.T. Fiske (Eds.), *Affect and Cognition*. Hillsdale, NJ: Lawrence Erlbaum Associates, 1982. **143, 144**

Isen, A.M., Shalker, T.E., Clark, M., & Karp, L. Affect accessibility of material in memory and behavior: A cognitive loop? *Journal of Personality and Social Psychology*, 1978, *36*, 1-12. **143**

Ishiki, D.M., **562**

Isner, J.M., **351**

Ison, J.R., & Hoffman, H.S. Reflex modification in the domain of startle: II. The anomalous history of a robust and ubiquitous phenomenon. *Psychological Bulletin*, 1983, *1*, 3-17. **156**

Ivanov-Smolenski, A.G. On the methods of examining the conditional food reflexes in children and mental defectives. *Brain*, 1927, *50*, 138-141. **152**

Ivanov-Smolenski, A.G. [On the interaction of the first and second signal systems in some physiological and pathological conditions], *Fiziologicheskii Zhurnal SSSR*, 1949, *35*, 271-281. **152**

Ivanys, E., **525**

Iversen, K. *Temporary rise in the frequency of thyrotoxicosis in Denmark, 1941-1945.* Copenhagen: Rosenkilde & Bagger, 1948. **352**

Iversen, K. An epidemic wave of thyrotoxicosis in Denmark during World War II. *American Journal of the Medical Sciences*, 1949, *217*, 121-132. **352**

Iversen, L.L., & Schon, F. The use of autoradiographic techniques for the identification and mapping of transmitter-specific neurons in CNS. In A. Mandell & D. Segal, (Eds.), *New concepts of transmitter regulation*. New York: Plenum Press, 1973. **538, 539**

Iversen, S.D., **20**

Ives, J.O., **543**

Iwahara, S., Oishi, H., Yamazaki, S., & Sakai, K. Effects of chlordiazepoxide upon spontaneous alternation and hippocampal electrical activity in white rats. *Psychopharmacologia*, 1972, *24*, 497-507. **31**

Iwawaki, S., Sumida, K., Okuno, S., & Cowen, E. Manifest anxiety in Japanese, French, and United States children. *Child Development*, 1967, *38*, 713-722. **300-01**

Izard, C.E., **116, 122, 123, 124, 125, 126, 179, 180, 415, 417, 688, 689**

Izard, C.E. *The face of emotion*. Meredith, NY: Appleton-Century-Crofts, 1971. **111, 112, 114, 116, 416**

Izard, C.E. Anxiety: A variable combination of interacting fundamental emotion. In C.D. Spielberger (Ed.), *Anxiety: Current trends in research and theory*. New York: Academic Press, 1972. **112, 114, 117, 119, 123, 124, 125, 126, 135, 140, 486, 689**

Izard, C.E. *Human emotions*. New York: Plenum Press, 1977. **110, 114, 116, 118, 123, 689**

Izard, C.E. *The maximally discriminative facial movement coding system (Max)*.

Newark, DE: University of Delaware, Instructional Resources Center, 1979. **116**

Izard, C.E. Measuring emotions in human development. In C. Izard (Ed.) *Measuring emotions in infants and children.* Cambridge: Cambridge University Press, 1982. **417**

Izard, C.E. The primacy of emotions in emotion-cognition relationships and human development. In C.E. Izard, J. Kagan & R. Zajonc (Eds.) *Emotions, cognition, & behavior,* in press. **171-72, 178**

Izard, C.E., Dougherty, F.E., Bloxom, B.M., & Kotsch, W.E. *The differential emotions scale: A method of measuring the subjective experience of discrete emotions.* Nashville, TN: Vanderbilt University, 1974. **126**

Izard, C.E., Hembree, E.A., Dougherty, L.M., & Spizzirri, C.L. Changes in two- to nineteen-month-old infants' facial expressions following acute pain. *Developmental Psychology,* 1983, *19,* 418-426. **114**

Izard, C.E., Huebner, R., Risser, D., McGinnis, G., & Dougherty, L. The young infant's ability to produce discrete emotional expressions. *Developmental Psychology,* 1980, *16,* 132-140. **417**

Izard, C.E., Kagan, J., & Zajonc, R.B. *Emotions, cognition & behavior.* New York: Cambridge University Press, in press. **110, 123**

Izard, C.E., & Malatesta, C.Z. A developmental theory of the emotions. *Behavioral and Brain Sciences,* in press. **109, 122, 123**

Izard, C.E., & Schwartz, G.E. *Depression and depressive disorders: Developmental perspective.* New York: Guilford Press, in press. **119**

Izard, C.E., & Tomkins, S.S. Affect and behavior: Anxiety as a negative affect. In C.D. Spielberger (Ed.), *Anxiety and Behavior (Vol. 1).* New York: Academic Press, 1966. **122**

Jablensky, A., **325, 578, 688, 746, 753, 775, 776, 778, 783, 785, 788**

Jablensky, A., Sartorius, N., Gulbinat, W., & Ernberg, G. Characteristics of depressive patients contacting psychiatric services in four cultures. *Acta psychiatrica scandinavica,* 1981, *63,* 367-383. **746**

Jackson, D.N. The dynamics of structured personality tests: 1971. *Psychological Review,* 1971, *78,* 229-248. **682, 683**

Jackson, D.N. *Personality Research Form manual.* Goshen, NY: Research Psychologists Press, 1974. **696**

Jackson, D.N., & Paunonen, S.V. Personality structure and assessment. *Annual Review of Psychology,* 1980, *31,* 503-551. **682**

Jackson, R.L., **211, 239, 243**

Jackson, R.L., Maier, S.F., & Rapoport, P.M. Exposure to inescapable shock produces both activity and associative deficits. *Learning and Motivation,* 1978, *9,* 69-98. **17**

Jacobsen, E. *Progressive relaxation.* Chicago: University of Chicago, 1929. **111**

Jacobson, A., **519, 522, 540**

Jacobson, E. *The self and object world.* New York: International Universities Press, 1964. **624**

Jacobson, G., **513, 543**

Jaeger, J.J., **351**

Jaffe, J.H. Drug addiction and drug abuse. In A.G. Gilman, L.S. Goodman, A. Gilman, S.E. Mayer & K.L. Melmon (Eds.), *Goodman and Gilman's the pharmacological basis of therapeutics* (6 ed.). New York: Macmillan, 1980. **549, 552**

Jaffe, J.H., & Martin, W.R. Opioid Analgesics and Antagonists. In A.G. Gilman, L.S. Goodman, A. Gilman, S.E. Mayer & K.L. Melmon (Eds.), *Goodman and Gilman's the pharmacological basis of therapeutics* (6 ed.). New York: Macmillan, 1980. **541, 542**

James, N.McI., **66, 67**

James, W. What is emotion? *Mind*, 1884, *19*, 188-205. **111, 136**

James, W. *The principles of psychiatry.* New York: Holt, Rinehart, & Winston, 1890. (Reprinted, New York: Dover Press, 1950.). **111, 114, 117, 138**

Jameson, J.S., **428**

Jamieson, R., **440**

Janda, L., **213, 442**

Janet, P. *Les obsessions et la psychasthenie.* Paris: Bailliere, 1903. **577**

Janis, I. *Stress and frustration.* New York: Harcourt, Brace, Jovanovitch, 1969. **622**

Jannoun, L., **428**

Jannoun, L., Munby, M., Catalan, J., & Gelder, M. A home-based treatment programme for agoraphobia: Replication and controlled evaluation. *Behavior Therapy*, 1980, *11*, 294-305. **433**

Janowsky, D.S., Berens, S.C., & Davis, J.M. Correlations between mood, weight, and electrolytes during menstrual cycle: A renin-angiotensin-aldosterone hypothesis of premenstrual tension. *Psychosomatic Medicine*, 1973, *35*, 143-154. **74, 75**

Jansson, L., & Òst, L.G. Behavioral treatment for agoraphobia: An evaluative review. *Clinical Psychology Review*, 1982, *2*, 311-336. **425**

Janzen, J. *The quest for therapy in lower Zaire.* Berkeley, CA: University of California Press, 1978. **307**

Jaskir, J., **377**

Jaspers, K. *General psychopathology.* Translated by J. Hoenig and M.W. Hamilton. Manchester: Manchester University Press, 1963. **736, 741**

Javaid, J., **67, 544, 545**

Jeans, J., **392, 393, 511, 513**

Jegede, R.O. Outpatient psychiatry in an urban clinic in a developing country. *Social Psychiatry*, 1978, *13*, 93-98. **307**

Jenike, M. Rapid response of severe obsessive-compulsive disorder to tranylcypromine. *American Journal of Psychiatry*, 1981, *138*, 1249-1250. **505, 508**

Jenkins, C., **359**

Jenkins, D., **55**

Jenkins, R.L., & Boyer, A. Types of delinquent behavior and background factors. *International Journal of Social Psychiatry*, 1968, *14*, 65-76. **720**

Jenner, F.A., **349**

Jensen, C.C., & Ek, J.I. The excretion of certain adrenal steroids during mental stress in healthy persons. *Acta Psychiatrica Scandinavica*, 1962, *38*, 302-306. **58**

Jensen, L.H., **30, 42**

Jerremalm, A., **426, 496**

Jersild, A.T., & Holmes, F.B. Children's fears. *Child Development Monograph*, 1935, No. 20. **374, 707**

Jersild, A.T., & Thomas, W.S. The influence of adrenal extract on behavior and mental efficiency. *American Journal of Psychology*, 1931, *43*, 447-456. **534, 550**

Jevning, R., Wilson, A.F., & Vanderlaan, E.F. Plasma prolactin and growth hormone during meditation. *Psychosomatic Medicine* 1978, *40*, 329-333. **71, 72**

Jimerson, D.C., **547, 563, 564, 567, 570, 574, 588, 795**

Jobert, A., **7, 11**

Jobin, M., **359**

Joffe, J., Rawson, R., & Mulick, J. Control of their environment reduces emotionality in rats. *Science*, 1973, *180*, 1383-1384. **212**

Johanson, C.E., **676**

Johanson, C.E., & Uhlenhuth, E.H. Drug preferences in humans. *Federation Proceedings*, 1982, *41*, 228-233. **677**

Johansson, J., **426, 496**

Johansson, S., Levi, L., & Lindstedt, S. Reports from the laboratory for clinical stress research. Stockholm, 1970, pp. 17-25. **71**

Johnson, A.M., Falstein, E.L., Szursk, S., & Svendsen, M. School phobia. *American Journal of Orthopsychiatry*, 1941, *11*, 702-711. **746**

Johnson, R., **379**

Johnson, S.B., & Melamed, B.G. The assessment and treatment of children's fears. In B.B. Lahey & A.E. Kazdin (Eds.), *Advances in clinical child psychology* (Vol. 2). New York: Plenum, 1979. **370, 376, 709, 711, 712**

Johnston, D.W., **216, 217, 218, 220, 425, 428**

Johnston, D.W., Lancashire, M., Matthews, A.M., Munby, M., Shaw, P.M., & Gelder, M.G. Imaginal flooding and exposure to real phobic situations: Changes during treatment. *British Journal of Psychiatry*, 1976, *129*, 372-377. **428**

Johnston, G.A.R., **36**

Johnston, J., **230, 242, 375, 459**

Johnstone, E., Owens, D., Frith, C., McPherson, K., Dowie, C., Riley, G., &

Gold, A. Neurotic illness and its response to anxiolytic and antidepressant treatment. *Psychological Medicine*, 1980, *10*, 321-328. **521, 544**

Jones, E. Fear, guilt and hate. *International Journal of Psychoanalysis*, 1929, *10*, 383-385. **624**

Jones, G.B., **343**

Jones, I.H., **304**

Jones, I.H. Psychiatric disorders among Aborigines of the Australian Western Desert. *Social Science and Medicine*, 1972, *6*, 263-267. **304**

Jones, I.H., & Horne, D.J. Diagnosis of psychiatric illness among tribal Aborigines. *Medical Journal of Australia*, 1972, *1*, 345-349. **304**

Jones, I.H., & Horne, D.J. Psychiatric disorders among the Aborigines of the Australian Western Desert: Further data and discussion. *Social Science and Medicine*, 1973, *7*, 219-228. **304, 305**

Jones, J.G., **661**

Jones, L.G., **71**

Jones, L.M., **444**

Jones, M.C. A laboratory study of fear: The case of Peter. *Pedagogical Seminary*, 1924, *31*, 308-315. **218, 707**

Jones, M.C. Physiological and psychological response to stress in neurotic patients. *Journal of Mental Science*, 1948, *44*, 392-404. **564**

Jones, M.T., **58, 61**

Jones, R.B., **434**

Jones, R.S.G., **540, 573**

Jones, R.T. Marihuana: human effects. In L.L. Iversen, S.D. Iversen, & S.H. Snyder (Eds.), *Handbook of psychopharmacology. Drugs of abuse.* New York: Plenum Press, 1978. **549**

Jornestedt, L., **503, 529, 585, 586**

Joslin, J., Fletcher, H., Emlen, J. A comparison of the responses to snakes of lab- and wild-reared rhesus monkeys. *Animal Behavior*, 1964, *12*, 348-352. **201, 215**

Julius, S., **348**

Julius, S., & Esler, M. Autonomic nervous cardiovascular regulation in borderline hypertension. *American Journal of Cardiology*, 1975, *36*, 685-692. **347, 348**

Kabler, J.D., **137**

Kafka, M.S., **563**

Kafka, M.S., van Kammen, D.P., Kleinman, J.E., Nurnberger, J.I., Siever, L.J., Uhde, T.W., & Polinsky, R.J. Alpha-adrenergic receptor function in schizophrenia, affective disorder and some neurological diseases. *Communications in Psychopharmacology*, 1981, *4*, 477-486. **563**

Kagan, J., **110, 123**

Kagan, J. Discrepancy, temperament and infant distress. In M. Lewis & L.A.

Rosenblum (Eds.), *The origins of fear*. New York: John Wiley, 1974, pp. 229-248. **113, 156**

Kagan, J. *The second year*. Cambridge: Harvard University Press, 1981. **418**

Kagan, J., Kearsley, R., & Zelaso, P. *Infancy, Its place in human development*. Cambridge: Harvard University Press, 1978. **414**

Kagan, J., & Moss, H.A. *Birth to maturity*. New York: Wiley, 1962. **378**

Kagan, J., Reznick, J.S., Clarke, C., Snidman, N., & Coll, C.G. Behavioral inhibition to the unfamiliar. *Child Development*, In press. **420**

Kahn, R.J., **510, 511, 538**

Kaiser, H.F., **654**

Kalat, J.W., **206, 208**

Kalbak, K. Incidence of arteriosclerosis in patients with rheumatoid arthritis receiving long-term corticosteroid therapy. *Annals of Rheumatic Diseases*, 1972, *31*, 196-200. **346**

Kalimo, E., Bice, T., & Novosel, M. Cross-cultural analysis of selected emotional questions from the Cornell Medical Index. *British Journal of Preventive Social Medicine*, 1970, *24*, 229-240. **302**

Kalin, N.H., **588**

Kallstrom, D.W., **659**

Kaloupek, D.G., **427**

Kaltreider, N.B., **622, 624, 627, 772**

Kaltreider, N.B., Dewitt, K.N., Weiss, D.S., & Horowitz, M.J. Patterns of individual change scales. *Archives of General Psychiatry*, 1981, 1263-1269. **614, 615**

Kamin, L.J., **203, 205, 220, 223**

Kamin, L.J. Psychodynamic changes through systematic desensitization. *Journal of Abnormal Psychology*, 1970, *76*, 199-205. **617**

Kamin, L.J., Brimer, C.J., & Black, A.H. Conditioned suppression as a monitor of fear of the CS in the course of avoidance training. *Journal of Comparative and Physiological Psychology*, 1963, *56*, 497-501. **205**

Kaminski, G. *Verhaltenstheorie und verhaltensmodifikation*. Stuttgart: Klett, 1970. **247, 259**

Kandel, E. From meta psychology to molecular biology: Explorations into the nature of anxiety. *American Journal of Psychiatry*, 1983, *140*, 1277-1292. **630**

Kane, J.M., **66**

Kanfer, F.H., **xxii, 254**

Kanfer, F.H. Self-regulation: Research, issues and speculations. In C. Neuringer & J.L. Michael (Eds.), *Behavior modification in clinical psychology*. New York: Appleton-Century, 1970. **254**

Kanfer, F.H. Self-management methods. In F.H. Kanfer & A.P. Goldstein (Eds.), *Helping people change: A textbook of methods*. New York: Pergamon Press, 1975. pp. 309-356. **248**

Kanfer, F.H. Target selection for clinical change program. *Behavioral Assessment*, in press. **259**

Kanfer, F.H., & Busemeyer, J.P. The use of problem-solving and decision-making in behavior therapy. *Clinical Psychology Review*, 1982, *2*, 239-266. **259**

Kanfer, F.H., & Goldfoot, D.A. Self-control and the tolerance of noxious stimulation. *Psychological Reports*, 1966, *18*, 79-85. **254**

Kanfer, F.H., & Goldstein, A.P. (Eds.). *Helping people change: A textbook of methods* (2 ed.). New York: Pergamon Press, 1980. **249**

Kanfer, F.H., & Hagerman, S. The role of self-regulation. In L.P. Rehm (Ed.), *Behavioral therapy for depression: Present status and future direction*. New York: Academic Press, 1980. **254**

Kanfer, F.H., Karoly, P., & Newman, A. Reduction of children's fear of the dark by competence-related and situational threat-related verbal cues. *Journal of Consulting and Clinical Psychology*, 1975, *43*, 251-258. **254**

Kanfer, F.H., & Seidner, M.L. Self-control: Factors enhancing tolerance of noxious stimulation. *Journal of Personality and Social Psychology*, 1973, *25*, 381-389. **254**

Kanner, A.D., **112, 114, 119**

Kanner, L. *Child psychiatry* (3rd ed.). Springfield: Charles C. Thomas, 1957. **411**

Kanno, P.H., **655**

Kantor, J., Zitrin, C.M., & Zeldis, S. Mitral valve prolapse syndrome in agoraphobic patients. *American Journal of Psychiatry*, 1980, *100*, 302-305. **365**

Kaplan, P.M., Smith, A., Grobstein, R., & Fischman, S.E. Family mediation of stress. *Social Work*, 1973, *18*, 60-69. **378**

Kaplowitz, C., **418**

Kapur, M., **309**

Kapur, R.L., Kapur, M., & Carstairs, G.M. Indian psychiatric interview schedule. *Social Psychiatry*, 1974, *9*, 61-69. **309**

Karabanow, O. Double-blind controlled study in phobias and obsessions. *Journal of International Medical Research*, 1977, *5*, 42-48. **504, 507**

Karas, G.G., **62**

Kàrker, A., **208**

Karlsson, E.S., **351**

Karniol, I.G., **547, 549**

Karno, M., **xxx**

Karobath, M., & Supavilai, P. Distinction of benzodiazepine agonists from antagonists by photoaffinity labelling of benzodiazepine receptors in vitro. *Neuroscience Letters*, 1982, *31*, 65-69. **33**

Karoly, P., **254, 433**

Karp, L., **143**

Kasahara, Y. Fear of eye-to-eye confrontation among neurotic patients in Japan.

In T.K. Lebra & W.P. Lebra (Eds.), *Japanese culture and behavior*. Honolulu: University of Hawaii Press, 1976. **316, 317**

Kashima, T., **348**

Kastrup, M. Psychic disorders among pre-school children in a geographically delimited area of Aarhus County, Denmark. *Acta Psychiatrica Scandinavica*, 1976, *54*, 29-42. **284**

Kataoka, Y., Gutman, Y., Costa, E., & Guidotti, A. Benzodiazepine and muscimol binding sites in adrenal medulla: Receptors or drug acceptor sites. *Society for Neuroscience Abstracts*, 1983, *9*, 1041. **38**

Kataoka, Y., Gutman, Y., Guidotti, A., Panula, P., Wrobleski, J., Cosenza-Murphy, D., Wu, J.-Y., & Costa, E. Intrinsic GABAergic system of adrenal chromaffin cells. *Proceedings of the National Academy of Science. USA*, 1984, *81*, 3218-3222. **39**

Katcher, A.H., **149**

Katkin, E.S., **647**

Katon, W., Kleinman, A., & Rosen, G. Depression and somatization: A review. Parts I and II. *American Journal of Medicine*, 1982, *72*, 127-134, 241-247. **319**

Katz, E.R., Kellerman, J., & Siegel, S.E. Anxiety as an affective focus in the clinical study of acute behavioral distress: A reply to Shacham and Daut. *Journal of Consulting and Clinical Psychology*, 1981, *49*, 470-471. **372, 712**

Katz, J., **62, 384**

Katz, J., Weiner, H., Gallagher, T.E., & Hellman, L. Stress, distress, and ego defenses: Psychoendocrine responses to impending breast tumor biopsy. *Archives of General Psychiatry*, 1970, *23*, 131-142. **62**

Katz, L., **530**

Katz, M.M., Robins, E., Croughan, J., Secunda, S., & Swann, A. Behavioural measurement and drug response characteristics of unipolar and bipolar depression. *Psychological Medicine*, 1982, *12*, 25-36. **65, 544**

Katzev, R.D., **234**

Kay, B., **392, 393, 511, 513**

Kazdin, A.E., **432**

Kazdin, A.E. Drawing valid inferences from case studies. *Journal of Consulting and Clinical Psychology*, 1981, *49*, 183-192. **643**

Kazdin, A.E. Single-case experimental designs. In P. Kendall & J. Butcher (Eds.), *Handbook of research methods in clinical psychology*. New York: Wiley, 1982. **643**

Kazdin, A.E., & Wilcoxon, L.A. Systematic desensitization and nonspecific treatment effects: A methodological evaluation. *Psychological Bulletin*, 1976, *83*, 229-258. **432**

Keane, T.M., **427**

Keane, T.M., & Kaloupek, D.G. Imaginal flooding in the treatment of a post-traumatic stress disorder. *Journal of Consulting and Clinical Psychology*, 1982, *50*, 138-140. **427**

Kearsley, R., **414**

Keir, R., **201, 202, 215, 216, 222, 243**

Kelleher, R.T., **238**

Keller, M.B., **293**

Kellerman, H., **112, 114, 119, 417**

Kellerman, J., **372, 712**

Kellett, J., **426**

Kellner, R., **678**

Kellner, R., Collins, C., Shulman, R.S., & Pathak, D. The short-term antianxiety effects of propranolol HCL. *Journal of Clinical Pharmacology*, 1974, *14*, 301-304. **546**

Kellner, R., Rada, R.T., Andersen, T., & Pathak, D. The effects of chlordiazepoxide on self-rated depression, anxiety and well-being. *Psychopharmacology*, 1979, *64*, 185-191. **676**

Kelly, D. *Anxiety and emotions*. Springfield, IL: Charles C. Thomas Co., 1980. **183, 581**

Kelly, D., Guirguis, W., Frommer, E., Mitchell-Heggs, N., & Sargant, W. Treatment of phobic states with antidepressants. A retrospective study of 246 patients. *British Journal of Psychiatry*, 1970, *116*, 387-398. **750**

Kelly, D., Mitchell-Heggs, N., & Sherman, D. Anxiety and the effects of sodium lactate assessed clinically and physiologically. *British Journal of Psychiatry*, 1971, *119*, 129-141. **82, 586, 749**

Kelly, D., & Walter, C.J.S. A clinical and physiological relationship between anxiety and depression. *British Journal of Psychiatry*. 1969, *115*, 401-406. **747, 749**

Kelly, D.H., & Walter, C.J.S. The relationship between clinical diagnosis and anxiety assessed by forearm blood flow and other measurements. *British Journal of Psychiatry*, 1968, *114*, 611-626. **82**

Kelly, G. *The psychology of personal constructs*. New York: Norton, 1955. **89**

Kelly, J., & Grossman, S.P. GABA and hypothalamic feeding systems. II. A comparison of GABA, glycine and acetylcholine agonists and antagonists. *Pharmacology, Biochemistry and Behavior*. 1979, *11*, 647-652. **31**

Kendall, P.C., **659, 702, 709**

Kendall, P.C., Finch, A.J., Jr., Auerbach, S.M., Hooke, J.F., & Mikulka, P.J. The state-trait anxiety inventory: A systematic evaluation. *Journal of Consulting and Clinical Psychology*, 1976, *44* (3), 406-412. **660**

Kendall, P.C., & Hollon, S.D. Assessing self-referent speech: Methods in the measurement of self-statements. In P.C. Kendall & S.D. Hollon (Eds.), *Assessment strategies for cognitive-behavioral interventions*. New York: Academic Press, 1981. **704**

Kendall, P.C., & Korgeski, G.P. Assessment and cognitive-behavioral interventions. *Cognitive Therapy and Research*, 1979, *3*, 1-21. **92**

Kendrick, M.J., Craig, K.D., Lawson, D.M., & Davidson, P.O. Cognitive and behavioral therapy for musical-performance anxiety. *Journal of Consulting and Clinical Psychology*, 1982, *50*, 353-362. **434**

Kennedy, W.A. School phobia: Rapid treatment of fifty cases. *Journal of Abnormal Psychology*, 1965, *70*, 285-289. **373, 714, 715**

Kenny, M. Latah: The symbolism of a putative mental disorder. *Culture, Medicine and Psychiatry*, 1978, *2*, 209-231. **313**

Kenny, M. Paradox Lost: The latah problem revisited. *Journal of Nervous and Mental Disease*, 1983, *171*, 159-167. **313**

Kenway, A. A double-blind comparison of pimozide and haloperidol in the treatment of recurrent anxiety states. *British Journal of Clinical Practice*, 1973, *27*, 67-68. **520, 523**

Kenyon, F.E. Hypochondriacal states. *British Journal of Psychiatry*, 1976, *129*, 1-14. **747**

Kenyon, P., **349**

Keren, A., **350**

Kernberg, O. *The borderline conditions in pathological narcissism*. New York: Aronson, 1975. **624**

Kerr, T.A., **66, 328, 366, 747, 773**

Kerr, T.A., Roth, M., & Shapira, K. Prediction of outcome in anxiety states and depressive illnesses. *British Journal of Psychiatry*, 1974, *124*, 125-133. **747, 754**

Kessler, K.A. Tricyclic antidepressants: Mode of action and clinical use. In M.A. Lipton, A. DiMascio & K.F. Killam (Eds.), *Psychopharmacology: A generation of progress*. New York: Raven Press, 1978. **544**

Kettler, R., **28**

Kety, S.S., **115-116**

Kety, S.S. Cerebral circulation and metabolism in health and disease. *American Journal of Medicine*, 1950, *8*, 205-217. **337**

Kety, S.S. Toward hypotheses for a biochemical component in the vulnerability to schizophrenia. *Seminars in Psychiatry*, 1972, *4*, 233-237. **115**

Keyser, M.L., **548**

Kidd, C.B., **519, 523, 540**

Kidd, K.K., **286, 292, 293, 394, 395**

Kidson, M.A., & Jones, I.H. Psychiatric disorders among the Aborigines of the Australian western desert. *Archives of General Psychiatry*, 1968, *19*, 413-417. **304**

Kielholz, P., **746**

Kielholz, P. Genetische und Nosologische Aspekte der Angst. *Das ärztliche Gespräch*, (Tropon, Kòln), 1971, No. 15, 3-6. **752**

Kielholz, P. *Beta-blockers and the central nervous system*. Baltimore: University Park Press, 1977. **546**

Kieras, D. Beyond pictures and words: Alternate information processing models for imagery effects in verbal memory. *Psychological Bulletin*, 1978, *5*, 532-554. **158**

Kierkegaard, S. *The concept of dread*. (W. Lowrie, trans.). Princeton, N.J.: Princeton University Press, 1944. **533, 736, 779**

Kierkegaard, S. *The concept of anxiety* and *The sickness unto death*. Edited and translated by H.V. Hong & E.H. Hong. Guilford, Surrey: Princeton University Press, 1980. **172, 736, 779**

Kiev, A. *Transcultural psychiatry*. New York: Free Press, 1972. pp. 78-108. **312, 315**

Kilgore, K., **676**

Kilpatrick, A., **285**

Kilts, C., **586**

Kimmel, H. Conditions of fear and anxiety. In C.D. Spielberger & I.G. Sarason (Eds.), *Stress and anxiety* (Vol. I). New York: Halsted Press, 1975, pp. 189-210. **237**

King, A.C., **565**

King, B.D., Sokoloff, L., & Wechsler, R.L. The effects of L-epinephrine and L-norepinephrine upon cerebral circulation and metabolism in man. *Journal of Clinical Investigation*, 1952, *31*, 273-279. **534, 550**

King, D., **568, 586, 786, 793, 794**

King, F.J., & Heinrich, D.L. An investigation of the casual influence of trait and state anxiety on academic achievement. *Journal of Educational psychology*, 1976, *68*, 330-334. **660**

King, J., **202**

Kinsman, R.A., **650, 652**

Kinsman, R.A., Dirks, J.F., Dahlem, N.W., & Heller, A.S. Anxiety in asthma: Panic-fear symptomatology and personality in relation to manifest anxiety. *Psychological Reports*, 1980, *46* (1), 196-198. **652**

Kintsch, W. *The representation of meaning in memory*. Hillsdale, NJ: Lawrence Erlbaum Associates, 1974. **160**

Kipper, D.A. Behavior therapy for fears brought on by war experiences. *Journal of Consulting and Clinical Psychology*, 1977, *45*, 216-221. **427**

Kirsch, I., **194**

Kirsher, N., **341**

Kisch, E.S., **61**

Kistler, K., **59, 71**

Kleber, H.D., **15, 526, 529, 542, 548, 552**

Kleber, R.J. A double-blind comparative study of desipramine hydrochloride and diazepam in the control of mixed anxiety/depression symptomatology. *Journal of Clinical Psychiatry*, 1979, *40*, 165-170. **521, 544**

Kleiger, J.H., **650, 652**

Klein, D.F., xxi-xxii, xxiii, xxxiv, 83, 241, 293, 328, 359, 366, 390, 391, 392, 393, 397, 401, 403, 404, 406, 407, 409, 453, 456, 486, 511, 512, 513, 514, 515, 524, 527, 540, 543, 544, 547, 551, 552, 557, 562, 586, 591, 670, 762, 768

Klein, D.F. Delineation of two drug-responsive anxiety syndromes. *Psychopharmacologia*, 1964, *5*, 397-408. **82, 293, 397, 400, 511, 534, 538, 543, 762**

Klein, D.F. Importance of psychiatric diagnosis in prediction of clinical drug effects. *Archives of General Psychiatry*, 1967, *16*, 118-126. **82**

Klein, D.F. Non-scientific constraints on psychiatric treatment research produced by the organization of clinical services. In Merlis, S. (Ed.), *Non-scientific constraints on medical research*. Raven Press, 1970, New York: pp. 69-90. **531**

Klein, D.F. Drug therapy as a means of syndromal identification and nosological revision. In Cole, J.O., Freedman, A.M., & Friedhoff, A.J. (Eds.), *Psychopathology and psychopharmacology*. Baltimore: The John Hopkins Press, 1973, pp. 143-160. **501**

Klein, D.F. Anxiety reconceptualized. *Comprehensive Psychiatry*, 1980, *21*, 411-427. **557, 776, 780**

Klein, D.F. Anxiety reconceptualized. In D.F. Klein, & J. Rabkin (Eds)., *Anxiety: New research and changing concepts*. New York: Raven Press, 1981. pp. 235-265. **133, 169, 275, 366, 486, 502, 510, 524, 606, 607, 611, 627, 761**

Klein, D.F., & Davis, J.M. *Diagnosis and drug treatment of psychiatric disorder*. (1 ed.). Baltimore, MD: Williams and Wilkins, 1969. **531, 669**

Klein, D.F., & Fink, M. Psychiatric reaction patterns to imipramine. *American Journal of Psychiatry*, 1962, *119*, 432-438. **390, 512, 534, 543, 560**

Klein, D.F., Gittelman, R., Quitkin, F.M., & Rifkin, A. Diagnosis and drug treatment of psychiatric disorders: Adults and children (2 ed.). Baltimore: Williams & Wilkins, 1980. **502, 512, 513, 540, 585**

Klein, D.F., & Gittelman-Klein, R. Drug treatment of separation anxious and depressive illness in children. In *Advances in Biological psychiatry* (Vol. 2). Basel: S. Karger, 1978. **291**

Klein, D.F., & Rabkin, J.G. *Anxiety: New research and changing concepts*. New York: Raven Press, 1981. **297, 760**

Klein, D.F., Zitrin, C.M., & Woerner, M. Antidepressants, anxiety, panic, and phobia. In M.A. Lipton, A. DiMascio & R.F. Killam (Eds.), *Psychopharmacology: A generation of progress*. New York: Raven Press, 1978. **543**

Klein, D.F., Zitrin, C.M., Woerner, M.G., & Ross, D.C. Treatment of phobias: II. Behavior therapy and supportive psychotherapy: Are there any specific ingredients? *Archives of General Psychiatry*, 1983, *40*, 139-145. **397, 400**

Klein, M. On the theory of anxiety and guilt. In J. Riviere (Ed.), *Developments in psychoanalysis*. London: Hogarth Press, 1952. **602**

Kleinknecht, R. The origins and remission of fear in a group of tarantula enthusiasts. *Behaviour Research and Therapy*, 1982, *20*, 437-444. **458**

Kleinknecht, R., Klepac, R., & Alexander, L. Origins and characteristics of fear of dentistry. *Journal of the American Dental Association*, 1973, *86*, 842-848. **371**

Kleinman, A. Depression, somatization and the new cross-cultural psychiatry. *Social Science and Medicine*, 1977, *11*, 3-10. **298**

Kleinman, A., Eisenberg, L., & Good, B. Culture, illness and care. *Annals of Internal Medicine*, 1977, *88*, 251-258. **299**

Kleinman, A., & Kleinman, J. The interconnections among depressive experiences, the meanings of pain, and culture. In A. Kleinman & B. Good (Eds.),

Culture and depression: Toward an anthropology of dysphoric affect and affective disorders. Berkeley: University of California Press, in press. **319**

Kleinman, A.M., **298, 319, 325, 326, 327, 485, 688**

Kleinman, A.M. *Patients and healers in the context of culture.* Berkeley: University of California Press, 1980. **317**

Kleinman, A.M. Neurasthenia and Depression. *Culture, Medicine and Psychiatry,* 1982, *6,* 117-190. **311, 317, 318**

Kleinman, A.M. Somatization. *Foreign Referential Journal of Psychiatry.* Peoples Republic of China, in press. **319**

Kleinman, J.E., **319, 563**

Klepac, R., **371**

Klepner, C.A., Lippa, S.A., Benson, D.I., Sano, M.C., & Beer, B. Resolution of two biochemically and pharmacologically distinct benzodiazepine receptors. *Pharmacology, Biochemistry and Behavior,* 1979, *11,* 457-462. **12**

Klerman, G.L., **114, 116, 118, 240, 293, 297, 304, 613**

Klerman, J.L., **116**

Klevan, T., **68**

Kligman, D.H., **416, 417**

Klinedinst, J.D., **708**

Klinger, E. Dimensions of thought and imagery in normal waking states. *Journal of Altered States of Consciousness,* 1978, *4,* 97-113. **702**

Klinger, E., Barta, S.G., & Maxeiner, M.E. Current concerns: Assessing therapeutically relevant motivation. In P.C. Kendall & S.D. Hollon (Eds.), *Assessment strategies for cognitive-behavioral interventions.* New York: Academic Press, 1981, pp. 97-120. **92**

Klinnert, M.D., **417**

Klinnert, M.D., Campos, J., Sorce, J.F., Emde, R.N., & Svejda, M.J. Social referencing: Emotional expressions as behavior regulators. In R. Plutchik & H. Kellerman (Eds.), *Emotions in early development.* New York: Academic Press, 1982. **417**

Klinnert, M.D., Sorce, J.F., Emde, R.N., Stenberg, C., & Gaensbauer, T.J. Continuities and change in early emotional life: Maternal perceptions of surprise, fear and anger. In R. Emde & R. Harmon (Eds.), *Continuities and discontinuities in development.* New York: Plenum Publishing Corp., 1984. **418**

Klosko, J.S., **494**

Knight, R., Atkins, A., Eagle, C., Evans, N., Finklestein, J.W., Fukushima, D., Katz, J., & Weiner, H. Psychological stress, ego defenses, and cortisol production in children hospitalized for elective surgery. *Psychosomatic Medicine,* 1979, *41,* 40-49. **62, 384**

Knott, V.J., **780**

Ko, G.N., Elsworth, J.D., Roth, R.H., Rifkin, B.G., Leigh, H., & Redmond, D.E., Jr. Panic-induced elevation of plasma MHPG levels in phobic-anxious patients. *Archives of General Psychiatry,* 1983, *40,* 425-430. **548, 570**

Kobasa, S.C., **676**

Koenigsberg, S., & Johnson, R. Child behavior during sequential dental visits. *Journal of the American Dental Association*, 1972, *85*, 128-132. **379**

Kohlstrom, J., **229, 235, 239, 240, 454**

Kohout, J., **561-62**

Kohut, H. *Analysis of the self.* New York: International Universities Press, 1971. **624**

Kolb, L.C., Burris, B.C., & Griffiths, S. *Propranolol and clonidine in treatment of the chronic post traumatic stress disorders of war.* Paper presented at the American Psychiatric Association Meeting, New York, N.Y., May, 1983. **548**

Kolvin, I., **392, 393, 511, 513**

Kondo, A. Morita therapy: A Japanese therapy for neurosis. *American Journal of Psychoanalysis*, 1953, *13*, 31-37. **316**

Konincyx, P. Stress hyperprolactinemia in clinical practice. *Lancet*, 1978, *2*, 273. **71**

Konkel, D.R., **39, 41, 43, 44, 45, 50**

Kontos, H.A., Richardson, D.W., Raper, A.J., Zubair-Ul-Hassan, & Patterson, J.L., Jr. Mechanism of action of hypocapnic alkalosis on limb blood vessels in man and dog. *American Journal of Physiology*, 1972, *223*, 1296-1303. **350**

Kopin, I.J. Catecholamines, adrenal hormones and stress. In D.T. Krieger & J.C. Hughs (Eds.), *Neuroendocrinology.* New York: H.P. Publishing, 1980. **346**

Koppanyi, T. The effect of subcutaneously injected epinephrine in normal human subjects. *Proceedings of the Society for Experimental Biology in Medicine*, 1928, *25*, 744-745. **534, 550**

Korchin, S.J., **60, 65, 534, 550**

Korgeski, G.P., **92**

Korn, S., **376**

Kornetsky, C. Animal models: Promises and problems. In I. Hanin & E. Usdin (Eds.), *Animal models in psychiatry and neurology.* New York: Pergamon, 1977. **79**

Kornhaber, R.C., & Schroeder, H.E. Importance of model similarity in extinction of avoidance behavior in children. *Journal of Consulting and Clinical Psychology*, 1975, *43*, 601-607. **708**

Korson, L., **543**

Kositchek, R., **365**

Koslow, S.H., **58, 60, 66, 67**

Koslow, S.H., Maas, J.W., Bowden, C.L., Davis, J.M., Hanin, I., & Javaid, J. CSF and urinary biogenic amines and metabolites in depression and mania: a controlled, univariate analysis. *Archives of General Psychiatry*, 1983, *40*, 999-1010. **67, 544, 545**

Koslow, S.H., Stokes, P.E., Mendels, J., Ramsey, A., & Casper, R. Insulin tolerance test: Human growth hormone response and insulin resistance in primary unipolar depressed, bipolar depressed, and control subjects. *Psychological Medicine*, 1982, *12*, 45-55. **58**

Koss, M.P., & Butcher, J.N. A comparison of psychiatric patients' self-report with other sources of clinical information. *Journal of Research in Personality*, 1973, *7*, 225-236. **683**

Kotchen, T.A., **71**

Kotsch, W.E., **126**

Kovacs, M., & Beck, A. An empirical clinical approach towards a definition of childhood depression. In J.G. Schulterbrandt & A. Raskin (Eds.), *Depression in children: Diagnosis, treatment and conceptual models*. New York: Raven Press, 1977. **126**

Kovacs, M., & Beck, A.T. Cognitive-affective processes in depression. In C.E. Izard (Ed.), *Emotions in personality and psychopathology*. New York: Plenum, 1979. **144**

Kowalski, A.A., **569**

Kozak, M.H., **161, 164, 437, 444**

Kozak, M.J., **xxxv, 136, 161, 218, 219, 220, 233, 241, 366, 435, 436, 437, 453, 454, 455, 457, 458, 460, 463, 466, 479, 494, 498, 500**

Kozak, M.J. *The psychophysiological effects of training on variously elicited imaginings*. Unpublished doctoral dissertation. University of Wisconsin, Madison, 1982. **436**

Kraanen, J., **428**

Kracht, J. Fright-thyrotoxicosis in the wild rabbit: A model of thyrotrophic alarm-reaction. *Acta Endocrinologia (Kbh)*, 1954, *15*, 355-362. **341**

Kraemer, G.W., **236**

Kraepelin, E. *Dementia praecox paraphrenia* (1919). G.M. Robertson (ed.) New York: Krieger, 1971. **775, 778**

Kraepelin, E. *Psychiatrie*. 5. Auflage. Leipzig: Barth, 1896. **737, 741**

Kramer, J.C., Klein, D.F., & Fink, M. Withdrawal symptoms following discontinuation of imipramine therapy. *American Journal of Psychiatry*, 1961, *118*, 549-550. **552**

Kramer, M., **281, 282, 283, 719**

Kramer, M., Sartorius, N., Jablensky, A., & Gulbinat, W. The ICD-9 classification of mental disorders. *Acta Psychiatrica Scandinavica*, 1979, *59*, 241-262. **753**

Krantz, S., & Hammen, C. Assessment of cognitive bias in depression. *Journal of Abnormal Psychology*, 1979, *88*, 611-619. **92**

Kratochwill, T.R., **372, 373, 374**

Kreisberg, R. Diabetic ketoacidosis: New concepts and trends in pathogenesis and management. *Annals of Internal Medicine*, 1978, *88*, 681-699. **350**

Kremen, I., **132**

Kremer, M.W., **614**

Kreuz, L.E., & Rose, R.M. Assessment of aggressive behavior and plasma testosterone in young criminal population. *Psychosomatic Medicine*, 1972, *26*, 479-482. **74**

Krieger, D.T. Neuroendocrine physiology. In P. Felig, J.D. Baxter, A.E. Broadus & L.A. Frohman (Eds.), *Endocrinology and Metabolism*. New York: McGraw Hill. 1981, pp. 125-149. **54**

Krieger, D.T., & Glick, S.M. Growth hormone and cortisol responsiveness in Cushing's syndrome: Relation to a possible central nervous system etiology. *American Journal of Medicine*, 1972, *52*, 25-40. **68**

Krietman, N., **293, 562**

Kringlen, E. Obsessional neurotics: A long term follow-up. *British Journal of Psychiatry*, 1965, *111*, 709-722. **579**

Krohn, A. (Ed.). *Hysteria, the elusive neurosis*. New York: International Universities Press, 1978. **669**

Kronfol, Z., **66, 67**

Krsiak, M., **525**

Krsiak, M. Effects of drugs on behaviour of aggressive mice. *British Journal of Pharmacology*, 1979, *65*, 525-533. **30**

Krug, S.E., & Laughlin, J.E. Second-order factors among normal and pathological primary personality traits. *Journal of Consulting Psychology*, 1977, *45* (4), 575-582. **654**

Krupnick, J., **624, 627**

Krutzsch, H., **41, 43, 44, 45**

Krystal, J.H., **542, 552**

Kubena, R.K., **11**

Kubie, L.S. A physiological approach to the concept of anxiety. *Psychosomatic Medicine*, 1941, *3*, 263-276. **603**

Kuchel, O. Autonomic nervous system in hypertension: clinical aspects. In J. Genest., E. Koiw & O. Kuchel (Eds.), *Hypertension*. New York: McGraw-Hill, 1977. **347**

Kuhn, C., **63, 358, 776, 779**

Kuhn, T.S. *The structure of scientific revolutions* (2nd ed.). Chicago: University of Chicago Press, 1970. **777**

Kuipers, A.C.M., **428, 433, 745**

Kukla, A., **121**

Kulcsar, A., **28, 538, 563**

Kuller, L.H., **325, 327**

Kupfer, D.J., **567, 786, 795**

Kupfer, D.J., & Thase, M.E. The use of the sleep laboratory in the diagnosis of affective disorders. *The Psychiatric Clinics of North America*, 1983, 6, 1-13. **568**

Kurokawa, N., Suematsu, H., Tamai, J., Esaki, M., Hiroyuki, A., & Yujiro, I. Effect of emotional stress on human growth secretion. *Journal of Psychosomatic Research*, 1971, *21*, 231-235. **67, 68**

Kwee, K.G., **426**

Labrie, A., **359**
LaBrie, R., **677**
Labrum, A.H., **335, 337**
Lacey, B.C., **334**
Lacey, J.I. Somatic response patterning and stress: Some revisions of activation theory. In M.H. Appley & R. Trumbull (Eds.), *Psychological stress: Issues in research*. New York: Appleton-Century-Crofts, 1967. **156, 335, 336**
Lacey, J.I., & Lacey, B.C. On heart rate responses and behavior: A reply to Elliott. *Journal of Personality and Social Psychology*, 1974, *30*, 1-18. **334**
Lachar, D., **708**
Lader, M.H., **81, 167, 194, 278, 280, 348, 349, 525, 538, 546, 746**
Lader, M.H. Palmar skin conductance measures in anxiety and phobic states. *Journal of Psychosomatic Research*, 1967, *11*, 271-281. **581**
Lader, M.H. Psychosomatic and psychophysiological aspects of anxiety. In O.W. Hill (Ed.), *Modern trends in psychosomatic medicine-2*. New York: Appleton-Century-Crofts, 1970. **338**
Lader, M.H. The nature of anxiety. *British Journal of Psychiatry*, 1972, *121*, 481-491. **740**
Lader, M.H. The peripheral and central role of catecholamines in the mechanisms of anxiety. *International Pharmacopsychiatry*, 1974, *9*, 125-137. **553**
Lader, M.H. Psychophysiology of clinical anxiety. In T. Silverstone & B. Barraclough (Eds.), *Contemporary psychiatry*. British Journal of Psychiatry Special Publication, 1975, *9*, 127-132. **793, 795**
Lader, M.H. *The psychophysiology of mental illness*. London: Routledge and Kegan Paul, 1975. **81, 583, 793, 795**
Lader, M.H. Psychophysiological studies in anxiety. In G.D. Burrows & B. Davies (Eds.) *Handbook of studies in anxiety*. Amsterdam: Elsevier/North Holland, 1980. **564, 581**
Lader, M.H. A psychophysiological approach to pathological anxiety. In A. Okasha (Ed.), *Proceedings of symposium on psychopathology of anxiety and its management*. World Psychiatric Association, Cairo, Jan. 11-13, 1981. **741**
Lader, M.H. Biological differentiation of anxiety, arousal, and stress. In R.J. Matthew (Ed.), *The Biology of anxiety*. New York: Brunner/Mazel, 1982. **334, 337**
Lader, M.H., Gelder, M.G., & Marks, I.M. Palmar skin conductance measures of predictions of response to desensitization. *Journal of Psychosomatic Research*, 1967, *11*, 283-290. **439**
Lader, M.H., & Marks, I. *Clinical anxiety*. New York: Grune and Stratton, 1971. **236, 241, 789**
Lader, M.H., & Mathews, A.M. A physiological model of phobic anxiety and desensitization. *Behaviour Research and Therapy*, 1968, *6*, 411-421. **219, 439**

Lader, M.H., & Tyrer, P.J. Central and peripheral effects of propranolol and sotalol in normal human subjects. *British Journal of Pharmacology*, 1972, *45*, 557-560. **546**

Lader, M.H., & Wing, L. *Physiological measures, sedative drugs, and morbid anxiety.* New York: Oxford University Press, 1966. **132, 167, 168, 365, 439, 444, 445, 494, 498**

Lader, M.H., & Wing, L. Physiologic measures in agitated and retarded depressed patients. *Journal of Psychiatric Research*, 1969, *7*, 89-95. **583**

Lahmeyer, H.W., Miller, M., & DeLeon-Jones, F. Anxiety and mood fluctuations during normal menstrual cycle. *Psychosomatic Medicine*, 1982, *44*, 183-194. **75**

Laidlaw, J.C., **55**

Laird, J.D., Wagener, J.J., Halal, M., & Szegda, M. Remembering what you feel: Effects of emotion on memory. *Journal of Personality and Social Psychology*, 1982, *42*, 646-657. **146-47, 169**

Laitsch, K., **216**

Lake, C.R., **563, 564, 570, 588**

Lakin, M.L., **49**

Lal, H., **543**

Lal, H., & Shearman, G.T. Interceptive discriminative stimuli in the development of CNS drugs and a case of an animal model of anxiety. *Annual Reports in Medicinal Chemistry*, 1980, *15*, 51-58. **36**

Lalouel, J.M., **325**

Lamarck, **599**

Lamb, M.E., **389**

Lamb, T.A., **74**

Lambert, C., **426**

Lambo, T.A., **305, 307**

Lambo, T.A. Malignant anxiety: A syndrome associated with criminal conduct in Africans. *Journal of Mental Science*, 1962, *108*, 256-264. **307**

Lamborn, K.R., **543, 555**

Lammintaustra, R., **67, 341**

Lampert, R.P., **555**

Lancashire, M., **428**

Lancaster, D., **213, 442**

Landis, C., & Hunt, W.A. Adrenalin and emotion. *Psychological Reviews*, 1932, *39*, 467-485. **534, 550**

Landis, D.H., **563**

Lane, J., **63, 358**

Lane, T.W., **472**

Lang, P.J., xxiv, xxxv, **109, 136, 153, 154, 155, 159, 162, 163, 164, 165, 166, 171-72, 178, 181-82, 208, 264, 364, 385, 437, 453, 454, 457, 461, 466, 485, 494, 496, 498, 679, 683, 691, 708**

Lang, P.J. Experimental studies of desensitization psychotherapy. In J. Wolpe

(Ed.), *The conditioning therapies*. New York: Holt, Rhinehart, & Winston, 1964. **xxiv, 132, 133, 363**

Lang, P.J. Fear reduction and fear behavior: Problems in treating a construct. In J.M. Shlien (Ed.), *Research in psychotherapy* (Vol. III). Washington, D.C.: American Psychological Association, 1968. pp. 90-103. **xxiv, 133, 201, 205, 221, 493**

Lang, P.J. The mechanics of desensitization and the laboratory study of human fear. In C.M. Franks (Ed.), *Behavior therapy: Appraisal and status*. New York: McGraw-Hill, 1969. **91, 252**

Lang, P.J. Autonomic control or learning to play the internal organs. *Psychology Today*, October 1970, 37-41. **156, 157**

Lang, P.J. The application of psychophysiological methods to the study of psychotherapy and behavior modification. In A.E. Bergin & S.L. Garfield (Eds.), *Handbook of psychotherapy and behavior change*. New York: Wiley, 1971. **201, 205, 221, 334, 743, 751**

Lang, P.J. Psychophysiological assessment of anxiety and fear. In J.D. Cone & R.P. Hawkins (Eds.), *Behavioral assessment: New directions in clinical psychology*. New York: Bruner/Mazel, 1977. **133, 144, 151, 152, 158, 435, 463**

Lang, P.J. Anxiety: Toward a psychophysiological definition. In H.S. Akiskal & W.L. Webb (Eds.), *Psychiatric diagnosis: Exploration of biological predictors*. New York: Spectrum Publications, 1978. pp. 365-389. **xxiv, 152, 789**

Lang, P.J. A bio-informational theory of emotional imagery. *Psychophysiology*, 1979, *16*, 495-512. **91, 114, 144, 151, 157, 158, 164, 187, 435**

Lang, P.J. Behavioral treatment and bio-behavioral assessment: Computer applications. In J.P. Sidowski, J.H. Johnson & T.A. Williams, *Technology in mental health care delivery systems*. Norwood, NJ: Ablex, 1980. **155**

Lang, P.J. Cognition in emotion: Concept and action. In C. Izard, J. Kagan & Zajonc (Eds.), *Emotion, cognition and behavior*. New York: Cambridge University Press, 1984, pp. 192-225. **146**

Lang, P.J., Kozak, M.J., Miller, G.A., Levin, D.N., & McLean, A., Jr. Emotional imagery: Conceptual structure and pattern of somato-visceral response. *Psychophysiology*, 1980, *17*, 179-192. **161, 437**

Lang, P.J., & Lazovik, A.D. Experimental desensitization of a phobia. *Journal of Abnormal and Social Psychology*, 1963, *66*, 519-525. **252**

Lang, P.J., Lazovik, A.D., & Reynolds, D.J. Desensitization, suggestibility and pseudotherapy. *Journal of Abnormal Psychology*, 70, 1965, 395-402. **252**

Lang, P.J., Levin, D.N., Miller, G.A., & Kozak, M.H. Fear behavior, fear imagery, and the psychophysiology of emotion: The problem of affective response integration. *Journal of Abnormal Psychology*, 1983, *92*, 276-306. **161, 164, 437, 444**

Lang, P.J., Melamed, B.G., & Hart, J.D. A psychophysiological analysis of fear modification using an automated desensitization procedure. *Journal of Abnormal Psychology*, 1970, *76*, 220-234. **162, 164, 219, 439**

Lang, P.J., Öhman, A., & Simons, R.F. The psychophysiology of anticipation.

In J. Requin (Ed.), *Attention and performance* (Vol. 7). New York: Academic Press, 1978. **153**

Lange, K. *The emotions.* Denmark, 1885. Trans. by Istar A. Haupt for K. Dunlap (Ed.), *The emotions.* Baltimore: Williams & Wilkins, 1922. **111, 115**

Langer, S.Z., **563**

Langner, T.S., **306**

Lanyon, R.I., **614**

Lapierre, Y.D., Knott, V.J., & Gray, R. Psychophysiological correlates of sodium lactate. *Psychopharmacology Bulletin,* 1984, *20,* 50-57. **780**

Lapin, I.P. Non-specific, non-selective and mild increase in the latency of pentylenetetrazol seizures produced by large doses of the putative endogenous ligands of the benzodiazepine receptor. *Neuropharmacology,* 1981, *20,* 781-786. **48**

Lapouse, R., & Monk, M.A. An epidemiologic study of behavior characteristics in children. *American Journal of Public Health,* 1958, *48,* 1134-1144. **284**

Lapouse, R., & Monk, M.A. Fears and worries in a representative sample of children. *American Journal of Orthopsychiatry,* 1959, *29,* 803-818. **374**

La Rocco, J.M., **135**

Larousse, C., **31**

Larsson, H., **702**

Latimer, P.R., **106, 692**

Laude, R., **194, 494, 625**

Laughlin, J.E., **654**

Laurent, J.-P., **13, 28, 29, 32, 33, 34, 35, 38**

Laverty, R., **539**

Laverty, S.G., **206**

Lawson, D.M., **434**

Lazare, A., Klerman, G.L., & Armor, D.J. Oral, obsessive, and hysterical personality patterns. *Archives of General Psychiatry,* 1966, *14,* 624-630. **613**

Lazarus, A.A., **246**

Lazarus, A.A. *Multimodal therapy.* New York: Springer, 1976. **430**

Lazarus, R.S. *Psychological stress and the coping process.* New York: McGraw-Hill, 1966. **177, 238, 622**

Lazarus, R.S. Emotions and adaptation: Conceptual & empirical relations. In W.J. Arnold (Ed.), *Nebraska symposium on motivation: 1968.* Lincoln, NE: University of Nebraska Press, 1968. **118, 119, 139**

Lazarus, R.S. Cognitive and coping processes in emotion. In B. Weiner (Ed.), *Cognitive views of human motivation.* New York: Academic Press, 1974. **114**

Lazarus, R.S., & Averill, J.R. Emotion and Cognition: With special reference to anxiety. In C.D. Spielberger (Ed.), *Anxiety: Current trends in theory and research* (Vol. 2). New York: Academic Press, 1972. pp. 241-283. **112, 119-20, 238**

Lazarus, R.S., & DeLongis, A. Psychological stress and coping in aging. *American Psychologist,* 1983, *38,* 245-254. **110, 119**

Lazarus, R.S., Kanner, A.D., & Folkman, S. Emotions: A cognitive-phenomenological analysis. In R. Plutchik & H. Kellerman (Eds.), *Emotion: Theory, research, and experience* (Vol. 1). New York: Academic Press, 1980. **112, 114, 119**

Lazovik, A.D., **252**

Lazowick, L.M. On the nature of identification. *Journal of Abnormal Psychology*, 1955, *51*, 175-183. **647**

Leaf, P.J., **282, 283**

Leak, D.A., **61**

Leake, C.D. Prologue and epilogue of carbon dioxide therapy: Carbon dioxide as a physiological agent. *Behavioral Neuropsychiatry*, 1973, *4*, 10-12. **551**

Leary, M.R. Social anxiety. In L. Wheeler (Ed.) *Review of personality and social psychology* (Vol. 3), Beverly Hills, CA: Sage Publications, 1982. **90, 95**

Leblanc, J., Cote, J., Jobin, M., & Labrie, A. Plasma catecholamines and cardiovascular response to cold and mental activity. *Journal of Applied Physiology*, 1979, *47*, 1207-1211. **359**

Leckman, J.F., **40, 286, 288, 290, 292, 293, 294, 394, 396**

Leckman, J.F., Maas, J.W., Redmond, D.E., Jr., & Heninger, G.R. Effects of oral clonidine on plasma 3-methoxy-4-hydroxy phenylethylene glycol (MHPG) in man: Preliminary report. *Life Sciences*, 1980, *26*, 2179-2185. **547, 571**

Leckman, J.F., Merikangas, K.R., Pauls, D.L., Prusoff, B.A., & Weissman, M.M. Anxiety disorders and depression: Contradictions between family study data and DSM-III conventions. *American Journal of Psychiatry*, 1983, *140*, 880-882. **286, 289, 290, 294, 483, 569**

Leckman, J.F., Weissman, M.M., Merikangas, K.R., Pauls, D.L., & Prusoff, B.A. Panic disorder and major depression: Increased risk of depression, alcoholism, panic, and phobic disorders in families of depressed probands with panic disorder. *Archives of Psychiatry*, 1983, *40*, 1055-1060. **286, 287, 288, 764, 780, 793**

Lecrubier, Y., **791**

Ledwidge, B. Cognitive behavior modification: A step in the wrong direction? *Psychological Bulletin*, 1978, *85*, 353-375. **432**

Lee, R.L.M. Structure and anti-structure in the culture-bound syndromes: The Malay Case. *Culture, Medicine and Psychiatry*, 1981, *5*, 233-248. **313**

Leeb-Lundberg, F., **540**

Lefkowitz, R.J., **346**

Le Goc, Y., **791**

Lehmann, H.E., **746**

Leibovici, H., **350**

Leigh, H., **548, 570**

Leighton, A.H., **309**

Leighton, A.H., Lambo, T.A., Hughes, C.A., Leighton, D.C., Murphy, J.M., & Macklin, D.B. *Psychiatric disorder among the Yoruba*. Ithaca, NY: Cornell University Press, 1966. **305, 307**

Levine, S., Haltmeyer, G.C., Karas, G.G., & Dennenberg, V.H. Physiological and behavioral effects of infantile stimulation. *Physiology and Behavior*, 1967, *2*, 55-59. **62**

Levis, D.J., **220, 226, 456, 469**

Levis, D.J., & Boyd, T.L. Symptom maintenance: An infrahuman analysis and extension of the conservation of anxiety principle. *Journal of Abnormal Psychology*, 1979, *88*, 107-120. **211, 218, 226**

Levitt, E.E., **159**

Levitt, E.E. *The psychology of anxiety*. Indianapolis: Bobbs-Merrill, 1967. **109**

Levitt, M., **83, 359**

Levy, D.M. *Maternal overprotection*. New York: Columbia University Press, 1943. **378**

Levy, G.F., **65, 551**

Levy, R., **429**

Lewin, B.D. Reflections on affect. In M. Schur (Ed.), *Drives, affects, behavior* (Vol. 2). New York: International Universities Press, 1965. **598**

✳ Lewis, A. States of depression: Clinical and aetiological differentiation. *British Medical Journal*, 1938, *2*, 875-878. **xviii, 790, 791**

✳ Lewis, A. A note on classifying phobia. *Psychological Medicine*, 1976, *6*, 21-22. **735, 743**

Lewis, B.I. Chronic hyperventilation syndrome. *Journal of the American Medical Association*, 1954, *155*, 1204-1207. **350**

Lewis, J.K., **527**

Lewis, M., **417**

Lewis, M., & Brooks, J. Self, other and fear: Infants' reactions to people. In M. Lewis & L.A. Rosenblum (Eds.), *The origins of fear*. New York: John Wiley, 1974. **605**

Lewis, M., & Brooks-Gunn, J. *Social cognition and the acquisition of self*. New York: Plenum Publishing Corp., 1979. **418**

Lewis, M., Feiring, C., McGuffey, C., & Jaskir, J. Predicting psychopathology in six-year-olds from early social relations. *Child Development*, 1984, *55*, 123-136. **377**

Lewis, M., & Michalson, L. The measurement of emotional state. In C. Izard (Ed.), *Measurement of emotion in infants and children*. New York: Cambridge University Press, 1981. **378**

Lewis, M., & Michalson, L. *Children's emotions and moods*. New York: Plenum Press, 1983. **109**

Lewis, Sir A.J. *Price's textbook of the practice of medicine*. London: Oxford University Press, 1966. **562, 747**

Lewis, Sir A.J. The ambiguous word "anxiety". *International Journal of Psychiatry*, 1970, *9*, 62-79. **740**

Lewis, T. *Report upon soldiers returned as cases of 'disordered action of the heart' (DAH) or 'valvular disease of the heart' (VDH)*. Medical Research Committee, Special Report Series No. 8, London, 1917. **737**

Libretti, A., **349**

Lidbrink, P., **539, 540**

Lidbrink, P., Corrodi, H., Fuxe, K., & Olson, L. The effects of benzo-
diazepines, meprobamate, and barbiturates on central monoamine neurons. In
S. Garattini, E. Mussini & L.O. Randall, (Eds.), *The benzodiazepines*. New
York: Raven Press, 1973. **7, 15**

Lieberman, A.F. Preschoolers' competence with a peer: Relations with attachment and peer experience. *Child Development*, 1977, *48*, 1277-1287. **713-14**

Lieberman, J.A., Brenner, R., Lesser, M., Coccaro, E., Borenstern, M., &
Kane, J.M. Dexamethasone suppression tests in patients with panic disorder.
American Journals of Psychiatry, 1983, *140*, 917-919. **66**

Lieberman, K.W., Stokes, P.E., Fanelli, C., & Klevan, T. Reuptake of biogenic
amines by brain slices: Effects of hydrocortisone. *Psychopharmacology*, 59-
61, *70*, 1980. **68**

Liebowitz, M.R., **551**

Liebowitz, M.R., Fyer, A.J., McGrath, P., & Klein, D.F. Clonidine treatment
of panic disorder. *Psychopharmacology Bulletin*, 1981, *17*, 122-123. **527,
547**

Liebowitz, M.R., Quitkin, F.M., & Stewart, J. *Atypical depression: Description
and treatment*. Paper presented at 136th annual meeting of the American
Psychiatric Association, NYC, May 6, 1983. **508**

Liebowitz, M.R., Quitkin, F.M., Stewart, J., McGrath, P., Harrison, W., Rabkin, J., Tricamo, E., Markowitz, J., & Klein, D.F. Phenelzine versus imipramine in atypical depression. *Archives of General Psychiatry*, 1984, *41*,
669-677. **670**

Light, K.C., **116**

Lighthall, F.F., **708**

Lindemann, E., & Finesinger, J.E. The effect of adrenaline and mecholyl in
states of anxiety in psychoneurotic patients. *American Journal of Psychiatry*,
1938, *95*, 353-370. **82**

Lindemann, E., & Finesinger, J.E. Subjective responses of psychoneurotic
patients to adrenaline and mecholyl. *Psychosomatic Medicine*, 1940, *2*, 231-
248. **82**

Linden, D.R. Attenuation and reestablishment of the CER by discriminated
avoidance conditioning in rats. *Journal of Comparative and Physiological
Psychology*, 1969, *69*, 573-578. **205**

Lindsley, D.B. Emotion. In S.S. Stevens (Ed.), *Handbook of experimental
psychology*. New York: John Wiley, 1951. **115, 138, 139**

Lindsley, D.B. Psychological phenomena & the electroencephalogram.
Electroencephalography & Clinical Neurophysiology, 1952, *4*, 443-456. **138**

Lindsley, D.B. The role of nonspecific reticulo-thalamo-cortical systems in emotion. In P. Black (Ed.), *Physiological correlates of emotion*. New York:
Academic Press, 1970. **115**

Lindstedt, S., **71**

Ling, N., **68**

Linnolla, M., **552, 558**

Lipman, R.S., **240**

✻ Lipman, R.S. Differentiating anxiety and depression in anxiety disorders: Use of rating scales. *Psychopharmacology Bulletin*, 1982, *18* (4), 69-77. **677, 749**

Lipman, R.S., Cole, J.O., Park, L.C., & Rickels, K. Sensitivity of symptom and non-symptom focused criteria of outpatient drug efficacy. *American Journal of Psychiatry*, 1965, *122*, 24-27. **677**

Lipman, R.S., Covi, L., & Shapiro, A.K. The Hopkins symptom checklist (HSCL): Factors derived from the HSCL-90. *Journal of Affective Disorders*, 1979, *1*, 9-24. **677**

Lippa, S.A., **12**

Lippman, D., **63-64, 64, 65, 66, 67, 72, 339, 340, 357, 359**

Lipsedge, M., **293, 397, 746**

Lira, T., White, M.J., & Finch, A.J., Jr. Anxiety and mood states in delinquent adolescents. *Journal of Personality Assessment*, 1977, *41* (5), 532-536. **661**

Litchfield, N.B. Intravenous sedation in oral surgery. A report on 1,142 cases using diazepam. *Australian Dental Journal*, 1972, *17*, 429-433. **538**

Litner, J.S., **227**

Little, K.B., **649**

Livingston, L., **74**

Ljungdahl, A., **539, 540**

Lo, L.U.M. A followup study of obsessional neurotics in Hong Kong Chinese. *British Journal of Psychiatry*, *113*, 823-832, 1967. **579**

Locke, B.Z., **281, 282**

Locke, E. Behavior modification is not cognitive—and other myths. A reply to Ledwidge. *Cognitive Therapy and Research*, 1979, *3*, 119-125. **432**

Loevinger, J. Objective tests as instruments of psychological theory. *Psychological Reports*, 1957, *3*, 635-694. **686**

Loewenstein, R.J., **588**

Lofft, J.G., & Demars, J.P. A chemotherapeutic alternative to the extended treatment of psychoneurosis. *Diseases of the Nervous System*, 1974, *35*, 409-415. **520, 523, 540**

Lohr, N., **66, 67**

Lojtha, A., **49**

LoLordo, V.M., **227, 228-29**

LoLordo, V.M. Similarity of conditioned fear responses based upon different aversive events. *Journal of Comparative and Physiological Psychology*, 1967, *64*, 154-158. **228**

LoLordo, V.M. Selective associations. In A. Dickinson & R. Boakes (Eds.), *Mechanisms of learning and motivation: A memorial to Jerzy Konorski*. Hillsdale, NJ: Lawrence Erlbaum Associates, 1978, pp. 367-398. **208**

LoLordo, V.M. Constraints on learning. In M. Bitterman, V. LoLordo, J.B. Overmier, & M. Rashotte (Eds.), *Animal learning: Survey and analysis*. New York: Plenum, 1979, pp. 473-504. **208**

Lomborn, K.R., **543**

Long, C.N. The relation of cholesterol and ascorbic acid to the secretion of the adrenal cortex. *Recent Progress in Hormone Research*, 1947, *1*, 99-122. **55**

Lord, D.J., & Kidd, C.B. Haloperidol versus diazepam: A double-blind crossover clinical trial. *Medical Journal of Australia*, 1973, *1*, 586-568. **519, 523, 540**

Lorr, M., **135, 677, 689**

Lorr, M., & McNair, D. *Profile of mood states: Bi-polar form (POMS-BI)*. San Diego: Educational and Industrial Testing Service, 1982. **689**

Lossen, P.T., Kistler, K., & Prange, A.J. Use of TSH response to TRH as an independent variable. *American Journal of Psychiatry*, 1983, *140*, 700-703. **59, 71**

Low, S. The meaning of *Nervios*: A sociocultural analysis of symptom presentation in San Jose, Costa Rica. *Culture, Medicine and Psychiatry*, 1981, *5*, 25-48. **319**

Lowenstein, E., **243**

Lubetsky, M., **551, 573**

Lubin, B., **176, 658, 689**

Luborsky, L. Momentary forgetting during psychotherapy and psychoanalysis. In R. Holt (Ed.), *Motives and thought*. Psychological issues (Monograph 18/19). New York: International Universities Press, 1967. **643**

Luborsky, L. Forgetting and remembering (momentary forgetting) during psychotherapy. In M. Mayman (Ed.), *Psychoanalytic research. Psychological issues* (Monograph 30). New York: International Universities Press, 1973. **643**

Luborsky, L. Measuring a pervasive psychic structure in psychotherapy: The core conflictual relationship theme. In N. Freedman & S. Grand (Eds.), *Communicative structures and psychic structures*. New York: Plenum, 1977. **614**

Luborsky, L., Bachrach, H., Graff, H., Pulver, S., & Christoph, P. Preconditions and consequences of transference interpretations: A clinical-quantitative investigation. *Journal of Nervous and Mental Disease*, 1979, *167*, 391-401. **643**

Luborsky, L., & Mintz, J. What sets off momentary forgetting during a psychoanalysis? *Psychoanalysis and Contemporary Science*, 1974, *3*, 233-268. **643**

Ludwig, A. A sociomedical diagnosis . . . of sorts. *American Journal of Psychotherapy*, 1982, *3*, 350-356. **319**

Lum, L.C. The syndrome of chronic habitual hyperventilation. In O.W. Hill (Ed.), *Modern trends in psychosomatic medicine-3*. London: Butterworth, 1976. **349, 350**

Lum, L.C. Hyperventilation and anxiety state. *Journal of the Royal Society of Medicine*, 1981, *74*, 1-4. **551**

Lumia, A.R., **203**

Lummis, S.C., **40**

Lundberg, U., **57**

Lunmus, W.F., **569**

Luria, A.R. The role of language in the formulation of temporary connections. In E. Simon, (Ed.), *Psychology in the Soviet Union*. Stanford, CA: Stanford University Press, 1957. **152**

Lushene, R.E., **126, 300, 565, 571, 657, 684, 689**

Luthe, W. *Autogenic therapy*. New York: Grune & Stratton, 1970. **475**

Lykken, D.T. Research with twins: The concept of emergenesis. *Psychophysiology*, 1982, *19*, 361-373. **685**

Lynn, R. National differences in anxiety and extroversion. *Progress in Experimental Personality Research*, 1982, *11*, 213-258. **301**

Maas, J.W., **58, 60, 66, 67, 542, 544, 545, 547, 553, 570, 571**

Maas, J.W., & Mednieks, M. Hydrocortisone mediated increase of norepinephrine uptake by brain slices. *Science* 1971, *171*, 178-179. **57, 68**

McCall, R.B., **545**

McCall, R.B. The development of intellectual functioning in infancy and the prediction of later I.Q. In J. Osofsky (Ed.), *Handbook of infant development*. New York: John Wiley, 1979. **414**

McCandless, B.R., **708**

McLean, A., Jr., **136, 437**

McClure, J.M., **82, 534, 551, 586, 749**

Maccoby, E., & Masters, J.C. Attachment and dependency. In P.H. Mussen (Ed.), *Charmichael's manual of child psychology* (Vol. 2). New York: Wiley, 1970. **378**

McCrae, R.R. Consensual validation of personality traits: Evidence from self-reports and ratings. *Journal of Personality and Social Psychology*, 1982, *43*, 293-303. **681**

McCrae, R.R., & Costa, P.T. Updating Norman's "Adequate Taxonomy": Intelligence and personality dimensions in natural language and in questionnaires. *Journal of Personality and Social Psychology*, in press. **696**

McCutcheon, B.A., & Adams, H.E. The physiological basis of implosive therapy. *Behaviour Research and Therapy*, 1975, *13*, 93-100. **438**

McDermott, J., **299**

McDonald, R., **506, 507, 586**

MacDonald, R.L., & Barker, J.L. Enhancement of GABA-mediated postsynaptic inhibition in cultured mammalian spinal cord neurons: A common mode of anticonvulsant action. *Brain Research* 1979, *167*, 323-336. **540**

MacDougall, J.M., **365**

McDougall, W. *An introduction to social psychology*. London: Methuen, 1923. **114**

McEvoy, L., **xxx**

McFadden, E.R., Jr., **351**

McFall, R.M., & Twentyman, C.T. Four experiments on the relative contributions of rehearsal, modeling, and coaching to assertion training. *Journal of Abnormal Psychology*, 1973, *81*, 199-218. **169**

MacFarlane, J.W., Allen, L., & Honzik, M.P. *A developmental study of the behavior problems of normal children between 21 months and 14 years.* Berkeley: University of California Press, 1954. **373, 408, 411, 712**

McGinnis, G., **417**

McGlynn, F.D., **227, 242**

McGrath, P.J., **527, 547, 551, 670**

McGuffey, C., **377**

McGuire, R., **293, 397, 746**

McKillen, B.A., **545, 592**

McKinley, J.C., **645, 666**

McKinley, J.C., Hathaway, S.R., & Meehl, P.E. The MMPI VI, the K-scale. *Journal of Consulting Psychology,* 1948, *12,* 20-31. **650**

McKinney, W.T., Jr., **xxi, 200, 527, 793**

McKinney, W.T., Jr. Animal models in psychiatry. *Perspectives in Biology and Medicine,* 1974, *17,* 529-541. **xxi, 79, 199, 242**

Mackintosh, N.J. Stimulus selection: Learning to ignore stimuli that predict no change in reinforcement. In R.A. Hinde & J. Stevenson-Hinde (Eds.), *Constraints on learning.* New York: Academic Press, 1973. pp. 75-100. **239**

Mackintosh, N.J. *The psychology of animal learning.* London: Academic Press, 1974. **208, 242, 244**

Macklin, D.B., **305, 307**

McKoon, G., **169**

McLaren, S., **428**

McLean, A., Jr., **161, 437**

McLean, A., Jr. *Emotional imagery: Stimulus information, imagery ability, and patterns of physiological response.* Unpublished doctoral dissertation, University of Wisconsin, Madison, 1981. **162, 436**

MacLean, P.D. Implications of microelectrode findings on exteroceptive inputs to the limbic cortex. In C.H. Hockman (Ed.), *Limbic system mechanisms and autonomic function.* Springfield, IL: Charles C. Thomas, 1972. **115**

McClean, V., **278**

McLendon, D.M., **538**

McLennan & Miller, J.J. Gamma-aminobutyric acid and the inhibition of the septal nuclei of the rat. *Journal of Physiology (London),* 1974, *237,* 625-633. **14**

McMillen, B.A., Warnack, W., German, D.C., & Shore, P.A. Effects of chronic desipramine treatment on rat brain noradrenergic responses to alpha-adrenergic drugs. *European Journal of Pharmacology,* 1980, *61,* 239-246. **544**

McMurtry, M., **58**

McNair, D., **689**

McNair, D.M., & Kahn, R.J. Imipramine with a benzodiazepine for agoraphobia. In D.F. Klein & J.G. Rabkin (Eds.), Anxiety: *New research and changing concepts.* New York: Raven Press, 1981. pp. 69-79. **510, 511, 538**

McNair, D.M., **549**

McNair, D.M., & Lorr, M. An analysis of mood in neurotics. *Journal of Abnormal and Social Psychology*, 1964, *69*, 620-627. **135**

McNair, D.M., Lorr, M., & Droppleman, L.F. *Manual: Profile of mood states.* San Diego, CA: Educational and Industrial Testing Services, 1971. **135, 677, 689**

McNally, R.J., & Reiss, S. The preparedness theory of phobias and human safety-signal conditioning. *Behaviour Research and Therapy*, 1983, *20*, 153-159. **376**

McNamee, B., **15, 541**

McNaughton, N., **12, 14, 20, 21**

McNeil, D.W., Melamed, B.G., Cuthbert, B.N., & Lang, P.J. Emotional imagery and psychophysiological responsivity in simple phobia and agoraphobia. *Psychophysiology*, 1983, *20*, 459. (Abstract). **165, 166**

McPherson, F.M., Brougham, L., & McLaren, S. Maintenance of improvement in agoraphobic patients treated by behavioural methods—a four-year follow-up. *Behaviour Research and Therapy*, 1980, *18*, 150-152. **428**

McPherson, K., **521, 544**

Mafucci, R.J., **529**

Magarey, C.J., Todd, P.B., & Blizard, P.J. Psycho-social factors influencing delay and breast self-examination in women with symptoms of breast cancer. *Social Science and Medicine*, 1977, *11* (4), 229-232. **661**

Magarian, G.J. Hyperventilation syndromes: infrequently recognized common expressions of anxiety and stress. *Medicine*, 1982, *61*, 219-236. **348**

Magnus, R., & Schiff, A. Once daily treatment for mixed anxiety/depressive states: A comparison of slow release amitriptyline and fluphenazine with nortriptyline. *Journal of International Medical Research*, 1977, *5*, 109-113. **521**

Magnusson, D., **122, 659**

Magnusson, D., & Stattin, H. Stability of cross-sectional patterns of behavior. *Journal of Research in Personality*, 1981, *15*, 488-496. **122**

Mahal, A., Malik, S., & Srinivasamurthy, U. Evaluation of loxapine succinate as an anxiolytic in comparison with chlordiazepoxide. *Current Therapeutic Research*, 1976, *20*, 84-93. **519**

Mahler, M. *On human symbiosis and the vicissitudes of individuation.* New York: International Universities Press, 1968. **603**

Mahler, M., Pine, F., & Bergman, A. *The psychological birth of the human infant.* New York: Basic Books, 1975. **417, 418**

Mahoney, M. A critical analysis of rational-emotive theory and practice. In A. Ellis & J.M. Whiteley (Eds.), *Theoretical and empirical foundations of rational-emotive therapy.* Monterey, CA: Brooks/Cole, 1979. **430, 431**

Mahoney, M.J., & Kazdin, A.E. Misconceptions and premature evacuations. *Psychological Bulletin*, 1979, *86*, 1044-1049. **432**

Maier, N.R.F. *Frustration: The study of behavior without a goal.* New York: McGraw-Hill, 1949. **223, 224**

Maier, S.F., **xxi, 17**

Maier, S.F., & Jackson, R.L. Learned helplessness: All of us were right (and wrong): Inescapable shock has multiple effects. In G. Bower (Ed.), *Advances in learning and motivation* (Vol. 13). New York: Academic Press, 1979, pp. 155-218. **239**

Maier, S.F., & Seligman, M.E.P. Learned helplessness: Theory and evidence. *Journal of Experimental Psychology: General*, 1976, *105*, 3-45. **16, 17, 239**

Maier, S.F., Seligman, M.E.P., & Solomon, R.L. Pavlovian fear conditioning and learned helplessness. In B. Campbell & R. Church (Eds.), *Punishment and aversive behavior*. New York: Appleton-Century, 1969, pp. 299-342. **242**

Majewska, M.D., Chuang, D.M., & Costa, E. Stimulation by benzodiazepines of the prostaglandin D_2 release in C^6 glioma cells. *Society for Neuroscience Abstracts*, 1983, *9*, 1042. **40**

Malamed, **xxviii**

Malan, D.H. *A study of brief psychotherapy*. Springfield, IL: Charles C. Thomas, 1963. **614, 615**

Malan, D.H. *Toward the validation of dynamic psychotherapy*. New York: Plenum, 1976. **614, 615**

Malatesta, C.Z., **109, 122, 123**

Maletzky, B.M. Anxiolytic efficacy of alprazolam compared to diazepam and placebo. *Journal of International Medical Research*, 1980, *8*, 139-143. **518, 522, 538**

Malik, S., **519**

Mallorga, P., **40**

Mandel, M.R., **114, 116**

Mandler, G. Helplessness: Theory and research in anxiety. In C.D. Spielberger (Ed.), *Anxiety: Current trends in theory and research* (Vol. 2). New York: Academic Press, 1972, pp. 359-374. **119, 238**

Mandler, G. *Mind and emotion*. New York: John Wiley & Sons, 1975. **109, 110, 111, 112, 114, 115, 116, 119, 139, 140**

Mandler, G. The generation of emotion: A psychological theory. In R. Plutchik & H. Kellerman (Eds.), *Emotion: Theory, research, and experience*. New York: Academic Press, 1980. **119, 120**

Mandler, G., Mandler, J.M., Kremen, I., & Sholiton, R. The response to threat: Relations among verbal and physiological indices. *Psychological Monographs*, 1961, *75*, Whole No. 513. **132**

Mandler, G., Mandler, J.M., & Uviller, E.T. Autonomic feedback: The perceptions of autonomic activity. *Journal of Abnormal and Social Psychology*, 1958, *56*, 367-373. **132, 468**

Mandler, G., & Sarason, S.B. A study of anxiety and learning. *Journal of Abnormal and Social Psychology*, 1952, *47*, 166-173. **120, 660**

Mandler, G., & Watson, D.L. Anxiety and the interruption of behavior. In C.D. Spielberger (Ed.), *Anxiety and behavior*. New York: Academic Press, 1966, pp. 263-288. **113, 225, 238**

Mandler, J.M., **132, 468**

Manian, A.A., **541**

Manicas, P.T., & Secord, P.F. Implications for psychology of the new philosophy of science. *American Psychologist*, 1983, *38*, 399-413. **247**

Manosevitz, M., & Lanyon, R.I. Fear survey schedule: A normative study. *Psychological Reports*, 1965, *17*, 699-703. **614**

Manson, S., Shore, J., & Bloom, J. The depressive experience in American Indian communities: A challenge for psychiatric theory and diagnosis. In B.J. Good & A.M. Kleinman (Eds.), *Culture and depression: Toward an anthropology of dysphoric affect and affective disorders*. Berkeley: University of California Press, in press. **310**

Manyam, N.V.B., More, T.A., & Katz, L. Effect of isoniazid on cerebrospinal fluid and plasma GABA levels in Huntington's Disease. *Life Sciences*, 1980, *26*, 1303-1308. **530**

Mao, C.C., **28, 33, 35, 538**

Marangos, P.J., **31, 48, 575**

Marangos, P.J., Matino, A.M., Paul, S.M., & Skolnick, P. The benzodiazepines and inosine antagonize caffeine-induced seizures. *Psychopharmacology*, 1981, *72*, 269-273. **49**

Marangos, P.J., Patel, J., Hirata, F., Sondhein, D., Paul, S.M., Skolnick, P., & Godwin, F.K. Inhibition of diazepam binding by tryptophan derivatives including melatonin and its brain metabolite N-acetyl-5-methoxy kynurenamine. *Life Sciences*, 1981, *29*, 259-276. **49**

Marangos, P.J., Paul, S.M., Parma, A.M., Goodwin, F.K., Syapin, P., & Skolnick, P. Purinergic inhibition of diazepam binding to rat brain (in vitro). *Life Science*, 1979, *24*, 851-858. **28, 48, 573**

Marañon, G. La reacción emotiva a la adrénalina. *Medicina Ibera*, 1920, *12*, 353-357. **534, 550**

Marañon, G. Contribution à l'étude de l'action émotive de l'adrénaline. *Revue Francaise Endocrinologie*, 1924, *2*, 301-325. **534, 550**

Marcucci, R., **30**

Margalit, D., & Segal, M. A pharmacologic study of analgesia produced by stimulation of the nucleus locus coeruleus. *Psychopharmacology*, 1979, *62*, 169-173. **542**

Margolis, S., **569**

Mariani, F., **346**

Mark, A.L., **349**

Markette, J., **521, 544**

Markiewicz, W., Hunt, S., Harrison, D.C., & Alderman, E.L. Circulatory effects of diazepam in heart disease. *Journal of Clinical Pharmacology*, 1976, *16*, 637-644. **538**

Markowitz, J., **670**

Marks, I.M., **64, 233, 236, 241, 293, 397, 425, 426, 427, 428, 429, 434, 436, 438, 439, 440, 456, 485, 746, 789**

Marks, I.M. *Fears and phobias.* New York: Academic Press, 1969. **186, 195, 214, 376, 460, 600**

Marks, I.M. The classification of phobic disorders. *British Journal of Psychiatry,* 1970, *116,* 377-386. **745, 749, 761**

Marks, I.M. Phobic disorders four years after treatment: a prospective followup. *British Journal of Psychiatry,* 1971, *118,* 682-688. **749**

Marks, I.M. Perspective on flooding. *Seminars in Psychiatry,* 1972, *4,* 129-138. **64, 220, 221**

Marks, I.M. Phobias and obsessions: Clinical phenomena in search of a laboratory model. In J. Maser & M. Seligman (Eds.), *Psychopathology: Experimental models.* San Francisco: Freeman, 1977. pp. 174-213. **200, 213, 217**

Marks, I.M. Behavioral psychotherapy of adult neurosis. In S.L. Garfield & A.E. Bergin (Eds.), *Handbook of psychotherapy and behavior change.* New York: Wiley, 1978. **421, 422, 432, 438, 440**

Marks, I.M. *Cure and care of neuroses.* New York: Wiley, 1981. **99, 585, 750**

Marks, I.M. Behavioral concepts and treatment of neuroses. In M. Rosenbaum, C.M. Franks & Y. Jaffe (Eds.), *Perspectives on behavior therapy in the eighties.* New York: Springer, 1983. pp. 112-137. **256**

Marks, I.M., Boulougouris, J.C., & Marset, P. Flooding versus desensitization in the treatment of phobic patients: A cross-over study. *British Journal of Psychiatry,* 1971, *119,* 353-375. **220, 425**

Marks, I.M., & Gelder, M.G. A controlled retrospective study of behaviour therapy in phobic patients. *British Journal of Psychiatry,* 1965, *111,* 571-573. **425**

Marks, I.M., Gray, S., Cohen, D., Hill, R., Mawson, D., Ramm, R., & Stern, R.S. Imipramine and brief therapist aided exposure in agoraphobics having self-exposure homework. *Archives of General Psychiatry,* 1983, *40,* 153-162. **368**

Marks, I.M., Hodgson, R.J., & Rachman, S. Treatment of chronic obsessive-compulsive neurosis by *in vivo* exposure. *British Journal of Psychiatry,* 1975, *127,* 349-364. **429**

Marks, I.M., & Lader, M. Anxiety states (anxiety neurosis): a review. *Journal of Nervous and Mental Disease,* 1973, *156,* 3-18. **278, 280, 348, 349, 746**

Marks, I.M., Rachman, S., & Hodgson, R.J. Clomipramine and exposure for obsessive-compulsive rituals I & II. *British Journal of Psychiatry,* 1980, *136,* 1-25. **144, 505, 507**

Marks, I.M., Stern, R.S., Mawson, D., Cobb, J., & McDonald, R. Clomipramine and exposure for obsessive-compulsive rituals: I. *British Journal of Psychiatry,* 1980, *136,* 1-25. **506, 507, 586**

Markus, H., **151**

Marmar, C., **624, 627**

Marmor, J., & Woods, S.M. *The interface between the psychodynamic and behavioral therapies.* New York: Plenum, 1980. **603**

Marsella, A. Depressive experience and disorder across cultures. In H. Triandis & J. Dragus (Eds.), *Handbook of cross-cultural psychology: Psychopathology* (Vol. 6). Boston: Allyn and Bacon, 1980. pp. 237-290. **299**

Marset, P., **220, 425**

Marshall, G.D., & Zimbardo, P.G. Affective consequences of inadequately explained physiological arousal. *Journal of Personality and Social Psychology*, 1979, *37*, 970-988. **113**

Martens, R., & Simon, J.A. Comparison of three predictors of state anxiety competitive situations. *Research Quarterly*, 1976, *47* (3), 381-387. **661**

Martin, B., **120**

Martin, B. Parent-child relations. In F.D. Horwitz (Ed.), *Review of child development research* (Vol. 4). Chicago: University of Chicago Press, 1975. **378**

Martin, I.L., **34**

Martin, R.B., Shaw, M.A., & Taylor, P.P. The influence of prior surgical experience on the child's behavior at the initial dental visit. *Journal of Dentistry for Children*, 1977, *44*, 35-39. **372**

Martin, R.L., **771, 793**

Martin, W.R., **541, 542**

Martuza, V.R., & Kallstrom, D.W. Validity of the state-trait anxiety inventory in an academic setting. *Psychological Reports*, 1974, *35*, 363-366. **659**

Maruyama, G.M., **121**

Marzillier, J.S., Lambert, C., & Kellett, J. A controlled evaluation of systematic desensitization and social skills training for social inadequate psychiatric patients. *Behavior Research and Therapy*, 1976, *14*, 225-228. **426**

Maser, J.D., **489**

Maslach, C. Negative emotional biasing of unexplained arousal. *Journal of Personality and Social Psychology*, 1979, *37*, 953-959. **113**

Mason, J.W., **56, 58, 59, 61, 62, 63, 345**

Mason, J.W. A review of psychoendocrine research on the pituitary-adrenal cortical system. *Psychosomatic Medicine*, 1968, *30*, 576-607. **61, 63, 69**

Mason, J.W. Strategy in psychosomatic research. *Psychosomatic Medicine*, 1970, *32*, 427-439. **56**

Mason, J.W. Emotion as reflected in patterns of endocrine integration. I. some theoretical aspects of psychoendocrine studies of emotions. In L. Levi (Ed.), *Emotions—their parameters and measurement*. New York: Raven Press, 1975. **115, 116, 118, 334, 359**

Mason, J.W., & Brady, J.V. The sensitivity of psychoendocrine systems to social and physical environment. In P.H. Leiderman & D. Shapiro (Eds.), *Psychobiological approaches to social behavior*. Stanford, CA: Stanford University Press, 1964, pp. 4-23. **55**

Mason, J.W., Hartley, L.H., Kotchen, T.A., Wherry, F.E., Pennington, L.L., & Jones, L.G. Plasma thyroid stimulating hormone response in anticipation of muscular exercise in the human. *Journal Clinical Endocrinology Metabolism*, 1972, *37*, 403-406. **71**

Mason, J.W., Harwood, C.T., & Rosenthal, N.R. Influence of some environmental factors on plasma and urinary 17-hydroxycorticosteroid levels in the rhesus monkey. *American Journal Physiology*, 1957, *190*, 429-433. **55, 65**

Mason, J.W., Sachar, E.J., Fishman, J.R., Hamburg, D.A., & Handlon, J.H. Corticosteroid responses to hospital admission. *Archives of General Psychiatry*, 1965, *13*, 1-8. **58, 61**

Mason, S.T., & Iversen, S.D. Theories of the dorsal bundle extinction effect. *Brain Research Reviews*, 1979, *1*, 107-137. **20**

Masserman, **xxi**

Masserman, J.H. *Behavior and neurosis: An experimental psychoanalytic approach to psychobiologic principles.* Chicago: University of Chicago Press, 1943. **202, 220**

Massotti, M., Guidotti, A., & Costa, E. Characterization of benzodiazepines and gamma-aminobutyric recognition sites and their endogenous modulators. *Journal of Neuroscience*, 1981, *1*, 409-418. **49**

Massry, S.G., **350**

Masters, J.C., **378**

Masui, T., **284**

Matas, L., **140**

Mather, M.D., **224, 234**

Mather, M.D. Obsessions and compulsions. In C. Costello (Ed.), *Symptoms of psychopathology.* New York: Wiley, 1970. **226**

Mathew, R.J., Weinman, M.L., & Claghorn, J.L. Anxiety and cerebral blood flow. In R.J. Mathew (Ed.), *The biology of anxiety.* New York: Brunner/Mazel, 1982. **337**

Mathews, A.M., **167, 194, 219, 220, 425, 439**

Mathews, A.M. Psychophysiological approaches to the investigation of desensitization. *Psychological Bulletin*, 1971, *76*, 73-91. **219**

Mathews, A.M. Fear reduction research and clinical phobias. *Psychological Bulletin*, 1978, *85*, 390-404. **10, 20, 427, 439**

Mathews, A.M., Gelder, M.G., & Johnston, D.W. *Agoraphobia: Nature and treatment.* New York: Guilford Press, 1981. **216, 217, 218, 428**

Mathews, A.M., Jannoun, L., & Gelder, M. *Self-help methods in agoraphobia.* Paper presented at the conference of the European Association of Behavior Therapy, Paris, September, 1979. **428**

Mathews, A.M., Johnston, D.W., Lancashire, M., Munby, D., Shaw, P.M., & Gelder, M.G. Imaginal flooding and exposure to real phobic situations: Treatment outcome with agoraphobic patients. *British Journal of Psychiatry*, 1976, *129*, 362-371. **428**

Mathews, A.M., & Shaw, P.M. Emotional arousal and persuasion effects in flooding. *Behaviour Research and Therapy*, 1973, *11*, 587-598. **438**

Mathews, A.M., & Shaw, P.M. Cognitions related to anxiety: A pilot study of treatment. *Behavior Research and Therapy*, 1977, *15*, 503-505. **194**

Matino, A.M., **49**

Matthews, A.M., **428**

Mattingly, B.A., **212**

Matussek, N., Ackenheil, M., Hippius, H., Muller, F., Schroder, H.-Th., Schultes, H., & Wasilewski, B. Effect of clonidine on growth hormone release in psychiatric patients and controls. *Psychiatry Res.*, 1980, *2*, 25-36. **563**

Maudsley, H. *The pathology of the mind.* London: MacMillan, 1895. **577**

Mavissakalian, M.R., **132, 165, 363, 455, 497, 790**

Mavissakalian, M.R., & Barlos, D.H. Assessment of obsessive-compulsive disorders. In D.H. Barlow (Ed.), *Behavioral assessment of adult disorders.* New York: Guilford Press, 1981, pp. 209-239. **493, 494**

Mawson, D., **368, 506, 507, 586**

Maxeiner, M.E., **92**

May, M.A., **682**

May, R. *The meaning of anxiety.* New York: Ronald Press Company, 1950. **533, 737**

May, R. *The meaning of anxiety* (rev. ed.). New York: W.W. Norton, 1977. **172**

✳ Mayr, E. *Evolution and the diversity of life.* Cambridge, MA: Belknap Press, 1976. **323**

Mazur, A., & Lamb, T.A. Testosterone, status and mood in human males. *Hormones and Behavior*, 1980, *14*, 236-246. **74**

Means, B., **143, 144**

Meares, R.A., **583**

Meddis, R. Bipolar factors in mood adjective checklists. *British Journal of Social and Clinical Psychology*, 1972, *11*, 178-184. **135, 689**

Mednieks, M., **57, 68**

Medoff, N.J., **149**

Meehl, P.E., **650, 684**

Meehl, P.E. Hedonic capacity: Some conjectures. *Bulletin of the Menninger Clinic*, 1975, *39*, 295-307. **700**

Meehl, P.E., & Golden, R.R. Taxometric methods. In P.C. Kendall & J.N. Butcher (Eds.), *Handbook of research methods in clinical psychology.* New York: Wiley, 1982. **723**

Meehl, P.H., **667**

Meek, J.L., **41, 43, 44, 45**

Mehrabian, A., **135, 136**

Mehrabian, A., & Russell, J.A. *An approach to environmental psychology.* Cambridge, MA: MIT Press, 1974. **135, 136, 155, 485**

Meichenbaum, D., **106, 384**

Meichenbaum, D. *Cognitive-behavior modification: An integrative approach.* New York: Plenum Press, 1977. **167, 169, 241, 425**

Meichenbaum, D. Cognitive behavior modification: The need for a fairer assessment. *Cognitive Therapy and Research*, 1979, *3*, 127-132. **430, 432**

Meichenbaum, D., & Gilmore, J.B. The nature of unconscious processes: A cognitive-behavioral perspective. In K. Bower & D. Meichenbaum (Eds.), *The unconscious reconsidered.* New York: John Wiley, in press. **106**

Meichenbaum, D., & Turk, D. The cognitive-behavioral management of anxiety, anger, and pain. In P.O. Davidson (Ed.), *The behavioral management of anxiety, depression, and pain*. New York: Brunner/Mazel, 1976. **429**

Mekulka, P.J., **660**

Melamed, B.G., **162, 164, 165, 166, 219, 370, 371, 376, 384, 385, 439, 709, 711, 712**

Melamed, B.G., & Bush, J.P. Family factors in children with acute illness. In S. Auerbach & A. Stoberg (Eds.), *Crises in families*. New York: Hemisphere Publishing Co., in press. **372, 379**

Melamed, B.G., Dearborn, M., & Hermecz, D.A. Necessary considerations for surgery preparation: Age and previous experience. *Psychosomatic Medicine*, 1983, *45*(6), 517-525. **384**

Melamed, B.G., Robbins, S., & Graves, S. Preparation for surgery and medical procedures. In C. Russo & J. Varni (Eds.), *Behavioral pediatrics*. New York: Plenum, 1982. **374**

Melamed, B.G., & Siegel, L.J. Reduction of anxiety in children facing hospitalization and surgery by use of filmed modeling. *Journal of Consulting and Clinical Psychology*, 1975, *43*, 511-521. **708**

Mellanby, J., **7, 8, 11, 12, 13, 15**

Mellanby, J., Gray, J.A., Quintero, S., Holt, L., & McNaughton, N. Septal driving of hippocampal thetal rhythm: a role for gamma-amino-butyrate in the effects of minor tranquilizers. *Neuroscience*, 1981, *6*, 1413-1421. **12**

Mellinger, G.D., **281**

Mellstrom, M., Cicala, G.A., & Zuckerman, M. General versus specific trait anxiety measures in the prediction of fear of snakes, heights, and darkness. *Journal of Consulting and Clinical Psychology*, 1976, *44* (1), 83-91. **657**

Melosh, W., **63, 358**

Mendels, J., **58**

Mendels, J., & Weinstein, N. The relationship between depression and anxiety. *Archives of General Psychiatry*, 1972, *27*, 649-653. **240**

Mendelson, W.B., **32, 34, 568, 569, 588**

Mendlowitz, M., **82, 534, 550**

Menkes, D.B., **528, 544**

Menkes, D.B., Aghajanian, G.K., & McCall, R.B. Chronic antidepressant treatment enhances alpha-adrenergic and serotonergic responses in the facial nucleus. *Life Sciences*, 1980, *27*, 45-55. **545**

Menlove, F.L., **375, 708**

Menninger, S., **455**

Merchant, A.F., **548**

Merideth, C., **516, 517**

Merikangas, K.R., **40, 286, 287, 288, 289, 290, 292, 293, 294, 394, 396, 483, 569, 764, 780, 793**

Mersch, P., **433**

Merteus, C., **309**

Metzger, R.L., Miller, M., Sofka, M., Cohen, M., & Pennock, M. *Information processing and worrying*. Paper presented at the Association for the Advancement of Behavior Therapy, Washington, D.C., December, 1983. **471**

Metzner, R. Some experimental analogues of obsession. *Behaviour Research and Therapy*, 1963, *1*, 231-236. **224**

Meyer, R.E., **15, 541**

Meyer, R.E. Behavioral pharmacology of marihuana. In M.A. Lipton, A. DeMascio & K.F. Killam (Eds.), *Psychopharmacology: A generation of progress*. New York: Raven Press, 1978. **549**

Meyer, R.E., & Mirin, S.M. *The heroin stimulus: Implications for a theory of addiction*. New York: Plenum Press, 1979. **542**

Meyer, V. Modification of expectations in cases with obsessional rituals. *Behaviour Research and Therapy*, 1966, *4*, 273-280. **429**

Meyer, V., Levy, R., & Schnurer, A. The behavioural treatment of obsessive-compulsive disorder. In H.R. Beech (Ed.), *Obsessional states*. London: Methuen, 1974. **429**

Mezzich, J., **235, 243**

Michael, S.T., **306**

Michalson, L., **109, 378**

Michels, R., **370, 377, 619, 624, 641, 642, 700**

Michelson, L., Mavissakalian, M., & Menninger, S. Prognostic utility of locus of control in treatment of agoraphobia. *Behaviour Research and Therapy*, 1983, *21*, 309-314. **455**

Middlemiss, D.N., **13, 15, 40**

Migeon, C.J., **56, 58, 59**

Mikkelsen, E., **504, 506**

Mikulka, P.J., **660**

Milavsky, B., **149**

Milberg, S., **147, 148, 149**

Milby, J.B., **429**

Milcarek, B.I., **80**

Miller, B.V., & Bernstein, D.A. Instructional demand in a behavioral avoidance test for claustrophic fears. *Journal of Abnormal Psychology*, 1972, *80*, 206-210. **258, 336**

Miller, B.V., & Levis, D.J. The effects of varying short visual exposure times to a phobic test stimulus on subsequent avoidance behavior. *Behaviour Research and Therapy*, 1971, *9*, 17-21. **469**

Miller, G.A., **161, 164, 437, 444**

Miller, G.A., Levin, D.N., Kozak, M.J., Cook, E.W., III, McLean, A., Jr., Carroll, J., & Lang, P.J. *Emotional imagery: Individual differences in imagery ability and physiological response. Psychophysiology*, 1981, *18*, 196. (Abstract). **437**

Miller, G.A., Levin, D.N., Kozak, M.J., Cook, E.W., III, McLean, A., Jr., & Lang, P.J. Emotional imagery: Effects of individual differences in perceptual imagery on physiological response. Manuscript in preparation. **136**

Miller, L.C., **713**

Miller, L.C. Louisville Behavior Checklist for males, 6-12 years of age. *Psychological Reports*, 1967, *21*, 885-896. **716, 717**

Miller, L.C. *Louisville Behavior Checklist Manual*. Los Angeles: Western Psychological Services, 1977. **708**

Miller, L.C. Fears and anxiety in children. In C.E. Walder & M.C. Roberts (Eds.), *Handbook of clinical child psychology*. New York: Wiley, 1983. **373, 374, 384**

Miller, L.C., Barrett, C.L., & Hampe, E. Phobias of childhood in a prescientific era. In A. Davids (Ed.), *Child personality and psychopathology: Current topics* (Vol. 1). New York: Wiley, 1974. **373, 712, 714, 715**

Miller, L.C., Barrett, C.L., Hampe, E., & Noble, H. Factor structure of childhood fears. *Journal of Consulting and Clinical Psychology*, 1972, *39*, 264-268. **373, 708, 709**

Miller, M., **75, 471**

Miller, N.E., **100, 203, 214, 224, 225, 237, 263, 267, 603, 707**

Miller, N.E. Learning of visceral and glandular responses. *Science*, 1969, *163*, 434-445. **237**

Miller, N.E. Motivation and psychological stress. In R. Pfaff (Ed.), *The physiological mechanism of motivation*. New York: Springer-Verlag, Inc., 1982, pp. 409-432. **74, 270**

Miller, R.C., **345**

Miller, R.C., & Berman, J.S. The efficacy of cognitive behavior therapies: A quantitative review of the research evidence. *Psychological Bulletin*, 1983, *94*, 39-53. **102**

Miller, R.G., Rubin, R.T., Clark, B.R., Poland, R.E., & Arthur, R.J. The stress of aircraft carrier landings. In: Corticosteroid responses in naval aviators. *Psychosomatic Medicine*, 1970, *32*, 581-588. **344**

Miller, S., **212, 227, 234, 236, 238, 240, 242**

Miller, S., Mineka, S., & Cook, M. Comparison of various flooding procedures in reducing fear and in extinguishing jump-up avoidance responding. *Animal learning and Behavior*, 1982, *10*, 390-400. **234**

Miller, T.I., **612**

Millet, P., **65**

Millon, T. *Million Multiaxial Clinical Inventory Manual*. Minneapolis: National Computer Systems, 1977. **662, 663**

Mills, H., Agras, W.S., Barlow, D.H., & Mills, J. Compulsive rituals treated by response prevention. *Archives of General Psychiatry*, 1973, *28*, 524-529. **233, 234**

Mills, J., **233, 234**

Minard, J., **120**

Mindra, V., **523, 540**

Mineka, S., **xxi, 205, 212, 216, 227, 234, 243, 257, 258, 638**

Mineka, S. New perspectives on conditioning models and incubation theory. A review of H. Eysenck's "The conditioning model of neurosis." *The Behavioral and Brain Sciences*, 1979, *2*, 178. (a). **204, 205, 210, 221, 233, 234**

Mineka, S. The role of fear in theories of avoidance learning, flooding, and extinction. *Psychological Bulletin*, 1979, *86*, 985-1010. (b). **204, 221**

Mineka, S. Depression and helplessness in primates. In H. Fitzgerald, J. Mullins, & P. Gage (Eds.), *Child nurturance series, Vol. 3: Primate behavior and child nurturance* New York: Plenum, 1982. pp. 197-242. **235, 243**

Mineka, S. The frightful complexity of the origins of fears. In J.B. Overmier & F.R. Brush (Eds.), *Affect, conditioning, and cognition: Essays on the determinants of behavior*. Hillsdale, NJ: Lawrence Erlbaum Associates, in press. **148, 242, 251, 252, 253, 268, 383, 454, 455, 458, 459, 465, 466, 476**

Mineka, S., Cook, M., & Miller, S. Fear conditioned with escapable and inescapable shock: The effects of a feedback stimulus. *Journal of Experimental Psychology: Animal Behavior Processes*, accepted pending revision, 1984a. **212, 227, 242**

Mineka, S., Davidson, M., Cook, M., & Keir, R. Observational conditioning of snake fear in rhesus monkeys. *Journal of Abnormal Psychology*, 1984b. **215, 216, 243**

Mineka, S., & Gino, A. Dissociative effects of different types and amounts of non-reinforced CS exposure on avoidance extinction and the CER. *Learning and Motivation*, 1979, *10*, 141-160. **221, 234**

Mineka, S., & Gino, A. Dissociation between CER and extended avoidance performance. *Learning and Motivation*, 1980, *11*, 476-502. **205**

Mineka, S., Gunnar, M., & Champoux, M. The effects of control in the early social and emotional development of rhesus monkeys. Manuscript submitted for publication. **212, 242**

Mineka, S., & Keir, R. The effects of flooding on reducing snake fear in rhesus monkeys: Six month follow-up and further flooding. *Behaviour Research and Therapy*, 1983, *21*, 517-535. **201, 222**

Mineka, S., Keir, R., & Price, V. Fear of snakes in wild- and lab-reared rhesus monkeys. *Animal Learning and Behavior*, 1980, *8*, 653-663. **201, 202, 222**

Mineka, S., & Kohlstrom, J. Unpredictable and uncontrollable aversive events. *Journal of Abnormal Psychology*, 1978, *87*, 256-271. **229, 235, 239, 240, 454**

Mineka, S., Miller, S., Gino, A., & Giencke, L. Dissociative effects of flooding on a multivariate assessment of fear reduction and on jump-up avoidance extinction. *Learning and Motivation*, 1981, *12*, 435-461. **234, 236**

Mineka, S., & Suomi, S.J. Social separation in monkeys. *Psychological Bulletin*, 1978, *85*, 1376-1400. **236**

Mineka, S., Suomi, S.J., & Delizio, R. Multiple peer separations in adolescent monkeys: An opponent process interpretation. *Journal of Experimental Psychology: General*, 1981, *110*, 56-85. **224**

Miner, G.D. The evidence of genetic components in the neurosis: A review. *Archives of General Psychiatry*, 1973, *29*, 111-118. **286**

Minor, T., **433**

Mintz, J., **643**

Mirin, S.M., **542**

Mirin, S.M., Meyer, R.E., & McNamee, B. Psychopathology and mood during heroin abuse: Acute vs. chronic. *Archives of General Psychiatry*, 1976, *33*, 1503-1508. **15, 541**

Mirman, M., **518, 522**

Mischel, W. *Personality and assessment*. New York: Wiley, 1968. **681**

Mitchell-Heggs, N., **82, 586, 749, 750**

Miura, M., & Usa, S. Morita Therapy. *Psychologia*, 1970, *13*, 18-34. **317**

Miura, Y., **347**

Miyabo, S. Prolactin and growth hormone responses to psychological stress in normal and neurotic subjects. *Journal Clinical Endocrinology Metabolism*, 1977, *44*, 947-951. **71**

Mobley, P.L., **544**

Modigh, K. Long-term effects of electroconvulsive shock therapy on synthesis, turnover and uptake of brain monoamines. *Psychopharmacology*, 1976, *49*, 179-185. **24**

Moerdyk, A., & Spinks, P. Preliminary cross-cultural validity study of taylor manifest anxiety scale. *Psychological Reports*, 1979, *45*, 663-664. **302**

Mòhler, H., **28, 29, 33, 34, 35, 538**

Mòhler, H., & Okada, T. Benzodiazepine receptors: Demonstration in the central nervous system. *Science*, 1977, *198*, 849-851 (a). **537-38**

Mòhler, H., & Okada, T. Properties of H-3 diazepam binding to benzodiazepine receptors in rat cerebral cortex. *Life Sciences*, 1977, *20*, 2101-2110 (c). **28**

Mòhler, H., & Okada, T. Benzodiazepine receptors in normal and pathological human brain. *British Journal of Psychiatry*, 1978, *133*, 261-268 (a). **28, 31**

Mòhler, H., & Okada, T. Biochemical identification of the site of action of benzodiazepines in human brain by ^{3}H-diazepam binding. *Life Sciences*, 1978, *22*, 985-996 (b). **28, 31**

Mòhler, H., Polc, P., Cumin, R., Pieri, L., & Kettler, R. Nicotinamide is a brain constituent with benzodiazepine-like actions. *Nature*, 1979, *278*, 563-565. **28**

Mòhler, H., Richards, J.G., & Wu, J.-Y. Autoradiographic localization of benzodiazepine receptors in immunocytochemically identified Y-aminobutyric synapses. *Proceedings of the National Academy of Sciences, U.S.A.*, 1981, *78*, 1935-1938. **33**

Moncada, V., **48, 81**

Monk, M.A., **374**

Monroe, J.J., **671**

Montgomery, L.E., **709**

Montgomery, M.A., Clayton, P.J., & Friedhoff, A.J. Psychiatric illness in Tourette Syndrome patients and first degree relatives. In A.J. Friedhoff & T. Chase, *Gilles de la Tourette Syndrome*. New York, Raven Press, 1982. **587**

Montgomery, S.A. Clomipramine in obsessional neurosis: a placebo controlled trial. *Pharmaceutical Medicine*, 1980, *1*, 189-192. **585, 586**

Monti, J.M., Altier, H., Prandro, M. The actions of flunitrazepam on heart and respiratory rates and skin potential fluctuations during the sleep cycle in normal volunteers and neurotic patients with insomnia. *Psychopharmacologia*, 1975, *43*, 187-190. **581**

Montouri, J., **126**

Mook, D.G. In defense of external invalidity. *American Psychologist*, 1983, *38*, 379-387. **247**

Moore, A., **588**

Moore E.M.C., **61**

More, T.A., **530**

Morel, B.A. *Traite des maladies mentales*. Paris: Masson, 1860. **736, 737**

Morgan, M.J. Resistance to satiation. *Animal Behavior*, 1974, *22*, 449-466. **31**

Morison, R.A., **737**

Morokoff, P., **140**

Morris, L.W., Davis, M.A., & Hutchings, C.H. Cognitive and emotional components of anxiety: Literature review and a revised Worry-Emotionality Scale. *Journal of Educational Psychology*, 1981, *73*, 541-555. **95**

Morris, R.J., & Kratochwill, T.R. *Treating children's fears and phobias: A behavioral approach*. New York: Pergamon Press, 1983. **372, 373, 374**

Morrow, B.R., & Labrum, A.H. The relationship between psychological and physiological measure of anxiety. *Psychological Medicine*, 1978, *8, 95-101*. **335, 337**

Morse, W.H., **238**

Mortensen, S.A., Vilhelmson, R., & Sande, E. Prinzmetal's variant angina (PVA). Circadian variation in response to hyperventilation. *Acta Medica Scandinavica*. Supplement., 1981, *644*, 38-49. **350**

Morton, N.E. *Outline of genetic epidemiology*. Basel: Karger, 1982. **325, 327**

Morton, N.E., & Chung, C.S. *Genetic epidemiology*. New York: Academic Press, 1978. **277**

Morton, N.E., Rao, D.C., & Lalouel, J.M. *Methods in genetic epidemiology*. Basel: Karger, 1983. **325**

Moss, H.A., **378**

Moss, H.B., **562**

Moss, J., **342, 358, 359**

Mountjoy, C.Q., **748, 750, 789, 790, 795**

Mowrer, O.H., **467, 653**

Mowrer, O.H. On the dual nature of learning: A reinterpretation of "conditioning" and "problem-solving." *Harvard Educational Review*, 1947, *17*, 102-148. **203, 465**

Mowrer, O.H. *Learning theory and behavior*. New York: John Wiley & Sons, 1960. **213, 227, 375, 421, 458, 603**

Mowrer, O.H., & Viek, P. An experimental analogue of fear from a sense of helplessness. *Journal of Abnormal Social Psychology*, 1948, *83*, 193-200. **212**

Moyer, K.E. *The physiology of hostility.* Chicago, IL: Markham Publishing Co., 1971. **118**

Mueller, C.W., & Donnerstein, E. Film-facilitated arousal and prosocial behavior. *Journal of Experimental Social Psychology*, 1981, *17*, 31-41. **149**

Mueller, E.A., **588**

Muers, J.K., **281, 282**

Mulick, J., **212**

Muller, F., **563**

Munby, D., **428**

Munby, M., **428, 433**

Munby, M., & Johnston, D.W. Agoraphobia: The long-term follow-up of behavioural treatment. *British Journal of Psychiatry*, 1980, *137*, 418-427. **428**

Mundim, F.D., **519, 540**

Munjack, D.J., Kanno, P.H., & Oziel, L.J. Ejaculatory disorders: Some psychometric data. *Psychological Reports*, 1978, *43* (3, Part 1), 783-787. **655**

Munjack, D.J., & Moss, H.B. Affective disorders and alcoholism in families of agoraphobics. *Archives of General Psychiatry*, 1981, *38*, 869-871. **562**

Munoz, R., **60, 762**

Murausku, B., **59**

Murburg, M., **542**

Murphy, D.L., **503, 504, 507, 508, 509, 547, 563, 564, 568, 569, 581, 583, 586, 588**

Murphy, D.L., Campbell, I., & Costa, J.L. Current status of the indoleamine hypothesis of the affective disorders. In M.A. Lipton, A. DiMascio & K.F. Killam (Eds.), *Psychopharmacology: A generation of progress.* New York: Raven Press, 1978. **544**

Murphy, G.E., **195, 793**

Murphy, H.B.M. *Comparative psychiatry: The international and intercultural distribution of mental illness.* New York: Springer-Verlag, 1982. **299, 304, 306, 317**

Murphy, J.M., **305, 307**

Murray, E., & Foote, F. The origins of fear of snakes. *Behaviour Research and Therapy*, 1979, *17*, 489-493. **213, 214**

Murray, S., & King, J. Snake avoidance in feral and laboratory reared squirrel monkeys. *Behaviour*, 1973, *47*, 281-289. **202**

Myers, J.K., **279, 280, 579**

Myers, J.K., Weissman, M.M., Tischler, G.L., Holzer, C.E., Leaf, P.J., Orvaschel, H., Anthony, J., Boyd, J.H., Burke, J.D., Kramer, M., & Stoltzman, R. Six-month prevalence of psychiatric disorders in three communities: 1980-1982. *Archives of General Psychiatry*, 1984. **282, 283**

Mynett, C.R., **406, 411**

Myrhed, M., **555**

Myrsten, A.L., **335**

Nachmias, H., **203**
Nagy, A., & Lojtha, A. Thyroid hormones and derivatives inhibit flunitrazepam binding. *Journal of Neurochemistry*, 1983, *40*, 414-417. **49**
Nahl, M., **213, 442**
Nakamura, C.Y., **708, 709**
Napias, Ch. **40**
Naraghi, M., **746**
Nasera, H. Children's reactions to hospitalization and illness. *Child Psychiatry and Human Development*, 1978, *9*, 3-19. **377**
Nathanson, J., **518, 522**
Natsoulas, T. What are perceptual reports about? *Psychological Bulletin*, 1967, *4*, 249-272. **703**
Nee, L.R., Caine, E.D., & Polinsky, R.J. Gilles de la Tourette Syndrome: Clinical and family study of 50 cases. *Annals of Neurology*, *7*, 40-49, 1980. **587**
Neef, G., **32, 34**
Neese, R.M., **66**
Neill, W.A., & Hattenhauer, M. Impairment of myocardial O_2 supply due to hyperventilation. *Circulation*, 1975, *52*, 854-859. **350**
Neisser, U., **203**
Neisser, U. *Cognitive Psychology*. New York: Appleton-Century-Crofts, 1967. **622**
Nelbach, J.H., **55**
Nelsen, J.M., **549**
Nemeroff, C.B., & Evans, D.L. Concurrent use of anti-depressants and propanolol: Case report and theoretical considerations. *Biological Psychiatry*, 1983, *18*, 237-241. **530**
Nemiah, J. Obsessive-compulsive neurosis. In A.M. Freedman & H.I. Kaplan (Eds.), *A comprehensive textbook of psychiatry*. Baltimore: Williams and Wilkens, 1967. **224**
Nemiah, J.L. The psychoanalytic view of anxiety. In D.F. Klein & J.G. Rabkin (Eds.), *Anxiety: New research and changing concepts*. New York: Raven Press, 1981. **607**
Nemiah, T., Freyberger, H., & Sifneos, P.M. Alexithymia: A view of the psychosomatic process. In Oscar Hill (Ed.), *Modern trends in psychosomatic medicine* (Vol. 3). London: Butterworths, 1976, pp. 430-439. **167**
Nesse, R.M., **63-64, 64, 65, 66, 67, 72, 339, 340, 357, 359**
Nesse, R.M., Curtis, G.C., Brown, G.M., & Rubin, R.T. Anxiety induced by flooding therapy for phobias does not elicit a prolactin secretory response. *Psychosomatic Medicine*, 1980, *42*, 25-31. **71, 339**
Nessleroade, J.R. *Some implications of the trait-state distinction for the study of adult development and aging: "Still labile after all these years."* Presidential

address, Division 20, annual meeting of the American Psychological Association, 1983. **684**

Nestadt, G., **xxx**

Nestoros, J.N. Ethanol selectively potentiates GABA-mediated inhibition of single feline cortical neurons. *Life Sciences*, 1980, *26*, 519-523. **11**

Newell, A. Production systems: Models of control structures. In W.G. Chase (Ed.), *Visual information processing*. New York: Academic Press, 1973, pp. 463-526. **158**

Newman, A., **212, 242, 254**

Newmark, C.S. Stability of state and trait anxiety. *Psychological Reports*, 1972, *30*, 196-198. **658**

Newmark, C.S., Faschingbauer, T.R., Finch, A.J., Jr., & Kendall, P.C. Factor analysis of the MMPI-STAI. *Journal of Clinical Psychology*, 1975, *31* (3), 449-452. **659**

Newmark, C.S., Hetzel, W., & Frerking, R.A. The effects of personality tests on state and trait anxiety. *Journal of Personality Assessment*, 1974, *38*, 17-20. **659**

Newton, K., **505, 508, 509, 585**

Newton, T.F., **567, 786, 795**

Nichols, K., **746**

Nicholson, A.N., & Wright, C.M. Comparative studies with thieno and benzodiazepines: Spatial delayed alternation behaviour in the monkeys (Macaca mulatta). *Neuropharmacology*, 1980, *19*, 491-495. **31**

Nicoll, R. Selective actions of barbiturates on synaptic transmission. In M.A. Lipton, A. DiMascio, & K.F. Killam, (Eds.), *Psychopharmacology: A generation of progress*. New York: Raven Press, 1978. **539**

Nielsen, M., **7, 13, 30, 32, 34, 41, 42, 50**

Nies, A., **543**

Nies, A., Robinson, D.S., Lamborn, K.R., & Lampert, R.P. Genetic control of platelet and plasma monoamine oxidase activity. *Archives of General Psychiatry*, 1973, *28*, 834-838. **555**

Ninan, P.T., **552**

Ninan, P.T., Insel, T.R., Cohen, R.M., Cook, J.M., Skolnick, P., & Paul, S.M. Benzodiazepine receptor mediated experimental "anxiety" in primates. *Science*, 1982, *218*, 1332-1334. **38, 39**

Nisbett, R., & Ross, L. *Human inference: Strategies and shortcomings of social judgment*. Englewood Cliffs, NJ: Prentice-Hall, 1980. **702**

Nisbett, R.E., & Wilson, T.P. Telling more than we know: Verbal reports on mental processes. *Psychological Review*, 1977, *84*, 231-279. **441**

Noble, H., **373, 708, 709, 713**

Noel, G.L., Dimond, R.C., Earll, J.M., & Frantz, A.G. Prolactin, thyrotropin, and growth hormone release during stress associated with parachute jumping. *Aviation, Space and Environmental Medicine*, 1976, *47*, 543-547. **69, 70, 343**

Noel, G.L., Suh, H.K., Stone, J.G., & Frantz, A.G. Human prolaction and growth hormone release during surgery and other conditions of stress. *Journal Clinical Endocrinology Metabolism.* 1972, *34*, 840-851. **69**

Nogeire, C., **65**

Noirot, E. Ultrasounds and maternal behavior in small rodents. *Developmental Psychobiology*, 1972, *5*, 371-387. **524**

Noland, W.A., & Parkes, M.W. The effects of benzodiazepines on the behaviour of mice on a hole-board. *Psychopharmacologia*, 1973, *29*, 277-288. **31**

Nordheden, B., **335**

Norman, W.T. Personality measurement, faking, and detection: An assessment method for use in personnel selection. *Journal of Applied Psychology*, 1963, *47*, 225-241. **682, 683**

Norman, W.T. "To see ourselves as others see us!": Relations among self-perceptions, peer-perceptions, and expected peer-perceptions of personality attributes. *Multivariate Behavioral Research*, 1969, *4*, 417-443. **681, 682, 696**

Norstad, N., **516, 517, 538, 545**

Norton, J.A., **58**

Novick, W.J., Jr., **543**

Novosel, M., **302**

Nowicki, G., **143, 144**

Nowlis, H., **135, 689**

Nowlis, V., & Green, R.F. *Factor analytic studies of mood.* Technical Report, Office of Naval Research, 1964. **658**

Nowlis, V., & Nowlis, H. The description and analysis of mood. *Annals, New York Academy of Science*, 1956, *65*, 345-355. **135, 689**

Noyes, R., Jr., **285, 286, 288, 294, 328, 329, 357, 365, 366, 780, 793**

Noyes, R., Jr. Beta-blocking drugs and anxiety. *Psychosomatics*, 1982, *23*, 155-170. **514**

Noyes, R., Jr., Anderson, D.J., Clancy, J., Crowe, R.R., Slymen, D.J., Ghoneim, M.M., & Hinrichs, J.V. Diazepam and propranolol in panic disorder and agoraphobia, *Archives of General Psychiatry*, 1984, *41*, 287-292. **538, 682**

Noyes, R., Jr., Clancy, J., Crowe, R., Hoenk, P.R., & Slymen, D.J. The familial prevalence of anxiety neurosis. *Archives of General Psychiatry*, 1978, *35*, 1057-1059. **325**

Nurnberger, J.I., **563**

Nurnberger, J.R., **558-59, 563**

Nutt, D.J., **34**

Nuun, W.D., **65**

Nyback, H., Walters, J.R., & Aghajanian, G.K. Tricyclic antidepressants: effects on the firing rate of brain noradrenergic neurons. *European Journal of Pharmacology*, 1975, *32*, 302-312. **544**

Nyback, H.V., Walters, J.R., Aghajanian, G.K., & Roth, R.H. Tricyclic antidepressants: effects on firing rate of brain noradrenergic neurons. *European Journal of Pharmacology*, 1975, *32*302-312. **571**

Obeyesekere, G. Depression, Buddhism and the Work of Culture in Sri Lanka. In A. Kleinman & B. Good (Eds.), *Culture and depression: Toward an anthropology of dysphoric affect and affective disorders*. Berkeley: University of California Press, in press. **320**

Obmascher, P., **389**

O'Brien, G.T., **386, 434-35, 480, 481, 486, 487, 488, 768, 773**

Obrist, P.A. *Cardiovascular psychophysiology: A perspective*. New York: Plenum Press, 1981. **153, 168**

Obrist, P.A., Light, K.C., & Hastrup, J.L. Emotion and the cardiovascular system—A critical perspective. In C.E. Izard (Ed.), *Measuring emotions in infants and children*. New York: Cambridge University Press, 1982. **116**

Oertel, W., **40**

Ogg, G., **505, 508, 509, 585**

O'Gorman, J., & Jamieson, R. The incremental stimulus intensity effect and habituation of autonomic responses in man. *Physiological Psychology*, 1975, *3*, 385-389. **440**

Ogren, S.-O., **539, 540**

O'Hearn, T.P., Jr., **660**

Òhman, A., **153, 208, 376**

Òhman, A. Fear relevance, autonomic conditioning, and phobias: A laboratory model. In P.O. Sjoden & S. Bates (Eds.), *Trends in behavior therapy*. New York: Academic Press, 1979. **156**

Òhman, A. The role of experimental psychology in the scientific analysis of psychopathology. *International Journal of Psychology*, 1981, *16*, 299-321. **218**

Òhman, A., & Dimberg, U. Facial expressions as conditioned stimuli for electrodermal responses: A case of "preparedness"? *Journal of Personality and Social Psychology*, 1978, *36*, 251-258. **208, 216**

Òhman, A., Ericksson, A., & Olofsson, C. One-trial learning and superior resistance to extinction of autonomic responses conditioned to potentially phobic stimuli. *Journal of Comparative and Physiological Psychology*, 1975, *88*, 619-627. **207, 209, 268, 376**

Òhman, A., Fredrikson, M., & Hugdahl, K. Toward an experimental model for simple phobic reactions. *Behavioural Analysis and Modification*, 1978, *2*, 97-114. (a). **207**

Òhman, A., Fredrikson, M., & Hugdahl, K. Orienting and defensive responding in the electrodermal system: Palmar-dorsal differences and recovery rate during conditioning to potentially phobic stimuli. *Psychophysiology*, 1978, *15*, 93-101. (b). **207, 209**

Òhman, A., Fredrikson, M., Hugdahl, K., & Rimino, P.-A. The premise of equipotentiality in human classical conditioning: Conditioned electrodermal responses to potentially phobic stimuli. *Journal of Experimental Psychology: General*, 1976, *105*, 313-337. **207**

Oishi, H., **31**

Okada, M., **659**

Okada, T., **28, 31, 537-38**

Okasha, A., & Ashour, A. Psycho-demographic study of anxiety in Egypt: The PSE in its Arabic version. *British Journal of Psychiatry*, 1981, *139*, 70-73. **310**

Okel, B.B., & Hurst, J.W. Prolonged hyperventilation in man: associated electrolyte changes and subjective symptoms. *Archives of internal Medicine*, 1961, *108*, 157-163. **349**

Oken, D., **534, 550**

Okuno, S., **300-01**

O'Leary, K.D., & Borkovec, T.D. Conceptual, ethical, and methodological problems of placebo groups in psychotherapy research. *American Psychologist*, 1978, *33*, 821-830. **473**

Oliveau, D.C., **165, 279, 284, 293, 372, 444, 713, 747**

Olivier, A., **558**

Olofsson, C., **207, 209, 268, 376**

Olpe, H.R., & Jones, R.S.G. The action of anti-convulsant drugs on the firing of locus coeruleus neurons: Selective activating effect of carbamazepine. *European Journal of Pharmacology*, 1983, *91*, 107-110. **540**

Olpe, H.R., Jones, R.S.G., & Steinman, M.W. The locus coeruleus: Actions of psychoactive drugs. *Experientia*, 1983, *39*, 242-249. **573**

Olsen, R.W. GABA-benzodiazepine-barbiturate receptor interactions. *Journal of Neurochemistry*, 1981, *37*, 1-13. **11, 12, 41**

Olsen, R.W., Bergman, M.D., Van Ness, P.C., Lummis, S.C., Watkins, A.E., Napias, Ch., & Greenlee, D.V. Aminobutyric acid receptor binding in mammalian brain: Heterogeneity of binding sites. *Molecular Pharmacology*, 1980, *19*, 217-227. **40**

Olsen, R.W., Leeb-Lundberg, F., Snowman, A.S., & Stephenson, F.A. Barbiturate interactions with the benzodiazepine receptor complex in mammalian brain. In E. Usdin, P. Skolnick, J.F. Tallman, Jr., D. Greenblatt & S.M. Paul (Eds.), *Pharmacology of benzodiazepines*. London: MacMillan, 1982. **540**

Olson, L., **7, 15, 539**

O'Neil, H.F., Jr., **659**

O'Nell, C., **315**

O'Nell, C.W. An investigation of reported "fright" as a factor in the etiology of susto, "magical fright." *Ethos*, 1975, *3*, 268-283. **315**

O'Nell, C.W., & Rubel, A. The meaning of susto (magical fright). *Actas del XLI Congreso Internacional de Americanistas*, 1976, *3*, 342-349. **315**

Oppenheim, H. quoted after Kraepeline (1896). **737**

Oppenheimer, B.S., Levine, S.A., Morison, R.A., Rothschild, M.A., St. Lawrence, W., & Wilson, F.N. Report on neurocirculatory asthenia and its management. *Military Surgeon*, 1918, *42*, 409-426 and 711-719. **737**

Opter, M.K., **306**

Orley, J., & Wing, J.K. Psychiatric disorders in two African villages. *Archives of General Psychiatry*, 1979, *36*, 513-520. **309**

Ornstein, H., & Carr, J. Implosion therapy by tape-recording. *Behaviour Research and Therapy*, 1975, *13*, 177-182. **438**

Orvaschel, H., **282, 283**

Orvaschel, H. Parental depression and child psychopathology. In S.B. Guze, F.J. Earls & J.E. Barret (Eds.), *Childhood psychopathology and development*. New York: Raven Press, 1983. **293**

Orvaschel, H., & Weissman, M.M. Epidemiology of anxiety disorders in children: A review. In R. Gittelman (Ed.), *Anxiety disorders of childhood*. New York: Guilford Press, in press. **283, 284**

Orvin, G. Treatment of the phobic obsessive compulsive patients with oxazepam. *Psychosomatics*, 1967, *8*, 278-280. **585**

Osanalos, I., **518, 522**

Osborne, F.H., Mattingly, B.A., Redmon, W.K., & Osborne, J.S. Factors affecting the measurement of classically conditioned fear in rats following exposure to escapable versus inescapable signaled shock. *Journal of Experimental Psychology: Animal Behavior Processes*, 1975, *1*, 364-373. **212**

Osborne, J.S., **212**

Osgood, C., **653**

Osgood, C. Dimensionality of the semantic space for communication via facial expression. *Scandinavian Journal of Psychology*, 1966, *7*, 1-30. **416**

Òst, L.-G., **425**

Òst, L.-G., & Hugdahl, K. Acquisition of phobias and anxiety response patterns in clinical patients. *Behaviour Research and Therapy*, 1981, *19*, 439-447. **213**

Òst, L.-G., & Hugdahl, K. Acquisition of agoraphobia, mode of onset and anxiety response patterns. *Behaviour Research and Therapy*, 1983, *21*, 623-631. **217**

Òst, L.-G., Jerremalm, A., & Johansson, J. Individual response patterns and the effects of differential behavioral methods in the treatment of social phobia. *Behaviour Research and Therapy*, 1981, *19*, 1-16. **426, 496**

Overall, J.E., **521, 544**

Overmier, J., Patterson, J., & Wielciwicz, R. Environmental contingencies as sources of stress in animals. In S. Levine & H. Ursin (Ed.), *Coping and health*. New York: Plenum, 1980, pp. 1-38. **239**

Owen, S., **14**

Owen, S., Boarder, M.R., Gray, J.A., & Fillenz, M. Acquisition and extinction of continuously and partially reinforced running in rats with lesions of the dorsal noradrenergic bundle. *Behavioral Brain Research*, 1982, *5*, 11-41. **20**

Owens, D., **521, 544**

Ozarow, B.J., **423, 429, 446**

Oziel, L.J., **655**

Page, C.W., **647, 649**

Page, H., & Hall, J. Experimental extinction as a function of the prevention of a response. *Journal of Comparative and Physiological Psychology*, 1953, *46*, 33-34. **220**

Page, H.A., **221**

Page, H.A. The facilitation of experimental extinction by response prevention as a function of the acquisition of a new response. *Journal of Comparative and Physiological Psychology*, 1955, *48*, 14-16. **220**

Page, I.H., **82, 546, 551**

Paget, K.D., **709**

Paivio, A. Imagery and verbal processes. New York: Holt, Rinehart and Winston, 1971 [Reprinted by Lawrence Erlbaum Associates, Hillsdale, N.J., 1979. **158**

Palermo, D.S., **708**

Pancake, V.R., **377**

Pankratz, L.D., **295**

Panksepp, J., **526**

Panksepp, J., Herman, B.M., Vilberg, T., Bishop, P., & DeEskinazi, F.G. Endogenous opiates and social behavior. *Neuroscience and Behavior Reviews*, 1980, *4*, 473-487. **526**

Panula, P., **39**

Papez, J.W. A proposed mechanism of emotion. *Archives of Neurology and Psychiatry*, 1937, *38*, 725-743. **139**

Parad, H.W., **243**

Parish, L., **518, 522**

Park, L.C., **677**

Parker, R.R., **17**

Parks, M.W., **31**

Parkinson, S., C., & Gillis, J.S. The subjective effects of selected phenothiazines. *Research Communications in Psychology, Psychiatry and Behavior*, 1977, *2* (5-6), 297-312. **648**

Parma, A.M., **28, 48, 573, 575**

Pascal, B., **172**

Paschelke, G., **34, 35, 36, 551**

Patal, M.K., **349**

Patel, J., **49, 575**

Pathak, D., **546, 676**

Patrick, R., **143, 144**

Patterson, J.M., **211, 239, 243**

Paugh, B.A., **48, 81**

Paul, G.L., **256**

Paul, N., **593**

Paul, S.M., **28, 31, 38, 39, 48, 49, 538, 539, 552, 573**

Paul, S.M., Syapin, P.J., Paugh, B.A., Moncada, V., & Skolnick, P. Correlation between benzodiazepine receptor occupation and anticonvulsant effects of diazepam. *Nature*, 1979, *281*, 688-689. **81**

Pauley, J.D., **236, 389**

Pauls, D.L., **285, 286, 287, 288, 289, 290, 294, 328, 329, 483, 569, 764, 780, 793**

Pauls, D.L., Bucher, K.D., Crowe, R.R., & Noyes, R. A genetic study of panic disorder pedigrees. *American Journal of Human Genetics*, 1980, *32*, 639-644. **286**

Pauls, D.L., Noyes, R., Jr., & Crowe, R.R. The familial prevalence in second-degree relatives of patients with anxiety neurosis (panic disorder). *Journal of Affective Disorders*, 1979, *1*, 279-285. **286**

Pauls, O.L., **365**

Paunonen, S.V., **682**

Pavlov, I.J. *Conditional reflexes and psychiatry*. (Trans. W.H. Gantt). London: Lawrence and Wishart, 1941. **55, 152**

Pavlov, I.P. *Conditioned reflexes*. (Translated by G. Anrep). New York: Oxford University Press, 1927. **xxi, 199, 208, 554, 623, 738, 739, 779**

Paykel, E.S., **323**

Paykel, E.S., Parker, R.R., Penrose, R.J.J., & Rassaby, E.R. Depressive classification and prediction of response to phenelzine. *British Journal of Psychiatry*, 1979, *134*, 572-581. **17**

Payne, L.L., **428**

Peabody, F.W., Sturgis, C.C., & Tompkins, E.H. Epinephrine hypersensitiveness and its relation to hyperthyroidism. *American Journal of Medical Science*, 1921, *161*, 508-517. **534, 550**

Pearson, J.S., & Swenson, W.M. *A user's guide to the Mayo Clinic automated MMPI program*. New York: The Psychological Corporation, 1967. **646**

Pecknold, J., **504, 506, 586**

Peeke, H.V.S., **489, 607, 610, 771**

Peffer, K.E., **475**

Pekkarinen, A., **67, 341**

Penia, C., **350**

Pennebaker, J.W. *The psychology of physical symptoms*. New York: Springer, 1982. **251**

Pennington, L.L., **71**

Pennock, M., **471**

Penrose, R.J.J., **17**

Peplau, L.A., & Perlman, D. (Eds.). *Loneliness: A sourcebook of current theory, research and therapy*. New York: Wiley-Interscience, 1982. **106**

Pepper, C.M., & Henderson, G. Opiates and opioid peptides hyperpolarize locus coeruleus neurons *in vitro*. *Science*, 1980, *209*, 394-396. **542**

Pereira-Ogan, J., **518, 522**

Perigault, F., **231**

Perlman, D., **106**

Peronnet, F., **71**

Peroutka, S.J., U'Prichard, D.C., Greenberg, D.A., & Snyder, S.H. Neuroleptic drug interactions with norepinephrine alpha receptor binding sites in rat brain. *Neuropharmacology*, 1977, *16*, 549-556. **541**

Perrott, M.C., **560**

Persky, H., Grinker, R.R., Hamburg, D.A., Sabshin, M.A., Korchin, S.J., Basowitz, H., & Chevalier, J.A. Adrenal cortisol function in anxious human subjects: Plasma level and urinary excretion of hydrocortisone. *Archives of Neurology and Psychiatry*, 1956, *76*, 549-558. **60, 65**

Persky, H., Grosz, H.J., Norton, J.A., & McMurtry, M. Effect of hypnotically-induced anxiety on plasma hydrocortisone level of normal subjects. *Journal of Clinical Endocrinology*, 1959, *19*, 700-710. **58**

Persson, R., **547**

Pert, C.B., & Snyder, S.H. Opiate receptor: Demonstration in nervous tissue. *Science (New York)*, 1973, *179*, 111-114. **15**

Petersen, E.N., **30, 32, 34, 41, 42**

Petersen, S.C., **49**

Peterson, D.R. Behavior problems of middle childhood. *Journal of Consulting Psychology*, 1961, *25*, 205-209. **716, 717**

Peterson, D.R. *The clinical study of social behavior.* New York: Appleton-Century-Crofts, 1968. **681**

Petrie, W.M., Mafucci, R.J., & Woolsky, R.L. Propanolol and depression. *American Journal of Psychiatry*, 1982, *139*, 92-94. **529**

Petty, F., **17, 19**

Petty, F., & Sherman, A.D. GABA-ergic modulation of learned helplessness. *Pharmacology, Biochemistry and Behavior*, 1981, *15*, 567-570. **18**

Petursson, H., Bhattacharya, S.K., Glover, V., Sandler, M., & Lader, M.H. Urinary monoamine oxidase inhibitor and benzodiazepine withdrawal. *British Journal of Psychiatry*, 1982, *140*, 7-10. **538**

Pfeffer, J.M. The aetiology of the hyperventilation syndrome. *Psychotherapy and psychosomatics*, 1978, *30*, 47-56. **350**

Phares, E.J. Test anxiety, expectancies, and expectancy changes. *Psychological Reports*, 1968, *22*, 259-265, 488-496. **120**

Phillips, J., **544**

Phillipszoon, E., **416**

Piaget, J., **410**

Pick, G.R., **65**

Pickar, D., **552**

Pieri, L., **11, 13, 14, 28, 29, 32, 33, 34, 35, 38, 538**

Pillard, R.C., Mcnair, D.M., & Fisher, S. Does marijuana enhance experimentally induced anxiety? *Psychopharmacologia*, 1974, *40*, 205-210. **549**

Pilling, V.B., **327**

Pincus, G., **55**

Pincus, G., & Hoagland, H. Steroid excretion and the stress of flying. *Journal of Aviation Medicine*, 1943, *14*, 173-188. **55**

Pinder, R.M., **521**

Pine, F., **417, 418**

Pinkster, H., **489, 607, 610, 771**

Piotrowski, Z. Quoted after Campbell, R.J. (1981) *Psychiatric Dictionary* (5th ed.). London: Oxford University Press, 1957. **741**

Pitcher, E.G., & Prelinger, E. *Children tell stories: An analysis of fantasy*. New York: International Universities Press, 1963. **614**

Pitres, A., & Régis, E. *Les obsessions et les impulsions*. Paris: Doin 1902. **744**

Pitts, F.N., Jr. The biochemistry of anxiety. *Scientific American*, 1969, *220*, 69-75. **534, 551**

Pitts, F.N., Jr., & Allen, R.E. Beta adrenergic blockade in the treatment of anxiety. In R.J. Mathew (Ed.), *The biology of anxiety*. New York: Brunner/Mazel, 1980. **81**

Pitts, F.N., Jr., & McClure, J.N. Lactate metabolism in anxiety neurosis. *New England Journal of Medicine*, 1967, *227*, 1329-1336. **82, 534, 551, 586, 749**

Platt, J. Strong inference. *Science*, 1964, *146*, 247-353. **642-43**

Platzek, D., **126**

Plochg, I., **433**

Plomin, R. Childhood temperament. In B. Lahey & A. Kazdin (Eds.), *Advances in clinical child psychology* (Vol. 6). New York: Plenum Press, 1983, pp. 45-92. **414, 415**

Plum, F., **350**

Plutchik, R., **135, 146**

Plutchik, R. *Emotion: A psychoevolutionary synthesis*. New York: Harper & Row, 1980. **110, 118, 185**

Pohorecky, L.A., **17, 18, 19, 20, 25**

Pohorecky, L.A., & Brick, J. Activity of neurons in the locus coeruleus of the rat: inhibition by ethanol. *Brain Research*, 1977, *131*, 174-179. **571**

Poland, R.E., **344, 345**

Polc, P., **11, 13, 14, 28, 29, 32, 33, 34, 35, 38, 538, 540**

Polc, P., Robert, N., & Wright, D.M. Ethyl Beta-carboline-3-carboxylate antagonizes the action of GABA and benzodiazepines in the hippocampus. *Brain Research*, 1981, *217*, 216. **34, 36**

Poldinger, W. Application of the neuroleptic pimozide (ORAP-R 6238) for tranquilizer indications in a controlled study. *International Pharmacopsychiatry*, 1976, *11*, 16-24. **520, 523, 540**

Polin, A.T. The effect of flooding and physical suppression as extinction techniques on an anxiety motivated avoidance locomotor response. *Journal of Psychology*, 1959, *47*, 253-255. **220, 234**

Polinsky, R.J., **563, 587**

Pollin, W., & Goldin, S. The physiological and psychological effects of intravenously administered epinephrine and its metabolism in normal and schizophrenic men. *Journal of Psychiatric Research*, 1961, *1*, 50-67. **534, 550**

Pollitt, J., & Young, J. Anxiety state or masked depression? A study based on the action of monoamine oxidase inhibitors. *British Journal of Psychiatry*, 1971, *199*, 143-149. **750**

Pollock, S., **278**

Poole, C., **660**

Pope, H.G., **677**

Porot, M. Normal and pathological anxiety. In A. Okasha (Ed.), *Proceedings of symposium on psychopathology of anxiety and its management*. World Psychiatric Association, Cairo, Jan. 11-13, 1981. **740**

Post, B., **335**

Post, R.M., **547, 551, 558, 558-59, 559, 561, 562, 563, 565, 567, 568, 569, 570, 571, 572, 573, 574, 575, 795**

Post, R.M., Ballenger, J.C., & Goodwin, F.K. Cerebrospinal fluid studies of neurotransmitter function in manic and depressive illness. In J.H. Wood (Ed.), *Neurobiology of Cerebrospinal Fluid*. New York, Plenum Press, 1980. **570**

Potkin, S.G., **401**

Pottash, A.L.C., **15**

Powell, A., & Lumia, A.R. Avoidance conditioning and behavior therapies: A reply to Costello. *Psychological Review*, 1971, *78*, 344-347. **203**

Powell, G.E. *Brain and personality*. London: Saxon House, 1979. **10**

Prandro, M., **581**

Prange, A.J., **59, 71**

Prelinger, E., **614**

Presley, A.S., **293, 562**

Price, D.B., Thaler, M., & Mason, J.W. Preoperative emotional states and adrenal cortical activity: Studies on cardiac and pulmonary surgery patients, *Archives of Neurology and Psychiatry*, 1957, *77*, 646-656. **56, 58, 62**

Price, V., **201, 202, 222**

Primavera, L.H., Simon, W., & Camiza, J. An investigation of personality and caffeine use. *British Journal of Addiction*, 1975, *70*, 213-215. **573**

Prince, R. Functional symptoms associated with study in Nigerian students. *West African Medical Journal*, 1960, *11*, 198-206. **308**

Pritchard, C., **746**

Pritchard, J., **293, 395, 400**

Proffer, C.R. *The unpublished Dostoevsky, diaries and notebooks* (Vol. 1). Ann Arbor, MI: Ardis 1973. **593**

Proffer, C.R. *The unpublished Dostoevsky, diaries and notebooks* (Vol. 2). Ann Arbor, MI: Ardis 1975. **593**

Proffer, C.R. *The unpublished Dostoevsky, diaries and notebooks* (Vol. 3). Ann Arbor, MI: Ardis 1976. **593**

Prudo, R., **278**

Prusoff, B.A., **286, 287, 288, 289, 290, 292, 293, 294, 394, 395, 483, 569, 764, 780, 793**

Pruzinsky, T., **95, 252, 467, 468, 469**

Pruzinsky, T., & Borkovec, T.D. *Cognitive characteristics of chronic worriers.* Paper presented at the Association for the Advancement of Behavior Therapy, Washington, D.C., December, 1983. **470**

Puig-Antich, J. Major depression and conduct disorder in prepuberty. *Journal of American Academy of Child Psychiatry*, 1982, *2*, 118-128. **125**

Pulver, S., **643**

Puzantian, V., **791**

Quay, H.C., **284**

Quay, H.C. Classification. In H.C. Quay & J. Werry (Eds.), *Psychopathological disorders of childhood* (2nd ed.). New York: Wiley, 1979. **708, 716**

Quesney, L.F., **558**

Quillian, M.R. Semantic memory. In M.L. Minsky (Ed.), *Semantic information processing*. Cambridge, MA: MIT Press, 1966. **158**

Quintero, S., **7, 8, 11, 12, 13, 15**

Quitkin, F.M., **502, 508, 512, 513, 540, 585, 670**

Quitkin, F.M., & Klein, D.F. Two behavioral syndromes in young adults related to possible minimal brain dysfunction. *Journal of Psychiatric Research*, 1969, *7*, 131-142. **401**

Quitkin, F.M., Rifkin, A.H., & Klein, D.F. Neurologic soft signs in schizophrenia and character disorders. *Archives of General Psychiatry*, 1976, *33*, 845-853. **401**

Raab, W. *Preventive myocardiology*. Springfield: Thomas, 1970. **346**

Rabavilas, A.D., Boulougouris, J.C., & Stefanis, C. Duration of flooding sessions in the treatment of obsessive-compulsive patients. *Behaviour Research and Therapy*, 1976, *14*, 249-355. **428**

Rabkin, J.G., **xxxiii, 241, 297, 328, 366, 453, 456, 540, 552, 586, 591, 670, 760**

Rachman, S., **132, 144, 201, 203, 209, 220, 222, 225, 231-32, 334, 363, 367, 425, 428, 429, 438, 446, 454, 455, 456, 459, 465, 497, 505, 507**

Rachman, S. Primary obsessional slowness. *Behavioral Research and Therapy*, 1974, *111*, 463-471. **578**

Rachman, S. Obsessional-compulsive checking. *Behaviour Research and Therapy*, 1976, *14*, 269-277. **201, 421, 459**

Rachman, S. The conditioning theory of fear acquisition: A critical examination. *Behaviour Research and Therapy*, 1977, *15*, 375-388. **209, 214**

Rachman, S. *Fear and courage*. San Francisco: W.H. Freeman, 1978. **91, 143, 209, 213, 214, 222, 457, 459**

Rachman, S. Emotional processing. *Behaviour Research and Therapy*, 1980, *18*, 51-60. **436, 457**

Rachman, S. The primacy of affect. *Behaviour Research and Therapy*, 1981, *19*, 27-290. **458**

Rachman, S. The modification of agoraphobic behavior: Some fresh possibilities. *Behaviour Research and Therapy*, 1983, *21*, 567-574. **455, 457**

Rachman, S. Agoraphobia: A safety signal perspective. *Behaviour Research and Therapy*, 1984, *22*, 59-70. **455, 457, 459**

Rachman, S., & DeSilva, P. Abnormal and normal obsessions. *Behaviour Research and Therapy*, 1978, *16*, 233-248. **475**

Rachman, S., Hodgson, R., & Marks, I. The treatment of chronic obsessional neurosis. *Behaviour Research and Therapy*, 1971, *9*, 231-247. **233**

Rachman, S., & Hodgson, R.J. Synchrony and desynchrony in fear and avoidance. *Behavior Research and Therapy*, 1974, *12*, 311-318. **xxiv, 10, 133, 201, 334, 363, 376, 454, 459, 497, 683**

Rachman, S., & Hodgson, R.J. *Obsessions and compulsions*. Englewood Cliffs, NJ: Prentice Hall, 1980. **89, 204, 223, 224, 226, 227, 230-31, 232, 233, 234, 456, 459, 460**

Rachman, S., Marks, I.M., & Hodgson, R. The treatment of obsessive-compulsive neurotics by modelling and flooding *in vivo*. *Behaviour Research and Therapy*, 1973, *11*, 463-471. **233, 429**

Rachman, S., & Seligman, M.E.P. Unprepared phobias: "Be prepared." *Behaviour Research and Therapy*, 1976, *14*, 333-338. **209**

Rada, R.T., **676**

Radcliffe, W.N., **444**

Radke-Yarrow, M., **419**

Rado, S. Psychodynamics and depression from the etiological point of view. In W. Gaylin (Ed.), *The meaning of despair*. New York: Science House, 1968. **125**

Rae, D.S., **xxx**

Rahe, R.H., **344**

Raichle, M.E., & Plum, F. Hyperventilation and cerebral blood flow. *Stroke*, 1972, *3*, 566-572. **350**

Raisman, R., **563**

Rajecki, D.W., Lamb, M.E., & Obmascher, P. Toward a general theory of infantile attachment. A comparative review of aspects of the social bond. *Behavioral and Brain Sciences*, 1978, *1*, 417-464. **389**

Ramesh, S., **523, 540**

Ramm, E., Marks, I.M., Yuksel, S., & Stern, R.S. *Anxiety management training for anxiety states, comparing positive with negative self statements*. Unpublished manuscript, 1983. **434**

Ramm, R., **368**

Ramsay, I., **742**

Ramsey, A., **58**

Randall, O.S., **348**

Ransom, B.R., **7, 11, 12**

Rao, A.V. A controlled trial with Valium in obsessive compulsive state. *Journal of the Indian Medical Association*, 1964, *42*, 564-567. **575**

Rao, D.C., **325**

Rao, D.C., Elston, R.C., Kuller, L.H., Feinleib, N., Carter, C., & Havlik, R. *Genetic epidemiology of coronary heart disease: Parts, present, and future.* New York: Alan R. Liss, 1983. **325, 327**

Rapaport, C. *Character, anxiety and social affiliation.* Unpublished doctoral dissertation, New York University, 1963. **613**

Rapaport, D. The structure of psychoanalytic theory (1959). *Psychological Issues* (Monograph 6). New York: International Press, 1960. **641, 642**

Raper, A.J., **350**

Rapoport, J.L., **584**

Rapoport, P.M., **17**

Rappaport, H., & Katkin, E.S. Relationships among manifest anxiety, response to stress, and the perception of autonomic activity. *Journal of Consulting & Clinical Psychology*, 1972, *38* (2), 219-224. **647**

Rappaport, J., Elkins, R., Mikkelsen, E., & et al. Clinical controlled trial of chlorimipramine in adolescents with obsessive-compulsive disorder. *Psychopharmacology Bulletin*, 1980, *16* (3), 61-63. **504, 506**

Rashotte, M.G., **230**

Raskin, A., **689**

Raskin, M. Decreased skin conductance response habituation in chronically anxious patients. *Biological Psychiatry*, 1975, *2*, 309-319. **583**

Raskin, M., Peeke, H.V.S., Dickman, W., & Pinkster, H. Panic and generalized anxiety disorders: Developmental antecedents and precipitants. *Archives of General Psychiatry*, 1982, *39*, 687-689. **489, 607, 610, 771**

Rassaby, E.R., **17**

Ratcliff, R., & McKoon, G. Does activation really spread? *Psychological Review*, 1981, *88*, (5), 454-462. **169**

Ratcliffe, K., **281, 282, 310, 677**

Rauste von Wright, M., **66**

Ravaris, C.L., **543**

Ravaris, C.L., Nies, A., Robinson, D.S., Ives, J.O., Lamborn, K.R., & Korson, L. A multiple dose, controlled study of pheneizine in depression-anxiety states. *Archives of General Psychiatry*, 1976, *33*, 347-350. **543**

Ravel, J., **309**

Ravindranath, P.A., **523, 540**

Rawlins, J.N.P., **14, 21**

Rawlins, J.N.P., Feldon, J., & Gray, J.A. Septo-hippocampal connections and the hippocampal theta rhythm. *Experimental Brain Research*, 1979, *37*, 49-63. **14**

Rawson, R., **212**

Raymond, F.A., **555**

Rayner, R., **202, 218, 707**

Razran, G. The observable unconscious and the inferable conscious in current Soviet psychophysiology: Interoceptive conditioning, semantic conditioning, and the orienting reflex. *Psychological Review*, 1961, *68*, 81-150. **217, 237**

Reatig, N., **689**

Reddy, W., **55**

Redfering, D.L., & Jones, J.G. Effects of defensiveness on the state-trait anxiety inventory. *Psychological Reports*, 1978, *43* (1), 83-89. **661**

Redmon, W.K., **212**

Redmond, D.E., Jr., **114, 526, 529, 539, 542, 546, 547, 548, 550, 551, 552, 554, 562, 570, 571, 572, 591, 592, 635**

Redmond, D.E., Jr. Alterations in the function of the nucleus locus coeruleus: A possible model for studies of anxiety. In I. Hanin & E. Usdin (Eds.), *Animal models in psychiatry and neurology*. New York: Pergamon Press, 1977. **539, 542, 547, 553, 554, 570, 571**

Redmond, D.E., Jr. New and old evidence for the involvement of a brain norepinephrine system in anxiety. In W.E. Fann, I. Karacan, A.D. Pokorny & R.L. Williams (Eds.), *Phenomenology and treatment of anxiety*. New York: Spectrum, 1979. **14, 15, 18, 21, 81, 541, 554**

Redmond, D.E., Jr. Clonidine and the primate locus coeruleus: Evidence suggesting anxiolytic and anti-withdrawal effects. In H. Lal & S. Fielding, *Psychopharmacology of clonidine*. New York: Alan R. Liss, 1981. **542, 552, 554**

Redmond, D.E., Jr. Central mechanisms and alpha-adrenergic receptors in opiate withdrawal and other psychiatric syndromes: New studies with clonidine. *Journal of Clinical Psychiatry*, 1982, *43* (Supplement), 1-48. **547**

Redmond, D.E., Jr., & Huang, Y.H. Current concepts II. New evidence for a locus coeruleus-norepinephrine connection with anxiety. *Life Science*, 1979, *25*, 2149-2162. **542, 543, 553, 570, 797**

Redmond, D.E., Jr., Huang, Y.H., Snyder, D.R., & Maas, J.W. Behavioral effects of stimulation of the nucleus locus coeruleus in the stump-tailed monkey (*Macaca arctoides*). *Brain Research*, 1976b, *116*, 502-510. **542, 553, 570**

Redmond, D.E., Jr., Huang, Y.H., Snyder, D.R., Maas, J.W., & Baulu, J. Behavioral changes following lesions of the locus coeruleus in Macaca arctoides. *Neuroscience Abstracts*, 1976a, *1*, 472. **553**

Redmond, D.E., Jr., & Krystal, J.H. Multiple mechanisms of withdrawal from opioid drugs. In W.M. Cowan (Ed.), *Annual review of neuroscience*, 1984, *7*, 443-478. **542, 552**

Reed, E.W., **285, 314, 353**

Reed, L., **121**

Regestein, Q.E., **61**

Regier, D.A., Muers, J.K., Kramer, M., Robins, L.N., Blazer, D.G., Hough, R.L., Eaton, W.W., & Locke, B.Z. Th NIMH epidemiologic catchment area

(ECA) program: Historical context, major objectives, and study population characteristics. *Archives of General Psychiatry*, 1984. **281, 282**

Régis, E., **744**

Reich, J.H., **416, 417**

Reich, T., **586, 587**

Reichlin, S., **67**

Rein, A., **365**

Reiser, M.F., **335**

Reiss, S., **376**

Reite, M., Short, R., Seiler, C., & Pauley, J.D. Attachment, loss, and depression. *Journal of Child Psychology and Psychiatry*, 1981, *22*, 141-169. **236, 389**

Rennie, T.A.C., **306**

Reppucci, N.D., & Saunders, J.T. Social psychology of behavior modification. *American Psychologist*, 1974, *29*, 649-660. **247**

Rescorla, R.A., **213**

Rescorla, R.A. Second-order conditioning: Implications for theories of learning. In F.J. McGuigan & D.B. Lumsden (Eds.), *Contemporary approaches to conditioning and learning*. New York: Winston, 1973, pp. 127-150. **214**

Rescorla, R.A. Effect of inflation of the unconditioned stimulus value following conditioning. *Journal of Comparative and Physiological Psychology*, 1974, *86*, 101-106. **210, 243**

Rescorla, R.A. Some implications of a cognitive perspective on Pavlovian conditioning. In S.H. Hulje, H. Fowler & W.K. Honig (Eds.), *Cognitive processes in animal behavior*. Hillsdale, NJ: Lawrence Erlbaum Associates, 1978. **153**

Rescorla, R.A., & Heth, C.D. Reinstatement of fear to an extinguished conditioned stimulus. *Journal of Experimental Psychology: Animal Behavior Processes*, 1975, *104*, 88-96. **210**

Rescorla, R.A., & LoLordo, V.M. Inhibition of avoidance behavior. *Journal of Comparative and Physiological Psychology*, 1965, *59*, 406-412. **227, 228-29**

Rest, S., **121**

Reynolds, C.F., III, Shaw, D.H., Newton, T.F., Coble, P.A., & Kupfer, D.J. EEG Sleep in outpatients with generalized anxiety: A preliminary comparison with depressed outpatients. *Psychiatry Research*, 1983, *8*, 81-89. **567, 786, 795**

Reynolds, C.R., & Paget, K.D. Factor analysis of the Revised Children's Manifest Anxiety Scale for blacks, whites, males and females with a national normative sample. *Journal of Consulting and Clinical Psychology*, 1981, *49*, 352-359. **709**

Reynolds, C.R., & Richmond, B.O. What I think and feel: A revised measure of children's manifest anxiety. *Journal of Abnormal Psychology*, 1978, *6*, 271-280. **708**

Reynolds, D. *Morita psychotherapy*. Berkeley: University of California Press, 1976. **316, 317**

Reynolds, D.J., **252**

Reyntjens, A.M., & van Mierlo, F.P. A comparative double-blind trial of pimoxide in stress-induced psychic and functional disorders. *Current Medical Research and Opinion*, 1972, *1*, 116-122. **540**

Reznicek, V., **525**

Reznick, J.S., **420**

Rhead, C. The role of pregenital fixations in agoraphobia. *Journal of the American Psychoanalytic Association*, 1969, *17*, 848-861. **603**

Rhoads, J.M., **617**

Rhymes, J., **379**

Riccio, D.C., **212, 221, 469**

Riccio, D.C., & Silvestri, R. Extinction of avoidance behavior and the problem of residual fear. *Behaviour Research and Therapy*, 1973, *11*, 1-9. **233**

Rice, K.M., & Blanchard, E.B. Biofeedback in the treatment of anxiety disorder. *Clinical Psychology Review*, 1982, *2*, 557-577. **441**

Richards, C.S., & Siegel, L.F. Behavioral treatment of anxiety states and avoidance behaviors in children. In D. Margolin II (Ed.), *Child behavior therapy*. New York: Gardner Press, Inc., 1978. **372, 373**

Richards, J.G., **29, 33, 34, 35**

Richardson, D.W., **350**

Richardson, F., **429**

Richman, N., Stevenson, J.E., & Graham, P.J. Prevalence of behavior problems in three-year old children: An epidemiologic study in a London borough. *Journal of Child Psychology and Psychiatry*, 1975, *16*, 277-287. **284**

Richmond, B.O., **708**

Rick, D.F., **658**

Rickels, K., **677**

Rickels, K. Use of anti-anxiety agents in anxious outpatients. *Psychopharmacology*, 1978, *58*, 1-17. **12, 585**

Rickels, K. Recent advances in anxiolytic therapy. *Journal of Clinical Psychiatry*, 1981, *42*, (section 2), 40-44. **516, 517**

Rickels, K., Downing, R.W., & Winokur, A. Antianxiety drugs: Clinical use in psychiatry. In L.L. Iversen, S.D. Iversen & S.H. Snyder (Eds.), *Handbook of psychopharmacology* (Vol. 13). New York: Plenum, 1978. **79**

Rickels, K., Pereira-Ogan, J., Case, W., Osanalos, I., Mirman, M., Nathanson, J., & Parish, L. Chlormezanone in anxiety: A drug rediscovered? *American Journal of Psychiatry*, 1974, *131*, 592-595. **518, 522**

Rickels, K., Weisman, K., Norstad, N., Singer, M., Stoltz, D., Brown, A., & Danton, J. Buspirone and diazepam in anxiety: A controlled study. *Journal of Clinical Psychiatry*, 1982, *43*, 12 (Part 2), 81-86. **516, 517, 538, 545**

Rickels, K., Weisse, C., Feldman, H., Fee, E.M., & Wiswesser, G. Loxapine

Robins, L.N. *The Vietnam drug user returns: Final report, Sept. 1973.* Washington, D.C.: Special Action Office Monograph, Ser. A, No. 2, U.S. Government Printing Office, 1974. **541**

Robins, L.N., Helzer, J.E., Croughan, J., & Ratcliffe, K. National institute of mental health diagnostic interview schedule: Its history, characteristics and validity. *Archives of General Psychiatry,* 1981, *38,* 381-389. **281, 282, 310, 677**

Robinson, D.S., **543, 555**

Robinson, D.S., Nies, A., Ravaris, C.L., & Lomborn, K.R. The monoamine oxidase inhibitor pheneizine in the treatment of depressive-anxiety states. *Archives of General Psychiatry,* 1973, *29,* 407-413. **543**

Robinson, E., **95, 252, 467, 468, 469**

Robinson, J.S., **414**

Robson, R.D., **34**

Rocha, A.V., **519, 540**

Rodin, E. Metrazol tolerance in a "normal" volunteer population. *Electroencephalography and clinical neurophysiology.* 1958, *10,* 433-446. **551**

Rodriguez, A., Rodriguez, M., & Eisenberg, L. The outcome of school phobia. *American Journal of Psychiatry,* 1959, *116,* 540-544. **400**

Rodriguez, M., **400**

Roffwarg, H., **65**

Rohrbaugh, M., & Riccio, D. Paradoxical enhancement of learned fear. *Journal of Abnormal Psychology,* 1970, *75,* 210-216. **469**

Ronan, J.A., **351**

Ròper, G., & Rachman, S. Obsessional-compulsive checking: Replication and development. *Behaviour Research and Therapy,* 1975, *14,* 25-32. **225**

Ròper, G., Rachman, S., & Hodgson, R. An experiment on obsessional checking. *Behaviour Research and Therapy,* 1973, *11,* 271-277. **225**

Ròper, G., Rachman, S., & Marks, I.M. Passive and participant modeling in exposure treatment of obsessive-compulsive neurotics. *Behaviour Research and Therapy,* 1975, *13,* 271-279. **428**

Roscoe, B., **538**

Rose, R.M., **59, 61, 63, 74, 345**

Rose, R.M., & Hurst, M.W. Plasma cortisol and growth hormone responses to intravenous catheterization. *Journal of Human Stress,* 1975, *1,* 22-36. **62, 63, 65, 68**

Rose, R., Jenkins, C., Hurst, M. *Air Traffic Controller Health Change Study.* Boston, Boston University School of Medicine, 1978. **359**

Rosen, B.M., Bahn, A.K., & Kramer, M. Demographic and diagnostic characteristics of psychiatric clinic outpatients in the U.S.A., 1961. *American Journal of Orthopsychiatry,* 1964, *34,* 455-468. **719**

Rosen, G., **319**

Rosenbaum, J.F. The drug treatment of anxiety. *New England Journal of Medicine,* 1982, *306,* 401-404. **79**

Rosenbaum, R.M., **121**

Rosenberg, C. Family aspects of obsessional neurosis. *British Journal of psychiatry*, 1967, *113*, 405-413. **584**

Rosenblatt, A.D., & Thickstun, J.T. Modern psychoanalytic concepts in a general psychology. *Psychological Issues*, 1977, *11* (2/3) (Monograph 42/43). **602**

Rosencrans, J.A., **543**

Rosenman, R.H., **68, 365**

Rosenman, R.H., Friedman, M., Straus, R., Wurm, R., Kositchek, R., Hahn, W., & Werthessen, N.T. A predictive study of coronary heart disease. The western collaborative group study. *Journal of the American Medical Association*, 1964, *189*, 15-22. **365**

Rosenthal, D. *Genetics of Psychopathology*. New York: McGraw-Hill, 1971. **236**

Rosenthal, N.R., **55, 65**

Rosenthal, S., & Bowden, C.L. A double-blind comparison of thioridazine (Mellaril) versus diazepam (Valium) in patients with chronic mixed anxiety and depressive symptoms. *Current Therapeutic Research*, 1973, *15*, 261-267. **520, 523, 540**

Rosenthal, T., **375, 791**

Rosenwald, G.C. Effectiveness of defenses against anal impulse arousal. *Journal of Consulting and Clinical Psychology*, 1972, *39*, 292-298. **613**

Rosie, R., **65**

Ross, D.C., **397, 400, 486, 511, 512, 514, 515**

Ross, J., **147, 148, 149**

Ross, L., **702**

Ross, R.R. Positive and negative partial-reinforcement extinction effects carried through continuous reinforcement, changed motivation, and changed response. *Journal of Experimental Psychology*, 1964, *68*, 492-502. **229, 230**

Ross, W.B., Wetterberg, L., & Myrhed, M. Genetic control of plasma dopamine-beta-hydroxylase. *Life Sciences*, 1973, *12*, 529-532. **555**

Roth, M., **66, 747, 754, 773**

Roth, M. The phobic anxiety-depersonalization syndrome. *Proceedings of the Royal Society of Medicine*, 1959, *52*, 587-595. **xviii, 560**

Roth, M. The phobic anxiety-depersonalization syndrome and some general aetiological problems in psychiatry. *Journal of Neuropsychiatry*, 1960, *1*, 293-306. **293, 558**

Roth, M. A classification of affective disorders based on a synthesis of new and old concepts. In E. Meyer III & J.V. Brady (Eds.), *Research in the psychobiology of human behavior*. Baltimore: Johns Hopkins University Press, 1979. **16, 17, 19**

Roth, M. Agoraphobia, panic disorder and generalized anxiety disorder: Some implications of recent advances. *Psychiatric Developments*, 1984, *2*, 31-52. **775, 778**

Roth, M., Gurney, C., Garside, R.F., & Kerr, T.A. Studies in the classification of affective disorder. The relationship between anxiety states and depressive illnesses -I. *British Journal of Psychiatry*, 1972, *121*, 147-161. **328, 366, 747**

Roth, M., & Harper, M. Temporal lobe epilepsy and the phobic anxiety, depersonalization syndrome. Part II. Protetical and theoretical considerations. *Comprehensive Psychiatry*, 1962, *3*, 215-226. **558**

✳ Roth, M., & Mountjoy, C.Q. The distinction between anxiety states and depressive disorders. In E.S. Paykel (Ed.), *Handbook of affective disorders*. New York: Guilford Press, 1982, pp. 70-92. **748, 750, 789, 790, 795**

Roth, R.H., **536, 548, 570, 571**

Roth, W.T., **367**

Rothballer, A.M. The effects of catecholamines on CNS. *Pharmacological Reviews*, 1959, *2*, 494-547. **550**

Rothschild, M.A., **737**

Routh, D.K., **372**

Routenberg, A. The two-arousal hypothesis: Reticular formation and limbic system. *Psychological Review*, 1968, *75*, 51-80. **139**

Roy, A. (Ed.) *Hysteria*. New York: Wiley, 1982. **669**

Roy-Byrne, P.P., **558, 559, 561, 568, 569**

Roy-Byrne, P.P., Uhde, T.W., Post, R.M., King, A.C., & Buchsbaum, M.S. Normal pain sensitivity in patients with panic disorder. *Psychiatry Research*, in press. **565**

Rozin, P., & Kalat, J.W. Specific hungers and poison avoidance as adaptive specializations of learning. *Psychological Review*, 1971, *78*, 459-487. **206, 208**

Rubel, A., **315**

Rubel, A., O'Nell, C., & Collada-Ardon, R.C. *Susto, A folk illness*. Berkeley, CA: University of California Press, in press. **315**

Rubin, R.T., **71, 339, 344**

Rubin, R.T., Miller, R.C., Clark, B.R., Poland, R.E., & Arthur, R.J. The stress of aircraft carrier landings. II: 3-methoxy-4-hydroxyphanyl-glycol excretion in naval aviators. *Psychosomatic Medicine*, 1970, *32*, 589-597. **345**

Rubin, R.T., Rahe, R.H., Arthur, R.J., & Clark, B.R. Adrenal cortical activity changes during underwater demolition team training. *Psychosomatic Medicine*, 1969, *31*, 553-564. **344**

Rudzik, A.D., Hesster, J.B., Tang, A.H., Straw, R.N., & Friis, W. Triazolobenzodiazepines, a new class of central nervous system-depressant compounds. In S. Garattini, E. Mussini & L.O. Randall (Eds.), *The benzodiazepines*. New York: Raven Press, 1973, pp. 285-297. **539**

Ruebush, B.K., **708**

Rusalova, M.N., Izard, C.E., & Simonov, P.V. Comparative analysis of mimical and autonomic components of man's emotional state. *Aviation, Space, and Environmental Medicine*, 1975, *46*, 1132-1134. **116**

Rush, A.J., **431, 705**

Rushmer, R.F. *Cardiovascular dynamics*. Philadelphia: Saunders, 1970. **335**

Ruskin, A., Beard, O.W., & Schaffer, R.L. "Blast hypertension": elevated arterial pressure in victims of the Texas City disaster. *American Journal of Medicine*, 1948, *4*, 228-235. **347**

Russell, D.C. Clinical clues of neurohumoral interpretation of the genesis of arrhythmias. Paper presented at workshop on: *Acute effect of psychological stress on functional cardiovascular system. Models and clinical assessment.* Pisa, Italy, 1983. **346**

Russell, J.A., **135, 136, 155, 485**

Russell, J.A. Affective space is bipolar. *Journal of Personality and Social Psychology*, 1979, *37* (3), 345-356. **115, 135, 485**

Russell, J.A. A circumplex model of affect. *Journal of Personality and Social Psychology*, 1980, *39*, 1161-1178. **135, 136, 168, 690**

Russell, J.A., & Mehrabian, A. Evidence for a three-factor theory of emotions. *Journal of Research in Personality*, 1977, *11*, 273-294. **135, 136**

Russell, J.A., & Ridgeway, D. Dimensions underlying children's emotional concepts. *Developmental Psychology*, 1983, *19*, 795-804. **416**

Rutter, M., **370, 386**

Rutter, M. *Children of Sick Parents: An Environmental and Psychiatric Study.* Maudsley Monographs 16, Institute of Psychiatry. London: Oxford University Press, 1966. **293**

Rutter, M. *Maternal deprivation reassessed* (2nd ed.) New York: Penguin Books, 1981. **377**

Rutter, M., Tizard, J., & Whitmore, K. *Education, health, and behavior.* New York: Wiley, 1970. **373, 712**

Ryle, J.A. Nosophobia. *Journal of Mental Science*, 1948, *94*, 1-17. **744**

Ryman, D.H., Biersner, R.J., & La Rocco, J.M. Reliabilities and validities of the mood questionnaire. *Psychological Reports*, 1974, *35*, 479-484. **135**

Sabshin, M.A., **60, 65**

Sachar, E.J., **58, 61, 83, 359, 780**

Sachar, E.J., Fishman, J.R., & Mason, J.W. Influence of hypnotic trance on plasma 17-hydroxycorticosteroid concentration. *Psychosomatic Medicine*, 1965, *27*, 330-341. **58**

Sackett, G.P. Monkeys reared in isolation with pictures as visual inputs: Evidence for an innate releasing mechanism. *Science*, 1966, *154*, 1468-1472. **217**

Sahley, T.L., Panksepp, J., & Slovick, A.J. Cholinergic modulation of separation distress in the domestic chick. *European Journal of Pharmacology*, 1981, *72*, 261-264. **526**

St. George, S., **365**

St. Lawrence, W., **737**

Sakai, K., **31**

Sakheim, D.K., **150, 499, 500**

Salapetek, P., **605**

Salis, M., **36**

Salman, S., **17, 18, 19, 20**

Salmon, P. *The effect of propranolol on emotional behaviour in rats.* Unpublished doctoral dissertation, Oxford University, 1983. **21**

Salmon, P., & Gray, J.A. Opposing acute (anxiolytic?) and chronic (anxiogenic?) behavioural effects of a beta-blocker, propranolol, in the rat. *Psychopharmacology,* in press. **21, 22**

Salt, P., **114, 116**

Saltzman, H.A., Heyman, A., & Sieber, H.O. Correlation of clinical and physiologic manifestations of hyperventilation. *New England Journal of Medicine,* 1963, *268,* 1431-1433. **350**

Salzer, H.M. Relative hypoglycemia as a cause of neuropsychiatric illness. *Journal of the National Medical Association,* 1966, *58,* 12-17. **569**

Salzman, L., & Thaler, F. Obsessive-compulsive disorders: A review of the literature. *American Journal of Psychiatry,* 1981, *138,* 286-296. **507, 508, 585**

Sameroff, A.J., & Chandler, M. Reproductive risk and the continuum of caretaking casualty. In F.D. Horowitz (Ed.), *Review of the child development research, Volume 4.* Chicago: University of Chicago Press, 1976, pp. 187-244. **414, 415**

Sampson, H., **612**

Samuel, J.R., Grange, R.A., & Hawkins, T.D. Anesthetic technique for carotid angiography. *Anaesthesia,* 1968, *23,* 543-546. **350**

Samuels, L.T., **56, 58, 59**

Sande, E., **350**

Sanderson, R., **206**

Sandler, J., & Hazari, A. The obsessional: On the psychological classification of obsessional character traits and symptoms. *British Journal of Medical psychology,* 1960, *33,* 113-122. **470**

Sandler, M., **538**

Sandwisch, D., **74**

Sanghera, M.K., McKillen, B.A., German, D.C. Buspirone, a non-benzodiazepine anxiolytic, increases locus coeruleus noradrenergic neuronal activity. *European Journal of Pharmacology,* 1983, *86,* 107-110. **545, 592**

Sano, M.C., **12**

Santrock, J.W., **149**

Sarason, B.R., **94, 97**

Sarason, I.G., **94, 120, 132, 171-72, 176, 178, 179-81, 241, 533**

Sarason, I.G. The relationship of anxiety and "lack of defensiveness" to intellectual performance. *Journal of Consulting Psychology,* 1956, *20,* 220-222. **120**

Sarason, I.G. Interrelationships among individual difference variables, behavior in psychotherapy, and verbal conditioning. *Journal of Abnormal and Social Psychology,* 1958, *56,* 339-344. **180**

Sarason, I.G. Test anxiety and cognitive modeling. *Journal of Personality and Social Psychology*, 1973, *28*, 58-61. **96**

Sarason, I.G. The Test Anxiety Scale: Concept and research. In C.D. Spielberger & I.G. Sarason (Eds.), *Stress and Anxiety* (Vol. 5). Washington: Hemisphere, 1978, pp. 193-216. **180**

Sarason, I.G. Three lacunae of cognitive therapy. *Cognitive Therapy and Research*, 1979, *3*, 223-235. **102**

Sarason, I.G. *Stress, anxiety, and cognitive interference: Reactions to tests*. Arlington, VA: Office of Naval Research, 1982. **498**

Sarason, I.G. *Worry and attentional orientation*. Unpublished study. Seattle, WA: University of Washington, 1983. **97**

Sarason, I.G. Stress, anxiety, and cognitive interference: Reactions to tests. *Journal of Personality and Social Psychology*, 1984, *46*, 929-938. **93, 704, 705**

Sarason, I.G., & Basham, R.B. Unpublished study. Seattle, WA: University of Washington, 1983. **94**

Sarason, I.G., & Ganzer, V.J. Anxiety, reinforcement and experimental instructions in a free verbal situation. *Journal of Abnormal and Social Psychology*, 1962, *65*, 300-307. **180**

Sarason, I.G., & Minard, J. Test anxiety, experimental instructions, and the Wechsler Adult Intelligence Scale. *Journal of Educational Psychology*, 1962, *53*, 299-302. **120**

Sarason, I.G., & Sarason, B.R. Teaching cognitive and social skills to high school students. *Journal of Consulting and Clinical Psychology*, 1981, *49*, 908-918. **97**

Sarason, I.G., & Stoops, R. Test anxiety and the passage of time. *Journal of Consulting and Clinical Psychology*, 1978, *46*, 102-109. **94**

Sarason, S.B., **120, 660**

Sarason, S.B. Anxiety, intervention, and the culture of the school. In C.D. Spielberger (Ed.), *Anxiety: Current trends in theory and research*. New York: Academic Press, 1972. **109, 120**

Sarason, S.B., Davidson, K.S., Lighthall, F.F., Waite, P.R., & Ruebush, B.K. *Anxiety in elementary school children: A report of research*. New York: Wiley, 1960. **120, 708**

Sargant, W., **750**

Sarnoff, I., & Corwin, S.M. Castration anxiety and the fear of death. *Journal of Personality*, 1959, *27*, 374-385. **614**

Sarnoff, I., & Zimbardo, P.G. Anxiety, fear and social affiliation. *Journal of Abnormal and Social Psychology*, 1961, *62*, 356-363. **613**

Sartorius, N., **742, 746, 753**

Sartorius, N. Epidemiology of anxiety. *Pharmakopsychiatrie Neuropsychopharmakologie* (Stuttgart), 1980, *13*, 249-253. **304, 557, 735**

Sartorius, N., Davidian, H., Ernberg, G., Fenton, F.R., Fujii, I., Gastpar, M., Gulbinat, W., Jablensky, A., Kielholz, P., Lehmann, H.E., Naraghi, M.,

Shimizu, M., Shinfuku, N., & Takahashi, R. *Depressive disorders in different cultures.* Report on the WHO collaborative study on standardized assessment of depressive disorders. WHO, Geneva, 1983. **746**

Sartory, G., **454, 456, 497**

Sartory, G. Some psychophysiological issues in behavioral psychotherapy, *Behavioral Psychotherapy*, 1981, *9*, 215-230. **134**

Sartory, G., Rachman, S., & Grey, S.J. Return of fear: The role of rehearsal. *Behaviour Research and Therapy*, 1982, *20*, 123-136. **363, 438, 465**

Sartory, G., Rachman, S.J., & Grey, S.J. An investigation of the relation between reported fear and heart rate. *Behaviour Research and Therapy*, 1977, *15*, 425-438. **132**

Saunders, J.T., **247**

Saxena, B., **505, 507**

Scarr, S., & Salapetek, P. Patterns of fear development during infancy. *Merrill Palmer Quarterly*, 1970, *16*, 53-90. **605**

Scarth, L., **392, 393, 511, 513**

Schachter, J. Pain, fear and anger in hypertensives and normotensives. *Psychosomatic Medicine*, 1957, *19*, 17-28. **137**

Schachter, S. The interaction of cognitive and physiological determinants of emotional state. In L. Berkowitz (Ed.), *Advances in experimental social psychology* (Vol. 1). New York: Academic Press, 1964. **139, 157**

Schachter, S. The interaction of cognitive and physiological determinants of emotional state. In C.D. Spielberger (Ed.), *Anxiety and behavior*. New York: Academic Press, 1966. **499**

Schachter, S. *Emotion, obesity and crime.* New York: Academic Press, 1971. **110, 112, 114**

Schacter, S., & Singer, J.E. Cognitive, social, and physiological determinants of emotional state. *Psychological Review*, 1962, *69*, 379-399. **111, 113, 534, 550**

Schacter, S., & Singer, J.E. Cognitive, social, and physiological determinants of emotional state. In C.D. Spielberger (Ed.), *Anxiety and behavior*. New York: Academic Press, 1966. **534, 550**

Schaefer, E.S., & Plutchik, R. Interrelationships of emotions, traits, and diagnostic constructs. *Psychological Reports*, 1966, *18*, 399-419. **135, 146**

Schafer, R. The termination of brief psychotherapy. *International Journal of Psychoanalytic Psychotherapy*, 1973, *2*, 135-148. **615**

Schaffer, H.R. Cognitive components of the infant's response to strangers. In M. Lewis & L.A. Rosenblum (Eds.), *The origins of fear*. New York: Wiley, 1974. **113**

Schaffer, R.L., **347**

Schaffner, R., **11, 13, 14, 28, 29, 32, 33, 34, 35, 38, 538**

Schalch, D.S., **67, 68, 340**

Schaneberg, S., **63, 358**

Schlesser, M.A., Winokur, G., & Sherman, B.M. Hypothalamic-pituitary-adrenal axis activity in depressive illness: Its relationship to classification. *Archives of General Psychiatry*, 1980, *37*, 737-743. **66**

Schlosberg, H.S., **416**

Schlosberg, H.S. The description of facial expression in terms of two dimensions. *Journal of Experimental Psychology*, 1952, *44*, 229-237. **135**

Schlosberg, H.S. Three dimensions of emotion. *Psychological Review*, 1954, *61*, 81-88. **117**

Schmid, P.G., Eckstein, J.W., & Abboud, F.M. Effects of 9-alpha-fluro-hydrocortisone on forearm vascular responses to norepinephrine. *Circulation*, 1966, *34*, 620-626. **346**

Schmid, R.G., **349**

Schmidt, M.I., **569**

Schmiechen, R., **32, 34**

Schneirla, T.C. An evolutionary and developmental theory of bi-phasic processes underlying approach and withdrawal. In M.R. Jones (Ed.), *Nebraska symposium on motivation*. Lincoln: University of Nebraska Press, 1959. **139, 156**

Schnurer, A., **429**

Schofield, L., **132, 165, 363, 497**

Schon, F., **538, 539**

Schork, M.A., **347**

Schotistaedt, W.W., **58**

Schraa, J.C., **650, 652**

Schreiner, B.F., **67, 68, 340**

Schroder, H.-Th., **563**

Schroeder, H.E., **708**

Schull, W.J., **347**

Schulman, A.H., & Kaplowitz, C. Mirror-image response during the first two years of life. *Developmental Psychobiology*, 1977, *10*, 133-142. **418**

Schulman, J., **369, 371, 379**

Schulterbrandt, J.B., Raskin, A., & Reatig, N. Further replication of factors of psychopathology in the interview, ward behavior and self-reported ratings of hospitalized depressed patients. *Psychological Reports*, 1974, *34*, 23-32. **689**

Schultes, H., **563**

Schur, M. The ego in anxiety. In R.M. Loewenstein (Ed.), *Drives, affects, behavior*. New York: International Universities Press, 1953. **603**

Schwank, A., **551**

Schwartz, B. On going back to nature: A review of Seligman and Hager's biological boundaries of learning. *Journal of the Experimental Analysis of Behavior*, 1974, *21*, 183-198. **206, 208**

Schwartz, B.J. The measurement of castration anxiety and anxiety over loss of love. *Journal of Personality*, 1955, *24*, 204-219. **614**

Schwartz, G.E., **114, 119, 383**

Schwartz, G.E. Psychophysiological patterning and emotion revisited: A systems perspective. In C.E. Izard (Ed.), *measuring emotions in infants and children*. New York: Cambridge University Press, 1982. **109, 113, 116**

Schwartz, G.E., Brown, S.L., & Shern, G.L. Facial muscle patterning and subjective experience during affective imagery: Sex differences. *Psychophysiology*, 1980, *17*, 75-82. **138**

Schwartz, G.E., Fair, P.L., Greenberg, P.S., Freedman, M., & Klerman, J.L. Facial electromyography in the assessment of emotion. *Psychophysiology*, 1974, *11*, 237. **116**

Schwartz, G.E., Fair, P.L., Salt, P., Mandel, M.R., & Klerman, G.L. Facial muscle patterning to affective imagery in depressed and non-depressed subjects. *Science*, 1976, *192*, 489-491. **114, 116**

Schwartz, G.E., Weinberger, D.A., & Singer, B.A. Cardiovascular differentiation of happiness, sadness, anger, and fear following imagery and exercise. *Psychosomatic Medicine*, 1981, *43*, 343-364. **338**

Schwartz, J.P., **43**

Schwartz, S., **71**

Schwartz, W.B., **349**

Scott, J.P. Effects of psychotropic drugs on separation distress in dogs. *Neuropsychopharmacology*. Proceedings IX Congress CINP 1981. Paris, Excerpta Medica, Amsterdam. **527**

Scuvee-Moreau, J.J., & Dresse, A.E. Effect of various antidepressant drugs on the spontaneous firing rates of locus coeruleus and dorsal raphe neurons of the rat. *European Journal of Pharmacology*, 1979, *57*, 219-225. **545**

Seaman, S.F., **527**

Seat, P.D., **708**

Sechter, D., **563**

Secord, P.F., **247**

Secunda, S., **65, 544**

Sedvall, G., **66**

Sega, R., **349**

Segal, M., **542**

Segal, M. The effects of brainstem priming stimulation on interhemispheric hippocampal responses in the awake rat. *Experimental Brain Research*, 1977a, *28*, 529-541. **9**

Segal, M. Excitability changes in rat hippocampus during conditioning. *Experimental Neurology*, 1977b, *55*, 67-73. **9**

Segi, J., **349**

Seidner, M.L., **254**

Seifter, J., **14, 32, 541**

Seiler, C., **236, 389**

Seligman, M.E.P., **16, 17, 121, 203, 209, 231-32, 239, 240, 242**

Seligman, M.E.P. Chronic fear produced by unpredictable electric shock. *Journal of Comparative and Physiological Psychology*, 1968, *66*, 402-411. **239, 240**

Seligman, M.E.P. On the generality of the laws of learning. *Psychological Review*, 1970, *77*, 408-418. **206, 207, 208**

Seligman, M.E.P. Phobias and preparedness. *Behavior Therapy*, 1971, *2*, 307-320. **200, 204, 206, 209, 242, 267, 376**

Seligman, M.E.P. Depression and learned helplessness. In R.J. Friedman & M.M. Katz (Eds.), *The psychology of depression: Contemporary theory and research*. Washington: Winston-Wiley, 1974, pp. 83-113. **xxi, 200, 239, 242**

Seligman, M.E.P. *Helplessness: On depression, development, and death*. San Francisco: W.H. Freeman, 1975. **xxi, 17, 120, 156, 238, 239, 240, 477, 623**

Seligman, M.E.P., & Binik, Y. Safety signal hypothesis. In H. Davis & H. Hurwitz (Eds.), *Operant-Pavlovian interactions*. Hillsdale, NJ: Lawrence Erlbaum Associates, 1977, pp. 165-180. **239, 240**

Seligman, M.E.P., & Hager, J. (Eds.). *Biological boundaries of learning*. New York: Appleton-Century-Crofts, 1972. **114, 206, 265, 600**

Seligman, M.E.P., & Johnston, J. A cognitive theory of avoidance learning. In F.J. McGuigan & D.B. Lumsden (Eds.), *Contemporary approaches to conditioning and learning*. New York: Wiley, 1973, pp. 69-110. **230, 242, 375, 459**

Selye, H. Thymus and adrenals in the response of the organism to injuries and intoxications. *British Journal of Experimental Pathology*, 1936, *17*, 234-248. **55**

Selye, H. *The stress of life* (rev. ed.). New York: McGraw-Hill, 1956. **173**

Selye, H. The stress concept and some of its implications. In V. Hamilton & D.M. Warburton (Eds.), *Human stress and cognition*. New York: Wiley & Sons, 1979. **115**

Sepinwall, J., **539**

Seraganian, P., **71**

Sergeant, H.G.S., **425**

Sergi, J., **349**

Sermat, V., **416**

Sermet, O. Emotional and medical factors in child dental anxiety. *Journal of Child Psychology and Psychiatry*, 1974, *15*, 313-321. **371**

Serra, M., **36**

Sethy, V.H., & Hodges, D.H. Role of beta-adrenergic receptors in the antidepressant activity of alprazolam. *Research Communications in Chemical Pathology and Pharmacology*, 1982, *36*, 329-332. **530**

Sewitch, T.S., & Kirsch, I. The cognitive content of anxiety: naturalistic evidence for the predominance of threat-related thoughts. *Cognitive Therapy and Research*, 1984, *8*, 49-58. **194**

Shader, R.I., **79, 538, 546, 552**

Shader, R.I., Goodman, M., & Gever, J. Panic disorders: Current perspectives. *Journal of Clinical Psychopharmacology*, 1982, *1*, 8s. **288**

Shader, R.I. *Journal of Clinical Psychopharmacology*, 1984, *4*, in press. **593**

Shalker, T.E., **143**

Shapira, K., **747, 754, 773**

Shapira, K., Roth, M., Kerr, T.A., & Gurney, C. The prognosis of affective disorders: The differentiation of anxiety from depressive illness. *British Journal of Psychiatry*, 1972, *121*, 175-181. **747**

Shapiro, A.K., **677**

Shapiro, A.K., Struening, E.L., Shapiro, E., & Milcarek, B.I. Diazepam: How much better than placebo. *Journal of Psychiatric Research*, 1983, *17*, 51-73. **80**

Shapiro, E., **80**

Shapiro, M. A method of measuring psychological changes specific to the individual psychiatric patient. *British Journal of Medical Psychology*, 1961, *34*, 151-155. **643**

Shapiro, M. A clinical approach to fundamental research with special reference to the study of the single patient. In P. Sainsbury & N. Kreitman (Eds.), *Methods of psychiatric research*. New York: Oxford University Press, 1963. **643**

Shapiro, M. The single case in clinical-psychological research. *Journal of General Psychology*, 1966, *74*, 3-23. **643**

Shapiro, T., & Stern, D. Psychoanalytic perspectives on the first year of life: The establishment of the object in an affective field. In S. Greenspan & G. Pollock (Eds.), *The course of life: Vol. I, Infancy and early childhood*. Adelphi, MD: National Institute of Mental Health (Mental Health Study Center), 1980. **605**

Sharma, S. Cross-cultural comparisons of anxiety: Methodological problems. *Topics in Culture Learning*, 1977, *5*, 166-173. **299, 302**

Shattan, S., **534, 550**

Shaw, B.F., **431, 705**

Shaw, D.H., **567, 786, 795**

Shaw, E.G., & Rought, D.K. Effects of mothers' presence on children's reactions to aversive procedures. *Journal of Pediatric Psychology*, 1982, *7*, 33-42. **372**

Shaw, J., **13, 15, 40**

Shaw, M.A., **372**

Shaw, O. Dental anxiety in children. *British Dental Journal*, 1975, *139*, 134-139. **371, 375**

Shaw, P. A comparison of three behaviour therapies in the treatment of social phobia. *British Journal of Psychiatry*, 1979, *134*, 620-623. **426**

Shaw, P.M., **194, 220, 425, 426, 428, 438**

Shear, M.K., **370, 377, 619, 641, 642, 700**

Shearman, G.T., **36**

Sheehan, D.V., **780**

＊ Sheehan, D.V. Current concepts in psychiatry: Panic attacks and phobias. *New England Journal of Medicine*, 1982, *307*, 156-158. **509, 510, 512**

Sheehan, D.V., Ballenger, J., & Jacobson, G. Treatment of endogeneous anxiety with phobic, hysterical and hypochondriacal symptoms. *Archives of General Psychiatry*, 1980, *37*, 51-59. **511, 513, 543**

Sheehan, D.V., Ballenger, J., & Jacobson, G. Relative efficacy of monoamine oxidase inhibitors and tricyclic antidepressants in the treatment of endogenous anxiety. In D. Klein & J. Rabkin (Eds.), *Anxiety: New research and changing concepts*. New York: Raven Press, 1981. **513**

＊ Sheehan, D.V., & Sheehan, K.H. The classification of anxiety and hysterical states. Part I. Historical review and empirical delineation. *Journal of Clinical Psychopharmacology*, 1982, *2*, 235-243. **749**

＊ Sheehan, D.V., & Sheehan, K.H. The classification of phobic disorders. *International Journal of Psychiatry in Medicine*, 1983, *12*, 243-266. **787, 789, 790**

Sheehan, K.H., **779, 787, 789, 790**

Sheehan, M.B., Clavcomb, J.B., Surman, O.S., Baer,L., Coleman, J., & Gelles, L. Panic attacks and the dexamethasone suppression test. *American Journal of Psychiatry*, 1983, *140*, 1063-1064. **67**

Shemer, A., **20**

Shepherd, M. Contributions of epidemiological research to the classification and diagnosis of mental disorders. In *Proceedings of the WHO/ADAMHA international conference on classification and diagnosis of mental disorders and alcohol- and drug-related problems, Copenhagen, 13-17 April 1982* (in press). **735**

Sherman, A.D., **18**

Sherman, A.D., & Petty, F. Specificity of the learned helplessness animal model of depression. *Pharmacology, Biochemistry and Behavior*, 1982, *16*, 449-454. **17**

Sherman, B.M., **66**

Sherman, D., **82, 586, 749**

Shern, G.L., **138**

Sheth, A., **523, 540**

Shettleworth, S. Constraints on learning. In D.S. Lehrman, R.A. Hinde & E. Shaw (Eds.), *Advances in the study of behavior* (Vol. 4). New York: Academic Press, 1972. **206**

Sheward, J., **65**

Shields, J.M., **236, 286, 325, 365**

Shigetomi, C., **372**

Shih, J., **563**

Shimizu, M., **746**

Shinfuku, N., **746**

Shipley, R.H., Butt, J.H., & Horwitz, B.A. Preparation to re-experience a stressful medical examination: Effect of repetitious videotape exposure and coping style. *Journal of Consulting and Clinical Psychology*, 1978, *46*, 499-507. **384**

Shirakawa, I., **547, 549**

Sholiton, R., **132**

Shore, J., **310**

Shore, P.A., **544**

Short, J., **505, 508, 509, 585**

Short, R., **236, 389**

Shulman, R.S., **546**

Shur, E., **563**

Sides, J.K., **438, 466**

Sidman, M. Some properties of warning stimulus in avoidance behavior. *Journal of Comparative and Physiological Psychology*, 1955, *48*, 444-450. **226**

Sidman, M. *Tactics of scientific research*. New York: Basic Books, 1960. **643**

Sidman, M. Avoidance behavior. In W. K. Honig (Ed.), *Operant behavior: Areas of research and application*. New York: Appleton-Century-Crofts, 1966, pp. 448-498. **228**

Sieber, H.O., **350**

Siegel, L.F., **xviii, 372, 373**

Siegel, L.J., **708**

Siegel, L.J., & Harkavy, J. The effects of filmed modeling as a prehospital preparatory on children with previous hospital experience. *Journal of Consulting and Clinical Psychology*, submitted for publication. **384**

Siegel, S.E., **372, 712**

Siever, L.J., **547, 562, 563, 565, 567, 570, 571, 588**

Siever, L.J., Insel, T.R., Jimerson, D.C., Lake, C.R., Uhde, T.W., Aloi, J., & Murphy, D.L. Growth hormone response to clonidine in obsessive-compulsive patients. *British Journal of Psychiatry*, 1983, *142*, 184-187. **563, 564, 588**

Siever, L.J., & Uhde, T.W. New studies and perspectives on the noradrenergic receptor system in depression: effects of the alpha-2 adrenergic agonist clonidine. *Biological Psychiatry*, 1984, *19*, 131-156. **563, 571, 572**

Sifneos, P.M., **167**

Sifneos, P.M. *Short-term psychotherapy and emotional crisis*. Cambridge: Harvard University Press, 1972. **703**

Silberman, E.K., **547**

Silberman, E.K., Post, R.M., Nurnberger, J.R., Theodore, W., & Boulenger, J.-P. Transient sensory, cognitive and affective phenomena in affective illness: a comparison with complex partial epilepsy. *British Journal of Psychiatry*, 1984, in press. **558-59**

Silverstone, T., **514, 515, 546, 750**

Silvestri, R., **233**

Simon, J.A., **661**

Simon, P., **11, 31**

Simon, P., & Soubrié, P. Behavioral studies to differentiate anxiolytic and sedative activity of the tranquilizing drugs. In J.R. Boissier (Ed.), *Modern problems in pharmacopsychiatry* (Vol. 14). Basel: Karger, 1979. **30**

Simon, W., **573**

Simonov, P.V., **116**

Simons, A.D., Garfield, S.L., & Murphy, G.E. The process of change in cognitive therapy and pharmacotherapy for depression. *Archives of General Psychiatry*, 1984, *41*, 45-54. **195**

Simons, R. The resolution of the latah paradox. *Journal of Nervous and Mental Disease*, 1980, *168*, 195-206. **313**

Simons, R. Latah II - Problems with a purely symbolic interpretation: A reply to Michael Kenny. *Journal of Nervous and Mental Disease*, 1983, *171*, 168-175. **313**

Simons, R.F., **153, 159**

Sine, L.F., **499**

Singer, B.A., **338**

Singer, J.E., **111, 113, 534, 550**

Singer, J.L. *Imagery and daydream methods in psychotherapy and behavior modification*. New York: Academic Press, 1974. **159**

Singer, J.L., & Antrobus, J.S. Daydreaming, imaginal processes, and personality: A normative study. In P. Sheehan (Ed.), *The function and nature of imagery*. New York: Academic Press, 1972. **470**

Singer, M., **516, 517, 538, 545**

Singer, M.T., **335**

Singh, A.N., & Saxena, B. Clomipramine (Anafranil) in depressive patients with obsessive neurosis. *Journal of International Medical Research*, 1977, *5*, Suppl. 5, 25-32. **505, 507**

Singleton, W., **514, 515, 546, 750**

Sinyor, D., Schwartz, S., Peronnet, F., Brisson, G., & Seraganian, P. Aerobic fitness level and reactivity to psychosocial stress: physiological, biochemical and subjective measures. *Psychosomatic Medicine*, 1983, *45*, 205-217. **71**

Sitaram, N., **568, 569, 795**

Sjostrand, I.-G., **519, 522, 540**

Skeeters, D.E., **646**

Skerritt, J.H., Johnston, G.A.R., & Braestrup, C. Modulation of GABA binding to rat brain membranes by alkyl β-carboline-3-carboxylate esters. *European Journal of Pharmacology*, 1983, *86*, 299-302. **36**

Skerritt, P.W. Anxiety and the heart - a historical review. *Psychological Medicine*, 1983, *13*, 17-25. **737**

Skipper, J.K., Jr., Leonard, R.G., & Rhymes, J. Child hospitalization and social interaction: An experimental study of mothers' feelings of stress, adaptation, and satisfaction. *Medical Care*, 1968, *6*(6), 496-506. **379**

Sklair, F., **561**

Skolnick, P., **28, 31, 38, 39, 40, 48, 49, 81, 538, 539, 552, 573**

Skolnick, P., Syapin, P.J., Paugh, B.A., Moncada, V., Marangos, P.J., & Paul, S.M. Inosine, an endogenous ligand of the brain benzodiazepine receptor, antagonizes pentylenetetrazole-evoked seizures. *Proceedings of the National Academy of Sciences USA*, 1979, *76*, 1515-1518. **48**

Slade, A.P., **563**

Slater, E. The neurotic constitution. *Journal of Neurology and Psychiatry*, 1943, *6*, 1. **749**

Slater, E., & Shields, J. Genetical aspects of anxiety. *The British Journal of Psychiatry*. Special Publication No. 3, M.H. Lader (Ed.), *Studies of Anxiety*. 1969, 62-71. **236, 286, 325**

Sletten, I., **571**

Sloane, R.B., Staples, F.R., Cristol, A.H., Yorkston, N.J., & Whipple, K. *Psychotherapy versus behavior therapy*. Cambridge, MA: Harvard University Press, 1975. **612**

Slovick, A.J., **526**

Slymen, D., **285, 288, 294, 325, 328, 329, 538, 682, 780, 793**

Smart, J.V., **546**

Smith, A., **378**

Smith, D.F., **646**

Smith, E., **235, 243**

Smith, M.L., Glass, G.V., & Miller, T.I. *The benefits of psychotherapy*. Baltimore: Johns Hopkins University Press, 1980. **612**

Smith, T., Ingram, R.E., & Brehm, S.S. Social anxiety, anxious self-preoccupation, and recall of self-relevant information. *Journal of Personality and Social Psychology*, 1983, *44*, 1276-1283. **95**

Smith, T.C., Cooperman, L.H., & Wollman, H. The therapeutic gases: oxygen, carbon dioxide, helium and water vapor. In A.G. Gilman, L.S. Goodman, A. Gilman, S.E. Mayer & K.L. Melmon, (Eds.), *Goodman and Gilman's the pharmacological basis of therapeutics* (6 ed.). New York: Macmillan Publishing Col., 1980. **551**

Smith, T.W. Change in irrational beliefs and the outcome of rational-emotive psychotherapy. *Journal of Consulting and Clinical Psychology*, 1983, *51*, 156-157. **93**

Smith, V.K., **548**

Snezhnevsky, A.V. (Ed.). *Handbook of Psychiatry* (Vol. I and II). Moscow: Medicina, 1983. **739**

Snidman, N., **420**

Snowman, A.S., **540**

Snyder, D.R., **542, 553, 570**

Snyder, S.H., **15, 541, 550**

Snyder, S.M., **541**

Sobisky, R., **34**

Soeldner, J.S., **569**

Sofka, M., **471**

Sokoloff, L., **534, 550**

Sokolov, Y.N. *Perception and the conditioned reflex.* New York: Macmillan, 1963. **156, 168**

Solano, C., **681**

Solomon, H.C., **137**

Solomon, K., & Hart, R. Pitfalls and prospects in clinical research on antianxiety drugs: Benzodiazepines and placebo - a research review. *Journal of Clinical Psychiatry*, 1978, *39*, 823-831. **79**

Solomon, R.L., **242**

Solomon, R.L., Kamin, L.J., & Wynne, L.C. Traumatic avoidance learning: The outcomes of several extinction procedures with dogs. *Journal of Abnormal and Social psychology*, 1953, *48*, 291-302. **203, 205, 220, 223**

Solomon, R.L., & Turner, L.H. Discriminative classical conditioning in dogs paralyzed by curare can later control discriminative avoidance responses in the normal state. *Psychological Review*, 1962, *69*, 202-219. **229**

Solyom, C., **375, 376**

Solyom, L., **538**

Solyom, L., Beck, P., Solyom, C., & Hugel, R. Some etiological factors in phobic neurosis. *Canadian Psychiatric Association Journal*, 1974, *19*, 69-78. **375, 376**

Solyom, L., & Sookman, D.A. Comparison of clomipramine hydrochloride (Anafranil) and behavior therapy in the treatment of obsessive neurosis. *Journal of International Medical Research*, 1977, *5*, Suppl. 5, 49-61. **505, 507**

Somerville, W., **342**

Sondheim, D., **49**

Sonnenschein, R.R., **137**

Sookman, D.A., **505, 507**

Sorce, J.F., **417, 418**

Sorce, J.F., & Emde, R.N. Mother's presence is not enough: The effect of emotional availability on infant exploration. *Developmental Psychology*, 1981, *17*, 737-745. **417**

Sorce, J.F., Emde, R.N., Campos, J., & Klinnert, M.D. Maternal emotional signaling: Its effect on the visual cliff behavior of one-year-olds. *Developmental Psychology*, in press. **417**

Soubrié, P., **7, 11, 30**

Soubrié, P., Thiebot, M.H., & Simon, P. Enhanced suppressive effects of aversive events induced in rats by picrotoxin: possibility of a GABA control on behavioral inhibition. *Pharmacology, Biochemistry and Behavior*, 1979, *10*, 463-469. **11**

Sparr, L., & Pankratz, L.D. Factitious post-traumatic stress disorder. *American Journal of Psychiatry*, 1983, *140*, 1016-1019. **295**

Spence, J.T., & Spence, K.W. The motivational components of manifest anxiety: Drive and drive stimuli. In C.D. Speilberger (Ed.), *Anxiety and behavior*. London: Academic Press, 1966. **138**

Spence, K.W., **138, 646**

Spencer, H. *The principles of psychology* (Vol. I) (1855). New York: Appleton, 1890. **111, 117**

Sperry, R. Neurology and the mind-brain problem. *American Scientist*, 1952, *40*, 291-312. **151**

Spiegel, J.P., **427, 611**

Spielberger, C.D., **177, 647, 649, 660, 662**

Spielberger, C.D. Theory and research on anxiety. In C.D. Spielberger (Ed.), *Anxiety and behavior*. New York: Academic Press, 1966, pp. 3-20. **176, 177, 657**

Spielberger, C.D. Anxiety as an emotional state. In C.D. Spielberger (Ed.), *Anxiety: Current trends in theory and research* (Vol. 1). New York: Academic Press, 1972, pp. 23-49. (a). **90, 120, 139, 168, 175, 176, 177, 655, 658, 664**

Spielberger, C.D. Conceptual and methodological issues in anxiety research. In C.D. Spielberger (Ed.), *Anxiety: Current trends in theory & research* (Vol. II). New York: Academic Press, 1972. (b). **176, 177, 658**

Spielberger, C.D. Emotional reactions to surgery. *Journal of Consulting and Clinical Psychology*, 1973, *40* (1), 33-38. (a). **659, 708**

Spielberger, C.D. Anxiety: State-trait process. In C.D. Spielberger & I.G. Sarason (Eds.), *Stress and anxiety* (Vol. 1). Washington, DC: Hemisphere/Wiley, 1975a, pp. 115-141. **176, 177**

Spielberger, C.D. The measurement of state and trait anxiety: Conceptual and methodological issues. In L. Levi (Ed.), *Emotions-their parameters and measurement*. New York: Raven Press, 1975b. **176, 177**

Spielberger, C.D. Stress anxiety and cardiovascular disease. *Journal of the South Carolina Medical Association*, 1976a, (no vol.) 15-22. **177, 660, 655**

Spielberger, C.D. State-trait anxiety and interactional psychology. In D. Magnusson & N.S. Endler (Eds.), *Personality at the crossroads: Current issues in interaction psychology*. Hillsdale, NJ: Lawrence Erlbaum Associates, 1977. pp. 173-184. **176, 660**

Spielberger, C.D. *Understanding stress and anxiety*. New York: Harper & Row, 1979. **176, 177**

Spielberger, C.D. *Test anxiety inventory: Preliminary professional manual*. Palo Alto, CA: Consulting Psychologists Press, 1980. **95, 180**

Spielberger, C.D. *Manual for the state-trait anxiety inventory (STAI Form Y)*. Palo Alto, CA: Consulting Psychologists Press, 1983. **176**

Spielberger, C.D. *State-trait anxiety inventory: A comprehensive bibliography*. Palo Alto, CA: Consulting Psychologists Press, 1984. **176, 177**

Spielberger, C.D., Anton, W.D., & Bedell, J. The nature and treatment of test anxiety. In M. Zuckerman & C.D. Spielberger (Eds.), *Emotions and anxiety: New concepts, methods, and applications*. New York: Lawrence Erlbaum Associates/Wiley, 1976. **660**

Spielberger, C.D., Auerbach, S.M., Wadsworth, A.P., Dunn, T.M., & Taulbee, E.S. Emotional reactions to surgery. *Journal of Consulting and Clinical Psychology*, 1973, *40*,33-38. **177**

Spielberger, C.D., & Diaz-Guerrero, R. (Eds.). *Cross-cultural anxiety*. Washington, D.C.: John Wiley and Sons, 1976. **300, 303**

Spielberger, C.D., Edwards, C.D., Lushene, R.E., Montouri, J., & Platzek, D. *STAIC: Preliminary manual*. Palo Alto, CA: Consulting Psychologists Press, 1973. **126**

Spielberger, C.D., Gorsuch, R.L., & Lushene, R.E. *Manual for the state-trait anxiety inventory*. Palo Alto, CA: Consulting Psychologist Press, 1970. **300, 565, 571, 657, 684, 689**

Spielberger, C.D., O'Neil, H.F., Jr., & Hansen, D.N. Anxiety, drive theory and computer assisted learning. In B.A. Maher (Ed.), *Progress in experimental personality research, Spielberger* (Vol. 6). 1972. **659**

Spielberger, C.D., Vagg, P.R., Barker, L.R., Donham, G.W., & Westberry, L.G. The factor structure of the state-trait Anxiety Inventory. In I.G. Sarason & C.D. Spielberger (Eds.), *Stress and anxiety*, (Vol. 7). Washington, D.C.: Hemisphere Press, 1980. **660**

Spinks, P., **302**

Spira, N., **512**

Spitz, R. *A genetic field theory of ego formation*. New York: International Universities Press, 1959. **414**

Spitz, R.A. Anxiety in infancy: A study of its manifestations in the first year of life. *International Journal of Psychoanalysis*, 1950, *31*, 138-143. **377, 605**

Spitzer, R.L., **328, 480, 676, 784, 786, 787, 788, 790, 796**

Spitzer, R.L., & Cantwell, D.P. The DSM-III classification of the psychiatric disorders of infancy,childhood, and adolescence. *Journal of the American Academy of Child Psychiatry*, 1980, *19*, 356-370. **720**

Spitzer, R.L., & Endicott, J. *Schedule for affective disorder and schizophrenia — lifetime version (3rd ed.)*. New York: Research Assessment and Training Unit New York State Psychiatric Institute, 1979. **394, 402**

Spitzer, R.L., Endicott, J., & Robins, E. *Research Diagnostic Criteria (RDC) for a selected group of functional disorders* (3rd ed). New York: Biometrics Research, New York State Psychiatric Institute, 1978. **60, 275**

Spitzer, R.L., & Williams, J.B.W. *Instruction manual for the structured clinical interview for DSM-III (SCID)*, revision of 2/14/1983. New York: Biometrics Research, New York State Psychiatric Institute, 1983. **677, 773, 783**

Spizzirri, C.L., **114**

Springer, K.J., **614**

Squires, R.F., **28, 537**

Squires, R.F., & Braestrup, C. Benzodiazepine receptors in rat brain. *Nature (London)*, 1977, *266*, 732-734. **538**

Srinivasamurthy, U., **519**

Srole, L., Langner, T.S., Michael, S.T., Opter, M.K., & Rennie, T.A.C. *Mental health in the metropolis: The midtown manhattan study.* New York: McGraw-Hill, 1962. **306**

Sroufe, L.A. Wariness of strangers and the study of infant development. *Child Development*, 1977, *48*, 731-746. **605**

Sroufe, L.A. The coherence of individual development. *American Psychologist*, 1979, *34*, 834-841. **377**

Sroufe, L.A., Fox, N., & Pancake, V.R. Attachment and dependency in developmental perspective. *Child Development*, 1983, *54*, 1615-1627. **377**

Sroufe, L.A., & Rutter, M. The domain of developmental psychopathology. *Child Development*, 1984, *55*, 17-29. **370, 386**

Sroufe, L.A., Waters, E., & Matas, L. Contextual determinants of infant affective response. In M. Lewis & L.A. Rosenblum (Eds.), *The origins of fear*. New York: Wiley, 1974. **140**

Stampfl, T.G. Implosive therapy: The theory, the subhuman analogue, the strategy, and the technique, Part 1: The theory. In S.G. Armitage (Ed.), *Behavior modification techniques in the treatment of emotional disorders*. Battle Creek, MI: V.A. Publications, 1967. **426**

Stampfl, T.G., & Levis, D.J. Essentials of implosive therapy: A learning-theory-based psychodynamic behavioural therapy. *Journal of Abnormal Psychology*, 1967, *72*, 496-530. **220**

Stanfield, C.A., **351**

Stanley, J., **643**

Staples, F.R., **612**

Stark, C.G., **49**

Starr, M.D., & Mineka, S. Determinants of fear over the course of avoidance learning. *Learning and Motivation*, 1977, *8*, 332-350. **205, 212, 227, 243**

Stattin, H., **122**

Stattin, H., & Magnusson, D. Stability of perceptions of own reactions across a variety of anxiety-provoking situations. *Perceptual and Motor Skills*, 1980, *51*, 959-967. **122**

Staub, E., Tursky, B., & Schwartz, G.E. Self-control and predictability: Their effects on reactions to aversive stimulation. *Journal of Personality and Social Psychology*, 1971, *18*, 157-162. **383**

Stefanis, C., **428**

Stein, A., **350**

Stein, L., Wise, C.D., & Belluzzi, J.D. Effects of benzodiazepines on central serotonergic mechanisms. In E. Costa & P. Greengard (Eds.), *Mechanism of action of benzodiazepines*. New York: Raven Press, 1975. **35, 36, 539**

Steinbook, R., **519, 522, 540**

Steiner, M., **66, 67**

Steinman, M.W., **573**

Steketee, G., **98, 106, 144, 423, 428, 429, 438, 439, 446, 465, 585, 692**

Steketee, G., & Foa, E.B. Obsessive-compulsive disorders. In D.H. Barlow (Ed.), *Behavioral treatment of adult disorders*. New York: Guilford Press, 1981. **496**

Steketee, G., Foa, E.B., & Grayson, J.B. Recent advances in the behavioral treatment of obsessive-compulsives. *Archives of General Psychiatry*, 1982, *39*, 1365-1371. **428, 429**

Stenberg, C., **114, 417, 418**

Stenberg, C. *The development of anger expressions in infancy*. Unpublished dissertation, 1982. **417**

Stenberg, C., Campos, J., & Emde, R.N. The facial expression of anger in infancy. *Child Development*, 1983, *54*, 178-184. **417**

Stephens, J., **525**

Stephenson, F.A., **540**

Stern, D., **605**

Stern, D.N. General issues in the study of fear. In M. Lewis & L.A. Rosenblum (Eds.), *The origins of fear*. New York: Wiley, 1974. **605**

Stern, D.N. Affect attunement. In J. Call, E. Galenson & R. Tyson (Eds.), *Frontiers of infant psychiatry - II*. New York: Basic Books, 1984. **420**

Stern, R.M., **372**

Stern, R.S., **368, 434, 506, 507, 586**

Stern, R.S. Obsessive thoughts: the problem of therapy. *British Journal of Psychiatry*, 1978, *132*, 200-205. **426**

Stern, R.S., & Cobb, J.P. Phenomenology of obsessive - compulsive neurosis. *British Journal of Psychiatry*, 1978, *132*, 233-239. **747**

Stern, R.S., & Marks, I.M. Brief and prolonged flooding: A comparison in agoraphobic patients. *Archives of General Psychiatry*, 1973, *28*, 270-276. **428, 438**

Stern, S., **350**

Sternbach, L.H. The discovery of CNS active 1,4 benzodiazepines. In E. Costa (Ed.), *The benzodiazepines: From molecular biology to clinical practice*. New York: Raven Press, 1983. **27**

Sternberg, D.E., **529, 542, 548, 552, 563, 571**

Stevenson, J., Burrows, G., & Chiu, E. Comparison of low doses of haloperidol and diazepam in anxiety states. *Medical Journal of Australia*, 1976, *1*, 451-459. **519, 523, 540**

Stevenson, J.E., **284**

Stevenson, M.K., Kanfer, F.H., & Higgins, J.M. Effects of goal specificity and time cues on pain tolerance. *Cognitive Research and Therapy*, in press. **254**

Stewart, J., **508, 670**

Stewart, L.H. Manifest anxiety and mother-son identification. *Journal of Clinical Psychology*, 1958, *14*, 382-384. **647**

Stewart, W. *Psychoanalysis: The first ten years, 1888-1898*. New York: MacMillan, 1967. **602, 610**

Stockham, M.A., **58**

Stokes, P.E., **58, 68**

Stokes, P.E. Studies on the control of adrenocortical function in depression. In T. Williams, M. Katz & J.A. Shields (Eds.) *Recent advances in the psychobiology of the depressive illnesses*. U.S. Government Printing Office, Washington, D.C., 1972. **60, 65**

Stokes, P.E., Pick, G.R., Stoll, P.M., & Nuun, W.D. Pituitary adrenal function in depressed patients: resistance to dexamethasone suppression. *Journal of Psychiatric Research*, 1975, *12*, 275-281. **65**

Stokes, P.E., Stoll, P.M., Koslow, S.H., Maas, J.W., Swann, A.C., & Robins, E. Pretreatment hypothalamic-pituitary-adrenocortical function in depressed patients and comparison groups: A multi-center study. *Archives of General Psychiatry*, 1984, *41*, 257-267. **58, 60, 66, 67**

Stoll, P.M., **58, 60, 65, 66, 67**

Stoltz, D., **516, 517, 538, 545**

Stoltzman, R., **xxx, 282, 283**

Stone, E.A. Subsensitivity to norepinephrine as a link between adaptation to stress and antidepressant therapy: an hypothesis. *Research Communications in Psychology, Psychiatry and Behavior*, 1979, *4*, 241-255. **16, 19**

Stone, J.G., **69**

Stone, N.M., & Borkovec, T.D. The paradoxical effect of brief CS exposure on analogue phobic subjects. *Behaviour Research and Therapy*, 1975, *13*, 51-54. **469**

Stone, W.N., **546**

Stone, W.N., Gleser, G.C., & Gottschalk, L.A. Anxiety and beta-adrenergic blockade. *Archives of General Psychiatry*, 1973, *29*, 620-622. **546**

Stoops, R., **94**

Stout, R.W. *Hormones in atherosclerosis*. Lancaster: MTP Press, 1982. **346**

Stoyva, J.M., **475**

Strahlendorf, H.K., & Strahlendorf, J.C. Iontophoretically applied benzodiazepines inhibit locus coeruleus unit activity. *Neuroscience Abstracts*, 1981, *7*, 793. **539**

Strahlendorf, J.C., **539**

Straus, E. On obsession: a clinical and methodological study. *Nervous and Mental Disorders Monograph No. 73*, 1948. **579**

Straus, R., **365**

Straw, R.N., **539**

Strober, M., **125, 126**

Strom, G., **82**

Strombom, U., **552**

Strong, E.K., **653**

Strosahl, K.D., & Ascough, J.C. Clinical uses of mental imagery: Experimental foundations, theoretical misconceptions, and research issues. *Psychological Bulletin*, 1981, *89*, 422-438. **159**

Struening, E.L., **80**

Study, R.E., & Barker, J.L. Diazepam and (-)pentobarbital: Fluctuation analysis reveals different mechanisms for potentiation of gamma amino butyric acid responses in cultured central neurons. *Proceedings of the National Academy of Sciences* 1981, *78*, 7180-7184. **28, 40, 540**

Sturgis, C.C., **81, 534, 550**

Suematsu, H., **67, 68**

Suh, H.K., **69**

Suhayl, N., **512**

Suinn, R.M., & Richardson, F. Anxiety management training: A non-specific behavior therapy program for anxiety control. *Behavior Therapy*, 1971, *2*, 498-511. **429**

Sullivan, H.S. In H.S. Perry & M.L. Gawel (Eds.), *Interpersonal theory of psychiatry*. New York: W.W. Norton, 1953. **603**

Sulser, F., **544**

Sulser, F. Tricyclic antidepressants: animal pharmacology (biochemical and metabolic aspects). In L.L. Iversen, S.D. Iversen & S.H. Snyder (Eds.), *Handbook of psychopharmacology, Vol. 14: Affective disorders: drug action in animals and man*. New York: Plenum Press, 1978. **16, 18**

Sulser, F. Pharmacology: Current antidepressants. *Psychiatric Annals*, 1980, *9*, 381-386. **797**

Sulser, F., Vetulani, J., & Mobley, P.L. Mode of action of antidepressant drugs. *Biochemical Pharmacology*, 1978, *27*, 257-261. **544**

Sumida, K., **300-01**

Sunland, D.M., **571**

Suomi, S.J., **224, 236**

Suomi, S.J., & Harlow, H.F. Production and alleviation of depressive behaviors in monkeys. In J. Maser & M.E.P. Seligman (Eds.), *Psychopathology: Experimental models*. San Francisco: Freeman, 1977, pp. 131-173. **xxi, 200**

Suomi, S.J., Kraemer, G.W., Baysinger, C.M., & DeLizio, R.D. Inherited and experiential factors associated with individual differences in anxious behavior displayed by rhesus monkeys. In D.F. Klein & J. Rabkin (Eds.), *Anxiety: New research and changing concepts*. New York: Raven Press, 1981, pp. 179-200. **236**

Suomi, S.J., Seaman, S.F., Lewis, J.K., DeLizio, R.D., & McKinney, W.T., Jr. Effects of imipramine treatment of separation-induced social disorders in rhesus monkeys. *Archives of General Psychiatry*, 1978, *35*, 321-325. **527**

Supavilai, P., **33**

Suria, A., **28, 33, 35**

Surman, O.S., **67**

Surman, O.S., Sheehan, D.V., Fuller, T.C., & Gallo, J. Panic disorder in genotypic HLA identical sibling pairs. *American Journal of Psychiatry*, 1983, *104*, 237-238. **780**

Suzman, M.M. Propranolol in the treatment of anxiety. *Postgraduate Medicine Journal*, 1976, *52*, 168-174. **546**

Svejda, M.J., **417**
Svendsen, M., **746**
Svensson, T.H., **547, 550, 551**
Svensson, T.H., Bunney, B.S., & Aghajanian, G.K. Inhibition of both noradrenergic and serotonergic neurons in brain by the alpha-adrenergic agonist clonidine. *Brain Research*, 1975, *92*, 291-306. **547**
Svensson, T.H., Persson, R., Wallin, L., & Walinder, J. Anxiolytic action of clonidine. *Nordisk Psykiatrisk Tidsskrift*, 1978, *32*, 439-441. **547**
Svensson, T.H., & Strombom, U. Discontinuation of chronic clonidine treatment. Evidence for facilitated brain noradrenergic neurotransmission. *Naunyn-Schmiedebergs Archiv für Pharmakologie*, 1977, *299*, 83-87. **552**
Svensson, T.H., & Usdin, T. Feedback inhibition of brain noradrenalin neurons by tricyclic antidepressants: Alpha-receptor mediation. *Science*, 1978, *202*, 1089-1091. **528, 544**
Swahn, C.G., **66**
Swann, A., **58, 60, 65, 66, 67, 544**
Swanson, B.M., **382**
Sweeney, D.R., **15**
Swenson, W.M., **646**
Syapin, P.J., **28, 48, 81, 573**
Syapin, P.J., & Skolnick, P. Characterization of benzodiazepine binding sites in cultured cells of neural origin. *Journal of Neurochemistry*, 1979, *32*, 1047-1051. **40**
Sylvester, D., **165, 279, 284, 293, 372, 747**
Syvalahti, E., Lammintausta, R., & Pekkarinen, A. Effect of psychic stress of examination on serum growth hormone, serum insulin, and plasma renin activity. *Acta Pharmacologia et Toxicologica*, 1976, *38*, 344-352. **67, 341**
Szeda, M., **146-47, 169**
Szewczak, M., **543**
Szursk, S., **746**

Taggart, P., & Carruthers, M. Endogenous hyperlipedemia induced by emotional stress of racing driving. *Lancet*, 1971, *1*, 363-366. **342**
Taggart, P., Carruthers, M., & Somerville, W. Electrocardiogram, plasma catecholamines, and lipids, and their modification by oxprenolol when speaking before an audience. *Lancet*, 1973, *2*, 341-346. **342**
Takahashi, R., **746**
Takemoto-Chock, N.K., **696**
Talbot, A., **379**
Tallman, J.F., **40**
Tallman, J.F., Paul, S.M., Skolnick, P., & Gallager, D.W. Receptors for the age of anxiety. *Science*, 1980, *207*, 274-281. **538, 539**
Tallman, J.F., Thomas, J.W., & Gallager, D.W. GABAergic modulation of benzodiazepine binding site sensitivity. *Nature*, 1978, *274*, 383-385. **33**

Tamai, J., **67, 68**

Tang, A.H., **539**

Tarazi, R.C., **82, 546, 551**

Tarika, J., **66, 67**

Tatsuoka, M.M., **696**

Taulbee, E.S., **177**

Taylor, C.B., **367, 456**

Taylor, J.A., **646, 662, 666, 667**

Taylor, J.A. The relationship of anxiety to the conditioned eyelid response. *Journal of Experimental Psychology*, 1951, *42*, 183-188. **708**

Taylor, K.M., & Laverty, R. The effect of chlordiazepoxide, diazepam and nitrazepam on catecholamine metabolism in regions of the rat brain. *European Journal of Pharmacology*, 1969, *8*, 296-301. **539**

Taylor, M., **82, 780**

Taylor, P.P., **372, 379**

Tearman, B., **456**

Teasdale, J.D., **121, 239, 240**

Teasdale, J.D. Learning models of obsessional-compulsive disorder. In H.R. Beech (Ed.), *Obsessional states*. London: Methuen and Co., 1974, pp. 197-229. **224, 226, 227, 228, 229**

Teasdale, J.D., & Fogarty, S.J. Differential effect of induced mood on retrieval of pleasant and unpleasant events from episodic memory. *Journal of Abnormal Psychology*, 1979, *88*, 248-257. **143**

Telch, M., Tearman, B., & Taylor, C.B. Antidepressant medication in the treatment of agoraphobia. *Behaviour Research and Therapy*, 1983, *21*, 505-518. **456**

Telch, M.J., Agras, W.S., Taylor, C.B., Roth, W.T., & Gallen, C.C. Combined pharmacological and behavioral treatment for agoraphobia: A controlled trial. In preparation. **367**

Tellegen, A., **xxiii, 485, 486, 500, 689, 690, 691, 703**

Tellegen, A. *Brief manual for the differential personality questionnaire*. Unpublished manuscript, University of Minnesota. **682, 694**

Tengblad, C.F., **351**

Tennes, K., Downey, K., & Vernadakis, A. Urinary cortisol excretion rates and anxiety in normal 1-year old infants. *Psychosomatic Medicine*, 1977, *39*, 178-187. **62, 63**

Tennyson, R.D., & Boutwell, R.C. Pretask versus within-task anxiety measures in predicting performance on a concept acquisition task. *Journal of Educational Psychology*, 1973, *65* (1), 88-92. **659**

Terwilliger, J.S., & Fiedler, F.E. An investigation of determinant inducing individuals to seek personal counseling. *Journal of Consulting Psychology*, 1958, *22*, 288. **647**

Tessman, E., **405, 411**

Teste, D.V., **523, 540**

Thaler, F., **507, 508, 585**

Thaler, M., **56, 58, 62**

Thase, M.E., **568**

Thayer, R.E. Measurement of activation through self-report. *Psychological Reports*, 1967, *20*, 663-678. **689**

Thayer, R.E. Activation states as assessed by verbal report and four psychophysiological variables. *Psychophysiology*, 1970, *7*, 86-94. **682**

Thein, S.G., **518, 522**

Theodore, W., **558-59**

Thickstun, J.T., **602**

Thiebot, M.H., **11**

Thiebot, M.H., Jobert, A., & Soubrie, P. Effets compares du muscimol et du diazepam sur les inhibitions du comportement, induites chez le rat par la nouveaute, la punition et le non-renforcement. *Psychopharmacology*, 1979, *61*, 85-89. **7, 11**

Thomas, A., & Chess, S. *Temperament and development*. New York: Brunner/ Mazal, 1977. **382, 415**

Thomas, A., & Chess, S. Genesis and evolution of behavioral disorders: From infancy to early adult life. *American Journal of Psychiatry*, 1984, 141(1), 1-9. **415**

Thomas, A., Chess, S., & Birch, H.G. *Temperament and behavior disorders in children*. New York: New York University Press, 1968. **382, 383, 409, 411, 733**

Thomas, A., Chess, S., Birch, H.G., Hertzig, M., & Korn, S. *Behavioral individuality in early childhood*. New York: New York University Press, 1963. **376**

Thomas, D. Retention of conditioned inhibition in a bar-press suppression paradigm. *Learning and Motivation*, 1979, *10*, 161-177. **211**

Thomas, J.W., **33**

Thomas, W.S., **534, 550**

Thompson, R.F., **439**

Thompson, S.C. Will it hurt less if I can control it? A complex answer to a simple question. *Psychological Bulletin*, 1981, *90*, 89-101. **383**

Thompson, W.D., **286**

Thoren, P., **550, 551, 588**

Thoren, P., Asberg, M., Cronholm, B., Jornestedt, L., & Traskman, L. Clomipramine treatment of obsessive compulsive disorder: A controlled clinical trial. *Archives of General psychiatry*, 1980, *37*, 1281-1289. **503, 504, 529, 585, 586**

Thorn, G.W., Jenkins, D., Laidlaw, J.C., Goetz, F.C., & Reddy, W. Response of the adrenal cortex to stress in man. *Transactions Association of the American Physicians*, 1953, *66*, 48-64. **55**

Thorndike, E. *Fundamentals of learning*. New York: Teachers College, 1932. **208, 265, 268**

Thorpe, G., & Burns, S. *The agoraphobic syndrome.* Chichester: John Wiley, 1983. **367**

Ticku, M.K. The effects of acute and chronic ethanol administration and its withdrawal on GABA receptor binding in rat brain. *British Journal of Pharmacology,* 1980, *70,* 403-410. **11**

Tinbergen, N. *The study of instincts.* New York: Oxford University Press, 1951. **140**

Tischler, G.L., **282, 283**

Tizard, J., **373, 712**

Todd, P.B., **661**

Toffano, G., **7, 28, 538**

Toffano, G., Guidotti, A., & Costa, E. Purification of an endogenous protein inhibitor for the high affinity binding of gamma aminobutyric acid to synaptic membranes of rat brain. *Proceedings of the National Academy of Sciences U.S.A.,* 1978, *75,* 4024-4028. **43**

Tomkins, S.S., **122**

Tomkins, S.S. *Affect, imagery, and consciousness* (Vol. 1). *The positive affects.* New York: Springer, 1962. **110, 111, 114, 118**

Tomkins, S.S. *Affect, imagery, and consciousness* (Vol. 2). *The negative affects.* New York, Springer, 1963. **119**

Tomkins, S.S. Affect as amplification: Some modifications in theory. In P. Plutchik & Kellerman (Eds), *Emotion: theory, research, and experience* (Vol. 1). New York: Academic Press, 1980. **110**

Tompkins, E.H., **534, 550**

Tompkins, E.H., Sturgis, C.C., & Wearn, J.T. Studies in epinephrine. II. *Archives of Internal Medicine,* 1919, *24,* 247-268. **81**

Toolan, J.M. Masked depression in children and adolescents. In S. Lesse (Ed.), *Masked depression.* New York: Jason Aronson, 1974. **125**

Torgersen, S. The nature and origin of common phobic fears. *British Journal of Psychiatry,* 1979, *134,* 343-351. **168, 744, 749**

Torgersen, S. Genetic factors in anxiety disorders. *Archives of General Psychiatry,* 1983, *40,* 1085-1089. **329, 585, 793**

Traskman, L., **503, 529, 585, 586**

Traughber, B., & Cataldo, M. Biobehavioral effects of pediatric hospitalization. In J. Tuma (Ed.), *Handbook for the practice of pediatric psychology.* New York: Wiley, 1982. **371**

Tricamo, E., **670**

Trout, D.L., **341**

Trower, P., Yardley, K., Bryant, B.M., & Shaw, P. The treatment of social failure: A comparison of anxiety-reduction and skills acquisition procedures on two social problems. *Behavior Modification,* 1978, *2,* 41-60. **426**

Trumble, D., **205, 227, 243**

Tsaltas, E., **20**

Tseng, W., & Hsu, F. Minor psychological disturbances of everyday life. In H.

Triandis & J. Draguns (Eds.), *Handbook of cross-cultural psychology: Psychopathology* (Vol. 6). Boston: Allyn and Bacon, 1980. pp. 61-98. **299**

Tseng, W., & McDermott, J. *Culture, mind and therapy.* New York: Brunner/ Mazel, 1981. **299**

Tsivoni, D., Stein, A., Keren, A., & Stern, S. Electrocardiographic characteristics of neurocirculatory asthenia during everyday activities. *British Heart Journal*, 1980, *44*, 426-431. **350**

Tsujioka, B., & Cattell, R. A cross-cultural comparison of the second stratum questionnaire personality factor structures-anxiety and extraversion - in America and Japan. *Journal of Social Psychology*, 1965, *65*, 205-219. **300**

Tsukamoto, T., **529**

Turk, D., **429**

Turnbull, M.J., **13, 15, 40**

Turner, L.H., **229**

Turner, P., **546**

Turner, P., Granville-Grossman, K.L., & Smart, J.V. Effect of adrenergic receptor blockade on the tachycardia of thyrotoxicosis and anxiety states. *Lancet*, 1965, *2*, 1316-1318. **546**

Turner, R.H., **106, 692**

Turner, R.M., **428**

Turner, V. *The forest of symbols.* Ithaca, NY: Cornell University Press, 1967. **307**

Tursky, B., **383**

Tweney, R.D., Doherty, M.E., & Mynett, C.R. Null hypothesis testing. *On scientific thinking.* New York: Columbia University Press, 1981. **406, 411**

Twentyman, C.T., **169**

Tyl, M.M., **658**

Tyrer, P.J., **546**

Tyrer, P.J. *The role of bodily feelings in anxiety* (Maudsley Monographs, No. 23). London: Oxford University Press, 1976. **21, 82**

Tyrer, P.J. Anxiety states. In E.S. Paykel (Ed.), *Handbook of affective disorders.* Edinburgh: Churchill Livingston, 1982. **755**

Tyrer, P.J., & Lader, M.H. Response to propranolol and diazepam in somatic and psychic anxiety. *British Medical Journal*, 1974, *2*, 14-16. **525, 546**

Tyrer, P.J., & Lader, M.H. Central and peripheral correlates of anxiety: A comparative study. *Journal of Nervous and Mental Diseases*, 1976, *162*, 99-104. **741**

Tyrer, P.J., & Tyrer, S. School refusal, truancy, and adult neurotic illness. *Psychological Medicine*, 1974, *4*, 416-421. **293, 716**

Tyrer, S., **293, 716**

Uddenberg, C.E., **702**

Uhde, T.W., **551, 558, 563, 564, 565, 571, 572, 573, 574, 588**

Uhde, T.W., Boulenger, J.-P., Jimerson, D.C., & Post, R.M. Caffeine:

Relationship to human anxiety, plasma MHPG and cortisol. *Psychopharmacology Bulletin*, 1984, *20*, 426-430. **574, 795**

Uhde, T.W., Boulenger, J.-P., & Post, R.M. Psychopathological effects of caffeine in psychiatric patients and normal controls. *American College of Psychopharmacology Abstracts*, 1983, p. 35. **551**

Uhde, T.W., Boulenger, J.-P., Roy-Byrne, P.P., Geraci, M.F., Vittone, B.J., & Post, R.M. Longitudinal course of panic disorder: Clinical and biological considerations. *Progress in Neuro-Psychopharmacology and Biological Psychiatry*, in press. **558, 559, 561, 569**

Uhde, T.W., Boulenger, J.-P., Siever, L.J., DuPont, R.L., & Post, R.M. Animal models of anxiety: Implications for research in humans. *Psychopharmacology Bulletin*, 1982, *18*, 47-52. **565, 570, 571**

Uhde, T.W., Boulenger, J.-P., Vittone, B.J., & Post, R.M. Historical and modern concepts of anxiety: A focus on adrenergic function. In J.C. Ballenger (Ed.), *Biology of agoraphobia*. Washington, D.C.: American Psychiatric Press, 1984. **570, 571, 572**

Uhde, T.W., Boulenger, J.-P., Vittone, B.J., Siever, L.J., & Post, R.M. Human anxiety and noradrenergic function: Preliminary studies with caffeine, clonidine and yohimbine. *Proceedings of the 7th world congress of psychiatry*. New York: Plenum Press, 1984. **562**

Uhde, T.W., Post, R.M., Siever, L.J., & Buchsbaum, M.S. Clonidine and psychophysical pain. *Lancet*, 1980, *2*, 1375. **547**

Uhde, T.W., Post, R.M., Siever, L.J., Buchsbaum, M.S., Jimerson, D.C., Silberman, E.K., Murphy, D.L., & Bunney, W.E., Jr. Clonidine: Effects on mood, anxiety, and pain. *Psychopharmacology Bulletin*, 1981, *17*, 125-126. **547**

Uhde, T.W., Roy-Byrne, P.P., Gillin, J.C., Mendelson, W.B., Boulenger, J.-P., Vittone, B.J., & Post, R.M. The sleep of patients with panic disorder: A preliminary report. *Psychiatry Research*, 1984. **568**

Uhde, T.W., Siever, L.J., & Post, R.M. Clonidine: Acute challenge and clinical trial paradigms for the investigation and treatment of anxiety disorders, affective illness and pain syndromes. In R.M. Post & J.C. Ballenger (Eds.), *Neurobiology of mood disorders*. Baltimore: Williams & Wilkins, 1984. **563, 567, 570, 571**

Uhde, T.W., Siever, L.J., Post, R.M., Jimerson, D.C., Boulenger, J.-P., & Buchsbaum, M.S. The relationship of plasma-free MHPG to anxiety and psychophysical pain in normal volunteers. *Psychopharmacology Bulletin*, 1982, *18*, 129-132. **567, 570**

Uhde, T.W., Vittone, B.J., & Post, R.M. Glucose tolerance testing induces somatic symptoms but not panic attacks in patients with panic disorder. *American Journal of Psychiatry*, 1984. **569**

Uhlenhuth, E.H., **677, 678**

Uhlenhuth, E.H., Balter, M.B., Mellinger, G.D., Cisin, I.H., & Clinthorne, J. Symptom checklist syndromes in the general population: Correlations with psychotherapeutic drug use. *Archives of General Psychiatry*, 1983, *40*, 1167-1173. **281**

Uhlenhuth, E.H., Johanson, C.E., Kilgore, K., & Kobasa, S.C. Drug preference and mood in humans: Preference for d-amphetamine and subject characteristics. *Psychopharmacology*, 1981, *74*, 191-194. **676**

Uhlenhuth, E.H., Stephens, J., Dim, B., & Covi, L. Diphenylhydantoin and phenobarbitol in the relief of psychoneurotic symptoms. *Psychopharmacologia*, 1972, *27*, 67-84. **525**

Ultee, K.A., **427**

Unger, M. *Defensiveness in children as it influences acquisition of fear-relevant information.* Unpublished masters thesis, University of Florida, 1982. **384**

Uno, T. Effect of general excitement and of fighting on some ductless glands of male albino rats. *American Journal of Physiology*, 1922, *61*, 203-214. **55**

U'Prichard, D.C., **541**

Urwin, H., Baade, E., & Levine, S. *Psychobiology of stress. A study of coping men.* New York: Academic Press, 1978. **266, 334, 335, 343, 344**

Usa, S., **317**

Usdin, T., **528, 544**

Uviller, E.T., **132, 468**

Uzgiris, I. *Organization of sensorimotor intelligence.* New York: Plenum Publishing Corp., 1976. **414**

Vaccarino, F., **36**

Vaccarino, F., Costa, E., & Guidotti, A. Synaptosomal basic proteins: Differences from myelin basic proteins. *Society for Neuroscience Abstracts*, 1983, *9*, 1042. **44**

Vagg, P.R., **649, 660**

Vagg, P.R., Spielberger, C.D., & O'Hearn, T.P., Jr. Is the state-trait anxiety inventory multidimensional? *Personality and Individual Differences*, 1980, *1*, 207-214. **660**

Vaisanen, E. Psychiatric disorders in Finland. In T. Anderson, C. Astrup, & A. Forsdahl (Eds.), Social Somatic and Psychiatric Studies of Geographically Defined Populations. *Acta-Psychiatrica Scandinavica*, 1976, Supplement 263. **278**

Valentino, R.J., Foote, S.L., & Aston-Jones, G. Corticotropin-releasing factor activates noradrenergic neurons of the locus coeruleus. *Brain Research*, 1983, *270*, 363-367. **550**

Van de Helm, H., **433**

Van den Hout, M.A., **551**

Van den Hout, M.A., & Griez, E. Cardiovascular and subjective responses to inhalation of carbon dioxide: A controlled test with anxious patients. *Psychotherapy and Psychosomatics*, 1982, *37*, 75-82. **551**

Van den Steen, N., **504, 506, 586**

Vanderlaan, E.F., **71, 72**

Vander Maelen, C.P., **542**

Vanderveer, A. The psychopathology of physical illness and hospital residence. *Quarterly Journal of Child Behavior*, 1949, *1*, 55-71. **378**

Van Doren, T., **586, 587**

Van Kammen, D.P., **563**

Van Luijk, J.N., **304**

van Mierlo, F.P., **540**

Van Ness, P.C., **40**

Van Oot, P., Lane, T.W., & Borkovec, T.D. Sleep disturbance. In H.E. Adams & P.B. Sutker (Eds.), *Comprehensive handbook of psychopathology*. New York: Plenum, 1984. **472**

Van Valkenburg, C., **568, 786, 793, 794**

Van Valkenburg, C., Akiskal, H.S., Puzantian, V., & Rosenthal, T. Anxious depression: Clinical, family history, and naturalistic outcome comparisons with panic and major depressive disorders. *Journal of Affective Disorders*, 1984, *6*, 67-82. **791**

Van Zanten, B., **433**

Vaughan, M., **426**

Vaughan, M. The relationship between obsessional personality, obsession in depression and symptoms of depression. *British Journal of Psychiatry*, 1976, *129*, 36-39. **587**

Velley, L., Cardo, B., & Bockaert, J. Modulation of rat brain alpha-adrenoceptor populations four weeks after stimulation of the nucleus locus coeruleus. *Psychopharmacology*, 1981, *74*, 226-231. **555**

Velten, E. A laboratory task for induction of mood states. *Behaviour Research and Therapy*, 1968, *6*, 473-482. **143**

Velucci, S.V., & Webster, R.A. Modification of diazepam's antileptazol activity by endogenous tryptophan-like compounds. *European Journal of Pharmacology*, 1981, *76*, 255-259. **49**

Venham, L., Bengston, D., & Cipes, M. Children's responses to sequential dental visits. *Journal of Dental Research*, 1977, *56*, 454-459. **372**

Venkatesh, A., Pauls, O.L., & Crowe, R. Mitral valve prolapse in anxiety neurosis (panic disorder). *American Heart Journal*, 1980, *100*, 302-305. **365**

Venning, E.H., Dyrenfurth, I., & Beck, J.C. Effect of anxiety upon aldosterone excretion in man. *Journal of Clinical Endocrinology*, 1957, *17*, 1005-1007. **58**

Vermilyea, B.B., **482, 483, 489, 494**

Vermilyea, J.A., **482, 483, 489**

Vermilyea, J.A., Boice, R., & Barlow, D.H. Rachman and Hodgson (1974) a decade later: How do desynchronous response systems relate to the treatment of agoraphobia? *Behaviour Research and Therapy*, in press. **454, 496, 497**

Vernadakis, A., **62, 63**

Vernon, D.T.A., Foley, J., & Schulman, J. Effect of mother-child separation and birth order on young children's responses to two potentially stressful experiences. *Journal of Personality and Social Psychology*, 1967, *5*(2), 162-164. **369, 371, 379**

Versiani, M., Bueno, J., & Mundim, F. A double-blind comparison between loxapine and chlordiazepoxide in the treatment of anxiety. *Psychopharmacology Bulletin*, 1977, *13*, 22-24. **519**

Versiani, M., Bueno, J.R., Mundim, F.D., Dasilva, J.A.R., & Rocha, A.V. A double-blind comparison between loxapine and chlordiazepoxide in the treatment of neurotic anxiety. *Current Therapeutic Research*, 1976, *20*, 701-715. **519, 540**

Vetulani, J., **544**

Vetulani, J., & Sulser, F. Action of various antidepressant treatments reduces reactivity of noradrenergic cyclic AMP-generating system in limbic forebrain. *Nature* (London), 1975, *257*, 495-496. **544**

Vickers, M.D., **538**

Videbech, T. The psychopathology of anancastic endogenous depression. *Acta Psychiatrica Scandinavica*, 1975, *52*, 336-373. **587**

Viek, P., **212**

Vilberg, T., **526**

Vilhelmson, R., **350**

Vinar, O., Dostalova, J., Krsiak, M., Reznicek, V., & Ivanys, E. Controlled comparison of the therapeutic effects of natrium oxybutyrate and oxazepam. *Activa Nervosa Supplement*, (Praha) 1979, *21*, 156-159. **525**

Vinogradova, O.S. Functional organization of the limbic system in the process of registration of information: Facts and hypotheses. In R.L. Isaacson & K.H. Pribram (Eds.), *The Hippocampus: 2. Neurophysiology and Behavior*. New York: Plenum Press, 1975. **10**

Vittone, B.J., **559, 561, 562, 568, 569, 570, 571, 572**

Vlachakis, N.D., de Guia, D., Mendlowitz, M., Antram, S., & Wolf, R.L. Hypertension and anxiety. A trial with epinephrine and norepinephrine infusion. *Mount Sinai Journal of Medicine of New York*, 1974, *41*, 615-625. **82, 534, 550**

Vogel, C., **512**

Vogel, J.R., Beer, B., & Clody, D.E. A simple and reliable conflict procedure for testing antianxiety agents. *Psychopharmacologia*, 1971, *21*, 1-7. **32, 34, 37, 50**

Volavka, J., **82, 780**

Von Gebsattel, F. Quoted after Jaspers (1963). **737**

Von Uexküll, T., & Wick, E. Die Situationshypertonia. *Archiv für Kreislauf Forschung*, 1962, *39*, 236-242. **341**

Von Wright, J.M., **66**

Waddell, M.T., **480, 481, 494, 768, 773**

Waddell, M.T., Barlow, D.H., & O'Brien, G.T. A preliminary investigation of cognitive and relaxation treatment of panic disorder: Effects on intense anxiety versus "background" anxiety. *Behaviour Research and Therapy*, 1984. **386, 434-35, 486, 487, 488**

Waddington, C.H. *New patterns in genetics and development*. New York: Columbia University Press, 1962. **414**

Wade, T.D., **416, 417**

Wadeson, R.W., **58**

Wadeson, R.W., Mason, J.W., Hamburg, D.A., & Handlon, J.H. Plasma and urinary 17-OH-CS responses to motion pictures. *Archives of General Psychiatry*, 1963, *9*, 146-156. **58**

Wadsworth, A.P., **177, 660**

Wadsworth, A.P., Barker, H.R., & Barker, M. Factor structure of the state-trait anxiety inventory under conditions of variable stress. *Journal of Clinical Psychology*, 1976, *32* (3), 576-579. **660**

Wadzisz, F.J. A comparison of oxypertine and diazepam in anxiety neurosis seen in hospital outpatients. *British Journal of Psychiatry*, 1972, *121*, 507-508. **520**

Waeber, R., Adler, R.H., Schwank, A., Galeazzi, R.L. Dyspnea proneness to CO_2 stimulation and personality (neuroticism, extraversion, MMPI factors). *Psychotherapy and Psychosomatics*, 1982, *37*, 119-123. **551**

Wagener, J.J., **146-47, 169**

Wagner, A.R., **20, 213, 439**

Waite, P.R., **708**

Waldofogel, S., **405, 411**

Waldron, S. The significance of childhood neurosis for adult mental health: A follow-up study. *American Journal of Psychiatry*, 1976, *133*, 532-538. **716**

Walinder, J., **547**

Walker, C.E., **382**

Walker, R.N. Body build and behavior in young children. *Monographs of the Society for Research in Child Development*, 1962, *127*(3), 1-94. **411**

Walker, R.N. Body build and behavior in young children. *Monographs of the Society for Research in Child Development*, 1963, *34*, 1-23. **405, 411**

Wallerstein, R.S., **624, 627**

Wallerstein, R.S., & Sampson, H. Issues in research in the psychoanalytic process. *International Journal of Psycho-Analysis*, 1971, *52*, 11-50. **612**

Wallin, L., **547**

Walter, C.J.S., **82, 747, 749**

Walters, J.R., **544, 571**

Walton, D., & Mather, M.D. The application of learning principles to the treatment of obsessive compulsive state in the acute and chronic phases of illness. *Behaviour Research and Therapy*, 1963, *1*, 163-174. **224, 234**

Warburton, F.W., **300**

Warnack, W., **544**

Warr, P., Barter, J., & Brownbridge, G. On the independence of positive and negative affect. *Journal of Personality and Social Psychology*, 1983, *44*, 644-651. **698, 699**

Wasilewski, B., **563**

Waters, E., **140**

Watkins, A.E., **40**

Watson, D., Clark, L.A., & Tellegen, A. Cross-cultural convergence in the structure of mood: A Japanese replication and a comparison with U.S. findings. *Journal of Personality and Social Psychology*, 1984, *47*, 127-144. **689**

Watson, D., & Friend, R. Measurement of social-evaluative anxiety. *Journal of Consulting and Clinical Psychology*, 1969, *33*, 448-457. **120**

Watson, D., & Tellegen, A. *Toward a consensual structure of mood*. Unpublished manuscript, University of Minnesota. **690**

Watson, D.L., **113, 225, 238**

Watson, J.B., & Rayner, R. Conditioned emotional reactions. *Journal of Experimental Psychology*, 1920, *3*, 1-14. **202, 218, 707**

Watson, J.P., Gaind, R., & Marks, I.M. Physiological habituation to continuous phobic stimulation. *Behaviour Research and Therapy*, 1972, *10*, 269-278. **427, 436, 438**

Watson, J.P., & Marks, I.M. Relevant and irrelevant fear in flooding—A crossover study of phobic patients. *Behavior Therapy*, 1971, *2*, 275-293. **426, 456**

Watts, A.G., **65**

Watts, C.A.H. *Depressive disorders in the community*. Bristol: John Wright & Sons, 1966. **791**

Watts, F.N. Habituation model of systematic desensitization. *Psychological Bulletin*, 1979, *86*, 627-637. **10**

Waxman, D. A clinical trial of clomipramine and diazepam in the treatment of phobic and obsessional illness. *Journal of International Medical Research*, 1977, *5*, 99-109. **503, 504, 508, 585**

Wearn, J.T., **81**

Wearn, J.T., & Sturgis, C.C. Studies on epinephrine. *Archives of Internal Medicine*, 1919, *24*, 247. **534, 550**

Webster, R.A., **49**

Wechsler, R.L., **534, 550**

Weerts, T.C., **138, 164**

Weerts, T.C., Cuthbert, B.N., Simons, R.F., & Lang, P.J. *Eye movement and the memory image*. In preparation. **159**

Weerts, T.C., & Lang, P.J. The psychophysiology of fear imagery: Differences between focal phobia and social-performance anxiety. *Journal of Consulting and Clinical Psychology*, 1978, *46*, 1157-1159. **164**

Wehr, T., **568, 569**

Wehrenberg, W.B., Baird, A., & Ling, N. Potent interaction between glucocorticoid and growth hormone releasing factor in vivo. *Science*, 1983, *222*, 556-558. **68**

Weidman, W.H., **555**

Weil, A.T., Zinberg, N.E., & Nelsen, J.M. Clinical and psychological effects of marihuana in man. *Science*, 1968, *162*, 1234-1242. **549**

Weimer, W.B. A conceptual framework for cognitive psychology: Motor theories of the mind. In R. Shaw & J. Bransford (Eds.), *Perceiving, acting, and knowing*. Hillsdale, NJ: Lawrence Erlbaum Associates, 1977. **151**

Weinberg, J., & Levine, S. Psychobiology of coping in animals: The effects of predictability. In S. Levine & H. Ursin (Eds.), *Coping and health*. New York: Plenum Press, 1980. **239**

Weinberger, D.A., **338**

Weinberger, D.R., Cannon-Spoor, H.E., Potkin, S.G., & Wyatt, R.J. Poor premorbid adjustment and CT scan abnormalities in chronic schizophrenia. *American Journal of Psychiatry*, 1980, *137*, 1410-1413. **401**

Weinberger, N. Effect of detainment on extinction of avoidance responses. *Journal of Comparative and Physiological Psychology*, 1965, *60*, 135-138. **220**

Weiner, A.A. Fear-anxiety: Rx: intravenous diazepam sedation. *General Dentistry*, 1979, *27*, 27-32. **538**

Weiner, B., Frieze, L., Kukla, A., Reed, L., Rest, S., & Rosenbaum, R.M. *Perceiving the causes of success and failure*. Morristown, NJ: General Learning Press, 1971. **121**

Weiner, B., & Graham, S. An attributional approach to emotional development. In C. Izard, J. Kagan & R. Zajonc (Eds.), *Emotions, cognition, & behavior*. New York: Cambridge University Press, in press. **121**

Weiner, H., **62, 357, 358, 360, 363, 364, 384**

Weiner, H. *Psychobiology and human disease*. New York: Elsevier, 1977. **353**

Weiner, H. *What the future holds for psychosomatic medicine*. Address to the plenary session of the VII world congress of the international college of psychosomatic medicine. In press, 1983. **345, 354**

Weiner, H., Singer, M.T., & Reiser, M.F. Cardiovascular responses and their psychophysiologic correlates. A study in healthy young adults and patients with peptic ulcer and hypertension. *Psychosomatic Medicine*, 1962, *24*, 477-498. **335**

Weiner, I.W. Psychological factors related to result of subtotal gastrectomy. *Psychosomatic Medicine*, 1956, *18*, 486-491. **647**

Weiner, N. Drugs that inhibit adrenergic nerves and block adrenergic receptors. In A.G. Gilman, L.S. Goodman, A. Gilman, S.E. Mayer & K.L. Melmon (Eds.), *Goodman and Gilman's the pharmacological basis of therapeutics* (6th ed.) New York: Macmillan, 1980. **550, 551**

Weingarten, C.H., **529**

Weinman, M.L., **337**

Weinshilboum, R.M., Raymond, F.A., Elveback, L.R., & Weidman, W.H.

Serum dopamine-beta-hydroxylase activity: Sibling-sibling correlation. *Science*, 1973, *181*, 943-945. **555**

Weinstein, H., **317**

Weinstein, N., **240**

Weisman, K., **xxx, 516, 517, 538, 545**

Weisman, R.G., & Litner, J.S. Positive conditioned reinforcement of Sidman avoidance behavior in rats. *Journal of Comparative and Physiological Psychology*, 1969, *68*, 597-603. **227**

Weisman, R.G., & Litner, J.S. The role of Pavlovian events in avoidance training. In R.A. Boakes & M.S. Halliday (Eds.), *Inhibition and learning*. New York: Academic Press, 1972, pp. 253-270. **227**

Weiss, D.S., **614, 615, 622**

Weiss, J., **270**

Weiss, J.M. Psychological and behavioral influences on gastrointestinal lesions in animal models. In J. Maser & M. Seligman (Eds.), *Psychopathology: Experimental models*. San Francisco: Freeman, 1977, pp. 232-269. **239**

Weiss, J.M., Bailey, W.H., Goodman, P.A., Hoffman, L.J., Ambrose, M.J., Salman, S., & Charry, J.M. A model for neurochemical study of depression. In M.Y. Spiegelstein & A. Levy (Eds.), *Behavioral models and the analysis of drug action*. Amsterdam: Elsevier, 1982. **17, 18, 19, 20**

Weiss, J.M., Glazer, H.I., & Pohorecky, L.A. Coping behavior and neurochemical changes: An alternative explanation for the original 'learned helplessness' experiments. In A. Serban & A. Kling (Eds.), *Animal Models in Human Psychobiology*. New York: Plenum Press, 1976. **17, 18, 19, 20, 25**

Weiss, M., & Burke, G. A five to ten year follow-up of hospitalized school phobic children and adolescents. *American Journal of Orthopsychiatry*, 1970, *40*, 672-676. **400**

Weisse, C., **519, 522, 540**

Weissman, M., & Klerman, G. Epidemiology of Mental Disorders. *Archives of General Psychiatry*, 1978, *35*, 705-712. **297, 304**

Weissman, M.M., **240, 282, 283, 284, 286, 289, 290, 294, 327, 366, 483, 569, 764, 780, 785, 793, 795**

Weissman, M.M., Gershon, E.S., Kidd, K.K., Prusoff, B.A., Leckman, J.F., Dibble, E., Hamovit, J., Thompson, W.D., Pauls, D.L., & Guroff, J.J. Psychiatric disorders in the relatives of probands with affective disorders: The Yale-NIMH collaborative family study. *Archives of General Psychiatry*, 1984, *41*, 13-21. **286**

Weissman, M.M., Kidd, K.K., & Prusoff, B.A. Variability in rates of affective disorders in relatives of depressed and normal probands. *Archives of General Psychiatry*, 1982, *39*, 1397-1403. **286, 394, 395**

Weissman, M.M., Leckman, J.F., Merikangas, K.R., Prusoff, B.A., & Gammon, G.D. Depression and anxiety disorders in parents and children: Results from the Yale family study, 1983, *38*, 139-152. **40, 286, 288, 290, 292, 294, 394, 396**

Weissman, M.M., Myers, J.K., & Harding, P.S. Psychiatric disorders in a U.S. urban community. *American Journal of Psychiatry*, 1978, *135*, 459-462. **279, 280, 579**

Weissman, M.M., & Paykel, E.S. *The depressed woman: A study of social relationships*. Chicago: University of Chicago Press, 1974. **323**

Weissman, M.M., Prusoff, B.A., Gammon, G.D., Merikangas, K.R., Leckman, J., Kidd, K.K. Psychopathology in the children (ages 6-18) of depressed and normal parents. *Journal of the American Academy of Child Psychiatry*, 1984, *23*, 78-84. **286, 292, 293**

Weisstub, E., **512**

Weisz, J.R., **708**

Weitzman, E.D., Fukushima, D., Nogeire, C., Roffwarg, H., Gallagher, T.F., & Hellman, L. Twenty-four hour pattern of the episodic secretion of cortisol in normal subjects. *Journal of Clinical Endocrinology and Metabolism*, 1971, *33*, 14-22. **65**

Welch, B.L. Adrenals of deer as indicators of population condition for purposes of management. *Proceedings of the First National Deer Disease Symposium*. Athens, GA: University of Georgia Center for Continuing Education, 1962. **55**

Welner, A., Reich, T., Robins, E., Fishman, R., & Van Doren, T. Obsessive compulsive neurosis: Record, family, and follow-up studies. *Comprehensive Psychiatry*, 1976, *17*, 527-539. **586, 587**

Welsh, G.S., **646, 649, 663, 666, 667, 681**

Welsh, G.S., An anxiety index and an internalization ratio for the MMPI. *Journal of Consulting Psychology*, 1952, *16*, 65-72. **648-49**

Welsh, G.S. Factor dimensions A and R. In G.S. Welsh & W.G. Dahlstrom, (Eds.), *Basic readings on the MMPI in psychology and medicine*. Minneapolis: University of Minnesota Press, 1956, pp. 264-281. **648-649**

Wendlandt, S., & File, S.E. Behavioral effects of lesions of the locus coeruleus noradrenaline system combined with adrenalectomy. *Behavioral and Neural Biology*, 1979, *26*, 189-201. **550**

Wenger, M.A., Clemens, T.L., Darsie, M.L., Engel, B.T., Estess, F.M., & Sonnenschein, R.R. Autonomic response patterns during intravenous infusion of epinephrine and norepinephrine. *Psychosomatic Medicine*, 1960, *22*, 294-307. **137**

Werry, J.S., & Quay, H.C. The prevalence of behavior symptoms in younger elementary school children. *American Journal of Orthopsychiatry*, 1971, *41*, 136-143. **284**

Werthessen, N.T., **365**

Wessels, H., **427-28**

Wessman, A.E., Rick, D.F., & Tyl, M.M. Characteristics and concomitants of mood fluctuations in college women. *Journal of Abnormal and Social Psychology*, 1960, *60*, 117-126. **658**

Westberry, L.G., **660**

Westphal, C. Ueber Zwangsvorstellungen. *Archive fuer Psychiatrie und Nervenkrankheiten*, 1878, *8*, 734-750. **577**

Wetterberg, L., **555**

Whalley, L.J., Dick, H., Watts, A.G., Christie, J.E., Rosie, R., Levy, G., Sheward, J., & Fink, G. Immediate increases in plasma prolactin and neurophysin but no other hormones after electroconclusive therapy. *Lancet*, 1982, *2*, 1064-1068. **65**

Wheatley, D. Comparative effects of propanolol and chlordiazepoxide in anxiety states. *British Journal of Psychiatry*, 1969, *115*, 1411-1412. **525, 546**

Wheatley, D. Buspirone: A multicenter efficacy study. *Journal of Clinical Psychiatry*, 1982, *43*, 92-94. **518, 522, 545**

Wheeler, E.O., White, P.D., Reed, E.W., & Cohen, M.E. Neurocirculatory asthenia (anxiety neurosis, effort syndrome, neurasthenia): A twenty year follow-up study of one hundred and seventy-three patients. *Journal of the American Medical Association*, 1950, *142*, 878-889. **314, 353**

Wheeler, R.C., **349**

Wherry, F.E., **71**

Whipple, K., **612**

White, A., **63, 358**

White, M.J., **661**

White, P.D., **82, 285, 314, 353, 564**

Whiting, J.W., & Child, I.L. *Child training and personality: A cross-cultural study*. New Haven: Yale University Press, 1953. **613**

Whitmore, K., **373, 712**

Wick, E., **341**

Wielciwicz, R., **239**

Wiggins, J.S. Personality structure. *Annual Review of Psychology*, 1968, *19*, 293-350. **697**

Wilbur, C.B., **614**

Wilcoxon, L.A., **432**

Wilker, J., **543**

Wilkinson, G.R., **538**

Wilkinson, L., **473**

Willer, M.L., **405, 411**

Williams, E.W., **58**

Williams, J.B.W., **677, 773, 783, 784**

Williams, R.B., Lane, J., Kuhn, C., Melosh, W., White, A., Schaneberg, S. Type A behavior and elevated physiological and neuroendocrine responses to cognitive tasks. *Science*, 1982, *218*, 483-485. **63, 358**

Williams, R.H. (Ed.) *Textbook of endocrinology*. Philadelphia, PA: Saunders, 1974. **53**

Willis, D.J., Swanson, B.M., & Walker, C.E. Etiological factors. In T.H. Ollendick & M. Hersen (Eds.), *Handbook of child psychopathology*. New York: Plenum Press, 1983. **382**

Wills, U., **746**

Wilner, N., **622, 624, 627, 772**

Wilson, A.F., **71, 72**

Wilson, F.N., **737**

Wilson, G.T., **99, 434**

Wilson, G.T. Adult disorders. In G.T. Wilson & C.M. Franks (Eds.), *Contemporary behavior therapy: Conceptual and empirical foundations.* New York: Guilford, 1982. **102**

Wilson, G.T., & Davison, G. Processes of fear reduction in systematic desensitization. *Psychological Bulletin,* 1971, *76,* 1-14. **220**

Wilson, H.K., **339**

Wilson, L.G., **562**

Wilson, T.P., **441**

Wincze, J.P., **132, 149-50, 334, 339, 363, 364, 427**

Winer, G.A. A review and analysis of children's fearful behavior in dental settings. *Child Development,* 1982, *53,* 1111-1133. **374, 711**

Wing, J.K., **309**

Wing, J.K., Cooper, J.E., & Sartorius, N. *The measurement and classification of psychiatric symptoms.* London: Cambridge University Press, 1979. **742**

Wing, L., **132, 167, 168, 365, 439, 444, 445, 494, 498, 583**

Winokur, A., **79**

Winokur, G., **60, 66, 762**

Winstead, D.K. Coffee consumption among psychiatric inpatients. *American Journal of Psychiatry,* 1976, *133,* 1447-1450. **551, 573**

Winters, V.P., **49**

Wirt, R.D., Lachar, D., Klinedinst, J.D., & Seat, P.D. *Multidimensional description of personality.* Los Angeles: Western Psychological Services, 1977. **708**

Wise, B.C., **36, 41, 43, 44, 45**

Wise, B.C., Guidotti, A., & Costa, E. Phosphorylation induces a decrease in the biological activity of the protein inhibitor (GABA-modulin) of γ-aminobutyric acid binding sites. *Proceedings of the National Academy of Sciences, U.S.A.,* 1983, *80,* 886-890. **41, 43, 44**

Wise, C.D., **35, 36, 539**

Wise, E.H., & Haynes, S.N. Cognitive treatment of test anxiety: Rational restructuring versus attentional training. *Cognitive Therapy and Research,* 1983, *7,* 69-78. **98**

Wiswesser, G., **519, 522, 540**

Wober, M. Distinguishing centri-culture from cross-cultural tests and research. *Perceptual and Motor Skills,* 1969, *28,* 488. **302**

Woerner, M.G., **397, 400, 486, 511, 512, 514, 515, 543, 544, 557, 762**

Wojnilower, D.A., **372**

Wolf, R.L., **82, 534, 550**

Wolf, S., & Wolff, H.G. Evidence on the genesis of peptic ulcer in men. *Journal of American Medical Association*, 1942, *120*, 670-675. **113**

Wolf, S., & Wolff, H.G. *Human gastric function*. New York: Oxford University Press, 1943. **137**

Wolf, S., & Wolff, H.G. *Human gastric function: An experimental study of a man and his stomach* (2nd ed.). New York: Oxford University Press, 1947. **137**

Wolfe, B., **99**

Wolff, C.T., **59**

Wolff, C.T., Friedman, S.B., Hofer, M.A., & Mason, J.W. Relationship between psychological defenses and mean urinary 17-hydroxycorticosteroid excretion rates: I. A Predictive study of parents of fatally ill children. *Psychosomatic Medicine*, 1964, *26*, 576-591. **59**

Wolff, E.A., **573**

Wolff, H.G., **58, 113, 137**

Wolff, H.H., **425**

Wolff, S., & Chick, J. Schizoid personality in childhood: A controlled follow-up study. *Psychological Medicine*, in press. **401**

Wolkenstein, B., **216**

Wollman, H., **551**

Wolpe, J. *Psychotherapy by reciprocal inhibition*. Stanford: Stanford University Press, 1958. **xxi, 169, 200, 202, 213, 219, 229, 233, 237, 242, 375, 425**

Wolpe, J. The behavioristic conception of neurosis: A reply to two critics. *Psychological Review*, 1971, *78*, 341-343. **203**

Wolpe, J. *The practice of behavior therapy*. New York: Pergamon Press, 1973. **427**

Wolpe, J., & Lang, P.G. A fear survey schedule for use in behavior therapy. *Behavior Research and Therapy*, 1964, *2*, 27-30. **708**

Wolpe, J., & Lazarus, A.A. *Behavior therapy techniques*. New York: Pergamon Press, 1966. **246**

Wood, A.J., Robertson, D., Robertson, R.M., Wilkinson, G.R., & Wood, M. Elevated plasma free drug concentrations of propranolol and diazepam during cardiac catheterization. *Circulation*, 1980, *62*, 1119-1122. **538**

Wood, M., **538**

Wood, P. Aetiology of DaCosto's syndrome. *British Medical Journal*, 1941, *1*, 845-851. **285**

Woodruff, R.A., **60, 762, 793**

Woods, S.M., **603**

Woodward, R., & Jones, R.B. Cognitive restructuring treatment: A controlled trial with anxious patients. *Behaviour Research and Therapy*, 1980, *18*, 401-407. **434**

Woodworth, R.W., & Schlosberg, H.S. *Experimental psychology*. New York: Holt, 1954. **416**

Woolsky, R.L., **529**

World Health Organization. *International classification of diseases—clinical modification* (9th ed.). Ann Arbor: Edwards Brothers, 1978. **578, 762**

World Health Organization. *Schizophrenia: An international follow-up study.* New York: Wiley, 1979. **310**

World Health Organization. *Report of the Sixth WHO Seminar on Psychiatric Diagnosis, Classification and Statistics, Basel, 2-8 December 1970.* WHO document MH 71.7, Geneva, 1970. **739-40**

Wright, C.M., **31**

Wright, D.M., **34, 36**

Wright, J.C., **63-64, 65, 243, 339**

Wrobleski, J., **39**

Wu, J.-Y., **33, 39**

Wuay, H.C., **284**

Wundt, W.W. *Outlines of psychology.* Leipzig: Wilhelm Englemann, 1907. **111, 117**

Wurm, R., **365**

Wurmser, L. *The mask of shame.* Baltimore: Johns Hopkins University Press, 1981. **106**

Wyatt, R.J., **401**

Wyatt, R.M., **568, 569**

Wynne, L.C., **203, 205, 220, 223**

Yamamoto, J., Kline, F., & Burgoyne, R. The treatment of severe anxiety in outpatients: A controlled study comparing chlordiazepoxide and chlorpromazine. *Psychosomatics*, 1973, *14*, 46-51. **520**

Yamamura, H.I., Manian, A.A., & Snyder, S.H. Muscarinic cholinergic receptor: Influence of pimozide and chlorpromazine metabolites. *Life Sciences*, 1976, *18*, 685-692. **541**

Yamazaki, S., **31**

Yao, T., **550, 551**

Yap, P.M. *Comparative psychiatry.* Toronto: University of Toronto Press, 1974, pp. 84-104. **312, 315**

Yardley, K., **426**

Yaryura-Tobias, J., & Bhagavan, H. L-Tryptophan in obsessive-compulsive disorders. *American Journal of Psychiatry*, 1977, *134*, 1298-1299. **505, 508**

Yerevanian, B., **568, 786, 793, 794**

Yerkes, A., **201, 208**

Yerkes, R.M., & Dodson, J.D. The relation of strength of stimulus to rapidity of habit-formation. *Journal of Comparative Neurology*, 1908, *18*, 459-82. **442**

Yerkes, R.M., & Yerkes, A. Nature and conditions of avoidance (fear) responses in chimpanzees. *Journal of Comparative Psychology*, 1936, *21*, 53-66. **201, 208**

Yim, B.J., **351**

Yorkston, NJ, **612**

Yorkston, NJ, Sergeant, H.G.S., & Rachman, S. Methodexitone relaxation for desensitizing agoraphobic patients. *Lancet*, 1968, 2, 651-653. **425**

Young, E., **66, 67**

Young, J.E., **587, 750**

Young, J.E., & Beck, A.T. Cognitive therapy: Clinical applications. In A.J. Rush (Ed.), *Short-term psychotherapies for depression*. Chichester: Wiley, 1982. **431**

Young, M., **423**

Young, P.A., **685**

Yu, P.N., Yim, B.J., & Stanfield, C.A. Hyperventilation syndrome: changes in the electrocardiogram, blood gases, and electrolytes during voluntary hyperventilation: possible mechanisms and clinical implications. *Archives of Internal Medicine*, 1959, *103*, 902-911. **351**

Yuijiro, I., **67, 68**

Yuksel, S., **434**

Yule, W., & Fernando, P. Blood phobia—beware. *Behaviour Research and Therapy*, 1980, *18*, 587-590. **485**

Zacharko, R.M., **797**

Zahn, T., Insel, T.R., & Murphy, D.L. Psychophysiologic changes during pharmacologic treatment of obsessive compulsive disorder. *British Journal of Psychiatry*, in press. **581, 583**

Zahn-Waxler, C., & Radke-Yarrow, M. The development of altruism: Alternative research strategies. In N. Eisenberg (Ed.), *The development of prosocial behavior*. New York: Academic Press, 1982. **419**

Zajonc, R.B., **110, 123**

Zajonc, R.B. Feeling and thinking: Preferences need no inferences. *American Psychologist*, 1980, *35*(2), 151-175. **111, 118, 157**

Zajonc, R.B., & Markus, H. Affect and cognition: The hard interface. In C. Izard, J. Kagan, & R. Zajonc (Eds.), *Emotion, cognition, & behavior*. New York: Cambridge University Press, 1984, pp. 73-102. **151**

Zarifian, E., **563**

Zautra, A., & Goodhart, D. Quality of life indicators: A review of the literature. *Community Mental Health Review*, 1979, *4*, 1-10. **251**

Zelaso, P., **414**

Zeldis, S., **365**

Zetzel, E.R. The concept of anxiety in relation to the development of psychoanalysis. *Journal of the American Psychoanalytic Association*, 1955, *3*, 369-388. **602**

Zevon, M.A., & Tellegen, A. The structure of mood change: An idiographic/ nomothetic analysis. *Journal of Personality and Social Psychology*, 1982, *43*, 111-122. **485, 486, 500, 689, 691, 703**

Zielinski, K. Short latency avoidance responses. A review of H. Eysenck's "The conditioning model of neurosis." *Behavioral and Brain Sciences*, 1979, *2*, 186-187. **218**

Zilberg, N., **624**

Zilberg, N., Weiss, D.S., & Horowitz, M.J. Impact of event scale: A cross validation study and some empirical evidence. *Journal of Consulting and Clinical Psychology*, 1982, *50*, 407-414. **622**

Zillmann, D., **149**

Zillmann, D. Anatomy of suspense. In P.H. Tannenbaum (Ed.), *The entertainment functions of television*. Hillsdale, NJ: Lawrence Erlbaum Associates, 1980. **149**

Zillmann, D. Treatment of excitation in emotional behavior. In J.T. Cacioppo & R.E. Petty (Eds.), *Perspectives in psychophysiology*. New York: Guilford Press, 1983. **149, 157, 168, 499**

Zillmann, D., & Bryant, J. Effect of residual excitation on the emotional response to provocation and delayed aggressive behavior. *Journal of Personality and Social Psychology*, 1974, *30*, 782-791. **149**

Zillmann, D., Bryant, J., Comisky, P.W., & Medoff, NJ Excitation and hedonic valence in the affect of erotica on motivated intermale aggression. *European Journal of Social Psychology*, 1981, *11*, 233-252. **149**

Zillmann, D., Katcher, A.H., & Milavsky, B. Excitation transfer from physical exercise to subsequent aggressive behavior. *Journal of Experimental Social Psychology*, 1972, *8*, 247-259. **149**

Zimbardo, P.G., **113, 613**

Zinberg, N.E., **549**

Zitrin, C.M., **365, 397, 400, 543**

Zitrin, C.M. Combined pharmacologic and psychotherapeutic treatment of phobias. In M.R. Mavissakalian & D.H. Barlow (Eds.), *Phobia: Psychological and pharmacological treatment*. New York: Guilford Press, 1981. pp. 145-175. **486, 514**

Zitrin, C.M., Klein, D.F., & Woerner, M.G. Behavior therapy, supportive psychotherapy, imipramine, and phobias. *Archives of General Psychiatry*, 1978, *35*, 307-316. **512, 514, 543, 544, 762**

Zitrin, C.M., Klein, D.F., & Woerner, M.G. Treatment of agoraphobia with group exposure *in vivo* and imipramine. *Archives of General Psychiatry*, 1980, *37*, 63-72. **486, 512, 514, 544**

Zitrin, C.M., Klein, D.F., Woerner, M.G., & Ross, D.C. Treatment of phobias: I. Comparison of imipramine hydrocholoride and placebo. *Archives of General Psychiatry*, 1983, *40*, 125-138. **397, 486, 511, 512, 514, 515**

Zitrin, C.M., Woerner, M.G., & Klein, D.F. Differentiation of panic anxiety from anticipatory anxiety and avoidance behavior. In D.F. Klein & J. Rabkin (Eds.), *Anxiety: New research and changing concepts*. New York: Raven Press, 1981. **514, 557**

Zuardi, A.W., Shirakawa, I., Finkelfarb, E., & Karniol, I.G. Action of Cannabidiol on the anxiety and other effects produced by delta-9-THC in normal subjects. *Psychopharmacology*, 1982, *76*, 245-250. **547, 549**

Zubair-Ul-Hassan Patterson, J.L., Jr., **350**

Zubin, J. Clinical phenomenological and biometric assessment of psychopathology with special reference to diagnosis. In S.B. Sells (Ed), *The definition and measurement of mental health*. Washington, D.C.: U.S. Department of Health, Education & Welfare, 1968. pp. 67-98. **xxiii**

Zubin, J. Research in clinical diagnosis. In B.B. Wolman (Ed.) *Clinical diagnosis of mental disorders*. New York: Plenum Publishing Corporation, 1978. **xxiii**

Zuckerman, M., **570, 657**

Zuckerman, M. The development of an Affect Adjective Check List for the measurement of anxiety. *Journal of Consulting Psychology*, 1960, *24*, 475-462. **176, 658**

Zuckerman, M., & Lubin, B. *Manual for the multiple affect adjective check list*. San Diego, CA: Educational and Industrial Testing Service, 1965. **176, 658, 689**

Zung, W.W.K. A rating instrument for anxiety disorders. *Psychosomatics*, 1971, *12*, 371-379. **688**

Zweifler, A., **348**

Subject Index